The Python 3
Standard Library
by Example

Developer's Library

Linux
for Developers
Jumpstart your Linux Programming Skills

PHP and **MySQL**
Web Development
Fifth Edition

Python
in Practice
Create Better Programs Using
Concurrency, Libraries, and Patterns

Developer's Library

The
Swift
Developer's Cookbook

Visit **informit.com/devlibrary** for a complete list of available publications.

The **Developer's Library** series from Addison-Wesley provides practicing programmers with unique, high-quality references and tutorials on the latest programming languages and technologies they use in their daily work. All books in the Developer's Library are written by expert technology practioners who are exceptionally skilled at organizing and presenting information in a way that is useful for other programmers.

Developer's Library titles cover a wide range of topics, from open source programming languages and technologies, mobile application development, and web development to Java programming and more.

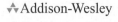

The Python 3 Standard Library by Example

Doug Hellmann

✦✦Addison-Wesley

Boston • Columbus • Indianapolis • New York • San Francisco • Amsterdam • Cape Town
Dubai • London • Madrid • Milan • Munich • Paris • Montreal • Toronto • Delhi • Mexico City
São Paulo • Sydney • Hong Kong • Seoul • Singapore • Taipei • Tokyo

For information about buying this title in bulk quantities, or for special sales opportunities (which may include electronic versions; custom cover designs; and content particular to your business, training goals, marketing focus, or branding interests), please contact our corporate sales department at corpsales@pearsoned.com or (800) 382-3419.

For government sales inquiries, please contact governmentsales@pearsoned.com.

For questions about sales outside the U.S., please contact intlcs@pearson.com.

Visit us on the Web: informit.com/aw

Library of Congress Control Number: 2017932317

ISBN-13: 978-0-13-429105-5
ISBN-10: 0-13-429105-0

1 17

For Theresa,
my one true love.

Contents at a Glance

Introduction		*xxxi*
Acknowledgments		*xxxiii*
About the Author		*xxxv*
Chapter 1	**Text**	1
Chapter 2	**Data Structures**	65
Chapter 3	**Algorithms**	143
Chapter 4	**Dates and Times**	211
Chapter 5	**Mathematics**	239
Chapter 6	**The File System**	295
Chapter 7	**Data Persistence and Exchange**	395
Chapter 8	**Data Compression and Archiving**	477
Chapter 9	**Cryptography**	523
Chapter 10	**Concurrency with Processes, Threads, and Coroutines**	535
Chapter 11	**Networking**	687
Chapter 12	**The Internet**	753
Chapter 13	**Email**	841
Chapter 14	**Application Building Blocks**	887
Chapter 15	**Internationalization and Localization**	1003
Chapter 16	**Developer Tools**	1023
Chapter 17	**Runtime Features**	1169
Chapter 18	**Language Tools**	1279

Chapter 19 Modules and Packages   **1329**

Appendix A Porting Notes   **1351**

Appendix B Outside of the Standard Library   **1367**

Index of Python Modules   *1373*

Index   *1375*

Contents

Introduction   *xxxi*

Acknowledgments   *xxxiii*

About the Author   *xxxv*

Chapter 1 Text   1
1.1   string: Text Constants and Templates   1
    1.1.1   Functions   1
    1.1.2   Templates   2
    1.1.3   Advanced Templates   4
    1.1.4   Formatter   6
    1.1.5   Constants   6
1.2   textwrap: Formatting Text Paragraphs   7
    1.2.1   Example Data   8
    1.2.2   Filling Paragraphs   8
    1.2.3   Removing Existing Indentation   8
    1.2.4   Combining Dedent and Fill   9
    1.2.5   Indenting Blocks   10
    1.2.6   Hanging Indents   12
    1.2.7   Truncating Long Text   12
1.3   re: Regular Expressions   13
    1.3.1   Finding Patterns in Text   14
    1.3.2   Compiling Expressions   15
    1.3.3   Multiple Matches   16
    1.3.4   Pattern Syntax   17
    1.3.5   Constraining the Search   28
    1.3.6   Dissecting Matches with Groups   30
    1.3.7   Search Options   36
    1.3.8   Looking Ahead or Behind   44
    1.3.9   Self-referencing Expressions   48
    1.3.10 Modifying Strings with Patterns   53
    1.3.11 Splitting with Patterns   55
1.4   difflib: Compare Sequences   58
    1.4.1   Comparing Bodies of Text   58
    1.4.2   Junk Data   61
    1.4.3   Comparing Arbitrary Types   62

Chapter 2   Data Structures   **65**
2.1   enum: Enumeration Type   66
        2.1.1   Creating Enumerations   66
        2.1.2   Iteration   67
        2.1.3   Comparing Enums   67
        2.1.4   Unique Enumeration Values   69
        2.1.5   Creating Enumerations Programmatically   71
        2.1.6   Non-integer Member Values   72
2.2   collections: Container Data Types   75
        2.2.1   ChainMap: Search Multiple Dictionaries   75
        2.2.2   Counter: Count Hashable Objects   79
        2.2.3   defaultdict: Missing Keys Return a Default Value   83
        2.2.4   deque: Double-Ended Queue   84
        2.2.5   namedtuple: Tuple Subclass with Named Fields   89
        2.2.6   OrderedDict: Remember the Order Keys Are Added to a Dictionary 94
        2.2.7   collections.abc: Abstract Base Classes for Containers   97
2.3   array: Sequence of Fixed-Type Data   98
        2.3.1   Initialization   98
        2.3.2   Manipulating Arrays   99
        2.3.3   Arrays and Files   100
        2.3.4   Alternative Byte Ordering   101
2.4   heapq: Heap Sort Algorithm   103
        2.4.1   Example Data   103
        2.4.2   Creating a Heap   104
        2.4.3   Accessing the Contents of a Heap   105
        2.4.4   Data Extremes from a Heap   107
        2.4.5   Efficiently Merging Sorted Sequences   108
2.5   bisect: Maintain Lists in Sorted Order   109
        2.5.1   Inserting in Sorted Order   109
        2.5.2   Handling Duplicates   110
2.6   queue: Thread-Safe FIFO Implementation   111
        2.6.1   Basic FIFO Queue   112
        2.6.2   LIFO Queue   112
        2.6.3   Priority Queue   113
        2.6.4   Building a Threaded Podcast Client   114
2.7   struct: Binary Data Structures   117
        2.7.1   Functions Versus Struct Class   117
        2.7.2   Packing and Unpacking   117
        2.7.3   Endianness   118
        2.7.4   Buffers   120
2.8   weakref: Impermanent References to Objects   121
        2.8.1   References   122
        2.8.2   Reference Callbacks   122
        2.8.3   Finalizing Objects   123
        2.8.4   Proxies   126
        2.8.5   Caching Objects   127

2.9   copy: Duplicate Objects   130
        2.9.1   Shallow Copies   130
        2.9.2   Deep Copies   131
        2.9.3   Customizing Copy Behavior   132
        2.9.4   Recursion in Deep Copy   133
2.10   pprint: Pretty-Print Data Structures   136
        2.10.1   Printing   136
        2.10.2   Formatting   137
        2.10.3   Arbitrary Classes   138
        2.10.4   Recursion   139
        2.10.5   Limiting Nested Output   139
        2.10.6   Controlling Output Width   140

Chapter 3   Algorithms   **143**
3.1   functools: Tools for Manipulating Functions   143
        3.1.1   Decorators   143
        3.1.2   Comparison   151
        3.1.3   Caching   155
        3.1.4   Reducing a Data Set   158
        3.1.5   Generic Functions   161
3.2   itertools: Iterator Functions   163
        3.2.1   Merging and Splitting Iterators   164
        3.2.2   Converting Inputs   167
        3.2.3   Producing New Values   169
        3.2.4   Filtering   172
        3.2.5   Grouping Data   175
        3.2.6   Combining Inputs   176
3.3   operator: Functional Interface to Built-in Operators   183
        3.3.1   Logical Operations   183
        3.3.2   Comparison Operators   184
        3.3.3   Arithmetic Operators   184
        3.3.4   Sequence Operators   186
        3.3.5   In-Place Operators   187
        3.3.6   Attribute and Item "Getters"   188
        3.3.7   Combining Operators and Custom Classes   190
3.4   contextlib: Context Manager Utilities   191
        3.4.1   Context Manager API   191
        3.4.2   Context Managers as Function Decorators   194
        3.4.3   From Generator to Context Manager   196
        3.4.4   Closing Open Handles   198
        3.4.5   Ignoring Exceptions   199
        3.4.6   Redirecting Output Streams   201
        3.4.7   Dynamic Context Manager Stacks   202

Chapter 4   Dates and Times   **211**
4.1   time: Clock Time   211
    4.1.1   Comparing Clocks   211
    4.1.2   Wall Clock Time   213
    4.1.3   Monotonic Clocks   214
    4.1.4   Processor Clock Time   214
    4.1.5   Performance Counter   216
    4.1.6   Time Components   217
    4.1.7   Working with Time Zones   218
    4.1.8   Parsing and Formatting Times   219
4.2   datetime: Date and Time Value Manipulation   221
    4.2.1   Times   221
    4.2.2   Dates   222
    4.2.3   timedeltas   225
    4.2.4   Date Arithmetic   226
    4.2.5   Comparing Values   228
    4.2.6   Combining Dates and Times   228
    4.2.7   Formatting and Parsing   230
    4.2.8   Time Zones   231
4.3   calendar: Work with Dates   233
    4.3.1   Formatting Examples   233
    4.3.2   Locales   236
    4.3.3   Calculating Dates   236

Chapter 5   Mathematics   **239**
5.1   decimal: Fixed- and Floating-Point Math   239
    5.1.1   Decimal   239
    5.1.2   Formatting   241
    5.1.3   Arithmetic   242
    5.1.4   Special Values   243
    5.1.5   Context   244
5.2   fractions: Rational Numbers   250
    5.2.1   Creating Fraction Instances   250
    5.2.2   Arithmetic   252
    5.2.3   Approximating Values   253
5.3   random: Pseudorandom Number Generators   254
    5.3.1   Generating Random Numbers   254
    5.3.2   Seeding   255
    5.3.3   Saving State   255
    5.3.4   Random Integers   257
    5.3.5   Picking Random Items   258
    5.3.6   Permutations   258
    5.3.7   Sampling   260
    5.3.8   Multiple Simultaneous Generators   261
    5.3.9   SystemRandom   262
    5.3.10   Non-uniform Distributions   263

5.4   math: Mathematical Functions   264
        5.4.1   Special Constants   265
        5.4.2   Testing for Exceptional Values   265
        5.4.3   Comparing   267
        5.4.4   Converting Floating-Point Values to Integers   270
        5.4.5   Alternative Representations of Floating-Point Values   271
        5.4.6   Positive and Negative Signs   272
        5.4.7   Commonly Used Calculations   274
        5.4.8   Exponents and Logarithms   278
        5.4.9   Angles   282
        5.4.10   Trigonometry   284
        5.4.11   Hyperbolic Functions   288
        5.4.12   Special Functions   289
5.5   statistics: Statistical Calculations   290
        5.5.1   Averages   290
        5.5.2   Variance   292

Chapter 6   The File System   295
6.1   os.path: Platform-Independent Manipulation of Filenames   296
        6.1.1   Parsing Paths   296
        6.1.2   Building Paths   300
        6.1.3   Normalizing Paths   301
        6.1.4   File Times   302
        6.1.5   Testing Files   303
6.2   pathlib: File System Paths as Objects   305
        6.2.1   Path Representations   305
        6.2.2   Building Paths   305
        6.2.3   Parsing Paths   307
        6.2.4   Creating Concrete Paths   309
        6.2.5   Directory Contents   309
        6.2.6   Reading and Writing Files   312
        6.2.7   Manipulating Directories and Symbolic Links   312
        6.2.8   File Types   313
        6.2.9   File Properties   315
        6.2.10   Permissions   317
        6.2.11   Deleting   318
6.3   glob: Filename Pattern Matching   319
        6.3.1   Example Data   320
        6.3.2   Wildcards   320
        6.3.3   Single-Character Wildcard   321
        6.3.4   Character Ranges   322
        6.3.5   Escaping Meta-characters   322
6.4   fnmatch: Unix-Style Glob Pattern Matching   323
        6.4.1   Simple Matching   323
        6.4.2   Filtering   325
        6.4.3   Translating Patterns   325

6.5   linecache: Read Text Files Efficiently   326
         6.5.1   Test Data   326
         6.5.2   Reading Specific Lines   327
         6.5.3   Handling Blank Lines   328
         6.5.4   Error Handling   328
         6.5.5   Reading Python Source Files   329
6.6   tempfile: Temporary File System Objects   330
         6.6.1   Temporary Files   331
         6.6.2   Named Files   333
         6.6.3   Spooled Files   333
         6.6.4   Temporary Directories   335
         6.6.5   Predicting Names   335
         6.6.6   Temporary File Location   336
6.7   shutil: High-Level File Operations   337
         6.7.1   Copying Files   337
         6.7.2   Copying File Metadata   340
         6.7.3   Working with Directory Trees   342
         6.7.4   Finding Files   345
         6.7.5   Archives   346
         6.7.6   File System Space   350
6.8   filecmp: Compare Files   351
         6.8.1   Example Data   351
         6.8.2   Comparing Files   353
         6.8.3   Comparing Directories   355
         6.8.4   Using Differences in a Program   357
6.9   mmap: Memory-Map Files   361
         6.9.1   Reading   361
         6.9.2   Writing   362
         6.9.3   Regular Expressions   364
6.10   codecs: String Encoding and Decoding   365
         6.10.1   Unicode Primer   365
         6.10.2   Working with Files   368
         6.10.3   Byte Order   370
         6.10.4   Error Handling   372
         6.10.5   Encoding Translation   376
         6.10.6   Non-Unicode Encodings   377
         6.10.7   Incremental Encoding   378
         6.10.8   Unicode Data and Network Communication   380
         6.10.9   Defining a Custom Encoding   383
6.11   io: Text, Binary, and Raw Stream I/O Tools   390
         6.11.1   In-Memory Streams   390
         6.11.2   Wrapping Byte Streams for Text Data   392

Chapter 7   Data Persistence and Exchange   **395**
7.1   pickle: Object Serialization   396
     7.1.1   Encoding and Decoding Data in Strings   396
     7.1.2   Working with Streams   397
     7.1.3   Problems Reconstructing Objects   399
     7.1.4   Unpicklable Objects   400
     7.1.5   Circular References   402
7.2   shelve: Persistent Storage of Objects   405
     7.2.1   Creating a New Shelf   405
     7.2.2   Writeback   406
     7.2.3   Specific Shelf Types   408
7.3   dbm: Unix Key–Value Databases   408
     7.3.1   Database Types   408
     7.3.2   Creating a New Database   409
     7.3.3   Opening an Existing Database   410
     7.3.4   Error Cases   411
7.4   sqlite3: Embedded Relational Database   412
     7.4.1   Creating a Database   412
     7.4.2   Retrieving Data   415
     7.4.3   Query Metadata   417
     7.4.4   Row Objects   417
     7.4.5   Using Variables with Queries   419
     7.4.6   Bulk Loading   421
     7.4.7   Defining New Column Types   422
     7.4.8   Determining Types for Columns   426
     7.4.9   Transactions   428
     7.4.10   Isolation Levels   431
     7.4.11   In-Memory Databases   434
     7.4.12   Exporting the Contents of a Database   435
     7.4.13   Using Python Functions in SQL   436
     7.4.14   Querying with Regular Expressions   439
     7.4.15   Custom Aggregation   440
     7.4.16   Threading and Connection Sharing   441
     7.4.17   Restricting Access to Data   442
7.5   xml.etree.ElementTree: XML Manipulation API   445
     7.5.1   Parsing an XML Document   445
     7.5.2   Traversing the Parsed Tree   446
     7.5.3   Finding Nodes in a Document   447
     7.5.4   Parsed Node Attributes   449
     7.5.5   Watching Events While Parsing   451
     7.5.6   Creating a Custom Tree Builder   453
     7.5.7   Parsing Strings   455
     7.5.8   Building Documents With Element Nodes   457
     7.5.9   Pretty-Printing XML   458
     7.5.10   Setting Element Properties   459

	7.5.11	Building Trees from Lists of Nodes	461
	7.5.12	Serializing XML to a Stream	464
7.6	csv: Comma-Separated Value Files		466
	7.6.1	Reading	466
	7.6.2	Writing	467
	7.6.3	Dialects	469
	7.6.4	Using Field Names	474

Chapter 8   Data Compression and Archiving   **477**

8.1	zlib: GNU zlib Compression		477
	8.1.1	Working with Data in Memory	477
	8.1.2	Incremental Compression and Decompression	479
	8.1.3	Mixed Content Streams	480
	8.1.4	Checksums	481
	8.1.5	Compressing Network Data	482
8.2	gzip: Read and Write GNU zip Files		486
	8.2.1	Writing Compressed Files	486
	8.2.2	Reading Compressed Data	489
	8.2.3	Working with Streams	490
8.3	bz2: bzip2 Compression		491
	8.3.1	One-Shot Operations in Memory	492
	8.3.2	Incremental Compression and Decompression	493
	8.3.3	Mixed-Content Streams	494
	8.3.4	Writing Compressed Files	495
	8.3.5	Reading Compressed Files	497
	8.3.6	Reading and Writing Unicode Data	498
	8.3.7	Compressing Network Data	499
8.4	tarfile: Tar Archive Access		503
	8.4.1	Testing Tar Files	503
	8.4.2	Reading Metadata from an Archive	504
	8.4.3	Extracting Files from an Archive	506
	8.4.4	Creating New Archives	508
	8.4.5	Using Alternative Archive Member Names	508
	8.4.6	Writing Data from Sources Other Than Files	509
	8.4.7	Appending to Archives	510
	8.4.8	Working with Compressed Archives	510
8.5	zipfile: ZIP Archive Access		511
	8.5.1	Testing ZIP Files	512
	8.5.2	Reading Metadata from an Archive	512
	8.5.3	Extracting Archived Files From an Archive	514
	8.5.4	Creating New Archives	514
	8.5.5	Using Alternative Archive Member Names	516
	8.5.6	Writing Data from Sources Other Than Files	517
	8.5.7	Writing with a ZipInfo Instance	517
	8.5.8	Appending to Files	518

8.5.9   Python ZIP Archives   519
8.5.10   Limitations   521

Chapter 9   Cryptography   **523**
9.1   hashlib: Cryptographic Hashing   523
       9.1.1   Hash Algorithms   523
       9.1.2   Sample Data   524
       9.1.3   MD5 Example   524
       9.1.4   SHA1 Example   525
       9.1.5   Creating a Hash by Name   525
       9.1.6   Incremental Updates   526
9.2   hmac: Cryptographic Message Signing and Verification   528
       9.2.1   Signing Messages   528
       9.2.2   Alternative Digest Types   528
       9.2.3   Binary Digests   529
       9.2.4   Applications of Message Signatures   530

Chapter 10 Concurrency with Processes, Threads, and Coroutines **535**
10.1   subprocess: Spawning Additional Processes   535
       10.1.1   Running External Command   536
       10.1.2   Working with Pipes Directly   542
       10.1.3   Connecting Segments of a Pipe   545
       10.1.4   Interacting with Another Command   546
       10.1.5   Signaling Between Processes   548
10.2   signal: Asynchronous System Events   553
       10.2.1   Receiving Signals   554
       10.2.2   Retrieving Registered Handlers   555
       10.2.3   Sending Signals   556
       10.2.4   Alarms   556
       10.2.5   Ignoring Signals   557
       10.2.6   Signals and Threads   558
10.3   threading: Manage Concurrent Operations Within a Process   560
       10.3.1   Thread Objects   560
       10.3.2   Determining the Current Thread   562
       10.3.3   Daemon Versus Non-daemon Threads   564
       10.3.4   Enumerating All Threads   567
       10.3.5   Subclassing Thread   568
       10.3.6   Timer Threads   570
       10.3.7   Signaling Between Threads   571
       10.3.8   Controlling Access to Resources   572
       10.3.9   Synchronizing Threads   578
       10.3.10 Limiting Concurrent Access to Resources   581
       10.3.11 Thread Specific Data   583
10.4   multiprocessing: Manage Processes Like Threads   586
       10.4.1   multiprocessing Basics   586
       10.4.2   Importable Target Functions   587

	10.4.3	Determining the Current Process	588
	10.4.4	Daemon Processes	589
	10.4.5	Waiting for Processes	591
	10.4.6	Terminating Processes	593
	10.4.7	Process Exit Status	594
	10.4.8	Logging	596
	10.4.9	Subclassing Process	597
	10.4.10	Passing Messages to Processes	598
	10.4.11	Signaling Between Processes	602
	10.4.12	Controlling Access to Resources	603
	10.4.13	Synchronizing Operations	604
	10.4.14	Controlling Concurrent Access to Resources	605
	10.4.15	Managing Shared State	608
	10.4.16	Shared Namespaces	608
	10.4.17	Process Pools	611
	10.4.18	Implementing MapReduce	613
10.5	asyncio: Asynchronous I/O, Event Loop, and Concurrency Tools		617
	10.5.1	Asynchronous Concurrency Concepts	618
	10.5.2	Cooperative Multitasking with Coroutines	618
	10.5.3	Scheduling Calls to Regular Functions	622
	10.5.4	Producing Results Asynchronously	625
	10.5.5	Executing Tasks Concurrently	628
	10.5.6	Composing Coroutines with Control Structures	632
	10.5.7	Synchronization Primitives	637
	10.5.8	Asynchronous I/O with Protocol Class Abstractions	644
	10.5.9	Asynchronous I/O Using Coroutines and Streams	650
	10.5.10	Using SSL	656
	10.5.11	Interacting with Domain Name Services	658
	10.5.12	Working with Subprocesses	661
	10.5.13	Receiving Unix Signals	668
	10.5.14	Combining Coroutines with Threads and Processes	670
	10.5.15	Debugging with asyncio	673
10.6	concurrent.futures: Manage Pools of Concurrent Tasks		677
	10.6.1	Using map() with a Basic Thread Pool	677
	10.6.2	Scheduling Individual Tasks	678
	10.6.3	Waiting for Tasks in Any Order	679
	10.6.4	Future Callbacks	680
	10.6.5	Canceling Tasks	681
	10.6.6	Exceptions in Tasks	683
	10.6.7	Context Manager	683
	10.6.8	Process Pools	684

Chapter 11 Networking **687**
11.1   ipaddress: Internet Addresses   687
        11.1.1   Addresses   687
        11.1.2   Networks   688
        11.1.3   Interfaces   692
11.2   socket: Network Communication   693
        11.2.1   Addressing, Protocol Families, and Socket Types   693
        11.2.2   TCP/IP Client and Server   704
        11.2.3   User Datagram Client and Server   711
        11.2.4   Unix Domain Sockets   714
        11.2.5   Multicast   717
        11.2.6   Sending Binary Data   721
        11.2.7   Non-blocking Communication and Timeouts   723
11.3   selectors: I/O Multiplexing Abstractions   724
        11.3.1   Operating Model   724
        11.3.2   Echo Server   724
        11.3.3   Echo Client   726
        11.3.4   Server and Client Together   727
11.4   select: Wait for I/O Efficiently   728
        11.4.1   Using select()   729
        11.4.2   Non-blocking I/O with Timeouts   734
        11.4.3   Using poll()   737
        11.4.4   Platform-Specific Options   742
11.5   socketserver: Creating Network Servers   742
        11.5.1   Server Types   742
        11.5.2   Server Objects   743
        11.5.3   Implementing a Server   743
        11.5.4   Request Handlers   743
        11.5.5   Echo Example   744
        11.5.6   Threading and Forking   749

Chapter 12 The Internet **753**
12.1   urllib.parse: Split URLs into Components   753
        12.1.1   Parsing   754
        12.1.2   Unparsing   756
        12.1.3   Joining   758
        12.1.4   Encoding Query Arguments   759
12.2   urllib.request: Network Resource Access   761
        12.2.1   HTTP GET   761
        12.2.2   Encoding Arguments   763
        12.2.3   HTTP POST   764
        12.2.4   Adding Outgoing Headers   765
        12.2.5   Posting Form Data from a Request   766
        12.2.6   Uploading Files   767
        12.2.7   Creating Custom Protocol Handlers   770

12.3   urllib.robotparser: Internet Spider Access Control   773
         12.3.1   robots.txt   773
         12.3.2   Testing Access Permissions   774
         12.3.3   Long-Lived Spiders   775
12.4   base64: Encode Binary Data with ASCII   776
         12.4.1   Base 64 Encoding   777
         12.4.2   Base64 Decoding   778
         12.4.3   URL-Safe Variations   778
         12.4.4   Other Encodings   779
12.5   http.server: Base Classes for Implementing Web Servers   781
         12.5.1   HTTP GET   781
         12.5.2   HTTP POST   784
         12.5.3   Threading and Forking   786
         12.5.4   Handling Errors   787
         12.5.5   Setting Headers   788
         12.5.6   Command-Line Use   789
12.6   http.cookies: HTTP Cookies   790
         12.6.1   Creating and Setting a Cookie   790
         12.6.2   Morsels   791
         12.6.3   Encoded Values   793
         12.6.4   Receiving and Parsing Cookie Headers   794
         12.6.5   Alternative Output Formats   795
12.7   webbrowser: Displays Web Pages   796
         12.7.1   Simple Example   796
         12.7.2   Windows Versus Tabs   796
         12.7.3   Using a Specific Browser   796
         12.7.4   BROWSER Variable   797
         12.7.5   Command-Line Interface   797
12.8   uuid: Universally Unique Identifiers   797
         12.8.1   UUID 1: IEEE 802 MAC Address   798
         12.8.2   UUID 3 and 5: Name-Based Values   800
         12.8.3   UUID 4: Random Values   802
         12.8.4   Working with UUID Objects   802
12.9   json: JavaScript Object Notation   803
         12.9.1   Encoding and Decoding Simple Data Types   804
         12.9.2   Human-Consumable Versus Compact Output   805
         12.9.3   Encoding Dictionaries   807
         12.9.4   Working with Custom Types   807
         12.9.5   Encoder and Decoder Classes   810
         12.9.6   Working with Streams and Files   813
         12.9.7   Mixed Data Streams   813
         12.9.8   JSON at the Command Line   815
12.10   xmlrpc.client: Client Library for XML-RPC   816
         12.10.1   Connecting to a Server   817
         12.10.2   Data Types   819

	12.10.3	Passing Objects	822
	12.10.4	Binary Data	823
	12.10.5	Exception Handling	825
	12.10.6	Combining Calls into One Message	826
12.11		xmlrpc.server: An XML-RPC Server	827
	12.11.1	A Simple Server	828
	12.11.2	Alternate API Names	829
	12.11.3	Dotted API Names	830
	12.11.4	Arbitrary API Names	831
	12.11.5	Exposing Methods of Objects	832
	12.11.6	Dispatching Calls	834
	12.11.7	Introspection API	837

Chapter 13 Email **841**

13.1		smtplib: Simple Mail Transfer Protocol Client	841
	13.1.1	Sending an Email Message	841
	13.1.2	Authentication and Encryption	843
	13.1.3	Verifying an Email Address	846
13.2		smtpd: Sample Mail Servers	847
	13.2.1	Mail Server Base Class	847
	13.2.2	Debugging Server	850
	13.2.3	Proxy Server	851
13.3		mailbox: Manipulate Email Archives	852
	13.3.1	mbox	852
	13.3.2	Maildir	855
	13.3.3	Message Flags	862
	13.3.4	Other Formats	864
13.4		imaplib: IMAP4 Client Library	864
	13.4.1	Variations	864
	13.4.2	Connecting to a Server	864
	13.4.3	Example Configuration	866
	13.4.4	Listing Mailboxes	866
	13.4.5	Mailbox Status	869
	13.4.6	Selecting a Mailbox	871
	13.4.7	Searching for Messages	872
	13.4.8	Search Criteria	872
	13.4.9	Fetching Messages	874
	13.4.10	Whole Messages	880
	13.4.11	Uploading Messages	881
	13.4.12	Moving and Copying Messages	883
	13.4.13	Deleting Messages	884

Chapter 14 Application Building Blocks   **887**
14.1   argparse: Command-Line Option and Argument Parsing   888
       14.1.1   Setting Up a Parser   888
       14.1.2   Defining Arguments   888
       14.1.3   Parsing a Command Line   889
       14.1.4   Simple Examples   889
       14.1.5   Help Output   897
       14.1.6   Parser Organization   901
       14.1.7   Advanced Argument Processing   908
14.2   getopt: Command-Line Option Parsing   916
       14.2.1   Function Arguments   916
       14.2.2   Short-Form Options   917
       14.2.3   Long-Form Options   917
       14.2.4   A Complete Example   918
       14.2.5   Abbreviating Long-Form Options   920
       14.2.6   GNU-Style Option Parsing   920
       14.2.7   Ending Argument Processing   922
14.3   readline: The GNU readline Library   922
       14.3.1   Configuring readline   923
       14.3.2   Completing Text   924
       14.3.3   Accessing the Completion Buffer   927
       14.3.4   Input History   931
       14.3.5   Hooks   934
14.4   getpass: Secure Password Prompt   935
       14.4.1   Example   935
       14.4.2   Using getpass Without a Terminal   937
14.5   cmd: Line-Oriented Command Processors   938
       14.5.1   Processing Commands   938
       14.5.2   Command Arguments   940
       14.5.3   Live Help   941
       14.5.4   Auto-Completion   942
       14.5.5   Overriding Base Class Methods   944
       14.5.6   Configuring Cmd Through Attributes   946
       14.5.7   Running Shell Commands   947
       14.5.8   Alternative Inputs   948
       14.5.9   Commands from sys.argv   950
14.6   shlex: Parse Shell-Style Syntaxes   951
       14.6.1   Parsing Quoted Strings   951
       14.6.2   Making Safe Strings for Shells   953
       14.6.3   Embedded Comments   954
       14.6.4   Splitting Strings into Tokens   954
       14.6.5   Including Other Sources of Tokens   955
       14.6.6   Controlling the Parser   956
       14.6.7   Error Handling   957
       14.6.8   POSIX Versus Non-POSIX Parsing   959

14.7   configparser: Work with Configuration Files   960
        14.7.1   Configuration File Format   961
        14.7.2   Reading Configuration Files   961
        14.7.3   Accessing Configuration Settings   963
        14.7.4   Modifying Settings   970
        14.7.5   Saving Configuration Files   972
        14.7.6   Option Search Path   972
        14.7.7   Combining Values with Interpolation   975
14.8   logging: Report Status, Error, and Informational Messages   980
        14.8.1   Logging Components   980
        14.8.2   Logging in Applications Versus Libraries   980
        14.8.3   Logging to a File   981
        14.8.4   Rotating Log Files   981
        14.8.5   Verbosity Levels   982
        14.8.6   Naming Logger Instances   984
        14.8.7   The Logging Tree   984
        14.8.8   Integration with the warnings Module   985
14.9   fileinput: Command-Line Filter Framework   986
        14.9.1   Converting M3U Files to RSS   987
        14.9.2   Progress Metadata   989
        14.9.3   In-Place Filtering   990
14.10   atexit: Program Shutdown Callbacks   993
        14.10.1   Registering Exit Callbacks   993
        14.10.2   Decorator Syntax   994
        14.10.3   Canceling Callbacks   994
        14.10.4   When Are atexit Callbacks Not Called?   995
        14.10.5   Handling Exceptions   997
14.11   sched: Timed Event Scheduler   998
        14.11.1   Running Events with a Delay   999
        14.11.2   Overlapping Events   1000
        14.11.3   Event Priorities   1001
        14.11.4   Canceling Events   1001

Chapter 15 Internationalization and Localization   **1003**
15.1   gettext: Message Catalogs   1003
        15.1.1   Translation Workflow Overview   1003
        15.1.2   Creating Message Catalogs from Source Code   1004
        15.1.3   Finding Message Catalogs at Runtime   1007
        15.1.4   Plural Values   1008
        15.1.5   Application Versus Module Localization   1011
        15.1.6   Switching Translations   1012
15.2   locale: Cultural Localization API   1012
        15.2.1   Probing the Current Locale   1013
        15.2.2   Currency   1018
        15.2.3   Formatting Numbers   1019

        15.2.4   Parsing Numbers   1021
        15.2.5   Dates and Times   1022

Chapter 16 Developer Tools   **1023**
16.1   pydoc: Online Help for Modules   1024
        16.1.1   Plain Text Help   1024
        16.1.2   HTML Help   1025
        16.1.3   Interactive Help   1026
16.2   doctest: Testing Through Documentation   1026
        16.2.1   Getting Started   1026
        16.2.2   Handling Unpredictable Output   1028
        16.2.3   Tracebacks   1032
        16.2.4   Working Around Whitespace   1034
        16.2.5   Test Locations   1039
        16.2.6   External Documentation   1042
        16.2.7   Running Tests   1044
        16.2.8   Test Context   1048
16.3   unittest: Automated Testing Framework   1051
        16.3.1   Basic Test Structure   1051
        16.3.2   Running Tests   1051
        16.3.3   Test Outcomes   1052
        16.3.4   Asserting Truth   1054
        16.3.5   Testing Equality   1054
        16.3.6   Almost Equal?   1055
        16.3.7   Containers   1056
        16.3.8   Testing for Exceptions   1061
        16.3.9   Test Fixtures   1062
        16.3.10 Repeating Tests with Different Inputs   1065
        16.3.11 Skipping Tests   1066
        16.3.12 Ignoring Failing Tests   1068
16.4   trace: Follow Program Flow   1069
        16.4.1   Example Program   1069
        16.4.2   Tracing Execution   1069
        16.4.3   Code Coverage   1070
        16.4.4   Calling Relationships   1073
        16.4.5   Programming Interface   1074
        16.4.6   Saving Result Data   1076
        16.4.7   Options   1077
16.5   traceback: Exceptions and Stack Traces   1078
        16.5.1   Supporting Functions   1079
        16.5.2   Examining the Stack   1079
        16.5.3   TracebackException   1081
        16.5.4   Low-Level Exception APIs   1082
        16.5.5   Low-Level Stack APIs   1086

16.6   cgitb: Detailed Traceback Reports   1089
        16.6.1   Standard Traceback Dumps   1089
        16.6.2   Enabling Detailed Tracebacks   1090
        16.6.3   Local Variables in Tracebacks   1093
        16.6.4   Exception Properties   1096
        16.6.5   HTML Output   1098
        16.6.6   Logging Tracebacks   1098
16.7   pdb: Interactive Debugger   1101
        16.7.1   Starting the Debugger   1101
        16.7.2   Controlling the Debugger   1104
        16.7.3   Breakpoints   1117
        16.7.4   Changing Execution Flow   1129
        16.7.5   Customizing the Debugger with Aliases   1136
        16.7.6   Saving Configuration Settings   1137
16.8   profile and pstats: Performance Analysis   1140
        16.8.1   Running the Profiler   1140
        16.8.2   Running in a Context   1143
        16.8.3   pstats: Saving and Working with Statistics   1144
        16.8.4   Limiting Report Contents   1145
        16.8.5   Caller/Callee Graphs   1146
16.9   timeit: Time the Execution of Small Bits of Python Code   1148
        16.9.1   Module Contents   1148
        16.9.2   Basic Example   1148
        16.9.3   Storing Values in a Dictionary   1149
        16.9.4   From the Command Line   1152
16.10   tabnanny: Indentation Validator   1153
        16.10.1 Running from the Command Line   1153
16.11   compileall: Byte-Compile Source Files   1155
        16.11.1 Compiling One Directory   1155
        16.11.2 Ignoring Files   1156
        16.11.3 Compiling sys.path   1157
        16.11.4 Compiling Individual Files   1157
        16.11.5 From the Command Line   1158
16.12   pyclbr: Class Browser   1160
        16.12.1 Scanning for Classes   1161
        16.12.2 Scanning for Functions   1162
16.13   venv: Create Virtual Environments   1163
        16.13.1 Creating Environments   1163
        16.13.2 Contents of a Virtual Environment   1164
        16.13.3 Using Virtual Environments   1165
16.14   ensurepip: Install the Python Package Installer   1167
        16.14.1 Installing pip   1167

Chapter 17 Runtime Features   **1169**
17.1   site: Site-wide Configuration   1169
    17.1.1   Import Path   1169
    17.1.2   User Directories   1171
    17.1.3   Path Configuration Files   1172
    17.1.4   Customizing Site Configuration   1175
    17.1.5   Customizing User Configuration   1176
    17.1.6   Disabling the site Module   1177
17.2   sys: System-Specific Configuration   1178
    17.2.1   Interpreter Settings   1178
    17.2.2   Runtime Environment   1185
    17.2.3   Memory Management and Limits   1187
    17.2.4   Exception Handling   1194
    17.2.5   Low-Level Thread Support   1197
    17.2.6   Modules and Imports   1200
    17.2.7   Tracing a Program As It Runs   1221
17.3   os: Portable Access to Operating System–Specific Features   1227
    17.3.1   Examining the File System Contents   1228
    17.3.2   Managing File System Permissions   1230
    17.3.3   Creating and Deleting Directories   1233
    17.3.4   Working with Symbolic Links   1234
    17.3.5   Safely Replacing an Existing File   1234
    17.3.6   Detecting and Changing the Process Owner   1235
    17.3.7   Managing the Process Environment   1237
    17.3.8   Managing the Process Working Directory   1238
    17.3.9   Running External Commands   1239
    17.3.10 Creating Processes with os.fork()   1240
    17.3.11 Waiting for Child Processes   1242
    17.3.12 Spawning New Processes   1244
    17.3.13 Operating System Error Codes   1245
17.4   platform: System Version Information   1246
    17.4.1   Interpreter   1246
    17.4.2   Platform   1247
    17.4.3   Operating System and Hardware Information   1248
    17.4.4   Executable Architecture   1250
17.5   resource: System Resource Management   1251
    17.5.1   Current Usage   1251
    17.5.2   Resource Limits   1252
17.6   gc: Garbage Collector   1254
    17.6.1   Tracing References   1255
    17.6.2   Forcing Garbage Collection   1258
    17.6.3   Finding References to Objects That Cannot Be Collected   1259
    17.6.4   Collection Thresholds and Generations   1261
    17.6.5   Debugging   1265

17.7   sysconfig: Interpreter Compile-Time Configuration   1270
    17.7.1   Configuration Variables   1270
    17.7.2   Installation Paths   1272
    17.7.3   Python Version and Platform   1276

Chapter 18 Language Tools   1279
18.1   warnings: Non-fatal Alerts   1279
    18.1.1   Categories and Filtering   1280
    18.1.2   Generating Warnings   1280
    18.1.3   Filtering with Patterns   1281
    18.1.4   Repeated Warnings   1283
    18.1.5   Alternative Message Delivery Functions   1284
    18.1.6   Formatting   1285
    18.1.7   Stack Level in Warnings   1286
18.2   abc: Abstract Base Classes   1287
    18.2.1   How ABCs Work   1287
    18.2.2   Registering a Concrete Class   1287
    18.2.3   Implementation Through Subclassing   1288
    18.2.4   Helper Base Class   1289
    18.2.5   Incomplete Implementations   1290
    18.2.6   Concrete Methods in ABCs   1291
    18.2.7   Abstract Properties   1292
    18.2.8   Abstract Class and Static Methods   1295
18.3   dis: Python Byte-Code Disassembler   1296
    18.3.1   Basic Disassembly   1297
    18.3.2   Disassembling Functions   1297
    18.3.3   Classes   1300
    18.3.4   Source Code   1301
    18.3.5   Using Disassembly to Debug   1302
    18.3.6   Performance Analysis of Loops   1303
    18.3.7   Compiler Optimizations   1309
18.4   inspect: Inspect Live Objects   1311
    18.4.1   Example Module   1311
    18.4.2   Inspecting Modules   1312
    18.4.3   Inspecting Classes   1314
    18.4.4   Inspecting Instances   1316
    18.4.5   Documentation Strings   1316
    18.4.6   Retrieving Source   1318
    18.4.7   Method and Function Signatures   1319
    18.4.8   Class Hierarchies   1322
    18.4.9   Method Resolution Order   1323
    18.4.10   The Stack and Frames   1324
    18.4.11   Command-Line Interface   1327

Chapter 19 Modules and Packages   **1329**
19.1   importlib: Python's Import Mechanism   1329
        19.1.1   Example Package   1329
        19.1.2   Module Types   1330
        19.1.3   Importing Modules   1331
        19.1.4   Loaders   1332
19.2   pkgutil: Package Utilities   1334
        19.2.1   Package Import Paths   1334
        19.2.2   Development Versions of Packages   1336
        19.2.3   Managing Paths with PKG Files   1338
        19.2.4   Nested Packages   1340
        19.2.5   Package Data   1341
19.3   zipimport: Load Python Code from ZIP Archives   1344
        19.3.1   Example   1344
        19.3.2   Finding a Module   1345
        19.3.3   Accessing Code   1345
        19.3.4   Source   1346
        19.3.5   Packages   1348
        19.3.6   Data   1348

Appendix A Porting Notes   **1351**
A.1   References   1351
A.2   New Modules   1352
A.3   Renamed Modules   1352
A.4   Removed Modules   1354
        A.4.1   bsddb   1354
        A.4.2   commands   1354
        A.4.3   compiler   1354
        A.4.4   dircache   1354
        A.4.5   EasyDialogs   1354
        A.4.6   exceptions   1354
        A.4.7   htmllib   1354
        A.4.8   md5   1354
        A.4.9   mimetools, MimeWriter, mimify, multifile, and rfc822   1354
        A.4.10   popen2   1354
        A.4.11   posixfile   1355
        A.4.12   sets   1355
        A.4.13   sha   1355
        A.4.14   sre   1355
        A.4.15   statvfs   1355
        A.4.16   thread   1355
        A.4.17   user   1355
A.5   Deprecated Modules   1355
        A.5.1   asyncore and asynchat   1355
        A.5.2   formatter   1355

Contents

A.5.3	imp		1356
A.5.4	optparse		1356
A.6	Summary of Changes to Modules		1356
A.6.1	abc		1356
A.6.2	anydbm		1356
A.6.3	argparse		1356
A.6.4	array		1357
A.6.5	atexit		1357
A.6.6	base64		1357
A.6.7	bz2		1357
A.6.8	collections		1357
A.6.9	comands		1357
A.6.10	configparser		1358
A.6.11	contextlib		1358
A.6.12	csv		1358
A.6.13	datetime		1358
A.6.14	decimal		1358
A.6.15	fractions		1358
A.6.16	gc		1358
A.6.17	gettext		1359
A.6.18	glob		1359
A.6.19	http.cookies		1359
A.6.20	imaplib		1359
A.6.21	inspect		1359
A.6.22	itertools		1359
A.6.23	json		1359
A.6.24	locale		1359
A.6.25	logging		1360
A.6.26	mailbox		1360
A.6.27	mmap		1360
A.6.28	operator		1360
A.6.29	os		1360
A.6.30	os.path		1361
A.6.31	pdb		1361
A.6.32	pickle		1361
A.6.33	pipes		1362
A.6.34	platform		1362
A.6.35	random		1362
A.6.36	re		1362
A.6.37	shelve		1362
A.6.38	signal		1362
A.6.39	socket		1362
A.6.40	socketserver		1363
A.6.41	string		1363
A.6.42	struct		1363

A.6.43   subprocess   1363
A.6.44   sys   1363
A.6.45   threading   1364
A.6.46   time   1364
A.6.47   unittest   1364
A.6.48   UserDict, UserList, and UserString   1365
A.6.49   uuid   1365
A.6.50   whichdb   1365
A.6.51   xml.etree.ElementTree   1365
A.6.52   zipimport   1365

Appendix B Outside of the Standard Library   **1367**
B.1   Text   1367
B.2   Algorithms   1367
B.3   Dates and Times   1368
B.4   Mathematics   1368
B.5   Data Persistence and Exchange   1368
B.6   Cryptography   1369
B.7   Concurrency with Processes, Threads, and Coroutines   1369
B.8   The Internet   1369
B.9   Email   1370
B.10   Application Building Blocks   1370
B.11   Developer Tools   1371

Index of Python Modules   *1373*

Index   *1375*

Introduction

Distributed with every copy of Python, the standard library contains hundreds of modules that provide tools for interacting with the operating system, interpreter, and Internet—all of them tested and ready to be used to jump-start the development of your applications. This book presents selected examples demonstrating how to use the most commonly used features of the modules that support Python's "batteries included" slogan, taken from the popular *Python Module of the Week* (PyMOTW) blog series.

This Book's Target Audience

The audience for this book consists of intermediate-level Python programmers. Thus, although all of the source code is presented with discussion, only a few cases include line-by-line explanations. Every section focuses on the features of the modules, illustrated by the source code and output from fully independent example programs. Each feature is presented as concisely as possible, so the reader can focus on the module or function being demonstrated without being distracted by the supporting code.

An experienced programmer who is familiar with other languages may be able to learn Python from this book, but the text is not intended to be an introduction to the language. Some prior experience writing Python programs will be useful when studying the examples.

Several sections, such as the description of network programming with sockets or hmac encryption, require domain-specific knowledge. The basic information needed to explain the examples is included here, but the range of topics covered by the modules in the standard library makes it impossible to cover every topic comprehensively in a single volume. The discussion of each module is followed by a list of suggested sources for more information and further reading, including online resources, RFC standards documents, and related books.

Python 3 Versus 2

The Python community is currently undergoing a transition from Python version 2 to Python version 3. As the major version number change implies, there are many incompatibilities between Python 2 and 3, and not just in the language. Quite a few of the standard library modules have been renamed or otherwise reorganized in Python 3.

The Python development community recognized that those incompatibilities would require an extended transition period, while the ecosystem of Python libraries and tools was updated to work with Python 3. Although many projects still rely on Python 2, it is only receiving security updates and is scheduled to be completely deprecated by 2020. All new-feature work is happening in the Python 3 releases.

It can be challenging, though not impossible, to write programs that work with both versions. Doing so often requires examining the version of Python under which a program is running and using different module names for imports or different arguments to classes or functions. A variety of tools, available outside of the standard library, can simplify this process. To keep the examples in this book as concise as possible, while still relying only on the standard library, they are focused on Python 3. All of the examples have been tested under Python 3.5 (the current release of the 3.x series at the time they were written), and may not work with Python 2 without modification. For examples designed to work with Python 2, refer to the Python 2 edition of the book, called *The Python Standard Library by Example*.

In an effort to maintain clear and concise descriptions for each example, the differences between Python 2 and 3 are not highlighted in each chapter. The Porting Notes appendix summarizes some of the biggest differences between these versions, and is organized to be useful as an aid when porting from Python 2 to 3.

How This Book Is Organized

This book supplements the comprehensive reference guide (available at `http://docs.python.org`), providing fully functional example programs to demonstrate the features described there. The modules are grouped into chapters to make it easy to find an individual module for reference and browse by subject for more leisurely exploration. In the unlikely event that you want to read it through from cover to cover, it is organized to minimize "forward references" to modules not yet covered, although it was not possible to eliminate them entirely.

Downloading the Example Code

The original versions of the articles and the sample code are available at `https://pymotw.com/3/`. Errata for the book can be found on the author's website: `https://doughellmann.com/blog/the-python-3-standard-library-by-example/`.

Register your copy of *The Python 3 Standard Library by Example* at informit.com for convenient access to downloads, updates, and corrections as they become available. To start the registration process, go to informit.com/register and log in or create an account. Enter the product ISBN (9780134291055) and click Submit. Once the process is complete, you will find any available bonus content under "Registered Products."

Acknowledgments

This book would not have come into being without the contributions and support of many other people.

I was first introduced to Python around 1997 by Dick Wall, while we were working together on GIS software at ERDAS. I remember being simultaneously happy that I had found a new tool language that was so easy to use, and sad that the company did not let us use it for "real work." I have used Python extensively at all of my subsequent jobs, and I have Dick to thank for the many happy hours I have spent working on software since then.

The Python core development team has created a robust ecosystem of language, tools, and libraries that continue to grow in popularity and find new application areas. Without the continued investment in time and resources they have given us, we would all still be spending our energy reinventing wheel after wheel.

The material in this book started out as a series of blog posts. Without the exceptionally positive response of the readers of the blog, those articles would never have been updated to work with Python 3, and this new book would not exist. Each of those posts has been reviewed and commented on by members of the Python community, with corrections, suggestions, and questions that led to the refinements and improvements that appear in this book. Thank you all for reading along week after week, and contributing your time and attention.

The technical reviewers for the book—Diana Clarke, Ian Cordasco, Mark McClain, Paul McLanahan, and Ryan Petrello—spent many hours looking for issues with the example code and accompanying explanations. Thanks to their diligence, the resulting text is stronger than I could have produced on my own.

Jim Baker provided helpful insight when documenting the `readline` module, especially by pointing out the gnureadline package for platforms where GNU libraries are old or not installed by default.

Patrick Kettner helped to collect the output for the platform module examples on Windows.

A special thanks goes to the editors, production staff, and marketing team at Addison-Wesley for all of their hard work and assistance in helping me realize my vision for this book and make it a success.

Finally, I want to thank my wife, Theresa Flynn, who has gracefully accepted all of the lost nights and weekends over the course of this new project. Thank you for your advice, encouragement, and support.

About the Author

 **Doug Hellmann** is currently employed by Red Hat to work on OpenStack. He is on the OpenStack Technical Committee and contributes to many aspects of the project. He has been programming in Python since version 1.4, and has worked on a variety of Unix and non-Unix platforms for projects in fields such as mapping, medical news publishing, banking, and data center automation. Doug is a Fellow of the Python Software Foundation, and served as its Communications Director from 2010 to 2012. After a year as a regular columnist for *Python Magazine*, he served as Editor-in-Chief from 2008 to 2009. Between 2007 and 2011, Doug published the popular *Python Module of the Week* series on his blog, and an earlier version of this book for Python 2 called *The Python Standard Library by Example*. He lives in Athens, Georgia.

Chapter 1

Text

The `str` class is the most obvious text processing tool available to Python programmers, but there are plenty of other tools in the standard library to make advanced text manipulation simple.

Programs may use `string.Template` as a simple way to parameterize strings beyond the features of `str` objects. While not as feature-rich as templates defined by many of the web frameworks or extension modules available from the Python Package Index, `string.Template` is a good middle ground for user-modifiable templates in which dynamic values need to be inserted into otherwise static text.

The `textwrap` (page 7) module includes tools for formatting text from paragraphs by limiting the width of output, adding indentation, and inserting line breaks to wrap lines consistently.

The standard library includes two modules for comparing text values that go beyond the built-in equality and sort comparison supported by string objects. `re` (page 13) provides a complete regular expression library, implemented in C for speed. Regular expressions are well suited for finding substrings within a larger data set, comparing strings against a pattern more complex than another fixed string, and mild parsing.

`difflib` (page 58), in contrast, computes the actual differences between sequences of text in terms of the parts added, removed, or changed. The output of the comparison functions in `difflib` can be used to provide more detailed feedback to the user about where changes occur in two inputs, how a document has changed over time, and so on.

1.1 string: Text Constants and Templates

The `string` module dates from the earliest versions of Python. Many of the functions previously implemented in the module have been moved to methods of `str` objects, but the module retains several useful constants and classes for working with `str` objects. This discussion will concentrate on them.

1.1.1 Functions

The function `capwords()` capitalizes all of the words in a string.

Listing 1.1: **string_capwords.py**

```
import string

s = 'The quick brown fox jumped over the lazy dog.'
```

```
print(s)
print(string.capwords(s))
```

The results are the same as those obtained by calling `split()`, capitalizing the words in the resulting list, and then calling `join()` to combine the results.

```
$ python3 string_capwords.py

The quick brown fox jumped over the lazy dog.
The Quick Brown Fox Jumped Over The Lazy Dog.
```

1.1.2 Templates

String templates were added as part of **PEP 292**[1] and are intended as an alternative to the built-in interpolation syntax. With `string.Template` interpolation, variables are identified by prefixing the name with $ (e.g., $var). Alternatively, if necessary to set them off from surrounding text, they can be wrapped with curly braces (e.g., ${var}).

This example compares a simple template with similar string interpolation using the % operator and the new format string syntax using `str.format()`.

Listing 1.2: **string_template.py**

```
import string

values = {'var': 'foo'}

t = string.Template("""
Variable         : $var
Escape           : $$
Variable in text: ${var}iable
""")

print('TEMPLATE:', t.substitute(values))

s = """
Variable         : %(var)s
Escape           : %%
Variable in text: %(var)siable
"""

print('INTERPOLATION:', s % values)

s = """
Variable         : {var}
Escape           : {{}}
```

---

[1] www.python.org/dev/peps/pep-0292

```
Variable in text: {var}iable
"""

print('FORMAT:', s.format(**values))
```

In the first two cases, the trigger character ($ or %) is escaped by repeating it twice. For the format syntax, both { and } need to be escaped by repeating them.

```
$ python3 string_template.py

TEMPLATE:
Variable          : foo
Escape            : $
Variable in text: fooiable

INTERPOLATION:
Variable          : foo
Escape            : %
Variable in text: fooiable

FORMAT:
Variable          : foo
Escape            : {}
Variable in text: fooiable
```

One key difference between templates and string interpolation or formatting is that the type of the arguments is not taken into account. The values are converted to strings, and the strings are inserted into the result. No formatting options are available. For example, there is no way to control the number of digits used to represent a floating-point value.

A benefit, though, is that use of the safe_substitute() method makes it possible to avoid exceptions if not all of the values needed by the template are provided as arguments.

Listing 1.3: string_template_missing.py

```
import string

values = {'var': 'foo'}

t = string.Template("$var is here but $missing is not provided")

try:
    print('substitute()      :', t.substitute(values))
except KeyError as err:
    print('ERROR:', str(err))

print('safe_substitute():', t.safe_substitute(values))
```

Since there is no value for `missing` in the values dictionary, a `KeyError` is raised by `substitute()`. Instead of raising the error, `safe_substitute()` catches it and leaves the variable expression alone in the text.

```
$ python3 string_template_missing.py

ERROR: 'missing'
safe_substitute(): foo is here but $missing is not provided
```

1.1.3   Advanced Templates

The default syntax for `string.Template` can be changed by adjusting the regular expression patterns it uses to find the variable names in the template body. A simple way to do that is to change the `delimiter` and `idpattern` class attributes.

Listing 1.4: **string_template_advanced.py**

```python
import string


class MyTemplate(string.Template):
    delimiter = '%'
    idpattern = '[a-z]+_[a-z]+'


template_text = '''
  Delimiter : %%
  Replaced  : %with_underscore
  Ignored   : %notunderscored
'''

d = {
    'with_underscore': 'replaced',
    'notunderscored': 'not replaced',
}

t = MyTemplate(template_text)
print('Modified ID pattern:')
print(t.safe_substitute(d))
```

In this example, the substitution rules are changed so that the delimiter is `%` instead of `$` and variable names must include an underscore somewhere in the middle. The pattern `%notunderscored` is not replaced by anything, because it does not include an underscore character.

```
$ python3 string_template_advanced.py

Modified ID pattern:
```

```
Delimiter : %
Replaced  : replaced
Ignored   : %notunderscored
```

For even more complex changes, it is possible to override the `pattern` attribute and define an entirely new regular expression. The pattern provided must contain four named groups for capturing the escaped delimiter, the named variable, a braced version of the variable name, and invalid delimiter patterns.

Listing 1.5: string_template_defaultpattern.py

```python
import string

t = string.Template('$var')
print(t.pattern.pattern)
```

The value of `t.pattern` is a compiled regular expression, but the original string is available via its `pattern` attribute.

```
\$(?:
  (?P<escaped>\$) |              # Two delimiters
  (?P<named>[_a-z][_a-z0-9]*)   | # Identifier
  {(?P<braced>[_a-z][_a-z0-9]*)} | # Braced identifier
  (?P<invalid>)                  # Ill-formed delimiter exprs
)
```

This example defines a new pattern to create a new type of template, using `{{var}}` as the variable syntax.

Listing 1.6: string_template_newsyntax.py

```python
import re
import string


class MyTemplate(string.Template):
    delimiter = '{{'
    pattern = r'''
    \{\{(?:
    (?P<escaped>\{\{)|
    (?P<named>[_a-z][_a-z0-9]*)\}\}|
    (?P<braced>[_a-z][_a-z0-9]*)\}\}|
    (?P<invalid>)
    )
    '''


t = MyTemplate('''
{{{{
```

```
{{var}}
''')

print('MATCHES:', t.pattern.findall(t.template))
print('SUBSTITUTED:', t.safe_substitute(var='replacement'))
```

Both the `named` and `braced` patterns must be provided separately, even though they are the same. Running the sample program generates the following output:

```
$ python3 string_template_newsyntax.py

MATCHES: [('{{', '', '', ''), ('', 'var', '', '')]
SUBSTITUTED:
{{
replacement
```

1.1.4 Formatter

The `Formatter` class implements the same layout specification language as the `format()` method of `str`. Its features include type coercion, alignment, attribute and field references, named and positional template arguments, and type-specific formatting options. Most of the time the `format()` method is a more convenient interface to these features, but `Formatter` is provided as a way to build subclasses, for cases where variations are needed.

1.1.5 Constants

The `string` module includes a number of constants related to ASCII and numerical character sets.

Listing 1.7: **string_constants.py**

```
import inspect
import string


def is_str(value):
    return isinstance(value, str)


for name, value in inspect.getmembers(string, is_str):
    if name.startswith('_'):
        continue
    print('%s=%r\n' % (name, value))
```

These constants are useful when working with ASCII data, but since it is increasingly common to encounter non-ASCII text in some form of Unicode, their application is limited.

```
$ python3 string_constants.py

ascii_letters='abcdefghijklmnopqrstuvwxyzABCDEFGHIJKLMNOPQRSTUVW
XYZ'

ascii_lowercase='abcdefghijklmnopqrstuvwxyz'

ascii_uppercase='ABCDEFGHIJKLMNOPQRSTUVWXYZ'

digits='0123456789'

hexdigits='0123456789abcdefABCDEF'

octdigits='01234567'

printable='0123456789abcdefghijklmnopqrstuvwxyzABCDEFGHIJKLMNOPQ
RSTUVWXYZ!"#$%&\'()*+,-./:;<=>?@[\\]^_`{|}~ \t\n\r\x0b\x0c'

punctuation='!"#$%&\'()*+,-./:;<=>?@[\\]^_`{|}~'

whitespace=' \t\n\r\x0b\x0c'
```

TIP

Related Reading

- Standard library documentation for `string`.[2]
- String Methods[3]: Methods of `str` objects that replace the deprecated functions in `string`.
- **PEP 292**[4]: Simpler String Substitutions.
- Format String Syntax[5]: The formal definition of the layout specification language used by Formatter and `str.format()`.

1.2   textwrap: Formatting Text Paragraphs

The `textwrap` module can be used to format text for output in situations where pretty-printing is desired. It offers programmatic functionality similar to the paragraph wrapping or filling features found in many text editors and word processors.

---

[2] https://docs.python.org/3.5/library/string.html
[3] https://docs.python.org/3/library/stdtypes.html#string-methods
[4] www.python.org/dev/peps/pep-0292
[5] https://docs.python.org/3.5/library/string.html#format-string-syntax

1.2.1   Example Data

The examples in this section use the module `textwrap_example.py`, which contains a string
`sample_text`.

Listing 1.8: **textwrap_example.py**

```
sample_text = '''
    The textwrap module can be used to format text for output in
    situations where pretty-printing is desired.  It offers
    programmatic functionality similar to the paragraph wrapping
    or filling features found in many text editors.
    '''
```

1.2.2   Filling Paragraphs

The `fill()` function takes text as input and produces formatted text as output.

Listing 1.9: **textwrap_fill.py**

```
import textwrap
from textwrap_example import sample_text

print(textwrap.fill(sample_text, width=50))
```

The results are something less than desirable. The text is now left justified, but the first
line retains its indent and the spaces from the front of each subsequent line are embedded
in the paragraph.

```
$ python3 textwrap_fill.py

    The textwrap module can be used to format
text for output in     situations where pretty-
printing is desired.  It offers      programmatic
functionality similar to the paragraph wrapping
or filling features found in many text editors.
```

1.2.3   Removing Existing Indentation

The previous example has embedded tabs and extra spaces mixed into the middle of the
output, so it is not formatted very cleanly. Removing the common whitespace prefix from
all of the lines in the sample text with `dedent()` produces better results and allows the use
of docstrings or embedded multiline strings straight from Python code while removing the
formatting of the code itself. The sample string has an artificial indent level introduced for
illustrating this feature.

Listing 1.10: textwrap_dedent.py

```
import textwrap
from textwrap_example import sample_text

dedented_text = textwrap.dedent(sample_text)
print('Dedented:')
print(dedented_text)
```

The results are starting to look better.

```
$ python3 textwrap_dedent.py

Dedented:

The textwrap module can be used to format text for output in
situations where pretty-printing is desired.  It offers
programmatic functionality similar to the paragraph wrapping
or filling features found in many text editors.
```

Since "dedent" is the opposite of "indent," the result is a block of text with the common initial whitespace from each line removed. If one line is already indented more than another, some of the whitespace will not be removed.

Input like

```
 Line one.
   Line two.
 Line three.
```

becomes

```
Line one.
  Line two.
Line three.
```

1.2.4 Combining Dedent and Fill

Next, the dedented text can be passed through fill() with a few different width values.

Listing 1.11: textwrap_fill_width.py

```
import textwrap
from textwrap_example import sample_text

dedented_text = textwrap.dedent(sample_text).strip()
for width in [45, 60]:
    print('{} Columns:\n'.format(width))
```

```
        print(textwrap.fill(dedented_text, width=width))
        print()
```

This produces outputs in the specified widths.

```
$ python3 textwrap_fill_width.py

45 Columns:

The textwrap module can be used to format
text for output in situations where pretty-
printing is desired.  It offers programmatic
functionality similar to the paragraph
wrapping or filling features found in many
text editors.

60 Columns:

The textwrap module can be used to format text for output in
situations where pretty-printing is desired.  It offers
programmatic functionality similar to the paragraph wrapping
or filling features found in many text editors.
```

1.2.5   Indenting Blocks

Use the indent() function to add consistent prefix text to all of the lines in a string. This
example formats the same example text as though it was part of an email message being
quoted in the reply, using > as the prefix for each line.

Listing 1.12: **textwrap_indent.py**

```
import textwrap
from textwrap_example import sample_text

dedented_text = textwrap.dedent(sample_text)
wrapped = textwrap.fill(dedented_text, width=50)
wrapped += '\n\nSecond paragraph after a blank line.'
final = textwrap.indent(wrapped, '> ')

print('Quoted block:\n')
print(final)
```

The block of text is split on newlines, the prefix is added to each line that contains text,
and then the lines are combined back into a new string and returned.

```
$ python3 textwrap_indent.py

Quoted block:
```

```
>   The textwrap module can be used to format text
> for output in situations where pretty-printing is
> desired.  It offers programmatic functionality
> similar to the paragraph wrapping or filling
> features found in many text editors.

> Second paragraph after a blank line.
```

To control which lines receive the new prefix, pass a callable as the predicate argument to indent(). The callable will be invoked for each line of text in turn and the prefix will be added for lines where the return value is true.

Listing 1.13: **textwrap_indent_predicate.py**

```python
import textwrap
from textwrap_example import sample_text


def should_indent(line):
    print('Indent {!r}?'.format(line))
    return len(line.strip()) % 2 == 0


dedented_text = textwrap.dedent(sample_text)
wrapped = textwrap.fill(dedented_text, width=50)
final = textwrap.indent(wrapped, 'EVEN ',
                        predicate=should_indent)

print('\nQuoted block:\n')
print(final)
```

This example adds the prefix EVEN to lines that contain an even number of characters.

```
$ python3 textwrap_indent_predicate.py

Indent ' The textwrap module can be used to format text\n'?
Indent 'for output in situations where pretty-printing is\n'?
Indent 'desired.  It offers programmatic functionality\n'?
Indent 'similar to the paragraph wrapping or filling\n'?
Indent 'features found in many text editors.'?

Quoted block:

EVEN  The textwrap module can be used to format text
for output in situations where pretty-printing is
EVEN desired.  It offers programmatic functionality
EVEN similar to the paragraph wrapping or filling
EVEN features found in many text editors.
```

1.2.6   Hanging Indents

In the same way that it is possible to set the width of the output, the indent of the first
line can be controlled independently of subsequent lines.

Listing 1.14: textwrap_hanging_indent.py

```
import textwrap
from textwrap_example import sample_text

dedented_text = textwrap.dedent(sample_text).strip()
print(textwrap.fill(dedented_text,
                    initial_indent='',
                    subsequent_indent=' ' * 4,
                    width=50,
                    ))
```

This ability makes it possible to produce a hanging indent, where the first line is indented
less than the other lines.

```
$ python3 textwrap_hanging_indent.py

The textwrap module can be used to format text for
    output in situations where pretty-printing is
    desired.  It offers programmatic functionality
    similar to the paragraph wrapping or filling
    features found in many text editors.
```

The indent values can include non-whitespace characters, too. The hanging indent can be
prefixed with * to produce bullet points, for example.

1.2.7   Truncating Long Text

To truncate text to create a summary or preview, use shorten(). All existing whitespace,
such as tabs, newlines, and series of multiple spaces, will be standardized to a single space.
Then the text will be truncated to a length less than or equal to what is requested, between
word boundaries so that no partial words are included.

Listing 1.15: textwrap_shorten.py

```
import textwrap
from textwrap_example import sample_text

dedented_text = textwrap.dedent(sample_text)
original = textwrap.fill(dedented_text, width=50)

print('Original:\n')
print(original)
```

```
shortened = textwrap.shorten(original, 100)
shortened_wrapped = textwrap.fill(shortened, width=50)

print('\nShortened:\n')
print(shortened_wrapped)
```

If non-whitespace text is removed from the original text as part of the truncation, it is replaced with a placeholder value. The default value [...] can be replaced by providing a placeholder argument to shorten().

```
$ python3 textwrap_shorten.py

Original:

 The textwrap module can be used to format text
for output in situations where pretty-printing is
desired.  It offers programmatic functionality
similar to the paragraph wrapping or filling
features found in many text editors.

Shortened:

The textwrap module can be used to format text for
output in situations where pretty-printing [...]
```

TIP

Related Reading

- Standard library documentation for textwrap.[6]

1.3   re: Regular Expressions

Regular expressions are text matching patterns described with a formal syntax. The patterns are interpreted as a set of instructions, which are then executed with a string as input to produce a matching subset or modified version of the original. The term "regular expressions" is frequently shortened to "regex" or "regexp" in conversation. Expressions can include literal text matching, repetition, pattern composition, branching, and other sophisticated rules. A large number of parsing problems are easier to solve with a regular expression than by creating a special-purpose lexer and parser.

---

[6] https://docs.python.org/3.5/library/textwrap.html

Regular expressions are typically used in applications that involve a lot of text processing. For example, they are commonly used as search patterns in text editing programs used by developers, including vi, emacs, and modern IDEs. They are also an integral part of Unix command-line utilities such as sed, grep, and awk. Many programming languages include support for regular expressions in the language syntax (Perl, Ruby, Awk, and Tcl). Other languages, such as C, C++, and Python, support regular expressions through extension libraries.

Multiple open source implementations of regular expressions exist, each sharing a common core syntax but with different extensions or modifications to their advanced features. The syntax used in Python's re module is based on the syntax used for regular expressions in Perl, with a few Python-specific enhancements.

NOTE

Although the formal definition of "regular expression" is limited to expressions that describe regular languages, some of the extensions supported by re go beyond describing regular languages. The term "regular expression" is used here in a more general sense to mean any expression that can be evaluated by Python's re module.

1.3.1 Finding Patterns in Text

The most common use for re is to search for patterns in text. The search() function takes the pattern and text to scan, and returns a Match object when the pattern is found. If the pattern is not found, search() returns None.

Each Match object holds information about the nature of the match, including the original input string, the regular expression used, and the location within the original string where the pattern occurs.

Listing 1.16: re_simple_match.py

```
import re

pattern = 'this'
text = 'Does this text match the pattern?'

match = re.search(pattern, text)

s = match.start()
e = match.end()

print('Found "{}"\nin "{}"\nfrom {} to {} ("{}")'.format(
    match.re.pattern, match.string, s, e, text[s:e]))
```

The start() and end() methods give the indexes into the string showing where the text matched by the pattern occurs.

```
$ python3 re_simple_match.py

Found "this"
in "Does this text match the pattern?"
from 5 to 9 ("this")
```

1.3.2 Compiling Expressions

Although re includes module-level functions for working with regular expressions as text strings, it is more efficient to *compile* the expressions a program uses frequently. The compile() function converts an expression string into a RegexObject.

Listing 1.17: **re_simple_compiled.py**

```
import re

# Precompile the patterns.
regexes = [
    re.compile(p)
    for p in ['this', 'that']
]
text = 'Does this text match the pattern?'

print('Text: {!r}\n'.format(text))

for regex in regexes:
    print('Seeking "{}" ->'.format(regex.pattern),
            end=' ')

    if regex.search(text):
        print('match!')
    else:
        print('no match')
```

The module-level functions maintain a cache of compiled expressions, but the size of the cache is limited and using compiled expressions directly avoids the overhead associated with cache lookup. Another advantage of using compiled expressions is that by precompiling all of the expressions when the module is loaded, the compilation work is shifted to application start time, instead of occurring at a point where the program may be responding to a user action.

```
$ python3 re_simple_compiled.py

Text: 'Does this text match the pattern?'

Seeking "this" -> match!
Seeking "that" -> no match
```

1.3.3 Multiple Matches

So far, the example patterns have all used `search()` to look for single instances of literal text strings. The `findall()` function returns all of the substrings of the input that match the pattern without overlapping.

Listing 1.18: re_findall.py

```
import re

text = 'abbaaabbbbaaaaa'

pattern = 'ab'

for match in re.findall(pattern, text):
    print('Found {!r}'.format(match))
```

There are two instances of `ab` in the input string.

```
$ python3 re_findall.py

Found 'ab'
Found 'ab'
```

`finditer()` returns an iterator that produces `Match` instances instead of the strings returned by `findall()`.

Listing 1.19: re_finditer.py

```
import re

text = 'abbaaabbbbaaaaa'

pattern = 'ab'

for match in re.finditer(pattern, text):
    s = match.start()
    e = match.end()
    print('Found {!r} at {:d}:{:d}'.format(
        text[s:e], s, e))
```

This example finds the same two occurrences of `ab`, and the `Match` instance shows where they are found in the original input.

```
$ python3 re_finditer.py

Found 'ab' at 0:2
Found 'ab' at 5:7
```

1.3.4   Pattern Syntax

Regular expressions support more powerful patterns than simple literal text strings. Patterns can repeat, can be anchored to different logical locations within the input, and can be expressed in compact forms that do not require every literal character to be present in the pattern. All of these features are used by combining literal text values with *meta-characters* that are part of the regular expression pattern syntax implemented by re.

Listing 1.20: re_test_patterns.py

```python
import re


def test_patterns(text, patterns):
    """Given source text and a list of patterns, look for
    matches for each pattern within the text and print
    them to stdout.
    """
    # Look for each pattern in the text and print the results.
    for pattern, desc in patterns:
        print("'{}' ({})\n".format(pattern, desc))
        print("  '{}'".format(text))
        for match in re.finditer(pattern, text):
            s = match.start()
            e = match.end()
            substr = text[s:e]
            n_backslashes = text[:s].count('\\')
            prefix = '.' * (s + n_backslashes)
            print("  {}'{}'".format(prefix, substr))
        print()
    return


if __name__ == '__main__':
    test_patterns('abbaaabbbbaaaaa',
                  [('ab', "'a' followed by 'b'"),
                   ])
```

The following examples use test_patterns() to explore how variations in patterns change the way they match the same input text. The output shows the input text and the substring range from each portion of the input that matches the pattern.

```
$ python3 re_test_patterns.py

'ab' ('a' followed by 'b')

  'abbaaabbbbaaaaa'
  'ab'
  .....'ab'
```

1.3.4.1   Repetition

There are five ways to express repetition in a pattern. A pattern followed by the meta-character * is repeated zero or more times (allowing a pattern to repeat zero times means it does not need to appear at all to match). If the * is replaced with +, the pattern must appear at least once. Using ? means the pattern appears zero or one time. For a specific number of occurrences, use {m} after the pattern, where m is the number of times the pattern should repeat. Finally, to allow a variable but limited number of repetitions, use {m,n}, where m is the minimum number of repetitions and n is the maximum. Leaving out n ({m,}) means the value must appear at least m times, with no maximum.

Listing 1.21: `re_repetition.py`

```
from re_test_patterns import test_patterns

test_patterns(
    'abbaabbba',
    [('ab*', 'a followed by zero or more b'),
     ('ab+', 'a followed by one or more b'),
     ('ab?', 'a followed by zero or one b'),
     ('ab{3}', 'a followed by three b'),
     ('ab{2,3}', 'a followed by two to three b')],
)
```

In this example, there are more matches for ab* and ab? than ab+.

```
$ python3 re_repetition.py

'ab*' (a followed by zero or more b)

  'abbaabbba'
  'abb'
  ...'a'
  ....'abbb'
  ........'a'

'ab+' (a followed by one or more b)

  'abbaabbba'
  'abb'
  ....'abbb'

'ab?' (a followed by zero or one b)

  'abbaabbba'
  'ab'
  ...'a'
  ....'ab'
  ........'a'
```

```
'ab{3}' (a followed by three b)

  'abbaabbba'
  ....'abbb'

'ab{2,3}' (a followed by two to three b)

  'abbaabbba'
  'abb'
  ....'abbb'
```

When processing a repetition instruction, re will usually consume as much of the input as possible while matching the pattern. This so-called *greedy* behavior may result in fewer individual matches, or the matches may include more of the input text than intended. Greediness can be turned off by following the repetition instruction with ?.

Listing 1.22: re_repetition_non_greedy.py

```python
from re_test_patterns import test_patterns

test_patterns(
    'abbaabbba',
    [('ab*?', 'a followed by zero or more b'),
     ('ab+?', 'a followed by one or more b'),
     ('ab??', 'a followed by zero or one b'),
     ('ab{3}?', 'a followed by three b'),
     ('ab{2,3}?', 'a followed by two to three b')],
)
```

Disabling greedy consumption of the input for any of the patterns where zero occurrences of b are allowed means the matched substring does not include any b characters.

```
$ python3 re_repetition_non_greedy.py

'ab*?' (a followed by zero or more b)

  'abbaabbba'
  'a'
  ...'a'
  ....'a'
  ........'a'

'ab+?' (a followed by one or more b)

  'abbaabbba'
  'ab'
  ....'ab'

'ab??' (a followed by zero or one b)
```

```
'abbaabbba'
'a'
...'a'
....'a'
........'a'
```

```
'ab{3}?' (a followed by three b)
```

```
'abbaabbba'
....'abbb'
```

```
'ab{2,3}?' (a followed by two to three b)
```

```
'abbaabbba'
'abb'
....'abb'
```

1.3.4.2 Character Sets

A *character set* is a group of characters, any one of which can match at that point in the pattern. For example, [ab] would match either a or b.

Listing 1.23: re_charset.py

```python
from re_test_patterns import test_patterns

test_patterns(
    'abbaabbba',
    [('[ab]', 'either a or b'),
     ('a[ab]+', 'a followed by 1 or more a or b'),
     ('a[ab]+?', 'a followed by 1 or more a or b, not greedy')],
)
```

The greedy form of the expression (a[ab]+) consumes the entire string because the first letter is a and every subsequent character is either a or b.

```
$ python3 re_charset.py

'[ab]' (either a or b)

'abbaabbba'
'a'
.'b'
..'b'
...'a'
....'a'
.....'b'
```

```
......'b'
.......'b'
........'a'
```

'a[ab]+' (a followed by 1 or more a or b)

```
'abbaabbba'
'abbaabbba'
```

'a[ab]+?' (a followed by 1 or more a or b, not greedy)

```
'abbaabbba'
'ab'
...'aa'
```

A character set can also be used to exclude specific characters. The carat (^) means to look for characters that are not in the set following the carat.

Listing 1.24: `re_charset_exclude.py`

```
from re_test_patterns import test_patterns

test_patterns(
    'This is some text -- with punctuation.',
    [('[^-. ]+', 'sequences without -, ., or space')],
)
```

This pattern finds all of the substrings that do not contain the characters -, ., or a space.

```
$ python3 re_charset_exclude.py

'[^-. ]+' (sequences without -, ., or space)

  'This is some text -- with punctuation.'
  'This'
  .....'is'
  ........'some'
  ............'text'
  ....................'with'
  ........................'punctuation'
```

As character sets grow larger, typing every character that should (or should not) match becomes tedious. A more compact format using *character ranges* can be used to define a character set to include all of the contiguous characters between the specified start and stop points.

Listing 1.25: `re_charset_ranges.py`

```
from re_test_patterns import test_patterns

test_patterns(
    'This is some text -- with punctuation.',
    [('[a-z]+', 'sequences of lowercase letters'),
     ('[A-Z]+', 'sequences of uppercase letters'),
     ('[a-zA-Z]+', 'sequences of lower- or uppercase letters'),
     ('[A-Z][a-z]+', 'one uppercase followed by lowercase')],
)
```

Here the range a-z includes the lowercase ASCII letters, and the range A-Z includes the uppercase ASCII letters. The ranges can also be combined into a single character set.

```
$ python3 re_charset_ranges.py

'[a-z]+' (sequences of lowercase letters)

  'This is some text -- with punctuation.'
  .'his'
  .....'is'
  ........'some'
  ............'text'
  ....................'with'
  ........................'punctuation'

'[A-Z]+' (sequences of uppercase letters)

  'This is some text -- with punctuation.'
  'T'

'[a-zA-Z]+' (sequences of lower- or uppercase letters)

  'This is some text -- with punctuation.'
  'This'
  .....'is'
  ........'some'
  ............'text'
  ....................'with'
  ........................'punctuation'

'[A-Z][a-z]+' (one uppercase followed by lowercase)

  'This is some text -- with punctuation.'
  'This'
```

As a special case of a character set, the meta-character dot, or period (.), indicates that the pattern should match any single character in that position.

Listing 1.26: `re_charset_dot.py`

```
from re_test_patterns import test_patterns

test_patterns(
    'abbaabbba',
    [('a.', 'a followed by any one character'),
     ('b.', 'b followed by any one character'),
     ('a.*b', 'a followed by anything, ending in b'),
     ('a.*?b', 'a followed by anything, ending in b')],
)
```

Combining the dot with repetition can result in very long matches, unless the non-greedy form is used.

```
$ python3 re_charset_dot.py

'a.' (a followed by any one character)

  'abbaabbba'
  'ab'
  ...'aa'

'b.' (b followed by any one character)

  'abbaabbba'
  .'bb'
  .....'bb'
  .......'ba'

'a.*b' (a followed by anything, ending in b)

  'abbaabbba'
  'abbaabbb'

'a.*?b' (a followed by anything, ending in b)

  'abbaabbba'
  'ab'
  ...'aab'
```

1.3.4.3   Escape Codes

An even more compact representation uses escape codes for several predefined character sets. The escape codes recognized by re are listed in Table 1.1.

Table 1.1: Regular Expression Escape Codes

Code	Meaning
\d	A digit
\D	A non-digit
\s	Whitespace (tab, space, newline, etc.)
\S	Non-whitespace
\w	Alphanumeric
\W	Non-alphanumeric

NOTE

Escapes are indicated by prefixing the character with a backslash (\). Unfortunately, a backslash must itself be escaped in normal Python strings, and that results in difficult-to-read expressions. Using *raw* strings, which are created by prefixing the literal value with r, eliminates this problem and maintains readability.

Listing 1.27: re_escape_codes.py

```
from re_test_patterns import test_patterns

test_patterns(
    'A prime #1 example!',
    [(r'\d+', 'sequence of digits'),
     (r'\D+', 'sequence of non-digits'),
     (r'\s+', 'sequence of whitespace'),
     (r'\S+', 'sequence of non-whitespace'),
     (r'\w+', 'alphanumeric characters'),
     (r'\W+', 'non-alphanumeric')],
)
```

These sample expressions combine escape codes with repetition to find sequences of like characters in the input string.

```
$ python3 re_escape_codes.py

'\d+' (sequence of digits)

  'A prime #1 example!'
  .........'1'

'\D+' (sequence of non-digits)

  'A prime #1 example!'
  'A prime #'
  .........' example!'
```

```
'\s+' (sequence of whitespace)

  'A prime #1 example!'
  .' '
  .......' '
  ..........' '

'\S+' (sequence of non-whitespace)

  'A prime #1 example!'
  'A'
  ..'prime'
  ........'#1'
  ...........'example!'

'\w+' (alphanumeric characters)

  'A prime #1 example!'
  'A'
  ..'prime'
  .........'1'
  ...........'example'

'\W+' (non-alphanumeric)

  'A prime #1 example!'
  .' '
  .......' #'
  ..........' '
  .................'!'
```

To match the characters that are part of the regular expression syntax, escape the characters in the search pattern.

Listing 1.28: re_escape_escapes.py

```python
from re_test_patterns import test_patterns

test_patterns(
    r'\d+ \D+ \s+',
    [(r'\\.\+', 'escape code')],
)
```

The pattern in this example escapes the backslash and plus characters, since both are meta-characters and have special meaning in a regular expression.

```
$ python3 re_escape_escapes.py

'\\.\+' (escape code)

  '\d+ \D+ \s+'
  '\d+'
  .....'\D+'
  ..........'\s+'
```

1.3.4.4   Anchoring

In addition to describing the content of a pattern to match, the relative location can be
specified in the input text where the pattern should appear by using *anchoring* instructions.
Table 1.2 lists valid anchoring codes.

Listing 1.29: `re_anchoring.py`

```
from re_test_patterns import test_patterns

test_patterns(
    'This is some text -- with punctuation.',
    [(r'^\w+', 'word at start of string'),
     (r'\A\w+', 'word at start of string'),
     (r'\w+\S*$', 'word near end of string'),
     (r'\w+\S*\Z', 'word near end of string'),
     (r'\w*t\w*', 'word containing t'),
     (r'\bt\w+', 't at start of word'),
     (r'\w+t\b', 't at end of word'),
     (r'\Bt\B', 't, not start or end of word')],
)
```

The patterns in the example for matching words at the beginning and the end of the
string are different because the word at the end of the string is followed by punctuation
to terminate the sentence. The pattern \w+$ would not match, since . is not considered an
alphanumeric character.

Table 1.2: Regular Expression Anchoring Codes

Code	Meaning
^	Start of string, or line
$	End of string, or line
\A	Start of string
\Z	End of string
\b	Empty string at the beginning or end of a word
\B	Empty string not at the beginning or end of a word

```
$ python3 re_anchoring.py

'^\w+' (word at start of string)

   'This is some text -- with punctuation.'
   'This'

'\A\w+' (word at start of string)

   'This is some text -- with punctuation.'
   'This'

'\w+\S*$' (word near end of string)

   'This is some text -- with punctuation.'
   .........................'punctuation.'

'\w+\S*\Z' (word near end of string)

   'This is some text -- with punctuation.'
   .........................'punctuation.'

'\w*t\w*' (word containing t)

   'This is some text -- with punctuation.'
   .............'text'
   ...................'with'
   ........................'punctuation'

'\bt\w+' (t at start of word)

   'This is some text -- with punctuation.'
   .............'text'

'\w+t\b' (t at end of word)

   'This is some text -- with punctuation.'
   .............'text'

'\Bt\B' (t, not start or end of word)

   'This is some text -- with punctuation.'
   ......................'t'
   ............................'t'
   ...............................'t'
```

1.3.5   Constraining the Search

In situations where it is known in advance that only a subset of the full input should be searched, the regular expression match can be further constrained by telling re to limit the search range. For example, if the pattern must appear at the front of the input, then using `match()` instead of `search()` will anchor the search without having to explicitly include an anchor in the search pattern.

Listing 1.30: re_match.py

```
import re

text = 'This is some text -- with punctuation.'
pattern = 'is'

print('Text    :', text)
print('Pattern:', pattern)

m = re.match(pattern, text)
print('Match   :', m)
s = re.search(pattern, text)
print('Search  :', s)
```

Since the literal text is does not appear at the start of the input text, it is not found using `match()`. The sequence appears two other times in the text, though, so `search()` finds it.

```
$ python3 re_match.py

Text    : This is some text -- with punctuation.
Pattern: is
Match   : None
Search  : <_sre.SRE_Match object; span=(2, 4), match='is'>
```

The `fullmatch()` method requires that the entire input string match the pattern.

Listing 1.31: re_fullmatch.py

```
import re

text = 'This is some text -- with punctuation.'
pattern = 'is'

print('Text       :', text)
print('Pattern    :', pattern)

m = re.search(pattern, text)
print('Search     :', m)
```

```
s = re.fullmatch(pattern, text)
print('Full match :', s)
```

Here search() shows that the pattern does appear in the input, but it does not consume all of the input so fullmatch() does not report a match.

```
$ python3 re_fullmatch.py

Text        : This is some text -- with punctuation.
Pattern     : is
Search      : <_sre.SRE_Match object; span=(2, 4), match='is'>
Full match : None
```

The search() method of a compiled regular expression accepts optional start and end position parameters to limit the search to a substring of the input.

Listing 1.32: **re_search_substring.py**

```
import re

text = 'This is some text -- with punctuation.'
pattern = re.compile(r'\b\w*is\w*\b')

print('Text:', text)
print()

pos = 0
while True:
    match = pattern.search(text, pos)
    if not match:
        break
    s = match.start()
    e = match.end()
    print('  {:>2d} : {:>2d} = "{}"'.format(
        s, e - 1, text[s:e]))
    # Move forward in text for the next search.
    pos = e
```

This example implements a less efficient form of iterall(). Each time a match is found, the end position of that match is used for the next search.

```
$ python3 re_search_substring.py

Text: This is some text -- with punctuation.

   0 :  3 = "This"
   5 :  6 = "is"
```

1.3.6   Dissecting Matches with Groups

Searching for pattern matches is the basis of the powerful capabilities provided by regular expressions. Adding *groups* to a pattern isolates parts of the matching text, expanding those capabilities to create a parser. Groups are defined by enclosing patterns in parentheses.

Listing 1.33: **re_groups.py**

```
from re_test_patterns import test_patterns

test_patterns(
    'abbaaabbbbaaaaa',
    [('a(ab)', 'a followed by literal ab'),
     ('a(a*b*)', 'a followed by 0-n a and 0-n b'),
     ('a(ab)*', 'a followed by 0-n ab'),
     ('a(ab)+', 'a followed by 1-n ab')],
)
```

Any complete regular expression can be converted to a group and nested within a larger expression. All of the repetition modifiers can be applied to a group as a whole, requiring the entire group pattern to repeat.

```
$ python3 re_groups.py

'a(ab)' (a followed by literal ab)

  'abbaaabbbbaaaaa'
  ....'aab'

'a(a*b*)' (a followed by 0-n a and 0-n b)

  'abbaaabbbbaaaaa'
  'abb'
  ...'aaabbbb'
  ..........'aaaaa'

'a(ab)*' (a followed by 0-n ab)

  'abbaaabbbbaaaaa'
  'a'
  ...'a'
  ....'aab'
  ..........'a'
  ...........'a'
  ............'a'
  .............'a'
  ..............'a'
```

```
'a(ab)+' (a followed by 1-n ab)

  'abbaaabbbbaaaaa'
  ....'aab'
```

To access the substrings matched by the individual groups within a pattern, use the groups() method of the Match object.

Listing 1.34: re_groups_match.py

```python
import re

text = 'This is some text -- with punctuation.'

print(text)
print()

patterns = [
    (r'^(\w+)', 'word at start of string'),
    (r'(\w+)\S*$', 'word at end, with optional punctuation'),
    (r'(\bt\w+)\W+(\w+)', 'word starting with t, another word'),
    (r'(\w+t)\b', 'word ending with t'),
]

for pattern, desc in patterns:
    regex = re.compile(pattern)
    match = regex.search(text)
    print("'{}' ({})\n".format(pattern, desc))
    print('  ', match.groups())
    print()
```

Match.groups() returns a sequence of strings in the order of the groups within the expression that matches the string.

```
$ python3 re_groups_match.py

This is some text -- with punctuation.

'^(\w+)' (word at start of string)

    ('This',)

'(\w+)\S*$' (word at end, with optional punctuation)

    ('punctuation',)

'(\bt\w+)\W+(\w+)' (word starting with t, another word)
```

```
    ('text', 'with')

'(\w+t)\b' (word ending with t)

    ('text',)
```

To ask for the match of a single group, use the `group()` method. This is useful when grouping is being used to find parts of the string, but some of the parts matched by groups are not needed in the results.

Listing 1.35: **re_groups_individual.py**

```python
import re

text = 'This is some text -- with punctuation.'

print('Input text            :', text)

# Word starting with 't' then another word
regex = re.compile(r'(\bt\w+)\W+(\w+)')
print('Pattern               :', regex.pattern)

match = regex.search(text)
print('Entire match          :', match.group(0))
print('Word starting with "t":', match.group(1))
print('Word after "t" word   :', match.group(2))
```

Group 0 represents the string matched by the entire expression, and subgroups are numbered starting with 1 in the order that their left parenthesis appears in the expression.

```
$ python3 re_groups_individual.py

Input text            : This is some text -- with punctuation.
Pattern               : (\bt\w+)\W+(\w+)
Entire match          : text -- with
Word starting with "t": text
Word after "t" word   : with
```

Python extends the basic grouping syntax to add *named groups*. Using names to refer to groups makes it easier to modify the pattern over time, without having to also modify the code using the match results. To set the name of a group, use the syntax `(?P<name>pattern)`.

Listing 1.36: **re_groups_named.py**

```python
import re

text = 'This is some text -- with punctuation.'

print(text)
```

```
    print()

patterns = [
    r'^(?P<first_word>\w+)',
    r'(?P<last_word>\w+)\S*$',
    r'(?P<t_word>\bt\w+)\W+(?P<other_word>\w+)',
    r'(?P<ends_with_t>\w+t)\b',
]

for pattern in patterns:
    regex = re.compile(pattern)
    match = regex.search(text)
    print("'{}'".format(pattern))
    print('  ', match.groups())
    print('  ', match.groupdict())
    print()
```

Use `groupdict()` to retrieve the dictionary mapping group names to substrings from the match. Named patterns are included in the ordered sequence returned by `groups()` as well.

```
$ python3 re_groups_named.py

This is some text -- with punctuation.

'^(?P<first_word>\w+)'
   ('This',)
   {'first_word': 'This'}

'(?P<last_word>\w+)\S*$'
   ('punctuation',)
   {'last_word': 'punctuation'}

'(?P<t_word>\bt\w+)\W+(?P<other_word>\w+)'
   ('text', 'with')
   {'t_word': 'text', 'other_word': 'with'}

'(?P<ends_with_t>\w+t)\b'
   ('text',)
   {'ends_with_t': 'text'}
```

An updated version of `test_patterns()` that shows the numbered and named groups matched by a pattern will make the following examples easier to follow.

Listing 1.37: re_test_patterns_groups.py

```
import re


def test_patterns(text, patterns):
```

```
"""Given source text and a list of patterns, look for
matches for each pattern within the text and print
them to stdout.
"""
# Look for each pattern in the text and print the results.
for pattern, desc in patterns:
    print('{!r} ({})\n'.format(pattern, desc))
    print('  {!r}'.format(text))
    for match in re.finditer(pattern, text):
        s = match.start()
        e = match.end()
        prefix = ' ' * (s)
        print(
            '  {}{!r}{} '.format(prefix,
                                 text[s:e],
                                 ' ' * (len(text) - e)),
            end=' ',
        )
        print(match.groups())
        if match.groupdict():
            print('{}{}'.format(
                ' ' * (len(text) - s),
                match.groupdict()),
            )
    print()
return
```

Since a group is itself a complete regular expression, groups can be nested within other groups to build even more complicated expressions.

Listing 1.38: re_groups_nested.py

```
from re_test_patterns_groups import test_patterns

test_patterns(
    'abbaabbba',
    [(r'a((a*)(b*))', 'a followed by 0-n a and 0-n b')],
)
```

In this case, the group (a*) matches an empty string, so the return value from `groups()` includes that empty string as the matched value.

```
$ python3 re_groups_nested.py

'a((a*)(b*))' (a followed by 0-n a and 0-n b)

  'abbaabbba'
  'abb'         ('bb', '', 'bb')
     'aabbb'    ('abbb', 'a', 'bbb')
          'a'   ('', '', '')
```

Groups are also useful for specifying alternative patterns. Use the pipe symbol (|) to indicate that either pattern should match. Consider the placement of the pipe carefully, though. The first expression in this example matches a sequence of a followed by a sequence consisting entirely of a single letter, a or b. The second pattern matches a followed by a sequence that may include *either* a or b. The patterns are similar, but the resulting matches are completely different.

Listing 1.39: `re_groups_alternative.py`

```
from re_test_patterns_groups import test_patterns

test_patterns(
    'abbaabbba',
    [(r'a((a+)|(b+))', 'a then seq. of a or seq. of b'),
     (r'a((a|b)+)', 'a then seq. of [ab]')],
)
```

When an alternative group is not matched, but the entire pattern does match, the return value of `groups()` includes a `None` value at the point in the sequence where the alternative group should appear.

```
$ python3 re_groups_alternative.py

'a((a+)|(b+))' (a then seq. of a or seq. of b)

  'abbaabbba'
  'abb'        ('bb', None, 'bb')
    'aa'       ('a', 'a', None)

'a((a|b)+)' (a then seq. of [ab])

  'abbaabbba'
  'abbaabbba'  ('bbaabbba', 'a')
```

Defining a group containing a subpattern is also useful in cases where the string matching the subpattern is not part of what should be extracted from the full text. These kinds of groups are called *non-capturing*. Non-capturing groups can be used to describe repetition patterns or alternatives, without isolating the matching portion of the string in the value returned. To create a non-capturing group, use the syntax (?:pattern).

Listing 1.40: `re_groups_noncapturing.py`

```
from re_test_patterns_groups import test_patterns

test_patterns(
    'abbaabbba',
    [(r'a((a+)|(b+))', 'capturing form'),
     (r'a((?:a+)|(?:b+))', 'noncapturing')],
)
```

In the following example, compare the groups returned for the capturing and non-capturing forms of a pattern that matches the same results.

```
$ python3 re_groups_noncapturing.py

'a((a+)|(b+))' (capturing form)

  'abbaabbba'
  'abb'          ('bb', None, 'bb')
     'aa'        ('a', 'a', None)

'a((?:a+)|(?:b+))' (noncapturing)

  'abbaabbba'
  'abb'          ('bb',)
     'aa'        ('a',)
```

1.3.7 Search Options

Option flags are used to change the way the matching engine processes an expression. The flags can be combined using a bitwise OR operation, then passed to `compile()`, `search()`, `match()`, and other functions that accept a pattern for searching.

1.3.7.1 Case-Insensitive Matching

`IGNORECASE` causes literal characters and character ranges in the pattern to match both uppercase and lowercase characters.

Listing 1.41: **re_flags_ignorecase.py**

```python
import re

text = 'This is some text -- with punctuation.'
pattern = r'\bT\w+'
with_case = re.compile(pattern)
without_case = re.compile(pattern, re.IGNORECASE)

print('Text:\n  {!r}'.format(text))
print('Pattern:\n  {}'.format(pattern))
print('Case-sensitive:')
for match in with_case.findall(text):
    print('  {!r}'.format(match))
print('Case-insensitive:')
for match in without_case.findall(text):
    print('  {!r}'.format(match))
```

Since the pattern includes the literal T, if `IGNORECASE` is not set, the only match is the word This. When case is ignored, text also matches.

```
$ python3 re_flags_ignorecase.py

Text:
  'This is some text -- with punctuation.'
Pattern:
  \bT\w+
Case-sensitive:
  'This'
Case-insensitive:
  'This'
  'text'
```

1.3.7.2 Input with Multiple Lines

Two flags affect how searching in multiline input works: `MULTILINE` and `DOTALL`. The
`MULTILINE` flag controls how the pattern matching code processes anchoring instructions
for text containing newline characters. When multiline mode is turned on, the anchor rules
for ^ and $ apply at the beginning and end of each line, in addition to the entire string.

Listing 1.42: re_flags_multiline.py

```
import re

text = 'This is some text -- with punctuation.\nA second line.'
pattern = r'(^\w+)|(\w+\S*$)'
single_line = re.compile(pattern)
multiline = re.compile(pattern, re.MULTILINE)

print('Text:\n  {!r}'.format(text))
print('Pattern:\n  {}'.format(pattern))
print('Single Line :')
for match in single_line.findall(text):
    print('  {!r}'.format(match))
print('Multline    :')
for match in multiline.findall(text):
    print('  {!r}'.format(match))
```

The pattern in the example matches the first or last word of the input. It matches `line.`
at the end of the string, even though there is no newline.

```
$ python3 re_flags_multiline.py

Text:
  'This is some text -- with punctuation.\nA second line.'
Pattern:
  (^\w+)|(\w+\S*$)
Single Line :
  ('This', '')
```

```
    ('', 'line.')
Multline    :
  ('This', '')
  ('', 'punctuation.')
  ('A', '')
  ('', 'line.')
```

DOTALL is the other flag related to multiline text. Normally, the dot character (.) matches everything in the input text except a newline character. The flag allows the dot to match newlines as well.

Listing 1.43: `re_flags_dotall.py`

```
import re

text = 'This is some text -- with punctuation.\nA second line.'
pattern = r'.+'
no_newlines = re.compile(pattern)
dotall = re.compile(pattern, re.DOTALL)

print('Text:\n  {!r}'.format(text))
print('Pattern:\n  {}'.format(pattern))
print('No newlines :')
for match in no_newlines.findall(text):
    print('  {!r}'.format(match))
print('Dotall      :')
for match in dotall.findall(text):
    print('  {!r}'.format(match))
```

Without the flag, each line of the input text matches the pattern separately. Adding the flag causes the entire string to be consumed.

```
$ python3 re_flags_dotall.py

Text:
  'This is some text -- with punctuation.\nA second line.'
Pattern:
  .+
No newlines :
  'This is some text -- with punctuation.'
  'A second line.'
Dotall      :
  'This is some text -- with punctuation.\nA second line.'
```

1.3.7.3   Unicode

Under Python 3, str objects use the full Unicode character set, and regular expression processing on a str assumes that the pattern and input text are both Unicode. The escape

codes described earlier are defined in terms of Unicode by default. Those assumptions mean
that the pattern \w+ will match both the words "French" and "Français". To restrict escape
codes to the ASCII character set, as was the default in Python 2, use the ASCII flag when
compiling the pattern or when calling the module-level functions search() and match().

Listing 1.44: **re_flags_ascii.py**

```
import re

text = u'Français łzoty Österreich'
pattern = r'\w+'
ascii_pattern = re.compile(pattern, re.ASCII)
unicode_pattern = re.compile(pattern)

print('Text    :', text)
print('Pattern :', pattern)
print('ASCII   :', list(ascii_pattern.findall(text)))
print('Unicode :', list(unicode_pattern.findall(text)))
```

The other escape sequences (\W, \b, \B, \d, \D, \s, and \S) are also processed differently
for ASCII text. Instead of consulting the Unicode database to find the properties of each
character, re uses the ASCII definition of the character set identified by the escape sequence.

```
$ python3 re_flags_ascii.py

Text    : Français łzoty Österreich
Pattern : \w+
ASCII   : ['Fran', 'ais', 'z', 'oty', 'sterreich']
Unicode : ['Français', 'łzoty', 'Österreich']
```

1.3.7.4   Verbose Expression Syntax

The compact format of regular expression syntax can become a hindrance as expressions
grow more complicated. As the number of groups in an expression increases, it will be more
work to keep track of why each element is needed and how exactly the parts of the expression
interact. Using named groups helps mitigate these issues, but a better solution is to use
verbose mode expressions, which allow comments and extra whitespace to be embedded in
the pattern.

A pattern to validate email addresses will illustrate how verbose mode makes working
with regular expressions easier. The first version recognizes addresses that end in one of
three top-level domains: .com, .org, or .edu.

Listing 1.45: **re_email_compact.py**

```
import re

address = re.compile('[\w\d.+-]+@([\w\d.]+\.)+(com|org|edu)')
```

```
candidates = [
    u'first.last@example.com',
    u'first.last+category@gmail.com',
    u'valid-address@mail.example.com',
    u'not-valid@example.foo',
]

for candidate in candidates:
    match = address.search(candidate)
    print('{:<30}  {}'.format(
        candidate, 'Matches' if match else 'No match')
    )
```

This expression is already complex. There are several character classes, groups, and repetition expressions.

```
$ python3 re_email_compact.py

first.last@example.com           Matches
first.last+category@gmail.com    Matches
valid-address@mail.example.com   Matches
not-valid@example.foo            No match
```

Converting the expression to a more verbose format will make it easier to extend.

Listing 1.46: re_email_verbose.py

```
import re

address = re.compile(
    '''
    [\w\d.+-]+       # Username
    @
    ([\w\d.]+\.)+    # Domain name prefix
    (com|org|edu)    # TODO: support more top-level domains
    ''',
    re.VERBOSE)

candidates = [
    u'first.last@example.com',
    u'first.last+category@gmail.com',
    u'valid-address@mail.example.com',
    u'not-valid@example.foo',
]

for candidate in candidates:
    match = address.search(candidate)
    print('{:<30}  {}'.format(
        candidate, 'Matches' if match else 'No match'),
    )
```

The expression matches the same inputs, but in this extended format it is easier to read. The comments also help identify different parts of the pattern so that it can be expanded to match more inputs.

```
$ python3 re_email_verbose.py

first.last@example.com              Matches
first.last+category@gmail.com       Matches
valid-address@mail.example.com      Matches
not-valid@example.foo               No match
```

This expanded version parses inputs that include a person's name and email address, as might appear in an email header. The name comes first and stands on its own, and the email address follows, surrounded by angle brackets (< and >).

Listing 1.47: `re_email_with_name.py`

```python
import re

address = re.compile(
    '''

    # A name is made up of letters, and may include "."
    # for title abbreviations and middle initials.
    ((?P<name>
       ([\w.,]+\s+)*[\w.,]+)
       \s*
       # Email addresses are wrapped in angle
       # brackets < >, but only if a name is
       # found, so keep the start bracket in this
       # group.
       <
    )? # The entire name is optional.

    # The address itself: username@domain.tld
    (?P<email>
      [\w\d.+-]+       # Username
      @
      ([\w\d.]+\.)+    # Domain name prefix
      (com|org|edu)    # Limit the allowed top-level domains.
    )

    >? # Optional closing angle bracket.
    ''',
    re.VERBOSE)

candidates = [
    u'first.last@example.com',
    u'first.last+category@gmail.com',
    u'valid-address@mail.example.com',
```

```
            u'not-valid@example.foo',
            u'First Last <first.last@example.com>',
            u'No Brackets first.last@example.com',
            u'First Last',
            u'First Middle Last <first.last@example.com>',
            u'First M. Last <first.last@example.com>',
            u'<first.last@example.com>',
        ]

        for candidate in candidates:
            print('Candidate:', candidate)
            match = address.search(candidate)
            if match:
                print('  Name :', match.groupdict()['name'])
                print('  Email:', match.groupdict()['email'])
            else:
                print('  No match')
```

As with other programming languages, the ability to insert comments into verbose regular expressions helps with their maintainability. This final version includes implementation notes to future maintainers and whitespace to separate the groups from each other and highlight their nesting level.

```
$ python3 re_email_with_name.py

Candidate: first.last@example.com
  Name : None
  Email: first.last@example.com
Candidate: first.last+category@gmail.com
  Name : None
  Email: first.last+category@gmail.com
Candidate: valid-address@mail.example.com
  Name : None
  Email: valid-address@mail.example.com
Candidate: not-valid@example.foo
  No match
Candidate: First Last <first.last@example.com>
  Name : First Last
  Email: first.last@example.com
Candidate: No Brackets first.last@example.com
  Name : None
  Email: first.last@example.com
Candidate: First Last
  No match
Candidate: First Middle Last <first.last@example.com>
  Name : First Middle Last
  Email: first.last@example.com
Candidate: First M. Last <first.last@example.com>
```

```
Name : First M. Last
Email: first.last@example.com
Candidate: <first.last@example.com>
Name : None
Email: first.last@example.com
```

1.3.7.5   Embedding Flags in Patterns

In situations where flags cannot be added when compiling an expression, such as when a pattern is passed as an argument to a library function that will compile it later, the flags can be embedded inside the expression string itself. For example, to turn case-insensitive matching on, add (?i) to the beginning of the expression.

Listing 1.48: **re_flags_embedded.py**

```
import re

text = 'This is some text -- with punctuation.'
pattern = r'(?i)\bT\w+'
regex = re.compile(pattern)

print('Text       :', text)
print('Pattern    :', pattern)
print('Matches    :', regex.findall(text))
```

Because the options control the way the entire expression is evaluated or parsed, they should always appear at the beginning of the expression.

```
$ python3 re_flags_embedded.py

Text       : This is some text -- with punctuation.
Pattern    : (?i)\bT\w+
Matches    : ['This', 'text']
```

The abbreviations for all of the flags are listed in Table 1.3.

Embedded flags can be combined by placing them within the same group. For example, (?im) turns on case-insensitive matching for multiline strings.

Table 1.3: Regular Expression Flag Abbreviations

Flag	Abbreviation
ASCII	a
IGNORECASE	i
MULTILINE	m
DOTALL	s
VERBOSE	x

1.3.8   Looking Ahead or Behind

In many cases, it is useful to match a part of a pattern only if some other part will also match. For example, in the email parsing expression, the angle brackets were marked as optional. Realistically, the brackets should be paired, and the expression should match only if both are present, or neither is. This modified version of the expression uses a *positive look ahead* assertion to match the pair. The look ahead assertion syntax is (?=pattern).

Listing 1.49: `re_look_ahead.py`

```
import re

address = re.compile(
    '''
    # A name is made up of letters, and may include "."
    # for title abbreviations and middle initials.
    ((?P<name>
       ([\w.,]+\s+)*[\w.,]+
     )
     \s+
    ) # The name is no longer optional.

    # LOOKAHEAD
    # Email addresses are wrapped in angle brackets, but only
    # if both are present or neither is.
    (?= (<.*>$)          # Remainder wrapped in angle brackets
        |
        ([^<].*[^>]$) # Remainder *not* wrapped in angle brackets
      )

    <? # Optional opening angle bracket

    # The address itself: username@domain.tld
    (?P<email>
      [\w\d.+-]+         # Username
      @
      ([\w\d.]+\.)+      # Domain name prefix
      (com|org|edu)      # Limit the allowed top-level domains.
    )

    >? # Optional closing angle bracket
    ''',
    re.VERBOSE)

candidates = [
    u'First Last <first.last@example.com>',
    u'No Brackets first.last@example.com',
    u'Open Bracket <first.last@example.com',
    u'Close Bracket first.last@example.com>',
]
```

```
for candidate in candidates:
    print('Candidate:', candidate)
    match = address.search(candidate)
    if match:
        print('  Name :', match.groupdict()['name'])
        print('  Email:', match.groupdict()['email'])
    else:
        print('  No match')
```

There are several important changes in this version of the expression. First, the name portion is no longer optional. That means stand-alone addresses do not match, but it also prevents improperly formatted name/address combinations from matching. The positive look ahead rule after the "name" group asserts that either the remainder of the string is wrapped with a pair of angle brackets, or there is not a mismatched bracket; either both or neither of the brackets is present. The look ahead is expressed as a group, but the match for a look ahead group does not consume any of the input text, so the rest of the pattern picks up from the same spot after the look ahead matches.

```
$ python3 re_look_ahead.py

Candidate: First Last <first.last@example.com>
  Name : First Last
  Email: first.last@example.com
Candidate: No Brackets first.last@example.com
  Name : No Brackets
  Email: first.last@example.com
Candidate: Open Bracket <first.last@example.com
  No match
Candidate: Close Bracket first.last@example.com>
  No match
```

A *negative look ahead* assertion (`(?!pattern)`) says that the pattern does not match the text following the current point. For example, the email recognition pattern could be modified to ignore the `noreply` mailing addresses commonly used by automated systems.

Listing 1.50: re_negative_look_ahead.py

```
import re

address = re.compile(
    '''
    ^

    # An address: username@domain.tld

    # Ignore noreply addresses.
    (?!noreply@.*$)
```

```
    [\w\d.+-]+          # Username
    @
    ([\w\d.]+\.)+       # Domain name prefix
    (com|org|edu)       # Limit the allowed top-level domains.

    $
    ''',
    re.VERBOSE)

candidates = [
    u'first.last@example.com',
    u'noreply@example.com',
]

for candidate in candidates:
    print('Candidate:', candidate)
    match = address.search(candidate)
    if match:
        print('  Match:', candidate[match.start():match.end()])
    else:
        print('  No match')
```

The address starting with `noreply` does not match the pattern, since the look ahead
assertion fails.

```
$ python3 re_negative_look_ahead.py

Candidate: first.last@example.com
  Match: first.last@example.com
Candidate: noreply@example.com
  No match
```

Instead of looking ahead for `noreply` in the username portion of the email address,
the pattern can alternatively be written using a *negative look behind* assertion after the
username is matched using the syntax (?<!pattern).

Listing 1.51: **re_negative_look_behind.py**

```
import re

address = re.compile(
    '''
    ^

    # An address: username@domain.tld

    [\w\d.+-]+          # Username

    # Ignore noreply addresses.
```

```
    (?<!noreply)

    @
    ([\w\d.]+\.)+      # Domain name prefix
    (com|org|edu)      # Limit the allowed top-level domains.

    $
    ''',
    re.VERBOSE)

candidates = [
    u'first.last@example.com',
    u'noreply@example.com',
]

for candidate in candidates:
    print('Candidate:', candidate)
    match = address.search(candidate)
    if match:
        print('  Match:', candidate[match.start():match.end()])
    else:
        print('  No match')
```

Looking backward works a little differently than looking ahead, in that the expression must use a fixed-length pattern. Repetitions are allowed, as long as there is a fixed number of them (no wildcards or ranges).

```
$ python3 re_negative_look_behind.py

Candidate: first.last@example.com
  Match: first.last@example.com
Candidate: noreply@example.com
  No match
```

A *positive look behind* assertion can be used to find text following a pattern using the syntax (?<=pattern). In the following example, the expression finds Twitter handles.

Listing 1.52: re_look_behind.py

```
import re

twitter = re.compile(
    '''
    # A twitter handle: @username
    (?<=@)
    ([\w\d_]+)         # Username
    ''',
    re.VERBOSE)
```

```
text = '''This text includes two Twitter handles.
One for @ThePSF, and one for the author, @doughellmann.
'''

print(text)
for match in twitter.findall(text):
    print('Handle:', match)
```

The pattern matches sequences of characters that can make up a Twitter handle, as long as they are preceded by an @.

```
$ python3 re_look_behind.py

This text includes two Twitter handles.
One for @ThePSF, and one for the author, @doughellmann.

Handle: ThePSF
Handle: doughellmann
```

1.3.9 Self-Referencing Expressions

Matched values can be used in later parts of an expression. For example, the email example can be updated to match only addresses composed of the first and last names of the person by including back-references to those groups. The easiest way to achieve this is by referring to the previously matched group by ID number, using \num.

Listing 1.53: **re_refer_to_group.py**

```
import re

address = re.compile(
    r'''

    # The regular name
    (\w+)                 # First name
    \s+
    (([\w.]+)\s+)?        # Optional middle name or initial
    (\w+)                 # Last name

    \s+

    <

    # The address: first_name.last_name@domain.tld
    (?P<email>
        \1                # First name
        \.
        \4                # Last name
        @
```

```
        ([\w\d.]+\.)+    # Domain name prefix
        (com|org|edu)    # Limit the allowed top-level domains.
    )

    >
    ''',
    re.VERBOSE | re.IGNORECASE)

candidates = [
    u'First Last <first.last@example.com>',
    u'Different Name <first.last@example.com>',
    u'First Middle Last <first.last@example.com>',
    u'First M. Last <first.last@example.com>',
]

for candidate in candidates:
    print('Candidate:', candidate)
    match = address.search(candidate)
    if match:
        print('  Match name :', match.group(1), match.group(4))
        print('  Match email:', match.group(5))
    else:
        print('  No match')
```

Although the syntax is simple, creating back-references by numerical ID has a few disadvantages. From a practical standpoint, as the expression changes, the groups must be counted again and every reference may need to be updated. Another disadvantage is that only 99 references can be made using the standard back-reference syntax \n, because if the ID number is three digits long, it will be interpreted as an octal character value instead of a group reference. Of course, if there are more than 99 groups in an expression, there will be more serious maintenance challenges than simply not being able to refer to all of them.

```
$ python3 re_refer_to_group.py

Candidate: First Last <first.last@example.com>
  Match name : First Last
  Match email: first.last@example.com
Candidate: Different Name <first.last@example.com>
  No match
Candidate: First Middle Last <first.last@example.com>
  Match name : First Last
  Match email: first.last@example.com
Candidate: First M. Last <first.last@example.com>
  Match name : First Last
  Match email: first.last@example.com
```

Python's expression parser includes an extension that uses (?P=name) to refer to the value of a named group matched earlier in the expression.

Listing 1.54: **re_refer_to_named_group.py**

```python
import re

address = re.compile(
    '''

    # The regular name
    (?P<first_name>\w+)
    \s+
    (([\w.]+)\s+)?          # Optional middle name or initial
    (?P<last_name>\w+)

    \s+

    <

    # The address: first_name.last_name@domain.tld
    (?P<email>
      (?P=first_name)
      \.
      (?P=last_name)
      @
      ([\w\d.]+\.)+      # Domain name prefix
      (com|org|edu)      # Limit the allowed top-level domains.
    )

    >
    ''',
    re.VERBOSE | re.IGNORECASE)

candidates = [
    u'First Last <first.last@example.com>',
    u'Different Name <first.last@example.com>',
    u'First Middle Last <first.last@example.com>',
    u'First M. Last <first.last@example.com>',
]

for candidate in candidates:
    print('Candidate:', candidate)
    match = address.search(candidate)
    if match:
        print('  Match name :', match.groupdict()['first_name'],
                end=' ')
        print(match.groupdict()['last_name'])
        print('  Match email:', match.groupdict()['email'])
    else:
        print('  No match')
```

The address expression is compiled with the `IGNORECASE` flag on, since proper names are normally capitalized but email addresses are not.

```
$ python3 re_refer_to_named_group.py

Candidate: First Last <first.last@example.com>
  Match name : First Last
  Match email: first.last@example.com
Candidate: Different Name <first.last@example.com>
  No match
Candidate: First Middle Last <first.last@example.com>
  Match name : First Last
  Match email: first.last@example.com
Candidate: First M. Last <first.last@example.com>
  Match name : First Last
  Match email: first.last@example.com
```

The other mechanism for using back-references in expressions chooses a different pattern based on whether a previous group matched. The email pattern can be corrected so that the angle brackets are required if a name is present, and not required if the email address is by itself. The syntax for testing whether a group has matched is `(?(id)yes-expression|no-expression)`, where `id` is the group name or number, `yes-expression` is the pattern to use if the group has a value, and `no-expression` is the pattern to use otherwise.

Listing 1.55: `re_id.py`

```
import re

address = re.compile(
    '''
    ^

    # A name is made up of letters, and may include "."
    # for title abbreviations and middle initials.
    (?P<name>
       ([\w.]+\s+)*[\w.]+
    )?
    \s*

    # Email addresses are wrapped in angle brackets, but
    # only if a name is found.
    (?(name)
       # Remainder wrapped in angle brackets because
       # there is a name
       (?P<brackets>(?=(<.*>$)))
       |
       # Remainder does not include angle brackets without name
       (?=([^<].*[^>]$))
    )
```

```
        # Look for a bracket only if the look-ahead assertion
        # found both of them.
        (?(brackets)<|\s*)

        # The address itself: username@domain.tld
        (?P<email>
          [\w\d.+-]+        # Username
          @
          ([\w\d.]+\.)+     # Domain name prefix
          (com|org|edu)     # Limit the allowed top-level domains.
         )

        # Look for a bracket only if the look-ahead assertion
        # found both of them.
        (?(brackets)>|\s*)

        $
        ''',
        re.VERBOSE)

candidates = [
    u'First Last <first.last@example.com>',
    u'No Brackets first.last@example.com',
    u'Open Bracket <first.last@example.com',
    u'Close Bracket first.last@example.com>',
    u'no.brackets@example.com',
]

for candidate in candidates:
    print('Candidate:', candidate)
    match = address.search(candidate)
    if match:
        print('  Match name :', match.groupdict()['name'])
        print('  Match email:', match.groupdict()['email'])
    else:
        print('  No match')
```

This version of the email address parser uses two tests. If the name group matches, then the look ahead assertion requires both angle brackets and sets up the brackets group. If name is not matched, the assertion requires the rest of the text to not have angle brackets around it. Later, if the brackets group is set, the actual pattern matching code consumes the brackets in the input using literal patterns; otherwise, it consumes any blank space.

```
$ python3 re_id.py

Candidate: First Last <first.last@example.com>
  Match name : First Last
  Match email: first.last@example.com
```

```
Candidate: No Brackets first.last@example.com
  No match
Candidate: Open Bracket <first.last@example.com
  No match
Candidate: Close Bracket first.last@example.com>
  No match
Candidate: no.brackets@example.com
  Match name : None
  Match email: no.brackets@example.com
```

1.3.10 Modifying Strings with Patterns

In addition to searching through text, re supports modifying text using regular expressions as the search mechanism, and the replacements can reference groups matched in the pattern as part of the substitution text. Use sub() to replace all occurrences of a pattern with another string.

Listing 1.56: **re_sub.py**

```
import re

bold = re.compile(r'\*{2}(.*?)\*{2}')

text = 'Make this **bold**.  This **too**.'

print('Text:', text)
print('Bold:', bold.sub(r'<b>\1</b>', text))
```

References to the text matched by the pattern can be inserted using the \num syntax used for back-references.

```
$ python3 re_sub.py

Text: Make this **bold**.  This **too**.
Bold: Make this <b>bold</b>.  This <b>too</b>.
```

To use named groups in the substitution, use the syntax \g<name>.

Listing 1.57: **re_sub_named_groups.py**

```
import re

bold = re.compile(r'\*{2}(?P<bold_text>.*?)\*{2}')

text = 'Make this **bold**.  This **too**.'

print('Text:', text)
print('Bold:', bold.sub(r'<b>\g<bold_text></b>', text))
```

The \g<name> syntax also works with numbered references, and using it eliminates any ambiguity between group numbers and surrounding literal digits.

```
$ python3 re_sub_named_groups.py

Text: Make this **bold**.  This **too**.
Bold: Make this <b>bold</b>.  This <b>too</b>.
```

Pass a value to count to limit the number of substitutions performed.

Listing 1.58: `re_sub_count.py`

```python
import re

bold = re.compile(r'\*{2}(.*?)\*{2}')

text = 'Make this **bold**.  This **too**.'

print('Text:', text)
print('Bold:', bold.sub(r'<b>\1</b>', text, count=1))
```

Only the first substitution is made because count is 1.

```
$ python3 re_sub_count.py

Text: Make this **bold**.  This **too**.
Bold: Make this <b>bold</b>.  This **too**.
```

subn() works just like sub() except that it returns both the modified string and the count of substitutions made.

Listing 1.59: `re_subn.py`

```python
import re

bold = re.compile(r'\*{2}(.*?)\*{2}')

text = 'Make this **bold**.  This **too**.'

print('Text:', text)
print('Bold:', bold.subn(r'<b>\1</b>', text))
```

The search pattern matches twice in the example.

```
$ python3 re_subn.py

Text: Make this **bold**.  This **too**.
Bold: ('Make this <b>bold</b>.  This <b>too</b>.', 2)
```

1.3.11 Splitting with Patterns

`str.split()` is one of the most frequently used methods for breaking apart strings to parse them. It supports only the use of literal values as separators, though, and sometimes a regular expression is necessary if the input is not consistently formatted. For example, many plain text markup languages define paragraph separators as two or more newline (\n) characters. In this case, `str.split()` cannot be used because of the "or more" part of the definition.

A strategy for identifying paragraphs using `findall()` would use a pattern like `(.+?)\n{2,}`.

Listing 1.60: re_paragraphs_findall.py

```python
import re

text = '''Paragraph one
on two lines.

Paragraph two.


Paragraph three.'''

for num, para in enumerate(re.findall(r'(.+?)\n{2,}',
                                      text,
                                      flags=re.DOTALL)
                           ):
    print(num, repr(para))
    print()
```

That pattern fails for paragraphs at the end of the input text, as illustrated by the fact that "Paragraph three." is not part of the output.

```
$ python3 re_paragraphs_findall.py

0 'Paragraph one\non two lines.'

1 'Paragraph two.'
```

Extending the pattern to say that a paragraph ends with two or more newlines or the end of input fixes the problem, but makes the pattern more complicated. Converting to `re.split()` instead of `re.findall()` handles the boundary condition automatically and keeps the pattern simpler.

Listing 1.61: re_split.py

```python
import re

text = '''Paragraph one
on two lines.
```

```
    Paragraph two.


    Paragraph three.'''

    print('With findall:')
    for num, para in enumerate(re.findall(r'(.+?)(\n{2,}|$)',
                                           text,
                                           flags=re.DOTALL)):
        print(num, repr(para))
        print()

    print()
    print('With split:')
    for num, para in enumerate(re.split(r'\n{2,}', text)):
        print(num, repr(para))
        print()
```

The pattern argument to `split()` expresses the markup specification more precisely. Two or more newline characters mark a separator point between paragraphs in the input string.

```
$ python3 re_split.py

With findall:
0 ('Paragraph one\non two lines.', '\n\n')

1 ('Paragraph two.', '\n\n\n')

2 ('Paragraph three.', '')


With split:
0 'Paragraph one\non two lines.'

1 'Paragraph two.'

2 'Paragraph three.'
```

Enclosing the expression in parentheses to define a group causes `split()` to work more like `str.partition()`, so it returns the separator values as well as the other parts of the string.

Listing 1.62: `re_split_groups.py`

```
import re

text = '''Paragraph one
on two lines.
```

```
    Paragraph two.


    Paragraph three.'''

print('With split:')
for num, para in enumerate(re.split(r'(\n{2,})', text)):
    print(num, repr(para))
    print()
```

The output now includes each paragraph, as well as the sequence of newlines separating them.

```
$ python3 re_split_groups.py

With split:
0 'Paragraph one\non two lines.'

1 '\n\n'

2 'Paragraph two.'

3 '\n\n\n'

4 'Paragraph three.'
```

TIP

Related Reading

- Standard library documentation for re.[7]
- Regular Expression HOWTO[8]: Andrew Kuchling's introduction to regular expressions for Python developers.
- Kodos[9]: An interactive regular expression testing tool by Phil Schwartz.
- pythex[10]: A web-based tool for testing regular expressions created by Gabriel Rodríguez. Inspired by Rubular.
- Wikipedia: Regular expression[11]: General introduction to regular expression concepts and techniques.
- locale (page 1012): Use the locale module to set the language configuration when working with Unicode text.
- unicodedata: Programmatic access to the Unicode character property database.

---

[7] https://docs.python.org/3.5/library/re.html
[8] https://docs.python.org/3.5/howto/regex.html
[9] http://kodos.sourceforge.net
[10] http://pythex.org
[11] https://en.wikipedia.org/wiki/Regular_expression

1.4   difflib: Compare Sequences

The difflib module contains tools for computing and working with differences between sequences. It is especially useful for comparing text, and includes functions that produce reports using several common difference formats.

The examples in this section will all use the following common test data in the difflib_data.py module.

Listing 1.63: difflib_data.py

```
text1 = """Lorem ipsum dolor sit amet, consectetuer adipiscing
elit. Integer eu lacus accumsan arcu fermentum euismod. Donec
pulvinar porttitor tellus. Aliquam venenatis. Donec facilisis
pharetra tortor.  In nec mauris eget magna consequat
convalis. Nam sed sem vitae odio pellentesque interdum. Sed
consequat viverra nisl. Suspendisse arcu metus, blandit quis,
rhoncus ac, pharetra eget, velit. Mauris urna. Morbi nonummy
molestie orci. Praesent nisi elit, fringilla ac, suscipit non,
tristique vel, mauris. Curabitur vel lorem id nisl porta
adipiscing. Suspendisse eu lectus. In nunc. Duis vulputate
tristique enim. Donec quis lectus a justo imperdiet tempus."""

text1_lines = text1.splitlines()

text2 = """Lorem ipsum dolor sit amet, consectetuer adipiscing
elit. Integer eu lacus accumsan arcu fermentum euismod. Donec
pulvinar, porttitor tellus. Aliquam venenatis. Donec facilisis
pharetra tortor. In nec mauris eget magna consequat
convalis. Nam cras vitae mi vitae odio pellentesque interdum. Sed
consequat viverra nisl. Suspendisse arcu metus, blandit quis,
rhoncus ac, pharetra eget, velit. Mauris urna. Morbi nonummy
molestie orci. Praesent nisi elit, fringilla ac, suscipit non,
tristique vel, mauris. Curabitur vel lorem id nisl porta
adipiscing. Duis vulputate tristique enim. Donec quis lectus a
justo imperdiet tempus.  Suspendisse eu lectus. In nunc."""

text2_lines = text2.splitlines()
```

1.4.1   Comparing Bodies of Text

The Differ class works on sequences of text lines and produces human-readable *deltas*, or change instructions, including differences within individual lines. The default output produced by Differ is similar to the diff command-line tool under Unix. It includes the original input values from both lists, including common values, and markup data to indicate which changes were made.

- Lines prefixed with - were in the first sequence, but not the second.

- Lines prefixed with + were in the second sequence, but not the first.

- If a line has an incremental difference between versions, an extra line prefixed with ?
  is used to highlight the change within the new version.

- If a line has not changed, it is printed with an extra blank space on the left column
  so that it is aligned with the other output that may have differences.

Breaking the text up into a sequence of individual lines before passing it to `compare()`
produces more readable output than passing in large strings.

Listing 1.64: difflib_differ.py

```
import difflib
from difflib_data import *

d = difflib.Differ()
diff = d.compare(text1_lines, text2_lines)
print('\n'.join(diff))
```

The beginning of both text segments in the sample data is the same, so the first line is
printed without any extra annotation.

```
  Lorem ipsum dolor sit amet, consectetuer adipiscing
  elit. Integer eu lacus accumsan arcu fermentum euismod. Donec
```

The third line of the data has been changed to include a comma in the modified text. Both
versions of the line are printed, with the extra information on line 5 showing the column
where the text was modified, including the fact that the , character was added.

```
- pulvinar porttitor tellus. Aliquam venenatis. Donec facilisis
+ pulvinar, porttitor tellus. Aliquam venenatis. Donec facilisis
?        +
```

The next few lines of the output show that an extra space was removed.

```
- pharetra tortor.  In nec mauris eget magna consequat
?                 -

+ pharetra tortor. In nec mauris eget magna consequat
```

Next, a more complex change was made, replacing several words in a phrase.

```
- convalis. Nam sed sem vitae odio pellentesque interdum. Sed
?              - --

+ convalis. Nam cras vitae mi vitae odio pellentesque interdum. Sed
?               +++ +++++   +
```

The last sentence in the paragraph was changed significantly, so the difference is represented by removing the old version and adding the new.

```
  consequat viverra nisl. Suspendisse arcu metus, blandit quis,
  rhoncus ac, pharetra eget, velit. Mauris urna. Morbi nonummy
  molestie orci. Praesent nisi elit, fringilla ac, suscipit non,
  tristique vel, mauris. Curabitur vel lorem id nisl porta
- adipiscing. Suspendisse eu lectus. In nunc. Duis vulputate
- tristique enim. Donec quis lectus a justo imperdiet tempus.
+ adipiscing. Duis vulputate tristique enim. Donec quis lectus a
+ justo imperdiet tempus.  Suspendisse eu lectus. In nunc.
```

The `ndiff()` function produces essentially the same output. The processing is specifically tailored for working with text data and eliminating "noise" in the input.

1.4.1.1   Other Output Formats

While the `Differ` class shows all of the input lines, a *unified diff* includes only the modified lines and a bit of context. The `unified_diff()` function produces this sort of output.

Listing 1.65: <code>difflib_unified.py</code>

```python
import difflib
from difflib_data import *

diff = difflib.unified_diff(
    text1_lines,
    text2_lines,
    lineterm='',
)
print('\n'.join(list(diff)))
```

The `lineterm` argument is used to tell `unified_diff()` to skip appending newlines to the control lines that it returns because the input lines do not include them. Newlines are added to all of the lines when they are printed. The output should look familiar to users of many popular version-control tools.

```
$ python3 difflib_unified.py

---
+++
@@ -1,11 +1,11 @@
 Lorem ipsum dolor sit amet, consectetuer adipiscing
 elit. Integer eu lacus accumsan arcu fermentum euismod. Donec
-pulvinar porttitor tellus. Aliquam venenatis. Donec facilisis
-pharetra tortor.  In nec mauris eget magna consequat
-convalis. Nam sed sem vitae odio pellentesque interdum. Sed
+pulvinar, porttitor tellus. Aliquam venenatis. Donec facilisis
```

```
+pharetra tortor. In nec mauris eget magna consequat
+convalis. Nam cras vitae mi vitae odio pellentesque interdum. S
ed
 consequat viverra nisl. Suspendisse arcu metus, blandit quis,
 rhoncus ac, pharetra eget, velit. Mauris urna. Morbi nonummy
 molestie orci. Praesent nisi elit, fringilla ac, suscipit non,
 tristique vel, mauris. Curabitur vel lorem id nisl porta
-adipiscing. Suspendisse eu lectus. In nunc. Duis vulputate
-tristique enim. Donec quis lectus a justo imperdiet tempus.
+adipiscing. Duis vulputate tristique enim. Donec quis lectus a
+justo imperdiet tempus.  Suspendisse eu lectus. In nunc.
```

Using `context_diff()` produces similar readable output.

1.4.2 Junk Data

All of the functions that produce difference sequences accept arguments to indicate which lines should be ignored and which characters within a line should be ignored. These parameters can be used to skip over markup or whitespace changes in two versions of a file, for example.

Listing 1.66: `difflib_junk.py`

```python
# This example is adapted from the source for difflib.py.

from difflib import SequenceMatcher


def show_results(match):
    print('  a    = {}'.format(match.a))
    print('  b    = {}'.format(match.b))
    print('  size = {}'.format(match.size))
    i, j, k = match
    print('  A[a:a+size] = {!r}'.format(A[i:i + k]))
    print('  B[b:b+size] = {!r}'.format(B[j:j + k]))


A = " abcd"
B = "abcd abcd"

print('A = {!r}'.format(A))
print('B = {!r}'.format(B))

print('\nWithout junk detection:')
s1 = SequenceMatcher(None, A, B)
match1 = s1.find_longest_match(0, len(A), 0, len(B))
show_results(match1)

print('\nTreat spaces as junk:')
```

```
s2 = SequenceMatcher(lambda x: x == " ", A, B)
match2 = s2.find_longest_match(0, len(A), 0, len(B))
show_results(match2)
```

The default for `Differ` is to not ignore any lines or characters explicitly, but rather to rely on the ability of `SequenceMatcher` to detect noise. The default for `ndiff()` is to ignore space and tab characters.

```
$ python3 difflib_junk.py

A = ' abcd'
B = 'abcd abcd'

Without junk detection:
  a    = 0
  b    = 4
  size = 5
  A[a:a+size] = ' abcd'
  B[b:b+size] = ' abcd'

Treat spaces as junk:
  a    = 1
  b    = 0
  size = 4
  A[a:a+size] = 'abcd'
  B[b:b+size] = 'abcd'
```

1.4.3 Comparing Arbitrary Types

The `SequenceMatcher` class compares two sequences of any types, as long as the values are hashable. It uses an algorithm to identify the longest contiguous matching blocks from the sequences, eliminating "junk" values that do not contribute to the real data.

The funct `get_opcodes()` returns a list of instructions for modifying the first sequence to make it match the second. The instructions are encoded as five-element tuples, including a string instruction (the "opcode") and two pairs of start and stop indexes into the sequences (denoted as `i1`, `i2`, `j1`, and `j2`) as shown in Table 1.4.

Table 1.4: `difflib.get_opcodes()` Instructions

Opcode	Definition
`'replace'`	Replace a[i1:i2] with b[j1:j2].
`'delete'`	Remove a[i1:i2] entirely.
`'insert'`	Insert b[j1:j2] at a[i1:i1].
`'equal'`	The subsequences are already equal.

Listing 1.67: difflib_seq.py

```python
import difflib

s1 = [1, 2, 3, 5, 6, 4]
s2 = [2, 3, 5, 4, 6, 1]

print('Initial data:')
print('s1 =', s1)
print('s2 =', s2)
print('s1 == s2:', s1 == s2)
print()

matcher = difflib.SequenceMatcher(None, s1, s2)
for tag, i1, i2, j1, j2 in reversed(matcher.get_opcodes()):

    if tag == 'delete':
        print('Remove {} from positions [{}:{}]'.format(
            s1[i1:i2], i1, i2))
        print('  before =', s1)
        del s1[i1:i2]

    elif tag == 'equal':
        print('s1[{}:{}] and s2[{}:{}] are the same'.format(
            i1, i2, j1, j2))

    elif tag == 'insert':
        print('Insert {} from s2[{}:{}] into s1 at {}'.format(
            s2[j1:j2], j1, j2, i1))
        print('  before =', s1)
        s1[i1:i2] = s2[j1:j2]

    elif tag == 'replace':
        print(('Replace {} from s1[{}:{}] '
               'with {} from s2[{}:{}]').format(
                   s1[i1:i2], i1, i2, s2[j1:j2], j1, j2))
        print('  before =', s1)
        s1[i1:i2] = s2[j1:j2]

    print('   after =', s1, '\n')

print('s1 == s2:', s1 == s2)
```

This example compares two lists of integers and uses get_opcodes() to derive the instructions for converting the original list into the newer version. The modifications are applied in reverse order so that the list indexes remain accurate after items are added and removed.

```
$ python3 difflib_seq.py

Initial data:
s1 = [1, 2, 3, 5, 6, 4]
s2 = [2, 3, 5, 4, 6, 1]
s1 == s2: False

Replace [4] from s1[5:6] with [1] from s2[5:6]
  before = [1, 2, 3, 5, 6, 4]
   after = [1, 2, 3, 5, 6, 1]

s1[4:5] and s2[4:5] are the same
   after = [1, 2, 3, 5, 6, 1]

Insert [4] from s2[3:4] into s1 at 4
  before = [1, 2, 3, 5, 6, 1]
   after = [1, 2, 3, 5, 4, 6, 1]

s1[1:4] and s2[0:3] are the same
   after = [1, 2, 3, 5, 4, 6, 1]

Remove [1] from positions [0:1]
  before = [1, 2, 3, 5, 4, 6, 1]
   after = [2, 3, 5, 4, 6, 1]

s1 == s2: True
```

SequenceMatcher works with custom classes, as well as built-in types, as long as they are hashable.

TIP

Related Reading

- Standard library documentation for difflib.[12]
- "Pattern Matching: The Gestalt Approach"[13]: Discussion of a similar algorithm by John W. Ratcliff and D. E. Metzener published in *Dr. Dobb's Journal* in July 1988.

---

[12] https://docs.python.org/3.5/library/difflib.html
[13] www.drdobbs.com/database/pattern-matching-the-gestalt-approach/184407970

Chapter 2

Data Structures

Python includes several standard programming data structures, such as `list`, `tuple`, `dict`, and `set`, as part of its built-in types. Many applications do not require other structures, but when they do, the standard library provides powerful and well-tested versions that are ready to be used.

The `enum` (page 66) module provides an implementation of an *enumeration* type, with iteration and comparison capabilities. It can be used to create well-defined symbols for values, instead of using literal strings or integers.

The `collections` (page 75) module includes implementations of several data structures that extend those found in other modules. For example, `Deque` is a double-ended queue, which allows the addition or removal of items from either end. The `defaultdict` is a dictionary that responds with a default value if a key is missing, while `OrderedDict` remembers the sequence in which items are added to it. `namedtuple` extends the normal `tuple` to give each member item an attribute name in addition to a numeric index.

For large amounts of data, an `array` (page 98) may make more efficient use of memory than a `list`. Since the `array` is limited to a single data type, it can use a more compact memory representation than a general-purpose `list`. At the same time, `array` instances can be manipulated using many of the same methods as a `list`, so it may be possible to replace a `list` with an `array` in an application without a lot of other changes.

Sorting items in a sequence is a fundamental aspect of data manipulation. Python's `list` includes a `sort()` method, but sometimes it is more efficient to maintain a list in sorted order without re-sorting it each time its contents are changed. The functions in `heapq` (page 103) modify the contents of a list while preserving the sort order of the list with low overhead.

Another option for building sorted lists or arrays is `bisect` (page 109). It uses a binary search to find the insertion point for new items, and is an alternative to repeatedly sorting a list that changes frequently.

Although the built-in `list` can simulate a queue using the `insert()` and `pop()` methods, it is not thread-safe. For true ordered communication between threads use the `queue` (page 111) module. `multiprocessing` (page 586) includes a version of a `Queue` that works between processes, making it easier to convert a multithreaded program to use processes instead.

`struct` (page 117) is useful for decoding data from another application, perhaps coming from a binary file or stream of data, into Python's native types for easier manipulation.

This chapter covers two modules related to memory management. For highly interconnected data structures, such as graphs and trees, use `weakref` (page 121) to maintain references while still allowing the garbage collector to clean up objects after they are no longer needed. Use the functions in `copy` (page 130) for duplicating data structures and their contents, including making recursive copies with `deepcopy()`.

Debugging data structures can be time consuming, especially when wading through printed output of large sequences or dictionaries. Use `pprint` (page 136) to create easy-to-read representations that can be printed to the console or written to a log file for easier debugging.

Finally, if the available types do not meet the requirements, subclass one of the native types and customize it, or build a new container type using one of the abstract base classes defined in `collections` (page 75) as a starting point.

2.1   enum: Enumeration Type

The `enum` module defines an enumeration type with iteration and comparison capabilities. It can be used to create well-defined symbols for values, instead of using literal integers or strings.

2.1.1   Creating Enumerations

A new enumeration is defined using the `class` syntax by subclassing `Enum` and adding class attributes describing the values.

Listing 2.1: enum_create.py

```
import enum


class BugStatus(enum.Enum):

    new = 7
    incomplete = 6
    invalid = 5
    wont_fix = 4
    in_progress = 3
    fix_committed = 2
    fix_released = 1


print('\nMember name: {}'.format(BugStatus.wont_fix.name))
print('Member value: {}'.format(BugStatus.wont_fix.value))
```

The members of the `Enum` are converted to instances as the class is parsed. Each instance has a `name` property corresponding to the member name and a `value` property corresponding to the value assigned to the name in the class definition.

```
$ python3 enum_create.py


Member name: wont_fix
Member value: 4
```

2.1.2 Iteration

Iterating over the enum *class* produces the individual members of the enumeration.

Listing 2.2: **enum_iterate.py**

```
import enum


class BugStatus(enum.Enum):

    new = 7
    incomplete = 6
    invalid = 5
    wont_fix = 4
    in_progress = 3
    fix_committed = 2
    fix_released = 1


for status in BugStatus:
    print('{:15} = {}'.format(status.name, status.value))
```

The members are produced in the order they are declared in the class definition. The names and values are not used to sort them in any way.

```
$ python3 enum_iterate.py

new             = 7
incomplete      = 6
invalid         = 5
wont_fix        = 4
in_progress     = 3
fix_committed   = 2
fix_released    = 1
```

2.1.3 Comparing Enums

Because enumeration members are not ordered, they support only comparison by identity and equality.

Listing 2.3: **enum_comparison.py**

```
import enum


class BugStatus(enum.Enum):

    new = 7
    incomplete = 6
```

```
    invalid = 5
    wont_fix = 4
    in_progress = 3
    fix_committed = 2
    fix_released = 1


actual_state = BugStatus.wont_fix
desired_state = BugStatus.fix_released

print('Equality:',
      actual_state == desired_state,
      actual_state == BugStatus.wont_fix)
print('Identity:',
      actual_state is desired_state,
      actual_state is BugStatus.wont_fix)
print('Ordered by value:')
try:
    print('\n'.join('  ' + s.name for s in sorted(BugStatus)))
except TypeError as err:
    print('  Cannot sort: {}'.format(err))
```

The greater-than and less-than comparison operators raise `TypeError` exceptions.

```
$ python3 enum_comparison.py

Equality: False True
Identity: False True
Ordered by value:
  Cannot sort: unorderable types: BugStatus() < BugStatus()
```

Use the `IntEnum` class for enumerations where the members need to behave more like numbers—for example, to support comparisons.

Listing 2.4: enum_intenum.py

```
import enum


class BugStatus(enum.IntEnum):

    new = 7
    incomplete = 6
    invalid = 5
    wont_fix = 4
    in_progress = 3
    fix_committed = 2
    fix_released = 1
```

```
print('Ordered by value:')
print('\n'.join('  ' + s.name for s in sorted(BugStatus)))
```

```
$ python3 enum_intenum.py

Ordered by value:
  fix_released
  fix_committed
  in_progress
  wont_fix
  invalid
  incomplete
  new
```

2.1.4   Unique Enumeration Values

Enum members with the same value are tracked as alias references to the same member object. Aliases do not cause repeated values to be present in the iterator for the Enum.

Listing 2.5: **enum_aliases.py**

```
import enum


class BugStatus(enum.Enum):

    new = 7
    incomplete = 6
    invalid = 5
    wont_fix = 4
    in_progress = 3
    fix_committed = 2
    fix_released = 1

    by_design = 4
    closed = 1


for status in BugStatus:
    print('{:15} = {}'.format(status.name, status.value))

print('\nSame: by_design is wont_fix: ',
      BugStatus.by_design is BugStatus.wont_fix)
print('Same: closed is fix_released: ',
      BugStatus.closed is BugStatus.fix_released)
```

Because by_design and closed are aliases for other members, they do not appear separately
in the output when iterating over the Enum. The canonical name for a member is the first
name attached to the value.

```
$ python3 enum_aliases.py

new            = 7
incomplete     = 6
invalid        = 5
wont_fix       = 4
in_progress    = 3
fix_committed  = 2
fix_released   = 1

Same: by_design is wont_fix:  True
Same: closed is fix_released:  True
```

To require all members to have unique values, add the @unique decorator to the Enum.

Listing 2.6: **enum_unique_enforce.py**

```
import enum


@enum.unique
class BugStatus(enum.Enum):

    new = 7
    incomplete = 6
    invalid = 5
    wont_fix = 4
    in_progress = 3
    fix_committed = 2
    fix_released = 1

    # This will trigger an error with unique applied.
    by_design = 4
    closed = 1
```

Members with repeated values trigger a ValueError exception when the Enum class is
being interpreted.

```
$ python3 enum_unique_enforce.py

Traceback (most recent call last):
  File "enum_unique_enforce.py", line 11, in <module>
    class BugStatus(enum.Enum):
```

```
File ".../lib/python3.5/enum.py", line 573, in unique
    (enumeration, alias_details))
ValueError: duplicate values found in <enum 'BugStatus'>:
by_design -> wont_fix, closed -> fix_released
```

2.1.5 Creating Enumerations Programmatically

In some cases, it is more convenient to create enumerations programmatically, rather than hard-coding them in a class definition. For those situations, Enum also supports passing the member names and values to the class constructor.

Listing 2.7: **enum_programmatic_create.py**

```python
import enum


BugStatus = enum.Enum(
    value='BugStatus',
    names=('fix_released fix_committed in_progress '
           'wont_fix invalid incomplete new'),
)

print('Member: {}'.format(BugStatus.new))

print('\nAll members:')
for status in BugStatus:
    print('{:15} = {}'.format(status.name, status.value))
```

The value argument is the name of the enumeration, which is used to build the representation of members. The names argument lists the members of the enumeration. When a single string is passed, it is split on whitespace and commas, and the resulting tokens are used as names for the members, which are automatically assigned values starting with 1.

```
$ python3 enum_programmatic_create.py

Member: BugStatus.new

All members:
fix_released    = 1
fix_committed   = 2
in_progress     = 3
wont_fix        = 4
invalid         = 5
incomplete      = 6
new             = 7
```

For more control over the values associated with members, the `names` string can be replaced with a sequence of two-part tuples or a dictionary mapping names to values.

Listing 2.8: **enum_programmatic_mapping.py**

```python
import enum


BugStatus = enum.Enum(
    value='BugStatus',
    names=[
        ('new', 7),
        ('incomplete', 6),
        ('invalid', 5),
        ('wont_fix', 4),
        ('in_progress', 3),
        ('fix_committed', 2),
        ('fix_released', 1),
    ],
)

print('All members:')
for status in BugStatus:
    print('{:15} = {}'.format(status.name, status.value))
```

In this example, a list of two-part tuples is given instead of a single string containing only the member names. This makes it possible to reconstruct the `BugStatus` enumeration with the members in the same order as the version defined in `enum_create.py`.

```
$ python3 enum_programmatic_mapping.py

All members:
new             = 7
incomplete      = 6
invalid         = 5
wont_fix        = 4
in_progress     = 3
fix_committed   = 2
fix_released    = 1
```

2.1.6   Non-integer Member Values

Enum member values are not restricted to integers. In fact, any type of object can be associated with a member. If the value is a tuple, the members are passed as individual arguments to `__init__()`.

Listing 2.9: enum_tuple_values.py

```python
import enum


class BugStatus(enum.Enum):

    new = (7, ['incomplete',
               'invalid',
               'wont_fix',
               'in_progress'])
    incomplete = (6, ['new', 'wont_fix'])
    invalid = (5, ['new'])
    wont_fix = (4, ['new'])
    in_progress = (3, ['new', 'fix_committed'])
    fix_committed = (2, ['in_progress', 'fix_released'])
    fix_released = (1, ['new'])

    def __init__(self, num, transitions):
        self.num = num
        self.transitions = transitions

    def can_transition(self, new_state):
        return new_state.name in self.transitions


print('Name:', BugStatus.in_progress)
print('Value:', BugStatus.in_progress.value)
print('Custom attribute:', BugStatus.in_progress.transitions)
print('Using attribute:',
      BugStatus.in_progress.can_transition(BugStatus.new))
```

In this example, each member value is a tuple containing the numerical ID (such as might be stored in a database) and a list of valid transitions away from the current state.

```
$ python3 enum_tuple_values.py

Name: BugStatus.in_progress
Value: (3, ['new', 'fix_committed'])
Custom attribute: ['new', 'fix_committed']
Using attribute: True
```

For more complex cases, tuples might become unwieldy. Since member values can be any type of object, dictionaries can be used for cases where there are a lot of separate attributes to track for each enum value. Complex values are passed directly to __init__() as the only argument other than self.

Listing 2.10: **enum_complex_values.py**

```python
import enum


class BugStatus(enum.Enum):

    new = {
        'num': 7,
        'transitions': [
            'incomplete',
            'invalid',
            'wont_fix',
            'in_progress',
        ],
    }
    incomplete = {
        'num': 6,
        'transitions': ['new', 'wont_fix'],
    }
    invalid = {
        'num': 5,
        'transitions': ['new'],
    }
    wont_fix = {
        'num': 4,
        'transitions': ['new'],
    }
    in_progress = {
        'num': 3,
        'transitions': ['new', 'fix_committed'],
    }
    fix_committed = {
        'num': 2,
        'transitions': ['in_progress', 'fix_released'],
    }
    fix_released = {
        'num': 1,
        'transitions': ['new'],
    }

    def __init__(self, vals):
        self.num = vals['num']
        self.transitions = vals['transitions']

    def can_transition(self, new_state):
        return new_state.name in self.transitions


print('Name:', BugStatus.in_progress)
print('Value:', BugStatus.in_progress.value)
```

```
print('Custom attribute:', BugStatus.in_progress.transitions)
print('Using attribute:',
      BugStatus.in_progress.can_transition(BugStatus.new))
```

This example expresses the same data as the previous example, using dictionaries rather than tuples.

```
$ python3 enum_complex_values.py

Name: BugStatus.in_progress
Value: {'transitions': ['new', 'fix_committed'], 'num': 3}
Custom attribute: ['new', 'fix_committed']
Using attribute: True
```

TIP

Related Reading

- Standard library documentation for enum.[1]
- **PEP 435**[2]: Adding an Enum type to the Python standard library.
- `flufl.enum`[3]: The original inspiration for enum, by Barry Warsaw.

2.2 collections: Container Data Types

The `collections` module includes container data types beyond the built-in types `list`, `dict`, and `tuple`.

2.2.1 ChainMap: Search Multiple Dictionaries

The `ChainMap` class manages a sequence of dictionaries, and searches through them in the order they appear to find values associated with keys. A `ChainMap` makes a good "context" container, since it can be treated as a stack for which changes happen as the stack grows, with these changes being discarded again as the stack shrinks.

2.2.1.1 Accessing Values

The `ChainMap` supports the same API as a regular dictionary for accessing existing values.

Listing 2.11: **collections_chainmap_read.py**

```
import collections

a = {'a': 'A', 'c': 'C'}
```

---

[1] https://docs.python.org/3.5/library/enum.html
[2] www.python.org/dev/peps/pep-0435
[3] http://pythonhosted.org/flufl.enum/

```
b = {'b': 'B', 'c': 'D'}

m = collections.ChainMap(a, b)

print('Individual Values')
print('a = {}'.format(m['a']))
print('b = {}'.format(m['b']))
print('c = {}'.format(m['c']))
print()

print('Keys = {}'.format(list(m.keys())))
print('Values = {}'.format(list(m.values())))
print()

print('Items:')
for k, v in m.items():
    print('{} = {}'.format(k, v))
print()

print('"d" in m: {}'.format(('d' in m)))
```

The child mappings are searched in the order they are passed to the constructor, so the value reported for the key 'c' comes from the a dictionary.

```
$ python3 collections_chainmap_read.py

Individual Values
a = A
b = B
c = C

Keys = ['c', 'b', 'a']
Values = ['C', 'B', 'A']

Items:
c = C
b = B
a = A

"d" in m: False
```

2.2.1.2 Reordering

The ChainMap stores the list of mappings over which it searches in a list in its maps attribute. This list is mutable, so it is possible to add new mappings directly or to change the order of the elements to control lookup and update behavior.

Listing 2.12: **collections_chainmap_reorder.py**

```
import collections

a = {'a': 'A', 'c': 'C'}
b = {'b': 'B', 'c': 'D'}

m = collections.ChainMap(a, b)

print(m.maps)
print('c = {}\n'.format(m['c']))

# Reverse the list.
m.maps = list(reversed(m.maps))

print(m.maps)
print('c = {}'.format(m['c']))
```

When the list of mappings is reversed, the value associated with `'c'` changes.

```
$ python3 collections_chainmap_reorder.py

[{'c': 'C', 'a': 'A'}, {'c': 'D', 'b': 'B'}]
c = C

[{'c': 'D', 'b': 'B'}, {'c': 'C', 'a': 'A'}]
c = D
```

2.2.1.3 Updating Values

A `ChainMap` does not cache the values in the child mappings. Thus, if their contents are modified, the results are reflected when the `ChainMap` is accessed.

Listing 2.13: **collections_chainmap_update_behind.py**

```
import collections

a = {'a': 'A', 'c': 'C'}
b = {'b': 'B', 'c': 'D'}

m = collections.ChainMap(a, b)
print('Before: {}'.format(m['c']))
a['c'] = 'E'
print('After : {}'.format(m['c']))
```

Changing the values associated with existing keys and adding new elements works the same way.

```
$ python3 collections_chainmap_update_behind.py

Before: C
After : E
```

It is also possible to set values through the `ChainMap` directly, although only the first mapping in the chain is actually modified.

Listing 2.14: **collections_chainmap_update_directly.py**

```
import collections

a = {'a': 'A', 'c': 'C'}
b = {'b': 'B', 'c': 'D'}

m = collections.ChainMap(a, b)
print('Before:', m)
m['c'] = 'E'
print('After :', m)
print('a:', a)
```

When the new value is stored using m, the a mapping is updated.

```
$ python3 collections_chainmap_update_directly.py

Before: ChainMap({'c': 'C', 'a': 'A'}, {'c': 'D', 'b': 'B'})
After : ChainMap({'c': 'E', 'a': 'A'}, {'c': 'D', 'b': 'B'})
a: {'c': 'E', 'a': 'A'}
```

`ChainMap` provides a convenience method for creating a new instance with one extra mapping at the front of the `maps` list to make it easy to avoid modifying the existing underlying data structures.

Listing 2.15: **collections_chainmap_new_child.py**

```
import collections

a = {'a': 'A', 'c': 'C'}
b = {'b': 'B', 'c': 'D'}

m1 = collections.ChainMap(a, b)
m2 = m1.new_child()

print('m1 before:', m1)
print('m2 before:', m2)

m2['c'] = 'E'

print('m1 after:', m1)
print('m2 after:', m2)
```

This stacking behavior is what makes it convenient to use `ChainMap` instances as template or application contexts. Specifically, it is easy to add or update values in one iteration, then discard the changes for the next iteration.

```
$ python3 collections_chainmap_new_child.py

m1 before: ChainMap({'c': 'C', 'a': 'A'}, {'c': 'D', 'b': 'B'})
m2 before: ChainMap({}, {'c': 'C', 'a': 'A'}, {'c': 'D', 'b':
'B'})
m1 after: ChainMap({'c': 'C', 'a': 'A'}, {'c': 'D', 'b': 'B'})
m2 after: ChainMap({'c': 'E'}, {'c': 'C', 'a': 'A'}, {'c': 'D',
'b': 'B'})
```

For situations where the new context is known or built in advance, it is also possible to pass a mapping to `new_child()`.

Listing 2.16: `collections_chainmap_new_child_explicit.py`

```
import collections

a = {'a': 'A', 'c': 'C'}
b = {'b': 'B', 'c': 'D'}
c = {'c': 'E'}

m1 = collections.ChainMap(a, b)
m2 = m1.new_child(c)

print('m1["c"] = {}'.format(m1['c']))
print('m2["c"] = {}'.format(m2['c']))
```

This is the equivalent of

```
m2 = collections.ChainMap(c, *m1.maps)
```

and produces

```
$ python3 collections_chainmap_new_child_explicit.py

m1["c"] = C
m2["c"] = E
```

2.2.2 Counter: Count Hashable Objects

A `Counter` is a container that keeps track of how many times equivalent values are added. It can be used to implement the same algorithms for which other languages commonly use bag or multiset data structures.

2.2.2.1   Initializing

Counter supports three forms of initialization. Its constructor can be called with a sequence of items, a dictionary containing keys and counts, or using keyword arguments that map string names to counts.

Listing 2.17: **collections_counter_init.py**

```
import collections

print(collections.Counter(['a', 'b', 'c', 'a', 'b', 'b']))
print(collections.Counter({'a': 2, 'b': 3, 'c': 1}))
print(collections.Counter(a=2, b=3, c=1))
```

The results of all three forms of initialization are the same.

```
$ python3 collections_counter_init.py

Counter({'b': 3, 'a': 2, 'c': 1})
Counter({'b': 3, 'a': 2, 'c': 1})
Counter({'b': 3, 'a': 2, 'c': 1})
```

An empty Counter can be constructed with no arguments and populated via the update() method.

Listing 2.18: **collections_counter_update.py**

```
import collections

c = collections.Counter()
print('Initial :', c)

c.update('abcdaab')
print('Sequence:', c)

c.update({'a': 1, 'd': 5})
print('Dict    :', c)
```

The count values are increased based on the new data, rather than replaced. In the preceding example, the count for a goes from 3 to 4.

```
$ python3 collections_counter_update.py

Initial : Counter()
Sequence: Counter({'a': 3, 'b': 2, 'c': 1, 'd': 1})
Dict    : Counter({'d': 6, 'a': 4, 'b': 2, 'c': 1})
```

2.2.2.2   Accessing Counts

Once a `Counter` is populated, its values can be retrieved using the dictionary API.

Listing 2.19: `collections_counter_get_values.py`

```
import collections

c = collections.Counter('abcdaab')

for letter in 'abcde':
    print('{} : {}'.format(letter, c[letter]))
```

`Counter` does not raise `KeyError` for unknown items. If a value has not been seen in the input (as with `e` in this example), its count is `0`.

```
$ python3 collections_counter_get_values.py

a : 3
b : 2
c : 1
d : 1
e : 0
```

The `elements()` method returns an iterator that produces all of the items known to the `Counter`.

Listing 2.20: `collections_counter_elements.py`

```
import collections

c = collections.Counter('extremely')
c['z'] = 0
print(c)
print(list(c.elements()))
```

The order of elements is not guaranteed, and items with counts less than or equal to zero are not included.

```
$ python3 collections_counter_elements.py

Counter({'e': 3, 'x': 1, 'm': 1, 't': 1, 'y': 1, 'l': 1, 'r': 1,
'z': 0})
['x', 'm', 't', 'e', 'e', 'e', 'y', 'l', 'r']
```

Use `most_common()` to produce a sequence of the n most frequently encountered input values and their respective counts.

Listing 2.21: **collections_counter_most_common.py**

```
import collections

c = collections.Counter()
with open('/usr/share/dict/words', 'rt') as f:
    for line in f:
        c.update(line.rstrip().lower())

print('Most common:')
for letter, count in c.most_common(3):
    print('{}: {:>7}'.format(letter, count))
```

This example counts the letters appearing in all of the words in the system dictionary to produce a frequency distribution, then prints the three most common letters. Leaving out the argument to most_common() produces a list of all the items, in order of frequency.

```
$ python3 collections_counter_most_common.py

Most common:
e:   235331
i:   201032
a:   199554
```

2.2.2.3   Arithmetic

Counter instances support arithmetic and set operations for aggregating results. This example shows the standard operators for creating new Counter instances, but the in-place operators +=, -=, &=, and |= are also supported.

Listing 2.22: **collections_counter_arithmetic.py**

```
import collections

c1 = collections.Counter(['a', 'b', 'c', 'a', 'b', 'b'])
c2 = collections.Counter('alphabet')

print('C1:', c1)
print('C2:', c2)

print('\nCombined counts:')
print(c1 + c2)

print('\nSubtraction:')
print(c1 - c2)

print('\nIntersection (taking positive minimums):')
```

```
print(c1 & c2)

print('\nUnion (taking maximums):')
print(c1 | c2)
```

Each time a new `Counter` is produced through an operation, any items with zero or negative counts are discarded. The count for `a` is the same in `c1` and `c2`, so subtraction leaves it at zero.

```
$ python3 collections_counter_arithmetic.py

C1: Counter({'b': 3, 'a': 2, 'c': 1})
C2: Counter({'a': 2, 'b': 1, 'p': 1, 't': 1, 'l': 1, 'e': 1, 'h': 1})

Combined counts:
Counter({'b': 4, 'a': 4, 'p': 1, 't': 1, 'c': 1, 'e': 1, 'l': 1, 'h': 1})

Subtraction:
Counter({'b': 2, 'c': 1})

Intersection (taking positive minimums):
Counter({'a': 2, 'b': 1})

Union (taking maximums):
Counter({'b': 3, 'a': 2, 'p': 1, 't': 1, 'c': 1, 'e': 1, 'l': 1, 'h': 1})
```

2.2.3 defaultdict: Missing Keys Return a Default Value

The standard dictionary includes the method `setdefault()` for retrieving a value and establishing a default if the value does not exist. By contrast, `defaultdict` lets the caller specify the default up front when the container is initialized.

Listing 2.23: **collections_defaultdict.py**

```
import collections


def default_factory():
    return 'default value'

d = collections.defaultdict(default_factory, foo='bar')
print('d:', d)
print('foo =>', d['foo'])
print('bar =>', d['bar'])
```

This method works well as long as it is appropriate for all keys to have the same default. It can be especially useful if the default is a type used for aggregating or accumulating

values, such as a `list`, `set`, or even `int`. The standard library documentation includes
several examples in which `defaultdict` is used in this way.

```
$ python3 collections_defaultdict.py

d: defaultdict(<function default_factory at 0x101921950>,
{'foo': 'bar'})
foo => bar
bar => default value
```

TIP

Related Reading

- `defaultdict` examples[4]: Examples of using `defaultdict` from the standard library documentation.
- Evolution of Default Dictionaries in Python[5]: James Tauber's discussion of how `defaultdict` relates to other means of initializing dictionaries.

2.2.4   deque: Double-Ended Queue

A double-ended queue, or `deque`, supports adding and removing elements from either end
of the queue. The more commonly used stacks and queues are degenerate forms of deques,
where the inputs and outputs are restricted to a single end.

Listing 2.24: **collections_deque.py**

```
import collections

d = collections.deque('abcdefg')
print('Deque:', d)
print('Length:', len(d))
print('Left end:', d[0])
print('Right end:', d[-1])

d.remove('c')
print('remove(c):', d)
```

Since deques are a type of sequence container, they support some of the same operations as `list`, such as examining the contents with `__getitem__()`, determining length, and removing elements from the middle of the queue by matching identity.

---

[4] https://docs.python.org/3.5/library/collections.html#defaultdict-examples
[5] http://jtauber.com/blog/2008/02/27/evolution_of_default_dictionaries_in_python/

```
$ python3 collections_deque.py

Deque: deque(['a', 'b', 'c', 'd', 'e', 'f', 'g'])
Length: 7
Left end: a
Right end: g
remove(c): deque(['a', 'b', 'd', 'e', 'f', 'g'])
```

2.2.4.1   Populating

A deque can be populated from either end, termed "left" and "right" in the Python implementation.

Listing 2.25: **collections_deque_populating.py**

```
import collections

# Add to the right.
d1 = collections.deque()
d1.extend('abcdefg')
print('extend     :', d1)
d1.append('h')
print('append     :', d1)

# Add to the left.
d2 = collections.deque()
d2.extendleft(range(6))
print('extendleft:', d2)
d2.appendleft(6)
print('appendleft:', d2)
```

The `extendleft()` function iterates over its input and performs the equivalent of an `appendleft()` for each item. The end result is that the `deque` contains the input sequence in reverse order.

```
$ python3 collections_deque_populating.py

extend     : deque(['a', 'b', 'c', 'd', 'e', 'f', 'g'])
append     : deque(['a', 'b', 'c', 'd', 'e', 'f', 'g', 'h'])
extendleft: deque([5, 4, 3, 2, 1, 0])
appendleft: deque([6, 5, 4, 3, 2, 1, 0])
```

2.2.4.2   Consuming

Similarly, the elements of the `deque` can be consumed from both ends or either end, depending on the algorithm being applied.

Listing 2.26: **collections_deque_consuming.py**

```
import collections

print('From the right:')
d = collections.deque('abcdefg')
while True:
    try:
        print(d.pop(), end='')
    except IndexError:
        break
print

print('\nFrom the left:')
d = collections.deque(range(6))
while True:
    try:
        print(d.popleft(), end='')
    except IndexError:
        break
print
```

Use pop() to remove an item from the "right" end of the deque and popleft() to take an item from the "left" end.

```
$ python3 collections_deque_consuming.py

From the right:
gfedcba
From the left:
012345
```

Since deques are thread-safe, the contents can even be consumed from both ends at the same time from separate threads.

Listing 2.27: **collections_deque_both_ends.py**

```
import collections
import threading
import time

candle = collections.deque(range(5))


def burn(direction, nextSource):
    while True:
        try:
            next = nextSource()
        except IndexError:
```

```
                    break
           else:
               print('{:>8}: {}'.format(direction, next))
               time.sleep(0.1)
       print('{:>8} done'.format(direction))
       return

left = threading.Thread(target=burn,
                        args=('Left', candle.popleft))
right = threading.Thread(target=burn,
                         args=('Right', candle.pop))

left.start()
right.start()

left.join()
right.join()
```

The threads in this example alternate between each end, removing items until the deque is empty.

```
$ python3 collections_deque_both_ends.py

 Left: 0
Right: 4
Right: 3
 Left: 1
Right: 2
 Left done
Right done
```

2.2.4.3 Rotating

Another useful aspect of the deque is the ability to rotate it in either direction, so as to skip over some items.

Listing 2.28: **collections_deque_rotate.py**

```
import collections

d = collections.deque(range(10))
print('Normal        :', d)

d = collections.deque(range(10))
d.rotate(2)
print('Right rotation:', d)

d = collections.deque(range(10))
```

```
d.rotate(-2)
print('Left rotation :', d)
```

Rotating the `deque` to the right (using a positive rotation) takes items from the right end and moves them to the left end. Rotating to the left (with a negative value) takes items from the left end and moves them to the right end. It may help to visualize the items in the deque as being engraved along the edge of a dial.

```
$ python3 collections_deque_rotate.py

Normal         : deque([0, 1, 2, 3, 4, 5, 6, 7, 8, 9])
Right rotation: deque([8, 9, 0, 1, 2, 3, 4, 5, 6, 7])
Left rotation : deque([2, 3, 4, 5, 6, 7, 8, 9, 0, 1])
```

2.2.4.4   Constraining the Queue Size

A `deque` instance can be configured with a maximum length so that it never grows beyond that size. When the queue reaches the specified length, existing items are discarded as new items are added. This behavior is useful for finding the last n items in a stream of undetermined length.

Listing 2.29: **collections_deque_maxlen.py**

```
import collections
import random

# Set the random seed so we see the same output each time
# the script is run.
random.seed(1)

d1 = collections.deque(maxlen=3)
d2 = collections.deque(maxlen=3)

for i in range(5):
    n = random.randint(0, 100)
    print('n =', n)
    d1.append(n)
    d2.appendleft(n)
    print('D1:', d1)
    print('D2:', d2)
```

The deque length is maintained regardless of which end the items are added to.

```
$ python3 collections_deque_maxlen.py

n = 17
D1: deque([17], maxlen=3)
D2: deque([17], maxlen=3)
```

```
n = 72
D1: deque([17, 72], maxlen=3)
D2: deque([72, 17], maxlen=3)
n = 97
D1: deque([17, 72, 97], maxlen=3)
D2: deque([97, 72, 17], maxlen=3)
n = 8
D1: deque([72, 97, 8], maxlen=3)
D2: deque([8, 97, 72], maxlen=3)
n = 32
D1: deque([97, 8, 32], maxlen=3)
D2: deque([32, 8, 97], maxlen=3)
```

TIP

Related Reading

- Wikipedia: Deque[6]: A discussion of the deque data structure.
- deque Recipes[7]: Examples of using deques in algorithms from the standard library documentation.

2.2.5 namedtuple: Tuple Subclass with Named Fields

The standard tuple uses numerical indexes to access its members.

Listing 2.30: `collections_tuple.py`

```python
bob = ('Bob', 30, 'male')
print('Representation:', bob)

jane = ('Jane', 29, 'female')
print('\nField by index:', jane[0])

print('\nFields by index:')
for p in [bob, jane]:
    print('{} is a {} year old {}'.format(*p))
```

This makes tuples convenient containers for simple uses.

```
$ python3 collections_tuple.py

Representation: ('Bob', 30, 'male')

Field by index: Jane
```

---

[6] https://en.wikipedia.org/wiki/Deque
[7] https://docs.python.org/3.5/library/collections.html#deque-recipes

```
Fields by index:
Bob is a 30 year old male
Jane is a 29 year old female
```

In contrast, remembering which index should be used for each value can lead to errors, especially if the `tuple` has a lot of fields and is constructed far from where it is used. A `namedtuple` assigns names, as well as the numerical index, to each member.

2.2.5.1 Defining

`namedtuple` instances are just as memory efficient as regular tuples because they do not have per-instance dictionaries. Each kind of `namedtuple` is represented by its own class, which is created by using the `namedtuple()` factory function. The arguments are the name of the new class and a string containing the names of the elements.

Listing 2.31: `collections_namedtuple_person.py`

```python
import collections

Person = collections.namedtuple('Person', 'name age')

bob = Person(name='Bob', age=30)
print('\nRepresentation:', bob)

jane = Person(name='Jane', age=29)
print('\nField by name:', jane.name)

print('\nFields by index:')
for p in [bob, jane]:
    print('{} is {} years old'.format(*p))
```

As the example illustrates, it is possible to access the fields of the `namedtuple` by name using dotted notation (`obj.attr`) as well as by using the positional indexes of standard tuples.

```
$ python3 collections_namedtuple_person.py


Representation: Person(name='Bob', age=30)

Field by name: Jane

Fields by index:
Bob is 30 years old
Jane is 29 years old
```

Just like a regular `tuple`, a `namedtuple` is immutable. This restriction allows `tuple` instances to have a consistent hash value, which makes it possible to use them as keys in dictionaries and to be included in sets.

Listing 2.32: collections_namedtuple_immutable.py

```
import collections

Person = collections.namedtuple('Person', 'name age')

pat = Person(name='Pat', age=12)
print('\nRepresentation:', pat)

pat.age = 21
```

Trying to change a value through its named attribute results in an `AttributeError`.

```
$ python3 collections_namedtuple_immutable.py


Representation: Person(name='Pat', age=12)
Traceback (most recent call last):
  File "collections_namedtuple_immutable.py", line 17, in
<module>
    pat.age = 21
AttributeError: can't set attribute
```

2.2.5.2   Invalid Field Names

Field names are invalid if they are repeated or conflict with Python keywords.

Listing 2.33: collections_namedtuple_bad_fields.py

```
import collections

try:
    collections.namedtuple('Person', 'name class age')
except ValueError as err:
    print(err)

try:
    collections.namedtuple('Person', 'name age age')
except ValueError as err:
    print(err)
```

As the field names are parsed, invalid values cause `ValueError` exceptions.

```
$ python3 collections_namedtuple_bad_fields.py

Type names and field names cannot be a keyword: 'class'
Encountered duplicate field name: 'age'
```

In situations where a `namedtuple` is created based on values outside the control of the program (such as to represent the rows returned by a database query, where the schema is not known in advance), the `rename` option should be set to `True` so the invalid fields are renamed.

Listing 2.34: **collections_namedtuple_rename.py**

```python
import collections

with_class = collections.namedtuple(
    'Person', 'name class age',
    rename=True)
print(with_class._fields)

two_ages = collections.namedtuple(
    'Person', 'name age age',
    rename=True)
print(two_ages._fields)
```

The new names for renamed fields depend on their index in the tuple, so the field with name `class` becomes `_1` and the duplicate `age` field is changed to `_2`.

```
$ python3 collections_namedtuple_rename.py

('name', '_1', 'age')
('name', 'age', '_2')
```

2.2.5.3   Special Attributes

`namedtuple` provides several useful attributes and methods for working with subclasses and instances. All of these built-in properties have names prefixed with an underscore (`_`), which by convention in most Python programs indicates a private attribute. For `namedtuple`, however, the prefix is intended to protect the name from collision with user-provided attribute names.

The names of the fields passed to `namedtuple` to define the new class are saved in the `_fields` attribute.

Listing 2.35: **collections_namedtuple_fields.py**

```python
import collections

Person = collections.namedtuple('Person', 'name age')

bob = Person(name='Bob', age=30)
print('Representation:', bob)
print('Fields:', bob._fields)
```

Although the argument is a single space-separated string, the stored value is the sequence of individual names.

```
$ python3 collections_namedtuple_fields.py

Representation: Person(name='Bob', age=30)
Fields: ('name', 'age')
```

namedtuple instances can be converted to OrderedDict instances using _asdict().

Listing 2.36: collections_namedtuple_asdict.py

```
import collections

Person = collections.namedtuple('Person', 'name age')

bob = Person(name='Bob', age=30)
print('Representation:', bob)
print('As Dictionary:', bob._asdict())
```

The keys of the OrderedDict are in the same order as the fields for the namedtuple.

```
$ python3 collections_namedtuple_asdict.py

Representation: Person(name='Bob', age=30)
As Dictionary: OrderedDict([('name', 'Bob'), ('age', 30)])
```

The _replace() method builds a new instance, replacing the values of some fields in the process.

Listing 2.37: collections_namedtuple_replace.py

```
import collections

Person = collections.namedtuple('Person', 'name age')

bob = Person(name='Bob', age=30)
print('\nBefore:', bob)
bob2 = bob._replace(name='Robert')
print('After:', bob2)
print('Same?:', bob is bob2)
```

Although the name implies it is modifying the existing object, because namedtuple instances are immutable the method actually returns a new object.

```
$ python3 collections_namedtuple_replace.py


Before: Person(name='Bob', age=30)
After: Person(name='Robert', age=30)
Same?: False
```

2.2.6 OrderedDict: Remember the Order Keys Are Added to a Dictionary

An OrderedDict is a dictionary subclass that remembers the order in which its contents are added.

Listing 2.38: collections_ordereddict_iter.py

```
import collections

print('Regular dictionary:')
d = {}
d['a'] = 'A'
d['b'] = 'B'
d['c'] = 'C'

for k, v in d.items():
    print(k, v)

print('\nOrderedDict:')
d = collections.OrderedDict()
d['a'] = 'A'
d['b'] = 'B'
d['c'] = 'C'

for k, v in d.items():
    print(k, v)
```

A regular dict does not track the insertion order, and iterating over it produces the values in order based on how the keys are stored in the hash table, which is in turn influenced by a random value to reduce collisions. In an OrderedDict, by contrast, the order in which the items are inserted is remembered and used when creating an iterator.

```
$ python3 collections_ordereddict_iter.py

Regular dictionary:
c C
b B
a A

OrderedDict:
```

```
a A
b B
c C
```

2.2.6.1 Equality

A regular `dict` looks at its contents when testing for equality. An `OrderedDict` also considers the order in which the items were added.

Listing 2.39: collections_ordereddict_equality.py

```python
import collections

print('dict       :', end=' ')
d1 = {}
d1['a'] = 'A'
d1['b'] = 'B'
d1['c'] = 'C'

d2 = {}
d2['c'] = 'C'
d2['b'] = 'B'
d2['a'] = 'A'

print(d1 == d2)

print('OrderedDict:', end=' ')

d1 = collections.OrderedDict()
d1['a'] = 'A'
d1['b'] = 'B'
d1['c'] = 'C'

d2 = collections.OrderedDict()
d2['c'] = 'C'
d2['b'] = 'B'
d2['a'] = 'A'

print(d1 == d2)
```

In this case, since the two ordered dictionaries are created from values in a different order, they are considered to be different.

```
$ python3 collections_ordereddict_equality.py

dict       : True
OrderedDict: False
```

2.2.6.2   Reordering

It is possible to change the order of the keys in an `OrderedDict` by moving them to either
the beginning or the end of the sequence using `move_to_end()`.

Listing 2.40: collections_ordereddict_move_to_end.py

```
import collections

d = collections.OrderedDict(
    [('a', 'A'), ('b', 'B'), ('c', 'C')]
)

print('Before:')
for k, v in d.items():
    print(k, v)

d.move_to_end('b')

print('\nmove_to_end():')
for k, v in d.items():
    print(k, v)

d.move_to_end('b', last=False)

print('\nmove_to_end(last=False):')
for k, v in d.items():
    print(k, v)
```

The `last` argument tells `move_to_end()` whether to move the item to be the last item in
the key sequence (when `True`) or the first (when `False`).

```
$ python3 collections_ordereddict_move_to_end.py

Before:
a A
b B
c C

move_to_end():
a A
c C
b B

move_to_end(last=False):
b B
a A
c C
```

TIP

Related Reading

- PYTHONHASHSEED[8]: Environment variable to control the random seed value added to the hash algorithm for key locations in the dictionary.

2.2.7 collections.abc: Abstract Base Classes for Containers

The `collections.abc` module contains abstract base classes that define the APIs for container data structures built into Python and provided by the `collections` module. Refer to Table 2.1 for a list of the classes and their purposes.

Table 2.1: Abstract Base Classes

Class	Base Class(es)	API Purpose
Container		Basic container features, such as the `in` operator
Hashable		Adds support for providing a hash value for the container instance
Iterable		Can create an iterator over the container contents
Iterator	Iterable	Is an iterator over the container contents
Generator	Iterator	Extends iterators with the generator protocol from PEP 342
Sized		Adds methods for containers that know how big they are
Callable		For containers that can be invoked as a function
Sequence	Sized, Iterable, Container	Supports retrieving individual items, iterating, and changing the order of items
MutableSequence	Sequence	Supports adding and removing items to an instance after it has been created
ByteString	Sequence	Combined API of `bytes` and `bytearray`
Set	Sized, Iterable, Container	Supports set operations such as intersection and union
MutableSet	Set	Adds methods for manipulating the set contents after it is created
Mapping	Sized, Iterable, Container	Defines the read-only API used by `dict`
MutableMapping	Mapping	Defines the methods for manipulating the contents of a mapping after it is created
MappingView	Sized	Defines the view API for accessing a mapping from an iterator

continues

---

[8] https://docs.python.org/3.5/using/cmdline.html#envvar-PYTHONHASHSEED

Table 2.1: Abstract Base Classes, *continued*

Class	Base Class(es)	API Purpose
ItemsView	MappingView, Set	Part of the view API
KeysView	MappingView, Set	Part of the view API
ValuesView	MappingView	Part of the view API
Awaitable		API for objects that can be used in await expressions, such as coroutines
Coroutine	Awaitable	API for classes that implement the coroutine protocol
AsyncIterable		API for iterables compatible with async for, as defined in **PEP 492**
AsyncIterator	AsyncIterable	API for asynchronous iterators

In addition to clearly defining the APIs for containers with different semantics, these abstract base classes can be used to test whether an object supports an API before invoking it using isinstance(). Some of the classes also provide implementations of methods, and they can be used as mix-ins to build up custom container types without implementing every method from scratch.

TIP

Related Reading

- Standard library documentation for collections.[9]
- Python 2 to 3 porting notes for collections (page 1357).
- **PEP 342**[10]: Coroutines via Enhanced Generators.
- **PEP 492**[11]: Coroutines with async and await syntax.

2.3   array: Sequence of Fixed-Type Data

The array module defines a sequence data structure that looks very much like a list, except that all of the members have to be of the same primitive type. The types supported are all numeric or other fixed-size primitive types such as bytes.

Refer to Table 2.2 for some of the supported types. The standard library documentation for array includes a complete list of type codes.

2.3.1   Initialization

An array is instantiated with an argument describing the type of data to be allowed, and possibly an initial sequence of data to store in the array.

---

[9] https://docs.python.org/3.5/library/collections.html
[10] www.python.org/dev/peps/pep-0342
[11] www.python.org/dev/peps/pep-0492

Table 2.2: Type Codes for **array** Members

Code	Type	Minimum Size (Bytes)
b	Int	1
B	Int	1
h	Signed short	2
H	Unsigned short	2
i	Signed int	2
I	Unsigned int	2
l	Signed long	4
L	Unsigned long	4
q	Signed long long	8
Q	Unsigned long long	8
f	Float	4
d	Double float	8

Listing 2.41: **array_string.py**

```
import array
import binascii

s = b'This is the array.'
a = array.array('b', s)

print('As byte string:', s)
print('As array       :', a)
print('As hex         :', binascii.hexlify(a))
```

In this example, the array is configured to hold a sequence of bytes and is initialized with a simple byte string.

```
$ python3 array_string.py

As byte string: b'This is the array.'
As array       : array('b', [84, 104, 105, 115, 32, 105, 115, 32,
 116, 104, 101, 32, 97, 114, 114, 97, 121, 46])
As hex         : b'546869732069732074686520617272617921792e'
```

2.3.2 Manipulating Arrays

An array can be extended and otherwise manipulated in the same ways as other Python sequences.

Listing 2.42: **array_sequence.py**

```
import array
import pprint

a = array.array('i', range(3))
```

```
print('Initial :', a)

a.extend(range(3))
print('Extended:', a)

print('Slice    :', a[2:5])

print('Iterator:')
print(list(enumerate(a)))
```

The supported operations include slicing, iterating, and adding elements to the end.

```
$ python3 array_sequence.py

Initial : array('i', [0, 1, 2])
Extended: array('i', [0, 1, 2, 0, 1, 2])
Slice    : array('i', [2, 0, 1])
Iterator:
[(0, 0), (1, 1), (2, 2), (3, 0), (4, 1), (5, 2)]
```

2.3.3   Arrays and Files

The contents of an array can be written to and read from files using built-in methods coded efficiently for that purpose.

Listing 2.43: array_file.py

```
import array
import binascii
import tempfile

a = array.array('i', range(5))
print('A1:', a)

# Write the array of numbers to a temporary file.
output = tempfile.NamedTemporaryFile()
a.tofile(output.file)  # Must pass an *actual* file
output.flush()

# Read the raw data.
with open(output.name, 'rb') as input:
    raw_data = input.read()
    print('Raw Contents:', binascii.hexlify(raw_data))

    # Read the data into an array.
    input.seek(0)
    a2 = array.array('i')
    a2.fromfile(input, len(a))
    print('A2:', a2)
```

This example illustrates reading the data "raw," meaning directly from the binary file, versus reading it into a new array and converting the bytes to the appropriate types.

```
$ python3 array_file.py

A1: array('i', [0, 1, 2, 3, 4])
Raw Contents: b'0000000001000000020000000300000004000000'
A2: array('i', [0, 1, 2, 3, 4])
```

tofile() uses tobytes() to format the data, and fromfile() uses frombytes() to convert it back to an array instance.

Listing 2.44: array_tobytes.py

```python
import array
import binascii

a = array.array('i', range(5))
print('A1:', a)

as_bytes = a.tobytes()
print('Bytes:', binascii.hexlify(as_bytes))

a2 = array.array('i')
a2.frombytes(as_bytes)
print('A2:', a2)
```

Both tobytes() and frombytes() work on byte strings, not Unicode strings.

```
$ python3 array_tobytes.py

A1: array('i', [0, 1, 2, 3, 4])
Bytes: b'0000000001000000020000000300000004000000'
A2: array('i', [0, 1, 2, 3, 4])
```

2.3.4 Alternative Byte Ordering

If the data in the array is not in the native byte order, or if the data needs to be swapped before being sent to a system with a different byte order (or over the network), it is possible to convert the entire array without iterating over the elements from Python.

Listing 2.45: array_byteswap.py

```python
import array
import binascii


def to_hex(a):
    chars_per_item = a.itemsize * 2  # 2 hex digits
```

```
        hex_version = binascii.hexlify(a)
        num_chunks = len(hex_version) // chars_per_item
        for i in range(num_chunks):
            start = i * chars_per_item
            end = start + chars_per_item
            yield hex_version[start:end]

    start = int('0x12345678', 16)
    end = start + 5
    a1 = array.array('i', range(start, end))
    a2 = array.array('i', range(start, end))
    a2.byteswap()

    fmt = '{:>12} {:>12} {:>12} {:>12}'
    print(fmt.format('A1 hex', 'A1', 'A2 hex', 'A2'))
    print(fmt.format('-' * 12, '-' * 12, '-' * 12, '-' * 12))
    fmt = '{!r:>12} {:12} {!r:>12} {:12}'
    for values in zip(to_hex(a1), a1, to_hex(a2), a2):
        print(fmt.format(*values))
```

The `byteswap()` method switches the byte order of the items in the array from within C, so it is much more efficient than looping over the data in Python.

```
$ python3 array_byteswap.py

      A1 hex            A1       A2 hex            A2
------------  ------------  ------------  ------------
b'78563412'     305419896  b'12345678'    2018915346
b'79563412'     305419897  b'12345679'    2035692562
b'7a563412'     305419898  b'1234567a'    2052469778
b'7b563412'     305419899  b'1234567b'    2069246994
b'7c563412'     305419900  b'1234567c'    2086024210
```

TIP

Related Reading

- Standard library documentation for `array`.[12]
- `struct` (page 117): The `struct` module.
- Numerical Python[13]: NumPy is a Python library for working with large data sets efficiently.
- Python 2 to 3 porting notes for `array` (page 1357).

---

[12] https://docs.python.org/3.5/library/array.html
[13] www.scipy.org

2.4   heapq: Heap Sort Algorithm

A *heap* is a tree-like data structure in which the child nodes have a sort-order relationship with the parents. *Binary heaps* can be represented using a list or array organized so that the children of element N are at positions $2*N+1$ and $2*N+2$ (for zero-based indexes). This layout makes it possible to rearrange heaps in place, so it is not necessary to reallocate as much memory when adding or removing items.

A max-heap ensures that the parent is larger than or equal to both of its children. A min-heap requires that the parent be less than or equal to its children. Python's heapq module implements a min-heap.

2.4.1   Example Data

The examples in this section use the data in heapq_heapdata.py.

Listing 2.46: heapq_heapdata.py

```
# This data was generated with the random module.

data = [19, 9, 4, 10, 11]
```

The heap output is printed using heapq_showtree.py.

Listing 2.47: heapq_showtree.py

```
import math
from io import StringIO


def show_tree(tree, total_width=36, fill=' '):
    """Pretty-print a tree."""
    output = StringIO()
    last_row = -1
    for i, n in enumerate(tree):
        if i:
            row = int(math.floor(math.log(i + 1, 2)))
        else:
            row = 0
        if row != last_row:
            output.write('\n')
        columns = 2 ** row
        col_width = int(math.floor(total_width / columns))
        output.write(str(n).center(col_width, fill))
        last_row = row
    print(output.getvalue())
    print('-' * total_width)
    print()
```

2.4.2 Creating a Heap

There are two basic ways to create a heap: heappush() and heapify().

Listing 2.48: heapq_heappush.py

```
import heapq
from heapq_showtree import show_tree
from heapq_heapdata import data

heap = []
print('random :', data)
print()

for n in data:
    print('add {:>3}:'.format(n))
    heapq.heappush(heap, n)
    show_tree(heap)
```

When heappush() is used, the heap sort order of the elements is maintained as new items are added from a data source.

```
$ python3 heapq_heappush.py

random : [19, 9, 4, 10, 11]

add  19:

                        19
------------------------------------------

add   9:

                         9
            19
------------------------------------------

add   4:

                         4
            19                    9
------------------------------------------

add  10:

                         4
            10                    9
      19
------------------------------------------
```

```
add  11:

                    4
        10                    9
    19        11
-------------------------------------
```

If the data is already in memory, it is more efficient to use `heapify()` to rearrange the items of the list in place.

Listing 2.49: heapq_heapify.py

```
import heapq
from heapq_showtree import show_tree
from heapq_heapdata import data

print('random    :', data)
heapq.heapify(data)
print('heapified :')
show_tree(data)
```

The result of building a list in heap order one item at a time is the same as building an unordered list and then calling `heapify()`.

```
$ python3 heapq_heapify.py

random    : [19, 9, 4, 10, 11]
heapified :

                    4
        9                    19
    10        11
-------------------------------------
```

2.4.3   Accessing the Contents of a Heap

Once the heap is organized correctly, use `heappop()` to remove the element with the lowest value.

Listing 2.50: heapq_heappop.py

```
import heapq
from heapq_showtree import show_tree
from heapq_heapdata import data

print('random    :', data)
heapq.heapify(data)
```

```
print('heapified :')
show_tree(data)
print

for i in range(2):
    smallest = heapq.heappop(data)
    print('pop    {:>3}:'.format(smallest))
    show_tree(data)
```

In this example, adapted from the standard library documentation, `heapify()` and `heappop()` are used to sort a list of numbers.

```
$ python3 heapq_heappop.py

random     : [19, 9, 4, 10, 11]
heapified :

                        4
            9                       19
      10          11
------------------------------------

pop      4:

                        9
           10                       19
      11
------------------------------------

pop      9:

                       10
           11                       19
------------------------------------
```

To remove existing elements and replace them with new values in a single operation, use `heapreplace()`.

Listing 2.51: **heapq_heapreplace.py**

```
import heapq
from heapq_showtree import show_tree
from heapq_heapdata import data

heapq.heapify(data)
print('start:')
show_tree(data)

for n in [0, 13]:
```

```
        smallest = heapq.heapreplace(data, n)
        print('replace {:>2} with {:>2}:'.format(smallest, n))
        show_tree(data)
```

Replacing elements in place makes it possible to maintain a fixed-size heap, such as a queue of jobs ordered by priority.

```
$ python3 heapq_heapreplace.py

start:

                         4
           9                         19
      10        11
------------------------------------

replace  4 with  0:

                         0
           9                         19
      10        11
------------------------------------

replace  0 with 13:

                         9
          10                         19
      13        11
------------------------------------
```

2.4.4   Data Extremes from a Heap

heapq also includes two functions to examine an iterable and find a range of the largest or smallest values it contains.

Listing 2.52: heapq_extremes.py

```
import heapq
from heapq_heapdata import data

print('all       :', data)
print('3 largest :', heapq.nlargest(3, data))
print('from sort :', list(reversed(sorted(data)[-3:])))
print('3 smallest:', heapq.nsmallest(3, data))
print('from sort :', sorted(data)[:3])
```

Using nlargest() and nsmallest() is efficient only for relatively small values of $n > 1$, but can still come in handy in a few cases.

```
$ python3 heapq_extremes.py

all        : [19, 9, 4, 10, 11]
3 largest  : [19, 11, 10]
from sort  : [19, 11, 10]
3 smallest : [4, 9, 10]
from sort  : [4, 9, 10]
```

2.4.5   Efficiently Merging Sorted Sequences

Combining several sorted sequences into one new sequence is easy for small data sets.

```
list(sorted(itertools.chain(*data)))
```

For larger data sets, this technique can use a considerable amount of memory. Instead of sorting the entire combined sequence, merge() uses a heap to generate a new sequence one item at a time, determining the next item using a fixed amount of memory.

Listing 2.53: heapq_merge.py

```python
import heapq
import random


random.seed(2016)

data = []
for i in range(4):
    new_data = list(random.sample(range(1, 101), 5))
    new_data.sort()
    data.append(new_data)

for i, d in enumerate(data):
    print('{}: {}'.format(i, d))

print('\nMerged:')
for i in heapq.merge(*data):
    print(i, end=' ')
print()
```

Because the implementation of merge() uses a heap, it consumes memory based on the number of sequences being merged, rather than the number of items in those sequences.

```
$ python3 heapq_merge.py

0: [33, 58, 71, 88, 95]
1: [10, 11, 17, 38, 91]
```

```
2: [13, 18, 39, 61, 63]
3: [20, 27, 31, 42, 45]

Merged:
10 11 13 17 18 20 27 31 33 38 39 42 45 58 61 63 71 88 91 95
```

TIP

Related Reading

- Standard library documentation for heapq.[14]
- Wikipedia: Heap (data structure)[15]: A general description of heap data structures.
- Section 2.6.3, "Priority Queue" (page 113): A priority queue implementation from Queue in the standard library.

2.5 bisect: Maintain Lists in Sorted Order

The bisect module implements an algorithm for inserting elements into a list while maintaining the list in sorted order.

2.5.1 Inserting in Sorted Order

Here is a simple example in which insort() is used to insert items into a list in sorted order.

Listing 2.54: bisect_example.py

```python
import bisect

# A series of random numbers
values = [14, 85, 77, 26, 50, 45, 66, 79, 10, 3, 84, 77, 1]

print('New  Pos  Contents')
print('---  ---  --------')

l = []
for i in values:
    position = bisect.bisect(l, i)
    bisect.insort(l, i)
    print('{:3}  {:3}'.format(i, position), l)
```

The first column of the output shows the new random number. The second column shows the position where the number will be inserted into the list. The remainder of each line is the current sorted list.

---

[14] https://docs.python.org/3.5/library/heapq.html
[15] https://en.wikipedia.org/wiki/Heap_(data_structure)

```
$ python3 bisect_example.py

New  Pos  Contents
---  ---  --------
 14    0  [14]
 85    1  [14, 85]
 77    1  [14, 77, 85]
 26    1  [14, 26, 77, 85]
 50    2  [14, 26, 50, 77, 85]
 45    2  [14, 26, 45, 50, 77, 85]
 66    4  [14, 26, 45, 50, 66, 77, 85]
 79    6  [14, 26, 45, 50, 66, 77, 79, 85]
 10    0  [10, 14, 26, 45, 50, 66, 77, 79, 85]
  3    0  [3, 10, 14, 26, 45, 50, 66, 77, 79, 85]
 84    9  [3, 10, 14, 26, 45, 50, 66, 77, 79, 84, 85]
 77    8  [3, 10, 14, 26, 45, 50, 66, 77, 77, 79, 84, 85]
  1    0  [1, 3, 10, 14, 26, 45, 50, 66, 77, 77, 79, 84, 85]
```

This is a simple example. In fact, given the amount of data being manipulated, it might be faster to simply build the list and then sort it once. By contrast, for long lists, significant time and memory savings can be achieved using an insertion sort algorithm such as this, especially when the operation to compare two members of the list requires expensive computation.

2.5.2 Handling Duplicates

The result set shown previously includes a repeated value, 77. The `bisect` module provides two ways to handle repeats: New values can be inserted either to the left of existing values, or to the right. The `insort()` function is actually an alias for `insort_right()`, which inserts an item after the existing value. The corresponding function `insort_left()` inserts an item before the existing value.

Listing 2.55: **bisect_example2.py**

```python
import bisect

# A series of random numbers
values = [14, 85, 77, 26, 50, 45, 66, 79, 10, 3, 84, 77, 1]

print('New  Pos  Contents')
print('---  ---  --------')

# Use bisect_left and insort_left.
l = []
for i in values:
    position = bisect.bisect_left(l, i)
    bisect.insort_left(l, i)
    print('{:3}  {:3}'.format(i, position), l)
```

When the same data is manipulated using `bisect_left()` and `insort_left()`, the results are the same sorted list but the insert positions are different for the duplicate values.

```
$ python3 bisect_example2.py

New  Pos  Contents
---  ---  --------
 14   0  [14]
 85   1  [14, 85]
 77   1  [14, 77, 85]
 26   1  [14, 26, 77, 85]
 50   2  [14, 26, 50, 77, 85]
 45   2  [14, 26, 45, 50, 77, 85]
 66   4  [14, 26, 45, 50, 66, 77, 85]
 79   6  [14, 26, 45, 50, 66, 77, 79, 85]
 10   0  [10, 14, 26, 45, 50, 66, 77, 79, 85]
  3   0  [3, 10, 14, 26, 45, 50, 66, 77, 79, 85]
 84   9  [3, 10, 14, 26, 45, 50, 66, 77, 79, 84, 85]
 77   7  [3, 10, 14, 26, 45, 50, 66, 77, 77, 79, 84, 85]
  1   0  [1, 3, 10, 14, 26, 45, 50, 66, 77, 77, 79, 84, 85]
```

TIP

Related Reading

- Standard library documentation for `bisect`.[16]
- Wikipedia: Insertion Sort[17]: A description of the insertion sort algorithm.

2.6   queue: Thread-Safe FIFO Implementation

The queue module provides a first-in, first-out (FIFO) data structure suitable for multi-threaded programming. It can be used to pass messages or other data between producer and consumer threads safely. Locking is handled for the caller, so many threads can work with the same Queue instance safely and easily. The size of a Queue (the number of elements it contains) may be restricted to throttle memory usage or processing.

NOTE

This discussion assumes you already understand the general nature of a queue. If you do not, you may want to read some of the references before continuing.

---

[16] https://docs.python.org/3.5/library/bisect.html
[17] https://en.wikipedia.org/wiki/Insertion_sort

2.6.1   Basic FIFO Queue

The `Queue` class implements a basic first-in, first-out container. Elements are added to one
"end" of the sequence using `put()`, and removed from the other end using `get()`.

Listing 2.56: **queue_fifo.py**

```
import queue

q = queue.Queue()

for i in range(5):
    q.put(i)

while not q.empty():
    print(q.get(), end=' ')
print()
```

This example uses a single thread to illustrate that elements are removed from the queue
in the same order in which they are inserted.

```
$ python3 queue_fifo.py

0 1 2 3 4
```

2.6.2   LIFO Queue

In contrast to the standard FIFO implementation of `Queue`, the `LifoQueue` uses last-in,
first-out ordering (normally associated with a stack data structure).

Listing 2.57: **queue_lifo.py**

```
import queue

q = queue.LifoQueue()

for i in range(5):
    q.put(i)

while not q.empty():
    print(q.get(), end=' ')
print()
```

The item most recently `put` into the queue is removed by `get`.

```
$ python3 queue_lifo.py

4 3 2 1 0
```

2.6.3 Priority Queue

Sometimes the processing order of the items in a queue needs to be based on characteristics of those items, rather than just the order they are created or added to the queue. For example, print jobs from the payroll department may take precedence over a code listing that a developer wants to print. PriorityQueue uses the sort order of the contents of the queue to decide which item to retrieve.

Listing 2.58: `queue_priority.py`

```python
import functools
import queue
import threading


@functools.total_ordering
class Job:

    def __init__(self, priority, description):
        self.priority = priority
        self.description = description
        print('New job:', description)
        return

    def __eq__(self, other):
        try:
            return self.priority == other.priority
        except AttributeError:
            return NotImplemented

    def __lt__(self, other):
        try:
            return self.priority < other.priority
        except AttributeError:
            return NotImplemented


q = queue.PriorityQueue()

q.put(Job(3, 'Mid-level job'))
q.put(Job(10, 'Low-level job'))
q.put(Job(1, 'Important job'))


def process_job(q):
    while True:
        next_job = q.get()
        print('Processing job:', next_job.description)
        q.task_done()
```

```
workers = [
    threading.Thread(target=process_job, args=(q,)),
    threading.Thread(target=process_job, args=(q,)),
]
for w in workers:
    w.setDaemon(True)
    w.start()

q.join()
```

This example has multiple threads consuming the jobs, which are processed based on the priority of items in the queue at the time `get()` was called. The order of processing for items added to the queue while the consumer threads are running depends on thread context switching.

```
$ python3 queue_priority.py

New job: Mid-level job
New job: Low-level job
New job: Important job
Processing job: Important job
Processing job: Mid-level job
Processing job: Low-level job
```

2.6.4   Building a Threaded Podcast Client

The source code for the podcasting client in this section demonstrates how to use the `Queue` class with multiple threads. The program reads one or more RSS feeds, queues up the enclosures for the five most recent episodes from each feed to be downloaded, and processes several downloads in parallel using threads. It does not have enough error handling for production use, but the skeleton implementation illustrates the use of the `queue` module.

First, some operating parameters are established. Usually, these would come from user inputs (e.g., preferences or a database). The example uses hard-coded values for the number of threads and list of URLs to fetch.

Listing 2.59: **fetch_podcasts.py**

```
from queue import Queue
import threading
import time
import urllib
from urllib.parse import urlparse

import feedparser

# Set up some global variables.
num_fetch_threads = 2
enclosure_queue = Queue()
```

```
    # A real app wouldn't use hard-coded data.
    feed_urls = [
        'http://talkpython.fm/episodes/rss',
    ]


    def message(s):
        print('{}: {}'.format(threading.current_thread().name, s))
```

The function `download_enclosures()` runs in the worker thread and processes the downloads using `urllib`.

```
    def download_enclosures(q):
        """This is the worker thread function.
        It processes items in the queue one after
        another.  These daemon threads go into an
        infinite loop, and exit only when
        the main thread ends.
        """
        while True:
            message('looking for the next enclosure')
            url = q.get()
            filename = url.rpartition('/')[-1]
            message('downloading {}'.format(filename))
            response = urllib.request.urlopen(url)
            data = response.read()
            # Save the downloaded file to the current directory.
            message('writing to {}'.format(filename))
            with open(filename, 'wb') as outfile:
                outfile.write(data)
            q.task_done()
```

Once the target function for the threads is defined, the worker threads can be started. When `download_enclosures()` processes the statement `url = q.get()`, it blocks and waits until the queue has something to return. That means it is safe to start the threads before there is anything in the queue.

```
    # Set up some threads to fetch the enclosures.
    for i in range(num_fetch_threads):
        worker = threading.Thread(
            target=download_enclosures,
            args=(enclosure_queue,),
            name='worker-{}'.format(i),
        )
        worker.setDaemon(True)
        worker.start()
```

The next step is to retrieve the feed contents using the `feedparser` module and enqueue the URLs of the enclosures. As soon as the first URL is added to the queue, one of the worker threads picks it up and starts downloading it. The loop continues to add items until the feed is exhausted, and the worker threads take turns dequeuing URLs to download them.

```python
# Download the feed(s) and put the enclosure URLs into
# the queue.
for url in feed_urls:
    response = feedparser.parse(url, agent='fetch_podcasts.py')
    for entry in response['entries'][:5]:
        for enclosure in entry.get('enclosures', []):
            parsed_url = urlparse(enclosure['url'])
            message('queuing {}'.format(
                parsed_url.path.rpartition('/')[-1]))
            enclosure_queue.put(enclosure['url'])
```

The only thing left to do is wait for the queue to empty out again, using `join()`.

```python
# Now wait for the queue to be empty, indicating that we have
# processed all of the downloads.
message('*** main thread waiting')
enclosure_queue.join()
message('*** done')
```

Running the sample script produces output similar to the following.

```
$ python3 fetch_podcasts.py

worker-0: looking for the next enclosure
worker-1: looking for the next enclosure
MainThread: queuing turbogears-and-the-future-of-python-web-framework
s.mp3
MainThread: queuing continuum-scientific-python-and-the-business-of-o
pen-source.mp3
MainThread: queuing openstack-cloud-computing-built-on-python.mp3
MainThread: queuing pypy.js-pypy-python-in-your-browser.mp3
MainThread: queuing machine-learning-with-python-and-scikit-learn.mp3
MainThread: *** main thread waiting
worker-0: downloading turbogears-and-the-future-of-python-web-framewo
rks.mp3
worker-1: downloading continuum-scientific-python-and-the-business-of
-open-source.mp3
worker-0: looking for the next enclosure
worker-0: downloading openstack-cloud-computing-built-on-python.mp3
worker-1: looking for the next enclosure
worker-1: downloading pypy.js-pypy-python-in-your-browser.mp3
worker-0: looking for the next enclosure
worker-0: downloading machine-learning-with-python-and-scikit-learn.m
p3
```

```
worker-1: looking for the next enclosure
worker-0: looking for the next enclosure
MainThread: *** done
```

The actual output will depend on the contents of the RSS feed used.

TIP

Related Reading

- Standard library documentation for queue.[18]
- deque: Double-ended queue (page 84) from collections (page 75).
- Queue data structures[19]: Wikipedia article explaining queues.
- FIFO[20]: Wikipedia article explaining first-in, first-out data structures.
- feedparser module[21]: A module for parsing RSS and Atom feeds, created by Mark Pilgrim and maintained by Kurt McKee.

2.7   struct: Binary Data Structures

The struct module includes functions for converting between strings of bytes and native Python data types such as numbers and strings.

2.7.1   Functions Versus Struct Class

A set of module-level functions is available for working with structured values, as well as the Struct class. Format specifiers are converted from their string format to a compiled representation, similar to the way regular expressions are handled. The conversion takes some resources, so it is typically more efficient to do it once when creating a Struct instance and call methods on the instance instead of using the module-level functions. All of the following examples use the Struct class.

2.7.2   Packing and Unpacking

Structs support *packing* data into strings, and *unpacking* data from strings using format specifiers made up of characters representing the type of the data and optional count and endianness indicators. Refer to the standard library documentation for a complete list of the supported format specifiers.

In this example, the specifier calls for an integer or long integer value, a two-byte string, and a floating-point number. The spaces in the format specifier are included to separate the type indicators, and are ignored when the format is compiled.

---

[18] https://docs.python.org/3.5/library/queue.html
[19] https://en.wikipedia.org/wiki/Queue_(abstract_data_type)
[20] https://en.wikipedia.org/wiki/FIFO_(computing_and_electronics)
[21] https://pypi.python.org/pypi/feedparser

Listing 2.60: **struct_pack.py**

Listing 2.60: **struct_pack.py**

```
import struct
import binascii

values = (1, 'ab'.encode('utf-8'), 2.7)
s = struct.Struct('I 2s f')
packed_data = s.pack(*values)

print('Original values:', values)
print('Format string  :', s.format)
print('Uses           :', s.size, 'bytes')
print('Packed Value   :', binascii.hexlify(packed_data))
```

The example converts the packed value to a sequence of hex bytes for printing with
binascii.hexlify(), since some of the characters are nulls.

```
$ python3 struct_pack.py

Original values: (1, b'ab', 2.7)
Format string  : b'I 2s f'
Uses           : 12 bytes
Packed Value   : b'0100000061620000cdcc2c40'
```

Use unpack() to extract data from its packed representation.

Listing 2.61: **struct_unpack.py**

```
import struct
import binascii

packed_data = binascii.unhexlify(b'0100000061620000cdcc2c40')

s = struct.Struct('I 2s f')
unpacked_data = s.unpack(packed_data)
print('Unpacked Values:', unpacked_data)
```

Passing the packed value to unpack(), gives basically the same values back (note the discrepancy in the floating point value).

```
$ python3 struct_unpack.py

Unpacked Values: (1, b'ab', 2.700000047683716)
```

2.7.3 Endianness

By default, values are encoded using the native C library notion of *endianness*. It is easy
to override that choice by providing an explicit endianness directive in the format string.

Table 2.3: Byte Order Specifiers for Struct

Code	Meaning
@	Native order
=	Native standard
<	Little-endian
>	Big-endian
!	Network order

Listing 2.62: struct_endianness.py

```python
import struct
import binascii

values = (1, 'ab'.encode('utf-8'), 2.7)
print('Original values:', values)

endianness = [
    ('@', 'native, native'),
    ('=', 'native, standard'),
    ('<', 'little-endian'),
    ('>', 'big-endian'),
    ('!', 'network'),
]

for code, name in endianness:
    s = struct.Struct(code + ' I 2s f')
    packed_data = s.pack(*values)
    print()
    print('Format string  :', s.format, 'for', name)
    print('Uses           :', s.size, 'bytes')
    print('Packed Value   :', binascii.hexlify(packed_data))
    print('Unpacked Value :', s.unpack(packed_data))
```

Table 2.3 lists the byte order specifiers used by Struct.

```
$ python3 struct_endianness.py

Original values: (1, b'ab', 2.7)

Format string  : b'@ I 2s f' for native, native
Uses           : 12 bytes
Packed Value   : b'0100000061620000cdcc2c40'
Unpacked Value : (1, b'ab', 2.700000047683716)

Format string  : b'= I 2s f' for native, standard
Uses           : 10 bytes
Packed Value   : b'010000006162cdcc2c40'
```

```
Unpacked Value : (1, b'ab', 2.700000047683716)

Format string  : b'< I 2s f' for little-endian
Uses           : 10 bytes
Packed Value   : b'010000006162cdcc2c40'
Unpacked Value : (1, b'ab', 2.700000047683716)

Format string  : b'> I 2s f' for big-endian
Uses           : 10 bytes
Packed Value   : b'000000016162402ccccd'
Unpacked Value : (1, b'ab', 2.700000047683716)

Format string  : b'! I 2s f' for network
Uses           : 10 bytes
Packed Value   : b'000000016162402ccccd'
Unpacked Value : (1, b'ab', 2.700000047683716)
```

2.7.4   Buffers

Working with binary packed data is typically reserved for performance-sensitive situations or passing data into and out of extension modules. These cases can be optimized by avoiding the overhead of allocating a new buffer for each packed structure. The pack_into() and unpack_from() methods support writing to pre-allocated buffers directly.

Listing 2.63: **struct_buffers.py**

```python
import array
import binascii
import ctypes
import struct

s = struct.Struct('I 2s f')
values = (1, 'ab'.encode('utf-8'), 2.7)
print('Original:', values)

print()
print('ctypes string buffer')

b = ctypes.create_string_buffer(s.size)
print('Before   :', binascii.hexlify(b.raw))
s.pack_into(b, 0, *values)
print('After    :', binascii.hexlify(b.raw))
print('Unpacked:', s.unpack_from(b, 0))

print()
print('array')

a = array.array('b', b'\0' * s.size)
```

```
print('Before   :', binascii.hexlify(a))
s.pack_into(a, 0, *values)
print('After    :', binascii.hexlify(a))
print('Unpacked:', s.unpack_from(a, 0))
```

The size attribute of the Struct tells us how big the buffer needs to be.

```
$ python3 struct_buffers.py

Original: (1, b'ab', 2.7)

ctypes string buffer
Before   : b'00000000000000000000000000'
After    : b'0100000061620000cdcc2c40'
Unpacked: (1, b'ab', 2.700000047683716)

array
Before   : b'00000000000000000000000000'
After    : b'0100000061620000cdcc2c40'
Unpacked: (1, b'ab', 2.700000047683716)
```

TIP

Related Reading

- Standard library documentation for struct.[22]
- Python 2 to 3 porting notes for struct (page 1363).
- array (page 98): The array module, for working with sequences of fixed-type values.
- binascii: The binascii module, for producing ASCII representations of binary data.
- WikiPedia: Endianness[23]: Explanation of byte order and endianness in encoding.

2.8   weakref: Impermanent References to Objects

The weakref module supports weak references to objects. A normal reference increments the reference count on the object and prevents it from being garbage collected. This outcome is not always desirable, especially when a circular reference might be present or when a cache of objects should be deleted when memory is needed. A weak reference is a handle to an object that does not keep it from being cleaned up automatically.

---

[22] https://docs.python.org/3.5/library/struct.html
[23] https://en.wikipedia.org/wiki/Endianness

2.8.1   References

Weak references to objects are managed through the `ref` class. To retrieve the original object, call the reference object.

Listing 2.64: **weakref_ref.py**

```
import weakref


class ExpensiveObject:

    def __del__(self):
        print('(Deleting {})'.format(self))


obj = ExpensiveObject()
r = weakref.ref(obj)

print('obj:', obj)
print('ref:', r)
print('r():', r())

print('deleting obj')
del obj
print('r():', r())
```

In this case, since `obj` is deleted before the second call to the reference, the `ref` returns None.

```
$ python3 weakref_ref.py

obj: <__main__.ExpensiveObject object at 0x1007b1a58>
ref: <weakref at 0x1007a92c8; to 'ExpensiveObject' at
0x1007b1a58>
r(): <__main__.ExpensiveObject object at 0x1007b1a58>
deleting obj
(Deleting <__main__.ExpensiveObject object at 0x1007b1a58>)
r(): None
```

2.8.2   Reference Callbacks

The `ref` constructor accepts an optional callback function that is invoked when the referenced object is deleted.

Listing 2.65: **weakref_ref_callback.py**

```
import weakref


class ExpensiveObject:

    def __del__(self):
        print('(Deleting {})'.format(self))


def callback(reference):
    """Invoked when referenced object is deleted"""
    print('callback({!r})'.format(reference))


obj = ExpensiveObject()
r = weakref.ref(obj, callback)

print('obj:', obj)
print('ref:', r)
print('r():', r())

print('deleting obj')
del obj
print('r():', r())
```

The callback receives the reference object as an argument after the reference is "dead"
and no longer refers to the original object. One use for this feature is to remove the weak
reference object from a cache.

```
$ python3 weakref_ref_callback.py

obj: <__main__.ExpensiveObject object at 0x1010b1978>
ref: <weakref at 0x1010a92c8; to 'ExpensiveObject' at
0x1010b1978>
r(): <__main__.ExpensiveObject object at 0x1010b1978>
deleting obj
(Deleting <__main__.ExpensiveObject object at 0x1010b1978>)
callback(<weakref at 0x1010a92c8; dead>)
r(): None
```

2.8.3   Finalizing Objects

For more robust management of resources when weak references are cleaned up, use `finalize`
to associate callbacks with objects. A `finalize` instance is retained until the attached object
is deleted, even if the application does not retain a reference to the finalizer.

Listing 2.66: **weakref_finalize.py**

```
import weakref


class ExpensiveObject:

    def __del__(self):
        print('(Deleting {})'.format(self))


def on_finalize(*args):
    print('on_finalize({!r})'.format(args))


obj = ExpensiveObject()
weakref.finalize(obj, on_finalize, 'extra argument')

del obj
```

The arguments to `finalize` are the object to track, a callable to invoke when the object is garbage collected, and any positional or named arguments to pass to the callable.

```
$ python3 weakref_finalize.py

(Deleting <__main__.ExpensiveObject object at 0x1019b10f0>)
on_finalize(('extra argument',))
```

The `finalize` instance has a writable property `atexit` to control whether the callback is invoked as a program is exiting, if it hasn't already been called.

Listing 2.67: **weakref_finalize_atexit.py**

```
import sys
import weakref


class ExpensiveObject:

    def __del__(self):
        print('(Deleting {})'.format(self))


def on_finalize(*args):
    print('on_finalize({!r})'.format(args))


obj = ExpensiveObject()
f = weakref.finalize(obj, on_finalize, 'extra argument')
f.atexit = bool(int(sys.argv[1]))
```

The default is to invoke the callback. Setting `atexit` to false disables that behavior.

```
$ python3 weakref_finalize_atexit.py 1

on_finalize(('extra argument',))
(Deleting <__main__.ExpensiveObject object at 0x1007b10f0>)

$ python3 weakref_finalize_atexit.py 0
```

Giving the `finalize` instance a reference to the object it tracks causes a reference to be retained, so the object is never garbage collected.

Listing 2.68: **weakref_finalize_reference.py**

```python
import gc
import weakref


class ExpensiveObject:

    def __del__(self):
        print('(Deleting {})'.format(self))


def on_finalize(*args):
    print('on_finalize({!r})'.format(args))


obj = ExpensiveObject()
obj_id = id(obj)

f = weakref.finalize(obj, on_finalize, obj)
f.atexit = False

del obj

for o in gc.get_objects():
    if id(o) == obj_id:
        print('found uncollected object in gc')
```

As this example shows, even though the explicit reference to `obj` is deleted, the object is retained and visible to the garbage collector through `f`.

```
$ python3 weakref_finalize_reference.py

found uncollected object in gc
```

Using a bound method of a tracked object as the callable can also prevent an object from being finalized properly.

Listing 2.69: **weakref_finalize_reference_method.py**

```python
import gc
import weakref


class ExpensiveObject:

    def __del__(self):
        print('(Deleting {})'.format(self))

    def do_finalize(self):
        print('do_finalize')


obj = ExpensiveObject()
obj_id = id(obj)

f = weakref.finalize(obj, obj.do_finalize)
f.atexit = False

del obj

for o in gc.get_objects():
    if id(o) == obj_id:
        print('found uncollected object in gc')
```

Because the callable given to `finalize` is a bound method of the instance `obj`, the finalize object holds a reference to `obj`, which cannot be deleted and garbage collected.

```
$ python3 weakref_finalize_reference_method.py

found uncollected object in gc
```

2.8.4   Proxies

It is sometimes more convenient to use a proxy, rather than a weak reference. Proxies can be used as though they were the original object, and do not need to be called before the object is accessible. As a consequence, they can be passed to a library that does not know it is receiving a reference instead of the real object.

Listing 2.70: **weakref_proxy.py**

```python
import weakref


class ExpensiveObject:

    def __init__(self, name):
```

```
        self.name = name

    def __del__(self):
        print('(Deleting {})'.format(self))


obj = ExpensiveObject('My Object')
r = weakref.ref(obj)
p = weakref.proxy(obj)

print('via obj:', obj.name)
print('via ref:', r().name)
print('via proxy:', p.name)
del obj
print('via proxy:', p.name)
```

If the proxy is accessed after the referent object is removed, a `ReferenceError` exception is raised.

```
$ python3 weakref_proxy.py

via obj: My Object
via ref: My Object
via proxy: My Object
(Deleting <__main__.ExpensiveObject object at 0x1007aa7b8>)
Traceback (most recent call last):
  File "weakref_proxy.py", line 30, in <module>
    print('via proxy:', p.name)
ReferenceError: weakly-referenced object no longer exists
```

2.8.5 Caching Objects

The `ref` and `proxy` classes are considered "low level." While they are useful for maintaining weak references to individual objects and allowing cycles to be garbage collected, the `WeakKeyDictionary` and `WeakValueDictionary` classes provide a more appropriate API for creating a cache of several objects.

The `WeakValueDictionary` class uses weak references to the values it holds, allowing them to be garbage collected when other code is not actually using them. Using explicit calls to the garbage collector illustrates the difference between memory handling with a regular dictionary and `WeakValueDictionary`:

Listing 2.71: weakref_valuedict.py

```
import gc
from pprint import pprint
import weakref

gc.set_debug(gc.DEBUG_UNCOLLECTABLE)
```

```python
class ExpensiveObject:

    def __init__(self, name):
        self.name = name

    def __repr__(self):
        return 'ExpensiveObject({})'.format(self.name)

    def __del__(self):
        print('    (Deleting {})'.format(self))


def demo(cache_factory):
    # Hold objects so any weak references
    # are not removed immediately.
    all_refs = {}
    # Create the cache using the factory.
    print('CACHE TYPE:', cache_factory)
    cache = cache_factory()
    for name in ['one', 'two', 'three']:
        o = ExpensiveObject(name)
        cache[name] = o
        all_refs[name] = o
        del o  # decref

    print('  all_refs =', end=' ')
    pprint(all_refs)
    print('\n  Before, cache contains:', list(cache.keys()))
    for name, value in cache.items():
        print('    {} = {}'.format(name, value))
        del value  # decref

    # Remove all references to the objects except the cache.
    print('\n  Cleanup:')
    del all_refs
    gc.collect()

    print('\n  After, cache contains:', list(cache.keys()))
    for name, value in cache.items():
        print('    {} = {}'.format(name, value))
    print('  demo returning')
    return


demo(dict)
print()

demo(weakref.WeakValueDictionary)
```

Any loop variables that refer to the values being cached must be cleared explicitly so the reference count of the object is decremented. Otherwise, the garbage collector will not remove the objects and they will remain in the cache. Similarly, the `all_refs` variable is used to hold references to prevent them from being garbage collected prematurely.

```
$ python3 weakref_valuedict.py

CACHE TYPE: <class 'dict'>
  all_refs = {'one': ExpensiveObject(one),
 'three': ExpensiveObject(three),
 'two': ExpensiveObject(two)}

  Before, cache contains: ['one', 'three', 'two']
    one = ExpensiveObject(one)
    three = ExpensiveObject(three)
    two = ExpensiveObject(two)

  Cleanup:

  After, cache contains: ['one', 'three', 'two']
    one = ExpensiveObject(one)
    three = ExpensiveObject(three)
    two = ExpensiveObject(two)
  demo returning
    (Deleting ExpensiveObject(one))
    (Deleting ExpensiveObject(three))
    (Deleting ExpensiveObject(two))

CACHE TYPE: <class 'weakref.WeakValueDictionary'>
  all_refs = {'one': ExpensiveObject(one),
 'three': ExpensiveObject(three),
 'two': ExpensiveObject(two)}

  Before, cache contains: ['one', 'three', 'two']
    one = ExpensiveObject(one)
    three = ExpensiveObject(three)
    two = ExpensiveObject(two)

  Cleanup:
    (Deleting ExpensiveObject(one))
    (Deleting ExpensiveObject(three))
    (Deleting ExpensiveObject(two))

  After, cache contains: []
  demo returning
```

The `WeakKeyDictionary` works similarly but uses weak references for the keys instead of the values in the dictionary.

WARNING

The library documentation for weakref contains this warning:

> **Caution:** Because a WeakValueDictionary is built on top of a Python dictionary, it must not change size when iterating over it. This can be difficult to ensure for a WeakValueDictionary because actions performed by the program during iteration may cause items in the dictionary to vanish "by magic" (as a side effect of garbage collection).

TIP

Related Reading

- Standard library documentation for weakref.[24]
- gc (page 1254): The gc module is the interface to the interpreter's garbage collector.
- **PEP 205**[25]: Weak References enhancement proposal.

2.9   copy: Duplicate Objects

The copy module includes two functions, copy() and deepcopy(), for duplicating existing objects.

2.9.1   Shallow Copies

The *shallow copy* created by copy() is a new container populated with references to the contents of the original object. When making a shallow copy of a list object, a new list is constructed and the elements of the original object are appended to it.

Listing 2.72: **copy_shallow.py**

```
import copy
import functools


@functools.total_ordering
class MyClass:

    def __init__(self, name):
        self.name = name

    def __eq__(self, other):
        return self.name == other.name

    def __gt__(self, other):
```

---

[24] https://docs.python.org/3.5/library/weakref.html
[25] www.python.org/dev/peps/pep-0205

```
        return self.name > other.name


a = MyClass('a')
my_list = [a]
dup = copy.copy(my_list)

print('             my_list:', my_list)
print('                 dup:', dup)
print('      dup is my_list:', (dup is my_list))
print('      dup == my_list:', (dup == my_list))
print('dup[0] is my_list[0]:', (dup[0] is my_list[0]))
print('dup[0] == my_list[0]:', (dup[0] == my_list[0]))
```

For a shallow copy, the MyClass instance is not duplicated, so the reference in the dup list is to the same object that is in my_list.

```
$ python3 copy_shallow.py

             my_list: [<__main__.MyClass object at 0x1007a87b8>]
                 dup: [<__main__.MyClass object at 0x1007a87b8>]
      dup is my_list: False
      dup == my_list: True
dup[0] is my_list[0]: True
dup[0] == my_list[0]: True
```

2.9.2 Deep Copies

The *deep copy* created by deepcopy() is a new container populated with copies of the contents of the original object. To make a deep copy of a list, a new list is constructed, the elements of the original list are copied, and then those copies are appended to the new list.

Replacing the call to copy() with deepcopy() makes the difference in the output apparent.

Listing 2.73: copy_deep.py

```
import copy
import functools


@functools.total_ordering
class MyClass:

    def __init__(self, name):
        self.name = name

    def __eq__(self, other):
```

```
            return self.name == other.name

        def __gt__(self, other):
            return self.name > other.name


a = MyClass('a')
my_list = [a]
dup = copy.deepcopy(my_list)

print('           my_list:', my_list)
print('               dup:', dup)
print('     dup is my_list:', (dup is my_list))
print('     dup == my_list:', (dup == my_list))
print('dup[0] is my_list[0]:', (dup[0] is my_list[0]))
print('dup[0] == my_list[0]:', (dup[0] == my_list[0]))
```

The first element of the list is no longer the same object reference, but when the two objects are compared they still evaluate as being equal.

```
$ python3 copy_deep.py

            my_list: [<__main__.MyClass object at 0x1018a87b8>]
                dup: [<__main__.MyClass object at 0x1018b1b70>]
     dup is my_list: False
     dup == my_list: True
dup[0] is my_list[0]: False
dup[0] == my_list[0]: True
```

2.9.3 Customizing Copy Behavior

It is possible to control how copies are made using the __copy__() and __deepcopy__() special methods.

- __copy__() is called without any arguments and should return a shallow copy of the object.

- __deepcopy__() is called with a memo dictionary and should return a deep copy of the object. Any member attributes that need to be deep-copied should be passed to copy.deepcopy(), along with the memo dictionary, to control for recursion. (The memo dictionary is explained in more detail later.)

The following example illustrates how the methods are called.

Listing 2.74: copy_hooks.py

```python
import copy
import functools


@functools.total_ordering
class MyClass:

    def __init__(self, name):
        self.name = name

    def __eq__(self, other):
        return self.name == other.name

    def __gt__(self, other):
        return self.name > other.name

    def __copy__(self):
        print('__copy__()')
        return MyClass(self.name)

    def __deepcopy__(self, memo):
        print('__deepcopy__({})'.format(memo))
        return MyClass(copy.deepcopy(self.name, memo))


a = MyClass('a')

sc = copy.copy(a)
dc = copy.deepcopy(a)
```

The memo dictionary is used to keep track of the values that have been copied already, so as to avoid infinite recursion.

```
$ python3 copy_hooks.py

__copy__()
__deepcopy__({})
```

2.9.4 Recursion in Deep Copy

To avoid problems with duplicating recursive data structures, deepcopy() uses a dictionary to track objects that have already been copied. This dictionary is passed to the __deepcopy__() method so it can be examined there as well.

The next example shows how an interconnected data structure such as a directed graph can help protect against recursion by implementing a __deepcopy__() method.

Listing 2.75: `copy_recursion.py`

```python
import copy


class Graph:

    def __init__(self, name, connections):
        self.name = name
        self.connections = connections

    def add_connection(self, other):
        self.connections.append(other)

    def __repr__(self):
        return 'Graph(name={}, id={})'.format(
            self.name, id(self))

    def __deepcopy__(self, memo):
        print('\nCalling __deepcopy__ for {!r}'.format(self))
        if self in memo:
            existing = memo.get(self)
            print('  Already copied to {!r}'.format(existing))
            return existing
        print('  Memo dictionary:')
        if memo:
            for k, v in memo.items():
                print('    {}: {}'.format(k, v))
        else:
            print('    (empty)')
        dup = Graph(copy.deepcopy(self.name, memo), [])
        print('  Copying to new object {}'.format(dup))
        memo[self] = dup
        for c in self.connections:
            dup.add_connection(copy.deepcopy(c, memo))
        return dup


root = Graph('root', [])
a = Graph('a', [root])
b = Graph('b', [a, root])
root.add_connection(a)
root.add_connection(b)

dup = copy.deepcopy(root)
```

The `Graph` class includes a few basic directed graph methods. An instance can be initialized with a name and a list of existing nodes to which it is connected. The `add_connection()` method is used to set up bidirectional connections. It is also used by the deep copy operator.

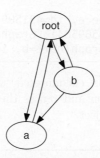

Figure 2.1: Deep Copy for an Object Graph with Cycles

The __deepcopy__() method prints messages to show how it is called, and manages the memo dictionary contents as needed. Instead of copying the entire connection list wholesale, it creates a new list and appends copies of the individual connections to it. That ensures that the memo dictionary is updated as each new node is duplicated, and it avoids recursion issues or extra copies of nodes. As before, the method returns the copied object when it is done.

The graph shown in Figure 2.1 includes several cycles, but handling the recursion with the memo dictionary prevents the traversal from causing a stack overflow error. When the *root* node is copied, it produces the following output.

```
$ python3 copy_recursion.py


Calling __deepcopy__ for Graph(name=root, id=4314569528)
  Memo dictionary:
    (empty)
  Copying to new object Graph(name=root, id=4315093592)

Calling __deepcopy__ for Graph(name=a, id=4314569584)
  Memo dictionary:
    Graph(name=root, id=4314569528): Graph(name=root,
id=4315093592)
  Copying to new object Graph(name=a, id=4315094208)

Calling __deepcopy__ for Graph(name=root, id=4314569528)
  Already copied to Graph(name=root, id=4315093592)

Calling __deepcopy__ for Graph(name=b, id=4315092248)
  Memo dictionary:
    4314569528: Graph(name=root, id=4315093592)
    4315692808: [Graph(name=root, id=4314569528), Graph(name=a,
id=4314569584)]
    Graph(name=root, id=4314569528): Graph(name=root,
id=4315093592)
```

```
4314569584: Graph(name=a, id=4315094208)
  Graph(name=a, id=4314569584): Graph(name=a, id=4315094208)
Copying to new object Graph(name=b, id=4315177536)
```

The second time the *root* node is encountered, while the *a* node is being copied, __deepcopy__() detects the recursion and reuses the existing value from the memo dictionary instead of creating a new object.

TIP

Related Reading

- Standard library documentation for copy.[26]

2.10   pprint: Pretty-Print Data Structures

The pprint module contains a "pretty printer" for producing aesthetically pleasing views of data structures. The formatter produces representations of data structures that can be parsed correctly by the interpreter, and that are also easy for a human to read. The output is kept on a single line, if possible, and indented when split across multiple lines.

The examples in this section all depend on pprint_data.py, which is shown here.

Listing 2.76: **pprint_data.py**

```
data = [
    (1, {'a': 'A', 'b': 'B', 'c': 'C', 'd': 'D'}),
    (2, {'e': 'E', 'f': 'F', 'g': 'G', 'h': 'H',
         'i': 'I', 'j': 'J', 'k': 'K', 'l': 'L'}),
    (3, ['m', 'n']),
    (4, ['o', 'p', 'q']),
    (5, ['r', 's', 't''u', 'v', 'x', 'y', 'z']),
]
```

2.10.1   Printing

The simplest way to use the module is through the pprint() function.

Listing 2.77: **pprint_pprint.py**

```
from pprint import pprint

from pprint_data import data

print('PRINT:')
```

---
[26] https://docs.python.org/3.5/library/copy.html

```
print(data)
print()
print('PPRINT:')
pprint(data)
```

pprint() formats an object and writes it to the data stream passed in as an argument (or sys.stdout by default).

```
$ python3 pprint_pprint.py

PRINT:
[(1, {'c': 'C', 'b': 'B', 'd': 'D', 'a': 'A'}), (2, {'k': 'K', 'i':
'I', 'g': 'G', 'f': 'F', 'e': 'E', 'h': 'H', 'l': 'L', 'j': 'J'}), (
3, ['m', 'n']), (4, ['o', 'p', 'q']), (5, ['r', 's', 'tu', 'v', 'x',
 'y', 'z'])]

PPRINT:
[(1, {'a': 'A', 'b': 'B', 'c': 'C', 'd': 'D'}),
 (2,
  {'e': 'E',
   'f': 'F',
   'g': 'G',
   'h': 'H',
   'i': 'I',
   'j': 'J',
   'k': 'K',
   'l': 'L'}),
 (3, ['m', 'n']),
 (4, ['o', 'p', 'q']),
 (5, ['r', 's', 'tu', 'v', 'x', 'y', 'z'])]
```

2.10.2   Formatting

To format a data structure without writing it directly to a stream (for example, for logging), use pformat() to build a string representation.

Listing 2.78: pprint_pformat.py

```
import logging
from pprint import pformat
from pprint_data import data

logging.basicConfig(
    level=logging.DEBUG,
    format='%(levelname)-8s %(message)s',
)

logging.debug('Logging pformatted data')
```

```
formatted = pformat(data)
for line in formatted.splitlines():
    logging.debug(line.rstrip())
```

The formatted string can then be printed or logged independently.

```
$ python3 pprint_pformat.py

DEBUG      Logging pformatted data
DEBUG      [(1, {'a': 'A', 'b': 'B', 'c': 'C', 'd': 'D'}),
DEBUG       (2,
DEBUG        {'e': 'E',
DEBUG         'f': 'F',
DEBUG         'g': 'G',
DEBUG         'h': 'H',
DEBUG         'i': 'I',
DEBUG         'j': 'J',
DEBUG         'k': 'K',
DEBUG         'l': 'L'}),
DEBUG       (3, ['m', 'n']),
DEBUG       (4, ['o', 'p', 'q']),
DEBUG       (5, ['r', 's', 'tu', 'v', 'x', 'y', 'z'])]
```

2.10.3   Arbitrary Classes

The PrettyPrinter class used by pprint() can also work with custom classes, if they define a __repr__() method.

Listing 2.79: pprint_arbitrary_object.py

```
from pprint import pprint


class node:

    def __init__(self, name, contents=[]):
        self.name = name
        self.contents = contents[:]

    def __repr__(self):
        return (
            'node(' + repr(self.name) + ', ' +
            repr(self.contents) + ')'
        )


trees = [
    node('node-1'),
    node('node-2', [node('node-2-1')]),
```

```
            node('node-3', [node('node-3-1')]),
    ]
    pprint(trees)
```

The representations of the nested objects are combined by the `PrettyPrinter` to return the full string representation.

```
$ python3 pprint_arbitrary_object.py

[node('node-1', []),
 node('node-2', [node('node-2-1', [])]),
 node('node-3', [node('node-3-1', [])])]]
```

2.10.4   Recursion

Recursive data structures are represented with a reference to the original source of the data, given in the format `<Recursion on typename with id=number>`.

Listing 2.80: **pprint_recursion.py**

```
from pprint import pprint

local_data = ['a', 'b', 1, 2]
local_data.append(local_data)

print('id(local_data) =>', id(local_data))
pprint(local_data)
```

In this example, the list `local_data` is added to itself, creating a recursive reference.

```
$ python3 pprint_recursion.py

id(local_data) => 4324368136
['a', 'b', 1, 2, <Recursion on list with id=4324368136>]
```

2.10.5   Limiting Nested Output

For very deep data structures, it may not be desirable for the output to include all of the details. The data may not be formatted properly, the formatted text might be too large to manage, or some of the data may be extraneous.

Listing 2.81: **pprint_depth.py**

```
from pprint import pprint

from pprint_data import data

pprint(data, depth=1)
pprint(data, depth=2)
```

Use the `depth` argument to control how far down into the nested data structure the pretty printer recurses. Levels not included in the output are represented by ellipses.

```
$ python3 pprint_depth.py

[(...), (...), (...), (...), (...)]
[(1, {...}), (2, {...}), (3, [...]), (4, [...]), (5, [...])]
```

2.10.6   Controlling Output Width

The default output width for the formatted text is 80 columns. To adjust that width, use the `width` argument to `pprint()`.

Listing 2.82: pprint_width.py

```
from pprint import pprint

from pprint_data import data

for width in [80, 5]:
    print('WIDTH =', width)
    pprint(data, width=width)
    print()
```

When the width is too small to accommodate the formatted data structure, the lines are not truncated or wrapped if doing so would introduce invalid syntax.

```
$ python3 pprint_width.py

WIDTH = 80
[(1, {'a': 'A', 'b': 'B', 'c': 'C', 'd': 'D'}),
 (2,
  {'e': 'E',
   'f': 'F',
   'g': 'G',
   'h': 'H',
   'i': 'I',
   'j': 'J',
   'k': 'K',
   'l': 'L'}),
 (3, ['m', 'n']),
 (4, ['o', 'p', 'q']),
 (5, ['r', 's', 'tu', 'v', 'x', 'y', 'z'])]

WIDTH = 5
[(1,
  {'a': 'A',
   'b': 'B',
```

```
        'c': 'C',
        'd': 'D'}),
      (2,
       {'e': 'E',
        'f': 'F',
        'g': 'G',
        'h': 'H',
        'i': 'I',
        'j': 'J',
        'k': 'K',
        'l': 'L'}),
      (3,
       ['m',
        'n']),
      (4,
       ['o',
        'p',
        'q']),
      (5,
       ['r',
        's',
        'tu',
        'v',
        'x',
        'y',
        'z'])]
```

The compact flag tells pprint() to try to fit more data on each individual line, rather than spreading complex data structures across lines.

Listing 2.83: pprint_compact.py

```
from pprint import pprint

from pprint_data import data

print('DEFAULT:')
pprint(data, compact=False)
print('\nCOMPACT:')
pprint(data, compact=True)
```

This example shows that when a data structure does not fit on a line, it is split up (as with the second item in the data list). When multiple elements can fit on a line, as with the third and fourth members, they are placed that way.

```
$ python3 pprint_compact.py

[(1, {'a': 'A', 'b': 'B', 'c': 'C', 'd': 'D'}),
 (2,
```

```
 {'e': 'E',
  'f': 'F',
  'g': 'G',
  'h': 'H',
  'i': 'I',
  'j': 'J',
  'k': 'K',
  'l': 'L'}),
 (3, ['m', 'n']),
 (4, ['o', 'p', 'q']),
 (5, ['r', 's', 'tu', 'v', 'x', 'y', 'z'])]
[(1, {'a': 'A', 'b': 'B', 'c': 'C', 'd': 'D'}),
 (2,
  {'e': 'E',
   'f': 'F',
   'g': 'G',
   'h': 'H',
   'i': 'I',
   'j': 'J',
   'k': 'K',
   'l': 'L'}),
 (3, ['m', 'n']), (4, ['o', 'p', 'q']),
 (5, ['r', 's', 'tu', 'v', 'x', 'y', 'z'])]
```

TIP

Related Reading

- Standard library documentation for pprint.[27]

---

[27] https://docs.python.org/3.5/library/pprint.html

Chapter 3

Algorithms

Python includes several modules for implementing algorithms elegantly and concisely using whatever style is most appropriate for the task. It supports purely procedural, object-oriented, and functional styles, and all three styles are frequently mixed within different parts of the same program.

`functools` (page 143) includes functions for creating function decorators, enabling aspect-oriented programming and code reuse beyond what a traditional object-oriented approach supports. It also provides a class decorator for implementing all of the rich comparison APIs using a shortcut, and `partial` objects for creating references to functions with their arguments included.

The `itertools` (page 163) module includes functions for creating and working with iterators and generators used in functional programming. The `operator` (page 183) module eliminates the need for many trivial lambda functions when using a functional programming style by providing function-based interfaces to built-in operations such as arithmetic or item lookup.

No matter which style is used in a program, `contextlib` (page 191) makes resource management easier, more reliable, and more concise. Combining context managers and the `with` statement reduces the number of `try:finally` blocks and indentation levels needed, while ensuring that files, sockets, database transactions, and other resources are closed and released at the right time.

3.1 functools: Tools for Manipulating Functions

The `functools` module provides tools for adapting or extending functions and other callable objects, without completely rewriting them.

3.1.1 Decorators

The primary tool supplied by the `functools` module is the class `partial`, which can be used to "wrap" a callable object with default arguments. The resulting object is itself callable and can be treated as though it is the original function. It takes all of the same arguments as the original, and can be invoked with extra positional or named arguments as well. A `partial` can be used instead of a `lambda` to provide default arguments to a function, while leaving some arguments unspecified.

3.1.1.1   Partial Objects

The first example shows two simple `partial` objects for the function `myfunc()`. The output of `show_details()` includes the func, args, and keywords attributes of the partial object.

Listing 3.1: <code>functools_partial.py</code>

```python
import functools


def myfunc(a, b=2):
    "Docstring for myfunc()."
    print('  called myfunc with:', (a, b))


def show_details(name, f, is_partial=False):
    "Show details of a callable object."
    print('{}:'.format(name))
    print('  object:', f)
    if not is_partial:
        print('  __name__:', f.__name__)
    if is_partial:
        print('  func:', f.func)
        print('  args:', f.args)
        print('  keywords:', f.keywords)
    return


show_details('myfunc', myfunc)
myfunc('a', 3)
print()

# Set a different default value for 'b', but require
# the caller to provide 'a'.
p1 = functools.partial(myfunc, b=4)
show_details('partial with named default', p1, True)
p1('passing a')
p1('override b', b=5)
print()

# Set default values for both 'a' and 'b'.
p2 = functools.partial(myfunc, 'default a', b=99)
show_details('partial with defaults', p2, True)
p2()
p2(b='override b')
print()

print('Insufficient arguments:')
p1()
```

At the end of the example, the first `partial` created is invoked without passing a value for a, causing an exception.

```
$ python3 functools_partial.py

myfunc:
    object: <function myfunc at 0x1007a6a60>
    __name__: myfunc
    called myfunc with: ('a', 3)

partial with named default:
    object: functools.partial(<function myfunc at 0x1007a6a60>,
b=4)
    func: <function myfunc at 0x1007a6a60>
    args: ()
    keywords: {'b': 4}
    called myfunc with: ('passing a', 4)
    called myfunc with: ('override b', 5)

partial with defaults:
    object: functools.partial(<function myfunc at 0x1007a6a60>,
'default a', b=99)
    func: <function myfunc at 0x1007a6a60>
    args: ('default a',)
    keywords: {'b': 99}
    called myfunc with: ('default a', 99)
    called myfunc with: ('default a', 'override b')

Insufficient arguments:
Traceback (most recent call last):
    File "functools_partial.py", line 51, in <module>
        p1()
TypeError: myfunc() missing 1 required positional argument: 'a'
```

3.1.1.2 Acquiring Function Properties

The `partial` object does not have `__name__` or `__doc__` attributes by default, and without those attributes, decorated functions are more difficult to debug. `update_wrapper()` can be used to copy or add attributes from the original function to the `partial` object.

Listing 3.2: `functools_update_wrapper.py`

```
import functools


def myfunc(a, b=2):
    "Docstring for myfunc()."
    print('  called myfunc with:', (a, b))
```

```
def show_details(name, f):
    "Show details of a callable object."
    print('{}:'.format(name))
    print('  object:', f)
    print('  __name__:', end=' ')
    try:
        print(f.__name__)
    except AttributeError:
        print('(no __name__)')
    print('  __doc__', repr(f.__doc__))
    print()


show_details('myfunc', myfunc)

p1 = functools.partial(myfunc, b=4)
show_details('raw wrapper', p1)

print('Updating wrapper:')
print('  assign:', functools.WRAPPER_ASSIGNMENTS)
print('  update:', functools.WRAPPER_UPDATES)
print()

functools.update_wrapper(p1, myfunc)
show_details('updated wrapper', p1)
```

The attributes added to the wrapper are defined in WRAPPER_ASSIGNMENTS, while
WRAPPER_UPDATES lists values to be modified.

```
$ python3 functools_update_wrapper.py

myfunc:
  object: <function myfunc at 0x1018a6a60>
  __name__: myfunc
  __doc__ 'Docstring for myfunc().'

raw wrapper:
  object: functools.partial(<function myfunc at 0x1018a6a60>,
b=4)
  __name__: (no __name__)
  __doc__ 'partial(func, *args, **keywords) - new function with
partial application\n    of the given arguments and keywords.\n'

Updating wrapper:
  assign: ('__module__', '__name__', '__qualname__', '__doc__',
'__annotations__')
  update: ('__dict__',)
```

```
updated wrapper:
  object: functools.partial(<function myfunc at 0x1018a6a60>,
b=4)
  __name__: myfunc
  __doc__ 'Docstring for myfunc().'
```

3.1.1.3 Other Callables

Partials work with any callable object, not just with stand-alone functions.

Listing 3.3: **functools_callable.py**

```
import functools


class MyClass:
    "Demonstration class for functools"

    def __call__(self, e, f=6):
        "Docstring for MyClass.__call__"
        print('  called object with:', (self, e, f))


def show_details(name, f):
    "Show details of a callable object."
    print('{}:'.format(name))
    print('  object:', f)
    print('  __name__:', end=' ')
    try:
        print(f.__name__)
    except AttributeError:
        print('(no __name__)')
    print('  __doc__', repr(f.__doc__))
    return


o = MyClass()

show_details('instance', o)
o('e goes here')
print()

p = functools.partial(o, e='default for e', f=8)
functools.update_wrapper(p, o)
show_details('instance wrapper', p)
p()
```

This example creates partials from an instance of a class with a `__call__()` method.

```
$ python3 functools_callable.py

instance:
  object: <__main__.MyClass object at 0x1011b1cf8>
  __name__: (no __name__)
  __doc__ 'Demonstration class for functools'
  called object with: (<__main__.MyClass object at 0x1011b1cf8>,
'e goes here', 6)

instance wrapper:
  object: functools.partial(<__main__.MyClass object at
0x1011b1cf8>, f=8, e='default for e')
  __name__: (no __name__)
  __doc__ 'Demonstration class for functools'
  called object with: (<__main__.MyClass object at 0x1011b1cf8>,
'default for e', 8)
```

3.1.1.4   Methods and Functions

While `partial()` returns a callable ready to be used directly, `partialmethod()` returns a callable ready to be used as an unbound method of an object. In the following example, the same stand-alone function is added as an attribute of `MyClass` twice, once using `partialmethod()` as `method1()` and again using `partial()` as `method2()`.

Listing 3.4: **functools_partialmethod.py**

```
import functools


def standalone(self, a=1, b=2):
    "Standalone function"
    print(' called standalone with:', (self, a, b))
    if self is not None:
        print(' self.attr =', self.attr)


class MyClass:
    "Demonstration class for functools"

    def __init__(self):
        self.attr = 'instance attribute'

    method1 = functools.partialmethod(standalone)
    method2 = functools.partial(standalone)


o = MyClass()
```

```
print('standalone')
standalone(None)
print()

print('method1 as partialmethod')
o.method1()
print()

print('method2 as partial')
try:
    o.method2()
except TypeError as err:
    print('ERROR: {}'.format(err))
```

method1() can be called from an instance of MyClass, and the instance is passed as the first argument, just as with methods that are defined in the usual way. method2() is not set up as a bound method, so the self argument must be passed explicitly; otherwise, the call will result in a TypeError.

```
$ python3 functools_partialmethod.py

standalone
  called standalone with: (None, 1, 2)

method1 as partialmethod
  called standalone with: (<__main__.MyClass object at
0x1007b1d30>, 1, 2)
  self.attr = instance attribute

method2 as partial
ERROR: standalone() missing 1 required positional argument:
'self'
```

3.1.1.5 Acquiring Function Properties for Decorators

Updating the properties of a wrapped callable is especially useful for decorators, because the transformed function ends up with properties of the original "bare" function.

Listing 3.5: **functools_wraps.py**

```
import functools


def show_details(name, f):
    "Show details of a callable object."
    print('{}:'.format(name))
    print('  object:', f)
    print('  __name__:', end=' ')
```

```
    try:
        print(f.__name__)
    except AttributeError:
        print('(no __name__)')
    print('  __doc__', repr(f.__doc__))
    print()


def simple_decorator(f):
    @functools.wraps(f)
    def decorated(a='decorated defaults', b=1):
        print('  decorated:', (a, b))
        print('  ', end=' ')
        return f(a, b=b)
    return decorated


def myfunc(a, b=2):
    "myfunc() is not complicated"
    print('  myfunc:', (a, b))
    return


# The raw function
show_details('myfunc', myfunc)
myfunc('unwrapped, default b')
myfunc('unwrapped, passing b', 3)
print()

# Wrap explicitly.
wrapped_myfunc = simple_decorator(myfunc)
show_details('wrapped_myfunc', wrapped_myfunc)
wrapped_myfunc()
wrapped_myfunc('args to wrapped', 4)
print()


# Wrap with decorator syntax.
@simple_decorator
def decorated_myfunc(a, b):
    myfunc(a, b)
    return

show_details('decorated_myfunc', decorated_myfunc)
decorated_myfunc()
decorated_myfunc('args to decorated', 4)
```

---

functools provides a decorator, wraps(), that applies update_wrapper() to the decorated function.

```
$ python3 functools_wraps.py

myfunc:
    object: <function myfunc at 0x101241b70>
    __name__: myfunc
    __doc__ 'myfunc() is not complicated'

    myfunc: ('unwrapped, default b', 2)
    myfunc: ('unwrapped, passing b', 3)

wrapped_myfunc:
    object: <function myfunc at 0x1012e62f0>
    __name__: myfunc
    __doc__ 'myfunc() is not complicated'

    decorated: ('decorated defaults', 1)
       myfunc: ('decorated defaults', 1)
    decorated: ('args to wrapped', 4)
       myfunc: ('args to wrapped', 4)

decorated_myfunc:
    object: <function decorated_myfunc at 0x1012e6400>
    __name__: decorated_myfunc
    __doc__ None

    decorated: ('decorated defaults', 1)
       myfunc: ('decorated defaults', 1)
    decorated: ('args to decorated', 4)
       myfunc: ('args to decorated', 4)
```

3.1.2   Comparison

Under Python 2, classes could define a __cmp__() method that returns -1, 0, or 1 based on whether the object is less than, equal to, or greater than, respectively, the item being compared. Python 2.1 introduced the *rich comparison* methods API (__lt__(), __le__(), __eq__(), __ne__(), __gt__(), and __ge__()), which perform a single comparison operation and return a boolean value. Python 3 deprecated __cmp__() in favor of these new methods, and functools provides tools to make it easier to write classes that comply with the new comparison requirements in Python 3.

3.1.2.1   Rich Comparison

The rich comparison API is designed to allow classes with complex comparisons to implement each test in the most efficient way possible. However, for classes where comparison is relatively simple, there is no point in manually creating each of the rich comparison methods. The total_ordering() class decorator takes a class that provides some of the methods, and adds the rest of them.

Listing 3.6: **functools_total_ordering.py**

```python
import functools
import inspect
from pprint import pprint


@functools.total_ordering
class MyObject:

    def __init__(self, val):
        self.val = val

    def __eq__(self, other):
        print('  testing __eq__({}, {})'.format(
            self.val, other.val))
        return self.val == other.val

    def __gt__(self, other):
        print('  testing __gt__({}, {})'.format(
            self.val, other.val))
        return self.val > other.val


print('Methods:\n')
pprint(inspect.getmembers(MyObject, inspect.isfunction))

a = MyObject(1)
b = MyObject(2)

print('\nComparisons:')
for expr in ['a < b', 'a <= b', 'a == b', 'a >= b', 'a > b']:
    print('\n{:<6}:'.format(expr))
    result = eval(expr)
    print('  result of {}: {}'.format(expr, result))
```

The class must provide implementation of __eq__() and one other rich comparison method. The decorator adds implementations of the rest of the methods that work by using the comparisons provided. If a comparison cannot be made, the method should return NotImplemented so the comparison can be tried using the reverse comparison operators on the other object, before failing entirely.

```
$ python3 functools_total_ordering.py

Methods:

[('__eq__', <function MyObject.__eq__ at 0x10139a488>),
 ('__ge__', <function _ge_from_gt at 0x1012e2510>),
```

```
    ('__gt__', <function MyObject.__gt__ at 0x10139a510>),
    ('__init__', <function MyObject.__init__ at 0x10139a400>),
    ('__le__', <function _le_from_gt at 0x1012e2598>),
    ('__lt__', <function _lt_from_gt at 0x1012e2488>)]

Comparisons:

a < b :
  testing __gt__(1, 2)
  testing __eq__(1, 2)
  result of a < b: True

a <= b:
  testing __gt__(1, 2)
  result of a <= b: True

a == b:
  testing __eq__(1, 2)
  result of a == b: False

a >= b:
  testing __gt__(1, 2)
  testing __eq__(1, 2)
  result of a >= b: False

a > b :
  testing __gt__(1, 2)
  result of a > b: False
```

3.1.2.2 Collation Order

Since old-style comparison functions are deprecated in Python 3, the cmp argument to functions like sort() is also no longer supported. Older programs that use comparison functions can use cmp_to_key() to convert them to a function that returns a *collation key*, which is used to determine the position in the final sequence.

Listing 3.7: functools_cmp_to_key.py

```
import functools


class MyObject:

    def __init__(self, val):
        self.val = val

    def __str__(self):
        return 'MyObject({})'.format(self.val)
```

```
def compare_obj(a, b):
    """Old-style comparison function.
    """
    print('comparing {} and {}'.format(a, b))
    if a.val < b.val:
        return -1
    elif a.val > b.val:
        return 1
    return 0

# Make a key function using cmp_to_key().
get_key = functools.cmp_to_key(compare_obj)


def get_key_wrapper(o):
    "Wrapper function for get_key to allow for print statements."
    new_key = get_key(o)
    print('key_wrapper({}) -> {!r}'.format(o, new_key))
    return new_key

objs = [MyObject(x) for x in range(5, 0, -1)]

for o in sorted(objs, key=get_key_wrapper):
    print(o)
```

Normally `cmp_to_key()` would be used directly, but in this example an extra wrapper function is introduced to print out more information as the key function is being called.

The output shows that `sorted()` starts by calling `get_key_wrapper()` for each item in the sequence to produce a key. The keys returned by `cmp_to_key()` are instances of a class defined in `functools` that implements the rich comparison API using the old-style comparison function passed in. After all of the keys are created, the sequence is sorted by comparing the keys.

```
$ python3 functools_cmp_to_key.py

key_wrapper(MyObject(5)) -> <functools.KeyWrapper object at
0x1011c5530>
key_wrapper(MyObject(4)) -> <functools.KeyWrapper object at
0x1011c5510>
key_wrapper(MyObject(3)) -> <functools.KeyWrapper object at
0x1011c54f0>
key_wrapper(MyObject(2)) -> <functools.KeyWrapper object at
0x1011c5390>
key_wrapper(MyObject(1)) -> <functools.KeyWrapper object at
0x1011c5710>
comparing MyObject(4) and MyObject(5)
comparing MyObject(3) and MyObject(4)
comparing MyObject(2) and MyObject(3)
comparing MyObject(1) and MyObject(2)
```

```
MyObject(1)
MyObject(2)
MyObject(3)
MyObject(4)
MyObject(5)
```

3.1.3 Caching

The lru_cache() decorator wraps a function in a "least recently used" cache. Arguments to the function are used to build a hash key, which is then mapped to the result. Subsequent calls with the same arguments will fetch the value from the cache instead of calling the function. The decorator also adds methods to the function to examine the state of the cache (cache_info()) and empty the cache (cache_clear()).

Listing 3.8: **functools_lru_cache.py**

```
import functools


@functools.lru_cache()
def expensive(a, b):
    print('expensive({}, {})'.format(a, b))
    return a * b


MAX = 2

print('First set of calls:')
for i in range(MAX):
    for j in range(MAX):
        expensive(i, j)
print(expensive.cache_info())

print('\nSecond set of calls:')
for i in range(MAX + 1):
    for j in range(MAX + 1):
        expensive(i, j)
print(expensive.cache_info())

print('\nClearing cache:')
expensive.cache_clear()
print(expensive.cache_info())

print('\nThird set of calls:')
for i in range(MAX):
    for j in range(MAX):
        expensive(i, j)
print(expensive.cache_info())
```

This example makes several calls to `expensive()` in a set of nested loops. The second time those calls are made with the same values, the results appear in the cache. When the cache is cleared and the loops are run again, the values must be recomputed.

```
$ python3 functools_lru_cache.py

First set of calls:
expensive(0, 0)
expensive(0, 1)
expensive(1, 0)
expensive(1, 1)
CacheInfo(hits=0, misses=4, maxsize=128, currsize=4)

Second set of calls:
expensive(0, 2)
expensive(1, 2)
expensive(2, 0)
expensive(2, 1)
expensive(2, 2)
CacheInfo(hits=4, misses=9, maxsize=128, currsize=9)

Clearing cache:
CacheInfo(hits=0, misses=0, maxsize=128, currsize=0)

Third set of calls:
expensive(0, 0)
expensive(0, 1)
expensive(1, 0)
expensive(1, 1)
CacheInfo(hits=0, misses=4, maxsize=128, currsize=4)
```

To prevent the cache from growing without bounds in a long-running process, it is given a maximum size. The default is 128 entries, but that size can be changed for each cache using the `maxsize` argument.

Listing 3.9: functools_lru_cache_expire.py

```
import functools


@functools.lru_cache(maxsize=2)
def expensive(a, b):
    print('called expensive({}, {})'.format(a, b))
    return a * b


def make_call(a, b):
    print('({}, {})'.format(a, b), end=' ')
    pre_hits = expensive.cache_info().hits
```

```
        expensive(a, b)
        post_hits = expensive.cache_info().hits
        if post_hits > pre_hits:
            print('cache hit')


print('Establish the cache')
make_call(1, 2)
make_call(2, 3)

print('\nUse cached items')
make_call(1, 2)
make_call(2, 3)

print('\nCompute a new value, triggering cache expiration')
make_call(3, 4)

print('\nCache still contains one old item')
make_call(2, 3)

print('\nOldest item needs to be recomputed')
make_call(1, 2)
```

In this example, the cache size is set to 2 entries. When the third set of unique arguments (3,4) is used, the oldest item in the cache is dropped and replaced with the new result.

```
$ python3 functools_lru_cache_expire.py

Establish the cache
(1, 2) called expensive(1, 2)
(2, 3) called expensive(2, 3)

Use cached items
(1, 2) cache hit
(2, 3) cache hit

Compute a new value, triggering cache expiration
(3, 4) called expensive(3, 4)

Cache still contains one old item
(2, 3) cache hit

Oldest item needs to be recomputed
(1, 2) called expensive(1, 2)
```

The keys for the cache managed by lru_cache() must be hashable, so all of the arguments to the function wrapped with the cache lookup must be hashable.

Listing 3.10: **functools_lru_cache_arguments.py**

```
import functools


@functools.lru_cache(maxsize=2)
def expensive(a, b):
    print('called expensive({}, {})'.format(a, b))
    return a * b


def make_call(a, b):
    print('({}, {})'.format(a, b), end=' ')
    pre_hits = expensive.cache_info().hits
    expensive(a, b)
    post_hits = expensive.cache_info().hits
    if post_hits > pre_hits:
        print('cache hit')


make_call(1, 2)

try:
    make_call([1], 2)
except TypeError as err:
    print('ERROR: {}'.format(err))

try:
    make_call(1, {'2': 'two'})
except TypeError as err:
    print('ERROR: {}'.format(err))
```

If an object that cannot be hashed is passed in to the function, a `TypeError` is raised.

```
$ python3 functools_lru_cache_arguments.py

(1, 2) called expensive(1, 2)
([1], 2) ERROR: unhashable type: 'list'
(1, {'2': 'two'}) ERROR: unhashable type: 'dict'
```

3.1.4 Reducing a Data Set

The `reduce()` function takes a callable and a sequence of data as input. It produces a single value as output based on invoking the callable with the values from the sequence and accumulating the resulting output.

Listing 3.11: `functools_reduce.py`

```
import functools


def do_reduce(a, b):
    print('do_reduce({}, {})'.format(a, b))
    return a + b


data = range(1, 5)
print(data)
result = functools.reduce(do_reduce, data)
print('result: {}'.format(result))
```

This example adds up the numbers in the input sequence.

```
$ python3 functools_reduce.py

range(1, 5)
do_reduce(1, 2)
do_reduce(3, 3)
do_reduce(6, 4)
result: 10
```

The optional `initializer` argument is placed at the front of the sequence and processed along with the other items. This can be used to update a previously computed value with new inputs.

Listing 3.12: `functools_reduce_initializer.py`

```
import functools


def do_reduce(a, b):
    print('do_reduce({}, {})'.format(a, b))
    return a + b


data = range(1, 5)
print(data)
result = functools.reduce(do_reduce, data, 99)
print('result: {}'.format(result))
```

In this example, a previous sum of 99 is used to initialize the value computed by `reduce()`.

```
$ python3 functools_reduce_initializer.py

range(1, 5)
```

```
do_reduce(99, 1)
do_reduce(100, 2)
do_reduce(102, 3)
do_reduce(105, 4)
result: 109
```

Sequences with a single item automatically reduce to that value when no initializer is present. Empty lists generate an error, unless an initializer is provided.

Listing 3.13: **functools_reduce_short_sequences.py**

```
import functools


def do_reduce(a, b):
    print('do_reduce({}, {})'.format(a, b))
    return a + b


print('Single item in sequence:',
      functools.reduce(do_reduce, [1]))

print('Single item in sequence with initializer:',
      functools.reduce(do_reduce, [1], 99))

print('Empty sequence with initializer:',
      functools.reduce(do_reduce, [], 99))

try:
    print('Empty sequence:', functools.reduce(do_reduce, []))
except TypeError as err:
    print('ERROR: {}'.format(err))
```

Because the initializer argument serves as a default, but is also combined with the new values if the input sequence is not empty, it is important to consider carefully whether its use is appropriate. When it does not make sense to combine the default with new values, it is better to catch the TypeError rather than passing an initializer.

```
$ python3 functools_reduce_short_sequences.py

Single item in sequence: 1
do_reduce(99, 1)
Single item in sequence with initializer: 100
Empty sequence with initializer: 99
ERROR: reduce() of empty sequence with no initial value
```

3.1.5   Generic Functions

In a dynamically typed language like Python, there is often a need to perform slightly different operations based on the type of an argument, especially when dealing with the difference between a list of items and a single item. It is simple enough to check the type of an argument directly, but in cases where the behavioral difference can be isolated into separate functions, functools provides the singledispatch() decorator to register a set of *generic functions* for automatic switching based on the type of the first argument to a function.

Listing 3.14: functools_singledispatch.py

```
import functools


@functools.singledispatch
def myfunc(arg):
    print('default myfunc({!r})'.format(arg))


@myfunc.register(int)
def myfunc_int(arg):
    print('myfunc_int({})'.format(arg))


@myfunc.register(list)
def myfunc_list(arg):
    print('myfunc_list()')
    for item in arg:
        print('  {}'.format(item))


myfunc('string argument')
myfunc(1)
myfunc(2.3)
myfunc(['a', 'b', 'c'])
```

The register() attribute of the new function serves as another decorator for registering alternative implementations. The first function wrapped with singledispatch() is the default implementation if no other type-specific function is found, as with the float case in this example.

```
$ python3 functools_singledispatch.py

default myfunc('string argument')
myfunc_int(1)
default myfunc(2.3)
```

```
myfunc_list()
  a
  b
  c
```

When no exact match is found for the type, the inheritance order is evaluated and the closest matching type is used.

Listing 3.15: **functools_singledispatch_mro.py**

```
import functools


class A:
    pass


class B(A):
    pass


class C(A):
    pass


class D(B):
    pass


class E(C, D):
    pass


@functools.singledispatch
def myfunc(arg):
    print('default myfunc({})'.format(arg.__class__.__name__))


@myfunc.register(A)
def myfunc_A(arg):
    print('myfunc_A({})'.format(arg.__class__.__name__))


@myfunc.register(B)
def myfunc_B(arg):
    print('myfunc_B({})'.format(arg.__class__.__name__))


@myfunc.register(C)
```

```
def myfunc_C(arg):
    print('myfunc_C({})'.format(arg.__class__.__name__))


myfunc(A())
myfunc(B())
myfunc(C())
myfunc(D())
myfunc(E())
```

In this example, classes D and E do not match exactly with any registered generic functions, and the function selected depends on the class hierarchy.

```
$ python3 functools_singledispatch_mro.py

myfunc_A(A)
myfunc_B(B)
myfunc_C(C)
myfunc_B(D)
myfunc_C(E)
```

TIP

Related Reading

- Standard library documentation for functools.[1]
- Rich comparison methods[2]: Description of the rich comparison methods from the Python Reference Guide.
- Isolated @memoize[3]: Article on creating memoizing decorators that work well with unit tests, by Ned Batchelder.
- **PEP 443**[4]: Single-dispatch generic functions.
- inspect (page 1311): Introspection API for live objects.

3.2 itertools: Iterator Functions

The itertools module includes a set of functions for working with sequence data sets. The functions provided are inspired by similar features of functional programming languages such as Clojure, Haskell, APL, and SML. They are intended to be fast and use memory

---

[1] https://docs.python.org/3.5/library/functools.html
[2] https://docs.python.org/reference/datamodel.html#object.__lt__
[3] http://nedbatchelder.com/blog/201601/isolated_memoize.html
[4] www.python.org/dev/peps/pep-0443

efficiently. They can also be hooked together to express more complicated iteration-based algorithms.

Iterator-based code offers better memory consumption characteristics than code that uses lists. Since data is not produced from the iterator until it is needed, all of the data does not need to be stored in memory at the same time. This "lazy" processing model can reduce swapping and other side effects of large data sets, improving performance.

In addition to the functions defined in `itertools`, the examples in this section rely on some of the built-in functions for iteration.

3.2.1 Merging and Splitting Iterators

The `chain()` function takes several iterators as arguments and returns a single iterator that produces the contents of all of the inputs as though they came from a single iterator.

Listing 3.16: **`itertools_chain.py`**

```
from itertools import *

for i in chain([1, 2, 3], ['a', 'b', 'c']):
    print(i, end=' ')
print()
```

`chain()` makes it easy to process several sequences without constructing one large list.

```
$ python3 itertools_chain.py

1 2 3 a b c
```

If the iterables to be combined are not all known in advance, or if they need to be evaluated lazily, `chain.from_iterable()` can be used to construct the chain instead.

Listing 3.17: **`itertools_chain_from_iterable.py`**

```
from itertools import *


def make_iterables_to_chain():
    yield [1, 2, 3]
    yield ['a', 'b', 'c']


for i in chain.from_iterable(make_iterables_to_chain()):
    print(i, end=' ')
print()
```

```
$ python3 itertools_chain_from_iterable.py

1 2 3 a b c
```

The built-in function `zip()` returns an iterator that combines the elements of several iterators into tuples.

Listing 3.18: **itertools_zip.py**

```
for i in zip([1, 2, 3], ['a', 'b', 'c']):
    print(i)
```

As with the other functions in this module, the return value is an iterable object that produces values one at a time.

```
$ python3 itertools_zip.py

(1, 'a')
(2, 'b')
(3, 'c')
```

`zip()` stops when the first input iterator is exhausted. To process all of the inputs, even if the iterators produce different numbers of values, use `zip_longest()`.

Listing 3.19: **itertools_zip_longest.py**

```
from itertools import *

r1 = range(3)
r2 = range(2)

print('zip stops early:')
print(list(zip(r1, r2)))

r1 = range(3)
r2 = range(2)

print('\nzip_longest processes all of the values:')
print(list(zip_longest(r1, r2)))
```

By default, `zip_longest()` substitutes `None` for any missing values. Use the `fillvalue` argument to use a different substitute value.

```
$ python3 itertools_zip_longest.py

zip stops early:
[(0, 0), (1, 1)]

zip_longest processes all of the values:
[(0, 0), (1, 1), (2, None)]
```

The `islice()` function returns an iterator that returns selected items from the input iterator, by index.

Listing 3.20: **`itertools_islice.py`**

```
from itertools import *

print('Stop at 5:')
for i in islice(range(100), 5):
    print(i, end=' ')
print('\n')

print('Start at 5, Stop at 10:')
for i in islice(range(100), 5, 10):
    print(i, end=' ')
print('\n')

print('By tens to 100:')
for i in islice(range(100), 0, 100, 10):
    print(i, end=' ')
print('\n')
```

`islice()` takes the same arguments as the slice operator for lists: `start`, `stop`, and `step`. The start and step arguments are optional.

```
$ python3 itertools_islice.py

Stop at 5:
0 1 2 3 4

Start at 5, Stop at 10:
5 6 7 8 9

By tens to 100:
0 10 20 30 40 50 60 70 80 90
```

The `tee()` function returns several independent iterators (defaults to 2) based on a single original input.

Listing 3.21: **`itertools_tee.py`**

```
from itertools import *

r = islice(count(), 5)
i1, i2 = tee(r)

print('i1:', list(i1))
print('i2:', list(i2))
```

tee() has semantics similar to the Unix tee utility, which repeats the values it reads from its input and writes them to a named file and standard output. The iterators returned by tee() can be used to feed the same set of data into multiple algorithms to be processed in parallel.

```
$ python3 itertools_tee.py

i1: [0, 1, 2, 3, 4]
i2: [0, 1, 2, 3, 4]
```

The new iterators created by tee() share their input, so the original iterator should not be used after the new ones are created.

Listing 3.22: **itertools_tee_error.py**

```
from itertools import *

r = islice(count(), 5)
i1, i2 = tee(r)

print('r:', end=' ')
for i in r:
    print(i, end=' ')
    if i > 1:
        break
print()

print('i1:', list(i1))
print('i2:', list(i2))
```

If values are consumed from the original input, the new iterators will not produce those values.

```
$ python3 itertools_tee_error.py

r: 0 1 2
i1: [3, 4]
i2: [3, 4]
```

3.2.2 Converting Inputs

The built-in map() function returns an iterator that calls a function on the values in the input iterators, and returns the results. It stops when any input iterator is exhausted.

Listing 3.23: `itertools_map.py`

```python
def times_two(x):
    return 2 * x


def multiply(x, y):
    return (x, y, x * y)


print('Doubles:')
for i in map(times_two, range(5)):
    print(i)

print('\nMultiples:')
r1 = range(5)
r2 = range(5, 10)
for i in map(multiply, r1, r2):
    print('{:d} * {:d} = {:d}'.format(*i))

print('\nStopping:')
r1 = range(5)
r2 = range(2)
for i in map(multiply, r1, r2):
    print(i)
```

In the first example, the lambda function multiplies the input values by 2. In the second example, the lambda function multiplies two arguments, taken from separate iterators, and returns a tuple with the original arguments and the computed value. The third example stops after producing two tuples because the second range is exhausted.

```
$ python3 itertools_map.py

Doubles:
0
2
4
6
8

Multiples:
0 * 5 = 0
1 * 6 = 6
2 * 7 = 14
3 * 8 = 24
4 * 9 = 36

Stopping:
```

```
(0, 0, 0)
(1, 1, 1)
```

The starmap() function is similar to map(), but instead of constructing a tuple from multiple iterators, it splits up the items in a single iterator as arguments to the mapping function using the * syntax.

Listing 3.24: **itertools_starmap.py**

```
from itertools import *

values = [(0, 5), (1, 6), (2, 7), (3, 8), (4, 9)]

for i in starmap(lambda x, y: (x, y, x * y), values):
    print('{} * {} = {}'.format(*i))
```

Where the mapping function to map() is called f(i1,i2), the mapping function passed to starmap() is called f(*i).

```
$ python3 itertools_starmap.py

0 * 5 = 0
1 * 6 = 6
2 * 7 = 14
3 * 8 = 24
4 * 9 = 36
```

3.2.3 Producing New Values

The count() function returns an iterator that produces consecutive integers, indefinitely. The first number can be passed as an argument (the default is zero). There is no upper bound argument (see the built-in range() for more control over the result set).

Listing 3.25: **itertools_count.py**

```
from itertools import *

for i in zip(count(1), ['a', 'b', 'c']):
    print(i)
```

This example stops because the list argument is consumed.

```
$ python3 itertools_count.py

(1, 'a')
(2, 'b')
(3, 'c')
```

The start and step arguments to `count()` can be any numerical values that can be added together.

Listing 3.26: itertools_count_step.py

```python
import fractions
from itertools import *

start = fractions.Fraction(1, 3)
step = fractions.Fraction(1, 3)

for i in zip(count(start, step), ['a', 'b', 'c']):
    print('{}: {}'.format(*i))
```

In this example, the start point and steps are `Fraction` objects from the `fraction` module.

```
$ python3 itertools_count_step.py

1/3: a
2/3: b
1: c
```

The `cycle()` function returns an iterator that repeats the contents of the arguments it is given indefinitely. Because it has to remember the entire contents of the input iterator, it may consume quite a bit of memory if the iterator is long.

Listing 3.27: itertools_cycle.py

```python
from itertools import *

for i in zip(range(7), cycle(['a', 'b', 'c'])):
    print(i)
```

A counter variable is used to break out of the loop after a few cycles in this example.

```
$ python3 itertools_cycle.py

(0, 'a')
(1, 'b')
(2, 'c')
(3, 'a')
(4, 'b')
(5, 'c')
(6, 'a')
```

The `repeat()` function returns an iterator that produces the same value each time it is accessed.

Listing 3.28: **itertools_repeat.py**

```
from itertools import *

for i in repeat('over-and-over', 5):
    print(i)
```

The iterator returned by `repeat()` keeps returning data forever, unless the optional `times` argument is provided to limit it.

```
$ python3 itertools_repeat.py

over-and-over
over-and-over
over-and-over
over-and-over
over-and-over
```

It is useful to combine `repeat()` with `zip()` or `map()` when invariant values should be included with the values from the other iterators.

Listing 3.29: **itertools_repeat_zip.py**

```
from itertools import *

for i, s in zip(count(), repeat('over-and-over', 5)):
    print(i, s)
```

A counter value is combined with the constant returned by `repeat()` in this example.

```
$ python3 itertools_repeat_zip.py

0 over-and-over
1 over-and-over
2 over-and-over
3 over-and-over
4 over-and-over
```

This example uses `map()` to multiply the numbers in the range 0 through 4 by 2.

Listing 3.30: **itertools_repeat_map.py**

```
from itertools import *

for i in map(lambda x, y: (x, y, x * y), repeat(2), range(5)):
    print('{:d} * {:d} = {:d}'.format(*i))
```

The `repeat()` iterator does not need to be explicitly limited, since `map()` stops processing when any of its inputs ends, and the `range()` returns only five elements.

```
$ python3 itertools_repeat_map.py

2 * 0 = 0
2 * 1 = 2
2 * 2 = 4
2 * 3 = 6
2 * 4 = 8
```

3.2.4   Filtering

The `dropwhile()` function returns an iterator that produces elements of the input iterator after a condition becomes false for the first time.

Listing 3.31: itertools_dropwhile.py

```
from itertools import *


def should_drop(x):
    print('Testing:', x)
    return x < 1

for i in dropwhile(should_drop, [-1, 0, 1, 2, -2]):
    print('Yielding:', i)
```

`dropwhile()` does not filter every item of the input. After the condition is false the first time, all of the remaining items in the input are returned.

```
$ python3 itertools_dropwhile.py

Testing: -1
Testing: 0
Testing: 1
Yielding: 1
Yielding: 2
Yielding: -2
```

The opposite of `dropwhile()` is `takewhile()`. It returns an iterator that itself returns items from the input iterator as long as the test function returns true.

Listing 3.32: itertools_takewhile.py

```
from itertools import *


def should_take(x):
```

```
    print('Testing:', x)
    return x < 2

for i in takewhile(should_take, [-1, 0, 1, 2, -2]):
    print('Yielding:', i)
```

As soon as should_take() returns false, takewhile() stops processing the input.

```
$ python3 itertools_takewhile.py

Testing: -1
Yielding: -1
Testing: 0
Yielding: 0
Testing: 1
Yielding: 1
Testing: 2
```

The built-in function filter() returns an iterator that includes only items for which the test function returns true.

Listing 3.33: `itertools_filter.py`

```
from itertools import *


def check_item(x):
    print('Testing:', x)
    return x < 1


for i in filter(check_item, [-1, 0, 1, 2, -2]):
    print('Yielding:', i)
```

filter() differs from dropwhile() and takewhile() in that every item is tested before it is returned.

```
$ python3 itertools_filter.py

Testing: -1
Yielding: -1
Testing: 0
Yielding: 0
Testing: 1
Testing: 2
Testing: -2
Yielding: -2
```

filterfalse() returns an iterator that includes only items where the test function returns false.

Listing 3.34: itertools_filterfalse.py

```
from itertools import *


def check_item(x):
    print('Testing:', x)
    return x < 1

for i in filterfalse(check_item, [-1, 0, 1, 2, -2]):
    print('Yielding:', i)
```

The test expression in check_item() is the same, so the results in this example with filterfalse() are the opposite of the results from the previous example.

```
$ python3 itertools_filterfalse.py

Testing: -1
Testing: 0
Testing: 1
Yielding: 1
Testing: 2
Yielding: 2
Testing: -2
```

compress() offers another way to filter the contents of an iterable. Instead of calling a function, it uses the values in another iterable to indicate when to accept a value and when to ignore it.

Listing 3.35: itertools_compress.py

```
from itertools import *

every_third = cycle([False, False, True])
data = range(1, 10)

for i in compress(data, every_third):
    print(i, end=' ')
print()
```

The first argument is the data iterable to process. The second argument is a selector iterable that produces boolean values indicating which elements to take from the data input (a true value causes the value to be produced; a false value causes it to be ignored).

```
$ python3 itertools_compress.py

3 6 9
```

3.2.5   Grouping Data

The groupby() function returns an iterator that produces sets of values organized by a common key. This example illustrates grouping of related values based on an attribute.

Listing 3.36: **itertools_groupby_seq.py**

```python
import functools
from itertools import *
import operator
import pprint


@functools.total_ordering
class Point:

    def __init__(self, x, y):
        self.x = x
        self.y = y

    def __repr__(self):
        return '({}, {})'.format(self.x, self.y)

    def __eq__(self, other):
        return (self.x, self.y) == (other.x, other.y)

    def __gt__(self, other):
        return (self.x, self.y) > (other.x, other.y)


# Create a data set of Point instances.
data = list(map(Point,
                cycle(islice(count(), 3)),
                islice(count(), 7)))
print('Data:')
pprint.pprint(data, width=35)
print()

# Try to group the unsorted data based on X values.
print('Grouped, unsorted:')
for k, g in groupby(data, operator.attrgetter('x')):
    print(k, list(g))
print()

# Sort the data.
data.sort()
print('Sorted:')
pprint.pprint(data, width=35)
print()
```

```
# Group the sorted data based on X values.
print('Grouped, sorted:')
for k, g in groupby(data, operator.attrgetter('x')):
    print(k, list(g))
print()
```

The input sequence needs to be sorted on the key value so that the groupings will work out as expected.

```
$ python3 itertools_groupby_seq.py

Data:
[(0, 0),
 (1, 1),
 (2, 2),
 (0, 3),
 (1, 4),
 (2, 5),
 (0, 6)]

Grouped, unsorted:
0 [(0, 0)]
1 [(1, 1)]
2 [(2, 2)]
0 [(0, 3)]
1 [(1, 4)]
2 [(2, 5)]
0 [(0, 6)]

Sorted:
[(0, 0),
 (0, 3),
 (0, 6),
 (1, 1),
 (1, 4),
 (2, 2),
 (2, 5)]

Grouped, sorted:
0 [(0, 0), (0, 3), (0, 6)]
1 [(1, 1), (1, 4)]
2 [(2, 2), (2, 5)]
```

3.2.6 Combining Inputs

The `accumulate()` function processes the input iterable, passing the nth and $n+1$st item to a function and producing the return value instead of either input. The default function used to combine the two values adds them, so `accumulate()` can be used to produce the cumulative sum of a series of numerical inputs.

Listing 3.37: `itertools_accumulate.py`

```
from itertools import *

print(list(accumulate(range(5))))
print(list(accumulate('abcde')))
```

When used with a sequence of non-integer values, the results depend on what it means to "add" two items together. The second example in this script shows that when `accumulate()` receives a string input, each response is a progressively longer prefix of that string.

```
$ python3 itertools_accumulate.py

[0, 1, 3, 6, 10]
['a', 'ab', 'abc', 'abcd', 'abcde']
```

`accumulate()` may be combined with any other function that takes two input values to achieve different results.

Listing 3.38: `itertools_accumulate_custom.py`

```
from itertools import *


def f(a, b):
    print(a, b)
    return b + a + b

print(list(accumulate('abcde', f)))
```

This example combines the string values in a way that makes a series of (nonsensical) palindromes. Each step of the way when `f()` is called, it prints the input values passed to it by `accumulate()`.

```
$ python3 itertools_accumulate_custom.py

a b
bab c
cbabc d
dcbabcd e
['a', 'bab', 'cbabc', 'dcbabcd', 'edcbabcde']
```

Nested `for` loops that iterate over multiple sequences can often be replaced with `product()`, which produces a single iterable whose values are the Cartesian product of the set of input values.

Listing 3.39: **itertools_product.py**

```
from itertools import *
import pprint

FACE_CARDS = ('J', 'Q', 'K', 'A')
SUITS = ('H', 'D', 'C', 'S')

DECK = list(
    product(
        chain(range(2, 11), FACE_CARDS),
        SUITS,
    )
)

for card in DECK:
    print('{:>2}{}'.format(*card), end=' ')
    if card[1] == SUITS[-1]:
        print()
```

The values produced by product() are tuples, with the members taken from each of the iterables passed in as arguments in the order they are passed. The first tuple returned includes the first value from each iterable. The *last* iterable passed to product() is processed first, followed by the next-to-last, and so on. The result is that the return values are in order based on the first iterable, then the next iterable, and so on.

In this example, the cards are ordered first by value and then by suit.

```
$ python3 itertools_product.py

 2H  2D  2C  2S
 3H  3D  3C  3S
 4H  4D  4C  4S
 5H  5D  5C  5S
 6H  6D  6C  6S
 7H  7D  7C  7S
 8H  8D  8C  8S
 9H  9D  9C  9S
10H 10D 10C 10S
 JH  JD  JC  JS
 QH  QD  QC  QS
 KH  KD  KC  KS
 AH  AD  AC  AS
```

To change the order of the cards, change the order of the arguments to product().

Listing 3.40: **itertools_product_ordering.py**

```
from itertools import *
import pprint
```

```
FACE_CARDS = ('J', 'Q', 'K', 'A')
SUITS = ('H', 'D', 'C', 'S')

DECK = list(
    product(
        SUITS,
        chain(range(2, 11), FACE_CARDS),
    )
)

for card in DECK:
    print('{:>2}{}'.format(card[1], card[0]), end=' ')
    if card[1] == FACE_CARDS[-1]:
        print()
```

The print loop in this example looks for an ace card, instead of the spade suit, and then adds a newline to break up the output.

```
$ python3 itertools_product_ordering.py

2H  3H  4H  5H  6H  7H  8H  9H 10H  JH  QH  KH  AH
2D  3D  4D  5D  6D  7D  8D  9D 10D  JD  QD  KD  AD
2C  3C  4C  5C  6C  7C  8C  9C 10C  JC  QC  KC  AC
2S  3S  4S  5S  6S  7S  8S  9S 10S  JS  QS  KS  AS
```

To compute the product of a sequence with itself, specify how many times the input should be repeated.

Listing 3.41: **itertools_product_repeat.py**

```
from itertools import *


def show(iterable):
    for i, item in enumerate(iterable, 1):
        print(item, end=' ')
        if (i % 3) == 0:
            print()
    print()


print('Repeat 2:\n')
show(list(product(range(3), repeat=2)))

print('Repeat 3:\n')
show(list(product(range(3), repeat=3)))
```

Since repeating a single iterable is like passing the same iterable multiple times, each tuple produced by `product()` will contain a number of items equal to the repeat counter.

```
$ python3 itertools_product_repeat.py

Repeat 2:

(0, 0) (0, 1) (0, 2)
(1, 0) (1, 1) (1, 2)
(2, 0) (2, 1) (2, 2)

Repeat 3:

(0, 0, 0) (0, 0, 1) (0, 0, 2)
(0, 1, 0) (0, 1, 1) (0, 1, 2)
(0, 2, 0) (0, 2, 1) (0, 2, 2)
(1, 0, 0) (1, 0, 1) (1, 0, 2)
(1, 1, 0) (1, 1, 1) (1, 1, 2)
(1, 2, 0) (1, 2, 1) (1, 2, 2)
(2, 0, 0) (2, 0, 1) (2, 0, 2)
(2, 1, 0) (2, 1, 1) (2, 1, 2)
(2, 2, 0) (2, 2, 1) (2, 2, 2)
```

The `permutations()` function produces items from the input iterable combined in the possible permutations of the given length. It defaults to producing the full set of all permutations.

Listing 3.42: `itertools_permutations.py`

```python
from itertools import *


def show(iterable):
    first = None
    for i, item in enumerate(iterable, 1):
        if first != item[0]:
            if first is not None:
                print()
            first = item[0]
        print(''.join(item), end=' ')
    print()

print('All permutations:\n')
show(permutations('abcd'))

print('\nPairs:\n')
show(permutations('abcd', r=2))
```

Use the r argument to limit the length and number of the individual permutations returned.

```
$ python3 itertools_permutations.py

All permutations:

abcd abdc acbd acdb adbc adcb
bacd badc bcad bcda bdac bdca
cabd cadb cbad cbda cdab cdba
dabc dacb dbac dbca dcab dcba

Pairs:

ab ac ad
ba bc bd
ca cb cd
da db dc
```

To limit the values to unique combinations rather than permutations, use
combinations(). As long as the members of the input are unique, the output will not
include any repeated values.

Listing 3.43: **itertools_combinations.py**

```
from itertools import *


def show(iterable):
    first = None
    for i, item in enumerate(iterable, 1):
        if first != item[0]:
            if first is not None:
                print()
            first = item[0]
        print(''.join(item), end=' ')
    print()

print('Unique pairs:\n')
show(combinations('abcd', r=2))
```

Unlike with permutations, the r argument to combinations() is required.

```
$ python3 itertools_combinations.py

Unique pairs:

ab ac ad
bc bd
cd
```

While `combinations()` does not repeat individual input elements, sometimes it is useful to consider combinations that do include repeated elements. For those cases, use `combinations_with_replacement()`.

Listing 3.44: `itertools_combinations_with_replacement.py`

```python
from itertools import *


def show(iterable):
    first = None
    for i, item in enumerate(iterable, 1):
        if first != item[0]:
            if first is not None:
                print()
            first = item[0]
        print(''.join(item), end=' ')
    print()


print('Unique pairs:\n')
show(combinations_with_replacement('abcd', r=2))
```

In this output, each input item is paired with itself as well as all of the other members of the input sequence.

```
$ python3 itertools_combinations_with_replacement.py

Unique pairs:

aa ab ac ad
bb bc bd
cc cd
dd
```

TIP

Related Reading

- Standard library documentation for `itertools`.[5]
- Python 2 to 3 porting notes for `itertools` (page 1359).
- The Standard ML Basis Library[6]: The library for SML.
- Definition of Haskell and the Standard Libraries[7]: Standard library specification for the functional language Haskell.
- Clojure[8]: Clojure is a dynamic functional language that runs on the Java Virtual Machine.

---

[5] https://docs.python.org/3.5/library/itertools.html
[6] www.standardml.org/Basis/
[7] www.haskell.org/definition/
[8] http://clojure.org

- tee[9]: Unix command-line tool for splitting one input into multiple identical output streams.
- Wikipedia: Cartesian product[10]: Mathematical definition of the Cartesian product of two sequences.

3.3 operator: Functional Interface to Built-In Operators

Programming using iterators occasionally requires creating small functions for simple expressions. Sometimes, these can be implemented as lambda functions, but for some operations new functions are not needed at all. The operator module defines functions that correspond to the built-in arithmetic, comparison, and other operations for the standard object APIs.

3.3.1 Logical Operations

Functions are provided for determining the boolean equivalent for a value, negating a value to create the opposite boolean value, and comparing objects to see if they are identical.

Listing 3.45: **operator_boolean.py**

```
from operator import *

a = -1
b = 5

print('a =', a)
print('b =', b)
print()

print('not_(a)     :', not_(a))
print('truth(a)    :', truth(a))
print('is_(a, b)   :', is_(a, b))
print('is_not(a, b):', is_not(a, b))
```

not_() includes a trailing underscore because not is a Python keyword. truth() applies the same logic used when testing an expression in an if statement or converting an expression to a bool. is_() implements the same check used by the is keyword, and is_not() does the same test and returns the opposite answer.

```
$ python3 operator_boolean.py

a = -1
b = 5
```

---

[9] http://man7.org/linux/man-pages/man1/tee.1.html
[10] https://en.wikipedia.org/wiki/Cartesian_product

```
not_(a)      : False
truth(a)     : True
is_(a, b)    : False
is_not(a, b): True
```

3.3.2 Comparison Operators

All of the rich comparison operators are supported.

Listing 3.46: operator_comparisons.py

```
from operator import *

a = 1
b = 5.0

print('a =', a)
print('b =', b)
for func in (lt, le, eq, ne, ge, gt):
    print('{}(a, b): {}'.format(func.__name__, func(a, b)))
```

The functions are equivalent to the expression syntax using <, <=, ==, >=, and >.

```
$ python3 operator_comparisons.py

a = 1
b = 5.0
lt(a, b): True
le(a, b): True
eq(a, b): False
ne(a, b): True
ge(a, b): False
gt(a, b): False
```

3.3.3 Arithmetic Operators

The arithmetic operators for manipulating numerical values are also supported.

Listing 3.47: operator_math.py

```
from operator import *

a = -1
b = 5.0
c = 2
d = 6

print('a =', a)
```

```
print('b =', b)
print('c =', c)
print('d =', d)

print('\nPositive/Negative:')
print('abs(a):', abs(a))
print('neg(a):', neg(a))
print('neg(b):', neg(b))
print('pos(a):', pos(a))
print('pos(b):', pos(b))

print('\nArithmetic:')
print('add(a, b)      :', add(a, b))
print('floordiv(a, b):', floordiv(a, b))
print('floordiv(d, c):', floordiv(d, c))
print('mod(a, b)      :', mod(a, b))
print('mul(a, b)      :', mul(a, b))
print('pow(c, d)      :', pow(c, d))
print('sub(b, a)      :', sub(b, a))
print('truediv(a, b) :', truediv(a, b))
print('truediv(d, c) :', truediv(d, c))

print('\nBitwise:')
print('and_(c, d)  :', and_(c, d))
print('invert(c)   :', invert(c))
print('lshift(c, d):', lshift(c, d))
print('or_(c, d)   :', or_(c, d))
print('rshift(d, c):', rshift(d, c))
print('xor(c, d)   :', xor(c, d))
```

Two different division operators are provided: `floordiv()` (integer division as implemented in Python before version 3.0) and `truediv()` (floating-point division).

```
$ python3 operator_math.py

a = -1
b = 5.0
c = 2
d = 6

Positive/Negative:
abs(a): 1
neg(a): 1
neg(b): -5.0
pos(a): -1
pos(b): 5.0

Arithmetic:
add(a, b)      : 4.0
```

```
floordiv(a, b): -1.0
floordiv(d, c): 3
mod(a, b)     : 4.0
mul(a, b)     : -5.0
pow(c, d)     : 64
sub(b, a)     : 6.0
truediv(a, b) : -0.2
truediv(d, c) : 3.0

Bitwise:
and_(c, d)   : 2
invert(c)    : -3
lshift(c, d): 128
or_(c, d)    : 6
rshift(d, c): 1
xor(c, d)    : 4
```

3.3.4 Sequence Operators

The operators for working with sequences can be organized into four groups: building up sequences, searching for items, accessing contents, and removing items from sequences.

Listing 3.48: operator_sequences.py

```python
from operator import *

a = [1, 2, 3]
b = ['a', 'b', 'c']

print('a =', a)
print('b =', b)

print('\nConstructive:')
print(' concat(a, b):', concat(a, b))

print('\nSearching:')
print(' contains(a, 1)  :', contains(a, 1))
print(' contains(b, "d"):', contains(b, "d"))
print(' countOf(a, 1)   :', countOf(a, 1))
print(' countOf(b, "d") :', countOf(b, "d"))
print(' indexOf(a, 5)   :', indexOf(a, 1))

print('\nAccess Items:')
print(' getitem(b, 1)                 :',
    getitem(b, 1))
print(' getitem(b, slice(1, 3))        :',
    getitem(b, slice(1, 3)))
```

```
print(' setitem(b, 1, "d")                  :', end=' ')
setitem(b, 1, "d")
print(b)
print(' setitem(a, slice(1, 3), [4, 5]):', end=' ')
setitem(a, slice(1, 3), [4, 5])
print(a)

print('\nDestructive:')
print(' delitem(b, 1)                :', end=' ')
delitem(b, 1)
print(b)
print(' delitem(a, slice(1, 3)):', end=' ')
delitem(a, slice(1, 3))
print(a)
```

Some of these operations, such as `setitem()` and `delitem()`, modify the sequence in place and do not return a value.

```
$ python3 operator_sequences.py

a = [1, 2, 3]
b = ['a', 'b', 'c']

Constructive:
  concat(a, b): [1, 2, 3, 'a', 'b', 'c']

Searching:
  contains(a, 1)  : True
  contains(b, "d"): False
  countOf(a, 1)   : 1
  countOf(b, "d") : 0
  indexOf(a, 5)   : 0

Access Items:
  getitem(b, 1)                 : b
  getitem(b, slice(1, 3))       : ['b', 'c']
  setitem(b, 1, "d")            : ['a', 'd', 'c']
  setitem(a, slice(1, 3), [4, 5]): [1, 4, 5]

Destructive:
  delitem(b, 1)           : ['a', 'c']
  delitem(a, slice(1, 3)): [1]
```

3.3.5 In-Place Operators

In addition to the standard operators, many types of objects support "in-place" modification through special operators such as `+=`. Equivalent functions are available for in-place modifications as well.

Listing 3.49: `operator_inplace.py`

```
from operator import *

a = -1
b = 5.0
c = [1, 2, 3]
d = ['a', 'b', 'c']
print('a =', a)
print('b =', b)
print('c =', c)
print('d =', d)
print()

a = iadd(a, b)
print('a = iadd(a, b) =>', a)
print()

c = iconcat(c, d)
print('c = iconcat(c, d) =>', c)
```

These examples demonstrate just a few of the functions. Refer to the standard library documentation for complete details.

```
$ python3 operator_inplace.py

a = -1
b = 5.0
c = [1, 2, 3]
d = ['a', 'b', 'c']

a = iadd(a, b) => 4.0

c = iconcat(c, d) => [1, 2, 3, 'a', 'b', 'c']
```

3.3.6   Attribute and Item "Getters"

One of the most unusual features of the `operator` module is the concept of *getters*. These callable objects are constructed at runtime and retrieve attributes of objects or contents from sequences. Getters are especially useful when working with iterators or generator sequences, as they incur less overhead than a `lambda` or Python function.

Listing 3.50: `operator_attrgetter.py`

```
from operator import *


class MyObj:
    """example class for attrgetter"""
```

```
    def __init__(self, arg):
        super().__init__()
        self.arg = arg

    def __repr__(self):
        return 'MyObj({})'.format(self.arg)


l = [MyObj(i) for i in range(5)]
print('objects    :', l)

# Extract the 'arg' value from each object.
g = attrgetter('arg')
vals = [g(i) for i in l]
print('arg values:', vals)

# Sort using arg.
l.reverse()
print('reversed   :', l)
print('sorted     :', sorted(l, key=g))
```

Attribute getters work like `lambda x,n='attrname': getattr(x,n)`:

```
$ python3 operator_attrgetter.py

objects    : [MyObj(0), MyObj(1), MyObj(2), MyObj(3), MyObj(4)]
arg values: [0, 1, 2, 3, 4]
reversed   : [MyObj(4), MyObj(3), MyObj(2), MyObj(1), MyObj(0)]
sorted     : [MyObj(0), MyObj(1), MyObj(2), MyObj(3), MyObj(4)]
```

Item getters work like `lambda x,y=5: x[y]`:

Listing 3.51: operator_itemgetter.py

```
from operator import *

l = [dict(val=-1 * i) for i in range(4)]
print('Dictionaries:')
print(' original:', l)
g = itemgetter('val')
vals = [g(i) for i in l]
print('   values:', vals)
print('   sorted:', sorted(l, key=g))

print
l = [(i, i * -2) for i in range(4)]
print('\nTuples:')
print(' original:', l)
g = itemgetter(1)
```

```
vals = [g(i) for i in l]
print('   values:', vals)
print('   sorted:', sorted(l, key=g))
```

Item getters work with mappings as well as sequences.

```
$ python3 operator_itemgetter.py

Dictionaries:
 original: [{'val': 0}, {'val': -1}, {'val': -2}, {'val': -3}]
    values: [0, -1, -2, -3]
    sorted: [{'val': -3}, {'val': -2}, {'val': -1}, {'val': 0}]

Tuples:
 original: [(0, 0), (1, -2), (2, -4), (3, -6)]
    values: [0, -2, -4, -6]
    sorted: [(3, -6), (2, -4), (1, -2), (0, 0)]
```

3.3.7   Combining Operators and Custom Classes

The functions in the operator module work via the standard Python interfaces when performing their operations. Thus, they work with user-defined classes as well as the built-in types.

Listing 3.52: operator_classes.py

```
from operator import *


class MyObj:
    """Example for operator overloading"""

    def __init__(self, val):
        super(MyObj, self).__init__()
        self.val = val

    def __str__(self):
        return 'MyObj({})'.format(self.val)

    def __lt__(self, other):
        """compare for less-than"""
        print('Testing {} < {}'.format(self, other))
        return self.val < other.val

    def __add__(self, other):
        """add values"""
        print('Adding {} + {}'.format(self, other))
        return MyObj(self.val + other.val)
```

```
a = MyObj(1)
b = MyObj(2)

print('Comparison:')
print(lt(a, b))

print('\nArithmetic:')
print(add(a, b))
```

Refer to the Python reference guide for a complete list of the special methods used by each operator.

```
$ python3 operator_classes.py

Comparison:
Testing MyObj(1) < MyObj(2)
True

Arithmetic:
Adding MyObj(1) + MyObj(2)
MyObj(3)
```

TIP

Related Reading

- Standard library documentation for operator.[11]
- functools (page 143): Functional programming tools, including the total_ordering() decorator for adding rich comparison methods to a class.
- itertools (page 163): Iterator operations.
- collections (page 75): Abstract types for collections.
- numbers: Abstract types for numerical values.

3.4   contextlib: Context Manager Utilities

The contextlib module contains utilities for working with context managers and the with statement.

3.4.1   Context Manager API

A *context manager* is responsible for a resource within a code block, possibly creating it when the block is entered and then cleaning it up after the block is exited. For example, files

---

[11] https://docs.python.org/3.5/library/operator.html

support the context manager API, which ensures that the files are closed after all reading or writing is done.

Listing 3.53: `contextlib_file.py`

```
with open('/tmp/pymotw.txt', 'wt') as f:
    f.write('contents go here')
# File is automatically closed
```

A context manager is enabled by the `with` statement, and the API involves two methods. The `__enter__()` method is run when execution flow enters the code block inside the `with` statement. It returns an object to be used within the context. When execution flow leaves the `with` block, the `__exit__()` method of the context manager is called to clean up any resources that were used.

Listing 3.54: `contextlib_api.py`

```
class Context:

    def __init__(self):
        print('__init__()')

    def __enter__(self):
        print('__enter__()')
        return self

    def __exit__(self, exc_type, exc_val, exc_tb):
        print('__exit__()')

with Context():
    print('Doing work in the context')
```

Combining a context manager and the `with` statement is a more compact way of writing a `try:finally` block, since the context manager's `__exit__()` method is always called, even if an exception is raised.

```
$ python3 contextlib_api.py

__init__()
__enter__()
Doing work in the context
__exit__()
```

The `__enter__()` method can return any object to be associated with a name specified in the `as` clause of the `with` statement. In this example, the `Context` returns an object that uses the open context.

Listing 3.55: **contextlib_api_other_object.py**

```python
class WithinContext:

    def __init__(self, context):
        print('WithinContext.__init__({})'.format(context))

    def do_something(self):
        print('WithinContext.do_something()')

    def __del__(self):
        print('WithinContext.__del__')


class Context:

    def __init__(self):
        print('Context.__init__()')

    def __enter__(self):
        print('Context.__enter__()')
        return WithinContext(self)

    def __exit__(self, exc_type, exc_val, exc_tb):
        print('Context.__exit__()')


with Context() as c:
    c.do_something()
```

The value associated with the variable c is the object returned by __enter__(), which is not necessarily the Context instance created in the with statement.

```
$ python3 contextlib_api_other_object.py

Context.__init__()
Context.__enter__()
WithinContext.__init__(<__main__.Context object at 0x1007b1c50>)
WithinContext.do_something()
Context.__exit__()
WithinContext.__del__
```

The __exit__() method receives arguments containing details of any exception raised in the with block.

Listing 3.56: **contextlib_api_error.py**

```python
class Context:

    def __init__(self, handle_error):
        print('__init__({})'.format(handle_error))
        self.handle_error = handle_error
```

```
        def __enter__(self):
            print('__enter__()')
            return self

        def __exit__(self, exc_type, exc_val, exc_tb):
            print('__exit__()')
            print('  exc_type =', exc_type)
            print('  exc_val  =', exc_val)
            print('  exc_tb   =', exc_tb)
            return self.handle_error

    with Context(True):
        raise RuntimeError('error message handled')

    print()

    with Context(False):
        raise RuntimeError('error message propagated')
```

If the context manager can handle the exception, __exit__() should return a true value to indicate that the exception does not need to be propagated. Returning a false value causes the exception to be raised again after __exit__() returns.

```
$ python3 contextlib_api_error.py

__init__(True)
__enter__()
__exit__()
  exc_type = <class 'RuntimeError'>
  exc_val  = error message handled
  exc_tb   = <traceback object at 0x10115cc88>

__init__(False)
__enter__()
__exit__()
  exc_type = <class 'RuntimeError'>
  exc_val  = error message propagated
  exc_tb   = <traceback object at 0x10115cc88>
Traceback (most recent call last):
  File "contextlib_api_error.py", line 33, in <module>
    raise RuntimeError('error message propagated')
RuntimeError: error message propagated
```

3.4.2   Context Managers as Function Decorators

The class ContextDecorator adds support to regular context manager classes so that they can be used as function decorators as well as context managers.

Listing 3.57: **contextlib_decorator.py**

```
import contextlib


class Context(contextlib.ContextDecorator):

    def __init__(self, how_used):
        self.how_used = how_used
        print('__init__({})'.format(how_used))

    def __enter__(self):
        print('__enter__({})'.format(self.how_used))
        return self

    def __exit__(self, exc_type, exc_val, exc_tb):
        print('__exit__({})'.format(self.how_used))


@Context('as decorator')
def func(message):
    print(message)


print()
with Context('as context manager'):
    print('Doing work in the context')

print()
func('Doing work in the wrapped function')
```

One difference that arises when using the context manager as a decorator is that the value returned by __enter__() is not available inside the function being decorated, unlike the case when with and as are used. Arguments passed to the decorated function are available in the usual way.

```
$ python3 contextlib_decorator.py

__init__(as decorator)

__init__(as context manager)
__enter__(as context manager)
Doing work in the context
__exit__(as context manager)

__enter__(as decorator)
Doing work in the wrapped function
__exit__(as decorator)
```

3.4.3   From Generator to Context Manager

Creating context managers the traditional way—that is, by writing a class with __enter__()
and __exit__() methods—is not difficult. Nevertheless, writing everything out fully creates
extra overhead when only a trivial bit of context is being managed. In those sorts of situations, the best approach is to use the contextmanager() decorator to convert a generator
function into a context manager.

Listing 3.58: contextlib_contextmanager.py

```
import contextlib


@contextlib.contextmanager
def make_context():
    print(' entering')
    try:
        yield {}
    except RuntimeError as err:
        print('  ERROR:', err)
    finally:
        print('  exiting')

print('Normal:')
with make_context() as value:
    print('  inside with statement:', value)

print('\nHandled error:')
with make_context() as value:
    raise RuntimeError('showing example of handling an error')

print('\nUnhandled error:')
with make_context() as value:
    raise ValueError('this exception is not handled')
```

The generator should initialize the context, invoke yield exactly one time, and then clean
up the context. The value yielded, if any, is bound to the variable in the as clause of the with
statement. Exceptions from within the with block are raised again inside the generator, so
they can be handled there.

```
$ python3 contextlib_contextmanager.py

Normal:
  entering
  inside with statement: {}
  exiting

Handled error:
  entering
```

```
  ERROR: showing example of handling an error
  exiting

Unhandled error:
  entering
  exiting
Traceback (most recent call last):
  File "contextlib_contextmanager.py", line 32, in <module>
    raise ValueError('this exception is not handled')
ValueError: this exception is not handled
```

The context manager returned by contextmanager() is derived from ContextDecorator, so it also works as a function decorator.

Listing 3.59: `contextlib_contextmanager_decorator.py`

```python
import contextlib


@contextlib.contextmanager
def make_context():
    print('  entering')
    try:
        # Yield control, but not a value, because any value
        # yielded is not available when the context manager
        # is used as a decorator.
        yield
    except RuntimeError as err:
        print('  ERROR:', err)
    finally:
        print('  exiting')


@make_context()
def normal():
    print('  inside with statement')


@make_context()
def throw_error(err):
    raise err


print('Normal:')
normal()

print('\nHandled error:')
throw_error(RuntimeError('showing example of handling an error'))

print('\nUnhandled error:')
throw_error(ValueError('this exception is not handled'))
```

As shown in the preceding `ContextDecorator` example, when the context manager is used as a decorator, the value yielded by the generator is not available inside the function being decorated. Arguments passed to the decorated function are still available, as demonstrated by `throw_error()` in this example.

```
$ python3 contextlib_contextmanager_decorator.py

Normal:
  entering
  inside with statement
  exiting

Handled error:
  entering
  ERROR: showing example of handling an error
  exiting

Unhandled error:
  entering
  exiting
Traceback (most recent call last):
  File "contextlib_contextmanager_decorator.py", line 43, in
<module>
    throw_error(ValueError('this exception is not handled'))
  File ".../lib/python3.5/contextlib.py", line 30, in inner
    return func(*args, **kwds)
  File "contextlib_contextmanager_decorator.py", line 33, in
throw_error
    raise err
ValueError: this exception is not handled
```

3.4.4 Closing Open Handles

The `file` class supports the context manager API directly, but some other objects that represent open handles do not. The example given in the standard library documentation for `contextlib` is the object returned from `urllib.urlopen()`. Some other legacy classes use a `close()` method but do not support the context manager API. To ensure that a handle is closed, use `closing()` to create a context manager for it.

Listing 3.60: **contextlib_closing.py**

```
import contextlib


class Door:

    def __init__(self):
        print('  __init__()')
        self.status = 'open'
```

```
        def close(self):
            print('  close()')
            self.status = 'closed'

print('Normal Example:')
with contextlib.closing(Door()) as door:
    print('  inside with statement: {}'.format(door.status))
print('  outside with statement: {}'.format(door.status))

print('\nError handling example:')
try:
    with contextlib.closing(Door()) as door:
        print('  raising from inside with statement')
        raise RuntimeError('error message')
except Exception as err:
    print('  Had an error:', err)
```

The handle is closed whether there is an error in the with block or not.

```
$ python3 contextlib_closing.py

Normal Example:
  __init__()
  inside with statement: open
  close()
  outside with statement: closed

Error handling example:
  __init__()
  raising from inside with statement
  close()
  Had an error: error message
```

3.4.5 Ignoring Exceptions

It is frequently useful to ignore exceptions raised by libraries, because the error indicates that the desired state has already been achieved or can otherwise be ignored. The most common way to ignore exceptions is with a try:except statement that includes only a pass statement in the except block.

Listing 3.61: contextlib_ignore_error.py

```
import contextlib


class NonFatalError(Exception):
    pass
```

```
def non_idempotent_operation():
    raise NonFatalError(
        'The operation failed because of existing state'
    )


try:
    print('trying non-idempotent operation')
    non_idempotent_operation()
    print('succeeded!')
except NonFatalError:
    pass

print('done')
```

In this case, the operation fails and the error is ignored.

```
$ python3 contextlib_ignore_error.py

trying non-idempotent operation
done
```

The try:except form can be replaced with contextlib.suppress() to more explicitly suppress a class of exceptions happening anywhere within the with block.

Listing 3.62: contextlib_suppress.py

```
import contextlib


class NonFatalError(Exception):
    pass


def non_idempotent_operation():
    raise NonFatalError(
        'The operation failed because of existing state'
    )


with contextlib.suppress(NonFatalError):
    print('trying non-idempotent operation')
    non_idempotent_operation()
    print('succeeded!')

print('done')
```

In this updated version, the exception is discarded entirely.

```
$ python3 contextlib_suppress.py

trying non-idempotent operation
done
```

3.4.6   Redirecting Output Streams

Poorly designed library code may write directly to sys.stdout or sys.stderr, without providing arguments to configure different output destinations. The redirect_stdout() and redirect_stderr() context managers can be used to capture output from these kinds of functions, for which the source cannot be changed to accept a new output argument.

Listing 3.63: contextlib_redirect.py

```
from contextlib import redirect_stdout, redirect_stderr
import io
import sys


def misbehaving_function(a):
    sys.stdout.write('(stdout) A: {!r}\n'.format(a))
    sys.stderr.write('(stderr) A: {!r}\n'.format(a))


capture = io.StringIO()
with redirect_stdout(capture), redirect_stderr(capture):
    misbehaving_function(5)

print(capture.getvalue())
```

In this example, misbehaving_function() writes to both stdout and stderr, but the two context managers send that output to the same io.StringIO instance, where it is saved for later use.

```
$ python3 contextlib_redirect.py

(stdout) A: 5
(stderr) A: 5
```

NOTE

Both redirect_stdout() and redirect_stderr() modify the global state by replacing objects in the sys (page 1178) module; for this reason, they should be used with care. The functions are not really thread-safe, so calling them in a multithreaded application will have nondeterministic results. They also may interfere with other operations that expect the standard output streams to be attached to terminal devices.

3.4.7   Dynamic Context Manager Stacks

Most context managers operate on one object at a time, such as a single file or database handle. In these cases, the object is known in advance and the code using the context manager can be built around that one object. In other cases, a program may need to create an unknown number of objects within a context, with all of those objects expected to be cleaned up when control flow exits the context. `ExitStack` was created to handle these more dynamic cases.

An `ExitStack` instance maintains a stack data structure of cleanup callbacks. The callbacks are populated explicitly within the context, and any registered callbacks are called in the reverse order when control flow exits the context. The result is similar to having multiple nested `with` statements, except they are established dynamically.

3.4.7.1   Stacking Context Managers

Several approaches may be used to populate the `ExitStack`. This example uses `enter_context()` to add a new context manager to the stack.

Listing 3.64: **contextlib_exitstack_enter_context.py**

```python
import contextlib


@contextlib.contextmanager
def make_context(i):
    print('{} entering'.format(i))
    yield {}
    print('{} exiting'.format(i))


def variable_stack(n, msg):
    with contextlib.ExitStack() as stack:
        for i in range(n):
            stack.enter_context(make_context(i))
        print(msg)


variable_stack(2, 'inside context')
```

`enter_context()` first calls `__enter__()` on the context manager. It then registers its `__exit__()` method as a callback to be invoked as the stack is undone.

```
$ python3 contextlib_exitstack_enter_context.py

0 entering
1 entering
inside context
1 exiting
0 exiting
```

The context managers given to ExitStack are treated as though they appear within a
series of nested with statements. Errors that happen anywhere within the context propagate
through the normal error handling of the context managers. The following context manager
classes illustrate the way errors propagate.

Listing 3.65: contextlib_context_managers.py

```python
import contextlib


class Tracker:
    "Base class for noisy context managers."

    def __init__(self, i):
        self.i = i

    def msg(self, s):
        print('  {}({}): {}'.format(
            self.__class__.__name__, self.i, s))

    def __enter__(self):
        self.msg('entering')


class HandleError(Tracker):
    "If an exception is received, treat it as handled."

    def __exit__(self, *exc_details):
        received_exc = exc_details[1] is not None
        if received_exc:
            self.msg('handling exception {!r}'.format(
                exc_details[1]))
        self.msg('exiting {}'.format(received_exc))
        # Return a boolean value indicating whether the exception
        # was handled.
        return received_exc


class PassError(Tracker):
    "If an exception is received, propagate it."

    def __exit__(self, *exc_details):
        received_exc = exc_details[1] is not None
        if received_exc:
            self.msg('passing exception {!r}'.format(
                exc_details[1]))
        self.msg('exiting')
        # Return False, indicating any exception was not handled.
        return False
```

```
class ErrorOnExit(Tracker):
    "Cause an exception."

    def __exit__(self, *exc_details):
        self.msg('throwing error')
        raise RuntimeError('from {}'.format(self.i))


class ErrorOnEnter(Tracker):
    "Cause an exception."

    def __enter__(self):
        self.msg('throwing error on enter')
        raise RuntimeError('from {}'.format(self.i))

    def __exit__(self, *exc_info):
        self.msg('exiting')
```

The following examples using these classes are based on `variable_stack()`, which uses the context managers passed to construct an `ExitStack`, building up the overall context in a step-by-step manner. The examples pass different context managers to explore the error handling behavior. The first example presents the normal case of no exceptions.

```
print('No errors:')
variable_stack([
    HandleError(1),
    PassError(2),
])
```

The next example illustrates handling exceptions within the context managers at the end of the stack, in which all of the open contexts are closed as the stack is unwound.

```
print('\nError at the end of the context stack:')
variable_stack([
    HandleError(1),
    HandleError(2),
    ErrorOnExit(3),
])
```

In the next example, exceptions are handled within the context managers in the middle of the stack. The error does not occur until some contexts are already closed, so those contexts do not see the error.

```
print('\nError in the middle of the context stack:')
variable_stack([
    HandleError(1),
    PassError(2),
```

```
        ErrorOnExit(3),
        HandleError(4),
    ])
```

The final example shows the case in which the exception remains unhandled and propagates up to the calling code.

```
try:
    print('\nError ignored:')
    variable_stack([
        PassError(1),
        ErrorOnExit(2),
    ])
except RuntimeError:
    print('error handled outside of context')
```

If any context manager in the stack receives an exception and returns a True value, it prevents that exception from propagating up to any other context managers.

```
$ python3 contextlib_exitstack_enter_context_errors.py

No errors:
  HandleError(1): entering
  PassError(2): entering
  PassError(2): exiting
  HandleError(1): exiting False
outside of stack, any errors were handled

Error at the end of the context stack:
  HandleError(1): entering
  HandleError(2): entering
  ErrorOnExit(3): entering
  ErrorOnExit(3): throwing error
  HandleError(2): handling exception RuntimeError('from 3',)
  HandleError(2): exiting True
  HandleError(1): exiting False
outside of stack, any errors were handled

Error in the middle of the context stack:
  HandleError(1): entering
  PassError(2): entering
  ErrorOnExit(3): entering
  HandleError(4): entering
  HandleError(4): exiting False
  ErrorOnExit(3): throwing error
  PassError(2): passing exception RuntimeError('from 3',)
  PassError(2): exiting
  HandleError(1): handling exception RuntimeError('from 3',)
```

```
    HandleError(1): exiting True
    outside of stack, any errors were handled

Error ignored:
  PassError(1): entering
  ErrorOnExit(2): entering
  ErrorOnExit(2): throwing error
  PassError(1): passing exception RuntimeError('from 2',)
  PassError(1): exiting
error handled outside of context
```

3.4.7.2   Arbitrary Context Callbacks

ExitStack also supports arbitrary callbacks for closing a context, making it easy to clean up resources that are not controlled via a context manager.

Listing 3.66: **contextlib_exitstack_callbacks.py**

```
import contextlib


def callback(*args, **kwds):
    print('closing callback({}, {})'.format(args, kwds))


with contextlib.ExitStack() as stack:
    stack.callback(callback, 'arg1', 'arg2')
    stack.callback(callback, arg3='val3')
```

Just as with the __exit__() methods of full context managers, the callbacks are invoked in the reverse order that they are registered.

```
$ python3 contextlib_exitstack_callbacks.py

closing callback((), {'arg3': 'val3'})
closing callback(('arg1', 'arg2'), {})
```

The callbacks are invoked regardless of whether an error occurred, and they are not given any information about whether an error occurred. Their return value is ignored.

Listing 3.67: **contextlib_exitstack_callbacks_error.py**

```
import contextlib


def callback(*args, **kwds):
    print('closing callback({}, {})'.format(args, kwds))
```

```
try:
    with contextlib.ExitStack() as stack:
        stack.callback(callback, 'arg1', 'arg2')
        stack.callback(callback, arg3='val3')
        raise RuntimeError('thrown error')
except RuntimeError as err:
    print('ERROR: {}'.format(err))
```

Because they do not have access to the error, callbacks are unable to prevent exceptions from propagating through the rest of the stack of context managers.

```
$ python3 contextlib_exitstack_callbacks_error.py

closing callback((), {'arg3': 'val3'})
closing callback(('arg1', 'arg2'), {})
ERROR: thrown error
```

Callbacks offer a convenient way to clearly define cleanup logic without the overhead of creating a new context manager class. To improve code readability, that logic can be encapsulated in an inline function, and callback() can be used as a decorator.

Listing 3.68: **contextlib_exitstack_callbacks_decorator.py**

```
import contextlib


with contextlib.ExitStack() as stack:

    @stack.callback
    def inline_cleanup():
        print('inline_cleanup()')
        print('local_resource = {!r}'.format(local_resource))

    local_resource = 'resource created in context'
    print('within the context')
```

There is no way to specify the arguments for functions registered using the decorator form of callback(). However, if the cleanup callback is defined inline, scope rules give it access to variables defined in the calling code.

```
$ python3 contextlib_exitstack_callbacks_decorator.py

within the context
inline_cleanup()
local_resource = 'resource created in context'
```

3.4.7.3 Partial Stacks

Sometimes when building complex contexts, it is useful to be able to abort an operation if
the context cannot be completely constructed, but to delay the cleanup of all resources until
a later time if they can all be set up properly. For example, if an operation needs several
long-lived network connections, it may be best to not start the operation if one connection
fails. However, if all of the connections can be opened, they need to stay open longer than
the duration of a single context manager. The `pop_all()` method of `ExitStack` can be used
in this scenario.

   `pop_all()` clears all of the context managers and callbacks from the stack on which it
is called, and returns a new stack prepopulated with those same context managers and
callbacks. The `close()` method of the new stack can be invoked later, after the original
stack is gone, to clean up the resources.

Listing 3.69: contextlib_exitstack_pop_all.py

```python
import contextlib

from contextlib_context_managers import *


def variable_stack(contexts):
    with contextlib.ExitStack() as stack:
        for c in contexts:
            stack.enter_context(c)
        # Return the close() method of a new stack as a clean-up
        # function.
        return stack.pop_all().close
    # Explicitly return None, indicating that the ExitStack could
    # not be initialized cleanly but that cleanup has already
    # occurred.
    return None


print('No errors:')
cleaner = variable_stack([
    HandleError(1),
    HandleError(2),
])
cleaner()

print('\nHandled error building context manager stack:')
try:
    cleaner = variable_stack([
        HandleError(1),
        ErrorOnEnter(2),
    ])
except RuntimeError as err:
    print('caught error {}'.format(err))
```

```
    else:
        if cleaner is not None:
            cleaner()
        else:
            print('no cleaner returned')

print('\nUnhandled error building context manager stack:')
try:
    cleaner = variable_stack([
        PassError(1),
        ErrorOnEnter(2),
    ])
except RuntimeError as err:
    print('caught error {}'.format(err))
else:
    if cleaner is not None:
        cleaner()
    else:
        print('no cleaner returned')
```

This example uses the same context manager classes defined earlier, but ErrorOnEnter produces an error on __enter__() instead of __exit__(). Inside variable_stack(), if all of the contexts are entered without error, then the close() method of a new ExitStack is returned. If a handled error occurs, variable_stack() returns None to indicate that the cleanup work has already been done. If an unhandled error occurs, the partial stack is cleaned up and the error is propagated.

```
$ python3 contextlib_exitstack_pop_all.py

No errors:
  HandleError(1): entering
  HandleError(2): entering
  HandleError(2): exiting False
  HandleError(1): exiting False

Handled error building context manager stack:
  HandleError(1): entering
  ErrorOnEnter(2): throwing error on enter
  HandleError(1): handling exception RuntimeError('from 2',)
  HandleError(1): exiting True
no cleaner returned

Unhandled error building context manager stack:
  PassError(1): entering
  ErrorOnEnter(2): throwing error on enter
  PassError(1): passing exception RuntimeError('from 2',)
  PassError(1): exiting
caught error from 2
```

TIP

Related Reading

- Standard library documentation for `contextlib`.[12]
- **PEP 343**[13]: The `with` statement.
- Context Manager Types[14]: Description of the context manager API from the standard library documentation.
- `with` Statement Context Managers[15]: Description of the context manager API from the Python Reference Guide.
- Resource management in Python 3.3, or `contextlib.ExitStack` FTW![16]: Description of using ExitStack to deploy safe code from Barry Warsaw.

[12] https://docs.python.org/3.5/library/contextlib.html
[13] www.python.org/dev/peps/pep-0343
[14] https://docs.python.org/library/stdtypes.html#typecontextmanager
[15] https://docs.python.org/reference/datamodel.html#context-managers
[16] www.wefearchange.org/2013/05/resource-management-in-python-33-or.html

Chapter 4

Dates and Times

Python does not include native types for dates and times as it does for `int`, `float`, and `str`, but it provides three modules for manipulating date and time values in several representations.

The `time` (page 211) module exposes the time-related functions from the underlying C library. It includes functions for retrieving the clock time and the processor run time, as well as basic parsing and string formatting tools.

The `datetime` (page 221) module provides a higher-level interface for date, time, and combined values. The classes in `datetime` support arithmetic, comparison, and time zone configuration.

The `calendar` (page 233) module creates formatted representations of weeks, months, and years. It can also be used to compute recurring events, the day of the week for a given date, and other calendar-based values.

4.1 time: Clock Time

The `time` module provides access to several types of clocks, each useful for different purposes. The standard system calls such as `time()` report the system "wall clock" time. The `monotonic()` clock can be used to measure elapsed time in a long-running process because it is guaranteed never to move backward, even if the system time is changed. For performance testing, `perf_counter()` provides access to the clock with the highest available resolution, which makes short time measurements more accurate. The CPU time is available through `clock()`, and `process_time()` returns the combined processor time and system time.

NOTE

The implementations expose C library functions for manipulating dates and times. Because they are tied to the underlying C implementation, some details (such as the start of the epoch and the maximum date value supported) are platform-specific. Refer to the library documentation for complete details.

4.1.1 Comparing Clocks

Implementation details for the clocks vary by platform. Use `get_clock_info()` to access basic information about the current implementation, including the clock's resolution.

Listing 4.1: **time_get_clock_info.py**

```python
import textwrap
import time

available_clocks = [
    ('clock', time.clock),
    ('monotonic', time.monotonic),
    ('perf_counter', time.perf_counter),
    ('process_time', time.process_time),
    ('time', time.time),
]

for clock_name, func in available_clocks:
    print(textwrap.dedent('''\
    {name}:
        adjustable    : {info.adjustable}
        implementation: {info.implementation}
        monotonic     : {info.monotonic}
        resolution    : {info.resolution}
        current       : {current}
    ''').format(
        name=clock_name,
        info=time.get_clock_info(clock_name),
        current=func())
    )
```

The following output for Mac OS X shows that the monotonic and perf_counter clocks are implemented using the same underlying system call.

```
$ python3 time_get_clock_info.py

clock:
    adjustable    : False
    implementation: clock()
    monotonic     : True
    resolution    : 1e-06
    current       : 0.028399

monotonic:
    adjustable    : False
    implementation: mach_absolute_time()
    monotonic     : True
    resolution    : 1e-09
    current       : 172336.002232467

perf_counter:
    adjustable    : False
    implementation: mach_absolute_time()
```

```
        monotonic      : True
        resolution     : 1e-09
        current        : 172336.002280763

process_time:
        adjustable     : False
        implementation: getrusage(RUSAGE_SELF)
        monotonic      : True
        resolution     : 1e-06
        current        : 0.028593

time:
        adjustable     : True
        implementation: gettimeofday()
        monotonic      : False
        resolution     : 1e-06
        current        : 1471198232.045526
```

4.1.2 Wall Clock Time

One of the core functions of the time module is time(), which returns the number of seconds since the start of the "epoch" as a floating-point value.

Listing 4.2: time_time.py

```
import time

print('The time is:', time.time())
```

The epoch is the start of measurement for time, which for Unix systems is 0:00 on January 1, 1970. Although the value is always a float, the actual precision is platform-dependent.

```
$ python3 time_time.py

The time is: 1471198232.091589
```

The float representation is highly useful when storing or comparing dates, but less useful for producing human-readable representations. For logging or printing times, ctime() can be a better choice.

Listing 4.3: time_ctime.py

```
import time

print('The time is      :', time.ctime())
later = time.time() + 15
print('15 secs from now :', time.ctime(later))
```

The second `print()` call in this example shows how to use `ctime()` to format a time value other than the current time.

```
$ python3 time_ctime.py

The time is      : Sun Aug 14 14:10:32 2016
15 secs from now : Sun Aug 14 14:10:47 2016
```

4.1.3   Monotonic Clocks

Because `time()` looks at the system clock, and because the system clock can be changed by the user or system services for synchronizing clocks across multiple computers, calling `time()` repeatedly may produce values that go forward and backward. This can result in unexpected behavior when trying to measure durations or otherwise use those times for computation. To avoid those situations, use `monotonic()`, which always returns values that go forward.

Listing 4.4: <code>time_monotonic.py</code>

```
import time

start = time.monotonic()
time.sleep(0.1)
end = time.monotonic()
print('start : {:>9.2f}'.format(start))
print('end   : {:>9.2f}'.format(end))
print('span  : {:>9.2f}'.format(end - start))
```

The start point for the monotonic clock is not defined, so return values are useful only for doing calculations with other clock values. In this example, the duration of the sleep is measured using `monotonic()`.

```
$ python3 time_monotonic.py

start : 172336.14
end   : 172336.24
span  :      0.10
```

4.1.4   Processor Clock Time

While `time()` returns a wall clock time, `clock()` returns a processor clock time. The values returned from `clock()` reflect the actual time used by the program as it runs.

Listing 4.5: <code>time_clock.py</code>

```
import hashlib
import time
```

```
# Data to use to calculate md5 checksums
data = open(__file__, 'rb').read()

for i in range(5):
    h = hashlib.sha1()
    print(time.ctime(), ': {:0.3f} {:0.3f}'.format(
        time.time(), time.clock()))
    for i in range(300000):
        h.update(data)
    cksum = h.digest()
```

In this example, the formatted ctime() is printed along with the floating-point values from time(), and clock() for each iteration through the loop.

NOTE

If you want to run the example on your system, you may have to add more cycles to the inner loop or work with a larger amount of data to actually see a difference in the times.

```
$ python3 time_clock.py

Sun Aug 14 14:10:32 2016 : 1471198232.327 0.033
Sun Aug 14 14:10:32 2016 : 1471198232.705 0.409
Sun Aug 14 14:10:33 2016 : 1471198233.086 0.787
Sun Aug 14 14:10:33 2016 : 1471198233.466 1.166
Sun Aug 14 14:10:33 2016 : 1471198233.842 1.540
```

Typically, the processor clock does not tick if a program is not doing anything.

Listing 4.6: **time_clock_sleep.py**

```
import time

template = '{} - {:0.2f} - {:0.2f}'

print(template.format(
    time.ctime(), time.time(), time.clock())
)

for i in range(3, 0, -1):
    print('Sleeping', i)
    time.sleep(i)
    print(template.format(
        time.ctime(), time.time(), time.clock())
    )
```

In this example, the loop does very little work by going to sleep after each iteration. The
time() value increases even while the application is asleep, but the clock() value does not.

```
$ python3 -u time_clock_sleep.py

Sun Aug 14 14:10:34 2016 - 1471198234.28 - 0.03
Sleeping 3
Sun Aug 14 14:10:37 2016 - 1471198237.28 - 0.03
Sleeping 2
Sun Aug 14 14:10:39 2016 - 1471198239.29 - 0.03
Sleeping 1
Sun Aug 14 14:10:40 2016 - 1471198240.29 - 0.03
```

Calling sleep() yields control from the current thread and asks that thread to wait for
the system to wake it back up. If a program has only one thread, this function effectively
blocks the app so that it does no work.

4.1.5   Performance Counter

A high-resolution monotonic clock is essential for measuring performance. Determining
the best clock data source requires platform-specific knowledge, which Python provides
in perf_counter().

Listing 4.7: **time_perf_counter.py**

```
import hashlib
import time

# Data to use to calculate md5 checksums
data = open(__file__, 'rb').read()

loop_start = time.perf_counter()

for i in range(5):
    iter_start = time.perf_counter()
    h = hashlib.sha1()
    for i in range(300000):
        h.update(data)
    cksum = h.digest()
    now = time.perf_counter()
    loop_elapsed = now - loop_start
    iter_elapsed = now - iter_start
    print(time.ctime(), ': {:0.3f} {:0.3f}'.format(
        iter_elapsed, loop_elapsed))
```

As with monotonic(), the epoch for perf_counter() is undefined, and the values are
meant to be used for comparing and computing values, not as absolute times.

```
$ python3 time_perf_counter.py

Sun Aug 14 14:10:40 2016 : 0.487 0.487
Sun Aug 14 14:10:41 2016 : 0.485 0.973
Sun Aug 14 14:10:41 2016 : 0.494 1.466
Sun Aug 14 14:10:42 2016 : 0.487 1.953
Sun Aug 14 14:10:42 2016 : 0.480 2.434
```

4.1.6 Time Components

Storing times as elapsed seconds is useful in some situations, but sometimes a program needs to have access to the individual fields of a date (e.g., year, month). The `time` module defines `struct_time` for holding date and time values, with the components being broken out so they are easy to access. Several functions work with `struct_time` values instead of floats.

Listing 4.8: `time_struct.py`

```python
import time


def show_struct(s):
    print('  tm_year :', s.tm_year)
    print('  tm_mon  :', s.tm_mon)
    print('  tm_mday :', s.tm_mday)
    print('  tm_hour :', s.tm_hour)
    print('  tm_min  :', s.tm_min)
    print('  tm_sec  :', s.tm_sec)
    print('  tm_wday :', s.tm_wday)
    print('  tm_yday :', s.tm_yday)
    print('  tm_isdst:', s.tm_isdst)

print('gmtime:')
show_struct(time.gmtime())
print('\nlocaltime:')
show_struct(time.localtime())
print('\nmktime:', time.mktime(time.localtime()))
```

The `gmtime()` function returns the current time in UTC. `localtime()` returns the current time with the current time zone applied. `mktime()` takes a `struct_time` and converts it to the floating-point representation.

```
$ python3 time_struct.py

gmtime:
  tm_year : 2016
  tm_mon  : 8
  tm_mday : 14
```

```
    tm_hour : 18
    tm_min  : 10
    tm_sec  : 42
    tm_wday : 6
    tm_yday : 227
    tm_isdst: 0

localtime:
    tm_year : 2016
    tm_mon  : 8
    tm_mday : 14
    tm_hour : 14
    tm_min  : 10
    tm_sec  : 42
    tm_wday : 6
    tm_yday : 227
    tm_isdst: 1

mktime: 1471198242.0
```

4.1.7   Working with Time Zones

The functions for determining the current time depend on having the time zone set, either by the program or by using a default time zone set for the system. Changing the time zone does not change the actual time, just the way it is represented.

To change the time zone, set the environment variable TZ, and then call `tzset()`. The time zone can be specified with a great deal of detail, right down to the start and stop times for daylight savings time. It is usually easier to use the time zone name and let the underlying libraries derive the other information, though.

The following example changes the time zone to a few different values and shows how the changes affect other settings in the time module.

Listing 4.9: **time_timezone.py**

```python
import time
import os


def show_zone_info():
    print('  TZ    :', os.environ.get('TZ', '(not set)'))
    print('  tzname:', time.tzname)
    print('  Zone  : {} ({})'.format(
        time.timezone, (time.timezone / 3600)))
    print('  DST   :', time.daylight)
    print('  Time  :', time.ctime())
    print()


print('Default :')
```

```
show_zone_info()

ZONES = [
    'GMT',
    'Europe/Amsterdam',
]

for zone in ZONES:
    os.environ['TZ'] = zone
    time.tzset()
    print(zone, ':')
    show_zone_info()
```

The default time zone on the system used to prepare the examples is U.S./Eastern. The other zones in the example change the tzname, daylight flag, and timezone offset value.

```
$ python3 time_timezone.py

Default :
  TZ    : (not set)
  tzname: ('EST', 'EDT')
  Zone  : 18000 (5.0)
  DST   : 1
  Time  : Sun Aug 14 14:10:42 2016

GMT :
  TZ    : GMT
  tzname: ('GMT', 'GMT')
  Zone  : 0 (0.0)
  DST   : 0
  Time  : Sun Aug 14 18:10:42 2016

Europe/Amsterdam :
  TZ    : Europe/Amsterdam
  tzname: ('CET', 'CEST')
  Zone  : -3600 (-1.0)
  DST   : 1
  Time  : Sun Aug 14 20:10:42 2016
```

4.1.8 Parsing and Formatting Times

The functions strptime() and strftime() convert between struct_time and string representations of time values. The long list of formatting directives supported by both functions enables input and output in different styles. The complete list is available in the library documentation for the time module.

The following example converts the current time from a string to a `struct_time` instance, and then back to a string.

Listing 4.10: `time_strptime.py`

```
import time


def show_struct(s):
    print('  tm_year :', s.tm_year)
    print('  tm_mon  :', s.tm_mon)
    print('  tm_mday :', s.tm_mday)
    print('  tm_hour :', s.tm_hour)
    print('  tm_min  :', s.tm_min)
    print('  tm_sec  :', s.tm_sec)
    print('  tm_wday :', s.tm_wday)
    print('  tm_yday :', s.tm_yday)
    print('  tm_isdst:', s.tm_isdst)

now = time.ctime(1483391847.433716)
print('Now:', now)

parsed = time.strptime(now)
print('\nParsed:')
show_struct(parsed)

print('\nFormatted:',
      time.strftime("%a %b %d %H:%M:%S %Y", parsed))
```

The output string is not exactly like the input, since the day of the month is prefixed with a zero.

```
$ python3 time_strptime.py

Now: Mon Jan  2 16:17:27 2017

Parsed:
  tm_year : 2017
  tm_mon  : 1
  tm_mday : 2
  tm_hour : 16
  tm_min  : 17
  tm_sec  : 27
  tm_wday : 0
  tm_yday : 2
  tm_isdst: -1

Formatted: Mon Jan 02 16:17:27 2017
```

TIP

Related Reading

- Standard library documentation for time.[1]
- Python 2 to 3 porting notes for time (page 1364).
- datetime (page 221): The datetime module includes other classes for doing calculations with dates and times.
- calendar (page 233): Work with higher-level date functions to produce calendars or calculate recurring events.

4.2 datetime: Date and Time Value Manipulation

datetime contains functions and classes for date and time parsing, formatting, and arithmetic.

4.2.1 Times

Time values are represented with the time class. A time instance has attributes for hour, minute, second, and microsecond; it can also include time zone information.

Listing 4.11: datetime_time.py

```
import datetime

t = datetime.time(1, 2, 3)
print(t)
print('hour        :', t.hour)
print('minute      :', t.minute)
print('second      :', t.second)
print('microsecond:', t.microsecond)
print('tzinfo      :', t.tzinfo)
```

The arguments to initialize a time instance are optional, but the default of 0 is unlikely to be correct.

```
$ python3 datetime_time.py

01:02:03
hour       : 1
minute     : 2
second     : 3
microsecond: 0
tzinfo     : None
```

---

[1] https://docs.python.org/3.5/library/time.html

A `time` instance holds only values of time; it does not include a date associated with the time.

Listing 4.12: <code>datetime_time_minmax.py</code>

```
import datetime

print('Earliest  :', datetime.time.min)
print('Latest    :', datetime.time.max)
print('Resolution:', datetime.time.resolution)
```

The `min` and `max` class attributes reflect the valid range of times in a single day.

```
$ python3 datetime_time_minmax.py

Earliest  : 00:00:00
Latest    : 23:59:59.999999
Resolution: 0:00:00.000001
```

The resolution for `time` is limited to whole microseconds.

Listing 4.13: <code>datetime_time_resolution.py</code>

```
import datetime

for m in [1, 0, 0.1, 0.6]:
    try:
        print('{:02.1f} :'.format(m),
              datetime.time(0, 0, 0, microsecond=m))
    except TypeError as err:
        print('ERROR:', err)
```

Floating-point values for microseconds cause a `TypeError`.

```
$ python3 datetime_time_resolution.py

1.0 : 00:00:00.000001
0.0 : 00:00:00
ERROR: integer argument expected, got float
ERROR: integer argument expected, got float
```

4.2.2 Dates

Calendar date values are represented with the `date` class. Instances have attributes for `year`, `month`, and `day`. It is easy to create a date representing the current date using the `today()` class method.

Listing 4.14: datetime_date.py

```
import datetime

today = datetime.date.today()
print(today)
print('ctime   :', today.ctime())
tt = today.timetuple()
print('tuple   : tm_year  =', tt.tm_year)
print('          tm_mon   =', tt.tm_mon)
print('          tm_mday  =', tt.tm_mday)
print('          tm_hour  =', tt.tm_hour)
print('          tm_min   =', tt.tm_min)
print('          tm_sec   =', tt.tm_sec)
print('          tm_wday  =', tt.tm_wday)
print('          tm_yday  =', tt.tm_yday)
print('          tm_isdst =', tt.tm_isdst)
print('ordinal:', today.toordinal())
print('Year    :', today.year)
print('Mon     :', today.month)
print('Day     :', today.day)
```

This example prints the current date in several formats.

```
$ python3 datetime_date.py

2016-07-10
ctime   : Sun Jul 10 00:00:00 2016
tuple   : tm_year  = 2016
          tm_mon   = 7
          tm_mday  = 10
          tm_hour  = 0
          tm_min   = 0
          tm_sec   = 0
          tm_wday  = 6
          tm_yday  = 192
          tm_isdst = -1
ordinal: 736155
Year    : 2016
Mon     : 7
Day     : 10
```

There are also class methods for creating instances from POSIX timestamps or integers representing date values from the Gregorian calendar, where January 1 of the year 1 is designated as having the value 1 and each subsequent day increments the value by 1.

Listing 4.15: **datetime_date_fromordinal.py**

```
import datetime
import time

o = 733114
print('o                :', o)
print('fromordinal(o)  :', datetime.date.fromordinal(o))

t = time.time()
print('t                :', t)
print('fromtimestamp(t):', datetime.date.fromtimestamp(t))
```

This example illustrates the different value types used by `fromordinal()` and `fromtimestamp()`.

```
$ python3 datetime_date_fromordinal.py

o                : 733114
fromordinal(o)  : 2008-03-13
t                : 1468161894.788508
fromtimestamp(t): 2016-07-10
```

As is true with the `time` class, the range of date values supported can be determined using the `min` and `max` attributes.

Listing 4.16: **datetime_date_minmax.py**

```
import datetime

print('Earliest   :', datetime.date.min)
print('Latest     :', datetime.date.max)
print('Resolution:', datetime.date.resolution)
```

The resolution for dates is whole days.

```
$ python3 datetime_date_minmax.py

Earliest   : 0001-01-01
Latest     : 9999-12-31
Resolution: 1 day, 0:00:00
```

Another way to create new `date` instances is to use the `replace()` method of an existing date.

Listing 4.17: datetime_date_replace.py

```
import datetime

d1 = datetime.date(2008, 3, 29)
print('d1:', d1.ctime())

d2 = d1.replace(year=2009)
print('d2:', d2.ctime())
```

This example changes the year, leaving the day and month unmodified.

```
$ python3 datetime_date_replace.py

d1: Sat Mar 29 00:00:00 2008
d2: Sun Mar 29 00:00:00 2009
```

4.2.3 timedeltas

Future and past dates can be calculated using basic arithmetic on two datetime objects, or by combining a datetime with a timedelta. Subtracting dates produces a timedelta, and a timedelta can be also added or subtracted from a date to produce another date. The internal values for a timedelta are stored in days, seconds, and microseconds.

Listing 4.18: datetime_timedelta.py

```
import datetime

print('microseconds:', datetime.timedelta(microseconds=1))
print('milliseconds:', datetime.timedelta(milliseconds=1))
print('seconds      :', datetime.timedelta(seconds=1))
print('minutes      :', datetime.timedelta(minutes=1))
print('hours        :', datetime.timedelta(hours=1))
print('days         :', datetime.timedelta(days=1))
print('weeks        :', datetime.timedelta(weeks=1))
```

Intermediate-level values passed to the constructor are converted into days, seconds, and microseconds.

```
$ python3 datetime_timedelta.py

microseconds: 0:00:00.000001
milliseconds: 0:00:00.001000
seconds      : 0:00:01
minutes      : 0:01:00
hours        : 1:00:00
days         : 1 day, 0:00:00
weeks        : 7 days, 0:00:00
```

The full duration of a timedelta can be retrieved as a number of seconds using total_seconds().

Listing 4.19: **datetime_timedelta_total_seconds.py**

```
import datetime

for delta in [datetime.timedelta(microseconds=1),
              datetime.timedelta(milliseconds=1),
              datetime.timedelta(seconds=1),
              datetime.timedelta(minutes=1),
              datetime.timedelta(hours=1),
              datetime.timedelta(days=1),
              datetime.timedelta(weeks=1),
              ]:
    print('{:15} = {:8} seconds'.format(
        str(delta), delta.total_seconds())
    )
```

The return value is a floating-point number, to accommodate durations of less than 1 second.

```
$ python3 datetime_timedelta_total_seconds.py

0:00:00.000001  =      1e-06 seconds
0:00:00.001000  =      0.001 seconds
0:00:01         =        1.0 seconds
0:01:00         =       60.0 seconds
1:00:00         =     3600.0 seconds
1 day, 0:00:00  =    86400.0 seconds
7 days, 0:00:00 =   604800.0 seconds
```

4.2.4   Date Arithmetic

Date math uses the standard arithmetic operators.

Listing 4.20: **datetime_date_math.py**

```
import datetime

today = datetime.date.today()
print('Today     :', today)

one_day = datetime.timedelta(days=1)
print('One day   :', one_day)

yesterday = today - one_day
print('Yesterday:', yesterday)

tomorrow = today + one_day
print('Tomorrow :', tomorrow)
```

```
print()
print('tomorrow - yesterday:', tomorrow - yesterday)
print('yesterday - tomorrow:', yesterday - tomorrow)
```

This example with date objects illustrates the use of timedelta objects to compute new dates. In addition, date instances are subtracted to produce timedelta objects (including a negative delta value).

```
$ python3 datetime_date_math.py

Today    : 2016-07-10
One day  : 1 day, 0:00:00
Yesterday: 2016-07-09
Tomorrow : 2016-07-11

tomorrow - yesterday: 2 days, 0:00:00
yesterday - tomorrow: -2 days, 0:00:00
```

A timedelta object also supports arithmetic with integers, floats, and other timedelta instances.

Listing 4.21: **datetime_timedelta_math.py**

```
import datetime

one_day = datetime.timedelta(days=1)
print('1 day     :', one_day)
print('5 days    :', one_day * 5)
print('1.5 days  :', one_day * 1.5)
print('1/4 day   :', one_day / 4)

# Assume an hour for lunch.
work_day = datetime.timedelta(hours=7)
meeting_length = datetime.timedelta(hours=1)
print('meetings per day :', work_day / meeting_length)
```

In this example, several multiples of a single day are computed, with the resulting timedelta holding the appropriate number of days or hours.

The final example demonstrates how to compute values by combining two timedelta objects. In this case, the result is a floating-point number.

```
$ python3 datetime_timedelta_math.py

1 day     : 1 day, 0:00:00
5 days    : 5 days, 0:00:00
1.5 days  : 1 day, 12:00:00
1/4 day   : 6:00:00
meetings per day : 7.0
```

4.2.5   Comparing Values

Both date and time values can be compared using the standard comparison operators to determine which is earlier or later.

Listing 4.22: **datetime_comparing.py**

```
import datetime
import time

print('Times:')
t1 = datetime.time(12, 55, 0)
print('  t1:', t1)
t2 = datetime.time(13, 5, 0)
print('  t2:', t2)
print('  t1 < t2:', t1 < t2)

print
print('Dates:')
d1 = datetime.date.today()
print('  d1:', d1)
d2 = datetime.date.today() + datetime.timedelta(days=1)
print('  d2:', d2)
print('  d1 > d2:', d1 > d2)
```

All comparison operators are supported.

```
$ python3 datetime_comparing.py

Times:
  t1: 12:55:00
  t2: 13:05:00
  t1 < t2: True
Dates:
  d1: 2016-07-10
  d2: 2016-07-11
  d1 > d2: False
```

4.2.6   Combining Dates and Times

Use the datetime class to hold values consisting of both date and time components. As with date, several convenient class methods are available for creating datetime instances from other common values.

Listing 4.23: **datetime_datetime.py**

```
import datetime

print('Now    :', datetime.datetime.now())
```

```
print('Today   :', datetime.datetime.today())
print('UTC Now:', datetime.datetime.utcnow())
print

FIELDS = [
    'year', 'month', 'day',
    'hour', 'minute', 'second',
    'microsecond',
]

d = datetime.datetime.now()
for attr in FIELDS:
    print('{:15}: {}'.format(attr, getattr(d, attr)))
```

As might be expected, the datetime instance has all of the attributes of both a date object and a time object.

```
$ python3 datetime_datetime.py

Now     : 2016-07-10 10:44:55.215677
Today   : 2016-07-10 10:44:55.215719
UTC Now: 2016-07-10 14:44:55.215732
year           : 2016
month          : 7
day            : 10
hour           : 10
minute         : 44
second         : 55
microsecond    : 216198
```

Just like date, datetime provides convenient class methods for creating new instances. It also includes fromordinal() and fromtimestamp().

Listing 4.24: datetime_datetime_combine.py

```
import datetime

t = datetime.time(1, 2, 3)
print('t :', t)

d = datetime.date.today()
print('d :', d)

dt = datetime.datetime.combine(d, t)
print('dt:', dt)
```

combine() creates datetime instances from one date and one time instance.

```
$ python3 datetime_datetime_combine.py

t : 01:02:03
d : 2016-07-10
dt: 2016-07-10 01:02:03
```

4.2.7 Formatting and Parsing

The default string representation of a datetime object uses the ISO-8601 format (YYYY-MM-DDTHH:MM:SS.mmmmmm). Alternative formats can be generated using strftime().

Listing 4.25: datetime_datetime_strptime.py

```
import datetime

format = "%a %b %d %H:%M:%S %Y"

today = datetime.datetime.today()
print('ISO      :', today)

s = today.strftime(format)
print('strftime:', s)

d = datetime.datetime.strptime(s, format)
print('strptime:', d.strftime(format))
```

Use datetime.strptime() to convert formatted strings to datetime instances.

```
$ python3 datetime_datetime_strptime.py

ISO      : 2016-07-10 10:44:55.325247
strftime: Sun Jul 10 10:44:55 2016
strptime: Sun Jul 10 10:44:55 2016
```

The same formatting codes can be used with Python's string formatting mini-language[2] by placing them after the : in the field specification of the format string.

Listing 4.26: datetime_format.py

```
import datetime

today = datetime.datetime.today()
print('ISO      :', today)
print('format(): {:%a %b %d %H:%M:%S %Y}'.format(today))
```

---

[2] https://docs.python.org/3.5/library/string.html#formatspec

Table 4.1: `strptime`/`strftime` Format Codes

Symbol	Meaning	Example
%a	Abbreviated weekday name	`'Wed'`
%A	Full weekday name	`'Wednesday'`
%w	Weekday number: 0 (Sunday) through 6 (Saturday)	`'3'`
%d	Day of the month (zero padded)	`'13'`
%b	Abbreviated month name	`'Jan'`
%B	Full month name	`'January'`
%m	Month of the year	`'01'`
%y	Year without century	`'16'`
%Y	Year with century	`'2016'`
%H	Hour from 24-hour clock	`'17'`
%I	Hour from 12-hour clock	`'05'`
%p	AM/PM	`'PM'`
%M	Minutes	`'00'`
%S	Seconds	`'00'`
%f	Microseconds	`'000000'`
%z	UTC offset for time zone–aware objects	`'-0500'`
%Z	Time zone name	`'EST'`
%j	Day of the year	`'013'`
%W	Week of the year	`'02'`
%c	Date and time representation for the current locale	`'Wed Jan 13 17:00:00 2016'`
%x	Date representation for the current locale	`'01/13/16'`
%X	Time representation for the current locale	`'17:00:00'`
%%	A literal % character	`'%'`

Each datetime format code must be prefixed with %, and subsequent colons are treated as literal characters to be included in the output.

```
$ python3 datetime_format.py

ISO     : 2016-07-10 10:44:55.389239
format(): Sun Jul 10 10:44:55 2016
```

Table 4.1 gives all of the formatting codes for 5:00 PM January 13, 2016, in the U.S./Eastern time zone.

4.2.8 Time Zones

Within `datetime`, time zones are represented by subclasses of `tzinfo`. Since `tzinfo` is an abstract base class, applications need to define a subclass and provide appropriate implementations for a few methods to make it useful.

`datetime` does include a somewhat naive implementation in the class `timezone` that uses a fixed offset from UTC. This implementation does not support different offset values on different days of the year, such as where daylight savings time applies, or where the offset from UTC has changed over time.

Listing 4.27: datetime_timezone.py

```
import datetime

min6 = datetime.timezone(datetime.timedelta(hours=-6))
plus6 = datetime.timezone(datetime.timedelta(hours=6))
d = datetime.datetime.now(min6)

print(min6, ':', d)
print(datetime.timezone.utc, ':',
      d.astimezone(datetime.timezone.utc))
print(plus6, ':', d.astimezone(plus6))

# Convert to the current system timezone.
d_system = d.astimezone()
print(d_system.tzinfo, '        :', d_system)
```

To convert a datetime value from one time zone to another, use astimezone(). In the preceding example, two separate time zones 6 hours on either side of UTC are shown, and the utc instance from datetime.timezone is also used for reference. The final output line shows the value in the system time zone, which was obtained by calling astimezone() with no argument.

```
$ python3 datetime_timezone.py

UTC-06:00 : 2016-07-10 08:44:55.495995-06:00
UTC+00:00 : 2016-07-10 14:44:55.495995+00:00
UTC+06:00 : 2016-07-10 20:44:55.495995+06:00
EDT       : 2016-07-10 10:44:55.495995-04:00
```

NOTE

The third-party module pytz[3] is a better implementation for time zones. It supports named time zones, and the offset database is kept up-to-date as changes are made by political bodies around the world.

TIP

Related Reading

- Standard library documentation for datetime.[4]
- Python 2 to 3 porting notes for datetime (page 1358).

---

[3] http://pytz.sourceforge.net/
[4] https://docs.python.org/3.5/library/datetime.html

- calendar (page 233): The calendar module.
- time (page 211): The time module.
- dateutil[5]: dateutil from Labix extends the datetime module with additional features.
- pytz[6]: World time zone database and classes for making datetime objects time zone-aware.
- Wikipedia: Proleptic Gregorian calendar[7]: A description of the Gregorian calendar system.
- Wikipedia: ISO 8601[8]: The standard for numeric representation of dates and times.

4.3 calendar: Work with Dates

The calendar module defines the Calendar class, which encapsulates calculations for values such as the dates of the weeks in a given month or year. In addition, the TextCalendar and HTMLCalendar classes can produce preformatted output.

4.3.1 Formatting Examples

The prmonth() method is a simple function that produces the formatted text output for a month.

Listing 4.28: **calendar_textcalendar.py**

```
import calendar

c = calendar.TextCalendar(calendar.SUNDAY)
c.prmonth(2017, 7)
```

The example configures TextCalendar to start weeks on Sunday, following the U.S. convention. The default is to use the European convention of starting a week on Monday. The example produces the following output.

```
$ python3 calendar_textcalendar.py

     July 2017
Su Mo Tu We Th Fr Sa
                   1
 2  3  4  5  6  7  8
 9 10 11 12 13 14 15
16 17 18 19 20 21 22
23 24 25 26 27 28 29
30 31
```

---

[5] http://labix.org/python-dateutil
[6] http://pytz.sourceforge.net/
[7] https://en.wikipedia.org/wiki/Proleptic_Gregorian_calendar
[8] https://en.wikipedia.org/wiki/ISO_8601

A similar HTML table can be produced with `HTMLCalendar` and `formatmonth()`. The rendered output looks roughly the same as the plain text version, but is wrapped with HTML tags. Each table cell has a class attribute corresponding to the day of the week, so the HTML can be styled through CSS.

To produce output in a format other than one of the defaults, use `calendar` to calculate the dates and organize the values into week and month ranges, then iterate over the result. The `weekheader()`, `monthcalendar()`, and `yeardays2calendar()` methods of `Calendar` are especially useful for this purpose.

Calling `yeardays2calendar()` produces a sequence of "month row" lists. Each list of months includes each month as another list of weeks. The weeks are lists of tuples made up of day number (1–31) and weekday number (0–6). Days that fall outside of the month have a day number of 0.

Listing 4.29: `calendar_yeardays2calendar.py`

```
import calendar
import pprint

cal = calendar.Calendar(calendar.SUNDAY)

cal_data = cal.yeardays2calendar(2017, 3)
print('len(cal_data)        :', len(cal_data))

top_months = cal_data[0]
print('len(top_months)      :', len(top_months))

first_month = top_months[0]
print('len(first_month)     :', len(first_month))

print('first_month:')
pprint.pprint(first_month, width=65)
```

Calling `yeardays2calendar(2017,3)` returns data for 2017, organized with three months per row.

```
$ python3 calendar_yeardays2calendar.py

len(cal_data)      : 4
len(top_months)    : 3
len(first_month)   : 5
first_month:
[[(1, 6), (2, 0), (3, 1), (4, 2), (5, 3), (6, 4), (7, 5)],
 [(8, 6), (9, 0), (10, 1), (11, 2), (12, 3), (13, 4), (14, 5)],
 [(15, 6), (16, 0), (17, 1), (18, 2), (19, 3), (20, 4), (21,
5)],
 [(22, 6), (23, 0), (24, 1), (25, 2), (26, 3), (27, 4), (28,
5)],
 [(29, 6), (30, 0), (31, 1), (0, 2), (0, 3), (0, 4), (0, 5)]]
```

This is equivalent to the data used by `formatyear()`.

Listing 4.30: `calendar_formatyear.py`

```
import calendar

cal = calendar.TextCalendar(calendar.SUNDAY)
print(cal.formatyear(2017, 2, 1, 1, 3))
```

When given the same arguments, `formatyear()` produces the following output.

```
$ python3 calendar_formatyear.py
                              2017

          January                February                March
   Su Mo Tu We Th Fr Sa   Su Mo Tu We Th Fr Sa   Su Mo Tu We Th Fr Sa
    1  2  3  4  5  6  7             1  2  3  4             1  2  3  4
    8  9 10 11 12 13 14    5  6  7  8  9 10 11    5  6  7  8  9 10 11
   15 16 17 18 19 20 21   12 13 14 15 16 17 18   12 13 14 15 16 17 18
   22 23 24 25 26 27 28   19 20 21 22 23 24 25   19 20 21 22 23 24 25
   29 30 31               26 27 28               26 27 28 29 30 31

           April                    May                   June
   Su Mo Tu We Th Fr Sa   Su Mo Tu We Th Fr Sa   Su Mo Tu We Th Fr Sa
                      1       1  2  3  4  5  6                1  2  3
    2  3  4  5  6  7  8    7  8  9 10 11 12 13    4  5  6  7  8  9 10
    9 10 11 12 13 14 15   14 15 16 17 18 19 20   11 12 13 14 15 16 17
   16 17 18 19 20 21 22   21 22 23 24 25 26 27   18 19 20 21 22 23 24
   23 24 25 26 27 28 29   28 29 30 31            25 26 27 28 29 30
   30

            July                  August               September
   Su Mo Tu We Th Fr Sa   Su Mo Tu We Th Fr Sa   Su Mo Tu We Th Fr Sa
                      1          1  2  3  4  5                   1  2
    2  3  4  5  6  7  8    6  7  8  9 10 11 12    3  4  5  6  7  8  9
    9 10 11 12 13 14 15   13 14 15 16 17 18 19   10 11 12 13 14 15 16
   16 17 18 19 20 21 22   20 21 22 23 24 25 26   17 18 19 20 21 22 23
   23 24 25 26 27 28 29   27 28 29 30 31         24 25 26 27 28 29 30
   30 31

          October               November               December
   Su Mo Tu We Th Fr Sa   Su Mo Tu We Th Fr Sa   Su Mo Tu We Th Fr Sa
    1  2  3  4  5  6  7             1  2  3  4                   1  2
    8  9 10 11 12 13 14    5  6  7  8  9 10 11    3  4  5  6  7  8  9
   15 16 17 18 19 20 21   12 13 14 15 16 17 18   10 11 12 13 14 15 16
   22 23 24 25 26 27 28   19 20 21 22 23 24 25   17 18 19 20 21 22 23
   29 30 31               26 27 28 29 30         24 25 26 27 28 29 30
                                                 31
```

The day_name, day_abbr, month_name, and month_abbr module attributes are useful for producing custom-formatted output (e.g., including links in the HTML output). They are automatically configured correctly for the current locale.

4.3.2   Locales

To produce a calendar formatted for a locale other than the current default, use Locale-TextCalendar or LocaleHTMLCalendar.

Listing 4.31: calendar_locale.py

```
import calendar

c = calendar.LocaleTextCalendar(locale='en_US')
c.prmonth(2017, 7)

print()

c = calendar.LocaleTextCalendar(locale='fr_FR')
c.prmonth(2017, 7)
```

The first day of the week is not part of the locale settings. Instead, its value is taken from the argument to the calendar class, just as occurs with the regular TextCalendar class.

```
$ python3 calendar_locale.py

      July 2017
Mo Tu We Th Fr Sa Su
                1  2
 3  4  5  6  7  8  9
10 11 12 13 14 15 16
17 18 19 20 21 22 23
24 25 26 27 28 29 30
31

     juillet 2017
Lu Ma Me Je Ve Sa Di
                1  2
 3  4  5  6  7  8  9
10 11 12 13 14 15 16
17 18 19 20 21 22 23
24 25 26 27 28 29 30
31
```

4.3.3   Calculating Dates

Although the calendar module focuses mostly on printing full calendars in various formats, it also provides functions useful for working with dates in other ways, such as calculating dates for a recurring event. For example, the Python Atlanta User's Group meets on the second Thursday of every month. To calculate the dates for the meetings for a year, use the return value of monthcalendar().

Listing 4.32: **calendar_monthcalendar.py**

```
import calendar
import pprint

pprint.pprint(calendar.monthcalendar(2017, 7))
```

Some days have a 0 value. Those days of the week overlap with the given month, but are part of another month.

```
$ python3 calendar_monthcalendar.py

[[0, 0, 0, 0, 0, 1, 2],
 [3, 4, 5, 6, 7, 8, 9],
 [10, 11, 12, 13, 14, 15, 16],
 [17, 18, 19, 20, 21, 22, 23],
 [24, 25, 26, 27, 28, 29, 30],
 [31, 0, 0, 0, 0, 0, 0]]
```

The first day of the week defaults to Monday. It is possible to change that value by calling setfirstweekday(). An even more convenient approach in this case is to skip that step, since the calendar module includes constants for indexing into the date ranges returned by monthcalendar().

To calculate the group meeting dates for a year, assuming they are always on the second Thursday of every month, look at the output of monthcalendar() to find the dates on which Thursdays fall. The first and last weeks of the month are padded with 0 values as placeholders for the days falling in the preceding and subsequent months, respectively. For example, if a month starts on a Friday, the value in the first week in the Thursday position will be 0.

Listing 4.33: **calendar_secondthursday.py**

```
import calendar
import sys

year = int(sys.argv[1])

# Show every month.
for month in range(1, 13):

    # Compute the dates for each week that overlaps the month.
    c = calendar.monthcalendar(year, month)
    first_week = c[0]
    second_week = c[1]
```

```
third_week = c[2]

# If there is a Thursday in the first week,
# the second Thursday is in the second week.
# Otherwise, the second Thursday must be in
# the third week.
if first_week[calendar.THURSDAY]:
    meeting_date = second_week[calendar.THURSDAY]
else:
    meeting_date = third_week[calendar.THURSDAY]

print('{:>3}: {:>2}'.format(calendar.month_abbr[month],
                            meeting_date))
```

Thus, the meeting schedule for the year is as follows:

```
$ python3 calendar_secondthursday.py 2017

Jan: 12
Feb:  9
Mar:  9
Apr: 13
May: 11
Jun:  8
Jul: 13
Aug: 10
Sep: 14
Oct: 12
Nov:  9
Dec: 14
```

TIP

Related Reading

- Standard library documentation for calendar.[9]
- time (page 211): Lower-level time functions.
- datetime (page 221): Manipulate date values, including timestamps and time zones.
- locale (page 1012): Locale settings.

---

[9] https://docs.python.org/3.5/library/calendar.html

Chapter 5

Mathematics

As a general-purpose programming language, Python is frequently used to solve mathematical problems. It includes built-in types for managing integer and floating-point numbers, which are suitable for the basic math that might appear in an average application. The standard library includes modules for more advanced needs.

Python's built-in floating-point numbers use the underlying `double` representation. They are sufficiently precise for most programs with mathematical requirements, but when more accurate representations of non-integer values are needed, the `decimal` (page 239) and `fractions` (page 250) modules will be useful. Arithmetic with decimal and fractional values retains precision, but is not as fast as the native `float`.

The `random` (page 254) module includes a uniform distribution pseudorandom number generator, as well as functions for simulating many common non-uniform distributions.

The `math` (page 264) module contains fast implementations of advanced mathematical functions such as logarithms and trigonometric functions. The full complement of IEEE functions usually found in the native-platform C libraries is available through the module.

5.1 decimal: Fixed- and Floating-Point Math

The `decimal` module implements fixed- and floating-point arithmetic using the model familiar to most people, rather than the IEEE floating-point version implemented by most computer hardware and familiar to programmers. A `Decimal` instance can represent any number exactly, be rounded up or down, and apply a limit to the number of significant digits.

5.1.1 Decimal

Decimal values are represented as instances of the `Decimal` class. As its argument, the constructor takes one integer or string. Floating-point numbers can be converted to a string before being used to create a `Decimal`, thereby letting the caller explicitly deal with the number of digits for values that cannot be expressed exactly using hardware floating-point representations. Alternatively, the class method `from_float()` converts a floating-point number to its exact decimal representation.

Listing 5.1: `decimal_create.py`

```
import decimal

fmt = '{0:<25} {1:<25}'
```

```
print(fmt.format('Input', 'Output'))
print(fmt.format('-' * 25, '-' * 25))

# Integer
print(fmt.format(5, decimal.Decimal(5)))

# String
print(fmt.format('3.14', decimal.Decimal('3.14')))

# Float
f = 0.1
print(fmt.format(repr(f), decimal.Decimal(str(f))))
print('{:<0.23g} {:<25}'.format(
    f,
    str(decimal.Decimal.from_float(f))[:25])
)
```

The floating-point value of `0.1` is not represented as an exact value in binary, so its representation as a `float` is different from the `Decimal` value. The full string representation is truncated to 25 characters in the last line of this output.

```
$ python3 decimal_create.py

Input                       Output
------------------------    ------------------------
5                           5
3.14                        3.14
0.1                         0.1
0.1000000000000000055112    0.1000000000000000055111
```

`Decimals` can also be created from tuples containing a sign flag (`0` for positive, `1` for negative), a `tuple` of digits, and an integer exponent.

Listing 5.2: decimal_tuple.py

```
import decimal

# Tuple
t = (1, (1, 1), -2)
print('Input  :', t)
print('Decimal:', decimal.Decimal(t))
```

The tuple-based representation is less convenient to create, but offers a portable way of exporting decimal values without losing precision. The tuple form can be transmitted through the network or stored in a database that does not support accurate decimal values, then turned back into a `Decimal` instance later.

```
$ python3 decimal_tuple.py

Input  : (1, (1, 1), -2)
Decimal: -0.11
```

5.1.2 Formatting

Decimal responds to Python's string formatting protocol[1] by using the same syntax and options as other numerical types.

Listing 5.3: **decimal_format.py**

```
import decimal

d = decimal.Decimal(1.1)
print('Precision:')
print('{:.1}'.format(d))
print('{:.2}'.format(d))
print('{:.3}'.format(d))
print('{:.18}'.format(d))

print('\nWidth and precision combined:')
print('{:5.1f} {:5.1g}'.format(d, d))
print('{:5.2f} {:5.2g}'.format(d, d))
print('{:5.2f} {:5.2g}'.format(d, d))

print('\nZero padding:')
print('{:05.1}'.format(d))
print('{:05.2}'.format(d))
print('{:05.3}'.format(d))
```

The format strings can control the width of the output, the precision (i.e., the number of significant digits), and the means of padding the value to fill the width.

```
$ python3 decimal_format.py

Precision:
1
1.1
1.10
1.10000000000000009

Width and precision combined:
  1.1     1
 1.10   1.1
 1.10   1.1
```

---

[1] https://docs.python.org/3.5/library/string.html#formatspec

```
Zero padding:
00001
001.1
01.10
```

5.1.3   Arithmetic

`Decimal` overloads the simple arithmetic operators so instances can be manipulated in much the same way as the built-in numeric types.

Listing 5.4: `decimal_operators.py`

```python
import decimal

a = decimal.Decimal('5.1')
b = decimal.Decimal('3.14')
c = 4
d = 3.14

print('a      =', repr(a))
print('b      =', repr(b))
print('c      =', repr(c))
print('d      =', repr(d))
print()

print('a + b =', a + b)
print('a - b =', a - b)
print('a * b =', a * b)
print('a / b =', a / b)
print()

print('a + c =', a + c)
print('a - c =', a - c)
print('a * c =', a * c)
print('a / c =', a / c)
print()

print('a + d =', end=' ')
try:
    print(a + d)
except TypeError as e:
    print(e)
```

`Decimal` operators also accept integer arguments. In contrast, floating-point values must be converted to `Decimal` instances before they can be used by these operators.

```
$ python3 decimal_operators.py

a      = Decimal('5.1')
b      = Decimal('3.14')
```

```
c       = 4
d       = 3.14

a + b = 8.24
a - b = 1.96
a * b = 16.014
a / b = 1.6242038216560650955414012739

a + c = 9.1
a - c = 1.1
a * c = 20.4
a / c = 1.275

a + d = unsupported operand type(s) for +: 'decimal.Decimal' and
'float'
```

Beyond basic arithmetic, `Decimal` includes methods to find base 10 logarithms and natural logarithms. The return values from `log10()` and `ln()` are `Decimal` instances, so they can be used directly in formulas with other values.

5.1.4 Special Values

In addition to the expected numerical values, `Decimal` can represent several special values, including positive and negative values for infinity, "not a number" (`NaN`), and zero.

Listing 5.5: decimal_special.py

```python
import decimal

for value in ['Infinity', 'NaN', '0']:
    print(decimal.Decimal(value), decimal.Decimal('-' + value))
print()

# Math with infinity
print('Infinity + 1:', (decimal.Decimal('Infinity') + 1))
print('-Infinity + 1:', (decimal.Decimal('-Infinity') + 1))

# Print comparing NaN
print(decimal.Decimal('NaN') == decimal.Decimal('Infinity'))
print(decimal.Decimal('NaN') != decimal.Decimal(1))
```

Adding to infinite values returns another infinite value. Comparing for equality with `NaN` always returns false, whereas comparing for inequality with this value always returns true. Comparing for sort order against `NaN` is undefined and results in an error.

```
$ python3 decimal_special.py

Infinity -Infinity
NaN -NaN
0 -0
```

```
Infinity + 1: Infinity
-Infinity + 1: -Infinity
False
True
```

5.1.5 Context

So far, all of the examples have used the default behaviors of the `decimal` module. It is possible to override settings such as the precision maintained, the way in which rounding is performed, and error handling by using a *context*. Contexts can be applied for all `Decimal` instances in a thread or locally within a small code region.

5.1.5.1 Current Context

To retrieve the current global context, use `getcontext`.

Listing 5.6: **decimal_getcontext.py**

```python
import decimal

context = decimal.getcontext()

print('Emax     =', context.Emax)
print('Emin     =', context.Emin)
print('capitals =', context.capitals)
print('prec     =', context.prec)
print('rounding =', context.rounding)
print('flags    =')
for f, v in context.flags.items():
    print('  {}: {}'.format(f, v))
print('traps    =')
for t, v in context.traps.items():
    print('  {}: {}'.format(t, v))
```

The example script shows the public properties of a `Context`.

```
$ python3 decimal_getcontext.py

Emax     = 999999
Emin     = -999999
capitals = 1
prec     = 28
rounding = ROUND_HALF_EVEN
flags    =
  <class 'decimal.InvalidOperation'>: False
  <class 'decimal.FloatOperation'>: False
  <class 'decimal.DivisionByZero'>: False
  <class 'decimal.Overflow'>: False
```

```
        <class 'decimal.Underflow'>: False
        <class 'decimal.Subnormal'>: False
        <class 'decimal.Inexact'>: False
        <class 'decimal.Rounded'>: False
        <class 'decimal.Clamped'>: False
traps    =
        <class 'decimal.InvalidOperation'>: True
        <class 'decimal.FloatOperation'>: False
        <class 'decimal.DivisionByZero'>: True
        <class 'decimal.Overflow'>: True
        <class 'decimal.Underflow'>: False
        <class 'decimal.Subnormal'>: False
        <class 'decimal.Inexact'>: False
        <class 'decimal.Rounded'>: False
        <class 'decimal.Clamped'>: False
```

5.1.5.2 Precision

The prec attribute of the context controls the precision maintained for new values created as a result of arithmetic. Literal values are maintained as described.

Listing 5.7: `decimal_precision.py`

```python
import decimal

d = decimal.Decimal('0.123456')

for i in range(1, 5):
    decimal.getcontext().prec = i
    print(i, ':', d, d * 1)
```

To change the precision, assign a new value between 1 and decimal.MAX_PREC directly to the attribute.

```
$ python3 decimal_precision.py

1 : 0.123456 0.1
2 : 0.123456 0.12
3 : 0.123456 0.123
4 : 0.123456 0.1235
```

5.1.5.3 Rounding

There are several options for rounding to keep values within the desired precision.

ROUND_CEILING Always round upward toward infinity.

ROUND_DOWN Always round toward zero.

ROUND_FLOOR Always round down toward negative infinity.

ROUND_HALF_DOWN Round away from zero if the last significant digit is greater than or equal to 5; otherwise, round toward zero.

ROUND_HALF_EVEN Like ROUND_HALF_DOWN except that if the value is 5, then the preceding digit is examined. Even digits cause the result to be rounded down, and odd digits cause the result to be rounded up.

ROUND_HALF_UP Like ROUND_HALF_DOWN except that if the last significant digit is 5, the value is rounded away from zero.

ROUND_UP Round away from zero.

ROUND_05UP Round away from zero if the last digit is 0 or 5; otherwise, round toward zero.

Listing 5.8: `decimal_rounding.py`

```
import decimal

context = decimal.getcontext()

ROUNDING_MODES = [
    'ROUND_CEILING',
    'ROUND_DOWN',
    'ROUND_FLOOR',
    'ROUND_HALF_DOWN',
    'ROUND_HALF_EVEN',
    'ROUND_HALF_UP',
    'ROUND_UP',
    'ROUND_05UP',
]

header_fmt = '{:10} ' + ' '.join(['{:^8}'] * 6)

print(header_fmt.format(
    ' ',
    '1/8 (1)', '-1/8 (1)',
    '1/8 (2)', '-1/8 (2)',
    '1/8 (3)', '-1/8 (3)',
))
for rounding_mode in ROUNDING_MODES:
    print('{0:10}'.format(rounding_mode.partition('_')[-1]),
          end=' ')
    for precision in [1, 2, 3]:
        context.prec = precision
        context.rounding = getattr(decimal, rounding_mode)
        value = decimal.Decimal(1) / decimal.Decimal(8)
        print('{0:^8}'.format(value), end=' ')
```

```
        value = decimal.Decimal(-1) / decimal.Decimal(8)
        print('{0:^8}'.format(value), end=' ')
    print()
```

This program shows the effect of rounding the same value to different levels of precision using the different algorithms.

```
$ python3 decimal_rounding.py
```

	1/8 (1)	-1/8 (1)	1/8 (2)	-1/8 (2)	1/8 (3)	-1/8 (3)
CEILING	0.2	-0.1	0.13	-0.12	0.125	-0.125
DOWN	0.1	-0.1	0.12	-0.12	0.125	-0.125
FLOOR	0.1	-0.2	0.12	-0.13	0.125	-0.125
HALF_DOWN	0.1	-0.1	0.12	-0.12	0.125	-0.125
HALF_EVEN	0.1	-0.1	0.12	-0.12	0.125	-0.125
HALF_UP	0.1	-0.1	0.13	-0.13	0.125	-0.125
UP	0.2	-0.2	0.13	-0.13	0.125	-0.125
05UP	0.1	-0.1	0.12	-0.12	0.125	-0.125

5.1.5.4 Local Context

The context can be applied to a block of code using the with statement.

Listing 5.9: **decimal_context_manager.py**

```
import decimal

with decimal.localcontext() as c:
    c.prec = 2
    print('Local precision:', c.prec)
    print('3.14 / 3 =', (decimal.Decimal('3.14') / 3))

print()
print('Default precision:', decimal.getcontext().prec)
print('3.14 / 3 =', (decimal.Decimal('3.14') / 3))
```

The Context supports the context manager API used by with, so the settings apply only within the block.

```
$ python3 decimal_context_manager.py

Local precision: 2
```

```
3.14 / 3 = 1.0

Default precision: 28
3.14 / 3 = 1.04666666666666666666666667
```

5.1.5.5   Per-Instance Context

Contexts also can be used to construct `Decimal` instances, which then inherit the precision and rounding arguments of the conversion from the context.

Listing 5.10: **decimal_instance_context.py**

```python
import decimal

# Set up a context with limited precision.
c = decimal.getcontext().copy()
c.prec = 3

# Create our constant.
pi = c.create_decimal('3.1415')

# The constant value is rounded off.
print('PI     :', pi)

# The result of using the constant uses the global context.
print('RESULT:', decimal.Decimal('2.01') * pi)
```

This approach lets an application select the precision of constant values separately from the precision of user data, for example.

```
$ python3 decimal_instance_context.py

PI     : 3.14
RESULT: 6.3114
```

5.1.5.6   Threads

The "global" context is actually thread-local, so each thread can potentially be configured using different values.

Listing 5.11: **decimal_thread_context.py**

```python
import decimal
import threading
from queue import PriorityQueue


class Multiplier(threading.Thread):
    def __init__(self, a, b, prec, q):
```

```
            self.a = a
            self.b = b
            self.prec = prec
            self.q = q
            threading.Thread.__init__(self)

    def run(self):
        c = decimal.getcontext().copy()
        c.prec = self.prec
        decimal.setcontext(c)
        self.q.put((self.prec, a * b))


a = decimal.Decimal('3.14')
b = decimal.Decimal('1.234')
# A PriorityQueue will return values sorted by precision,
# no matter in which order the threads finish.
q = PriorityQueue()
threads = [Multiplier(a, b, i, q) for i in range(1, 6)]
for t in threads:
    t.start()

for t in threads:
    t.join()

for i in range(5):
    prec, value = q.get()
    print('{}  {}'.format(prec, value))
```

This example creates a new context using the specified values, then installs it within each
thread.

```
$ python3 decimal_thread_context.py

1  4
2  3.9
3  3.87
4  3.875
5  3.8748
```

TIP

Related Reading

- Standard library documentation for decimal.[2]
- Python 2 to 3 porting notes for decimal (page 1358).

---

[2] https://docs.python.org/3.5/library/decimal.html

- Wikipedia: Floating Point[3]: Article on floating-point representations and arithmetic.
- Floating Point Arithmetic: Issues and Limitations[4]: Article from the Python tutorial describing floating-point math representation issues.

5.2   fractions: Rational Numbers

The `Fraction` class implements numerical operations for rational numbers based on the API defined by `Rational` in the `numbers` module.

5.2.1   Creating Fraction Instances

As with the `decimal` (page 239) module, new values can be created in several ways. One easy way is to create them from separate numerator and denominator values.

Listing 5.12: **fractions_create_integers.py**

```
import fractions

for n, d in [(1, 2), (2, 4), (3, 6)]:
    f = fractions.Fraction(n, d)
    print('{}/{} = {}'.format(n, d, f))
```

The lowest common denominator is maintained as new values are computed.

```
$ python3 fractions_create_integers.py

1/2 = 1/2
2/4 = 1/2
3/6 = 1/2
```

Another way to create a `Fraction` is using a string representation of `<numerator>` / `<denominator>`.

Listing 5.13: **fractions_create_strings.py**

```
import fractions

for s in ['1/2', '2/4', '3/6']:
    f = fractions.Fraction(s)
    print('{} = {}'.format(s, f))
```

---

[3] https://en.wikipedia.org/wiki/Floating_point
[4] https://docs.python.org/tutorial/floatingpoint.html

The string is parsed to find the numerator and denominator values.

```
$ python3 fractions_create_strings.py

1/2 = 1/2
2/4 = 1/2
3/6 = 1/2
```

Strings can also use the more usual decimal or floating-point notation of series of digits separated by a period. Any string that can be parsed by `float()` and that does not represent NaN or an infinite value is supported.

Listing 5.14: **fractions_create_strings_floats.py**

```
import fractions

for s in ['0.5', '1.5', '2.0', '5e-1']:
    f = fractions.Fraction(s)
    print('{0:>4} = {1}'.format(s, f))
```

The numerator and denominator values represented by the floating-point value are computed automatically.

```
$ python3 fractions_create_strings_floats.py

 0.5 = 1/2
 1.5 = 3/2
 2.0 = 2
5e-1 = 1/2
```

It is also possible to create `Fraction` instances directly from other representations of rational values, such as `float` or `Decimal`.

Listing 5.15: **fractions_from_float.py**

```
import fractions

for v in [0.1, 0.5, 1.5, 2.0]:
    print('{} = {}'.format(v, fractions.Fraction(v)))
```

Floating-point values that cannot be expressed exactly may yield unexpected results.

```
$ python3 fractions_from_float.py

0.1 = 3602879701896397/36028797018963968
0.5 = 1/2
1.5 = 3/2
2.0 = 2
```

Using `Decimal` representations of the values gives the expected results.

Listing 5.16: `fractions_from_decimal.py`

```
import decimal
import fractions

values = [
    decimal.Decimal('0.1'),
    decimal.Decimal('0.5'),
    decimal.Decimal('1.5'),
    decimal.Decimal('2.0'),
]

for v in values:
    print('{} = {}'.format(v, fractions.Fraction(v)))
```

The internal implementation of `Decimal` does not suffer from the precision errors of the standard floating-point representation.

```
$ python3 fractions_from_decimal.py

0.1 = 1/10
0.5 = 1/2
1.5 = 3/2
2.0 = 2
```

5.2.2   Arithmetic

Once the fractions are instantiated, they can be used in mathematical expressions.

Listing 5.17: `fractions_arithmetic.py`

```
import fractions

f1 = fractions.Fraction(1, 2)
f2 = fractions.Fraction(3, 4)

print('{} + {} = {}'.format(f1, f2, f1 + f2))
print('{} - {} = {}'.format(f1, f2, f1 - f2))
print('{} * {} = {}'.format(f1, f2, f1 * f2))
print('{} / {} = {}'.format(f1, f2, f1 / f2))
```

All of the standard operators are supported.

```
$ python3 fractions_arithmetic.py

1/2 + 3/4 = 5/4
1/2 - 3/4 = -1/4
```

```
1/2 * 3/4 = 3/8
1/2 / 3/4 = 2/3
```

5.2.3 Approximating Values

A useful feature of Fraction is the ability to convert a floating-point number to an approximate rational value.

Listing 5.18: fractions_limit_denominator.py

```python
import fractions
import math

print('PI       =', math.pi)

f_pi = fractions.Fraction(str(math.pi))
print('No limit =', f_pi)

for i in [1, 6, 11, 60, 70, 90, 100]:
    limited = f_pi.limit_denominator(i)
    print('{0:8} = {1}'.format(i, limited))
```

The value of the fraction can be controlled by limiting the size of the denominator.

```
$ python3 fractions_limit_denominator.py

PI       = 3.141592653589793
No limit = 3141592653589793/1000000000000000
       1 = 3
       6 = 19/6
      11 = 22/7
      60 = 179/57
      70 = 201/64
      90 = 267/85
     100 = 311/99
```

TIP

Related Reading

- Standard library documentation for fractions.[5]
- decimal (page 239): The decimal module provides an API for fixed- and floating-point math.
- numbers: Numeric abstract base classes.
- Python 2 to 3 porting notes for fractions (page 1358).

---

[5] https://docs.python.org/3.5/library/fractions.html

5.3   random: Pseudorandom Number Generators

The random module provides a fast pseudorandom number generator based on the *Mersenne Twister* algorithm. Originally developed to produce inputs for Monte Carlo simulations, Mersenne Twister generates numbers with nearly uniform distribution and a large period, making it suited to a wide range of applications.

5.3.1   Generating Random Numbers

The random() function returns the next random floating-point value from the generated sequence. All of the return values fall within the range 0 <= n < 1.0.

Listing 5.19: **random_random.py**

```python
import random

for i in range(5):
    print('%04.3f' % random.random(), end=' ')
print()
```

Running the program repeatedly produces different sequences of numbers.

```
$ python3 random_random.py

0.859 0.297 0.554 0.985 0.452

$ python3 random_random.py

0.797 0.658 0.170 0.297 0.593
```

To generate numbers in a specific numerical range, use uniform() instead.

Listing 5.20: **random_uniform.py**

```python
import random

for i in range(5):
    print('{:04.3f}'.format(random.uniform(1, 100)), end=' ')
print()
```

Pass minimum and maximum values, and uniform() adjusts the return values from random() using the formula min + (max -min) * random().

```
$ python3 random_uniform.py

12.428 93.766 95.359 39.649 88.983
```

5.3.2 Seeding

random() produces different values each time it is called and has a very large period before it repeats any numbers. This is useful for producing unique values or variations, but sometimes having the same data set available to be processed in different ways is useful. One technique is to use a program to generate random values and save them to be processed by a separate step. That may not be practical for large amounts of data, though, so random includes the seed() function for initializing the pseudorandom generator so that it produces an expected set of values.

Listing 5.21: random_seed.py

```
import random

random.seed(1)

for i in range(5):
    print('{:04.3f}'.format(random.random()), end=' ')
print()
```

The seed value controls the first value produced by the formula, which is used to generate pseudorandom numbers. Since the formula is deterministic, it also sets the full sequence produced after the seed is changed. The argument to seed() can be any hashable object. The default is to use a platform-specific source of randomness, if one is available. Otherwise, the current time is used.

```
$ python3 random_seed.py

0.134 0.847 0.764 0.255 0.495

$ python3 random_seed.py

0.134 0.847 0.764 0.255 0.495
```

5.3.3 Saving State

The internal state of the pseudorandom algorithm used by random() can be saved and used to control the numbers produced in subsequent runs. Restoring the previous state before continuing reduces the likelihood of repeating values or sequences of values from the earlier input. The getstate() function returns data that can be used to reinitialize the random number generator later with setstate().

Listing 5.22: random_state.py

```
import random
import os
import pickle
```

```
if os.path.exists('state.dat'):
    # Restore the previously saved state.
    print('Found state.dat, initializing random module')
    with open('state.dat', 'rb') as f:
        state = pickle.load(f)
    random.setstate(state)
else:
    # Use a well-known start state.
    print('No state.dat, seeding')
    random.seed(1)

# Produce random values.
for i in range(3):
    print('{:04.3f}'.format(random.random()), end=' ')
print()

# Save state for next time.
with open('state.dat', 'wb') as f:
    pickle.dump(random.getstate(), f)

# Produce more random values.
print('\nAfter saving state:')
for i in range(3):
    print('{:04.3f}'.format(random.random()), end=' ')
print()
```

The data returned by `getstate()` is an implementation detail, so this example saves the data to a file with `pickle` (page 396); otherwise, it treats the pseudorandom number generator as a black box. If the file exists when the program starts, it loads the old state and continues. Each run produces a few numbers before and after saving the state, to show that restoring the state causes the generator to produce the same values again.

```
$ python3 random_state.py

No state.dat, seeding
0.134 0.847 0.764

After saving state:
0.255 0.495 0.449

$ python3 random_state.py

Found state.dat, initializing random module
0.255 0.495 0.449

After saving state:
0.652 0.789 0.094
```

5.3.4 Random Integers

random() generates floating-point numbers. It is possible to convert the results to integers, but using randint() to generate integers directly is more convenient.

Listing 5.23: **random_randint.py**

```python
import random

print('[1, 100]:', end=' ')

for i in range(3):
    print(random.randint(1, 100), end=' ')

print('\n[-5, 5]:', end=' ')
for i in range(3):
    print(random.randint(-5, 5), end=' ')
print()
```

The arguments to randint() are the ends of the inclusive range for the values. The numbers can be positive or negative, but the first value should be less than the second.

```
$ python3 random_randint.py

[1, 100]: 98 75 34
[-5, 5]: 4 0 5
```

randrange() is a more general form of selecting values from a range.

Listing 5.24: **random_randrange.py**

```python
import random

for i in range(3):
    print(random.randrange(0, 101, 5), end=' ')
print()
```

randrange() supports a step argument, in addition to start and stop values, so it is fully equivalent to selecting a random value from range(start,stop,step). It is more efficient, because the range is not actually constructed.

```
$ python3 random_randrange.py

15 20 85
```

5.3.5   Picking Random Items

One common use for random number generators is to select a random item from a sequence of enumerated values, even if those values are not numbers. random includes the `choice()` function for making a random selection from a sequence. This example simulates flipping a coin 10,000 times to count how many times it comes up heads and how many times it comes up tails.

Listing 5.25: `random_choice.py`

```python
import random
import itertools

outcomes = {
    'heads': 0,
    'tails': 0,
}
sides = list(outcomes.keys())

for i in range(10000):
    outcomes[random.choice(sides)] += 1

print('Heads:', outcomes['heads'])
print('Tails:', outcomes['tails'])
```

Only two outcomes are allowed. Thus, rather than use numbers and convert them, the words "heads" and "tails" are used with `choice()`. The results are tabulated in a dictionary using the outcome names as keys.

```
$ python3 random_choice.py

Heads: 5091
Tails: 4909
```

5.3.6   Permutations

A simulation of a card game needs to mix up the deck of cards and then deal the cards to the players, without using the same card more than once. Using `choice()` could result in the same card being dealt twice. Instead, the deck can be mixed up with `shuffle()` and then individual cards removed as they are dealt.

Listing 5.26: `random_shuffle.py`

```python
import random
import itertools

FACE_CARDS = ('J', 'Q', 'K', 'A')
SUITS = ('H', 'D', 'C', 'S')
```

```
def new_deck():
    return [
        # Always use 2 places for the value, so the strings
        # are a consistent width.
        '{:>2}{}'.format(*c)
        for c in itertools.product(
            itertools.chain(range(2, 11), FACE_CARDS),
            SUITS,
        )
    ]


def show_deck(deck):
    p_deck = deck[:]
    while p_deck:
        row = p_deck[:13]
        p_deck = p_deck[13:]
        for j in row:
            print(j, end=' ')
        print()

# Make a new deck, with the cards in order.
deck = new_deck()
print('Initial deck:')
show_deck(deck)

# Shuffle the deck to randomize the order.
random.shuffle(deck)
print('\nShuffled deck:')
show_deck(deck)

# Deal 4 hands of 5 cards each.
hands = [[], [], [], []]

for i in range(5):
    for h in hands:
        h.append(deck.pop())

# Show the hands.
print('\nHands:')
for n, h in enumerate(hands):
    print('{}:'.format(n + 1), end=' ')
    for c in h:
        print(c, end=' ')
    print()

# Show the remaining deck.
print('\nRemaining deck:')
show_deck(deck)
```

The cards are represented as strings with the face value and a letter indicating the suit. The dealt "hands" are created by adding one card at a time to each of four lists, and removing that card from the deck so it cannot be dealt again.

```
$ python3 random_shuffle.py

Initial deck:
2H   2D   2C   2S   3H   3D   3C   3S   4H   4D   4C   4S   5H
5D   5C   5S   6H   6D   6C   6S   7H   7D   7C   7S   8H   8D
8C   8S   9H   9D   9C   9S  10H  10D  10C  10S   JH   JD   JC
JS   QH   QD   QC   QS   KH   KD   KC   KS   AH   AD   AC   AS

Shuffled deck:
QD   8C   JD   2S   AC   2C   6S   6D   6C   7H   JC   QS   QC
KS   4D  10C   KH   5S   9C  10S   5C   7C   AS   6H   3C   9H
4S   7S  10H   2D   8S   AH   9S   8H   QH   5D   5H   KD   8D
10D  4C   3S   3H   7D   AD   4H   9D   3D   2H   KC   JH   JS

Hands:
1:   JS   3D   7D  10D   5D
2:   JH   9D   3H   8D   QH
3:   KC   4H   3S   KD   8H
4:   2H   AD   4C   5H   9S

Remaining deck:
QD   8C   JD   2S   AC   2C   6S   6D   6C   7H   JC   QS   QC
KS   4D  10C   KH   5S   9C  10S   5C   7C   AS   6H   3C   9H
4S   7S  10H   2D   8S   AH
```

5.3.7 Sampling

Many simulations need random samples from a population of input values. The sample() function generates samples without repeating values and without modifying the input sequence. This example prints a random sample of words from the system dictionary.

Listing 5.27: random_sample.py

```
import random

with open('/usr/share/dict/words', 'rt') as f:
    words = f.readlines()
words = [w.rstrip() for w in words]

for w in random.sample(words, 5):
    print(w)
```

The algorithm for producing the result set takes into account the sizes of the input and the sample requested to produce the result as efficiently as possible.

```
$ python3 random_sample.py

streamlet
impestation
violaquercitrin
mycetoid
plethoretical

$ python3 random_sample.py

nonseditious
empyemic
ultrasonic
Kyurinish
amphide
```

5.3.8 Multiple Simultaneous Generators

In addition to module-level functions, random includes a Random class to manage the internal state for several random number generators. All of the functions described earlier are available as methods of the Random instances, and each instance can be initialized and used separately, without interfering with the values returned by other instances.

Listing 5.28: **random_random_class.py**

```python
import random
import time

print('Default initializiation:\n')

r1 = random.Random()
r2 = random.Random()

for i in range(3):
    print('{:04.3f}  {:04.3f}'.format(r1.random(), r2.random()))

print('\nSame seed:\n')

seed = time.time()
r1 = random.Random(seed)
r2 = random.Random(seed)

for i in range(3):
    print('{:04.3f}  {:04.3f}'.format(r1.random(), r2.random()))
```

On a system with good native random value seeding, the instances start out in unique states. However, if a good platform random value generator is lacking, the instances are likely to have been seeded with the current time and, in turn, will produce the same values.

```
$ python3 random_random_class.py

Default initializiation:

0.862   0.390
0.833   0.624
0.252   0.080

Same seed:

0.466   0.466
0.682   0.682
0.407   0.407
```

5.3.9 SystemRandom

Some operating systems provide a random number generator that has access to more sources of entropy that can be introduced into the generator. random exposes this feature through the SystemRandom class. It has the same API as Random but uses os.urandom() to generate the values that form the basis of all the other algorithms.

Listing 5.29: random_system_random.py

```
import random
import time

print('Default initializiation:\n')

r1 = random.SystemRandom()
r2 = random.SystemRandom()

for i in range(3):
    print('{:04.3f}   {:04.3f}'.format(r1.random(), r2.random()))

print('\nSame seed:\n')

seed = time.time()
r1 = random.SystemRandom(seed)
r2 = random.SystemRandom(seed)

for i in range(3):
    print('{:04.3f}   {:04.3f}'.format(r1.random(), r2.random()))
```

Sequences produced by SystemRandom are not reproducible because the randomness is coming from the system, rather than the software state. (In fact, seed() and setstate() have no effect at all.)

```
$ python3 random_system_random.py

Default initializiation:

0.110  0.481
0.624  0.350
0.378  0.056

Same seed:

0.634  0.731
0.893  0.843
0.065  0.177
```

5.3.10 Non-uniform Distributions

While the uniform distribution of the values produced by `random()` is useful for many purposes, other distributions more accurately model specific situations. The `random` module includes functions to produce values in those distributions, too. They are listed here, but not covered in detail because their uses tend to be specialized and require more complex examples.

5.3.10.1 Normal

The *normal* distribution is commonly used for non-uniform continuous values such as grades, heights, and weights. The curve produced by the distribution has a distinctive shape that has led to it being nicknamed a "bell curve." `random` includes two functions for generating values with a normal distribution: `normalvariate()` and the slightly faster `gauss()` (the normal distribution is also called the Gaussian distribution).

The related function, `lognormvariate()`, produces pseudorandom values where the logarithm of the values is distributed normally. Log-normal distributions are useful for values that are the product of several random variables that do not interact.

5.3.10.2 Approximation

The *triangular* distribution is used as an approximate distribution for small sample sizes. The "curve" of a triangular distribution has low points at known minimum and maximum values, and a high point at the mode, which is estimated based on a "most likely" outcome (reflected by the mode argument to `triangular()`).

5.3.10.3 Exponential

`expovariate()` produces an exponential distribution useful for simulating arrival or interval time values for homogeneous Poisson processes such as the rate of radioactive decay or requests coming into a web server.

The Pareto, or power law, distribution matches many observable phenomena and was popularized in *The Long Tail* by Chris Anderson. The `paretovariate()` function is useful for simulating allocation of resources to individuals (e.g., wealth to people, demand for musicians, attention to blogs).

5.3.10.4　Angular

The von Mises, or circular normal, distribution (produced by `vonmisesvariate()`) is used for computing probabilities of cyclic values such as angles, calendar days, and times.

5.3.10.5　Sizes

`betavariate()` generates values with the Beta distribution, which is commonly used in Bayesian statistics and applications such as task duration modeling.

The Gamma distribution produced by `gammavariate()` is used for modeling the sizes of things such as waiting times, rainfall amounts, and computational errors.

The Weibull distribution computed by `weibullvariate()` is used in failure analysis, industrial engineering, and weather forecasting. It describes the distribution of sizes of particles or other discrete objects.

TIP

Related Reading

- Standard library documentation for `random`.[6]
- Mersenne Twister: A 623-dimensionally equidistributed uniform pseudorandom number generator: Article by M. Matsumoto and T. Nishimura from *ACM Transactions on Modeling and Computer Simulation* Vol. 8, No. 1, January 1998, pp. 3–30.
- Wikipedia: Mersenne Twister[7]: Article about the pseudorandom generator algorithm used by Python.
- Wikipedia: Uniform distribution[8]: Article about continuous uniform distributions in statistics.

5.4　math: Mathematical Functions

The `math` module implements many of the specialized IEEE functions that would normally be found in the native-platform C libraries for complex mathematical operations using floating-point values, including logarithms and trigonometric operations.

---

[6] https://docs.python.org/3.5/library/random.html
[7] https://en.wikipedia.org/wiki/Mersenne_twister
[8] https://en.wikipedia.org/wiki/Uniform_distribution_(continuous)

5.4.1 Special Constants

Many math operations depend on special constants. math includes values for π (pi), e, nan (not a number), and infinity.

Listing 5.30: math_constants.py

```
import math

print(' π : {:.30f}'.format(math.pi))
print('  e: {:.30f}'.format(math.e))
print('nan: {:.30f}'.format(math.nan))
print('inf: {:.30f}'.format(math.inf))
```

Both π and e are limited in precision only by the platform's floating-point C library.

```
$ python3 math_constants.pyπ

  : 3.141592653589793115997963468544
  e: 2.718281828459045090795598298428
nan: nan
inf: inf
```

5.4.2 Testing for Exceptional Values

Floating-point calculations can result in two types of exceptional values. The first of these, inf (infinity), appears when the double used to hold a floating-point value overflows from a value with a large absolute value.

Listing 5.31: math_isinf.py

```
import math

print('{:^3} {:6} {:6} {:6}'.format(
    'e', 'x', 'x**2', 'isinf'))
print('{:-^3} {:-^6} {:-^6} {:-^6}'.format(
    '', '', '', ''))

for e in range(0, 201, 20):
    x = 10.0 ** e
    y = x * x
    print('{:3d} {:<6g} {:<6g} {!s:6}'.format(
        e, x, y, math.isinf(y),
    ))
```

When the exponent in this example grows large enough, the square of x no longer fits inside a double, and the value is recorded as infinite.

```
$ python3 math_isinf.py

  e   x        x**2     isinf
 --- ------   ------   ------
   0 1        1        False
  20 1e+20    1e+40    False
  40 1e+40    1e+80    False
  60 1e+60    1e+120   False
  80 1e+80    1e+160   False
 100 1e+100   1e+200   False
 120 1e+120   1e+240   False
 140 1e+140   1e+280   False
 160 1e+160   inf      True
 180 1e+180   inf      True
 200 1e+200   inf      True
```

Not all floating-point overflows result in `inf` values, however. Calculating an exponent with floating-point values, in particular, raises `OverflowError` instead of preserving the `inf` result.

Listing 5.32: **math_overflow.py**

```
x = 10.0 ** 200

print('x     =', x)
print('x*x   =', x * x)
print('x**2 =', end=' ')
try:
    print(x ** 2)
except OverflowError as err:
    print(err)
```

This discrepancy is caused by an implementation difference in the library used by C Python.

```
$ python3 math_overflow.py

x     = 1e+200
x*x   = inf
x**2 = (34, 'Result too large')
```

Division operations using infinite values are undefined. The result of dividing a number by infinity is `nan` (not a number).

Listing 5.33: **math_isnan.py**

```
import math

x = (10.0 ** 200) * (10.0 ** 200)
y = x / x
```

```
print('x =', x)
print('isnan(x) =', math.isnan(x))
print('y = x / x =', x / x)
print('y == nan =', y == float('nan'))
print('isnan(y) =', math.isnan(y))
```

nan does not compare as equal to any value, even itself. Thus, to check for nan, use `isnan()`.

```
$ python3 math_isnan.py

x = inf
isnan(x) = False
y = x / x = nan
y == nan = False
isnan(y) = True
```

Use `isfinite()` to check for regular numbers or either of the special values `inf` or `nan`.

Listing 5.34: math_isfinite.py

```
import math

for f in [0.0, 1.0, math.pi, math.e, math.inf, math.nan]:
    print('{:5.2f} {!s}'.format(f, math.isfinite(f)))
```

`isfinite()` returns false for either of the exceptional cases, and true otherwise.

```
$ python3 math_isfinite.py

 0.00 True
 1.00 True
 3.14 True
 2.72 True
  inf False
  nan False
```

5.4.3   Comparing

Comparisons involving floating-point values can be error prone, with each step of the computation potentially introducing errors due to the numerical representation. The `isclose()` function uses a stable algorithm to minimize these errors and perform both relative and absolute comparisons. The formula used is equivalent to

```
abs(a-b) <= max(rel_tol * max(abs(a), abs(b)), abs_tol)
```

By default, `isclose()` performs relative comparisons with the tolerance set to `1e-09`, meaning that the difference between the values must be less than or equal to `1e-09` times the larger absolute value between a and b. Passing the keyword argument `rel_tol` to `isclose()` changes the tolerance. In this example, the values must be within 10% of each other.

Listing 5.35: `math_isclose.py`

```
import math

INPUTS = [
    (1000, 900, 0.1),
    (100, 90, 0.1),
    (10, 9, 0.1),
    (1, 0.9, 0.1),
    (0.1, 0.09, 0.1),
]

print('{:^8} {:^8} {:^8} {:^8} {:^8} {:^8}'.format(
    'a', 'b', 'rel_tol', 'abs(a-b)', 'tolerance', 'close')
)
print('{:-^8} {:-^8} {:-^8} {:-^8} {:-^8} {:-^8}'.format(
    '-', '-', '-', '-', '-', '-'),
)

fmt = '{:8.2f} {:8.2f} {:8.2f} {:8.2f} {:8.2f} {!s:>8}'

for a, b, rel_tol in INPUTS:
    close = math.isclose(a, b, rel_tol=rel_tol)
    tolerance = rel_tol * max(abs(a), abs(b))
    abs_diff = abs(a - b)
    print(fmt.format(a, b, rel_tol, abs_diff, tolerance, close))
```

The comparison between `0.1` and `0.09` fails because of the error representing `0.1`.

```
$ python3 math_isclose.py

    a         b      rel_tol  abs(a-b) tolerance  close
 --------  --------  --------  --------  --------  --------
 1000.00   900.00     0.10    100.00    100.00     True
  100.00    90.00     0.10     10.00     10.00     True
   10.00     9.00     0.10      1.00      1.00     True
    1.00     0.90     0.10      0.10      0.10     True
    0.10     0.09     0.10      0.01      0.01     False
```

To use a fixed or "absolute" tolerance, pass `abs_tol` instead of `rel_tol`.

Listing 5.36: `math_isclose_abs_tol.py`

```
import math

INPUTS = [
```

```
        (1.0, 1.0 + 1e-07, 1e-08),
        (1.0, 1.0 + 1e-08, 1e-08),
        (1.0, 1.0 + 1e-09, 1e-08),
]

print('{:^8} {:^11} {:^8} {:^10} {:^8}'.format(
    'a', 'b', 'abs_tol', 'abs(a-b)', 'close')
)
print('{:-^8} {:-^11} {:-^8} {:-^10} {:-^8}'.format(
    '-', '-', '-', '-', '-'),
)

for a, b, abs_tol in INPUTS:
    close = math.isclose(a, b, abs_tol=abs_tol)
    abs_diff = abs(a - b)
    print('{:8.2f} {:11} {:8} {:0.9f} {!s:>8}'.format(
        a, b, abs_tol, abs_diff, close))
```

For an absolute tolerance, the difference between the input values must be less than the tolerance given.

```
$ python3 math_isclose_abs_tol.py

    a         b       abs_tol   abs(a-b)   close
--------  -----------  --------  ----------  --------
   1.00   1.0000001    1e-08  0.000000100   False
   1.00   1.00000001   1e-08  0.000000010   True
   1.00  1.000000001   1e-08  0.000000001   True
```

nan and inf are special cases.

Listing 5.37: math_isclose_inf.py

```
import math

print('nan, nan:', math.isclose(math.nan, math.nan))
print('nan, 1.0:', math.isclose(math.nan, 1.0))
print('inf, inf:', math.isclose(math.inf, math.inf))
print('inf, 1.0:', math.isclose(math.inf, 1.0))
```

nan is never close to another value, including itself. inf is close to only itself.

```
$ python3 math_isclose_inf.py

nan, nan: False
nan, 1.0: False
inf, inf: True
inf, 1.0: False
```

5.4.4   Converting Floating-Point Values to Integers

The math module includes three functions for converting floating-point values to whole
numbers. Each takes a different approach, and will be useful in different circumstances.

The simplest is trunc(), which truncates the digits following the decimal, leaving only
the significant digits making up the whole-number portion of the value. floor() converts
its input to the largest preceding integer, and ceil() (ceiling) produces the largest integer
following sequentially after the input value.

Listing 5.38: math_integers.py

```
import math

HEADINGS = ('i', 'int', 'trunk', 'floor', 'ceil')
print('{:^5} {:^5} {:^5} {:^5} {:^5}'.format(*HEADINGS))
print('{:-^5} {:-^5} {:-^5} {:-^5} {:-^5}'.format(
    '', '', '', '', '',
))

fmt = '{:5.1f} {:5.1f} {:5.1f} {:5.1f} {:5.1f}'

TEST_VALUES = [
    -1.5,
    -0.8,
    -0.5,
    -0.2,
    0,
    0.2,
    0.5,
    0.8,
    1,
]

for i in TEST_VALUES:
    print(fmt.format(
        i,
        int(i),
        math.trunc(i),
        math.floor(i),
        math.ceil(i),
    ))
```

trunc() is equivalent to converting to int directly.

```
$ python3 math_integers.py

  i    int  trunk floor ceil
----- ----- ----- ----- -----
-1.5  -1.0  -1.0  -2.0  -1.0
```

```
-0.8    0.0    0.0   -1.0    0.0
-0.5    0.0    0.0   -1.0    0.0
-0.2    0.0    0.0   -1.0    0.0
 0.0    0.0    0.0    0.0    0.0
 0.2    0.0    0.0    0.0    1.0
 0.5    0.0    0.0    0.0    1.0
 0.8    0.0    0.0    0.0    1.0
 1.0    1.0    1.0    1.0    1.0
```

5.4.5 Alternative Representations of Floating-Point Values

modf() takes a single floating-point number and returns a tuple containing the fractional and whole-number parts of the input value.

Listing 5.39: math_modf.py

```
import math

for i in range(6):
    print('{}/2 = {}'.format(i, math.modf(i / 2.0)))
```

Both numbers in the return value are floats.

```
$ python3 math_modf.py

0/2 = (0.0, 0.0)
1/2 = (0.5, 0.0)
2/2 = (0.0, 1.0)
3/2 = (0.5, 1.0)
4/2 = (0.0, 2.0)
5/2 = (0.5, 2.0)
```

frexp() returns the mantissa and exponent of a floating-point number. This function can be used to create a more portable representation of the value.

Listing 5.40: math_frexp.py

```
import math

print('{:^7} {:^7} {:^7}'.format('x', 'm', 'e'))
print('{:-^7} {:-^7} {:-^7}'.format('', '', ''))

for x in [0.1, 0.5, 4.0]:
    m, e = math.frexp(x)
    print('{:7.2f} {:7.2f} {:7d}'.format(x, m, e))
```

frexp() uses the formula $x = m * 2**e$, and returns the values m and e.

```
$ python3 math_frexp.py

   x        m        e
------- ------- -------
  0.10    0.80      -3
  0.50    0.50       0
  4.00    0.50       3
```

ldexp() is the inverse of frexp().

Listing 5.41: math_ldexp.py

```
import math

print('{:^7} {:^7} {:^7}'.format('m', 'e', 'x'))
print('{:-^7} {:-^7} {:-^7}'.format('', '', ''))

INPUTS = [
    (0.8, -3),
    (0.5, 0),
    (0.5, 3),
]

for m, e in INPUTS:
    x = math.ldexp(m, e)
    print('{:7.2f} {:7d} {:7.2f}'.format(m, e, x))
```

Using the same formula as frexp(), ldexp() takes the mantissa and exponent values as arguments and returns a floating-point number.

```
$ python3 math_ldexp.py

   m        e        x
------- ------- -------
  0.80      -3    0.10
  0.50       0    0.50
  0.50       3    4.00
```

5.4.6   Positive and Negative Signs

The absolute value of a number is its value without a sign. Use fabs() to calculate the absolute value of a floating-point number.

Listing 5.42: math_fabs.py

```
import math

print(math.fabs(-1.1))
print(math.fabs(-0.0))
```

```
print(math.fabs(0.0))
print(math.fabs(1.1))
```

In practical terms, the absolute value of a float is represented as a positive value.

```
$ python3 math_fabs.py

1.1
0.0
0.0
1.1
```

To determine the sign of a value, either to give a set of values the same sign or to compare two values, use copysign() to set the sign of a known good value.

Listing 5.43: math_copysign.py

```
import math

HEADINGS = ('f', 's', '< 0', '> 0', '= 0')
print('{:^5} {:^5} {:^5} {:^5} {:^5}'.format(*HEADINGS))
print('{:-^5} {:-^5} {:-^5} {:-^5} {:-^5}'.format(
    '', '', '', '', '',
))

VALUES = [
    -1.0,
    0.0,
    1.0,
    float('-inf'),
    float('inf'),
    float('-nan'),
    float('nan'),
]

for f in VALUES:
    s = int(math.copysign(1, f))
    print('{:5.1f} {:5d} {!s:5} {!s:5} {!s:5}'.format(
        f, s, f < 0, f > 0, f == 0,
    ))
```

An extra function like copysign() is needed because comparing nan and -nan directly with other values does not work.

```
$ python3 math_copysign.py

  f     s    < 0   > 0   = 0
----- ----- ----- ----- -----
 -1.0    -1 True  False False
```

```
0.0      1 False False True
1.0      1 False True  False
-inf    -1 True  False False
inf      1 False True  False
nan     -1 False False False
nan      1 False False False
```

5.4.7 Commonly Used Calculations

Representing precise values in binary floating-point memory is challenging. Some values cannot be represented exactly. In addition, the more often a value is manipulated through repeated calculations, the more likely it is that a representation error will be introduced. math includes a function for computing the sum of a series of floating-point numbers using an efficient algorithm that minimizes such errors.

Listing 5.44: math_fsum.py

```
import math

values = [0.1] * 10

print('Input values:', values)

print('sum()       : {:.20f}'.format(sum(values)))

s = 0.0
for i in values:
    s += i
print('for-loop    : {:.20f}'.format(s))

print('math.fsum() : {:.20f}'.format(math.fsum(values)))
```

Given a sequence of 10 values, each equal to 0.1, the expected value for the sum of the sequence is 1.0. Since 0.1 cannot be represented exactly as a floating-point value, however, errors are introduced into the sum unless it is calculated with fsum().

```
$ python3 math_fsum.py

Input values: [0.1, 0.1, 0.1, 0.1, 0.1, 0.1, 0.1, 0.1, 0.1, 0.1]
sum()       : 0.99999999999999988898
for-loop    : 0.99999999999999988898
math.fsum() : 1.00000000000000000000
```

factorial() is commonly used to calculate the number of permutations and combinations of a series of objects. The factorial of a positive integer n, expressed as n!, is defined recursively as (n-1)! * n and stops with 0! == 1.

Listing 5.45: math_factorial.py

```python
import math

for i in [0, 1.0, 2.0, 3.0, 4.0, 5.0, 6.1]:
    try:
        print('{:2.0f} {:6.0f}'.format(i, math.factorial(i)))
    except ValueError as err:
        print('Error computing factorial({}): {}'.format(i, err))
```

factorial() works only with whole numbers, but does accept `float` arguments as long as they can be converted to an integer without losing value.

```
$ python3 math_factorial.py

 0       1
 1       1
 2       2
 3       6
 4      24
 5     120
Error computing factorial(6.1): factorial() only accepts integral
values
```

gamma() is like factorial(), except that it works with real numbers and the value is shifted down by 1 (gamma is equal to (n - 1)!).

Listing 5.46: math_gamma.py

```python
import math

for i in [0, 1.1, 2.2, 3.3, 4.4, 5.5, 6.6]:
    try:
        print('{:2.1f} {:6.2f}'.format(i, math.gamma(i)))
    except ValueError as err:
        print('Error computing gamma({}): {}'.format(i, err))
```

Since zero causes the start value to be negative, it is not allowed.

```
$ python3 math_gamma.py

Error computing gamma(0): math domain error
1.1    0.95
2.2    1.10
3.3    2.68
4.4   10.14
5.5   52.34
6.6  344.70
```

`lgamma()` returns the natural logarithm of the absolute value of gamma for the input value.

Listing 5.47: `math_lgamma.py`

```
import math

for i in [0, 1.1, 2.2, 3.3, 4.4, 5.5, 6.6]:
    try:
        print('{:2.1f} {:.20f} {:.20f}'.format(
            i,
            math.lgamma(i),
            math.log(math.gamma(i)),
        ))
    except ValueError as err:
        print('Error computing lgamma({}): {}'.format(i, err))
```

Using `lgamma()` retains more precision than calculating the logarithm separately using the results of `gamma()`.

```
$ python3 math_lgamma.py

Error computing lgamma(0): math domain error
1.1 -0.04987244125984036103 -0.04987244125983997245
2.2 0.09694746679063825923 0.09694746679063866168
3.3 0.98709857789473387513 0.98709857789473409717
4.4 2.31610349142485727469 2.31610349142485727469
5.5 3.95781396761871651080 3.95781396761871606671
6.6 5.84268005527463252236 5.84268005527463252236
```

The modulo operator (%) computes the remainder of a division expression (i.e., 5 % 2 = 1). The operator built into the language works well with integers but, as with so many other floating-point operations, intermediate calculations cause representational issues that result in a loss of data. `fmod()` provides a more accurate implementation for floating-point values.

Listing 5.48: `math_fmod.py`

```
import math

print('{:^4} {:^4} {:^5} {:^5}'.format(
    'x', 'y', '%', 'fmod'))
print('{:-^4} {:-^4} {:-^5} {:-^5}'.format(
    '-', '-', '-', '-'))

INPUTS = [
    (5, 2),
    (5, -2),
```

```
        (-5, 2),
]

for x, y in INPUTS:
    print('{:4.1f} {:4.1f} {:5.2f} {:5.2f}'.format(
        x,
        y,
        x % y,
        math.fmod(x, y),
    ))
```

A potentially more frequent source of confusion is the fact that the algorithm used by fmod() for computing modulo is also different from that used by %, so the sign of the result is different.

```
$ python3 math_fmod.py

 x     y      %    fmod
----  ----  -----  -----
 5.0   2.0   1.00   1.00
 5.0  -2.0  -1.00   1.00
-5.0   2.0   1.00  -1.00
```

Use gcd() to find the largest integer that can divide evenly into two integers—that is, the greatest common divisor.

Listing 5.49: math_gcd.py

```
import math

print(math.gcd(10, 8))
print(math.gcd(10, 0))
print(math.gcd(50, 225))
print(math.gcd(11, 9))
print(math.gcd(0, 0))
```

If both values are 0, the result is 0.

```
$ python3 math_gcd.py

2
10
25
1
0
```

5.4.8   Exponents and Logarithms

Exponential growth curves appear in economics, physics, and other sciences. Python has a built-in exponentiation operator (**), but `pow()` can be useful when a callable function is needed as an argument to another function.

Listing 5.50: `math_pow.py`

```python
import math

INPUTS = [
    # Typical uses
    (2, 3),
    (2.1, 3.2),

    # Always 1
    (1.0, 5),
    (2.0, 0),

    # Not a number
    (2, float('nan')),

    # Roots
    (9.0, 0.5),
    (27.0, 1.0 / 3),
]

for x, y in INPUTS:
    print('{:5.1f} ** {:5.3f} = {:6.3f}'.format(
        x, y, math.pow(x, y)))
```

Raising `1` to any power always returns `1.0`, as does raising any value to a power of `0.0`. Most operations on `nan` (not a number) return `nan`. If the exponent is less than 1, `pow()` computes a root.

```
$ python3 math_pow.py

 2.0 ** 3.000 =  8.000
 2.1 ** 3.200 = 10.742
 1.0 ** 5.000 =  1.000
 2.0 ** 0.000 =  1.000
 2.0 **   nan =    nan
 9.0 ** 0.500 =  3.000
27.0 ** 0.333 =  3.000
```

Since square roots (exponent of 1/2) are used so frequently, a separate function is provided for computing them.

Listing 5.51: `math_sqrt.py`

```
import math

print(math.sqrt(9.0))
print(math.sqrt(3))
try:
    print(math.sqrt(-1))
except ValueError as err:
    print('Cannot compute sqrt(-1):', err)
```

Computing the square roots of negative numbers requires *complex numbers*, which are not handled by math. Any attempt to calculate a square root of a negative value results in a ValueError.

```
$ python3 math_sqrt.py

3.0
1.7320508075688772
Cannot compute sqrt(-1): math domain error
```

The logarithm function finds y, where x = b ** y. By default, log() computes the natural logarithm (the base is *e*). If a second argument is provided, that value is used as the base.

Listing 5.52: `math_log.py`

```
import math

print(math.log(8))
print(math.log(8, 2))
print(math.log(0.5, 2))
```

Logarithms where x is less than 1 yield negative results.

```
$ python3 math_log.py

2.0794415416798357
3.0
-1.0
```

Three variations of log() are available. Given floating-point representation and rounding errors, the computed value produced by log(x,b) has limited accuracy, especially for some bases. log10() computes log(x,10), using a more accurate algorithm than log().

Listing 5.53: math_log10.py

```python
import math

print('{:2} {:^12} {:^10} {:^20} {:8}'.format(
    'i', 'x', 'accurate', 'inaccurate', 'mismatch',
))
print('{:-^2} {:-^12} {:-^10} {:-^20} {:-^8}'.format(
    '', '', '', '', '',
))

for i in range(0, 10):
    x = math.pow(10, i)
    accurate = math.log10(x)
    inaccurate = math.log(x, 10)
    match = '' if int(inaccurate) == i else '*'
    print('{:2d} {:12.1f} {:10.8f} {:20.18f} {:^5}'.format(
        i, x, accurate, inaccurate, match,
    ))
```

The lines in the output with trailing ∗ highlight the inaccurate values.

```
$ python3 math_log10.py

i       x        accurate      inaccurate          mismatch
-- ------------ ---------- -------------------- --------
 0          1.0 0.00000000 0.000000000000000000
 1         10.0 1.00000000 1.000000000000000000
 2        100.0 2.00000000 2.000000000000000000
 3       1000.0 3.00000000 2.999999999999999556    *
 4      10000.0 4.00000000 4.000000000000000000
 5     100000.0 5.00000000 5.000000000000000000
 6    1000000.0 6.00000000 5.999999999999999112    *
 7   10000000.0 7.00000000 7.000000000000000000
 8  100000000.0 8.00000000 8.000000000000000000
 9 1000000000.0 9.00000000 8.999999999999998224    *
```

Similar to log10(), log2() calculates the equivalent of math.log(x,2).

Listing 5.54: math_log2.py

```python
import math

print('{:>2} {:^5} {:^5}'.format(
    'i', 'x', 'log2',
))
print('{:-^2} {:-^5} {:-^5}'.format(
    '', '', '',
))
```

```
for i in range(0, 10):
    x = math.pow(2, i)
    result = math.log2(x)
    print('{:2d} {:5.1f} {:5.1f}'.format(
        i, x, result,
    ))
```

Depending on the underlying platform, the built-in and special-purpose function can offer better performance and accuracy by taking advantage of special-purpose algorithms for base 2 that are not found in the more general-purpose function.

```
$ python3 math_log2.py

 i   x    log2
-- ----- -----
 0   1.0   0.0
 1   2.0   1.0
 2   4.0   2.0
 3   8.0   3.0
 4  16.0   4.0
 5  32.0   5.0
 6  64.0   6.0
 7 128.0   7.0
 8 256.0   8.0
 9 512.0   9.0
```

log1p() calculates the Newton-Mercator series (the natural logarithm of 1 + x).

Listing 5.55: math_log1p.py

```
import math

x = 0.0000000000000000000000001
print('x        :', x)
print('1 + x    :', 1 + x)
print('log(1+x):', math.log(1 + x))
print('log1p(x):', math.log1p(x))
```

log1p() is more accurate for values of x very close to zero because it uses an algorithm that compensates for round-off errors from the initial addition.

```
$ python3 math_log1p.py

x        : 1e-25
1 + x    : 1.0
log(1+x): 0.0
log1p(x): 1e-25
```

`exp()` computes the exponential function (e∗∗x).

Listing 5.56: math_exp.py

```
import math

x = 2

fmt = '{:.20f}'
print(fmt.format(math.e ** 2))
print(fmt.format(math.pow(math.e, 2)))
print(fmt.format(math.exp(2)))
```

Like the other special-case functions, it uses an algorithm that produces more accurate results than the general-purpose equivalent `math.pow(math.e,x)`.

```
$ python3 math_exp.py

7.38905609893064951876
7.38905609893064951876
7.38905609893065040694
```

`expm1()` is the inverse of `log1p()`, and calculates `e∗∗x - 1`.

Listing 5.57: math_expm1.py

```
import math

x = 0.0000000000000000000000001

print(x)
print(math.exp(x) - 1)
print(math.expm1(x))
```

Small values of x lose precision when the subtraction is performed separately, just as occurs with `log1p()`.

```
$ python3 math_expm1.py

1e-25
0.0
1e-25
```

5.4.9   Angles

Although degrees are more commonly used in everyday discussions of angles, radians are the standard unit of angular measure in science and math. A radian is the angle created when two lines intersect at the center of a circle, with their ends on the circumference of the circle spaced one radius apart.

The circumference is calculated as $2\pi r$, so there is a relationship between radians and π—a value that shows up frequently in trigonometric calculations. That relationship leads to radians being used in trigonometry and calculus, because they result in more compact formulas.

To convert from degrees to radians, use `radians()`.

Listing 5.58: math_radians.py

```python
import math

print('{:^7} {:^7} {:^7}'.format(
    'Degrees', 'Radians', 'Expected'))
print('{:-^7} {:-^7} {:-^7}'.format(
    '', '', ''))

INPUTS = [
    (0, 0),
    (30, math.pi / 6),
    (45, math.pi / 4),
    (60, math.pi / 3),
    (90, math.pi / 2),
    (180, math.pi),
    (270, 3 / 2.0 * math.pi),
    (360, 2 * math.pi),
]

for deg, expected in INPUTS:
    print('{:7d} {:7.2f} {:7.2f}'.format(
        deg,
        math.radians(deg),
        expected,
    ))
```

The formula for the conversion is `rad = deg * π / 180`.

```
$ python3 math_radians.py

Degrees Radians Expected
------- ------- -------
      0    0.00    0.00
     30    0.52    0.52
     45    0.79    0.79
     60    1.05    1.05
     90    1.57    1.57
    180    3.14    3.14
    270    4.71    4.71
    360    6.28    6.28
```

To convert from radians to degrees, use `degrees()`.

Listing 5.59: `math_degrees.py`

```
import math

INPUTS = [
    (0, 0),
    (math.pi / 6, 30),
    (math.pi / 4, 45),
    (math.pi / 3, 60),
    (math.pi / 2, 90),
    (math.pi, 180),
    (3 * math.pi / 2, 270),
    (2 * math.pi, 360),
]

print('{:^8} {:^8} {:^8}'.format(
    'Radians', 'Degrees', 'Expected'))
print('{:-^8} {:-^8} {:-^8}'.format('', '', ''))
for rad, expected in INPUTS:
    print('{:8.2f} {:8.2f} {:8.2f}'.format(
        rad,
        math.degrees(rad),
        expected,
    ))
```

The formula is `deg = rad * 180 / π`.

```
$ python3 math_degrees.py

Radians  Degrees  Expected
-------- -------- --------
    0.00     0.00     0.00
    0.52    30.00    30.00
    0.79    45.00    45.00
    1.05    60.00    60.00
    1.57    90.00    90.00
    3.14   180.00   180.00
    4.71   270.00   270.00
    6.28   360.00   360.00
```

5.4.10 Trigonometry

Trigonometric functions relate angles in a triangle to the lengths of its sides. They show up in formulas with periodic properties such as harmonics, in circular motion, or when dealing with angles. All of the trigonometric functions in the standard library take angles expressed as radians.

Given an angle in a right triangle, the *sine* is the ratio of the length of the side opposite the angle to the hypotenuse (`sin A = opposite/hypotenuse`). The *cosine* is the ratio of the length of the adjacent side to the hypotenuse (`cos A = adjacent/hypotenuse`). The *tangent* is the ratio of the opposite side to the adjacent side (`tan A = opposite/adjacent`).

Listing 5.60: `math_trig.py`

```python
import math

print('{:^7} {:^7} {:^7} {:^7} {:^7}'.format(
    'Degrees', 'Radians', 'Sine', 'Cosine', 'Tangent'))
print('{:-^7} {:-^7} {:-^7} {:-^7} {:-^7}'.format(
    '-', '-', '-', '-', '-'))

fmt = '{:7.2f} {:7.2f} {:7.2f} {:7.2f} {:7.2f}'

for deg in range(0, 361, 30):
    rad = math.radians(deg)
    if deg in (90, 270):
        t = float('inf')
    else:
        t = math.tan(rad)
    print(fmt.format(deg, rad, math.sin(rad), math.cos(rad), t))
```

The tangent can also be defined as the ratio of the sine of the angle to its cosine. Since the cosine is 0 for $\pi/2$ and $3\pi/2$ radians, the tangent is infinite.

```
$ python3 math_trig.py

Degrees Radians  Sine   Cosine  Tangent
------- -------  ------- ------- -------
   0.00    0.00    0.00    1.00    0.00
  30.00    0.52    0.50    0.87    0.58
  60.00    1.05    0.87    0.50    1.73
  90.00    1.57    1.00    0.00     inf
 120.00    2.09    0.87   -0.50   -1.73
 150.00    2.62    0.50   -0.87   -0.58
 180.00    3.14    0.00   -1.00   -0.00
 210.00    3.67   -0.50   -0.87    0.58
 240.00    4.19   -0.87   -0.50    1.73
 270.00    4.71   -1.00   -0.00     inf
 300.00    5.24   -0.87    0.50   -1.73
 330.00    5.76   -0.50    0.87   -0.58
 360.00    6.28   -0.00    1.00   -0.00
```

Given a point (x,y), the length of the hypotenuse for the triangle between the points $[(0, 0), (x, 0), (x, y)]$ is `(x**2 + y**2) ** 1/2`. It can be computed with `hypot()`.

Listing 5.61: **math_hypot.py**

```
import math

print('{:^7} {:^7} {:^10}'.format('X', 'Y', 'Hypotenuse'))
print('{:-^7} {:-^7} {:-^10}'.format('', '', ''))

POINTS = [
    # Simple points
    (1, 1),
    (-1, -1),
    (math.sqrt(2), math.sqrt(2)),
    (3, 4),   # 3-4-5 triangle
    # On the circle
    (math.sqrt(2) / 2, math.sqrt(2) / 2),   # pi/4 rads
    (0.5, math.sqrt(3) / 2),   # pi/3 rads
]

for x, y in POINTS:
    h = math.hypot(x, y)
    print('{:7.2f} {:7.2f} {:7.2f}'.format(x, y, h))
```

Points on the circle always have hypotenuse equal to 1.

```
$ python3 math_hypot.py

   X       Y     Hypotenuse
------- ------- ----------
   1.00    1.00    1.41
  -1.00   -1.00    1.41
   1.41    1.41    2.00
   3.00    4.00    5.00
   0.71    0.71    1.00
   0.50    0.87    1.00
```

The same function can be used to find the distance between two points.

Listing 5.62: **math_distance_2_points.py**

```
import math

print('{:^8} {:^8} {:^8} {:^8} {:^8}'.format(
    'X1', 'Y1', 'X2', 'Y2', 'Distance',
))
print('{:-^8} {:-^8} {:-^8} {:-^8} {:-^8}'.format(
    '', '', '', '', '',
))

POINTS = [
    ((5, 5), (6, 6)),
```

```
        ((-6, -6), (-5, -5)),
        ((0, 0), (3, 4)),    # 3-4-5 triangle
        ((-1, -1), (2, 3)),  # 3-4-5 triangle
]

for (x1, y1), (x2, y2) in POINTS:
    x = x1 - x2
    y = y1 - y2
    h = math.hypot(x, y)
    print('{:8.2f} {:8.2f} {:8.2f} {:8.2f} {:8.2f}'.format(
        x1, y1, x2, y2, h,
    ))
```

Use the difference in the x and y values to move one endpoint to the origin, and then pass the results to hypot().

```
$ python3 math_distance_2_points.py

    X1       Y1       X2       Y2     Distance
--------  -------- -------- -------- --------
    5.00     5.00     6.00     6.00     1.41
   -6.00    -6.00    -5.00    -5.00     1.41
    0.00     0.00     3.00     4.00     5.00
   -1.00    -1.00     2.00     3.00     5.00
```

math also defines inverse trigonometric functions.

Listing 5.63: math_inverse_trig.py

```
import math

for r in [0, 0.5, 1]:
    print('arcsine({:.1f})    = {:5.2f}'.format(r, math.asin(r)))
    print('arccosine({:.1f})  = {:5.2f}'.format(r, math.acos(r)))
    print('arctangent({:.1f}) = {:5.2f}'.format(r, math.atan(r)))
    print()
```

The value 1.57 is roughly equal to $\pi/2$, or 90 degrees, the angle at which the sine is 1 and the cosine is 0.

```
$ python3 math_inverse_trig.py

arcsine(0.0)    =  0.00
arccosine(0.0)  =  1.57
arctangent(0.0) =  0.00

arcsine(0.5)    =  0.52
arccosine(0.5)  =  1.05
```

```
arctangent(0.5) =  0.46

arcsine(1.0)    =  1.57
arccosine(1.0)  =  0.00
arctangent(1.0) =  0.79
```

5.4.11   Hyperbolic Functions

Hyperbolic functions appear in linear differential equations and are used when working with electromagnetic fields, fluid dynamics, special relativity, and other advanced physics and mathematics.

Listing 5.64: `math_hyperbolic.py`

```python
import math

print('{:^6} {:^6} {:^6} {:^6}'.format(
    'X', 'sinh', 'cosh', 'tanh',
))
print('{:-^6} {:-^6} {:-^6} {:-^6}'.format('', '', '', ''))

fmt = '{:6.4f} {:6.4f} {:6.4f} {:6.4f}'

for i in range(0, 11, 2):
    x = i / 10.0
    print(fmt.format(
        x,
        math.sinh(x),
        math.cosh(x),
        math.tanh(x),
    ))
```

Whereas the cosine and sine functions enscribe a circle, the hyperbolic cosine and hyperbolic sine form half of a hyperbola.

```
$ python3 math_hyperbolic.py

  X     sinh   cosh   tanh
------ ------ ------ ------
0.0000 0.0000 1.0000 0.0000
0.2000 0.2013 1.0201 0.1974
0.4000 0.4108 1.0811 0.3799
0.6000 0.6367 1.1855 0.5370
0.8000 0.8881 1.3374 0.6640
1.0000 1.1752 1.5431 0.7616
```

The inverse hyperbolic functions `acosh()`, `asinh()`, and `atanh()` are also available.

5.4.12   Special Functions

The Gauss error function is used in statistics.

Listing 5.65: <code>math_erf.py</code>

```
import math

print('{:^5} {:7}'.format('x', 'erf(x)'))
print('{:-^5} {:-^7}'.format('', ''))

for x in [-3, -2, -1, -0.5, -0.25, 0, 0.25, 0.5, 1, 2, 3]:
    print('{:5.2f} {:7.4f}'.format(x, math.erf(x)))
```

For the error function, `erf(-x) == -erf(x)`.

```
$ python3 math_erf.py

  x    erf(x)
----- --------
-3.00 -1.0000
-2.00 -0.9953
-1.00 -0.8427
-0.50 -0.5205
-0.25 -0.2763
 0.00  0.0000
 0.25  0.2763
 0.50  0.5205
 1.00  0.8427
 2.00  0.9953
 3.00  1.0000
```

The complementary error function `erfc()` produces values equivalent to `1 - erf(x)`.

Listing 5.66: <code>math_erfc.py</code>

```
import math

print('{:^5} {:7}'.format('x', 'erfc(x)'))
print('{:-^5} {:-^7}'.format('', ''))

for x in [-3, -2, -1, -0.5, -0.25, 0, 0.25, 0.5, 1, 2, 3]:
    print('{:5.2f} {:7.4f}'.format(x, math.erfc(x)))
```

The implementation of `erfc()` avoids precision errors for small values of x when subtracting from 1.

```
$ python3 math_erfc.py

   x   erfc(x)
-----  -------
-3.00  2.0000
-2.00  1.9953
-1.00  1.8427
-0.50  1.5205
-0.25  1.2763
 0.00  1.0000
 0.25  0.7237
 0.50  0.4795
 1.00  0.1573
 2.00  0.0047
 3.00  0.0000
```

TIP

Related Reading

- Standard library documentation for math.[9]
- IEEE floating-point arithmetic in Python[10]: Blog post by John Cook about how special values arise and are dealt with when doing math in Python.
- SciPy[11]: Open source libraries for scientific and mathematical calculations in Python.
- **PEP 485**[12]: A Function for testing approximate equality.

5.5 statistics: Statistical Calculations

The statistics module implements many common statistical formulas that allow for efficient calculations using Python's various numerical types (int, float, Decimal, and Fraction).

5.5.1 Averages

Three forms of averages are supported: the mean, the median, and the mode. Calculate the arithmetic mean with mean().

---

[9] https://docs.python.org/3.5/library/math.html
[10] www.johndcook.com/blog/2009/07/21/ieee-arithmetic-python/
[11] http://scipy.org
[12] www.python.org/dev/peps/pep-0485

Listing 5.67: statistics_mean.py

```
from statistics import *

data = [1, 2, 2, 5, 10, 12]

print('{:0.2f}'.format(mean(data)))
```

The return value for integers and floats is always a `float`. For `Decimal` and `Fraction` input data, the result is of the same type as the inputs.

```
$ python3 statistics_mean.py

5.33
```

Calculate the most common data point in a data set using `mode()`.

Listing 5.68: statistics_mode.py

```
from statistics import *

data = [1, 2, 2, 5, 10, 12]

print(mode(data))
```

The return value is always a member of the input data set. Because `mode()` treats the input as a set of discrete values, and counts the recurrences, the inputs do not actually need to be numerical values.

```
$ python3 statistics_mode.py

2
```

There are four variations for calculating the median, or middle, value. The first three are straightforward versions of the usual algorithm, with different solutions for handling data sets with an even number of elements.

Listing 5.69: statistics_median.py

```
from statistics import *

data = [1, 2, 2, 5, 10, 12]

print('median    : {:0.2f}'.format(median(data)))
print('low       : {:0.2f}'.format(median_low(data)))
print('high      : {:0.2f}'.format(median_high(data)))
```

median() finds the center value. If the data set contains an even number of values, it averages the two middle items. median_low() always returns a value from the input data set, using the lower of the two middle items for data sets with an even number of items. median_high() similarly returns the higher of the two middle items.

```
$ python3 statistics_median.py

median    : 3.50
low       : 2.00
high      : 5.00
```

The fourth version of the median calculation, median_grouped(), treats the inputs as continuous data. It calculates the 50% percentile median by first finding the median range using the provided interval width, and then interpolating within that range using the position of the actual values from the data set that fall in that range.

Listing 5.70: statistics_median_grouped.py

```
from statistics import *

data = [10, 20, 30, 40]

print('1: {:0.2f}'.format(median_grouped(data, interval=1)))
print('2: {:0.2f}'.format(median_grouped(data, interval=2)))
print('3: {:0.2f}'.format(median_grouped(data, interval=3)))
```

As the interval width increases, the median computed for the same data set changes.

```
$ python3 statistics_median_grouped.py

1: 29.50
2: 29.00
3: 28.50
```

5.5.2 Variance

Statistics uses two values to express how disperse a set of values is relative to the mean. The *variance* is the average of the square of the difference of each value and the mean, and the *standard deviation* is the square root of the variance (which is useful because taking the square root allows the standard deviation to be expressed in the same units as the input data). A large value for the variance or the standard deviation indicate that a set of data is disperse, while a small value indicates that the data is clustered closer to the mean.

Listing 5.71: statistics_variance.py

```
from statistics import *
import subprocess
```

```
def get_line_lengths():
    cmd = 'wc -l ../[a-z]*/*.py'
    out = subprocess.check_output(
        cmd, shell=True).decode('utf-8')
    for line in out.splitlines():
        parts = line.split()
        if parts[1].strip().lower() == 'total':
            break
        nlines = int(parts[0].strip())
        if not nlines:
            continue  # Skip empty files.
        yield (nlines, parts[1].strip())


data = list(get_line_lengths())

lengths = [d[0] for d in data]
sample = lengths[::2]

print('Basic statistics:')
print('  count     : {:3d}'.format(len(lengths)))
print('  min       : {:6.2f}'.format(min(lengths)))
print('  max       : {:6.2f}'.format(max(lengths)))
print('  mean      : {:6.2f}'.format(mean(lengths)))

print('\nPopulation variance:')
print('  pstdev    : {:6.2f}'.format(pstdev(lengths)))
print('  pvariance : {:6.2f}'.format(pvariance(lengths)))

print('\nEstimated variance for sample:')
print('  count     : {:3d}'.format(len(sample)))
print('  stdev     : {:6.2f}'.format(stdev(sample)))
print('  variance  : {:6.2f}'.format(variance(sample)))
```

Python includes two sets of functions for computing variance and standard deviation, depending on whether the data set represents the entire population or a sample of the population. This example first uses wc to count the number of lines in the input files for all of the example programs. It then uses pvariance() and pstdev() to compute the variance and standard deviation for the entire population. Finally, it uses variance() and stddev() to compute the sample variance and standard deviation for a subset created by using the length of every second file found.

```
$ python3 statistics_variance.py

Basic statistics:
  count   : 959
  min     :   4.00
  max     : 228.00
  mean    :  28.62
```

```
Population variance:
  pstdev    :  18.52
  pvariance : 342.95

Estimated variance for sample:
  count    : 480
  stdev    :  21.09
  variance : 444.61
```

TIP

Related Reading

- Standard library documentation for statistics.[13]
- Median for Discrete and Continuous Frequency Type Data (grouped data)[14]: Discussion of median for continuous data.
- **PEP 450**[15]: Adding a Statistics Module to the Standard Library.

---

[13] https://docs.python.org/3.5/library/statistics.html
[14] www.mathstips.com/statistics/median-for-discrete-and-continuous-frequency-type.html
[15] www.python.org/dev/peps/pep-0450

Chapter 6

The File System

Python's standard library includes a large range of tools for working with files on the file system, building and parsing filenames, and examining file contents.

The first step in working with files is to determine the name of the file to work on. Python represents filenames as simple strings, but provides tools for building them from standard, platform-independent components in os.path (page 296).

The pathlib (page 305) module provides an object-oriented API for working with file system paths. Using it instead of os.path offers greater convenience because it operates at a higher level of abstraction.

List the contents of a directory with listdir() from os (page 1227), or use glob (page 319) to build a list of filenames from a pattern.

The filename pattern matching used by glob is also exposed directly through fnmatch (page 323), so it can be used in other contexts.

After the name of the file is identified, other characteristics, such as permissions or the file size, can be checked using os.stat() and the constants in stat.

When an application needs random access to files, linecache (page 326) makes it easy to read lines by their line number. The contents of the file are maintained in a cache, so be careful of memory consumption.

tempfile (page 330) is useful for cases that need to create scratch files to hold data temporarily, or before moving data to a permanent location. It provides classes to create temporary files and directories safely and securely. Names are guaranteed to be unique, and include random components so they are not easily guessable.

Frequently, programs need to work on files as a whole, without regard to their content. The shutil (page 337) module includes high-level file operations such as copying files and directories, and creating or extracting archives of files.

The filecmp (page 351) module compares files and directories by looking at the bytes they contain, but without any special knowledge about their format.

The built-in file class can be used to read and write files that are visible on local file systems. A program's performance can suffer when it accesses large files through the read() and write() interfaces, though, because both of them involve copying the data multiple times as it is moved from the disk to memory the application can see. Using mmap (page 361) tells the operating system to use its virtual memory subsystem to map a file's contents directly into memory accessible by a program, avoiding a copy step between the operating system and the internal buffer for the file object.

Text data using characters not available in ASCII is usually saved in a Unicode data format. Since the standard file handle assumes each byte of a text file represents one character, reading Unicode text with multibyte encodings requires extra processing. The codecs (page 365) module handles the encoding and decoding automatically, so that in many cases a non-ASCII file can be used without any other changes to the program.

The io (page 390) module provides access to the classes used to implement Python's file-based input and output. For testing code that depends on reading or writing data from files, io provides an in-memory stream object that behaves like a file, but does not reside on disk.

6.1   os.path: Platform-Independent Manipulation of Filenames

Writing code to work with files on multiple platforms is easy using the functions included in the os.path module. Even programs not intended to be ported between platforms should use os.path for reliable filename parsing.

6.1.1   Parsing Paths

The first set of functions in os.path can be used to parse strings representing filenames into their component parts. These functions do not depend on the paths actually existing; rather, they operate solely on the strings.

Path parsing depends on a few variables defined in os (page 1227):

- os.sep: The separator between portions of the path (e.g., "/" or "\").

- os.extsep: The separator between a filename and the file "extension" (e.g., ".").

- os.pardir: The path component that means traverse the directory tree up one level (e.g., "..").

- os.curdir: The path component that refers to the current directory (e.g., ".").

The split() function breaks the path into two separate parts and returns a tuple with the results. The second element of the tuple is the last component of the path, and the first element is everything that comes before it.

Listing 6.1: **ospath_split.py**

```
import os.path

PATHS = [
    '/one/two/three',
    '/one/two/three/',
    '/',
    '.',
    '',
]

for path in PATHS:
    print('{!r:>17} : {}'.format(path, os.path.split(path)))
```

When the input argument ends in `os.sep`, the last element of the path is an empty string.

```
$ python3 ospath_split.py

   '/one/two/three' : ('/one/two', 'three')
  '/one/two/three/' : ('/one/two/three', '')
                '/' : ('/', '')
                '.' : ('', '.')
                 '' : ('', '')
```

The `basename()` function returns a value equivalent to the second part of the `split()` value.

Listing 6.2: ospath_basename.py

```python
import os.path

PATHS = [
    '/one/two/three',
    '/one/two/three/',
    '/',
    '.',
    '',
]

for path in PATHS:
    print('{!r:>17} : {!r}'.format(path, os.path.basename(path)))
```

The full path is stripped down to the last element, whether that refers to a file or a directory. If the path ends in the directory separator (`os.sep`), the base portion is considered to be empty.

```
$ python3 ospath_basename.py

   '/one/two/three' : 'three'
  '/one/two/three/' : ''
                '/' : ''
                '.' : '.'
                 '' : ''
```

The `dirname()` function returns the first part of the split path.

Listing 6.3: ospath_dirname.py

```python
import os.path

PATHS = [
    '/one/two/three',
    '/one/two/three/',
```

```
        '/',
        '.',
        '',
    ]

    for path in PATHS:
        print('{!r:>17} : {!r}'.format(path, os.path.dirname(path)))
```

Combining the results of `basename()` with `dirname()` gives the original path.

```
$ python3 ospath_dirname.py

    '/one/two/three' : '/one/two'
   '/one/two/three/' : '/one/two/three'
                 '/' : '/'
                 '.' : ''
                  '' : ''
```

`splitext()` works like `split()`, but divides the path on the extension separator, rather than the directory separator.

Listing 6.4: ospath_splitext.py

```
import os.path

PATHS = [
    'filename.txt',
    'filename',
    '/path/to/filename.txt',
    '/',
    '',
    'my-archive.tar.gz',
    'no-extension.',
]

for path in PATHS:
    print('{!r:>21} : {!r}'.format(path, os.path.splitext(path)))
```

Only the last occurrence of `os.extsep` is used when looking for the extension. Thus, if a filename has multiple extensions, the results of splitting it leaves part of the extension on the prefix.

```
$ python3 ospath_splitext.py

         'filename.txt' : ('filename', '.txt')
             'filename' : ('filename', '')
 '/path/to/filename.txt' : ('/path/to/filename', '.txt')
                    '/' : ('/', '')
                     '' : ('', '')
```

```
'my-archive.tar.gz' : ('my-archive.tar', '.gz')
'no-extension.' : ('no-extension', '.')
```

commonprefix() takes a list of paths as an argument and returns a single string that represents a common prefix present in all of the paths. The value may represent a path that does not actually exist, and the path separator is not included in the consideration. As a consequence, the prefix might not stop on a separator boundary.

Listing 6.5: ospath_commonprefix.py

```
import os.path

paths = ['/one/two/three/four',
         '/one/two/threefold',
         '/one/two/three/',
         ]
for path in paths:
    print('PATH:', path)

print()
print('PREFIX:', os.path.commonprefix(paths))
```

In this example, the common prefix string is /one/two/three, even though one path does not include a directory named three.

```
$ python3 ospath_commonprefix.py

PATH: /one/two/three/four
PATH: /one/two/threefold
PATH: /one/two/three/

PREFIX: /one/two/three
```

commonpath() does honor path separators. It returns a prefix that does not include partial path values.

Listing 6.6: ospath_commonpath.py

```
import os.path

paths = ['/one/two/three/four',
         '/one/two/threefold',
         '/one/two/three/',
         ]
for path in paths:
    print('PATH:', path)

print()
print('PREFIX:', os.path.commonpath(paths))
```

Because "threefold" does not have a path separator after "three", the common prefix is /one/two.

```
$ python3 ospath_commonpath.py

PATH: /one/two/three/four
PATH: /one/two/threefold
PATH: /one/two/three/

PREFIX: /one/two
```

6.1.2   Building Paths

Besides taking existing paths apart, it is frequently necessary to build paths from other strings. To combine several path components into a single value, use join().

Listing 6.7: ospath_join.py

```
import os.path

PATHS = [
    ('one', 'two', 'three'),
    ('/', 'one', 'two', 'three'),
    ('/one', '/two', '/three'),
]

for parts in PATHS:
    print('{} : {!r}'.format(parts, os.path.join(*parts)))
```

If any argument to join begins with os.sep, all of the previous arguments are discarded and the new one becomes the beginning of the return value.

```
$ python3 ospath_join.py

('one', 'two', 'three') : 'one/two/three'
('/', 'one', 'two', 'three') : '/one/two/three'
('/one', '/two', '/three') : '/three'
```

It is also possible to work with paths that include "variable" components that can be expanded automatically. For example, expanduser() converts the tilde (~) character to the name of a user's home directory.

Listing 6.8: ospath_expanduser.py

```
import os.path

for user in ['', 'dhellmann', 'nosuchuser']:
    lookup = '~' + user
```

```
    print('{!r:>15} : {!r}'.format(
        lookup, os.path.expanduser(lookup)))
```

If the user's home directory cannot be found, the string is returned unchanged, as with ~nosuchuser in this example.

```
$ python3 ospath_expanduser.py

            '~' : '/Users/dhellmann'
   '~dhellmann' : '/Users/dhellmann'
 '~nosuchuser' : '~nosuchuser'
```

expandvars() is more general, and expands any shell environment variables present in the path.

Listing 6.9: ospath_expandvars.py

```
import os.path
import os

os.environ['MYVAR'] = 'VALUE'

print(os.path.expandvars('/path/to/$MYVAR'))
```

No validation is performed to ensure that the variable value results in the name of a file that already exists.

```
$ python3 ospath_expandvars.py

/path/to/VALUE
```

6.1.3 Normalizing Paths

Paths assembled from separate strings using join() or with embedded variables might end up with extra separators or relative path components. Use normpath() to clean them up.

Listing 6.10: ospath_normpath.py

```
import os.path

PATHS = [
    'one//two//three',
    'one/./two/./three',
    'one/../alt/two/three',
]

for path in PATHS:
    print('{!r:>22} : {!r}'.format(path, os.path.normpath(path)))
```

Path segments made up of `os.curdir` and `os.pardir` are evaluated and collapsed.

```
$ python3 ospath_normpath.py

      'one//two//three' : 'one/two/three'
   'one/./two/./three' : 'one/two/three'
'one/../alt/two/three' : 'alt/two/three'
```

To convert a relative path to an absolute filename, use `abspath()`.

Listing 6.11: ospath_abspath.py

```
import os
import os.path

os.chdir('/usr')

PATHS = [
    '.',
    '..',
    './one/two/three',
    '../one/two/three',
]

for path in PATHS:
    print('{!r:>21} : {!r}'.format(path, os.path.abspath(path)))
```

The result is a complete path, starting at the top of the file system tree.

```
$ python3 ospath_abspath.py

                    '.' : '/usr'
                   '..' : '/'
      './one/two/three' : '/usr/one/two/three'
     '../one/two/three' : '/one/two/three'
```

6.1.4   File Times

Besides working with paths, `os.path` includes functions for retrieving file properties, similar to the ones returned by `os.stat()`.

Listing 6.12: ospath_properties.py

```
import os.path
import time

print('File         :', __file__)
print('Access time  :', time.ctime(os.path.getatime(__file__)))
```

```
print('Modified time:', time.ctime(os.path.getmtime(__file__)))
print('Change time  :', time.ctime(os.path.getctime(__file__)))
print('Size         :', os.path.getsize(__file__))
```

os.path.getatime() returns the access time, os.path.getmtime() returns the modification time, and os.path.getctime() returns the creation time. os.path.getsize() returns the amount of data in the file, represented in bytes.

```
$ python3 ospath_properties.py

File          : ospath_properties.py
Access time   : Fri Aug 26 16:38:05 2016
Modified time: Fri Aug 26 15:50:48 2016
Change time   : Fri Aug 26 15:50:49 2016
Size          : 481
```

6.1.5 Testing Files

When a program encounters a path name, it often needs to know whether the path refers to a file, directory, or symlink and whether it exists. os.path includes functions for testing all of these conditions.

Listing 6.13: ospath_tests.py

```
import os.path

FILENAMES = [
    __file__,
    os.path.dirname(__file__),
    '/',
    './broken_link',
]

for file in FILENAMES:
    print('File         : {!r}'.format(file))
    print('Absolute     :', os.path.isabs(file))
    print('Is File?     :', os.path.isfile(file))
    print('Is Dir?      :', os.path.isdir(file))
    print('Is Link?     :', os.path.islink(file))
    print('Mountpoint?  :', os.path.ismount(file))
    print('Exists?      :', os.path.exists(file))
    print('Link Exists?:', os.path.lexists(file))
    print()
```

All of the test functions return boolean values.

```
$ ln -s /does/not/exist broken_link
$ python3 ospath_tests.py
```

```
File         : 'ospath_tests.py'
Absolute     : False
Is File?     : True
Is Dir?      : False
Is Link?     : False
Mountpoint?  : False
Exists?      : True
Link Exists?: True

File         : ''
Absolute     : False
Is File?     : False
Is Dir?      : False
Is Link?     : False
Mountpoint?  : False
Exists?      : False
Link Exists?: False

File         : '/'
Absolute     : True
Is File?     : False
Is Dir?      : True
Is Link?     : False
Mountpoint?  : True
Exists?      : True
Link Exists?: True

File         : './broken_link'
Absolute     : False
Is File?     : False
Is Dir?      : False
Is Link?     : True
Mountpoint?  : False
Exists?      : False
Link Exists?: True
```

TIP

Related Reading

- Standard library documentation for os.path.[1]
- Python 2 to 3 porting notes for os.path (page 1361).
- pathlib (page 305): Paths as objects.
- os (page 1227): The os module is a parent of os.path.
- time (page 211): The time module includes functions to convert between the representation used by the time property functions in os.path and easy-to-read strings.

---

[1] https://docs.python.org/3.5/library/os.path.html

6.2 pathlib: File System Paths as Objects

The `pathlib` module provides an object-oriented API for parsing, building, testing, and otherwise working on filenames and paths, instead of using low-level string operations.

6.2.1 Path Representations

`pathlib` includes classes for managing file system paths formatted using either the POSIX standard or Microsoft Windows syntax. It includes "pure" classes, which operate on strings but do not interact with an actual file system, and "concrete" classes, which extend the API to include operations that reflect or modify data on the local file system.

The pure classes `PurePosixPath` and `PureWindowsPath` can be instantiated and used on any operating system, since they work only on names. To instantiate the correct class for working with a real file system, use `Path` to get either a `PosixPath` or a `WindowsPath`, depending on the platform.

6.2.2 Building Paths

To instantiate a new path, give a string as the first argument. The string representation of the path object is this name value. To create a new path referring to a value relative to an existing path, use the / operator to extend the path. The argument to the operator can either be a string or another path object.

Listing 6.14: `pathlib_operator.py`

```
import pathlib

usr = pathlib.PurePosixPath('/usr')
print(usr)

usr_local = usr / 'local'
print(usr_local)

usr_share = usr / pathlib.PurePosixPath('share')
print(usr_share)

root = usr / '..'
print(root)

etc = root / '/etc/'
print(etc)
```

As the value for `root` in the example output shows, the operator combines the path values as they are given, and does not normalize the result when it contains the parent directory reference `".."`. If a segment begins with the path separator, however, it is interpreted as a new "root" reference in the same way as `os.path.join()`. Extra path separators are removed from the middle of the path value, as in the `etc` example here.

```
$ python3 pathlib_operator.py

/usr
/usr/local
/usr/share
/usr/..
/etc
```

The concrete path classes include a `resolve()` method for normalizing a path by looking at the file system for directories and symbolic links and producing the absolute path referred to by a name.

Listing 6.15: pathlib_resolve.py

```
import pathlib

usr_local = pathlib.Path('/usr/local')
share = usr_local / '..' / 'share'
print(share.resolve())
```

Here the relative path is converted to the absolute path to `/usr/share`. If the input path includes symlinks, those are expanded as well to allow the resolved path to refer directly to the target.

```
$ python3 pathlib_resolve.py

/usr/share
```

To build paths when the segments are not known in advance, use `joinpath()`, passing each path segment as a separate argument.

Listing 6.16: pathlib_joinpath.py

```
import pathlib

root = pathlib.PurePosixPath('/')
subdirs = ['usr', 'local']
usr_local = root.joinpath(*subdirs)
print(usr_local)
```

As with the / operator, calling `joinpath()` creates a new instance.

```
$ python3 pathlib_joinpath.py

/usr/local
```

Given an existing path object, it is easy to build a new one with minor differences such as referring to a different file in the same directory. Use `with_name()` to create a new path that replaces the name portion of a path with a different filename. Use `with_suffix()` to create a new path that replaces the filename's extension with a different value.

Listing 6.17: **pathlib_from_existing.py**

```
import pathlib

ind = pathlib.PurePosixPath('source/pathlib/index.rst')
print(ind)

py = ind.with_name('pathlib_from_existing.py')
print(py)

pyc = py.with_suffix('.pyc')
print(pyc)
```

Both methods return new objects, and the original is left unchanged.

```
$ python3 pathlib_from_existing.py

source/pathlib/index.rst
source/pathlib/pathlib_from_existing.py
source/pathlib/pathlib_from_existing.pyc
```

6.2.3   Parsing Paths

Path objects have methods and properties for extracting partial values from the name. For example, the `parts` property produces a sequence of path segments parsed based on the path separator value.

Listing 6.18: **pathlib_parts.py**

```
import pathlib

p = pathlib.PurePosixPath('/usr/local')
print(p.parts)
```

The sequence is a tuple, reflecting the immutability of the path instance.

```
$ python3 pathlib_parts.py

('/', 'usr', 'local')
```

There are two ways to navigate "up" the file system hierarchy from a given path object. The `parent` property refers to a new path instance for the directory containing the path, the value returned by `os.path.dirname()`. The `parents` property is an iterable that produces parent directory references, continually going "up" the path hierarchy until it reaches the root.

Listing 6.19: pathlib_parents.py

```python
import pathlib

p = pathlib.PurePosixPath('/usr/local/lib')

print('parent: {}'.format(p.parent))

print('\nhierarchy:')
for up in p.parents:
    print(up)
```

The example iterates over the `parents` property and prints the member values.

```
$ python3 pathlib_parents.py

parent: /usr/local

hierarchy:
/usr/local
/usr
/
```

Other parts of the path can be accessed through properties of the path object. The `name` property holds the last part of the path, after the final path separator (the same value that `os.path.basename()` produces). The `suffix` property holds the value after the extension separator, and the `stem` property holds the portion of the name before the suffix.

Listing 6.20: pathlib_name.py

```python
import pathlib

p = pathlib.PurePosixPath('./source/pathlib/pathlib_name.py')
print('path  : {}'.format(p))
print('name  : {}'.format(p.name))
print('suffix: {}'.format(p.suffix))
print('stem  : {}'.format(p.stem))
```

Although the `suffix` and `stem` values are similar to the values produced by `os.path.splitext()`, the values are based on only the value of `name`, not on the full path.

```
$ python3 pathlib_name.py

path  : source/pathlib/pathlib_name.py
name  : pathlib_name.py
suffix: .py
stem  : pathlib_name
```

6.2.4   Creating Concrete Paths

Instances of the concrete `Path` class can be created from string arguments referring to the name (or potential name) of a file, directory, or symbolic link on the file system. The class also provides several convenient methods for building instances using commonly used locations that change, such as the current working directory and the user's home directory.

Listing 6.21: `pathlib_convenience.py`

```
import pathlib

home = pathlib.Path.home()
print('home: ', home)

cwd = pathlib.Path.cwd()
print('cwd : ', cwd)
```

Both methods create `Path` instances prepopulated with an absolute file system reference.

```
$ python3 pathlib_convenience.py

home:   /Users/dhellmann
cwd :   /Users/dhellmann/PyMOTW
```

6.2.5   Directory Contents

Three methods can be used to access the directory listings and discover the names of files available on the file system. `iterdir()` is a generator, yielding a new `Path` instance for each item in the containing directory.

Listing 6.22: `pathlib_iterdir.py`

```
import pathlib

p = pathlib.Path('.')

for f in p.iterdir():
    print(f)
```

If the `Path` does not refer to a directory, `iterdir()` raises `NotADirectoryError`.

```
$ python3 pathlib_iterdir.py

example_link
index.rst
pathlib_chmod.py
pathlib_convenience.py
pathlib_from_existing.py
```

```
pathlib_glob.py
pathlib_iterdir.py
pathlib_joinpath.py
pathlib_mkdir.py
pathlib_name.py
pathlib_operator.py
pathlib_ownership.py
pathlib_parents.py
pathlib_parts.py
pathlib_read_write.py
pathlib_resolve.py
pathlib_rglob.py
pathlib_rmdir.py
pathlib_stat.py
pathlib_symlink_to.py
pathlib_touch.py
pathlib_types.py
pathlib_unlink.py
```

Use `glob()` to find only files matching a pattern.

Listing 6.23: `pathlib_glob.py`

```python
import pathlib

p = pathlib.Path('..')

for f in p.glob('*.rst'):
    print(f)
```

This example shows all of the reStructuredText[2] input files in the parent directory of the script.

```
$ python3 pathlib_glob.py

../about.rst
../algorithm_tools.rst
../book.rst
../compression.rst
../concurrency.rst
../cryptographic.rst
../data_structures.rst
../dates.rst
../dev_tools.rst
../email.rst
../file_access.rst
../frameworks.rst
```

---

[2] http://docutils.sourceforge.net/

```
../i18n.rst
../importing.rst
../index.rst
../internet_protocols.rst
../language.rst
../networking.rst
../numeric.rst
../persistence.rst
../porting_notes.rst
../runtime_services.rst
../text.rst
../third_party.rst
../unix.rst
```

The glob processor supports recursive scanning using the pattern prefix ** or by calling rglob() instead of glob().

Listing 6.24: pathlib_rglob.py

```python
import pathlib

p = pathlib.Path('..')

for f in p.rglob('pathlib_*.py'):
    print(f)
```

Because this example starts from the parent directory, a recursive search is necessary to find the example files matching pathlib_*.py.

```
$ python3 pathlib_rglob.py

../pathlib/pathlib_chmod.py
../pathlib/pathlib_convenience.py
../pathlib/pathlib_from_existing.py
../pathlib/pathlib_glob.py
../pathlib/pathlib_iterdir.py
../pathlib/pathlib_joinpath.py
../pathlib/pathlib_mkdir.py
../pathlib/pathlib_name.py
../pathlib/pathlib_operator.py
../pathlib/pathlib_ownership.py
../pathlib/pathlib_parents.py
../pathlib/pathlib_parts.py
../pathlib/pathlib_read_write.py
../pathlib/pathlib_resolve.py
../pathlib/pathlib_rglob.py
../pathlib/pathlib_rmdir.py
../pathlib/pathlib_stat.py
../pathlib/pathlib_symlink_to.py
```

```
../pathlib/pathlib_touch.py
../pathlib/pathlib_types.py
../pathlib/pathlib_unlink.py
```

6.2.6   Reading and Writing Files

Each `Path` instance includes methods for working with the contents of the file to which it refers. For immediately retrieving the contents, use `read_bytes()` or `read_text()`. To write to the file, use `write_bytes()` or `write_text()`. Use the `open()` method to open the file and retain the file handle, instead of passing the name to the built-in `open()` function.

Listing 6.25: pathlib_read_write.py

```python
import pathlib

f = pathlib.Path('example.txt')

f.write_bytes('This is the content'.encode('utf-8'))

with f.open('r', encoding='utf-8') as handle:
    print('read from open(): {!r}'.format(handle.read()))

print('read_text(): {!r}'.format(f.read_text('utf-8')))
```

The convenience methods do some type checking before opening the file and writing to it, but otherwise they are equivalent to doing the operation directly.

```
$ python3 pathlib_read_write.py

read from open(): 'This is the content'
read_text(): 'This is the content'
```

6.2.7   Manipulating Directories and Symbolic Links

Paths representing directories or symbolic links that do not exist can be used to create the associated file system entries.

Listing 6.26: pathlib_mkdir.py

```python
import pathlib

p = pathlib.Path('example_dir')

print('Creating {}'.format(p))
p.mkdir()
```

If the path already exists, `mkdir()` raises a `FileExistsError`.

```
$ python3 pathlib_mkdir.py

Creating example_dir

$ python3 pathlib_mkdir.py

Creating example_dir
Traceback (most recent call last):
  File "pathlib_mkdir.py", line 16, in <module>
    p.mkdir()
  File ".../lib/python3.5/pathlib.py", line 1214, in mkdir
    self._accessor.mkdir(self, mode)
  File ".../lib/python3.5/pathlib.py", line 371, in wrapped
    return strfunc(str(pathobj), *args)
FileExistsError: [Errno 17] File exists: 'example_dir'
```

Use `symlink_to()` to create a symbolic link. The link will be named based on the path's value and will refer to the name given as an argument to `symlink_to()`.

Listing 6.27: **pathlib_symlink_to.py**

```
import pathlib

p = pathlib.Path('example_link')

p.symlink_to('index.rst')

print(p)
print(p.resolve().name)
```

This example first creates a symbolic link, then uses `resolve()` to read the link to find what it points to and print the name.

```
$ python3 pathlib_symlink_to.py

example_link
index.rst
```

6.2.8 File Types

A `Path` instance includes several methods for testing the type of file refered to by the path. This example creates several files of different types and tests those as well as a few other device-specific files available on the local operating system.

Listing 6.28: **pathlib_types.py**

```
import itertools
import os
import pathlib
```

```
root = pathlib.Path('test_files')

# Clean up from previous runs.
if root.exists():
    for f in root.iterdir():
        f.unlink()
else:
    root.mkdir()

# Create test files.
(root / 'file').write_text(
    'This is a regular file', encoding='utf-8')
(root / 'symlink').symlink_to('file')
os.mkfifo(str(root / 'fifo'))

# Check the file types.
to_scan = itertools.chain(
    root.iterdir(),
    [pathlib.Path('/dev/disk0'),
     pathlib.Path('/dev/console')],
)
hfmt = '{:18s}' + ('  {:>5}' * 6)
print(hfmt.format('Name', 'File', 'Dir', 'Link', 'FIFO', 'Block',
                  'Character'))
print()

fmt = '{:20s}  ' + ('{!r:>5}  ' * 6)
for f in to_scan:
    print(fmt.format(
        str(f),
        f.is_file(),
        f.is_dir(),
        f.is_symlink(),
        f.is_fifo(),
        f.is_block_device(),
        f.is_char_device(),
    ))
```

Each of the methods—is_dir(), is_file(), is_symlink(), is_socket(), is_fifo(), is_block_device(), and is_char_device()—takes no arguments.

```
$ python3 pathlib_types.py

Name                    File    Dir    Link    FIFO   Block  Character

test_files/fifo         False  False  False    True  False  False
test_files/file          True  False  False   False  False  False
test_files/symlink       True  False   True   False  False  False
```

```
/dev/disk0          False  False  False  False   True  False
/dev/console        False  False  False  False  False   True
```

6.2.9   File Properties

Detailed information about a file can be accessed using the methods `stat()` and `lstat()` (for checking the status of something that might be a symbolic link). These methods produce the same results as `os.stat()` and `os.lstat()`, respectively.

Listing 6.29: `pathlib_stat.py`

```python
import pathlib
import sys
import time

if len(sys.argv) == 1:
    filename = __file__
else:
    filename = sys.argv[1]

p = pathlib.Path(filename)
stat_info = p.stat()

print('{}:'.format(filename))
print('  Size:', stat_info.st_size)
print('  Permissions:', oct(stat_info.st_mode))
print('  Owner:', stat_info.st_uid)
print('  Device:', stat_info.st_dev)
print('  Created       :', time.ctime(stat_info.st_ctime))
print('  Last modified:', time.ctime(stat_info.st_mtime))
print('  Last accessed:', time.ctime(stat_info.st_atime))
```

The output will vary depending on how the example code was installed. Try passing different filenames on the command line to `pathlib_stat.py`.

```
$ python3 pathlib_stat.py

pathlib_stat.py:
  Size: 607
  Permissions: 0o100644
  Owner: 527
  Device: 16777218
  Created       : Thu Dec 29 12:25:25 2016
  Last modified: Thu Dec 29 12:25:25 2016
  Last accessed: Thu Dec 29 12:25:34 2016

$ python3 pathlib_stat.py index.rst
```

```
index.rst:
  Size: 19363
  Permissions: 0o100644
  Owner: 527
  Device: 16777218
  Created       : Thu Dec 29 11:27:58 2016
  Last modified: Thu Dec 29 11:27:58 2016
  Last accessed: Thu Dec 29 12:25:33 2016
```

For simpler access to information about the owner of a file, use owner() and group().

Listing 6.30: pathlib_ownership.py

```
import pathlib

p = pathlib.Path(__file__)

print('{} is owned by {}/{}'.format(p, p.owner(), p.group()))
```

While stat() returns numerical system ID values, these methods look up the name associated with the IDs.

```
$ python3 pathlib_ownership.py

pathlib_ownership.py is owned by dhellmann/dhellmann
```

The touch() method works like the Unix command touch to create a file or update an existing file's modification time and permissions.

Listing 6.31: pathlib_touch.py

```
import pathlib
import time

p = pathlib.Path('touched')
if p.exists():
    print('already exists')
else:
    print('creating new')

p.touch()
start = p.stat()

time.sleep(1)

p.touch()
end = p.stat()

print('Start:', time.ctime(start.st_mtime))
print('End  :', time.ctime(end.st_mtime))
```

Running this example more than once updates the existing file on subsequent runs.

```
$ python3 pathlib_touch.py

creating new
Start: Thu Dec 29 12:25:34 2016
End  : Thu Dec 29 12:25:35 2016

$ python3 pathlib_touch.py

already exists
Start: Thu Dec 29 12:25:35 2016
End  : Thu Dec 29 12:25:36 2016
```

6.2.10 Permissions

On Unix-like systems, file permissions can be changed using chmod(), passing the mode as
an integer. Mode values can be constructed using constants defined in the stat module.
This example toggles the user's execute permission bit.

Listing 6.32: **pathlib_chmod.py**

```
import os
import pathlib
import stat

# Create a fresh test file.
f = pathlib.Path('pathlib_chmod_example.txt')
if f.exists():
    f.unlink()
f.write_text('contents')

# Determine which permissions are already set using stat.
existing_permissions = stat.S_IMODE(f.stat().st_mode)
print('Before: {:o}'.format(existing_permissions))

# Decide which way to toggle them.
if not (existing_permissions & os.X_OK):
    print('Adding execute permission')
    new_permissions = existing_permissions | stat.S_IXUSR
else:
    print('Removing execute permission')
    # Use xor to remove the user execute permission.
    new_permissions = existing_permissions ^ stat.S_IXUSR

# Make the change and show the new value.
f.chmod(new_permissions)
after_permissions = stat.S_IMODE(f.stat().st_mode)
print('After: {:o}'.format(after_permissions))
```

The script assumes it has the permissions necessary to modify the mode of the file when run.

```
$ python3 pathlib_chmod.py

Before: 644
Adding execute permission
After: 744
```

6.2.11 Deleting

Two methods are available for removing things from the file system, depending on the type. To remove an empty directory, use `rmdir()`.

Listing 6.33: **pathlib_rmdir.py**

```
import pathlib

p = pathlib.Path('example_dir')

print('Removing {}'.format(p))
p.rmdir()
```

A `FileNotFoundError` exception is raised if the post-conditions are already met and the directory does not exist. An error also occurs in case of an attempt to remove a directory that is not empty.

```
$ python3 pathlib_rmdir.py

Removing example_dir

$ python3 pathlib_rmdir.py

Removing example_dir
Traceback (most recent call last):
  File "pathlib_rmdir.py", line 16, in <module>
    p.rmdir()
  File ".../lib/python3.5/pathlib.py", line 1262, in rmdir
    self._accessor.rmdir(self)
  File ".../lib/python3.5/pathlib.py", line 371, in wrapped
    return strfunc(str(pathobj), *args)
FileNotFoundError: [Errno 2] No such file or directory:
'example_dir'
```

For files, symbolic links, and most other path types, use `unlink()`.

Listing 6.34: **pathlib_unlink.py**

```
import pathlib

p = pathlib.Path('touched')

p.touch()

print('exists before removing:', p.exists())

p.unlink()

print('exists after removing:', p.exists())
```

The user must have permission to remove the file, symbolic link, socket, or other file system object.

```
$ python3 pathlib_unlink.py

exists before removing: True
exists after removing: False
```

TIP

Related Reading

- Standard library documentation for `pathlib`.[3]
- `os.path` (page 296): Platform-independent manipulation of filenames.
- Managing File System Permissions (page 1230): Discussion of `os.stat()` and `os.lstat()`.
- `glob` (page 319): Unix shell pattern matching for filenames.
- **PEP 428**[4]: The `pathlib` module.

6.3 glob: Filename Pattern Matching

Even though the `glob` API is small, this module packs a lot of power. It is useful in any situation where a program needs to look for a list of files on the file system with names matching a pattern. To create a list of filenames that all have a certain extension, prefix, or string in the middle, use `glob` instead of writing custom code to scan the directory contents.

The pattern rules for `glob` are not the same as the rules for the regular expressions used by the `re` (page 13) module. Instead, they follow standard Unix path expansion rules. Only

---

[3] https://docs.python.org/3.5/library/pathlib.html
[4] www.python.org/dev/peps/pep-0428

a few special characters are used to implement two different wildcards and character ranges. The pattern rules are applied to segments of the filename (stopping at the path separator, /). Paths in the pattern can be relative or absolute. Shell variable names and tildes (~) are not expanded.

6.3.1   Example Data

The examples in this section assume the following test files are present in the current working directory.

```
$ python3 glob_maketestdata.py

dir
dir/file.txt
dir/file1.txt
dir/file2.txt
dir/filea.txt
dir/fileb.txt
dir/file?.txt
dir/file*.txt
dir/file[.txt
dir/subdir
dir/subdir/subfile.txt
```

If these files do not exist, use `glob_maketestdata.py` in the sample code to create them before running the following examples.

6.3.2   Wildcards

An asterisk (*) matches zero or more characters in a segment of a name—for example, `dir/*`.

Listing 6.35: glob_asterisk.py

```
import glob
for name in sorted(glob.glob('dir/*')):
    print(name)
```

This pattern matches every path name (file or directory) in the directory dir, without recursing further into subdirectories. The data returned by `glob()` is not sorted, so the examples here sort it to facilitate studying the results.

```
$ python3 glob_asterisk.py

dir/file*.txt
dir/file.txt
dir/file1.txt
dir/file2.txt
dir/file?.txt
```

```
dir/file[.txt
dir/filea.txt
dir/fileb.txt
dir/subdir
```

To list files in a subdirectory, the subdirectory must be included in the pattern.

Listing 6.36: glob_subdir.py

```python
import glob

print('Named explicitly:')
for name in sorted(glob.glob('dir/subdir/*')):
    print('  {}'.format(name))

print('Named with wildcard:')
for name in sorted(glob.glob('dir/*/*')):
    print('  {}'.format(name))
```

The first case shown earlier lists the subdirectory name explicitly, while the second case depends on a wildcard to find the directory.

```
$ python3 glob_subdir.py

Named explicitly:
  dir/subdir/subfile.txt
Named with wildcard:
  dir/subdir/subfile.txt
```

The results, in this case, are the same. If there was another subdirectory, the wildcard would match both subdirectories and the filenames from both would appear in the results.

6.3.3 Single-Character Wildcard

A question mark (?) is another wildcard character. It matches any single character in that position in the name.

Listing 6.37: glob_question.py

```python
import glob

for name in sorted(glob.glob('dir/file?.txt')):
    print(name)
```

This example matches all filenames that begin with file, have one more character of any type, and end with .txt.

```
$ python3 glob_question.py

dir/file*.txt
```

```
dir/file1.txt
dir/file2.txt
dir/file?.txt
dir/file[.txt
dir/filea.txt
dir/fileb.txt
```

6.3.4   Character Ranges

Use a character range ([a-z]) instead of a question mark to match one of several characters. The following example finds all files with a digit in the name before the extension.

Listing 6.38: **glob_charrange.py**

```
import glob
for name in sorted(glob.glob('dir/*[0-9].*')):
    print(name)
```

The character range [0-9] matches any single digit. The range is ordered based on the character code for each letter/digit, and the dash indicates an unbroken range of sequential characters. The same range value could be written [0123456789].

```
$ python3 glob_charrange.py

dir/file1.txt
dir/file2.txt
```

6.3.5   Escaping Meta-characters

Sometimes it is necessary to search for files with names containing the special meta-characters glob uses for its patterns. The escape() function builds a suitable pattern in which the special characters are "escaped" so they are not expanded or interpreted as special by glob.

Listing 6.39: **glob_escape.py**

```
import glob

specials = '?*['

for char in specials:
    pattern = 'dir/*' + glob.escape(char) + '.txt'
    print('Searching for: {!r}'.format(pattern))
    for name in sorted(glob.glob(pattern)):
        print(name)
    print()
```

Each special character is escaped by building a character range containing a single entry.

```
$ python3 glob_escape.py

Searching for: 'dir/*[?].txt'
dir/file?.txt

Searching for: 'dir/*[*].txt'
dir/file*.txt

Searching for: 'dir/*[[].txt'
dir/file[.txt
```

TIP

Related Reading

- Standard library documentation for glob.[5]
- Pattern Matching Notation[6]: An explanation of globbing from The Open Group's Shell Command Language specification.
- fnmatch (page 323): Filename matching implementation.
- Python 2 to 3 porting notes for glob (page 1359).

6.4 fnmatch: Unix-Style Glob Pattern Matching

The fnmatch module is used to compare filenames against glob-style patterns such as those used by Unix shells.

6.4.1 Simple Matching

fnmatch() compares a single filename against a pattern and returns a boolean value, indicating whether they match. The comparison is case-sensitive when the operating system uses a case-sensitive file system.

Listing 6.40: fnmatch_fnmatch.py

```
import fnmatch
import os

pattern = 'fnmatch_*.py'
print('Pattern :', pattern)
print()
```

---

[5] https://docs.python.org/3.5/library/glob.html
[6] www.opengroup.org/onlinepubs/000095399/utilities/xcu_chap02.html#tag_02_13

```
files = os.listdir('.')
for name in files:
    print('Filename: {:<25} {}'.format(
        name, fnmatch.fnmatch(name, pattern)))
```

In this example, the pattern matches all files starting with 'fnmatch_' and ending in '.py'.

```
$ python3 fnmatch_fnmatch.py

Pattern : fnmatch_*.py

Filename: fnmatch_filter.py         True
Filename: fnmatch_fnmatch.py        True
Filename: fnmatch_fnmatchcase.py    True
Filename: fnmatch_translate.py      True
Filename: index.rst                 False
```

To force a case-sensitive comparison, regardless of the file system and operating system settings, use fnmatchcase().

Listing 6.41: **fnmatch_fnmatchcase.py**

```
import fnmatch
import os

pattern = 'FNMATCH_*.PY'
print('Pattern :', pattern)
print()

files = os.listdir('.')

for name in files:
    print('Filename: {:<25} {}'.format(
        name, fnmatch.fnmatchcase(name, pattern)))
```

Since the OS X system used to test this program uses a case-sensitive file system, no files match the modified pattern.

```
$ python3 fnmatch_fnmatchcase.py

Pattern : FNMATCH_*.PY

Filename: fnmatch_filter.py         False
Filename: fnmatch_fnmatch.py        False
Filename: fnmatch_fnmatchcase.py    False
Filename: fnmatch_translate.py      False
Filename: index.rst                 False
```

6.4.2 Filtering

To test a sequence of filenames, use `filter()`, which returns a list of the names that match the pattern argument.

Listing 6.42: `fnmatch_filter.py`

```
import fnmatch
import os
import pprint

pattern = 'fnmatch_*.py'
print('Pattern :', pattern)

files = os.listdir('.')

print('\nFiles   :')
pprint.pprint(files)

print('\nMatches :')
pprint.pprint(fnmatch.filter(files, pattern))
```

In this example, `filter()` returns the list of names of the example source files associated with this section.

```
$ python3 fnmatch_filter.py

Pattern : fnmatch_*.py

Files   :
['fnmatch_filter.py',
 'fnmatch_fnmatch.py',
 'fnmatch_fnmatchcase.py',
 'fnmatch_translate.py',
 'index.rst']

Matches :
['fnmatch_filter.py',
 'fnmatch_fnmatch.py',
 'fnmatch_fnmatchcase.py',
 'fnmatch_translate.py']
```

6.4.3 Translating Patterns

Internally, `fnmatch` converts the `glob` pattern to a regular expression and uses the `re` (page 13) module to compare the name and pattern. The `translate()` function is the public API for converting `glob` patterns to regular expressions.

Listing 6.43: `fnmatch_translate.py`

```
import fnmatch

pattern = 'fnmatch_*.py'
print('Pattern :', pattern)
print('Regex   :', fnmatch.translate(pattern))
```

Some of the characters are escaped to make a valid expression.

```
$ python3 fnmatch_translate.py

Pattern : fnmatch_*.py
Regex   : fnmatch_.*\.py\Z(?ms)
```

TIP

Related Reading

- Standard library documentation for `fnmatch`.[7]
- `glob` (page 319): The `glob` module combines `fnmatch` matching with `os.listdir()` to produce lists of files and directories matching patterns.
- `re` (page 13): Regular expression pattern matching.

6.5   linecache: Read Text Files Efficiently

The `linecache` module is used within other parts of the Python standard library when dealing with Python source files. The implementation of the cache holds the contents of files, parsed into separate lines, in memory. The API returns the requested line(s) by indexing into a `list`, and saves time over repeatedly reading the file and parsing lines to find the one desired. This module is especially useful when looking for multiple lines from the same file, such as when producing a traceback for an error report.

6.5.1   Test Data

The following text, which was produced by a Lorem Ipsum generator, is used as sample input.

Listing 6.44: `linecache_data.py`

```
import os
import tempfile
```

---

[7] https://docs.python.org/3.5/library/fnmatch.html

```
lorem = '''Lorem ipsum dolor sit amet, consectetuer
adipiscing elit.  Vivamus eget elit. In posuere mi non
risus. Mauris id quam posuere lectus sollicitudin
varius. Praesent at mi. Nunc eu velit. Sed augue massa,
fermentum id, nonummy a, nonummy sit amet, ligula. Curabitur
eros pede, egestas at, ultricies ac, apellentesque eu,
tellus.

Sed sed odio sed mi luctus mollis. Integer et nulla ac augue
convallis accumsan. Ut felis. Donec lectus sapien, elementum
nec, condimentum ac, interdum non, tellus. Aenean viverra,
mauris vehicula semper porttitor, ipsum odio consectetuer
lorem, ac imperdiet eros odio a sapien. Nulla mauris tellus,
aliquam non, egestas a, nonummy et, erat. Vivamus sagittis
porttitor eros.'''


def make_tempfile():
    fd, temp_file_name = tempfile.mkstemp()
    os.close(fd)
    with open(temp_file_name, 'wt') as f:
        f.write(lorem)
    return temp_file_name


def cleanup(filename):
    os.unlink(filename)
```

6.5.2   Reading Specific Lines

The line numbers of files read by the linecache module start with 1, but normally lists
start indexing the array from 0.

Listing 6.45: `linecache_getline.py`

```
import linecache
from linecache_data import *

filename = make_tempfile()

# Pick out the same line from source and cache.
# (Notice that linecache counts from 1.)
print('SOURCE:')
print('{!r}'.format(lorem.split('\n')[4]))
print()
print('CACHE:')
print('{!r}'.format(linecache.getline(filename, 5)))

cleanup(filename)
```

Each line returned includes a trailing newline.

```
$ python3 linecache_getline.py

SOURCE:
'fermentum id, nonummy a, nonummy sit amet, ligula. Curabitur'

CACHE:
'fermentum id, nonummy a, nonummy sit amet, ligula. Curabitur\n'
```

6.5.3   Handling Blank Lines

The return value always includes the newline at the end of the line. Thus, if the line is empty, the return value is just the newline.

Listing 6.46: <code>linecache_empty_line.py</code>

```
import linecache
from linecache_data import *

filename = make_tempfile()

# Blank lines include the newline.
print('BLANK : {!r}'.format(linecache.getline(filename, 8)))

cleanup(filename)
```

Line 8 of the input file contains no text.

```
$ python3 linecache_empty_line.py

BLANK : '\n'
```

6.5.4   Error Handling

If the requested line number falls out of the range of valid lines in the file, `getline()` returns an empty string.

Listing 6.47: <code>linecache_out_of_range.py</code>

```
import linecache
from linecache_data import *

filename = make_tempfile()

# The cache always returns a string, and uses
# an empty string to indicate a line that does
```

```
# not exist.
not_there = linecache.getline(filename, 500)
print('NOT THERE: {!r} includes {} characters'.format(
    not_there, len(not_there)))

cleanup(filename)
```

The input file has only 15 lines, so requesting line 500 is like trying to read past the end of the file.

```
$ python3 linecache_out_of_range.py

NOT THERE: '' includes 0 characters
```

Reading from a file that does not exist is handled in the same way.

Listing 6.48: **linecache_missing_file.py**

```
import linecache

# Errors are even hidden if linecache cannot find the file.
no_such_file = linecache.getline(
    'this_file_does_not_exist.txt', 1,
)
print('NO FILE: {!r}'.format(no_such_file))
```

The module never raises an exception when the caller tries to read data.

```
$ python3 linecache_missing_file.py

NO FILE: ''
```

6.5.5   Reading Python Source Files

Since linecache is used so heavily when producing tracebacks, one of its key features is the ability to find Python source modules in the import path by specifying the base name of the module.

Listing 6.49: **linecache_path_search.py**

```
import linecache
import os

# Look for the linecache module using
# the built-in sys.path search.
module_line = linecache.getline('linecache.py', 3)
print('MODULE:')
print(repr(module_line))
```

```
# Look at the linecache module source directly.
file_src = linecache.__file__
if file_src.endswith('.pyc'):
    file_src = file_src[:-1]
print('\nFILE:')
with open(file_src, 'r') as f:
    file_line = f.readlines()[2]
print(repr(file_line))
```

The cache population code in `linecache` searches `sys.path` for the named module if it cannot find a file with that name in the current directory. This example looks for `linecache.py`. Since there is no copy in the current directory, the file from the standard library is found instead.

```
$ python3 linecache_path_search.py

MODULE:
'This is intended to read lines from modules imported -- hence
if a filename\n'

FILE:
'This is intended to read lines from modules imported -- hence
if a filename\n'
```

TIP

Related Reading

- Standard library documentation for `linecache`.[8]

6.6   tempfile: Temporary File System Objects

Creating temporary files with unique names securely, so they cannot be guessed by someone wanting to break the application or steal the data, is challenging. The `tempfile` module provides several functions for creating temporary file system resources securely. `TemporaryFile()` opens and returns an unnamed file, `NamedTemporaryFile()` opens and returns a named file, `SpooledTemporaryFile` holds its contents in memory before writing to disk, and `TemporaryDirectory` is a context manager that removes the directory when the context is closed.

---

[8] https://docs.python.org/3.5/library/linecache.html

6.6.1 Temporary Files

Applications that need temporary files to store data, without needing to share that file with other programs, should use the TemporaryFile() function to create the files. This function creates a file, and on platforms where it is possible, unlinks the new file immediately. As a consequence, another program cannot find or open the file, since there is no reference to it in the file system table. The file created by TemporaryFile() is removed automatically when it is closed, whether by calling close() or by using the context manager API and with statement.

Listing 6.50: tempfile_TemporaryFile.py

```
import os
import tempfile

print('Building a filename with PID:')
filename = '/tmp/guess_my_name.{}.txt'.format(os.getpid())
with open(filename, 'w+b') as temp:
    print('temp:')
    print('  {!r}'.format(temp))
    print('temp.name:')
    print('  {!r}'.format(temp.name))

# Clean up the temporary file yourself.
os.remove(filename)

print()
print('TemporaryFile:')
with tempfile.TemporaryFile() as temp:
    print('temp:')
    print('  {!r}'.format(temp))
    print('temp.name:')
    print('  {!r}'.format(temp.name))

# Automatically cleans up the file
```

This example illustrates the difference in creating a temporary file using a common pattern for making up a name versus using the TemporaryFile() function. The file returned by TemporaryFile() has no name.

```
$ python3 tempfile_TemporaryFile.py

Building a filename with PID:
temp:
  <_io.BufferedRandom name='/tmp/guess_my_name.12151.txt'>
temp.name:
  '/tmp/guess_my_name.12151.txt'
```

```
TemporaryFile:
temp:
  <_io.BufferedRandom name=4>
temp.name:
  4
```

By default, the file handle is created with mode `'w+b'` so that it behaves consistently on all platforms, and so that the caller can write to it and read from it.

Listing 6.51: `tempfile_TemporaryFile_binary.py`

```
import os
import tempfile

with tempfile.TemporaryFile() as temp:
    temp.write(b'Some data')

    temp.seek(0)
    print(temp.read())
```

After writing, the file handle must be "rewound" using `seek()` to read the data back from it.

```
$ python3 tempfile_TemporaryFile_binary.py

b'Some data'
```

To open the file in text mode, set `mode` to `'w+t'` when the file is created.

Listing 6.52: `tempfile_TemporaryFile_text.py`

```
import tempfile

with tempfile.TemporaryFile(mode='w+t') as f:
    f.writelines(['first\n', 'second\n'])

    f.seek(0)
    for line in f:
        print(line.rstrip())
```

The file handle treats the data as text.

```
$ python3 tempfile_TemporaryFile_text.py

first
second
```

6.6.2 Named Files

In some situations, having a named temporary file is important. For applications spanning multiple processes, or even hosts, naming the file is the simplest way to pass it between parts of the application. The `NamedTemporaryFile()` function creates a file without unlinking it, so it retains its name (accessed with the `name` attribute).

Listing 6.53: tempfile_NamedTemporaryFile.py

```
import os
import pathlib
import tempfile

with tempfile.NamedTemporaryFile() as temp:
    print('temp:')
    print('  {!r}'.format(temp))
    print('temp.name:')
    print('  {!r}'.format(temp.name))

    f = pathlib.Path(temp.name)

print('Exists after close:', f.exists())
```

The file is removed after the handle is closed.

```
$ python3 tempfile_NamedTemporaryFile.py

temp:
  <tempfile._TemporaryFileWrapper object at 0x1011b2d30>
temp.name:
  '/var/folders/5q/8gk0wq888xlggz008k8dr7180000hg/T/tmps4qh5zde'
Exists after close: False
```

6.6.3 Spooled Files

For temporary files containing relatively small amounts of data, it is likely to be more efficient to use a `SpooledTemporaryFile` because it holds the file contents in memory using an `io.BytesIO` or `io.StringIO` buffer until the data reaches a threshold size. When the amount of data passes the threshold, it is "rolled over" and written to disk, and then the buffer is replaced with a normal `TemporaryFile()`.

Listing 6.54: tempfile_SpooledTemporaryFile.py

```
import tempfile

with tempfile.SpooledTemporaryFile(max_size=100,
                                   mode='w+t',
                                   encoding='utf-8') as temp:
```

```
    print('temp: {!r}'.format(temp))

    for i in range(3):
        temp.write('This line is repeated over and over.\n')
        print(temp._rolled, temp._file)
```

This example uses private attributes of the `SpooledTemporaryFile` to determine when the rollover to disk has happened. It is rarely necessary to check this status except when tuning the buffer size.

```
$ python3 tempfile_SpooledTemporaryFile.py

temp: <tempfile.SpooledTemporaryFile object at 0x1007b2c88>
False <_io.StringIO object at 0x1007a3d38>
False <_io.StringIO object at 0x1007a3d38>
True <_io.TextIOWrapper name=4 mode='w+t' encoding='utf-8'>
```

To explicitly cause the buffer to be written to disk, call the `rollover()` or `fileno()` method.

Listing 6.55: **tempfile_SpooledTemporaryFile_explicit.py**

```
import tempfile

with tempfile.SpooledTemporaryFile(max_size=1000,
                                   mode='w+t',
                                   encoding='utf-8') as temp:
    print('temp: {!r}'.format(temp))

    for i in range(3):
        temp.write('This line is repeated over and over.\n')
        print(temp._rolled, temp._file)
    print('rolling over')
    temp.rollover()
    print(temp._rolled, temp._file)
```

In this example, because the buffer size is so much larger than the amount of data, no file would be created on disk unless `rollover()` is called.

```
$ python3 tempfile_SpooledTemporaryFile_explicit.py

temp: <tempfile.SpooledTemporaryFile object at 0x1007b2c88>
False <_io.StringIO object at 0x1007a3d38>
False <_io.StringIO object at 0x1007a3d38>
False <_io.StringIO object at 0x1007a3d38>
rolling over
True <_io.TextIOWrapper name=4 mode='w+t' encoding='utf-8'>
```

6.6.4 Temporary Directories

When several temporary files are needed, it may be more convenient to create a single temporary directory with `TemporaryDirectory` and open all of the files in that directory.

Listing 6.56: tempfile_TemporaryDirectory.py

```python
import pathlib
import tempfile

with tempfile.TemporaryDirectory() as directory_name:
    the_dir = pathlib.Path(directory_name)
    print(the_dir)
    a_file = the_dir / 'a_file.txt'
    a_file.write_text('This file is deleted.')

print('Directory exists after?', the_dir.exists())
print('Contents after:', list(the_dir.glob('*')))
```

The context manager produces the name of the directory, which can then be used within the context block to build other filenames.

```
$ python3 tempfile_TemporaryDirectory.py

/var/folders/5q/8gk0wq888xlggz008k8dr7180000hg/T/tmp_urhiioj
Directory exists after? False
Contents after: []
```

6.6.5 Predicting Names

While less secure than strictly anonymous temporary files, including a predictable portion in the name makes it possible to find the file and examine it for debugging purposes. All of the functions described so far take three arguments to control the filenames to some degree. Names are generated using the following formula:

```
dir + prefix + random + suffix
```

All of the values except `random` can be passed as arguments to the functions for creating temporary files or directories.

Listing 6.57: tempfile_NamedTemporaryFile_args.py

```python
import tempfile

with tempfile.NamedTemporaryFile(suffix='_suffix',
                                 prefix='prefix_',
                                 dir='/tmp') as temp:
    print('temp:')
    print('  ', temp)
```

```
print('temp.name:')
print('  ', temp.name)
```

The `prefix` and `suffix` arguments are combined with a random string of characters to build the filename, and the `dir` argument is taken as is and used as the location of the new file.

```
$ python3 tempfile_NamedTemporaryFile_args.py

temp:
   <tempfile._TemporaryFileWrapper object at 0x1018b2d68>
temp.name:
   /tmp/prefix_q6wd5czl_suffix
```

6.6.6   Temporary File Location

If an explicit destination is not given using the `dir` argument, the path used for the temporary files will vary based on the current platform and settings. The `tempfile` module includes two functions for querying the settings being used at runtime.

Listing 6.58: tempfile_settings.py

```
import tempfile

print('gettempdir():', tempfile.gettempdir())
print('gettempprefix():', tempfile.gettempprefix())
```

`gettempdir()` returns the default directory that will hold all of the temporary files, and `gettempprefix()` returns the string prefix for new file and directory names.

```
$ python3 tempfile_settings.py

gettempdir(): /var/folders/5q/8gk0wq888xlggz008k8dr7180000hg/T
gettempprefix(): tmp
```

The value returned by `gettempdir()` is set based on a straightforward algorithm of looking through a list of locations for the first place where the current process can create a file. The search list has the following order:

1. The environment variable `TMPDIR`.

2. The environment variable `TEMP`.

3. The environment variable `TMP`.

4. A fallback, based on the platform. (Windows uses the first available of `C:\temp`, `C:\tmp`, `\temp`, or `\tmp`. Other platforms use `/tmp`, `/var/tmp`, or `/usr/tmp`.)

5. If no other directory can be found, the current working directory is used.

Listing 6.59: `tempfile_tempdir.py`

```
import tempfile

tempfile.tempdir = '/I/changed/this/path'
print('gettempdir():', tempfile.gettempdir())
```

Programs that need to use a global location for all temporary files without using any of these environment variables should set `tempfile.tempdir` directly by assigning a value to the variable.

```
$ python3 tempfile_tempdir.py

gettempdir(): /I/changed/this/path
```

TIP

Related Reading

- Standard library documentation for `tempfile`.[9]
- random (page 254): Pseudorandom number generators, used to introduce random values into temporary filenames.

6.7 shutil: High-Level File Operations

The `shutil` module includes high-level file operations such as copying and archiving.

6.7.1 Copying Files

`copyfile()` copies the contents of the source to the destination. It raises `IOError` if it does not have permission to write to the destination file.

Listing 6.60: `shutil_copyfile.py`

```
import glob
import shutil

print('BEFORE:', glob.glob('shutil_copyfile.*'))

shutil.copyfile('shutil_copyfile.py', 'shutil_copyfile.py.copy')

print('AFTER:', glob.glob('shutil_copyfile.*'))
```

---

[9] https://docs.python.org/3.5/library/tempfile.html

Because the function opens the input file for reading, regardless of its type, special files (such as Unix device nodes) cannot be copied as new special files with `copyfile()`.

```
$ python3 shutil_copyfile.py

BEFORE: ['shutil_copyfile.py']
AFTER: ['shutil_copyfile.py', 'shutil_copyfile.py.copy']
```

The implementation of `copyfile()` uses the lower-level function `copyfileobj()`. While the arguments to `copyfile()` are filenames, the arguments to `copyfileobj()` are open file handles. The optional third argument is a buffer length to use for reading in blocks.

Listing 6.61: **shutil_copyfileobj.py**

```python
import io
import os
import shutil
import sys


class VerboseStringIO(io.StringIO):

    def read(self, n=-1):
        next = io.StringIO.read(self, n)
        print('read({}) got {} bytes'.format(n, len(next)))
        return next


lorem_ipsum = '''Lorem ipsum dolor sit amet, consectetuer
adipiscing elit.  Vestibulum aliquam mollis dolor. Donec
vulputate nunc ut diam. Ut rutrum mi vel sem. Vestibulum
ante ipsum.'''

print('Default:')
input = VerboseStringIO(lorem_ipsum)
output = io.StringIO()
shutil.copyfileobj(input, output)

print()

print('All at once:')
input = VerboseStringIO(lorem_ipsum)
output = io.StringIO()
shutil.copyfileobj(input, output, -1)

print()

print('Blocks of 256:')
input = VerboseStringIO(lorem_ipsum)
```

```
output = io.StringIO()
shutil.copyfileobj(input, output, 256)
```

The default behavior is to read using large blocks. Use -1 to read all of the input at one time or another positive integer to set a specific block size. This example uses several different block sizes to show the effect.

```
$ python3 shutil_copyfileobj.py

Default:
read(16384) got 166 bytes
read(16384) got 0 bytes

All at once:
read(-1) got 166 bytes
read(-1) got 0 bytes

Blocks of 256:
read(256) got 166 bytes
read(256) got 0 bytes
```

The copy() function interprets the output name in the same way that the Unix command-line tool cp does. If the named destination refers to a directory instead of a file, a new file is created in the directory using the base name of the source.

Listing 6.62: **shutil_copy.py**

```
import glob
import os
import shutil

os.mkdir('example')
print('BEFORE:', glob.glob('example/*'))

shutil.copy('shutil_copy.py', 'example')

print('AFTER :', glob.glob('example/*'))
```

The permissions of the file are copied along with the contents.

```
$ python3 shutil_copy.py

BEFORE: []
AFTER : ['example/shutil_copy.py']
```

copy2() works like copy(), but includes the access and modification times in the metadata copied to the new file.

Listing 6.63: **shutil_copy2.py**

```
import os
import shutil
import time


def show_file_info(filename):
    stat_info = os.stat(filename)
    print('  Mode    :', oct(stat_info.st_mode))
    print('  Created :', time.ctime(stat_info.st_ctime))
    print('  Accessed:', time.ctime(stat_info.st_atime))
    print('  Modified:', time.ctime(stat_info.st_mtime))


os.mkdir('example')
print('SOURCE:')
show_file_info('shutil_copy2.py')

shutil.copy2('shutil_copy2.py', 'example')

print('DEST:')
show_file_info('example/shutil_copy2.py')
```

The new file has all of the same characteristics as the old version.

```
$ python3 shutil_copy2.py

SOURCE:
  Mode    : 0o100644
  Created : Wed Dec 28 19:03:12 2016
  Accessed: Wed Dec 28 19:03:49 2016
  Modified: Wed Dec 28 19:03:12 2016
DEST:
  Mode    : 0o100644
  Created : Wed Dec 28 19:03:49 2016
  Accessed: Wed Dec 28 19:03:49 2016
  Modified: Wed Dec 28 19:03:12 2016
```

6.7.2   Copying File Metadata

By default, when a new file is created under Unix, it receives permissions based on the umask of the current user. To copy the permissions from one file to another, use copymode().

Listing 6.64: **shutil_copymode.py**

```
import os
import shutil
import subprocess
```

```
with open('file_to_change.txt', 'wt') as f:
    f.write('content')
os.chmod('file_to_change.txt', 0o444)

print('BEFORE:', oct(os.stat('file_to_change.txt').st_mode))

shutil.copymode('shutil_copymode.py', 'file_to_change.txt')

print('AFTER :', oct(os.stat('file_to_change.txt').st_mode))
```

This example script creates a file to be modified, then uses `copymode()` to duplicate the permissions of the script to the example file.

```
$ python3 shutil_copymode.py

BEFORE: 0o100444
AFTER : 0o100644
```

To copy other metadata for the file, use `copystat()`.

Listing 6.65: shutil_copystat.py

```
import os
import shutil
import time


def show_file_info(filename):
    stat_info = os.stat(filename)
    print('  Mode    :', oct(stat_info.st_mode))
    print('  Created :', time.ctime(stat_info.st_ctime))
    print('  Accessed:', time.ctime(stat_info.st_atime))
    print('  Modified:', time.ctime(stat_info.st_mtime))


with open('file_to_change.txt', 'wt') as f:
    f.write('content')
os.chmod('file_to_change.txt', 0o444)

print('BEFORE:')
show_file_info('file_to_change.txt')

shutil.copystat('shutil_copystat.py', 'file_to_change.txt')

print('AFTER:')
show_file_info('file_to_change.txt')
```

Only the permissions and dates associated with the file are duplicated with `copystat()`.

```
$ python3 shutil_copystat.py

BEFORE:
  Mode    : 0o100444
  Created : Wed Dec 28 19:03:49 2016
  Accessed: Wed Dec 28 19:03:49 2016
  Modified: Wed Dec 28 19:03:49 2016
AFTER:
  Mode    : 0o100644
  Created : Wed Dec 28 19:03:49 2016
  Accessed: Wed Dec 28 19:03:49 2016
  Modified: Wed Dec 28 19:03:46 2016
```

6.7.3   Working with Directory Trees

shutil includes three functions for working with directory trees. To copy a directory from one place to another, use copytree(). This function recurses through the source directory tree, copying files to the destination. The destination directory must not exist in advance.

Listing 6.66: shutil_copytree.py

```python
import glob
import pprint
import shutil

print('BEFORE:')
pprint.pprint(glob.glob('/tmp/example/*'))

shutil.copytree('../shutil', '/tmp/example')

print('\nAFTER:')
pprint.pprint(glob.glob('/tmp/example/*'))
```

The symlinks argument controls whether symbolic links are copied as links or as files. The default is to copy the contents to new files. If the option is true, new symlinks are created within the destination tree.

```
$ python3 shutil_copytree.py

BEFORE:
[]

AFTER:
['/tmp/example/example',
 '/tmp/example/example.out',
 '/tmp/example/file_to_change.txt',
 '/tmp/example/index.rst',
```

```
'/tmp/example/shutil_copy.py',
'/tmp/example/shutil_copy2.py',
'/tmp/example/shutil_copyfile.py',
'/tmp/example/shutil_copyfile.py.copy',
'/tmp/example/shutil_copyfileobj.py',
'/tmp/example/shutil_copymode.py',
'/tmp/example/shutil_copystat.py',
'/tmp/example/shutil_copytree.py',
'/tmp/example/shutil_copytree_verbose.py',
'/tmp/example/shutil_disk_usage.py',
'/tmp/example/shutil_get_archive_formats.py',
'/tmp/example/shutil_get_unpack_formats.py',
'/tmp/example/shutil_make_archive.py',
'/tmp/example/shutil_move.py',
'/tmp/example/shutil_rmtree.py',
'/tmp/example/shutil_unpack_archive.py',
'/tmp/example/shutil_which.py',
'/tmp/example/shutil_which_regular_file.py']
```

copytree() accepts two callable arguments to control its behavior. The ignore argument
is called with the name of each directory or subdirectory being copied, along with a list
of the contents of the directory. The function should return a list of items that should be
copied. The copy_function argument is called to actually copy the file.

Listing 6.67: shutil_copytree_verbose.py

```python
import glob
import pprint
import shutil


def verbose_copy(src, dst):
    print('copying\n {!r}\n to {!r}'.format(src, dst))
    return shutil.copy2(src, dst)


print('BEFORE:')
pprint.pprint(glob.glob('/tmp/example/*'))
print()

shutil.copytree(
    '../shutil', '/tmp/example',
    copy_function=verbose_copy,
    ignore=shutil.ignore_patterns('*.py'),
)

print('\nAFTER:')
pprint.pprint(glob.glob('/tmp/example/*'))
```

In the example, ignore_patterns() is used to create an ignore function to skip copying
Python source files. verbose_copy() first prints the names of files as they are copied; it then
uses copy2(), the default copy function, to make the copies.

```
$ python3 shutil_copytree_verbose.py

BEFORE:
[]

copying
 '../shutil/example.out'
 to '/tmp/example/example.out'
copying
 '../shutil/file_to_change.txt'
 to '/tmp/example/file_to_change.txt'
copying
 '../shutil/index.rst'
 to '/tmp/example/index.rst'

AFTER:
['/tmp/example/example',
 '/tmp/example/example.out',
 '/tmp/example/file_to_change.txt',
 '/tmp/example/index.rst']
```

To remove a directory and its contents, use rmtree().

Listing 6.68: **shutil_rmtree.py**

```
import glob
import pprint
import shutil

print('BEFORE:')
pprint.pprint(glob.glob('/tmp/example/*'))

shutil.rmtree('/tmp/example')

print('\nAFTER:')
pprint.pprint(glob.glob('/tmp/example/*'))
```

Errors are raised as exceptions by default, but can be ignored if the second argument is
true. A special error handler function can be provided in the third argument.

```
$ python3 shutil_rmtree.py

BEFORE:
['/tmp/example/example',
 '/tmp/example/example.out',
```

```
    '/tmp/example/file_to_change.txt',
    '/tmp/example/index.rst']

AFTER:
[]
```

To move a file or directory from one place to another, use move().

Listing 6.69: shutil_move.py

```
import glob
import shutil

with open('example.txt', 'wt') as f:
    f.write('contents')

print('BEFORE: ', glob.glob('example*'))

shutil.move('example.txt', 'example.out')

print('AFTER : ', glob.glob('example*'))
```

The semantics are similar to those of the Unix command mv. If the source and the destination are within the same file system, the source is renamed. Otherwise, the source is copied to the destination and then the source is removed.

```
$ python3 shutil_move.py

BEFORE:  ['example.txt']
AFTER :  ['example.out']
```

6.7.4 Finding Files

The which() function scans a search path looking for a named file. The typical use case is to find an executable program on the shell's search path defined in the environment variable PATH.

Listing 6.70: shutil_which.py

```
import shutil

print(shutil.which('virtualenv'))
print(shutil.which('tox'))
print(shutil.which('no-such-program'))
```

If no file matching the search parameters can be found, which() returns None.

```
$ python3 shutil_which.py

/Users/dhellmann/Library/Python/3.5/bin/virtualenv
/Users/dhellmann/Library/Python/3.5/bin/tox
None
```

which() takes arguments to filter based on the permissions the file has and the search path to examine. The `path` argument defaults to `os.environ('PATH')`, but can be any string containing directory names separated by `os.pathsep`. The `mode` argument should be a bit-mask matching the permissions of the file. By default, the mask looks for executable files, but the following example uses a readable bitmask and an alternative search path to find a configuration file.

Listing 6.71: **shutil_which_regular_file.py**

```
import os
import shutil

path = os.pathsep.join([
    '.',
    os.path.expanduser('~/pymotw'),
])

mode = os.F_OK | os.R_OK

filename = shutil.which(
    'config.ini',
    mode=mode,
    path=path,
)

print(filename)
```

A race condition may still occur when searching for readable files in this way, because in the time between finding the file and actually trying to use it, the file can be deleted or its permissions can be changed.

```
$ touch config.ini
$ python3 shutil_which_regular_file.py

./config.ini
```

6.7.5   Archives

Python's standard library includes many modules for managing archive files, such as `tarfile` (page 503) and `zipfile` (page 511). In addition, several higher-level functions are available for creating and extracting archives in `shutil`. `get_archive_formats()` returns a sequence of names and descriptions for formats supported on the current system.

Listing 6.72: **shutil_get_archive_formats.py**

```
import shutil

for format, description in shutil.get_archive_formats():
    print('{:<5}: {}'.format(format, description))
```

The formats supported depend on which modules and underlying libraries are available. Thus, the output for this example may change based on where it is run.

```
$ python3 shutil_get_archive_formats.py

bztar: bzip2'ed tar-file
gztar: gzip'ed tar-file
tar  : uncompressed tar file
xztar: xz'ed tar-file
zip  : ZIP file
```

Use `make_archive()` to create a new archive file. Its inputs are designed to best support archiving an entire directory and all of its contents, recursively. By default, it uses the current working directory, so that all of the files and subdirectories appear at the top level of the archive. To change that behavior, use the `root_dir` argument to move to a new relative position on the file system and the `base_dir` argument to specify a directory to add to the archive.

Listing 6.73: **shutil_make_archive.py**

```
import logging
import shutil
import sys
import tarfile

logging.basicConfig(
    format='%(message)s',
    stream=sys.stdout,
    level=logging.DEBUG,
)
logger = logging.getLogger('pymotw')

print('Creating archive:')
shutil.make_archive(
    'example', 'gztar',
    root_dir='..',
    base_dir='shutil',
    logger=logger,
)
```

```
    print('\nArchive contents:')
    with tarfile.open('example.tar.gz', 'r') as t:
        for n in t.getnames():
            print(n)
```

This example starts within the source directory for the examples for shutil and moves up one level in the file system; it then adds the shutil directory to a tar archive compressed with gzip. The logging (page 980) module is configured to show messages from make_archive() about what it is doing.

```
$ python3 shutil_make_archive.py

Creating archive:
changing into '..'
Creating tar archive
changing back to '...'

Archive contents:
shutil
shutil/config.ini
shutil/example.out
shutil/file_to_change.txt
shutil/index.rst
shutil/shutil_copy.py
shutil/shutil_copy2.py
shutil/shutil_copyfile.py
shutil/shutil_copyfileobj.py
shutil/shutil_copymode.py
shutil/shutil_copystat.py
shutil/shutil_copytree.py
shutil/shutil_copytree_verbose.py
shutil/shutil_disk_usage.py
shutil/shutil_get_archive_formats.py
shutil/shutil_get_unpack_formats.py
shutil/shutil_make_archive.py
shutil/shutil_move.py
shutil/shutil_rmtree.py
shutil/shutil_unpack_archive.py
shutil/shutil_which.py
shutil/shutil_which_regular_file.py
```

shutil maintains a registry of formats that can be unpacked on the current system; this registry is accessible via get_unpack_formats().

Listing 6.74: shutil_get_unpack_formats.py

```
import shutil

for format, exts, description in shutil.get_unpack_formats():
```

```
print('{:<5}: {}, names ending in {}'.format(
    format, description, exts))
```

The shutil-managed registry is different from the registry for creating archives because it also includes common file extensions used for each format. The function for extracting an archive uses the registry to guess which format it should use based on the file extension.

```
$ python3 shutil_get_unpack_formats.py

bztar: bzip2'ed tar-file, names ending in ['.tar.bz2', '.tbz2']
gztar: gzip'ed tar-file, names ending in ['.tar.gz', '.tgz']
tar  : uncompressed tar file, names ending in ['.tar']
xztar: xz'ed tar-file, names ending in ['.tar.xz', '.txz']
zip  : ZIP file, names ending in ['.zip']
```

Extract the archive with unpack_archive(), passing the archive filename and optionally the directory where it should be extracted. If no directory is given, the current directory is used.

Listing 6.75: **shutil_unpack_archive.py**

```python
import pathlib
import shutil
import sys
import tempfile

with tempfile.TemporaryDirectory() as d:
    print('Unpacking archive:')
    shutil.unpack_archive(
        'example.tar.gz',
        extract_dir=d,
    )

    print('\nCreated:')
    prefix_len = len(d) + 1
    for extracted in pathlib.Path(d).rglob('*'):
        print(str(extracted)[prefix_len:])
```

In this example, unpack_archive() is able to determine the format of the archive because the filename ends with tar.gz, and that value is associated with the gztar format in the unpack format registry.

```
$ python3 shutil_unpack_archive.py

Unpacking archive:

Created:
shutil
```

```
shutil/config.ini
shutil/example.out
shutil/file_to_change.txt
shutil/index.rst
shutil/shutil_copy.py
shutil/shutil_copy2.py
shutil/shutil_copyfile.py
shutil/shutil_copyfileobj.py
shutil/shutil_copymode.py
shutil/shutil_copystat.py
shutil/shutil_copytree.py
shutil/shutil_copytree_verbose.py
shutil/shutil_disk_usage.py
shutil/shutil_get_archive_formats.py
shutil/shutil_get_unpack_formats.py
shutil/shutil_make_archive.py
shutil/shutil_move.py
shutil/shutil_rmtree.py
shutil/shutil_unpack_archive.py
shutil/shutil_which.py
shutil/shutil_which_regular_file.py
```

6.7.6   File System Space

It can be useful to examine the local file system to see how much space is available before performing a long-running operation that may exhaust that space. disk_usage() returns a tuple consisting of the total space, the amount currently being used, and the amount remaining unused (free space).

Listing 6.76: **shutil_disk_usage.py**

```
import shutil

total_b, used_b, free_b = shutil.disk_usage('.')

gib = 2 ** 30   # GiB == gibibyte
gb = 10 ** 9    # GB == gigabyte

print('Total: {:6.2f} GB  {:6.2f} GiB'.format(
    total_b / gb, total_b / gib))
print('Used : {:6.2f} GB  {:6.2f} GiB'.format(
    used_b / gb, used_b / gib))
print('Free : {:6.2f} GB  {:6.2f} GiB'.format(
    free_b / gb, free_b / gib))
```

The values returned by disk_usage() are given in bytes, so the example program converts them to more readable units before printing them.

```
$ python3 shutil_disk_usage.py

Total: 499.42 GB   465.12 GiB
Used : 246.68 GB   229.73 GiB
Free : 252.48 GB   235.14 GiB
```

TIP
Related Reading

- Standard library documentation for `shutil`.[10]
- Chapter 8, "Data Compression and Archiving" (page 477): Modules for dealing with archive and compression formats.

6.8 filecmp: Compare Files

The `filecmp` module includes functions and a class for comparing files and directories on the file system.

6.8.1 Example Data

The examples in this discussion use a set of test files created by `filecmp_mkexamples.py`.

Listing 6.77: **filecmp_mkexamples.py**

```python
import os


def mkfile(filename, body=None):
    with open(filename, 'w') as f:
        f.write(body or filename)
    return


def make_example_dir(top):
    if not os.path.exists(top):
        os.mkdir(top)
    curdir = os.getcwd()
    os.chdir(top)

    os.mkdir('dir1')
    os.mkdir('dir2')
```

---

[10] https://docs.python.org/3.5/library/shutil.html

```
        mkfile('dir1/file_only_in_dir1')
        mkfile('dir2/file_only_in_dir2')

        os.mkdir('dir1/dir_only_in_dir1')
        os.mkdir('dir2/dir_only_in_dir2')

        os.mkdir('dir1/common_dir')
        os.mkdir('dir2/common_dir')

        mkfile('dir1/common_file', 'this file is the same')
        mkfile('dir2/common_file', 'this file is the same')

        mkfile('dir1/not_the_same')
        mkfile('dir2/not_the_same')

        mkfile('dir1/file_in_dir1', 'This is a file in dir1')
        os.mkdir('dir2/file_in_dir1')

        os.chdir(curdir)
        return

if __name__ == '__main__':
    os.chdir(os.path.dirname(__file__) or os.getcwd())
    make_example_dir('example')
    make_example_dir('example/dir1/common_dir')
    make_example_dir('example/dir2/common_dir')
```

Running the script produces a tree of files under the directory example.

```
$ find example

example
example/dir1
example/dir1/common_dir
example/dir1/common_dir/dir1
example/dir1/common_dir/dir1/common_dir
example/dir1/common_dir/dir1/common_file
example/dir1/common_dir/dir1/dir_only_in_dir1
example/dir1/common_dir/dir1/file_in_dir1
example/dir1/common_dir/dir1/file_only_in_dir1
example/dir1/common_dir/dir1/not_the_same
example/dir1/common_dir/dir2
example/dir1/common_dir/dir2/common_dir
example/dir1/common_dir/dir2/common_file
example/dir1/common_dir/dir2/dir_only_in_dir2
example/dir1/common_dir/dir2/file_in_dir1
example/dir1/common_dir/dir2/file_only_in_dir2
example/dir1/common_dir/dir2/not_the_same
example/dir1/common_file
```

```
example/dir1/dir_only_in_dir1
example/dir1/file_in_dir1
example/dir1/file_only_in_dir1
example/dir1/not_the_same
example/dir2
example/dir2/common_dir
example/dir2/common_dir/dir1
example/dir2/common_dir/dir1/common_dir
example/dir2/common_dir/dir1/common_file
example/dir2/common_dir/dir1/dir_only_in_dir1
example/dir2/common_dir/dir1/file_in_dir1
example/dir2/common_dir/dir1/file_only_in_dir1
example/dir2/common_dir/dir1/not_the_same
example/dir2/common_dir/dir2
example/dir2/common_dir/dir2/common_dir
example/dir2/common_dir/dir2/common_file
example/dir2/common_dir/dir2/dir_only_in_dir2
example/dir2/common_dir/dir2/file_in_dir1
example/dir2/common_dir/dir2/file_only_in_dir2
example/dir2/common_dir/dir2/not_the_same
example/dir2/common_file
example/dir2/dir_only_in_dir2
example/dir2/file_in_dir1
example/dir2/file_only_in_dir2
example/dir2/not_the_same
```

The same directory structure is repeated one time under the common_dir directories to give interesting recursive comparison options.

6.8.2 Comparing Files

cmp() compares two files on the file system.

Listing 6.78: **filecmp_cmp.py**

```python
import filecmp

print('common_file :', end=' ')
print(filecmp.cmp('example/dir1/common_file',
                  'example/dir2/common_file'),
      end=' ')
print(filecmp.cmp('example/dir1/common_file',
                  'example/dir2/common_file',
                  shallow=False))

print('not_the_same:', end=' ')
print(filecmp.cmp('example/dir1/not_the_same',
                  'example/dir2/not_the_same'),
      end=' ')
```

```
print(filecmp.cmp('example/dir1/not_the_same',
                  'example/dir2/not_the_same',
                  shallow=False))

print('identical    :', end=' ')
print(filecmp.cmp('example/dir1/file_only_in_dir1',
                  'example/dir1/file_only_in_dir1'),
      end=' ')
print(filecmp.cmp('example/dir1/file_only_in_dir1',
                  'example/dir1/file_only_in_dir1',
                  shallow=False))
```

The `shallow` argument tells `cmp()` whether to look at the contents of the file, in addition to its metadata. The default is to perform a shallow comparison using the information available from `os.stat()`. If the results are the same, the files are considered the same. Thus, files of the same size that were created at the same time are reported as the same, even if their contents differ. When `shallow` is `False`, the contents of the file are always compared.

```
$ python3 filecmp_cmp.py

common_file : True True
not_the_same: True False
identical    : True True
```

To compare a set of files in two directories without recursing, use `cmpfiles()`. The arguments are the names of the directories and a list of files to be checked in the two locations. The list of common files passed in should contain only filenames (directories always result in a mismatch), and the files must be present in both locations. The next example shows a simple way to build the common list. The comparison also takes the `shallow` flag, just as with `cmp()`.

Listing 6.79: filecmp_cmpfiles.py

```
import filecmp
import os

# Determine the items that exist in both directories.
d1_contents = set(os.listdir('example/dir1'))
d2_contents = set(os.listdir('example/dir2'))
common = list(d1_contents & d2_contents)
common_files = [
    f
    for f in common
    if os.path.isfile(os.path.join('example/dir1', f))
]
print('Common files:', common_files)
```

```
# Compare the directories.
match, mismatch, errors = filecmp.cmpfiles(
    'example/dir1',
    'example/dir2',
    common_files,
)
print('Match      :', match)
print('Mismatch   :', mismatch)
print('Errors     :', errors)
```

cmpfiles() returns three lists of filenames containing files that match, files that do not match, and files that could not be compared (due to permission problems or for any other reason).

```
$ python3 filecmp_cmpfiles.py

Common files: ['not_the_same', 'file_in_dir1', 'common_file']
Match       : ['not_the_same', 'common_file']
Mismatch    : ['file_in_dir1']
Errors      : []
```

6.8.3 Comparing Directories

The functions described earlier are suitable for relatively simple comparisons. For recursive comparison of large directory trees or for more complete analysis, the dircmp class is more useful. In its simplest use case, report() prints a report comparing two directories.

Listing 6.80: **filecmp_dircmp_report.py**

```
import filecmp

dc = filecmp.dircmp('example/dir1', 'example/dir2')
dc.report()
```

The output is a plain-text report showing the results of just the contents of the directories given, without recursing. In this case, the file not_the_same is thought to be the same because the contents are not being compared. There is no way to have dircmp compare the contents of files in the same way that cmp() does.

```
$ python3 filecmp_dircmp_report.py

diff example/dir1 example/dir2
Only in example/dir1 : ['dir_only_in_dir1', 'file_only_in_dir1']
Only in example/dir2 : ['dir_only_in_dir2', 'file_only_in_dir2']
Identical files : ['common_file', 'not_the_same']
Common subdirectories : ['common_dir']
Common funny cases : ['file_in_dir1']
```

For more detail, and to make a recursive comparison, use `report_full_closure()`.

Listing 6.81: **`filecmp_dircmp_report_full_closure.py`**

```python
import filecmp

dc = filecmp.dircmp('example/dir1', 'example/dir2')
dc.report_full_closure()
```

The output includes comparisons of all parallel subdirectories.

```
$ python3 filecmp_dircmp_report_full_closure.py

diff example/dir1 example/dir2
Only in example/dir1 : ['dir_only_in_dir1', 'file_only_in_dir1']
Only in example/dir2 : ['dir_only_in_dir2', 'file_only_in_dir2']
Identical files : ['common_file', 'not_the_same']
Common subdirectories : ['common_dir']
Common funny cases : ['file_in_dir1']

diff example/dir1/common_dir example/dir2/common_dir
Common subdirectories : ['dir1', 'dir2']

diff example/dir1/common_dir/dir1 example/dir2/common_dir/dir1
Identical files : ['common_file', 'file_in_dir1',
'file_only_in_dir1', 'not_the_same']
Common subdirectories : ['common_dir', 'dir_only_in_dir1']

diff example/dir1/common_dir/dir1/dir_only_in_dir1
example/dir2/common_dir/dir1/dir_only_in_dir1

diff example/dir1/common_dir/dir1/common_dir
example/dir2/common_dir/dir1/common_dir

diff example/dir1/common_dir/dir2 example/dir2/common_dir/dir2
Identical files : ['common_file', 'file_only_in_dir2',
'not_the_same']
Common subdirectories : ['common_dir', 'dir_only_in_dir2',
'file_in_dir1']

diff example/dir1/common_dir/dir2/common_dir
example/dir2/common_dir/dir2/common_dir

diff example/dir1/common_dir/dir2/file_in_dir1
example/dir2/common_dir/dir2/file_in_dir1

diff example/dir1/common_dir/dir2/dir_only_in_dir2
example/dir2/common_dir/dir2/dir_only_in_dir2
```

6.8.4 Using Differences in a Program

Besides producing printed reports, dircmp calculates lists of files that can be used in programs directly. Each of the following attributes is calculated only when requested, so creating a dircmp instance does not incur overhead for unused data.

Listing 6.82: filecmp_dircmp_list.py

```
import filecmp
import pprint

dc = filecmp.dircmp('example/dir1', 'example/dir2')
print('Left:')
pprint.pprint(dc.left_list)

print('\nRight:')
pprint.pprint(dc.right_list)
```

The files and subdirectories contained in the directories being compared are listed in left_list and right_list.

```
$ python3 filecmp_dircmp_list.py

Left:
['common_dir',
 'common_file',
 'dir_only_in_dir1',
 'file_in_dir1',
 'file_only_in_dir1',
 'not_the_same']

Right:
['common_dir',
 'common_file',
 'dir_only_in_dir2',
 'file_in_dir1',
 'file_only_in_dir2',
 'not_the_same']
```

The inputs can be filtered by passing a list of names to ignore to the constructor. By default, the names RCS, CVS, and tags are ignored.

Listing 6.83: filecmp_dircmp_list_filter.py

```
import filecmp
import pprint

dc = filecmp.dircmp('example/dir1', 'example/dir2',
                    ignore=['common_file'])
```

```
print('Left:')
pprint.pprint(dc.left_list)

print('\nRight:')
pprint.pprint(dc.right_list)
```

In this case, `common_file` is left out of the list of files to be compared.

```
$ python3 filecmp_dircmp_list_filter.py

Left:
['common_dir',
 'dir_only_in_dir1',
 'file_in_dir1',
 'file_only_in_dir1',
 'not_the_same']

Right:
['common_dir',
 'dir_only_in_dir2',
 'file_in_dir1',
 'file_only_in_dir2',
 'not_the_same']
```

The names of files common to both input directories are saved in `common`, and the files unique to each directory are listed in `left_only` and `right_only`.

Listing 6.84: `filecmp_dircmp_membership.py`

```
import filecmp
import pprint

dc = filecmp.dircmp('example/dir1', 'example/dir2')
print('Common:')
pprint.pprint(dc.common)

print('\nLeft:')
pprint.pprint(dc.left_only)

print('\nRight:')
pprint.pprint(dc.right_only)
```

The "left" directory is the first argument to `dircmp()` and the "right" directory is the second.

```
$ python3 filecmp_dircmp_membership.py

Common:
['file_in_dir1', 'common_file', 'common_dir', 'not_the_same']
```

```
Left:
['dir_only_in_dir1', 'file_only_in_dir1']

Right:
['file_only_in_dir2', 'dir_only_in_dir2']
```

The common members can be further broken down into files, directories, and "funny" items (anything that has a different type in the two directories or for which there is an error from os.stat()).

Listing 6.85: filecmp_dircmp_common.py

```python
import filecmp
import pprint

dc = filecmp.dircmp('example/dir1', 'example/dir2')
print('Common:')
pprint.pprint(dc.common)

print('\nDirectories:')
pprint.pprint(dc.common_dirs)

print('\nFiles:')
pprint.pprint(dc.common_files)

print('\nFunny:')
pprint.pprint(dc.common_funny)
```

In the example data, the file_in_dir1 item is a file in one directory and a subdirectory in the other, so it shows up in the "funny" list.

```
$ python3 filecmp_dircmp_common.py

Common:
['file_in_dir1', 'common_file', 'common_dir', 'not_the_same']

Directories:
['common_dir']

Files:
['common_file', 'not_the_same']

Funny:
['file_in_dir1']
```

The differences between files are broken down similarly.

Listing 6.86: **filecmp_dircmp_diff.py**

```
import filecmp

dc = filecmp.dircmp('example/dir1', 'example/dir2')
print('Same       :', dc.same_files)
print('Different :', dc.diff_files)
print('Funny      :', dc.funny_files)
```

The file not_the_same is being compared via os.stat(), and the contents are not examined, so it is included in the same_files list.

```
$ python3 filecmp_dircmp_diff.py

Same       : ['common_file', 'not_the_same']
Different : []
Funny      : []
```

Finally, the subdirectories are saved to allow easy recursive comparison.

Listing 6.87: **filecmp_dircmp_subdirs.py**

```
import filecmp

dc = filecmp.dircmp('example/dir1', 'example/dir2')
print('Subdirectories:')
print(dc.subdirs)
```

The attribute subdirs is a dictionary mapping the directory name to new dircmp objects.

```
$ python3 filecmp_dircmp_subdirs.py

Subdirectories:
{'common_dir': <filecmp.dircmp object at 0x1019b2be0>}
```

TIP

Related Reading

- Standard library documentation for filecmp.[11]
- difflib (page 58): Computing the differences between two sequences.

---

[11] https://docs.python.org/3.5/library/filecmp.html

6.9   mmap: Memory-Map Files

Memory-mapping a file uses the operating system's virtual memory to access the data on the file system directly, instead of accessing the data with the normal I/O functions. Memory-mapping typically improves I/O performance because it does not require either making a separate system call for each access or copying data between buffers; instead, the memory is accessed directly by both the kernel and the user application.

Memory-mapped files can be treated as mutable strings or file-like objects, depending on the need. A mapped file supports the expected file API methods, such as `close()`, `flush()`, `read()`, `readline()`, `seek()`, `tell()`, and `write()`. It also supports the string API, with features such as slicing and methods like `find()`.

The examples in this section use the text file `lorem.txt`, which contains a bit of Lorem Ipsum. For reference, the text of the file is shown in the following listing.

Listing 6.88: `lorem.txt`

```
Lorem ipsum dolor sit amet, consectetuer adipiscing elit.
Donec egestas, enim et consectetuer ullamcorper, lectus ligula
rutrum leo, a elementum elit tortor eu quam. Duis tincidunt nisi ut
ante. Nulla facilisi. Sed tristique eros eu libero. Pellentesque vel
arcu. Vivamus purus orci, iaculis ac, suscipit sit amet, pulvinar eu,
lacus. Praesent placerat tortor sed nisl. Nunc blandit diam egestas
dui. Pellentesque habitant morbi tristique senectus et netus et
malesuada fames ac turpis egestas. Aliquam viverra fringilla
leo. Nulla feugiat augue eleifend nulla. Vivamus mauris. Vivamus sed
mauris in nibh placerat egestas. Suspendisse potenti. Mauris
massa. Ut eget velit auctor tortor blandit sollicitudin. Suspendisse
imperdiet justo.
```

NOTE

The arguments and behaviors for `mmap()` differ between Unix and Windows, but those differences are not fully discussed here. For more details, refer to the standard library documentation.

6.9.1   Reading

Use the `mmap()` function to create a memory-mapped file. The first argument is a file descriptor, either from the `fileno()` method of a `file` object or from `os.open()`. The caller is responsible for opening the file before invoking `mmap()`, and closing it after it is no longer needed.

The second argument to `mmap()` is a size in bytes indicating the portion of the file to map. If the value is `0`, the entire file is mapped. If the size is larger than the current size of the file, the file is extended.

NOTE

Windows does not support creating a zero-length mapping.

An optional keyword argument, `access`, is supported by both platforms. Use `ACCESS_READ` for read-only access, `ACCESS_WRITE` for write-through access (assignments to the memory go directly to the file), and `ACCESS_COPY` for copy-on-write access (assignments to memory are not written to the file).

Listing 6.89: mmap_read.py

```python
import mmap

with open('lorem.txt', 'r') as f:
    with mmap.mmap(f.fileno(), 0,
                   access=mmap.ACCESS_READ) as m:
        print('First 10 bytes via read :', m.read(10))
        print('First 10 bytes via slice:', m[:10])
        print('2nd   10 bytes via read :', m.read(10))
```

The file pointer tracks the last byte accessed through a slice operation. In this example, the pointer moves ahead 10 bytes after the first read. It is then reset to the beginning of the file by the slice operation, and moved ahead 10 bytes again by the slice. After the slice operation, calling `read()` again gives bytes 11–20 in the file.

```
$ python3 mmap_read.py

First 10 bytes via read : b'Lorem ipsu'
First 10 bytes via slice: b'Lorem ipsu'
2nd   10 bytes via read : b'm dolor si'
```

6.9.2 Writing

To set up the memory-mapped file to receive updates, open it for appending with mode `'r+'` (not `'w'`) before mapping it. Then use any of the API methods that change the data (e.g., `write()`, assignment to a slice).

The next example uses the default access mode of `ACCESS_WRITE` and assignment to a slice to modify part of a line in place.

Listing 6.90: mmap_write_slice.py

```python
import mmap
import shutil

# Copy the example file.
shutil.copyfile('lorem.txt', 'lorem_copy.txt')

word = b'consectetuer'
```

```
    reversed = word[::-1]
    print('Looking for    :', word)
    print('Replacing with :', reversed)

    with open('lorem_copy.txt', 'r+') as f:
        with mmap.mmap(f.fileno(), 0) as m:
            print('Before:\n{}'.format(m.readline().rstrip()))
            m.seek(0)  # Rewind

            loc = m.find(word)
            m[loc:loc + len(word)] = reversed
            m.flush()

            m.seek(0)  # Rewind
            print('After :\n{}'.format(m.readline().rstrip()))

            f.seek(0)  # Rewind
            print('File  :\n{}'.format(f.readline().rstrip()))
```

The word "consectetuer" is replaced in the middle of the first line in memory and in the file.

```
$ python3 mmap_write_slice.py

Looking for    : b'consectetuer'
Replacing with : b'reutetcesnoc'
Before:
b'Lorem ipsum dolor sit amet, consectetuer adipiscing elit.'
After :
b'Lorem ipsum dolor sit amet, reutetcesnoc adipiscing elit.'
File  :
Lorem ipsum dolor sit amet, reutetcesnoc adipiscing elit.
```

6.9.2.1 Copy Mode

With the access setting ACCESS_COPY, changes are not written to the file on disk.

Listing 6.91: **mmap_write_copy.py**

```
import mmap
import shutil

# Copy the example file.
shutil.copyfile('lorem.txt', 'lorem_copy.txt')

word = b'consectetuer'
reversed = word[::-1]
```

```
with open('lorem_copy.txt', 'r+') as f:
    with mmap.mmap(f.fileno(), 0,
                   access=mmap.ACCESS_COPY) as m:
        print('Memory Before:\n{}'.format(
            m.readline().rstrip()))
        print('File Before  :\n{}\n'.format(
            f.readline().rstrip()))

        m.seek(0)  # Rewind
        loc = m.find(word)
        m[loc:loc + len(word)] = reversed

        m.seek(0)  # Rewind
        print('Memory After :\n{}'.format(
            m.readline().rstrip()))

        f.seek(0)
        print('File After   :\n{}'.format(
            f.readline().rstrip()))
```

The file handle in this example must be rewound separately from the `mmap` handle, because the internal states of the two objects are maintained separately.

```
$ python3 mmap_write_copy.py

Memory Before:
b'Lorem ipsum dolor sit amet, consectetuer adipiscing elit.'
File Before  :
Lorem ipsum dolor sit amet, consectetuer adipiscing elit.

Memory After :
b'Lorem ipsum dolor sit amet, reutetcesnoc adipiscing elit.'
File After   :
Lorem ipsum dolor sit amet, consectetuer adipiscing elit.
```

6.9.3   Regular Expressions

Since a memory-mapped file can act like a string, it can be used with other modules that operate on strings, such as regular expressions. This example finds all of the sentences with "nulla" in them.

Listing 6.92: **mmap_regex.py**

```
import mmap
import re

pattern = re.compile(rb'(\.\W+)?([^.]?nulla[^.]*?\.)',
                     re.DOTALL | re.IGNORECASE | re.MULTILINE)
```

```
with open('lorem.txt', 'r') as f:
    with mmap.mmap(f.fileno(), 0,
                   access=mmap.ACCESS_READ) as m:
        for match in pattern.findall(m):
            print(match[1].replace(b'\n', b' '))
```

Because the pattern includes two groups, the return value from `findall()` is a sequence of tuples. The `print` statement pulls out the matching sentence and replaces newlines with spaces so that each result prints on a single line.

```
$ python3 mmap_regex.py

b'Nulla facilisi.'
b'Nulla feugiat augue eleifend nulla.'
```

TIP

Related Reading

- Standard library documentation for mmap.[12]
- Python 2 to 3 porting notes for mmap (page 1360).
- os (page 1227): The os module.
- re (page 13): Regular expressions.

6.10   codecs: String Encoding and Decoding

The `codecs` module provides stream and file interfaces for transcoding text data between different representations. It is most commonly used to work with Unicode text, but other encodings are available for other purposes.

6.10.1   Unicode Primer

CPython 3.x differentiates between *text* and *byte* strings. `bytes` instances use a sequence of 8-bit byte values. In contrast, `str` strings are managed internally as a sequence of Unicode *code points*. The code point values are represented using 2 or 4 bytes each, depending on the options given when Python was compiled.

When `str` values are output, they are encoded using one of several standard schemes, so that the sequence of bytes can be reconstructed as the same string of text later. The bytes of the encoded value are not necessarily the same as the code point values, and the encoding defines a way to translate between the two sets of values. Reading Unicode data

---

[12] https://docs.python.org/3.5/library/mmap.html

also requires knowing the encoding so that the incoming bytes can be converted to the internal representation used by the `unicode` class.

The most commonly used encodings for Western languages are `UTF-8` and `UTF-16`, which use sequences of 1- and 2-byte values, respectively, to represent each code point. Other encodings can be more efficient for storing languages in which most of the characters are represented by code points that do not fit into 2 bytes.

TIP

Related Reading

For more introductory information about Unicode, refer to the list of references at the end of this section. The Python Unicode HOWTO is especially helpful.

6.10.1.1   Encodings

The best way to understand encodings is to look at the different series of bytes produced by encoding the same string in different ways. The following examples use this function to format the byte string to make it easier to read.

Listing 6.93: **codecs_to_hex.py**

```
import binascii


def to_hex(t, nbytes):
    """Format text t as a sequence of nbyte long values
    separated by spaces.
    """
    chars_per_item = nbytes * 2
    hex_version = binascii.hexlify(t)
    return b' '.join(
        hex_version[start:start + chars_per_item]
        for start in range(0, len(hex_version), chars_per_item)
    )


if __name__ == '__main__':
    print(to_hex(b'abcdef', 1))
    print(to_hex(b'abcdef', 2))
```

The function uses `binascii` to get a hexadecimal representation of the input byte string, then inserts a space between every `nbytes` bytes before returning the value.

```
$ python3 codecs_to_hex.py

b'61 62 63 64 65 66'
b'6162 6364 6566'
```

The first encoding example begins by printing the text 'français' using the raw representation of the unicode class, followed by the name of each character from the Unicode database. The next two lines encode the string as UTF-8 and UTF-16, respectively, and show the hexadecimal values resulting from the encoding.

Listing 6.94: **codecs_encodings.py**

```
import unicodedata
from codecs_to_hex import to_hex

text = 'français'

print('Raw    : {!r}'.format(text))
for c in text:
    print('  {!r}: {}'.format(c, unicodedata.name(c, c)))
print('UTF-8 : {!r}'.format(to_hex(text.encode('utf-8'), 1)))
print('UTF-16: {!r}'.format(to_hex(text.encode('utf-16'), 2)))
```

The result of encoding a str is a bytes object.

```
$ python3 codecs_encodings.py

Raw    : 'français'
  'f': LATIN SMALL LETTER F
  'r': LATIN SMALL LETTER R
  'a': LATIN SMALL LETTER A
  'n': LATIN SMALL LETTER N
  'ç': LATIN SMALL LETTER C WITH CEDILLA
  'a': LATIN SMALL LETTER A
  'i': LATIN SMALL LETTER I
  's': LATIN SMALL LETTER S
UTF-8 : b'66 72 61 6e c3 a7 61 69 73'
UTF-16: b'fffe 6600 7200 6100 6e00 e700 6100 6900 7300'
```

Given a sequence of encoded bytes as a bytes instance, the decode() method translates them to code points and returns the sequence as a str instance.

Listing 6.95: **codecs_decode.py**

```
from codecs_to_hex import to_hex

text = 'français'
encoded = text.encode('utf-8')
decoded = encoded.decode('utf-8')

print('Original :', repr(text))
print('Encoded  :', to_hex(encoded, 1), type(encoded))
print('Decoded  :', repr(decoded), type(decoded))
```

The choice of encoding used does not change the output type.

```
$ python3 codecs_decode.py

Original : 'français'
Encoded  : b'66 72 61 6e c3 a7 61 69 73' <class 'bytes'>
Decoded  : 'français' <class 'str'>
```

NOTE

The default encoding is set during the interpreter start-up process, when site (page 1169) is loaded. Refer to Section 17.2.1.4, "Unicode Defaults" (page 1181) section in the discussion of sys (page 1178) for a description of the default encoding settings.

6.10.2   Working with Files

Encoding and decoding strings is especially important when dealing with I/O operations. Whether writing to a file, socket, or other stream, the data must use the proper encoding. In general, all text data needs to be decoded from its byte representation as it is read, and encoded from the internal values to a specific representation as it is written. A program can explicitly encode and decode data, but depending on the encoding used it can be a nontrivial task to determine whether enough bytes have been read to fully decode the data. codecs provides classes that manage the data encoding and decoding, so applications do not have to do that work.

The simplest interface provided by codecs is an alternative to the built-in open() function. The new version works just like the built-in, but adds two new arguments to specify the encoding and desired error handling technique.

Listing 6.96: **codecs_open_write.py**

```
from codecs_to_hex import to_hex

import codecs
import sys

encoding = sys.argv[1]
filename = encoding + '.txt'

print('Writing to', filename)
with codecs.open(filename, mode='w', encoding=encoding) as f:
    f.write('français')

# Determine the byte grouping to use for to_hex().
nbytes = {
    'utf-8': 1,
    'utf-16': 2,
```

```
    'utf-32': 4,
}.get(encoding, 1)

# Show the raw bytes in the file.
print('File contents:')
with open(filename, mode='rb') as f:
    print(to_hex(f.read(), nbytes))
```

This example starts with a `unicode` string with "ç" and saves the text to a file using an encoding specified on the command line.

```
$ python3 codecs_open_write.py utf-8

Writing to utf-8.txt
File contents:
b'66 72 61 6e c3 a7 61 69 73'

$ python3 codecs_open_write.py utf-16

Writing to utf-16.txt
File contents:
b'fffe 6600 7200 6100 6e00 e700 6100 6900 7300'

$ python3 codecs_open_write.py utf-32

Writing to utf-32.txt
File contents:
b'fffe0000 66000000 72000000 61000000 6e000000 e7000000 61000000
69000000 73000000'
```

Reading the data with `open()` is straightforward, with one catch: The encoding must be known in advance, so as to set up the decoder correctly. Some data formats, such as XML, specify the encoding as part of the file, but usually it is left to the application to manage. `codecs` simply takes the encoding as an argument and assumes it is correct.

Listing 6.97: codecs_open_read.py

```
import codecs
import sys

encoding = sys.argv[1]
filename = encoding + '.txt'

print('Reading from', filename)
with codecs.open(filename, mode='r', encoding=encoding) as f:
    print(repr(f.read()))
```

This example reads the files created by the previous program, and prints the representation of the resulting `unicode` object to the console.

```
$ python3 codecs_open_read.py utf-8

Reading from utf-8.txt
'français'

$ python3 codecs_open_read.py utf-16

Reading from utf-16.txt
'français'

$ python3 codecs_open_read.py utf-32

Reading from utf-32.txt
'français'
```

6.10.3   Byte Order

Multibyte encodings such as UTF-16 and UTF-32 pose a problem when transferring the data between different computer systems, either by copying the file directly or with network communication. Different systems use different ordering of the high- and low-order bytes. This characteristic of the data, known as its *endianness*, depends on factors such as the hardware architecture and choices made by the operating system and application developer. There is not always a way to know in advance which byte order should be used for a given set of data, so the multibyte encodings include a *byte-order marker* (BOM) as the first few bytes of encoded output. For example, UTF-16 is defined in such a way that 0xFFFE and 0xFEFF are not valid characters, and can be used to indicate the byte order. codecs defines constants for the byte-order markers used by UTF-16 and UTF-32.

Listing 6.98: codecs_bom.py

```python
import codecs
from codecs_to_hex import to_hex

BOM_TYPES = [
    'BOM', 'BOM_BE', 'BOM_LE',
    'BOM_UTF8',
    'BOM_UTF16', 'BOM_UTF16_BE', 'BOM_UTF16_LE',
    'BOM_UTF32', 'BOM_UTF32_BE', 'BOM_UTF32_LE',
]

for name in BOM_TYPES:
    print('{:12} : {}'.format(
        name, to_hex(getattr(codecs, name), 2)))
```

BOM, BOM_UTF16, and BOM_UTF32 are automatically set to the appropriate big-endian or little-endian values depending on the current system's native byte order.

```
$ python3 codecs_bom.py

BOM           : b'fffe'
BOM_BE        : b'feff'
BOM_LE        : b'fffe'
BOM_UTF8      : b'efbb bf'
BOM_UTF16     : b'fffe'
BOM_UTF16_BE  : b'feff'
BOM_UTF16_LE  : b'fffe'
BOM_UTF32     : b'fffe 0000'
BOM_UTF32_BE  : b'0000 feff'
BOM_UTF32_LE  : b'fffe 0000'
```

Byte ordering is detected and handled automatically by the decoders in codecs, but an explicit ordering can be specified when encoding.

Listing 6.99: **codecs_bom_create_file.py**

```python
import codecs
from codecs_to_hex import to_hex

# Pick the non-native version of UTF-16 encoding.
if codecs.BOM_UTF16 == codecs.BOM_UTF16_BE:
    bom = codecs.BOM_UTF16_LE
    encoding = 'utf_16_le'
else:
    bom = codecs.BOM_UTF16_BE
    encoding = 'utf_16_be'

print('Native order  :', to_hex(codecs.BOM_UTF16, 2))
print('Selected order:', to_hex(bom, 2))

# Encode the text.
encoded_text = 'français'.encode(encoding)
print('{:14}: {}'.format(encoding, to_hex(encoded_text, 2)))

with open('nonnative-encoded.txt', mode='wb') as f:
    # Write the selected byte-order marker.  It is not included
    # in the encoded text because the byte order was given
    # explicitly when selecting the encoding.
    f.write(bom)
    # Write the byte string for the encoded text.
    f.write(encoded_text)
```

codecs_bom_create_file.py figures out the native byte ordering, then uses the alternate form explicitly so the next example can demonstrate auto-detection while reading.

```
$ python3 codecs_bom_create_file.py

Native order  : b'fffe'
Selected order: b'feff'
utf_16_be     : b'0066 0072 0061 006e 00e7 0061 0069 0073'
```

codecs_bom_detection.py does not specify a byte order when opening the file, so the
decoder uses the BOM value in the first 2 bytes of the file to determine it.

Listing 6.100: codecs_bom_detection.py

```
import codecs
from codecs_to_hex import to_hex

# Look at the raw data.
with open('nonnative-encoded.txt', mode='rb') as f:
    raw_bytes = f.read()

print('Raw    :', to_hex(raw_bytes, 2))

# Reopen the file and let codecs detect the BOM.
with codecs.open('nonnative-encoded.txt',
                 mode='r',
                 encoding='utf-16',
                 ) as f:
    decoded_text = f.read()

print('Decoded:', repr(decoded_text))
```

Since the first 2 bytes of the file are used for byte order detection, they are not included
in the data returned by read().

```
$ python3 codecs_bom_detection.py

Raw    : b'feff 0066 0072 0061 006e 00e7 0061 0069 0073'
Decoded: 'français'
```

6.10.4   Error Handling

The previous sections pointed out the need to know the encoding being used when reading
and writing Unicode files. Setting the encoding correctly is important for two reasons. First,
if the encoding is configured incorrectly while reading from a file, the data will be interpreted
incorrectly and may be corrupted or simply fail to decode. Second, not all Unicode characters
can be represented in all encodings; thus, if the wrong encoding is used while writing, then
an error will be generated and data may be lost.

codecs uses the same five error handling options that are provided by the encode()
method of str and the decode() method of bytes, listed in Table 6.1.

Table 6.1: Codec Error Handling Modes

Error Mode	Description
strict	Raises an exception if the data cannot be converted
replace	Substitutes a special marker character for data that cannot be encoded
ignore	Skips the data
xmlcharrefreplace	XML character (encoding only)
backslashreplace	Escape sequence (encoding only)

6.10.4.1   Encoding Errors

The most common error condition is receiving a UnicodeEncodeError when writing Unicode data to an ASCII output stream, such as a regular file or sys.stdout without a more robust encoding set. The sample program in Listing 6.101 can be used to experiment with the different error handling modes.

Listing 6.101: codecs_encode_error.py

```
import codecs
import sys

error_handling = sys.argv[1]

text = 'français'

try:
    # Save the data, encoded as ASCII, using the error
    # handling mode specified on the command line.
    with codecs.open('encode_error.txt', 'w',
                     encoding='ascii',
                     errors=error_handling) as f:
        f.write(text)

except UnicodeEncodeError as err:
    print('ERROR:', err)

else:
    # If there was no error writing to the file,
    # show the file's contents.
    with open('encode_error.txt', 'rb') as f:
        print('File contents: {!r}'.format(f.read()))
```

While strict mode is the safest choice for ensuring an application explicitly sets the correct encoding for all I/O operations, it can lead to program crashes when an exception is raised.

```
$ python3 codecs_encode_error.py strict

ERROR: 'ascii' codec can't encode character '\xe7' in position
4: ordinal not in range(128)
```

Some of the other error modes are more flexible. For example, `replace` ensures that no error is raised, at the expense of possibly losing data that cannot be converted to the requested encoding. The Unicode character for pi still cannot be encoded in ASCII, but instead of raising an exception, the pi character is replaced with ? in the output.

```
$ python3 codecs_encode_error.py replace

File contents: b'fran?ais'
```

To just skip over problem data, use `ignore`. Any data that cannot be encoded will then be discarded.

```
$ python3 codecs_encode_error.py ignore

File contents: b'franais'
```

Two lossless error handling options are available, both of which replace the character with an alternate representation defined by a standard separate from the encoding. `xmlchar-refreplace` uses an XML character reference as a substitute (the list of character references is specified in the W3C document "XML Entity Definitions for Characters").

```
$ python3 codecs_encode_error.py xmlcharrefreplace

File contents: b'fran&#231;ais'
```

The other lossless error handling scheme is `backslashreplace`, which produces an output format like the value returned when `repr()` of a `unicode` object is printed. Unicode characters are replaced with \u followed by the hexadecimal value of the code point.

```
$ python3 codecs_encode_error.py backslashreplace

File contents: b'fran\\xe7ais'
```

6.10.4.2 Decoding Errors

Errors may also occur when decoding data, especially if the wrong encoding is used.

Listing 6.102: `codecs_decode_error.py`

```
import codecs
import sys

from codecs_to_hex import to_hex

error_handling = sys.argv[1]

text = 'français'
```

```
print('Original       :', repr(text))

# Save the data with one encoding.
with codecs.open('decode_error.txt', 'w',
                 encoding='utf-16') as f:
    f.write(text)

# Dump the bytes from the file.
with open('decode_error.txt', 'rb') as f:
    print('File contents:', to_hex(f.read(), 1))

# Try to read the data with the wrong encoding.
with codecs.open('decode_error.txt', 'r',
                 encoding='utf-8',
                 errors=error_handling) as f:
    try:
        data = f.read()
    except UnicodeDecodeError as err:
        print('ERROR:', err)
    else:
        print('Read          :', repr(data))
```

As with encoding, the strict error handling mode raises an exception if the byte stream cannot be properly decoded. In this case, a UnicodeDecodeError results from trying to convert part of the UTF-16 BOM to a character using the UTF-8 decoder.

```
$ python3 codecs_decode_error.py strict

Original    : 'français'
File contents: b'ff fe 66 00 72 00 61 00 6e 00 e7 00 61 00 69 00
73 00'
ERROR: 'utf-8' codec can't decode byte 0xff in position 0:
invalid start byte
```

Switching to ignore causes the decoder to skip over the invalid bytes. The result is still not quite what is expected, though, since it includes embedded null bytes.

```
$ python3 codecs_decode_error.py ignore

Original    : 'français'
File contents: b'ff fe 66 00 72 00 61 00 6e 00 e7 00 61 00 69 00
73 00'
Read          : 'f\x00r\x00a\x00n\x00\x00a\x00i\x00s\x00'
```

In replace mode, invalid bytes are replaced with \uFFFD, the official Unicode replacement character, which looks like a diamond with a black background containing a white question mark.

```
$ python3 codecs_decode_error.py replace

Original      : 'français'
File contents: b'ff fe 66 00 72 00 61 00 6e 00 e7 00 61 00 69 00
73 00'
Read          : 'f\x00r\x00a\x00n\x00\x00a\x00i\x00s\x00'
```

6.10.5   Encoding Translation

Although most applications will work with str data internally, decoding or encoding it as part of an I/O operation, the ability to change a file's encoding without holding on to that intermediate data format is sometimes useful. EncodedFile() takes an open file handle using one encoding and wraps it with a class that translates the data to another encoding as the I/O occurs.

Listing 6.103: **codecs_encodedfile.py**

```
from codecs_to_hex import to_hex

import codecs
import io

# Raw version of the original data
data = 'français'

# Manually encode it as UTF-8.
utf8 = data.encode('utf-8')
print('Start as UTF-8   :', to_hex(utf8, 1))

# Set up an output buffer, then wrap it as an EncodedFile.
output = io.BytesIO()
encoded_file = codecs.EncodedFile(output, data_encoding='utf-8',
                                  file_encoding='utf-16')
encoded_file.write(utf8)

# Fetch the buffer contents as a UTF-16 encoded byte string.
utf16 = output.getvalue()
print('Encoded to UTF-16:', to_hex(utf16, 2))

# Set up another buffer with the UTF-16 data for reading,
# and wrap it with another EncodedFile.
buffer = io.BytesIO(utf16)
encoded_file = codecs.EncodedFile(buffer, data_encoding='utf-8',
                                  file_encoding='utf-16')

# Read the UTF-8 encoded version of the data.
recoded = encoded_file.read()
print('Back to UTF-8     :', to_hex(recoded, 1))
```

This example shows reading from and writing to separate handles returned by Encoded-File(). No matter whether the handle is used for reading or writing, the file_encoding always refers to the encoding used by the open file handle that is passed as the first argument, and the data_encoding value refers to the encoding used by the data that passes through the read() and write() calls.

```
$ python3 codecs_encodedfile.py

Start as UTF-8    : b'66 72 61 6e c3 a7 61 69 73'
Encoded to UTF-16: b'fffe 6600 7200 6100 6e00 e700 6100 6900
7300'
Back to UTF-8     : b'66 72 61 6e c3 a7 61 69 73'
```

6.10.6 Non-Unicode Encodings

Although most of the earlier examples used Unicode encodings, codecs can be used for many other data translations. For example, Python includes codecs for working with base 64, bzip2, ROT-13, ZIP, and other data formats.

Listing 6.104: <code>codecs_rot13.py</code>

```
import codecs
import io

buffer = io.StringIO()
stream = codecs.getwriter('rot_13')(buffer)

text = 'abcdefghijklmnopqrstuvwxyz'

stream.write(text)
stream.flush()

print('Original:', text)
print('ROT-13   :', buffer.getvalue())
```

Any transformation that can be expressed as a function taking a single input argument and returning a byte or Unicode string can be registered as a codec. For the 'rot_13' codec, the input should be a Unicode string; the output will also be a Unicode string.

```
$ python3 codecs_rot13.py

Original: abcdefghijklmnopqrstuvwxyz
ROT-13   : nopqrstuvwxyzabcdefghijklm
```

Using codecs to wrap a data stream provides a simpler interface than working directly with zlib (page 477).

Listing 6.105: `codecs_zlib.py`

```python
import codecs
import io

from codecs_to_hex import to_hex

buffer = io.BytesIO()
stream = codecs.getwriter('zlib')(buffer)

text = b'abcdefghijklmnopqrstuvwxyz\n' * 50

stream.write(text)
stream.flush()

print('Original length :', len(text))
compressed_data = buffer.getvalue()
print('ZIP compressed  :', len(compressed_data))

buffer = io.BytesIO(compressed_data)
stream = codecs.getreader('zlib')(buffer)

first_line = stream.readline()
print('Read first line :', repr(first_line))

uncompressed_data = first_line + stream.read()
print('Uncompressed     :', len(uncompressed_data))
print('Same             :', text == uncompressed_data)
```

Not all compression or encoding systems support reading a portion of the data through the stream interface with `readline()` or `read()`, because they need to find the end of a compressed segment so as to expand it. If a program cannot hold the entire uncompressed data set in memory, the incremental access features of the compression library should be used, instead of `codecs`.

```
$ python3 codecs_zlib.py

Original length : 1350
ZIP compressed  : 48
Read first line : b'abcdefghijklmnopqrstuvwxyz\n'
Uncompressed    : 1350
Same            : True
```

6.10.7   Incremental Encoding

Some of the encodings provided, especially `bz2` and `zlib`, may dramatically change the length of the data stream as they work on it. For large data sets, these encodings operate better incrementally, working on one small chunk of data at a time. The `IncrementalEncoder`/ `IncrementalDecoder` API is designed for this purpose.

Listing 6.106: <code>codecs_incremental_bz2.py</code>

```python
import codecs
import sys

from codecs_to_hex import to_hex

text = b'abcdefghijklmnopqrstuvwxyz\n'
repetitions = 50

print('Text length :', len(text))
print('Repetitions :', repetitions)
print('Expected len:', len(text) * repetitions)

# Encode the text several times to build up a
# large amount of data.
encoder = codecs.getincrementalencoder('bz2')()
encoded = []

print()
print('Encoding:', end=' ')
last = repetitions - 1
for i in range(repetitions):
    en_c = encoder.encode(text, final=(i == last))
    if en_c:
        print('\nEncoded : {} bytes'.format(len(en_c)))
        encoded.append(en_c)
    else:
        sys.stdout.write('.')

all_encoded = b''.join(encoded)
print()
print('Total encoded length:', len(all_encoded))
print()

# Decode the byte string one byte at a time.
decoder = codecs.getincrementaldecoder('bz2')()
decoded = []

print('Decoding:', end=' ')
for i, b in enumerate(all_encoded):
    final = (i + 1) == len(text)
    c = decoder.decode(bytes([b]), final)
    if c:
        print('\nDecoded : {} characters'.format(len(c)))
        print('Decoding:', end=' ')
        decoded.append(c)
    else:
        sys.stdout.write('.')
print()
```

```
restored = b''.join(decoded)

print()
print('Total uncompressed length:', len(restored))
```

Each time data is passed to the encoder or decoder, its internal state is updated. When the state is consistent (as defined by the codec), data is returned and the state resets. Until that point, calls to `encode()` and `decode()` will not return any data. When the last bit of data is passed in, the argument `final` should be set to `True` so the codec knows to flush any remaining buffered data.

```
$ python3 codecs_incremental_bz2.py

Text length : 27
Repetitions : 50
Expected len: 1350

Encoding: ...............................................
Encoded : 99 bytes

Total encoded length: 99

Decoding: ...................................................
...............................
Decoded : 1350 characters
Decoding: ..........

Total uncompressed length: 1350
```

6.10.8   Unicode Data and Network Communication

Network sockets are byte streams, and unlike the standard input and output streams, they do not support encoding by default. As a consequence, programs that want to send or receive Unicode data over the network must encode the data into bytes before it is written to a socket. The server in the next example tries to echo the data it receives back to the sender.

Listing 6.107: `codecs_socket_fail.py`

```
import sys
import socketserver


class Echo(socketserver.BaseRequestHandler):

    def handle(self):
        # Get some bytes and echo them back to the client.
        data = self.request.recv(1024)
```

```
            self.request.send(data)
            return


if __name__ == '__main__':
    import codecs
    import socket
    import threading

    address = ('localhost', 0)  # Let the kernel assign a port.
    server = socketserver.TCPServer(address, Echo)
    ip, port = server.server_address  # Which port was assigned?

    t = threading.Thread(target=server.serve_forever)
    t.setDaemon(True)  # Don't hang on exit.
    t.start()

    # Connect to the server.
    s = socket.socket(socket.AF_INET, socket.SOCK_STREAM)
    s.connect((ip, port))

    # Send the data.
    # WRONG: Not encoded first!
    text = 'français'
    len_sent = s.send(text)

    # Receive a response.
    response = s.recv(len_sent)
    print(repr(response))

    # Clean up.
    s.close()
    server.socket.close()
```

The data could be encoded explicitly before each call to send(), but missing one call to
send() would result in an encoding error.

```
$ python3 codecs_socket_fail.py

Traceback (most recent call last):
  File "codecs_socket_fail.py", line 43, in <module>
    len_sent = s.send(text)
TypeError: a bytes-like object is required, not 'str'
```

Using makefile() to get a file-like handle for the socket, and then wrapping that handle
with a stream-based reader or writer, ensures that Unicode strings will be encoded on the
way into and out of the socket.

Listing 6.108: `codecs_socket.py`

```python
import sys
import socketserver


class Echo(socketserver.BaseRequestHandler):

    def handle(self):
        """Get some bytes and echo them back to the client.

        There is no need to decode them, since they are not used.

        """
        data = self.request.recv(1024)
        self.request.send(data)


class PassThrough:

    def __init__(self, other):
        self.other = other

    def write(self, data):
        print('Writing :', repr(data))
        return self.other.write(data)

    def read(self, size=-1):
        print('Reading :', end=' ')
        data = self.other.read(size)
        print(repr(data))
        return data

    def flush(self):
        return self.other.flush()

    def close(self):
        return self.other.close()


if __name__ == '__main__':
    import codecs
    import socket
    import threading

    address = ('localhost', 0)  # Let the kernel assign a port.
    server = socketserver.TCPServer(address, Echo)
    ip, port = server.server_address  # Which port was assigned?

    t = threading.Thread(target=server.serve_forever)
```

```
        t.setDaemon(True)  # Don't hang on exit.
        t.start()

        # Connect to the server.
        s = socket.socket(socket.AF_INET, socket.SOCK_STREAM)
        s.connect((ip, port))

        # Wrap the socket with a reader and a writer.
        read_file = s.makefile('rb')
        incoming = codecs.getreader('utf-8')(PassThrough(read_file))
        write_file = s.makefile('wb')
        outgoing = codecs.getwriter('utf-8')(PassThrough(write_file))

        # Send the data.
        text = 'français'
        print('Sending :', repr(text))
        outgoing.write(text)
        outgoing.flush()

        # Receive a response.
        response = incoming.read()
        print('Received:', repr(response))

        # Clean up.
        s.close()
        server.socket.close()
```

This example uses `PassThrough` to show that the data is encoded before being sent, and the response is decoded after it is received in the client.

```
$ python3 codecs_socket.py

Sending : 'français'
Writing : b'fran\xc3\xa7ais'
Reading : b'fran\xc3\xa7ais'
Reading : b''
Received: 'français'
```

6.10.9 Defining a Custom Encoding

Since Python comes with a large number of standard codecs, an application is unlikely to need to define a custom encoder or decoder. When this step is necessary, though, several base classes in `codecs` can make the process easier.

The first step is to understand the nature of the transformation described by the encoding. The examples in this section will use an "invertcaps" encoding that converts uppercase letters to lowercase, and lowercase letters to uppercase. Following is a simple definition of an encoding function that performs this transformation on an input string.

Listing 6.109: **codecs_invertcaps.py**

```python
import string


def invertcaps(text):
    """Return new string with the case of all letters switched.
    """
    return ''.join(
        c.upper() if c in string.ascii_lowercase
        else c.lower() if c in string.ascii_uppercase
        else c
        for c in text
    )

if __name__ == '__main__':
    print(invertcaps('ABCdef'))
    print(invertcaps('abcDEF'))
```

In this case, the encoder and the decoder are the same function (as is also the case with ROT-13).

```
$ python3 codecs_invertcaps.py

abcDEF
ABCdef
```

Although it is easy to understand, this implementation is not efficient, especially for very large text strings. Fortunately, codecs includes some helper functions for creating *character map*–based codecs such as invertcaps. A character map encoding is made up of two dictionaries. The *encoding map* converts character values from the input string to byte values in the output, while the *decoding map* goes the other way. Create the decoding map first, and then use make_encoding_map() to convert it to an encoding map. The C functions charmap_encode() and charmap_decode() use the maps to convert their input data efficiently.

Listing 6.110: **codecs_invertcaps_charmap.py**

```python
import codecs
import string

# Map every character to itself.
decoding_map = codecs.make_identity_dict(range(256))

# Make a list of pairs of ordinal values for the
# lowercase and uppercase letters.
pairs = list(zip(
    [ord(c) for c in string.ascii_lowercase],
    [ord(c) for c in string.ascii_uppercase],
))
```

```
    # Modify the mapping to convert upper to lower and
    # lower to upper.
    decoding_map.update({
        upper: lower
        for (lower, upper)
        in pairs
    })
    decoding_map.update({
        lower: upper
        for (lower, upper)
        in pairs
    })

    # Create a separate encoding map.
    encoding_map = codecs.make_encoding_map(decoding_map)

    if __name__ == '__main__':
        print(codecs.charmap_encode('abcDEF', 'strict',
                                    encoding_map))
        print(codecs.charmap_decode(b'abcDEF', 'strict',
                                    decoding_map))
        print(encoding_map == decoding_map)
```

Although the encoding and decoding maps for invertcaps are the same, that may not always be the case. make_encoding_map() detects situations where more than one input character is encoded to the same output byte and replaces the encoding value with None to mark the encoding as undefined.

```
$ python3 codecs_invertcaps_charmap.py

(b'ABCdef', 6)
('ABCdef', 6)
True
```

The character map encoder and decoder support all of the standard error handling methods described earlier, so no extra work is needed to comply with that part of the API.

Listing 6.111: `codecs_invertcaps_error.py`

```
import codecs
from codecs_invertcaps_charmap import encoding_map

text = 'pi: \u03c0'

for error in ['ignore', 'replace', 'strict']:
    try:
        encoded = codecs.charmap_encode(
            text, error, encoding_map)
```

```
    except UnicodeEncodeError as err:
        encoded = str(err)
    print('{:7}: {}'.format(error, encoded))
```

Because the Unicode code point for π is not in the encoding map, the strict error handling mode raises an exception.

```
$ python3 codecs_invertcaps_error.py

ignore : (b'PI: ', 5)
replace: (b'PI: ?', 5)
strict : 'charmap' codec can't encode character '\u03c0' in
position 4: character maps to <undefined>
```

After the encoding and decoding maps are defined, a few additional classes need to be set up, and the encoding should be registered. register() adds a search function to the registry so that when a user wants to use the encoding, codecs can locate it. The search function must take a single string argument with the name of the encoding, and return a CodecInfo object if it knows the encoding, or None if it does not.

Listing 6.112: codecs_register.py

```
import codecs
import encodings


def search1(encoding):
    print('search1: Searching for:', encoding)
    return None


def search2(encoding):
    print('search2: Searching for:', encoding)
    return None

codecs.register(search1)
codecs.register(search2)

utf8 = codecs.lookup('utf-8')
print('UTF-8:', utf8)

try:
    unknown = codecs.lookup('no-such-encoding')
except LookupError as err:
    print('ERROR:', err)
```

Multiple search functions can be registered, and each will be called in turn until one returns a CodecInfo or the list is exhausted. The internal search function registered by codecs knows how to load the standard codecs such as UTF-8 from encodings, so those names will never be passed to custom search functions.

```
$ python3 codecs_register.py

UTF-8: <codecs.CodecInfo object for encoding utf-8 at
0x1007773a8>
search1: Searching for: no-such-encoding
search2: Searching for: no-such-encoding
ERROR: unknown encoding: no-such-encoding
```

The CodecInfo instance returned by the search function tells codecs how to encode and decode using all of the different mechanisms supported: stateless, incremental, and stream. codecs includes base classes to help with setting up a character map encoding. This example puts all of the pieces together to register a search function that returns a CodecInfo instance configured for the invertcaps codec.

Listing 6.113: codecs_invertcaps_register.py

```
import codecs

from codecs_invertcaps_charmap import encoding_map, decoding_map


class InvertCapsCodec(codecs.Codec):
    "Stateless encoder/decoder"

    def encode(self, input, errors='strict'):
        return codecs.charmap_encode(input, errors, encoding_map)

    def decode(self, input, errors='strict'):
        return codecs.charmap_decode(input, errors, decoding_map)


class InvertCapsIncrementalEncoder(codecs.IncrementalEncoder):
    def encode(self, input, final=False):
        data, nbytes = codecs.charmap_encode(input,
                                             self.errors,
                                             encoding_map)
        return data


class InvertCapsIncrementalDecoder(codecs.IncrementalDecoder):
    def decode(self, input, final=False):
        data, nbytes = codecs.charmap_decode(input,
                                             self.errors,
                                             decoding_map)
        return data
```

```
    class InvertCapsStreamReader(InvertCapsCodec,
                                 codecs.StreamReader):
        pass


    class InvertCapsStreamWriter(InvertCapsCodec,
                                 codecs.StreamWriter):
        pass


    def find_invertcaps(encoding):
        """Return the codec for 'invertcaps'.
        """
        if encoding == 'invertcaps':
            return codecs.CodecInfo(
                name='invertcaps',
                encode=InvertCapsCodec().encode,
                decode=InvertCapsCodec().decode,
                incrementalencoder=InvertCapsIncrementalEncoder,
                incrementaldecoder=InvertCapsIncrementalDecoder,
                streamreader=InvertCapsStreamReader,
                streamwriter=InvertCapsStreamWriter,
            )
        return None


    codecs.register(find_invertcaps)

    if __name__ == '__main__':

        # Stateless encoder/decoder
        encoder = codecs.getencoder('invertcaps')
        text = 'abcDEF'
        encoded_text, consumed = encoder(text)
        print('Encoded "{}" to "{}", consuming {} characters'.format(
            text, encoded_text, consumed))

        # Stream writer
        import io
        buffer = io.BytesIO()
        writer = codecs.getwriter('invertcaps')(buffer)
        print('StreamWriter for io buffer: ')
        print('  writing "abcDEF"')
        writer.write('abcDEF')
        print('  buffer contents: ', buffer.getvalue())

        # Incremental decoder
        decoder_factory = codecs.getincrementaldecoder('invertcaps')
        decoder = decoder_factory()
        decoded_text_parts = []
```

```
    for c in encoded_text:
        decoded_text_parts.append(
            decoder.decode(bytes([c]), final=False)
        )
    decoded_text_parts.append(decoder.decode(b'', final=True))
    decoded_text = ''.join(decoded_text_parts)
    print('IncrementalDecoder converted {!r} to {!r}'.format(
        encoded_text, decoded_text))
```

The stateless encoder/decoder base class is Codec. Override encode() and decode() with the new implementation (in this case, calling charmap_encode() and charmap_decode(), respectively). Each method must return a tuple containing the transformed data and the number of the input bytes or characters consumed. Conveniently, charmap_encode() and charmap_decode() already return that information.

IncrementalEncoder and IncrementalDecoder serve as base classes for the incremental interfaces. The encode() and decode() methods of the incremental classes are defined in such a way that they return only the actual transformed data. Any information about buffering is maintained as internal state. The invertcaps encoding does not need to buffer data (it uses a one-to-one mapping). For encodings that produce a different amount of output depending on the data being processed, such as compression algorithms, BufferedIncrementalEncoder and BufferedIncrementalDecoder are more appropriate base classes, since they manage the unprocessed portion of the input.

StreamReader and StreamWriter need encode() and decode() methods, too. Because they are expected to return the same value as the version from Codec, multiple inheritance can be used for the implementation.

```
$ python3 codecs_invertcaps_register.py

Encoded "abcDEF" to "b'ABCdef'", consuming 6 characters
StreamWriter for io buffer:
  writing "abcDEF"
  buffer contents:  b'ABCdef'
IncrementalDecoder converted b'ABCdef' to 'abcDEF'
```

TIP

Related Reading

- Standard library documentation for codecs.[13]
- locale (page 1012): Accessing and managing the localization-based configuration settings and behaviors.
- io (page 390): The io module includes file and stream wrappers that handle encoding and decoding, too.
- socketserver (page 742): For a more detailed example of an echo server, see the socketserver module.

[13] https://docs.python.org/3.5/library/codecs.html

- encodings: Package in the standard library containing the encoder/decoder implementations provided by Python.
- **PEP 100**[14]: Python Unicode Integration.
- Unicode HOWTO[15]: The official guide to using Unicode with Python.
- Text vs. Data Instead of Unicode vs. 8-bit[16]: Section of the "What's New" article for Python 3.0 covering the text handling changes.
- Python Unicode Objects[17]: Fredrik Lundh's article about using non-ASCII character sets in Python 2.0.
- How to Use UTF-8 with Python[18]: Evan Jones's quick guide to working with Unicode, including XML data and the byte-order marker.
- On the Goodness of Unicode[19]: Introduction to internationalization and Unicode by Tim Bray.
- On Character Strings[20]: A look at the history of string processing in programming languages, by Tim Bray.
- Characters vs. Bytes[21]: Part 1 of Tim Bray's essay on modern character string processing for computer programmers. This installment covers in-memory representation of text in formats other than ASCII bytes.
- Wikipedia: Endianness[22]: Explanation of endianness.
- W3C XML Entity Definitions for Characters[23]: Specification for XML representations of character references that cannot be represented in an encoding.

6.11   io: Text, Binary, and Raw Stream I/O Tools

The io module implements the classes behind the interpreter's built-in open() for file-based input and output operations. The classes are decomposed in such a way that they can be recombined for alternative purposes—for example, to enable writing Unicode data to a network socket.

6.11.1   In-Memory Streams

StringIO provides a convenient means of working with text in memory using the file API (e.g., read(), write()). Using StringIO to build large strings can offer performance savings

---

[14] www.python.org/dev/peps/pep-0100
[15] https://docs.python.org/3/howto/unicode.html
[16] https://docs.python.org/3.0/whatsnew/3.0.html#text-vs-data-instead-of-unicode-vs-8-bit
[17] http://effbot.org/zone/unicode-objects.htm
[18] http://evanjones.ca/python-utf8.html
[19] www.tbray.org/ongoing/When/200x/2003/04/06/Unicode
[20] www.tbray.org/ongoing/When/200x/2003/04/13/Strings
[21] www.tbray.org/ongoing/When/200x/2003/04/26/UTF
[22] https://en.wikipedia.org/wiki/Endianness
[23] www.w3.org/TR/xml-entity-names/

over some other string concatenation techniques in some cases. In-memory stream buffers are also useful for testing, where writing to a real file on disk may slow down the test suite.

A few standard examples of using `StringIO` buffers follow.

Listing 6.114: io_stringio.py

```
import io

# Write to a buffer.
output = io.StringIO()
output.write('This goes into the buffer. ')
print('And so does this.', file=output)

# Retrieve the value written.
print(output.getvalue())

output.close()  # Discard buffer memory.

# Initialize a read buffer.
input = io.StringIO('Inital value for read buffer')

# Read from the buffer.
print(input.read())
```

This example uses `read()`, but the `readline()` and `readlines()` methods are also available. The `StringIO` class provides a `seek()` method for jumping around in a buffer while reading, which can be useful for rewinding if a look-ahead parsing algorithm is being used.

```
$ python3 io_stringio.py

This goes into the buffer. And so does this.

Inital value for read buffer
```

To work with raw bytes instead of Unicode text, use `BytesIO`.

Listing 6.115: io_bytesio.py

```
import io

# Write to a buffer.
output = io.BytesIO()
output.write('This goes into the buffer. '.encode('utf-8'))
output.write('ÁÇÊ'.encode('utf-8'))

# Retrieve the value written.
print(output.getvalue())

output.close()  # Discard buffer memory.
```

```
# Initialize a read buffer.
input = io.BytesIO(b'Inital value for read buffer')

# Read from the buffer.
print(input.read())
```

The values written to the `BytesIO` instance must be `bytes` rather than `str`.

```
$ python3 io_bytesio.py

b'This goes into the buffer. \xc3\x81\xc3\x87\xc3\x8a'
b'Inital value for read buffer'
```

6.11.2   Wrapping Byte Streams for Text Data

Raw byte streams such as sockets can be wrapped with a layer to handle string encoding and decoding, making it easier to use them with text data. The `TextIOWrapper` class supports both writing and reading. The `write_through` argument disables buffering, and flushes all data written to the wrapper through to the underlying buffer immediately.

Listing 6.116: **io_textiowrapper.py**

```
import io

# Write to a buffer.
output = io.BytesIO()
wrapper = io.TextIOWrapper(
    output,
    encoding='utf-8',
    write_through=True,
)
wrapper.write('This goes into the buffer. ')
wrapper.write('ÁÇÊ')

# Retrieve the value written.
print(output.getvalue())

output.close()  # Discard buffer memory.

# Initialize a read buffer.
input = io.BytesIO(
    b'Inital value for read buffer with unicode characters ' +
    'ÁÇÊ'.encode('utf-8')
)
wrapper = io.TextIOWrapper(input, encoding='utf-8')

# Read from the buffer.
print(wrapper.read())
```

This example uses a `BytesIO` instance as the stream. Examples for `bz2` (page 491), `http.server` (page 781), and `subprocess` (page 535) demonstrate using `TextIOWrapper` with other types of file-like objects.

```
$ python3 io_textiowrapper.py

b'This goes into the buffer. \xc3\x81\xc3\x87\xc3\x8a'
Inital value for read buffer with unicode characters ÁÇÊ
```

TIP

Related Reading

- Standard library documentation for io.[24]
- Section 12.2.3, "HTTP POST" (page 784): Uses the `detach()` of `TextIOWrapper` to manage the wrapper separately from the wrapped socket.
- Efficient String Concatenation in Python[25]: Examines various methods of combining strings and their relative merits.

---

[24] https://docs.python.org/3.5/library/io.html
[25] www.skymind.com/%7Eocrow/python_string/

Chapter 7
Data Persistence and Exchange

There are two aspects to preserving data for long-term use: converting the data back and forth between the object in-memory and the storage format, and working with the storage of the converted data. The standard library includes a variety of modules that handle both aspects in different situations.

Two modules convert objects into a format that can be transmitted or stored (a process known as *serializing*). It is most common to use `pickle` (page 396) for persistence—it is integrated with some of the other standard library modules that actually store the serialized data, such as `shelve`. `json` is more frequently used for web-based applications, however, since it integrates better with existing web service storage tools.

Once the in-memory object is converted to a format that can be saved, the next step is to decide how to store the data. A simple flat file with serialized objects written one after the other works for data that does not need to be indexed in any way. Python includes a collection of modules for storing key–value pairs in a simple database using one of the DBM format variants when an indexed lookup is needed.

The most straightforward way to take advantage of the DBM format is to use `shelve` (page 405). Open the shelve file, and access it through a dictionary-like API. Objects saved to the database are automatically pickled and saved without any extra work by the caller.

One drawback of `shelve` is that when using the default interface there is no way to predict which DBM format will be used: `shelve` selects one based on the libraries available on the system where the database is created. The format does not matter if an application will not need to share the database files between hosts with different libraries, but if portability is a requirement, use one of the classes in the module to ensure a specific format is selected.

For web applications that work with data in JSON already, use of `json` (page 803) and `dbm` (page 408) provides another persistence mechanism. Using `dbm` directly requires a little more work than using `shelve` because the DBM database keys and values must be strings, and the objects will not be re-created automatically when the value is accessed in the database.

The `sqlite3` (page 412) in-process relational database is available with most Python distributions for storing data in more complex arrangements than key–value pairs. The database is stored in memory or in a local file, and all access occurs from within the same process so there is no network communication lag. The compact nature of `sqlite3` makes it especially well suited for embedding in desktop applications or development versions of web apps.

Other modules are available for parsing more formally defined formats, an ability that is useful for exchanging data between Python programs and applications written in other languages. `xml.etree.ElementTree` (page 445) can parse XML documents and provides several operating modes for different applications. Besides the parsing tools, `ElementTree` includes an interface for creating well-formed XML documents from objects in memory. The csv (page 466) module can read and write tabular data in formats produced by spreadsheets or database applications, making it useful for bulk loading data or for converting the data from one format to another.

7.1   pickle: Object Serialization

The pickle module implements an algorithm for turning an arbitrary Python object into a series of bytes. This process is also called *serializing* the object. The byte stream representing the object can then be transmitted or stored, and later reconstructed to create a new object with the same characteristics.

WARNING

The documentation for pickle makes clear that it offers no security guarantees. In fact, unpickling data can execute arbitrary code. Be careful when using pickle for interprocess communication or data storage, and do not trust data that cannot be verified as secure. See the hmac (page 528) module for an example of a secure way to verify the source of a pickled data source.

7.1.1   Encoding and Decoding Data in Strings

This first example uses dumps() to encode a data structure as a string, then prints the string to the console. It uses a data structure made up of entirely built-in types. Instances of any class can be pickled, as will be illustrated in a later example.

Listing 7.1: **pickle_string.py**

```python
import pickle
import pprint

data = [{'a': 'A', 'b': 2, 'c': 3.0}]
print('DATA:', end=' ')
pprint.pprint(data)

data_string = pickle.dumps(data)
print('PICKLE: {!r}'.format(data_string))
```

By default, the pickle will be written in a binary format that is most compatible when sharing between Python 3 programs.

```
$ python3 pickle_string.py

DATA: [{'a': 'A', 'b': 2, 'c': 3.0}]
PICKLE: b'\x80\x03]q\x00}q\x01(X\x01\x00\x00\x00cq\x02G@\x08\x00
\x00\x00\x00\x00\x00\x00X\x01\x00\x00\x00bq\x03K\x02X\x01\x00\x00\x0
0aq\x04X\x01\x00\x00\x00Aq\x05ua.'
```

After the data is serialized, it can be written to a file, socket, pipe, or other location. Later, the file can be read and the data unpickled to construct a new object with the same values.

Listing 7.2: **pickle_unpickle.py**

```python
import pickle
import pprint

data1 = [{'a': 'A', 'b': 2, 'c': 3.0}]
print('BEFORE: ', end=' ')
pprint.pprint(data1)

data1_string = pickle.dumps(data1)

data2 = pickle.loads(data1_string)
print('AFTER : ', end=' ')
pprint.pprint(data2)

print('SAME? :', (data1 is data2))
print('EQUAL?:', (data1 == data2))
```

The newly constructed object is equal to, but not the same object as, the original.

```
$ python3 pickle_unpickle.py

BEFORE:  [{'a': 'A', 'b': 2, 'c': 3.0}]
AFTER :  [{'a': 'A', 'b': 2, 'c': 3.0}]
SAME? : False
EQUAL?: True
```

7.1.2 Working with Streams

In addition to dumps() and loads(), pickle provides convenience functions for working with file-like streams. It is possible to write multiple objects to a stream, and then read them from the stream without knowing in advance how many objects are written or how big they are.

Listing 7.3: **pickle_stream.py**

```python
import io
import pickle
import pprint


class SimpleObject:

    def __init__(self, name):
        self.name = name
```

```
        self.name_backwards = name[::-1]
        return


data = []
data.append(SimpleObject('pickle'))
data.append(SimpleObject('preserve'))
data.append(SimpleObject('last'))

# Simulate a file.
out_s = io.BytesIO()

# Write to the stream.
for o in data:
    print('WRITING : {} ({})'.format(o.name, o.name_backwards))
    pickle.dump(o, out_s)
    out_s.flush()

# Set up a readable stream.
in_s = io.BytesIO(out_s.getvalue())

# Read the data.
while True:
    try:
        o = pickle.load(in_s)
    except EOFError:
        break
    else:
        print('READ    : {} ({})'.format(
            o.name, o.name_backwards))
```

This example simulates streams using two `BytesIO` buffers. The first buffer receives the pickled objects, and its value is fed to a second buffer from which `load()` reads. A simple database format could use pickles to store objects, too. The `shelve` (page 405) module is one such implementation.

```
$ python3 pickle_stream.py

WRITING : pickle (elkcip)
WRITING : preserve (evreserp)
WRITING : last (tsal)
READ    : pickle (elkcip)
READ    : preserve (evreserp)
READ    : last (tsal)
```

Besides storing data, pickles are handy for interprocess communication. For example, `os.fork()` and `os.pipe()` can be used to establish worker processes that read job instructions from one pipe and write the results to another pipe. The core code for managing the worker pool and sending jobs in and receiving responses can be reused, since the job and response objects do not have to be based on a particular class. When using pipes or sockets, do not forget to flush after dumping each object, so as to push the data through the connection to the other end. See the `multiprocessing` (page 586) module for a reusable worker pool manager.

7.1.3 Problems Reconstructing Objects

When working with custom classes, the class being pickled must appear in the namespace of the process reading the pickle. Only the data for the instance is pickled, not the class definition. The class name is used to find the constructor to create the new object when unpickling. The following example writes instances of a class to a file.

Listing 7.4: `pickle_dump_to_file_1.py`

```python
import pickle
import sys


class SimpleObject:

    def __init__(self, name):
        self.name = name
        l = list(name)
        l.reverse()
        self.name_backwards = ''.join(l)


if __name__ == '__main__':
    data = []
    data.append(SimpleObject('pickle'))
    data.append(SimpleObject('preserve'))
    data.append(SimpleObject('last'))

    filename = sys.argv[1]

    with open(filename, 'wb') as out_s:
        for o in data:
            print('WRITING: {} ({})'.format(
                o.name, o.name_backwards))
            pickle.dump(o, out_s)
```

When run, the script creates a file based on the name given as an argument on the command line.

```
$ python3 pickle_dump_to_file_1.py test.dat

WRITING: pickle (elkcip)
WRITING: preserve (evreserp)
WRITING: last (tsal)
```

A simplistic attempt to load the resulting pickled objects fails.

Listing 7.5: `pickle_load_from_file_1.py`

```
import pickle
import pprint
import sys

filename = sys.argv[1]

with open(filename, 'rb') as in_s:
    while True:
        try:
            o = pickle.load(in_s)
        except EOFError:
            break
        else:
            print('READ: {} ({})'.format(
                o.name, o.name_backwards))
```

This version fails because there is no `SimpleObject` class available.

```
$ python3 pickle_load_from_file_1.py test.dat

Traceback (most recent call last):
  File "pickle_load_from_file_1.py", line 15, in <module>
    o = pickle.load(in_s)
AttributeError: Can't get attribute 'SimpleObject' on <module '_
_main__' from 'pickle_load_from_file_1.py'>
```

The corrected version, which imports `SimpleObject` from the original script, succeeds. Adding this import statement to the end of the import list allows the script to find the class and construct the object.

```
from pickle_dump_to_file_1 import SimpleObject
```

Running the modified script now produces the desired results.

```
$ python3 pickle_load_from_file_2.py test.dat

READ: pickle (elkcip)
READ: preserve (evreserp)
READ: last (tsal)
```

7.1.4 Unpicklable Objects

Not all objects can be pickled. Sockets, file handles, database connections, and other objects with runtime state that depends on the operating system or another process may not be

able to be saved in a meaningful way. Objects that have non-picklable attributes can define
`__getstate__()` and `__setstate__()` to return a subset of the state of the instance to be
pickled.

The `__getstate__()` method must return an object containing the internal state of the
object. One convenient way to represent that state is with a dictionary, but the value can
be any picklable object. The state is stored, and then passed to `__setstate__()` when the
object is loaded from the pickle.

Listing 7.6: pickle_state.py

```python
import pickle


class State:

    def __init__(self, name):
        self.name = name

    def __repr__(self):
        return 'State({!r})'.format(self.__dict__)


class MyClass:

    def __init__(self, name):
        print('MyClass.__init__({})'.format(name))
        self._set_name(name)

    def _set_name(self, name):
        self.name = name
        self.computed = name[::-1]

    def __repr__(self):
        return 'MyClass({!r}) (computed={!r})'.format(
            self.name, self.computed)

    def __getstate__(self):
        state = State(self.name)
        print('__getstate__ -> {!r}'.format(state))
        return state

    def __setstate__(self, state):
        print('__setstate__({!r})'.format(state))
        self._set_name(state.name)


inst = MyClass('name here')
print('Before:', inst)
```

```
dumped = pickle.dumps(inst)

reloaded = pickle.loads(dumped)
print('After:', reloaded)
```

This example uses a separate `State` object to hold the internal state of `MyClass`. When an instance of `MyClass` is loaded from a pickle, `__setstate__()` is passed a `State` instance that it uses to initialize the object.

```
$ python3 pickle_state.py

MyClass.__init__(name here)
Before: MyClass('name here') (computed='ereh eman')
__getstate__ -> State({'name': 'name here'})
__setstate__(State({'name': 'name here'}))
After: MyClass('name here') (computed='ereh eman')
```

WARNING

If the return value is false, then `__setstate__()` is not called when the object is unpickled.

7.1.5   Circular References

The pickle protocol automatically handles circular references between objects, so complex data structures do not need any special handling. Consider the directed graph in Figure 7.1. It includes several cycles, yet the correct structure can be pickled and then reloaded.

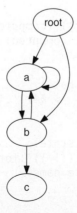

Figure 7.1: Pickling a Data Structure with Cycles

Listing 7.7: `pickle_cycle.py`

```python
import pickle


class Node:
    """A simple digraph
    """
    def __init__(self, name):
        self.name = name
        self.connections = []

    def add_edge(self, node):
        "Create an edge between this node and the other."
        self.connections.append(node)

    def __iter__(self):
        return iter(self.connections)


def preorder_traversal(root, seen=None, parent=None):
    """Generator function to yield the edges in a graph.
    """
    if seen is None:
        seen = set()
    yield (parent, root)
    if root in seen:
        return
    seen.add(root)
    for node in root:
        recurse = preorder_traversal(node, seen, root)
        for parent, subnode in recurse:
            yield (parent, subnode)


def show_edges(root):
    "Print all the edges in the graph."
    for parent, child in preorder_traversal(root):
        if not parent:
            continue
        print('{:>5} -> {:>2} ({})'.format(
            parent.name, child.name, id(child)))


# Set up the nodes.
root = Node('root')
a = Node('a')
b = Node('b')
c = Node('c')
```

```
# Add edges between them.
root.add_edge(a)
root.add_edge(b)
a.add_edge(b)
b.add_edge(a)
b.add_edge(c)
a.add_edge(a)

print('ORIGINAL GRAPH:')
show_edges(root)

# Pickle and unpickle the graph to create
# a new set of nodes.
dumped = pickle.dumps(root)
reloaded = pickle.loads(dumped)

print('\nRELOADED GRAPH:')
show_edges(reloaded)
```

The reloaded nodes are not the same object, but the relationship between the nodes is maintained and only one copy of the object with multiple references is reloaded. Both of these statements can be verified by examining the id() values for the nodes before and after they are passed through pickle.

```
$ python3 pickle_cycle.py

ORIGINAL GRAPH:
  root ->  a  (4315798272)
     a ->  b  (4315798384)
     b ->  a  (4315798272)
     b ->  c  (4315799112)
     a ->  a  (4315798272)
  root ->  b  (4315798384)

RELOADED GRAPH:
  root ->  a  (4315904096)
     a ->  b  (4315904152)
     b ->  a  (4315904096)
     b ->  c  (4315904208)
     a ->  a  (4315904096)
  root ->  b  (4315904152)
```

TIP

Related Reading

- Standard library documentation for pickle.[1]
- **PEP 3154**[2]: Pickle protocol version 4.

---

[1] https://docs.python.org/3.5/library/pickle.html
[2] www.python.org/dev/peps/pep-3154

- shelve (page 405): The shelve module uses pickle to store data in a DBM database.
- Pickle: An interesting stack language[3]: Tutorial by Alexandre Vassalotti.

7.2 shelve: Persistent Storage of Objects

The shelve module can be used as a simple persistent storage option for Python objects when a relational database is not required. The shelf is accessed by keys, just as with a dictionary. The values are pickled and written to a database that is created and managed by dbm (page 408).

7.2.1 Creating a New Shelf

The simplest way to use shelve is via the DbfilenameShelf class. It uses dbm (page 408) to store the data. The class can be used either directly or by calling shelve.open().

Listing 7.8: **shelve_create.py**

```
import shelve

with shelve.open('test_shelf.db') as s:
    s['key1'] = {
        'int': 10,
        'float': 9.5,
        'string': 'Sample data',
    }
```

To access the data again, open the shelf and use it like a dictionary.

Listing 7.9: **shelve_existing.py**

```
import shelve

with shelve.open('test_shelf.db') as s:
    existing = s['key1']

print(existing)
```

Running both sample scripts produces the following output.

```
$ python3 shelve_create.py
$ python3 shelve_existing.py

{'string': 'Sample data', 'int': 10, 'float': 9.5}
```

---

[3] http://peadrop.com/blog/2007/06/18/pickle-an-interesting-stack-language/

The dbm (page 408) module does not support multiple applications writing to the same database at the same time, but it does support concurrent read-only clients. If a client will not be modifying the shelf, tell shelve to open the database read-only by passing flag='r'.

Listing 7.10: **shelve_readonly.py**

```
import dbm
import shelve

with shelve.open('test_shelf.db', flag='r') as s:
    print('Existing:', s['key1'])
    try:
        s['key1'] = 'new value'
    except dbm.error as err:
        print('ERROR: {}'.format(err))
```

If the program tries to modify the database while it is opened as a read-only source, an access error exception is generated. The exception type depends on the database module selected by dbm (page 408) when the database was created.

```
$ python3 shelve_readonly.py

Existing: {'string': 'Sample data', 'int': 10, 'float': 9.5}
ERROR: cannot add item to database
```

7.2.2 Writeback

Shelves do not track modifications to volatile objects, by default. Thus, if the contents of an item stored in the shelf are changed, the shelf must be updated explicitly by storing the entire item again.

Listing 7.11: **shelve_withoutwriteback.py**

```
import shelve

with shelve.open('test_shelf.db') as s:
    print(s['key1'])
    s['key1']['new_value'] = 'this was not here before'

with shelve.open('test_shelf.db', writeback=True) as s:
    print(s['key1'])
```

In this example, the dictionary at 'key1' is not stored again. Thus, when the shelf is re-opened, the changes have not been preserved.

```
$ python3 shelve_create.py
$ python3 shelve_withoutwriteback.py
```

```
{'string': 'Sample data', 'int': 10, 'float': 9.5}
{'string': 'Sample data', 'int': 10, 'float': 9.5}
```

To automatically catch changes to volatile objects stored in the shelf, open the shelf with writeback enabled. The `writeback` flag causes the shelf to remember all of the objects retrieved from the database using an in-memory cache. Each cache object is also written back to the database when the shelf is closed.

Listing 7.12: **shelve_writeback.py**

```
import shelve
import pprint

with shelve.open('test_shelf.db', writeback=True) as s:
    print('Initial data:')
    pprint.pprint(s['key1'])

    s['key1']['new_value'] = 'this was not here before'
    print('\nModified:')
    pprint.pprint(s['key1'])

with shelve.open('test_shelf.db', writeback=True) as s:
    print('\nPreserved:')
    pprint.pprint(s['key1'])
```

Although it reduces the chance of programmer error, and can make object persistence more transparent, using writeback mode may not be desirable in every situation. The cache consumes extra memory while the shelf is open, and pausing to write every cached object back to the database when it is closed slows down the application. All of the cached objects are written back to the database because there is no way to tell if they have been modified. If the application reads data more than it writes, writeback will impact performance unnecessarily.

```
$ python3 shelve_create.py
$ python3 shelve_writeback.py

Initial data:
{'float': 9.5, 'int': 10, 'string': 'Sample data'}

Modified:
{'float': 9.5,
 'int': 10,
 'new_value': 'this was not here before',
 'string': 'Sample data'}

Preserved:
{'float': 9.5,
```

```
'int': 10,
'new_value': 'this was not here before',
'string': 'Sample data'}
```

7.2.3 Specific Shelf Types

The earlier examples all used the default shelf implementation. Using `shelve.open()` instead of one of the shelf implementations directly is a common usage pattern, especially if the type of database used to store the data does not matter. At other times, however, the database format is important. In those situations, use `DbfilenameShelf` or `BsdDbShelf` directly, or even subclass `Shelf` for a custom solution.

TIP

Related Reading

- Standard library documentation for `shelve`.[4]
- dbm (page 408): The dbm module finds an available DBM library to create a new database.
- feedcache[5]: The `feedcache` module uses `shelve` as a default storage option.
- shove[6]: The `shove` module implements a similar API with more back-end formats.

7.3   dbm: Unix Key–Value Databases

`dbm` is a front-end for DBM-style databases that use simple string values as keys to access records containing strings. It uses `whichdb()` to identify databases, then opens them with the appropriate module. `dbm` is used as a back-end for `shelve` (page 405), which stores objects in a DBM database using `pickle` (page 396).

7.3.1 Database Types

Python comes with several modules for accessing DBM-style databases. The default implementation selected depends on the libraries available on the current system and the options used when Python was compiled. Separate interfaces to the specific implementations allow Python programs to exchange data with programs in other languages that do not automatically switch between available formats, and to write portable data files that will work on multiple platforms.

---

[4] https://docs.python.org/3.5/library/shelve.html
[5] https://bitbucket.org/dhellmann/feedcache
[6] http://pypi.python.org/pypi/shove/

7.3.1.1 dbm.gnu

dbm.gnu is an interface to the version of the dbm library from the GNU project. It works the same way as the other DBM implementations described here, with a few changes to the flags supported by open().

Besides the standard 'r', 'w', 'c', and 'n' flags, dbm.gnu.open() supports:

- 'f' to open the database in *fast* mode. In fast mode, writes to the database are not synchronized.

- 's' to open the database in *synchronized* mode. Changes to the database are written to the file as they are made, rather than being delayed until the database is closed or synced explicitly.

- 'u' to open the database in an unlocked state.

7.3.1.2 dbm.ndbm

The dbm.ndbm module provides an interface to the Unix ndbm implementations of the dbm format, depending on how the module was configured during compilation. The module attribute library identifies the name of the library that configure was able to find when the extension module was compiled.

7.3.1.3 dbm.dumb

The dbm.dumb module is a portable fallback implementation of the DBM API when no other implementations are available. No external dependencies are required to use dbm.dumb, but it works more slowly than most other implementations.

7.3.2 Creating a New Database

The storage format for new databases is selected by looking for usable versions of each of the submodules in order.

- dbm.gnu

- dbm.ndbm

- dbm.dumb

The open() function takes flags to control how the database file is managed. To create a new database when necessary, use 'c'. Using 'n' always creates a new database, overwriting an existing file.

Listing 7.13: dbm_new.py

```
import dbm

with dbm.open('/tmp/example.db', 'n') as db:
    db['key'] = 'value'
```

```
db['today'] = 'Sunday'
db['author'] = 'Doug'
```

In this example, the file is always reinitialized.

```
$ python3 dbm_new.py
```

whichdb() reports the type of database that was created.

Listing 7.14: `dbm_whichdb.py`

```
import dbm

print(dbm.whichdb('/tmp/example.db'))
```

Output from the example program will vary, depending on which modules are installed on the system.

```
$ python3 dbm_whichdb.py

dbm.ndbm
```

7.3.3 Opening an Existing Database

To open an existing database, use flags of either 'r' (for read-only) or 'w' (for read-write). Existing databases are automatically given to whichdb() to identify. Thus, as long as a file can be identified, the appropriate module is used to open it.

Listing 7.15: `dbm_existing.py`

```
import dbm

with dbm.open('/tmp/example.db', 'r') as db:
    print('keys():', db.keys())
    for k in db.keys():
        print('iterating:', k, db[k])
    print('db["author"] =', db['author'])
```

Once opened, db is a dictionary-like object. New keys are always converted to byte strings when added to the database, and returned as byte strings.

```
$ python3 dbm_existing.py

keys(): [b'key', b'today', b'author']
iterating: b'key' b'value'
iterating: b'today' b'Sunday'
iterating: b'author' b'Doug'
db["author"] = b'Doug'
```

7.3.4 Error Cases

The keys of the database need to be strings.

Listing 7.16: dbm_intkeys.py

```
import dbm

with dbm.open('/tmp/example.db', 'w') as db:
    try:
        db[1] = 'one'
    except TypeError as err:
        print(err)
```

Passing another type results in a `TypeError`.

```
$ python3 dbm_intkeys.py

dbm mappings have bytes or string keys only
```

Values must be strings or `None`.

Listing 7.17: dbm_intvalue.py

```
import dbm

with dbm.open('/tmp/example.db', 'w') as db:
    try:
        db['one'] = 1
    except TypeError as err:
        print(err)
```

A similar `TypeError` is raised if a value is not a string.

```
$ python3 dbm_intvalue.py

dbm mappings have byte or string elements only
```

TIP

Related Reading

- Standard library documentation for dbm.[7]
- Python 2 to 3 porting notes for anydbm (page 1356).
- Python 2 to 3 porting notes for whichdb (page 1365).
- shelve (page 405): Examples for the shelve module, which uses dbm to store data.

---

[7] https://docs.python.org/3.5/library/dbm.html

7.4   sqlite3: Embedded Relational Database

The `sqlite3` module implements a Python DB-API 2.0[8] compliant interface to SQLite, an in-process relational database. SQLite is designed to be embedded in applications, instead of using a separate database server program such as MySQL, PostgreSQL, or Oracle. It is fast, rigorously tested, and flexible, making it suitable for prototyping and production deployment for some applications.

7.4.1   Creating a Database

An SQLite database is stored as a single file on the file system. The library manages access to the file, including locking it to prevent corruption when multiple writers use it. The database is created the first time the file is accessed, but the application is responsible for managing the table definitions, or *schema*, within the database.

This example looks for the database file before opening it with `connect()` so it knows when to create the schema for new databases.

Listing 7.18: `sqlite3_createdb.py`

```
import os
import sqlite3

db_filename = 'todo.db'

db_is_new = not os.path.exists(db_filename)

conn = sqlite3.connect(db_filename)

if db_is_new:
    print('Need to create schema')
else:
    print('Database exists; assume schema does, too.')

conn.close()
```

Running the script twice shows that it creates the empty file if one does not exist.

```
$ ls *.db

ls: *.db: No such file or directory

$ python3 sqlite3_createdb.py

Need to create schema
```

---

[8] www.python.org/dev/peps/pep-0249/

```
$ ls *.db

todo.db

$ python3 sqlite3_createdb.py

Database exists; assume schema does, too.
```

After creating the new database file, the next step is to create the schema to define the tables within the database. The remaining examples in this section all use the same database schema with tables for managing tasks. The details of the database schema are presented in Table 7.1 and Table 7.2.

The *data definition language* (DDL) statements to create the tables are shown in the following listing.

Listing 7.19: todo_schema.sql

```
-- Schema for to-do application examples

-- Projects are high-level activities made up of tasks
create table project (
    name        text primary key,
    description text,
    deadline    date
);

-- Tasks are steps that can be taken to complete a project
create table task (
    id          integer primary key autoincrement not null,
    priority    integer default 1,
```

Table 7.1: The Project Table

Column	Type	Description
name	text	Project name
description	text	Long project description
deadline	date	Due date for the entire project

Table 7.2: The Task Table

Column	Type	Description
id	number	Unique task identifier
priority	integer	Numerical priority, lower is more important
details	text	Full task details
status	text	Task status (one of new, pending, done, or canceled)
deadline	date	Due date for this task
completed_on	date	When the task was completed
project	text	The name of the project for this task

```
    details      text,
    status       text,
    deadline     date,
    completed_on date,
    project      text not null references project(name)
);
```

The `executescript()` method of the `Connection` can be used to run the DDL instructions to create the schema.

Listing 7.20: **sqlite3_create_schema.py**

```python
import os
import sqlite3

db_filename = 'todo.db'
schema_filename = 'todo_schema.sql'

db_is_new = not os.path.exists(db_filename)

with sqlite3.connect(db_filename) as conn:
    if db_is_new:
        print('Creating schema')
        with open(schema_filename, 'rt') as f:
            schema = f.read()
        conn.executescript(schema)

        print('Inserting initial data')

        conn.executescript("""
        insert into project (name, description, deadline)
        values ('pymotw', 'Python Module of the Week',
                '2016-11-01');

        insert into task (details, status, deadline, project)
        values ('write about select', 'done', '2016-04-25',
                'pymotw');

        insert into task (details, status, deadline, project)
        values ('write about random', 'waiting', '2016-08-22',
                'pymotw');

        insert into task (details, status, deadline, project)
        values ('write about sqlite3', 'active', '2017-07-31',
                'pymotw');
        """)
    else:
        print('Database exists, assume schema does, too.')
```

After the tables are created, a few `insert` statements create a sample project and related tasks. The `sqlite3` command-line program can be used to examine the contents of the database.

```
$ rm -f todo.db
$ python3 sqlite3_create_schema.py

Creating schema
Inserting initial data

$ sqlite3 todo.db 'select * from task'

1|1|write about select|done|2016-04-25||pymotw
2|1|write about random|waiting|2016-08-22||pymotw
3|1|write about sqlite3|active|2017-07-31||pymotw
```

7.4.2   Retrieving Data

To retrieve the values saved in the `task` table from within a Python program, create a `Cursor` from a database connection. A cursor produces a consistent view of the data, and is the primary means of interacting with a transactional database system like SQLite.

Listing 7.21: **sqlite3_select_tasks.py**

```python
import sqlite3

db_filename = 'todo.db'

with sqlite3.connect(db_filename) as conn:
    cursor = conn.cursor()

    cursor.execute("""
    select id, priority, details, status, deadline from task
    where project = 'pymotw'
    """)

    for row in cursor.fetchall():
        task_id, priority, details, status, deadline = row
        print('{:2d} [{:d}] {:<25} [{:<8}] ({})'.format(
            task_id, priority, details, status, deadline))
```

Querying is a two-step process. First, run the query with the cursor's `execute()` method to tell the database engine which data to collect. Then, use `fetchall()` to retrieve the results. The return value is a sequence of tuples containing the values for the columns included in the `select` clause of the query.

```
$ python3 sqlite3_select_tasks.py

1 [1] write about select        [done    ] (2016-04-25)
2 [1] write about random        [waiting ] (2016-08-22)
3 [1] write about sqlite3       [active  ] (2017-07-31)
```

The results can be retrieved one at a time with `fetchone()`, or in fixed-size batches with `fetchmany()`.

Listing 7.22: **sqlite3_select_variations.py**

```python
import sqlite3

db_filename = 'todo.db'

with sqlite3.connect(db_filename) as conn:
    cursor = conn.cursor()

    cursor.execute("""
    select name, description, deadline from project
    where name = 'pymotw'
    """)
    name, description, deadline = cursor.fetchone()

    print('Project details for {} ({})\n  due {}'.format(
        description, name, deadline))

    cursor.execute("""
    select id, priority, details, status, deadline from task
    where project = 'pymotw' order by deadline
    """)

    print('\nNext 5 tasks:')
    for row in cursor.fetchmany(5):
        task_id, priority, details, status, deadline = row
        print('{:2d} [{:d}] {:<25} [{:<8}] ({})'.format(
            task_id, priority, details, status, deadline))
```

The value passed to `fetchmany()` is the maximum number of items to return. If fewer items are available, the sequence returned will be smaller than the maximum value.

```
$ python3 sqlite3_select_variations.py

Project details for Python Module of the Week (pymotw)
   due 2016-11-01

Next 5 tasks:
  1 [1] write about select        [done    ] (2016-04-25)
```

```
2 [1] write about random        [waiting ] (2016-08-22)
3 [1] write about sqlite3       [active  ] (2017-07-31)
```

7.4.3   Query Metadata

The DB-API 2.0 specification says that after `execute()` has been called, the `Cursor` should set its `description` attribute to hold information about the data that will be returned by the fetch methods. The API specification defines the description value as a sequence of tuples containing the column name, type, display size, internal size, precision, scale, and a flag that says whether null values are accepted.

Listing 7.23: `sqlite3_cursor_description.py`

```python
import sqlite3

db_filename = 'todo.db'

with sqlite3.connect(db_filename) as conn:
    cursor = conn.cursor()

    cursor.execute("""
    select * from task where project = 'pymotw'
    """)

    print('Task table has these columns:')
    for colinfo in cursor.description:
        print(colinfo)
```

Because `sqlite3` does not enforce type or size constraints on data inserted into a database, only the column name value is filled in.

```
$ python3 sqlite3_cursor_description.py

Task table has these columns:
('id', None, None, None, None, None, None)
('priority', None, None, None, None, None, None)
('details', None, None, None, None, None, None)
('status', None, None, None, None, None, None)
('deadline', None, None, None, None, None, None)
('completed_on', None, None, None, None, None, None)
('project', None, None, None, None, None, None)
```

7.4.4   Row Objects

By default, the values returned by the fetch methods as "rows" from the database are tuples. The caller is responsible for knowing the order of the columns in the query and extracting individual values from the tuple. When the number of values in a query grows, or when the code working with the data is spread out in a library, it is usually easier to work with an object and access values using their column names. That way, the number and order of the tuple contents can change over time as the query is edited, and code depending on the query results is less likely to break.

Connection objects have a row_factory property that allows the calling code to control the type of object created to represent each row in the query result set. sqlite3 also includes a Row class that is intended to be used as a row factory. Column values can be accessed through Row instances by using the column index or name.

Listing 7.24: sqlite3_row_factory.py

```python
import sqlite3

db_filename = 'todo.db'

with sqlite3.connect(db_filename) as conn:
    # Change the row factory to use Row.
    conn.row_factory = sqlite3.Row

    cursor = conn.cursor()

    cursor.execute("""
    select name, description, deadline from project
    where name = 'pymotw'
    """)
    name, description, deadline = cursor.fetchone()

    print('Project details for {} ({})\n  due {}'.format(
        description, name, deadline))

    cursor.execute("""
    select id, priority, status, deadline, details from task
    where project = 'pymotw' order by deadline
    """)

    print('\nNext 5 tasks:')
    for row in cursor.fetchmany(5):
        print('{:2d} [{:d}] {:<25} [{:<8}] ({})'.format(
            row['id'], row['priority'], row['details'],
            row['status'], row['deadline'],
        ))
```

This version of the sqlite3_select_variations.py example has been rewritten using Row instances instead of tuples. The row from the project table is still printed by accessing the column values through position, but the print statement for tasks uses keyword lookup instead. As a consequence, it does not matter that the order of the columns in the query has changed.

```
$ python3 sqlite3_row_factory.py

Project details for Python Module of the Week (pymotw)
  due 2016-11-01

Next 5 tasks:
 1 [1] write about select          [done    ] (2016-04-25)
 2 [1] write about random          [waiting ] (2016-08-22)
 3 [1] write about sqlite3         [active  ] (2017-07-31)
```

7.4.5   Using Variables with Queries

The use of queries defined as literal strings embedded in a program is inflexible. For example, when another project is added to the database, the query to show the top five tasks should be updated to work with either project. One way to increase the flexibility is to build an SQL statement with the desired query by combining values in Python. However, building a query string in this way is dangerous, and should be avoided. Failing to correctly escape special characters in the variable parts of the query can result in SQL parsing errors or—even worse—a class of security vulnerabilities known as *SQL-injection attacks*, which allow intruders to execute arbitrary SQL statements in the database.

The proper way to use dynamic values with queries is through *host variables* passed to execute() along with the SQL instruction. A placeholder value in the SQL is replaced with the value of the host variable when the statement executes. Using host variables instead of inserting arbitrary values into the SQL before it is parsed avoids injection attacks because there is no chance that the untrusted values will affect how the SQL is parsed. SQLite supports two forms for queries with placeholders: positional and named.

7.4.5.1   Positional Parameters

A question mark (?) denotes a positional argument, passed to execute() as a member of a tuple.

Listing 7.25: **sqlite3_argument_positional.py**

```
import sqlite3
import sys

db_filename = 'todo.db'
project_name = sys.argv[1]

with sqlite3.connect(db_filename) as conn:
    cursor = conn.cursor()

    query = """
    select id, priority, details, status, deadline from task
    where project = ?
    """
```

```
cursor.execute(query, (project_name,))

for row in cursor.fetchall():
    task_id, priority, details, status, deadline = row
    print('{:2d} [{:d}] {:<25} [{:<8}] ({})'.format(
        task_id, priority, details, status, deadline))
```

The command-line argument is passed safely to the query as a positional argument, and bad data will not corrupt the database.

```
$ python3 sqlite3_argument_positional.py pymotw

 1 [1] write about select        [done    ] (2016-04-25)
 2 [1] write about random        [waiting ] (2016-08-22)
 3 [1] write about sqlite3       [active  ] (2017-07-31)
```

7.4.5.2 Named Parameters

Use named parameters for more complex queries with a lot of parameters, or where some parameters are repeated multiple times within the query. Named parameters are prefixed with a colon (e.g., :param_name).

Listing 7.26: **sqlite3_argument_named.py**

```
import sqlite3
import sys

db_filename = 'todo.db'
project_name = sys.argv[1]

with sqlite3.connect(db_filename) as conn:
    cursor = conn.cursor()

    query = """
    select id, priority, details, status, deadline from task
    where project = :project_name
    order by deadline, priority
    """

    cursor.execute(query, {'project_name': project_name})

    for row in cursor.fetchall():
        task_id, priority, details, status, deadline = row
        print('{:2d} [{:d}] {:<25} [{:<8}] ({})'.format(
            task_id, priority, details, status, deadline))
```

Neither positional nor named parameters need to be quoted or escaped, since they are given special treatment by the query parser.

```
$ python3 sqlite3_argument_named.py pymotw

1 [1] write about select          [done    ] (2016-04-25)
2 [1] write about random          [waiting ] (2016-08-22)
3 [1] write about sqlite3         [active  ] (2017-07-31)
```

Query parameters can be used with select, insert, and update statements. They can appear in any part of the query where a literal value is legal.

Listing 7.27: **sqlite3_argument_update.py**

```python
import sqlite3
import sys

db_filename = 'todo.db'
id = int(sys.argv[1])
status = sys.argv[2]

with sqlite3.connect(db_filename) as conn:
    cursor = conn.cursor()
    query = "update task set status = :status where id = :id"
    cursor.execute(query, {'status': status, 'id': id})
```

This update statement uses two named parameters. The id value is used to find the right row to modify, and the status value is written to the table.

```
$ python3 sqlite3_argument_update.py 2 done
$ python3 sqlite3_argument_named.py pymotw

1 [1] write about select          [done    ] (2016-04-25)
2 [1] write about random          [done    ] (2016-08-22)
3 [1] write about sqlite3         [active  ] (2017-07-31)
```

7.4.6 Bulk Loading

To apply the same SQL instruction to a large set of data, use executemany(). This method is useful for loading data, since it avoids looping over the inputs in Python and lets the underlying library apply loop optimizations. This example program reads a list of tasks from a comma-separated value file using the csv (page 466) module and loads them into the database.

Listing 7.28: **sqlite3_load_csv.py**

```python
import csv
import sqlite3
import sys

db_filename = 'todo.db'
```

```
data_filename = sys.argv[1]

SQL = """
insert into task (details, priority, status, deadline, project)
values (:details, :priority, 'active', :deadline, :project)
"""

with open(data_filename, 'rt') as csv_file:
    csv_reader = csv.DictReader(csv_file)

    with sqlite3.connect(db_filename) as conn:
        cursor = conn.cursor()
        cursor.executemany(SQL, csv_reader)
```

The file `tasks.csv` contains the following sample data:

```
deadline,project,priority,details
2016-11-30,pymotw,2,"finish reviewing markup"
2016-08-20,pymotw,2,"revise chapter intros"
2016-11-01,pymotw,1,"subtitle"
```

Running the program produces the following output.

```
$ python3 sqlite3_load_csv.py tasks.csv
$ python3 sqlite3_argument_named.py pymotw

1 [1] write about select         [done   ] (2016-04-25)
5 [2] revise chapter intros      [active ] (2016-08-20)
2 [1] write about random         [done   ] (2016-08-22)
6 [1] subtitle                   [active ] (2016-11-01)
4 [2] finish reviewing markup    [active ] (2016-11-30)
3 [1] write about sqlite3        [active ] (2017-07-31)
```

7.4.7   Defining New Column Types

SQLite has native support for integer, floating-point, and text columns. Data of these types is converted automatically by `sqlite3` from Python's representation to values that can be stored in the database, and back again, as needed. Integer values are loaded from the database into `int` or `long` variables, depending on the size of the value. Text is saved and retrieved as `str`, unless the `text_factory` for the `Connection` has been changed.

Although SQLite supports only a few data types internally, `sqlite3` includes facilities for defining custom types to allow a Python application to store any type of data in a column. Conversion for types beyond those supported by default is enabled in the database connection using the `detect_types` flag. Use `PARSE_DECLTYPES` if the column was declared using the desired type when the table was defined.

Listing 7.29: sqlite3_date_types.py

```python
import sqlite3
import sys

db_filename = 'todo.db'

sql = "select id, details, deadline from task"


def show_deadline(conn):
    conn.row_factory = sqlite3.Row
    cursor = conn.cursor()
    cursor.execute(sql)
    row = cursor.fetchone()
    for col in ['id', 'details', 'deadline']:
        print('  {:<8}  {!r:<26} {}'.format(
            col, row[col], type(row[col])))
    return


print('Without type detection:')
with sqlite3.connect(db_filename) as conn:
    show_deadline(conn)

print('\nWith type detection:')
with sqlite3.connect(db_filename,
                     detect_types=sqlite3.PARSE_DECLTYPES,
                     ) as conn:
    show_deadline(conn)
```

sqlite3 provides converters for date and timestamp columns, using the classes `date` and `datetime`, respectively, from the `datetime` (page 221) module to represent the values in Python. Both date-related converters are enabled automatically when type detection is turned on.

```
$ python3 sqlite3_date_types.py

Without type detection:
  id        1                          <class 'int'>
  details   'write about select'       <class 'str'>
  deadline  '2016-04-25'               <class 'str'>

With type detection:
  id        1                          <class 'int'>
  details   'write about select'       <class 'str'>
  deadline  datetime.date(2016, 4, 25) <class 'datetime.date'>
```

Two functions need to be registered to define a new type. The *adapter* takes the Python object as input and returns a byte string that can be stored in the database. The *converter* receives the string from the database and returns a Python object. Use `register_adapter()` to define an adapter function, and `register_converter()` for a converter function.

Listing 7.30: `sqlite3_custom_type.py`

```
import pickle
import sqlite3

db_filename = 'todo.db'


def adapter_func(obj):
    """Convert from in-memory to storage representation.
    """
    print('adapter_func({})\n'.format(obj))
    return pickle.dumps(obj)


def converter_func(data):
    """Convert from storage to in-memory representation.
    """
    print('converter_func({!r})\n'.format(data))
    return pickle.loads(data)


class MyObj:

    def __init__(self, arg):
        self.arg = arg

    def __str__(self):
        return 'MyObj({!r})'.format(self.arg)

# Register the functions for manipulating the type.
sqlite3.register_adapter(MyObj, adapter_func)
sqlite3.register_converter("MyObj", converter_func)

# Create some objects to save.  Use a list of tuples so
# the sequence can be passed directly to executemany().
to_save = [
    (MyObj('this is a value to save'),),
    (MyObj(42),),
]

with sqlite3.connect(
        db_filename,
        detect_types=sqlite3.PARSE_DECLTYPES) as conn:
```

```
# Create a table with column of type "MyObj".
conn.execute("""
create table if not exists obj (
    id    integer primary key autoincrement not null,
    data  MyObj
)
""")
cursor = conn.cursor()

# Insert the objects into the database.
cursor.executemany("insert into obj (data) values (?)",
                   to_save)

# Query the database for the objects just saved.
cursor.execute("select id, data from obj")
for obj_id, obj in cursor.fetchall():
    print('Retrieved', obj_id, obj)
    print('  with type', type(obj))
    print()
```

This example uses pickle (page 396) to save an object to a string that can be stored in the database, a useful technique for storing arbitrary objects, but one that does not allow querying based on object attributes. A real *object-relational mapper*, such as SQLAlchemy,[9] that stores attribute values in their own columns will be more useful for large amounts of data.

```
$ python3 sqlite3_custom_type.py

adapter_func(MyObj('this is a value to save'))

adapter_func(MyObj(42))

converter_func(b'\x80\x03c__main__\nMyObj\nq\x00)\x81q\x01}q\x02X\x0
3\x00\x00\x00argq\x03X\x17\x00\x00\x00this is a value to saveq\x04sb
.')

converter_func(b'\x80\x03c__main__\nMyObj\nq\x00)\x81q\x01}q\x02X\x0
3\x00\x00\x00argq\x03K*sb.')

Retrieved 1 MyObj('this is a value to save')
  with type <class '__main__.MyObj'>

Retrieved 2 MyObj(42)
  with type <class '__main__.MyObj'>
```

---

[9] www.sqlalchemy.org

7.4.8   Determining Types for Columns

There are two sources for information about the types of data for a query. The original table declaration can be used to identify the type of a real column, as shown earlier. Alternatively, a type specifier can be included in the select clause of the query itself using the form as "name [type]".

Listing 7.31: `sqlite3_custom_type_column.py`

```python
import pickle
import sqlite3

db_filename = 'todo.db'


def adapter_func(obj):
    """Convert from in-memory to storage representation.
    """
    print('adapter_func({})\n'.format(obj))
    return pickle.dumps(obj)


def converter_func(data):
    """Convert from storage to in-memory representation.
    """
    print('converter_func({!r})\n'.format(data))
    return pickle.loads(data)


class MyObj:

    def __init__(self, arg):
        self.arg = arg

    def __str__(self):
        return 'MyObj({!r})'.format(self.arg)

# Register the functions for manipulating the type.
sqlite3.register_adapter(MyObj, adapter_func)
sqlite3.register_converter("MyObj", converter_func)

# Create some objects to save.  Use a list of tuples so we
# can pass this sequence directly to executemany().
to_save = [
    (MyObj('this is a value to save'),),
    (MyObj(42),),
]

with sqlite3.connect(
```

```
            db_filename,
            detect_types=sqlite3.PARSE_COLNAMES) as conn:
        # Create a table with column of type "text".
        conn.execute("""
        create table if not exists obj2 (
            id      integer primary key autoincrement not null,
            data    text
        )
        """)
        cursor = conn.cursor()

        # Insert the objects into the database.
        cursor.executemany("insert into obj2 (data) values (?)",
                           to_save)

        # Query the database for the objects just saved,
        # using a type specifier to convert the text
        # to objects.
        cursor.execute(
            'select id, data as "pickle [MyObj]" from obj2',
        )
        for obj_id, obj in cursor.fetchall():
            print('Retrieved', obj_id, obj)
            print('  with type', type(obj))
            print()
```

Use the `detect_types` flag `PARSE_COLNAMES` when the type is part of the query instead of the original table definition.

```
$ python3 sqlite3_custom_type_column.py

adapter_func(MyObj('this is a value to save'))

adapter_func(MyObj(42))

converter_func(b'\x80\x03c__main__\nMyObj\nq\x00)\x81q\x01}q\x02X\x0
3\x00\x00\x00argq\x03X\x17\x00\x00\x00this is a value to saveq\x04sb
.')

converter_func(b'\x80\x03c__main__\nMyObj\nq\x00)\x81q\x01}q\x02X\x0
3\x00\x00\x00argq\x03K*sb.')

Retrieved 1 MyObj('this is a value to save')
  with type <class '__main__.MyObj'>

Retrieved 2 MyObj(42)
  with type <class '__main__.MyObj'>
```

7.4.9   Transactions

One of the key features of relational databases is the use of *transactions* to maintain a consistent internal state. With transactions enabled, several changes can be made through one connection without affecting any other users until the results are *committed* and flushed to the actual database.

7.4.9.1   Preserving Changes

Changes to the database, made through either `insert` or `update` statements, need to be saved by explicitly calling `commit()`. This requirement gives an application an opportunity to make several related changes together, so they are stored *atomically* instead of incrementally. Such an approach avoids the situation where partial updates are seen by different clients connecting to the database simultaneously.

The effect of calling `commit()` can be seen with a program that uses several connections to the database. A new row is inserted with the first connection, and then two attempts are made to read it back using separate connections.

Listing 7.32: `sqlite3_transaction_commit.py`

```
import sqlite3

db_filename = 'todo.db'


def show_projects(conn):
    cursor = conn.cursor()
    cursor.execute('select name, description from project')
    for name, desc in cursor.fetchall():
        print('  ', name)


with sqlite3.connect(db_filename) as conn1:
    print('Before changes:')
    show_projects(conn1)

    # Insert in one cursor.
    cursor1 = conn1.cursor()
    cursor1.execute("""
    insert into project (name, description, deadline)
    values ('virtualenvwrapper', 'Virtualenv Extensions',
            '2011-01-01')
    """)

    print('\nAfter changes in conn1:')
    show_projects(conn1)

    # Select from another connection, without committing first.
    print('\nBefore commit:')
```

```
with sqlite3.connect(db_filename) as conn2:
    show_projects(conn2)

# Commit, then select from another connection.
conn1.commit()
print('\nAfter commit:')
with sqlite3.connect(db_filename) as conn3:
    show_projects(conn3)
```

When show_projects() is called before conn1 has been committed, the results depend
on which connection is used. Since the change was made through conn1, this connection
sees the altered data. Conversely, conn2 does not. After committing, the new connection
conn3 sees the inserted row.

```
$ python3 sqlite3_transaction_commit.py

Before changes:
    pymotw

After changes in conn1:
    pymotw
    virtualenvwrapper

Before commit:
    pymotw

After commit:
    pymotw
    virtualenvwrapper
```

7.4.9.2   Discarding Changes

Uncommitted changes can also be discarded entirely using rollback(). The commit() and
rollback() methods are usually called from different parts of the same try:except block,
with errors triggering a rollback.

Listing 7.33: **sqlite3_transaction_rollback.py**

```
import sqlite3

db_filename = 'todo.db'


def show_projects(conn):
    cursor = conn.cursor()
    cursor.execute('select name, description from project')
    for name, desc in cursor.fetchall():
        print('  ', name)
```

```
with sqlite3.connect(db_filename) as conn:

    print('Before changes:')
    show_projects(conn)

    try:

        # Insert
        cursor = conn.cursor()
        cursor.execute("""delete from project
                    where name = 'virtualenvwrapper'
                    """)

        # Show the settings.
        print('\nAfter delete:')
        show_projects(conn)

        # Pretend the processing caused an error.
        raise RuntimeError('simulated error')

    except Exception as err:
        # Discard the changes.
        print('ERROR:', err)
        conn.rollback()

    else:
        # Save the changes.
        conn.commit()

    # Show the results.
    print('\nAfter rollback:')
    show_projects(conn)
```

After calling rollback(), the changes to the database are no longer present.

```
$ python3 sqlite3_transaction_rollback.py

Before changes:
    pymotw
    virtualenvwrapper

After delete:
    pymotw
ERROR: simulated error

After rollback:
    pymotw
    virtualenvwrapper
```

7.4.10   Isolation Levels

sqlite3 supports three locking modes, called *isolation levels*, that control the technique used to prevent incompatible changes between connections. The isolation level is set by passing a string as the isolation_level argument when a connection is opened, so different connections can use different values.

This program demonstrates the effect of different isolation levels on the order of events in threads using separate connections to the same database. Four threads are created: two that write changes to the database by updating existing rows, and two that attempt to read all of the rows from the task table.

Listing 7.34: **sqlite3_isolation_levels.py**

```python
import logging
import sqlite3
import sys
import threading
import time

logging.basicConfig(
    level=logging.DEBUG,
    format='%(asctime)s (%(threadName)-10s) %(message)s',
)

db_filename = 'todo.db'
isolation_level = sys.argv[1]


def writer():
    with sqlite3.connect(
            db_filename,
            isolation_level=isolation_level) as conn:
        cursor = conn.cursor()
        cursor.execute('update task set priority = priority + 1')
        logging.debug('waiting to synchronize')
        ready.wait()  # Synchronize threads
        logging.debug('PAUSING')
        time.sleep(1)
        conn.commit()
        logging.debug('CHANGES COMMITTED')


def reader():
    with sqlite3.connect(
            db_filename,
            isolation_level=isolation_level) as conn:
        cursor = conn.cursor()
        logging.debug('waiting to synchronize')
        ready.wait()  # Synchronize threads
```

```
            logging.debug('wait over')
            cursor.execute('select * from task')
            logging.debug('SELECT EXECUTED')
            cursor.fetchall()
            logging.debug('results fetched')


if __name__ == '__main__':
    ready = threading.Event()

    threads = [
        threading.Thread(name='Reader 1', target=reader),
        threading.Thread(name='Reader 2', target=reader),
        threading.Thread(name='Writer 1', target=writer),
        threading.Thread(name='Writer 2', target=writer),
    ]

    [t.start() for t in threads]

    time.sleep(1)
    logging.debug('setting ready')
    ready.set()

    [t.join() for t in threads]
```

The threads are synchronized using an `Event` object from the `threading` (page 560) module. The `writer()` function connects and make changes to the database, but does not commit before the event fires. The `reader()` function connects, then waits to query the database until after the synchronization event occurs.

7.4.10.1 Deferred

The default isolation level is `DEFERRED`. Using deferred mode locks the database, but only once a change is begun. All of the earlier examples used deferred mode.

```
$ python3 sqlite3_isolation_levels.py DEFERRED

2016-08-20 17:46:26,972 (Reader 1  ) waiting to synchronize
2016-08-20 17:46:26,972 (Reader 2  ) waiting to synchronize
2016-08-20 17:46:26,973 (Writer 1  ) waiting to synchronize
2016-08-20 17:46:27,977 (MainThread) setting ready
2016-08-20 17:46:27,979 (Reader 1  ) wait over
2016-08-20 17:46:27,979 (Writer 1  ) PAUSING
2016-08-20 17:46:27,979 (Reader 2  ) wait over
2016-08-20 17:46:27,981 (Reader 1  ) SELECT EXECUTED
2016-08-20 17:46:27,982 (Reader 1  ) results fetched
2016-08-20 17:46:27,982 (Reader 2  ) SELECT EXECUTED
2016-08-20 17:46:27,982 (Reader 2  ) results fetched
```

```
2016-08-20 17:46:28,985 (Writer 1  ) CHANGES COMMITTED
2016-08-20 17:46:29,043 (Writer 2  ) waiting to synchronize
2016-08-20 17:46:29,043 (Writer 2  ) PAUSING
2016-08-20 17:46:30,044 (Writer 2  ) CHANGES COMMITTED
```

7.4.10.2 Immediate

Immediate mode locks the database as soon as a change starts and prevents other cursors from making changes until the transaction is committed. It is suitable for a database with complicated writes, but more readers than writers, because the readers are not blocked while the transaction is ongoing.

```
$ python3 sqlite3_isolation_levels.py IMMEDIATE

2016-08-20 17:46:30,121 (Reader 1  ) waiting to synchronize
2016-08-20 17:46:30,121 (Reader 2  ) waiting to synchronize
2016-08-20 17:46:30,123 (Writer 1  ) waiting to synchronize
2016-08-20 17:46:31,122 (MainThread) setting ready
2016-08-20 17:46:31,122 (Reader 1  ) wait over
2016-08-20 17:46:31,122 (Reader 2  ) wait over
2016-08-20 17:46:31,122 (Writer 1  ) PAUSING
2016-08-20 17:46:31,124 (Reader 1  ) SELECT EXECUTED
2016-08-20 17:46:31,124 (Reader 2  ) SELECT EXECUTED
2016-08-20 17:46:31,125 (Reader 2  ) results fetched
2016-08-20 17:46:31,125 (Reader 1  ) results fetched
2016-08-20 17:46:32,128 (Writer 1  ) CHANGES COMMITTED
2016-08-20 17:46:32,199 (Writer 2  ) waiting to synchronize
2016-08-20 17:46:32,199 (Writer 2  ) PAUSING
2016-08-20 17:46:33,200 (Writer 2  ) CHANGES COMMITTED
```

7.4.10.3 Exclusive

Exclusive mode locks the database to all readers and writers. Its use should be limited in situations where database performance is important, because each exclusive connection blocks all other users.

```
$ python3 sqlite3_isolation_levels.py EXCLUSIVE

2016-08-20 17:46:33,320 (Reader 1  ) waiting to synchronize
2016-08-20 17:46:33,320 (Reader 2  ) waiting to synchronize
2016-08-20 17:46:33,324 (Writer 2  ) waiting to synchronize
2016-08-20 17:46:34,323 (MainThread) setting ready
2016-08-20 17:46:34,323 (Reader 1  ) wait over
2016-08-20 17:46:34,323 (Writer 2  ) PAUSING
2016-08-20 17:46:34,323 (Reader 2  ) wait over
2016-08-20 17:46:35,327 (Writer 2  ) CHANGES COMMITTED
```

```
2016-08-20 17:46:35,368 (Reader 2  ) SELECT EXECUTED
2016-08-20 17:46:35,368 (Reader 2  ) results fetched
2016-08-20 17:46:35,369 (Reader 1  ) SELECT EXECUTED
2016-08-20 17:46:35,369 (Reader 1  ) results fetched
2016-08-20 17:46:35,385 (Writer 1  ) waiting to synchronize
2016-08-20 17:46:35,385 (Writer 1  ) PAUSING
2016-08-20 17:46:36,386 (Writer 1  ) CHANGES COMMITTED
```

Because the first writer has started making changes, the readers and the second writer block until it commits. The sleep() call introduces an artificial delay in the writer thread to highlight the fact that the other connections are blocking.

7.4.10.4 Autocommit

The isolation_level parameter for the connection can also be set to None to enable autocommit mode. With autocommit enabled, each execute() call is committed immediately when the statement finishes. Autocommit mode is suited for short-duration transactions, such as those that insert a small amount of data into a single table. The database is locked for as little time as possible, so contention for resources between threads is less likely.

In sqlite3_autocommit.py, the explicit call to commit() has been removed and the isolation level is set to None; otherwise, this method is the same as sqlite3_isolation_levels.py. The output is different, however, since both writer threads finish their work before either reader starts querying.

```
$ python3 sqlite3_autocommit.py

2016-08-20 17:46:36,451 (Reader 1  ) waiting to synchronize
2016-08-20 17:46:36,451 (Reader 2  ) waiting to synchronize
2016-08-20 17:46:36,455 (Writer 1  ) waiting to synchronize
2016-08-20 17:46:36,456 (Writer 2  ) waiting to synchronize
2016-08-20 17:46:37,452 (MainThread) setting ready
2016-08-20 17:46:37,452 (Reader 1  ) wait over
2016-08-20 17:46:37,452 (Writer 2  ) PAUSING
2016-08-20 17:46:37,452 (Reader 2  ) wait over
2016-08-20 17:46:37,453 (Writer 1  ) PAUSING
2016-08-20 17:46:37,453 (Reader 1  ) SELECT EXECUTED
2016-08-20 17:46:37,454 (Reader 2  ) SELECT EXECUTED
2016-08-20 17:46:37,454 (Reader 1  ) results fetched
2016-08-20 17:46:37,454 (Reader 2  ) results fetched
```

7.4.11 In-Memory Databases

SQLite supports managing an entire database in RAM, instead of relying on a disk file. In-memory databases are useful for automated testing, where the database does not need to be preserved between test runs, or when experimenting with a schema or other database features. To open an in-memory database, use the string ':memory:' instead of a filename when creating the Connection. Each ':memory:' connection creates a separate database instance, so changes made by a cursor in one connection do not affect other connections.

7.4.12 Exporting the Contents of a Database

The contents of an in-memory database can be saved using the iterdump() method of the Connection. The iterator returned by iterdump() produces a series of strings that together build SQL instructions to re-create the state of the database.

Listing 7.35: **sqlite3_iterdump.py**

```
import sqlite3

schema_filename = 'todo_schema.sql'

with sqlite3.connect(':memory:') as conn:
    conn.row_factory = sqlite3.Row

    print('Creating schema')
    with open(schema_filename, 'rt') as f:
        schema = f.read()
    conn.executescript(schema)

    print('Inserting initial data')
    conn.execute("""
    insert into project (name, description, deadline)
    values ('pymotw', 'Python Module of the Week',
            '2010-11-01')
    """)
    data = [
        ('write about select', 'done', '2010-10-03',
         'pymotw'),
        ('write about random', 'waiting', '2010-10-10',
         'pymotw'),
        ('write about sqlite3', 'active', '2010-10-17',
         'pymotw'),
    ]
    conn.executemany("""
    insert into task (details, status, deadline, project)
    values (?, ?, ?, ?)
    """, data)

    print('Dumping:')
    for text in conn.iterdump():
        print(text)
```

iterdump() can also be used with databases saved to files, but it is most useful for preserving a database that would not otherwise be saved. Here, its output has been edited to fit on the page yet remain syntactically correct.

```
$ python3 sqlite3_iterdump.py

Creating schema
Inserting initial data
Dumping:
BEGIN TRANSACTION;
CREATE TABLE project (
    name        text primary key,
    description text,
    deadline    date
);
INSERT INTO "project" VALUES('pymotw','Python Module of the
Week','2010-11-01');
DELETE FROM "sqlite_sequence";
INSERT INTO "sqlite_sequence" VALUES('task',3);
CREATE TABLE task (
    id           integer primary key autoincrement not null,
    priority     integer default 1,
    details      text,
    status       text,
    deadline     date,
    completed_on date,
    project      text not null references project(name)
);
INSERT INTO "task" VALUES(1,1,'write about
select','done','2010-10-03',NULL,'pymotw');
INSERT INTO "task" VALUES(2,1,'write about
random','waiting','2010-10-10',NULL,'pymotw');
INSERT INTO "task" VALUES(3,1,'write about
sqlite3','active','2010-10-17',NULL,'pymotw');
COMMIT;
```

7.4.13   Using Python Functions in SQL

SQL syntax supports calling functions during queries, either in the column list or in the
where clause of the select statement. This feature makes it possible to process data before
returning it from the query. It can be used to convert between different formats, perform
calculations that would be clumsy in pure SQL, and reuse application code.

Listing 7.36: **sqlite3_create_function.py**

```
import codecs
import sqlite3

db_filename = 'todo.db'
```

```
def encrypt(s):
    print('Encrypting {!r}'.format(s))
    return codecs.encode(s, 'rot-13')


def decrypt(s):
    print('Decrypting {!r}'.format(s))
    return codecs.encode(s, 'rot-13')


with sqlite3.connect(db_filename) as conn:

    conn.create_function('encrypt', 1, encrypt)
    conn.create_function('decrypt', 1, decrypt)
    cursor = conn.cursor()

    # Raw values
    print('Original values:')
    query = "select id, details from task"
    cursor.execute(query)
    for row in cursor.fetchall():
        print(row)

    print('\nEncrypting...')
    query = "update task set details = encrypt(details)"
    cursor.execute(query)

    print('\nRaw encrypted values:')
    query = "select id, details from task"
    cursor.execute(query)
    for row in cursor.fetchall():
        print(row)

    print('\nDecrypting in query...')
    query = "select id, decrypt(details) from task"
    cursor.execute(query)
    for row in cursor.fetchall():
        print(row)

    print('\nDecrypting...')
    query = "update task set details = decrypt(details)"
    cursor.execute(query)
```

Functions are exposed using the `create_function()` method of the `Connection`. The parameters are the name of the function (as it should be used from within SQL), the number of arguments that the function takes, and the Python function to expose.

```
$ python3 sqlite3_create_function.py

Original values:
(1, 'write about select')
(2, 'write about random')
(3, 'write about sqlite3')
(4, 'finish reviewing markup')
(5, 'revise chapter intros')
(6, 'subtitle')

Encrypting...
Encrypting 'write about select'
Encrypting 'write about random'
Encrypting 'write about sqlite3'
Encrypting 'finish reviewing markup'
Encrypting 'revise chapter intros'
Encrypting 'subtitle'

Raw encrypted values:
(1, 'jevgr nobhg fryrpg')
(2, 'jevgr nobhg enaqbz')
(3, 'jevgr nobhg fdyvgr3')
(4, 'svavfu erivrjvat znexhc')
(5, 'erivfr puncgre vagebf')
(6, 'fhogvgyr')

Decrypting in query...
Decrypting 'jevgr nobhg fryrpg'
Decrypting 'jevgr nobhg enaqbz'
Decrypting 'jevgr nobhg fdyvgr3'
Decrypting 'svavfu erivrjvat znexhc'
Decrypting 'erivfr puncgre vagebf'
Decrypting 'fhogvgyr'
(1, 'write about select')
(2, 'write about random')
(3, 'write about sqlite3')
(4, 'finish reviewing markup')
(5, 'revise chapter intros')
(6, 'subtitle')

Decrypting...
Decrypting 'jevgr nobhg fryrpg'
Decrypting 'jevgr nobhg enaqbz'
Decrypting 'jevgr nobhg fdyvgr3'
Decrypting 'svavfu erivrjvat znexhc'
Decrypting 'erivfr puncgre vagebf'
Decrypting 'fhogvgyr'
```

7.4.14 Querying with Regular Expressions

SQLite supports several special user functions that are associated with SQL syntax. For example, the function regexp can be used in a query to check whether a column's string value matches a regular expression using the following syntax.

```
SELECT * FROM table
WHERE column REGEXP '.*pattern.*'
```

The following example associates a function with regexp() to test values using Python's re (page 13) module.

Listing 7.37: sqlite3_regex.py

```python
import re
import sqlite3

db_filename = 'todo.db'


def regexp(pattern, input):
    return bool(re.match(pattern, input))


with sqlite3.connect(db_filename) as conn:
    conn.row_factory = sqlite3.Row
    conn.create_function('regexp', 2, regexp)
    cursor = conn.cursor()

    pattern = '.*[wW]rite [aA]bout.*'

    cursor.execute(
        """
        select id, priority, details, status, deadline from task
        where details regexp :pattern
        order by deadline, priority
        """,
        {'pattern': pattern},
    )

    for row in cursor.fetchall():
        task_id, priority, details, status, deadline = row
        print('{:2d} [{:d}] {:<25} [{:<8}] ({})'.format(
            task_id, priority, details, status, deadline))
```

The output is all of the tasks where the details column matches the pattern.

```
$ python3 sqlite3_regex.py

1 [9] write about select        [done    ] (2016-04-25)
2 [9] write about random        [done    ] (2016-08-22)
3 [9] write about sqlite3       [active  ] (2017-07-31)
```

7.4.15 Custom Aggregation

An aggregation function collects many pieces of individual data and summarizes it in some way. Examples of built-in aggregation functions include avg() (average), min(), max(), and count().

The API for aggregators used by sqlite3 is defined in terms of a class with two methods. The step() method is called once for each data value as the query is processed. The finalize() method is called one time at the end of the query and should return the aggregate value. This example implements an aggregator for the arithmetic *mode*. It returns the value that appears most frequently in the input.

Listing 7.38: **sqlite3_create_aggregate.py**

```python
import sqlite3
import collections

db_filename = 'todo.db'


class Mode:

    def __init__(self):
        self.counter = collections.Counter()

    def step(self, value):
        print('step({!r})'.format(value))
        self.counter[value] += 1

    def finalize(self):
        result, count = self.counter.most_common(1)[0]
        print('finalize() -> {!r} ({} times)'.format(
            result, count))
        return result


with sqlite3.connect(db_filename) as conn:
    conn.create_aggregate('mode', 1, Mode)

    cursor = conn.cursor()
    cursor.execute("""
    select mode(deadline) from task where project = 'pymotw'
    """)
```

```
        row = cursor.fetchone()
        print('mode(deadline) is:', row[0])
```

The aggregator class is registered with the `create_aggregate()` method of the `Connection`. The parameters are the name of the function (as it should be used from within SQL), the number of arguments that the `step()` method takes, and the class to use.

```
$ python3 sqlite3_create_aggregate.py

step('2016-04-25')
step('2016-08-22')
step('2017-07-31')
step('2016-11-30')
step('2016-08-20')
step('2016-11-01')
finalize() -> '2016-11-01' (1 times)
mode(deadline) is: 2016-11-01
```

7.4.16 Threading and Connection Sharing

For historical reasons having to do with old versions of SQLite, `Connection` objects cannot be shared between threads. Each thread must create its own connection to the database.

Listing 7.39: **sqlite3_threading.py**

```
import sqlite3
import sys
import threading
import time

db_filename = 'todo.db'
isolation_level = None  # Autocommit mode


def reader(conn):
    print('Starting thread')
    try:
        cursor = conn.cursor()
        cursor.execute('select * from task')
        cursor.fetchall()
        print('results fetched')
    except Exception as err:
        print('ERROR:', err)


if __name__ == '__main__':
    with sqlite3.connect(db_filename,
                         isolation_level=isolation_level,
```

```
            ) as conn:
    t = threading.Thread(name='Reader 1',
                        target=reader,
                        args=(conn,),
                        )
    t.start()
    t.join()
```

Attempts to share a connection between threads result in an exception.

```
$ python3 sqlite3_threading.py

Starting thread
ERROR: SQLite objects created in a thread can only be used in that
same thread.The object was created in thread id 140735234088960
and this is thread id 123145307557888
```

7.4.17   Restricting Access to Data

Although SQLite does not have user access controls found in other, larger relational databases, it does have a mechanism for limiting access to columns. Each connection can install an *authorizer function* to grant or deny access to columns at runtime based on any desired criteria. The authorizer function is invoked during the parsing of SQL statements. It is passed five arguments: The first is an action code indicating the type of operation being performed (e.g., reading, writing, deleting), and the rest depend on the action code. For SQLITE_READ operations, the arguments are the name of the table, the name of the column, the location in the SQL where the access is occurring (e.g., main query, trigger), and None.

Listing 7.40: sqlite3_set_authorizer.py

```
import sqlite3

db_filename = 'todo.db'


def authorizer_func(action, table, column, sql_location, ignore):
    print('\nauthorizer_func({}, {}, {}, {}, {})'.format(
        action, table, column, sql_location, ignore))

    response = sqlite3.SQLITE_OK  # Be permissive by default.

    if action == sqlite3.SQLITE_SELECT:
        print('requesting permission to run a select statement')
        response = sqlite3.SQLITE_OK

    elif action == sqlite3.SQLITE_READ:
        print('requesting access to column {}.{} from {}'.format(
```

```
            table, column, sql_location))
        if column == 'details':
            print('  ignoring details column')
            response = sqlite3.SQLITE_IGNORE
        elif column == 'priority':
            print('  preventing access to priority column')
            response = sqlite3.SQLITE_DENY

    return response


with sqlite3.connect(db_filename) as conn:
    conn.row_factory = sqlite3.Row
    conn.set_authorizer(authorizer_func)

    print('Using SQLITE_IGNORE to mask a column value:')
    cursor = conn.cursor()
    cursor.execute("""
    select id, details from task where project = 'pymotw'
    """)
    for row in cursor.fetchall():
        print(row['id'], row['details'])

    print('\nUsing SQLITE_DENY to deny access to a column:')
    cursor.execute("""
    select id, priority from task where project = 'pymotw'
    """)
    for row in cursor.fetchall():
        print(row['id'], row['details'])
```

This example uses `SQLITE_IGNORE` to cause the strings from the `task.details` column to be replaced with null values in the query results. It also prevents all access to the `task.priority` column by returning `SQLITE_DENY`, which in turn causes SQLite to raise an exception.

```
$ python3 sqlite3_set_authorizer.py

Using SQLITE_IGNORE to mask a column value:

authorizer_func(21, None, None, None, None)
requesting permission to run a select statement

authorizer_func(20, task, id, main, None)
requesting access to column task.id from main

authorizer_func(20, task, details, main, None)
requesting access to column task.details from main
  ignoring details column
```

```
authorizer_func(20, task, project, main, None)
requesting access to column task.project from main
1 None
2 None
3 None
4 None
5 None
6 None

Using SQLITE_DENY to deny access to a column:

authorizer_func(21, None, None, None, None)
requesting permission to run a select statement

authorizer_func(20, task, id, main, None)
requesting access to column task.id from main

authorizer_func(20, task, priority, main, None)
requesting access to column task.priority from main
  preventing access to priority column
Traceback (most recent call last):
  File "sqlite3_set_authorizer.py", line 53, in <module>
    """)
sqlite3.DatabaseError: access to task.priority is prohibited
```

The possible action codes are available as constants in `sqlite3`, with names prefixed `SQLITE_`. Each type of SQL statement can be flagged, and access to individual columns can be controlled as well.

TIP

Related Reading

- Standard library documentation for `sqlite3`.[10]

- **PEP 249**[11]: DB API 2.0 Specification (a standard interface for modules that provide access to relational databases).

- SQLite[12]: The official site of the SQLite library.

- shelve (page 405): Key–value store for saving arbitrary Python objects.

- SQLAlchemy[13]: A popular object-relational mapper that supports SQLite, among many other relational databases.

---

[10] https://docs.python.org/3.5/library/sqlite3.html
[11] www.python.org/dev/peps/pep-0249
[12] www.sqlite.org
[13] www.sqlalchemy.org

7.5   xml.etree.ElementTree: XML Manipulation API

The ElementTree library includes tools for parsing XML using event-based and document-based APIs, searching parsed documents with XPath expressions, and creating new or modifying existing documents.

7.5.1   Parsing an XML Document

Parsed XML documents are represented in memory by ElementTree and Element objects connected in a tree structure based on the way the nodes in the XML document are nested.

Parsing an entire document with parse() returns an ElementTree instance. The tree knows about all of the data in the input document, and the nodes of the tree can be searched or manipulated in place. While this flexibility can make working with the parsed document more convenient, this approach typically takes more memory than an event-based parsing approach because the entire document must be loaded at one time.

The memory footprint of small, simple documents, such as the following list of podcasts represented as an OPML outline, is not significant.

Listing 7.41: podcasts.opml

```
<?xml version="1.0" encoding="UTF-8"?>
<opml version="1.0">
<head>
    <title>My Podcasts</title>
    <dateCreated>Sat, 06 Aug 2016 15:53:26 GMT</dateCreated>
    <dateModified>Sat, 06 Aug 2016 15:53:26 GMT</dateModified>
</head>
<body>
  <outline text="Non-tech">
    <outline
        text="99% Invisible" type="rss"
        xmlUrl="http://feeds.99percentinvisible.org/99percentinvisible"
        htmlUrl="http://99percentinvisible.org" />
  </outline>
  <outline text="Python">
    <outline
        text="Talk Python to Me" type="rss"
        xmlUrl="https://talkpython.fm/episodes/rss"
        htmlUrl="https://talkpython.fm" />
    <outline
        text="Podcast.__init__" type="rss"
        xmlUrl="http://podcastinit.podbean.com/feed/"
        htmlUrl="http://podcastinit.com" />
  </outline>
</body>
</opml>
```

To parse the file, pass an open file handle to `parse()`.

Listing 7.42: ElementTree_parse_opml.py

```
from xml.etree import ElementTree

with open('podcasts.opml', 'rt') as f:
    tree = ElementTree.parse(f)

print(tree)
```

This method will read the data, parse the XML, and return an `ElementTree` object.

```
$ python3 ElementTree_parse_opml.py

<xml.etree.ElementTree.ElementTree object at 0x1013e5630>
```

7.5.2 Traversing the Parsed Tree

To visit all of the children in order, use `iter()` to create a generator that iterates over the `ElementTree` instance.

Listing 7.43: ElementTree_dump_opml.py

```
from xml.etree import ElementTree
import pprint

with open('podcasts.opml', 'rt') as f:
    tree = ElementTree.parse(f)

for node in tree.iter():
    print(node.tag)
```

This example prints the entire tree, one tag at a time.

```
$ python3 ElementTree_dump_opml.py

opml
head
title
dateCreated
dateModified
body
outline
outline
outline
outline
outline
```

To print only the groups of names and feed URLs for the podcasts, leave out all of the data in the header section by iterating over only the `outline` nodes, and print the `text` and `xmlUrl` attributes by looking up the values in the `attrib` dictionary.

Listing 7.44: **ElementTree_show_feed_urls.py**

```
from xml.etree import ElementTree

with open('podcasts.opml', 'rt') as f:
    tree = ElementTree.parse(f)

for node in tree.iter('outline'):
    name = node.attrib.get('text')
    url = node.attrib.get('xmlUrl')
    if name and url:
        print('  %s' % name)
        print('    %s' % url)
    else:
        print(name)
```

The `'outline'` argument to `iter()` means processing is limited to only nodes with the tag `'outline'`.

```
$ python3 ElementTree_show_feed_urls.py

Non-tech
  99% Invisible
    http://feeds.99percentinvisible.org/99percentinvisible
Python
  Talk Python to Me
    https://talkpython.fm/episodes/rss
  Podcast.__init__
    http://podcastinit.podbean.com/feed/
```

7.5.3   Finding Nodes in a Document

Walking through the entire tree, searching for relevant nodes, can be error prone. The previous example had to look at each outline node to determine if it was a group (nodes with only a `text` attribute) or a podcast (with both `text` and `xmlUrl`). To produce a simple list of the podcast-feed URLs, without names or groups, the logic could be simplified by using `findall()` to look for nodes with more descriptive search characteristics.

As a first pass at converting the first version, an XPath argument can be used to look for all outline nodes.

Listing 7.45: **ElementTree_find_feeds_by_tag.py**

```
from xml.etree import ElementTree

with open('podcasts.opml', 'rt') as f:
```

```
        tree = ElementTree.parse(f)

    for node in tree.findall('.//outline'):
        url = node.attrib.get('xmlUrl')
        if url:
            print(url)
```

The logic in this version is not substantially different from the version using `getiterator()`. It still has to check for the presence of the URL, except that it does not print the group name when the URL is not found.

```
$ python3 ElementTree_find_feeds_by_tag.py

http://feeds.99percentinvisible.org/99percentinvisible
https://talkpython.fm/episodes/rss
http://podcastinit.podbean.com/feed/
```

It is possible to take advantage of the fact that the outline nodes are nested only two levels deep. Changing the search path to `.//outline/outline` means the loop will process only the second level of outline nodes.

Listing 7.46: **ElementTree_find_feeds_by_structure.py**

```
from xml.etree import ElementTree

with open('podcasts.opml', 'rt') as f:
    tree = ElementTree.parse(f)

for node in tree.findall('.//outline/outline'):
    url = node.attrib.get('xmlUrl')
    print(url)
```

All of the outline nodes nested two levels deep in the input are expected to have the `xmlURL` attribute referring to the podcast feed, so the loop can skip checking for the attribute before using it.

```
$ python3 ElementTree_find_feeds_by_structure.py

http://feeds.99percentinvisible.org/99percentinvisible
https://talkpython.fm/episodes/rss
http://podcastinit.podbean.com/feed/
```

This version is limited to the existing structure, though, so if the outline nodes are ever rearranged into a deeper tree, it will stop working.

7.5.4 Parsed Node Attributes

The items returned by findall() and iter() are Element objects, each representing a node in the XML parse tree. Each Element has attributes for accessing data pulled out of the XML. This behavior can be illustrated with a somewhat more contrived example input file, data.xml.

Listing 7.47: data.xml

```
1  <?xml version="1.0" encoding="UTF-8"?>
2  <top>
3    <child>Regular text.</child>
4    <child_with_tail>Regular text.</child_with_tail>"Tail" text.
5    <with_attributes name="value" foo="bar" />
6    <entity_expansion attribute="This &#38; That">
7      That &#38; This
8    </entity_expansion>
9  </top>
```

The XML attributes of a node are available in the attrib property, which acts like a dictionary.

Listing 7.48: ElementTree_node_attributes.py

```
from xml.etree import ElementTree

with open('data.xml', 'rt') as f:
    tree = ElementTree.parse(f)

node = tree.find('./with_attributes')
print(node.tag)
for name, value in sorted(node.attrib.items()):
    print('  %-4s = "%s"' % (name, value))
```

The node on line 5 of the input file has two attributes, name and foo.

```
$ python3 ElementTree_node_attributes.py

with_attributes
  foo  = "bar"
  name = "value"
```

The text content of the nodes is available, along with the *tail* text, which comes after the end of a close tag.

Listing 7.49: ElementTree_node_text.py

```
from xml.etree import ElementTree

with open('data.xml', 'rt') as f:
```

```
        tree = ElementTree.parse(f)

    for path in ['./child', './child_with_tail']:
        node = tree.find(path)
        print(node.tag)
        print('  child node text:', node.text)
        print('  and tail text  :', node.tail)
```

The `child` node on line 3 contains embedded text, and the node on line 4 has text with a tail (including whitespace).

```
$ python3 ElementTree_node_text.py

child
  child node text: Regular text.
  and tail text  :

child_with_tail
  child node text: Regular text.
  and tail text  : "Tail" text.
```

XML entity references embedded in the document are converted to the appropriate characters before values are returned.

Listing 7.50: ElementTree_entity_references.py

```
from xml.etree import ElementTree

with open('data.xml', 'rt') as f:
    tree = ElementTree.parse(f)

node = tree.find('entity_expansion')
print(node.tag)
print('  in attribute:', node.attrib['attribute'])
print('  in text     :', node.text.strip())
```

The automatic conversion means the implementation detail of representing certain characters in an XML document can be ignored.

```
$ python3 ElementTree_entity_references.py

entity_expansion
  in attribute: This & That
  in text     : That & This
```

7.5.5   Watching Events While Parsing

The other API for processing XML documents is event based. The parser generates `start`
events for opening tags and `end` events for closing tags. Data can be extracted from the
document during the parsing phase by iterating over the event stream, which is convenient
if it is not necessary to manipulate the entire document afterward and there is no need to
hold the entire parsed document in memory.

Events can be one of the following types:

`start` A new tag is encountered. The closing angle bracket of the tag is processed, but not
the contents.

`end` The closing angle bracket of a closing tag is processed. All of the children were already
processed.

`start-ns` Start a namespace declaration.

`end-ns` End a namespace declaration.

`iterparse()` returns an iterable that produces tuples containing the name of the event
and the node triggering the event.

Listing 7.51: **ElementTree_show_all_events.py**

```
from xml.etree.ElementTree import iterparse

depth = 0
prefix_width = 8
prefix_dots = '.' * prefix_width
line_template = ''.join([
    '{prefix:<0.{prefix_len}}',
    '{event:<8}',
    '{suffix:<{suffix_len}} ',
    '{node.tag:<12} ',
    '{node_id}',
])

EVENT_NAMES = ['start', 'end', 'start-ns', 'end-ns']

for (event, node) in iterparse('podcasts.opml', EVENT_NAMES):
    if event == 'end':
        depth -= 1

    prefix_len = depth * 2

    print(line_template.format(
        prefix=prefix_dots,
        prefix_len=prefix_len,
        suffix='',
        suffix_len=(prefix_width - prefix_len),
```

```
        node=node,
        node_id=id(node),
        event=event,
    ))

    if event == 'start':
        depth += 1
```

By default, only `end` events are generated. To see other events, pass the list of desired event names to `iterparse()`, as in this example.

```
$ python3 ElementTree_show_all_events.py

start          opml           4312612200
..start        head           4316174520
....start      title          4316254440
....end        title          4316254440
....start      dateCreated    4316254520
....end        dateCreated    4316254520
....start      dateModified   4316254680
....end        dateModified   4316254680
..end          head           4316174520
..start        body           4316254840
....start      outline        4316254920
......start    outline        4316255080
......end      outline        4316255080
....end        outline        4316254920
....start      outline        4316255160
......start    outline        4316255240
......end      outline        4316255240
......start    outline        4316255320
......end      outline        4316255320
....end        outline        4316255160
..end          body           4316254840
end            opml           4312612200
```

Event-style processing is more natural for some operations, such as converting XML input to some other format. This technique can be used to convert the list of podcasts from the earlier examples from an XML file to a CSV file, so they can be loaded into a spreadsheet or database application.

Listing 7.52: ElementTree_write_podcast_csv.py

```
import csv
from xml.etree.ElementTree import iterparse
import sys

writer = csv.writer(sys.stdout, quoting=csv.QUOTE_NONNUMERIC)
```

```
    group_name = ''

    parsing = iterparse('podcasts.opml', events=['start'])

    for (event, node) in parsing:
        if node.tag != 'outline':
            # Ignore anything not part of the outline.
            continue
        if not node.attrib.get('xmlUrl'):
            # Remember the current group.
            group_name = node.attrib['text']
        else:
            # Output a podcast entry.
            writer.writerow(
                (group_name, node.attrib['text'],
                 node.attrib['xmlUrl'],
                 node.attrib.get('htmlUrl', ''))
            )
```

This conversion program does not need to hold the entire parsed input file in memory, and processing each node as it is encountered in the input is more efficient.

```
$ python3 ElementTree_write_podcast_csv.py

"Non-tech","99% Invisible","http://feeds.99percentinvisible.org/\
99percentinvisible","http://99percentinvisible.org"
"Python","Talk Python to Me","https://talkpython.fm/episodes/rss\
","https://talkpython.fm"
"Python","Podcast.__init__","http://podcastinit.podbean.com/feed\
/","http://podcastinit.com"
```

NOTE

The output from ElementTree_write_podcast_csv.py has been reformatted to fit on this page. The output lines ending with \ indicate an artificial line break.

7.5.6   Creating a Custom Tree Builder

A potentially more efficient means of handling parse events is to replace the standard tree builder behavior with a custom version. The XMLParser parser uses a TreeBuilder to process the XML and call methods on a target class to save the results. The usual output is an ElementTree instance created by the default TreeBuilder class. Replacing TreeBuilder with another class allows it to receive the events before the Element nodes are instantiated, saving that portion of the overhead.

The XML-to-CSV converter from the previous section can be reimplemented as a tree builder.

Listing 7.53: **ElementTree_podcast_csv_treebuilder.py**

```python
import csv
import io
from xml.etree.ElementTree import XMLParser
import sys


class PodcastListToCSV(object):

    def __init__(self, outputFile):
        self.writer = csv.writer(
            outputFile,
            quoting=csv.QUOTE_NONNUMERIC,
        )
        self.group_name = ''

    def start(self, tag, attrib):
        if tag != 'outline':
            # Ignore anything not part of the outline.
            return
        if not attrib.get('xmlUrl'):
            # Remember the current group.
            self.group_name = attrib['text']
        else:
            # Output a podcast entry.
            self.writer.writerow(
                (self.group_name,
                 attrib['text'],
                 attrib['xmlUrl'],
                 attrib.get('htmlUrl', ''))
            )

    def end(self, tag):
        "Ignore closing tags"

    def data(self, data):
        "Ignore data inside nodes"

    def close(self):
        "Nothing special to do here"


target = PodcastListToCSV(sys.stdout)
parser = XMLParser(target=target)
with open('podcasts.opml', 'rt') as f:
    for line in f:
        parser.feed(line)
parser.close()
```

PodcastListToCSV implements the TreeBuilder protocol. Each time a new XML tag is encountered, start() is called with the tag name and attributes. When a closing tag is seen, end() is called with the name. In between, data() is called when a node has content (the tree builder is expected to keep up with the "current" node). When all of the input is processed, close() is called. It can return a value, which will be returned to the user of the TreeBuilder.

```
$ python3 ElementTree_podcast_csv_treebuilder.py

"Non-tech","99% Invisible","http://feeds.99percentinvisible.org/\
99percentinvisible","http://99percentinvisible.org"
"Python","Talk Python to Me","https://talkpython.fm/episodes/rss\
","https://talkpython.fm"
"Python","Podcast.__init__","http://podcastinit.podbean.com/feed\
/","http://podcastinit.com"
```

NOTE

The output from ElementTree_podcast_csv_treebuidler.py has been reformatted to fit on this page. The output lines ending with \ indicate an artificial line break.

7.5.7 Parsing Strings

To work with smaller bits of XML text, especially string literals that might be embedded in the source of a program, use XML() and the string containing the XML to be parsed as the only argument.

Listing 7.54: **ElementTree_XML.py**

```python
from xml.etree.ElementTree import XML


def show_node(node):
    print(node.tag)
    if node.text is not None and node.text.strip():
        print('  text: "%s"' % node.text)
    if node.tail is not None and node.tail.strip():
        print('  tail: "%s"' % node.tail)
    for name, value in sorted(node.attrib.items()):
        print('  %-4s = "%s"' % (name, value))
    for child in node:
        show_node(child)


parsed = XML('''
<root>
  <group>
```

```
      <child id="a">This is child "a".</child>
      <child id="b">This is child "b".</child>
    </group>
    <group>
      <child id="c">This is child "c".</child>
    </group>
</root>
''')

print('parsed =', parsed)

for elem in parsed:
    show_node(elem)
```

Unlike with parse(), the return value is an Element instance instead of an ElementTree. An Element supports the iterator protocol directly, so there is no need to call getiterator().

```
$ python3 ElementTree_XML.py

parsed = <Element 'root' at 0x10079eef8>
group
child
  text: "This is child "a"."
  id   = "a"
child
  text: "This is child "b"."
  id   = "b"
group
child
  text: "This is child "c"."
  id   = "c"
```

For structured XML that uses the id attribute to identify unique nodes of interest, XMLID() is a convenient way to access the parse results.

Listing 7.55: ElementTree_XMLID.py

```
from xml.etree.ElementTree import XMLID

tree, id_map = XMLID('''
<root>
  <group>
    <child id="a">This is child "a".</child>
    <child id="b">This is child "b".</child>
  </group>
  <group>
    <child id="c">This is child "c".</child>
  </group>
```

```
</root>
''')

for key, value in sorted(id_map.items()):
    print('%s = %s' % (key, value))
```

XMLID() returns the parsed tree as an Element object, along with a dictionary mapping the id attribute strings to the individual nodes in the tree.

```
$ python3 ElementTree_XMLID.py

a = <Element 'child' at 0x10133aea8>
b = <Element 'child' at 0x10133aef8>
c = <Element 'child' at 0x10133af98>
```

7.5.8 Building Documents with Element Nodes

In addition to its parsing capabilities, xml.etree.ElementTree supports creating well-formed XML documents from Element objects constructed in an application. The Element class used when a document is parsed also knows how to generate a serialized form of its contents, which can then be written to a file or other data stream.

Three helper functions are useful for creating a hierarchy of Element nodes. Element() creates a standard node, SubElement() attaches a new node to a parent, and Comment() creates a node that serializes data using XML's comment syntax.

Listing 7.56: ElementTree_create.py

```
from xml.etree.ElementTree import (
    Element, SubElement, Comment, tostring,
)

top = Element('top')

comment = Comment('Generated for PyMOTW')
top.append(comment)

child = SubElement(top, 'child')
child.text = 'This child contains text.'

child_with_tail = SubElement(top, 'child_with_tail')
child_with_tail.text = 'This child has text.'
child_with_tail.tail = 'And "tail" text.'

child_with_entity_ref = SubElement(top, 'child_with_entity_ref')
child_with_entity_ref.text = 'This & that'

print(tostring(top))
```

The output contains only the XML nodes in the tree—not the XML declaration with version and encoding.

```
$ python3 ElementTree_create.py

b'<top><!--Generated for PyMOTW--><child>This child contains text.</
child><child_with_tail>This child has text.</child_with_tail>And "ta
il" text.<child_with_entity_ref>This &amp; that</child_with_entity_r
ef></top>'
```

The & character in the text of `child_with_entity_ref` is converted to the entity reference `&amp;` automatically.

7.5.9   Pretty-Printing XML

`ElementTree` makes no effort to format the output of `tostring()` to make it easy to read, because adding extra whitespace changes the contents of the document. To make the output easier to follow, the rest of the examples will use `xml.dom.minidom` to parse the XML before using its `toprettyxml()` method.

Listing 7.57: `ElementTree_pretty.py`

```
from xml.etree import ElementTree
from xml.dom import minidom


def prettify(elem):
    """Return a pretty-printed XML string for the Element.
    """
    rough_string = ElementTree.tostring(elem, 'utf-8')
    reparsed = minidom.parseString(rough_string)
    return reparsed.toprettyxml(indent="  ")
```

The updated example is shown in the following listing.

Listing 7.58: `ElementTree_create_pretty.py`

```
from xml.etree.ElementTree import Element, SubElement, Comment
from ElementTree_pretty import prettify

top = Element('top')

comment = Comment('Generated for PyMOTW')
top.append(comment)

child = SubElement(top, 'child')
child.text = 'This child contains text.'

child_with_tail = SubElement(top, 'child_with_tail')
```

```
child_with_tail.text = 'This child has text.'
child_with_tail.tail = 'And "tail" text.'

child_with_entity_ref = SubElement(top, 'child_with_entity_ref')
child_with_entity_ref.text = 'This & that'

print(prettify(top))
```

The output is also easier to read.

```
$ python3 ElementTree_create_pretty.py

<?xml version="1.0" ?>
<top>
  <!--Generated for PyMOTW-->
  <child>This child contains text.</child>
  <child_with_tail>This child has text.</child_with_tail>
  And &quot;tail&quot; text.
  <child_with_entity_ref>This &amp; that</child_with_entity_ref>
</top>
```

In addition to the extra whitespace for formatting, the `xml.dom.minidom` pretty-printer adds an XML declaration to the output.

7.5.10 Setting Element Properties

The previous example created nodes with tags and text content, but did not set any attributes of the nodes. Many of the examples from Section 7.5.1, "Parsing an XML Document" (page 445) worked with an OPML file listing podcasts and their feeds. The `outline` nodes in the tree used attributes for the group names and podcast properties. ElementTree can be used to construct a similar XML file from a CSV input file, setting all of the element attributes as the tree is constructed.

Listing 7.59: **ElementTree_csv_to_xml.py**

```
import csv
from xml.etree.ElementTree import (
    Element, SubElement, Comment, tostring,
)
import datetime
from ElementTree_pretty import prettify

generated_on = str(datetime.datetime.now())

# Configure one attribute with set().
root = Element('opml')
root.set('version', '1.0')

root.append(
```

```
    Comment('Generated by ElementTree_csv_to_xml.py for PyMOTW')
)

head = SubElement(root, 'head')
title = SubElement(head, 'title')
title.text = 'My Podcasts'
dc = SubElement(head, 'dateCreated')
dc.text = generated_on
dm = SubElement(head, 'dateModified')
dm.text = generated_on

body = SubElement(root, 'body')

with open('podcasts.csv', 'rt') as f:
    current_group = None
    reader = csv.reader(f)
    for row in reader:
        group_name, podcast_name, xml_url, html_url = row
        if (current_group is None or
                group_name != current_group.text):
            # Start a new group.
            current_group = SubElement(
                body, 'outline',
                {'text': group_name},
            )
        # Add this podcast to the group,
        # setting all its attributes at
        # once.
        podcast = SubElement(
            current_group, 'outline',
            {'text': podcast_name,
             'xmlUrl': xml_url,
             'htmlUrl': html_url},
        )

print(prettify(root))
```

This example uses two techniques to set the attribute values of new nodes. The root node is configured using set() to change one attribute at a time. The podcast nodes are given all of their attributes at once by passing a dictionary to the node factory.

```
$ python3 ElementTree_csv_to_xml.py

<?xml version="1.0" ?>
<opml version="1.0">
  <!--Generated by ElementTree_csv_to_xml.py for PyMOTW-->
  <head>
    <title>My Podcasts</title>
    <dateCreated>2016-08-06 17:09:00.524979</dateCreated>
    <dateModified>2016-08-06 17:09:00.524979</dateModified>
```

```
    </head>
    <body>
      <outline text="Non-tech">
        <outline htmlUrl="http://99percentinvisible.org" text="99%\
  Invisible" xmlUrl="http://feeds.99percentinvisible.org/99percen\
  tinvisible"/>
      </outline>
      <outline text="Python">
        <outline htmlUrl="https://talkpython.fm" text="Talk Python\
  to Me" xmlUrl="https://talkpython.fm/episodes/rss"/>
      </outline>
      <outline text="Python">
        <outline htmlUrl="http://podcastinit.com" text="Podcast.__\
  init__" xmlUrl="http://podcastinit.podbean.com/feed/"/>
      </outline>
    </body>
</opml>
```

7.5.11   Building Trees from Lists of Nodes

Multiple children can be added to an Element instance together with the extend() method. The argument to extend() is any iterable, including a list or another Element instance.

Listing 7.60: ElementTree_extend.py

```python
from xml.etree.ElementTree import Element, tostring
from ElementTree_pretty import prettify

top = Element('top')

children = [
    Element('child', num=str(i))
    for i in range(3)
]

top.extend(children)

print(prettify(top))
```

When a list is given, the nodes in the list are added directly to the new parent.

```
$ python3 ElementTree_extend.py

<?xml version="1.0" ?>
<top>
  <child num="0"/>
  <child num="1"/>
  <child num="2"/>
</top>
```

When another `Element` instance is given, the children of that node are added to the new parent.

Listing 7.61: **ElementTree_extend_node.py**

```python
from xml.etree.ElementTree import (
    Element, SubElement, tostring, XML,
)
from ElementTree_pretty import prettify

top = Element('top')

parent = SubElement(top, 'parent')

children = XML(
    '<root><child num="0" /><child num="1" />'
    '<child num="2" /></root>'
)
parent.extend(children)

print(prettify(top))
```

In this case, the node with tag `root` created by parsing the XML string has three children, which are added to the `parent` node. The `root` node is not part of the output tree.

```
$ python3 ElementTree_extend_node.py

<?xml version="1.0" ?>
<top>
  <parent>
    <child num="0"/>
    <child num="1"/>
    <child num="2"/>
  </parent>
</top>
```

It is important to understand that `extend()` does not modify any existing parent–child relationships with the nodes. If the values passed to `extend()` exist somewhere in the tree already, they will still be there, and will be repeated in the output.

Listing 7.62: **ElementTree_extend_node_copy.py**

```python
from xml.etree.ElementTree import (
    Element, SubElement, tostring, XML,
)
from ElementTree_pretty import prettify

top = Element('top')
```

```
parent_a = SubElement(top, 'parent', id='A')
parent_b = SubElement(top, 'parent', id='B')

# Create children.
children = XML(
    '<root><child num="0" /><child num="1" />'
    '<child num="2" /></root>'
)

# Set the id to the Python object id of the node
# to make duplicates easier to spot.
for c in children:
    c.set('id', str(id(c)))

# Add to first parent.
parent_a.extend(children)

print('A:')
print(prettify(top))
print()

# Copy nodes to second parent.
parent_b.extend(children)

print('B:')
print(prettify(top))
print()
```

Setting the `id` attribute of these children to the Python unique object identifier highlights the fact that the same node objects appear in the output tree more than once.

```
$ python3 ElementTree_extend_node_copy.py

A:
<?xml version="1.0" ?>
<top>
  <parent id="A">
    <child id="4316789880" num="0"/>
    <child id="4316789960" num="1"/>
    <child id="4316790040" num="2"/>
  </parent>
  <parent id="B"/>
</top>


B:
<?xml version="1.0" ?>
<top>
  <parent id="A">
```

```
        <child id="4316789880" num="0"/>
        <child id="4316789960" num="1"/>
        <child id="4316790040" num="2"/>
    </parent>
    <parent id="B">
        <child id="4316789880" num="0"/>
        <child id="4316789960" num="1"/>
        <child id="4316790040" num="2"/>
    </parent>
</top>
```

7.5.12   Serializing XML to a Stream

tostring() is implemented by writing to an in-memory file-like object, then returning a
string representing the entire element tree. When working with large amounts of data, it
will take less memory and make more efficient use of the I/O libraries to write directly to
a file handle using the write() method of ElementTree.

Listing 7.63: **ElementTree_write.py**

```python
import io
import sys
from xml.etree.ElementTree import (
    Element, SubElement, Comment, ElementTree,
)

top = Element('top')

comment = Comment('Generated for PyMOTW')
top.append(comment)

child = SubElement(top, 'child')
child.text = 'This child contains text.'

child_with_tail = SubElement(top, 'child_with_tail')
child_with_tail.text = 'This child has regular text.'
child_with_tail.tail = 'And "tail" text.'

child_with_entity_ref = SubElement(top, 'child_with_entity_ref')
child_with_entity_ref.text = 'This & that'

empty_child = SubElement(top, 'empty_child')

ElementTree(top).write(sys.stdout.buffer)
```

The example uses sys.stdout.buffer to write to the console instead of sys.stdout
because ElementTree produces encoded bytes instead of a Unicode string. It could also
write to a file opened in binary mode or socket.

```
$ python3 ElementTree_write.py

<top><!--Generated for PyMOTW--><child>This child contains text.</ch
ild><child_with_tail>This child has regular text.</child_with_tail>A
nd "tail" text.<child_with_entity_ref>This &amp; that</child_with_en
tity_ref><empty_child /></top>
```

The last node in the tree contains no text or subnodes, so it is written as an empty tag, `<empty_child />`. `write()` takes a method argument to control the handling for empty nodes.

Listing 7.64: **ElementTree_write_method.py**

```
import io
import sys
from xml.etree.ElementTree import (
    Element, SubElement, ElementTree,
)

top = Element('top')

child = SubElement(top, 'child')
child.text = 'Contains text.'

empty_child = SubElement(top, 'empty_child')

for method in ['xml', 'html', 'text']:
    print(method)
    sys.stdout.flush()
    ElementTree(top).write(sys.stdout.buffer, method=method)
    print('\n')
```

Three methods are supported:

xml The default method, produces `<empty_child />`.

html Produces the tag pair, as is required in HTML documents (`<empty_child>`
`</empty_child>`).

text Prints only the text of nodes, and skips empty tags entirely.

```
$ python3 ElementTree_write_method.py

xml
<top><child>Contains text.</child><empty_child /></top>

html
<top><child>Contains text.</child><empty_child></empty_child></t
```

```
op>

text
Contains text.
```

TIP

Related Reading

- Standard library documentation for xml.etree.ElementTree.[14]
- csv (page 466): Read and write comma-separated value files.
- defusedxml[15]: A package with fixes for various entity-expansion denial-of-service vulnerabilities useful for working with untrusted XML data.
- Pretty print xml with python: indenting xml[16]: A tip from Rene Dudfield for pretty-printing XML in Python.
- ElementTree Overview[17]: Fredrick Lundh's original documentation and links to the development versions of the ElementTree library.
- Process XML in Python with ElementTree[18]: IBM DeveloperWorks article by David Mertz.
- Outline Processor Markup Language (OPML)[19]: Dave Winer's OPML specification and documentation.
- XML Path Language (XPath)[20]: A syntax for identifying parts of an XML document.
- XPath Support in ElementTree[21]: Part of Fredrick Lundh's original documentation for ElementTree.

7.6   csv: Comma-Separated Value Files

The csv module can be used to work with data exported from spreadsheets and databases into text files formatted with fields and records, commonly referred to as *comma-separated value* (CSV) format because commas are often used to separate the fields in a record.

7.6.1   Reading

Use reader() to create a an object for reading data from a CSV file. The reader can be used as an iterator to process the rows of the file in order.

---

[14] https://docs.python.org/3.5/library/xml.etree.elementtree.html
[15] https://pypi.python.org/pypi/defusedxml
[16] http://renesd.blogspot.com/2007/05/pretty-print-xml-with-python.html
[17] http://effbot.org/zone/element-index.htm
[18] www.ibm.com/developerworks/library/x-matters28/
[19] www.opml.org
[20] www.w3.org/TR/xpath/
[21] http://effbot.org/zone/element-xpath.htm

Listing 7.65: `csv_reader.py`

```
import csv
import sys

with open(sys.argv[1], 'rt') as f:
    reader = csv.reader(f)
    for row in reader:
        print(row)
```

The first argument to `reader()` is the source of text lines. In this case, it is a file, but any iterable is accepted (e.g., a `StringIO` instance, `list`). Other optional arguments can be given to control how the input data is parsed.

```
"Title 1","Title 2","Title 3","Title 4"
1,"a",08/18/07,"å"
2,"bʃ",08/19/07,""
3,"c",08/20/07,"ç"
```

As it is read, each row of the input data is parsed and converted to a `list` of strings.

```
$ python3 csv_reader.py testdata.csv

['Title 1', 'Title 2', 'Title 3', 'Title 4']
['1', 'a', '08/18/07', 'å']
['2', 'b', '08/19/07', ʃ'']
['3', 'c', '08/20/07', 'ç']
```

The parser handles line breaks embedded within strings in a row, which is why a "row" is not always the same as a "line" of input from the file.

```
"Title 1","Title 2","Title 3"
1,"first line
second line",08/18/07
```

Fields with line breaks in the input retain the internal line breaks when they are returned by the parser.

```
$ python3 csv_reader.py testlinebreak.csv

['Title 1', 'Title 2', 'Title 3']
['1', 'first line\nsecond line', '08/18/07']
```

7.6.2 Writing

Writing CSV files is just as easy as reading them. Use `writer()` to create an object for writing, then iterate over the rows, using `writerow()` to print them.

Listing 7.66: <code>csv_writer.py</code>

```
import csv
import sys

unicode_chars = 'ʃåç'

with open(sys.argv[1], 'wt') as f:
    writer = csv.writer(f)
    writer.writerow(('Title 1', 'Title 2', 'Title 3', 'Title 4'))
    for i in range(3):
        row = (
            i + 1,
            chr(ord('a') + i),
            '08/{:02d}/07'.format(i + 1),
            unicode_chars[i],
        )
        writer.writerow(row)

print(open(sys.argv[1], 'rt').read())
```

The output does not look exactly like the exported data used in the reader example because it lacks quotes around some of the values.

```
$ python3 csv_writer.py testout.csv

Title 1,Title 2,Title 3,Title 4
1,a,08/01/07,å
2,bʃ,08/02/07,
3,c,08/03/07,ç
```

7.6.2.1 Quoting

The default quoting behavior is different for the writer, so the second and third columns in the previous example are not quoted. To add quoting, set the `quoting` argument to one of the other quoting modes.

```
writer = csv.writer(f, quoting=csv.QUOTE_NONNUMERIC)
```

In this case, `QUOTE_NONNUMERIC` adds quotes around all columns that contain values that are not numbers.

```
$ python3 csv_writer_quoted.py testout_quoted.csv

"Title 1","Title 2","Title 3","Title 4"
1,"a","08/01/07","å"
2,"bʃ","08/02/07",""
3,"c","08/03/07","ç"
```

Four different quoting options are available, defined as constants in the `csv` module.

`QUOTE_ALL` Quote everything, regardless of type.

`QUOTE_MINIMAL` Quote fields with special characters (anything that would confuse a parser configured with the same dialect and options). This is the default.

`QUOTE_NONNUMERIC` Quote all fields that are not integers or floats. When used with the reader, input fields that are not quoted are converted to floats.

`QUOTE_NONE` Do not quote anything on output. When used with the reader, quote characters are included in the field values (normally, they are treated as delimiters and stripped).

7.6.3 Dialects

There is no well-defined standard for comma-separated value files, so the parser needs to be flexible. To provide this flexibility, many parameters are used to control how `csv` parses or writes data. Rather than passing each of these parameters to the reader and the writer separately, they are grouped together into a *dialect* object.

Dialect classes can be registered by name, so that callers of the `csv` module do not need to know the parameter settings in advance. The complete list of registered dialects can be retrieved with `list_dialects()`.

Listing 7.67: `csv_list_dialects.py`

```
import csv

print(csv.list_dialects())
```

The standard library includes three dialects: `excel`, `excel-tabs`, and `unix`. The `excel` dialect is intended for working with data in the default export format for Microsoft Excel; it also works with LibreOffice.[22] The `unix` dialect quotes all fields with double quotes and uses \n as the record separator.

```
$ python3 csv_list_dialects.py

['excel', 'excel-tab', 'unix']
```

7.6.3.1 Creating a Dialect

If, instead of using commas to delimit fields, the input file uses pipes (|), a new dialect can be registered using the appropriate delimiter.

```
"Title 1"|"Title 2"|"Title 3"
1|"first line
second line"|08/18/07
```

---

[22] www.libreoffice.org

Listing 7.68: **csv_dialect.py**

```
import csv

csv.register_dialect('pipes', delimiter='|')

with open('testdata.pipes', 'r') as f:
    reader = csv.reader(f, dialect='pipes')
    for row in reader:
        print(row)
```

Using the "pipes" dialect, the file can be read just as with the comma-delimited file.

```
$ python3 csv_dialect.py

['Title 1', 'Title 2', 'Title 3']
['1', 'first line\nsecond line', '08/18/07']
```

7.6.3.2 Dialect Parameters

A dialect specifies all of the tokens used when parsing or writing a data file. Table 7.3 lists the aspects of the file format that can be specified, from the way columns are delimited to the character used to escape a token.

Listing 7.69: **csv_dialect_variations.py**

```
import csv
import sys

csv.register_dialect('escaped',
                     escapechar='\\',
                     doublequote=False,
                     quoting=csv.QUOTE_NONE,
                     )
```

Table 7.3: CSV Dialect Parameters

Attribute	Default	Meaning
delimiter	,	Field separator (one character)
doublequote	True	Flag controlling whether quotechar instances are doubled
escapechar	None	Character used to indicate an escape sequence
lineterminator	\r\n	String used by writer to terminate a line
quotechar	"	String to surround fields containing special values (one character)
quoting	QUOTE_MINIMAL	Controls quoting behavior described earlier
skipinitialspace	False	Ignore whitespace after the field delimiter

```
csv.register_dialect('singlequote',
                     quotechar="'",
                     quoting=csv.QUOTE_ALL,
                     )

quoting_modes = {
    getattr(csv, n): n
    for n in dir(csv)
    if n.startswith('QUOTE_')
}

TEMPLATE = '''\
Dialect: "{name}"

  delimiter      = {dl!r:<6}    skipinitialspace = {si!r}
  doublequote    = {dq!r:<6}    quoting          = {qu}
  quotechar      = {qc!r:<6}    lineterminator   = {lt!r}
  escapechar     = {ec!r:<6}
'''

for name in sorted(csv.list_dialects()):
    dialect = csv.get_dialect(name)

    print(TEMPLATE.format(
        name=name,
        dl=dialect.delimiter,
        si=dialect.skipinitialspace,
        dq=dialect.doublequote,
        qu=quoting_modes[dialect.quoting],
        qc=dialect.quotechar,
        lt=dialect.lineterminator,
        ec=dialect.escapechar,
    ))

    writer = csv.writer(sys.stdout, dialect=dialect)
    writer.writerow(
        ('col1', 1, '10/01/2010',
         'Special chars: " \' {} to parse'.format(
             dialect.delimiter))
    )
    print()
```

This program shows how the same data appears when formatted using several different dialects.

```
$ python3 csv_dialect_variations.py

Dialect: "escaped"
```

```
   delimiter   = ','          skipinitialspace = 0
   doublequote = 0            quoting          = QUOTE_NONE
   quotechar   = '"'          lineterminator   = '\r\n'
   escapechar  = '\\'
```

col1,1,10/01/2010,Special chars: \" ' \, to parse

Dialect: "excel"

```
   delimiter   = ','          skipinitialspace = 0
   doublequote = 1            quoting          = QUOTE_MINIMAL
   quotechar   = '"'          lineterminator   = '\r\n'
   escapechar  = None
```

col1,1,10/01/2010,"Special chars: "" ' , to parse"

Dialect: "excel-tab"

```
   delimiter   = '\t'         skipinitialspace = 0
   doublequote = 1            quoting          = QUOTE_MINIMAL
   quotechar   = '"'          lineterminator   = '\r\n'
   escapechar  = None
```

col1   1   10/01/2010   "Special chars: "" '   to parse"

Dialect: "singlequote"

```
   delimiter   = ','          skipinitialspace = 0
   doublequote = 1            quoting          = QUOTE_ALL
   quotechar   = "'"          lineterminator   = '\r\n'
   escapechar  = None
```

'col1','1','10/01/2010','Special chars: " '' , to parse'

Dialect: "unix"

```
   delimiter   = ','          skipinitialspace = 0
   doublequote = 1            quoting          = QUOTE_ALL
   quotechar   = '"'          lineterminator   = '\n'
   escapechar  = None
```

"col1","1","10/01/2010","Special chars: "" ' , to parse"

7.6.3.3   Automatically Detecting Dialects

The best way to configure a dialect for parsing an input file is to know the correct settings
in advance. For data for which the dialect parameters are unknown, the Sniffer class can
be used to make an educated guess. The sniff() method takes a sample of the input data
and an optional argument giving the possible delimiter characters.

Listing 7.70: `csv_dialect_sniffer.py`

```
import csv
from io import StringIO
import textwrap

csv.register_dialect('escaped',
                     escapechar='\\',
                     doublequote=False,
                     quoting=csv.QUOTE_NONE)
csv.register_dialect('singlequote',
                     quotechar="'",
                     quoting=csv.QUOTE_ALL)

# Generate sample data for all known dialects.
samples = []
for name in sorted(csv.list_dialects()):
    buffer = StringIO()
    dialect = csv.get_dialect(name)
    writer = csv.writer(buffer, dialect=dialect)
    writer.writerow(
        ('col1', 1, '10/01/2010',
         'Special chars " \' {} to parse'.format(
            dialect.delimiter))
    )
    samples.append((name, dialect, buffer.getvalue()))

# Guess the dialect for a given sample, and then use the results
# to parse the data.
sniffer = csv.Sniffer()
for name, expected, sample in samples:
    print('Dialect: "{}"'.format(name))
    print('In: {}'.format(sample.rstrip()))
    dialect = sniffer.sniff(sample, delimiters=',\t')
    reader = csv.reader(StringIO(sample), dialect=dialect)
    print('Parsed:\n  {}\n'.format(
        '\n  '.join(repr(r) for r in next(reader))))
```

`sniff()` returns a `Dialect` instance with the settings to be used for parsing the data. The results are not always perfect, as demonstrated by the "escaped" dialect in the example.

```
$ python3 csv_dialect_sniffer.py

Dialect: "escaped"
In: col1,1,10/01/2010,Special chars \" ' \, to parse
Parsed:
  'col1'
  '1'
  '10/01/2010'
```

```
'Special chars \\" \' \\'
' to parse'
```

```
Dialect: "excel"
In: col1,1,10/01/2010,"Special chars "" ' , to parse"
Parsed:
  'col1'
  '1'
  '10/01/2010'
  'Special chars " \' , to parse'
```

```
Dialect: "excel-tab"
In: col1        1       10/01/2010      "Special chars "" '     to parse"
Parsed:
  'col1'
  '1'
  '10/01/2010'
  'Special chars " \' \t to parse'
```

```
Dialect: "singlequote"
In: 'col1','1','10/01/2010','Special chars " '' , to parse'
Parsed:
  'col1'
  '1'
  '10/01/2010'
  'Special chars " \' , to parse'
```

```
Dialect: "unix"
In: "col1","1","10/01/2010","Special chars "" ' , to parse"
Parsed:
  'col1'
  '1'
  '10/01/2010'
  'Special chars " \' , to parse'
```

7.6.4 Using Field Names

In addition to working with sequences of data, the csv module includes classes for working with rows as dictionaries so that the fields can be named. The DictReader and DictWriter classes translate rows to dictionaries instead of lists. Keys for the dictionary can be passed in, or inferred from the first row in the input (when the row contains headers).

Listing 7.71: csv_dictreader.py

```
import csv
import sys
```

```
with open(sys.argv[1], 'rt') as f:
    reader = csv.DictReader(f)
    for row in reader:
        print(row)
```

The dictionary-based reader and writer are implemented as wrappers around the sequence-based classes, and use the same methods and arguments. The only difference in the reader API is that rows are returned as dictionaries instead of lists or tuples.

```
$ python3 csv_dictreader.py testdata.csv

{'Title 2': 'a', 'Title 3': '08/18/07', 'Title 4': 'å', 'Title 1
': '1'}
{'Title 2': 'b', 'Title 3': '08/19/07', 'Title 4': 'ʃ'', 'Title 1
': '2'}
{'Title 2': 'c', 'Title 3': '08/20/07', 'Title 4': 'ç', 'Title 1
': '3'}
```

The DictWriter must be given a list of field names so it knows how to order the columns in the output.

Listing 7.72: **csv_dictwriter.py**

```
import csv
import sys

fieldnames = ('Title 1', 'Title 2', 'Title 3', 'Title 4')
headers = {
    n: n
    for n in fieldnames
}
unicode_chars = 'ʃåç'

with open(sys.argv[1], 'wt') as f:

    writer = csv.DictWriter(f, fieldnames=fieldnames)
    writer.writeheader()

    for i in range(3):
        writer.writerow({
            'Title 1': i + 1,
            'Title 2': chr(ord('a') + i),
            'Title 3': '08/{:02d}/07'.format(i + 1),
            'Title 4': unicode_chars[i],
        })

print(open(sys.argv[1], 'rt').read())
```

The field names are not written to the file automatically, but they can be written explicitly using the `writeheader()` method.

```
$ python3 csv_dictwriter.py testout.csv

Title 1,Title 2,Title 3,Title 4
1,a,08/01/07,å
2,bʃ,08/02/07,
3,c,08/03/07,ç
```

TIP

Related Reading

- Standard library documentation for `csv`.[23]
- **PEP 305**[24]: CSV File API.
- Python 2 to 3 porting notes for `csv` (page 1358).

---

[23] https://docs.python.org/3.5/library/csv.html
[24] www.python.org/dev/peps/pep-0305

Chapter 8

Data Compression and Archiving

Although modern computer systems have an ever-increasing storage capacity, the growth in the amount of data being produced is unrelenting. Lossless compression algorithms make up for some of the shortfall in capacity by trading time spent compressing or decompressing data for the space needed to store it. Python includes interfaces to the most popular compression libraries so it can read and write files interchangeably.

zlib (page 477) and gzip (page 486) expose the GNU zip library, and bz2 (page 491) provides access to the more recent bzip2 format. Both formats work on streams of data, without regard to input format, and provide interfaces for reading and writing compressed files transparently. Use these modules for compressing a single file or data source.

The standard library also includes modules to manage *archive* formats, for combining several files into a single file that can be managed as a unit. tarfile (page 503) reads and writes the Unix tape archive format—an old standard still widely used today because of its flexibility. zipfile (page 511) works with archives based on the format popularized by the PC program PKZIP, originally used under MS-DOS and Windows, but now also used on other platforms because of the simplicity of its API and the easy portability of the format.

8.1 zlib: GNU zlib Compression

The zlib module provides a lower-level interface to many of the functions in the zlib compression library from the GNU project.

8.1.1 Working with Data in Memory

The simplest way of working with zlib requires holding all of the data to be compressed or decompressed in memory.

Listing 8.1: `zlib_memory.py`

```python
import zlib
import binascii

original_data = b'This is the original text.'
print('Original     :', len(original_data), original_data)

compressed = zlib.compress(original_data)
print('Compressed   :', len(compressed),
      binascii.hexlify(compressed))
```

```
decompressed = zlib.decompress(compressed)
print('Decompressed :', len(decompressed), decompressed)
```

The `compress()` and `decompress()` functions both take a byte sequence argument and return a byte sequence.

```
$ python3 zlib_memory.py

Original     : 26 b'This is the original text.'
Compressed   : 32 b'789c0bc9c82c5600a2928c5485fca2ccf4ccbcc41c85
92d48a123d007f2f097e'
Decompressed : 26 b'This is the original text.'
```

The previous example demonstrates that the compressed version of small amounts of data can be larger than the uncompressed version. While the actual results depend on the input data, it is interesting to observe the compression overhead for small data sets.

Listing 8.2: `zlib_lengths.py`

```
import zlib

original_data = b'This is the original text.'

template = '{:>15}  {:>15}'
print(template.format('len(data)', 'len(compressed)'))
print(template.format('-' * 15, '-' * 15))

for i in range(5):
    data = original_data * i
    compressed = zlib.compress(data)
    highlight = '*' if len(data) < len(compressed) else ''
    print(template.format(len(data), len(compressed)), highlight)
```

The * characters in the output highlight the lines where the compressed data takes up more memory than the uncompressed version.

```
$ python3 zlib_lengths.py

      len(data)  len(compressed)
---------------  ---------------
              0                8 *
             26               32 *
             52               35
             78               35
            104               36
```

zlib supports several different compression levels, allowing a balance between computational cost and the amount of space reduction. The default compression level, zlib.Z_DEFAULT_COMPRESSION, is -1 and corresponds to a hard-coded value that represents a compromise between performance and compression outcome. This currently corresponds to level 6.

Listing 8.3: **zlib_compresslevel.py**

```python
import zlib

input_data = b'Some repeated text.\n' * 1024
template = '{:>5}  {:>5}'

print(template.format('Level', 'Size'))
print(template.format('-----', '----'))

for i in range(0, 10):
    data = zlib.compress(input_data, i)
    print(template.format(i, len(data)))
```

A level of 0 means no compression at all. A level of 9 requires the most computation and produces the smallest output. As this example shows, the same size reduction may be achieved with multiple compression levels for a given input.

```
$ python3 zlib_compresslevel.py

Level   Size
-----   ----
    0  20491
    1    172
    2    172
    3    172
    4     98
    5     98
    6     98
    7     98
    8     98
    9     98
```

8.1.2 Incremental Compression and Decompression

The in-memory approach has drawbacks that make it impractical for real-world use cases. Its major drawback is that the system needs enough memory to hold both the uncompressed and compressed versions resident in memory at the same time. The alternative is to use Compress and Decompress objects to manipulate data incrementally, so that the entire data set does not have to fit into memory.

Listing 8.4: **`zlib_incremental.py`**

```
import zlib
import binascii

compressor = zlib.compressobj(1)

with open('lorem.txt', 'rb') as input:
    while True:
        block = input.read(64)
        if not block:
            break
        compressed = compressor.compress(block)
        if compressed:
            print('Compressed: {}'.format(
                binascii.hexlify(compressed)))
        else:
            print('buffering...')
    remaining = compressor.flush()
    print('Flushed: {}'.format(binascii.hexlify(remaining)))
```

This example reads small blocks of data from a plain text file and passes the data set to `compress()`. The compressor maintains an internal buffer of compressed data. Since the compression algorithm depends on checksums and minimum block sizes, the compressor may not be ready to return data each time it receives more input. If it does not have an entire compressed block ready, it returns an empty byte string. When all of the data is fed in, the `flush()` method forces the compressor to close the final block and return the rest of the compressed data.

```
$ python3 zlib_incremental.py

Compressed: b'7801'
buffering...
buffering...
buffering...
buffering...
buffering...
Flushed: b'55904b6ac4400c44f73e451da0f129b20c2110c85e696b8c40dde
dd167ce1f7915025a087daa9ef4be8c07e4f21c38962e834b800647435fd3b90
747b2810eb9c4bbcc13ac123bded6e4bef1c91ee40d3c6580e3ff52aad2e8cb2
eb6062dad74a89ca904cbb0f2545e0db4b1f2e01955b8c511cb2ac08967d228a
f1447c8ec72e40c4c714116e60cdef171bb6c0feaa255dff1c507c2c4439ec96
05b7e0ba9fc54bae39355cb89fd6ebe5841d673c7b7bc68a46f575a312eebd22
0d4b32441bdc1b36ebf0aedef3d57ea4b26dd986dd39af57dfb05d32279de'
```

8.1.3   Mixed Content Streams

The `Decompress` class returned by `decompressobj()` can also be used in situations where compressed data and uncompressed data are mixed together.

Listing 8.5: `zlib_mixed.py`

```
import zlib

lorem = open('lorem.txt', 'rb').read()
compressed = zlib.compress(lorem)
combined = compressed + lorem

decompressor = zlib.decompressobj()
decompressed = decompressor.decompress(combined)

decompressed_matches = decompressed == lorem
print('Decompressed matches lorem:', decompressed_matches)

unused_matches = decompressor.unused_data == lorem
print('Unused data matches lorem :', unused_matches)
```

After decompressing all of the data, the `unused_data` attribute contains any data not used.

```
$ python3 zlib_mixed.py

Decompressed matches lorem: True
Unused data matches lorem : True
```

8.1.4 Checksums

In addition to compression and decompression functions, `zlib` includes two functions for computing checksums of data, `adler32()` and `crc32()`. Neither checksum is cryptographically secure, and they are intended for use only for data integrity verification.

Listing 8.6: `zlib_checksums.py`

```
import zlib

data = open('lorem.txt', 'rb').read()

cksum = zlib.adler32(data)
print('Adler32: {:12d}'.format(cksum))
print('        : {:12d}'.format(zlib.adler32(data, cksum)))

cksum = zlib.crc32(data)
print('CRC-32 : {:12d}'.format(cksum))
print('        : {:12d}'.format(zlib.crc32(data, cksum)))
```

Both functions take the same arguments: a byte string containing the data and an optional value to be used as a starting point for the checksum. They return a 32-bit signed integer value that can also be passed back on subsequent calls as a new starting-point argument to produce a *running* checksum.

```
$ python3 zlib_checksums.py

Adler32:   3542251998
      :    669447099
CRC-32 :   3038370516
      :    2870078631
```

8.1.5   Compressing Network Data

The server in the next listing uses the stream compressor to respond to requests consisting of filenames by writing a compressed version of the file to the socket used to communicate with the client.

Listing 8.7: zlib_server.py

```python
import zlib
import logging
import socketserver
import binascii

BLOCK_SIZE = 64


class ZlibRequestHandler(socketserver.BaseRequestHandler):

    logger = logging.getLogger('Server')

    def handle(self):
        compressor = zlib.compressobj(1)

        # Find out which file the client wants.
        filename = self.request.recv(1024).decode('utf-8')
        self.logger.debug('client asked for: %r', filename)

        # Send chunks of the file as they are compressed.
        with open(filename, 'rb') as input:
            while True:
                block = input.read(BLOCK_SIZE)
                if not block:
                    break
                self.logger.debug('RAW %r', block)
                compressed = compressor.compress(block)
                if compressed:
                    self.logger.debug(
                        'SENDING %r',
                        binascii.hexlify(compressed))
                    self.request.send(compressed)
                else:
                    self.logger.debug('BUFFERING')
```

```
        # Send any data being buffered by the compressor.
        remaining = compressor.flush()
        while remaining:
            to_send = remaining[:BLOCK_SIZE]
            remaining = remaining[BLOCK_SIZE:]
            self.logger.debug('FLUSHING %r',
                               binascii.hexlify(to_send))
            self.request.send(to_send)
        return


if __name__ == '__main__':
    import socket
    import threading
    from io import BytesIO

    logging.basicConfig(
        level=logging.DEBUG,
        format='%(name)s: %(message)s',
    )
    logger = logging.getLogger('Client')

    # Set up a server, running in a separate thread.
    address = ('localhost', 0)  # Let the kernel assign a port.
    server = socketserver.TCPServer(address, ZlibRequestHandler)
    ip, port = server.server_address  # What port was assigned?

    t = threading.Thread(target=server.serve_forever)
    t.setDaemon(True)
    t.start()

    # Connect to the server as a client.
    logger.info('Contacting server on %s:%s', ip, port)
    s = socket.socket(socket.AF_INET, socket.SOCK_STREAM)
    s.connect((ip, port))

    # Ask for a file.
    requested_file = 'lorem.txt'
    logger.debug('sending filename: %r', requested_file)
    len_sent = s.send(requested_file.encode('utf-8'))

    # Receive a response.
    buffer = BytesIO()
    decompressor = zlib.decompressobj()
    while True:
        response = s.recv(BLOCK_SIZE)
        if not response:
            break
        logger.debug('READ %r', binascii.hexlify(response))
```

```
        # Include any unconsumed data when
        # feeding the decompressor.
        to_decompress = decompressor.unconsumed_tail + response
        while to_decompress:
            decompressed = decompressor.decompress(to_decompress)
            if decompressed:
                logger.debug('DECOMPRESSED %r', decompressed)
                buffer.write(decompressed)
                # Look for unconsumed data due to buffer overflow.
                to_decompress = decompressor.unconsumed_tail
            else:
                logger.debug('BUFFERING')
                to_decompress = None

    # Deal with data reamining inside the decompressor buffer.
    remainder = decompressor.flush()
    if remainder:
        logger.debug('FLUSHED %r', remainder)
        buffer.write(remainder)

    full_response = buffer.getvalue()
    lorem = open('lorem.txt', 'rb').read()
    logger.debug('response matches file contents: %s',
                 full_response == lorem)

    # Clean up.
    s.close()
    server.socket.close()
```

This listing includes some artificial chunking to illustrate the buffering behavior that happens when passing the data to `compress()` or `decompress()` does not result in a complete block of compressed or uncompressed output.

The client connects to the socket and requests a file. Then it loops, receiving blocks of compressed data. Since a block may not always contain all of the information needed to decompress it entirely, the remainder of any data received earlier is combined with the new data and passed to the decompressor. As the data is decompressed, it is appended to a buffer, which is compared against the file contents at the end of the processing loop.

WARNING

This server has obvious security implications. Do not run it on a system on the open Internet or in any environment where security might be an issue.

```
$ python3 zlib_server.py

Client: Contacting server on 127.0.0.1:53658
Client: sending filename: 'lorem.txt'
Server: client asked for: 'lorem.txt'
```

```
Server: RAW b'Lorem ipsum dolor sit amet, consectetuer adipiscin
g elit. Donec\n'
Server: SENDING b'7801'
Server: RAW b'egestas, enim et consectetuer ullamcorper, lectus
ligula rutrum '
Server: BUFFERING
Server: RAW b'leo, a\nelementum elit tortor eu quam. Duis tincid
unt nisi ut ant'
Server: BUFFERING
Server: RAW b'e. Nulla\nfacilisi. Sed tristique eros eu libero.
Pellentesque ve'
Server: BUFFERING
Server: RAW b'l arcu. Vivamus\npurus orci, iaculis ac, suscipit
sit amet, pulvi'
Client: READ b'7801'
Client: BUFFERING
Server: BUFFERING
Server: RAW b'nar eu,\nlacus.\n'
Server: BUFFERING
Server: FLUSHING b'55904b6ac4400c44f73e451da0f129b20c2110c85e696
b8c40ddedd167ce1f7915025a087daa9ef4be8c07e4f21c38962e834b8006474
35fd3b90747b2810eb9'
Server: FLUSHING b'c4bbcc13ac123bded6e4bef1c91ee40d3c6580e3ff52a
ad2e8cb2eb6062dad74a89ca904cbb0f2545e0db4b1f2e01955b8c511cb2ac08
967d228af1447c8ec72'
Client: READ b'55904b6ac4400c44f73e451da0f129b20c2110c85e696b8c4
0ddedd167ce1f7915025a087daa9ef4be8c07e4f21c38962e834b800647435fd
3b90747b2810eb9'
Server: FLUSHING b'e40c4c714116e60cdef171bb6c0feaa255dff1c507c2c
4439ec9605b7e0ba9fc54bae39355cb89fd6ebe5841d673c7b7bc68a46f575a3
12eebd220d4b32441bd'
Client: DECOMPRESSED b'Lorem ipsum dolor sit amet, consectetuer
adi'
Client: READ b'c4bbcc13ac123bded6e4bef1c91ee40d3c6580e3ff52aad2e
8cb2eb6062dad74a89ca904cbb0f2545e0db4b1f2e01955b8c511cb2ac08967d
228af1447c8ec72'
Client: DECOMPRESSED b'piscing elit. Donec\negestas, enim et con
sectetuer ullamcorper, lectus ligula rutrum leo, a\nelementum el
it tortor eu quam. Duis tinci'
Client: READ b'e40c4c714116e60cdef171bb6c0feaa255dff1c507c2c4439
ec9605b7e0ba9fc54bae39355cb89fd6ebe5841d673c7b7bc68a46f575a312ee
bd220d4b32441bd'
Client: DECOMPRESSED b'dunt nisi ut ante. Nulla\nfacilisi. Sed t
ristique eros eu libero. Pellentesque vel arcu. Vivamus\npurus o
rci, iaculis ac'
Server: FLUSHING b'c1b36ebf0aedef3d57ea4b26dd986dd39af57dfb05d32
279de'
Client: READ b'c1b36ebf0aedef3d57ea4b26dd986dd39af57dfb05d32279d
e'
```

```
Client: DECOMPRESSED b', suscipit sit amet, pulvinar eu,\nlacus.
\n'
Client: response matches file contents: True
```

TIP

Related Reading

- Standard library documentation for zlib.[1]
- gzip (page 486): The gzip module includes a higher-level (file-based) interface to the zlib library.
- zlib: A Massively Spiffy Yet Delicately Unobtrusive Compression Library[2]: Home page for zlib library.
- zlib 1.2.11 Manual[3]: Complete zlib documentation.
- bz2 (page 491): The bz2 module provides a similar interface to the bzip2 compression library.

8.2   gzip: Read and Write GNU zip Files

The gzip module provides a file-like interface to GNU zip files, using zlib (page 477) to compress and uncompress the data.

8.2.1   Writing Compressed Files

The module-level function open() creates an instance of the file-like class GzipFile. The usual methods for writing and reading bytes are provided.

Listing 8.8: gzip_write.py

```python
import gzip
import io
import os

outfilename = 'example.txt.gz'
with gzip.open(outfilename, 'wb') as output:
    with io.TextIOWrapper(output, encoding='utf-8') as enc:
        enc.write('Contents of the example file go here.\n')

print(outfilename, 'contains', os.stat(outfilename).st_size,
      'bytes')
os.system('file -b --mime {}'.format(outfilename))
```

---

[1] https://docs.python.org/3.5/library/zlib.html
[2] www.zlib.net
[3] www.zlib.net/manual.html

To write data into a compressed file, open the file with mode `'wb'`. This example wraps the `GzipFile` with a `TextIOWrapper` from the `io` (page 390) module to encode Unicode text to bytes suitable for compression.

```
$ python3 gzip_write.py

application/x-gzip; charset=binary
example.txt.gz contains 75 bytes
```

Different amounts of compression can be used by passing a `compresslevel` argument. Valid values range from 0 to 9, inclusive. Lower values lead to faster processing and result in less compression. Higher values lead to slower processing and compress more, up to a point.

Listing 8.9: gzip_compresslevel.py

```python
import gzip
import io
import os
import hashlib


def get_hash(data):
    return hashlib.md5(data).hexdigest()


data = open('lorem.txt', 'r').read() * 1024
cksum = get_hash(data.encode('utf-8'))


print('Level  Size       Checksum')
print('-----  ---------- ----------------------------------')
print('data   {:>10} {}'.format(len(data), cksum))

for i in range(0, 10):
    filename = 'compress-level-{}.gz'.format(i)
    with gzip.open(filename, 'wb', compresslevel=i) as output:
        with io.TextIOWrapper(output, encoding='utf-8') as enc:
            enc.write(data)
    size = os.stat(filename).st_size
    cksum = get_hash(open(filename, 'rb').read())
    print('{:>5d}  {:>10d}  {}'.format(i, size, cksum))
```

The center column of numbers in the output shows the size (in bytes) of the files produced by compressing the input. For this input data, the higher compression values do not necessarily pay off with decreased storage space. Results will vary, depending on the input data.

```
$ python3 gzip_compresslevel.py

Level  Size       Checksum
-----  ---------- --------------------------------
data      754688  e4c0f9433723971563f08a458715119c
   0      754848  7f050dafb281c7b9d30e5fccf4e0cf19
   1        9846  3b1708684b3655d136b8dca292f5bbba
   2        8267  48ceb436bf10bc6bbd60489eb285de27
   3        8227  4217663bf275f4241a8b73b1a1cfd734
   4        4167  1a5d9b968520d64ed10a4c125735d8b4
   5        4167  90d85bf6457c2eaf20307deb90d071c6
   6        4167  1798ac0cbd77d79973efd8e222bf85d8
   7        4167  7fe834b01c164a14c2d2d8e5560402e6
   8        4167  03795b47b899384cdb95f99c1b7f9f71
   9        4167  a33be56e455f8c787860f23c3b47b6f1
```

A `GzipFile` instance also includes a `writelines()` method that can be used to write a sequence of strings.

Listing 8.10: gzip_writelines.py

```python
import gzip
import io
import itertools
import os

with gzip.open('example_lines.txt.gz', 'wb') as output:
    with io.TextIOWrapper(output, encoding='utf-8') as enc:
        enc.writelines(
            itertools.repeat('The same line, over and over.\n',
                             10)
        )

os.system('gzcat example_lines.txt.gz')
```

As with a regular file, the input lines need to include a newline character.

```
$ python3 gzip_writelines.py

The same line, over and over.
The same line, over and over.
The same line, over and over.
The same line, over and over.
The same line, over and over.
The same line, over and over.
The same line, over and over.
The same line, over and over.
The same line, over and over.
The same line, over and over.
```

8.2.2   Reading Compressed Data

To read data back from previously compressed files, open the file with binary read mode
('rb') so no text-based translation of line endings or Unicode decoding is performed.

Listing 8.11: gzip_read.py

```
import gzip
import io

with gzip.open('example.txt.gz', 'rb') as input_file:
    with io.TextIOWrapper(input_file, encoding='utf-8') as dec:
        print(dec.read())
```

This example reads the file written by gzip_write.py from the previous section, using a
TextIOWrapper to decode the text after it is decompressed.

```
$ python3 gzip_read.py

Contents of the example file go here.
```

While reading a file, it is also possible to seek and read only part of the data.

Listing 8.12: gzip_seek.py

```
import gzip

with gzip.open('example.txt.gz', 'rb') as input_file:
    print('Entire file:')
    all_data = input_file.read()
    print(all_data)

    expected = all_data[5:15]

    # Rewind to beginning
    input_file.seek(0)

    # Move ahead 5 bytes
    input_file.seek(5)
    print('Starting at position 5 for 10 bytes:')
    partial = input_file.read(10)
    print(partial)

    print()
    print(expected == partial)
```

The seek() position is relative to the *uncompressed* data, so the caller does not need to
know that the data file is compressed.

```
$ python3 gzip_seek.py

Entire file:
b'Contents of the example file go here.\n'
Starting at position 5 for 10 bytes:
b'nts of the'

True
```

8.2.3   Working with Streams

The GzipFile class can be used to wrap other types of data streams so they can use compression as well. This approach is useful when data is being transmitted over a socket or an existing (already open) file handle. A BytesIO buffer can also be used with GzipFile for operations on data in memory.

Listing 8.13: **gzip_BytesIO.py**

```
import gzip
from io import BytesIO
import binascii

uncompressed_data = b'The same line, over and over.\n' * 10
print('UNCOMPRESSED:', len(uncompressed_data))
print(uncompressed_data)

buf = BytesIO()
with gzip.GzipFile(mode='wb', fileobj=buf) as f:
    f.write(uncompressed_data)

compressed_data = buf.getvalue()
print('COMPRESSED:', len(compressed_data))
print(binascii.hexlify(compressed_data))

inbuffer = BytesIO(compressed_data)
with gzip.GzipFile(mode='rb', fileobj=inbuffer) as f:
    reread_data = f.read(len(uncompressed_data))

print('\nREREAD:', len(reread_data))
print(reread_data)
```

One benefit of using GzipFile over zlib (page 477) is that the former supports the file API. However, when rereading the previously compressed data, an explicit length is passed to read(). Omitting the length results in a CRC error, possibly because BytesIO returns an empty string before reporting EOF. When working with streams of compressed data, either prefix the data with an integer representing the actual amount of data to be read or use the incremental decompression API in zlib.

```
$ python3 gzip_BytesIO.py

UNCOMPRESSED: 300
b'The same line, over and over.\nThe same line, over and over.\nT
he same line, over and over.\nThe same line, over and over.\nThe
same line, over and over.\nThe same line, over and over.\nThe sam
e line, over and over.\nThe same line, over and over.\nThe same l
ine, over and over.\nThe same line, over and over.\n'
COMPRESSED: 51
b'1f8b08006149aa5702ff0bc94855284ecc4d55c8c9cc4bd551c82f4b2d5248c
c4b0133f4b8424665916401d3e717802c010000'

REREAD: 300
b'The same line, over and over.\nThe same line, over and over.\nT
he same line, over and over.\nThe same line, over and over.\nThe
same line, over and over.\nThe same line, over and over.\nThe sam
e line, over and over.\nThe same line, over and over.\nThe same l
ine, over and over.\nThe same line, over and over.\n'
```

TIP

Related Reading

- Standard library documentation for gzip.[4]
- zlib (page 477): The zlib module is a lower-level interface to gzip compression.
- zipfile (page 511): The zipfile module gives access to ZIP archives.
- bz2 (page 491): The bz2 module uses the bzip2 compression format.
- tarfile (page 503): The tarfile module includes built-in support for reading compressed tar archives.
- io (page 390): Building blocks for creating input and output pipelines.

8.3   bz2: bzip2 Compression

The bz2 module is an interface for the bzip2 library, used to compress data for storage or transmission. Three APIs are provided for this purpose:

- "One shot" compression/decompression functions for operating on a blob of data
- Iterative compression/decompression objects for working with streams of data
- A file-like class that supports reading and writing as with an uncompressed file

---

[4] https://docs.python.org/3.5/library/gzip.html

8.3.1   One-Shot Operations in Memory

The simplest way to work with bz2 is to load all of the data to be compressed or decompressed in memory, and then use compress() and decompress(), respectively, to transform it.

Listing 8.14: bz2_memory.py

```
import bz2
import binascii

original_data = b'This is the original text.'
print('Original     : {} bytes'.format(len(original_data)))
print(original_data)

print()
compressed = bz2.compress(original_data)
print('Compressed   : {} bytes'.format(len(compressed)))
hex_version = binascii.hexlify(compressed)
for i in range(len(hex_version) // 40 + 1):
    print(hex_version[i * 40:(i + 1) * 40])

print()
decompressed = bz2.decompress(compressed)
print('Decompressed : {} bytes'.format(len(decompressed)))
print(decompressed)
```

The compressed data contains non-ASCII characters, so it needs to be converted to its hexadecimal representation before it can be printed. In the output from these examples, the hexadecimal version is reformatted to have at most 40 characters on each line.

```
$ python3 bz2_memory.py

Original     : 26 bytes
b'This is the original text.'

Compressed   : 62 bytes
b'425a683931415926535916be35a6000002938040'
b'01040022e59c402000314c000111e93d434da223'
b'028cf9e73148cae0a0d6ed7f17724538509016be'
b'35a6'

Decompressed : 26 bytes
b'This is the original text.'
```

For short text, the compressed version can be significantly longer than the original. While the actual results depend on the input data, it is interesting to observe the compression overhead.

Listing 8.15: bz2_lengths.py

```
import bz2

original_data = b'This is the original text.'

fmt = '{:>15}  {:>15}'
print(fmt.format('len(data)', 'len(compressed)'))
print(fmt.format('-' * 15, '-' * 15))

for i in range(5):
    data = original_data * i
    compressed = bz2.compress(data)
    print(fmt.format(len(data), len(compressed)), end='')
    print('*' if len(data) < len(compressed) else '')
```

The output lines ending with * show the points where the compressed data is longer than the raw input.

```
$ python3 bz2_lengths.py

      len(data)  len(compressed)
---------------  ---------------
              0  14*
             26  62*
             52  68*
             78  70
            104  72
```

8.3.2 Incremental Compression and Decompression

The in-memory approach has obvious drawbacks that make it impractical for real-world use cases. The alternative is to use BZ2Compressor and BZ2Decompressor objects to manipulate data incrementally so that the entire data set does not have to fit into memory.

Listing 8.16: bz2_incremental.py

```
import bz2
import binascii
import io

compressor = bz2.BZ2Compressor()

with open('lorem.txt', 'rb') as input:
    while True:
        block = input.read(64)
        if not block:
            break
        compressed = compressor.compress(block)
```

```
        if compressed:
            print('Compressed: {}'.format(
                binascii.hexlify(compressed)))
        else:
            print('buffering...')
    remaining = compressor.flush()
    print('Flushed: {}'.format(binascii.hexlify(remaining)))
```

This example reads small blocks of data from a plain text file and passes it to `compress()`.
The compressor maintains an internal buffer of compressed data. Since the compression
algorithm depends on checksums and minimum block sizes, the compressor may not be ready
to return data each time it receives more input. If it does not have an entire compressed
block ready, it returns an empty string. When all of the data is fed in, the `flush()` method
forces the compressor to close the final block and return the rest of the compressed data.

```
$ python3 bz2_incremental.py

buffering...
buffering...
buffering...
buffering...
Flushed: b'425a6839314159265359ba83a48c000014d5800010400504052fa
7fe003000ba9112793d4ca789068698a0d1a341901a0d53f4d1119a8d4c9e812
d755a67c10798387682c7ca7b5a3bb75da77755eb81c1cb1ca94c4b6faf209c5
2a90aaa4d16a4a1b9c167a01c8d9ef32589d831e77df7a5753a398b11660e392
126fc18a72a1088716cc8dedda5d489da410748531278043d70a8a131c2b8adc
d6a221bdb8c7ff76b88c1d5342ee48a70a12175074918'
```

8.3.3 Mixed-Content Streams

`BZ2Decompressor` can also be used in situations where compressed data and uncompressed
data are mixed together.

Listing 8.17: bz2_mixed.py

```
import bz2

lorem = open('lorem.txt', 'rt').read().encode('utf-8')
compressed = bz2.compress(lorem)
combined = compressed + lorem

decompressor = bz2.BZ2Decompressor()
decompressed = decompressor.decompress(combined)

decompressed_matches = decompressed == lorem
print('Decompressed matches lorem:', decompressed_matches)

unused_matches = decompressor.unused_data == lorem
print('Unused data matches lorem :', unused_matches)
```

After decompressing all of the data, the `unused_data` attribute contains any data not used.

```
$ python3 bz2_mixed.py

Decompressed matches lorem: True
Unused data matches lorem : True
```

8.3.4 Writing Compressed Files

`BZ2File` can be used to write to and read from bzip2-compressed files using the usual methods for writing and reading data.

Listing 8.18: bz2_file_write.py

```
import bz2
import io
import os

data = 'Contents of the example file go here.\n'

with bz2.BZ2File('example.bz2', 'wb') as output:
    with io.TextIOWrapper(output, encoding='utf-8') as enc:
        enc.write(data)

os.system('file example.bz2')
```

To write data into a compressed file, open the file with mode `'wb'`. This example wraps the `BZ2File` with a `TextIOWrapper` from the `io` (page 390) module to encode Unicode text to bytes suitable for compression.

```
$ python3 bz2_file_write.py

example.bz2: bzip2 compressed data, block size = 900k
```

Different compression levels can be used by passing a `compresslevel` argument. Valid values range from 1 to 9, inclusive. Lower values lead to faster processing and result in less compression. Higher values lead to slower processing and compress more, up to a point.

Listing 8.19: bz2_file_compresslevel.py

```
import bz2
import io
import os

data = open('lorem.txt', 'r', encoding='utf-8').read() * 1024
print('Input contains {} bytes'.format(
    len(data.encode('utf-8'))))
```

```
for i in range(1, 10):
    filename = 'compress-level-{}.bz2'.format(i)
    with bz2.BZ2File(filename, 'wb', compresslevel=i) as output:
        with io.TextIOWrapper(output, encoding='utf-8') as enc:
            enc.write(data)
    os.system('cksum {}'.format(filename))
```

The center column of numbers in the output of the script is the size in bytes of the files produced. For this input data, the higher compression values do not always pay off in decreased storage space for the same input data. Results will vary for other inputs.

```
$ python3 bz2_file_compresslevel.py

3018243926 8771 compress-level-1.bz2
1942389165 4949 compress-level-2.bz2
2596054176 3708 compress-level-3.bz2
1491394456 2705 compress-level-4.bz2
1425874420 2705 compress-level-5.bz2
2232840816 2574 compress-level-6.bz2
447681641  2394 compress-level-7.bz2
3699654768 1137 compress-level-8.bz2
3103658384 1137 compress-level-9.bz2
Input contains 754688 bytes
```

A BZ2File instance also includes a writelines() method that can be used to write a sequence of strings.

Listing 8.20: **bz2_file_writelines.py**

```
import bz2
import io
import itertools
import os

data = 'The same line, over and over.\n'

with bz2.BZ2File('lines.bz2', 'wb') as output:
    with io.TextIOWrapper(output, encoding='utf-8') as enc:
        enc.writelines(itertools.repeat(data, 10))

os.system('bzcat lines.bz2')
```

The lines should end in a newline character, as when writing to a regular file.

```
$ python3 bz2_file_writelines.py

The same line, over and over.
The same line, over and over.
```

```
The same line, over and over.
The same line, over and over.
The same line, over and over.
The same line, over and over.
The same line, over and over.
The same line, over and over.
The same line, over and over.
The same line, over and over.
```

8.3.5 Reading Compressed Files

To read data back from previously compressed files, open the file in read mode (`'rb'`). The value returned from `read()` will be a byte string.

Listing 8.21: bz2_file_read.py

```python
import bz2
import io

with bz2.BZ2File('example.bz2', 'rb') as input:
    with io.TextIOWrapper(input, encoding='utf-8') as dec:
        print(dec.read())
```

This example reads the file written by `bz2_file_write.py` from the previous section. The `BZ2File` is wrapped with a `TextIOWrapper` to decode bytes read to Unicode text.

```
$ python3 bz2_file_read.py

Contents of the example file go here.
```

While reading a file, it is also possible to jump ahead using `seek()` and then to read only part of the data.

Listing 8.22: bz2_file_seek.py

```python
import bz2
import contextlib

with bz2.BZ2File('example.bz2', 'rb') as input:
    print('Entire file:')
    all_data = input.read()
    print(all_data)

    expected = all_data[5:15]

    # Rewind to beginning
    input.seek(0)
```

```
# Move ahead 5 bytes
input.seek(5)
print('Starting at position 5 for 10 bytes:')
partial = input.read(10)
print(partial)

print()
print(expected == partial)
```

The seek() position is relative to the *uncompressed* data, so the caller does not need to be aware that the data file is compressed. This allows a BZ2File instance to be passed to a function expecting a regular uncompressed file.

```
$ python3 bz2_file_seek.py

Entire file:
b'Contents of the example file go here.\n'
Starting at position 5 for 10 bytes:
b'nts of the'

True
```

8.3.6   Reading and Writing Unicode Data

The previous examples used BZ2File directly and managed the encoding and decoding of Unicode text strings with an io.TextIOWrapper, where necessary. These extra steps can be avoided by using bz2.open(), which sets up an io.TextIOWrapper to handle the encoding or decoding automatically.

Listing 8.23: bz2_unicode.py

```
import bz2
import os

data = 'Character with an åccent.'

with bz2.open('example.bz2', 'wt', encoding='utf-8') as output:
    output.write(data)

with bz2.open('example.bz2', 'rt', encoding='utf-8') as input:
    print('Full file: {}'.format(input.read()))

# Move to the beginning of the accented character.
with bz2.open('example.bz2', 'rt', encoding='utf-8') as input:
    input.seek(18)
    print('One character: {}'.format(input.read(1)))

# Move to the middle of the accented character.
with bz2.open('example.bz2', 'rt', encoding='utf-8') as input:
```

```
            input.seek(19)
            try:
                print(input.read(1))
            except UnicodeDecodeError:
                print('ERROR: failed to decode')
```

The file handle returned by open() supports seek(), but use care because the file pointer moves by *bytes*—not *characters*—and may end up in the middle of an encoded character.

```
$ python3 bz2_unicode.py

Full file: Character with an åccent.
One character: å
ERROR: failed to decode
```

8.3.7 Compressing Network Data

The code in the next example responds to requests consisting of filenames by writing a compressed version of the file to the socket used to communicate with the client. It has some artificial chunking in place to illustrate the buffering that occurs when the data passed to compress() or decompress() does not result in a complete block of compressed or uncompressed output.

Listing 8.24: **bz2_server.py**

```python
import bz2
import logging
import socketserver
import binascii

BLOCK_SIZE = 32


class Bz2RequestHandler(socketserver.BaseRequestHandler):

    logger = logging.getLogger('Server')

    def handle(self):
        compressor = bz2.BZ2Compressor()

        # Find out which file the client wants.
        filename = self.request.recv(1024).decode('utf-8')
        self.logger.debug('client asked for: "%s"', filename)

        # Send chunks of the file as they are compressed.
        with open(filename, 'rb') as input:
            while True:
                block = input.read(BLOCK_SIZE)
```

```
            if not block:
                break
            self.logger.debug('RAW %r', block)
            compressed = compressor.compress(block)
            if compressed:
                self.logger.debug(
                    'SENDING %r',
                    binascii.hexlify(compressed))
                self.request.send(compressed)
            else:
                self.logger.debug('BUFFERING')

    # Send any data being buffered by the compressor.
    remaining = compressor.flush()
    while remaining:
        to_send = remaining[:BLOCK_SIZE]
        remaining = remaining[BLOCK_SIZE:]
        self.logger.debug('FLUSHING %r',
                          binascii.hexlify(to_send))
        self.request.send(to_send)
    return
```

The main program starts a server in a thread, combining SocketServer and Bz2RequestHandler.

```
if __name__ == '__main__':
    import socket
    import sys
    from io import StringIO
    import threading

    logging.basicConfig(level=logging.DEBUG,
                        format='%(name)s: %(message)s',
                        )

    # Set up a server, running in a separate thread.
    address = ('localhost', 0)  # Let the kernel assign a port.
    server = socketserver.TCPServer(address, Bz2RequestHandler)
    ip, port = server.server_address  # What port was assigned?

    t = threading.Thread(target=server.serve_forever)
    t.setDaemon(True)
    t.start()

    logger = logging.getLogger('Client')

    # Connect to the server.
    logger.info('Contacting server on %s:%s', ip, port)
    s = socket.socket(socket.AF_INET, socket.SOCK_STREAM)
    s.connect((ip, port))
```

```
        # Ask for a file.
        requested_file = (sys.argv[0]
                          if len(sys.argv) > 1
                          else 'lorem.txt')
        logger.debug('sending filename: "%s"', requested_file)
        len_sent = s.send(requested_file.encode('utf-8'))

        # Receive a response.
        buffer = StringIO()
        decompressor = bz2.BZ2Decompressor()
        while True:
            response = s.recv(BLOCK_SIZE)
            if not response:
                break
            logger.debug('READ %r', binascii.hexlify(response))

            # Include any unconsumed data when feeding the
            # decompressor.
            decompressed = decompressor.decompress(response)
            if decompressed:
                logger.debug('DECOMPRESSED %r', decompressed)
                buffer.write(decompressed.decode('utf-8'))
            else:
                logger.debug('BUFFERING')

        full_response = buffer.getvalue()
        lorem = open(requested_file, 'rt').read()
        logger.debug('response matches file contents: %s',
                     full_response == lorem)

        # Clean up.
        server.shutdown()
        server.socket.close()
        s.close()
```

The program then opens a socket to communicate with the server as a client, and requests the file (defaulting to lorem.txt).

```
Lorem ipsum dolor sit amet, consectetuer adipiscing elit. Donec
egestas, enim et consectetuer ullamcorper, lectus ligula rutrum leo,
a elementum elit tortor eu quam. Duis tincidunt nisi ut ante. Nulla
facilisi.
```

WARNING

This implementation has obvious security implications. Do not run it on a server on the open Internet or in any environment where security might be an issue.

Running bz2_server.py produces the following output.

```
$ python3 bz2_server.py

Client: Contacting server on 127.0.0.1:57364
Client: sending filename: "lorem.txt"
Server: client asked for: "lorem.txt"
Server: RAW b'Lorem ipsum dolor sit amet, cons'
Server: BUFFERING
Server: RAW b'ectetuer adipiscing elit. Donec\n'
Server: BUFFERING
Server: RAW b'egestas, enim et consectetuer ul'
Server: BUFFERING
Server: RAW b'lamcorper, lectus ligula rutrum '
Server: BUFFERING
Server: RAW b'leo,\na elementum elit tortor eu '
Server: BUFFERING
Server: RAW b'quam. Duis tincidunt nisi ut ant'
Server: BUFFERING
Server: RAW b'e. Nulla\nfacilisi.\n'
Server: BUFFERING
Server: FLUSHING b'425a6839314159265359ba83a48c000014d5800010400
504052fa7fe003000ba'
Server: FLUSHING b'9112793d4ca789068698a0d1a341901a0d53f4d1119a8
d4c9e812d755a67c107'
Client: READ b'425a6839314159265359ba83a48c000014d58000104005040
52fa7fe003000ba'
Server: FLUSHING b'98387682c7ca7b5a3bb75da77755eb81c1cb1ca94c4b6
faf209c52a90aaa4d16'
Client: BUFFERING
Server: FLUSHING b'a4a1b9c167a01c8d9ef32589d831e77df7a5753a398b1
1660e392126fc18a72a'
Client: READ b'9112793d4ca789068698a0d1a341901a0d53f4d1119a8d4c9
e812d755a67c107'
Server: FLUSHING b'1088716cc8dedda5d489da410748531278043d70a8a13
1c2b8adcd6a221bdb8c'
Client: BUFFERING
Server: FLUSHING b'7ff76b88c1d5342ee48a70a12175074918'
Client: READ b'98387682c7ca7b5a3bb75da77755eb81c1cb1ca94c4b6faf2
09c52a90aaa4d16'
Client: BUFFERING
Client: READ b'a4a1b9c167a01c8d9ef32589d831e77df7a5753a398b11660
e392126fc18a72a'
Client: BUFFERING
Client: READ b'1088716cc8dedda5d489da410748531278043d70a8a131c2b
8adcd6a221bdb8c'
Client: BUFFERING
Client: READ b'7ff76b88c1d5342ee48a70a12175074918'
Client: DECOMPRESSED b'Lorem ipsum dolor sit amet, consectetuer
```

```
adipiscing elit. Donec\negestas, enim et consectetuer ullamcorpe
r, lectus ligula rutrum leo,\na elementum elit tortor eu quam. D
uis tincidunt nisi ut ante. Nulla\nfacilisi.\n'
Client: response matches file contents: True
```

TIP

Related Reading

- Standard library documentation for bz2.[5]
- bzip2[6]: The home page for bzip2.
- zlib (page 477): The zlib module for GNU zip compression.
- gzip (page 486): A file-like interface to GNU zip-compressed files.
- io (page 390): Building blocks for creating input and output pipelines.
- Python 2 to 3 porting notes for bz2 (page 1357).

8.4 tarfile: Tar Archive Access

The tarfile module provides read and write access to Unix tar archives, including compressed files. In addition to the POSIX standards, several GNU tar extensions are supported. Unix special file types, such as hard and soft links, and device nodes are handled as well.

NOTE

Although tarfile implements a Unix format, it can be used to create and read tar archives under Microsoft Windows, too.

8.4.1 Testing Tar Files

The is_tarfile() function returns a boolean value indicating whether the filename passed as an argument refers to a valid tar archive.

Listing 8.25: **tarfile_is_tarfile.py**

```
import tarfile

for filename in ['README.txt', 'example.tar',
                 'bad_example.tar', 'notthere.tar']:
```

---

[5] https://docs.python.org/3.5/library/bz2.html
[6] www.bzip.org

```
try:
    print('{:>15}  {}'.format(filename, tarfile.is_tarfile(
        filename)))
except IOError as err:
    print('{:>15}  {}'.format(filename, err))
```

If the file does not exist, is_tarfile() raises an IOError.

```
$ python3 tarfile_is_tarfile.py

   README.txt  False
  example.tar  True
bad_example.tar  False
  notthere.tar  [Errno 2] No such file or directory:
'notthere.tar'
```

8.4.2 Reading Metadata from an Archive

Use the TarFile class to work directly with a tar archive. This class supports methods for reading data about existing archives as well as modifying the archives by adding more files.

To read the names of the files in an existing archive, use getnames().

Listing 8.26: tarfile_getnames.py

```
import tarfile

with tarfile.open('example.tar', 'r') as t:
    print(t.getnames())
```

The return value is a list of strings with the names of the archive contents.

```
$ python3 tarfile_getnames.py

['index.rst', 'README.txt']
```

In addition to names, metadata about the archive members is available as instances of TarInfo objects.

Listing 8.27: tarfile_getmembers.py

```
import tarfile
import time

with tarfile.open('example.tar', 'r') as t:
    for member_info in t.getmembers():
        print(member_info.name)
        print('  Modified:', time.ctime(member_info.mtime))
```

```
            print(' Mode    :', oct(member_info.mode))
            print(' Type    :', member_info.type)
            print(' Size    :', member_info.size, 'bytes')
            print()
```

Load the metadata via getmembers() and getmember().

```
$ python3 tarfile_getmembers.py

index.rst
  Modified: Fri Aug 19 16:27:54 2016
  Mode    : 0o644
  Type    : b'0'
  Size    : 9878 bytes

README.txt
  Modified: Fri Aug 19 16:27:54 2016
  Mode    : 0o644
  Type    : b'0'
  Size    : 75 bytes
```

If the name of the archive member is known in advance, its TarInfo object can be retrieved with getmember().

Listing 8.28: tarfile_getmember.py

```
import tarfile
import time

with tarfile.open('example.tar', 'r') as t:
    for filename in ['README.txt', 'notthere.txt']:
        try:
            info = t.getmember(filename)
        except KeyError:
            print('ERROR: Did not find {} in tar archive'.format(
                filename))
        else:
            print('{} is {:d} bytes'.format(
                info.name, info.size))
```

If the archive member is not present, getmember() raises a KeyError.

```
$ python3 tarfile_getmember.py

README.txt is 75 bytes
ERROR: Did not find notthere.txt in tar archive
```

8.4.3   Extracting Files from an Archive

To access the data from an archive member within a program, use the extractfile()
method, passing the member's name.

Listing 8.29: **tarfile_extractfile.py**

```python
import tarfile

with tarfile.open('example.tar', 'r') as t:
    for filename in ['README.txt', 'notthere.txt']:
        try:
            f = t.extractfile(filename)
        except KeyError:
            print('ERROR: Did not find {} in tar archive'.format(
                filename))
        else:
            print(filename, ':')
            print(f.read().decode('utf-8'))
```

The return value is a file-like object from which the contents of the archive member can be
read.

```
$ python3 tarfile_extractfile.py

README.txt :
The examples for the tarfile module use this file and
example.tar as data.

ERROR: Did not find notthere.txt in tar archive
```

To unpack the archive and write the files to the file system, use extract() or
extractall() instead.

Listing 8.30: **tarfile_extract.py**

```python
import tarfile
import os

os.mkdir('outdir')
with tarfile.open('example.tar', 'r') as t:
    t.extract('README.txt', 'outdir')
print(os.listdir('outdir'))
```

The member or members are read from the archive and written to the file system, starting
in the directory named in the arguments.

```
$ python3 tarfile_extract.py

['README.txt']
```

The standard library documentation includes a note stating that `extractall()` is safer than `extract()`, especially for working with streaming data where rewinding to read an earlier part of the input is not possible. It should be used in most cases.

Listing 8.31: **tarfile_extractall.py**

```
import tarfile
import os

os.mkdir('outdir')
with tarfile.open('example.tar', 'r') as t:
    t.extractall('outdir')
print(os.listdir('outdir'))
```

With `extractall()`, the first argument is the name of the directory where the files should be written.

```
$ python3 tarfile_extractall.py

['README.txt', 'index.rst']
```

To extract specific files from the archive, pass their names or `TarInfo` metadata containers to `extractall()`.

Listing 8.32: **tarfile_extractall_members.py**

```
import tarfile
import os

os.mkdir('outdir')
with tarfile.open('example.tar', 'r') as t:
    t.extractall('outdir',
                 members=[t.getmember('README.txt')],
                 )
print(os.listdir('outdir'))
```

When a `members` list is provided, only the named files are extracted.

```
$ python3 tarfile_extractall_members.py

['README.txt']
```

8.4.4   Creating New Archives

To create a new archive, open the `TarFile` with a mode of `'w'`.

Listing 8.33: `tarfile_add.py`

```
import tarfile

print('creating archive')
with tarfile.open('tarfile_add.tar', mode='w') as out:
    print('adding README.txt')
    out.add('README.txt')

print()
print('Contents:')
with tarfile.open('tarfile_add.tar', mode='r') as t:
    for member_info in t.getmembers():
        print(member_info.name)
```

Any existing file is truncated and a new archive is started. To add files, use the `add()` method.

```
$ python3 tarfile_add.py

creating archive
adding README.txt

Contents:
README.txt
```

8.4.5   Using Alternative Archive Member Names

It is possible to add a file to an archive using a name other than the original filename by constructing a `TarInfo` object with an alternative `arcname` and passing it to `addfile()`.

Listing 8.34: `tarfile_addfile.py`

```
import tarfile

print('creating archive')
with tarfile.open('tarfile_addfile.tar', mode='w') as out:
    print('adding README.txt as RENAMED.txt')
    info = out.gettarinfo('README.txt', arcname='RENAMED.txt')
    out.addfile(info)

print()
print('Contents:')
with tarfile.open('tarfile_addfile.tar', mode='r') as t:
    for member_info in t.getmembers():
        print(member_info.name)
```

The archive includes only the changed filename.

```
$ python3 tarfile_addfile.py

creating archive
adding README.txt as RENAMED.txt

Contents:
RENAMED.txt
```

8.4.6 Writing Data from Sources Other Than Files

Sometimes it is necessary to write data into an archive directly from memory. Rather than writing the data to a file and then adding that file to the archive, you can use `addfile()` to add data from an open file-like handle that returns bytes.

Listing 8.35: **tarfile_addfile_string.py**

```python
import io
import tarfile

text = 'This is the data to write to the archive.'
data = text.encode('utf-8')

with tarfile.open('addfile_string.tar', mode='w') as out:
    info = tarfile.TarInfo('made_up_file.txt')
    info.size = len(data)
    out.addfile(info, io.BytesIO(data))

print('Contents:')
with tarfile.open('addfile_string.tar', mode='r') as t:
    for member_info in t.getmembers():
        print(member_info.name)
        f = t.extractfile(member_info)
        print(f.read().decode('utf-8'))
```

When a `TarInfo` object is constructed first, the archive member can be given any name desired. After setting the size, the data is written to the archive using `addfile()` and a `BytesIO` buffer as a source of the data.

```
$ python3 tarfile_addfile_string.py

Contents:
made_up_file.txt
This is the data to write to the archive.
```

8.4.7   Appending to Archives

In addition to creating new archives, it is possible to append to an existing file by using mode 'a'.

Listing 8.36: **tarfile_append.py**

```
import tarfile

print('creating archive')
with tarfile.open('tarfile_append.tar', mode='w') as out:
    out.add('README.txt')

print('contents:',)
with tarfile.open('tarfile_append.tar', mode='r') as t:
    print([m.name for m in t.getmembers()])

print('adding index.rst')
with tarfile.open('tarfile_append.tar', mode='a') as out:
    out.add('index.rst')

print('contents:',)
with tarfile.open('tarfile_append.tar', mode='r') as t:
    print([m.name for m in t.getmembers()])
```

The resulting archive ends up with two members.

```
$ python3 tarfile_append.py

creating archive
contents:
['README.txt']
adding index.rst
contents:
['README.txt', 'index.rst']
```

8.4.8   Working with Compressed Archives

Besides regular tar archive files, the tarfile module can work with archives compressed via the gzip and bzip2 protocols. To open a compressed archive, modify the mode string passed to open() to include ":gz" or ":bz2", depending on the desired compression method.

Listing 8.37: **tarfile_compression.py**

```
import tarfile
import os

fmt = '{:<30} {:<10}'
print(fmt.format('FILENAME', 'SIZE'))
print(fmt.format('README.txt', os.stat('README.txt').st_size))
```

```
FILES = [
    ('tarfile_compression.tar', 'w'),
    ('tarfile_compression.tar.gz', 'w:gz'),
    ('tarfile_compression.tar.bz2', 'w:bz2'),
]

for filename, write_mode in FILES:
    with tarfile.open(filename, mode=write_mode) as out:
        out.add('README.txt')

    print(fmt.format(filename, os.stat(filename).st_size),
          end=' ')
    print([
        m.name
        for m in tarfile.open(filename, 'r:*').getmembers()
    ])
```

When opening an existing archive for reading, specify "r:*" to have `tarfile` determine the compression method to use automatically.

```
$ python3 tarfile_compression.py

FILENAME                         SIZE
README.txt                       75
tarfile_compression.tar          10240      ['README.txt']
tarfile_compression.tar.gz       213        ['README.txt']
tarfile_compression.tar.bz2      199        ['README.txt']
```

TIP

Related Reading

- Standard library documentation for `tarfile`.[7]
- GNU tar manual[8]: Documentation of the tar format, including extensions.
- `zipfile` (page 511): Similar access for ZIP archives.
- `gzip` (page 486): GNU zip compression.
- `bz2` (page 491): Bzip2 compression.

8.5 zipfile: ZIP Archive Access

The `zipfile` module can be used to read and write ZIP archive files, the format popularized by the PC program PKZIP.

---

[7] https://docs.python.org/3.5/library/tarfile.html
[8] www.gnu.org/software/tar/manual/html_node/Standard.html

8.5.1   Testing ZIP Files

The `is_zipfile()` function returns a boolean value indicating whether the filename passed as an argument refers to a valid ZIP archive.

Listing 8.38: `zipfile_is_zipfile.py`

```
import zipfile

for filename in ['README.txt', 'example.zip',
                 'bad_example.zip', 'notthere.zip']:
    print('{:>15}  {}'.format(
        filename, zipfile.is_zipfile(filename)))
```

If the file does not exist at all, `is_zipfile()` returns `False`.

```
$ python3 zipfile_is_zipfile.py

     README.txt  False
    example.zip  True
bad_example.zip  False
   notthere.zip  False
```

8.5.2   Reading Metadata from an Archive

Use the `ZipFile` class to work directly with a ZIP archive. This class supports methods for reading data about existing archives as well as modifying the archives by adding more files.

Listing 8.39: `zipfile_namelist.py`

```
import zipfile

with zipfile.ZipFile('example.zip', 'r') as zf:
    print(zf.namelist())
```

The `namelist()` method returns the names of the files in an existing archive.

```
$ python3 zipfile_namelist.py

['README.txt']
```

The list of names is only part of the information available from the archive, though. To access all of the metadata about the ZIP contents, use the `infolist()` and `getinfo()` methods.

Listing 8.40: `zipfile_infolist.py`

```
import datetime
import zipfile
```

```
def print_info(archive_name):
    with zipfile.ZipFile(archive_name) as zf:
        for info in zf.infolist():
            print(info.filename)
            print('  Comment     :', info.comment)
            mod_date = datetime.datetime(*info.date_time)
            print('  Modified    :', mod_date)
            if info.create_system == 0:
                system = 'Windows'
            elif info.create_system == 3:
                system = 'Unix'
            else:
                system = 'UNKNOWN'
            print('  System      :', system)
            print('  ZIP version :', info.create_version)
            print('  Compressed  :', info.compress_size, 'bytes')
            print('  Uncompressed:', info.file_size, 'bytes')
            print()


if __name__ == '__main__':
    print_info('example.zip')
```

There are additional fields other than those printed here, but deciphering the values into anything useful requires careful reading of the *PKZIP Application Note* with the ZIP file specification.

```
$ python3 zipfile_infolist.py

README.txt
  Comment     : b''
  Modified    : 2010-11-15 06:48:02
  System      : Unix
  ZIP version : 30
  Compressed  : 65 bytes
  Uncompressed: 76 bytes
```

If the name of the archive member is known in advance, its `ZipInfo` object can be retrieved directly with `getinfo()`.

Listing 8.41: zipfile_getinfo.py

```
import zipfile

with zipfile.ZipFile('example.zip') as zf:
    for filename in ['README.txt', 'notthere.txt']:
        try:
            info = zf.getinfo(filename)
        except KeyError:
            print('ERROR: Did not find {} in zip file'.format(
                filename))
```

```
else:
    print('{} is {} bytes'.format(
        info.filename, info.file_size))
```

If the archive member is not present, `getinfo()` raises a `KeyError`.

```
$ python3 zipfile_getinfo.py

README.txt is 76 bytes
ERROR: Did not find notthere.txt in zip file
```

8.5.3 Extracting Archived Files From an Archive

To access the data from an archive member, use the `read()` method, passing the member's name.

Listing 8.42: `zipfile_read.py`

```
import zipfile

with zipfile.ZipFile('example.zip') as zf:
    for filename in ['README.txt', 'notthere.txt']:
        try:
            data = zf.read(filename)
        except KeyError:
            print('ERROR: Did not find {} in zip file'.format(
                filename))
        else:
            print(filename, ':')
            print(data)
        print()
```

The data is automatically decompressed, if necessary.

```
$ python3 zipfile_read.py

README.txt :
b'The examples for the zipfile module use \nthis file and exampl
e.zip as data.\n'

ERROR: Did not find notthere.txt in zip file
```

8.5.4 Creating New Archives

To create a new archive, instantiate the `ZipFile` with a mode of `'w'`. Any existing file is truncated and a new archive is started. To add files, use the `write()` method.

Listing 8.43: **zipfile_write.py**

```
from zipfile_infolist import print_info
import zipfile

print('creating archive')
with zipfile.ZipFile('write.zip', mode='w') as zf:
    print('adding README.txt')
    zf.write('README.txt')

print()
print_info('write.zip')
```

By default, the contents of the archive are not compressed.

```
$ python3 zipfile_write.py

creating archive
adding README.txt

README.txt
    Comment     : b''
    Modified    : 2016-08-07 13:31:24
    System      : Unix
    ZIP version : 20
    Compressed  : 76 bytes
    Uncompressed: 76 bytes
```

To add compression, the zlib (page 477) module is required. If zlib is available, the compression mode for individual files or for the archive as a whole can be set using zipfile.ZIP_DEFLATED. The default compression mode is zipfile.ZIP_STORED, which adds the input data to the archive without compressing it.

Listing 8.44: **zipfile_write_compression.py**

```
from zipfile_infolist import print_info
import zipfile
try:
    import zlib
    compression = zipfile.ZIP_DEFLATED
except:
    compression = zipfile.ZIP_STORED

modes = {
    zipfile.ZIP_DEFLATED: 'deflated',
    zipfile.ZIP_STORED: 'stored',
}

print('creating archive')
```

```
with zipfile.ZipFile('write_compression.zip', mode='w') as zf:
    mode_name = modes[compression]
    print('adding README.txt with compression mode', mode_name)
    zf.write('README.txt', compress_type=compression)

print()
print_info('write_compression.zip')
```

This time, the archive member is compressed.

```
$ python3 zipfile_write_compression.py

creating archive
adding README.txt with compression mode deflated

README.txt
    Comment    : b''
    Modified   : 2016-08-07 13:31:24
    System     : Unix
    ZIP version : 20
    Compressed : 65 bytes
    Uncompressed: 76 bytes
```

8.5.5 Using Alternative Archive Member Names

Pass an arcname value to write() to add a file to an archive using a name other than the original filename.

Listing 8.45: zipfile_write_arcname.py

```
from zipfile_infolist import print_info
import zipfile

with zipfile.ZipFile('write_arcname.zip', mode='w') as zf:
    zf.write('README.txt', arcname='NOT_README.txt')

print_info('write_arcname.zip')
```

There is no sign of the original filename in the archive.

```
$ python3 zipfile_write_arcname.py

NOT_README.txt
    Comment    : b''
    Modified   : 2016-08-07 13:31:24
    System     : Unix
    ZIP version : 20
    Compressed : 76 bytes
    Uncompressed: 76 bytes
```

8.5.6 Writing Data from Sources Other Than Files

Sometimes it is necessary to write to a ZIP archive using data that did not come from an existing file. Rather than writing the data to a file and then adding that file to the ZIP archive, use the writestr() method to add a string of bytes to the archive directly.

Listing 8.46: zipfile_writestr.py

```python
from zipfile_infolist import print_info
import zipfile

msg = 'This data did not exist in a file.'
with zipfile.ZipFile('writestr.zip',
                     mode='w',
                     compression=zipfile.ZIP_DEFLATED,
                     ) as zf:
    zf.writestr('from_string.txt', msg)

print_info('writestr.zip')

with zipfile.ZipFile('writestr.zip', 'r') as zf:
    print(zf.read('from_string.txt'))
```

In this case, the compress_type argument to ZipFile was used to compress the data, since writestr() does not take an argument to specify the compression.

```
$ python3 zipfile_writestr.py

from_string.txt
  Comment     : b''
  Modified    : 2016-12-29 12:14:42
  System      : Unix
  ZIP version : 20
  Compressed  : 36 bytes
  Uncompressed: 34 bytes

b'This data did not exist in a file.'
```

8.5.7 Writing with a ZipInfo Instance

Normally, the modification date is computed when a file or string is added to the archive. A ZipInfo instance can be passed to writestr() to define the modification date and other metadata.

Listing 8.47: zipfile_writestr_zipinfo.py

```python
import time
import zipfile
from zipfile_infolist import print_info
```

```
msg = b'This data did not exist in a file.'

with zipfile.ZipFile('writestr_zipinfo.zip',
                     mode='w',
                     ) as zf:
    info = zipfile.ZipInfo('from_string.txt',
                           date_time=time.localtime(time.time()),
                           )
    info.compress_type = zipfile.ZIP_DEFLATED
    info.comment = b'Remarks go here'
    info.create_system = 0
    zf.writestr(info, msg)

print_info('writestr_zipinfo.zip')
```

In this example, the modified time is set to the current time, the data is compressed, and
false value for `create_system` is used. A simple comment is also associated with the new
file.

```
$ python3 zipfile_writestr_zipinfo.py

from_string.txt
    Comment     : b'Remarks go here'
    Modified    : 2016-12-29 12:14:42
    System      : Windows
    ZIP version : 20
    Compressed  : 36 bytes
    Uncompressed: 34 bytes
```

8.5.8 Appending to Files

In addition to creating new archives, it is possible to append to an existing archive or add
an archive at the end of an existing file (such as a `.exe` file for a self-extracting archive). To
open a file to append to it, use mode `'a'`.

Listing 8.48: `zipfile_append.py`

```
from zipfile_infolist import print_info
import zipfile

print('creating archive')
with zipfile.ZipFile('append.zip', mode='w') as zf:
    zf.write('README.txt')

print()
print_info('append.zip')
```

```
print('appending to the archive')
with zipfile.ZipFile('append.zip', mode='a') as zf:
    zf.write('README.txt', arcname='README2.txt')

print()
print_info('append.zip')
```

The resulting archive contains two members.

```
$ python3 zipfile_append.py

creating archive

README.txt
  Comment    : b''
  Modified   : 2016-08-07 13:31:24
  System     : Unix
  ZIP version : 20
  Compressed  : 76 bytes
  Uncompressed: 76 bytes

appending to the archive

README.txt
  Comment    : b''
  Modified   : 2016-08-07 13:31:24
  System     : Unix
  ZIP version : 20
  Compressed  : 76 bytes
  Uncompressed: 76 bytes

README2.txt
  Comment    : b''
  Modified   : 2016-08-07 13:31:24
  System     : Unix
  ZIP version : 20
  Compressed  : 76 bytes
  Uncompressed: 76 bytes
```

8.5.9 Python ZIP Archives

Python can import modules from inside ZIP archives using zipimport (page 1344), if those archives appear in sys.path. The PyZipFile class can be used to construct a module suitable for use in this way. The extra method writepy() tells PyZipFile to scan a directory for .py files and add the corresponding .pyo or .pyc file to the archive. If neither compiled form exists, a .pyc file is created and added.

Listing 8.49: `zipfile_pyzipfile.py`

```python
import sys
import zipfile

if __name__ == '__main__':
    with zipfile.PyZipFile('pyzipfile.zip', mode='w') as zf:
        zf.debug = 3
        print('Adding python files')
        zf.writepy('.')
    for name in zf.namelist():
        print(name)

    print()
    sys.path.insert(0, 'pyzipfile.zip')
    import zipfile_pyzipfile
    print('Imported from:', zipfile_pyzipfile.__file__)
```

With the debug attribute of the `PyZipFile` set to 3, verbose debugging is enabled and output is produced as the program compiles each .py file it finds.

```
$ python3 zipfile_pyzipfile.py

Adding python files
Adding files from directory .
Compiling ./zipfile_append.py
Adding zipfile_append.pyc
Compiling ./zipfile_getinfo.py
Adding zipfile_getinfo.pyc
Compiling ./zipfile_infolist.py
Adding zipfile_infolist.pyc
Compiling ./zipfile_is_zipfile.py
Adding zipfile_is_zipfile.pyc
Compiling ./zipfile_namelist.py
Adding zipfile_namelist.pyc
Compiling ./zipfile_printdir.py
Adding zipfile_printdir.pyc
Compiling ./zipfile_pyzipfile.py
Adding zipfile_pyzipfile.pyc
Compiling ./zipfile_read.py
Adding zipfile_read.pyc
Compiling ./zipfile_write.py
Adding zipfile_write.pyc
Compiling ./zipfile_write_arcname.py
Adding zipfile_write_arcname.pyc
Compiling ./zipfile_write_compression.py
Adding zipfile_write_compression.pyc
Compiling ./zipfile_writestr.py
Adding zipfile_writestr.pyc
```

```
Compiling ./zipfile_writestr_zipinfo.py
Adding zipfile_writestr_zipinfo.pyc
zipfile_append.pyc
zipfile_getinfo.pyc
zipfile_infolist.pyc
zipfile_is_zipfile.pyc
zipfile_namelist.pyc
zipfile_printdir.pyc
zipfile_pyzipfile.pyc
zipfile_read.pyc
zipfile_write.pyc
zipfile_write_arcname.pyc
zipfile_write_compression.pyc
zipfile_writestr.pyc
zipfile_writestr_zipinfo.pyc

Imported from: pyzipfile.zip/zipfile_pyzipfile.pyc
```

8.5.10   Limitations

The zipfile module does not support ZIP files with appended comments, or multi-disk archives. It does support ZIP files larger than 4 GB that use the ZIP64 extensions.

TIP

Related Reading

- Standard library documentation for zipfile.[9]
- zlib (page 477): ZIP compression library.
- tarfile (page 503): Read and write tar archives.
- zipimport (page 1344): Import Python modules from ZIP archive.
- PKZIP Application Note[10]: Official specification for the ZIP archive format.

---

[9] https://docs.python.org/3.5/library/zipfile.html
[10] www.pkware.com/documents/casestudies/APPNOTE.TXT

Chapter 9
Cryptography

Encryption secures messages so that they can be verified as accurate and protected from interception. Python's cryptography support includes `hashlib` (page 523) for generating signatures of message content using standard algorithms such as MD5 and SHA, and `hmac` (page 528) for verifying that a message has not been altered in transmission.

9.1 hashlib: Cryptographic Hashing

The `hashlib` module defines an API for accessing different cryptographic hashing algorithms. To work with a specific hash algorithm, use the appropriate constructor function or `new()` to create a hash object. From there, the objects use the same API, no matter which algorithm is being used.

9.1.1 Hash Algorithms

Since `hashlib` is "backed" by OpenSSL, all of the algorithms provided by that library are available, including the following:

- MD5
- SHA1
- SHA224
- SHA256
- SHA384
- SHA512

Some algorithms are available on all platforms, and some depend on the underlying libraries. For lists of each, look at `algorithms_guaranteed` and `algorithms_available`, respectively.

Listing 9.1: **hashlib_algorithms.py**

```
import hashlib


print('Guaranteed:\n{}\n'.format(
```

```
    ', '.join(sorted(hashlib.algorithms_guaranteed)))))
print('Available:\n{}'.format(
    ', '.join(sorted(hashlib.algorithms_available)))))
```

```
$ python3 hashlib_algorithms.py

Guaranteed:
md5, sha1, sha224, sha256, sha384, sha512

Available:
DSA, DSA-SHA, MD4, MD5, MDC2, RIPEMD160, SHA, SHA1, SHA224,
SHA256, SHA384, SHA512, dsaEncryption, dsaWithSHA,
ecdsa-with-SHA1, md4, md5, mdc2, ripemd160, sha, sha1, sha224,
sha256, sha384, sha512
```

9.1.2   Sample Data

All of the examples in this section use the same sample data, shown in the following listing.

Listing 9.2: **hashlib_data.py**

```
import hashlib

lorem = '''Lorem ipsum dolor sit amet, consectetur adipisicing
elit, sed do eiusmod tempor incididunt ut labore et dolore magna
aliqua. Ut enim ad minim veniam, quis nostrud exercitation
ullamco laboris nisi ut aliquip ex ea commodo consequat. Duis
aute irure dolor in reprehenderit in voluptate velit esse cillum
dolore eu fugiat nulla pariatur. Excepteur sint occaecat
cupidatat non proident, sunt in culpa qui officia deserunt
mollit anim id est laborum.'''
```

9.1.3   MD5 Example

To calculate the MD5 hash, or *digest*, for a block of data (here a Unicode string converted to a byte string), first create the hash object, then add the data, and finally call digest() or hexdigest().

Listing 9.3: **hashlib_md5.py**

```
import hashlib

from hashlib_data import lorem

h = hashlib.md5()
h.update(lorem.encode('utf-8'))
print(h.hexdigest())
```

This example uses the `hexdigest()` method instead of `digest()` because the output is formatted so it can be printed clearly. If a binary digest value is acceptable, use `digest()`.

```
$ python3 hashlib_md5.py

3f2fd2c9e25d60fb0fa5d593b802b7a8
```

9.1.4   SHA1 Example

A SHA1 digest is calculated in the same way.

Listing 9.4: **hashlib_sha1.py**

```
import hashlib

from hashlib_data import lorem

h = hashlib.sha1()
h.update(lorem.encode('utf-8'))
print(h.hexdigest())
```

The digest value is different in this example because the algorithm changed from MD5 to SHA1.

```
$ python3 hashlib_sha1.py

ea360b288b3dd178fe2625f55b2959bf1dba6eef
```

9.1.5   Creating a Hash by Name

Sometimes it is more convenient to refer to the algorithm by giving its name in a string rather than by using the constructor function directly. It is useful, for example, to be able to store the hash type in a configuration file. In those cases, use `new()` to create a hash calculator.

Listing 9.5: **hashlib_new.py**

```
import argparse
import hashlib
import sys

from hashlib_data import lorem

parser = argparse.ArgumentParser('hashlib demo')
parser.add_argument(
    'hash_name',
```

```
    choices=hashlib.algorithms_available,
    help='the name of the hash algorithm to use',
)
parser.add_argument(
    'data',
    nargs='?',
    default=lorem,
    help='the input data to hash, defaults to lorem ipsum',
)
args = parser.parse_args()

h = hashlib.new(args.hash_name)
h.update(args.data.encode('utf-8'))
print(h.hexdigest())
```

When run with a variety of arguments, this program produces the following output.

```
$ python3 hashlib_new.py sha1

ea360b288b3dd178fe2625f55b2959bf1dba6eef

$ python3 hashlib_new.py sha256

3c887cc71c67949df29568119cc646f46b9cd2c2b39d456065646bc2fc09ffd8

$ python3 hashlib_new.py sha512

a7e53384eb9bb4251a19571450465d51809e0b7046101b87c4faef96b9bc904cf7f90
035f444952dfd9f6084eeee2457433f3ade614712f42f80960b2fca43ff

$ python3 hashlib_new.py md5

3f2fd2c9e25d60fb0fa5d593b802b7a8
```

9.1.6   Incremental Updates

The update() method of the hash calculators can be called repeatedly. Each time, the digest is updated based on the additional text fed in. Updating incrementally is more efficient than reading an entire file into memory, and produces the same results.

Listing 9.6: hashlib_update.py

```
import hashlib

from hashlib_data import lorem

h = hashlib.md5()
```

```
    h.update(lorem.encode('utf-8'))
    all_at_once = h.hexdigest()


    def chunkize(size, text):
        "Return parts of the text in size-based increments."
        start = 0
        while start < len(text):
            chunk = text[start:start + size]
            yield chunk
            start += size
        return

    h = hashlib.md5()
    for chunk in chunkize(64, lorem.encode('utf-8')):
        h.update(chunk)
    line_by_line = h.hexdigest()

    print('All at once :', all_at_once)
    print('Line by line:', line_by_line)
    print('Same        :', (all_at_once == line_by_line))
```

This example demonstrates how to update a digest incrementally as data is read or otherwise produced.

```
$ python3 hashlib_update.py

All at once : 3f2fd2c9e25d60fb0fa5d593b802b7a8
Line by line: 3f2fd2c9e25d60fb0fa5d593b802b7a8
Same        : True
```

TIP

Related Reading

- Standard library documentation for hashlib.[1]
- hmac (page 528): The hmac module.
- OpenSSL[2]: An open source encryption toolkit.
- Cryptography[3] module: A Python package that provides cryptographic recipes and primitives.
- Voidspace: IronPython and hashlib[4]: A wrapper for hashlib that works with IronPython.

---

[1] https://docs.python.org/3.5/library/hashlib.html
[2] www.openssl.org
[3] https://pypi.python.org/pypi/cryptography
[4] www.voidspace.org.uk/python/weblog/arch_d7_2006_10_07.shtml#e497

9.2   hmac: **Cryptographic Message Signing and Verification**

The HMAC algorithm can be used to verify the integrity of information passed between applications or stored in a potentially vulnerable location. The basic idea is to generate a cryptographic hash of the actual data combined with a shared secret key. The resulting hash can then be used to check the transmitted or stored message to determine a level of trust, without transmitting the secret key.

WARNING

Disclaimer: I am not a security expert. For the full details on HMAC, check out **RFC 2104**.[5]

9.2.1   Signing Messages

The new() function creates a new object for calculating a message signature. This example uses the default MD5 hash algorithm.

Listing 9.7: **hmac_simple.py**

```python
import hmac

digest_maker = hmac.new(b'secret-shared-key-goes-here')

with open('lorem.txt', 'rb') as f:
    while True:
        block = f.read(1024)
        if not block:
            break
        digest_maker.update(block)

digest = digest_maker.hexdigest()
print(digest)
```

When run, the code reads a data file and computes an HMAC signature for it.

```
$ python3 hmac_simple.py

4bcb287e284f8c21e87e14ba2dc40b16
```

9.2.2   Alternative Digest Types

Although the default cryptographic algorithm for hmac is MD5, that option is not the most secure method. MD5 hashes have some weaknesses, such as collisions (where two different

---

[5] https://tools.ietf.org/html/rfc2104.html

messages produce the same hash). The SHA1 algorithm is considered to be stronger, and should be used instead.

Listing 9.8: hmac_sha.py

```python
import hmac
import hashlib

digest_maker = hmac.new(
    b'secret-shared-key-goes-here',
    b'',
    'sha1',
)

with open('hmac_sha.py', 'rb') as f:
    while True:
        block = f.read(1024)
        if not block:
            break
        digest_maker.update(block)

digest = digest_maker.hexdigest()
print(digest)
```

The new() function takes three arguments. The first is the secret key, which should be shared between the two endpoints that are communicating so both ends can use the same value. The second value is an initial message. If the message content that needs to be authenticated is small, such as a timestamp or HTTP POST, the entire body of the message can be passed to new() instead of using the update() method. The last argument is the digest module to be used. The default is hashlib.md5, but this example passes 'sha1', causing hmac to use hashlib.sha1 instead.

```
$ python3 hmac_sha.py

3c3992fa7aefb81b73a52f49713cf3faa272382a
```

9.2.3 Binary Digests

The previous examples used the hexdigest() method to produce printable digests. A hexdigest is a different representation of the value calculated by the digest() method, which is a binary value that may include unprintable characters, including NUL. Some web services (Google checkout, Amazon S3) use the base64 encoded version of the binary digest instead of the hexdigest.

Listing 9.9: hmac_base64.py

```python
import base64
import hmac
```

```
import hashlib

with open('lorem.txt', 'rb') as f:
    body = f.read()

hash = hmac.new(
    b'secret-shared-key-goes-here',
    body,
    hashlib.sha1,
)

digest = hash.digest()
print(base64.encodestring(digest))
```

The base64 encoded string ends in a newline, which frequently needs to be stripped off when embedding the string in HTTP headers or other formatting-sensitive contexts.

```
$ python3 hmac_base64.py

b'olW2DoXHGJEKGU0aE9fOwSVE/o4=\n'
```

9.2.4   Applications of Message Signatures

HMAC authentication should be used for any public network service, and anytime data is stored where security is important. For example, when sending data through a pipe or socket, that data should be signed and then the signature should be tested before the data is used. The extended example given here is available in the file hmac_pickle.py.

The first step is to establish a function to calculate a digest for a string, along with a simple class to be instantiated and passed through a communication channel.

Listing 9.10: `hmac_pickle.py`

```
import hashlib
import hmac
import io
import pickle
import pprint


def make_digest(message):
    "Return a digest for the message."
    hash = hmac.new(
        b'secret-shared-key-goes-here',
        message,
        hashlib.sha1,
    )
    return hash.hexdigest().encode('utf-8')
```

```
class SimpleObject:
    """Demonstrate checking digests before unpickling.
    """

    def __init__(self, name):
        self.name = name

    def __str__(self):
        return self.name
```

Next, create a `BytesIO` buffer to represent the socket or pipe. The example uses a naive, but easy-to-parse, format for the data stream. The digest and length of the data are written, followed by a newline. The serialized representation of the object, generated by `pickle` (page 396), follows. A real system would not want to depend on a length value—after all, if the digest is wrong, the length is probably wrong as well. Some sort of terminator sequence not likely to appear in the real data would be more appropriate.

The example program then writes two objects to the stream. The first is written using the correct digest value.

```
# Simulate a writable socket or pipe with a buffer.
out_s = io.BytesIO()

# Write a valid object to the stream:
#   digest\nlength\npickle
o = SimpleObject('digest matches')
pickled_data = pickle.dumps(o)
digest = make_digest(pickled_data)
header = b'%s %d\n' % (digest, len(pickled_data))
print('WRITING: {}'.format(header))
out_s.write(header)
out_s.write(pickled_data)
```

The second object is written to the stream with an invalid digest, produced by calculating the digest for some other data instead of the pickle.

```
# Write an invalid object to the stream.
o = SimpleObject('digest does not match')
pickled_data = pickle.dumps(o)
digest = make_digest(b'not the pickled data at all')
header = b'%s %d\n' % (digest, len(pickled_data))
print('\nWRITING: {}'.format(header))
out_s.write(header)
out_s.write(pickled_data)

out_s.flush()
```

Now that the data is in the `BytesIO` buffer, it can be read back out again. Start by reading the line of data with the digest and data length. Then read the remaining data, using the length value. `pickle.load()` could read directly from the stream—but that strategy assumes a trusted data stream, and this data is not yet trusted enough to unpickle it. Reading the pickle as a string from the stream, without actually unpickling the object, is safer.

```python
# Simulate a readable socket or pipe with a buffer.
in_s = io.BytesIO(out_s.getvalue())

# Read the data.
while True:
    first_line = in_s.readline()
    if not first_line:
        break
    incoming_digest, incoming_length = first_line.split(b' ')
    incoming_length = int(incoming_length.decode('utf-8'))
    print('\nREAD:', incoming_digest, incoming_length)
```

Once the pickled data is in memory, the digest value can be recalculated and compared against the data read using `compare_digest()`. If the digests match, it is safe to trust the data and unpickle it.

```python
    incoming_pickled_data = in_s.read(incoming_length)

    actual_digest = make_digest(incoming_pickled_data)
    print('ACTUAL:', actual_digest)

    if hmac.compare_digest(actual_digest, incoming_digest):
        obj = pickle.loads(incoming_pickled_data)
        print('OK:', obj)
    else:
        print('WARNING: Data corruption')
```

The output shows that the first object is verified and the second is deemed "corrupted," as expected.

```
$ python3 hmac_pickle.py

WRITING: b'f49cd2bf7922911129e8df37f76f95485a0b52ca 69\n'

WRITING: b'b01b209e28d7e053408ebe23b90fe5c33bc6a0ec 76\n'

READ: b'f49cd2bf7922911129e8df37f76f95485a0b52ca' 69
ACTUAL: b'f49cd2bf7922911129e8df37f76f95485a0b52ca'
OK: digest matches

READ: b'b01b209e28d7e053408ebe23b90fe5c33bc6a0ec' 76
ACTUAL: b'2ab061f9a9f749b8dd6f175bf57292e02e95c119'
WARNING: Data corruption
```

Comparing two digests with a simple string or bytes comparison can be used in a timing attack to expose part or all of the secret key by passing digests of different lengths. `compare_digest()` implements a fast but constant-time comparison function to protect against timing attacks.

TIP

Related Reading

- Standard library documentation for hmac.[6]
- **RFC 2104**[7]: HMAC: Keyed-Hashing for Message Authentication.
- hashlib (page 523): The hashlib module provides MD5 and SHA1 hash generators.
- pickle (page 396): Serialization library.
- Wikipedia: MD5[8]: Description of the MD5 hashing algorithm.
- Signing and Authenticating REST Requests (Amazon AWS)[9]: Instructions for authenticating to S3 using HMAC-SHA1 signed credentials.

---

[6] https://docs.python.org/3.5/library/hmac.html
[7] https://tools.ietf.org/html/rfc2104.html
[8] https://en.wikipedia.org/wiki/MD5
[9] http://docs.aws.amazon.com/AmazonS3/latest/dev/RESTAuthentication.html

Chapter 10

Concurrency with Processes, Threads, and Coroutines

Python includes sophisticated tools for managing concurrent operations using processes and threads. Even many relatively simple programs can be made to run faster by applying techniques for running parts of the job concurrently using these modules.

subprocess (page 535) provides an API for creating and communicating with secondary processes. It is especially good for running programs that produce or consume text, since the API supports passing data back and forth through the standard input and output channels of the new process.

The signal (page 553) module exposes the Unix signal mechanism for sending events to other processes. The signals are processed asynchronously, usually by interrupting what the program is doing at the time the signal arrives. Signaling is useful as a coarse messaging system, but other interprocess communication techniques are more reliable and can deliver more complicated messages.

threading (page 560) includes a high-level, object-oriented API for working with concurrency from Python. Thread objects run concurrently within the same process and share memory. Using threads is an easy way to scale for tasks that are more I/O bound than CPU bound.

The multiprocessing (page 586) module mirrors threading, except that instead of a Thread class it provides a Process. Each Process is a true system process without shared memory, but multiprocessing provides features for sharing data and passing messages so that in many cases converting from threads to processes is as simple as changing a few import statements.

asyncio (page 617) provides a framework for concurrency and asynchronous I/O management using either a class-based protocol system or coroutines. asyncio replaces the old asyncore and asynchat modules, which are still available but deprecated.

concurrent.futures (page 677) provides implementation of thread and process-based executors for managing resources pools for running concurrent tasks.

10.1 subprocess: Spawning Additional Processes

The subprocess module supports three APIs for working with processes. The run() function, added in Python 3.5, is a high-level API for running a process and optionally collecting its output. The functions call(), check_call(), and check_output() are the former high-level API, carried over from Python 2. They are still supported and widely used in existing programs. The class Popen is a low-level API used to build the other APIs and useful for more complex process interactions. The constructor for Popen takes arguments to set up the new process so the parent can communicate with it via pipes. It provides all of the functionality of the other modules and functions it replaces, and more. The API is consistent for all uses, and many of the extra steps of overhead needed (such as closing extra file descriptors and ensuring the pipes are closed) are "built in" instead of being handled separately by the application code.

The subprocess module is intended to replace functions such as os.system(), os.spawnv(), the variations of popen() in the os (page 1227) and popen2 modules, and the commands module. To make it easier to compare subprocess with those other modules, many of the examples in this section re-create the ones used for os and popen2.

NOTE

The API for working on Unix and Windows is roughly the same, but the underlying implementation is different because of differences in the process models in the operating systems. All of the examples shown here were tested on Mac OS X. Their behavior on a non-Unix OS may vary.

10.1.1   Running External Commands

To run an external command without interacting with it in the same way as os.system(), use the run() function.

Listing 10.1: **subprocess_os_system.py**

```
import subprocess

completed = subprocess.run(['ls', '-1'])
print('returncode:', completed.returncode)
```

The command-line arguments are passed as a list of strings, which avoids the need for escaping quotes or other special characters that might be interpreted by the shell. run() returns a CompletedProcess instance, with information about the process such as the exit code and output.

```
$ python3 subprocess_os_system.py

index.rst
interaction.py
repeater.py
signal_child.py
signal_parent.py
subprocess_check_output_error_trap_output.py
subprocess_os_system.py
subprocess_pipes.py
subprocess_popen2.py
```

```
subprocess_popen3.py
subprocess_popen4.py
subprocess_popen_read.py
subprocess_popen_write.py
subprocess_run_check.py
subprocess_run_output.py
subprocess_run_output_error.py
subprocess_run_output_error_suppress.py
subprocess_run_output_error_trap.py
subprocess_shell_variables.py
subprocess_signal_parent_shell.py
subprocess_signal_setpgrp.py
returncode: 0
```

Setting the `shell` argument to a true value causes `subprocess` to spawn an intermediate shell process, which then runs the command. The default is to run the command directly.

Listing 10.2: `subprocess_shell_variables.py`

```
import subprocess

completed = subprocess.run('echo $HOME', shell=True)
print('returncode:', completed.returncode)
```

Using an intermediate shell means that variables, glob patterns, and other special shell features in the command string are processed before the command is run.

```
$ python3 subprocess_shell_variables.py

/Users/dhellmann
returncode: 0
```

NOTE

Using `run()` without passing `check=True` is equivalent to using `call()`, which returns only the exit code from the process.

10.1.1.1 Error Handling

The `returncode` attribute of the `CompletedProcess` is the exit code of the program. The caller is responsible for interpreting it to detect errors. If the `check` argument to `run()` is `True`, the exit code is checked. If it indicates an error happened, then a `CalledProcessError` exception is raised.

Listing 10.3: **subprocess_run_check.py**

```
import subprocess

try:
    subprocess.run(['false'], check=True)
except subprocess.CalledProcessError as err:
    print('ERROR:', err)
```

The `false` command always exits with a non-zero status code, which `run()` interprets as an error.

```
$ python3 subprocess_run_check.py

ERROR: Command '['false']' returned non-zero exit status 1
```

NOTE

Passing check=True to run() makes it equivalent to using check_call().

10.1.1.2   Capturing Output

The standard input and output channels for the process started by `run()` are bound to the parent's input and output. As a consequence, the calling program cannot capture the output of the command. Pass `PIPE` for the `stdout` and `stderr` arguments to capture the output for later processing.

Listing 10.4: **subprocess_run_output.py**

```
import subprocess

completed = subprocess.run(
    ['ls', '-1'],
    stdout=subprocess.PIPE,
)
print('returncode:', completed.returncode)
print('Have {} bytes in stdout:\n{}'.format(
    len(completed.stdout),
    completed.stdout.decode('utf-8'))
)
```

The `ls -1` command runs successfully, so the text it prints to standard output is captured and returned.

```
$ python3 subprocess_run_output.py

returncode: 0
Have 522 bytes in stdout:
```

```
index.rst
interaction.py
repeater.py
signal_child.py
signal_parent.py
subprocess_check_output_error_trap_output.py
subprocess_os_system.py
subprocess_pipes.py
subprocess_popen2.py
subprocess_popen3.py
subprocess_popen4.py
subprocess_popen_read.py
subprocess_popen_write.py
subprocess_run_check.py
subprocess_run_output.py
subprocess_run_output_error.py
subprocess_run_output_error_suppress.py
subprocess_run_output_error_trap.py
subprocess_shell_variables.py
subprocess_signal_parent_shell.py
subprocess_signal_setpgrp.py
```

NOTE

Passing check=True and setting stdout to PIPE is equivalent to using check_output().

The next example runs a series of commands in a subshell. Messages are sent to standard output and standard error before the commands exit with an error code.

Listing 10.5: subprocess_run_output_error.py

```python
import subprocess

try:
    completed = subprocess.run(
        'echo to stdout; echo to stderr 1>&2; exit 1',
        check=True,
        shell=True,
        stdout=subprocess.PIPE,
    )
except subprocess.CalledProcessError as err:
    print('ERROR:', err)
else:
    print('returncode:', completed.returncode)
    print('Have {} bytes in stdout: {!r}'.format(
        len(completed.stdout),
        completed.stdout.decode('utf-8'))
    )
```

The message to standard error is printed to the console, but the message to standard output is hidden.

```
$ python3 subprocess_run_output_error.py

to stderr
ERROR: Command 'echo to stdout; echo to stderr 1>&2; exit 1'
returned non-zero exit status 1
```

To prevent error messages from commands run through run() from being written to the console, set the stderr parameter to the constant PIPE.

Listing 10.6: **subprocess_run_output_error_trap.py**

```
import subprocess

try:
    completed = subprocess.run(
        'echo to stdout; echo to stderr 1>&2; exit 1',
        shell=True,
        stdout=subprocess.PIPE,
        stderr=subprocess.PIPE,
    )
except subprocess.CalledProcessError as err:
    print('ERROR:', err)
else:
    print('returncode:', completed.returncode)
    print('Have {} bytes in stdout: {!r}'.format(
        len(completed.stdout),
        completed.stdout.decode('utf-8'))
    )
    print('Have {} bytes in stderr: {!r}'.format(
        len(completed.stderr),
        completed.stderr.decode('utf-8'))
    )
```

This example does not set check=True, so the output of the command is captured and printed.

```
$ python3 subprocess_run_output_error_trap.py

returncode: 1
Have 10 bytes in stdout: 'to stdout\n'
Have 10 bytes in stderr: 'to stderr\n'
```

To capture error messages when using check_output(), set stderr to STDOUT, and the messages will be merged with the rest of the output from the command.

Listing 10.7: **subprocess_check_output_error_trap_output.py**

```
import subprocess

try:
    output = subprocess.check_output(
        'echo to stdout; echo to stderr 1>&2',
        shell=True,
        stderr=subprocess.STDOUT,
    )
except subprocess.CalledProcessError as err:
    print('ERROR:', err)
else:
    print('Have {} bytes in output: {!r}'.format(
        len(output),
        output.decode('utf-8')))
    )
```

The order of output may vary, depending on how buffering is applied to the standard output stream and how much data is printed.

```
$ python3 subprocess_check_output_error_trap_output.py

Have 20 bytes in output: 'to stdout\nto stderr\n'
```

10.1.1.3 Suppressing Output

For cases where the output should not be shown or captured, use DEVNULL to suppress an output stream. The next example suppresses both the standard output and error streams.

Listing 10.8: **subprocess_run_output_error_suppress.py**

```
import subprocess

try:
    completed = subprocess.run(
        'echo to stdout; echo to stderr 1>&2; exit 1',
        shell=True,
        stdout=subprocess.DEVNULL,
        stderr=subprocess.DEVNULL,
    )
except subprocess.CalledProcessError as err:
    print('ERROR:', err)
else:
    print('returncode:', completed.returncode)
    print('stdout is {!r}'.format(completed.stdout))
    print('stderr is {!r}'.format(completed.stderr))
```

The name `DEVNULL` comes from the Unix special device file, `/dev/null`. It responds with end-of-file when opened for reading, and receives but ignores any amount of input when writing.

```
$ python3 subprocess_run_output_error_suppress.py

returncode: 1
stdout is None
stderr is None
```

10.1.2   Working with Pipes Directly

The functions `run()`, `call()`, `check_call()`, and `check_output()` are wrappers around the `Popen` class. Using `Popen` directly gives more control over how the command is run, and how its input and output streams are processed. For example, by passing different arguments for `stdin`, `stdout`, and `stderr`, it is possible to mimic the variations of `os.popen()`.

10.1.2.1   One-Way Communication with a Process

To run a process and read all of its output, set the `stdout` value to `PIPE` and call `communicate()`.

Listing 10.9: **subprocess_popen_read.py**

```
import subprocess

print('read:')
proc = subprocess.Popen(
    ['echo', '"to stdout"'],
    stdout=subprocess.PIPE,
)
stdout_value = proc.communicate()[0].decode('utf-8')
print('stdout:', repr(stdout_value))
```

This is similar to the way `popen()` works, except that the reading is managed internally by the `Popen` instance.

```
$ python3 subprocess_popen_read.py

read:
stdout: '"to stdout"\n'
```

To set up a pipe to allow the calling program to write data to it, set `stdin` to `PIPE`.

Listing 10.10: **subprocess_popen_write.py**

```
import subprocess

print('write:')
proc = subprocess.Popen(
```

```
    ['cat', '-'],
    stdin=subprocess.PIPE,
)
proc.communicate('stdin: to stdin\n'.encode('utf-8'))
```

To send data to the standard input channel of the process one time, pass the data to communicate(). This is similar to using popen() with mode 'w'.

```
$ python3 -u subprocess_popen_write.py

write:
stdin: to stdin
```

10.1.2.2 Bidirectional Communication with a Process

To set up the Popen instance for reading and writing at the same time, use a combination of the previous techniques.

Listing 10.11: **subprocess_popen2.py**

```
import subprocess

print('popen2:')

proc = subprocess.Popen(
    ['cat', '-'],
    stdin=subprocess.PIPE,
    stdout=subprocess.PIPE,
)
msg = 'through stdin to stdout'.encode('utf-8')
stdout_value = proc.communicate(msg)[0].decode('utf-8')
print('pass through:', repr(stdout_value))
```

This sets up the pipe to mimic popen2().

```
$ python3 -u subprocess_popen2.py

popen2:
pass through: 'through stdin to stdout'
```

10.1.2.3 Capturing Error Output

It is also possible to watch both of the streams for stdout and stderr, as with popen3().

Listing 10.12: **subprocess_popen3.py**

```
import subprocess

print('popen3:')
```

```
proc = subprocess.Popen(
    'cat -; echo "to stderr" 1>&2',
    shell=True,
    stdin=subprocess.PIPE,
    stdout=subprocess.PIPE,
    stderr=subprocess.PIPE,
)
msg = 'through stdin to stdout'.encode('utf-8')
stdout_value, stderr_value = proc.communicate(msg)
print('pass through:', repr(stdout_value.decode('utf-8')))
print('stderr      :', repr(stderr_value.decode('utf-8')))
```

Reading from `stderr` works the same way as reading from `stdout`. Passing `PIPE` tells `Popen` to attach to the channel, and `communicate()` reads all of the data from it before returning.

```
$ python3 -u subprocess_popen3.py

popen3:
pass through: 'through stdin to stdout'
stderr      : 'to stderr\n'
```

10.1.2.4   Combining Regular and Error Output

To direct the error output from the process to its standard output channel, use `STDOUT` for `stderr` instead of `PIPE`.

Listing 10.13: subprocess_popen4.py

```
import subprocess

print('popen4:')
proc = subprocess.Popen(
    'cat -; echo "to stderr" 1>&2',
    shell=True,
    stdin=subprocess.PIPE,
    stdout=subprocess.PIPE,
    stderr=subprocess.STDOUT,
)
msg = 'through stdin to stdout\n'.encode('utf-8')
stdout_value, stderr_value = proc.communicate(msg)
print('combined output:', repr(stdout_value.decode('utf-8')))
print('stderr value    :', repr(stderr_value))
```

Combining the output in this way is similar to how `popen4()` works.

```
$ python3 -u subprocess_popen4.py

popen4:
combined output: 'through stdin to stdout\nto stderr\n'
stderr value    : None
```

10.1.3 Connecting Segments of a Pipe

Multiple commands can be connected into a *pipeline*, similar to the way the Unix shell works, by creating separate Popen instances and chaining their inputs and outputs together. The stdout attribute of one Popen instance is used as the stdin argument for the next instance in the pipeline, instead of the constant PIPE. The output is read from the stdout handle for the final command in the pipeline.

Listing 10.14: **subprocess_pipes.py**

```python
import subprocess

cat = subprocess.Popen(
    ['cat', 'index.rst'],
    stdout=subprocess.PIPE,
)

grep = subprocess.Popen(
    ['grep', '.. literalinclude::'],
    stdin=cat.stdout,
    stdout=subprocess.PIPE,
)

cut = subprocess.Popen(
    ['cut', '-f', '3', '-d:'],
    stdin=grep.stdout,
    stdout=subprocess.PIPE,
)

end_of_pipe = cut.stdout

print('Included files:')
for line in end_of_pipe:
    print(line.decode('utf-8').strip())
```

This example reproduces the following command line:

```
$ cat index.rst | grep ".. literalinclude" | cut -f 3 -d:
```

The pipeline reads the reStructuredText source file for this section and finds all of the lines that include other files. It then prints the names of the files being included.

```
$ python3 -u subprocess_pipes.py

Included files:
subprocess_os_system.py
subprocess_shell_variables.py
subprocess_run_check.py
subprocess_run_output.py
subprocess_run_output_error.py
subprocess_run_output_error_trap.py
subprocess_check_output_error_trap_output.py
subprocess_run_output_error_suppress.py
subprocess_popen_read.py
subprocess_popen_write.py
subprocess_popen2.py
subprocess_popen3.py
subprocess_popen4.py
subprocess_pipes.py
repeater.py
interaction.py
signal_child.py
signal_parent.py
subprocess_signal_parent_shell.py
subprocess_signal_setpgrp.py
```

10.1.4   Interacting with Another Command

All of the previous examples assume a limited amount of interaction. The `communicate()` method reads all of the output and waits for the child process to exit before returning. It is also possible to write to and read from the individual pipe handles used by the `Popen` instance incrementally, as the program runs. A simple echo program that reads from standard input and writes to standard output illustrates this technique.

The script `repeater.py` is used as the child process in the next example. It reads from `stdin` and writes the values to `stdout`, one line at a time, until there is no more input. It also writes a message to `stderr` when it starts and stops, showing the lifetime of the child process.

Listing 10.15: repeater.py

```
import sys

sys.stderr.write('repeater.py: starting\n')
sys.stderr.flush()

while True:
    next_line = sys.stdin.readline()
```

```
            sys.stderr.flush()
            if not next_line:
                break
            sys.stdout.write(next_line)
            sys.stdout.flush()

        sys.stderr.write('repeater.py: exiting\n')
        sys.stderr.flush()
```

The next interaction example uses the `stdin` and `stdout` file handles owned by the `Popen` instance in different ways. In the first example, a sequence of five numbers is written to `stdin` of the process; after each write operation, the next line of output is read back. In the second example, the same five numbers are written, but the output is read all at once using `communicate()`.

Listing 10.16: `interaction.py`

```python
import io
import subprocess

print('One line at a time:')
proc = subprocess.Popen(
    'python3 repeater.py',
    shell=True,
    stdin=subprocess.PIPE,
    stdout=subprocess.PIPE,
)
stdin = io.TextIOWrapper(
    proc.stdin,
    encoding='utf-8',
    line_buffering=True,  # Send data on newline
)
stdout = io.TextIOWrapper(
    proc.stdout,
    encoding='utf-8',
)
for i in range(5):
    line = '{}\n'.format(i)
    stdin.write(line)
    output = stdout.readline()
    print(output.rstrip())
remainder = proc.communicate()[0].decode('utf-8')
print(remainder)

print()
print('All output at once:')
proc = subprocess.Popen(
    'python3 repeater.py',
    shell=True,
```

```
        stdin=subprocess.PIPE,
        stdout=subprocess.PIPE,
    )
    stdin = io.TextIOWrapper(
        proc.stdin,
        encoding='utf-8',
    )
    for i in range(5):
        line = '{}\n'.format(i)
        stdin.write(line)
    stdin.flush()

    output = proc.communicate()[0].decode('utf-8')
    print(output)
```

The "repeater.py: exiting" lines come at different points in the output for each loop style.

```
$ python3 -u interaction.py

One line at a time:
repeater.py: starting
0
1
2
3
4
repeater.py: exiting


All output at once:
repeater.py: starting
repeater.py: exiting
0
1
2
3
4
```

10.1.5   Signaling Between Processes

The process management examples for the os (page 1227) module include a demonstration of signaling between processes using os.fork() and os.kill(). Since each Popen instance provides a *pid* attribute with the process ID of the child process, it is possible to do something similar with subprocess.

The next example combines two scripts. This child process sets up a signal handler for the USR signal.

Listing 10.17: signal_child.py

```python
import os
import signal
import time
import sys

pid = os.getpid()
received = False


def signal_usr1(signum, frame):
    "Callback invoked when a signal is received"
    global received
    received = True
    print('CHILD {:>6}: Received USR1'.format(pid))
    sys.stdout.flush()


print('CHILD {:>6}: Setting up signal handler'.format(pid))
sys.stdout.flush()
signal.signal(signal.SIGUSR1, signal_usr1)
print('CHILD {:>6}: Pausing to wait for signal'.format(pid))
sys.stdout.flush()
time.sleep(3)

if not received:
    print('CHILD {:>6}: Never received signal'.format(pid))
```

This script runs as the parent process. It starts signal_child.py, then sends the USR1 signal.

Listing 10.18: signal_parent.py

```python
import os
import signal
import subprocess
import time
import sys

proc = subprocess.Popen(['python3', 'signal_child.py'])
print('PARENT      : Pausing before sending signal...')
sys.stdout.flush()
time.sleep(1)
print('PARENT      : Signaling child')
sys.stdout.flush()
os.kill(proc.pid, signal.SIGUSR1)
```

The output is shown here.

```
$ python3 signal_parent.py

PARENT       : Pausing before sending signal...
CHILD  26976: Setting up signal handler
CHILD  26976: Pausing to wait for signal
PARENT       : Signaling child
CHILD  26976: Received USR1
```

10.1.5.1   Process Groups/Sessions

If the process created by Popen spawns subprocesses, those children will not receive any signals sent to the parent. As a consequence, when using the shell argument to Popen, it will be difficult to force the command started in the shell to terminate by sending SIGINT or SIGTERM.

Listing 10.19: **subprocess_signal_parent_shell.py**

```
import os
import signal
import subprocess
import tempfile
import time
import sys

script = '''#!/bin/sh
echo "Shell script in process $$"
set -x
python3 signal_child.py
'''
script_file = tempfile.NamedTemporaryFile('wt')
script_file.write(script)
script_file.flush()

proc = subprocess.Popen(['sh', script_file.name])
print('PARENT      : Pausing before signaling {}...'.format(
    proc.pid))
sys.stdout.flush()
time.sleep(1)
print('PARENT      : Signaling child {}'.format(proc.pid))
sys.stdout.flush()
os.kill(proc.pid, signal.SIGUSR1)
time.sleep(3)
```

In this example, the pid used to send the signal does not match the pid of the child of the shell script waiting for the signal, because three separate processes are interacting:

- The program subprocess_signal_parent_shell.py

- The shell process running the script created by the main python program

- The program `signal_child.py`

```
$ python3 subprocess_signal_parent_shell.py

PARENT       : Pausing before signaling 26984...
Shell script in process 26984
+ python3 signal_child.py
CHILD  26985: Setting up signal handler
CHILD  26985: Pausing to wait for signal
PARENT       : Signaling child 26984
CHILD  26985: Never received signal
```

To send signals to descendants without knowing their process ID, use a *process group* to associate the children so they can be signaled together. The process group is created with `os.setpgrp()`, which sets the process group ID to the process ID of the current process. All child processes inherit their process group from their parent. Because this group should be set only in the shell created by `Popen` and its descendants, `os.setpgrp()` should not be called in the same process where the `Popen` is created. Instead, the function is passed to `Popen` as the `preexec_fn` argument so that it runs after the `fork()` inside the new process, before it uses `exec()` to run the shell. To signal the entire process group, use `os.killpg()` with the `pid` value from the `Popen` instance.

Listing 10.20: **subprocess_signal_setpgrp.py**

```python
import os
import signal
import subprocess
import tempfile
import time
import sys


def show_setting_prgrp():
    print('Calling os.setpgrp() from {}'.format(os.getpid()))
    os.setpgrp()
    print('Process group is now {}'.format(
        os.getpid(), os.getpgrp()))
    sys.stdout.flush()


script = '''#!/bin/sh
echo "Shell script in process $$"
set -x
python3 signal_child.py
'''

script_file = tempfile.NamedTemporaryFile('wt')
```

```
script_file.write(script)
script_file.flush()

proc = subprocess.Popen(
    ['sh', script_file.name],
    preexec_fn=show_setting_prgrp,
)
print('PARENT      : Pausing before signaling {}...'.format(
    proc.pid))
sys.stdout.flush()
time.sleep(1)
print('PARENT      : Signaling process group {}'.format(
    proc.pid))
sys.stdout.flush()
os.killpg(proc.pid, signal.SIGUSR1)
time.sleep(3)
```

The sequence of events is shown here:

1. The parent program instantiates `Popen`.

2. The `Popen` instance forks a new process.

3. The new process runs `os.setpgrp()`.

4. The new process runs `exec()` to start the shell.

5. The shell runs the shell script.

6. The shell script forks again, and that process execs Python.

7. Python runs `signal_child.py`.

8. The parent program signals the process group using the pid of the shell.

9. The shell and Python processes receive the signal.

10. The shell ignores the signal.

11. The Python process running `signal_child.py` invokes the signal handler.

```
$ python3 subprocess_signal_setpgrp.py

Calling os.setpgrp() from 26992
Process group is now 26992
PARENT      : Pausing before signaling 26992...
Shell script in process 26992
+ python3 signal_child.py
CHILD  26993: Setting up signal handler
```

```
CHILD   26993: Pausing to wait for signal
PARENT       : Signaling process group 26992
CHILD   26993: Received USR1
```

TIP

Related Reading

- Standard library documentation for subprocess.[1]

- os (page 1227): Although subprocess replaces many of them, the functions for working with processes found in the os module are still widely used in existing code.

- UNIX Signals and Process Groups[2]: A good description of Unix signaling and how process groups work.

- signal (page 553): More details about using the signal module.

- *Advanced Programming in the UNIX Environment, Third Edition*[3]: Covers working with multiple processes, such as handling signals and closing duplicated file descriptors.

- pipes: Unix shell command pipeline templates in the standard library.

10.2   signal: Asynchronous System Events

Signals are an operating system feature that provide a means of notifying a program of an event, and having it handled asynchronously. They can be generated by the system itself, or sent from one process to another. Since signals interrupt the regular flow of the program, it is possible that some operations (especially I/O) may produce errors if a signal is received while they are ongoing.

Signals are identified by integers and are defined in the operating system C headers. Python exposes the signals appropriate for the platform as symbols in the signal module. The examples in this section use SIGINT and SIGUSR1, both of which are typically defined for all Unix and Unix-like systems.

NOTE

Programming with Unix signal handlers is a nontrivial endeavor. This section presents an introduction to this complex topic, but does not include all of the details needed to use signals successfully on every platform. Some degree of standardization is apparent across versions of Unix, but some variation exists as well, so consult the operating system documentation if you run into trouble.

---

[1] https://docs.python.org/3.5/library/subprocess.html
[2] www.cs.ucsb.edu/~almeroth/classes/W99.276/assignment1/signals.html
[3] https://www.amazon.com/Advanced-Programming-UNIX-Environment-3rd/dp/0321637739/

10.2.1   Receiving Signals

As with other forms of event-based programming, signals are received by establishing a callback function, called a *signal handler*, that is invoked when the signal occurs. The arguments to the signal handler are the signal number and the stack frame from the point in the program that was interrupted by the signal.

Listing 10.21: signal_signal.py

```python
import signal
import os
import time


def receive_signal(signum, stack):
    print('Received:', signum)

# Register signal handlers.
signal.signal(signal.SIGUSR1, receive_signal)
signal.signal(signal.SIGUSR2, receive_signal)

# Print the process ID so it can be used with 'kill'
# to send this program signals.
print('My PID is:', os.getpid())

while True:
    print('Waiting...')
    time.sleep(3)
```

This example script loops indefinitely, pausing for a few seconds each time. When a signal comes in, the sleep() call is interrupted and the signal handler receive_signal prints the signal number. After the signal handler returns, the loop continues.

Send signals to the running program using os.kill() or the Unix command-line program kill.

```
$ python3 signal_signal.py

My PID is: 71387
Waiting...
Waiting...
Waiting...
Received: 30
Waiting...
Waiting...
Received: 31
Waiting...
Waiting...
Traceback (most recent call last):
  File "signal_signal.py", line 28, in <module>
```

```
    time.sleep(3)
KeyboardInterrupt
```

The previous output was produced by running `signal_signal.py` in one window, then executing the following commands in another window:

```
$ kill -USR1 $pid
$ kill -USR2 $pid
$ kill -INT $pid
```

10.2.2   Retrieving Registered Handlers

To see which signal handlers are registered for a signal, use `getsignal()`. Pass the signal number as an argument. The return value is the registered handler, or one of the special values `SIG_IGN` (if the signal is being ignored), `SIG_DFL` (if the default behavior is being used), or `None` (if the existing signal handler was registered from C, rather than Python).

Listing 10.22: **signal_getsignal.py**

```
import signal


def alarm_received(n, stack):
    return

signal.signal(signal.SIGALRM, alarm_received)

signals_to_names = {
    getattr(signal, n): n
    for n in dir(signal)
    if n.startswith('SIG') and '_' not in n
}

for s, name in sorted(signals_to_names.items()):
    handler = signal.getsignal(s)
    if handler is signal.SIG_DFL:
        handler = 'SIG_DFL'
    elif handler is signal.SIG_IGN:
        handler = 'SIG_IGN'
    print('{:<10} ({:2d}):'.format(name, s), handler)
```

Again, since each OS may have different signals defined, the output on other systems may vary. The following output is from OS X.

```
$ python3 signal_getsignal.py

SIGHUP     ( 1): SIG_DFL
SIGINT     ( 2): <built-in function default_int_handler>
```

```
SIGQUIT    ( 3): SIG_DFL
SIGILL     ( 4): SIG_DFL
SIGTRAP    ( 5): SIG_DFL
SIGIOT     ( 6): SIG_DFL
SIGEMT     ( 7): SIG_DFL
SIGFPE     ( 8): SIG_DFL
SIGKILL    ( 9): None
SIGBUS     (10): SIG_DFL
SIGSEGV    (11): SIG_DFL
SIGSYS     (12): SIG_DFL
SIGPIPE    (13): SIG_IGN
SIGALRM    (14): <function alarm_received at 0x100757f28>
SIGTERM    (15): SIG_DFL
SIGURG     (16): SIG_DFL
SIGSTOP    (17): None
SIGTSTP    (18): SIG_DFL
SIGCONT    (19): SIG_DFL
SIGCHLD    (20): SIG_DFL
SIGTTIN    (21): SIG_DFL
SIGTTOU    (22): SIG_DFL
SIGIO      (23): SIG_DFL
SIGXCPU    (24): SIG_DFL
SIGXFSZ    (25): SIG_IGN
SIGVTALRM  (26): SIG_DFL
SIGPROF    (27): SIG_DFL
SIGWINCH   (28): SIG_DFL
SIGINFO    (29): SIG_DFL
SIGUSR1    (30): SIG_DFL
SIGUSR2    (31): SIG_DFL
```

10.2.3   Sending Signals

The function used to send signals from within Python is `os.kill()`. Its use is covered in a later section on the `os` (page 1227) module, Section 17.3.10, "Creating Processes with os.fork()" (page 1240).

10.2.4   Alarms

Alarms are a special sort of signal, which are generated when the program asks the OS to notify it after some period of time has elapsed. As the standard module documentation for `os` (page 1227) points out, this approach is useful for avoiding blocking indefinitely on an I/O operation or other system call.

Listing 10.23: `signal_alarm.py`

```
import signal
import time


def receive_alarm(signum, stack):
```

```
    print('Alarm :', time.ctime())

# Call receive_alarm in 2 seconds.
signal.signal(signal.SIGALRM, receive_alarm)
signal.alarm(2)

print('Before:', time.ctime())
time.sleep(4)
print('After :', time.ctime())
```

In this example, the call to sleep() is interrupted, but then continues after the signal is
processed. The message printed after sleep() returns shows that the program was paused
for at least as long as the sleep duration.

```
$ python3 signal_alarm.py

Before: Sun Sep 11 11:31:18 2016
Alarm : Sun Sep 11 11:31:20 2016
After : Sun Sep 11 11:31:22 2016
```

10.2.5 Ignoring Signals

To ignore a signal, register SIG_IGN as the handler. This script replaces the default handler
for SIGINT with SIG_IGN, and registers a handler for SIGUSR1. It then uses signal.pause()
to wait for a signal to be received.

Listing 10.24: **signal_ignore.py**

```
import signal
import os
import time


def do_exit(sig, stack):
    raise SystemExit('Exiting')

signal.signal(signal.SIGINT, signal.SIG_IGN)
signal.signal(signal.SIGUSR1, do_exit)

print('My PID:', os.getpid())

signal.pause()
```

Normally SIGINT (the signal sent by the shell to a program when the user presses Ctrl-C)
raises a KeyboardInterrupt. This example ignores SIGINT and raises SystemExit when it sees
SIGUSR1. Each ^C in the output represents an attempt to use Ctrl-C to kill the script from the
terminal. Using kill -USR1 72598 from another terminal eventually causes the script to exit.

```
$ python3 signal_ignore.py

My PID: 72598
^C^C^C^CExiting
```

10.2.6   Signals and Threads

Mixing signals and threads rarely works well because only the main thread of a process will receive signals. The following example sets up a signal handler, waits for the signal in one thread, and sends the signal from another thread.

Listing 10.25: `signal_threads.py`

```python
import signal
import threading
import os
import time


def signal_handler(num, stack):
    print('Received signal {} in {}'.format(
        num, threading.currentThread().name))


signal.signal(signal.SIGUSR1, signal_handler)


def wait_for_signal():
    print('Waiting for signal in',
          threading.currentThread().name)
    signal.pause()
    print('Done waiting')

# Start a thread that will not receive the signal.
receiver = threading.Thread(
    target=wait_for_signal,
    name='receiver',
)
receiver.start()
time.sleep(0.1)


def send_signal():
    print('Sending signal in', threading.currentThread().name)
    os.kill(os.getpid(), signal.SIGUSR1)

sender = threading.Thread(target=send_signal, name='sender')
sender.start()
sender.join()
```

```
# Wait for the thread to see the signal (not going to happen!).
print('Waiting for', receiver.name)
signal.alarm(2)
receiver.join()
```

The signal handlers were all registered in the main thread because this is a requirement of the signal module implementation for Python, regardless of underlying platform support for mixing threads and signals. Although the receiver thread calls signal.pause(), it does not receive the signal. The signal.alarm(2) call near the end of the example prevents an infinite block, since the receiver thread will never exit.

```
$ python3 signal_threads.py

Waiting for signal in receiver
Sending signal in sender
Received signal 30 in MainThread
Waiting for receiver
Alarm clock
```

Although alarms can be set in any thread, they are always received by the main thread.

Listing 10.26: signal_threads_alarm.py

```
import signal
import time
import threading


def signal_handler(num, stack):
    print(time.ctime(), 'Alarm in',
          threading.currentThread().name)


signal.signal(signal.SIGALRM, signal_handler)


def use_alarm():
    t_name = threading.currentThread().name
    print(time.ctime(), 'Setting alarm in', t_name)
    signal.alarm(1)
    print(time.ctime(), 'Sleeping in', t_name)
    time.sleep(3)
    print(time.ctime(), 'Done with sleep in', t_name)


# Start a thread that will not receive the signal.
alarm_thread = threading.Thread(
    target=use_alarm,
    name='alarm_thread',
)
alarm_thread.start()
```

```
time.sleep(0.1)

# Wait for the thread to see the signal (not going to happen!).
print(time.ctime(), 'Waiting for', alarm_thread.name)
alarm_thread.join()

print(time.ctime(), 'Exiting normally')
```

In this example, the alarm does not abort the sleep() call in use_alarm().

```
$ python3 signal_threads_alarm.py

Sun Sep 11 11:31:22 2016 Setting alarm in alarm_thread
Sun Sep 11 11:31:22 2016 Sleeping in alarm_thread
Sun Sep 11 11:31:22 2016 Waiting for alarm_thread
Sun Sep 11 11:31:23 2016 Alarm in MainThread
Sun Sep 11 11:31:25 2016 Done with sleep in alarm_thread
Sun Sep 11 11:31:25 2016 Exiting normally
```

TIP

Related Reading

- Standard library documentation for signal.[4]
- **PEP 475**[5]: Retry system calls failing with EINTR.
- subprocess (page 535): More examples of sending signals to processes.
- Section 17.3.10, "Creating Processes with os.fork()" (page 1240): The kill() function can be used to send signals between processes.

10.3 threading: Manage Concurrent Operations Within a Process

The threading module provides APIs for managing several threads of execution, which allows a program to run multiple operations concurrently in the same process space.

10.3.1 Thread Objects

The simplest way to use a Thread is to instantiate it with a target function and call start() to let it begin working.

---

[4] https://docs.python.org/3.5/library/signal.html
[5] www.python.org/dev/peps/pep-0475

Listing 10.27: threading_simple.py

```python
import threading


def worker():
    """thread worker function"""
    print('Worker')


threads = []
for i in range(5):
    t = threading.Thread(target=worker)
    threads.append(t)
    t.start()
```

The output is five lines with "Worker" on each.

```
$ python3 threading_simple.py

Worker
Worker
Worker
Worker
Worker
```

It is useful to be able to spawn a thread and pass arguments that tell it which work to do. Any type of object can be passed as argument to the thread. The next example passes a number, which the thread then prints.

Listing 10.28: threading_simpleargs.py

```python
import threading


def worker(num):
    """thread worker function"""
    print('Worker: %s' % num)


threads = []
for i in range(5):
    t = threading.Thread(target=worker, args=(i,))
    threads.append(t)
    t.start()
```

The integer argument is now included in the message printed by each thread.

```
$ python3 threading_simpleargs.py

Worker: 0
Worker: 1
Worker: 2
Worker: 3
Worker: 4
```

10.3.2   Determining the Current Thread

Using arguments to identify or name the thread is cumbersome and unnecessary. Each
Thread instance has a name with a default value that can be changed as the thread is
created. Naming threads is useful in server processes in which multiple service threads
handle different operations.

Listing 10.29: threading_names.py

```
import threading
import time


def worker():
    print(threading.current_thread().getName(), 'Starting')
    time.sleep(0.2)
    print(threading.current_thread().getName(), 'Exiting')


def my_service():
    print(threading.current_thread().getName(), 'Starting')
    time.sleep(0.3)
    print(threading.current_thread().getName(), 'Exiting')


t = threading.Thread(name='my_service', target=my_service)
w = threading.Thread(name='worker', target=worker)
w2 = threading.Thread(target=worker)  # Use default name

w.start()
w2.start()
t.start()
```

The debug output includes the name of the current thread on each line. The lines with
"Thread-1" in the thread name column correspond to the unnamed thread w2.

```
$ python3 threading_names.py

worker Starting
Thread-1 Starting
my_service Starting
worker Exiting
Thread-1 Exiting
my_service Exiting
```

Most programs do not use `print` to debug. The `logging` (page 980) module supports embedding the thread name in every log message using the formatter code `%(threadName)s`. Including thread names in log messages makes it possible to trace those messages back to their source.

Listing 10.30: **threading_names_log.py**

```python
import logging
import threading
import time


def worker():
    logging.debug('Starting')
    time.sleep(0.2)
    logging.debug('Exiting')


def my_service():
    logging.debug('Starting')
    time.sleep(0.3)
    logging.debug('Exiting')


logging.basicConfig(
    level=logging.DEBUG,
    format='[%(levelname)s] (%(threadName)-10s) %(message)s',
)

t = threading.Thread(name='my_service', target=my_service)
w = threading.Thread(name='worker', target=worker)
w2 = threading.Thread(target=worker)  # Use default name

w.start()
w2.start()
t.start()
```

logging (page 980) is also thread-safe, so messages from different threads are kept distinct in the output.

```
$ python3 threading_names_log.py

[DEBUG] (worker    ) Starting
[DEBUG] (Thread-1  ) Starting
[DEBUG] (my_service) Starting
[DEBUG] (worker    ) Exiting
[DEBUG] (Thread-1  ) Exiting
[DEBUG] (my_service) Exiting
```

10.3.3 Daemon Versus Non-daemon Threads

Up to this point, the example programs have implicitly waited to exit until all threads have completed their work. Sometimes, however, programs spawn a thread as a *daemon* that runs without blocking the main program from exiting. Daemon threads are useful for services where there may not be an easy way to interrupt the thread, or where letting the thread die in the middle of its work does not lead to loss or corruption of data (for example, a thread that generates "heart-beats" for a service monitoring tool). To mark a thread as a daemon, pass daemon=True when constructing it or call its set_daemon() method with True. The default is for threads to not be daemons.

Listing 10.31: `threading_daemon.py`

```python
import threading
import time
import logging


def daemon():
    logging.debug('Starting')
    time.sleep(0.2)
    logging.debug('Exiting')


def non_daemon():
    logging.debug('Starting')
    logging.debug('Exiting')


logging.basicConfig(
    level=logging.DEBUG,
    format='(%(threadName)-10s) %(message)s',
)

d = threading.Thread(name='daemon', target=daemon, daemon=True)

t = threading.Thread(name='non-daemon', target=non_daemon)
```

```
d.start()
t.start()
```

The output from this code does not include the "Exiting" message from the daemon thread, since all of the non-daemon threads (including the main thread) exit before the daemon thread wakes up from the sleep() call.

```
$ python3 threading_daemon.py

(daemon     ) Starting
(non-daemon) Starting
(non-daemon) Exiting
```

To wait until a daemon thread has completed its work, use the join() method.

Listing 10.32: threading_daemon_join.py

```
import threading
import time
import logging


def daemon():
    logging.debug('Starting')
    time.sleep(0.2)
    logging.debug('Exiting')


def non_daemon():
    logging.debug('Starting')
    logging.debug('Exiting')


logging.basicConfig(
    level=logging.DEBUG,
    format='(%(threadName)-10s) %(message)s',
)

d = threading.Thread(name='daemon', target=daemon, daemon=True)

t = threading.Thread(name='non-daemon', target=non_daemon)

d.start()
t.start()

d.join()
t.join()
```

Waiting for the daemon thread to exit using `join()` means it has a chance to produce its "Exiting" message.

```
$ python3 threading_daemon_join.py

(daemon     ) Starting
(non-daemon) Starting
(non-daemon) Exiting
(daemon     ) Exiting
```

By default, `join()` blocks indefinitely. Alternatively, a float value may be passed that represents the number of seconds to wait for the thread to become inactive. If the thread does not complete within the timeout period, `join()` returns anyway.

Listing 10.33: **threading_daemon_join_timeout.py**

```python
import threading
import time
import logging


def daemon():
    logging.debug('Starting')
    time.sleep(0.2)
    logging.debug('Exiting')


def non_daemon():
    logging.debug('Starting')
    logging.debug('Exiting')


logging.basicConfig(
    level=logging.DEBUG,
    format='(%(threadName)-10s) %(message)s',
)

d = threading.Thread(name='daemon', target=daemon, daemon=True)

t = threading.Thread(name='non-daemon', target=non_daemon)

d.start()
t.start()

d.join(0.1)
print('d.isAlive()', d.isAlive())
t.join()
```

Since the timeout passed is less than the amount of time the daemon thread sleeps, the thread is still "alive" after join() returns.

```
$ python3 threading_daemon_join_timeout.py

(daemon    ) Starting
(non-daemon) Starting
(non-daemon) Exiting
d.isAlive() True
```

10.3.4   Enumerating All Threads

It is not necessary to retain an explicit handle to all of the daemon threads to ensure they have completed before exiting the main process. enumerate() returns a list of active Thread instances. The list includes the current thread, and since joining the current thread introduces a deadlock situation, it must be skipped.

Listing 10.34: **threading_enumerate.py**

```python
import random
import threading
import time
import logging


def worker():
    """thread worker function"""
    pause = random.randint(1, 5) / 10
    logging.debug('sleeping %0.2f', pause)
    time.sleep(pause)
    logging.debug('ending')


logging.basicConfig(
    level=logging.DEBUG,
    format='(%(threadName)-10s) %(message)s',
)

for i in range(3):
    t = threading.Thread(target=worker, daemon=True)
    t.start()

main_thread = threading.main_thread()
for t in threading.enumerate():
    if t is main_thread:
        continue
    logging.debug('joining %s', t.getName())
    t.join()
```

Because the worker is sleeping for a random amount of time, the output from this program may vary.

```
$ python3 threading_enumerate.py

(Thread-1  ) sleeping 0.20
(Thread-2  ) sleeping 0.30
(Thread-3  ) sleeping 0.40
(MainThread) joining Thread-1
(Thread-1  ) ending
(MainThread) joining Thread-3
(Thread-2  ) ending
(Thread-3  ) ending
(MainThread) joining Thread-2
```

10.3.5   Subclassing Thread

At start-up, a `Thread` does some basic initialization and then calls its `run()` method, which in turn calls the target function passed to the constructor. To create a subclass of `Thread`, override `run()` to do whatever is necessary.

Listing 10.35: **threading_subclass.py**

```
import threading
import logging


class MyThread(threading.Thread):

    def run(self):
        logging.debug('running')


logging.basicConfig(
    level=logging.DEBUG,
    format='(%(threadName)-10s) %(message)s',
)

for i in range(5):
    t = MyThread()
    t.start()
```

The return value of `run()` is ignored.

```
$ python3 threading_subclass.py

(Thread-1  ) running
(Thread-2  ) running
(Thread-3  ) running
```

```
(Thread-4  ) running
(Thread-5  ) running
```

Because the args and kwargs values passed to the Thread constructor are saved in private variables using names prefixed with '__', they are not easily accessed from a subclass. To pass arguments to a custom thread type, redefine the constructor to save the values in an instance attribute that can be seen in the subclass.

Listing 10.36: `threading_subclass_args.py`

```python
import threading
import logging


class MyThreadWithArgs(threading.Thread):

    def __init__(self, group=None, target=None, name=None,
                 args=(), kwargs=None, *, daemon=None):
        super().__init__(group=group, target=target, name=name,
                         daemon=daemon)
        self.args = args
        self.kwargs = kwargs

    def run(self):
        logging.debug('running with %s and %s',
                      self.args, self.kwargs)


logging.basicConfig(
    level=logging.DEBUG,
    format='(%(threadName)-10s) %(message)s',
)

for i in range(5):
    t = MyThreadWithArgs(args=(i,), kwargs={'a': 'A', 'b': 'B'})
    t.start()
```

MyThreadWithArgs uses the same API as Thread, but another class could easily change the constructor method to take more or different arguments more directly related to the purpose of the thread, as with any other class.

```
$ python3 threading_subclass_args.py

(Thread-1  ) running with (0,) and {'b': 'B', 'a': 'A'}
(Thread-2  ) running with (1,) and {'b': 'B', 'a': 'A'}
(Thread-3  ) running with (2,) and {'b': 'B', 'a': 'A'}
(Thread-4  ) running with (3,) and {'b': 'B', 'a': 'A'}
(Thread-5  ) running with (4,) and {'b': 'B', 'a': 'A'}
```

10.3.6   Timer Threads

One example of a reason to subclass `Thread` is provided by `Timer`, which is also included in `threading`. A `Timer` starts its work after a delay, and can be canceled at any point within that delay time period.

Listing 10.37: `threading_timer.py`

```
import threading
import time
import logging


def delayed():
    logging.debug('worker running')


logging.basicConfig(
    level=logging.DEBUG,
    format='(%(threadName)-10s) %(message)s',
)

t1 = threading.Timer(0.3, delayed)
t1.setName('t1')
t2 = threading.Timer(0.3, delayed)
t2.setName('t2')

logging.debug('starting timers')
t1.start()
t2.start()

logging.debug('waiting before canceling %s', t2.getName())
time.sleep(0.2)
logging.debug('canceling %s', t2.getName())
t2.cancel()
logging.debug('done')
```

The second timer in this example never runs, and the first timer appears to run after the rest of the main program is done. Since it is not a daemon thread, it is joined implicitly when the main thread is done.

```
$ python3 threading_timer.py

(MainThread) starting timers
(MainThread) waiting before canceling t2
(MainThread) canceling t2
(MainThread) done
(t1        ) worker running
```

10.3.7 Signaling Between Threads

Although the point of using multiple threads is to run separate operations concurrently, sometimes it is important to be able to synchronize the operations in two or more threads. Event objects are a simple way to communicate between threads safely. An Event manages an internal flag that callers can control with the set() and clear() methods. Other threads can use wait() to pause until the flag is set, effectively blocking progress until those threads are allowed to continue.

Listing 10.38: **threading_event.py**

```
import logging
import threading
import time


def wait_for_event(e):
    """Wait for the event to be set before doing anything"""
    logging.debug('wait_for_event starting')
    event_is_set = e.wait()
    logging.debug('event set: %s', event_is_set)


def wait_for_event_timeout(e, t):
    """Wait t seconds and then timeout"""
    while not e.is_set():
        logging.debug('wait_for_event_timeout starting')
        event_is_set = e.wait(t)
        logging.debug('event set: %s', event_is_set)
        if event_is_set:
            logging.debug('processing event')
        else:
            logging.debug('doing other work')


logging.basicConfig(
    level=logging.DEBUG,
    format='(%(threadName)-10s) %(message)s',
)

e = threading.Event()
t1 = threading.Thread(
    name='block',
    target=wait_for_event,
    args=(e,),
)
t1.start()

t2 = threading.Thread(
    name='nonblock',
```

```
        target=wait_for_event_timeout,
        args=(e, 2),
    )
    t2.start()

    logging.debug('Waiting before calling Event.set()')
    time.sleep(0.3)
    e.set()
    logging.debug('Event is set')
```

The `wait()` method takes an argument representing the number of seconds to wait for the event before timing out. It returns a boolean value indicating whether the event is set, so the caller knows why `wait()` returned. The `is_set()` method can be used separately on the event without fear of blocking.

In this example, `wait_for_event_timeout()` checks the event status without blocking indefinitely. The `wait_for_event()` blocks on the call to `wait()`, which does not return until the event status changes.

```
$ python3 threading_event.py

(block      ) wait_for_event starting
(nonblock   ) wait_for_event_timeout starting
(MainThread) Waiting before calling Event.set()
(MainThread) Event is set
(nonblock   ) event set: True
(nonblock   ) processing event
(block      ) event set: True
```

10.3.8   Controlling Access to Resources

In addition to synchronizing the operations of threads, it is important to be able to control access to shared resources to prevent corruption or missed data. Python's built-in data structures (e.g., lists, dictionaries) are thread-safe as a side effect of having atomic byte-codes for manipulating them (the global interpreter lock that protects Python's internal data structures is not released in the middle of an update). Other data structures implemented in Python, or simpler types like integers and floats, do not have that protection. To guard against simultaneous access to an object, use a `Lock` object.

Listing 10.39: `threading_lock.py`

```
import logging
import random
import threading
import time
```

```
class Counter:

    def __init__(self, start=0):
        self.lock = threading.Lock()
        self.value = start

    def increment(self):
        logging.debug('Waiting for lock')
        self.lock.acquire()
        try:
            logging.debug('Acquired lock')
            self.value = self.value + 1
        finally:
            self.lock.release()


def worker(c):
    for i in range(2):
        pause = random.random()
        logging.debug('Sleeping %0.02f', pause)
        time.sleep(pause)
        c.increment()
    logging.debug('Done')


logging.basicConfig(
    level=logging.DEBUG,
    format='(%(threadName)-10s) %(message)s',
)

counter = Counter()
for i in range(2):
    t = threading.Thread(target=worker, args=(counter,))
    t.start()

logging.debug('Waiting for worker threads')
main_thread = threading.main_thread()
for t in threading.enumerate():
    if t is not main_thread:
        t.join()
logging.debug('Counter: %d', counter.value)
```

In this example, the worker() function increments a Counter instance, which manages a Lock to prevent two threads from changing its internal state at the same time. If the Lock was not used, a change to the value attribute might potentially be missed.

```
$ python3 threading_lock.py

(Thread-1  ) Sleeping 0.18
(Thread-2  ) Sleeping 0.93
(MainThread) Waiting for worker threads
(Thread-1  ) Waiting for lock
(Thread-1  ) Acquired lock
(Thread-1  ) Sleeping 0.11
(Thread-1  ) Waiting for lock
(Thread-1  ) Acquired lock
(Thread-1  ) Done
(Thread-2  ) Waiting for lock
(Thread-2  ) Acquired lock
(Thread-2  ) Sleeping 0.81
(Thread-2  ) Waiting for lock
(Thread-2  ) Acquired lock
(Thread-2  ) Done
(MainThread) Counter: 4
```

To determine whether another thread has acquired the lock without holding up the current thread, pass `False` for the `blocking` argument to `acquire()`. In the next example, `worker()` tries to acquire the lock three separate times and counts how many attempts it has to make to do so. In the meantime, `lock_holder()` cycles between holding and releasing the lock, with short pauses in each state used to simulate load.

Listing 10.40: **threading_lock_noblock.py**

```python
import logging
import threading
import time


def lock_holder(lock):
    logging.debug('Starting')
    while True:
        lock.acquire()
        try:
            logging.debug('Holding')
            time.sleep(0.5)
        finally:
            logging.debug('Not holding')
            lock.release()
        time.sleep(0.5)


def worker(lock):
    logging.debug('Starting')
    num_tries = 0
```

```
        num_acquires = 0
        while num_acquires < 3:
            time.sleep(0.5)
            logging.debug('Trying to acquire')
            have_it = lock.acquire(0)
            try:
                num_tries += 1
                if have_it:
                    logging.debug('Iteration %d: Acquired',
                                  num_tries)
                    num_acquires += 1
                else:
                    logging.debug('Iteration %d: Not acquired',
                                  num_tries)
            finally:
                if have_it:
                    lock.release()
        logging.debug('Done after %d iterations', num_tries)


logging.basicConfig(
    level=logging.DEBUG,
    format='(%(threadName)-10s) %(message)s',
)

lock = threading.Lock()

holder = threading.Thread(
    target=lock_holder,
    args=(lock,),
    name='LockHolder',
    daemon=True,
)
holder.start()

worker = threading.Thread(
    target=worker,
    args=(lock,),
    name='Worker',
)
worker.start()
```

It takes worker() more than three iterations to acquire the lock three separate times.

```
$ python3 threading_lock_noblock.py

(LockHolder) Starting
(LockHolder) Holding
(Worker    ) Starting
```

```
(LockHolder) Not holding
(Worker    ) Trying to acquire
(Worker    ) Iteration 1: Acquired
(LockHolder) Holding
(Worker    ) Trying to acquire
(Worker    ) Iteration 2: Not acquired
(LockHolder) Not holding
(Worker    ) Trying to acquire
(Worker    ) Iteration 3: Acquired
(LockHolder) Holding
(Worker    ) Trying to acquire
(Worker    ) Iteration 4: Not acquired
(LockHolder) Not holding
(Worker    ) Trying to acquire
(Worker    ) Iteration 5: Acquired
(Worker    ) Done after 5 iterations
```

10.3.8.1   Re-entrant Locks

Normal `Lock` objects cannot be acquired more than once, even by the same thread. If a lock is accessed by more than one function in the same call chain, undesirable side effects may occur.

Listing 10.41: `threading_lock_reacquire.py`

```python
import threading

lock = threading.Lock()

print('First try :', lock.acquire())
print('Second try:', lock.acquire(0))
```

In this case, the second call to `acquire()` is given a zero timeout to prevent it from blocking because the lock has been obtained by the first call.

```
$ python3 threading_lock_reacquire.py

First try : True
Second try: False
```

In a situation where separate code from the same thread needs to "reacquire" the lock, use an `RLock` instead.

Listing 10.42: `threading_rlock.py`

```python
import threading

lock = threading.RLock()
```

```
print('First try :', lock.acquire())
print('Second try:', lock.acquire(0))
```

The only change to the code from the previous example was substituting RLock for Lock.

```
$ python3 threading_rlock.py

First try : True
Second try: True
```

10.3.8.2 Locks as Context Managers

Locks implement the context manager API and are compatible with the with statement. Using with removes the need to explicitly acquire and release the lock.

Listing 10.43: **threading_lock_with.py**

```
import threading
import logging


def worker_with(lock):
    with lock:
        logging.debug('Lock acquired via with')


def worker_no_with(lock):
    lock.acquire()
    try:
        logging.debug('Lock acquired directly')
    finally:
        lock.release()


logging.basicConfig(
    level=logging.DEBUG,
    format='(%(threadName)-10s) %(message)s',
)

lock = threading.Lock()
w = threading.Thread(target=worker_with, args=(lock,))
nw = threading.Thread(target=worker_no_with, args=(lock,))

w.start()
nw.start()
```

The two functions worker_with() and worker_no_with() manage the lock in equivalent ways.

```
$ python3 threading_lock_with.py

(Thread-1  ) Lock acquired via with
(Thread-2  ) Lock acquired directly
```

10.3.9   Synchronizing Threads

In addition to using Events, another way of synchronizing threads is by using a Condition object. Because the Condition uses a Lock, it can be tied to a shared resource, allowing multiple threads to wait for the resource to be updated. In the next example, the consumer() threads wait for the Condition to be set before continuing. The producer() thread is responsible for setting the condition and notifying the other threads that they can continue.

Listing 10.44: **threading_condition.py**

```
import logging
import threading
import time


def consumer(cond):
    """wait for the condition and use the resource"""
    logging.debug('Starting consumer thread')
    with cond:
        cond.wait()
        logging.debug('Resource is available to consumer')


def producer(cond):
    """set up the resource to be used by the consumer"""
    logging.debug('Starting producer thread')
    with cond:
        logging.debug('Making resource available')
        cond.notifyAll()


logging.basicConfig(
    level=logging.DEBUG,
    format='%(asctime)s (%(threadName)-2s) %(message)s',
)

condition = threading.Condition()
c1 = threading.Thread(name='c1', target=consumer,
                      args=(condition,))
c2 = threading.Thread(name='c2', target=consumer,
                      args=(condition,))
p = threading.Thread(name='p', target=producer,
                     args=(condition,))
```

```
c1.start()
time.sleep(0.2)
c2.start()
time.sleep(0.2)
p.start()
```

The threads use `with` to acquire the lock associated with the `Condition`. Using the `acquire()` and `release()` methods explicitly also works.

```
$ python3 threading_condition.py

2016-07-10 10:45:28,170 (c1) Starting consumer thread
2016-07-10 10:45:28,376 (c2) Starting consumer thread
2016-07-10 10:45:28,581 (p ) Starting producer thread
2016-07-10 10:45:28,581 (p ) Making resource available
2016-07-10 10:45:28,582 (c1) Resource is available to consumer
2016-07-10 10:45:28,582 (c2) Resource is available to consumer
```

Barriers are another thread synchronization mechanism. A `Barrier` establishes a control point, and all participating threads then block until all of the participating "parties" have reached that point. With this approach, threads can start up separately and then pause until they are all ready to proceed.

Listing 10.45: **threading_barrier.py**

```python
import threading
import time


def worker(barrier):
    print(threading.current_thread().name,
          'waiting for barrier with {} others'.format(
              barrier.n_waiting))
    worker_id = barrier.wait()
    print(threading.current_thread().name, 'after barrier',
          worker_id)


NUM_THREADS = 3

barrier = threading.Barrier(NUM_THREADS)

threads = [
    threading.Thread(
        name='worker-%s' % i,
        target=worker,
        args=(barrier,),
    )
    for i in range(NUM_THREADS)
]
```

```
for t in threads:
    print(t.name, 'starting')
    t.start()
    time.sleep(0.1)

for t in threads:
    t.join()
```

In this example, the `Barrier` is configured to block until three threads are waiting. When the condition is met, all of the threads are released past the control point at the same time. The return value from `wait()` indicates the number of the party being released, and can be used to limit some threads from taking an action such as cleaning up a shared resource.

```
$ python3 threading_barrier.py

worker-0 starting
worker-0 waiting for barrier with 0 others
worker-1 starting
worker-1 waiting for barrier with 1 others
worker-2 starting
worker-2 waiting for barrier with 2 others
worker-2 after barrier 2
worker-0 after barrier 0
worker-1 after barrier 1
```

The `abort()` method of `Barrier` causes all of the waiting threads to receive a `BrokenBarrierError`. This allows threads to clean up if processing stops while they are blocked on `wait()`.

Listing 10.46: threading_barrier_abort.py

```
import threading
import time


def worker(barrier):
    print(threading.current_thread().name,
          'waiting for barrier with {} others'.format(
              barrier.n_waiting))
    try:
        worker_id = barrier.wait()
    except threading.BrokenBarrierError:
        print(threading.current_thread().name, 'aborting')
    else:
        print(threading.current_thread().name, 'after barrier',
              worker_id)
```

```
NUM_THREADS = 3

barrier = threading.Barrier(NUM_THREADS + 1)

threads = [
    threading.Thread(
        name='worker-%s' % i,
        target=worker,
        args=(barrier,),
    )
    for i in range(NUM_THREADS)
]

for t in threads:
    print(t.name, 'starting')
    t.start()
    time.sleep(0.1)

barrier.abort()

for t in threads:
    t.join()
```

This example configures the `Barrier` to expect one more participating thread than is actually started so that processing in all of the threads is blocked. The `abort()` call raises an exception in each blocked thread.

```
$ python3 threading_barrier_abort.py

worker-0 starting
worker-0 waiting for barrier with 0 others
worker-1 starting
worker-1 waiting for barrier with 1 others
worker-2 starting
worker-2 waiting for barrier with 2 others
worker-0 aborting
worker-2 aborting
worker-1 aborting
```

10.3.10   Limiting Concurrent Access to Resources

Sometimes it is useful to allow more than one worker access to a resource at a time, while still limiting the overall number. For example, a connection pool might support a fixed number of simultaneous connections, or a network application might support a fixed number of concurrent downloads. A `Semaphore` is one way to manage those connections.

Listing 10.47: **threading_semaphore.py**

```python
import logging
import random
import threading
import time


class ActivePool:

    def __init__(self):
        super(ActivePool, self).__init__()
        self.active = []
        self.lock = threading.Lock()

    def makeActive(self, name):
        with self.lock:
            self.active.append(name)
            logging.debug('Running: %s', self.active)

    def makeInactive(self, name):
        with self.lock:
            self.active.remove(name)
            logging.debug('Running: %s', self.active)


def worker(s, pool):
    logging.debug('Waiting to join the pool')
    with s:
        name = threading.current_thread().getName()
        pool.makeActive(name)
        time.sleep(0.1)
        pool.makeInactive(name)


logging.basicConfig(
    level=logging.DEBUG,
    format='%(asctime)s (%(threadName)-2s) %(message)s',
)

pool = ActivePool()
s = threading.Semaphore(2)
for i in range(4):
    t = threading.Thread(
        target=worker,
        name=str(i),
        args=(s, pool),
    )
    t.start()
```

In this example, the `ActivePool` class simply serves as a convenient way to track which threads are able to run at a given moment. A real resource pool would allocate a connection or some other value to the newly active thread, and reclaim the value when the thread is done. Here, it is just used to hold the names of the active threads to show that at most two are running concurrently.

```
$ python3 threading_semaphore.py

2016-07-10 10:45:29,398 (0 ) Waiting to join the pool
2016-07-10 10:45:29,398 (0 ) Running: ['0']
2016-07-10 10:45:29,399 (1 ) Waiting to join the pool
2016-07-10 10:45:29,399 (1 ) Running: ['0', '1']
2016-07-10 10:45:29,399 (2 ) Waiting to join the pool
2016-07-10 10:45:29,399 (3 ) Waiting to join the pool
2016-07-10 10:45:29,501 (1 ) Running: ['0']
2016-07-10 10:45:29,501 (0 ) Running: []
2016-07-10 10:45:29,502 (3 ) Running: ['3']
2016-07-10 10:45:29,502 (2 ) Running: ['3', '2']
2016-07-10 10:45:29,607 (3 ) Running: ['2']
2016-07-10 10:45:29,608 (2 ) Running: []
```

10.3.11 Thread Specific Data

While some resources need to be locked so multiple threads can use them, others need to be protected so that they are hidden from threads that do not own them. The `local()` class creates an object capable of hiding values from view in separate threads.

Listing 10.48: threading_local.py

```python
import random
import threading
import logging


def show_value(data):
    try:
        val = data.value
    except AttributeError:
        logging.debug('No value yet')
    else:
        logging.debug('value=%s', val)


def worker(data):
    show_value(data)
    data.value = random.randint(1, 100)
    show_value(data)
```

```
logging.basicConfig(
    level=logging.DEBUG,
    format='(%(threadName)-10s) %(message)s',
)

local_data = threading.local()
show_value(local_data)
local_data.value = 1000
show_value(local_data)

for i in range(2):
    t = threading.Thread(target=worker, args=(local_data,))
    t.start()
```

The attribute `local_data.value` is not present for any thread until it is set in that thread.

```
$ python3 threading_local.py

(MainThread) No value yet
(MainThread) value=1000
(Thread-1  ) No value yet
(Thread-1  ) value=33
(Thread-2  ) No value yet
(Thread-2  ) value=74
```

To initialize the settings so all threads start with the same value, use a subclass and set the attributes in `__init__()`.

Listing 10.49: **threading_local_defaults.py**

```
import random
import threading
import logging


def show_value(data):
    try:
        val = data.value
    except AttributeError:
        logging.debug('No value yet')
    else:
        logging.debug('value=%s', val)


def worker(data):
    show_value(data)
    data.value = random.randint(1, 100)
    show_value(data)
```

```
class MyLocal(threading.local):

    def __init__(self, value):
        super().__init__()
        logging.debug('Initializing %r', self)
        self.value = value


logging.basicConfig(
    level=logging.DEBUG,
    format='(%(threadName)-10s) %(message)s',
)

local_data = MyLocal(1000)
show_value(local_data)

for i in range(2):
    t = threading.Thread(target=worker, args=(local_data,))
    t.start()
```

`__init__()` is invoked on the same object (note the `id()` value) once in each thread to set the default values.

```
$ python3 threading_local_defaults.py

(MainThread) Initializing <__main__.MyLocal object at
0x101c6c288>
(MainThread) value=1000
(Thread-1  ) Initializing <__main__.MyLocal object at
0x101c6c288>
(Thread-1  ) value=1000
(Thread-1  ) value=18
(Thread-2  ) Initializing <__main__.MyLocal object at
0x101c6c288>
(Thread-2  ) value=1000
(Thread-2  ) value=77
```

TIP

Related Reading

- Standard library documentation for `threading`.[6]
- Python 2 to 3 porting notes for `threading` (page 1364).
- `thread`: Lower-level thread API.

---

[6] https://docs.python.org/3.5/library/threading.html

- Queue: Thread-safe queue, useful for passing messages between threads.
- multiprocessing (page 586): An API for working with processes that mirrors the threading API.

10.4 multiprocessing: Manage Processes Like Threads

The multiprocessing module includes an API for dividing work between multiple processes based on the API for threading (page 560). In some cases, multiprocessing is a drop-in replacement, and can be used instead of threading to take advantage of multiple CPU cores and thereby avoid computational bottlenecks associated with Python's global interpreter lock.

Due to the similarity of the multiprocessing and threading modules, the first few examples here are modified from the threading examples. Features provided by multiprocessing but not available in threading are covered later.

10.4.1 multiprocessing Basics

The simplest way to spawn a second process is to instantiate a Process object with a target function and then call start() to let it begin working.

Listing 10.50: **multiprocessing_simple.py**

```
import multiprocessing


def worker():
    """worker function"""
    print('Worker')


if __name__ == '__main__':
    jobs = []
    for i in range(5):
        p = multiprocessing.Process(target=worker)
        jobs.append(p)
        p.start()
```

The output includes the word "Worker" printed five times, although it may not come out entirely clean, depending on the order of execution, because each process is competing for access to the output stream.

```
$ python3 multiprocessing_simple.py

Worker
Worker
```

```
Worker
Worker
Worker
```

In most cases, it is more useful to spawn a process with arguments to tell that process which work to do. Unlike with `threading`, to pass arguments to a `multiprocessing` `Process`, the arguments must be serialized using `pickle` (page 396). The next example passes each worker a number to be printed.

Listing 10.51: `multiprocessing_simpleargs.py`

```python
import multiprocessing


def worker(num):
    """thread worker function"""
    print('Worker:', num)


if __name__ == '__main__':
    jobs = []
    for i in range(5):
        p = multiprocessing.Process(target=worker, args=(i,))
        jobs.append(p)
        p.start()
```

The integer argument is now included in the message printed by each worker.

```
$ python3 multiprocessing_simpleargs.py

Worker: 0
Worker: 1
Worker: 2
Worker: 3
Worker: 4
```

10.4.2 Importable Target Functions

One difference between the `threading` and `multiprocessing` examples is the extra protection for `__main__` included in the `multiprocessing` examples. Due to the way the new processes are started, the child process needs to be able to import the script containing the target function. Wrapping the main part of the application in a check for `__main__` ensures that it does not run recursively in each child as the module is imported. Another approach is to import the target function from a separate script. For example, `multiprocessing_import_main.py` uses a worker function defined in a second module.

Listing 10.52: `multiprocessing_import_main.py`

```python
import multiprocessing
import multiprocessing_import_worker

if __name__ == '__main__':
    jobs = []
    for i in range(5):
        p = multiprocessing.Process(
            target=multiprocessing_import_worker.worker,
        )
        jobs.append(p)
        p.start()
```

The worker function is defined in `multiprocessing_import_worker.py`.

Listing 10.53: `multiprocessing_import_worker.py`

```python
def worker():
    """worker function"""
    print('Worker')
    return
```

Calling the main program produces output similar to the first example.

```
$ python3 multiprocessing_import_main.py

Worker
Worker
Worker
Worker
Worker
```

10.4.3 Determining the Current Process

Passing arguments to identify or name the process is both cumbersome and unnecessary. Each `Process` instance has a name with a default value that can be changed as the process is created. Naming processes is useful for keeping track of them, especially in applications where multiple types of processes are running simultaneously.

Listing 10.54: `multiprocessing_names.py`

```python
import multiprocessing
import time


def worker():
    name = multiprocessing.current_process().name
    print(name, 'Starting')
```

```
        time.sleep(2)
        print(name, 'Exiting')


def my_service():
    name = multiprocessing.current_process().name
    print(name, 'Starting')
    time.sleep(3)
    print(name, 'Exiting')


if __name__ == '__main__':
    service = multiprocessing.Process(
        name='my_service',
        target=my_service,
    )
    worker_1 = multiprocessing.Process(
        name='worker 1',
        target=worker,
    )
    worker_2 = multiprocessing.Process(  # Default name
        target=worker,
    )

    worker_1.start()
    worker_2.start()
    service.start()
```

The debug output includes the name of the current process on each line. The lines with
`Process-3` in the name column correspond to the unnamed process `worker_1`.

```
$ python3 multiprocessing_names.py

worker 1 Starting
worker 1 Exiting
Process-3 Starting
Process-3 Exiting
my_service Starting
my_service Exiting
```

10.4.4 Daemon Processes

By default, the main program will not exit until all of the children have exited. Sometimes
starting a background process that runs without blocking the main program from exiting
is useful, such as in services that lack an easy way to interrupt the worker, or when letting
it die in the middle of its work does not cause the loss or corruption of data (e.g., a task
that generates "heartbeats" for a service monitoring tool).

To mark a process as a daemon, set its `daemon` attribute to `True`. The default is for processes to not be daemons.

Listing 10.55: <code>multiprocessing_daemon.py</code>

```python
import multiprocessing
import time
import sys


def daemon():
    p = multiprocessing.current_process()
    print('Starting:', p.name, p.pid)
    sys.stdout.flush()
    time.sleep(2)
    print('Exiting :', p.name, p.pid)
    sys.stdout.flush()


def non_daemon():
    p = multiprocessing.current_process()
    print('Starting:', p.name, p.pid)
    sys.stdout.flush()
    print('Exiting :', p.name, p.pid)
    sys.stdout.flush()


if __name__ == '__main__':
    d = multiprocessing.Process(
        name='daemon',
        target=daemon,
    )
    d.daemon = True

    n = multiprocessing.Process(
        name='non-daemon',
        target=non_daemon,
    )
    n.daemon = False

    d.start()
    time.sleep(1)
    n.start()
```

The output does not include the "Exiting" message from the daemon process, since all of the non-daemon processes (including the main program) exit before the daemon process wakes up from its 2-second sleep.

```
$ python3 multiprocessing_daemon.py

Starting: daemon 70880
Starting: non-daemon 70881
Exiting : non-daemon 70881
```

The daemon process is terminated automatically before the main program exits, which avoids the case in which orphaned processes are left running. This behavior can be verified by looking for the process ID value that is printed when the program runs, and then checking for that process with a command such as ps.

10.4.5 Waiting for Processes

To wait until a process has completed its work and exited, use the join() method.

Listing 10.56: **multiprocessing_daemon_join.py**

```python
import multiprocessing
import time
import sys


def daemon():
    name = multiprocessing.current_process().name
    print('Starting:', name)
    time.sleep(2)
    print('Exiting :', name)


def non_daemon():
    name = multiprocessing.current_process().name
    print('Starting:', name)
    print('Exiting :', name)


if __name__ == '__main__':
    d = multiprocessing.Process(
        name='daemon',
        target=daemon,
    )
    d.daemon = True

    n = multiprocessing.Process(
        name='non-daemon',
        target=non_daemon,
    )
    n.daemon = False
```

```
    d.start()
    time.sleep(1)
    n.start()

    d.join()
    n.join()
```

Since the main process waits for the daemon to exit using `join()`, the "Exiting" message is printed this time.

```
$ python3 multiprocessing_daemon_join.py

Starting: non-daemon
Exiting : non-daemon
Starting: daemon
Exiting : daemon
```

By default, `join()` blocks indefinitely. Alternatively, a timeout argument (a float representing the number of seconds to wait for the process to become inactive) may be passed to the module. If the process does not complete within the timeout period, `join()` returns anyway.

Listing 10.57: multiprocessing_daemon_join_timeout.py

```python
import multiprocessing
import time
import sys


def daemon():
    name = multiprocessing.current_process().name
    print('Starting:', name)
    time.sleep(2)
    print('Exiting :', name)


def non_daemon():
    name = multiprocessing.current_process().name
    print('Starting:', name)
    print('Exiting :', name)


if __name__ == '__main__':
    d = multiprocessing.Process(
        name='daemon',
        target=daemon,
    )
    d.daemon = True
```

```
    n = multiprocessing.Process(
        name='non-daemon',
        target=non_daemon,
    )
    n.daemon = False

    d.start()
    n.start()

    d.join(1)
    print('d.is_alive()', d.is_alive())
    n.join()
```

Since the timeout passed is less than the amount of time the daemon sleeps, the process is still "alive" after join() returns.

```
$ python3 multiprocessing_daemon_join_timeout.py

Starting: non-daemon
Exiting : non-daemon
d.is_alive() True
```

10.4.6 Terminating Processes

Although it is better to use the *poison pill* method of signaling to a process that it should exit [see Section 10.4.10, "Passing Messages to Processes" (page 598), later in this chapter], if a process appears hung or deadlocked, it can be useful to be able to kill it forcibly. Calling terminate() on a process object kills the child process.

Listing 10.58: **multiprocessing_terminate.py**

```
import multiprocessing
import time


def slow_worker():
    print('Starting worker')
    time.sleep(0.1)
    print('Finished worker')


if __name__ == '__main__':
    p = multiprocessing.Process(target=slow_worker)
    print('BEFORE:', p, p.is_alive())

    p.start()
    print('DURING:', p, p.is_alive())
```

```
    p.terminate()
    print('TERMINATED:', p, p.is_alive())

    p.join()
    print('JOINED:', p, p.is_alive())
```

NOTE

It is important to join() the process after terminating it, so as to give the process management code enough time to update the status of the object to reflect the termination.

```
$ python3 multiprocessing_terminate.py

BEFORE: <Process(Process-1, initial)> False
DURING: <Process(Process-1, started)> True
TERMINATED: <Process(Process-1, started)> True
JOINED: <Process(Process-1, stopped[SIGTERM])> False
```

10.4.7   Process Exit Status

The status code produced when the process exits can be accessed via the exitcode attribute. The ranges allowed for this attribute are listed in Table 10.1.

Listing 10.59: **multiprocessing_exitcode.py**

```
import multiprocessing
import sys
import time


def exit_error():
    sys.exit(1)


def exit_ok():
    return
```

Table 10.1: Multiprocessing Exit Codes

Exit Code	Meaning
== 0	No error was produced
> 0	The process had an error, and exited with that code
< 0	The process was killed with a signal of -1 * exitcode

```
def return_value():
    return 1


def raises():
    raise RuntimeError('There was an error!')


def terminated():
    time.sleep(3)


if __name__ == '__main__':
    jobs = []
    funcs = [
        exit_error,
        exit_ok,
        return_value,
        raises,
        terminated,
    ]
    for f in funcs:
        print('Starting process for', f.__name__)
        j = multiprocessing.Process(target=f, name=f.__name__)
        jobs.append(j)
        j.start()

    jobs[-1].terminate()

    for j in jobs:
        j.join()
        print('{:>15}.exitcode = {}'.format(j.name, j.exitcode))
```

Processes that raise an exception automatically get an exitcode of 1.

```
$ python3 multiprocessing_exitcode.py

Starting process for exit_error
Starting process for exit_ok
Starting process for return_value
Starting process for raises
Starting process for terminated
Process raises:
Traceback (most recent call last):
  File ".../lib/python3.5/multiprocessing/process.py", line 249,
in _bootstrap
    self.run()
```

```
    File ".../lib/python3.5/multiprocessing/process.py", line 93,
in run
        self._target(*self._args, **self._kwargs)
    File "multiprocessing_exitcode.py", line 28, in raises
        raise RuntimeError('There was an error!')
RuntimeError: There was an error!
       exit_error.exitcode = 1
          exit_ok.exitcode = 0
     return_value.exitcode = 0
           raises.exitcode = 1
       terminated.exitcode = -15
```

10.4.8   Logging

When debugging concurrency issues, it can be useful to have access to the internals of
the objects provided by multiprocessing. A convenient module-level function is available
to enable logging; it is called log_to_stderr(). It sets up a logger object using logging
(page 980) and adds a handler so that log messages are sent to the standard error channel.

Listing 10.60: `multiprocessing_log_to_stderr.py`

```python
import multiprocessing
import logging
import sys


def worker():
    print('Doing some work')
    sys.stdout.flush()


if __name__ == '__main__':
    multiprocessing.log_to_stderr(logging.DEBUG)
    p = multiprocessing.Process(target=worker)
    p.start()
    p.join()
```

By default, the logging level is set to NOTSET, meaning that no messages are produced.
Pass a different level to initialize the logger to the level of detail desired.

```
$ python3 multiprocessing_log_to_stderr.py

[INFO/Process-1] child process calling self.run()
Doing some work
[INFO/Process-1] process shutting down
[DEBUG/Process-1] running all "atexit" finalizers with priority
>= 0
```

```
[DEBUG/Process-1] running the remaining "atexit" finalizers
[INFO/Process-1] process exiting with exitcode 0
[INFO/MainProcess] process shutting down
[DEBUG/MainProcess] running all "atexit" finalizers with
priority >= 0
[DEBUG/MainProcess] running the remaining "atexit" finalizers
```

To manipulate the logger directly (change its level setting or add handlers), use get_logger().

Listing 10.61: **multiprocessing_get_logger.py**

```python
import multiprocessing
import logging
import sys


def worker():
    print('Doing some work')
    sys.stdout.flush()


if __name__ == '__main__':
    multiprocessing.log_to_stderr()
    logger = multiprocessing.get_logger()
    logger.setLevel(logging.INFO)
    p = multiprocessing.Process(target=worker)
    p.start()
    p.join()
```

The logger can also be configured through the logging configuration file API, using the name multiprocessing.

```
$ python3 multiprocessing_get_logger.py

[INFO/Process-1] child process calling self.run()
Doing some work
[INFO/Process-1] process shutting down
[INFO/Process-1] process exiting with exitcode 0
[INFO/MainProcess] process shutting down
```

10.4.9 Subclassing Process

Although the simplest way to start a job in a separate process is to use Process and pass a target function, it is also possible to use a custom subclass.

Listing 10.62: **multiprocessing_subclass.py**

```
import multiprocessing


class Worker(multiprocessing.Process):

    def run(self):
        print('In {}'.format(self.name))
        return


if __name__ == '__main__':
    jobs = []
    for i in range(5):
        p = Worker()
        jobs.append(p)
        p.start()
    for j in jobs:
        j.join()
```

The derived class should override run() to do its work.

```
$ python3 multiprocessing_subclass.py

In Worker-1
In Worker-2
In Worker-3
In Worker-4
In Worker-5
```

10.4.10   Passing Messages to Processes

As with threads, a common use pattern for multiple processes is to divide a job up among several workers to run in parallel. Effective use of multiple processes usually requires some communication between them, so that work can be divided and results can be aggregated. A simple way to communicate between processes with multiprocessing is to use a Queue to pass messages back and forth. Any object that can be serialized with pickle (page 396) can pass through a Queue.

Listing 10.63: **multiprocessing_queue.py**

```
import multiprocessing


class MyFancyClass:

    def __init__(self, name):
        self.name = name
```

```
        def do_something(self):
            proc_name = multiprocessing.current_process().name
            print('Doing something fancy in {} for {}!'.format(
                proc_name, self.name))


    def worker(q):
        obj = q.get()
        obj.do_something()


    if __name__ == '__main__':
        queue = multiprocessing.Queue()

        p = multiprocessing.Process(target=worker, args=(queue,))
        p.start()

        queue.put(MyFancyClass('Fancy Dan'))

        # Wait for the worker to finish.
        queue.close()
        queue.join_thread()
        p.join()
```

This short example passes just a single message to a single worker, then the main process
waits for the worker to finish.

```
$ python3 multiprocessing_queue.py

Doing something fancy in Process-1 for Fancy Dan!
```

A more complex example shows how to manage several workers that are consuming
data from a `JoinableQueue` and passing results back to the parent process. The *poison pill*
technique is used to stop these workers. After setting up the real tasks, the main program
adds one "stop" value per worker to the job queue. When a worker encounters the special
value, it breaks out of its processing loop. The main process uses the task queue's `join()`
method to wait for all of the tasks to finish before processing the results.

Listing 10.64: **multiprocessing_producer_consumer.py**

```
import multiprocessing
import time


class Consumer(multiprocessing.Process):

    def __init__(self, task_queue, result_queue):
        multiprocessing.Process.__init__(self)
```

```
        self.task_queue = task_queue
        self.result_queue = result_queue

    def run(self):
        proc_name = self.name
        while True:
            next_task = self.task_queue.get()
            if next_task is None:
                # Poison pill means shutdown.
                print('{}: Exiting'.format(proc_name))
                self.task_queue.task_done()
                break
            print('{}: {}'.format(proc_name, next_task))
            answer = next_task()
            self.task_queue.task_done()
            self.result_queue.put(answer)


class Task:

    def __init__(self, a, b):
        self.a = a
        self.b = b

    def __call__(self):
        time.sleep(0.1)  # Pretend to take time to do the work.
        return '{self.a} * {self.b} = {product}'.format(
            self=self, product=self.a * self.b)

    def __str__(self):
        return '{self.a} * {self.b}'.format(self=self)


if __name__ == '__main__':
    # Establish communication queues.
    tasks = multiprocessing.JoinableQueue()
    results = multiprocessing.Queue()

    # Start consumers.
    num_consumers = multiprocessing.cpu_count() * 2
    print('Creating {} consumers'.format(num_consumers))
    consumers = [
        Consumer(tasks, results)
        for i in range(num_consumers)
    ]
    for w in consumers:
        w.start()
```

```
    # Enqueue jobs.
    num_jobs = 10
    for i in range(num_jobs):
        tasks.put(Task(i, i))

    # Add a poison pill for each consumer.
    for i in range(num_consumers):
        tasks.put(None)

    # Wait for all of the tasks to finish.
    tasks.join()

    # Start printing results.
    while num_jobs:
        result = results.get()
        print('Result:', result)
        num_jobs -= 1
```

Although the jobs enter the queue in order, their execution occurs in parallel. Thus, there is no guarantee about the order in which they will be completed.

```
$ python3 -u multiprocessing_producer_consumer.py

Creating 8 consumers
Consumer-1: 0 * 0
Consumer-2: 1 * 1
Consumer-3: 2 * 2
Consumer-4: 3 * 3
Consumer-5: 4 * 4
Consumer-6: 5 * 5
Consumer-7: 6 * 6
Consumer-8: 7 * 7
Consumer-3: 8 * 8
Consumer-7: 9 * 9
Consumer-4: Exiting
Consumer-1: Exiting
Consumer-2: Exiting
Consumer-5: Exiting
Consumer-6: Exiting
Consumer-8: Exiting
Consumer-7: Exiting
Consumer-3: Exiting
Result: 6 * 6 = 36
Result: 2 * 2 = 4
Result: 3 * 3 = 9
Result: 0 * 0 = 0
```

```
Result: 1 * 1 = 1
Result: 7 * 7 = 49
Result: 4 * 4 = 16
Result: 5 * 5 = 25
Result: 8 * 8 = 64
Result: 9 * 9 = 81
```

10.4.11   Signaling Between Processes

The Event class provides a simple way to communicate state information between processes. An event can be toggled between set and unset states. Users of the event object can wait for its state to change from unset to set, using an optional timeout value.

Listing 10.65: multiprocessing_event.py

```python
import multiprocessing
import time


def wait_for_event(e):
    """Wait for the event to be set before doing anything"""
    print('wait_for_event: starting')
    e.wait()
    print('wait_for_event: e.is_set()->', e.is_set())


def wait_for_event_timeout(e, t):
    """Wait t seconds and then timeout"""
    print('wait_for_event_timeout: starting')
    e.wait(t)
    print('wait_for_event_timeout: e.is_set()->', e.is_set())


if __name__ == '__main__':
    e = multiprocessing.Event()
    w1 = multiprocessing.Process(
        name='block',
        target=wait_for_event,
        args=(e,),
    )
    w1.start()

    w2 = multiprocessing.Process(
        name='nonblock',
        target=wait_for_event_timeout,
        args=(e, 2),
    )
    w2.start()
```

```
print('main: waiting before calling Event.set()')
time.sleep(3)
e.set()
print('main: event is set')
```

When wait() times out, it returns without an error. The caller is responsible for checking the state of the event using is_set().

```
$ python3 -u multiprocessing_event.py

main: waiting before calling Event.set()
wait_for_event: starting
wait_for_event_timeout: starting
wait_for_event_timeout: e.is_set()-> False
main: event is set
wait_for_event: e.is_set()-> True
```

10.4.12 Controlling Access to Resources

When a single resource needs to be shared between multiple processes, a Lock can be used to avoid conflicting accesses.

Listing 10.66: **multiprocessing_lock.py**

```
import multiprocessing
import sys


def worker_with(lock, stream):
    with lock:
        stream.write('Lock acquired via with\n')


def worker_no_with(lock, stream):
    lock.acquire()
    try:
        stream.write('Lock acquired directly\n')
    finally:
        lock.release()


lock = multiprocessing.Lock()
w = multiprocessing.Process(
    target=worker_with,
    args=(lock, sys.stdout),
)
nw = multiprocessing.Process(
    target=worker_no_with,
```

```
        args=(lock, sys.stdout),
    )

    w.start()
    nw.start()

    w.join()
    nw.join()
```

In this example, the messages printed to the console may be jumbled together if the two processes do not synchronize their accesses of the output stream with the lock.

```
$ python3 multiprocessing_lock.py

Lock acquired via with
Lock acquired directly
```

10.4.13 Synchronizing Operations

Condition objects can be used to synchronize parts of a workflow so that some run in parallel but others run sequentially, even if they are in separate processes.

Listing 10.67: `multiprocessing_condition.py`

```
import multiprocessing
import time


def stage_1(cond):
    """perform first stage of work,
    then notify stage_2 to continue
    """
    name = multiprocessing.current_process().name
    print('Starting', name)
    with cond:
        print('{} done and ready for stage 2'.format(name))
        cond.notify_all()


def stage_2(cond):
    """wait for the condition telling us stage_1 is done"""
    name = multiprocessing.current_process().name
    print('Starting', name)
    with cond:
        cond.wait()
        print('{} running'.format(name))
```

```python
if __name__ == '__main__':
    condition = multiprocessing.Condition()
    s1 = multiprocessing.Process(name='s1',
                                 target=stage_1,
                                 args=(condition,))
    s2_clients = [
        multiprocessing.Process(
            name='stage_2[{}]'.format(i),
            target=stage_2,
            args=(condition,),
        )
        for i in range(1, 3)
    ]

    for c in s2_clients:
        c.start()
        time.sleep(1)
    s1.start()

    s1.join()
    for c in s2_clients:
        c.join()
```

In this example, two processes run the second stage of a job in parallel, but only after the first stage is done.

```
$ python3 multiprocessing_condition.py

Starting s1
s1 done and ready for stage 2
Starting stage_2[2]
stage_2[2] running
Starting stage_2[1]
stage_2[1] running
```

10.4.14 Controlling Concurrent Access to Resources

Sometimes it is useful to allow multiple workers to access the same resource at the same time, while still limiting the overall number of workers with access. For example, a connection pool might support a fixed number of simultaneous connections, or a network application might support a fixed number of concurrent downloads. A Semaphore is one way to manage those connections.

Listing 10.68: **multiprocessing_semaphore.py**

```python
import random
import multiprocessing
import time
```

```python
class ActivePool:

    def __init__(self):
        super(ActivePool, self).__init__()
        self.mgr = multiprocessing.Manager()
        self.active = self.mgr.list()
        self.lock = multiprocessing.Lock()

    def makeActive(self, name):
        with self.lock:
            self.active.append(name)

    def makeInactive(self, name):
        with self.lock:
            self.active.remove(name)

    def __str__(self):
        with self.lock:
            return str(self.active)


def worker(s, pool):
    name = multiprocessing.current_process().name
    with s:
        pool.makeActive(name)
        print('Activating {} now running {}'.format(
            name, pool))
        time.sleep(random.random())
        pool.makeInactive(name)


if __name__ == '__main__':
    pool = ActivePool()
    s = multiprocessing.Semaphore(3)
    jobs = [
        multiprocessing.Process(
            target=worker,
            name=str(i),
            args=(s, pool),
        )
        for i in range(10)
    ]

    for j in jobs:
        j.start()

    while True:
        alive = 0
        for j in jobs:
```

```
            if j.is_alive():
                alive += 1
                j.join(timeout=0.1)
                print('Now running {}'.format(pool))
        if alive == 0:
            # All done
            break
```

In this example, the `ActivePool` class serves as a convenient way to track which processes are running at a given moment. A real resource pool would probably allocate a connection or some other value to the newly active process, and reclaim the value when the task is done. Here, the pool holds the names of the active processes and shows that only three are running concurrently.

```
$ python3 -u multiprocessing_semaphore.py

Activating 0 now running ['0', '1', '2']
Activating 1 now running ['0', '1', '2']
Activating 2 now running ['0', '1', '2']
Now running ['0', '1', '2']
Now running ['0', '1', '2']
Now running ['0', '1', '2']
Now running ['0', '1', '2']
Activating 3 now running ['0', '1', '3']
Activating 4 now running ['1', '3', '4']
Activating 6 now running ['1', '4', '6']
Now running ['1', '4', '6']
Now running ['1', '4', '6']
Activating 5 now running ['1', '4', '5']
Now running ['1', '4', '5']
Now running ['1', '4', '5']
Now running ['1', '4', '5']
Activating 8 now running ['4', '5', '8']
Now running ['4', '5', '8']
Now running ['4', '5', '8']
Now running ['4', '5', '8']
Now running ['4', '5', '8']
Now running ['4', '5', '8']
Activating 7 now running ['5', '8', '7']
Now running ['5', '8', '7']
Activating 9 now running ['8', '7', '9']
Now running ['8', '7', '9']
Now running ['8', '9']
Now running ['8', '9']
Now running ['9']
Now running ['9']
Now running ['9']
Now running ['9']
Now running []
```

10.4.15   Managing Shared State

In the previous example, the list of active processes is maintained centrally in the `ActivePool` instance via a special type of list object created by a `Manager`. The `Manager` is responsible for coordinating shared information state between all of its users.

Listing 10.69: `multiprocessing_manager_dict.py`

```
import multiprocessing
import pprint


def worker(d, key, value):
    d[key] = value


if __name__ == '__main__':
    mgr = multiprocessing.Manager()
    d = mgr.dict()
    jobs = [
        multiprocessing.Process(
            target=worker,
            args=(d, i, i * 2),
        )
        for i in range(10)
    ]
    for j in jobs:
        j.start()
    for j in jobs:
        j.join()
    print('Results:', d)
```

Because the list is created through the manager, it is shared and updates are seen in all processes. Dictionaries are also supported.

```
$ python3 multiprocessing_manager_dict.py

Results: {0: 0, 1: 2, 2: 4, 3: 6, 4: 8, 5: 10, 6: 12, 7: 14,
8: 16, 9: 18}
```

10.4.16   Shared Namespaces

In addition to dictionaries and lists, a `Manager` can create a shared `Namespace`.

Listing 10.70: `multiprocessing_namespaces.py`

```python
import multiprocessing


def producer(ns, event):
    ns.value = 'This is the value'
    event.set()


def consumer(ns, event):
    try:
        print('Before event: {}'.format(ns.value))
    except Exception as err:
        print('Before event, error:', str(err))
    event.wait()
    print('After event:', ns.value)


if __name__ == '__main__':
    mgr = multiprocessing.Manager()
    namespace = mgr.Namespace()
    event = multiprocessing.Event()
    p = multiprocessing.Process(
        target=producer,
        args=(namespace, event),
    )
    c = multiprocessing.Process(
        target=consumer,
        args=(namespace, event),
    )

    c.start()
    p.start()

    c.join()
    p.join()
```

Any named value added to the Namespace is visible to all of the clients that receive the Namespace instance.

```
$ python3 multiprocessing_namespaces.py

Before event, error: 'Namespace' object has no attribute 'value'
After event: This is the value
```

Updates to the contents of mutable values in the namespace are not propagated auto-matically, as shown in the next example.

Listing 10.71: **multiprocessing_namespaces_mutable.py**

```python
import multiprocessing


def producer(ns, event):
    # DOES NOT UPDATE GLOBAL VALUE!
    ns.my_list.append('This is the value')
    event.set()


def consumer(ns, event):
    print('Before event:', ns.my_list)
    event.wait()
    print('After event :', ns.my_list)


if __name__ == '__main__':
    mgr = multiprocessing.Manager()
    namespace = mgr.Namespace()
    namespace.my_list = []

    event = multiprocessing.Event()
    p = multiprocessing.Process(
        target=producer,
        args=(namespace, event),
    )
    c = multiprocessing.Process(
        target=consumer,
        args=(namespace, event),
    )

    c.start()
    p.start()

    c.join()
    p.join()
```

To update the list, attach it to the namespace object again.

```
$ python3 multiprocessing_namespaces_mutable.py

Before event: []
After event : []
```

10.4.17 Process Pools

The `Pool` class can be used to manage a fixed number of workers for simple cases where the work to be done can be broken up and distributed between workers independently. The return values from the jobs are collected and returned as a list. The pool arguments include the number of processes and a function to run when starting the task process (invoked once per child).

Listing 10.72: `multiprocessing_pool.py`

```
import multiprocessing


def do_calculation(data):
    return data * 2


def start_process():
    print('Starting', multiprocessing.current_process().name)


if __name__ == '__main__':
    inputs = list(range(10))
    print('Input   :', inputs)

    builtin_outputs = list(map(do_calculation, inputs))
    print('Built-in:', builtin_outputs)

    pool_size = multiprocessing.cpu_count() * 2
    pool = multiprocessing.Pool(
        processes=pool_size,
        initializer=start_process,
    )
    pool_outputs = pool.map(do_calculation, inputs)
    pool.close()  # No more tasks
    pool.join()  # Wrap up current tasks.

    print('Pool    :', pool_outputs)
```

The result of the `map()` method is functionally equivalent to the result of the built-in `map()`, except that individual tasks run in parallel. Since the pool processes its inputs in parallel, `close()` and `join()` can be used to synchronize the main process with the task processes, thereby ensuring proper cleanup.

```
$ python3 multiprocessing_pool.py

Input   : [0, 1, 2, 3, 4, 5, 6, 7, 8, 9]
Built-in: [0, 2, 4, 6, 8, 10, 12, 14, 16, 18]
```

```
Starting ForkPoolWorker-3
Starting ForkPoolWorker-4
Starting ForkPoolWorker-5
Starting ForkPoolWorker-6
Starting ForkPoolWorker-1
Starting ForkPoolWorker-7
Starting ForkPoolWorker-2
Starting ForkPoolWorker-8
Pool     : [0, 2, 4, 6, 8, 10, 12, 14, 16, 18]
```

By default, `Pool` creates a fixed number of worker processes and passes jobs to them until there are no more jobs. Setting the `maxtasksperchild` parameter tells the pool to restart a worker process after it has finished a few tasks, preventing long-running workers from consuming ever more system resources.

Listing 10.73: **multiprocessing_pool_maxtasksperchild.py**

```python
import multiprocessing


def do_calculation(data):
    return data * 2


def start_process():
    print('Starting', multiprocessing.current_process().name)


if __name__ == '__main__':
    inputs = list(range(10))
    print('Input   :', inputs)

    builtin_outputs = list(map(do_calculation, inputs))
    print('Built-in:', builtin_outputs)

    pool_size = multiprocessing.cpu_count() * 2
    pool = multiprocessing.Pool(
        processes=pool_size,
        initializer=start_process,
        maxtasksperchild=2,
    )
    pool_outputs = pool.map(do_calculation, inputs)
    pool.close()  # No more tasks
    pool.join()   # Wrap up current tasks.

    print('Pool    :', pool_outputs)
```

The pool restarts the workers when they have completed their allotted tasks, even if there is no more work. In the following output, eight workers are created, even though there are only 10 tasks, and each worker can complete two of them at a time.

```
$ python3 multiprocessing_pool_maxtasksperchild.py

Input   : [0, 1, 2, 3, 4, 5, 6, 7, 8, 9]
Built-in: [0, 2, 4, 6, 8, 10, 12, 14, 16, 18]
Starting ForkPoolWorker-1
Starting ForkPoolWorker-2
Starting ForkPoolWorker-4
Starting ForkPoolWorker-5
Starting ForkPoolWorker-6
Starting ForkPoolWorker-3
Starting ForkPoolWorker-7
Starting ForkPoolWorker-8
Pool    : [0, 2, 4, 6, 8, 10, 12, 14, 16, 18]
```

10.4.18   Implementing MapReduce

The `Pool` class can be used to create a simple single-server MapReduce implementation. Although it does not deliver the full benefits of distributed processing, this approach does illustrate how easy it is to break some problems down into distributable units of work.

In a MapReduce-based system, input data is broken down into chunks for processing by different worker instances. Each chunk of input data is *mapped* to an intermediate state using a simple transformation. The intermediate data is then collected together and partitioned based on a key value so that all of the related values are kept together. Finally, the partitioned data is *reduced* to a result set.

Listing 10.74: `multiprocessing_mapreduce.py`

```
import collections
import itertools
import multiprocessing


class SimpleMapReduce:

    def __init__(self, map_func, reduce_func, num_workers=None):
        """
        map_func

            Function to map inputs to intermediate data. Takes as
            argument one input value and returns a tuple with the
            key and a value to be reduced.
```

```
reduce_func

    Function to reduce partitioned version of intermediate
    data to final output. Takes as argument a key as
    produced by map_func and a sequence of the values
    associated with that key.

num_workers

    The number of workers to create in the pool. Defaults
    to the number of CPUs available on the current host.
    """
    self.map_func = map_func
    self.reduce_func = reduce_func
    self.pool = multiprocessing.Pool(num_workers)

def partition(self, mapped_values):
    """Organize the mapped values by their key.
    Returns an unsorted sequence of tuples with a key
    and a sequence of values.
    """
    partitioned_data = collections.defaultdict(list)
    for key, value in mapped_values:
        partitioned_data[key].append(value)
    return partitioned_data.items()

def __call__(self, inputs, chunksize=1):
    """Process the inputs through the map and reduce functions
    given.

    inputs
        An iterable containing the input data to be processed.

    chunksize=1
        The portion of the input data to hand to each worker.
        This can be used to tune performance during the mapping
        phase.
    """
    map_responses = self.pool.map(
        self.map_func,
        inputs,
        chunksize=chunksize,
    )
    partitioned_data = self.partition(
        itertools.chain(*map_responses)
    )
    reduced_values = self.pool.map(
        self.reduce_func,
```

```
            partitioned_data,
        )
        return reduced_values
```

The following example script uses SimpleMapReduce to count the "words" in the reStructuredText source for this article, ignoring some of the markup.

Listing 10.75: **multiprocessing_wordcount.py**

```
import multiprocessing
import string

from multiprocessing_mapreduce import SimpleMapReduce


def file_to_words(filename):
    """Read a file and return a sequence of
    (word, occurences) values.
    """
    STOP_WORDS = set([
        'a', 'an', 'and', 'are', 'as', 'be', 'by', 'for', 'if',
        'in', 'is', 'it', 'of', 'or', 'py', 'rst', 'that', 'the',
        'to', 'with',
    ])
    TR = str.maketrans({
        p: ' '
        for p in string.punctuation
    })

    print('{} reading {}'.format(
        multiprocessing.current_process().name, filename))
    output = []

    with open(filename, 'rt') as f:
        for line in f:
            # Skip comment lines.
            if line.lstrip().startswith('..'):
                continue
            line = line.translate(TR)  # Strip punctuation.
            for word in line.split():
                word = word.lower()
                if word.isalpha() and word not in STOP_WORDS:
                    output.append((word, 1))
    return output


def count_words(item):
    """Convert the partitioned data for a word to a
```

```
        tuple containing the word and the number of occurences.
        """
        word, occurences = item
        return (word, sum(occurences))


if __name__ == '__main__':
    import operator
    import glob

    input_files = glob.glob('*.rst')

    mapper = SimpleMapReduce(file_to_words, count_words)
    word_counts = mapper(input_files)
    word_counts.sort(key=operator.itemgetter(1))
    word_counts.reverse()

    print('\nTOP 20 WORDS BY FREQUENCY\n')
    top20 = word_counts[:20]
    longest = max(len(word) for word, count in top20)
    for word, count in top20:
        print('{word:<{len}}: {count:5}'.format(
            len=longest + 1,
            word=word,
            count=count)
        )
```

The file_to_words() function converts each input file to a sequence of tuples containing the word and the number 1 (representing a single occurrence). The data is divided up by partition() using the word as the key, so the resulting structure consists of a key and a sequence of 1 values representing each occurrence of the word. The partitioned data is converted to a set of tuples containing a word and the count for that word by count_words() during the reduction phase.

```
$ python3 -u multiprocessing_wordcount.py

ForkPoolWorker-1 reading basics.rst
ForkPoolWorker-2 reading communication.rst
ForkPoolWorker-3 reading index.rst
ForkPoolWorker-4 reading mapreduce.rst

TOP 20 WORDS BY FREQUENCY

process         :    83
running         :    45
multiprocessing :    44
worker          :    40
starting        :    37
now             :    35
```

```
after           :   34
processes       :   31
start           :   29
header          :   27
pymotw          :   27
caption         :   27
end             :   27
daemon          :   22
can             :   22
exiting         :   21
forkpoolworker  :   21
consumer        :   20
main            :   18
event           :   16
```

TIP

Related Reading

- Standard library documentation for `multiprocessing`.[7]
- `threading` (page 560): High-level API for working with threads.
- Wikipedia: MapReduce[8]: Overview of MapReduce on Wikipedia.
- MapReduce: Simplified Data Processing on Large Clusters[9]: Google Labs presentation and paper on MapReduce.
- `operator` (page 183): Operator tools such as `itemgetter`.

10.5 asyncio: Asynchronous I/O, Event Loop, and Concurrency Tools

The `asyncio` module provides tools for building concurrent applications using coroutines. While the `threading` (page 560) module implements concurrency through application threads, and `multiprocessing` (page 586) implements concurrency using system processes, `asyncio` uses a single-threaded, single-process approach in which parts of an application co-operate to switch tasks explicitly at optimal times. Most often this context switching occurs when the program would otherwise block while waiting to read or write data, but `asyncio` also includes support for scheduling code to run at a specific future time, to enable one coroutine to wait for another to complete, for handling system signals, and for recognizing other events that may be reasons for an application to change what it is working on.

---

[7] https://docs.python.org/3.5/library/multiprocessing.html
[8] https://en.wikipedia.org/wiki/MapReduce
[9] http://research.google.com/archive/mapreduce.html

10.5.1   Asynchronous Concurrency Concepts

Most programs using other concurrency models are written linearly, and rely on the underlying threading or process management of the language runtime or operating system to change context as appropriate. An application based on `asyncio` requires the application code to explicitly handle context changes, and using the techniques for doing that correctly depends on understanding several interrelated concepts.

The framework provided by `asyncio` centers on an *event loop*, a first-class object that is responsible for efficiently handling I/O events, system events, and application context changes. Several loop implementations are provided, to take advantage of the operating systems' capabilities efficiently. While a reasonable default is usually selected automatically, it is also possible to pick a particular event loop implementation from within the application. This is useful under Windows, for example, where some loop classes add support for external processes in a way that may trade some efficiencies in network I/O.

An application interacts with the event loop explicitly to register code to be run, and lets the event loop make the necessary calls into application code when resources are available. For example, a network server opens sockets and then registers them to be notified when input events occur on them. The event loop alerts the server code when a new incoming connection is established or when data is available to read. Application code is expected to yield control again after a short period of time when no more work can be done in the current context. For example, if there is no more data to read from a socket, the server should yield control back to the event loop.

The mechanism for yielding control back to the event loop depends on Python's *coroutines*, special functions that give up control to the caller without losing their state. Coroutines are quite similar to generator functions; in fact, generators can be used to implement coroutines in versions of Python earlier than 3.5 without native support for coroutine objects. `asyncio` also provides a class-based abstraction layer for *protocols* and *transports* for writing code using callbacks instead of writing coroutines directly. In both the class-based and coroutine models, explicitly changing context by re-entering the event loop takes the place of implicit context changes in Python's threading implementation.

A *future* is a data structure representing the result of work that has not been completed yet. The event loop can watch for a `Future` object to be set to done, thereby allowing one part of an application to wait for another part to finish some work. Besides futures, `asyncio` includes other concurrency primitives such as locks and semaphores.

A `Task` is a subclass of `Future` that knows how to wrap and manage the execution of a coroutine. An event loop schedules tasks to run when the resources they need are available, and to produce a result that can be consumed by other coroutines.

10.5.2   Cooperative Multitasking with Coroutines

Coroutines are a language construct designed for concurrent operation. A coroutine function creates a coroutine object when called, and the caller can then run the code of the function using the coroutine's `send()` method. A coroutine can pause execution using the `await` keyword with another coroutine. While it is paused, the coroutine's state is maintained, allowing it to resume where it left off the next time it is awakened.

10.5.2.1 Starting a Coroutine

The asyncio event loop can start a coroutine in several different ways. The simplest approach is to use run_until_complete(), passing the coroutine to this method directly.

Listing 10.76: asyncio_coroutine.py

```
import asyncio


async def coroutine():
    print('in coroutine')


event_loop = asyncio.get_event_loop()
try:
    print('starting coroutine')
    coro = coroutine()
    print('entering event loop')
    event_loop.run_until_complete(coro)
finally:
    print('closing event loop')
    event_loop.close()
```

The first step is to obtain a reference to the event loop. The default loop type can be used, or a specific loop class can be instantiated. In this example, the default loop is used. The run_until_complete() method starts the loop with the coroutine object; it stops the loop when the coroutine exits by returning.

```
$ python3 asyncio_coroutine.py

starting coroutine
entering event loop
in coroutine
closing event loop
```

10.5.2.2 Returning Values from Coroutines

The return value of a coroutine is passed back to the code that starts and waits for it.

Listing 10.77: asyncio_coroutine_return.py

```
import asyncio


async def coroutine():
    print('in coroutine')
    return 'result'
```

```
event_loop = asyncio.get_event_loop()
try:
    return_value = event_loop.run_until_complete(
        coroutine()
    )
    print('it returned: {!r}'.format(return_value))
finally:
    event_loop.close()
```

In this case, run_until_complete() also returns the result of the coroutine it is waiting for.

```
$ python3 asyncio_coroutine_return.py

in coroutine
it returned: 'result'
```

10.5.2.3   Chaining Coroutines

One coroutine can start another coroutine and wait for the results, which makes it easier to decompose a task into reusable parts. The following example has two phases that must be executed in order, but that can run concurrently with other operations.

Listing 10.78: **asyncio_coroutine_chain.py**

```
import asyncio


async def outer():
    print('in outer')
    print('waiting for result1')
    result1 = await phase1()
    print('waiting for result2')
    result2 = await phase2(result1)
    return (result1, result2)


async def phase1():
    print('in phase1')
    return 'result1'


async def phase2(arg):
    print('in phase2')
    return 'result2 derived from {}'.format(arg)


event_loop = asyncio.get_event_loop()
try:
```

```
        return_value = event_loop.run_until_complete(outer())
        print('return value: {!r}'.format(return_value))
    finally:
        event_loop.close()
```

The `await` keyword is used instead of adding the new coroutines to the loop. Because control flow is already inside of a coroutine being managed by the loop, it is not necessary to tell the loop to manage the new coroutines.

```
$ python3 asyncio_coroutine_chain.py

in outer
waiting for result1
in phase1
waiting for result2
in phase2
return value: ('result1', 'result2 derived from result1')
```

10.5.2.4 Generators Instead of Coroutines

Coroutine functions are a key component of the design of `asyncio`. They provide a language construct for stopping the execution of part of a program, preserving the state of that call, and re-entering the state at a later time. All of those actions are important capabilities for a concurrency framework.

Python 3.5 introduced new language features to define such coroutines natively using `async def` and to yield control using `await`, and the examples for `asyncio` take advantage of those new features. Earlier versions of Python 3 can use generator functions wrapped with the `asyncio.coroutine()` decorator and `yield from` to achieve the same effect.

Listing 10.79: asyncio_generator.py

```
import asyncio


@asyncio.coroutine
def outer():
    print('in outer')
    print('waiting for result1')
    result1 = yield from phase1()
    print('waiting for result2')
    result2 = yield from phase2(result1)
    return (result1, result2)


@asyncio.coroutine
def phase1():
    print('in phase1')
    return 'result1'
```

```
@asyncio.coroutine
def phase2(arg):
    print('in phase2')
    return 'result2 derived from {}'.format(arg)


event_loop = asyncio.get_event_loop()
try:
    return_value = event_loop.run_until_complete(outer())
    print('return value: {!r}'.format(return_value))
finally:
    event_loop.close()
```

The preceding example reproduces `asyncio_coroutine_chain.py` using generator functions instead of native coroutines.

```
$ python3 asyncio_generator.py

in outer
waiting for result1
in phase1
waiting for result2
in phase2
return value: ('result1', 'result2 derived from result1')
```

10.5.3   Scheduling Calls to Regular Functions

In addition to managing coroutines and I/O callbacks, the `asyncio` event loop can schedule calls to regular functions based on the timer value kept in the loop.

10.5.3.1   Scheduling a Callback "Soon"

If the timing of the callback does not matter, `call_soon()` can be used to schedule the call for the next iteration of the loop. Any extra positional arguments after the function are passed to the callback when it is invoked. To pass keyword arguments to the callback, use `partial()` from the `functools` (page 143) module.

Listing 10.80: asyncio_call_soon.py

```
import asyncio
import functools


def callback(arg, *, kwarg='default'):
    print('callback invoked with {} and {}'.format(arg, kwarg))


async def main(loop):
    print('registering callbacks')
```

```
        loop.call_soon(callback, 1)
        wrapped = functools.partial(callback, kwarg='not default')
        loop.call_soon(wrapped, 2)

        await asyncio.sleep(0.1)


event_loop = asyncio.get_event_loop()
try:
    print('entering event loop')
    event_loop.run_until_complete(main(event_loop))
finally:
    print('closing event loop')
    event_loop.close()
```

The callbacks are invoked in the order they are scheduled.

```
$ python3 asyncio_call_soon.py

entering event loop
registering callbacks
callback invoked with 1 and default
callback invoked with 2 and not default
closing event loop
```

10.5.3.2 Scheduling a Callback with a Delay

To postpone a callback until some time in the future, use `call_later()`. The first argument to this method is the delay in seconds, and the second argument is the callback.

Listing 10.81: **asyncio_call_later.py**

```
import asyncio


def callback(n):
    print('callback {} invoked'.format(n))


async def main(loop):
    print('registering callbacks')
    loop.call_later(0.2, callback, 1)
    loop.call_later(0.1, callback, 2)
    loop.call_soon(callback, 3)

    await asyncio.sleep(0.4)


event_loop = asyncio.get_event_loop()
try:
```

```
        print('entering event loop')
        event_loop.run_until_complete(main(event_loop))
    finally:
        print('closing event loop')
        event_loop.close()
```

In this example, the same callback function is scheduled for several different times with different arguments. The final instance, using `call_soon()`, invokes the callback with the argument 3 before any of the time-scheduled instances occur, showing that "soon" usually implies a minimal delay.

```
$ python3 asyncio_call_later.py

entering event loop
registering callbacks
callback 3 invoked
callback 2 invoked
callback 1 invoked
closing event loop
```

10.5.3.3 Scheduling a Callback for a Specific Time

It is also possible to schedule a call to occur at a specific time. The loop used for this purpose relies on a monotonic clock, rather than a wall-clock time, to ensure that the value of "now" never regresses. To choose a time for a scheduled callback, it is necessary to start from the internal state of that clock using the loop's `time()` method.

Listing 10.82: **asyncio_call_at.py**

```
import asyncio
import time


def callback(n, loop):
    print('callback {} invoked at {}'.format(n, loop.time()))


async def main(loop):
    now = loop.time()
    print('clock time: {}'.format(time.time()))
    print('loop  time: {}'.format(now))

    print('registering callbacks')
    loop.call_at(now + 0.2, callback, 1, loop)
    loop.call_at(now + 0.1, callback, 2, loop)
    loop.call_soon(callback, 3, loop)

    await asyncio.sleep(1)
```

```
event_loop = asyncio.get_event_loop()
try:
    print('entering event loop')
    event_loop.run_until_complete(main(event_loop))
finally:
    print('closing event loop')
    event_loop.close()
```

Note that the time according to the loop does not match the value returned by time.time().

```
$ python3 asyncio_call_at.py

entering event loop
clock time: 1479050248.66192
loop  time: 1008846.13856885
registering callbacks
callback 3 invoked at 1008846.13867956
callback 2 invoked at 1008846.239931555
callback 1 invoked at 1008846.343480996
closing event loop
```

10.5.4 Producing Results Asynchronously

A Future represents the result of work that has not been completed yet. The event loop can watch for a Future object's state to indicate that it is done, allowing one part of an application to wait for another part to finish some work.

10.5.4.1 Waiting for a Future

A Future acts like a coroutine, so any techniques useful for waiting for a coroutine can also be used to wait for the future to be marked done. The next example passes the future to the event loop's run_until_complete() method.

Listing 10.83: asyncio_future_event_loop.py

```
import asyncio


def mark_done(future, result):
    print('setting future result to {!r}'.format(result))
    future.set_result(result)


event_loop = asyncio.get_event_loop()
try:
    all_done = asyncio.Future()
```

```
        print('scheduling mark_done')
        event_loop.call_soon(mark_done, all_done, 'the result')

        print('entering event loop')
        result = event_loop.run_until_complete(all_done)
        print('returned result: {!r}'.format(result))
    finally:
        print('closing event loop')
        event_loop.close()

    print('future result: {!r}'.format(all_done.result()))
```

The state of the `Future` changes to done when `set_result()` is called, and the `Future` instance retains the result given to the method for later retrieval.

```
$ python3 asyncio_future_event_loop.py

scheduling mark_done
entering event loop
setting future result to 'the result'
returned result: 'the result'
closing event loop
future result: 'the result'
```

A `Future` can also be used with the `await` keyword, as in the next example.

Listing 10.84: asyncio_future_await.py

```
import asyncio


def mark_done(future, result):
    print('setting future result to {!r}'.format(result))
    future.set_result(result)


async def main(loop):
    all_done = asyncio.Future()

    print('scheduling mark_done')
    loop.call_soon(mark_done, all_done, 'the result')

    result = await all_done
    print('returned result: {!r}'.format(result))


event_loop = asyncio.get_event_loop()
try:
    event_loop.run_until_complete(main(event_loop))
```

```
    finally:
        event_loop.close()
```

The result of the Future is returned by await, so it is frequently possible to have the same code work with a regular coroutine and a Future instance.

```
$ python3 asyncio_future_await.py

scheduling mark_done
setting future result to 'the result'
returned result: 'the result'
```

10.5.4.2 Future Callbacks

In addition to working like a coroutine, a Future can invoke callbacks when it is completed. Callbacks are invoked in the order that they are registered.

Listing 10.85: **asyncio_future_callback.py**

```
import asyncio
import functools


def callback(future, n):
    print('{}: future done: {}'.format(n, future.result()))


async def register_callbacks(all_done):
    print('registering callbacks on future')
    all_done.add_done_callback(functools.partial(callback, n=1))
    all_done.add_done_callback(functools.partial(callback, n=2))


async def main(all_done):
    await register_callbacks(all_done)
    print('setting result of future')
    all_done.set_result('the result')


event_loop = asyncio.get_event_loop()
try:
    all_done = asyncio.Future()
    event_loop.run_until_complete(main(all_done))
finally:
    event_loop.close()
```

The callback should expect one argument, the Future instance. To pass additional arguments to the callbacks, use functools.partial() to create a wrapper.

```
$ python3 asyncio_future_callback.py

registering callbacks on future
setting result of future
1: future done: the result
2: future done: the result
```

10.5.5   Executing Tasks Concurrently

Tasks are one of the primary ways to interact with the event loop. Tasks wrap coroutines and track when they are complete. Because they are subclasses of `Future`, other coroutines can wait for tasks, and each task has a result that can be retrieved after it completes.

10.5.5.1   Starting a Task

To start a task, use `create_task()` to create a `Task` instance. The resulting task will run as part of the concurrent operations managed by the event loop as long as the loop is running and the coroutine does not return.

Listing 10.86: <code>asyncio_create_task.py</code>

```python
import asyncio


async def task_func():
    print('in task_func')
    return 'the result'


async def main(loop):
    print('creating task')
    task = loop.create_task(task_func())
    print('waiting for {!r}'.format(task))
    return_value = await task
    print('task completed {!r}'.format(task))
    print('return value: {!r}'.format(return_value))


event_loop = asyncio.get_event_loop()
try:
    event_loop.run_until_complete(main(event_loop))
finally:
    event_loop.close()
```

This example waits for the task to return a result before the `main()` function exits.

```
$ python3 asyncio_create_task.py

creating task
waiting for <Task pending coro=<task_func() running at
asyncio_create_task.py:12>>
in task_func
task completed <Task finished coro=<task_func() done, defined at
asyncio_create_task.py:12> result='the result'>
return value: 'the result'
```

10.5.5.2 Canceling a Task

By retaining the `Task` object returned from `create_task()`, it is possible to cancel the operation of the task before it completes.

Listing 10.87: asyncio_cancel_task.py

```python
import asyncio


async def task_func():
    print('in task_func')
    return 'the result'


async def main(loop):
    print('creating task')
    task = loop.create_task(task_func())

    print('canceling task')
    task.cancel()

    print('canceled task {!r}'.format(task))
    try:
        await task
    except asyncio.CancelledError:
        print('caught error from canceled task')
    else:
        print('task result: {!r}'.format(task.result()))


event_loop = asyncio.get_event_loop()
try:
    event_loop.run_until_complete(main(event_loop))
```

```
finally:
    event_loop.close()
```

This example creates and then cancels a task before starting the event loop. The result is a `CancelledError` exception thrown by the `run_until_complete()` method.

```
$ python3 asyncio_cancel_task.py

creating task
canceling task
canceled task <Task cancelling coro=<task_func() running at
asyncio_cancel_task.py:12>>
caught error from canceled task
```

If a task is canceled while it is waiting for another concurrent operation to finish, the task is notified of its cancellation through a `CancelledError` exception raised at the point where it is waiting.

Listing 10.88: asyncio_cancel_task2.py

```python
import asyncio


async def task_func():
    print('in task_func, sleeping')
    try:
        await asyncio.sleep(1)
    except asyncio.CancelledError:
        print('task_func was canceled')
        raise
    return 'the result'


def task_canceller(t):
    print('in task_canceller')
    t.cancel()
    print('canceled the task')


async def main(loop):
    print('creating task')
    task = loop.create_task(task_func())
    loop.call_soon(task_canceller, task)
    try:
        await task
    except asyncio.CancelledError:
        print('main() also sees task as canceled')
```

```
event_loop = asyncio.get_event_loop()
try:
    event_loop.run_until_complete(main(event_loop))
finally:
    event_loop.close()
```

Catching the exception provides an opportunity to clean up work already done, if necessary.

```
$ python3 asyncio_cancel_task2.py

creating task
in task_func, sleeping
in task_canceller
canceled the task
task_func was canceled
main() also sees task as canceled
```

10.5.5.3   Creating Tasks from Coroutines

The ensure_future() function returns a Task tied to the execution of a coroutine. That Task instance can then be passed to other code, which can wait for it without knowing how the original coroutine was constructed or called.

Listing 10.89: **asyncio_ensure_future.py**

```
import asyncio


async def wrapped():
    print('wrapped')
    return 'result'


async def inner(task):
    print('inner: starting')
    print('inner: waiting for {!r}'.format(task))
    result = await task
    print('inner: task returned {!r}'.format(result))


async def starter():
    print('starter: creating task')
    task = asyncio.ensure_future(wrapped())
    print('starter: waiting for inner')
    await inner(task)
    print('starter: inner returned')
```

```
event_loop = asyncio.get_event_loop()
try:
    print('entering event loop')
    result = event_loop.run_until_complete(starter())
finally:
    event_loop.close()
```

Note that the coroutine given to `ensure_future()` does not start until something uses `await`, which allows it to be executed.

```
$ python3 asyncio_ensure_future.py

entering event loop
starter: creating task
starter: waiting for inner
inner: starting
inner: waiting for <Task pending coro=<wrapped() running at
asyncio_ensure_future.py:12>>
wrapped
inner: task returned 'result'
starter: inner returned
```

10.5.6   Composing Coroutines with Control Structures

Linear control flow between a series of coroutines is easy to manage with the built-in language keyword `await`. More complicated structures allowing one coroutine to wait for several others to complete in parallel can also be created using tools in `asyncio`.

10.5.6.1   Waiting for Multiple Coroutines

It is often useful to divide one operation into many parts, which are then executed separately. For example, this approach is an efficient way of downloading several remote resources or querying remote APIs. In situations where the order of execution doesn't matter, and where there may be an arbitrary number of operations, `wait()` can be used to pause one coroutine until the other background operations complete.

Listing 10.90: asyncio_wait.py

```
import asyncio


async def phase(i):
    print('in phase {}'.format(i))
    await asyncio.sleep(0.1 * i)
    print('done with phase {}'.format(i))
    return 'phase {} result'.format(i)
```

```
async def main(num_phases):
    print('starting main')
    phases = [
        phase(i)
        for i in range(num_phases)
    ]
    print('waiting for phases to complete')
    completed, pending = await asyncio.wait(phases)
    results = [t.result() for t in completed]
    print('results: {!r}'.format(results))


event_loop = asyncio.get_event_loop()
try:
    event_loop.run_until_complete(main(3))
finally:
    event_loop.close()
```

Internally, wait() uses a set to hold the Task instances it creates, which means that the instances start, and finish, in an unpredictable order. The return value from wait() is a tuple containing two sets holding the finished and pending tasks.

```
$ python3 asyncio_wait.py

starting main
waiting for phases to complete
in phase 0
in phase 1
in phase 2
done with phase 0
done with phase 1
done with phase 2
results: ['phase 1 result', 'phase 0 result', 'phase 2 result']
```

If wait() is used with a timeout value, only pending operations will remain after the timeout occurs.

Listing 10.91: **asyncio_wait_timeout.py**

```
import asyncio


async def phase(i):
    print('in phase {}'.format(i))
    try:
        await asyncio.sleep(0.1 * i)
    except asyncio.CancelledError:
        print('phase {} canceled'.format(i))
        raise
```

```
        else:
            print('done with phase {}'.format(i))
            return 'phase {} result'.format(i)


async def main(num_phases):
    print('starting main')
    phases = [
        phase(i)
        for i in range(num_phases)
    ]
    print('waiting 0.1 for phases to complete')
    completed, pending = await asyncio.wait(phases, timeout=0.1)
    print('{} completed and {} pending'.format(
        len(completed), len(pending),
    ))
    # Cancel remaining tasks so they do not generate errors
    # as we exit without finishing them.
    if pending:
        print('canceling tasks')
        for t in pending:
            t.cancel()
    print('exiting main')


event_loop = asyncio.get_event_loop()
try:
    event_loop.run_until_complete(main(3))
finally:
    event_loop.close()
```

The remaining background operations should be handled explicitly for several reasons. Although pending tasks are suspended when `wait()` returns, they will resume as soon as control reverts to the event loop. Without another call to `wait()`, nothing will receive the output of the tasks; that is, the tasks will run and consume resources with no benefit. Also, `asyncio` emits a warning if there are pending tasks when the program exits. These warnings may be printed on the console, where users of the application will see them. Therefore, it is best either to cancel any remaining background operations, or to use `wait()` to let them finish running.

```
$ python3 asyncio_wait_timeout.py

starting main
waiting 0.1 for phases to complete
in phase 1
in phase 0
in phase 2
done with phase 0
```

```
1 completed and 2 pending
cancelling tasks
exiting main
phase 1 cancelled
phase 2 cancelled
```

10.5.6.2 Gathering Results from Coroutines

If the background phases are well defined, and only the results of those phases matter, then
gather() may be more useful for waiting for multiple operations.

Listing 10.92: asyncio_gather.py

```python
import asyncio


async def phase1():
    print('in phase1')
    await asyncio.sleep(2)
    print('done with phase1')
    return 'phase1 result'


async def phase2():
    print('in phase2')
    await asyncio.sleep(1)
    print('done with phase2')
    return 'phase2 result'


async def main():
    print('starting main')
    print('waiting for phases to complete')
    results = await asyncio.gather(
        phase1(),
        phase2(),
    )
    print('results: {!r}'.format(results))


event_loop = asyncio.get_event_loop()
try:
    event_loop.run_until_complete(main())
finally:
    event_loop.close()
```

The tasks created by gather() are not exposed, so they cannot be canceled. The return
value is a list of results presented in the same order as the arguments passed to gather(),
regardless of the order in which the background operations actually completed.

```
$ python3 asyncio_gather.py

starting main
waiting for phases to complete
in phase2
in phase1
done with phase2
done with phase1
results: ['phase1 result', 'phase2 result']
```

10.5.6.3   Handling Background Operations as They Finish

as_completed() is a generator that manages the execution of a list of coroutines given to it and produces their results one at a time as each coroutine finishes running. As with wait(), order is not guaranteed by as_completed(), but it is not necessary to wait for all of the background operations to complete before taking other action.

Listing 10.93: **asyncio_as_completed.py**

```python
import asyncio


async def phase(i):
    print('in phase {}'.format(i))
    await asyncio.sleep(0.5 - (0.1 * i))
    print('done with phase {}'.format(i))
    return 'phase {} result'.format(i)


async def main(num_phases):
    print('starting main')
    phases = [
        phase(i)
        for i in range(num_phases)
    ]
    print('waiting for phases to complete')
    results = []
    for next_to_complete in asyncio.as_completed(phases):
        answer = await next_to_complete
        print('received answer {!r}'.format(answer))
        results.append(answer)
    print('results: {!r}'.format(results))
    return results


event_loop = asyncio.get_event_loop()
try:
    event_loop.run_until_complete(main(3))
```

```
      finally:
          event_loop.close()
```

This example starts several background phases that finish in the reverse order from which
they start. As the generator is consumed, the loop waits for the result of the coroutine using
await.

```
$ python3 asyncio_as_completed.py

starting main
waiting for phases to complete
in phase 0
in phase 2
in phase 1
done with phase 2
received answer 'phase 2 result'
done with phase 1
received answer 'phase 1 result'
done with phase 0
received answer 'phase 0 result'
results: ['phase 2 result', 'phase 1 result', 'phase 0 result']
```

10.5.7 Synchronization Primitives

Although asyncio applications usually run as single-threaded processes, they are still built
as concurrent applications. Each coroutine or task may execute in an unpredictable order,
based on delays and interrupts from I/O and other external events. To support safe concurrency, asyncio includes implementations of some of the same low-level primitives found
in the threading (page 560) and multiprocessing (page 586) modules.

10.5.7.1 Locks

A Lock can be used to guard access to a shared resource. Only the holder of the lock can
use the resource. Multiple attempts to acquire the lock will block so that there is only one
holder at a time.

Listing 10.94: asyncio_lock.py

```
import asyncio
import functools


def unlock(lock):
    print('callback releasing lock')
    lock.release()


async def coro1(lock):
    print('coro1 waiting for the lock')
```

```
    with await lock:
        print('coro1 acquired lock')
    print('coro1 released lock')


async def coro2(lock):
    print('coro2 waiting for the lock')
    await lock
    try:
        print('coro2 acquired lock')
    finally:
        print('coro2 released lock')
        lock.release()


async def main(loop):
    # Create and acquire a shared lock.
    lock = asyncio.Lock()
    print('acquiring the lock before starting coroutines')
    await lock.acquire()
    print('lock acquired: {}'.format(lock.locked()))

    # Schedule a callback to unlock the lock.
    loop.call_later(0.1, functools.partial(unlock, lock))

    # Run the coroutines that want to use the lock.
    print('waiting for coroutines')
    await asyncio.wait([coro1(lock), coro2(lock)]),


event_loop = asyncio.get_event_loop()
try:
    event_loop.run_until_complete(main(event_loop))
finally:
    event_loop.close()
```

A lock can be invoked directly, using `await` to acquire it and calling the `release()` method when done, as in `coro2()` in this example. They also can be used as asynchronous context managers with the `with await` keywords, as in `coro1()`.

```
$ python3 asyncio_lock.py

acquiring the lock before starting coroutines
lock acquired: True
waiting for coroutines
coro1 waiting for the lock
coro2 waiting for the lock
callback releasing lock
coro1 acquired lock
coro1 released lock
```

```
coro2 acquired lock
coro2 released lock
```

10.5.7.2 Events

An `asyncio.Event` is based on a `threading.Event`. It allows multiple consumers to wait for something to happen without looking for a specific value to be associated with the notification.

Listing 10.95: **asyncio_event.py**

```
import asyncio
import functools


def set_event(event):
    print('setting event in callback')
    event.set()


async def coro1(event):
    print('coro1 waiting for event')
    await event.wait()
    print('coro1 triggered')


async def coro2(event):
    print('coro2 waiting for event')
    await event.wait()
    print('coro2 triggered')


async def main(loop):
    # Create a shared event.
    event = asyncio.Event()
    print('event start state: {}'.format(event.is_set()))

    loop.call_later(
        0.1, functools.partial(set_event, event)
    )

    await asyncio.wait([coro1(event), coro2(event)])
    print('event end state: {}'.format(event.is_set()))


event_loop = asyncio.get_event_loop()
try:
    event_loop.run_until_complete(main(event_loop))
finally:
    event_loop.close()
```

As with the `Lock`, both `coro1()` and `coro2()` wait for the event to be set. The difference is that both can start as soon as the event state changes, and they do not need to acquire a unique hold on the event object.

```
$ python3 asyncio_event.py

event start state: False
coro2 waiting for event
coro1 waiting for event
setting event in callback
coro2 triggered
coro1 triggered
event end state: True
```

10.5.7.3   Conditions

A `Condition` works similarly to an `Event` except that rather than notifying all waiting coroutines, the number of waiters awakened is controlled with an argument to `notify()`.

Listing 10.96: asyncio_condition.py

```python
import asyncio


async def consumer(condition, n):
    with await condition:
        print('consumer {} is waiting'.format(n))
        await condition.wait()
        print('consumer {} triggered'.format(n))
    print('ending consumer {}'.format(n))


async def manipulate_condition(condition):
    print('starting manipulate_condition')

    # Pause to let consumers start
    await asyncio.sleep(0.1)

    for i in range(1, 3):
        with await condition:
            print('notifying {} consumers'.format(i))
            condition.notify(n=i)
        await asyncio.sleep(0.1)

    with await condition:
        print('notifying remaining consumers')
        condition.notify_all()

    print('ending manipulate_condition')
```

```
async def main(loop):
    # Create a condition.
    condition = asyncio.Condition()

    # Set up tasks watching the condition.
    consumers = [
        consumer(condition, i)
        for i in range(5)
    ]

    # Schedule a task to manipulate the condition variable.
    loop.create_task(manipulate_condition(condition))

    # Wait for the consumers to be done.
    await asyncio.wait(consumers)


event_loop = asyncio.get_event_loop()
try:
    result = event_loop.run_until_complete(main(event_loop))
finally:
    event_loop.close()
```

This example starts five consumers of the Condition. Each uses the wait() method to wait for a notification that it can proceed. manipulate_condition() notifies one consumer, then two consumers, then all of the remaining consumers.

```
$ python3 asyncio_condition.py

starting manipulate_condition
consumer 3 is waiting
consumer 1 is waiting
consumer 2 is waiting
consumer 0 is waiting
consumer 4 is waiting
notifying 1 consumers
consumer 3 triggered
ending consumer 3
notifying 2 consumers
consumer 1 triggered
ending consumer 1
consumer 2 triggered
ending consumer 2
notifying remaining consumers
ending manipulate_condition
consumer 0 triggered
ending consumer 0
consumer 4 triggered
ending consumer 4
```

10.5.7.4   Queues

An `asyncio.Queue` provides a first-in, first-out data structure for coroutines, much like a `queue.Queue` does for threads or a `multiprocessing.Queue` does for processes.

Listing 10.97: asyncio_queue.py

```python
import asyncio


async def consumer(n, q):
    print('consumer {}: starting'.format(n))
    while True:
        print('consumer {}: waiting for item'.format(n))
        item = await q.get()
        print('consumer {}: has item {}'.format(n, item))
        if item is None:
            # None is the signal to stop.
            q.task_done()
            break
        else:
            await asyncio.sleep(0.01 * item)
            q.task_done()
    print('consumer {}: ending'.format(n))


async def producer(q, num_workers):
    print('producer: starting')
    # Add some numbers to the queue to simulate jobs.
    for i in range(num_workers * 3):
        await q.put(i)
        print('producer: added task {} to the queue'.format(i))
    # Add None entries in the queue
    # to signal the consumers to exit.
    print('producer: adding stop signals to the queue')
    for i in range(num_workers):
        await q.put(None)
    print('producer: waiting for queue to empty')
    await q.join()
    print('producer: ending')


async def main(loop, num_consumers):
    # Create the queue with a fixed size so the producer
    # will block until the consumers pull some items out.
    q = asyncio.Queue(maxsize=num_consumers)

    # Schedule the consumer tasks.
    consumers = [
        loop.create_task(consumer(i, q))
```

```
            for i in range(num_consumers)
        ]

        # Schedule the producer task.
        prod = loop.create_task(producer(q, num_consumers))

        # Wait for all of the coroutines to finish.
        await asyncio.wait(consumers + [prod])


    event_loop = asyncio.get_event_loop()
    try:
        event_loop.run_until_complete(main(event_loop, 2))
    finally:
        event_loop.close()
```

Adding items with put() and removing items with get() are both asynchronous operations, since the queue size might be fixed (blocking an addition) or the queue might be empty (blocking a call to fetch an item).

```
$ python3 asyncio_queue.py

consumer 0: starting
consumer 0: waiting for item
consumer 1: starting
consumer 1: waiting for item
producer: starting
producer: added task 0 to the queue
producer: added task 1 to the queue
consumer 0: has item 0
consumer 1: has item 1
producer: added task 2 to the queue
producer: added task 3 to the queue
consumer 0: waiting for item
consumer 0: has item 2
producer: added task 4 to the queue
consumer 1: waiting for item
consumer 1: has item 3
producer: added task 5 to the queue
producer: adding stop signals to the queue
consumer 0: waiting for item
consumer 0: has item 4
consumer 1: waiting for item
consumer 1: has item 5
producer: waiting for queue to empty
consumer 0: waiting for item
consumer 0: has item None
consumer 0: ending
consumer 1: waiting for item
```

```
consumer 1: has item None
consumer 1: ending
producer: ending
```

10.5.8   Asynchronous I/O with Protocol Class Abstractions

Up to this point, the examples have all avoided mingling concurrency and I/O operations to focus on one concept at a time. However, switching contexts when I/O blocks is one of the primary use cases for asyncio. Building on the concurrency concepts introduced earlier, this section examines two sample programs that implement a simple echo server and client, similar to the examples used in the socket (page 693) and socketserver (page 742) sections. A client can connect to the server, send some data, and then receive the same data as a response. Each time an I/O operation is initiated, the executing code gives up control to the event loop, allowing other tasks to run until the I/O is ready.

10.5.8.1   Echo Server

The server starts by importing the modules it needs to set up asyncio and logging (page 980), and then it creates an event loop object.

Listing 10.98: asyncio_echo_server_protocol.py

```python
import asyncio
import logging
import sys

SERVER_ADDRESS = ('localhost', 10000)

logging.basicConfig(
    level=logging.DEBUG,
    format='%(name)s: %(message)s',
    stream=sys.stderr,
)
log = logging.getLogger('main')

event_loop = asyncio.get_event_loop()
```

The server then defines a subclass of asyncio.Protocol to handle client communication. The protocol object's methods are invoked based on events associated with the server socket.

```python
class EchoServer(asyncio.Protocol):
```

Each new client connection triggers a call to connection_made(). The transport argument is an instance of asyncio.Transport, which provides an abstraction for doing asynchronous I/O using the socket. Different types of communication provide different transport implementations, all with the same API. For example, separate transport classes are used for working with sockets and for working with pipes to subprocesses. The address of the incoming client is available from the transport through `get_extra_info()`, an implementation-specific method.

```python
def connection_made(self, transport):
    self.transport = transport
    self.address = transport.get_extra_info('peername')
    self.log = logging.getLogger(
        'EchoServer_{}_{}'.format(*self.address)
    )
    self.log.debug('connection accepted')
```

After a connection is established, when data is sent from the client to the server, the `data_received()` method of the protocol is invoked to pass the data in for processing. Data is passed as a byte string, and it is up to the application to decode it in an appropriate way. In the code that follows, the results are logged, and then a response is sent back to the client immediately by calling `transport.write()`.

```python
def data_received(self, data):
    self.log.debug('received {!r}'.format(data))
    self.transport.write(data)
    self.log.debug('sent {!r}'.format(data))
```

Some transports support a special end-of-file indicator ("EOF"). When an EOF is encountered, the `eof_received()` method is called. In this implementation, the EOF is sent back to the client to indicate that it was received. Because not all transports support an explicit EOF, this protocol asks the transport first whether it is safe to send EOF.

```python
def eof_received(self):
    self.log.debug('received EOF')
    if self.transport.can_write_eof():
        self.transport.write_eof()
```

When a connection is closed, either normally or as the result of an error, the protocol's `connection_lost()` method is called. If an error occurred, the argument contains an appropriate exception object; otherwise, it is `None`.

```python
def connection_lost(self, error):
    if error:
        self.log.error('ERROR: {}'.format(error))
    else:
        self.log.debug('closing')
    super().connection_lost(error)
```

There are two steps to starting the server. First, the application tells the event loop to create a new server object using the protocol class and the hostname and socket on which to listen. The `create_server()` method is a coroutine, so the results must be processed by the event loop to actually start the server. Completing the coroutine produces an `asyncio.Server` instance tied to the event loop.

```
# Create the server and let the loop finish the coroutine before
# starting the real event loop.
factory = event_loop.create_server(EchoServer, *SERVER_ADDRESS)
server = event_loop.run_until_complete(factory)
log.debug('starting up on {} port {}'.format(*SERVER_ADDRESS))
```

Next, the event loop needs to be run to process events and handle client requests. For a long-running service, the `run_forever()` method is the simplest way to do this. When the event loop is stopped, either by the application code or by signaling the process, the server can be closed to clean up the socket properly. The event loop can then be closed to finish handling any other coroutines before the program exits.

```
# Enter the event loop permanently to handle all connections.
try:
    event_loop.run_forever()
finally:
    log.debug('closing server')
    server.close()
    event_loop.run_until_complete(server.wait_closed())
    log.debug('closing event loop')
    event_loop.close()
```

10.5.8.2 Echo Client

Constructing a client using a protocol class is very similar to constructing a server. The code again starts by importing the modules it needs to set up `asyncio` and `logging` (page 980), and then creating an event loop object.

Listing 10.99: `asyncio_echo_client_protocol.py`

```
import asyncio
import functools
import logging
import sys

MESSAGES = [
    b'This is the message. ',
    b'It will be sent ',
    b'in parts.',
]
SERVER_ADDRESS = ('localhost', 10000)

logging.basicConfig(
    level=logging.DEBUG,
    format='%(name)s: %(message)s',
```

```
        stream=sys.stderr,
    )
    log = logging.getLogger('main')

    event_loop = asyncio.get_event_loop()
```

The client protocol class defines the same methods as the server, but with different implementations. The class constructor accepts two arguments: a list of the messages to send and a Future instance to use to signal that the client has completed a cycle of work by receiving a response from the server.

```
class EchoClient(asyncio.Protocol):

    def __init__(self, messages, future):
        super().__init__()
        self.messages = messages
        self.log = logging.getLogger('EchoClient')
        self.f = future
```

When the client successfully connects to the server, it starts communicating immediately. The messages are sent one at a time, although the underlying networking code may combine multiple messages into one transmission. When the entire sequence of messages is exhausted, an EOF is sent.

Although it appears that all of the data is sent immediately, in fact the transport object buffers the outgoing data and sets up a callback to actually transmit when the socket's buffer is ready to receive data. This processing is handled transparently, so the application code can be written as though the I/O operation is happening right away.

```
    def connection_made(self, transport):
        self.transport = transport
        self.address = transport.get_extra_info('peername')
        self.log.debug(
            'connecting to {} port {}'.format(*self.address)
        )
        # This could be transport.writelines() except that
        # would make it harder to show each part of the message
        # being sent.
        for msg in self.messages:
            transport.write(msg)
            self.log.debug('sending {!r}'.format(msg))
        if transport.can_write_eof():
            transport.write_eof()
```

When the response from the server is received, it is logged.

```
    def data_received(self, data):
        self.log.debug('received {!r}'.format(data))
```

Finally, when either an end-of-file marker is received or the connection is closed from the server's side, the local transport object is closed and the future object is marked as done by setting a result.

```
def eof_received(self):
    self.log.debug('received EOF')
    self.transport.close()
    if not self.f.done():
        self.f.set_result(True)

def connection_lost(self, exc):
    self.log.debug('server closed connection')
    self.transport.close()
    if not self.f.done():
        self.f.set_result(True)
    super().connection_lost(exc)
```

Normally, the protocol class is passed to the event loop to create the connection. In this case, because the event loop has no facility for passing extra arguments to the protocol constructor, it is necessary to create a `partial` to wrap the client class and pass the list of messages to send and the `Future` instance. That new callable is then used in place of the class when calling `create_connection()` to establish the client connection.

```
client_completed = asyncio.Future()

client_factory = functools.partial(
    EchoClient,
    messages=MESSAGES,
    future=client_completed,
)
factory_coroutine = event_loop.create_connection(
    client_factory,
    *SERVER_ADDRESS,
)
```

To trigger the client to run, the event loop is called once with the coroutine for creating the client, and then again with the `Future` instance given to the client to communicate when it is finished. Using two calls in this way avoids the creation of an infinite loop in the client program, which likely wants to exit after it has finished communicating with the server. If only the first call was used to wait for the coroutine to create the client, it might not process all of the response data and clean up the connection to the server properly.

```
log.debug('waiting for client to complete')
try:
    event_loop.run_until_complete(factory_coroutine)
    event_loop.run_until_complete(client_completed)
```

```
        finally:
            log.debug('closing event loop')
            event_loop.close()
```

10.5.8.3 Output

Running the server in one window and the client in another window produces the following output.

```
$ python3 asyncio_echo_client_protocol.py
asyncio: Using selector: KqueueSelector
main: waiting for client to complete
EchoClient: connecting to ::1 port 10000
EchoClient: sending b'This is the message. '
EchoClient: sending b'It will be sent '
EchoClient: sending b'in parts.'
EchoClient: received b'This is the message. It will be sent in parts.'
EchoClient: received EOF
EchoClient: server closed connection
main: closing event loop

$ python3 asyncio_echo_client_protocol.py
asyncio: Using selector: KqueueSelector
main: waiting for client to complete
EchoClient: connecting to ::1 port 10000
EchoClient: sending b'This is the message. '
EchoClient: sending b'It will be sent '
EchoClient: sending b'in parts.'
EchoClient: received b'This is the message. It will be sent in parts.'
EchoClient: received EOF
EchoClient: server closed connection
main: closing event loop

$ python3 asyncio_echo_client_protocol.py
asyncio: Using selector: KqueueSelector
main: waiting for client to complete
EchoClient: connecting to ::1 port 10000
EchoClient: sending b'This is the message. '
EchoClient: sending b'It will be sent '
EchoClient: sending b'in parts.'
EchoClient: received b'This is the message. It will be sent in parts.'
EchoClient: received EOF
EchoClient: server closed connection
main: closing event loop
```

Although the client always sends the messages separately, the first time the client runs, the server receives one large message and echoes that back to the client. These results vary in subsequent runs, based on how busy the network is and whether the network buffers are flushed before all of the data is prepared.

```
$ python3 asyncio_echo_server_protocol.py
asyncio: Using selector: KqueueSelector
main: starting up on localhost port 10000
EchoServer_::1_63347: connection accepted
EchoServer_::1_63347: received b'This is the message. It will
be sent in parts.'
EchoServer_::1_63347: sent b'This is the message. It will be
sent in parts.'
EchoServer_::1_63347: received EOF
EchoServer_::1_63347: closing

EchoServer_::1_63387: connection accepted
EchoServer_::1_63387: received b'This is the message. '
EchoServer_::1_63387: sent b'This is the message. '
EchoServer_::1_63387: received b'It will be sent in parts.'
EchoServer_::1_63387: sent b'It will be sent in parts.'
EchoServer_::1_63387: received EOF
EchoServer_::1_63387: closing

EchoServer_::1_63389: connection accepted
EchoServer_::1_63389: received b'This is the message. It will
be sent '
EchoServer_::1_63389: sent b'This is the message. It will be sent '
EchoServer_::1_63389: received b'in parts.'
EchoServer_::1_63389: sent b'in parts.'
EchoServer_::1_63389: received EOF
EchoServer_::1_63389: closing
```

10.5.9   Asynchronous I/O Using Coroutines and Streams

This section examines alternative versions of the two sample programs implementing a simple echo server and client, using coroutines and the `asyncio` streams API instead of the protocol and transport class abstractions. The examples operate at a lower abstraction level than the `Protocol` API discussed previously, but the events being processed are similar.

10.5.9.1   Echo Server

The server starts by importing the modules it needs to set up `asyncio` and `logging` (page 980). It then creates an event loop object.

Listing 10.100: asyncio_echo_server_coroutine.py

```
import asyncio
import logging
import sys

SERVER_ADDRESS = ('localhost', 10000)
logging.basicConfig(
```

```
        level=logging.DEBUG,
        format='%(name)s: %(message)s',
        stream=sys.stderr,
    )
    log = logging.getLogger('main')

    event_loop = asyncio.get_event_loop()
```

The server then defines a coroutine to handle communication. Each time a client connects, a new instance of the coroutine is invoked; thus, within the function, the code communicates with only one client at a time. Python's language runtime manages the state for each coroutine instance, so the application code does not need to manage any extra data structures to track separate clients.

The arguments to the coroutine are `StreamReader` and `StreamWriter` instances associated with the new connection. As with the `Transport`, the client address can be accessed through the writer's method `get_extra_info()`.

```
async def echo(reader, writer):
    address = writer.get_extra_info('peername')
    log = logging.getLogger('echo_{}_{}'.format(*address))
    log.debug('connection accepted')
```

Although the coroutine is called when the connection is established, at this point there may not be any data to read. To avoid blocking while reading, the coroutine uses `await` with the `read()` call to allow the event loop to carry on processing other tasks until there is data to read.

```
    while True:
        data = await reader.read(128)
```

If the client sends data, it is returned from `await` and can be sent back to the client by passing it to the writer. Multiple calls to `write()` can be used to buffer outgoing data, and then `drain()` is used to flush the results. Since flushing network I/O can block, `await` is once again used to restore control to the event loop, which monitors the write socket and invokes the writer when it is possible to send more data.

```
        if data:
            log.debug('received {!r}'.format(data))
            writer.write(data)
            await writer.drain()
            log.debug('sent {!r}'.format(data))
```

If the client has not sent any data, `read()` returns an empty byte string to indicate that the connection is closed. The server needs to close the socket for writing to the client, and then the coroutine can return to indicate that it is finished.

```
    else:
        log.debug('closing')
        writer.close()
        return
```

There are two steps to starting the server. First, the application tells the event loop to create a new server object using the coroutine and the hostname and socket on which to listen. The `start_server()` method is itself a coroutine, so the results must be processed by the event loop to actually start the server. Completing the coroutine produces an `asyncio.Server` instance tied to the event loop.

```
# Create the server and let the loop finish the coroutine before
# starting the real event loop.
factory = asyncio.start_server(echo, *SERVER_ADDRESS)
server = event_loop.run_until_complete(factory)
log.debug('starting up on {} port {}'.format(*SERVER_ADDRESS))
```

Next, the event loop needs to be run to process events and handle client requests. For a long-running service, the `run_forever()` method is the simplest way to do this. When the event loop is stopped, either by the application code or by signaling the process, the server can be closed to clean up the socket properly. The event loop can then be closed to finish handling any other coroutines before the program exits.

```
# Enter the event loop permanently to handle all connections.
try:
    event_loop.run_forever()
except KeyboardInterrupt:
    pass
finally:
    log.debug('closing server')
    server.close()
    event_loop.run_until_complete(server.wait_closed())
    log.debug('closing event loop')
    event_loop.close()
```

10.5.9.2   Echo Client

Constructing a client using a coroutine is very similar to constructing a server. The code again starts by importing the modules it needs to set up `asyncio` and `logging` (page 980), and then creating an event loop object.

Listing 10.101: `asyncio_echo_client_coroutine.py`

```
import asyncio
import logging
import sys
```

```
MESSAGES = [
    b'This is the message. ',
    b'It will be sent ',
    b'in parts.',
]
SERVER_ADDRESS = ('localhost', 10000)

logging.basicConfig(
    level=logging.DEBUG,
    format='%(name)s: %(message)s',
    stream=sys.stderr,
)
log = logging.getLogger('main')

event_loop = asyncio.get_event_loop()
```

The `echo_client` coroutine takes arguments telling it where the server is and which messages to send.

```
async def echo_client(address, messages):
```

This coroutine is called when the task starts, but it has no active connection to work with. The first step, therefore, is to have the client establish its own connection. It uses `await` to avoid blocking other activity while the `open_connection()` coroutine runs.

```
log = logging.getLogger('echo_client')

log.debug('connecting to {} port {}'.format(*address))
reader, writer = await asyncio.open_connection(*address)
```

The `open_connection()` coroutine returns `StreamReader` and `StreamWriter` instances associated with the new socket. The next step is to use the writer to send data to the server. As in the server, the writer will buffer outgoing data until the socket is ready or `drain()` is used to flush the results. Since flushing network I/O can block, `await` is once again used to restore control to the event loop, which monitors the write socket and invokes the writer when it is possible to send more data.

```
# This could be writer.writelines() except that
# would make it harder to show each part of the message
# being sent.
for msg in messages:
    writer.write(msg)
    log.debug('sending {!r}'.format(msg))
if writer.can_write_eof():
    writer.write_eof()
await writer.drain()
```

Next, the client looks for a response from the server by trying to read data until there is nothing left to read. To avoid blocking on an individual `read()` call, `await` yields control back to the event loop. If the server has sent data, it is logged. If the server has not sent any data, `read()` returns an empty byte string to indicate that the connection is closed. The client needs to first close the socket for sending data to the server and then return to indicate that it is finished.

```
log.debug('waiting for response')
while True:
    data = await reader.read(128)
    if data:
        log.debug('received {!r}'.format(data))
    else:
        log.debug('closing')
        writer.close()
        return
```

To start the client, the event loop is called with the coroutine for creating the client. Using `run_until_complete()` for this purpose avoids the creation of an infinite loop in the client program. Unlike in the protocol example, no separate future is needed to signal when the coroutine is finished, because `echo_client()` contains all of the client logic and does not return until it has received a response and closed the server connection.

```
try:
    event_loop.run_until_complete(
        echo_client(SERVER_ADDRESS, MESSAGES)
    )
finally:
    log.debug('closing event loop')
    event_loop.close()
```

10.5.9.3   Output

Running the server in one window and the client in another window produces the following output.

```
$ python3 asyncio_echo_client_coroutine.py
asyncio: Using selector: KqueueSelector
echo_client: connecting to localhost port 10000
echo_client: sending b'This is the message. '
echo_client: sending b'It will be sent '
echo_client: sending b'in parts.'
echo_client: waiting for response
echo_client: received b'This is the message. It will be sent in parts.'
echo_client: closing
main: closing event loop
```

```
$ python3 asyncio_echo_client_coroutine.py
asyncio: Using selector: KqueueSelector
echo_client: connecting to localhost port 10000
echo_client: sending b'This is the message. '
echo_client: sending b'It will be sent '
echo_client: sending b'in parts.'
echo_client: waiting for response
echo_client: received b'This is the message. It will be sent in parts.'
echo_client: closing
main: closing event loop

$ python3 asyncio_echo_client_coroutine.py
asyncio: Using selector: KqueueSelector
echo_client: connecting to localhost port 10000
echo_client: sending b'This is the message. '
echo_client: sending b'It will be sent '
echo_client: sending b'in parts.'
echo_client: waiting for response
echo_client: received b'This is the message. It will be sent '
echo_client: received b'in parts.'
echo_client: closing
main: closing event loop
```

Although the client always sends the messages separately, the first two times the client
runs, the server receives one large message and echoes that back to the client. These results
vary in subsequent runs, based on how busy the network is and whether the network buffers
are flushed before all of the data is prepared.

```
$ python3 asyncio_echo_server_coroutine.py
asyncio: Using selector: KqueueSelector
main: starting up on localhost port 10000
echo_::1_64624: connection accepted
echo_::1_64624: received b'This is the message. It will be sent
in parts.'
echo_::1_64624: sent b'This is the message. It will be sent in parts.'
echo_::1_64624: closing

echo_::1_64626: connection accepted
echo_::1_64626: received b'This is the message. It will be sent
in parts.'
echo_::1_64626: sent b'This is the message. It will be sent in parts.'
echo_::1_64626: closing

echo_::1_64627: connection accepted
echo_::1_64627: received b'This is the message. It will be sent '
echo_::1_64627: sent b'This is the message. It will be sent '
echo_::1_64627: received b'in parts.'
echo_::1_64627: sent b'in parts.'
echo_::1_64627: closing
```

10.5.10   Using SSL

asyncio has built-in support for enabling SSL communication on sockets. Passing an SSLContext instance to the coroutines that create server or client connections enables the support and ensures that the SSL protocol setup is performed before the socket is presented as ready for the application to use.

The coroutine-based echo server and client from the previous section can be updated with a few small changes. The first step is to create the certificate and key files. A self-signed certificate can be created with a command like the following:

```
$ openssl req -newkey rsa:2048 -nodes -keyout pymotw.key \
-x509 -days 365 -out pymotw.crt
```

The openssl command will prompt for several values that are used to generate the certificate, and then produce the output files requested.

The insecure socket setup in the previous server example uses start_server() to create the listening socket.

```
factory = asyncio.start_server(echo, *SERVER_ADDRESS)
server = event_loop.run_until_complete(factory)
```

To add encryption, create an SSLContext with the certificate and key just generated and then pass the context to start_server().

```
# The certificate is created with pymotw.com as the hostname.
# This name will not match when the example code runs elsewhere,
# so disable hostname verification.
ssl_context = ssl.create_default_context(ssl.Purpose.CLIENT_AUTH)
ssl_context.check_hostname = False
ssl_context.load_cert_chain('pymotw.crt', 'pymotw.key')

# Create the server and let the loop finish the coroutine before
# starting the real event loop.
factory = asyncio.start_server(echo, *SERVER_ADDRESS,
                               ssl=ssl_context)
```

Similar changes are needed in the client. The old version uses open_connection() to create the socket connected to the server.

```
reader, writer = await asyncio.open_connection(*address)
```

An SSLContext is needed again to secure the client side of the socket. Client identity is not being enforced, so only the certificate needs to be loaded.

```
# The certificate is created with pymotw.com as the hostname.
# This name will not match when the example code runs
# elsewhere, so disable hostname verification.
ssl_context = ssl.create_default_context(
```

```
        ssl.Purpose.SERVER_AUTH,
    )
    ssl_context.check_hostname = False
    ssl_context.load_verify_locations('pymotw.crt')
    reader, writer = await asyncio.open_connection(
        *server_address, ssl=ssl_context)
```

One other small change is needed in the client. Because the SSL connection does not support sending an end-of-file (EOF) notification, the client uses a NULL byte as a message terminator instead. The old version of the client send loop uses `write_eof()`.

```
    # This could be writer.writelines() except that
    # would make it harder to show each part of the message
    # being sent.
    for msg in messages:
        writer.write(msg)
        log.debug('sending {!r}'.format(msg))
    if writer.can_write_eof():
        writer.write_eof()
    await writer.drain()
```

The new version sends a zero byte (`b'\x00'`) to indicate the end of the message.

```
    # This could be writer.writelines() except that
    # would make it harder to show each part of the message
    # being sent.
    for msg in messages:
        writer.write(msg)
        log.debug('sending {!r}'.format(msg))
    # SSL does not support EOF, so send a null byte to indicate
    # the end of the message.
    writer.write(b'\x00')
    await writer.drain()
```

The `echo()` coroutine in the server must look for the NULL byte and close the client connection when it is received.

```
async def echo(reader, writer):
    address = writer.get_extra_info('peername')
    log = logging.getLogger('echo_{}_{}'.format(*address))
    log.debug('connection accepted')
    while True:
        data = await reader.read(128)
        terminate = data.endswith(b'\x00')
        data = data.rstrip(b'\x00')
        if data:
            log.debug('received {!r}'.format(data))
            writer.write(data)
            await writer.drain()
```

```
        log.debug('sent {!r}'.format(data))
    if not data or terminate:
        log.debug('message terminated, closing connection')
        writer.close()
        return
```

Running the server in one window and the client in another window produces this output.

```
$ python3 asyncio_echo_server_ssl.py
asyncio: Using selector: KqueueSelector
main: starting up on localhost port 10000
echo_::1_53957: connection accepted
echo_::1_53957: received b'This is the message. '
echo_::1_53957: sent b'This is the message. '
echo_::1_53957: received b'It will be sent in parts.'
echo_::1_53957: sent b'It will be sent in parts.'
echo_::1_53957: message terminated, closing connection
```

```
$ python3 asyncio_echo_client_ssl.py
asyncio: Using selector: KqueueSelector
echo_client: connecting to localhost port 10000
echo_client: sending b'This is the message. '
echo_client: sending b'It will be sent '
echo_client: sending b'in parts.'
echo_client: waiting for response
echo_client: received b'This is the message. '
echo_client: received b'It will be sent in parts.'
echo_client: closing
main: closing event loop
```

10.5.11   Interacting with Domain Name Services

Applications use the network to communicate with servers for domain name service (DNS) operations such as converting between hostnames and IP addresses. asyncio event loops include convenience methods to take care of those operations in the background, so as to avoid blocking during the queries.

10.5.11.1   Address Lookup by Name

Use the coroutine getaddrinfo() to convert a hostname and port number to an IP or IPv6 address. As with the version of the function in the socket (page 693) module, the return value is a list of tuples containing five pieces of information:

- The address family
- The address type

- The protocol

- The canonical name for the server

- A socket address tuple suitable for opening a connection to the server on the port originally specified

Queries can be filtered by protocol. In the following example, a filter ensures that only TCP responses are returned.

Listing 10.102: **asyncio_getaddrinfo.py**

```python
import asyncio
import logging
import socket
import sys


TARGETS = [
    ('pymotw.com', 'https'),
    ('doughellmann.com', 'https'),
    ('python.org', 'https'),
]


async def main(loop, targets):
    for target in targets:
        info = await loop.getaddrinfo(
            *target,
            proto=socket.IPPROTO_TCP,
        )

        for host in info:
            print('{:20}: {}'.format(target[0], host[4][0]))


event_loop = asyncio.get_event_loop()
try:
    event_loop.run_until_complete(main(event_loop, TARGETS))
finally:
    event_loop.close()
```

The example program converts a hostname and protocol name to an IP address and port number.

```
$ python3 asyncio_getaddrinfo.py

pymotw.com          : 66.33.211.242
doughellmann.com    : 66.33.211.240
python.org          : 23.253.135.79
python.org          : 2001:4802:7901::e60a:1375:0:6
```

10.5.11.2   Name Lookup by Address

The coroutine `getnameinfo()` works in the reverse direction, converting an IP address to a hostname and a port number to a protocol name, where possible.

Listing 10.103: **asyncio_getnameinfo.py**

```python
import asyncio
import logging
import socket
import sys


TARGETS = [
    ('66.33.211.242', 443),
    ('104.130.43.121', 443),
]


async def main(loop, targets):
    for target in targets:
        info = await loop.getnameinfo(target)
        print('{:15}: {} {}'.format(target[0], *info))


event_loop = asyncio.get_event_loop()
try:
    event_loop.run_until_complete(main(event_loop, TARGETS))
finally:
    event_loop.close()
```

This example shows that the IP address for pymotw.com refers to a server at DreamHost, the hosting company where the site runs. The second IP address examined is for python.org, and it does not resolve back to a hostname.

```
$ python3 asyncio_getnameinfo.py

66.33.211.242  : apache2-echo.catalina.dreamhost.com https
104.130.43.121 : 104.130.43.121 https
```

TIP

Related Reading

- The socket (page 693) module discussion includes a more detailed examination of these operations.

10.5.12   Working with Subprocesses

It is frequently necessary to work with other programs and processes so as to take advantage of existing code without rewriting it or to access libraries or features not available from within Python. As with network I/O, asyncio includes two abstractions for starting another program and then interacting with it.

10.5.12.1   Using the Protocol Abstraction with Subprocesses

The next example uses a coroutine to launch a process to run the Unix command df, which finds the amount of free space on local disks. It uses subprocess_exec() to launch the process and tie it to a protocol class that knows how to read the df command output and parse it. The methods of the protocol class are called automatically based on I/O events for the subprocess. Because the stdin and stderr arguments are both set to None, those communication channels are not connected to the new process.

Listing 10.104: asyncio_subprocess_protocol.py

```python
import asyncio
import functools


async def run_df(loop):
    print('in run_df')

    cmd_done = asyncio.Future(loop=loop)
    factory = functools.partial(DFProtocol, cmd_done)
    proc = loop.subprocess_exec(
        factory,
        'df', '-hl',
        stdin=None,
        stderr=None,
    )
    try:
        print('launching process')
        transport, protocol = await proc
        print('waiting for process to complete')
        await cmd_done
    finally:
        transport.close()

    return cmd_done.result()
```

The class DFProtocol is derived from SubprocessProtocol, which defines the API that allows for a class to communicate with another process through pipes. The done argument is expected to be a Future that the caller will use to watch for the process to finish.

```
class DFProtocol(asyncio.SubprocessProtocol):

    FD_NAMES = ['stdin', 'stdout', 'stderr']

    def __init__(self, done_future):
        self.done = done_future
        self.buffer = bytearray()
        super().__init__()
```

As in socket communication, `connection_made()` is invoked when the input channels to the new process are set up. The `transport` argument is an instance of a subclass of `BaseSubprocessTransport`. It can read data output by the process and write data to the input stream for the process, if the process was configured to receive input.

```
def connection_made(self, transport):
    print('process started {}'.format(transport.get_pid()))
    self.transport = transport
```

When the process has generated output, `pipe_data_received()` is invoked with the file descriptor where the data was emitted and the actual data read from the pipe. The protocol class saves the output from the standard output channel of the process in a buffer for later processing.

```
def pipe_data_received(self, fd, data):
    print('read {} bytes from {}'.format(len(data),
                                          self.FD_NAMES[fd]))
    if fd == 1:
        self.buffer.extend(data)
```

When the process terminates, `process_exited()` is called. The exit code of the process is available from the transport object by calling `get_returncode()`. In this case, if no error is reported, the available output is decoded and parsed before being returned through the `Future` instance. Conversely, if an error is generated, the results are assumed to be empty. Setting the result of the future tells `run_df()` that the process has exited, so it first cleans up and then returns the results.

```
def process_exited(self):
    print('process exited')
    return_code = self.transport.get_returncode()
    print('return code {}'.format(return_code))
    if not return_code:
        cmd_output = bytes(self.buffer).decode()
        results = self._parse_results(cmd_output)
    else:
        results = []
    self.done.set_result((return_code, results))
```

The command output is parsed into a sequence of dictionaries mapping the header names to their values for each line of output, and the resulting list is returned.

```python
    def _parse_results(self, output):
        print('parsing results')
        # Output has one row of headers, all single words. The
        # remaining rows are one per file system, with columns
        # matching the headers (assuming that none of the
        # mount points has whitespace in the names).
        if not output:
            return []
        lines = output.splitlines()
        headers = lines[0].split()
        devices = lines[1:]
        results = [
            dict(zip(headers, line.split()))
            for line in devices
        ]
        return results
```

The run_df() coroutine is run using run_until_complete(). The results are then examined and the free space on each device is printed.

```python
event_loop = asyncio.get_event_loop()
try:
    return_code, results = event_loop.run_until_complete(
        run_df(event_loop)
    )
finally:
    event_loop.close()

if return_code:
    print('error exit {}'.format(return_code))
else:
    print('\nFree space:')
    for r in results:
        print('{Mounted:25}: {Avail}'.format(**r))
```

The following output shows the sequence of steps taken, and the free space on three drives on the system where the program was run.

```
$ python3 asyncio_subprocess_protocol.py

in run_df
launching process
process started 49675
waiting for process to complete
read 332 bytes from stdout
```

```
process exited
return code 0
parsing results

Free space:
/                       : 233Gi
/Volumes/hubertinternal : 157Gi
/Volumes/hubert-tm      : 2.3Ti
```

10.5.12.2   Calling Subprocesses with Coroutines and Streams

To use coroutines to run a process directly, instead of accessing it through a `Protocol` subclass, call `create_subprocess_exec()` and specify whether to connect `stdout`, `stderr`, and `stdin` to pipes. The result of the coroutine to spawn the subprocess is a `Process` instance that can be used to manipulate the subprocess or communicate with it.

Listing 10.105: **asyncio_subprocess_coroutine.py**

```
import asyncio
import asyncio.subprocess


async def run_df():
    print('in run_df')

    buffer = bytearray()

    create = asyncio.create_subprocess_exec(
        'df', '-hl',
        stdout=asyncio.subprocess.PIPE,
    )
    print('launching process')
    proc = await create
    print('process started {}'.format(proc.pid))
```

In this example, `df` does not need any input other than its command-line arguments, so the next step is to read all of the output. With the `Protocol`, there is no control over how much data is read at a time. This example uses `readline()`, but it could also call `read()` directly to read data that is not line oriented. The output of the command is buffered, as with the protocol example, so it can be parsed later.

```
    while True:
        line = await proc.stdout.readline()
        print('read {!r}'.format(line))
        if not line:
            print('no more output from command')
            break
        buffer.extend(line)
```

The `readline()` method returns an empty byte string when there is no more output because the program has finished. To ensure the process is cleaned up properly, the next step is to wait for the process to exit fully.

```
print('waiting for process to complete')
await proc.wait()
```

At that point, the exit status can be examined to determine whether to parse the output or to treat the error because it produced no output. The parsing logic is the same as in the previous example, but is found in a stand-alone function (not shown here) because there is no protocol class to hide it in. After the data is parsed, the results and exit code are returned to the caller.

```
return_code = proc.returncode
print('return code {}'.format(return_code))
if not return_code:
    cmd_output = bytes(buffer).decode()
    results = _parse_results(cmd_output)
else:
    results = []

return (return_code, results)
```

The main program looks similar to the protocol-based example, because the implementation changes are isolated in `run_df()`.

```
event_loop = asyncio.get_event_loop()
try:
    return_code, results = event_loop.run_until_complete(
        run_df()
    )
finally:
    event_loop.close()

if return_code:
    print('error exit {}'.format(return_code))
else:
    print('\nFree space:')
    for r in results:
        print('{Mounted:25}: {Avail}'.format(**r))
```

Since the output from `df` can be read one line at a time, it is echoed to show the progress of the program. Otherwise, the output looks similar to that produced in the previous example.

```
$ python3 asyncio_subprocess_coroutine.py

in run_df
launching process
```

```
process started 49678
read b'Filesystem       Size   Used  Avail Capacity    iused
ifree %iused  Mounted on\n'
read b'/dev/disk2s2  446Gi  213Gi  233Gi     48%  55955082
61015132   48%   /\n'
read b'/dev/disk1    465Gi  307Gi  157Gi     67%  80514922
41281172   66%   /Volumes/hubertinternal\n'
read b'/dev/disk3s2  3.6Ti  1.4Ti  2.3Ti     38% 181837749
306480579   37%   /Volumes/hubert-tm\n'
read b''
no more output from command
waiting for process to complete
return code 0
parsing results

Free space:
/                          : 233Gi
/Volumes/hubertinternal    : 157Gi
/Volumes/hubert-tm         : 2.3Ti
```

10.5.12.3   Sending Data to a Subprocess

Both of the previous examples used only a single communication channel to read data from
a second process. It is often necessary to send data into a command for processing. The
next example defines a coroutine to execute the Unix command tr for translating characters in its input stream. In this case, tr is used to convert lowercase letters to uppercase
letters.

The to_upper() coroutine takes as argument an event loop and an input string. It spawns
a second process running "tr [:lower:] [:upper:]".

Listing 10.106: asyncio_subprocess_coroutine_write.py

```
import asyncio
import asyncio.subprocess


async def to_upper(input):
    print('in to_upper')

    create = asyncio.create_subprocess_exec(
        'tr', '[:lower:]', '[:upper:]',
        stdout=asyncio.subprocess.PIPE,
        stdin=asyncio.subprocess.PIPE,
    )
    print('launching process')
    proc = await create
    print('pid {}'.format(proc.pid))
```

Next, to_upper() uses the communicate() method of the Process to send the input string to the command and read all of the resulting output, asynchronously. As with the subprocess.Popen version of the same method, communicate() returns all of the byte strings output by this method. If a command is likely to produce more data than can fit comfortably into memory, the input cannot be produced all at once, or the output must be processed incrementally, a better approach may be to use the stdin, stdout, and stderr handles of the Process directly instead of calling communicate().

```
print('communicating with process')
stdout, stderr = await proc.communicate(input.encode())
```

After the I/O is done, waiting for the process to completely exit ensures it is cleaned up properly.

```
print('waiting for process to complete')
await proc.wait()
```

The return code can then be examined, and the output byte string decoded, to prepare the return value from the coroutine.

```
return_code = proc.returncode
print('return code {}'.format(return_code))
if not return_code:
    results = bytes(stdout).decode()
else:
    results = ''

return (return_code, results)
```

The main part of the program establishes a message string to be transformed, sets up the event loop to run to_upper(), and prints the results.

```
MESSAGE = """
This message will be converted
to all caps.
"""

event_loop = asyncio.get_event_loop()
try:
    return_code, results = event_loop.run_until_complete(
        to_upper(MESSAGE)
    )
finally:
    event_loop.close()

if return_code:
    print('error exit {}'.format(return_code))
```

```
else:
    print('Original: {!r}'.format(MESSAGE))
    print('Changed : {!r}'.format(results))
```

The output shows the sequence of operations and the transformation of the simple text message.

```
$ python3 asyncio_subprocess_coroutine_write.py

in to_upper
launching process
pid 49684
communicating with process
waiting for process to complete
return code 0
Original: '\nThis message will be converted\nto all caps.\n'
Changed : '\nTHIS MESSAGE WILL BE CONVERTED\nTO ALL CAPS.\n'
```

10.5.13   Receiving Unix Signals

Unix system event notifications usually interrupt an application, triggering their handler. When used with `asyncio`, signal handler callbacks are interleaved with the other coroutines and callbacks managed by the event loop. This integration results in fewer interrupted functions, and minimizes the need to provide safeguards for cleaning up incomplete operations.

Signal handlers must be regular callables, not coroutines.

Listing 10.107: asyncio_signal.py

```
import asyncio
import functools
import os
import signal


def signal_handler(name):
    print('signal_handler({!r})'.format(name))
```

The signal handlers are registered using `add_signal_handler()`. The first argument is the signal; the second is the callback. Callbacks are not passed any arguments, so if arguments are needed, a function can be wrapped with `functools.partial()`.

```
event_loop = asyncio.get_event_loop()

event_loop.add_signal_handler(
    signal.SIGHUP,
    functools.partial(signal_handler, name='SIGHUP'),
)
```

```
event_loop.add_signal_handler(
    signal.SIGUSR1,
    functools.partial(signal_handler, name='SIGUSR1'),
)
event_loop.add_signal_handler(
    signal.SIGINT,
    functools.partial(signal_handler, name='SIGINT'),
)
```

This example program uses a coroutine to send signals to itself via os.kill(). After each signal is sent, the coroutine yields control to allow the handler to be run. In a real-world application, there would be more places where application code yields back to the event loop, so that no artificial yield (like that found in the example) would be needed.

```
async def send_signals():
    pid = os.getpid()
    print('starting send_signals for {}'.format(pid))

    for name in ['SIGHUP', 'SIGHUP', 'SIGUSR1', 'SIGINT']:
        print('sending {}'.format(name))
        os.kill(pid, getattr(signal, name))
        # Yield control to allow the signal handler to run,
        # since the signal does not interrupt the program
        # flow otherwise.
        print('yielding control')
        await asyncio.sleep(0.01)
    return
```

The main program runs send_signals() until it has sent all of the signals.

```
try:
    event_loop.run_until_complete(send_signals())
finally:
    event_loop.close()
```

The output shows how the handlers are called when send_signals() yields control after sending a signal.

```
$ python3 asyncio_signal.py

starting send_signals for 21772
sending SIGHUP
yielding control
signal_handler('SIGHUP')
sending SIGHUP
yielding control
signal_handler('SIGHUP')
sending SIGUSR1
```

```
yielding control
signal_handler('SIGUSR1')
sending SIGINT
yielding control
signal_handler('SIGINT')
```

TIP

Related Reading

- signal (page 553): Receive notification of asynchronous system events.

10.5.14   Combining Coroutines with Threads and Processes

Many predefined libraries are not ready to be used with asyncio natively. They may block, or they may depend on concurrency features not available through the module. It is still possible to use those libraries in an application based on asyncio by using an *executor* from concurrent.futures (page 677) to run the code in either a separate thread or a separate process.

10.5.14.1   Threads

The run_in_executor() method of the event loop takes an executor instance, a regular callable to invoke, and any arguments to be passed to the callable. It returns a Future that can be used to wait for the function to finish its work and return something. If no executor is passed in, a ThreadPoolExecutor is created. The next example explicitly creates an executor to limit the number of worker threads it will have available.

A ThreadPoolExecutor starts its worker threads and then calls each of the provided functions once in a thread. This example shows how to combine run_in_executor() and wait() to have a coroutine yield control to the event loop while blocking functions run in separate threads, and then wake back up when those functions are finished.

Listing 10.108: **asyncio_executor_thread.py**

```
import asyncio
import concurrent.futures
import logging
import sys
import time


def blocks(n):
    log = logging.getLogger('blocks({})'.format(n))
    log.info('running')
    time.sleep(0.1)
```

```
            log.info('done')
            return n ** 2


    async def run_blocking_tasks(executor):
        log = logging.getLogger('run_blocking_tasks')
        log.info('starting')

        log.info('creating executor tasks')
        loop = asyncio.get_event_loop()
        blocking_tasks = [
            loop.run_in_executor(executor, blocks, i)
            for i in range(6)
        ]
        log.info('waiting for executor tasks')
        completed, pending = await asyncio.wait(blocking_tasks)
        results = [t.result() for t in completed]
        log.info('results: {!r}'.format(results))

        log.info('exiting')


    if __name__ == '__main__':
        # Configure logging to show the name of the thread
        # where the log message originates.
        logging.basicConfig(
            level=logging.INFO,
            format='%(threadName)10s %(name)18s: %(message)s',
            stream=sys.stderr,
        )

        # Create a limited thread pool.
        executor = concurrent.futures.ThreadPoolExecutor(
            max_workers=3,
        )

        event_loop = asyncio.get_event_loop()
        try:
            event_loop.run_until_complete(
                run_blocking_tasks(executor)
            )
        finally:
            event_loop.close()
```

asyncio_executor_thread.py uses logging (page 980) to conveniently indicate which thread and function are producing each log message. Because a separate logger is used in each call to blocks(), the output clearly shows the same threads being reused to call multiple copies of the function with different arguments.

```
$ python3 asyncio_executor_thread.py

MainThread run_blocking_tasks: starting
MainThread run_blocking_tasks: creating executor tasks
  Thread-1         blocks(0): running
  Thread-2         blocks(1): running
  Thread-3         blocks(2): running
MainThread run_blocking_tasks: waiting for executor tasks
  Thread-1         blocks(0): done
  Thread-3         blocks(2): done
  Thread-1         blocks(3): running
  Thread-2         blocks(1): done
  Thread-3         blocks(4): running
  Thread-2         blocks(5): running
  Thread-1         blocks(3): done
  Thread-2         blocks(5): done
  Thread-3         blocks(4): done
MainThread run_blocking_tasks: results: [16, 4, 1, 0, 25, 9]
MainThread run_blocking_tasks: exiting
```

10.5.14.2   Processes

A `ProcessPoolExecutor` works in much the same way, creating a set of worker processes instead of threads. Although using separate processes requires more system resources, for computationally intensive operations it can make sense to run a separate task on each CPU core.

Listing 10.109: **asyncio_executor_process.py**

```python
# Changes from asyncio_executor_thread.py

if __name__ == '__main__':
    # Configure logging to show the ID of the process
    # where the log message originates.
    logging.basicConfig(
        level=logging.INFO,
        format='PID %(process)5s %(name)18s: %(message)s',
        stream=sys.stderr,
    )

    # Create a limited process pool.
    executor = concurrent.futures.ProcessPoolExecutor(
        max_workers=3,
    )

    event_loop = asyncio.get_event_loop()
    try:
        event_loop.run_until_complete(
```

```
            run_blocking_tasks(executor)
        )
    finally:
        event_loop.close()
```

The only change needed to move from threads to processes is to create a different type of executor. This example also changes the logging format string to include the process ID instead of the thread name, thereby demonstrating that the tasks are really running in separate processes.

```
$ python3 asyncio_executor_process.py

PID 16429 run_blocking_tasks: starting
PID 16429 run_blocking_tasks: creating executor tasks
PID 16429 run_blocking_tasks: waiting for executor tasks
PID 16430          blocks(0): running
PID 16431          blocks(1): running
PID 16432          blocks(2): running
PID 16430          blocks(0): done
PID 16432          blocks(2): done
PID 16431          blocks(1): done
PID 16430          blocks(3): running
PID 16432          blocks(4): running
PID 16431          blocks(5): running
PID 16431          blocks(5): done
PID 16432          blocks(4): done
PID 16430          blocks(3): done
PID 16429 run_blocking_tasks: results: [4, 0, 16, 1, 9, 25]
PID 16429 run_blocking_tasks: exiting
```

10.5.15 Debugging with asyncio

Several useful debugging features are built into `asyncio`. For example, the event loop uses `logging` (page 980) to generate status messages as it runs. Some of these messages are available if logging is enabled in an application; others can be turned on explicitly by telling the loop to generate more debugging messages. Call `set_debug()` and pass in a boolean value to indicate whether debugging should be enabled.

Because applications built on `asyncio` are highly sensitive to greedy coroutines that fail to yield control, support for detecting slow callbacks is built into the event loop. Turn on this feature by enabling debugging, and control the definition of "slow" by setting the `slow_callback_duration` property of the loop to the number of seconds after which a warning should be emitted.

Finally, if an application using `asyncio` exits without cleaning up some of the coroutines or other resources, that behavior may signal that a logic error is preventing some of the application code from running. Enabling `ResourceWarning` warnings causes these cases to be reported when the program exits.

Listing 10.110: **asyncio_debug.py**

```python
import argparse
import asyncio
import logging
import sys
import time
import warnings

parser = argparse.ArgumentParser('debugging asyncio')
parser.add_argument(
    '-v',
    dest='verbose',
    default=False,
    action='store_true',
)
args = parser.parse_args()

logging.basicConfig(
    level=logging.DEBUG,
    format='%(levelname)7s: %(message)s',
    stream=sys.stderr,
)
LOG = logging.getLogger('')


async def inner():
    LOG.info('inner starting')
    # Use a blocking sleep to simulate
    # doing work inside the function.
    time.sleep(0.1)
    LOG.info('inner completed')


async def outer(loop):
    LOG.info('outer starting')
    await asyncio.ensure_future(loop.create_task(inner()))
    LOG.info('outer completed')


event_loop = asyncio.get_event_loop()
if args.verbose:
    LOG.info('enabling debugging')

    # Enable debugging.
    event_loop.set_debug(True)

    # Make the threshold for "slow" tasks very very small for
    # illustration. The default is 0.1, or 100 milliseconds.
    event_loop.slow_callback_duration = 0.001
```

```
    # Report all mistakes managing asynchronous resources.
    warnings.simplefilter('always', ResourceWarning)

LOG.info('entering event loop')
event_loop.run_until_complete(outer(event_loop))
```

When run without debugging enabled, everything looks fine with this application.

```
$ python3 asyncio_debug.py

  DEBUG: Using selector: KqueueSelector
   INFO: entering event loop
   INFO: outer starting
   INFO: inner starting
   INFO: inner completed
   INFO: outer completed
```

Turning on debugging, however, exposes some of the problematic issues in the application. For example, although `inner()` finishes, it takes more time to do so than the `slow_callback_duration` that has been set. In addition, the event loop is not closed properly when the program exits.

```
$ python3 asyncio_debug.py -v

  DEBUG: Using selector: KqueueSelector
   INFO: enabling debugging
   INFO: entering event loop
   INFO: outer starting
   INFO: inner starting
   INFO: inner completed
WARNING: Executing <Task finished coro=<inner() done, defined at
asyncio_debug.py:34> result=None created at asyncio_debug.py:44>
took 0.102 seconds
   INFO: outer completed
.../lib/python3.5/asyncio/base_events.py:429: ResourceWarning:
unclosed event loop <_UnixSelectorEventLoop running=False
closed=False debug=True>
  DEBUG: Close <_UnixSelectorEventLoop running=False
closed=False debug=True>
```

NOTE

In Python 3.5, asyncio is still a *provisional* module. The API was stablized in Python 3.6, and most of the changes were backported to later patch releases of Python 3.5. As a result, the module may work slightly differently under different versions of Python 3.5.

TIP

Related Reading

- Standard library documentation for `asyncio`.[10]
- **PEP 3156**[11]: Asynchronous IO Support Rebooted: The "asyncio" Module.
- **PEP 380**[12]: Syntax for Delegating to a Subgenerator.
- **PEP 492**[13]: Coroutines with `async` and `await` syntax.
- `concurrent.futures` (page 677): Manage pools of concurrent tasks.
- `socket` (page 693): Low-level network communication.
- `select` (page 728): Low-level asynchronous I/O tools.
- `socketserver` (page 742): Framework for creating network servers.
- What's New in Python 3.6: asyncio[14]: Summary of the changes to `asyncio` as the API stablized in Python 3.6.
- trollius[15]: A port of Tulip, the original version of `asyncio`, to Python 2.
- The New asyncio Module in Python 3.4: Event Loops[16]: Article by Gastón Hillar in *Dr. Dobb's*.
- Exploring Python 3's Asyncio by Example[17]: Blog post by Chad Lung.
- A Web Crawler with Asyncio Coroutines[18]: An article in *The Architecture of Open Source Applications* by A. Jesse Jiryu Davis and Guido van Rossum.
- Playing with asyncio[19]: Blog post by Nathan Hoad.
- Async I/O and Python[20]: Blog post by Mark McLoughlin.
- A Curious Course on Coroutines and Concurrency[21]: PyCon 2009 tutorial by David Beazley.
- How the heck does async/await work in Python 3.5?[22]: Blog post by Brett Cannon.
- *Unix Network Programming, Volume 1: The Sockets Networking API, Third Edition*, by W. Richard Stevens, Bill Fenner, and Andrew M. Rudoff; Addison-Wesley Professional, 2004. ISBN-10: 0131411551.
- *Foundations of Python Network Programming, Third Edition*, by Brandon Rhodes and John Goerzen; Apress, 2014. ISBN-10: 1430258543.

---

[10] https://docs.python.org/3.5/library/asyncio.html
[11] www.python.org/dev/peps/pep-3156
[12] www.python.org/dev/peps/pep-0380
[13] www.python.org/dev/peps/pep-0492
[14] https://docs.python.org/3/whatsnew/3.6.html#asyncio
[15] https://pypi.python.org/pypi/trollius
[16] www.drdobbs.com/open-source/the-new-asyncio-module-in-python-34-even/240168401
[17] www.giantflyingsaucer.com/blog/?p=5557
[18] http://aosabook.org/en/500L/a-web-crawler-with-asyncio-coroutines.html
[19] www.getoffmalawn.com/blog/playing-with-asyncio
[20] https://blogs.gnome.org/markmc/2013/06/04/async-io-and-python/
[21] www.dabeaz.com/coroutines/
[22] www.snarky.ca/how-the-heck-does-async-await-work-in-python-3-5

10.6 concurrent.futures: Manage Pools of Concurrent Tasks

The `concurrent.futures` module provides interfaces for running tasks using pools of thread or process workers. The APIs are the same for both options, so applications can switch between threads and processes with minimal changes.

The module provides two types of classes for interacting with the pools. *Executors* are used for managing pools of workers, and *futures* are used for managing results computed by the workers. To use a pool of workers, an application creates an instance of the appropriate executor class and then submits tasks for it to run. When each task is started, a `Future` instance is returned. When the result of the task is needed, an application can use the `Future` to block until the result becomes available. Various APIs are provided that make it convenient to wait for tasks to complete, so the `Future` objects do not need to be managed directly.

10.6.1 Using map() with a Basic Thread Pool

The `ThreadPoolExecutor` manages a set of worker threads, passing tasks to them as they become available for more work. The next example uses `map()` to concurrently produce a set of results from an input iterable. The task uses `time.sleep()` to pause a different amount of time to demonstrate that, regardless of the order of execution of concurrent tasks, `map()` always returns the values in order based on the inputs.

Listing 10.111: `futures_thread_pool_map.py`

```
from concurrent import futures
import threading
import time


def task(n):
    print('{}: sleeping {}'.format(
        threading.current_thread().name,
        n)
    )
    time.sleep(n / 10)
    print('{}: done with {}'.format(
        threading.current_thread().name,
        n)
    )
    return n / 10


ex = futures.ThreadPoolExecutor(max_workers=2)
print('main: starting')
results = ex.map(task, range(5, 0, -1))
print('main: unprocessed results {}'.format(results))
print('main: waiting for real results')
```

```
real_results = list(results)
print('main: results: {}'.format(real_results))
```

The return value from `map()` is actually a special type of iterator that knows to wait for each response as the main program iterates over it.

```
$ python3 futures_thread_pool_map.py

main: starting
Thread-1: sleeping 5
Thread-2: sleeping 4
main: unprocessed results <generator object
Executor.map.<locals>.result_iterator at 0x1013c80a0>
main: waiting for real results
Thread-2: done with 4
Thread-2: sleeping 3
Thread-1: done with 5
Thread-1: sleeping 2
Thread-1: done with 2
Thread-1: sleeping 1
Thread-2: done with 3
Thread-1: done with 1
main: results: [0.5, 0.4, 0.3, 0.2, 0.1]
```

10.6.2   Scheduling Individual Tasks

In addition to using `map()`, it is possible to schedule an individual task with an executor using `submit()`. The `Future` instance returned can then be used to wait for that task's results.

Listing 10.112: **futures_thread_pool_submit.py**

```
from concurrent import futures
import threading
import time


def task(n):
    print('{}: sleeping {}'.format(
        threading.current_thread().name,
        n)
    )
    time.sleep(n / 10)
    print('{}: done with {}'.format(
        threading.current_thread().name,
        n)
    )
    return n / 10
```

```
ex = futures.ThreadPoolExecutor(max_workers=2)
print('main: starting')
f = ex.submit(task, 5)
print('main: future: {}'.format(f))
print('main: waiting for results')
result = f.result()
print('main: result: {}'.format(result))
print('main: future after result: {}'.format(f))
```

The status of the Future changes after the tasks are completed and the result is made available.

```
$ python3 futures_thread_pool_submit.py

main: starting
Thread-1: sleeping 5
main: future: <Future at 0x1010e6080 state=running>
main: waiting for results
Thread-1: done with 5
main: result: 0.5
main: future after result: <Future at 0x1010e6080 state=finished
  returned float>
```

10.6.3 Waiting for Tasks in Any Order

Invoking the result() method of a Future blocks until the task completes (either by returning a value or by raising an exception) or is canceled. The results of multiple tasks can be accessed in the order the tasks were scheduled using map(). If the order in which the results should be processed does not matter, use as_completed() to process them as each task finishes.

Listing 10.113: futures_as_completed.py

```
from concurrent import futures
import random
import time


def task(n):
    time.sleep(random.random())
    return (n, n / 10)


ex = futures.ThreadPoolExecutor(max_workers=5)
print('main: starting')

wait_for = [
    ex.submit(task, i)
```

```
        for i in range(5, 0, -1)
]

for f in futures.as_completed(wait_for):
    print('main: result: {}'.format(f.result()))
```

Because the pool has as many workers as tasks, all of the tasks can be started. They finish in a random order, so the values generated by as_completed() are different each time the example program runs.

```
$ python3 futures_as_completed.py

main: starting
main: result: (3, 0.3)
main: result: (5, 0.5)
main: result: (4, 0.4)
main: result: (2, 0.2)
main: result: (1, 0.1)
```

10.6.4   Future Callbacks

To take some action when a task completed, without explicitly waiting for the result, use add_done_callback() to specify a new function to call when the Future is done. The callback should be a callable taking a single argument, the Future instance.

Listing 10.114: futures_future_callback.py

```
from concurrent import futures
import time


def task(n):
    print('{}: sleeping'.format(n))
    time.sleep(0.5)
    print('{}: done'.format(n))
    return n / 10


def done(fn):
    if fn.cancelled():
        print('{}: canceled'.format(fn.arg))
    elif fn.done():
        error = fn.exception()
        if error:
            print('{}: error returned: {}'.format(
```

```
                fn.arg, error))
        else:
            result = fn.result()
            print('{}: value returned: {}'.format(
                fn.arg, result))


if __name__ == '__main__':
    ex = futures.ThreadPoolExecutor(max_workers=2)
    print('main: starting')
    f = ex.submit(task, 5)
    f.arg = 5
    f.add_done_callback(done)
    result = f.result()
```

The callback is invoked regardless of the reason the Future is considered "done," so it is necessary to check the status of the object passed to the callback before using it in any way.

```
$ python3 futures_future_callback.py

main: starting
5: sleeping
5: done
5: value returned: 0.5
```

10.6.5   Canceling Tasks

A Future can be canceled, if it has been submitted but not started, by calling its cancel() method.

Listing 10.115: **futures_future_callback_cancel.py**

```
from concurrent import futures
import time


def task(n):
    print('{}: sleeping'.format(n))
    time.sleep(0.5)
    print('{}: done'.format(n))
    return n / 10


def done(fn):
    if fn.cancelled():
        print('{}: canceled'.format(fn.arg))
```

```
        elif fn.done():
            print('{}: not canceled'.format(fn.arg))


    if __name__ == '__main__':
        ex = futures.ThreadPoolExecutor(max_workers=2)
        print('main: starting')
        tasks = []

        for i in range(10, 0, -1):
            print('main: submitting {}'.format(i))
            f = ex.submit(task, i)
            f.arg = i
            f.add_done_callback(done)
            tasks.append((i, f))

        for i, t in reversed(tasks):
            if not t.cancel():
                print('main: did not cancel {}'.format(i))

        ex.shutdown()
```

cancel() returns a boolean value indicating whether the task could be canceled.

```
$ python3 futures_future_callback_cancel.py

main: starting
main: submitting 10
10: sleeping
main: submitting 9
9: sleeping
main: submitting 8
main: submitting 7
main: submitting 6
main: submitting 5
main: submitting 4
main: submitting 3
main: submitting 2
main: submitting 1
1: canceled
2: canceled
3: canceled
4: canceled
5: canceled
6: canceled
7: canceled
8: canceled
main: did not cancel 9
main: did not cancel 10
```

```
10: done
10: not canceled
9: done
9: not canceled
```

10.6.6   Exceptions in Tasks

If a task raises an unhandled exception, it is saved to the Future for the task and made available through the result() or exception() method.

Listing 10.116: futures_future_exception.py

```python
from concurrent import futures


def task(n):
    print('{}: starting'.format(n))
    raise ValueError('the value {} is no good'.format(n))


ex = futures.ThreadPoolExecutor(max_workers=2)
print('main: starting')
f = ex.submit(task, 5)

error = f.exception()
print('main: error: {}'.format(error))

try:
    result = f.result()
except ValueError as e:
    print('main: saw error "{}" when accessing result'.format(e))
```

If result() is called after an unhandled exception is raised within a task function, the same exception is raised again in the current context.

```
$ python3 futures_future_exception.py

main: starting
5: starting
main: error: the value 5 is no good
main: saw error "the value 5 is no good" when accessing result
```

10.6.7   Context Manager

Executors work as context managers, running tasks concurrently and waiting for them all to complete. When the context manager exits, the shutdown() method of the executor is called.

```python
from concurrent import futures


def task(n):
    print(n)


with futures.ThreadPoolExecutor(max_workers=2) as ex:
    print('main: starting')
    ex.submit(task, 1)
    ex.submit(task, 2)
    ex.submit(task, 3)
    ex.submit(task, 4)

print('main: done')
```

This mode of using the executor is useful when the thread or process resources should be cleaned up when execution leaves the current scope.

```
$ python3 futures_context_manager.py

main: starting
1
2
3
4
main: done
```

10.6.8   Process Pools

The `ProcessPoolExecutor` works in the same way as `ThreadPoolExecutor`, but uses processes instead of threads. This approach allows CPU-intensive operations to use a separate CPU and not be blocked by the CPython interpreter's global interpreter lock.

```python
from concurrent import futures
import os


def task(n):
    return (n, os.getpid())


ex = futures.ProcessPoolExecutor(max_workers=2)
results = ex.map(task, range(5, 0, -1))
```

```
    for n, pid in results:
        print('ran task {} in process {}'.format(n, pid))
```

As with the thread pool, individual worker processes are reused for multiple tasks.

```
$ python3 futures_process_pool_map.py

ran task 5 in process 60245
ran task 4 in process 60246
ran task 3 in process 60245
ran task 2 in process 60245
ran task 1 in process 60245
```

If something happens to one of the worker processes that causes it to exit unexpectedly, the ProcessPoolExecutor is considered "broken" and will no longer schedule tasks.

Listing 10.119: **futures_process_pool_broken.py**

```
from concurrent import futures
import os
import signal


with futures.ProcessPoolExecutor(max_workers=2) as ex:
    print('getting the pid for one worker')
    f1 = ex.submit(os.getpid)
    pid1 = f1.result()

    print('killing process {}'.format(pid1))
    os.kill(pid1, signal.SIGHUP)

    print('submitting another task')
    f2 = ex.submit(os.getpid)
    try:
        pid2 = f2.result()
    except futures.process.BrokenProcessPool as e:
        print('could not start new tasks: {}'.format(e))
```

The BrokenProcessPool exception is actually thrown when the results are processed, rather than when the new task is submitted.

```
$ python3 futures_process_pool_broken.py

getting the pid for one worker
killing process 62059
submitting another task
could not start new tasks: A process in the process pool was
terminated abruptly while the future was running or pending.
```

TIP

Related Reading

- Standard library documentation for `concurrent.futures`.[23]
- **PEP 3148**[24]: The proposal for creating the `concurrent.futures` feature set.
- Section 10.5.14, "Combining Coroutines with Threads and Processes" (page 670).
- `threading` (page 560).
- `multiprocessing` (page 586).

---

[23] https://docs.python.org/3.5/library/concurrent.futures.html
[24] www.python.org/dev/peps/pep-3148

Chapter 11

Networking

Network communication is used to retrieve data needed for an algorithm running locally, to share information for distributed processing, and to manage cloud services. Python's standard library comes complete with modules for creating network services, as well as for accessing existing services remotely.

The `ipaddress` (page 687) module includes classes for validating, comparing, and otherwise operating on IPv4 and IPv6 network addresses.

The low-level `socket` (page 693) library provides direct access to the native C socket library, and can be used to communicate with any network service. `selectors` (page 724) provides a high-level interface for watching multiple sockets simultaneously, and is useful for allowing network servers to communicate with multiple clients simultaneously. `select` (page 728) provides the low-level APIs used by `selectors` (page 724).

The frameworks in `socketserver` (page 742) abstract out a significant portion of the repetitive work necessary to create a new network server. The classes can be combined to create servers that fork or use threads and support TCP or UDP. Only the actual message handling needs to be provided by the application.

11.1   ipaddress: Internet Addresses

The `ipaddress` module includes classes for working with IPv4 and IPv6 network addresses. The classes support validation, finding addresses and hosts on a network, and other common operations.

11.1.1   Addresses

The most basic object represents the network address itself. Pass a string, integer, or byte sequence to `ip_address()` to construct an address. The return value will be an `IPv4Address` or `IPv6Address` instance, depending on the type of address being used.

Listing 11.1: `ipaddress_addresses.py`

```
import binascii
import ipaddress


ADDRESSES = [
    '10.9.0.6',
```

```
                 'fdfd:87b5:b475:5e3e:b1bc:e121:a8eb:14aa',
    ]

    for ip in ADDRESSES:
        addr = ipaddress.ip_address(ip)
        print('{!r}'.format(addr))
        print('   IP version:', addr.version)
        print('   is private:', addr.is_private)
        print('  packed form:', binascii.hexlify(addr.packed))
        print('      integer:', int(addr))
        print()
```

Both classes can provide various representations of the address for different purposes, as well as answer basic assertions such as whether the address is reserved for multicast communication or whether it is on a private network.

```
$ python3 ipaddress_addresses.py

IPv4Address('10.9.0.6')
   IP version: 4
   is private: True
  packed form: b'0a090006'
      integer: 168361990

IPv6Address('fdfd:87b5:b475:5e3e:b1bc:e121:a8eb:14aa')
   IP version: 6
   is private: True
  packed form: b'fdfd87b5b4755e3eb1bce121a8eb14aa'
      integer: 337611086560236126439725644408160982186
```

11.1.2   Networks

A network is defined by a range of addresses. It is usually expressed with a base address and a mask indicating which portions of the address represent the network, and which portions represent addresses on that network. The mask can be expressed either explicitly or by using a prefix length value, as in the following example.

Listing 11.2: ipaddress_networks.py

```
import ipaddress

NETWORKS = [
    '10.9.0.0/24',
    'fdfd:87b5:b475:5e3e::/64',
]

for n in NETWORKS:
    net = ipaddress.ip_network(n)
```

```
    print('{!r}'.format(net))
    print('     is private:', net.is_private)
    print('      broadcast:', net.broadcast_address)
    print('     compressed:', net.compressed)
    print('   with netmask:', net.with_netmask)
    print('  with hostmask:', net.with_hostmask)
    print('  num addresses:', net.num_addresses)
    print()
```

As with addresses, there are two network classes for IPv4 and IPv6 networks. Each class provides properties or methods for accessing values associated with the network, such as the broadcast address and the addresses on the network available for hosts to use.

```
$ python3 ipaddress_networks.py

IPv4Network('10.9.0.0/24')
    is private: True
     broadcast: 10.9.0.255
    compressed: 10.9.0.0/24
  with netmask: 10.9.0.0/255.255.255.0
 with hostmask: 10.9.0.0/0.0.0.255
 num addresses: 256

IPv6Network('fdfd:87b5:b475:5e3e::/64')
    is private: True
     broadcast: fdfd:87b5:b475:5e3e:ffff:ffff:ffff:ffff
    compressed: fdfd:87b5:b475:5e3e::/64
  with netmask: fdfd:87b5:b475:5e3e::/ffff:ffff:ffff:ffff::
 with hostmask: fdfd:87b5:b475:5e3e::/::ffff:ffff:ffff:ffff
 num addresses: 18446744073709551616
```

A network instance is iterable and yields the addresses on the network.

Listing 11.3: **ipaddress_network_iterate.py**

```
import ipaddress

NETWORKS = [
    '10.9.0.0/24',
    'fdfd:87b5:b475:5e3e::/64',
]

for n in NETWORKS:
    net = ipaddress.ip_network(n)
    print('{!r}'.format(net))
    for i, ip in zip(range(3), net):
        print(ip)
    print()
```

This example prints only a few of the addresses, because an IPv6 network can contain far more addresses than fit in the output.

```
$ python3 ipaddress_network_iterate.py

IPv4Network('10.9.0.0/24')
10.9.0.0
10.9.0.1
10.9.0.2

IPv6Network('fdfd:87b5:b475:5e3e::/64')
fdfd:87b5:b475:5e3e::
fdfd:87b5:b475:5e3e::1
fdfd:87b5:b475:5e3e::2
```

Iterating over the network yields addresses, but not all of them are valid for hosts. For example, the base address of the network and the broadcast address are both included. To find the addresses that can be used by regular hosts on the network, use the `hosts()` method, which produces a generator.

Listing 11.4: **ipaddress_network_iterate_hosts.py**

```python
import ipaddress

NETWORKS = [
    '10.9.0.0/24',
    'fdfd:87b5:b475:5e3e::/64',
]

for n in NETWORKS:
    net = ipaddress.ip_network(n)
    print('{!r}'.format(net))
    for i, ip in zip(range(3), net.hosts()):
        print(ip)
    print()
```

Comparing the output of this example with the previous example shows that the host addresses do not include the first values produced when iterating over the entire network.

```
$ python3 ipaddress_network_iterate_hosts.py

IPv4Network('10.9.0.0/24')
10.9.0.1
10.9.0.2
10.9.0.3

IPv6Network('fdfd:87b5:b475:5e3e::/64')
fdfd:87b5:b475:5e3e::1
```

```
fdfd:87b5:b475:5e3e::2
fdfd:87b5:b475:5e3e::3
```

In addition to the iterator protocol, networks support the `in` operator, which is used to determine whether an address is part of a network.

Listing 11.5: `ipaddress_network_membership.py`

```
import ipaddress


NETWORKS = [
    ipaddress.ip_network('10.9.0.0/24'),
    ipaddress.ip_network('fdfd:87b5:b475:5e3e::/64'),
]

ADDRESSES = [
    ipaddress.ip_address('10.9.0.6'),
    ipaddress.ip_address('10.7.0.31'),
    ipaddress.ip_address(
        'fdfd:87b5:b475:5e3e:b1bc:e121:a8eb:14aa'
    ),
    ipaddress.ip_address('fe80::3840:c439:b25e:63b0'),
]


for ip in ADDRESSES:
    for net in NETWORKS:
        if ip in net:
            print('{}\nis on {}'.format(ip, net))
            break
    else:
        print('{}\nis not on a known network'.format(ip))
    print()
```

The implementation of `in` uses the network mask to test the address, so it is much more efficient than expanding the full list of addresses on the network.

```
$ python3 ipaddress_network_membership.py

10.9.0.6
is on 10.9.0.0/24

10.7.0.31
is not on a known network

fdfd:87b5:b475:5e3e:b1bc:e121:a8eb:14aa
is on fdfd:87b5:b475:5e3e::/64
```

```
fe80::3840:c439:b25e:63b0
is not on a known network
```

11.1.3   Interfaces

A network interface represents a specific address on a network and can be represented by a
host address and a network prefix or netmask.

Listing 11.6: ipaddress_interfaces.py

```python
import ipaddress


ADDRESSES = [
    '10.9.0.6/24',
    'fdfd:87b5:b475:5e3e:b1bc:e121:a8eb:14aa/64',
]


for ip in ADDRESSES:
    iface = ipaddress.ip_interface(ip)
    print('{!r}'.format(iface))
    print('network:\n  ', iface.network)
    print('ip:\n  ', iface.ip)
    print('IP with prefixlen:\n  ', iface.with_prefixlen)
    print('netmask:\n  ', iface.with_netmask)
    print('hostmask:\n  ', iface.with_hostmask)
    print()
```

The interface object has properties to access the full network and address separately, as
well as several different ways to express the interface and network mask.

```
$ python3 ipaddress_interfaces.py

IPv4Interface('10.9.0.6/24')
network:
   10.9.0.0/24
ip:
   10.9.0.6
IP with prefixlen:
   10.9.0.6/24
netmask:
   10.9.0.6/255.255.255.0
hostmask:
   10.9.0.6/0.0.0.255

IPv6Interface('fdfd:87b5:b475:5e3e:b1bc:e121:a8eb:14aa/64')
network:
   fdfd:87b5:b475:5e3e::/64
```

```
ip:
    fdfd:87b5:b475:5e3e:b1bc:e121:a8eb:14aa
IP with prefixlen:
    fdfd:87b5:b475:5e3e:b1bc:e121:a8eb:14aa/64
netmask:
    fdfd:87b5:b475:5e3e:b1bc:e121:a8eb:14aa/ffff:ffff:ffff:ffff::
hostmask:
    fdfd:87b5:b475:5e3e:b1bc:e121:a8eb:14aa/::ffff:ffff:ffff:ffff
```

TIP

Related Reading

- Standard library documentation for `ipaddress`.[1]
- **PEP 3144**[2]: IP Address Manipulation Library for the Python Standard Library.
- An introduction to the `ipaddress` module.[3]
- Wikipedia: IP address[4]: An introduction to IP addresses and networks.
- *Computer Networks, Fifth Edition*, by Andrew S. Tanenbaum and David J. Wetherall. Pearson, 2010. ISBN-10: 0132126958.

11.2   socket: Network Communication

The `socket` module exposes the low-level C API for communicating over a network using the BSD socket interface. It includes the `socket` class, for handling the actual data channel, as well as functions for network-related tasks such as converting a server's name to an address and formatting data to be sent across the network.

11.2.1   Addressing, Protocol Families, and Socket Types

A *socket* is one endpoint of a communication channel used by programs to pass data back and forth locally or across the Internet. Sockets have two primary properties controlling the way they send data: The *address family* controls the OSI network layer protocol used and the *socket type* controls the transport layer protocol.

Python supports three address families. The most common, `AF_INET`, is used for IPv4 Internet addressing. IPv4 addresses are 4 bytes long and are usually represented as a sequence of four numbers, one per octet, separated by dots (e.g., `10.1.1.5` and `127.0.0.1`).

---

[1] https://docs.python.org/3.5/library/ipaddress.html
[2] www.python.org/dev/peps/pep-3144
[3] https://docs.python.org/3.5/howto/ipaddress.html#ipaddress-howto
[4] https://en.wikipedia.org/wiki/IP_address

These values are more commonly referred to as "IP addresses." Almost all Internet networking is done using IPv4 at this time.

`AF_INET6` is used for IPv6 Internet addressing. IPv6 is the "next generation" version of the Internet protocol, and supports 128-bit addresses, traffic shaping, and routing features not available under IPv4. Adoption of IPv6 continues to grow, especially with the proliferation of cloud computing and the extra devices being added to the network because of Internet-of-things projects.

`AF_UNIX` is the address family for Unix Domain Sockets (UDS), an interprocess communication protocol available on POSIX-compliant systems. The implementation of UDS typically allows the operating system to pass data directly from process to process, without going through the network stack. This approach is more efficient than using `AF_INET`, but because the file system is used as the namespace for addressing, UDS is restricted to processes on the same system. The appeal of using UDS over other IPC mechanisms such as named pipes or shared memory is that the programming interface is the same as for IP networking, so the application can take advantage of efficient communication when running on a single host, yet use the same code when sending data across the network.

NOTE

The `AF_UNIX` constant is defined only on systems where UDS is supported.

The socket type is usually either `SOCK_DGRAM` for message-oriented datagram transport or `SOCK_STREAM` for stream-oriented transport. Datagram sockets are most often associated with UDP, the *user datagram protocol*. They provide unreliable delivery of individual messages. Stream-oriented sockets are associated with TCP, the *transmission control protocol*. They provide byte streams between the client and the server, ensuring message delivery or failure notification through timeout management, retransmission, and other features.

Most application protocols that deliver a large amount of data, such as HTTP, are built on top of TCP because it is simpler to create complex applications when message ordering and delivery are handled automatically. UDP is commonly used for protocols where order is less important (since the messages are self-contained and often small, such as name lookups via DNS), and for *multicasting* (sending the same data to several hosts). Both UDP and TCP can be used with either IPv4 or IPv6 addressing.

NOTE

Python's `socket` module supports other socket types but they are less commonly used, and so are not covered here. Refer to the standard library documentation for more details.

11.2.1.1   Looking Up Hosts on the Network

`socket` includes functions to interface with the domain name services on the network so that a program can convert the hostname of a server into its numerical network address. Applications do not need to convert addresses explicitly before using them to connect to a server. Nevertheless, when reporting errors, it can be useful to include both the numerical address and the name value being used.

To find the official name of the current host, use `gethostname()`.

Listing 11.7: socket_gethostname.py

```
import socket

print(socket.gethostname())
```

The name returned will depend on the network settings for the current system, and may change if it is on a different network (such as a laptop attached to a wireless LAN).

```
$ python3 socket_gethostname.py

apu.hellfly.net
```

Use `gethostbyname()` to consult the operating system hostname resolution API and convert the name of a server to its numerical address.

Listing 11.8: socket_gethostbyname.py

```
import socket

HOSTS = [
    'apu',
    'pymotw.com',
    'www.python.org',
    'nosuchname',
]

for host in HOSTS:
    try:
        print('{} : {}'.format(host, socket.gethostbyname(host)))
    except socket.error as msg:
        print('{} : {}'.format(host, msg))
```

If the DNS configuration of the current system includes one or more domains in the search, the name argument does not need to be a fully qualified name (i.e., it does not need to include the domain name as well as the base hostname). If the name cannot be found, an exception of type `socket.error` is raised.

```
$ python3 socket_gethostbyname.py

apu : 10.9.0.10
pymotw.com : 66.33.211.242
www.python.org : 151.101.32.223
nosuchname : [Errno 8] nodename nor servname provided, or not
known
```

For access to more naming information about a server, use gethostbyname_ex(). It returns the canonical hostname of the server, any aliases, and all of the available IP addresses that can be used to reach it.

Listing 11.9: socket_gethostbyname_ex.py

```python
import socket

HOSTS = [
    'apu',
    'pymotw.com',
    'www.python.org',
    'nosuchname',
]

for host in HOSTS:
    print(host)
    try:
        name, aliases, addresses = socket.gethostbyname_ex(host)
        print('  Hostname:', name)
        print('  Aliases :', aliases)
        print(' Addresses:', addresses)
    except socket.error as msg:
        print('ERROR:', msg)
    print()
```

Having all known IP addresses for a server lets a client implement its own load-balancing or fail-over algorithms.

```
$ python3 socket_gethostbyname_ex.py

apu
  Hostname: apu.hellfly.net
  Aliases : ['apu']
 Addresses: ['10.9.0.10']

pymotw.com
  Hostname: pymotw.com
  Aliases : []
 Addresses: ['66.33.211.242']

www.python.org
  Hostname: prod.python.map.fastlylb.net
  Aliases : ['www.python.org', 'python.map.fastly.net']
 Addresses: ['151.101.32.223']

nosuchname
ERROR: [Errno 8] nodename nor servname provided, or not known
```

Use `getfqdn()` to convert a partial name to a fully qualified domain name.

Listing 11.10: **socket_getfqdn.py**

```
import socket

for host in ['apu', 'pymotw.com']:
    print('{:>10} : {}'.format(host, socket.getfqdn(host)))
```

The name returned will not necessarily match the input argument in any way if the input is an alias, as www is here.

```
$ python3 socket_getfqdn.py

       apu : apu.hellfly.net
pymotw.com : apache2-echo.catalina.dreamhost.com
```

When the address of a server is available, use `gethostbyaddr()` to do a "reverse" lookup for the name.

Listing 11.11: **socket_gethostbyaddr.py**

```
import socket

hostname, aliases, addresses = socket.gethostbyaddr('10.9.0.10')

print('Hostname :', hostname)
print('Aliases  :', aliases)
print('Addresses:', addresses)
```

The return value is a tuple containing the full hostname, any aliases, and all IP addresses associated with the name.

```
$ python3 socket_gethostbyaddr.py

Hostname : apu.hellfly.net
Aliases  : ['apu']
Addresses: ['10.9.0.10']
```

11.2.1.2 Finding Service Information

In addition to an IP address, each socket address includes an integer *port number*. Many applications can run on the same host, listening on a single IP address, but only one socket at a time can use a port at that address. The combination of IP address, protocol, and port number uniquely identifies a communication channel and ensures that messages sent through a socket arrive at the correct destination.

Some of the port numbers are pre-allocated for a specific protocol. For example, communication between email servers using SMTP occurs over port number 25 using TCP, and web clients and servers use port 80 for HTTP. The port numbers for network services with standardized names can be looked up with `getservbyname()`.

Listing 11.12: **socket_getservbyname.py**

```
import socket
from urllib.parse import urlparse

URLS = [
    'http://www.python.org',
    'https://www.mybank.com',
    'ftp://prep.ai.mit.edu',
    'gopher://gopher.micro.umn.edu',
    'smtp://mail.example.com',
    'imap://mail.example.com',
    'imaps://mail.example.com',
    'pop3://pop.example.com',
    'pop3s://pop.example.com',
]

for url in URLS:
    parsed_url = urlparse(url)
    port = socket.getservbyname(parsed_url.scheme)
    print('{:>6} : {}'.format(parsed_url.scheme, port))
```

Although a standardized service is unlikely to change ports, looking up the value with a system call instead of hard-coding it is more flexible when new services are added in the future.

```
$ python3 socket_getservbyname.py

  http : 80
 https : 443
   ftp : 21
gopher : 70
  smtp : 25
  imap : 143
 imaps : 993
  pop3 : 110
 pop3s : 995
```

To reverse the service port lookup, use `getservbyport()`.

Listing 11.13: **socket_getservbyport.py**

```
import socket
from urllib.parse import urlunparse
```

```
for port in [80, 443, 21, 70, 25, 143, 993, 110, 995]:
    url = '{}://example.com/'.format(socket.getservbyport(port))
    print(url)
```

The reverse lookup is useful for constructing URLs to services from arbitrary addresses.

```
$ python3 socket_getservbyport.py

http://example.com/
https://example.com/
ftp://example.com/
gopher://example.com/
smtp://example.com/
imap://example.com/
imaps://example.com/
pop3://example.com/
pop3s://example.com/
```

To retrieve the number assigned to a transport protocol, use `getprotobyname()`.

Listing 11.14: socket_getprotobyname.py

```python
import socket


def get_constants(prefix):
    """Create a dictionary mapping socket module
    constants to their names.
    """
    return {
        getattr(socket, n): n
        for n in dir(socket)
        if n.startswith(prefix)
    }


protocols = get_constants('IPPROTO_')

for name in ['icmp', 'udp', 'tcp']:
    proto_num = socket.getprotobyname(name)
    const_name = protocols[proto_num]
    print('{:>4} -> {:2d} (socket.{:<12} = {:2d})'.format(
        name, proto_num, const_name,
        getattr(socket, const_name)))
```

The values for protocol numbers are standardized, and defined as constants in `socket` with the prefix `IPPROTO_`.

```
$ python3 socket_getprotobyname.py

icmp ->  1 (socket.IPPROTO_ICMP =  1)
 udp -> 17 (socket.IPPROTO_UDP  = 17)
 tcp ->  6 (socket.IPPROTO_TCP  =  6)
```

11.2.1.3 Looking Up Server Addresses

getaddrinfo() converts the basic address of a service into a list of tuples with all of the information necessary to make a connection. Each tuple may contain different network families or protocols.

Listing 11.15: socket_getaddrinfo.py

```python
import socket


def get_constants(prefix):
    """Create a dictionary mapping socket module
    constants to their names.
    """
    return {
        getattr(socket, n): n
        for n in dir(socket)
        if n.startswith(prefix)
    }


families = get_constants('AF_')
types = get_constants('SOCK_')
protocols = get_constants('IPPROTO_')

for response in socket.getaddrinfo('www.python.org', 'http'):

    # Unpack the response tuple.
    family, socktype, proto, canonname, sockaddr = response

    print('Family         :', families[family])
    print('Type           :', types[socktype])
    print('Protocol       :', protocols[proto])
    print('Canonical name:', canonname)
    print('Socket address:', sockaddr)
    print()
```

This program demonstrates how to look up the connection information for www.python.org.

```
$ python3 socket_getaddrinfo.py

Family          : AF_INET
Type            : SOCK_DGRAM
Protocol        : IPPROTO_UDP
Canonical name:
Socket address: ('151.101.32.223', 80)

Family          : AF_INET
Type            : SOCK_STREAM
Protocol        : IPPROTO_TCP
Canonical name:
Socket address: ('151.101.32.223', 80)

Family          : AF_INET6
Type            : SOCK_DGRAM
Protocol        : IPPROTO_UDP
Canonical name:
Socket address: ('2a04:4e42:8::223', 80, 0, 0)

Family          : AF_INET6
Type            : SOCK_STREAM
Protocol        : IPPROTO_TCP
Canonical name:
Socket address: ('2a04:4e42:8::223', 80, 0, 0)
```

getaddrinfo() takes several arguments for filtering the result list. The host and port values given in the example are required arguments. The optional arguments are family, socktype, proto, and flags. The optional values should be either 0 or one of the constants defined by socket.

Listing 11.16: socket_getaddrinfo_extra_args.py

```python
import socket


def get_constants(prefix):
    """Create a dictionary mapping socket module
    constants to their names.
    """
    return {
        getattr(socket, n): n
        for n in dir(socket)
        if n.startswith(prefix)
    }
```

```
    families = get_constants('AF_')
    types = get_constants('SOCK_')
    protocols = get_constants('IPPROTO_')

    responses = socket.getaddrinfo(
        host='www.python.org',
        port='http',
        family=socket.AF_INET,
        type=socket.SOCK_STREAM,
        proto=socket.IPPROTO_TCP,
        flags=socket.AI_CANONNAME,
    )

    for response in responses:
        # Unpack the response tuple.
        family, socktype, proto, canonname, sockaddr = response

        print('Family        :', families[family])
        print('Type          :', types[socktype])
        print('Protocol      :', protocols[proto])
        print('Canonical name:', canonname)
        print('Socket address:', sockaddr)
        print()
```

Since `flags` includes `AI_CANONNAME`, the canonical name of the server—which may be different from the value used for the lookup if the host has any aliases—is included in the results this time. Without the flag, the canonical name value is left empty.

```
$ python3 socket_getaddrinfo_extra_args.py

Family        : AF_INET
Type          : SOCK_STREAM
Protocol      : IPPROTO_TCP
Canonical name: prod.python.map.fastlylb.net
Socket address: ('151.101.32.223', 80)
```

11.2.1.4   IP Address Representations

Network programs written in C use the data type `struct sockaddr` to represent IP addresses as binary values (instead of the string addresses usually found in Python programs). To convert IPv4 addresses between the Python representation and the C representation, use `inet_aton()` and `inet_ntoa()`.

Listing 11.17: socket_address_packing.py

```
import binascii
import socket
import struct
```

```
import sys

for string_address in ['192.168.1.1', '127.0.0.1']:
    packed = socket.inet_aton(string_address)
    print('Original:', string_address)
    print('Packed  :', binascii.hexlify(packed))
    print('Unpacked:', socket.inet_ntoa(packed))
    print()
```

The 4 bytes in the packed format can be passed to C libraries, transmitted safely over the network, or saved to a database compactly.

```
$ python3 socket_address_packing.py

Original: 192.168.1.1
Packed  : b'c0a80101'
Unpacked: 192.168.1.1

Original: 127.0.0.1
Packed  : b'7f000001'
Unpacked: 127.0.0.1
```

The related functions inet_pton() and inet_ntop() work with both IPv4 and IPv6 addresses, producing the appropriate format based on the address family parameter passed in.

Listing 11.18: socket_ipv6_address_packing.py

```
import binascii
import socket
import struct
import sys

string_address = '2002:ac10:10a:1234:21e:52ff:fe74:40e'
packed = socket.inet_pton(socket.AF_INET6, string_address)

print('Original:', string_address)
print('Packed  :', binascii.hexlify(packed))
print('Unpacked:', socket.inet_ntop(socket.AF_INET6, packed))
```

An IPv6 address is already a hexadecimal value, so converting the packed version to a series of hex digits produces a string similar to the original value.

```
$ python3 socket_ipv6_address_packing.py

Original: 2002:ac10:10a:1234:21e:52ff:fe74:40e
Packed  : b'2002ac10010a1234021e52fffe74040e'
Unpacked: 2002:ac10:10a:1234:21e:52ff:fe74:40e
```

Related Reading

- Wikipedia: IPv6[5]: Article discussing Internet Protocol Version 6 (IPv6).
- Wikipedia: OSI model[6]: Article describing the seven-layer model of networking implementation.
- Assigned Internet Protocol Numbers[7]: List of standard protocol names and numbers.

11.2.2   TCP/IP Client and Server

Sockets can be configured to act as a *server* and listen for incoming messages, or they can connect to other applications as a *client*. After both ends of a TCP/IP socket are connected, communication is bidirectional.

11.2.2.1   Echo Server

This sample program, which is based on the one in the standard library documentation, receives incoming messages and echos them back to the sender. It starts by creating a TCP/IP socket, and then `bind()` is used to associate the socket with the server address. In this case, the address is `localhost`, referring to the current server, and the port number is 10000.

Listing 11.19: **socket_echo_server.py**

```
import socket
import sys

# Create a TCP/IP socket.
sock = socket.socket(socket.AF_INET, socket.SOCK_STREAM)

# Bind the socket to the port.
server_address = ('localhost', 10000)
print('starting up on {} port {}'.format(*server_address))
sock.bind(server_address)

# Listen for incoming connections.
sock.listen(1)

while True:
    # Wait for a connection.
    print('waiting for a connection')
    connection, client_address = sock.accept()
    try:
```

---

[5] https://en.wikipedia.org/wiki/IPv6
[6] https://en.wikipedia.org/wiki/OSI_model
[7] www.iana.org/assignments/protocol-numbers/protocol-numbers.xml

```
        print('connection from', client_address)

        # Receive the data in small chunks and retransmit it.
        while True:
            data = connection.recv(16)
            print('received {!r}'.format(data))
            if data:
                print('sending data back to the client')
                connection.sendall(data)
            else:
                print('no data from', client_address)
                break

    finally:
        # Clean up the connection.
        connection.close()
```

Calling `listen()` puts the socket into server mode, and `accept()` waits for an incoming connection. The integer argument is the number of connections the system should queue up in the background before rejecting new clients. This example expects to work with only one connection at a time.

`accept()` returns an open connection between the server and the client, along with the client's address. The connection is actually a different socket on another port (assigned by the kernel). Data is read from the connection with `recv()` and transmitted with `sendall()`.

When communication with a client ends, the connection needs to be cleaned up using `close()`. This example uses a `try:finally` block to ensure that `close()` is always called, even in the event of an error.

11.2.2.2 Echo Client

The client program sets up its `socket` differently from the way a server does. Instead of binding to a port and listening, it uses `connect()` to attach the socket directly to the remote address.

Listing 11.20: **socket_echo_client.py**

```
import socket
import sys

# Create a TCP/IP socket.
sock = socket.socket(socket.AF_INET, socket.SOCK_STREAM)

# Connect the socket to the port where the server is listening.
server_address = ('localhost', 10000)
print('connecting to {} port {}'.format(*server_address))
sock.connect(server_address)

try:
```

```
# Send data.
message = b'This is the message.  It will be repeated.'
print('sending {!r}'.format(message))
sock.sendall(message)

# Look for the response.
amount_received = 0
amount_expected = len(message)

while amount_received < amount_expected:
    data = sock.recv(16)
    amount_received += len(data)
    print('received {!r}'.format(data))

finally:
    print('closing socket')
    sock.close()
```

After the connection is established, data can be sent through the socket with `sendall()` and received with `recv()`, just as in the server. When the entire message is sent and a copy received, the socket is closed to free up the port.

11.2.2.3 Client and Server Together

The client and the server should run in separate terminal windows, so they can communicate with each other. The server output shows the incoming connection and data, as well as the response sent back to the client.

```
$ python3 socket_echo_server.py
starting up on localhost port 10000
waiting for a connection
connection from ('127.0.0.1', 65141)
received b'This is the mess'
sending data back to the client
received b'age.  It will be'
sending data back to the client
received b' repeated.'
sending data back to the client
received b''
no data from ('127.0.0.1', 65141)
waiting for a connection
```

The client output shows the outgoing message and the response from the server.

```
$ python3 socket_echo_client.py
connecting to localhost port 10000
sending b'This is the message.  It will be repeated.'
received b'This is the mess'
```

```
received b'age.  It will be'
received b' repeated.'
closing socket
```

11.2.2.4 Easy Client Connections

TCP/IP clients can save a few steps by using the convenience function `create_connection()`
to connect to a server. The function takes one argument, a two-value tuple containing the
address of the server, and derives the best address to use for the connection.

Listing 11.21: **socket_echo_client_easy.py**

```python
import socket
import sys


def get_constants(prefix):
    """Create a dictionary mapping socket module
    constants to their names.
    """
    return {
        getattr(socket, n): n
        for n in dir(socket)
        if n.startswith(prefix)
    }


families = get_constants('AF_')
types = get_constants('SOCK_')
protocols = get_constants('IPPROTO_')

# Create a TCP/IP socket.
sock = socket.create_connection(('localhost', 10000))

print('Family  :', families[sock.family])
print('Type    :', types[sock.type])
print('Protocol:', protocols[sock.proto])
print()

try:

    # Send data.
    message = b'This is the message.  It will be repeated.'
    print('sending {!r}'.format(message))
    sock.sendall(message)

    amount_received = 0
    amount_expected = len(message)
```

```
        while amount_received < amount_expected:
            data = sock.recv(16)
            amount_received += len(data)
            print('received {!r}'.format(data))

    finally:
        print('closing socket')
        sock.close()
```

create_connection() uses getaddrinfo() to find candidate connection parameters, and returns a socket opened with the first configuration that creates a successful connection. The family, type, and proto attributes can be examined to determine the type of socket being returned.

```
$ python3 socket_echo_client_easy.py
Family  : AF_INET
Type    : SOCK_STREAM
Protocol: IPPROTO_TCP

sending b'This is the message.  It will be repeated.'
received b'This is the mess'
received b'age.  It will be'
received b' repeated.'
closing socket
```

11.2.2.5 Choosing an Address for Listening

It is important to bind a server to the correct address, so that clients can communicate with it. The previous examples all used 'localhost' as the IP address, which limits connections to clients running on the same server. Use a public address of the server, such as the value returned by gethostname(), to allow other hosts to connect. The next example modifies the echo server to listen on an address specified via a command-line argument.

Listing 11.22: **socket_echo_server_explicit.py**

```
import socket
import sys

# Create a TCP/IP socket.
sock = socket.socket(socket.AF_INET, socket.SOCK_STREAM)

# Bind the socket to the address given on the command line.
server_name = sys.argv[1]
server_address = (server_name, 10000)
print('starting up on {} port {}'.format(*server_address))
sock.bind(server_address)
sock.listen(1)
```

```
while True:
    print('waiting for a connection')
    connection, client_address = sock.accept()
    try:
        print('client connected:', client_address)
        while True:
            data = connection.recv(16)
            print('received {!r}'.format(data))
            if data:
                connection.sendall(data)
            else:
                break
    finally:
        connection.close()
```

A similar modification to the client program is needed before the server can be tested.

Listing 11.23: **socket_echo_client_explicit.py**

```
import socket
import sys

# Create a TCP/IP socket.
sock = socket.socket(socket.AF_INET, socket.SOCK_STREAM)

# Connect the socket to the port on the server
# given by the caller.
server_address = (sys.argv[1], 10000)
print('connecting to {} port {}'.format(*server_address))
sock.connect(server_address)

try:

    message = b'This is the message.  It will be repeated.'
    print('sending {!r}'.format(message))
    sock.sendall(message)

    amount_received = 0
    amount_expected = len(message)
    while amount_received < amount_expected:
        data = sock.recv(16)
        amount_received += len(data)
        print('received {!r}'.format(data))

finally:
    sock.close()
```

After the server is started with the argument hubert, the netstat command shows that it is listening on the address for the named host.

```
$ host hubert.hellfly.net

hubert.hellfly.net has address 10.9.0.6

$ netstat -an | grep 10000

Active Internet connections (including servers)
Proto Recv-Q Send-Q  Local Address      Foreign Address     (state)
...
tcp4      0      0   10.9.0.6.10000     *.*                 LISTEN
...
```

Running the client on another host, and passing hubert.hellfly.net as the host where the server is running, produces the following output:

```
$ hostname

apu

$ python3 ./socket_echo_client_explicit.py hubert.hellfly.net
connecting to hubert.hellfly.net port 10000
sending b'This is the message.  It will be repeated.'
received b'This is the mess'
received b'age.  It will be'
received b' repeated.'
```

Here is the server output:

```
$ python3 socket_echo_server_explicit.py hubert.hellfly.net
starting up on hubert.hellfly.net port 10000
waiting for a connection
client connected: ('10.9.0.10', 33139)
received b''
waiting for a connection
client connected: ('10.9.0.10', 33140)
received b'This is the mess'
received b'age.  It will be'
received b' repeated.'
received b''
waiting for a connection
```

Many servers have more than one network interface and, therefore, more than one IP address. Rather than running separate copies of a service bound to each IP address, use the special address INADDR_ANY to listen on all addresses at the same time. Although socket defines a constant for INADDR_ANY, the value is an integer and must be converted to a dotted-notation string address before it can be passed to `bind()`. As a shortcut, use `0.0.0.0` or an empty string (`''`) instead of doing the conversion.

Listing 11.24: **socket_echo_server_any.py**

```python
import socket
import sys

# Create a TCP/IP socket.
sock = socket.socket(socket.AF_INET, socket.SOCK_STREAM)

# Bind the socket to the address given on the command line.
server_address = ('', 10000)
sock.bind(server_address)
print('starting up on {} port {}'.format(*sock.getsockname()))
sock.listen(1)

while True:
    print('waiting for a connection')
    connection, client_address = sock.accept()
    try:
        print('client connected:', client_address)
        while True:
            data = connection.recv(16)
            print('received {!r}'.format(data))
            if data:
                connection.sendall(data)
            else:
                break
    finally:
        connection.close()
```

To see the actual address being used by a socket, call its `getsockname()` method. After the service starts, running `netstat` again shows that it is listening for incoming connections on any address.

```
$ netstat -an

Active Internet connections (including servers)
Proto Recv-Q Send-Q  Local Address    Foreign Address  (state)
...
tcp4       0      0  *.10000          *.*              LISTEN
...
```

11.2.3 User Datagram Client and Server

The user datagram protocol (UDP) works differently from TCP/IP. Whereas TCP is a *stream-oriented* protocol, ensuring that all of the data is transmitted in the right order,

UDP is a *message-oriented* protocol. On the one hand, UDP does not require a long-lived connection, so setting up a UDP socket is a little simpler. On the other hand, UDP messages must fit within a single datagram (for IPv4, that means they can hold only 65,507 bytes because the 65,535-byte packet also includes header information) and delivery is not guaranteed as it is with TCP.

11.2.3.1 Echo Server

Since there is no connection per se, the server does not need to listen for and accept connections. Rather, it simply needs to use `bind()` to associate its socket with a port, and then wait for individual messages.

Listing 11.25: **socket_echo_server_dgram.py**

```python
import socket
import sys

# Create a UDP socket.
sock = socket.socket(socket.AF_INET, socket.SOCK_DGRAM)

# Bind the socket to the port.
server_address = ('localhost', 10000)
print('starting up on {} port {}'.format(*server_address))
sock.bind(server_address)

while True:
    print('\nwaiting to receive message')
    data, address = sock.recvfrom(4096)

    print('received {} bytes from {}'.format(
        len(data), address))
    print(data)

    if data:
        sent = sock.sendto(data, address)
        print('sent {} bytes back to {}'.format(
            sent, address))
```

Messages are read from the socket using `recvfrom()`, which returns the data as well as the address of the client from which it was sent.

11.2.3.2 Echo Client

The UDP echo client is similar the server, but it does not use `bind()` to attach its socket to an address. It uses `sendto()` to deliver its message directly to the server and `recvfrom()` to receive the response.

Listing 11.26: socket_echo_client_dgram.py

```python
import socket
import sys

# Create a UDP socket.
sock = socket.socket(socket.AF_INET, socket.SOCK_DGRAM)

server_address = ('localhost', 10000)
message = b'This is the message.  It will be repeated.'

try:

    # Send data.
    print('sending {!r}'.format(message))
    sent = sock.sendto(message, server_address)

    # Receive response.
    print('waiting to receive')
    data, server = sock.recvfrom(4096)
    print('received {!r}'.format(data))

finally:
    print('closing socket')
    sock.close()
```

11.2.3.3 Client and Server Together

Running the server produces the following output:

```
$ python3 socket_echo_server_dgram.py
starting up on localhost port 10000

waiting to receive message
received 42 bytes from ('127.0.0.1', 57870)
b'This is the message.  It will be repeated.'
sent 42 bytes back to ('127.0.0.1', 57870)

waiting to receive message
```

The client output is shown here:

```
$ python3 socket_echo_client_dgram.py
sending b'This is the message.  It will be repeated.'
waiting to receive
received b'This is the message.  It will be repeated.'
closing socket
```

11.2.4   Unix Domain Sockets

From the programmer's perspective, there are two essential differences between using a Unix domain socket and an TCP/IP socket. First, the address of the socket is a path on the file system, rather than a tuple containing the server name and port. Second, the node created in the file system to represent the socket persists after the socket is closed, so it needs to be removed each time the server starts. The echo server example given earlier can be updated to use UDS by making a few changes in the setup section.

The `socket` needs to be created with address family `AF_UNIX`. Binding the socket and managing the incoming connections works the same way as with TCP/IP sockets.

Listing 11.27: `socket_echo_server_uds.py`

```
import socket
import sys
import os

server_address = './uds_socket'

# Make sure the socket does not already exist.
try:
    os.unlink(server_address)
except OSError:
    if os.path.exists(server_address):
        raise

# Create a UDS socket.
sock = socket.socket(socket.AF_UNIX, socket.SOCK_STREAM)

# Bind the socket to the address.
print('starting up on {}'.format(server_address))
sock.bind(server_address)

# Listen for incoming connections.
sock.listen(1)

while True:
    # Wait for a connection.
    print('waiting for a connection')
    connection, client_address = sock.accept()
    try:
        print('connection from', client_address)

        # Receive the data in small chunks and retransmit it.
        while True:
            data = connection.recv(16)
            print('received {!r}'.format(data))
            if data:
                print('sending data back to the client')
```

```
                    connection.sendall(data)
            else:
                print('no data from', client_address)
                break

    finally:
        # Clean up the connection.
        connection.close()
```

The client setup also needs to be modified to work with UDS. The client should assume that the file system node for the socket exists, since the server creates it by binding to the address. Sending and receiving data works the same way in the UDS client as in the TCP/IP client described earlier.

Listing 11.28: **socket_echo_client_uds.py**

```
import socket
import sys

# Create a UDS socket.
sock = socket.socket(socket.AF_UNIX, socket.SOCK_STREAM)

# Connect the socket to the port where the server is listening.
server_address = './uds_socket'
print('connecting to {}'.format(server_address))
try:
    sock.connect(server_address)
except socket.error as msg:
    print(msg)
    sys.exit(1)

try:

    # Send data.
    message = b'This is the message.  It will be repeated.'
    print('sending {!r}'.format(message))
    sock.sendall(message)

    amount_received = 0
    amount_expected = len(message)

    while amount_received < amount_expected:
        data = sock.recv(16)
        amount_received += len(data)
        print('received {!r}'.format(data))

finally:
    print('closing socket')
    sock.close()
```

The program output is mostly the same, with appropriate updates for the address information. The server shows the messages received and sent back to the client.

```
$ python3 socket_echo_server_uds.py
starting up on ./uds_socket
waiting for a connection
connection from
received b'This is the mess'
sending data back to the client
received b'age.  It will be'
sending data back to the client
received b' repeated.'
sending data back to the client
received b''
no data from
waiting for a connection
```

The client sends the message all at once, and receives parts of it back incrementally.

```
$ python3 socket_echo_client_uds.py
connecting to ./uds_socket
sending b'This is the message.  It will be repeated.'
received b'This is the mess'
received b'age.  It will be'
received b' repeated.'
closing socket
```

11.2.4.1 Permissions

Since the UDS socket is represented by a node on the file system, standard file system permissions can be used to control access to the server.

```
$ ls -l ./uds_socket

srwxr-xr-x  1 dhellmann  dhellmann  0 Aug 21 11:19 uds_socket

$ sudo chown root ./uds_socket

$ ls -l ./uds_socket

srwxr-xr-x  1 root  dhellmann  0 Aug 21 11:19 uds_socket
```

Running the client as a user other than root now results in an error because the process does not have permission to open the socket.

```
$ python3 socket_echo_client_uds.py

connecting to ./uds_socket
[Errno 13] Permission denied
```

11.2.4.2 Communication Between Parent and Child Processes

The socketpair() function is useful for setting up UDS sockets for interprocess communication under Unix. It creates a pair of connected sockets that can be used to communicate between a parent process and a child process after the child is forked.

Listing 11.29: socket_socketpair.py

```python
import socket
import os

parent, child = socket.socketpair()

pid = os.fork()

if pid:
    print('in parent, sending message')
    child.close()
    parent.sendall(b'ping')
    response = parent.recv(1024)
    print('response from child:', response)
    parent.close()

else:
    print('in child, waiting for message')
    parent.close()
    message = child.recv(1024)
    print('message from parent:', message)
    child.sendall(b'pong')
    child.close()
```

By default, a UDS socket is created. Alternatively, the caller can pass address family, socket type, and even protocol options to specify how the sockets should be created.

```
$ python3 -u socket_socketpair.py

in parent, sending message
in child, waiting for message
message from parent: b'ping'
response from child: b'pong'
```

11.2.5 Multicast

Point-to-point connections suffice for many communication needs, but passing the same information between many peers becomes increasingly more challenging as the number of direct connections grows. Sending messages separately to each recipient consumes additional processing time and bandwidth, which can be a problem for applications that perform operations such as streaming video or audio. Using *multicast* to deliver messages to more than one endpoint at a time achieves better efficiency because the network infrastructure ensures that the packets are delivered to all recipients.

Multicast messages are always sent using UDP, since TCP assumes a pair of communicating systems are present. The addresses used for multicast, called *multicast groups*, are a subset of the regular IPv4 address range (224.0.0.0 through 230.255.255.255) that have been reserved for multicast traffic. These addresses are treated specially by network routers and switches, so messages sent to the group can be distributed over the Internet to all recipients that have joined the group.

NOTE

Some managed switches and routers have multicast traffic disabled by default. If you have trouble with the example programs, check your network configuration.

11.2.5.1 Sending Multicast Messages

The modified echo client in the next example will send a message to a multicast group, then report all of the responses it receives. Since it has no way of knowing how many responses to expect, it uses a timeout value for the socket to avoid blocking indefinitely while waiting for an answer.

The socket also needs to be configured with a *time-to-live* value (TTL) for the messages. The TTL controls how many networks will receive the packet. Set the TTL with the `IP_MULTICAST_TTL` option and `setsockopt()`. The default, 1, means that the packets are not forwarded by the router beyond the current network segment. The TTL value can range up to 255, and should be packed into a single byte.

Listing 11.30: **socket_multicast_sender.py**

```
import socket
import struct
import sys

message = b'very important data'
multicast_group = ('224.3.29.71', 10000)

# Create the datagram socket.
sock = socket.socket(socket.AF_INET, socket.SOCK_DGRAM)

# Set a timeout so the socket does not block
# indefinitely when trying to receive data.
sock.settimeout(0.2)

# Set the time-to-live for messages to 1 so they do not
# go past the local network segment.
ttl = struct.pack('b', 1)
sock.setsockopt(socket.IPPROTO_IP, socket.IP_MULTICAST_TTL, ttl)

try:

    # Send data to the multicast group.
    print('sending {!r}'.format(message))
```

```
        sent = sock.sendto(message, multicast_group)

        # Look for responses from all recipients.
        while True:
            print('waiting to receive')
            try:
                data, server = sock.recvfrom(16)
            except socket.timeout:
                print('timed out, no more responses')
                break
            else:
                print('received {!r} from {}'.format(
                    data, server))

finally:
    print('closing socket')
    sock.close()
```

The rest of the sender looks like the UDP echo client, except that it expects multiple responses. It uses a loop to call recvfrom() until it times out.

11.2.5.2 Receiving Multicast Messages

The first step when establishing a multicast receiver is to create the UDP socket. After the regular socket is created and bound to a port, it can be added to the multicast group by using setsockopt() to change the IP_ADD_MEMBERSHIP option. The option value is the 8-byte packed representation of the multicast group address, followed by the network interface on which the server should listen for the traffic, identified by its IP address. In this case, the receiver listens on all interfaces using INADDR_ANY.

Listing 11.31: socket_multicast_receiver.py

```
import socket
import struct
import sys

multicast_group = '224.3.29.71'
server_address = ('', 10000)

# Create the socket.
sock = socket.socket(socket.AF_INET, socket.SOCK_DGRAM)

# Bind to the server address.
sock.bind(server_address)

# Tell the operating system to add the socket to
# the multicast group on all interfaces.
group = socket.inet_aton(multicast_group)
mreq = struct.pack('4sL', group, socket.INADDR_ANY)
sock.setsockopt(
```

```
    socket.IPPROTO_IP,
    socket.IP_ADD_MEMBERSHIP,
    mreq)

# Receive/respond loop
while True:
    print('\nwaiting to receive message')
    data, address = sock.recvfrom(1024)

    print('received {} bytes from {}'.format(
        len(data), address))
    print(data)

    print('sending acknowledgement to', address)
    sock.sendto(b'ack', address)
```

The main loop for the receiver is just like the regular UDP echo server.

11.2.5.3 Example Output

This example shows the multicast receiver running on two different hosts. A has address 192.168.1.13, and B has address 192.168.1.14.

```
[A]$ python3 socket_multicast_receiver.py

waiting to receive message
received 19 bytes from ('192.168.1.14', 62650)
b'very important data'
sending acknowledgement to ('192.168.1.14', 62650)

waiting to receive message

[B]$ python3 source/socket/socket_multicast_receiver.py

waiting to receive message
received 19 bytes from ('192.168.1.14', 64288)
b'very important data'
sending acknowledgement to ('192.168.1.14', 64288)

waiting to receive message
```

The sender is running on host B.

```
[B]$ python3 socket_multicast_sender.py
sending b'very important data'
waiting to receive
received b'ack' from ('192.168.1.14', 10000)
waiting to receive
received b'ack' from ('192.168.1.13', 10000)
waiting to receive
```

```
timed out, no more responses
closing socket
```

The message is sent one time, and two acknowledgments of the outgoing message are received, one each from hosts A and B.

TIP

Related Reading

- Wikipedia: Multicast[8]: Article describing the technical details of multicasting.
- Wikipedia: IP multicast[9]: Article about IP multicasting, with information about addressing.

11.2.6 Sending Binary Data

Sockets transmit streams of bytes. Those bytes can contain text messages encoded as bytes, as in the previous examples, or they can be made up of binary data that has been packed into a buffer with struct (page 117) to prepare it for transmission.

This client program encodes an integer, a string of two characters, and a floating-point value into a sequence of bytes that can be passed to the socket for transmission.

Listing 11.32: **socket_binary_client.py**

```
import binascii
import socket
import struct
import sys

# Create a TCP/IP socket.
sock = socket.socket(socket.AF_INET, socket.SOCK_STREAM)
server_address = ('localhost', 10000)
sock.connect(server_address)

values = (1, b'ab', 2.7)
packer = struct.Struct('I 2s f')
packed_data = packer.pack(*values)

print('values =', values)

try:
    # Send data.
    print('sending {!r}'.format(binascii.hexlify(packed_data)))
    sock.sendall(packed_data)
finally:
    print('closing socket')
    sock.close()
```

---

[8] https://en.wikipedia.org/wiki/Multicast
[9] https://en.wikipedia.org/wiki/IP_multicast

When sending multibyte binary data between two systems, it is important to ensure that both sides of the connection know which order the bytes are in and how to assemble them back into the correct order for the local architecture. The server program uses the same Struct specifier to unpack the bytes it receives so they are interpreted in the correct order.

Listing 11.33: socket_binary_server.py

```
import binascii
import socket
import struct
import sys

# Create a TCP/IP socket.
sock = socket.socket(socket.AF_INET, socket.SOCK_STREAM)
server_address = ('localhost', 10000)
sock.bind(server_address)
sock.listen(1)

unpacker = struct.Struct('I 2s f')

while True:
    print('\nwaiting for a connection')
    connection, client_address = sock.accept()
    try:
        data = connection.recv(unpacker.size)
        print('received {!r}'.format(binascii.hexlify(data)))

        unpacked_data = unpacker.unpack(data)
        print('unpacked:', unpacked_data)

    finally:
        connection.close()
```

Running the client produces the following output.

```
$ python3 source/socket/socket_binary_client.py
values = (1, b'ab', 2.7)
sending b'0100000061620000cdcc2c40'
closing socket
```

The server shows the values it receives.

```
$ python3 socket_binary_server.py

waiting for a connection
received b'0100000061620000cdcc2c40'
unpacked: (1, b'ab', 2.700000047683716)

waiting for a connection
```

The floating point value loses some precision as it is packed and unpacked, but otherwise the data is transmitted as expected. One thing to keep in mind is that depending on the value of the integer, it may be more efficient to convert it to text and then transmit that data, instead of using `struct`. The integer 1 uses 1 byte when represented as a string, but 4 bytes when packed into the structure.

TIP

Related Reading

- `struct` (page 117): Converting between strings and other data types.

11.2.7   Non-blocking Communication and Timeouts

By default, a `socket` is configured so that sending or receiving data *blocks*, meaning that it stops program execution until the socket is ready. Calls to `send()` wait for buffer space to become available for the outgoing data, and calls to `recv()` wait for the other program to send data that can be read. This form of I/O operation is easy to understand, but can lead to inefficient operation and even deadlocks, if both programs end up waiting for the other to send or receive data.

There are a few ways to work around this situation. One approach is to use a separate thread for communicating with each socket. This can introduce other complexities, though, with communication between the threads. Another option is to change the socket to not block at all, and to return immediately if it is not ready to handle the operation. Use the `setblocking()` method to change the blocking flag for a socket. The default value is 1, which means to block; a value of 0 turns off blocking. If the socket has blocking turned off and it is not ready to perform the operation, then `socket.error` is raised.

A compromise solution is to set a timeout value for socket operations. Use `settimeout()` to change the timeout of a `socket` to a floating-point value representing the number of seconds to block before deciding the socket is not ready for the operation. When the timeout expires, a `timeout` exception is raised.

TIP

Related Reading

- Standard library documentation for `socket`.[10]
- Python 2 to 3 porting notes for `socket` (page 1362).
- `select` (page 728): Testing a socket to see if it is ready for reading or writing for non-blocking I/O.
- `SocketServer`: Framework for creating network servers.
- `asyncio` (page 617): Asynchronous I/O and concurrency tools.
- `urllib` and `urllib2`: Most network clients should use the more convenient libraries for accessing remote resources through a URL.

---

[10] https://docs.python.org/3.5/library/socket.html

- Socket Programming HOWTO[11]: An instructional guide by Gordon McMillan, included in the standard library documentation.

- *Foundations of Python Network Programming, Third Edition*, by Brandon Rhodes and John Goerzen. Apress, 2014. ISBN-10: 1430258543.

- *Unix Network Programming, Volume 1: The Sockets Networking API, Third Edition*, by W. Richard Stevens, Bill Fenner, and Andrew M. Rudoff. Addison-Wesley, 2004. ISBN-10: 0131411551.

11.3   selectors: I/O Multiplexing Abstractions

The `selectors` module provides a platform-independent abstraction layer on top of the platform-specific I/O monitoring functions in `select` (page 728).

11.3.1   Operating Model

The APIs in `selectors` are event based, similar to `poll()` from `select`. Several implementations exist, and the module automatically sets the alias `DefaultSelector` to refer to the most efficient one for the current system configuration.

A selector object provides methods for specifying which events to look for on a socket, and then lets the caller wait for events in a platform-independent way. Registering interest in an event creates a `SelectorKey`, which holds the socket, information about the events of interest, and optional application data. The owner of the selector calls its `select()` method to learn about events. The return value is a sequence of key objects and a bitmask indicating which events have occurred. A program using a selector should repeatedly call `select()`, and then handle the events appropriately.

11.3.2   Echo Server

The echo server example presented here uses the application data in the `SelectorKey` to register a callback function to be invoked on the new event. The main loop gets the callback from the key and passes the socket and event mask to it. As the server starts, it registers the `accept()` function to be called for read events on the main server socket. Accepting the connection produces a new socket, which is then registered with the `read()` function as a callback for read events.

Listing 11.34: selectors_echo_server.py

```
import selectors
import socket

mysel = selectors.DefaultSelector()
keep_running = True


def read(connection, mask):
```

---

[11] https://docs.python.org/3/howto/sockets.html

```
        "Callback for read events"
        global keep_running

        client_address = connection.getpeername()
        print('read({})'.format(client_address))
        data = connection.recv(1024)
        if data:
            # A readable client socket has data.
            print('  received {!r}'.format(data))
            connection.sendall(data)
        else:
            # Interpret empty result as closed connection.
            print('  closing')
            mysel.unregister(connection)
            connection.close()
            # Tell the main loop to stop.
            keep_running = False


    def accept(sock, mask):
        "Callback for new connections"
        new_connection, addr = sock.accept()
        print('accept({})'.format(addr))
        new_connection.setblocking(False)
        mysel.register(new_connection, selectors.EVENT_READ, read)


    server_address = ('localhost', 10000)
    print('starting up on {} port {}'.format(*server_address))
    server = socket.socket(socket.AF_INET, socket.SOCK_STREAM)
    server.setblocking(False)
    server.bind(server_address)
    server.listen(5)

    mysel.register(server, selectors.EVENT_READ, accept)

    while keep_running:
        print('waiting for I/O')
        for key, mask in mysel.select(timeout=1):
            callback = key.data
            callback(key.fileobj, mask)

    print('shutting down')
    mysel.close()
```

If read() does not receive any data from the socket, it interprets the read event as the other side of the connection being closed instead of sending data. Consequently, it removes the socket from the selector and closes it. Because it is only a example program, this server also shuts itself down after it has finished communicating with a single client.

11.3.3   Echo Client

The echo client example that follows processes all of the I/O events in the main loop, instead of using callbacks. It sets up the selector to report read events on the socket, and to report when the socket is ready to send data. Because it looks at two types of events, the client must check which occurred by examining the mask value. After all of its outgoing data has been sent, it changes the selector configuration to report only when there is data to read.

Listing 11.35: **selectors_echo_client.py**

```python
import selectors
import socket

mysel = selectors.DefaultSelector()
keep_running = True
outgoing = [
    b'It will be repeated.',
    b'This is the message.  ',
]
bytes_sent = 0
bytes_received = 0

# Connecting is a blocking operation, so call setblocking()
# after it returns.
server_address = ('localhost', 10000)
print('connecting to {} port {}'.format(*server_address))
sock = socket.socket(socket.AF_INET, socket.SOCK_STREAM)
sock.connect(server_address)
sock.setblocking(False)

# Set up the selector to watch for when the socket is ready
# to send data as well as when there is data to read.
mysel.register(
    sock,
    selectors.EVENT_READ | selectors.EVENT_WRITE,
)

while keep_running:
    print('waiting for I/O')
    for key, mask in mysel.select(timeout=1):
        connection = key.fileobj
        client_address = connection.getpeername()
        print('client({})'.format(client_address))

        if mask & selectors.EVENT_READ:
            print('  ready to read')
            data = connection.recv(1024)
            if data:
                # A readable client socket has data.
                print('  received {!r}'.format(data))
```

```
                        bytes_received += len(data)

                # Interpret empty result as closed connection,
                # and also close when we have received a copy
                # of all of the data sent.
                keep_running = not (
                    data or
                    (bytes_received and
                     (bytes_received == bytes_sent))
                )

            if mask & selectors.EVENT_WRITE:
                print('  ready to write')
                if not outgoing:
                    # We are out of messages, so we no longer need to
                    # write anything. Change our registration to let
                    # us keep reading responses from the server.
                    print('  switching to read-only')
                    mysel.modify(sock, selectors.EVENT_READ)
                else:
                    # Send the next message.
                    next_msg = outgoing.pop()
                    print('  sending {!r}'.format(next_msg))
                    sock.sendall(next_msg)
                    bytes_sent += len(next_msg)

print('shutting down')
mysel.unregister(connection)
connection.close()
mysel.close()
```

The client tracks both the amount of data it has sent and the amount it has received. When those values match and are non-zero, the client exits the processing loop and cleanly shuts down by removing the socket from the selector and closing both the socket and the selector.

11.3.4 Server and Client Together

The client and the server should be run in separate terminal windows, so they can communicate with each other. The server output shows the incoming connection and data, as well as the response sent back to the client.

```
$ python3 source/selectors/selectors_echo_server.py
starting up on localhost port 10000
waiting for I/O
waiting for I/O
accept(('127.0.0.1', 59850))
waiting for I/O
read(('127.0.0.1', 59850))
```

```
        received b'This is the message.  It will be repeated.'
waiting for I/O
read(('127.0.0.1', 59850))
  closing
shutting down
```

The client output shows the outgoing message and the response from the server.

```
$ python3 source/selectors/selectors_echo_client.py
connecting to localhost port 10000
waiting for I/O
client(('127.0.0.1', 10000))
  ready to write
  sending b'This is the message.  '
waiting for I/O
client(('127.0.0.1', 10000))
  ready to write
  sending b'It will be repeated.'
waiting for I/O
client(('127.0.0.1', 10000))
  ready to write
  switching to read-only
waiting for I/O
client(('127.0.0.1', 10000))
  ready to read
  received b'This is the message.  It will be repeated.'
shutting down
```

TIP

Related Reading

- Standard library documentation for selectors.[12]
- select (page 728): Lower-level APIs for handling I/O efficiently.

11.4   select: Wait for I/O Efficiently

The select module provides access to platform-specific I/O monitoring functions. The most portable interface is the POSIX function select(), which is available on Unix and Windows. The module also includes poll(), a Unix-only API, and several options that work only with specific variants of Unix.

---

[12] https://docs.python.org/3.5/library/selectors.html

NOTE

The new `selectors` (page 724) module provides a higher-level interface built on top of the APIs in `select`. It is easier to build portable code using `selectors`, so use that module unless the low-level APIs provided by `select` are somehow required.

11.4.1 Using select()

Python's `select()` function is a direct interface to the underlying operating system implementation. It monitors sockets, open files, and pipes—anything with a `fileno()` method that returns a valid file descriptor—until they become readable or writable or a communication error occurs. `select()` makes it easy to monitor multiple connections at the same time, and it is more efficient than writing a polling loop in Python using socket timeouts, because the monitoring happens in the operating system network layer, instead of the interpreter.

NOTE

Using Python's file objects with `select()` works for Unix, but is not supported under Windows.

The echo server example from the `socket` (page 693) section can be extended to watch for more than one connection at a time by using `select()`. The new version starts out by creating a non-blocking TCP/IP socket and configuring it to listen on an address.

Listing 11.36: **select_echo_server.py**

```
import select
import socket
import sys
import queue

# Create a TCP/IP socket.
server = socket.socket(socket.AF_INET, socket.SOCK_STREAM)
server.setblocking(0)

# Bind the socket to the port.
server_address = ('localhost', 10000)
print('starting up on {} port {}'.format(*server_address),
      file=sys.stderr)
server.bind(server_address)

# Listen for incoming connections.
server.listen(5)
```

The arguments to `select()` are three lists containing communication channels to monitor. The first is a list of the objects to be checked for incoming data to be read, the second contains objects that will receive outgoing data when there is room in their buffer, and the third includes those objects that may have an error (usually a combination of the input and output channel objects). The next step is to set up the lists containing input sources and output destinations to be passed to `select()`.

```
# Sockets from which we expect to read
inputs = [server]

# Sockets to which we expect to write
outputs = []
```

Connections are added to and removed from these lists by the server main loop. Since this version of the server will wait for a socket to become writable before sending any data (instead of immediately sending the reply), each output connection needs a queue to act as a buffer for the data to be sent through it.

```
# Outgoing message queues (socket:Queue)
message_queues = {}
```

The main portion of the server program loops, calling `select()` to block and wait for network activity.

```
while inputs:

    # Wait for at least one of the sockets to be
    # ready for processing.
    print('waiting for the next event', file=sys.stderr)
    readable, writable, exceptional = select.select(inputs,
                                                    outputs,
                                                    inputs)
```

`select()` returns three new lists, containing subsets of the contents of the lists passed in. The sockets in the `readable` list have incoming data buffered and available to be read; the sockets in the `writable` list have free space in their buffer and can be written to; and the sockets returned in `exceptional` have had an error (the actual definition of "exceptional condition" depends on the platform).

The "readable" sockets represent three possible cases. If the socket is the main "server" socket (i.e., the one being used to listen for connections), then the "readable" condition means it is ready to accept another incoming connection. In addition to adding the new connection to the list of inputs to monitor, this section sets the client socket to not block.

```
    # Handle inputs.
    for s in readable:

        if s is server:
            # A "readable" socket is ready to accept a connection.
            connection, client_address = s.accept()
            print('  connection from', client_address,
                  file=sys.stderr)
```

```
            connection.setblocking(0)
            inputs.append(connection)

            # Give the connection a queue for data
            # we want to send.
            message_queues[connection] = queue.Queue()
```

The next case is an established connection with a client that has sent data. The data is read with `recv()`, then placed on the queue so it can be sent through the socket and back to the client.

```
        else:
            data = s.recv(1024)
            if data:
                # A readable client socket has data.
                print('  received {!r} from {}'.format(
                    data, s.getpeername()), file=sys.stderr,
                )
                message_queues[s].put(data)
                # Add output channel for response.
                if s not in outputs:
                    outputs.append(s)
```

A readable socket that returns no data from `recv()` is from a client that has disconnected, and the stream is ready to be closed.

```
            else:
                # Interpret empty result as closed connection.
                print('  closing', client_address,
                    file=sys.stderr)
                # Stop listening for input on the connection.
                if s in outputs:
                    outputs.remove(s)
                inputs.remove(s)
                s.close()

                # Remove message queue.
                del message_queues[s]
```

There are fewer cases for the writable connections. If the queue holds data intended for a connection, the next message is sent. Otherwise, the connection is removed from the list of output connections so that the next time through the loop `select()` does not indicate that the socket is ready to send data.

```
    # Handle outputs.
    for s in writable:
        try:
            next_msg = message_queues[s].get_nowait()
```

```
except queue.Empty:
    # No messages waiting, so stop checking
    # for writability.
    print('  ', s.getpeername(), 'queue empty',
          file=sys.stderr)
    outputs.remove(s)
else:
    print('  sending {!r} to {}'.format(next_msg,
                                        s.getpeername()),
          file=sys.stderr)
    s.send(next_msg)
```

Finally, sockets in the exceptional list are closed.

```
# Handle "exceptional conditions."
for s in exceptional:
    print('exception condition on', s.getpeername(),
          file=sys.stderr)
    # Stop listening for input on the connection.
    inputs.remove(s)
    if s in outputs:
        outputs.remove(s)
    s.close()

    # Remove message queue.
    del message_queues[s]
```

The example client program uses two sockets to demonstrate how the server with select() manages multiple connections at the same time. The client starts by connecting each TCP/IP socket to the server.

Listing 11.37: select_echo_multiclient.py

```
import socket
import sys

messages = [
    'This is the message. ',
    'It will be sent ',
    'in parts.',
]
server_address = ('localhost', 10000)

# Create a TCP/IP socket.
socks = [
    socket.socket(socket.AF_INET, socket.SOCK_STREAM),
    socket.socket(socket.AF_INET, socket.SOCK_STREAM),
]
```

```
# Connect the socket to the port where the server is listening.
print('connecting to {} port {}'.format(*server_address),
      file=sys.stderr)
for s in socks:
    s.connect(server_address)
```

Next, it sends one piece of the message at a time via each socket and reads all responses available after writing new data.

```
for message in messages:
    outgoing_data = message.encode()

    # Send messages on both sockets.
    for s in socks:
        print('{}: sending {!r}'.format(s.getsockname(),
                                         outgoing_data),
              file=sys.stderr)
        s.send(outgoing_data)

    # Read responses on both sockets.
    for s in socks:
        data = s.recv(1024)
        print('{}: received {!r}'.format(s.getsockname(),
                                          data),
              file=sys.stderr)
        if not data:
            print('closing socket', s.getsockname(),
                  file=sys.stderr)
            s.close()
```

Run the server in one window and the client in another window. The output will look like that shown here, albeit with different port numbers.

```
$ python3 select_echo_server.py
starting up on localhost port 10000
waiting for the next event
  connection from ('127.0.0.1', 61003)
waiting for the next event
  connection from ('127.0.0.1', 61004)
waiting for the next event
  received b'This is the message. ' from ('127.0.0.1', 61003)
  received b'This is the message. ' from ('127.0.0.1', 61004)
waiting for the next event
  sending b'This is the message. ' to ('127.0.0.1', 61003)
  sending b'This is the message. ' to ('127.0.0.1', 61004)
waiting for the next event
    ('127.0.0.1', 61003) queue empty
    ('127.0.0.1', 61004) queue empty
```

```
waiting for the next event
  received b'It will be sent ' from ('127.0.0.1', 61003)
  received b'It will be sent ' from ('127.0.0.1', 61004)
waiting for the next event
  sending b'It will be sent ' to ('127.0.0.1', 61003)
  sending b'It will be sent ' to ('127.0.0.1', 61004)
waiting for the next event
  ('127.0.0.1', 61003) queue empty
  ('127.0.0.1', 61004) queue empty
waiting for the next event
  received b'in parts.' from ('127.0.0.1', 61003)
waiting for the next event
  received b'in parts.' from ('127.0.0.1', 61004)
  sending b'in parts.' to ('127.0.0.1', 61003)
waiting for the next event
  ('127.0.0.1', 61003) queue empty
  sending b'in parts.' to ('127.0.0.1', 61004)
waiting for the next event
  ('127.0.0.1', 61004) queue empty
waiting for the next event
  closing ('127.0.0.1', 61004)
  closing ('127.0.0.1', 61004)
waiting for the next event
```

The client output shows the data being sent and received using both sockets.

```
$ python3 select_echo_multiclient.py
connecting to localhost port 10000
('127.0.0.1', 61003): sending b'This is the message. '
('127.0.0.1', 61004): sending b'This is the message. '
('127.0.0.1', 61003): received b'This is the message. '
('127.0.0.1', 61004): received b'This is the message. '
('127.0.0.1', 61003): sending b'It will be sent '
('127.0.0.1', 61004): sending b'It will be sent '
('127.0.0.1', 61003): received b'It will be sent '
('127.0.0.1', 61004): received b'It will be sent '
('127.0.0.1', 61003): sending b'in parts.'
('127.0.0.1', 61004): sending b'in parts.'
('127.0.0.1', 61003): received b'in parts.'
('127.0.0.1', 61004): received b'in parts.'
```

11.4.2 Non-blocking I/O with Timeouts

select() also takes an optional fourth parameter—namely, the number of seconds to wait before ending the monitoring if no channels have become active. Using a timeout value lets a main program call select() as part of a larger processing loop, taking other actions in between checking for network input.

When the timeout expires, `select()` returns three empty lists. Updating the server example to use a timeout requires adding the extra argument to the `select()` call and handling the empty lists after `select()` returns.

Listing 11.38: **select_echo_server_timeout.py**

```
readable, writable, exceptional = select.select(inputs,
                                                 outputs,
                                                 inputs,
                                                 timeout)

if not (readable or writable or exceptional):
    print('  timed out, do some other work here',
          file=sys.stderr)
    continue
```

This "slow" version of the client program pauses after sending each message, to simulate latency or some other delay in transmission.

Listing 11.39: **select_echo_slow_client.py**

```python
import socket
import sys
import time

# Create a TCP/IP socket.
sock = socket.socket(socket.AF_INET, socket.SOCK_STREAM)

# Connect the socket to the port where the server is listening.
server_address = ('localhost', 10000)
print('connecting to {} port {}'.format(*server_address),
      file=sys.stderr)
sock.connect(server_address)

time.sleep(1)

messages = [
    'Part one of the message.',
    'Part two of the message.',
]
amount_expected = len(''.join(messages))

try:

    # Send data.
    for message in messages:
        data = message.encode()
        print('sending {!r}'.format(data), file=sys.stderr)
        sock.sendall(data)
```

```
        time.sleep(1.5)

    # Look for the response.
    amount_received = 0

    while amount_received < amount_expected:
        data = sock.recv(16)
        amount_received += len(data)
        print('received {!r}'.format(data), file=sys.stderr)

finally:
    print('closing socket', file=sys.stderr)
    sock.close()
```

Running the new server with the slow client produces the following output.

```
$ python3 select_echo_server_timeout.py
starting up on localhost port 10000
waiting for the next event
  timed out, do some other work here
waiting for the next event
  connection from ('127.0.0.1', 61144)
waiting for the next event
  timed out, do some other work here
waiting for the next event
  received b'Part one of the message.' from ('127.0.0.1', 61144)
waiting for the next event
  sending b'Part one of the message.' to ('127.0.0.1', 61144)
waiting for the next event
('127.0.0.1', 61144) queue empty
waiting for the next event
  timed out, do some other work here
waiting for the next event
  received b'Part two of the message.' from ('127.0.0.1', 61144)
waiting for the next event
  sending b'Part two of the message.' to ('127.0.0.1', 61144)
waiting for the next event
('127.0.0.1', 61144) queue empty
waiting for the next event
  timed out, do some other work here
waiting for the next event
closing ('127.0.0.1', 61144)
waiting for the next event
  timed out, do some other work here
```

The client output is shown here:

```
$ python3 select_echo_slow_client.py
connecting to localhost port 10000
```

```
sending b'Part one of the message.'
sending b'Part two of the message.'
received b'Part one of the '
received b'message.Part two'
received b' of the message.'
closing socket
```

11.4.3   Using poll()

The poll() function provides features similar to those offered by select(), but the under-lying implementation is more efficient. The trade-off is that poll() is not supported under Windows, so programs using poll() are less portable.

An echo server built on poll() starts with the same socket configuration code used in the other examples.

Listing 11.40: select_poll_echo_server.py

```python
import select
import socket
import sys
import queue

# Create a TCP/IP socket.
server = socket.socket(socket.AF_INET, socket.SOCK_STREAM)
server.setblocking(0)

# Bind the socket to the port.
server_address = ('localhost', 10000)
print('starting up on {} port {}'.format(*server_address),
      file=sys.stderr)
server.bind(server_address)

# Listen for incoming connections.
server.listen(5)

# Keep up with the queues of outgoing messages.
message_queues = {}
```

The timeout value passed to poll() is given in units of milliseconds, instead of seconds. Thus, to pause for a full second, the timeout must be set to 1000.

```python
# Do not block forever (milliseconds).
TIMEOUT = 1000
```

Python implements poll() with a class that manages the registered data channels being monitored. Channels are added by calling register() with flags indicating which events are interesting for that channel. The full set of flags is listed in Table 11.1.

Table 11.1: Event Flags for poll()

Event	Description
POLLIN	Input ready
POLLPRI	Priority input ready
POLLOUT	Able to receive output
POLLERR	Error
POLLHUP	Channel closed
POLLNVAL	Channel not open

The echo server will be setting up some sockets just for reading and others to be read from or written to. The appropriate combinations of flags are saved to the local variables `READ_ONLY` and `READ_WRITE`, respectively.

```
# Commonly used flag sets
READ_ONLY = (
    select.POLLIN |
    select.POLLPRI |
    select.POLLHUP |
    select.POLLERR
)
READ_WRITE = READ_ONLY | select.POLLOUT
```

The `server` socket is registered so that any incoming connections or data triggers an event.

```
# Set up the poller.
poller = select.poll()
poller.register(server, READ_ONLY)
```

Since `poll()` returns a list of tuples containing the file descriptor for the socket and the event flag, a mapping from file descriptor numbers to objects is needed to retrieve the `socket` to read or write from it.

```
# Map file descriptors to socket objects.
fd_to_socket = {
    server.fileno(): server,
}
```

The server's loop calls `poll()` and then processes the "events" returned by looking up the socket and taking action based on the flag in the event.

```
while True:

    # Wait for at least one of the sockets to be
    # ready for processing.
    print('waiting for the next event', file=sys.stderr)
    events = poller.poll(TIMEOUT)
```

```
for fd, flag in events:

    # Retrieve the actual socket from its file descriptor.
    s = fd_to_socket[fd]
```

As with `select()`, when the main server socket is "readable," that really means there is a pending connection from a client. The new connection is registered with the `READ_ONLY` flags to watch for new data to come through it.

```
# Handle inputs.
if flag & (select.POLLIN | select.POLLPRI):

    if s is server:
        # A readable socket is ready
        # to accept a connection.
        connection, client_address = s.accept()
        print('  connection', client_address,
              file=sys.stderr)
        connection.setblocking(0)
        fd_to_socket[connection.fileno()] = connection
        poller.register(connection, READ_ONLY)

        # Give the connection a queue for data to send.
        message_queues[connection] = queue.Queue()
```

Sockets other than the server are existing clients, and `recv()` is used to access the data waiting to be read.

```
else:
    data = s.recv(1024)
```

If `recv()` returns any data, it is placed into the outgoing queue for the socket. The flags for that socket are then changed using `modify()` so that `poll()` will watch for the socket to be ready to receive data.

```
if data:
    # A readable client socket has data.
    print('  received {!r} from {}'.format(
        data, s.getpeername()), file=sys.stderr,
    )
    message_queues[s].put(data)
    # Add output channel for response.
    poller.modify(s, READ_WRITE)
```

An empty string returned by `recv()` means the client disconnected, so `unregister()` is used to tell the `poll` object to ignore the socket.

```
        else:
            # Interpret empty result as closed connection.
            print('  closing', client_address,
                    file=sys.stderr)
            # Stop listening for input on the connection.
            poller.unregister(s)
            s.close()

            # Remove message queue.
            del message_queues[s]
```

The POLLHUP flag indicates a client that "hung up" the connection without closing it cleanly. The server stops polling clients that disappear.

```
    elif flag & select.POLLHUP:
        # Client hung up
        print('  closing', client_address, '(HUP)',
                file=sys.stderr)
        # Stop listening for input on the connection.
        poller.unregister(s)
        s.close()
```

The handling for writable sockets looks like the version used in the example for select(), except that modify() is used to change the flags for the socket in the poller, instead of removing it from the output list.

```
    elif flag & select.POLLOUT:
        # Socket is ready to send data,
        # if there is any to send.
        try:
            next_msg = message_queues[s].get_nowait()
        except queue.Empty:
            # No messages waiting, so stop checking.
            print(s.getpeername(), 'queue empty',
                    file=sys.stderr)
            poller.modify(s, READ_ONLY)
        else:
            print('  sending {!r} to {}'.format(
                next_msg, s.getpeername()), file=sys.stderr,
            )
            s.send(next_msg)
```

Finally, any events with a POLLERR error cause the server to close the socket.

```
    elif flag & select.POLLERR:
        print('  exception on', s.getpeername(),
                file=sys.stderr)
        # Stop listening for input on the connection.
        poller.unregister(s)
```

```
            s.close()

            # Remove message queue.
            del message_queues[s]
```

When the poll-based server is run together with `select_echo_multiclient.py` (the client program that uses multiple sockets), it produces the following output.

```
$ python3 select_poll_echo_server.py
starting up on localhost port 10000
waiting for the next event
waiting for the next event
waiting for the next event
waiting for the next event
  connection ('127.0.0.1', 61253)
waiting for the next event
  connection ('127.0.0.1', 61254)
waiting for the next event
  received b'This is the message. ' from ('127.0.0.1', 61253)
  received b'This is the message. ' from ('127.0.0.1', 61254)
waiting for the next event
  sending b'This is the message. ' to ('127.0.0.1', 61253)
  sending b'This is the message. ' to ('127.0.0.1', 61254)
waiting for the next event
('127.0.0.1', 61253) queue empty
('127.0.0.1', 61254) queue empty
waiting for the next event
  received b'It will be sent ' from ('127.0.0.1', 61253)
  received b'It will be sent ' from ('127.0.0.1', 61254)
waiting for the next event
  sending b'It will be sent ' to ('127.0.0.1', 61253)
  sending b'It will be sent ' to ('127.0.0.1', 61254)
waiting for the next event
('127.0.0.1', 61253) queue empty
('127.0.0.1', 61254) queue empty
waiting for the next event
  received b'in parts.' from ('127.0.0.1', 61253)
  received b'in parts.' from ('127.0.0.1', 61254)
waiting for the next event
  sending b'in parts.' to ('127.0.0.1', 61253)
  sending b'in parts.' to ('127.0.0.1', 61254)
waiting for the next event
('127.0.0.1', 61253) queue empty
('127.0.0.1', 61254) queue empty
waiting for the next event
  closing ('127.0.0.1', 61254)
waiting for the next event
  closing ('127.0.0.1', 61254)
waiting for the next event
```

11.4.4   Platform-Specific Options

Less portable options provided by `select` are `epoll`, the *edge polling* API supported by Linux; `kqueue`, which uses BSD's *kernel queue*; and `kevent`, BSD's *kernel event* interface. Refer to the operating system library documentation for more details on how they work.

TIP

Related Reading

- Standard library documentation for `select`.[13]
- `selectors` (page 724): Higher-level abstraction on top of `select`.
- Socket Programming HOWTO[14]: An instructional guide by Gordon McMillan, included in the standard library documentation.
- `socket` (page 693): Low-level network communication.
- `SocketServer`: Framework for creating network server applications.
- `asyncio` (page 617): Asynchronous I/O framework.
- *Unix Network Programming, Volume 1: The Sockets Networking API, Third Edition*, by W. Richard Stevens, Bill Fenner, and Andrew M. Rudoff. Addison-Wesley, 2004. ISBN-10: 0131411551.
- *Foundations of Python Network Programming, Third Edition*, by Brandon Rhodes and John Goerzen. Apress, 2014. ISBN-10: 1430258543.

11.5   socketserver: Creating Network Servers

The `socketserver` module is a framework for creating network servers. It defines classes for handling synchronous network requests (the server request handler blocks until the request is completed) over TCP, UDP, Unix streams, and Unix datagrams. It also provides mix-in classes for easily converting servers to use a separate thread or process for each request.

Responsibility for processing a request is split between a server class and a request handler class. The server deals with the communication issues, such as listening on a socket and accepting connections, and the request handler deals with the "protocol" issues, such as interpreting incoming data, processing it, and sending data back to the client. This division of responsibility means that many applications can use one of the existing server classes without any modifications, and provide a request handler class for it to work with the custom protocol.

11.5.1   Server Types

Five server classes are defined in `socketserver`. `BaseServer` defines the API, and is not intended to be instantiated and used directly. `TCPServer` uses TCP/IP sockets to commu-

---

[13] https://docs.python.org/3.5/library/select.html
[14] https://docs.python.org/howto/sockets.html

nicate. `UDPServer` uses datagram sockets. `UnixStreamServer` and `UnixDatagramServer` use Unix-domain sockets and are available only on Unix platforms.

11.5.2 Server Objects

To construct a server, pass it an address on which to listen for requests and a request handler *class* (not instance). The address format depends on the server type and the socket family used. Refer to the `socket` (page 693) module documentation for details.

Once the server object is instantiated, use either `handle_request()` or `serve_forever()` to process requests. The `serve_forever()` method calls `handle_request()` in an infinite loop. If an application needs to integrate the server with another event loop or use `select()` to monitor several sockets for different servers, however, it can call `handle_request()` directly.

11.5.3 Implementing a Server

When creating a server, it is usually sufficient to reuse one of the existing classes and provide a custom request handler class. For other cases, `BaseServer` includes several methods that can be overridden in a subclass.

- `verify_request(request,client_address)`: Returns `True` to process the request or `False` to ignore it. For example, a server could refuse requests from an IP range or if it is overloaded.

- `process_request(request,client_address)`: Calls `finish_request()` to actually do the work of handling the request. This method can also create a separate thread or process, as the mix-in classes do.

- `finish_request(request,client_address)`: Creates a request handler instance using the class given to the server's constructor. Calls `handle()` on the request handler to process the request.

11.5.4 Request Handlers

Request handlers do most of the work of receiving incoming requests and deciding which action to take. The handler is responsible for implementing the protocol on top of the socket layer (i.e., HTTP, XML-RPC, or AMQP). The request handler reads the request from the incoming data channel, processes it, and writes a response back out. Three methods are available to be overridden.

- `setup()`: Prepares the request handler for the request. In the `StreamRequestHandler`, the `setup()` method creates file-like objects for reading from and writing to the socket.

- `handle()`: Does the real work for the request. Parses the incoming request, processes the data, and sends a response.

- `finish()`: Cleans up anything created during `setup()`.

Many handlers can be implemented with only a `handle()` method.

11.5.5   Echo Example

This example implements a simple server/request handler pair that accepts TCP connections and echos back any data sent by the client. It starts with the request handler.

Listing 11.41: **socketserver_echo.py**

```
import logging
import sys
import socketserver

logging.basicConfig(level=logging.DEBUG,
                    format='%(name)s: %(message)s',
                    )


class EchoRequestHandler(socketserver.BaseRequestHandler):

    def __init__(self, request, client_address, server):
        self.logger = logging.getLogger('EchoRequestHandler')
        self.logger.debug('__init__')
        socketserver.BaseRequestHandler.__init__(self, request,
                                                 client_address,
                                                 server)
        return

    def setup(self):
        self.logger.debug('setup')
        return socketserver.BaseRequestHandler.setup(self)

    def handle(self):
        self.logger.debug('handle')

        # Echo the data back to the client.
        data = self.request.recv(1024)
        self.logger.debug('recv()->"%s"', data)
        self.request.send(data)
        return

    def finish(self):
        self.logger.debug('finish')
        return socketserver.BaseRequestHandler.finish(self)
```

The only method that actually needs to be implemented is EchoRequestHandler .handle(), but versions of all of the methods described earlier are included here to illustrate the sequence of calls made. The EchoServer class does nothing different from TCPServer, except log when each method is called.

```
class EchoServer(socketserver.TCPServer):

    def __init__(self, server_address,
                 handler_class=EchoRequestHandler,
                 ):
        self.logger = logging.getLogger('EchoServer')
        self.logger.debug('__init__')
        socketserver.TCPServer.__init__(self, server_address,
                                        handler_class)
        return

    def server_activate(self):
        self.logger.debug('server_activate')
        socketserver.TCPServer.server_activate(self)
        return

    def serve_forever(self, poll_interval=0.5):
        self.logger.debug('waiting for request')
        self.logger.info(
            'Handling requests, press <Ctrl-C> to quit'
        )
        socketserver.TCPServer.serve_forever(self, poll_interval)
        return

    def handle_request(self):
        self.logger.debug('handle_request')
        return socketserver.TCPServer.handle_request(self)

    def verify_request(self, request, client_address):
        self.logger.debug('verify_request(%s, %s)',
                          request, client_address)
        return socketserver.TCPServer.verify_request(
            self, request, client_address,
        )

    def process_request(self, request, client_address):
        self.logger.debug('process_request(%s, %s)',
                          request, client_address)
        return socketserver.TCPServer.process_request(
            self, request, client_address,
        )

    def server_close(self):
        self.logger.debug('server_close')
        return socketserver.TCPServer.server_close(self)

    def finish_request(self, request, client_address):
        self.logger.debug('finish_request(%s, %s)',
                          request, client_address)
```

```
        return socketserver.TCPServer.finish_request(
            self, request, client_address,
        )

    def close_request(self, request_address):
        self.logger.debug('close_request(%s)', request_address)
        return socketserver.TCPServer.close_request(
            self, request_address,
        )

    def shutdown(self):
        self.logger.debug('shutdown()')
        return socketserver.TCPServer.shutdown(self)
```

The last step is to add a main program that sets up the server to run in a thread, and sends it data to illustrate which methods are called as the data is echoed back.

```
if __name__ == '__main__':
    import socket
    import threading

    address = ('localhost', 0)  # Let the kernel assign a port.
    server = EchoServer(address, EchoRequestHandler)
    ip, port = server.server_address  # What port was assigned?

    # Start the server in a thread.
    t = threading.Thread(target=server.serve_forever)
    t.setDaemon(True)  # Don't hang on exit.
    t.start()

    logger = logging.getLogger('client')
    logger.info('Server on %s:%s', ip, port)

    # Connect to the server.
    logger.debug('creating socket')
    s = socket.socket(socket.AF_INET, socket.SOCK_STREAM)
    logger.debug('connecting to server')
    s.connect((ip, port))

    # Send the data.
    message = 'Hello, world'.encode()
    logger.debug('sending data: %r', message)
    len_sent = s.send(message)

    # Receive a response.
    logger.debug('waiting for response')
    response = s.recv(len_sent)
    logger.debug('response from server: %r', response)
```

```
        # Clean up.
        server.shutdown()
        logger.debug('closing socket')
        s.close()
        logger.debug('done')
        server.socket.close()
```

Running the program produces the following output.

```
$ python3 socketserver_echo.py

EchoServer: __init__
EchoServer: server_activate
EchoServer: waiting for request
EchoServer: Handling requests, press <Ctrl-C> to quit
client: Server on 127.0.0.1:55484
client: creating socket
client: connecting to server
client: sending data: b'Hello, world'
EchoServer: verify_request(<socket.socket fd=7, family=AddressFamily
.AF_INET, type=SocketKind.SOCK_STREAM, proto=0, laddr=('127.0.0.1',
55484), raddr=('127.0.0.1', 55485)>, ('127.0.0.1', 55485))
EchoServer: process_request(<socket.socket fd=7, family=AddressFamil
y.AF_INET, type=SocketKind.SOCK_STREAM, proto=0, laddr=('127.0.0.1',
 55484), raddr=('127.0.0.1', 55485)>, ('127.0.0.1', 55485))
EchoServer: finish_request(<socket.socket fd=7, family=AddressFamily
.AF_INET, type=SocketKind.SOCK_STREAM, proto=0, laddr=('127.0.0.1',
55484), raddr=('127.0.0.1', 55485)>, ('127.0.0.1', 55485))
EchoRequestHandler: __init__
EchoRequestHandler: setup
EchoRequestHandler: handle
client: waiting for response
EchoRequestHandler: recv()->"b'Hello, world'"
EchoRequestHandler: finish
client: response from server: b'Hello, world'
EchoServer: shutdown()
EchoServer: close_request(<socket.socket fd=7, family=AddressFamily.
AF_INET, type=SocketKind.SOCK_STREAM, proto=0, laddr=('127.0.0.1', 5
5484), raddr=('127.0.0.1', 55485)>)
client: closing socket
client: done
```

NOTE

The port number used will change each time the program runs because the kernel allocates an available port automatically. To make the server listen on a specific port each time, provide that number in the address tuple instead of the 0.

A condensed version of the same server, without the logging calls, is presented here. Only the handle() method in the request handler class needs to be provided.

Listing 11.42: socketserver_echo_simple.py

```python
import socketserver


class EchoRequestHandler(socketserver.BaseRequestHandler):

    def handle(self):
        # Echo the data back to the client.
        data = self.request.recv(1024)
        self.request.send(data)
        return


if __name__ == '__main__':
    import socket
    import threading

    address = ('localhost', 0)  # Let the kernel assign a port.
    server = socketserver.TCPServer(address, EchoRequestHandler)
    ip, port = server.server_address  # What port was assigned?

    t = threading.Thread(target=server.serve_forever)
    t.setDaemon(True)  # Don't hang on exit.
    t.start()

    # Connect to the server.
    s = socket.socket(socket.AF_INET, socket.SOCK_STREAM)
    s.connect((ip, port))

    # Send the data.
    message = 'Hello, world'.encode()
    print('Sending : {!r}'.format(message))
    len_sent = s.send(message)

    # Receive a response.
    response = s.recv(len_sent)
    print('Received: {!r}'.format(response))

    # Clean up.
    server.shutdown()
    s.close()
    server.socket.close()
```

In this case, no special server class is required because the TCPServer handles all of the server requirements.

```
$ python3 socketserver_echo_simple.py

Sending : b'Hello, world'
Received: b'Hello, world'
```

11.5.6 Threading and Forking

To add threading or forking support to a server, include the appropriate mix-in in the class hierarchy for the server. The mix-in classes override process_request() to start a new thread or process when a request is ready to be handled, and the work is done in the new child.

For threads, use ThreadingMixIn.

Listing 11.43: socketserver_threaded.py

```
import threading
import socketserver


class ThreadedEchoRequestHandler(
        socketserver.BaseRequestHandler,
):

    def handle(self):
        # Echo the data back to the client.
        data = self.request.recv(1024)
        cur_thread = threading.currentThread()
        response = b'%s: %s' % (cur_thread.getName().encode(),
                                data)
        self.request.send(response)
        return


class ThreadedEchoServer(socketserver.ThreadingMixIn,
                         socketserver.TCPServer,
                         ):
    pass


if __name__ == '__main__':
    import socket

    address = ('localhost', 0)  # Let the kernel assign a port.
    server = ThreadedEchoServer(address,
                                ThreadedEchoRequestHandler)
    ip, port = server.server_address  # What port was assigned?

    t = threading.Thread(target=server.serve_forever)
```

```
      t.setDaemon(True)  # Don't hang on exit.
      t.start()
      print('Server loop running in thread:', t.getName())

      # Connect to the server.
      s = socket.socket(socket.AF_INET, socket.SOCK_STREAM)
      s.connect((ip, port))

      # Send the data.
      message = b'Hello, world'
      print('Sending : {!r}'.format(message))
      len_sent = s.send(message)

      # Receive a response.
      response = s.recv(1024)
      print('Received: {!r}'.format(response))

      # Clean up.
      server.shutdown()
      s.close()
      server.socket.close()
```

The response from this threaded server includes the identifier of the thread where the request is handled.

```
$ python3 socketserver_threaded.py

Server loop running in thread: Thread-1
Sending : b'Hello, world'
Received: b'Thread-2: Hello, world'
```

For separate processes, use the `ForkingMixIn`.

Listing 11.44: socketserver_forking.py

```
import os
import socketserver


class ForkingEchoRequestHandler(socketserver.BaseRequestHandler):

    def handle(self):
        # Echo the data back to the client.
        data = self.request.recv(1024)
        cur_pid = os.getpid()
        response = b'%d: %s' % (cur_pid, data)
        self.request.send(response)
        return
```

```
    class ForkingEchoServer(socketserver.ForkingMixIn,
                            socketserver.TCPServer,
                            ):
        pass


    if __name__ == '__main__':
        import socket
        import threading

        address = ('localhost', 0)  # Let the kernel assign a port.
        server = ForkingEchoServer(address,
                                   ForkingEchoRequestHandler)
        ip, port = server.server_address  # What port was assigned?

        t = threading.Thread(target=server.serve_forever)
        t.setDaemon(True)  # Don't hang on exit.
        t.start()
        print('Server loop running in process:', os.getpid())

        # Connect to the server.
        s = socket.socket(socket.AF_INET, socket.SOCK_STREAM)
        s.connect((ip, port))

        # Send the data.
        message = 'Hello, world'.encode()
        print('Sending : {!r}'.format(message))
        len_sent = s.send(message)

        # Receive a response.
        response = s.recv(1024)
        print('Received: {!r}'.format(response))

        # Clean up.
        server.shutdown()
        s.close()
        server.socket.close()
```

In this case, the process ID of the child is included in the response from the server.

```
$ python3 socketserver_forking.py

Server loop running in process: 22599
Sending : b'Hello, world'
Received: b'22600: Hello, world'
```

TIP

Related Reading

- Standard library documentation for `socketserver`.[15]
- `socket` (page 693): Low-level network communication.
- `select` (page 728): Low-level asynchronous I/O tools.
- `asyncio` (page 617): Asynchronous I/O, event loop, and concurrency tools.
- `SimpleXMLRPCServer`: XML-RPC server built using `socketserver`.
- *Unix Network Programming, Volume 1: The Sockets Networking API, Third Edition*, by W. Richard Stevens, Bill Fenner, and Andrew M. Rudoff. Addison-Wesley, 2004. ISBN-10: 0131411551.
- *Foundations of Python Network Programming, Third Edition*, by Brandon Rhodes and John Goerzen. Apress, 2014. ISBN-10: 1430258543.

---

[15] https://docs.python.org/3.5/library/socketserver.html

Chapter 12

The Internet

The Internet is a pervasive aspect of modern computing. Even small, single-use scripts frequently interact with remote services to send or receive data. Python's rich set of tools for working with web protocols makes it well suited for programming web-based applications, either as a client or as a server.

The `urllib.parse` (page 753) module manipulates URL strings, splitting and combining their components, and is useful in clients and servers.

The `urllib.request` (page 761) module implements an API for retrieving content remotely.

HTTP POST requests are usually "form encoded" with `urllib`. Binary data sent through a POST should be encoded with `base64` (page 776) first, to comply with the message format standard.

Well-behaved clients that access many sites as a spider or crawler should use `urllib.robotparser` (page 773) to ensure they have permission before placing a heavy load on the remote server.

To create a custom web server with Python, without requiring any external frameworks, use `http.server` (page 781) as a starting point. It handles the HTTP protocol, so the only customization needed is the application code for responding to the incoming requests.

Session state in the server can be managed through cookies created and parsed by the `http.cookies` (page 790) module. Full support for expiration, path, domain, and other cookie settings makes it easy to configure the session.

The `uuid` (page 797) module is used for generating identifiers for resources that need unique values. UUIDs are good choices for automatically generating Uniform Resource Name (URN) values, where the name of the resource needs to be unique but does not need to convey any meaning.

Python's standard library includes support for two web-based remote procedure call mechanisms. The JavaScript Object Notation (JSON) encoding scheme used in AJAX communication and REST APIs are implemented in `json` (page 803). It works equally well in the client or the server. Complete XML-RPC client and server libraries are also included in `xmlrpc.client` (page 816) and `xmlrpc.server` (page 827), respectively.

12.1 urllib.parse: Split URLs into Components

The `urllib.parse` module provides functions for manipulating URLs and their component parts, to either break them down or build them up.

12.1.1 Parsing

The return value from the `urlparse()` function is a `ParseResult` object that acts like a tuple with six elements.

Listing 12.1: `urllib_parse_urlparse.py`

```
from urllib.parse import urlparse

url = 'http://netloc/path;param?query=arg#frag'
parsed = urlparse(url)
print(parsed)
```

The parts of the URL available through the tuple interface are the scheme, network location, path, path segment parameters (separated from the path by a semicolon), query, and fragment.

```
$ python3 urllib_parse_urlparse.py

ParseResult(scheme='http', netloc='netloc', path='/path',
params='param', query='query=arg', fragment='frag')
```

Although the return value acts like a tuple, it is really based on a `namedtuple`, a subclass of `tuple` that supports accessing the parts of the URL via named attributes as well as indexes. In addition to being easier to use for the programmer, the attribute API offers access to several values not available in the `tuple` API.

Listing 12.2: `urllib_parse_urlparseattrs.py`

```
from urllib.parse import urlparse

url = 'http://user:pwd@NetLoc:80/path;param?query=arg#frag'
parsed = urlparse(url)
print('scheme  :', parsed.scheme)
print('netloc  :', parsed.netloc)
print('path    :', parsed.path)
print('params  :', parsed.params)
print('query   :', parsed.query)
print('fragment:', parsed.fragment)
print('username:', parsed.username)
print('password:', parsed.password)
print('hostname:', parsed.hostname)
print('port    :', parsed.port)
```

The `username` and `password` are available when present in the input URL, and set to `None` when not. The `hostname` is the same value as `netloc`, in all lowercase and with the port value stripped. The `port` is converted to an integer when present and `None` when not.

```
$ python3 urllib_parse_urlparseattrs.py

scheme  : http
netloc  : user:pwd@NetLoc:80
path    : /path
params  : param
query   : query=arg
fragment: frag
username: user
password: pwd
hostname: netloc
port    : 80
```

The urlsplit() function is an alternative to urlparse(). It behaves a little differently, because it does not split the parameters from the URL. This is useful for URLs following **RFC 2396**,[1] which supports parameters for each segment of the path.

Listing 12.3: **urllib_parse_urlsplit.py**

```
from urllib.parse import urlsplit

url = 'http://user:pwd@NetLoc:80/p1;para/p2;para?query=arg#frag'
parsed = urlsplit(url)
print(parsed)
print('scheme  :', parsed.scheme)
print('netloc  :', parsed.netloc)
print('path    :', parsed.path)
print('query   :', parsed.query)
print('fragment:', parsed.fragment)
print('username:', parsed.username)
print('password:', parsed.password)
print('hostname:', parsed.hostname)
print('port    :', parsed.port)
```

Since the parameters are not split out, the tuple API will show five elements instead of six, and there is no params attribute.

```
$ python3 urllib_parse_urlsplit.py

SplitResult(scheme='http', netloc='user:pwd@NetLoc:80',
path='/p1;para/p2;para', query='query=arg', fragment='frag')
scheme  : http
netloc  : user:pwd@NetLoc:80
path    : /p1;para/p2;para
query   : query=arg
```

[1] https://tools.ietf.org/html/rfc2396.html

```
fragment: frag
username: user
password: pwd
hostname: netloc
port    : 80
```

To simply strip the fragment identifier from a URL, such as when finding a base page name from a URL, use urldefrag().

Listing 12.4: urllib_parse_urldefrag.py

```python
from urllib.parse import urldefrag

original = 'http://netloc/path;param?query=arg#frag'
print('original:', original)
d = urldefrag(original)
print('url      :', d.url)
print('fragment:', d.fragment)
```

The return value is a DefragResult, based on namedtuple, containing the base URL and the fragment.

```
$ python3 urllib_parse_urldefrag.py

original: http://netloc/path;param?query=arg#frag
url     : http://netloc/path;param?query=arg
fragment: frag
```

12.1.2   Unparsing

There are several ways to reassemble the parts of a split URL into a single string. The parsed URL object has a geturl() method.

Listing 12.5: urllib_parse_geturl.py

```python
from urllib.parse import urlparse

original = 'http://netloc/path;param?query=arg#frag'
print('ORIG  :', original)
parsed = urlparse(original)
print('PARSED:', parsed.geturl())
```

geturl() works only on the object returned by urlparse() or urlsplit().

```
$ python3 urllib_parse_geturl.py

ORIG  : http://netloc/path;param?query=arg#frag
PARSED: http://netloc/path;param?query=arg#frag
```

A regular tuple containing strings can be combined into a URL with urlunparse().

Listing 12.6: **urllib_parse_urlunparse.py**

```
from urllib.parse import urlparse, urlunparse

original = 'http://netloc/path;param?query=arg#frag'
print('ORIG  :', original)
parsed = urlparse(original)
print('PARSED:', type(parsed), parsed)
t = parsed[:]
print('TUPLE :', type(t), t)
print('NEW   :', urlunparse(t))
```

While the ParseResult returned by urlparse() can be used as a tuple, this example explicitly creates a new tuple to show that urlunparse() works with normal tuples, too.

```
$ python3 urllib_parse_urlunparse.py

ORIG  : http://netloc/path;param?query=arg#frag
PARSED: <class 'urllib.parse.ParseResult'>
ParseResult(scheme='http', netloc='netloc', path='/path',
params='param', query='query=arg', fragment='frag')
TUPLE : <class 'tuple'> ('http', 'netloc', '/path', 'param',
'query=arg', 'frag')
NEW   : http://netloc/path;param?query=arg#frag
```

If the input URL included superfluous parts, those may be dropped from the reconstructed URL.

Listing 12.7: **urllib_parse_urlunparseextra.py**

```
from urllib.parse import urlparse, urlunparse

original = 'http://netloc/path;?#'
print('ORIG  :', original)
parsed = urlparse(original)
print('PARSED:', type(parsed), parsed)
t = parsed[:]
print('TUPLE :', type(t), t)
print('NEW   :', urlunparse(t))
```

In this case, parameters, query, and fragment are all missing in the original URL. The new URL does not look the same as the original, but is equivalent according to the standard.

```
$ python3 urllib_parse_urlunparseextra.py

ORIG  : http://netloc/path;?#
PARSED: <class 'urllib.parse.ParseResult'>
```

```
ParseResult(scheme='http', netloc='netloc', path='/path',
params='', query='', fragment='')
TUPLE : <class 'tuple'> ('http', 'netloc', '/path', '', '', '')
NEW    : http://netloc/path
```

12.1.3   Joining

In addition to parsing URLs, urlparse includes urljoin() for constructing absolute URLs
from relative fragments.

Listing 12.8: **urllib_parse_urljoin.py**

```
from urllib.parse import urljoin

print(urljoin('http://www.example.com/path/file.html',
              'anotherfile.html'))
print(urljoin('http://www.example.com/path/file.html',
              '../anotherfile.html'))
```

In the example, the relative portion of the path ("../") is taken into account when the
second URL is computed.

```
$ python3 urllib_parse_urljoin.py

http://www.example.com/path/anotherfile.html
http://www.example.com/anotherfile.html
```

Nonrelative paths are handled in the same way as by os.path.join().

Listing 12.9: **urllib_parse_urljoin_with_path.py**

```
from urllib.parse import urljoin

print(urljoin('http://www.example.com/path/',
              '/subpath/file.html'))
print(urljoin('http://www.example.com/path/',
              'subpath/file.html'))
```

If the path being joined to the URL starts with a slash (/), urljoin() resets the URL's
path to the top level. If it does not start with a slash, the new path value is appended to
the end of the existing path for the URL.

```
$ python3 urllib_parse_urljoin_with_path.py

http://www.example.com/subpath/file.html
http://www.example.com/path/subpath/file.html
```

12.1.4 Encoding Query Arguments

Before arguments can be added to a URL, they need to be encoded.

Listing 12.10: **urllib_parse_urlencode.py**

```
from urllib.parse import urlencode

query_args = {
    'q': 'query string',
    'foo': 'bar',
}
encoded_args = urlencode(query_args)
print('Encoded:', encoded_args)
```

Encoding replaces special characters such as spaces to ensure they are passed to the server using a format that complies with the standard.

```
$ python3 urllib_parse_urlencode.py

Encoded: q=query+string&foo=bar
```

To pass a sequence of values using separate occurrences of the variable in the query string, set doseq to True when calling urlencode().

Listing 12.11: **urllib_parse_urlencode_doseq.py**

```
from urllib.parse import urlencode

query_args = {
    'foo': ['foo1', 'foo2'],
}
print('Single  :', urlencode(query_args))
print('Sequence:', urlencode(query_args, doseq=True))
```

The result is a query string with several values associated with the same name.

```
$ python3 urllib_parse_urlencode_doseq.py

Single  : foo=%5B%27foo1%27%2C+%27foo2%27%5D
Sequence: foo=foo1&foo=foo2
```

To decode the query string, use parse_qs() or parse_qsl().

Listing 12.12: **urllib_parse_parse_qs.py**

```
from urllib.parse import parse_qs, parse_qsl

encoded = 'foo=foo1&foo=foo2'
```

```
print('parse_qs :', parse_qs(encoded))
print('parse_qsl:', parse_qsl(encoded))
```

The return value from `parse_qs()` is a dictionary mapping names to values, while `parse_qsl()` returns a list of tuples containing a name and a value.

```
$ python3 urllib_parse_parse_qs.py

parse_qs : {'foo': ['foo1', 'foo2']}
parse_qsl: [('foo', 'foo1'), ('foo', 'foo2')]
```

Special characters within the query arguments that might cause parse problems with the URL on the server side are "quoted" when passed to `urlencode()`. To quote them locally to make safe versions of the strings, use the `quote()` or `quote_plus()` function directly.

Listing 12.13: urllib_parse_quote.py

```
from urllib.parse import quote, quote_plus, urlencode

url = 'http://localhost:8080/~hellmann/'
print('urlencode() :', urlencode({'url': url}))
print('quote()     :', quote(url))
print('quote_plus():', quote_plus(url))
```

The quoting implementation in `quote_plus()` is more aggressive about the characters it replaces.

```
$ python3 urllib_parse_quote.py

urlencode() : url=http%3A%2F%2Flocalhost%3A8080%2F%7Ehellmann%2F
quote()     : http%3A//localhost%3A8080/%7Ehellmann/
quote_plus(): http%3A%2F%2Flocalhost%3A8080%2F%7Ehellmann%2F
```

To reverse the quote operations, use `unquote()` or `unquote_plus()`, as appropriate.

Listing 12.14: urllib_parse_unquote.py

```
from urllib.parse import unquote, unquote_plus

print(unquote('http%3A//localhost%3A8080/%7Ehellmann/'))
print(unquote_plus(
    'http%3A%2F%2Flocalhost%3A8080%2F%7Ehellmann%2F'
))
```

The encoded value is converted back to a normal string URL.

```
$ python3 urllib_parse_unquote.py

http://localhost:8080/~hellmann/
http://localhost:8080/~hellmann/
```

Related Reading

- Standard library documentation for urllib.parse.[2]
- urllib.request (page 761): Retrieve the contents of a resource identified by a URL.
- **RFC 1738**[3]: Uniform Resource Locator (URL) syntax.
- **RFC 1808**[4]: Relative URLs.
- **RFC 2396**[5]: Uniform Resource Identifier (URI) generic syntax.
- **RFC 3986**[6]: Uniform Resource Identifier (URI) syntax.

12.2   urllib.request: Network Resource Access

The urllib.request module provides an API for using Internet resources identified by URLs. It is designed to be extended by individual applications to support new protocols or add variations to existing protocols (such as handling HTTP basic authentication).

12.2.1   HTTP GET

NOTE

The test server for these examples is found in http_server_GET.py, from the examples for the http.server (page 781) module. Start the server in one terminal window, and then run these examples in another.

An HTTP GET operation is the simplest use of urllib.request. Pass the URL to urlopen() to get a "file-like" handle to the remote data.

Listing 12.15: **urllib_request_urlopen.py**

```
from urllib import request

response = request.urlopen('http://localhost:8080/')
print('RESPONSE:', response)
print('URL     :', response.geturl())

headers = response.info()
print('DATE    :', headers['date'])
print('HEADERS :')
print('---------')
```

[2] https://docs.python.org/3.5/library/urllib.parse.html
[3] https://tools.ietf.org/html/rfc1738.html
[4] https://tools.ietf.org/html/rfc1808.html
[5] https://tools.ietf.org/html/rfc2396.html
[6] https://tools.ietf.org/html/rfc3986.html

```
print(headers)

data = response.read().decode('utf-8')
print('LENGTH  :', len(data))
print('DATA    :')
print('---------')
print(data)
```

The example server accepts the incoming values and formats a plain text response to send back. The return value from `urlopen()` gives access to the headers from the HTTP server through the `info()` method, and the data for the remote resource can be accessed via methods like `read()` and `readlines()`.

```
$ python3 urllib_request_urlopen.py

RESPONSE: <http.client.HTTPResponse object at 0x101744d68>
URL     : http://localhost:8080/
DATE    : Sat, 08 Oct 2016 18:08:54 GMT
HEADERS :
---------
Server: BaseHTTP/0.6 Python/3.5.2
Date: Sat, 08 Oct 2016 18:08:54 GMT
Content-Type: text/plain; charset=utf-8


LENGTH  : 349
DATA    :
---------
CLIENT VALUES:
client_address=('127.0.0.1', 58420) (127.0.0.1)
command=GET
path=/
real path=/
query=
request_version=HTTP/1.1

SERVER VALUES:
server_version=BaseHTTP/0.6
sys_version=Python/3.5.2
protocol_version=HTTP/1.0

HEADERS RECEIVED:
Accept-Encoding=identity
Connection=close
Host=localhost:8080
User-Agent=Python-urllib/3.5
```

The file-like object returned by `urlopen()` is iterable.

Listing 12.16: **urllib_request_urlopen_iterator.py**

```
from urllib import request

response = request.urlopen('http://localhost:8080/')
for line in response:
    print(line.decode('utf-8').rstrip())
```

This example strips the trailing newlines and carriage returns before printing the output.

```
$ python3 urllib_request_urlopen_iterator.py

CLIENT VALUES:
client_address=('127.0.0.1', 58444) (127.0.0.1)
command=GET
path=/
real path=/
query=
request_version=HTTP/1.1

SERVER VALUES:
server_version=BaseHTTP/0.6
sys_version=Python/3.5.2
protocol_version=HTTP/1.0

HEADERS RECEIVED:
Accept-Encoding=identity
Connection=close
Host=localhost:8080
User-Agent=Python-urllib/3.5
```

12.2.2 Encoding Arguments

Arguments can be passed to the server by encoding them with urllib.parse.urlencode()
and appending them to the URL.

Listing 12.17: **urllib_request_http_get_args.py**

```
from urllib import parse
from urllib import request

query_args = {'q': 'query string', 'foo': 'bar'}
encoded_args = parse.urlencode(query_args)
print('Encoded:', encoded_args)

url = 'http://localhost:8080/?' + encoded_args
print(request.urlopen(url).read().decode('utf-8'))
```

The list of client values returned in the example output contains the encoded query arguments.

```
$ python urllib_request_http_get_args.py
Encoded: q=query+string&foo=bar
CLIENT VALUES:
client_address=('127.0.0.1', 58455) (127.0.0.1)
command=GET
path=/?q=query+string&foo=bar
real path=/
query=q=query+string&foo=bar
request_version=HTTP/1.1

SERVER VALUES:
server_version=BaseHTTP/0.6
sys_version=Python/3.5.2
protocol_version=HTTP/1.0

HEADERS RECEIVED:
Accept-Encoding=identity
Connection=close
Host=localhost:8080
User-Agent=Python-urllib/3.5
```

12.2.3   HTTP POST

NOTE

The test server for these examples is found in `http_server_POST.py`, from the examples for the `http.server` (page 781) module. Start the server in one terminal window, and then run these examples in another.

To send form-encoded data to the remote server using POST instead GET, pass the encoded query arguments as data to `urlopen()`.

Listing 12.18: `urllib_request_urlopen_post.py`

```python
from urllib import parse
from urllib import request

query_args = {'q': 'query string', 'foo': 'bar'}
encoded_args = parse.urlencode(query_args).encode('utf-8')
url = 'http://localhost:8080/'
print(request.urlopen(url, encoded_args).read().decode('utf-8'))
```

The server can decode the form data and access the individual values by name.

```
$ python3 urllib_request_urlopen_post.py

Client: ('127.0.0.1', 58568)
User-agent: Python-urllib/3.5
Path: /
Form data:
    foo=bar
    q=query string
```

12.2.4   Adding Outgoing Headers

urlopen() is a convenience function that hides some of the details of how the request is made and handled. More precise control is possible by using a **Request** instance directly. For example, custom headers can be added to the outgoing request to control the format of data returned, specify the version of a document cached locally, and tell the remote server the name of the software client communicating with it.

As the output from the earlier examples shows, the default *User-agent* header value is made up of the constant **Python-urllib**, followed by the Python interpreter version. When creating an application that will access web resources owned by someone else, the courteous approach is to include real user agent information in the requests, so they can identify the source of the hits more easily. Using a custom agent also allows them to control crawlers with a robots.txt file (see the http.robotparser module).

Listing 12.19: urllib_request_request_header.py

```
from urllib import request

r = request.Request('http://localhost:8080/')
r.add_header(
    'User-agent',
    'PyMOTW (https://pymotw.com/)',
)

response = request.urlopen(r)
data = response.read().decode('utf-8')
print(data)
```

After creating a **Request** object, use add_header() to set the user agent value before opening the request. The last line of the output shows the custom value.

```
$ python3 urllib_request_request_header.py

CLIENT VALUES:
client_address=('127.0.0.1', 58585) (127.0.0.1)
command=GET
```

```
path=/
real path=/
query=
request_version=HTTP/1.1

SERVER VALUES:
server_version=BaseHTTP/0.6
sys_version=Python/3.5.2
protocol_version=HTTP/1.0

HEADERS RECEIVED:
Accept-Encoding=identity
Connection=close
Host=localhost:8080
User-Agent=PyMOTW (https://pymotw.com/)
```

12.2.5   Posting Form Data from a Request

When building the Request, the outgoing data can be specified so that it will be posted to the server.

Listing 12.20: **urllib_request_request_post.py**

```
from urllib import parse
from urllib import request

query_args = {'q': 'query string', 'foo': 'bar'}

r = request.Request(
    url='http://localhost:8080/',
    data=parse.urlencode(query_args).encode('utf-8'),
)
print('Request method :', r.get_method())
r.add_header(
    'User-agent',
    'PyMOTW (https://pymotw.com/)',
)

print()
print('OUTGOING DATA:')
print(r.data)

print()
print('SERVER RESPONSE:')
print(request.urlopen(r).read().decode('utf-8'))
```

The HTTP method used by the Request changes from GET to POST automatically after the data is added.

```
$ python3 urllib_request_request_post.py

Request method : POST

OUTGOING DATA:
b'q=query+string&foo=bar'

SERVER RESPONSE:
Client: ('127.0.0.1', 58613)
User-agent: PyMOTW (https://pymotw.com/)
Path: /
Form data:
    foo=bar
    q=query string
```

12.2.6   Uploading Files

Encoding files for upload requires a little more work than using simple forms. A complete
MIME message needs to be constructed in the body of the request, so that the server can
distinguish the incoming form fields from uploaded files.

Listing 12.21: urllib_request_upload_files.py

```python
import io
import mimetypes
from urllib import request
import uuid


class MultiPartForm:
    """Accumulate the data to be used when posting a form."""

    def __init__(self):
        self.form_fields = []
        self.files = []
        # Use a large random byte string to separate
        # parts of the MIME data.
        self.boundary = uuid.uuid4().hex.encode('utf-8')
        return

    def get_content_type(self):
        return 'multipart/form-data; boundary={}'.format(
            self.boundary.decode('utf-8'))

    def add_field(self, name, value):
        """Add a simple field to the form data."""
        self.form_fields.append((name, value))
```

```python
    def add_file(self, fieldname, filename, fileHandle,
                 mimetype=None):
        """Add a file to be uploaded."""
        body = fileHandle.read()
        if mimetype is None:
            mimetype = (
                mimetypes.guess_type(filename)[0] or
                'application/octet-stream'
            )
        self.files.append((fieldname, filename, mimetype, body))
        return

    @staticmethod
    def _form_data(name):
        return ('Content-Disposition: form-data; '
                'name="{}"\r\n').format(name).encode('utf-8')

    @staticmethod
    def _attached_file(name, filename):
        return ('Content-Disposition: file; '
                'name="{}"; filename="{}"\r\n').format(
                    name, filename).encode('utf-8')

    @staticmethod
    def _content_type(ct):
        return 'Content-Type: {}\r\n'.format(ct).encode('utf-8')

    def __bytes__(self):
        """Return a byte-string representing the form data,
        including attached files.
        """
        buffer = io.BytesIO()
        boundary = b'--' + self.boundary + b'\r\n'

        # Add the form fields.
        for name, value in self.form_fields:
            buffer.write(boundary)
            buffer.write(self._form_data(name))
            buffer.write(b'\r\n')
            buffer.write(value.encode('utf-8'))
            buffer.write(b'\r\n')

        # Add the files to upload.
        for f_name, filename, f_content_type, body in self.files:
            buffer.write(boundary)
            buffer.write(self._attached_file(f_name, filename))
            buffer.write(self._content_type(f_content_type))
            buffer.write(b'\r\n')
            buffer.write(body)
```

```
            buffer.write(b'\r\n')

        buffer.write(b'--' + self.boundary + b'--\r\n')
        return buffer.getvalue()


if __name__ == '__main__':
    # Create the form with simple fields.
    form = MultiPartForm()
    form.add_field('firstname', 'Doug')
    form.add_field('lastname', 'Hellmann')

    # Add a fake file.
    form.add_file(
        'biography', 'bio.txt',
        fileHandle=io.BytesIO(b'Python developer and blogger.'))

    # Build the request, including the byte-string
    # for the data to be posted.
    data = bytes(form)
    r = request.Request('http://localhost:8080/', data=data)
    r.add_header(
        'User-agent',
        'PyMOTW (https://pymotw.com/)',
    )
    r.add_header('Content-type', form.get_content_type())
    r.add_header('Content-length', len(data))

    print()
    print('OUTGOING DATA:')
    for name, value in r.header_items():
        print('{}: {}'.format(name, value))
    print()
    print(r.data.decode('utf-8'))

    print()
    print('SERVER RESPONSE:')
    print(request.urlopen(r).read().decode('utf-8'))
```

The MultiPartForm class can represent an arbitrary form as a multipart MIME message with attached files.

```
$ python3 urllib_request_upload_files.py

OUTGOING DATA:
User-agent: PyMOTW (https://pymotw.com/)
Content-type: multipart/form-data;
    boundary=d99b5dc60871491b9d63352eb24972b4
```

```
Content-length: 389

--d99b5dc60871491b9d63352eb24972b4
Content-Disposition: form-data; name="firstname"

Doug
--d99b5dc60871491b9d63352eb24972b4
Content-Disposition: form-data; name="lastname"

Hellmann
--d99b5dc60871491b9d63352eb24972b4
Content-Disposition: file; name="biography";
    filename="bio.txt"
Content-Type: text/plain

Python developer and blogger.
--d99b5dc60871491b9d63352eb24972b4--


SERVER RESPONSE:
Client: ('127.0.0.1', 59310)
User-agent: PyMOTW (https://pymotw.com/)
Path: /
Form data:
    Uploaded biography as 'bio.txt' (29 bytes)
    firstname=Doug
    lastname=Hellmann
```

12.2.7   Creating Custom Protocol Handlers

urllib.request has built-in support for HTTP(S), FTP, and local file access. To add support for other URL types, register another protocol handler. For example, to support URLs that point to arbitrary files on remote NFS servers, without requiring users to mount the path before accessing the file, create a class derived from BaseHandler and with a method nfs_open().

The protocol-specific open() method takes a single argument, the Request instance, and returns an object with a read() method to read the data, an info() method to return the response headers, and a geturl() method to return the actual URL of the file being read. A simple way to meet these requirements is to create an instance of urllib.response.addinfourl, and then pass the headers, URL, and open file handle in to the constructor.

Listing 12.22: **urllib_request_nfs_handler.py**

```
import io
import mimetypes
import os
import tempfile
```

```
from urllib import request
from urllib import response


class NFSFile:

    def __init__(self, tempdir, filename):
        self.tempdir = tempdir
        self.filename = filename
        with open(os.path.join(tempdir, filename), 'rb') as f:
            self.buffer = io.BytesIO(f.read())

    def read(self, *args):
        return self.buffer.read(*args)

    def readline(self, *args):
        return self.buffer.readline(*args)

    def close(self):
        print('\nNFSFile:')
        print('  unmounting {}'.format(
            os.path.basename(self.tempdir)))
        print('  when {} is closed'.format(
            os.path.basename(self.filename)))


class FauxNFSHandler(request.BaseHandler):

    def __init__(self, tempdir):
        self.tempdir = tempdir
        super().__init__()

    def nfs_open(self, req):
        url = req.full_url
        directory_name, file_name = os.path.split(url)
        server_name = req.host
        print('FauxNFSHandler simulating mount:')
        print('  Remote path: {}'.format(directory_name))
        print('  Server     : {}'.format(server_name))
        print('  Local path : {}'.format(
            os.path.basename(tempdir)))
        print('  Filename   : {}'.format(file_name))
        local_file = os.path.join(tempdir, file_name)
        fp = NFSFile(tempdir, file_name)
        content_type = (
            mimetypes.guess_type(file_name)[0] or
            'application/octet-stream'
        )
        stats = os.stat(local_file)
```

```
            size = stats.st_size
            headers = {
                'Content-type': content_type,
                'Content-length': size,
            }
            return response.addinfourl(fp, headers,
                                        req.get_full_url())


if __name__ == '__main__':
    with tempfile.TemporaryDirectory() as tempdir:
        # Populate the temporary file for the simulation.
        filename = os.path.join(tempdir, 'file.txt')
        with open(filename, 'w', encoding='utf-8') as f:
            f.write('Contents of file.txt')

        # Construct an opener with our NFS handler
        # and register it as the default opener.
        opener = request.build_opener(FauxNFSHandler(tempdir))
        request.install_opener(opener)

        # Open the file through a URL.
        resp = request.urlopen(
            'nfs://remote_server/path/to/the/file.txt'
        )
        print()
        print('READ CONTENTS:', resp.read())
        print('URL          :', resp.geturl())
        print('HEADERS:')
        for name, value in sorted(resp.info().items()):
            print('  {:<15} = {}'.format(name, value))
        resp.close()
```

The `FauxNFSHandler` and `NFSFile` classes print messages to illustrate where a real implementation would add mount and unmount calls. Since this is just a simulation, `FauxNFSHandler` is primed with the name of a temporary directory where it should look for all of its files.

```
$ python3 urllib_request_nfs_handler.py

FauxNFSHandler simulating mount:
  Remote path: nfs://remote_server/path/to/the
  Server     : remote_server
  Local path : tmprucom5sb
  Filename   : file.txt

READ CONTENTS: b'Contents of file.txt'
URL          : nfs://remote_server/path/to/the/file.txt
```

```
HEADERS:
  Content-length  = 20
  Content-type    = text/plain

NFSFile:
  unmounting tmprucom5sb
  when file.txt is closed
```

TIP

Related Reading

- Standard library documentation for `urllib.request`.[7]
- `urllib.parse` (page 753): Work with the URL string itself.
- Form content types[8]: W3C specification for posting files or large amounts of data via HTTP forms.
- `mimetypes`: Map filenames to mimetype.
- Requests[9]: Third-party HTTP library with better support for secure connections and an easier-to-use API. The Python core development team recommends that most developers use `requests`, in part because this module receives more frequent security updates than the standard library.

12.3   urllib.robotparser: Internet Spider Access Control

`robotparser` implements a parser for the `robots.txt` file format, including a function that checks whether a given user agent can access a resource. It is intended for use in well-behaved spiders, or other crawler applications that need to be throttled or otherwise restricted.

12.3.1   robots.txt

The `robots.txt` file format is a simple text-based access control system for computer programs that automatically access web resources ("spiders," "crawlers," and the like). The file is made up of records that specify the user agent identifier for the program, followed by a list of URLs (or URL prefixes) that the agent may not access.

The following listing shows the `robots.txt` file for `https://pymotw.com/`.

Listing 12.23: `robots.txt`

```
Sitemap: https://pymotw.com/sitemap.xml
User-agent: *
Disallow: /admin/
```

---

[7] https://docs.python.org/3.5/library/urllib.request.html
[8] www.w3.org/TR/REC-html40/interact/forms.html#h-17.13.4
[9] https://pypi.python.org/pypi/requests

```
Disallow: /downloads/
Disallow: /media/
Disallow: /static/
Disallow: /codehosting/
```

This file prevents access to some of the parts of the site that are expensive in terms of the necessary computing resources and would overload the server if a search engine tried to index them. For a more complete set of examples of `robots.txt`, refer to the Web Robots Page.[10]

12.3.2   Testing Access Permissions

Using the data presented earlier, a simple crawler can test whether it is allowed to download a page using RobotFileParser.can_fetch().

Listing 12.24: **urllib_robotparser_simple.py**

```python
from urllib import parse
from urllib import robotparser

AGENT_NAME = 'PyMOTW'
URL_BASE = 'https://pymotw.com/'
parser = robotparser.RobotFileParser()
parser.set_url(parse.urljoin(URL_BASE, 'robots.txt'))
parser.read()

PATHS = [
    '/',
    '/PyMOTW/',
    '/admin/',
    '/downloads/PyMOTW-1.92.tar.gz',
]

for path in PATHS:
    print('{!r:>6} : {}'.format(
        parser.can_fetch(AGENT_NAME, path), path))
    url = parse.urljoin(URL_BASE, path)
    print('{!r:>6} : {}'.format(
        parser.can_fetch(AGENT_NAME, url), url))
    print()
```

The URL argument to can_fetch() can be a path relative to the root of the site, or it can be a full URL.

```
$ python3 urllib_robotparser_simple.py

  True : /
```

---

[10] www.robotstxt.org/orig.html

```
   True  :  https://pymotw.com/

   True  :  /PyMOTW/
   True  :  https://pymotw.com/PyMOTW/

   False :  /admin/
   False :  https://pymotw.com/admin/

   False :  /downloads/PyMOTW-1.92.tar.gz
   False :  https://pymotw.com/downloads/PyMOTW-1.92.tar.gz
```

12.3.3   Long-Lived Spiders

An application that takes a long time to process the resources it downloads or that is throttled to pause between downloads should check for new `robots.txt` files periodically based on the age of the content it has already downloaded. The age is not managed automatically, but convenience methods are available to facilitate its tracking.

Listing 12.25: **urllib_robotparser_longlived.py**

```python
from urllib import robotparser
import time

AGENT_NAME = 'PyMOTW'
parser = robotparser.RobotFileParser()
# Use the local copy.
parser.set_url('file:robots.txt')
parser.read()
parser.modified()

PATHS = [
    '/',
    '/PyMOTW/',
    '/admin/',
    '/downloads/PyMOTW-1.92.tar.gz',
]

for path in PATHS:
    age = int(time.time() - parser.mtime())
    print('age:', age, end=' ')
    if age > 1:
        print('rereading robots.txt')
        parser.read()
        parser.modified()
    else:
        print()
    print('{!r:>6} : {}'.format(
        parser.can_fetch(AGENT_NAME, path), path))
```

```
# Simulate a delay in processing.
time.sleep(1)
print()
```

This extreme example downloads a new `robots.txt` file if the existing file is more than 1 second old.

```
$ python3 urllib_robotparser_longlived.py

age: 0
  True : /

age: 1
  True : /PyMOTW/

age: 2 rereading robots.txt
 False : /admin/

age: 1
 False : /downloads/PyMOTW-1.92.tar.gz
```

A nicer version of the long-lived application might request the modification time for the file before downloading the entire thing. The `robots.txt` files are usually fairly small, however, so it is not that especially expensive to just retrieve the entire document again.

TIP

Related Reading

- Standard library documentation for `urllib.robotparser`.[11]
- The Web Robots Page[12]: Description of `robots.txt` format.

12.4   base64: Encode Binary Data with ASCII

The `base64` module contains functions for translating binary data into a subset of ASCII suitable for transmission using plaintext protocols. The Base64, Base32, Base16, and Base85 encodings convert 8-bit bytes to values that fit inside the ASCII range of printable characters, trading more bits to represent the data for compatibility with systems that support only ASCII data, such as SMTP. The *base* values correspond to the length of the alphabet used in each encoding. URL-safe variations of the original encodings use slightly different alphabets.

---

[11] https://docs.python.org/3.5/library/urllib.robotparser.html
[12] www.robotstxt.org/orig.html

12.4.1 Base 64 Encoding

The following listing is a simple example in which some text is encoded.

Listing 12.26: base64_b64encode.py

```
import base64
import textwrap

# Load this source file and strip the header.
with open(__file__, 'r', encoding='utf-8') as input:
    raw = input.read()
    initial_data = raw.split('#end_pymotw_header')[1]

byte_string = initial_data.encode('utf-8')
encoded_data = base64.b64encode(byte_string)

num_initial = len(byte_string)

# There will never be more than 2 padding bytes.
padding = 3 - (num_initial % 3)

print('{} bytes before encoding'.format(num_initial))
print('Expect {} padding bytes'.format(padding))
print('{} bytes after encoding\n'.format(len(encoded_data)))
print(encoded_data)
```

The input must be a byte string, so the Unicode string is first encoded to UTF-8. The output shows that the 185 bytes of the UTF-8 source has expanded to 248 bytes after being encoded.

NOTE

There are no carriage returns in the encoded data produced by the library, but the output has been wrapped artificially to make it fit better on the page.

```
$ python3 base64_b64encode.py

185 bytes before encoding
Expect 1 padding bytes
248 bytes after encoding
```

b'CgppbXBvcnQgYmFzZTY0CmltcG9ydCB0ZXh0d3JhcAoKIyBMb2FkIHRoaXMgc2
91cmNlIGZpbGUgYW5kIHN0cmlwIHRoZSBoZWFkZXIuCndpdGggb3BlbihfX2ZpbG
VfXywgJ3InLCBlbmNvZGluZz0ndXRmLTgnKSBhcyBpbnB1dDoKICAgIHJhdyA9IG
lucHV0LnJlYWQoKQogICAgaW5pdGlhbF9kYXRhID0gcmF3LnNwbGl0KCc='

12.4.2　Base64 Decoding

`b64decode()` converts an encoded string back to the original form by taking 4 bytes and converting them to the original 3 bytes, using a lookup table.

Listing 12.27: base64_b64decode.py

```
import base64

encoded_data = b'VGhpcyBpcyB0aGUgZGF0YSwgaW4gdGhlIGNsZWFyLg=='
decoded_data = base64.b64decode(encoded_data)
print('Encoded :', encoded_data)
print('Decoded :', decoded_data)
```

The encoding process looks at each sequence of 24 bits in the input (3 bytes) and encodes those same 24 bits spread over 4 bytes in the output. The equals signs at the end of the output are padding inserted because the number of bits in the original string was not evenly divisible by 24, in this example.

```
$ python3 base64_b64decode.py

Encoded : b'VGhpcyBpcyB0aGUgZGF0YSwgaW4gdGhlIGNsZWFyLg=='
Decoded : b'This is the data, in the clear.'
```

The value returned from `b64decode()` is a byte string. If the contents are known to be text, the byte string can be converted to a Unicode object. Because the point of using Base64 encoding is to be able to transmit binary data, however, it is not always safe to assume that the decoded value is text.

12.4.3　URL-Safe Variations

Because the default Base64 alphabet may use + and /, and those two characters are used in URLs, it is often necessary to use an alternative encoding with substitutes for those characters.

Listing 12.28: base64_urlsafe.py

```
import base64

encodes_with_pluses = b'\xfb\xef'
encodes_with_slashes = b'\xff\xff'

for original in [encodes_with_pluses, encodes_with_slashes]:
    print('Original         :', repr(original))
    print('Standard encoding:',
          base64.standard_b64encode(original))
    print('URL-safe encoding:',
          base64.urlsafe_b64encode(original))
    print()
```

The + is replaced with a -, and / is replaced with underscore (_). Otherwise, the alphabet is the same.

```
$ python3 base64_urlsafe.py

Original         : b'\xfb\xef'
Standard encoding: b'++8='
URL-safe encoding: b'--8='

Original         : b'\xff\xff'
Standard encoding: b'//8='
URL-safe encoding: b'__8='
```

12.4.4 Other Encodings

Besides Base64, the module provides functions for working with Base85, Base32, and Base16 (hex) encoded data.

Listing 12.29: **base64_base32.py**

```python
import base64

original_data = b'This is the data, in the clear.'
print('Original:', original_data)

encoded_data = base64.b32encode(original_data)
print('Encoded :', encoded_data)

decoded_data = base64.b32decode(encoded_data)
print('Decoded :', decoded_data)
```

The Base32 alphabet includes the 26 uppercase letters from the ASCII set and the digits 2 through 7.

```
$ python3 base64_base32.py

Original: b'This is the data, in the clear.'
Encoded : b'KRUGS4ZANFZSA5DIMUQGIYLUMEWCA2LOEB2GQZJAMNWGKYLSFY==
===='
Decoded : b'This is the data, in the clear.'
```

The Base16 functions work with the hexadecimal alphabet.

Listing 12.30: **base64_base16.py**

```python
import base64

original_data = b'This is the data, in the clear.'
```

```
print('Original:', original_data)

encoded_data = base64.b16encode(original_data)
print('Encoded :', encoded_data)

decoded_data = base64.b16decode(encoded_data)
print('Decoded :', decoded_data)
```

Each time the number of encoding bits decreases, the output in the encoded format expands to take up more space.

```
$ python3 base64_base16.py

Original: b'This is the data, in the clear.'
Encoded  : b'5468697320697320746865206461746120696E207468652063
6C6561722E'
Decoded : b'This is the data, in the clear.'
```

The Base85 functions use an expanded alphabet that is more space-efficient than the one used for Base64 encoding.

Listing 12.31: base64_base85.py

```
import base64

original_data = b'This is the data, in the clear.'
print('Original     : {} bytes {!r}'.format(
    len(original_data), original_data))

b64_data = base64.b64encode(original_data)
print('b64 Encoded : {} bytes {!r}'.format(
    len(b64_data), b64_data))

b85_data = base64.b85encode(original_data)
print('b85 Encoded : {} bytes {!r}'.format(
    len(b85_data), b85_data))

a85_data = base64.a85encode(original_data)
print('a85 Encoded : {} bytes {!r}'.format(
    len(a85_data), a85_data))
```

Several Base85 encodings and variations are used in Mercurial, git, and the PDF file format. Python includes two implementations, b85encode() implements the version used in Git Mercurial, and a85encode() implements the Ascii85 variant used by PDF files.

```
$ python3 base64_base85.py

Original    : 31 bytes b'This is the data, in the clear.'
b64 Encoded : 44 bytes b'VGhpcyBpcyB0aGUgZGF0YSwgaW4gdGhlIGNsZWF
```

```
yLg=='
b85 Encoded : 39 bytes b'RA^~)AZc?TbZBKDWMOn+EFfuaAarPDAY*K0VR9}
'
a85 Encoded : 39 bytes b'<+oue+DGm>FD,5.A79Rg/0JYE+EV:.+Cf5!@<*t
'
```

TIP

Related Reading

- Standard library documentation for base64.[13]
- **RFC 3548**[14]: The Base16, Base32, and Base64 Data Encodings.
- **RFC 1924**[15]: A Compact Representation of IPv6 Addresses (suggests Base85 encoding for IPv6 network addresses).
- Wikipedia: Ascii85.[16]
- Python 2 to 3 porting notes for base64 (page 1357).

12.5 http.server: Base Classes for Implementing Web Servers

http.server uses classes from socketserver (page 742) to create base classes for making HTTP servers. HTTPServer can be used directly, but the BaseHTTPRequestHandler is intended to be extended to handle each protocol method (e.g., GET, POST).

12.5.1 HTTP GET

To add support for an HTTP method in a request handler class, implement the method do_METHOD(), replacing METHOD with the name of the HTTP method (e.g., do_GET(), do_POST()). For consistency, the request handler methods take no arguments. All of the parameters for the request are parsed by BaseHTTPRequestHandler and stored as instance attributes of the request instance.

The example request handler illustrates how to return a response to the client, and some of the local attributes that can be useful in building the response.

Listing 12.32: http_server_GET.py

```
from http.server import BaseHTTPRequestHandler
from urllib import parse
```

---

[13] https://docs.python.org/3.5/library/base64.html
[14] https://tools.ietf.org/html/rfc3548.html
[15] https://tools.ietf.org/html/rfc1924.html
[16] https://en.wikipedia.org/wiki/Ascii85

```python
class GetHandler(BaseHTTPRequestHandler):

    def do_GET(self):
        parsed_path = parse.urlparse(self.path)
        message_parts = [
            'CLIENT VALUES:',
            'client_address={} ({})'.format(
                self.client_address,
                self.address_string()),
            'command={}'.format(self.command),
            'path={}'.format(self.path),
            'real path={}'.format(parsed_path.path),
            'query={}'.format(parsed_path.query),
            'request_version={}'.format(self.request_version),
            '',
            'SERVER VALUES:',
            'server_version={}'.format(self.server_version),
            'sys_version={}'.format(self.sys_version),
            'protocol_version={}'.format(self.protocol_version),
            '',
            'HEADERS RECEIVED:',
        ]
        for name, value in sorted(self.headers.items()):
            message_parts.append(
                '{}={}'.format(name, value.rstrip())
            )
        message_parts.append('')
        message = '\r\n'.join(message_parts)
        self.send_response(200)
        self.send_header('Content-Type',
                         'text/plain; charset=utf-8')
        self.end_headers()
        self.wfile.write(message.encode('utf-8'))


if __name__ == '__main__':
    from http.server import HTTPServer
    server = HTTPServer(('localhost', 8080), GetHandler)
    print('Starting server, use <Ctrl-C> to stop')
    server.serve_forever()
```

The message text is assembled and then written to `wfile`, the file handle wrapping the response socket. Each response needs a response code, which is set via `send_response()`. If an error code is used (e.g., 404, 501), an appropriate default error message is included in the header, or a message can be passed with the error code.

To run the request handler in a server, pass it to the constructor of `HTTPServer`, as in the `__main__` processing portion of the sample script. Then start the server.

```
$ python3 http_server_GET.py

Starting server, use <Ctrl-C> to stop
```

In a separate terminal, use `curl` to access it.

```
$ curl -v -i http://127.0.0.1:8080/?foo=bar

*   Trying 127.0.0.1...
* Connected to 127.0.0.1 (127.0.0.1) port 8080 (#0)
> GET /?foo=bar HTTP/1.1
> Host: 127.0.0.1:8080
> User-Agent: curl/7.43.0
> Accept: */*
>
HTTP/1.0 200 OK
Content-Type: text/plain; charset=utf-8
Server: BaseHTTP/0.6 Python/3.5.2
Date: Thu, 06 Oct 2016 20:44:11 GMT

CLIENT VALUES:
client_address=('127.0.0.1', 52934) (127.0.0.1)
command=GET
path=/?foo=bar
real path=/
query=foo=bar
request_version=HTTP/1.1

SERVER VALUES:
server_version=BaseHTTP/0.6
sys_version=Python/3.5.2
protocol_version=HTTP/1.0

HEADERS RECEIVED:
Accept=*/*
Host=127.0.0.1:8080
User-Agent=curl/7.43.0
* Connection #0 to host 127.0.0.1 left intact
```

NOTE

The output produced by different versions of `curl` may vary. If running the examples produces different output, check the version number reported by `curl`.

12.5.2   HTTP POST

Supporting POST requests is a little more work, because the base class does not parse the
form data automatically. The `cgi` module provides the `FieldStorage` class, which knows
how to parse the form, if it is given the correct inputs.

Listing 12.33: http_server_POST.py

```python
import cgi
from http.server import BaseHTTPRequestHandler
import io


class PostHandler(BaseHTTPRequestHandler):

    def do_POST(self):
        # Parse the form data posted.
        form = cgi.FieldStorage(
            fp=self.rfile,
            headers=self.headers,
            environ={
                'REQUEST_METHOD': 'POST',
                'CONTENT_TYPE': self.headers['Content-Type'],
            }
        )

        # Begin the response.
        self.send_response(200)
        self.send_header('Content-Type',
                         'text/plain; charset=utf-8')
        self.end_headers()

        out = io.TextIOWrapper(
            self.wfile,
            encoding='utf-8',
            line_buffering=False,
            write_through=True,
        )

        out.write('Client: {}\n'.format(self.client_address))
        out.write('User-agent: {}\n'.format(
            self.headers['user-agent']))
        out.write('Path: {}\n'.format(self.path))
        out.write('Form data:\n')

        # Echo back information about what was posted in the form.
        for field in form.keys():
            field_item = form[field]
            if field_item.filename:
                # The field contains an uploaded file.
```

```
                    file_data = field_item.file.read()
                    file_len = len(file_data)
                    del file_data
                    out.write(
                        '\tUploaded {} as {!r} ({} bytes)\n'.format(
                            field, field_item.filename, file_len)
                    )
                else:
                    # Regular form value
                    out.write('\t{}={}\n'.format(
                        field, form[field].value))

        # Disconnect the encoding wrapper from the underlying
        # buffer so that deleting the wrapper doesn't close
        # the socket, which is still being used by the server.
        out.detach()


if __name__ == '__main__':
    from http.server import HTTPServer
    server = HTTPServer(('localhost', 8080), PostHandler)
    print('Starting server, use <Ctrl-C> to stop')
    server.serve_forever()
```

Run the server in one window.

```
$ python3 http_server_POST.py

Starting server, use <Ctrl-C> to stop
```

The arguments to curl can include form data that is posted to the server by using the -F option. The last argument, -F datafile=@http_server_GET.py, posts the contents of the file http_server_GET.py to illustrate reading file data from the form.

```
$ curl -v http://127.0.0.1:8080/ -F name=dhellmann -F foo=bar \
-F datafile=@http_server_GET.py

*   Trying 127.0.0.1...
* Connected to 127.0.0.1 (127.0.0.1) port 8080 (#0)
> POST / HTTP/1.1
> Host: 127.0.0.1:8080
> User-Agent: curl/7.43.0
> Accept: */*
> Content-Length: 1974
> Expect: 100-continue
> Content-Type: multipart/form-data;
boundary=------------------------a2b3c7485cf8def2
>
```

```
* Done waiting for 100-continue
HTTP/1.0 200 OK
Content-Type: text/plain; charset=utf-8
Server: BaseHTTP/0.6 Python/3.5.2
Date: Thu, 06 Oct 2016 20:53:48 GMT

Client: ('127.0.0.1', 53121)
User-agent: curl/7.43.0
Path: /
Form data:
    name=dhellmann
    Uploaded datafile as 'http_server_GET.py' (1612 bytes)
    foo=bar
* Connection #0 to host 127.0.0.1 left intact
```

12.5.3 Threading and Forking

HTTPServer is a simple subclass of socketserver.TCPServer, and does not use multiple threads or processes to handle requests. To add threading or forking, create a new class using the appropriate mix-in from socketserver (page 742).

Listing 12.34: http_server_threads.py

```python
from http.server import HTTPServer, BaseHTTPRequestHandler
from socketserver import ThreadingMixIn
import threading


class Handler(BaseHTTPRequestHandler):

    def do_GET(self):
        self.send_response(200)
        self.send_header('Content-Type',
                         'text/plain; charset=utf-8')
        self.end_headers()
        message = threading.currentThread().getName()
        self.wfile.write(message.encode('utf-8'))
        self.wfile.write(b'\n')


class ThreadedHTTPServer(ThreadingMixIn, HTTPServer):
    """Handle requests in a separate thread."""


if __name__ == '__main__':
    server = ThreadedHTTPServer(('localhost', 8080), Handler)
    print('Starting server, use <Ctrl-C> to stop')
    server.serve_forever()
```

Run the server in the same way as in the other examples.

```
$ python3 http_server_threads.py

Starting server, use <Ctrl-C> to stop
```

Each time the server receives a request, it starts a new thread or process to handle it.

```
$ curl http://127.0.0.1:8080/

Thread-1

$ curl http://127.0.0.1:8080/

Thread-2

$ curl http://127.0.0.1:8080/

Thread-3
```

Swapping `ForkingMixIn` for `ThreadingMixIn` would achieve similar results, using separate processes instead of threads.

12.5.4   Handling Errors

Handle errors by calling `send_error()`, passing the appropriate error code and an optional error message. The entire response (with headers, status code, and body) is generated automatically.

Listing 12.35: **http_server_errors.py**

```python
from http.server import BaseHTTPRequestHandler


class ErrorHandler(BaseHTTPRequestHandler):

    def do_GET(self):
        self.send_error(404)


if __name__ == '__main__':
    from http.server import HTTPServer
    server = HTTPServer(('localhost', 8080), ErrorHandler)
    print('Starting server, use <Ctrl-C> to stop')
    server.serve_forever()
```

In this case, a 404 error is always returned.

```
$ python3 http_server_errors.py

Starting server, use <Ctrl-C> to stop
```

The error message is reported to the client using an HTML document as well as the header to indicate an error code.

```
$ curl -i http://127.0.0.1:8080/

HTTP/1.0 404 Not Found
Server: BaseHTTP/0.6 Python/3.5.2
Date: Thu, 06 Oct 2016 20:58:08 GMT
Connection: close
Content-Type: text/html;charset=utf-8
Content-Length: 447

<!DOCTYPE HTML PUBLIC "-//W3C//DTD HTML 4.01//EN"
        "http://www.w3.org/TR/html4/strict.dtd">
<html>
    <head>
        <meta http-equiv="Content-Type"
        content="text/html;charset=utf-8">
        <title>Error response</title>
    </head>
    <body>
        <h1>Error response</h1>
        <p>Error code: 404</p>
        <p>Message: Not Found.</p>
        <p>Error code explanation: 404 - Nothing matches the
        given URI.</p>
    </body>
</html>
```

12.5.5 Setting Headers

The `send_header` method adds header data to the HTTP response. It takes two arguments: the name of the header and the value.

Listing 12.36: `http_server_send_header.py`

```python
from http.server import BaseHTTPRequestHandler
import time


class GetHandler(BaseHTTPRequestHandler):

    def do_GET(self):
        self.send_response(200)
        self.send_header(
            'Content-Type',
            'text/plain; charset=utf-8',
        )
        self.send_header(
            'Last-Modified',
```

```
            self.date_time_string(time.time())
        )
        self.end_headers()
        self.wfile.write('Response body\n'.encode('utf-8'))


if __name__ == '__main__':
    from http.server import HTTPServer
    server = HTTPServer(('localhost', 8080), GetHandler)
    print('Starting server, use <Ctrl-C> to stop')
    server.serve_forever()
```

This example sets the Last-Modified header to the current timestamp, formatted according to RFC 7231.

```
$ curl -i http://127.0.0.1:8080/

HTTP/1.0 200 OK
Server: BaseHTTP/0.6 Python/3.5.2
Date: Thu, 06 Oct 2016 21:00:54 GMT
Content-Type: text/plain; charset=utf-8
Last-Modified: Thu, 06 Oct 2016 21:00:54 GMT

Response body
```

The server logs the request to the terminal, as in the other examples.

```
$ python3 http_server_send_header.py

Starting server, use <Ctrl-C> to stop
127.0.0.1 - - [06/Oct/2016 17:00:54] "GET / HTTP/1.1" 200 -
```

12.5.6 Command-Line Use

http.server includes a built-in server for serving files from the local file system. Start it from the command line by using the -m option for the Python interpreter.

```
$ python3 -m http.server 8080

Serving HTTP on 0.0.0.0 port 8080 ...
127.0.0.1 - - [06/Oct/2016 17:12:48] "HEAD /index.rst HTTP/1.1" 200 -
```

The root directory of the server is the working directory where the server starts.

```
$ curl -I http://127.0.0.1:8080/index.rst

HTTP/1.0 200 OK
Server: SimpleHTTP/0.6 Python/3.5.2
```

```
Date: Thu, 06 Oct 2016 21:12:48 GMT
Content-type: application/octet-stream
Content-Length: 8285
Last-Modified: Thu, 06 Oct 2016 21:12:10 GMT
```

TIP

Related Reading

- Standard library documentation for http.server.[17]

- socketserver (page 742): The socketserver module provides the base class that handles the raw socket connection.

- **RFC 7231**[18]: Hypertext Transfer Protocol (HTTP/1.1): Semantics and Content. This RFC includes a specification for the format of HTTP headers and dates.

12.6   http.cookies: HTTP Cookies

The http.cookies module implements a parser for cookies that is mostly **RFC 2109**[19] compliant. The implementation is a little less strict than the standard because MSIE 3.0x does not support the entire standard.

12.6.1   Creating and Setting a Cookie

Cookies are used as state management for browser-based application. As such, they are usually set by the server to be stored and returned by the client. The most trivial example of creating a cookie sets a single name–value pair.

Listing 12.37: **http_cookies_setheaders.py**

```
from http import cookies


c = cookies.SimpleCookie()
c['mycookie'] = 'cookie_value'
print(c)
```

The output is a valid Set-Cookie header that can be passed to the client as part of the HTTP response.

---

[17] https://docs.python.org/3.5/library/http.server.html
[18] https://tools.ietf.org/html/rfc7231.html
[19] https://tools.ietf.org/html/rfc2109.html

```
$ python3 http_cookies_setheaders.py

Set-Cookie: mycookie=cookie_value
```

12.6.2 Morsels

It is also possible to control the other aspects of a cookie, such as the expiration, path, and
domain. In fact, all of the RFC attributes for cookies can be managed through the `Morsel`
object representing the cookie value.

Listing 12.38: `http_cookies_Morsel.py`

```python
from http import cookies
import datetime


def show_cookie(c):
    print(c)
    for key, morsel in c.items():
        print()
        print('key =', morsel.key)
        print('  value =', morsel.value)
        print('  coded_value =', morsel.coded_value)
        for name in morsel.keys():
            if morsel[name]:
                print('  {} = {}'.format(name, morsel[name]))


c = cookies.SimpleCookie()

# A cookie with a value that has to be encoded
# to fit into the header
c['encoded_value_cookie'] = '"cookie,value;"'
c['encoded_value_cookie']['comment'] = 'Has escaped punctuation'

# A cookie that applies to only part of a site
c['restricted_cookie'] = 'cookie_value'
c['restricted_cookie']['path'] = '/sub/path'
c['restricted_cookie']['domain'] = 'PyMOTW'
c['restricted_cookie']['secure'] = True

# A cookie that expires in 5 minutes
c['with_max_age'] = 'expires in 5 minutes'
c['with_max_age']['max-age'] = 300  # Seconds

# A cookie that expires at a specific time
c['expires_at_time'] = 'cookie_value'
```

```
time_to_live = datetime.timedelta(hours=1)
expires = (datetime.datetime(2009, 2, 14, 18, 30, 14) +
           time_to_live)

# Date format: Wdy, DD-Mon-YY HH:MM:SS GMT
expires_at_time = expires.strftime('%a, %d %b %Y %H:%M:%S')
c['expires_at_time']['expires'] = expires_at_time

show_cookie(c)
```

This example includes two different methods for setting stored cookies that expire. One sets the max-age to a number of seconds, while the other sets expires to a date and time when the cookie should be discarded.

```
$ python3 http_cookies_Morsel.py

Set-Cookie: encoded_value_cookie="\"cookie\054value\073\"";
Comment=Has escaped punctuation
Set-Cookie: expires_at_time=cookie_value; expires=Sat, 14 Feb
2009 19:30:14
Set-Cookie: restricted_cookie=cookie_value; Domain=PyMOTW;
Path=/sub/path; Secure
Set-Cookie: with_max_age="expires in 5 minutes"; Max-Age=300

key = with_max_age
  value = expires in 5 minutes
  coded_value = "expires in 5 minutes"
  max-age = 300

key = expires_at_time
  value = cookie_value
  coded_value = cookie_value
  expires = Sat, 14 Feb 2009 19:30:14

key = restricted_cookie
  value = cookie_value
  coded_value = cookie_value
  domain = PyMOTW
  path = /sub/path
  secure = True

key = encoded_value_cookie
  value = "cookie,value;"
  coded_value = "\"cookie\054value\073\""
  comment = Has escaped punctuation
```

Both the `Cookie` and `Morsel` objects act like dictionaries. A `Morsel` responds to a fixed set of keys:

- expires

- path

- comment

- domain

- max-age

- secure

- version

The keys for a `Cookie` instance are the names of the individual cookies being stored. That information is also available from the key attribute of the `Morsel`.

12.6.3 Encoded Values

The cookie header needs values to be encoded so they can be parsed properly.

Listing 12.39: **http_cookies_coded_value.py**

```
from http import cookies


c = cookies.SimpleCookie()
c['integer'] = 5
c['with_quotes'] = 'He said, "Hello, World!"'

for name in ['integer', 'with_quotes']:
    print(c[name].key)
    print('  {}'.format(c[name]))
    print('  value={!r}'.format(c[name].value))
    print('  coded_value={!r}'.format(c[name].coded_value))
    print()
```

`Morsel.value` is always the decoded value of the cookie, while `Morsel.coded_value` is always the representation to be used for transmitting the value to the client. Both values are always strings. Values saved to a cookie that are not strings are automatically converted to strings.

```
$ python3 http_cookies_coded_value.py

integer
```

```
      Set-Cookie: integer=5
      value='5'
      coded_value='5'

  with_quotes
      Set-Cookie: with_quotes="He said\054 \"Hello\054 World!\""
      value='He said, "Hello, World!"'
      coded_value='"He said\\054 \\"Hello\\054 World!\\""'
```

12.6.4   Receiving and Parsing Cookie Headers

Once the client receives the `Set-Cookie` headers, it returns those cookies to the server on subsequent requests using a `Cookie` header. An incoming `Cookie` header string may contain several cookie values, separated by semicolons (;).

```
Cookie: integer=5; with_quotes="He said, \"Hello, World!\""
```

Depending on the web server and framework, cookies are available directly from the headers or the `HTTP_COOKIE` environment variable.

Listing 12.40: http_cookies_parse.py

```python
from http import cookies


HTTP_COOKIE = '; '.join([
    r'integer=5',
    r'with_quotes="He said, \"Hello, World!\""',
])

print('From constructor:')
c = cookies.SimpleCookie(HTTP_COOKIE)
print(c)

print()
print('From load():')
c = cookies.SimpleCookie()
c.load(HTTP_COOKIE)
print(c)
```

To decode them, pass the string without the header prefix to `SimpleCookie` when instantiating it, or use the `load()` method.

```
$ python3 http_cookies_parse.py

From constructor:
Set-Cookie: integer=5
Set-Cookie: with_quotes="He said, \"Hello, World!\""
```

```
From load():
Set-Cookie: integer=5
Set-Cookie: with_quotes="He said, \"Hello, World!\""
```

12.6.5 Alternative Output Formats

Besides using the `Set-Cookie` header, servers may deliver JavaScript that adds cookies to a client. `SimpleCookie` and `Morsel` provide JavaScript output via the `js_output()` method.

Listing 12.41: http_cookies_js_output.py

```python
from http import cookies
import textwrap


c = cookies.SimpleCookie()
c['mycookie'] = 'cookie_value'
c['another_cookie'] = 'second value'
js_text = c.js_output()
print(textwrap.dedent(js_text).lstrip())
```

The result is a complete `script` tag with statements to set the cookies.

```
$ python3 http_cookies_js_output.py

<script type="text/javascript">
<!-- begin hiding
document.cookie = "another_cookie=\"second value\"";
// end hiding -->
</script>

<script type="text/javascript">
<!-- begin hiding
document.cookie = "mycookie=cookie_value";
// end hiding -->
</script>
```

TIP

Related Reading

- Standard library documentation for `http.cookies`.[20]
- `http.cookiejar`: The `cookielib` module, for working with cookies on the client side.
- **RFC 2109**[21]: HTTP State Management Mechanism.

---

[20] https://docs.python.org/3.5/library/http.cookies.html
[21] https://tools.ietf.org/html/rfc2109.html

12.7   webbrowser: Displays Web Pages

The webbrowser module includes functions to open URLs in interactive browser applications. It provides a registry of available browsers, in case multiple options are available on the system. The browser can also be controlled with the BROWSER environment variable.

12.7.1   Simple Example

To open a page in the browser, use the open() function.

Listing 12.42: **webbrowser_open.py**

```
import webbrowser

webbrowser.open(
    'https://docs.python.org/3/library/webbrowser.html'
)
```

The URL is opened in a browser window, and that window is raised to the top of the window stack. The documentation says that an existing window will be reused, if possible, but the actual behavior may depend on your browser's settings. If you use Firefox on Mac OS X, a new window is always created.

12.7.2   Windows Versus Tabs

If you always want a new window used, use open_new().

Listing 12.43: **webbrowser_open_new.py**

```
import webbrowser

webbrowser.open_new(
    'https://docs.python.org/3/library/webbrowser.html'
)
```

If you would rather create a new tab, use open_new_tab() instead.

12.7.3   Using a Specific Browser

If for some reason your application needs to use a specific browser, you can access the set of registered browser controllers using the get() function. The browser controller has open(), open_new(), and open_new_tab() methods. The next example forces the use of the lynx browser.

Listing 12.44: **webbrowser_get.py**

```
import webbrowser

b = webbrowser.get('lynx')
b.open('https://docs.python.org/3/library/webbrowser.html')
```

Refer to the module documentation for a list of available browser types.

12.7.4   BROWSER Variable

Users can control the `webbrowser` module from outside your application by setting the environment variable `BROWSER` to the browser names or commands to try. The value used should consist of a series of browser names separated by `os.pathsep`. If the name includes `%s`, the name is interpreted as a literal command and executed directly, with the `%s` being replaced by the URL. Otherwise, the name is passed to `get()` to obtain a controller object from the registry.

For example, the following command opens the web page in lynx, assuming it is available, no matter which other browsers are registered:

```
$ BROWSER=lynx python3 webbrowser_open.py
```

If none of the names in `BROWSER` works, `webbrowser` falls back to its default behavior.

12.7.5   Command-Line Interface

All of the features of the `webbrowser` module are available via the command line as well as from within your Python program.

```
$ python3 -m webbrowser

Usage: .../lib/python3.5/webbrowser.py [-n | -t] url
    -n: open new window
    -t: open new tab
```

TIP

Related Reading

- Standard library documentation for webbrowser.[22]
- What the What?[23]: Runs your Python program and then launches a Google search for any exception message produced.

12.8   uuid: Universally Unique Identifiers

The `uuid` module implements Universally Unique Identifiers as described in **RFC 4122**[24]; this RFC defines a system for creating unique identifiers for resources in a way that does not require a central registrar. UUID values are 128 bits long and, as the reference guide says, "can guarantee uniqueness across space and time." They are useful for generating identifiers

---

[22] https://docs.python.org/3.5/library/webbrowser.html
[23] https://github.com/dhellmann/whatthewhat
[24] https://tools.ietf.org/html/rfc4122.html

for documents, hosts, and application clients, and in other situations where a unique value is necessary. The RFC specifically focuses on the creation of a Uniform Resource Name namespace and covers three main algorithms:

- Using IEEE 802 MAC addresses as a source of uniqueness

- Using pseudorandom numbers

- Using well-known strings combined with cryptographic hashing

In all cases, the seed value is combined with the system clock and a clock sequence value used to maintain uniqueness in case the clock is set backward.

12.8.1   UUID 1: IEEE 802 MAC Address

UUID version 1 values are computed using the host's MAC address. The uuid module uses getnode() to retrieve the MAC value of the current system.

Listing 12.45: **uuid_getnode.py**

```
import uuid

print(hex(uuid.getnode()))
```

If a system has more than one network card, and so more than one MAC address, any one of the values may be returned.

```
$ python3 uuid_getnode.py

0xc82a14598875
```

To generate a UUID for a host that is identified by its MAC address, use the uuid1() function. The node identifier argument is optional; leave the field blank to use the value returned by getnode().

Listing 12.46: **uuid_uuid1.py**

```
import uuid

u = uuid.uuid1()

print(u)
print(type(u))
print('bytes    :', repr(u.bytes))
print('hex      :', u.hex)
print('int      :', u.int)
print('urn      :', u.urn)
print('variant  :', u.variant)
print('version  :', u.version)
print('fields   :', u.fields)
```

```
print('    time_low              : ', u.time_low)
print('    time_mid              : ', u.time_mid)
print('    time_hi_version       : ', u.time_hi_version)
print('    clock_seq_hi_variant: ', u.clock_seq_hi_variant)
print('    clock_seq_low         : ', u.clock_seq_low)
print('    node                  : ', u.node)
print('    time                  : ', u.time)
print('    clock_seq             : ', u.clock_seq)
```

The components of the UUID object returned can be accessed through read-only instance attributes. Some attributes, such as hex, int, and urn, are different representations of the UUID value.

```
$ python3 uuid_uuid1.py

335ea282-cded-11e6-9ede-c82a14598875
<class 'uuid.UUID'>
bytes   : b'3^\xa2\x82\xcd\xed\x11\xe6\x9e\xde\xc8*\x14Y\x88u'
hex     : 335ea282cded11e69edec82a14598875
int     : 68281999803480928707202152670695098485
urn     : urn:uuid:335ea282-cded-11e6-9ede-c82a14598875
variant : specified in RFC 4122
version : 1
fields  : (861840002, 52717, 4582, 158, 222, 220083055593589)
    time_low              : 861840002
    time_mid              : 52717
    time_hi_version       : 4582
    clock_seq_hi_variant: 158
    clock_seq_low         : 222
    node                  : 220083055593589
    time                  : 137023257334162050
    clock_seq             : 7902
```

Because of the time component, each call to uuid1() returns a new value.

Listing 12.47: uuid_uuid1_repeat.py

```
import uuid

for i in range(3):
    print(uuid.uuid1())
```

In this output, only the time component (at the beginning of the string) changes.

```
$ python3 uuid_uuid1_repeat.py

3369ab5c-cded-11e6-8d5e-c82a14598875
336eea22-cded-11e6-9943-c82a14598875
336eeb5e-cded-11e6-9e22-c82a14598875
```

Because each computer has a different MAC address, running the example program on different systems will produce entirely different values. The next example passes explicit node IDs to simulate running on different hosts.

Listing 12.48: uuid_uuid1_othermac.py

```
import uuid

for node in [0x1ec200d9e0, 0x1e5274040e]:
    print(uuid.uuid1(node), hex(node))
```

In addition to a different time value being returned, the node identifier at the end of the UUID changes.

```
$ python3 uuid_uuid1_othermac.py

337969be-cded-11e6-97fa-001ec200d9e0 0x1ec200d9e0
3379b7e6-cded-11e6-9d72-001e5274040e 0x1e5274040e
```

12.8.2   UUID 3 and 5: Name-Based Values

In some contexts, it is desirable to create UUID values from names instead of random or time-based values. Versions 3 and 5 of the UUID specification use cryptographic hash values (MD5 or SHA-1, respectively) to combine namespace-specific seed values with names. Several well-known namespaces, identified by predefined UUID values, are available for working with DNS, URLs, ISO OIDs, and X.500 Distinguished Names. New application-specific namespaces can be defined by generating and saving UUID values.

Listing 12.49: uuid_uuid3_uuid5.py

```
import uuid

hostnames = ['www.doughellmann.com', 'blog.doughellmann.com']

for name in hostnames:
    print(name)
    print('  MD5   :', uuid.uuid3(uuid.NAMESPACE_DNS, name))
    print('  SHA-1 :', uuid.uuid5(uuid.NAMESPACE_DNS, name))
    print()
```

To create a UUID from a DNS name, pass uuid.NAMESPACE_DNS as the namespace argument to uuid3() or uuid5().

```
$ python3 uuid_uuid3_uuid5.py

www.doughellmann.com
  MD5   : bcd02e22-68f0-3046-a512-327cca9def8f
```

```
SHA-1 : e3329b12-30b7-57c4-8117-c2cd34a87ce9

blog.doughellmann.com
  MD5   : 9bdabfce-dfd6-37ab-8a3f-7f7293bcf111
  SHA-1 : fa829736-7ef8-5239-9906-b4775a5abacb
```

The UUID value for a given name in a namespace is always the same, no matter when or where it is calculated.

Listing 12.50: uuid_uuid3_repeat.py

```python
import uuid

namespace_types = sorted(
    n
    for n in dir(uuid)
    if n.startswith('NAMESPACE_')
)
name = 'www.doughellmann.com'

for namespace_type in namespace_types:
    print(namespace_type)
    namespace_uuid = getattr(uuid, namespace_type)
    print(' ', uuid.uuid3(namespace_uuid, name))
    print(' ', uuid.uuid3(namespace_uuid, name))
    print()
```

Values for the same name in the namespaces are different.

```
$ python3 uuid_uuid3_repeat.py

NAMESPACE_DNS
  bcd02e22-68f0-3046-a512-327cca9def8f
  bcd02e22-68f0-3046-a512-327cca9def8f

NAMESPACE_OID
  e7043ac1-4382-3c45-8271-d5c083e41723
  e7043ac1-4382-3c45-8271-d5c083e41723

NAMESPACE_URL
  5d0fdaa9-eafd-365e-b4d7-652500dd1208
  5d0fdaa9-eafd-365e-b4d7-652500dd1208

NAMESPACE_X500
  4a54d6e7-ce68-37fb-b0ba-09acc87cabb7
  4a54d6e7-ce68-37fb-b0ba-09acc87cabb7
```

12.8.3   UUID 4: Random Values

Sometimes host-based and namespace-based UUID values are not "different enough." For
example, in cases where the UUID is intended to be used as a hash key, a more random
sequence of values with more differentiation is desirable to avoid collisions in the hash table.
Having values with fewer common digits also makes it easier to find them in log files. To
add greater differentiation in UUIDs, use `uuid4()` to generate them using random input
values.

Listing 12.51: **uuid_uuid4.py**

```
import uuid

for i in range(3):
    print(uuid.uuid4())
```

The source of randomness depends on which C libraries are available when `uuid` is
imported. If `libuuid` (or `uuid.dll`) can be loaded and it contains a function for generating
random values, that function is used. Otherwise, `os.urandom()` or the `random` (page 254)
module is used.

```
$ python3 uuid_uuid4.py

7821863a-06f0-4109-9b88-59ba1ca5cc04
44846e16-4a59-4a21-8c8e-008f169c2dd5
1f3cef3c-e2bc-4877-96c8-eba43bf15bb6
```

12.8.4   Working with UUID Objects

In addition to generating new UUID values, strings in standard formats can be parsed to
create UUID objects, thereby making it easier to handle comparisons and sorting operations.

Listing 12.52: **uuid_uuid_objects.py**

```
import uuid


def show(msg, l):
    print(msg)
    for v in l:
        print(' ', v)
    print()

input_values = [
    'urn:uuid:f2f84497-b3bf-493a-bba9-7c68e6def80b',
    '{417a5ebb-01f7-4ed5-aeac-3d56cd5037b0}',
    '2115773a-5bf1-11dd-ab48-001ec200d9e0',
]
```

```
show('input_values', input_values)

uuids = [uuid.UUID(s) for s in input_values]
show('converted to uuids', uuids)

uuids.sort()
show('sorted', uuids)
```

Surrounding curly braces are removed from the input, as are dashes (-). If the string has a prefix containing urn: and/or uuid:, it is also removed. The remaining text must be a string of 16 hexadecimal digits, which are then interpreted as a UUID value.

```
$ python3 uuid_uuid_objects.py

input_values
  urn:uuid:f2f84497-b3bf-493a-bba9-7c68e6def80b
  {417a5ebb-01f7-4ed5-aeac-3d56cd5037b0}
  2115773a-5bf1-11dd-ab48-001ec200d9e0

converted to uuids
  f2f84497-b3bf-493a-bba9-7c68e6def80b
  417a5ebb-01f7-4ed5-aeac-3d56cd5037b0
  2115773a-5bf1-11dd-ab48-001ec200d9e0

sorted
  2115773a-5bf1-11dd-ab48-001ec200d9e0
  417a5ebb-01f7-4ed5-aeac-3d56cd5037b0
  f2f84497-b3bf-493a-bba9-7c68e6def80b
```

TIP

Related Reading

- Standard library documentation for uuid.[25]
- Python 2 to 3 porting notes for uuid (page 1365).
- **RFC 4122**[26]: A Universally Unique Identifier (UUID) URN Namespace.

12.9   json: JavaScript Object Notation

The json module provides an API similar to pickle (page 396) for converting in-memory Python objects to a serialized representation known as JavaScript Object Notation (JSON). Unlike pickle, JSON has the benefit of having implementations in many languages

---

[25] https://docs.python.org/3.5/library/uuid.html
[26] https://tools.ietf.org/html/rfc4122.html

(especially JavaScript). It is most used for communicating between the web server and client in a REST API, but can also help meet other interapplication communication needs.

12.9.1   Encoding and Decoding Simple Data Types

The encoder understands Python's native types by default (i.e., `str`, `int`, `float`, `list`, `tuple`, and `dict`).

Listing 12.53: `json_simple_types.py`

```
import json

data = [{'a': 'A', 'b': (2, 4), 'c': 3.0}]
print('DATA:', repr(data))

data_string = json.dumps(data)
print('JSON:', data_string)
```

Values are encoded in a manner that is superficially similar to Python's `repr()` output.

```
$ python3 json_simple_types.py

DATA: [{'c': 3.0, 'b': (2, 4), 'a': 'A'}]
JSON: [{"c": 3.0, "b": [2, 4], "a": "A"}]
```

Encoding, and then re-decoding, may not give exactly the same type of object.

Listing 12.54: `json_simple_types_decode.py`

```
import json

data = [{'a': 'A', 'b': (2, 4), 'c': 3.0}]
print('DATA    :', data)

data_string = json.dumps(data)
print('ENCODED:', data_string)

decoded = json.loads(data_string)
print('DECODED:', decoded)

print('ORIGINAL:', type(data[0]['b']))
print('DECODED :', type(decoded[0]['b']))
```

In particular, tuples become lists.

```
$ python3 json_simple_types_decode.py

DATA    : [{'c': 3.0, 'b': (2, 4), 'a': 'A'}]
ENCODED: [{"c": 3.0, "b": [2, 4], "a": "A"}]
```

```
DECODED: [{'c': 3.0, 'b': [2, 4], 'a': 'A'}]
ORIGINAL: <class 'tuple'>
DECODED : <class 'list'>
```

12.9.2 Human-Consumable Versus Compact Output

Another benefit of JSON over `pickle` (page 396) is that JSON produces human-readable results. The `dumps()` function accepts several arguments to make the output even easier to decipher. For example, the `sort_keys` flag tells the encoder to output the keys of a dictionary in sorted—instead of random—order.

Listing 12.55: **json_sort_keys.py**

```python
import json

data = [{'a': 'A', 'b': (2, 4), 'c': 3.0}]
print('DATA:', repr(data))

unsorted = json.dumps(data)
print('JSON:', json.dumps(data))
print('SORT:', json.dumps(data, sort_keys=True))

first = json.dumps(data, sort_keys=True)
second = json.dumps(data, sort_keys=True)

print('UNSORTED MATCH:', unsorted == first)
print('SORTED MATCH   :', first == second)
```

Sorting makes it easier to scan the results by eye, and also makes it possible to compare JSON output in tests.

```
$ python3 json_sort_keys.py

DATA: [{'c': 3.0, 'b': (2, 4), 'a': 'A'}]
JSON: [{"c": 3.0, "b": [2, 4], "a": "A"}]
SORT: [{"a": "A", "b": [2, 4], "c": 3.0}]
UNSORTED MATCH: False
SORTED MATCH   : True
```

For highly nested data structures, specify a value for `indent` so the output is formatted nicely as well.

Listing 12.56: **json_indent.py**

```python
import json

data = [{'a': 'A', 'b': (2, 4), 'c': 3.0}]
print('DATA:', repr(data))
```

```
print('NORMAL:', json.dumps(data, sort_keys=True))
print('INDENT:', json.dumps(data, sort_keys=True, indent=2))
```

When indent is a non-negative integer, the output more closely resembles that of pprint (page 136), with leading spaces for each level of the data structure matching the indent level.

```
$ python3 json_indent.py

DATA: [{'c': 3.0, 'b': (2, 4), 'a': 'A'}]
NORMAL: [{"a": "A", "b": [2, 4], "c": 3.0}]
INDENT: [
  {
    "a": "A",
    "b": [
      2,
      4
    ],
    "c": 3.0
  }
]
```

Such verbose output increases the number of bytes needed to transmit the same amount of data; thus, it is not intended for use in a production environment. In fact, the settings for separating data in the encoded output can be adjusted to make it even more compact than the default.

Listing 12.57: `json_compact_encoding.py`

```
import json

data = [{'a': 'A', 'b': (2, 4), 'c': 3.0}]
print('DATA:', repr(data))

print('repr(data)             :', len(repr(data)))

plain_dump = json.dumps(data)
print('dumps(data)            :', len(plain_dump))

small_indent = json.dumps(data, indent=2)
print('dumps(data, indent=2)  :', len(small_indent))

with_separators = json.dumps(data, separators=(',', ':'))
print('dumps(data, separators):', len(with_separators))
```

The separators argument to dumps() should be a tuple containing the strings to separate the items in a list and to separate the keys from the values in a dictionary. The default is (',',': '). Removing the whitespace yields a more compact output.

```
$ python3 json_compact_encoding.py

DATA: [{'c': 3.0, 'b': (2, 4), 'a': 'A'}]
repr(data)              : 35
dumps(data)             : 35
dumps(data, indent=2)   : 73
dumps(data, separators): 29
```

12.9.3   Encoding Dictionaries

The JSON format expects the keys to a dictionary to be strings. Trying to encode a dictionary with non-string types as keys produces a TypeError. One way to work around that limitation is to tell the encoder to skip over non-string keys using the skipkeys argument.

Listing 12.58: json_skipkeys.py

```
import json

data = [{'a': 'A', 'b': (2, 4), 'c': 3.0, ('d',): 'D tuple'}]

print('First attempt')
try:
    print(json.dumps(data))
except TypeError as err:
    print('ERROR:', err)

print()
print('Second attempt')
print(json.dumps(data, skipkeys=True))
```

Rather than raising an exception, the non-string key is then ignored.

```
$ python3 json_skipkeys.py

First attempt
ERROR: keys must be a string

Second attempt
[{"c": 3.0, "b": [2, 4], "a": "A"}]
```

12.9.4   Working with Custom Types

All of the examples so far have used Python's built-in types because those are supported by json natively. Custom classes may need to be encoded as well, and there are two ways to do that.

Suppose the class in the following listing needs to be encoded.

```
class MyObj:

    def __init__(self, s):
        self.s = s

    def __repr__(self):
        return '<MyObj({})>'.format(self.s)
```

A simple way to encode a MyObj instance is to define a function to convert an unknown type to a known type. This function does not need to do the encoding; it should simply convert one type of object to another.

```
import json
import json_myobj

obj = json_myobj.MyObj('instance value goes here')

print('First attempt')
try:
    print(json.dumps(obj))
except TypeError as err:
    print('ERROR:', err)


def convert_to_builtin_type(obj):
    print('default(', repr(obj), ')')
    # Convert objects to a dictionary of their representation.
    d = {
        '__class__': obj.__class__.__name__,
        '__module__': obj.__module__,
    }
    d.update(obj.__dict__)
    return d

print()
print('With default')
print(json.dumps(obj, default=convert_to_builtin_type))
```

In convert_to_builtin_type(), instances of classes not recognized by json are converted to dictionaries with enough information to re-create the object if a program has access to the Python modules needed for this process.

```
$ python3 json_dump_default.py

First attempt
```

```
ERROR: <MyObj(instance value goes here)> is not JSON serializable

With default
default( <MyObj(instance value goes here)> )
{"s": "instance value goes here", "__module__": "json_myobj",
"__class__": "MyObj"}
```

To decode the results and create a `MyObj()` instance, use the `object_hook` argument to `loads()` to tie into the decoder so the class can be imported from the module and used to create the instance. The `object_hook` is called for each dictionary decoded from the incoming data stream, providing a chance to convert the dictionary to another type of object. The hook function should return the object that the calling application should receive instead of the dictionary.

Listing 12.61: `json_load_object_hook.py`

```
import json


def dict_to_object(d):
    if '__class__' in d:
        class_name = d.pop('__class__')
        module_name = d.pop('__module__')
        module = __import__(module_name)
        print('MODULE:', module.__name__)
        class_ = getattr(module, class_name)
        print('CLASS:', class_)
        args = {
            key: value
            for key, value in d.items()
        }
        print('INSTANCE ARGS:', args)
        inst = class_(**args)
    else:
        inst = d
    return inst


encoded_object = '''
    [{"s": "instance value goes here",
      "__module__": "json_myobj", "__class__": "MyObj"}]
    '''

myobj_instance = json.loads(
    encoded_object,
    object_hook=dict_to_object,
)
print(myobj_instance)
```

Since json converts string values to Unicode objects, those objects need to be re-encoded as ASCII strings before they can be used as keyword arguments to the class constructor.

```
$ python3 json_load_object_hook.py

MODULE: json_myobj
CLASS: <class 'json_myobj.MyObj'>
INSTANCE ARGS: {'s': 'instance value goes here'}
[<MyObj(instance value goes here)>]
```

Similar hooks are available for the built-in types: integers (parse_int), floating-point numbers (parse_float), and constants (parse_constant).

12.9.5   Encoder and Decoder Classes

Besides the convenience functions already covered, the json module provides classes for encoding and decoding. Using the classes directly opens up access to extra APIs for customizing their behavior.

The JSONEncoder uses an iterable interface to produce "chunks" of encoded data, making it easier to write to files or network sockets without having to represent an entire data structure in memory.

Listing 12.62: json_encoder_iterable.py

```
import json

encoder = json.JSONEncoder()
data = [{'a': 'A', 'b': (2, 4), 'c': 3.0}]

for part in encoder.iterencode(data):
    print('PART:', part)
```

The output is generated in logical units, rather than being based on any size value.

```
$ python3 json_encoder_iterable.py

PART: [
PART: {
PART: "c"
PART: :
PART: 3.0
PART: ,
PART: "b"
PART: :
PART: [2
PART: , 4
PART: ]
```

```
PART: ,
PART: "a"
PART: :
PART: "A"
PART: }
PART: ]
```

The `encode()` method is basically equivalent to `''.join(encoder.iterencode())`, with some extra error checking up front.

To encode arbitrary objects, override the `default()` method with an implementation similar to the one used in `convert_to_builtin_type()`.

Listing 12.63: json_encoder_default.py

```python
import json
import json_myobj


class MyEncoder(json.JSONEncoder):

    def default(self, obj):
        print('default(', repr(obj), ')')
        # Convert objects to a dictionary of their representation.
        d = {
            '__class__': obj.__class__.__name__,
            '__module__': obj.__module__,
        }
        d.update(obj.__dict__)
        return d


obj = json_myobj.MyObj('internal data')
print(obj)
print(MyEncoder().encode(obj))
```

The output is the same as the previous implementation.

```
$ python3 json_encoder_default.py

<MyObj(internal data)>
default( <MyObj(internal data)> )
{"s": "internal data", "__module__": "json_myobj", "__class__":
"MyObj"}
```

Decoding text, and then converting the dictionary into an object, takes a little more work to set up than the previous implementation, but not much.

Listing 12.64: **json_decoder_object_hook.py**

```python
import json


class MyDecoder(json.JSONDecoder):

    def __init__(self):
        json.JSONDecoder.__init__(
            self,
            object_hook=self.dict_to_object,
        )

    def dict_to_object(self, d):
        if '__class__' in d:
            class_name = d.pop('__class__')
            module_name = d.pop('__module__')
            module = __import__(module_name)
            print('MODULE:', module.__name__)
            class_ = getattr(module, class_name)
            print('CLASS:', class_)
            args = {
                key: value
                for key, value in d.items()
            }
            print('INSTANCE ARGS:', args)
            inst = class_(**args)
        else:
            inst = d
        return inst


encoded_object = '''
[{"s": "instance value goes here",
  "__module__": "json_myobj", "__class__": "MyObj"}]
'''

myobj_instance = MyDecoder().decode(encoded_object)
print(myobj_instance)
```

The output is the same as the earlier example.

```
$ python3 json_decoder_object_hook.py

MODULE: json_myobj
CLASS: <class 'json_myobj.MyObj'>
INSTANCE ARGS: {'s': 'instance value goes here'}
[<MyObj(instance value goes here)>]
```

12.9.6   Working with Streams and Files

All of the examples so far have assumed that the encoded version of the entire data structure could be held in memory at one time. With large data structures, it may be preferable to write the encoding directly to a file-like object. The convenience functions `load()` and `dump()` accept references to a file-like object to use for reading or writing.

Listing 12.65: json_dump_file.py

```python
import io
import json

data = [{'a': 'A', 'b': (2, 4), 'c': 3.0}]

f = io.StringIO()
json.dump(data, f)

print(f.getvalue())
```

A socket or normal file handle would work the same way as the `StringIO` buffer used in this example.

```
$ python3 json_dump_file.py

[{"c": 3.0, "b": [2, 4], "a": "A"}]
```

Although it is not optimized to read only part of the data at a time, the `load()` function still offers the benefit of encapsulating the logic of generating objects from the stream input.

Listing 12.66: json_load_file.py

```python
import io
import json

f = io.StringIO('[{"a": "A", "c": 3.0, "b": [2, 4]}]')
print(json.load(f))
```

Just as with `dump()`, any file-like object can be passed to `load()`.

```
$ python3 json_load_file.py

[{'c': 3.0, 'b': [2, 4], 'a': 'A'}]
```

12.9.7   Mixed Data Streams

`JSONDecoder` includes `raw_decode()`, a method for decoding a data structure followed by more data, such as JSON data with trailing text. The return value is the object created

by decoding the input data, along with an index into that data indicating where decoding
left off.

Listing 12.67: **json_mixed_data.py**

```python
import json

decoder = json.JSONDecoder()


def get_decoded_and_remainder(input_data):
    obj, end = decoder.raw_decode(input_data)
    remaining = input_data[end:]
    return (obj, end, remaining)


encoded_object = '[{"a": "A", "c": 3.0, "b": [2, 4]}]'
extra_text = 'This text is not JSON.'

print('JSON first:')
data = ' '.join([encoded_object, extra_text])
obj, end, remaining = get_decoded_and_remainder(data)

print('Object              :', obj)
print('End of parsed input :', end)
print('Remaining text      :', repr(remaining))

print()
print('JSON embedded:')
try:
    data = ' '.join([extra_text, encoded_object, extra_text])
    obj, end, remaining = get_decoded_and_remainder(data)
except ValueError as err:
    print('ERROR:', err)
```

Unfortunately, this approach works only if the object appears at the beginning of the input.

```
$ python3 json_mixed_data.py

JSON first:
Object              : [{'c': 3.0, 'b': [2, 4], 'a': 'A'}]
End of parsed input : 35
Remaining text      : ' This text is not JSON.'

JSON embedded:
ERROR: Expecting value: line 1 column 1 (char 0)
```

12.9.8   JSON at the Command Line

The `json.tool` module implements a command-line program for reformatting JSON data
to be easier to read.

```
[{"a": "A", "c": 3.0, "b": [2, 4]}]
```

The input file `example.json` contains a mapping with the keys out of alphabetical
order. The first example shows the data reformatted in order, and the second example uses
`--sort-keys` to sort the mapping keys before printing the output.

```
$ python3 -m json.tool example.json

[
    {
        "a": "A",
        "c": 3.0,
        "b": [
            2,
            4
        ]
    }
]

$ python3 -m json.tool --sort-keys example.json

[
    {
        "a": "A",
        "b": [
            2,
            4
        ],
        "c": 3.0
    }
]
```

TIP

Related Reading

- Standard library documentation for `json`.[27]
- Python 2 to 3 porting notes for `json` (page 1359).

---

[27] https://docs.python.org/3.5/library/json.html

- JavaScript Object Notation[28]: JSON home, with documentation and implementations in other languages.
- jsonpickle[29]: jsonpickle allows for any Python object to be serialized into JSON.

12.10   xmlrpc.client: Client Library for XML-RPC

XML-RPC is a lightweight remote procedure call protocol built on top of HTTP and XML. The xmlrpclib module lets a Python program communicate with an XML-RPC server written in any language.

All of the examples in this section use the server defined in xmlrpc_server.py, which is available in the source distribution and included here for reference.

Listing 12.68: xmlrpc_server.py

```
from xmlrpc.server import SimpleXMLRPCServer
from xmlrpc.client import Binary
import datetime


class ExampleService:

    def ping(self):
        """Simple function to respond when called
        to demonstrate connectivity.
        """
        return True

    def now(self):
        """Returns the server current date and time."""
        return datetime.datetime.now()

    def show_type(self, arg):
        """Illustrates how types are passed in and out of
        server methods.

        Accepts one argument of any type.

        Returns a tuple with string representation of the value,
        the name of the type, and the value itself.

        """
        return (str(arg), str(type(arg)), arg)
```

---

[28] http://json.org/
[29] https://jsonpickle.github.io

```
    def raises_exception(self, msg):
        "Always raises a RuntimeError with the message passed in."
        raise RuntimeError(msg)

    def send_back_binary(self, bin):
        """Accepts a single Binary argument, and unpacks and
        repacks it to return it."""
        data = bin.data
        print('send_back_binary({!r})'.format(data))
        response = Binary(data)
        return response


if __name__ == '__main__':
    server = SimpleXMLRPCServer(('localhost', 9000),
                                logRequests=True,
                                allow_none=True)
    server.register_introspection_functions()
    server.register_multicall_functions()

    server.register_instance(ExampleService())

    try:
        print('Use Control-C to exit')
        server.serve_forever()
    except KeyboardInterrupt:
        print('Exiting')
```

12.10.1   Connecting to a Server

The simplest way to connect a client to a server is to instantiate a `ServerProxy` object, giving it the URI of the server. For example, the demo server runs on port 9000 of localhost.

Listing 12.69: **xmlrpc_ServerProxy.py**

```
import xmlrpc.client

server = xmlrpc.client.ServerProxy('http://localhost:9000')
print('Ping:', server.ping())
```

In this case, the `ping()` method of the service takes no arguments and returns a single boolean value.

```
$ python3 xmlrpc_ServerProxy.py

Ping: True
```

Other options are available to support alternative transports for connecting to servers. Both HTTP and HTTPS are supported out of the box, both with basic authentication. To implement a new communication channel, only a new transport class is needed. It could be an interesting exercise, for example, to implement XML-RPC over SMTP.

Listing 12.70: xmlrpc_ServerProxy_verbose.py

```
import xmlrpc.client

server = xmlrpc.client.ServerProxy('http://localhost:9000',
                                   verbose=True)
print('Ping:', server.ping())
```

The verbose option generates debugging information that is useful for resolving communication errors.

```
$ python3 xmlrpc_ServerProxy_verbose.py

send: b'POST /RPC2 HTTP/1.1\r\nHost: localhost:9000\r\n
Accept-Encoding: gzip\r\nContent-Type: text/xml\r\n
User-Agent: Python-xmlrpc/3.5\r\nContent-Length: 98\r\n\r\n'
send: b"<?xml version='1.0'?>\n<methodCall>\n<methodName>
ping</methodName>\n<params>\n</params>\n</methodCall>\n"
reply: 'HTTP/1.0 200 OK\r\n'
header: Server header: Date header: Content-type header:
Content-length body: b"<?xml version='1.0'?>\n<methodResponse>\n
<params>\n<param>\n<value><boolean>1</boolean></value>\n</param>
\n</params>\n</methodResponse>\n"
Ping: True
```

The default encoding can be changed from UTF-8 if an alternative system is needed.

Listing 12.71: xmlrpc_ServerProxy_encoding.py

```
import xmlrpc.client

server = xmlrpc.client.ServerProxy('http://localhost:9000',
                                   encoding='ISO-8859-1')
print('Ping:', server.ping())
```

The server automatically detects the correct encoding.

```
$ python3 xmlrpc_ServerProxy_encoding.py

Ping: True
```

The allow_none option controls whether Python's None value is automatically translated to a nil value or whether it causes an error.

```
import xmlrpc.client

server = xmlrpc.client.ServerProxy('http://localhost:9000',
                                    allow_none=False)
try:
    server.show_type(None)
except TypeError as err:
    print('ERROR:', err)

server = xmlrpc.client.ServerProxy('http://localhost:9000',
                                    allow_none=True)
print('Allowed:', server.show_type(None))
```

The error is raised locally if the client does not allow None, but it can also be raised from within the server if it is not configured to allow None.

```
$ python3 xmlrpc_ServerProxy_allow_none.py

ERROR: cannot marshal None unless allow_none is enabled
Allowed: ['None', "<class 'NoneType'>", None]
```

12.10.2   Data Types

The XML-RPC protocol recognizes a limited set of common data types. These types can be passed as arguments or return values, and they can be combined to create more complex data structures.

```
import xmlrpc.client
import datetime

server = xmlrpc.client.ServerProxy('http://localhost:9000')

data = [
    ('boolean', True),
    ('integer', 1),
    ('float', 2.5),
    ('string', 'some text'),
    ('datetime', datetime.datetime.now()),
    ('array', ['a', 'list']),
    ('array', ('a', 'tuple')),
    ('structure', {'a': 'dictionary'}),
]

for t, v in data:
    as_string, type_name, value = server.show_type(v)
```

```
print('{:<12}: {}'.format(t, as_string))
print('{:12}  {}'.format('', type_name))
print('{:12}  {}'.format('', value))
```

The simple types are shown here.

```
$ python3 xmlrpc_types.py

boolean     : True
              <class 'bool'>
              True
integer     : 1
              <class 'int'>
              1
float       : 2.5
              <class 'float'>
              2.5
string      : some text
              <class 'str'>
              some text
datetime    : 20160618T19:31:47
              <class 'xmlrpc.client.DateTime'>
              20160618T19:31:47
array       : ['a', 'list']
              <class 'list'>
              ['a', 'list']
array       : ['a', 'tuple']
              <class 'list'>
              ['a', 'tuple']
structure   : {'a': 'dictionary'}
              <class 'dict'>
              {'a': 'dictionary'}
```

The supported types can be nested to create values of arbitrary complexity.

Listing 12.74: xmlrpc_types_nested.py

```
import xmlrpc.client
import datetime
import pprint

server = xmlrpc.client.ServerProxy('http://localhost:9000')

data = {
    'boolean': True,
    'integer': 1,
    'floating-point number': 2.5,
    'string': 'some text',
    'datetime': datetime.datetime.now(),
    'array': ['a', 'list'],
```

```
            'array': ('a', 'tuple'),
            'structure': {'a': 'dictionary'},
    }
    arg = []
    for i in range(3):
        d = {}
        d.update(data)
        d['integer'] = i
        arg.append(d)

    print('Before:')
    pprint.pprint(arg, width=40)

    print('\nAfter:')
    pprint.pprint(server.show_type(arg)[-1], width=40)
```

This program passes a list of dictionaries containing all of the supported types to the sample server, which returns the data. Tuples are converted to lists and datetime instances are converted to DateTime objects, but otherwise the data is unchanged.

```
$ python3 xmlrpc_types_nested.py

Before:
[{'array': ('a', 'tuple'),
  'boolean': True,
  'datetime': datetime.datetime(2016, 6, 18, 19, 27, 30, 45333),
  'floating-point number': 2.5,
  'integer': 0,
  'string': 'some text',
  'structure': {'a': 'dictionary'}},
 {'array': ('a', 'tuple'),
  'boolean': True,
  'datetime': datetime.datetime(2016, 6, 18, 19, 27, 30, 45333),
  'floating-point number': 2.5,
  'integer': 1,
  'string': 'some text',
  'structure': {'a': 'dictionary'}},
 {'array': ('a', 'tuple'),
  'boolean': True,
  'datetime': datetime.datetime(2016, 6, 18, 19, 27, 30, 45333),
  'floating-point number': 2.5,
  'integer': 2,
  'string': 'some text',
  'structure': {'a': 'dictionary'}}]

After:
[{'array': ['a', 'tuple'],
  'boolean': True,
  'datetime': <DateTime '20160618T19:27:30' at 0x101ecfac8>,
  'floating-point number': 2.5,
```

```
          'integer': 0,
          'string': 'some text',
          'structure': {'a': 'dictionary'}},
         {'array': ['a', 'tuple'],
          'boolean': True,
          'datetime': <DateTime '20160618T19:27:30' at 0x101ecfcc0>,
          'floating-point number': 2.5,
          'integer': 1,
          'string': 'some text',
          'structure': {'a': 'dictionary'}},
         {'array': ['a', 'tuple'],
          'boolean': True,
          'datetime': <DateTime '20160618T19:27:30' at 0x101ecfe10>,
          'floating-point number': 2.5,
          'integer': 2,
          'string': 'some text',
          'structure': {'a': 'dictionary'}}]
```

XML-RPC supports dates as a native type. `xmlrpclib` can use one of two classes to represent the date values either in the outgoing proxy or when they are received from the server.

Listing 12.75: xmlrpc_ServerProxy_use_datetime.py

```python
import xmlrpc.client

server = xmlrpc.client.ServerProxy('http://localhost:9000',
                                   use_datetime=True)
now = server.now()
print('With:', now, type(now), now.__class__.__name__)

server = xmlrpc.client.ServerProxy('http://localhost:9000',
                                   use_datetime=False)
now = server.now()
print('Without:', now, type(now), now.__class__.__name__)
```

By default, an internal version of `DateTime` is used, but the `use_datetime` option turns on support for using the classes in the `datetime` (page 221) module.

```
$ python3 source/xmlrpc.client/xmlrpc_ServerProxy_use_datetime.py

With: 2016-06-18 19:18:31 <class 'datetime.datetime'> datetime
Without: 20160618T19:18:31 <class 'xmlrpc.client.DateTime'> DateTime
```

12.10.3   Passing Objects

Instances of Python classes are treated as structures and passed as a dictionary, with the attributes of the object as values in the dictionary.

Listing 12.76: **xmlrpc_types_object.py**

```python
import xmlrpc.client
import pprint


class MyObj:

    def __init__(self, a, b):
        self.a = a
        self.b = b

    def __repr__(self):
        return 'MyObj({!r}, {!r})'.format(self.a, self.b)


server = xmlrpc.client.ServerProxy('http://localhost:9000')

o = MyObj(1, 'b goes here')
print('o  :', o)
pprint.pprint(server.show_type(o))

o2 = MyObj(2, o)
print('\no2 :', o2)
pprint.pprint(server.show_type(o2))
```

When the value is sent back to the client from the server, the result is a dictionary on the client. This result reflects the fact that there is nothing encoded in the values to tell the server (or client) that it should be instantiated as part of a class.

```
$ python3 xmlrpc_types_object.py

o  : MyObj(1, 'b goes here')
["{'b': 'b goes here', 'a': 1}", "<class 'dict'>",
{'a': 1, 'b': 'b goes here'}]

o2 : MyObj(2, MyObj(1, 'b goes here'))
["{'b': {'b': 'b goes here', 'a': 1}, 'a': 2}",
 "<class 'dict'>",
 {'a': 2, 'b': {'a': 1, 'b': 'b goes here'}}]
```

12.10.4 Binary Data

All values passed to the server are encoded and escaped automatically. However, some data types may contain characters that are not valid XML. For example, binary image data may include byte values in the ASCII control range 0 to 31. To pass binary data, it is best to use the Binary class to encode it for transport.

Listing 12.77: xmlrpc_Binary.py

```
import xmlrpc.client
import xml.parsers.expat

server = xmlrpc.client.ServerProxy('http://localhost:9000')

s = b'This is a string with control characters\x00'
print('Local string:', s)

data = xmlrpc.client.Binary(s)
response = server.send_back_binary(data)
print('As binary:', response.data)

try:
    print('As string:', server.show_type(s))
except xml.parsers.expat.ExpatError as err:
    print('\nERROR:', err)
```

If the string containing a NULL byte is passed to show_type(), an exception is raised in the XML parser as it processes the response.

```
$ python3 xmlrpc_Binary.py

Local string: b'This is a string with control characters\x00'
As binary: b'This is a string with control characters\x00'

ERROR: not well-formed (invalid token): line 6, column 55
```

Binary objects can also be used to send objects using pickle (page 396). The normal security issues related to sending what amounts to executable code over the wire apply here (i.e., do not do this unless the communication channel is secure).

```
import xmlrpc.client
import pickle
import pprint


class MyObj:

    def __init__(self, a, b):
        self.a = a
        self.b = b

    def __repr__(self):
        return 'MyObj({!r}, {!r})'.format(self.a, self.b)

server = xmlrpc.client.ServerProxy('http://localhost:9000')
```

```
o = MyObj(1, 'b goes here')
print('Local:', id(o))
print(o)

print('\nAs object:')
pprint.pprint(server.show_type(o))

p = pickle.dumps(o)
b = xmlrpc.client.Binary(p)
r = server.send_back_binary(b)

o2 = pickle.loads(r.data)
print('\nFrom pickle:', id(o2))
pprint.pprint(o2)
```

The data attribute of the `Binary` instance contains the pickled version of the object, which must be unpickled before it can be used. That step results in a different object (with a new ID value).

```
$ python3 xmlrpc_Binary_pickle.py

Local: 4327262304
MyObj(1, 'b goes here')

As object:
["{'a': 1, 'b': 'b goes here'}", "<class 'dict'>",
{'a': 1, 'b': 'b goes here'}]

From pickle: 4327262472
MyObj(1, 'b goes here')
```

12.10.5 Exception Handling

Given that the XML-RPC server could potentially be written in any language, exception classes cannot be transmitted directly. Instead, exceptions raised in the server are converted to `Fault` objects and raised as exceptions locally in the client.

Listing 12.78: **xmlrpc_exception.py**

```
import xmlrpc.client

server = xmlrpc.client.ServerProxy('http://localhost:9000')
try:
    server.raises_exception('A message')
except Exception as err:
    print('Fault code:', err.faultCode)
    print('Message   :', err.faultString)
```

The original error message is saved in the faultString attribute, and faultCode is set to an XML-RPC error number.

```
$ python3 xmlrpc_exception.py

Fault code: 1
Message   : <class 'RuntimeError'>:A message
```

12.10.6 Combining Calls into One Message

Multicall is an extension to the XML-RPC protocol that allows more than one call to be sent at the same time, with the responses being collected and returned to the caller.

Listing 12.79: xmlrpc_MultiCall.py

```
import xmlrpc.client

server = xmlrpc.client.ServerProxy('http://localhost:9000')

multicall = xmlrpc.client.MultiCall(server)
multicall.ping()
multicall.show_type(1)
multicall.show_type('string')

for i, r in enumerate(multicall()):
    print(i, r)
```

To use a MultiCall instance, invoke the methods on it in the same way as with a ServerProxy, then call the object with no arguments to actually run the remote functions. The return value is an iterator that yields the results from all of the calls.

```
$ python3 xmlrpc_MultiCall.py

0 True
1 ['1', "<class 'int'>", 1]
2 ['string', "<class 'str'>", 'string']
```

If one of the calls causes a Fault, the exception is raised when the result is produced from the iterator and no more results are available.

Listing 12.80: xmlrpc_MultiCall_exception.py

```
import xmlrpc.client

server = xmlrpc.client.ServerProxy('http://localhost:9000')

multicall = xmlrpc.client.MultiCall(server)
multicall.ping()
```

```
multicall.show_type(1)
multicall.raises_exception('Next-to-last call stops execution')
multicall.show_type('string')

try:
    for i, r in enumerate(multicall()):
        print(i, r)
except xmlrpc.client.Fault as err:
    print('ERROR:', err)
```

Since the third response, from raises_exception(), generates an exception, the response from show_type() is not accessible.

```
$ python3 xmlrpc_MultiCall_exception.py

0 True
1 ['1', "<class 'int'>", 1]
ERROR: <Fault 1: "<class 'RuntimeError'>:Next-to-last call stops
execution">
```

TIP

Related Reading

- Standard library documentation for xmlrpc.client.[30]
- xmlrpc.server (page 827): An XML-RPC server implementation.
- http.server (page 781): An HTTP server implementation.
- XML-RPC HOWTO[31]: Describes how to use XML-RPC to implement clients and servers in a variety of languages.

12.11 xmlrpc.server: An XML-RPC Server

The xmlrpc.server module contains classes for creating cross-platform, language-independent servers using the XML-RPC protocol. Client libraries exist for many other languages besides Python, making XML-RPC a good choice for building RPC-style services.

NOTE

All of the examples provided here include a client module that interacts with the demonstration server. To run the examples, use two separate shell windows, one for the server and one for the client.

---

[30] https://docs.python.org/3.5/library/xmlrpc.client.html
[31] www.tldp.org/HOWTO/XML-RPC-HOWTO/index.html

12.11.1 A Simple Server

This simple server example exposes a single function that takes the name of a directory and returns the contents. The first step is to create the `SimpleXMLRPCServer` instance and tell it where to listen for incoming requests (localhost on port 9000 in this case). A function is then defined to be part of the service, and registered so the server knows how to call it. The final step is to put the server into an infinite loop receiving and responding to requests.

WARNING

This implementation has obvious security implications. Do not run it on a server on the open Internet or in any environment where security might be an issue.

Listing 12.81: **xmlrpc_function.py**

```
from xmlrpc.server import SimpleXMLRPCServer
import logging
import os

# Set up logging.
logging.basicConfig(level=logging.INFO)

server = SimpleXMLRPCServer(
    ('localhost', 9000),
    logRequests=True,
)


# Expose a function.
def list_contents(dir_name):
    logging.info('list_contents(%s)', dir_name)
    return os.listdir(dir_name)
server.register_function(list_contents)

# Start the server.
try:
    print('Use Control-C to exit')
    server.serve_forever()
except KeyboardInterrupt:
    print('Exiting')
```

The server can be accessed at the URL `http://localhost:9000` using `xmlrpc.client` (page 816). The client code in the following listing illustrates how to call the `list_contents()` service from Python.

Listing 12.82: **xmlrpc_function_client.py**

```
import xmlrpc.client

proxy = xmlrpc.client.ServerProxy('http://localhost:9000')
print(proxy.list_contents('/tmp'))
```

The ServerProxy is connected to the server using its base URL, and then methods are
called directly on the proxy. Each method invoked on the proxy is translated into a request
to the server. The arguments are formatted using XML, and then sent to the server in a
POST message. The server unpacks the XML and determines which function to call based
on the method name invoked from the client. The arguments are passed to the function,
and the return value is translated back to XML to be returned to the client.

Starting the server gives the following output.

```
$ python3 xmlrpc_function.py

Use Control-C to exit
```

Running the client in a second window shows the contents of the /tmp directory.

```
$ python3 xmlrpc_function_client.py

['com.apple.launchd.aoGXonn8nV', 'com.apple.launchd.ilryIaQugf',
'example.db.db',
'KSOutOfProcessFetcher.501.ppfIhqX0vjaTSb8AJYobDV7Cu68=',
'pymotw_import_example.shelve.db']
```

After the request is finished, the log output appears in the server window.

```
$ python3 xmlrpc_function.py

Use Control-C to exit
INFO:root:list_contents(/tmp)
127.0.0.1 - - [18/Jun/2016 19:54:54] "POST /RPC2 HTTP/1.1" 200 -
```

The first line of output is from the logging.info() call inside list_contents(). The second
line is from the server logging the request because logRequests is True.

12.11.2   Alternate API Names

Sometimes the function names used inside a module or library are not the names that should
be used in the external API. Names may change because a platform-specific implementation
is loaded, the service API is built dynamically based on a configuration file, or real functions
can be replaced with stubs for testing. To register a function with an alternate name, pass
the name as the second argument to register_function().

Listing 12.83: xmlrpc_alternate_name.py

```
from xmlrpc.server import SimpleXMLRPCServer
import os

server = SimpleXMLRPCServer(('localhost', 9000))


def list_contents(dir_name):
```

```
    "Expose a function with an alternate name"
    return os.listdir(dir_name)
server.register_function(list_contents, 'dir')

try:
    print('Use Control-C to exit')
    server.serve_forever()
except KeyboardInterrupt:
    print('Exiting')
```

The client should now use the name `dir()` instead of `list_contents()`.

Listing 12.84: **xmlrpc_alternate_name_client.py**

```
import xmlrpc.client

proxy = xmlrpc.client.ServerProxy('http://localhost:9000')
print('dir():', proxy.dir('/tmp'))
try:
    print('\nlist_contents():', proxy.list_contents('/tmp'))
except xmlrpc.client.Fault as err:
    print('\nERROR:', err)
```

Calling `list_contents()` results in an error, since the server no longer has a handler registered by that name.

```
$ python3 xmlrpc_alternate_name_client.py

dir(): ['com.apple.launchd.aoGXonn8nV',
'com.apple.launchd.ilryIaQugf', 'example.db.db',
'KSOutOfProcessFetcher.501.ppfIhqX0vjaTSb8AJYobDV7Cu68=',
'pymotw_import_example.shelve.db']

ERROR: <Fault 1: '<class \'Exception\'>:method "list_contents"
is not supported'>
```

12.11.3   Dotted API Names

Individual functions can be registered with names that are not normally legal for Python identifiers. For example, a period (.) can be included in the names to separate the namespace in the service. The next example extends the "directory" service to add "create" and "remove" calls. All of the functions are registered using the prefix `dir.` so that the same server can provide other services using a different prefix. One other difference in this example is that some of the functions return `None`, so the server must be told to translate the `None` values to a nil value.

Listing 12.85: xmlrpc_dotted_name.py

```
from xmlrpc.server import SimpleXMLRPCServer
import os

server = SimpleXMLRPCServer(('localhost', 9000), allow_none=True)

server.register_function(os.listdir, 'dir.list')
server.register_function(os.mkdir, 'dir.create')
server.register_function(os.rmdir, 'dir.remove')

try:
    print('Use Control-C to exit')
    server.serve_forever()
except KeyboardInterrupt:
    print('Exiting')
```

To call the service functions in the client, simply refer to them with the dotted name.

Listing 12.86: xmlrpc_dotted_name_client.py

```
import xmlrpc.client

proxy = xmlrpc.client.ServerProxy('http://localhost:9000')
print('BEFORE       :', 'EXAMPLE' in proxy.dir.list('/tmp'))
print('CREATE       :', proxy.dir.create('/tmp/EXAMPLE'))
print('SHOULD EXIST :', 'EXAMPLE' in proxy.dir.list('/tmp'))
print('REMOVE       :', proxy.dir.remove('/tmp/EXAMPLE'))
print('AFTER        :', 'EXAMPLE' in proxy.dir.list('/tmp'))
```

Assuming there is no /tmp/EXAMPLE file on the current system, the sample client script produces the following output.

```
$ python3 xmlrpc_dotted_name_client.py

BEFORE       : False
CREATE       : None
SHOULD EXIST : True
REMOVE       : None
AFTER        : False
```

12.11.4 Arbitrary API Names

Another interesting feature is the ability to register functions with names that are otherwise invalid Python object attribute names. The next example service registers a function with the name multiply args.

Listing 12.87: **xmlrpc_arbitrary_name.py**

```
from xmlrpc.server import SimpleXMLRPCServer

server = SimpleXMLRPCServer(('localhost', 9000))


def my_function(a, b):
    return a * b
server.register_function(my_function, 'multiply args')

try:
    print('Use Control-C to exit')
    server.serve_forever()
except KeyboardInterrupt:
    print('Exiting')
```

Since the registered name contains a space, dot notation cannot be used to access it directly from the proxy. Using getattr() does work, however.

Listing 12.88: **xmlrpc_arbitrary_name_client.py**

```
import xmlrpc.client

proxy = xmlrpc.client.ServerProxy('http://localhost:9000')
print(getattr(proxy, 'multiply args')(5, 5))
```

Creating services with names like this is not recommended, though. This example is provided not necessarily because it is a good idea, but because existing services with arbitrary names exist, and new programs may need to be able to call them.

```
$ python3 xmlrpc_arbitrary_name_client.py

25
```

12.11.5   Exposing Methods of Objects

The earlier sections talked about techniques for establishing APIs using good naming conventions and namespaces. Another way to incorporate namespaces into an API is to use instances of classes and expose their methods. The first example can be re-created using an instance with a single method.

Listing 12.89: **xmlrpc_instance.py**

```
from xmlrpc.server import SimpleXMLRPCServer
import os
import inspect
```

```
    server = SimpleXMLRPCServer(
        ('localhost', 9000),
        logRequests=True,
    )


    class DirectoryService:
        def list(self, dir_name):
            return os.listdir(dir_name)

    server.register_instance(DirectoryService())

    try:
        print('Use Control-C to exit')
        server.serve_forever()
    except KeyboardInterrupt:
        print('Exiting')
```

A client can call the method directly.

Listing 12.90: **xmlrpc_instance_client.py**

```
import xmlrpc.client

proxy = xmlrpc.client.ServerProxy('http://localhost:9000')
print(proxy.list('/tmp'))
```

The output shows the contents of the directory.

```
$ python3 xmlrpc_instance_client.py

['com.apple.launchd.aoGXonn8nV', 'com.apple.launchd.ilryIaQugf',
'example.db.db',
'KSOutOfProcessFetcher.501.ppfIhqX0vjaTSb8AJYobDV7Cu68=',
'pymotw_import_example.shelve.db']
```

The dir. prefix for the service has been lost, though. It can be restored by defining a class to set up a service tree that can be invoked from clients.

Listing 12.91: **xmlrpc_instance_dotted_names.py**

```
from xmlrpc.server import SimpleXMLRPCServer
import os
import inspect

server = SimpleXMLRPCServer(
    ('localhost', 9000),
    logRequests=True,
)
```

```
class ServiceRoot:
    pass


class DirectoryService:

    def list(self, dir_name):
        return os.listdir(dir_name)


root = ServiceRoot()
root.dir = DirectoryService()

server.register_instance(root, allow_dotted_names=True)

try:
    print('Use Control-C to exit')
    server.serve_forever()
except KeyboardInterrupt:
    print('Exiting')
```

Because the instance of `ServiceRoot` is registered with `allow_dotted_names` enabled, the server has permission to walk the tree of objects when a request comes in to find the named method using `getattr()`.

Listing 12.92: xmlrpc_instance_dotted_names_client.py

```
import xmlrpc.client

proxy = xmlrpc.client.ServerProxy('http://localhost:9000')
print(proxy.dir.list('/tmp'))
```

The output of `dir.list()` is the same as with the previous implementations.

```
$ python3 xmlrpc_instance_dotted_names_client.py

['com.apple.launchd.aoGXonn8nV', 'com.apple.launchd.ilryIaQugf',
'example.db.db',
'KSOutOfProcessFetcher.501.ppfIhqX0vjaTSb8AJYobDV7Cu68=',
'pymotw_import_example.shelve.db']
```

12.11.6 Dispatching Calls

By default, `register_instance()` finds all callable attributes of the instance with names not starting with an underscore (_) and registers them with their name. To be more careful about the exposed methods, custom dispatching logic can be used.

Listing 12.93: xmlrpc_instance_with_prefix.py

```python
from xmlrpc.server import SimpleXMLRPCServer
import os
import inspect

server = SimpleXMLRPCServer(
    ('localhost', 9000),
    logRequests=True,
)


def expose(f):
    "Decorator to set exposed flag on a function."
    f.exposed = True
    return f


def is_exposed(f):
    "Test whether another function should be publicly exposed."
    return getattr(f, 'exposed', False)


class MyService:
    PREFIX = 'prefix'

    def _dispatch(self, method, params):
        # Remove our prefix from the method name.
        if not method.startswith(self.PREFIX + '.'):
            raise Exception(
                'method "{}" is not supported'.format(method)
            )

        method_name = method.partition('.')[2]
        func = getattr(self, method_name)
        if not is_exposed(func):
            raise Exception(
                'method "{}" is not supported'.format(method)
            )

        return func(*params)

    @expose
    def public(self):
        return 'This is public'

    def private(self):
        return 'This is private'
```

```
server.register_instance(MyService())

try:
    print('Use Control-C to exit')
    server.serve_forever()
except KeyboardInterrupt:
    print('Exiting')
```

The public() method of MyService is marked as exposed to the XML-RPC service, whereas the private() method is not. The _dispatch() method is invoked when the client tries to access a function that is part of MyService. It first enforces the use of a prefix (prefix. in this case, but any string can be used). Then it requires the function to have an attribute called exposed with a true value. The exposed flag is set on a function using a decorator for convenience. The following example includes a few sample client calls.

Listing 12.94: xmlrpc_instance_with_prefix_client.py

```
import xmlrpc.client

proxy = xmlrpc.client.ServerProxy('http://localhost:9000')
print('public():', proxy.prefix.public())
try:
    print('private():', proxy.prefix.private())
except Exception as err:
    print('\nERROR:', err)
try:
    print('public() without prefix:', proxy.public())
except Exception as err:
    print('\nERROR:', err)
```

The resulting output, with the expected error messages trapped and reported, follows.

```
$ python3 xmlrpc_instance_with_prefix_client.py

public(): This is public

ERROR: <Fault 1: '<class \'Exception\'>:method "prefix.private" is
not supported'>

ERROR: <Fault 1: '<class \'Exception\'>:method "public" is not
supported'>
```

There are several other ways to override the dispatching mechanism, including subclassing directly from SimpleXMLRPCServer. Refer to the docstrings in the module for more details.

12.11.7   Introspection API

As with many network services, an XML-RPC server can be queried to determine which methods it supports and to learn how to use them. SimpleXMLRPCServer includes a set of public methods for performing this introspection. By default, they are turned off, but they can be enabled with register_introspection_functions(). Support for system.listMethods() and system.methodHelp() can be added to a service by defining _listMethods() and _methodHelp(), respectively, on the service class.

Listing 12.95: xmlrpc_introspection.py

```python
from xmlrpc.server import (SimpleXMLRPCServer,
                           list_public_methods)
import os
import inspect

server = SimpleXMLRPCServer(
    ('localhost', 9000),
    logRequests=True,
)
server.register_introspection_functions()


class DirectoryService:

    def _listMethods(self):
        return list_public_methods(self)

    def _methodHelp(self, method):
        f = getattr(self, method)
        return inspect.getdoc(f)

    def list(self, dir_name):
        """list(dir_name) => [<filenames>]

        Returns a list containing the contents of
        the named directory.

        """
        return os.listdir(dir_name)


server.register_instance(DirectoryService())

try:
    print('Use Control-C to exit')
    server.serve_forever()
except KeyboardInterrupt:
    print('Exiting')
```

In this case, the convenience function `list_public_methods()` scans an instance to return the names of callable attributes that do not start with an underscore (_). Redefine `_listMethods()` to apply whatever rules are desired. Similarly, for this basic example `_methodHelp()` returns the docstring of the function, but it could be written to build a help string from another source.

This client queries the server and reports on all of the publicly callable methods.

Listing 12.96: **xmlrpc_introspection_client.py**

```python
import xmlrpc.client

proxy = xmlrpc.client.ServerProxy('http://localhost:9000')
for method_name in proxy.system.listMethods():
    print('=' * 60)
    print(method_name)
    print('-' * 60)
    print(proxy.system.methodHelp(method_name))
    print()
```

The system methods are included in the results.

```
$ python3 xmlrpc_introspection_client.py

============================================================
list
------------------------------------------------------------
list(dir_name) => [<filenames>]

Returns a list containing the contents of
the named directory.

============================================================
system.listMethods
------------------------------------------------------------
system.listMethods() => ['add', 'subtract', 'multiple']

Returns a list of the methods supported by the server.

============================================================
system.methodHelp
------------------------------------------------------------
system.methodHelp('add') => "Adds two integers together"

Returns a string containing documentation for the specified method.

============================================================
system.methodSignature
```

```
------------------------------------------------------------
system.methodSignature('add') => [double, int, int]
```

Returns a list describing the signature of the method. In the
above example, the add method takes two integers as arguments
and returns a double result.

This server does NOT support system.methodSignature.

TIP

Related Reading

- Standard library documentation for xmlrpc.server.[32]
- xmlrpc.client (page 816): XML-RPC client.
- XML-RPC HOWTO[33]: Describes how to use XML-RPC to implement clients and servers in a
  variety of languages.

---

[32] https://docs.python.org/3.5/library/xmlrpc.server.html
[33] www.tldp.org/HOWTO/XML-RPC-HOWTO/index.html

Chapter 13

Email

Email is one of the oldest forms of digital communication, but it is still one of the most popular. Python's standard library includes modules for sending, receiving, and storing email messages.

smtplib (page 841) communicates with a mail server to deliver a message. smtpd (page 847) can be used to create a custom mail server, and provides classes useful for debugging email transmission in other applications.

imaplib (page 864) uses the IMAP protocol to manipulate messages stored on a server. It provides a low-level API for IMAP clients, and can query, retrieve, move, and delete messages.

Local message archives can be created and modified with mailbox (page 852) using several standard formats including the popular mbox and Maildir formats used by many email client programs.

13.1 smtplib: Simple Mail Transfer Protocol Client

smtplib includes the class SMTP, which can be used to communicate with mail servers to send mail.

NOTE

The email addresses, hostnames, and IP addresses in the following examples have been obscured, but otherwise the transcripts illustrate the sequence of commands and responses accurately.

13.1.1 Sending an Email Message

The most common use of SMTP is to connect to a mail server and send a message. The mail server hostname and port can be passed to the constructor, or connect() can be invoked explicitly. Once connected, call sendmail() with the envelope parameters and body of the message. The message text should be fully formed and comply with **RFC 5322**,[1] since smtplib does not modify the contents or headers at all. That means the From and To headers need to be added by the caller.

Listing 13.1: smtplib_sendmail.py

```
import smtplib
import email.utils
from email.mime.text import MIMEText
```

---

[1] https://tools.ietf.org/html/rfc5322

```
# Create the message.
msg = MIMEText('This is the body of the message.')
msg['To'] = email.utils.formataddr(('Recipient',
                                    'recipient@example.com'))
msg['From'] = email.utils.formataddr(('Author',
                                      'author@example.com'))
msg['Subject'] = 'Simple test message'

server = smtplib.SMTP('localhost', 1025)
server.set_debuglevel(True)  # Show communication with the server.
try:
    server.sendmail('author@example.com',
                    ['recipient@example.com'],
                    msg.as_string())
finally:
    server.quit()
```

In this example, debugging is also turned on to show the communication between client and server. Otherwise, the example would produce no output at all.

```
$ python3 smtplib_sendmail.py

send: 'ehlo 1.0.0.0.0.0.0.0.0.0.0.0.0.0.0.0.0.0.0.0.0.0.0.0.0.0.0.
0.0.0.0.0.0.ip6.arpa\r\n'
reply: b'250-1.0.0.0.0.0.0.0.0.0.0.0.0.0.0.0.0.0.0.0.0.0.0.0.0.0.0
.0.0.0.0.0.0.ip6.arpa\r\n'
reply: b'250-SIZE 33554432\r\n'
reply: b'250 HELP\r\n'
reply: retcode (250); Msg: b'1.0.0.0.0.0.0.0.0.0.0.0.0.0.0.0.0.0.0
.0.0.0.0.0.0.0.0.0.0.0.0.0.0.ip6.arpa\nSIZE 33554432\nHELP'
send: 'mail FROM:<author@example.com> size=236\r\n'
reply: b'250 OK\r\n'
reply: retcode (250); Msg: b'OK'
send: 'rcpt TO:<recipient@example.com>\r\n'
reply: b'250 OK\r\n'
reply: retcode (250); Msg: b'OK'
send: 'data\r\n'
reply: b'354 End data with <CR><LF>.<CR><LF>\r\n'
reply: retcode (354); Msg: b'End data with <CR><LF>.<CR><LF>'
data: (354, b'End data with <CR><LF>.<CR><LF>')
send: b'Content-Type: text/plain; charset="us-ascii"\r\nMIME-Ver
sion: 1.0\r\nContent-Transfer-Encoding: 7bit\r\nTo: Recipient <r
ecipient@example.com>\r\nFrom: Author <author@example.com>\r\nSu
bject: Simple test message\r\n\r\nThis is the body of the messag
e.\r\n.\r\n'
reply: b'250 OK\r\n'
reply: retcode (250); Msg: b'OK'
data: (250, b'OK')
send: 'quit\r\n'
```

```
reply: b'221 Bye\r\n'
reply: retcode (221); Msg: b'Bye'
```

The second argument to `sendmail()`, the recipients, is passed as a list. Any number of addresses can be included in the list to have the message delivered to each of them in turn. Since the envelope information is separate from the message headers, it is possible to blind carbon-copy (BCC) someone by including their address in the method argument but not in the message header.

13.1.2 Authentication and Encryption

The `SMTP` class also handles authentication and TLS (transport layer security) encryption, when the server supports them. To determine whether the server supports TLS, call `ehlo()` directly to identify the client to the server and ask it which extensions are available. Then call `has_extn()` to check the results. After TLS is started, `ehlo()` must be called again before authenticating the user. Many mail hosting providers now support *only* TLS-based connections. For communicating with those servers, use `SMTP_SSL` to initiate an encrypted connection.

Listing 13.2: **smtplib_authenticated.py**

```python
import smtplib
import email.utils
from email.mime.text import MIMEText
import getpass

# Prompt the user for connection info.
to_email = input('Recipient: ')
servername = input('Mail server name: ')
serverport = input('Server port: ')
if serverport:
    serverport = int(serverport)
else:
    serverport = 25
use_tls = input('Use TLS? (yes/no): ').lower()
username = input('Mail username: ')
password = getpass.getpass("%s's password: " % username)

# Create the message.
msg = MIMEText('Test message from PyMOTW.')
msg.set_unixfrom('author')
msg['To'] = email.utils.formataddr(('Recipient', to_email))
msg['From'] = email.utils.formataddr(('Author',
                                      'author@example.com'))
msg['Subject'] = 'Test from PyMOTW'

if use_tls == 'yes':
    print('starting with a secure connection')
    server = smtplib.SMTP_SSL(servername, serverport)
```

```
else:
    print('starting with an insecure connection')
    server = smtplib.SMTP(servername, serverport)
try:
    server.set_debuglevel(True)

    # Identify ourselves, prompting server for supported features.
    server.ehlo()

    # If we can encrypt this session, do it.
    if server.has_extn('STARTTLS'):
        print('(starting TLS)')
        server.starttls()
        server.ehlo()  # Reidentify ourselves over TLS connection.
    else:
        print('(no STARTTLS)')

    if server.has_extn('AUTH'):
        print('(logging in)')
        server.login(username, password)
    else:
        print('(no AUTH)')

    server.sendmail('author@example.com',
                    [to_email],
                    msg.as_string())
finally:
    server.quit()
```

The STARTTLS extension does not appear in the reply to EHLO after TLS is enabled.

```
$ python3 source/smtplib/smtplib_authenticated.py
Recipient: doug@pymotw.com
Mail server name: localhost
Server port: 1025
Use TLS? (yes/no): no
Mail username: test
test's password:
starting with an insecure connection
send: 'ehlo 1.0.0.0.0.0.0.0.0.0.0.0.0.0.0.0.0.0.0.0.0.0.0.0.0.0.0.0.0
.0.0.0.0.0.ip6.arpa\r\n'
reply: b'250-1.0.0.0.0.0.0.0.0.0.0.0.0.0.0.0.0.0.0.0.0.0.0.0.0.0.0.0.
0.0.0.0.0.0.ip6.arpa\r\n'
reply: b'250-SIZE 33554432\r\n'
reply: b'250 HELP\r\n'
reply: retcode (250); Msg: b'1.0.0.0.0.0.0.0.0.0.0.0.0.0.0.0.0.0.0.
0.0.0.0.0.0.0.0.0.0.0.0.0.0.0.ip6.arpa\nSIZE 33554432\nHELP'
(no STARTTLS)
(no AUTH)
```

```
send: 'mail FROM:<author@example.com> size=220\r\n'
reply: b'250 OK\r\n'
reply: retcode (250); Msg: b'OK'
send: 'rcpt TO:<doug@pymotw.com>\r\n'
reply: b'250 OK\r\n'
reply: retcode (250); Msg: b'OK'
send: 'data\r\n'
reply: b'354 End data with <CR><LF>.<CR><LF>\r\n'
reply: retcode (354); Msg: b'End data with <CR><LF>.<CR><LF>'
data: (354, b'End data with <CR><LF>.<CR><LF>')
send: b'Content-Type: text/plain; charset="us-ascii"\r\n
MIME-Version: 1.0\r\nContent-Transfer-Encoding: 7bit\r\nTo:
Recipient <doug@pymotw.com>\r\nFrom: Author <author@example.com>
\r\nSubject: Test from PyMOTW\r\n\r\nTest message from PyMOTW.
\r\n.\r\n'
reply: b'250 OK\r\n'
reply: retcode (250); Msg: b'OK'
data: (250, b'OK')
send: 'quit\r\n'
reply: b'221 Bye\r\n'
reply: retcode (221); Msg: b'Bye'

$ python3 source/smtplib/smtplib_authenticated.py
Recipient: doug@pymotw.com
Mail server name: mail.isp.net
Server port: 465
Use TLS? (yes/no): yes
Mail username: doughellmann@isp.net
doughellmann@isp.net's password:
starting with a secure connection
send: 'ehlo 1.0.0.0.0.0.0.0.0.0.0.0.0.0.0.0.0.0.0.0.0.0.0.0.0.0.0.0.0
.0.0.0.0.0.ip6.arpa\r\n'
reply: b'250-mail.isp.net\r\n'
reply: b'250-PIPELINING\r\n'
reply: b'250-SIZE 71000000\r\n'
reply: b'250-ENHANCEDSTATUSCODES\r\n'
reply: b'250-8BITMIME\r\n'
reply: b'250-AUTH PLAIN LOGIN\r\n'
reply: b'250 AUTH=PLAIN LOGIN\r\n'
reply: retcode (250); Msg: b'mail.isp.net\nPIPELINING\nSIZE
71000000\nENHANCEDSTATUSCODES\n8BITMIME\nAUTH PLAIN LOGIN\n
AUTH=PLAIN LOGIN'
(no STARTTLS)
(logging in)
send: 'AUTH PLAIN AGRvdWdoZWxsbWFubkBmYXN0bWFpbC5mbQBUTUZ3MDBmZmF
zdG1haWw=\r\n'
reply: b'235 2.0.0 OK\r\n'
reply: retcode (235); Msg: b'2.0.0 OK'
send: 'mail FROM:<author@example.com> size=220\r\n'
```

```
reply: b'250 2.1.0 Ok\r\n'
reply: retcode (250); Msg: b'2.1.0 Ok'
send: 'rcpt TO:<doug@pymotw.com>\r\n'
reply: b'250 2.1.5 Ok\r\n'
reply: retcode (250); Msg: b'2.1.5 Ok'
send: 'data\r\n'
reply: b'354 End data with <CR><LF>.<CR><LF>\r\n'
reply: retcode (354); Msg: b'End data with <CR><LF>.<CR><LF>'
data: (354, b'End data with <CR><LF>.<CR><LF>')
send: b'Content-Type: text/plain; charset="us-ascii"\r\n
MIME-Version: 1.0\r\nContent-Transfer-Encoding: 7bit\r\nTo:
Recipient <doug@pymotw.com>\r\nFrom: Author <author@example.com>
\r\nSubject: Test from PyMOTW\r\n\r\nTest message from PyMOTW.
\r\n.\r\n'
reply: b'250 2.0.0 Ok: queued as A0EF7F2983\r\n'
reply: retcode (250); Msg: b'2.0.0 Ok: queued as A0EF7F2983'
data: (250, b'2.0.0 Ok: queued as A0EF7F2983')
send: 'quit\r\n'
reply: b'221 2.0.0 Bye\r\n'
reply: retcode (221); Msg: b'2.0.0 Bye'
```

13.1.3   Verifying an Email Address

The SMTP protocol includes a command to ask a server whether an address is valid. Usually VRFY is disabled to prevent spammers from finding legitimate email addresses. If it is enabled, however, a client can ask the server about an address and receive a status code indicating validity, along with the user's full name, if it is available.

Listing 13.3: smtplib_verify.py

```
import smtplib

server = smtplib.SMTP('mail')
server.set_debuglevel(True)  # Show communication with the server.
try:
    dhellmann_result = server.verify('dhellmann')
    notthere_result = server.verify('notthere')
finally:
    server.quit()

print('dhellmann:', dhellmann_result)
print('notthere :', notthere_result)
```

As the last two lines of the output show, the address dhellmann is valid but notthere is not.

```
$ python3 smtplib_verify.py

send: 'vrfy <dhellmann>\r\n'
```

```
reply: '250 2.1.5 Doug Hellmann <dhellmann@mail>\r\n'
reply: retcode (250); Msg: 2.1.5 Doug Hellmann <dhellmann@mail>
send: 'vrfy <notthere>\r\n'
reply: '550 5.1.1 <notthere>... User unknown\r\n'
reply: retcode (550); Msg: 5.1.1 <notthere>... User unknown
send: 'quit\r\n'
reply: '221 2.0.0 mail closing connection\r\n'
reply: retcode (221); Msg: 2.0.0 mail closing connection
dhellmann: (250, '2.1.5 Doug Hellmann <dhellmann@mail>')
notthere : (550, '5.1.1 <notthere>... User unknown')
```

TIP

Related Reading

- Standard library documentation for smtplib.[2]
- **RFC 821**[3]: The Simple Mail Transfer Protocol (SMTP) specification.
- **RFC 1869**[4]: SMTP Service Extensions to the base protocol.
- **RFC 822**[5]: Standard for the Format of ARPA Internet Text Messages; the original email message format specification.
- **RFC 5322**[6]: Internet Message Format; updates to the email message format.
- email: Standard library module for building and parsing email messages.
- smtpd (page 847): Implements a simple SMTP server.

13.2 smtpd: Sample Mail Servers

The smtpd module includes classes for building Simple Mail Transport Protocol (SMTP) servers. It is the server side of the protocol used by smtplib (page 841).

13.2.1 Mail Server Base Class

The base class for all of the provided example servers is SMTPServer. It handles communicating with the client and receiving incoming data, and it provides a convenient hook to override for processing the message once it is fully available.

The constructor arguments are the local address to listen for connections and the remote address where proxied messages should be delivered. The method process_message() is

---

[2] https://docs.python.org/3.5/library/smtplib.html
[3] https://tools.ietf.org/html/rfc821.html
[4] https://tools.ietf.org/html/rfc1869.html
[5] https://tools.ietf.org/html/rfc822.html
[6] https://tools.ietf.org/html/rfc5322.html

provided as a hook to be overridden by a derived class. It is called when the message is completely received, and given these arguments:

peer The client's address, a tuple containing the IP address and the incoming port.

mailfrom The "from" information found in the message envelope, which is given to the server by the client when the message is delivered. This does not necessarily match the From header in all cases.

rcpttos The list of recipients from the message envelope. Again, this does not always match the To header, especially if a recipient is being blind carbon copied.

data The full RFC 5322 message body.

The default implementation of process_message() raises NotImplementedError. The next example defines a subclass that overrides the method to print information about the messages it receives.

Listing 13.4: **smtpd_custom.py**

```python
import smtpd
import asyncore


class CustomSMTPServer(smtpd.SMTPServer):

    def process_message(self, peer, mailfrom, rcpttos, data):
        print('Receiving message from:', peer)
        print('Message addressed from:', mailfrom)
        print('Message addressed to  :', rcpttos)
        print('Message length        :', len(data))

server = CustomSMTPServer(('127.0.0.1', 1025), None)

asyncore.loop()
```

SMTPServer uses asyncore, so to run the server call asyncore.loop().

A client is needed to demonstrate the server. One of the examples from the section on smtplib (page 841) can be adapted to create a client to send data to the test server running locally on port 1025.

Listing 13.5: **smtpd_senddata.py**

```python
import smtplib
import email.utils
from email.mime.text import MIMEText

# Create the message.
```

```
msg = MIMEText('This is the body of the message.')
msg['To'] = email.utils.formataddr(('Recipient',
                                    'recipient@example.com'))
msg['From'] = email.utils.formataddr(('Author',
                                      'author@example.com'))
msg['Subject'] = 'Simple test message'

server = smtplib.SMTP('127.0.0.1', 1025)
server.set_debuglevel(True)  # Show communication with the server.
try:
    server.sendmail('author@example.com',
                    ['recipient@example.com'],
                    msg.as_string())
finally:
    server.quit()
```

To test the programs, run `smtpd_custom.py` in one terminal and `smtpd_senddata.py` in another.

```
$ python3 smtpd_custom.py

Receiving message from: ('127.0.0.1', 58541)
Message addressed from: author@example.com
Message addressed to  : ['recipient@example.com']
Message length        : 229
```

The debug output from `smtpd_senddata.py` shows all of the communication with the server.

```
$ python3 smtpd_senddata.py

send: 'ehlo 1.0.0.0.0.0.0.0.0.0.0.0.0.0.0.0.0.0.0.0.0.0.0.0.0.0.0.0.
0.0.0.0.0.0.ip6.arpa\r\n'
reply: b'250-1.0.0.0.0.0.0.0.0.0.0.0.0.0.0.0.0.0.0.0.0.0.0.0.0.0.0.0
.0.0.0.0.0.0.ip6.arpa\r\n'
reply: b'250-SIZE 33554432\r\n'
reply: b'250 HELP\r\n'
reply: retcode (250); Msg: b'1.0.0.0.0.0.0.0.0.0.0.0.0.0.0.0.0.0.0.0
.0.0.0.0.0.0.0.0.0.0.0.0.0.0.ip6.arpa\nSIZE 33554432\nHELP'
send: 'mail FROM:<author@example.com> size=236\r\n'
reply: b'250 OK\r\n'
reply: retcode (250); Msg: b'OK'
send: 'rcpt TO:<recipient@example.com>\r\n'
reply: b'250 OK\r\n'
reply: retcode (250); Msg: b'OK'
send: 'data\r\n'
reply: b'354 End data with <CR><LF>.<CR><LF>\r\n'
reply: retcode (354); Msg: b'End data with <CR><LF>.<CR><LF>'
data: (354, b'End data with <CR><LF>.<CR><LF>')
```

```
send: b'Content-Type: text/plain; charset="us-ascii"\r\nMIME-Ver
sion: 1.0\r\nContent-Transfer-Encoding: 7bit\r\nTo: Recipient <r
ecipient@example.com>\r\nFrom: Author <author@example.com>\r\nSu
bject: Simple test message\r\n\r\nThis is the body of the messag
e.\r\n.\r\n'
reply: b'250 OK\r\n'
reply: retcode (250); Msg: b'OK'
data: (250, b'OK')
send: 'quit\r\n'
reply: b'221 Bye\r\n'
reply: retcode (221); Msg: b'Bye'
```

To stop the server, press Ctrl-C.

13.2.2   Debugging Server

The previous example shows the arguments to process_message(), but smtpd also includes a
server specifically designed for more complete debugging, called DebuggingServer. It prints
the entire incoming message to the console and then stops processing (it does not proxy the
message to a real mail server).

Listing 13.6: smtpd_debug.py

```
import smtpd
import asyncore

server = smtpd.DebuggingServer(('127.0.0.1', 1025), None)

asyncore.loop()
```

Using the smtpd_senddata.py client program given earlier produces the following output
from the DebuggingServer.

```
---------- MESSAGE FOLLOWS ----------
Content-Type: text/plain; charset="us-ascii"
MIME-Version: 1.0
Content-Transfer-Encoding: 7bit
To: Recipient <recipient@example.com>
From: Author <author@example.com>
Subject: Simple test message
X-Peer: 127.0.0.1

This is the body of the message.
------------ END MESSAGE ------------
```

13.2.3   Proxy Server

The PureProxy class implements a straightforward proxy server. Incoming messages are forwarded upstream to the server given as an argument to the constructor.

WARNING

The standard library documentation for smtpd says, "running this has a good chance to make you into an open relay, so please be careful."

The steps for setting up the proxy server are similar to those for setting up the debug server.

Listing 13.7: smtpd_proxy.py

```
import smtpd
import asyncore

server = smtpd.PureProxy(('127.0.0.1', 1025), ('mail', 25))

asyncore.loop()
```

This program prints no output. Therefore, to verify that it is working, you should look at the mail server logs.

```
Aug 20 19:16:34 homer sendmail[6785]: m9JNGXJb006785:
from=<author@example.com>, size=248, class=0, nrcpts=1,
msgid=<200810192316.m9JNGXJb006785@homer.example.com>,
proto=ESMTP, daemon=MTA, relay=[192.168.1.17]
```

TIP

Related Reading

- Standard library documentation for smtpd.[7]
- smtplib (page 841): Provides a client interface.
- email: Parses email messages.
- asyncore: Base module for writing asynchronous servers.
- **RFC 2822**[8]: Internet Message Format; defines the email message format.
- **RFC 5322**[9]: Replacement for RFC 2822.

---

[7] https://docs.python.org/3.5/library/smtpd.html
[8] https://tools.ietf.org/html/rfc2822.html
[9] https://tools.ietf.org/html/rfc5322.html

13.3 mailbox: Manipulate Email Archives

The `mailbox` module defines a common API for accessing email messages stored in local disk formats, including

- Maildir

- mbox

- MH

- Babyl

- MMDF

There are base classes for `Mailbox` and `Message`, and each mailbox format includes a corresponding pair of subclasses to implement the details for that format.

13.3.1 mbox

The mbox format is the simplest to show in documentation, since it is entirely plain text. Each mailbox is stored as a single file, with all of the messages concatenated together. Each time a line starting with "`From `" ("From" followed by a single space) is encountered, it is treated as the beginning of a new message. Whenever those characters appear at the beginning of a line in the message body, they are escaped by prefixing the line with `>`.

13.3.1.1 Creating an mbox Mailbox

Instantiate the `mbox` class by passing the filename to the constructor. If the file does not exist, it is created when `add()` is used to append messages.

Listing 13.8: `mailbox_mbox_create.py`

```
import mailbox
import email.utils

from_addr = email.utils.formataddr(('Author',
                                    'author@example.com'))
to_addr = email.utils.formataddr(('Recipient',
                                  'recipient@example.com'))

payload = '''This is the body.
From (will not be escaped).
There are 3 lines.
'''

mbox = mailbox.mbox('example.mbox')
mbox.lock()
```

```
try:
    msg = mailbox.mboxMessage()
    msg.set_unixfrom('author Sat Feb  7 01:05:34 2009')
    msg['From'] = from_addr
    msg['To'] = to_addr
    msg['Subject'] = 'Sample message 1'
    msg.set_payload(payload)
    mbox.add(msg)
    mbox.flush()

    msg = mailbox.mboxMessage()
    msg.set_unixfrom('author')
    msg['From'] = from_addr
    msg['To'] = to_addr
    msg['Subject'] = 'Sample message 2'
    msg.set_payload('This is the second body.\n')
    mbox.add(msg)
    mbox.flush()
finally:
    mbox.unlock()

print(open('example.mbox', 'r').read())
```

The result of this script is a new mailbox file with two email messages.

```
$ python3 mailbox_mbox_create.py

From MAILER-DAEMON Thu Dec 29 17:23:56 2016
From: Author <author@example.com>
To: Recipient <recipient@example.com>
Subject: Sample message 1

This is the body.
>From (will not be escaped).
There are 3 lines.

From MAILER-DAEMON Thu Dec 29 17:23:56 2016
From: Author <author@example.com>
To: Recipient <recipient@example.com>
Subject: Sample message 2

This is the second body.
```

13.3.1.2 Reading an mbox Mailbox

To read an existing mailbox, open it and treat the mbox object like a dictionary. The keys are arbitrary values defined by the mailbox instance and are not necessary meaningful other than as internal identifiers for message objects.

Listing 13.9: mailbox_mbox_read.py

```python
import mailbox

mbox = mailbox.mbox('example.mbox')
for message in mbox:
    print(message['subject'])
```

The open mailbox supports the iterator protocol. Unlike with true dictionary objects, however, the default iterator for a mailbox works on the *values* instead of the *keys*.

```
$ python3 mailbox_mbox_read.py

Sample message 1
Sample message 2
```

13.3.1.3   Removing Messages from an mbox Mailbox

To remove an existing message from an mbox file, either use its key with `remove()` or use `del`.

Listing 13.10: mailbox_mbox_remove.py

```python
import mailbox

mbox = mailbox.mbox('example.mbox')
mbox.lock()
try:
    to_remove = []
    for key, msg in mbox.iteritems():
        if '2' in msg['subject']:
            print('Removing:', key)
            to_remove.append(key)
    for key in to_remove:
        mbox.remove(key)
finally:
    mbox.flush()
    mbox.close()

print(open('example.mbox', 'r').read())
```

The `lock()` and `unlock()` methods are used to prevent issues from simultaneous access to the file, and `flush()` forces the changes to be written to disk.

```
$ python3 mailbox_mbox_remove.py

Removing: 1
From MAILER-DAEMON Thu Dec 29 17:23:56 2016
From: Author <author@example.com>
```

```
To: Recipient <recipient@example.com>
Subject: Sample message 1

This is the body.
>From (will not be escaped).
There are 3 lines.
```

13.3.2 Maildir

The Maildir format was created to eliminate the problem of concurrent modification to an mbox file. Instead of using a single file, the mailbox is organized as a directory in which each message is contained in its own file. This scheme also allows mailboxes to be nested, so the API for a Maildir mailbox is extended with methods to work with subfolders.

13.3.2.1 Creating a Maildir Mailbox

The only real difference between creating a `Maildir` and an `mbox` is that the argument to the `Maildir` constructor is a directory name instead of a filename. As before, if the mailbox does not exist, it is created when messages are added.

Listing 13.11: `mailbox_maildir_create.py`

```python
import mailbox
import email.utils
import os

from_addr = email.utils.formataddr(('Author',
                                    'author@example.com'))
to_addr = email.utils.formataddr(('Recipient',
                                  'recipient@example.com'))

payload = '''This is the body.
From (will not be escaped).
There are 3 lines.
'''

mbox = mailbox.Maildir('Example')
mbox.lock()
try:
    msg = mailbox.mboxMessage()
    msg.set_unixfrom('author Sat Feb  7 01:05:34 2009')
    msg['From'] = from_addr
    msg['To'] = to_addr
    msg['Subject'] = 'Sample message 1'
    msg.set_payload(payload)
    mbox.add(msg)
    mbox.flush()

    msg = mailbox.mboxMessage()
```

```
        msg.set_unixfrom('author Sat Feb  7 01:05:34 2009')
        msg['From'] = from_addr
        msg['To'] = to_addr
        msg['Subject'] = 'Sample message 2'
        msg.set_payload('This is the second body.\n')
        mbox.add(msg)
        mbox.flush()
    finally:
        mbox.unlock()

    for dirname, subdirs, files in os.walk('Example'):
        print(dirname)
        print('  Directories:', subdirs)
        for name in files:
            fullname = os.path.join(dirname, name)
            print('\n***', fullname)
            print(open(fullname).read())
            print('*' * 20)
```

When messages are added to the mailbox, they go to the new subdirectory.

WARNING

Although it is safe to write to the same Maildir from multiple processes, add() is not thread-safe. Use a semaphore or other locking device to prevent simultaneous modifications to the mailbox from multiple threads of the same process.

```
$ python3 mailbox_maildir_create.py

Example
  Directories: ['cur', 'new', 'tmp']
Example/cur
  Directories: []
Example/new
  Directories: []

*** Example/new/1483032236.M378880P24253Q1.hubert.local
From: Author <author@example.com>
To: Recipient <recipient@example.com>
Subject: Sample message 1

This is the body.
From (will not be escaped).
There are 3 lines.

********************

*** Example/new/1483032236.M381366P24253Q2.hubert.local
```

```
From: Author <author@example.com>
To: Recipient <recipient@example.com>
Subject: Sample message 2

This is the second body.

********************
Example/tmp
  Directories: []
```

After they are read, a client could move the messages to the cur subdirectory using the set_subdir() method of the MaildirMessage.

Listing 13.12: **mailbox_maildir_set_subdir.py**

```python
import mailbox
import os

print('Before:')
mbox = mailbox.Maildir('Example')
mbox.lock()
try:
    for message_id, message in mbox.iteritems():
        print('{:6} "{}"'.format(message.get_subdir(),
                                 message['subject']))
        message.set_subdir('cur')
        # Tell the mailbox to update the message.
        mbox[message_id] = message
finally:
    mbox.flush()
    mbox.close()

print('\nAfter:')
mbox = mailbox.Maildir('Example')
for message in mbox:
    print('{:6} "{}"'.format(message.get_subdir(),
                             message['subject']))

print()
for dirname, subdirs, files in os.walk('Example'):
    print(dirname)
    print('  Directories:', subdirs)
    for name in files:
        fullname = os.path.join(dirname, name)
        print(fullname)
```

Although Maildir includes a tmp directory, the only valid arguments for set_subdir() are cur and new.

```
$ python3 mailbox_maildir_set_subdir.py

Before:
new     "Sample message 2"
new     "Sample message 1"

After:
cur     "Sample message 2"
cur     "Sample message 1"

Example
  Directories: ['cur', 'new', 'tmp']
Example/cur
  Directories: []
Example/cur/1483032236.M378880P24253Q1.hubert.local
Example/cur/1483032236.M381366P24253Q2.hubert.local
Example/new
  Directories: []
Example/tmp
  Directories: []
```

13.3.2.2   Reading from a Maildir Mailbox

Reading from an existing Maildir mailbox works just like reading from an mbox mailbox.

Listing 13.13: `mailbox_maildir_read.py`

```
import mailbox

mbox = mailbox.Maildir('Example')
for message in mbox:
    print(message['subject'])
```

The messages are not guaranteed to be read in any particular order.

```
$ python3 mailbox_maildir_read.py

Sample message 2
Sample message 1
```

13.3.2.3   Removing Messages from a Maildir Mailbox

To remove an existing message from a Maildir mailbox, either pass its key to `remove()` or use `del`.

Listing 13.14: `mailbox_maildir_remove.py`

```
import mailbox
import os

mbox = mailbox.Maildir('Example')
mbox.lock()
try:
    to_remove = []
    for key, msg in mbox.iteritems():
        if '2' in msg['subject']:
            print('Removing:', key)
            to_remove.append(key)
    for key in to_remove:
        mbox.remove(key)
finally:
    mbox.flush()
    mbox.close()

for dirname, subdirs, files in os.walk('Example'):
    print(dirname)
    print('  Directories:', subdirs)
    for name in files:
        fullname = os.path.join(dirname, name)
        print('\n***', fullname)
        print(open(fullname).read())
        print('*' * 20)
```

There is no way to compute the key for a message, so use `items()` or `iteritems()` to retrieve the key and the message object from the mailbox at the same time.

```
$ python3 mailbox_maildir_remove.py

Removing: 1483032236.M381366P24253Q2.hubert.local
Example
  Directories: ['cur', 'new', 'tmp']
Example/cur
  Directories: []

*** Example/cur/1483032236.M378880P24253Q1.hubert.local
From: Author <author@example.com>
To: Recipient <recipient@example.com>
Subject: Sample message 1

This is the body.
From (will not be escaped).
There are 3 lines.
```

```
********************
Example/new
   Directories: []
Example/tmp
   Directories: []
```

13.3.2.4 Maildir Folders

Subdirectories or *folders* of a Maildir mailbox can be managed directly through the methods of the Maildir class. Callers can list, retrieve, create, and remove subfolders for a given mailbox.

Listing 13.15: mailbox_maildir_folders.py

```
import mailbox
import os


def show_maildir(name):
    os.system('find {} -print'.format(name))


mbox = mailbox.Maildir('Example')
print('Before:', mbox.list_folders())
show_maildir('Example')

print('\n{:#^30}\n'.format(''))

mbox.add_folder('subfolder')
print('subfolder created:', mbox.list_folders())
show_maildir('Example')

subfolder = mbox.get_folder('subfolder')
print('subfolder contents:', subfolder.list_folders())

print('\n{:#^30}\n'.format(''))

subfolder.add_folder('second_level')
print('second_level created:', subfolder.list_folders())
show_maildir('Example')

print('\n{:#^30}\n'.format(''))

subfolder.remove_folder('second_level')
print('second_level removed:', subfolder.list_folders())
show_maildir('Example')
```

The directory name for the folder is constructed by prefixing the folder name with a period (.).

```
$ python3 mailbox_maildir_folders.py

Example
Example/cur
Example/cur/1483032236.M378880P24253Q1.hubert.local
Example/new
Example/tmp
Example
Example/.subfolder
Example/.subfolder/cur
Example/.subfolder/maildirfolder
Example/.subfolder/new
Example/.subfolder/tmp
Example/cur
Example/cur/1483032236.M378880P24253Q1.hubert.local
Example/new
Example/tmp
Example
Example/.subfolder
Example/.subfolder/.second_level
Example/.subfolder/.second_level/cur
Example/.subfolder/.second_level/maildirfolder
Example/.subfolder/.second_level/new
Example/.subfolder/.second_level/tmp
Example/.subfolder/cur
Example/.subfolder/maildirfolder
Example/.subfolder/new
Example/.subfolder/tmp
Example/cur
Example/cur/1483032236.M378880P24253Q1.hubert.local
Example/new
Example/tmp
Example
Example/.subfolder
Example/.subfolder/cur
Example/.subfolder/maildirfolder
Example/.subfolder/new
Example/.subfolder/tmp
Example/cur
Example/cur/1483032236.M378880P24253Q1.hubert.local
Example/new
Example/tmp
Before: []

##############################
```

```
subfolder created: ['subfolder']
subfolder contents: []

##############################

second_level created: ['second_level']

##############################

second_level removed: []
```

13.3.3 Message Flags

Messages in mailboxes have flags for tracking aspects such as whether the message has been
read, flagged as important by the reader, or marked for deletion later. Flags are stored as
a sequence of format-specific letter codes and the Message classes have methods to retrieve
and change the values of the flags. This example shows the flags on the messages in the
Example Maildir before adding the flag to indicate that the message is considered important.

Listing 13.16: mailbox_maildir_add_flag.py

```
import mailbox

print('Before:')
mbox = mailbox.Maildir('Example')
mbox.lock()
try:
    for message_id, message in mbox.iteritems():
        print('{:6} "{}"'.format(message.get_flags(),
                                 message['subject']))
        message.add_flag('F')
        # Tell the mailbox to update the message.
        mbox[message_id] = message
finally:
    mbox.flush()
    mbox.close()

print('\nAfter:')
mbox = mailbox.Maildir('Example')
for message in mbox:
    print('{:6} "{}"'.format(message.get_flags(),
                             message['subject']))
```

By default, messages have no flags. Adding a flag changes the message in memory, but
does not update the message on disk. To update the message on disk, store the message
object in the mailbox using its existing identifier.

```
$ python3 mailbox_maildir_add_flag.py

Before:
        "Sample message 1"

After:
F       "Sample message 1"
```

Adding flags with `add_flag()` preserves any existing flags. Using `set_flags()` writes over any existing set of flags, replacing it with the new values passed to the method.

Listing 13.17: **mailbox_maildir_set_flags.py**

```python
import mailbox

print('Before:')
mbox = mailbox.Maildir('Example')
mbox.lock()
try:
    for message_id, message in mbox.iteritems():
        print('{:6} "{}"'.format(message.get_flags(),
                                  message['subject']))
        message.set_flags('S')
        # Tell the mailbox to update the message.
        mbox[message_id] = message
finally:
    mbox.flush()
    mbox.close()

print('\nAfter:')
mbox = mailbox.Maildir('Example')
for message in mbox:
    print('{:6} "{}"'.format(message.get_flags(),
                             message['subject']))
```

The F flag added by the previous example is lost when `set_flags()` replaces the flags with S in this example.

```
$ python3 mailbox_maildir_set_flags.py

Before:
F       "Sample message 1"

After:
S       "Sample message 1"
```

13.3.4   Other Formats

`mailbox` supports a few other formats, but none is as popular as mbox or Maildir. MH is another multifile mailbox format used by some mail handlers. Babyl and MMDF are single-file formats that use different message separators than mbox. The single-file formats support the same API as mbox, and MH includes the folder-related methods found in the Maildir class.

TIP

Related Reading

- Standard library documentation for `mailbox`.[10]
- Python 2 to 3 porting notes for `mailbox` (page 1360).
- mbox manpage from qmail[11]: Documentation for the mbox format.
- Maildir manpage from qmail[12]: Documentation for the Maildir format.
- email: The `email` module.
- `imaplib` (page 864): The `imaplib` module can work with saved email messages on an IMAP server.

13.4   imaplib: IMAP4 Client Library

`imaplib` implements a client for communicating with Internet Message Access Protocol (IMAP) version 4 servers. The IMAP protocol defines a set of commands that are sent to the server and the responses that are delivered back to the client. Most of the commands are available as methods of the `IMAP4` object used to communicate with the server.

These examples discuss part of the IMAP protocol, but are by no means complete. Refer to **RFC 3501**[13] for complete details.

13.4.1   Variations

Three client classes are provided for communicating with servers using various mechanisms. The first, `IMAP4`, uses clear text sockets; `IMAP4_SSL` uses encrypted communication over SSL sockets; and `IMAP4_stream` uses the standard input and standard output of an external command. All of the examples here use `IMAP4_SSL`, but the APIs for the other classes are similar.

13.4.2   Connecting to a Server

There are two steps for establishing a connection with an IMAP server. First, set up the socket connection itself. Second, authenticate as a user with an account on the server. The following example code reads server and user information from a configuration file.

---

[10] https://docs.python.org/3.5/library/mailbox.html
[11] www.qmail.org/man/man5/mbox.html
[12] www.qmail.org/man/man5/maildir.html
[13] https://tools.ietf.org/html/rfc3501

Listing 13.18: **imaplib_connect.py**

```python
import imaplib
import configparser
import os


def open_connection(verbose=False):
    # Read the config file.
    config = configparser.ConfigParser()
    config.read([os.path.expanduser('~/.pymotw')])

    # Connect to the server.
    hostname = config.get('server', 'hostname')
    if verbose:
        print('Connecting to', hostname)
    connection = imaplib.IMAP4_SSL(hostname)

    # Log in to our account.
    username = config.get('account', 'username')
    password = config.get('account', 'password')
    if verbose:
        print('Logging in as', username)
    connection.login(username, password)
    return connection


if __name__ == '__main__':
    with open_connection(verbose=True) as c:
        print(c)
```

When run, open_connection() reads the configuration information from a file in the user's home directory, opens the IMAP4_SSL connection, and then authenticates the user.

```
$ python3 imaplib_connect.py

Connecting to pymotw.hellfly.net
Logging in as example
<imaplib.IMAP4_SSL object at 0x10421e320>
```

The other examples in this section reuse this module, to avoid duplicating the code.

13.4.2.1   Authentication Failure

If the connection is established but authentication fails, an exception is raised.

Listing 13.19: **imaplib_connect_fail.py**

```python
import imaplib
import configparser
```

```
import os

# Read the config file.
config = configparser.ConfigParser()
config.read([os.path.expanduser('~/.pymotw')])

# Connect to the server.
hostname = config.get('server', 'hostname')
print('Connecting to', hostname)
connection = imaplib.IMAP4_SSL(hostname)

# Log in to our account.
username = config.get('account', 'username')
password = 'this_is_the_wrong_password'
print('Logging in as', username)
try:
    connection.login(username, password)
except Exception as err:
    print('ERROR:', err)
```

This example uses the wrong password on purpose to trigger the exception.

```
$ python3 imaplib_connect_fail.py

Connecting to pymotw.hellfly.net
Logging in as example
ERROR: b'[AUTHENTICATIONFAILED] Authentication failed.'
```

13.4.3 Example Configuration

The example account has several mailboxes in a hierarchy:

- INBOX

- Deleted Messages

- Archive

- Example

  - 2016

There is one unread message in the INBOX folder, and one previously read message in Example/2016.

13.4.4 Listing Mailboxes

To retrieve the mailboxes available for an account, use the list() method.

Listing 13.20: imaplib_list.py

```python
import imaplib
from pprint import pprint
from imaplib_connect import open_connection

with open_connection() as c:
    typ, data = c.list()
    print('Response code:', typ)
    print('Response:')
    pprint(data)
```

The return value is a tuple containing a response code and the data returned by the server. The response code is OK, unless an error occurs. The data for list() is a sequence of strings containing *flags*, the *hierarchy delimiter*, and the *mailbox name* for each mailbox.

```
$ python3 imaplib_list.py

Response code: OK
Response:
[b'(\\HasChildren) "." Example',
 b'(\\HasNoChildren) "." Example.2016',
 b'(\\HasNoChildren) "." Archive',
 b'(\\HasNoChildren) "." "Deleted Messages"',
 b'(\\HasNoChildren) "." INBOX']
```

Each response string can be split into three parts using re (page 13) or csv (page 466) (see "IMAP Backup Script" in the references at the end of this section for an example using csv).

Listing 13.21: imaplib_list_parse.py

```python
import imaplib
import re

from imaplib_connect import open_connection

list_response_pattern = re.compile(
    r'\((?P<flags>.*?)\) "(?P<delimiter>.*)" (?P<name>.*)'
)


def parse_list_response(line):
    match = list_response_pattern.match(line.decode('utf-8'))
    flags, delimiter, mailbox_name = match.groups()
    mailbox_name = mailbox_name.strip('"')
    return (flags, delimiter, mailbox_name)
```

```
with open_connection() as c:
    typ, data = c.list()
print('Response code:', typ)

for line in data:
    print('Server response:', line)
    flags, delimiter, mailbox_name = parse_list_response(line)
    print('Parsed response:', (flags, delimiter, mailbox_name))
```

The server quotes the mailbox name if it includes spaces, but those quotes need to be stripped out to use the mailbox name later, in other calls to the server.

```
$ python3 imaplib_list_parse.py

Response code: OK
Server response: b'(\\HasChildren) "." Example'
Parsed response: ('\\HasChildren', '.', 'Example')
Server response: b'(\\HasNoChildren) "." Example.2016'
Parsed response: ('\\HasNoChildren', '.', 'Example.2016')
Server response: b'(\\HasNoChildren) "." Archive'
Parsed response: ('\\HasNoChildren', '.', 'Archive')
Server response: b'(\\HasNoChildren) "." "Deleted Messages"'
Parsed response: ('\\HasNoChildren', '.', 'Deleted Messages')
Server response: b'(\\HasNoChildren) "." INBOX'
Parsed response: ('\\HasNoChildren', '.', 'INBOX')
```

list() takes arguments to specify mailboxes in part of the hierarchy. For example, to list the subfolders in Example, pass "Example" as the directory argument.

Listing 13.22: imaplib_list_subfolders.py

```
import imaplib

from imaplib_connect import open_connection

with open_connection() as c:
    typ, data = c.list(directory='Example')

print('Response code:', typ)

for line in data:
    print('Server response:', line)
```

The parent and subfolders are returned.

```
$ python3 imaplib_list_subfolders.py

Response code: OK
```

```
Server response: b'(\\HasChildren) "." Example'
Server response: b'(\\HasNoChildren) "." Example.2016'
```

Alternatively, to list folders matching a pattern, pass the `pattern` argument.

Listing 13.23: **imaplib_list_pattern.py**

```python
import imaplib

from imaplib_connect import open_connection

with open_connection() as c:
    typ, data = c.list(pattern='*Example*')

print('Response code:', typ)

for line in data:
    print('Server response:', line)
```

In this case, both `Example` and `Example.2016` are included in the response.

```
$ python3 imaplib_list_pattern.py

Response code: OK
Server response: b'(\\HasChildren) "." Example'
Server response: b'(\\HasNoChildren) "." Example.2016'
```

13.4.5   Mailbox Status

Use `status()` to ask for aggregated information about the contents. Table 13.1 lists the status conditions defined by the standard.

The status conditions must be formatted as a space-separated string enclosed in parentheses—in other words, using the encoding for a "list" in the IMAP4 specification. The mailbox name is wrapped in " in case any of the names include spaces or other characters that would throw off the parser.

Table 13.1: IMAP 4 Mailbox Status Conditions

Condition	Meaning
MESSAGES	The number of messages in the mailbox
RECENT	The number of messages with the \Recent flag set
UIDNEXT	The next unique identifier value of the mailbox
UIDVALIDITY	The unique identifier validity value of the mailbox
UNSEEN	The number of messages that do not have the \Seen flag set

Listing 13.24: **imaplib_status.py**

```python
import imaplib
import re

from imaplib_connect import open_connection
from imaplib_list_parse import parse_list_response

with open_connection() as c:
    typ, data = c.list()
    for line in data:
        flags, delimiter, mailbox = parse_list_response(line)
        print('Mailbox:', mailbox)
        status = c.status(
            '"{}"'.format(mailbox),
            '(MESSAGES RECENT UIDNEXT UIDVALIDITY UNSEEN)',
        )
        print(status)
```

The return value is the usual tuple containing a response code and a list of information from the server. In this case, the list contains a single string formatted with the name of the mailbox in quotes, then the status conditions and values in parentheses.

```
$ python3 imaplib_status.py

Response code: OK
Server response: b'(\\HasChildren) "." Example'
Parsed response: ('\\HasChildren', '.', 'Example')
Server response: b'(\\HasNoChildren) "." Example.2016'
Parsed response: ('\\HasNoChildren', '.', 'Example.2016')
Server response: b'(\\HasNoChildren) "." Archive'
Parsed response: ('\\HasNoChildren', '.', 'Archive')
Server response: b'(\\HasNoChildren) "." "Deleted Messages"'
Parsed response: ('\\HasNoChildren', '.', 'Deleted Messages')
Server response: b'(\\HasNoChildren) "." INBOX'
Parsed response: ('\\HasNoChildren', '.', 'INBOX')
Mailbox: Example
('OK', [b'Example (MESSAGES 0 RECENT 0 UIDNEXT 2 UIDVALIDITY 145
7297771 UNSEEN 0)'])
Mailbox: Example.2016
('OK', [b'Example.2016 (MESSAGES 1 RECENT 0 UIDNEXT 3 UIDVALIDIT
Y 1457297772 UNSEEN 0)'])
Mailbox: Archive
('OK', [b'Archive (MESSAGES 0 RECENT 0 UIDNEXT 1 UIDVALIDITY 145
7297770 UNSEEN 0)'])
Mailbox: Deleted Messages
('OK', [b'"Deleted Messages" (MESSAGES 3 RECENT 0 UIDNEXT 4 UIDV
ALIDITY 1457297773 UNSEEN 0)'])
```

```
Mailbox: INBOX
('OK', [b'INBOX (MESSAGES 2 RECENT 0 UIDNEXT 6 UIDVALIDITY 14572
97769 UNSEEN 1)'])
```

13.4.6   Selecting a Mailbox

The basic mode of operation, once the client is authenticated, is to select a mailbox, then interrogate the server regarding messages in the mailbox. The connection is stateful, so after a mailbox is selected, all commands operate on messages in that mailbox until a new mailbox is selected.

Listing 13.25: **imaplib_select.py**

```python
import imaplib
import imaplib_connect

with imaplib_connect.open_connection() as c:
    typ, data = c.select('INBOX')
    print(typ, data)
    num_msgs = int(data[0])
    print('There are {} messages in INBOX'.format(num_msgs))
```

The response data contains the total number of messages in the mailbox.

```
$ python3 imaplib_select.py

OK [b'1']
There are 1 messages in INBOX
```

If an invalid mailbox is specified, the response code is NO.

Listing 13.26: **imaplib_select_invalid.py**

```python
import imaplib
import imaplib_connect

with imaplib_connect.open_connection() as c:
    typ, data = c.select('Does-Not-Exist')
    print(typ, data)
```

In this example, the data contains an error message describing the problem.

```
$ python3 imaplib_select_invalid.py

NO [b"Mailbox doesn't exist: Does-Not-Exist"]
```

13.4.7   Searching for Messages

After selecting the mailbox, use `search()` to retrieve the IDs of messages in the mailbox.

Listing 13.27: <code>imaplib_search_all.py</code>

```python
import imaplib
import imaplib_connect
from imaplib_list_parse import parse_list_response

with imaplib_connect.open_connection() as c:
    typ, mbox_data = c.list()
    for line in mbox_data:
        flags, delimiter, mbox_name = parse_list_response(line)
        c.select('"{}"'.format(mbox_name), readonly=True)
        typ, msg_ids = c.search(None, 'ALL')
        print(mbox_name, typ, msg_ids)
```

Message IDs are assigned by the server, and are implementation dependent. The IMAP4 protocol makes a distinction between sequential IDs for messages at a given point in time during a transaction and UID identifiers for messages, but not all servers implement both.

```
$ python3 imaplib_search_all.py

Response code: OK
Server response: b'(\\HasChildren) "." Example'
Parsed response: ('\\HasChildren', '.', 'Example')
Server response: b'(\\HasNoChildren) "." Example.2016'
Parsed response: ('\\HasNoChildren', '.', 'Example.2016')
Server response: b'(\\HasNoChildren) "." Archive'
Parsed response: ('\\HasNoChildren', '.', 'Archive')
Server response: b'(\\HasNoChildren) "." "Deleted Messages"'
Parsed response: ('\\HasNoChildren', '.', 'Deleted Messages')
Server response: b'(\\HasNoChildren) "." INBOX'
Parsed response: ('\\HasNoChildren', '.', 'INBOX')
Example OK [b'']
Example.2016 OK [b'1']
Archive OK [b'']
Deleted Messages OK [b'']
INBOX OK [b'1']
```

In this case, `INBOX` and `Example.2016` each have a different message with id `1`. The other mailboxes are empty.

13.4.8   Search Criteria

A variety of other search criteria can be used, including looking at dates for the message, flags, and other headers. Refer to section 6.4.4. of **RFC 3501**[14] for complete details.

---

[14] https://tools.ietf.org/html/rfc3501

To look for messages with `'Example message 2'` in the subject, the search criteria should be constructed as follows:

```
(SUBJECT "Example message 2")
```

This example finds all messages with the title "Example message 2" in all mailboxes.

Listing 13.28: imaplib_search_subject.py

```python
import imaplib
import imaplib_connect
from imaplib_list_parse import parse_list_response

with imaplib_connect.open_connection() as c:
    typ, mbox_data = c.list()
    for line in mbox_data:
        flags, delimiter, mbox_name = parse_list_response(line)
        c.select('"{}"'.format(mbox_name), readonly=True)
        typ, msg_ids = c.search(
            None,
            '(SUBJECT "Example message 2")',
        )
        print(mbox_name, typ, msg_ids)
```

There is only one such message in the account, and it is in the INBOX.

```
$ python3 imaplib_search_subject.py

Response code: OK
Server response: b'(\\HasChildren) "." Example'
Parsed response: ('\\HasChildren', '.', 'Example')
Server response: b'(\\HasNoChildren) "." Example.2016'
Parsed response: ('\\HasNoChildren', '.', 'Example.2016')
Server response: b'(\\HasNoChildren) "." Archive'
Parsed response: ('\\HasNoChildren', '.', 'Archive')
Server response: b'(\\HasNoChildren) "." "Deleted Messages"'
Parsed response: ('\\HasNoChildren', '.', 'Deleted Messages')
Server response: b'(\\HasNoChildren) "." INBOX'
Parsed response: ('\\HasNoChildren', '.', 'INBOX')
Example OK [b'']
Example.2016 OK [b'']
Archive OK [b'']
Deleted Messages OK [b'']
INBOX OK [b'1']
```

Search criteria can also be combined.

Listing 13.29: `imaplib_search_from.py`

```python
import imaplib
import imaplib_connect
from imaplib_list_parse import parse_list_response

with imaplib_connect.open_connection() as c:
    typ, mbox_data = c.list()
    for line in mbox_data:
        flags, delimiter, mbox_name = parse_list_response(line)
        c.select('"{}"'.format(mbox_name), readonly=True)
        typ, msg_ids = c.search(
            None,
            '(FROM "Doug" SUBJECT "Example message 2")',
        )
        print(mbox_name, typ, msg_ids)
```

The criteria are combined with a logical and operation.

```
$ python3 imaplib_search_from.py

Response code: OK
Server response: b'(\\HasChildren) "." Example'
Parsed response: ('\\HasChildren', '.', 'Example')
Server response: b'(\\HasNoChildren) "." Example.2016'
Parsed response: ('\\HasNoChildren', '.', 'Example.2016')
Server response: b'(\\HasNoChildren) "." Archive'
Parsed response: ('\\HasNoChildren', '.', 'Archive')
Server response: b'(\\HasNoChildren) "." "Deleted Messages"'
Parsed response: ('\\HasNoChildren', '.', 'Deleted Messages')
Server response: b'(\\HasNoChildren) "." INBOX'
Parsed response: ('\\HasNoChildren', '.', 'INBOX')
Example OK [b'']
Example.2016 OK [b'']
Archive OK [b'']
Deleted Messages OK [b'']
INBOX OK [b'1']
```

13.4.9 Fetching Messages

The identifiers returned by search() are used to retrieve the contents, or partial contents, of messages for further processing using the fetch() method. This function takes two arguments: the message IDs to fetch and the portion(s) of the message to retrieve.

The message_ids argument is a comma-separated list of IDs (e.g., "1", "1,2") or ID ranges (e.g., 1:2). The message_parts argument is an IMAP list of message segment names. As with the search criteria for search(), the IMAP protocol specifies named message segments so clients can efficiently retrieve only the parts of the message they actually need.

For example, to retrieve the headers of the messages in a mailbox, use `fetch()` with the argument `BODY.PEEK[HEADER]`.

NOTE

Another way to fetch the headers is to use BODY[HEADERS], but that form has a side effect of implicitly marking the message as read, which is undesirable in many cases.

Listing 13.30: `imaplib_fetch_raw.py`

```python
import imaplib
import pprint
import imaplib_connect

imaplib.Debug = 4
with imaplib_connect.open_connection() as c:
    c.select('INBOX', readonly=True)
    typ, msg_data = c.fetch('1', '(BODY.PEEK[HEADER] FLAGS)')
    pprint.pprint(msg_data)
```

In this example, the return value of `fetch()` has been partially parsed so it is somewhat harder to work with than the return value of `list()`. Turning on debugging shows the complete interaction between the client and the server to understand why this is so.

```
$ python3 imaplib_fetch_raw.py

  19:40.68 imaplib version 2.58
  19:40.68 new IMAP4 connection, tag=b'IIEN'
  19:40.70 < b'* OK [CAPABILITY IMAP4rev1 LITERAL+ SASL-IR LOGIN
-REFERRALS ID ENABLE IDLE AUTH=PLAIN] Dovecot (Ubuntu) ready.'
  19:40.70 > b'IIEN0 CAPABILITY'
  19:40.73 < b'* CAPABILITY IMAP4rev1 LITERAL+ SASL-IR LOGIN-REF
ERRALS ID ENABLE IDLE AUTH=PLAIN'
  19:40.73 < b'IIEN0 OK Pre-login capabilities listed, post-logi
n capabilities have more.'
  19:40.73 CAPABILITIES: ('IMAP4REV1', 'LITERAL+', 'SASL-IR', 'L
OGIN-REFERRALS', 'ID', 'ENABLE', 'IDLE', 'AUTH=PLAIN')
  19:40.73 > b'IIEN1 LOGIN example "TMFw00fpymotw"'
  19:40.79 < b'* CAPABILITY IMAP4rev1 LITERAL+ SASL-IR LOGIN-REF
ERRALS ID ENABLE IDLE SORT SORT=DISPLAY THREAD=REFERENCES THREAD
=REFS THREAD=ORDEREDSUBJECT MULTIAPPEND URL-PARTIAL CATENATE UNS
ELECT CHILDREN NAMESPACE UIDPLUS LIST-EXTENDED I18NLEVEL=1 CONDS
TORE QRESYNC ESEARCH ESORT SEARCHRES WITHIN CONTEXT=SEARCH LIST-
STATUS SPECIAL-USE BINARY MOVE'
  19:40.79 < b'IIEN1 OK Logged in'
  19:40.79 > b'IIEN2 EXAMINE INBOX'
  19:40.82 < b'* FLAGS (\\Answered \\Flagged \\Deleted \\Seen \\
```

```
Draft)'
    19:40.82 < b'* OK [PERMANENTFLAGS ()] Read-only mailbox.'
    19:40.82 < b'* 2 EXISTS'
    19:40.82 < b'* 0 RECENT'
    19:40.82 < b'* OK [UNSEEN 1] First unseen.'
    19:40.82 < b'* OK [UIDVALIDITY 1457297769] UIDs valid'
    19:40.82 < b'* OK [UIDNEXT 6] Predicted next UID'
    19:40.82 < b'* OK [HIGHESTMODSEQ 20] Highest'
    19:40.82 < b'IIEN2 OK [READ-ONLY] Examine completed (0.000 sec
s).'
    19:40.82 > b'IIEN3 FETCH 1 (BODY.PEEK[HEADER] FLAGS)'
    19:40.86 < b'* 1 FETCH (FLAGS () BODY[HEADER] {3108}'
    19:40.86 read literal size 3108
    19:40.86 < b')'
    19:40.89 < b'IIEN3 OK Fetch completed.'
    19:40.89 > b'IIEN4 LOGOUT'
    19:40.93 < b'* BYE Logging out'
    19:40.93 BYE response: b'Logging out'
[(b'1 (FLAGS () BODY[HEADER] {3108}',
  b'Return-Path: <doug@doughellmann.com>\r\nReceived: from compu
te4.internal ('
  b'compute4.nyi.internal [10.202.2.44])\r\n\t by sloti26t01 (Cy
rus 3.0.0-beta1'
  b'-git-fastmail-12410) with LMTPA;\r\n\t Sun, 06 Mar 2016 16:1
6:03 -0500\r'
  b'\nX-Sieve: CMU Sieve 2.4\r\nX-Spam-known-sender: yes, fadd1c
f2-dc3a-4984-a0'
  b'8b-02cef3cf1221="doug",\r\n   ea349ad0-9299-47b5-b632-6ff1e39
4cc7d="both he'
  b'llfly"\r\nX-Spam-score: 0.0\r\nX-Spam-hits: ALL_TRUSTED -1,
BAYES_00 -1.'
  b'9, LANGUAGES unknown, BAYES_USED global,\r\n   SA_VERSION 3.3
.2\r\nX-Spam'
  b"-source: IP='127.0.0.1', Host='unk', Country='unk', FromHead
er='com',\r\n "
  b" MailFrom='com'\r\nX-Spam-charsets: plain='us-ascii'\r\nX-Re
solved-to: d"
  b'oughellmann@fastmail.fm\r\nX-Delivered-to: doug@doughellmann
.com\r\nX-Ma'
  b'il-from: doug@doughellmann.com\r\nReceived: from mx5 ([10.20
2.2.204])\r'
  b'\n  by compute4.internal (LMTPProxy); Sun, 06 Mar 2016 16:16
:03 -0500\r\nRe'
  b'ceived: from mx5.nyi.internal (localhost [127.0.0.1])\r\n\tb
y mx5.nyi.inter'
  b'nal (Postfix) with ESMTP id 47CBA280DB3\r\n\tfor <doug@dough
ellmann.com>; S'
  b'un,  6 Mar 2016 16:16:03 -0500 (EST)\r\nReceived: from mx5.n
yi.internal (l'
```

```
    b'ocalhost [127.0.0.1])\r\n     by mx5.nyi.internal (Authentica
tion Milter) w'
    b'ith ESMTP\r\n     id A717886846E.30BA4280D81;\r\n     Sun, 6 M
ar 2016 16:1'
    b'6:03 -0500\r\nAuthentication-Results: mx5.nyi.internal;\r\n
  dkim=pass'
    b' (1024-bit rsa key) header.d=messagingengine.com header.i=@m
essagingengi'
    b'ne.com header.b=Jrsm+pCo;\r\n     x-local-ip=pass\r\nReceived
: from mailo'
    b'ut.nyi.internal (gateway1.nyi.internal [10.202.2.221])\r\n\t
(using TLSv1.2 '
    b'with cipher ECDHE-RSA-AES256-GCM-SHA384 (256/256 bits))\r\n\
t(No client cer'
    b'tificate requested)\r\n\tby mx5.nyi.internal (Postfix) with
ESMTPS id 30BA4'
    b'280D81\r\n\tfor <doug@doughellmann.com>; Sun,  6 Mar 2016 16
:16:03 -0500 (E'
    b'ST)\r\nReceived: from compute2.internal (compute2.nyi.intern
al [10.202.2.4'
    b'2])\r\n\tby mailout.nyi.internal (Postfix) with ESMTP id 174
0420D0A\r\n\tf'
    b'or <doug@doughellmann.com>; Sun,  6 Mar 2016 16:16:03 -0500
(EST)\r\nRecei'
    b'ved: from frontend2 ([10.202.2.161])\r\n     by compute2.intern
al (MEProxy); '
    b'Sun, 06 Mar 2016 16:16:03 -0500\r\nDKIM-Signature: v=1; a=rs
a-sha1; c=rela'
    b'xed/relaxed; d=\r\n\tmessagingengine.com; h=content-transfer
-encoding:conte'
    b'nt-type\r\n\t:date:from:message-id:mime-version:subject:to:x
-sasl-enc\r\n'
    b'\t:x-sasl-enc; s=smtpout; bh=P98NTsEo015suwJ4gk71knAWLa4=; b
=Jrsm+\r\n\t'
    b'pCovRIoQIRyp8Fl0L6JHOI8sbZy2obx7O28JF2iTlTWmX33Rhlq9403XRklw
N3JA\r\n\t7KSPq'
    b'MTp30Qdx6yIUaADwQqlO+QMuQq/QxBHdjeebmdhgVfjhqxrzTbSMww/ZNhL\
r\n\tYwv/QM/oDH'
    b'bXiLSUlB3Qrg+9wsE/0jU/EOisiU=\r\nX-Sasl-enc: 8ZJ+4ZRE8AGPzdL
RWQFivGymJb8pa'
    b'4G9JGcb7k4xKn+I 1457298962\r\nReceived: from [192.168.1.14]
(75-137-1-34.d'
    b'hcp.nwnn.ga.charter.com [75.137.1.34])\r\n\tby mail.messagin
gengine.com (Po'
    b'stfix) with ESMTPA id C0B366801CD\r\n\tfor <doug@doughellman
n.com>; Sun, 6'
    b' Mar 2016 16:16:02 -0500 (EST)\r\nFrom: Doug Hellmann <doug@
doughellmann.c'
    b'om>\r\nContent-Type: text/plain; charset=us-ascii\r\nContent
```

```
-Transfer-En'
  b'coding: 7bit\r\nSubject: PyMOTW Example message 2\r\nMessage
-Id: <00ABCD'
  b'46-DADA-4912-A451-D27165BC3A2F@doughellmann.com>\r\nDate: Su
n, 6 Mar 2016 '
  b'16:16:02 -0500\r\nTo: Doug Hellmann <doug@doughellmann.com>\
r\nMime-Vers'
  b'ion: 1.0 (Mac OS X Mail 9.2 \\(3112\\))\r\nX-Mailer: Apple M
ail (2.3112)'
  b'\r\n\r\n'),
 b')']
```

The response from the FETCH command starts with the flags, then indicates that the message includes 595 bytes of header data. The client constructs a tuple with the response for the message, and then closes the sequence with a single string containing the right paren-thesis ()) that the server sends at the end of the fetch response. Because of this formatting, it may be easier to fetch different pieces of information separately, or to recombine the response and parse it in the client.

Listing 13.31: **imaplib_fetch_separately.py**

```python
import imaplib
import pprint
import imaplib_connect

with imaplib_connect.open_connection() as c:
    c.select('INBOX', readonly=True)

    print('HEADER:')
    typ, msg_data = c.fetch('1', '(BODY.PEEK[HEADER])')
    for response_part in msg_data:
        if isinstance(response_part, tuple):
            print(response_part[1])

    print('\nBODY TEXT:')
    typ, msg_data = c.fetch('1', '(BODY.PEEK[TEXT])')
    for response_part in msg_data:
        if isinstance(response_part, tuple):
            print(response_part[1])

    print('\nFLAGS:')
    typ, msg_data = c.fetch('1', '(FLAGS)')
    for response_part in msg_data:
        print(response_part)
        print(imaplib.ParseFlags(response_part))
```

Fetching values separately has the added benefit of making it easy to use ParseFlags() to parse the flags from the response.

```
$ python3 imaplib_fetch_separately.py

HEADER:
b'Return-Path: <doug@doughellmann.com>\r\nReceived: from compute
4.internal (compute4.nyi.internal [10.202.2.44])\r\n\t by sloti2
6t01 (Cyrus 3.0.0-beta1-git-fastmail-12410) with LMTPA;\r\n\t Su
n, 06 Mar 2016 16:16:03 -0500\r\nX-Sieve: CMU Sieve 2.4\r\nX-Spa
m-known-sender: yes, fadd1cf2-dc3a-4984-a08b-02cef3cf1221="doug"
,\r\n  ea349ad0-9299-47b5-b632-6ff1e394cc7d="both hellfly"\r\nX-
Spam-score: 0.0\r\nX-Spam-hits: ALL_TRUSTED -1, BAYES_00 -1.9, L
ANGUAGES unknown, BAYES_USED global,\r\n  SA_VERSION 3.3.2\r\nX-
Spam-source: IP=\'127.0.0.1\', Host=\'unk\', Country=\'unk\', Fr
omHeader=\'com\',\r\n  MailFrom=\'com\'\r\nX-Spam-charsets: plai
n=\'us-ascii\'\r\nX-Resolved-to: doughellmann@fastmail.fm\r\nX-D
elivered-to: doug@doughellmann.com\r\nX-Mail-from: doug@doughell
mann.com\r\nReceived: from mx5 ([10.202.2.204])\r\n  by compute4
.internal (LMTPProxy); Sun, 06 Mar 2016 16:16:03 -0500\r\nReceiv
ed: from mx5.nyi.internal (localhost [127.0.0.1])\r\n\tby mx5.ny
i.internal (Postfix) with ESMTP id 47CBA280DB3\r\n\tfor <doug@do
ughellmann.com>; Sun,  6 Mar 2016 16:16:03 -0500 (EST)\r\nReceiv
ed: from mx5.nyi.internal (localhost [127.0.0.1])\r\n    by mx5.
nyi.internal (Authentication Milter) with ESMTP\r\n    id A71788
6846E.30BA4280D81;\r\n    Sun, 6 Mar 2016 16:16:03 -0500\r\nAuth
entication-Results: mx5.nyi.internal;\r\n    dkim=pass (1024-bit
 rsa key) header.d=messagingengine.com header.i=@messagingengine
.com header.b=Jrsm+pCo;\r\n    x-local-ip=pass\r\nReceived: from
 mailout.nyi.internal (gateway1.nyi.internal [10.202.2.221])\r\n
\t(using TLSv1.2 with cipher ECDHE-RSA-AES256-GCM-SHA384 (256/25
6 bits))\r\n\t(No client certificate requested)\r\n\tby mx5.nyi.
internal (Postfix) with ESMTPS id 30BA4280D81\r\n\tfor <doug@dou
ghellmann.com>; Sun,  6 Mar 2016 16:16:03 -0500 (EST)\r\nReceive
d: from compute2.internal (compute2.nyi.internal [10.202.2.42])\
r\n\tby mailout.nyi.internal (Postfix) with ESMTP id 1740420D0A\
r\n\tfor <doug@doughellmann.com>; Sun,  6 Mar 2016 16:16:03 -050
0 (EST)\r\nReceived: from frontend2 ([10.202.2.161])\r\n  by com
pute2.internal (MEProxy); Sun, 06 Mar 2016 16:16:03 -0500\r\nDKI
M-Signature: v=1; a=rsa-sha1; c=relaxed/relaxed; d=\r\n\tmessagi
ngengine.com; h=content-transfer-encoding:content-type\r\n\t:dat
e:from:message-id:mime-version:subject:to:x-sasl-enc\r\n\t:x-sas
l-enc; s=smtpout; bh=P98NTsEo015suwJ4gk71knAWLa4=; b=Jrsm+\r\n\t
pCovRIoQIRyp8Fl0L6JHOI8sbZy2obx7O28JF2iTlTWmX33Rhlq9403XRklwN3JA
\r\n\t7KSPqMTp30Qdx6yIUaADwQql0+QMuQq/QxBHdjeebmdhgVfjhqxrzTbSMw
w/ZNhL\r\n\tYwv/QM/oDHbXiLSUlB3Qrg+9wsE/0jU/EOisiU=\r\nX-Sasl-en
c: 8ZJ+4ZRE8AGPzdLRWQFivGymJb8pa4G9JGcb7k4xKn+I 1457298962\r\nRe
ceived: from [192.168.1.14] (75-137-1-34.dhcp.nwnn.ga.charter.co
m [75.137.1.34])\r\n\tby mail.messagingengine.com (Postfix) with
 ESMTPA id C0B366801CD\r\n\tfor <doug@doughellmann.com>; Sun,  6
 Mar 2016 16:16:02 -0500 (EST)\r\nFrom: Doug Hellmann <doug@doug
hellmann.com>\r\nContent-Type: text/plain; charset=us-ascii\r\nC
```

```
ontent-Transfer-Encoding: 7bit\r\nSubject: PyMOTW Example messag
e 2\r\nMessage-Id: <00ABCD46-DADA-4912-A451-D27165BC3A2F@doughel
lmann.com>\r\nDate: Sun, 6 Mar 2016 16:16:02 -0500\r\nTo: Doug H
ellmann <doug@doughellmann.com>\r\nMime-Version: 1.0 (Mac OS X M
ail 9.2 \\(3112\\))\r\nX-Mailer: Apple Mail (2.3112)\r\n\r\n'

BODY TEXT:
b'This is the second example message.\r\n'

FLAGS:
b'1 (FLAGS ())'
()
```

13.4.10   Whole Messages

As illustrated earlier, the client can ask the server for individual parts of the message separately. It is also possible to retrieve the entire message as an **RFC 822**[15]–formatted mail message and parse it with classes from the email module.

Listing 13.32: **imaplib_fetch_rfc822.py**

```
import imaplib
import email
import email.parser

import imaplib_connect


with imaplib_connect.open_connection() as c:
    c.select('INBOX', readonly=True)

    typ, msg_data = c.fetch('1', '(RFC822)')
    for response_part in msg_data:
        if isinstance(response_part, tuple):
            email_parser = email.parser.BytesFeedParser()
            email_parser.feed(response_part[1])
            msg = email_parser.close()
            for header in ['subject', 'to', 'from']:
                print('{:^8}: {}'.format(
                    header.upper(), msg[header]))
```

The parser in the email module makes it very easy to access and manipulate messages. This example prints just a few of the headers for each message.

```
$ python3 imaplib_fetch_rfc822.py

SUBJECT : PyMOTW Example message 2
```

_____

[15] https://tools.ietf.org/html/rfc822

```
    TO   : Doug Hellmann <doug@doughellmann.com>
    FROM : Doug Hellmann <doug@doughellmann.com>
```

13.4.11   Uploading Messages

To add a new message to a mailbox, construct a `Message` instance and pass it to the `append()` method, along with the timestamp for the message.

Listing 13.33: imaplib_append.py

```python
import imaplib
import time
import email.message
import imaplib_connect

new_message = email.message.Message()
new_message.set_unixfrom('pymotw')
new_message['Subject'] = 'subject goes here'
new_message['From'] = 'pymotw@example.com'
new_message['To'] = 'example@example.com'
new_message.set_payload('This is the body of the message.\n')

print(new_message)

with imaplib_connect.open_connection() as c:
    c.append('INBOX', '',
             imaplib.Time2Internaldate(time.time()),
             str(new_message).encode('utf-8'))

    # Show the headers for all messages in the mailbox.
    c.select('INBOX')
    typ, [msg_ids] = c.search(None, 'ALL')
    for num in msg_ids.split():
        typ, msg_data = c.fetch(num, '(BODY.PEEK[HEADER])')
        for response_part in msg_data:
            if isinstance(response_part, tuple):
                print('\n{}:'.format(num))
                print(response_part[1])
```

The `payload` used in this example is a simple plain text email body. `Message` also supports MIME-encoded multipart messages.

```
$ python3 imaplib_append.py

Subject: subject goes here
From: pymotw@example.com
To: example@example.com
```

This is the body of the message.

b'1':
b'Return-Path: <doug@doughellmann.com>\r\nReceived: from compute
4.internal (compute4.nyi.internal [10.202.2.44])\r\n\t by sloti2
6t01 (Cyrus 3.0.0-beta1-git-fastmail-12410) with LMTPA;\r\n\t Su
n, 06 Mar 2016 16:16:03 -0500\r\nX-Sieve: CMU Sieve 2.4\r\nX-Spa
m-known-sender: yes, fadd1cf2-dc3a-4984-a08b-02cef3cf1221="doug"
,\r\n ea349ad0-9299-47b5-b632-6ff1e394cc7d="both hellfly"\r\nX-
Spam-score: 0.0\r\nX-Spam-hits: ALL_TRUSTED -1, BAYES_00 -1.9, L
ANGUAGES unknown, BAYES_USED global,\r\n SA_VERSION 3.3.2\r\nX-
Spam-source: IP=\'127.0.0.1\', Host=\'unk\', Country=\'unk\', Fr
omHeader=\'com\',\r\n MailFrom=\'com\'\r\nX-Spam-charsets: plai
n=\'us-ascii\'\r\nX-Resolved-to: doughellmann@fastmail.fm\r\nX-D
elivered-to: doug@doughellmann.com\r\nX-Mail-from: doug@doughell
mann.com\r\nReceived: from mx5 ([10.202.2.204])\r\n by compute4
.internal (LMTPProxy); Sun, 06 Mar 2016 16:16:03 -0500\r\nReceiv
ed: from mx5.nyi.internal (localhost [127.0.0.1])\r\n\tby mx5.ny
i.internal (Postfix) with ESMTP id 47CBA280DB3\r\n\tfor <doug@do
ughellmann.com>; Sun, 6 Mar 2016 16:16:03 -0500 (EST)\r\nReceiv
ed: from mx5.nyi.internal (localhost [127.0.0.1])\r\n   by mx5.
nyi.internal (Authentication Milter) with ESMTP\r\n   id A71788
6846E.30BA4280D81;\r\n   Sun, 6 Mar 2016 16:16:03 -0500\r\nAuth
entication-Results: mx5.nyi.internal;\r\n   dkim=pass (1024-bit
 rsa key) header.d=messagingengine.com header.i=@messagingengine
.com header.b=Jrsm+pCo;\r\n   x-local-ip=pass\r\nReceived: from
 mailout.nyi.internal (gateway1.nyi.internal [10.202.2.221])\r\n
\t(using TLSv1.2 with cipher ECDHE-RSA-AES256-GCM-SHA384 (256/25
6 bits))\r\n\t(No client certificate requested)\r\n\tby mx5.nyi.
internal (Postfix) with ESMTPS id 30BA4280D81\r\n\tfor <doug@dou
ghellmann.com>; Sun, 6 Mar 2016 16:16:03 -0500 (EST)\r\nReceive
d: from compute2.internal (compute2.nyi.internal [10.202.2.42])\
r\n\tby mailout.nyi.internal (Postfix) with ESMTP id 1740420D0A\
r\n\tfor <doug@doughellmann.com>; Sun, 6 Mar 2016 16:16:03 -050
0 (EST)\r\nReceived: from frontend2 ([10.202.2.161])\r\n by com
pute2.internal (MEProxy); Sun, 06 Mar 2016 16:16:03 -0500\r\nDKI
M-Signature: v=1; a=rsa-sha1; c=relaxed/relaxed; d=\r\n\tmessagi
ngengine.com; h=content-transfer-encoding:content-type\r\n\t:dat
e:from:message-id:mime-version:subject:to:x-sasl-enc\r\n\t:x-sas
l-enc; s=smtpout; bh=P98NTsEo015suwJ4gk71knAWLa4=; b=Jrsm+\r\n\t
pCovRIoQIRyp8Fl0L6JHOI8sbZy2obx7O28JF2iTlTWmX33Rhlq9403XRklwN3JA
\r\n\t7KSPqMTp30Qdx6yIUaADwQqlO+QMuQq/QxBHdjeebmdhgVfjhqxrzTbSMw
w/ZNhL\r\n\tYwv/QM/oDHbXiLSUlB3Qrg+9wsE/0jU/EOisiU=\r\nX-Sasl-en
c: 8ZJ+4ZRE8AGPzdLRWQFivGymJb8pa4G9JGcb7k4xKn+I 1457298962\r\nRe
ceived: from [192.168.1.14] (75-137-1-34.dhcp.nwnn.ga.charter.co
m [75.137.1.34])\r\n\tby mail.messagingengine.com (Postfix) with
 ESMTPA id C0B366801CD\r\n\tfor <doug@doughellmann.com>; Sun, 6
 Mar 2016 16:16:02 -0500 (EST)\r\nFrom: Doug Hellmann <doug@doug

hellmann.com>\r\nContent-Type: text/plain; charset=us-ascii\r\nC
ontent-Transfer-Encoding: 7bit\r\nSubject: PyMOTW Example messag
e 2\r\nMessage-Id: <00ABCD46-DADA-4912-A451-D27165BC3A2F@doughel
lmann.com>\r\nDate: Sun, 6 Mar 2016 16:16:02 -0500\r\nTo: Doug H
ellmann <doug@doughellmann.com>\r\nMime-Version: 1.0 (Mac OS X M
ail 9.2 \\(3112\\))\r\nX-Mailer: Apple Mail (2.3112)\r\n\r\n'

b'2':
b'Subject: subject goes here\r\nFrom: pymotw@example.com\r\nTo:
example@example.com\r\n\r\n'

13.4.12 Moving and Copying Messages

Once a message is on the server, it can be moved or copied without downloading it by using move() or copy(), respectively. These methods operate on message ID ranges, just as fetch() does.

Listing 13.34: **imaplib_archive_read.py**

```
import imaplib
import imaplib_connect

with imaplib_connect.open_connection() as c:
    # Find the "SEEN" messages in INBOX.
    c.select('INBOX')
    typ, [response] = c.search(None, 'SEEN')
    if typ != 'OK':
        raise RuntimeError(response)
    msg_ids = ','.join(response.decode('utf-8').split(' '))

    # Create a new mailbox, "Example.Today".
    typ, create_response = c.create('Example.Today')
    print('CREATED Example.Today:', create_response)

    # Copy the messages.
    print('COPYING:', msg_ids)
    c.copy(msg_ids, 'Example.Today')

    # Look at the results.
    c.select('Example.Today')
    typ, [response] = c.search(None, 'ALL')
    print('COPIED:', response)
```

This example script creates a new mailbox under Example and copies the read messages from INBOX into it.

```
$ python3 imaplib_archive_read.py

CREATED Example.Today: [b'Completed']
```

```
COPYING: 2
COPIED: b'1'
```

Running the same script again shows the importance of checking return codes. Instead of raising an exception, the call to `create()` to make the new mailbox reports that the mailbox already exists.

```
$ python3 imaplib_archive_read.py

CREATED Example.Today: [b'[ALREADYEXISTS] Mailbox already exists
']
COPYING: 2
COPIED: b'1 2'
```

13.4.13   Deleting Messages

Although many modern mail clients use a "Trash folder" model for working with deleted messages, the messages are rarely moved into an actual folder. Instead, their flags are updated to add \Deleted. The operation for "emptying" the trash is implemented through the EXPUNGE command. The following example script finds the archived messages with "Lorem ipsum" in the subject, sets the deleted flag, and then shows that the messages are still present in the folder by querying the server again.

Listing 13.35: **imaplib_delete_messages.py**

```python
import imaplib
import imaplib_connect
from imaplib_list_parse import parse_list_response

with imaplib_connect.open_connection() as c:
    c.select('Example.Today')

    # Which IDs are in the mailbox?
    typ, [msg_ids] = c.search(None, 'ALL')
    print('Starting messages:', msg_ids)

    # Find the message(s).
    typ, [msg_ids] = c.search(
        None,
        '(SUBJECT "subject goes here")',
    )
    msg_ids = ','.join(msg_ids.decode('utf-8').split(' '))
    print('Matching messages:', msg_ids)

    # What are the current flags?
    typ, response = c.fetch(msg_ids, '(FLAGS)')
    print('Flags before:', response)

    # Change the Deleted flag.
```

```
        typ, response = c.store(msg_ids, '+FLAGS', r'(\Deleted)')

        # What are the flags now?
        typ, response = c.fetch(msg_ids, '(FLAGS)')
        print('Flags after:', response)

        # Really delete the message.
        typ, response = c.expunge()
        print('Expunged:', response)

        # Which IDs are left in the mailbox?
        typ, [msg_ids] = c.search(None, 'ALL')
        print('Remaining messages:', msg_ids)
```

Explicitly calling expunge() removes the messages, but calling close() has the same effect. The difference is the client is not notified about the deletions when close() is called.

```
$ python3 imaplib_delete_messages.py

Response code: OK
Server response: b'(\\HasChildren) "." Example'
Parsed response: ('\\HasChildren', '.', 'Example')
Server response: b'(\\HasNoChildren) "." Example.Today'
Parsed response: ('\\HasNoChildren', '.', 'Example.Today')
Server response: b'(\\HasNoChildren) "." Example.2016'
Parsed response: ('\\HasNoChildren', '.', 'Example.2016')
Server response: b'(\\HasNoChildren) "." Archive'
Parsed response: ('\\HasNoChildren', '.', 'Archive')
Server response: b'(\\HasNoChildren) "." "Deleted Messages"'
Parsed response: ('\\HasNoChildren', '.', 'Deleted Messages')
Server response: b'(\\HasNoChildren) "." INBOX'
Parsed response: ('\\HasNoChildren', '.', 'INBOX')
Starting messages: b'1 2'
Matching messages: 1,2
Flags before: [b'1 (FLAGS (\\Seen))', b'2 (FLAGS (\\Seen))']
Flags after: [b'1 (FLAGS (\\Deleted \\Seen))', b'2 (FLAGS (\\Del
eted \\Seen))']
Expunged: [b'2', b'1']
Remaining messages: b''
```

TIP

Related Reading

- Standard library documentation for imaplib.[16]
- rfc822: The rfc822 module includes an RFC 822/RFC 5322 parser.

---

[16] https://docs.python.org/3.5/library/imaplib.html

- email: The email module for parsing email messages.
- mailbox (page 852): Local mailbox parser.
- ConfigParser: Read and write configuration files.
- University of Washington IMAP Information Center[17]: Good resource for IMAP information, along with source code.
- **RFC 3501**[18]: Internet Message Access Protocol.
- **RFC 5322**[19]: Internet Message Format.
- IMAP Backup Script[20]: A script to back up email from an IMAP server.
- IMAPClient[21]: A higher-level client for talking to IMAP servers, written by Menno Smits.
- offlineimap[22]: A Python application for keeping a local set of mailboxes in sync with an IMAP server.
- Python 2 to 3 porting notes for imaplib (page 1359).

---

[17] www.washington.edu/imap/
[18] https://tools.ietf.org/html/rfc3501.html
[19] https://tools.ietf.org/html/rfc5322.html
[20] http://snipplr.com/view/7955/imap-backup-script/
[21] http://imapclient.freshfoo.com/
[22] www.offlineimap.org

Chapter 14

Application Building Blocks

The strength of Python's standard library is its size. It includes implementations of so many aspects of a program's structure that developers can concentrate on what makes their application unique, instead of having to write all of the basic pieces over and over again. This chapter covers some of the more frequently reused building blocks that solve problems common to so many applications.

`argparse` (page 888) is an interface for parsing and validating command-line arguments. It supports converting arguments from strings to integers and other types, running callbacks when an option is encountered, setting default values for options not provided by the user, and automatically producing usage instructions for a program. `getopt` (page 916) implements the low-level argument-processing model available to C programs and shell scripts. It has fewer features than other option parsing libraries, but that simplicity and familiarity make it a popular choice.

Interactive programs should use `readline` (page 922) to give the user a command prompt. This module includes tools for managing history, auto-completing parts of commands, and editing input interactively with `emacs` and `vi` key-bindings. To securely prompt the user for a password or other secret value, without echoing the value to the screen as it is typed, use `getpass` (page 935).

The `cmd` (page 938) module includes a framework for interactive, command-driven shell-style programs. It provides the main loop and handles the interaction with the user so the application just needs to implement the processing callbacks for the individual commands.

`shlex` (page 951) is a parser for shell-style syntax, with lines made up of tokens separated by whitespace. It is smart about quotes and escape sequences, so text with embedded spaces is treated as a single token. `shlex` works well as the tokenizer for domain-specific languages such as configuration files or programming languages.

It is easy to manage application configuration files with `configparser` (page 960). This module can save user preferences between program runs and read them the next time an application starts, or even serve as a simple data file format.

Applications being deployed in the real world need to give their users debugging information. Simple error messages and tracebacks are helpful, but when it is difficult to reproduce an issue, a full activity log can point directly to the chain of events that leads to a failure. The `logging` (page 980) module includes a full-featured API that manages log files, supports multiple threads, and even interfaces with remote logging daemons for centralized logging.

One of the most common patterns for programs in Unix environments is a line-by-line filter that reads data, modifies it, and writes it back out. Reading from files is simple enough, but there may not be an easier way to create a filter application than by using the `fileinput` (page 986) module. Its API is a line iterator that yields each input line, so the main body of the program is a simple `for` loop. The module handles parsing of command-line arguments for filenames to be processed, or falling back to reading directly from standard input, so tools built on `fileinput` can be run directly on a file or as part of a pipeline.

Use `atexit` (page 993) to schedule functions that should run as the interpreter is shutting down a program. Registering exit callbacks is useful for releasing resources by logging out of remote services, closing files, and other means.

The `sched` (page 998) module implements a scheduler for triggering events at set times in the future. The API does not dictate the definition of "time," so anything from true clock time to interpreter steps can be used for this purpose.

14.1   argparse: Command-Line Option and Argument Parsing

The `argparse` module includes tools for building command-line argument and option processors. It was added to Python 2.7 as a replacement for `optparse`. The implementation of `argparse` supports features that would not have been easy to add to `optparse` and that would have required backward-incompatible API changes, so a new module was brought into the library instead. `optparse` is now deprecated.

14.1.1   Setting Up a Parser

The first step when using `argparse` is to create a parser object and tell it which arguments to expect. The parser can then be used to process the command-line arguments when the program runs. The constructor for the parser class (`ArgumentParser`) takes several arguments to set up the description used in the help text for the program and other global behaviors or settings.

```
import argparse
parser = argparse.ArgumentParser(
    description='This is a PyMOTW sample program',
)
```

14.1.2   Defining Arguments

`argparse` is a complete argument-processing library. Arguments can trigger different actions, specified by the `action` argument to `add_argument()`. Supported actions include storing the argument (either singly or as part of a list), storing a constant value when the argument is encountered (including special handling for true/false values for Boolean switches), counting the number of times that an argument is seen, and calling a callback to use custom processing instructions.

The default action is to store the argument value. If a type is provided, the value is converted to that type before it is stored. If the `dest` argument is provided, the value is saved using that name when the command-line arguments are parsed.

14.1.3   Parsing a Command Line

After all of the arguments are defined, parse the command line by passing a sequence of argument strings to `parse_args()`. By default, the arguments are taken from `sys.argv[1:]`, but any list of strings can be used. The options are processed using the GNU/POSIX syntax, so option and argument values can be mixed in the sequence.

The return value from `parse_args()` is a `Namespace` containing the arguments to the command. The object holds the argument values as attributes. Thus, if the argument's `dest` is set to `"myoption"`, the value is accessible as `args.myoption`.

14.1.4   Simple Examples

Here is a simple example with three different options: a Boolean option (`-a`), a simple string option (`-b`), and an integer option (`-c`).

Listing 14.1: `argparse_short.py`

```
import argparse

parser = argparse.ArgumentParser(description='Short sample app')

parser.add_argument('-a', action="store_true", default=False)
parser.add_argument('-b', action="store", dest="b")
parser.add_argument('-c', action="store", dest="c", type=int)

print(parser.parse_args(['-a', '-bval', '-c', '3']))
```

There are a few ways to pass values to single character options. The previous example uses two different forms, `-bval` and `-c val`.

```
$ python3 argparse_short.py

Namespace(a=True, b='val', c=3)
```

The type of the value associated with `'c'` in the output is an integer, since the `ArgumentParser` was told to convert the argument before storing it.

"Long" option names, which include more than a single character in their name, are handled in the same way.

Listing 14.2: `argparse_long.py`

```
import argparse

parser = argparse.ArgumentParser(
    description='Example with long option names',
)

parser.add_argument('--noarg', action="store_true",
                    default=False)
```

```
parser.add_argument('--witharg', action="store",
                    dest="witharg")
parser.add_argument('--witharg2', action="store",
                    dest="witharg2", type=int)

print(
    parser.parse_args(
        ['--noarg', '--witharg', 'val', '--witharg2=3']
    )
)
```

The results are similar.

```
$ python3 argparse_long.py

Namespace(noarg=True, witharg='val', witharg2=3)
```

argparse is a full command-line argument parser tool. It handles both optional and required arguments.

Listing 14.3: **argparse_arguments.py**

```
import argparse

parser = argparse.ArgumentParser(
    description='Example with nonoptional arguments',
)

parser.add_argument('count', action="store", type=int)
parser.add_argument('units', action="store")

print(parser.parse_args())
```

In this example, the "count" argument is an integer and the "units" argument is saved as a string. If either is omitted from the command line, or if the value given cannot be converted to the right type, an error is reported.

```
$ python3 argparse_arguments.py 3 inches

Namespace(count=3, units='inches')

$ python3 argparse_arguments.py some inches

usage: argparse_arguments.py [-h] count units
argparse_arguments.py: error: argument count: invalid int value:
'some'

$ python3 argparse_arguments.py
```

```
usage: argparse_arguments.py [-h] count units
argparse_arguments.py: error: the following arguments are
required: count, units
```

14.1.4.1   Argument Actions

Any of six built-in actions can be triggered when an argument is encountered:

store Save the value, after optionally converting it to a different type. This is the default action taken if none is specified explicitly.

store_const Save a value defined as part of the argument specification, rather than a value that comes from the arguments being parsed. This is typically used to implement command-line flags that are not boolean values.

store_true/store_false Save the appropriate boolean value. These actions are used to implement Boolean switches.

append Save the value to a list. Multiple values are saved if the argument is repeated.

append_const Save a value defined in the argument specification to a list.

version Print the version details about the program and then exit.

The next example program demonstrates each of these action types, along with the minimum configuration needed for each to work.

Listing 14.4: **argparse_action.py**

```python
import argparse

parser = argparse.ArgumentParser()

parser.add_argument('-s', action='store',
                    dest='simple_value',
                    help='Store a simple value')

parser.add_argument('-c', action='store_const',
                    dest='constant_value',
                    const='value-to-store',
                    help='Store a constant value')

parser.add_argument('-t', action='store_true',
                    default=False,
                    dest='boolean_t',
                    help='Set a switch to true')
parser.add_argument('-f', action='store_false',
                    default=True,
                    dest='boolean_f',
                    help='Set a switch to false')
```

```
parser.add_argument('-a', action='append',
                     dest='collection',
                     default=[],
                     help='Add repeated values to a list')

parser.add_argument('-A', action='append_const',
                     dest='const_collection',
                     const='value-1-to-append',
                     default=[],
                     help='Add different values to list')
parser.add_argument('-B', action='append_const',
                     dest='const_collection',
                     const='value-2-to-append',
                     help='Add different values to list')

parser.add_argument('--version', action='version',
                     version='%(prog)s 1.0')

results = parser.parse_args()
print('simple_value     = {!r}'.format(results.simple_value))
print('constant_value   = {!r}'.format(results.constant_value))
print('boolean_t        = {!r}'.format(results.boolean_t))
print('boolean_f        = {!r}'.format(results.boolean_f))
print('collection       = {!r}'.format(results.collection))
print('const_collection = {!r}'.format(results.const_collection))
```

The -t and -f options are configured to modify different option values, with each storing either True or False. The dest values for -A and -B are the same, so their constant values are appended to the same list.

```
$ python3 argparse_action.py -h

usage: argparse_action.py [-h] [-s SIMPLE_VALUE] [-c] [-t] [-f]
                          [-a COLLECTION] [-A] [-B] [--version]

optional arguments:
  -h, --help       show this help message and exit
  -s SIMPLE_VALUE  Store a simple value
  -c               Store a constant value
  -t               Set a switch to true
  -f               Set a switch to false
  -a COLLECTION    Add repeated values to a list
  -A               Add different values to list
  -B               Add different values to list
  --version        show program's version number and exit

$ python3 argparse_action.py -s value

simple_value     = 'value'
```

```
constant_value   = None
boolean_t        = False
boolean_f        = True
collection       = []
const_collection = []

$ python3 argparse_action.py -c

simple_value     = None
constant_value   = 'value-to-store'
boolean_t        = False
boolean_f        = True
collection       = []
const_collection = []

$ python3 argparse_action.py -t

simple_value     = None
constant_value   = None
boolean_t        = True
boolean_f        = True
collection       = []
const_collection = []

$ python3 argparse_action.py -f

simple_value     = None
constant_value   = None
boolean_t        = False
boolean_f        = False
collection       = []
const_collection = []

$ python3 argparse_action.py -a one -a two -a three

simple_value     = None
constant_value   = None
boolean_t        = False
boolean_f        = True
collection       = ['one', 'two', 'three']
const_collection = []

$ python3 argparse_action.py -B -A

simple_value     = None
constant_value   = None
boolean_t        = False
boolean_f        = True
collection       = []
```

```
const_collection = ['value-2-to-append', 'value-1-to-append']

$ python3 argparse_action.py --version

argparse_action.py 1.0
```

14.1.4.2   Option Prefixes

The default syntax for options is based on the Unix convention of signifying command-line switches using a dash prefix (-). argparse supports other prefixes, so a program can conform to the local platform default (i.e., use / on Windows) or follow a different convention.

Listing 14.5: **argparse_prefix_chars.py**

```python
import argparse

parser = argparse.ArgumentParser(
    description='Change the option prefix characters',
    prefix_chars='-+/',
)

parser.add_argument('-a', action="store_false",
                    default=None,
                    help='Turn A off',
                    )
parser.add_argument('+a', action="store_true",
                    default=None,
                    help='Turn A on',
                    )
parser.add_argument('//noarg', '++noarg',
                    action="store_true",
                    default=False)

print(parser.parse_args())
```

Set the prefix_chars parameter for the ArgumentParser to a string containing all of the characters that should be allowed to signify options. Although prefix_chars establishes the allowed switch characters, the individual argument definitions specify the syntax for a given switch. This apparent redundancy gives explicit control over whether options using different prefixes are aliases (such as might be the case for platform-independent command-line syntax) or alternatives (e.g., using + to indicate turning a switch on and - to turn it off). In the previous example, +a and -a are separate arguments, and //noarg can also be given as ++noarg, but not --noarg.

```
$ python3 argparse_prefix_chars.py -h

usage: argparse_prefix_chars.py [-h] [-a] [+a] [//noarg]
```

```
Change the option prefix characters

optional arguments:
  -h, --help            show this help message and exit
  -a                    Turn A off
  +a                    Turn A on
  //noarg, ++noarg

$ python3 argparse_prefix_chars.py +a

Namespace(a=True, noarg=False)

$ python3 argparse_prefix_chars.py -a

Namespace(a=False, noarg=False)

$ python3 argparse_prefix_chars.py //noarg

Namespace(a=None, noarg=True)

$ python3 argparse_prefix_chars.py ++noarg

Namespace(a=None, noarg=True)

$ python3 argparse_prefix_chars.py --noarg

usage: argparse_prefix_chars.py [-h] [-a] [+a] [//noarg]
argparse_prefix_chars.py: error: unrecognized arguments: --noarg
```

14.1.4.3 Sources of Arguments

In the examples so far, the list of arguments given to the parser has either come from a list passed in explicitly or been taken implicitly from sys.argv. Passing the list explicitly is useful when using argparse to process command-line-like instructions that do not come from the command line (such as in a configuration file).

Listing 14.6: **argparse_with_shlex.py**

```
import argparse
from configparser import ConfigParser
import shlex

parser = argparse.ArgumentParser(description='Short sample app')

parser.add_argument('-a', action="store_true", default=False)
parser.add_argument('-b', action="store", dest="b")
parser.add_argument('-c', action="store", dest="c", type=int)

config = ConfigParser()
config.read('argparse_with_shlex.ini')
```

```
config_value = config.get('cli', 'options')
print('Config  :', config_value)

argument_list = shlex.split(config_value)
print('Arg List:', argument_list)

print('Results :', parser.parse_args(argument_list))
```

This example uses `configparser` (page 960) to read a configuration file.

```
[cli]
options = -a -b 2
```

`shlex` (page 951) makes it easy to split the string stored in the configuration file.

```
$ python3 argparse_with_shlex.py

Config  : -a -b 2
Arg List: ['-a', '-b', '2']
Results : Namespace(a=True, b='2', c=None)
```

An alternative to processing the configuration file in application code is to tell `argparse` how to recognize an argument that specifies an input file containing a set of arguments that should be processed using `fromfile_prefix_chars`.

Listing 14.7: **argparse_fromfile_prefix_chars.py**

```
import argparse
import shlex

parser = argparse.ArgumentParser(description='Short sample app',
                                 fromfile_prefix_chars='@',
                                 )

parser.add_argument('-a', action="store_true", default=False)
parser.add_argument('-b', action="store", dest="b")
parser.add_argument('-c', action="store", dest="c", type=int)

print(parser.parse_args(['@argparse_fromfile_prefix_chars.txt']))
```

This example stops when it finds an argument prefixed with @, then reads the named file to find more arguments. The file should contain one argument per line, as in the following listing.

Listing 14.8: **argparse_fromfile_prefix_chars.txt**

```
-a
-b
2
```

The output produced when processing `argparse_from_prefix_chars.txt` follows.

```
$ python3 argparse_fromfile_prefix_chars.py

Namespace(a=True, b='2', c=None)
```

14.1.5   Help Output

14.1.5.1   Automatically Generated Help

argparse will automatically add options to generate help, if configured to do so. The add_help argument to ArgumentParser controls the help-related options.

Listing 14.9: **argparse_with_help.py**

```python
import argparse

parser = argparse.ArgumentParser(add_help=True)

parser.add_argument('-a', action="store_true", default=False)
parser.add_argument('-b', action="store", dest="b")
parser.add_argument('-c', action="store", dest="c", type=int)

print(parser.parse_args())
```

The help options (-h and --help) are added by default, but can be disabled by setting add_help to false.

Listing 14.10: **argparse_without_help.py**

```python
import argparse

parser = argparse.ArgumentParser(add_help=False)

parser.add_argument('-a', action="store_true", default=False)
parser.add_argument('-b', action="store", dest="b")
parser.add_argument('-c', action="store", dest="c", type=int)

print(parser.parse_args())
```

Although -h and --help are de facto standard option names for requesting help, some applications or uses of argparse either do not need to provide help or need to use those option names for other purposes.

```
$ python3 argparse_with_help.py -h

usage: argparse_with_help.py [-h] [-a] [-b B] [-c C]

optional arguments:
  -h, --help  show this help message and exit
```

```
 -a
 -b B
 -c C

$ python3 argparse_without_help.py -h

usage: argparse_without_help.py [-a] [-b B] [-c C]
argparse_without_help.py: error: unrecognized arguments: -h
```

14.1.5.2   Customizing Help

For applications that need to handle the help output directly, some of the utility methods of ArgumentParser will be useful in creating custom actions (page 913) to print help with extra information.

Listing 14.11: **argparse_custom_help.py**

```python
import argparse

parser = argparse.ArgumentParser(add_help=True)

parser.add_argument('-a', action="store_true", default=False)
parser.add_argument('-b', action="store", dest="b")
parser.add_argument('-c', action="store", dest="c", type=int)

print('print_usage output:')
parser.print_usage()
print()

print('print_help output:')
parser.print_help()
```

print_usage() prints the short usage message for an argument parser, and print_help() prints the full help output.

```
$ python3 argparse_custom_help.py

print_usage output:
usage: argparse_custom_help.py [-h] [-a] [-b B] [-c C]

print_help output:
usage: argparse_custom_help.py [-h] [-a] [-b B] [-c C]

optional arguments:
  -h, --help  show this help message and exit
  -a
  -b B
  -c C
```

The ArgumentParser uses a formatter class to control the appearance of the help output. To change the class, pass formatter_class when instantiating the ArgumentParser.

For example, the RawDescriptionHelpFormatter bypasses the line wrapping provided by the default formatter.

Listing 14.12: **argparse_raw_description_help_formatter.py**

```
import argparse

parser = argparse.ArgumentParser(
    add_help=True,
    formatter_class=argparse.RawDescriptionHelpFormatter,
    description="""
description
    not
        wrapped""",
    epilog="""
epilog
  not
      wrapped""",
)

parser.add_argument(
    '-a', action="store_true",
    help="""argument
help is
wrapped
""",
)

parser.print_help()
```

All text in the description and epilog of the command will be left unchanged.

```
$ python3 argparse_raw_description_help_formatter.py

usage: argparse_raw_description_help_formatter.py [-h] [-a]

    description
        not
            wrapped

optional arguments:
  -h, --help  show this help message and exit
  -a          argument help is wrapped

    epilog
      not
          wrapped
```

The `RawTextHelpFormatter` treats all help text as if it were preformatted.

Listing 14.13: `argparse_raw_text_help_formatter.py`

```python
import argparse

parser = argparse.ArgumentParser(
    add_help=True,
    formatter_class=argparse.RawTextHelpFormatter,
    description="""
description
    not
        wrapped""",
    epilog="""
epilog
  not
      wrapped""",
)

parser.add_argument(
    '-a', action="store_true",
    help="""argument
help is not
wrapped
""",
)

parser.print_help()
```

The help text for the -a argument is no longer wrapped neatly.

```
$ python3 argparse_raw_text_help_formatter.py

usage: argparse_raw_text_help_formatter.py [-h] [-a]

    description
        not
            wrapped

optional arguments:
  -h, --help  show this help message and exit
  -a          argument
                help is not
                wrapped


    epilog
      not
          wrapped
```

Raw formatters may be useful for applications with examples in the description or epilog, where changing the format of the text may make the examples invalid.

The MetavarTypeHelpFormatter prints the name of the type for each option, instead of the destination variable, which can be useful for applications with lots of options of different types.

Listing 14.14: `argparse_metavar_type_help_formatter.py`

```
import argparse

parser = argparse.ArgumentParser(
    add_help=True,
    formatter_class=argparse.MetavarTypeHelpFormatter,
)

parser.add_argument('-i', type=int, dest='notshown1')
parser.add_argument('-f', type=float, dest='notshown2')

parser.print_help()
```

Rather than display the value of dest, the name of the type associated with the option is printed.

```
$ python3 argparse_metavar_type_help_formatter.py

usage: argparse_metavar_type_help_formatter.py [-h] [-i int] [-f
  float]

optional arguments:
  -h, --help  show this help message and exit
  -i int
  -f float
```

14.1.6   Parser Organization

argparse includes several features for organizing argument parsers, to make implementation easier or to improve the usability of the help output.

14.1.6.1   Sharing Parser Rules

Programmers commonly need to implement a suite of command-line tools that all take a set of arguments, and then perform some sort of specialized action. For example, if the programs all need to authenticate the user before taking any real action, they would all need to support --user and --password options. Rather than add the options explicitly to every ArgumentParser, it is possible to define a parent parser with the shared options, and then have the parsers for the individual programs inherit from its options.

The first step is to set up the parser with the shared argument definitions. Since each subsequent user of the parent parser will try to add the same help options, causing an exception, automatic help generation is turned off in the base parser.

Listing 14.15: **argparse_parent_base.py**

```
import argparse

parser = argparse.ArgumentParser(add_help=False)

parser.add_argument('--user', action="store")
parser.add_argument('--password', action="store")
```

Next, create another parser with parents set.

Listing 14.16: **argparse_uses_parent.py**

```
import argparse
import argparse_parent_base

parser = argparse.ArgumentParser(
    parents=[argparse_parent_base.parser],
)

parser.add_argument('--local-arg',
                    action="store_true",
                    default=False)

print(parser.parse_args())
```

The resulting program takes all three options.

```
$ python3 argparse_uses_parent.py -h

usage: argparse_uses_parent.py [-h] [--user USER]
                               [--password PASSWORD]
                               [--local-arg]

optional arguments:
  -h, --help           show this help message and exit
  --user USER
  --password PASSWORD
  --local-arg
```

14.1.6.2 Conflicting Options

The previous example pointed out that adding two argument handlers to a parser using the same argument name causes an exception. To change the conflict resolution behavior, pass a `conflict_handler`. The two built-in handlers are `error` (the default) and `resolve`, which picks a handler based on the order in which the handlers were added.

Listing 14.17: `argparse_conflict_handler_resolve.py`

```
import argparse

parser = argparse.ArgumentParser(conflict_handler='resolve')

parser.add_argument('-a', action="store")
parser.add_argument('-b', action="store", help='Short alone')
parser.add_argument('--long-b', '-b',
                    action="store",
                    help='Long and short together')

print(parser.parse_args(['-h']))
```

In this example, the last handler with a given argument name is used. As a result, the stand-alone option `-b` is masked by the alias for `--long-b`.

```
$ python3 argparse_conflict_handler_resolve.py

usage: argparse_conflict_handler_resolve.py [-h] [-a A]
[--long-b LONG_B]

optional arguments:
  -h, --help              show this help message and exit
  -a A
  --long-b LONG_B, -b LONG_B
                          Long and short together
```

Switching the order of the calls to `add_argument()` unmasks the stand-alone option.

Listing 14.18: `argparse_conflict_handler_resolve2.py`

```
import argparse

parser = argparse.ArgumentParser(conflict_handler='resolve')

parser.add_argument('-a', action="store")
parser.add_argument('--long-b', '-b',
                    action="store",
                    help='Long and short together')
parser.add_argument('-b', action="store", help='Short alone')

print(parser.parse_args(['-h']))
```

Now both options can be used together.

```
$ python3 argparse_conflict_handler_resolve2.py

usage: argparse_conflict_handler_resolve2.py [-h] [-a A]
                                             [--long-b LONG_B]
                                             [-b B]


optional arguments:
  -h, --help         show this help message and exit
  -a A
  --long-b LONG_B  Long and short together
  -b B               Short alone
```

14.1.6.3   Argument Groups

argparse combines the argument definitions into "groups." By default, it uses two groups: one for options and another for required position-based arguments.

Listing 14.19: `argparse_default_grouping.py`

```python
import argparse

parser = argparse.ArgumentParser(description='Short sample app')

parser.add_argument('--optional', action="store_true",
                    default=False)
parser.add_argument('positional', action="store")

print(parser.parse_args())
```

The grouping is reflected in the separate "positional arguments" and "optional arguments" sections of the help output.

```
$ python3 argparse_default_grouping.py -h

usage: argparse_default_grouping.py [-h] [--optional] positional

Short sample app

positional arguments:
  positional

optional arguments:
  -h, --help  show this help message and exit
  --optional
```

The grouping can be adjusted to organize the help more logically, with related options or values being documented together. For instance, the shared-option example that appeared earlier could be written using custom grouping so that the authentication options are shown together in the help.

Create the "authentication" group with add_argument_group() and then add each of the authentication-related options to the group, instead of the base parser.

Listing 14.20: **argparse_parent_with_group.py**

```
import argparse

parser = argparse.ArgumentParser(add_help=False)

group = parser.add_argument_group('authentication')

group.add_argument('--user', action="store")
group.add_argument('--password', action="store")
```

The program using the group-based parent lists it in the parents value, just as before.

Listing 14.21: **argparse_uses_parent_with_group.py**

```
import argparse
import argparse_parent_with_group

parser = argparse.ArgumentParser(
    parents=[argparse_parent_with_group.parser],
)

parser.add_argument('--local-arg',
                    action="store_true",
                    default=False)

print(parser.parse_args())
```

The help output now shows the authentication options together.

```
$ python3 argparse_uses_parent_with_group.py -h

usage: argparse_uses_parent_with_group.py [-h] [--user USER]
                                          [--password PASSWORD]
                                          [--local-arg]

optional arguments:
  -h, --help            show this help message and exit
  --local-arg

authentication:
  --user USER
  --password PASSWORD
```

14.1.6.4 Mutually Exclusive Options

Defining mutually exclusive options is a special case of the option grouping feature. It relies on add_mutually_exclusive_group() instead of add_argument_group().

Listing 14.22: `argparse_mutually_exclusive.py`

```
import argparse

parser = argparse.ArgumentParser()

group = parser.add_mutually_exclusive_group()
group.add_argument('-a', action='store_true')
group.add_argument('-b', action='store_true')

print(parser.parse_args())
```

argparse enforces the mutual exclusivity, so that only one of the options from the group can be given.

```
$ python3 argparse_mutually_exclusive.py -h

usage: argparse_mutually_exclusive.py [-h] [-a | -b]

optional arguments:
  -h, --help  show this help message and exit
  -a
  -b

$ python3 argparse_mutually_exclusive.py -a

Namespace(a=True, b=False)

$ python3 argparse_mutually_exclusive.py -b

Namespace(a=False, b=True)

$ python3 argparse_mutually_exclusive.py -a -b

usage: argparse_mutually_exclusive.py [-h] [-a | -b]
argparse_mutually_exclusive.py: error: argument -b: not allowed
with argument -a
```

14.1.6.5 Nesting Parsers

The parent parser approach described earlier is one way to share options between related commands. An alternative approach is to first combine the commands into a single program, and then use sub-parsers to handle each portion of the command line. The result works

in the same way as svn, hg, and other programs with multiple command-line actions, or
subcommands, do.

A program to work with directories on the file system might define commands for creating, deleting, and listing the contents of a directory.

Listing 14.23: `argparse_subparsers.py`

```python
import argparse

parser = argparse.ArgumentParser()

subparsers = parser.add_subparsers(help='commands')

# A list command
list_parser = subparsers.add_parser(
    'list', help='List contents')
list_parser.add_argument(
    'dirname', action='store',
    help='Directory to list')

# A create command
create_parser = subparsers.add_parser(
    'create', help='Create a directory')
create_parser.add_argument(
    'dirname', action='store',
    help='New directory to create')
create_parser.add_argument(
    '--read-only', default=False, action='store_true',
    help='Set permissions to prevent writing to the directory',
)

# A delete command
delete_parser = subparsers.add_parser(
    'delete', help='Remove a directory')
delete_parser.add_argument(
    'dirname', action='store', help='The directory to remove')
delete_parser.add_argument(
    '--recursive', '-r', default=False, action='store_true',
    help='Remove the contents of the directory, too',
)

print(parser.parse_args())
```

The help output shows the named sub-parsers as "commands" that can be specified on
the command line as positional arguments.

```
$ python3 argparse_subparsers.py -h

usage: argparse_subparsers.py [-h] {list,create,delete} ...
```

```
positional arguments:
  {list,create,delete}  commands
    list                List contents
    create              Create a directory
    delete              Remove a directory

optional arguments:
  -h, --help            show this help message and exit
```

Each sub-parser also has its own help, which describes the arguments and options for that command.

```
$ python3 argparse_subparsers.py create -h

usage: argparse_subparsers.py create [-h] [--read-only] dirname

positional arguments:
  dirname     New directory to create

optional arguments:
  -h, --help  show this help message and exit
  --read-only  Set permissions to prevent writing to the directory
```

When the arguments are parsed, the Namespace object returned by parse_args() includes only the values related to the command specified.

```
$ python3 argparse_subparsers.py delete -r foo

Namespace(dirname='foo', recursive=True)
```

14.1.7   Advanced Argument Processing

The examples presented so far have shown simple boolean flags, options with string or numerical arguments, and positional arguments. argparse also supports sophisticated argument specification of variable-length argument lists, enumerations, and constant values.

14.1.7.1   Variable Argument Lists

A single argument definition can be configured to account for multiple arguments on the command line being parsed. Set nargs to one of the flag values from Table 14.1, based on the number of required or expected arguments.

Listing 14.24: **argparse_nargs.py**

```
import argparse

parser = argparse.ArgumentParser()
```

Table 14.1: Flags for Variable Argument Definitions in argparse

Value	Meaning
N	The absolute number of arguments (e.g., 3)
?	0 or 1 arguments
*	0 or all arguments
+	All, and at least 1, argument

```
parser.add_argument('--three', nargs=3)
parser.add_argument('--optional', nargs='?')
parser.add_argument('--all', nargs='*', dest='all')
parser.add_argument('--one-or-more', nargs='+')

print(parser.parse_args())
```

The parser enforces the argument count instructions and generates an accurate syntax diagram as part of the command help text.

```
$ python3 argparse_nargs.py -h

usage: argparse_nargs.py [-h] [--three THREE THREE THREE]
                         [--optional [OPTIONAL]]
                         [--all [ALL [ALL ...]]]
                         [--one-or-more ONE_OR_MORE [ONE_OR_MORE ...]]

optional arguments:
  -h, --help            show this help message and exit
  --three THREE THREE THREE
  --optional [OPTIONAL]
  --all [ALL [ALL ...]]
  --one-or-more ONE_OR_MORE [ONE_OR_MORE ...]

$ python3 argparse_nargs.py

Namespace(all=None, one_or_more=None, optional=None, three=None)

$ python3 argparse_nargs.py --three

usage: argparse_nargs.py [-h] [--three THREE THREE THREE]
                         [--optional [OPTIONAL]]
                         [--all [ALL [ALL ...]]]
                         [--one-or-more ONE_OR_MORE [ONE_OR_MORE ...]]
argparse_nargs.py: error: argument --three: expected 3
argument(s)

$ python3 argparse_nargs.py --three a b c

Namespace(all=None, one_or_more=None, optional=None,
```

```
three=['a', 'b', 'c'])

$ python3 argparse_nargs.py --optional

Namespace(all=None, one_or_more=None, optional=None, three=None)

$ python3 argparse_nargs.py --optional with_value

Namespace(all=None, one_or_more=None, optional='with_value',
three=None)

$ python3 argparse_nargs.py --all with multiple values

Namespace(all=['with', 'multiple', 'values'], one_or_more=None,
optional=None, three=None)

$ python3 argparse_nargs.py --one-or-more with_value

Namespace(all=None, one_or_more=['with_value'], optional=None,
three=None)

$ python3 argparse_nargs.py --one-or-more with multiple values

Namespace(all=None, one_or_more=['with', 'multiple', 'values'],
optional=None, three=None)

$ python3 argparse_nargs.py --one-or-more

usage: argparse_nargs.py [-h] [--three THREE THREE THREE]
                         [--optional [OPTIONAL]]
                         [--all [ALL [ALL ...]]]
                         [--one-or-more ONE_OR_MORE [ONE_OR_MORE ...]]
argparse_nargs.py: error: argument --one-or-more: expected
at least one argument
```

14.1.7.2   Argument Types

argparse treats all argument values as strings, unless it is told to convert the string to another type. The type parameter to add_argument() defines a converter function, which the ArgumentParser uses to transform the argument value from a string to some other type.

Listing 14.25: argparse_type.py

```
import argparse

parser = argparse.ArgumentParser()

parser.add_argument('-i', type=int)
```

```
parser.add_argument('-f', type=float)
parser.add_argument('--file', type=open)

try:
    print(parser.parse_args())
except IOError as msg:
    parser.error(str(msg))
```

Any callable that takes a single string argument can be passed as type, including built-in types such as int and float or even open().

```
$ python3 argparse_type.py -i 1

Namespace(f=None, file=None, i=1)

$ python3 argparse_type.py -f 3.14

Namespace(f=3.14, file=None, i=None)

$ python3 argparse_type.py --file argparse_type.py

Namespace(f=None, file=<_io.TextIOWrapper
name='argparse_type.py' mode='r' encoding='UTF-8'>, i=None)
```

If the type conversion fails, argparse raises an exception. TypeError and ValueError exceptions are trapped automatically and converted to a simple error message for the user. Other exceptions, such as the IOError in the next example that is generated when the input file does not exist, must be handled by the caller.

```
$ python3 argparse_type.py -i a

usage: argparse_type.py [-h] [-i I] [-f F] [--file FILE]
argparse_type.py: error: argument -i: invalid int value: 'a'

$ python3 argparse_type.py -f 3.14.15

usage: argparse_type.py [-h] [-i I] [-f F] [--file FILE]
argparse_type.py: error: argument -f: invalid float value:
'3.14.15'

$ python3 argparse_type.py --file does_not_exist.txt

usage: argparse_type.py [-h] [-i I] [-f F] [--file FILE]
argparse_type.py: error: [Errno 2] No such file or directory:
'does_not_exist.txt'
```

To limit the values accepted as an input argument to a predefined set, use the choices parameter.

Listing 14.26: **argparse_choices.py**

```
import argparse

parser = argparse.ArgumentParser()

parser.add_argument(
    '--mode',
    choices=('read-only', 'read-write'),
)

print(parser.parse_args())
```

If the argument to `--mode` is not one of the allowed values, an error is generated and processing stops.

```
$ python3 argparse_choices.py -h

usage: argparse_choices.py [-h] [--mode {read-only,read-write}]

optional arguments:
  -h, --help            show this help message and exit
  --mode {read-only,read-write}

$ python3 argparse_choices.py --mode read-only

Namespace(mode='read-only')

$ python3 argparse_choices.py --mode invalid

usage: argparse_choices.py [-h] [--mode {read-only,read-write}]
argparse_choices.py: error: argument --mode: invalid choice:
'invalid' (choose from 'read-only', 'read-write')
```

14.1.7.3 File Arguments

Although `file` objects can be instantiated with a single string argument, that does not include the access mode argument. `FileType` provides a more flexible way of specifying that an argument should be a file, including the mode and buffer size.

Listing 14.27: **argparse_FileType.py**

```
import argparse

parser = argparse.ArgumentParser()

parser.add_argument('-i', metavar='in-file',
```

```
                              type=argparse.FileType('rt'))
    parser.add_argument('-o', metavar='out-file',
                              type=argparse.FileType('wt'))

    try:
        results = parser.parse_args()
        print('Input file:', results.i)
        print('Output file:', results.o)
    except IOError as msg:
        parser.error(str(msg))
```

The value associated with the argument name is the open file handle. The application is responsible for closing the file when it is no longer being used.

```
$ python3 argparse_FileType.py -h

usage: argparse_FileType.py [-h] [-i in-file] [-o out-file]

optional arguments:
  -h, --help    show this help message and exit
  -i in-file
  -o out-file

$ python3 argparse_FileType.py -i argparse_FileType.py -o tmp_\
file.txt

Input file: <_io.TextIOWrapper name='argparse_FileType.py'
mode='rt' encoding='UTF-8'>
Output file: <_io.TextIOWrapper name='tmp_file.txt' mode='wt'
encoding='UTF-8'>

$ python3 argparse_FileType.py -i no_such_file.txt

usage: argparse_FileType.py [-h] [-i in-file] [-o out-file]
argparse_FileType.py: error: argument -i: can't open
'no_such_file.txt': [Errno 2] No such file or directory:
'no_such_file.txt'
```

14.1.7.4 Custom Actions

In addition to the built-in actions described earlier, custom actions can be defined by providing an object that implements the Action API. The object passed to add_argument() as the action should take parameters describing the argument being defined (all of the same arguments that are given to add_argument()) and return a callable object that takes as parameters the parser processing the arguments, the namespace holding the parsing operation results, the value of the argument being acted on, and the option_string that triggered the action.

A class `Action` is provided as a convenient starting point for defining new actions. The constructor handles the argument definitions, so only __call__() needs to be overridden in the subclass.

Listing 14.28: **argparse_custom_action.py**

```python
import argparse


class CustomAction(argparse.Action):
    def __init__(self,
                 option_strings,
                 dest,
                 nargs=None,
                 const=None,
                 default=None,
                 type=None,
                 choices=None,
                 required=False,
                 help=None,
                 metavar=None):
        argparse.Action.__init__(self,
                                 option_strings=option_strings,
                                 dest=dest,
                                 nargs=nargs,
                                 const=const,
                                 default=default,
                                 type=type,
                                 choices=choices,
                                 required=required,
                                 help=help,
                                 metavar=metavar,
                                 )
        print('Initializing CustomAction')
        for name, value in sorted(locals().items()):
            if name == 'self' or value is None:
                continue
            print('  {} = {!r}'.format(name, value))
        print()
        return

    def __call__(self, parser, namespace, values,
                 option_string=None):
        print('Processing CustomAction for {}'.format(self.dest))
        print('  parser = {}'.format(id(parser)))
        print('  values = {!r}'.format(values))
        print('  option_string = {!r}'.format(option_string))

        # Do some arbitrary processing of the input values.
        if isinstance(values, list):
```

```
                        values = [v.upper() for v in values]
                    else:
                        values = values.upper()
                    # Save the results in the namespace using the destination
                    # variable given to our constructor.
                    setattr(namespace, self.dest, values)
                    print()

    parser = argparse.ArgumentParser()

    parser.add_argument('-a', action=CustomAction)
    parser.add_argument('-m', nargs='*', action=CustomAction)

    results = parser.parse_args(['-a', 'value',
                                 '-m', 'multivalue',
                                 'second'])
    print(results)
```

The type of values depends on the value of nargs. If the argument allows multiple values, values will be a list even if it contains only one item.

The value of option_string also depends on the original argument specification. For positional required arguments, option_string is always None.

```
$ python3 argparse_custom_action.py

Initializing CustomAction
  dest = 'a'
  option_strings = ['-a']
  required = False

Initializing CustomAction
  dest = 'm'
  nargs = '*'
  option_strings = ['-m']
  required = False

Processing CustomAction for a
  parser = 4315836992
  values = 'value'
  option_string = '-a'

Processing CustomAction for m
  parser = 4315836992
  values = ['multivalue', 'second']
  option_string = '-m'

Namespace(a='VALUE', m=['MULTIVALUE', 'SECOND'])
```

TIP

Related Reading

- Standard library documentation for `argparse`.[1]
- `configparser` (page 960): Read and write configuration files.
- `shlex` (page 951): Parse shell-like syntaxes.
- Python 2 to 3 porting notes for `argparse` (page 1356).

14.2   getopt: Command-Line Option Parsing

The `getopt` module is the original command-line option parser that supports the conventions established by the Unix function `getopt`. It parses an argument sequence, such as `sys.argv`, and returns a sequence of tuples containing (option, argument) pairs and a sequence of non-option arguments.

Supported option syntax includes short- and long-form options.

```
-a
-bval
-b val
--noarg
--witharg=val
--witharg val
```

NOTE

getopt is not deprecated, but `argparse` (page 888) is more actively maintained and should be used for new development.

14.2.1   Function Arguments

The `getopt()` function takes three arguments:

- The first parameter is the sequence of arguments to be parsed. This information usually comes from `sys.argv[1:]` (ignoring the program name in `sys.arg[0]`).

- The second argument is the option definition string for single-character options. If one of the options requires an argument, its letter is followed by a colon.

- The third argument, if used, is a sequence of the long-style option names. Long-style options can consist of more than one character, such as `--noarg` or `--witharg`. The

---

[1] https://docs.python.org/3.5/library/argparse.html

option names in the sequence should not include the -- prefix. If any long-form option requires an argument, its name should have a suffix of =.

Short- and long-form options can be combined in a single call.

14.2.2 Short-Form Options

The next example program accepts three options. The -a option is a simple flag, while -b and -c require an argument. The option definition string is "ab:c:".

Listing 14.29: getopt_short.py

```
import getopt

opts, args = getopt.getopt(['-a', '-bval', '-c', 'val'], 'ab:c:')

for opt in opts:
    print(opt)
```

This program passes a list of simulated option values to getopt() to show how they are processed.

```
$ python3 getopt_short.py

('-a', '')
('-b', 'val')
('-c', 'val')
```

14.2.3 Long-Form Options

For a program that takes two options, --noarg and --witharg, the long-argument sequence should be ['noarg','witharg='].

Listing 14.30: getopt_long.py

```
import getopt

opts, args = getopt.getopt(
    ['--noarg',
     '--witharg', 'val',
     '--witharg2=another'],
    '',
    ['noarg', 'witharg=', 'witharg2='],
)
for opt in opts:
    print(opt)
```

Since this sample program does not take any short-form options, the second argument to getopt() is an empty string.

```
$ python3 getopt_long.py

('--noarg', '')
('--witharg', 'val')
('--witharg2', 'another')
```

14.2.4   A Complete Example

The example in the following listing is a more complete program that takes five options:
-o, -v, --output, --verbose, and --version. The -o, --output, and --version options all
require an argument.

Listing 14.31: **getopt_example.py**

```python
import getopt
import sys

version = '1.0'
verbose = False
output_filename = 'default.out'

print('ARGV      :', sys.argv[1:])

try:
    options, remainder = getopt.getopt(
        sys.argv[1:],
        'o:v',
        ['output=',
         'verbose',
         'version=',
         ])
except getopt.GetoptError as err:
    print('ERROR:', err)
    sys.exit(1)

print('OPTIONS   :', options)

for opt, arg in options:
    if opt in ('-o', '--output'):
        output_filename = arg
    elif opt in ('-v', '--verbose'):
        verbose = True
    elif opt == '--version':
        version = arg

print('VERSION   :', version)
print('VERBOSE   :', verbose)
print('OUTPUT    :', output_filename)
print('REMAINING :', remainder)
```

This program can be called in a variety of ways. When it is called without any arguments, the default settings are used.

```
$ python3 getopt_example.py

ARGV      : []
OPTIONS   : []
VERSION   : 1.0
VERBOSE   : False
OUTPUT    : default.out
REMAINING : []
```

A single-letter option can be a separated from its argument by whitespace.

```
$ python3 getopt_example.py -o foo

ARGV      : ['-o', 'foo']
OPTIONS   : [('-o', 'foo')]
VERSION   : 1.0
VERBOSE   : False
OUTPUT    : foo
REMAINING : []
```

Alternatively, the option and the value can be combined into a single argument.

```
$ python3 getopt_example.py -ofoo

ARGV      : ['-ofoo']
OPTIONS   : [('-o', 'foo')]
VERSION   : 1.0
VERBOSE   : False
OUTPUT    : foo
REMAINING : []
```

A long-form option can similarly be separate from the value.

```
$ python3 getopt_example.py --output foo

ARGV      : ['--output', 'foo']
OPTIONS   : [('--output', 'foo')]
VERSION   : 1.0
VERBOSE   : False
OUTPUT    : foo
REMAINING : []
```

When a long-form option is combined with its value, the option name and the value should be separated by a single =.

```
$ python3 getopt_example.py --output=foo

ARGV      : ['--output=foo']
OPTIONS   : [('--output', 'foo')]
VERSION   : 1.0
VERBOSE   : False
OUTPUT    : foo
REMAINING : []
```

14.2.5   Abbreviating Long-Form Options

The long-form option does not have to be spelled out entirely on the command line, as long as a unique prefix is provided.

```
$ python3 getopt_example.py --o foo

ARGV      : ['--o', 'foo']
OPTIONS   : [('--output', 'foo')]
VERSION   : 1.0
VERBOSE   : False
OUTPUT    : foo
REMAINING : []
```

If a unique prefix is not provided, an exception is raised.

```
$ python3 getopt_example.py --ver 2.0

ARGV      : ['--ver', '2.0']
ERROR: option --ver not a unique prefix
```

14.2.6   GNU-Style Option Parsing

Normally, option processing stops as soon as the first non-option argument is encountered.

```
$ python3 getopt_example.py -v not_an_option --output foo

ARGV      : ['-v', 'not_an_option', '--output', 'foo']
OPTIONS   : [('-v', '')]
VERSION   : 1.0
VERBOSE   : True
OUTPUT    : default.out
REMAINING : ['not_an_option', '--output', 'foo']
```

To mix option and non-option arguments on the command line in any order, use gnu_getopt() instead.

Listing 14.32: getopt_gnu.py

```python
import getopt
import sys

version = '1.0'
verbose = False
output_filename = 'default.out'

print('ARGV      :', sys.argv[1:])

try:
    options, remainder = getopt.gnu_getopt(
        sys.argv[1:],
        'o:v',
        ['output=',
         'verbose',
         'version=',
         ])
except getopt.GetoptError as err:
    print('ERROR:', err)
    sys.exit(1)

print('OPTIONS   :', options)

for opt, arg in options:
    if opt in ('-o', '--output'):
        output_filename = arg
    elif opt in ('-v', '--verbose'):
        verbose = True
    elif opt == '--version':
        version = arg

print('VERSION   :', version)
print('VERBOSE   :', verbose)
print('OUTPUT    :', output_filename)
print('REMAINING :', remainder)
```

After changing the call in the previous example, the difference between the two approaches becomes clear.

```
$ python3 getopt_gnu.py -v not_an_option --output foo

ARGV       : ['-v', 'not_an_option', '--output', 'foo']
OPTIONS    : [('-v', ''), ('--output', 'foo')]
VERSION    : 1.0
VERBOSE    : True
```

```
OUTPUT    : foo
REMAINING : ['not_an_option']
```

14.2.7 Ending Argument Processing

If getopt() encounters -- in the input arguments, it stops processing the remaining arguments as options. This feature can be used to pass argument values that look like options,
such as filenames starting with a dash (-).

```
$ python3 getopt_example.py -v -- --output foo

ARGV      : ['-v', '--', '--output', 'foo']
OPTIONS   : [('-v', '')]
VERSION   : 1.0
VERBOSE   : True
OUTPUT    : default.out
REMAINING : ['--output', 'foo']
```

TIP

Related Reading

- Standard library documentation for getopt.[2]
- argparse (page 888): The argparse module replaces getopt for newer applications.

14.3 readline: The GNU readline Library

The readline module provides an interface to the GNU readline library. It can be used to
enhance interactive command-line programs to make them easier to use—for example, by
adding command-line text completion, or "tab completion."

NOTE

Because readline interacts with the console content, printing debug messages makes it difficult to see
what is happening in the sample code versus what readline is doing for free. The following examples
use the logging (page 980) module to write debug information to a separate file. The log output is
shown with each example.

---

[2] https://docs.python.org/3.5/library/getopt.html

NOTE

The GNU libraries needed for readline are not available on all platforms by default. If your system does not include them, you may need to recompile the Python interpreter to enable the module, after installing the dependencies. A stand-alone version of the library is also distributed from the Python Package Index under the name gnureadline.[3] The examples in this section first try to import gnureadline, and then fall back to readline.

14.3.1 Configuring readline

There are two ways to configure the underlying readline library: by using a configuration file or by using the parse_and_bind() function. Configuration options include the key-binding to invoke completion, editing modes (vi or emacs), and many other values. Refer to the documentation for the GNU readline library for details.

The easiest way to enable tab completion is through a call to parse_and_bind(). Other options can be set at the same time. This example changes the editing controls to use vi mode instead of the default of emacs. To edit the current input line, press ESC and then use the normal vi navigation keys, such as j, k, l, and h.

Listing 14.33: **readline_parse_and_bind.py**

```
try:
    import gnureadline as readline
except ImportError:
    import readline

readline.parse_and_bind('tab: complete')
readline.parse_and_bind('set editing-mode vi')

while True:
    line = input('Prompt ("stop" to quit): ')
    if line == 'stop':
        break
    print('ENTERED: {!r}'.format(line))
```

The same configuration can be stored as instructions in a file read by the library with a single call. If myreadline.rc contains

Listing 14.34: **myreadline.rc**

```
# Turn on tab completion.
tab: complete
```

---

[3] https://pypi.python.org/pypi/gnureadline

```
# Use vi editing mode instead of emacs.
set editing-mode vi
```

the file can be read with read_init_file().

Listing 14.35: **readline_read_init_file.py**

```
try:
    import gnureadline as readline
except ImportError:
    import readline

readline.read_init_file('myreadline.rc')

while True:
    line = input('Prompt ("stop" to quit): ')
    if line == 'stop':
        break
    print('ENTERED: {!r}'.format(line))
```

14.3.2   Completing Text

The next program has a built-in set of possible commands and uses tab completion when the user is entering instructions.

Listing 14.36: **readline_completer.py**

```
try:
    import gnureadline as readline
except ImportError:
    import readline
import logging

LOG_FILENAME = '/tmp/completer.log'
logging.basicConfig(
    format='%(message)s',
    filename=LOG_FILENAME,
    level=logging.DEBUG,
)


class SimpleCompleter:

    def __init__(self, options):
        self.options = sorted(options)

    def complete(self, text, state):
        response = None
```

```
        if state == 0:
            # This is the first time for this text,
            # so build a match list.
            if text:
                self.matches = [
                    s
                    for s in self.options
                    if s and s.startswith(text)
                ]
                logging.debug('%s matches: %s',
                              repr(text), self.matches)
            else:
                self.matches = self.options[:]
                logging.debug('(empty input) matches: %s',
                              self.matches)

        # Return the state'th item from the match list,
        # if that many items are present.
        try:
            response = self.matches[state]
        except IndexError:
            response = None
        logging.debug('complete(%s, %s) => %s',
                      repr(text), state, repr(response))
        return response


def input_loop():
    line = ''
    while line != 'stop':
        line = input('Prompt ("stop" to quit): ')
        print('Dispatch {}'.format(line))

# Register the completer function.
OPTIONS = ['start', 'stop', 'list', 'print']
readline.set_completer(SimpleCompleter(OPTIONS).complete)

# Use the tab key for completion.
readline.parse_and_bind('tab: complete')

# Prompt the user for text.
input_loop()
```

The input_loop() function in this program reads one line after another until the input value is "stop". A more sophisticated program could actually parse the input line and run the command.

The SimpleCompleter class keeps a list of "options" that are candidates for auto-completion. The complete() method for an instance is designed to be registered with readline as the source of completions. The arguments are a text string to complete and a state value that indicates how many times the function has been called with the same text. The function is called repeatedly, with the state being incremented upon each call. It should return a string if there is a candidate for that state value or None if there are no more candidates. The implementation of complete() in the previous listing looks for a set of matches when state is 0, and then returns all of the candidate matches one at a time on subsequent calls.

When the code in the previous listing is run, it produces the following initial output:

```
$ python3 readline_completer.py

Prompt ("stop" to quit):
```

Pressing tab twice causes a list of options to be printed.

```
$ python3 readline_completer.py

Prompt ("stop" to quit):
list   print  start  stop
Prompt ("stop" to quit):
```

The log file shows that complete() was called with two separate sequences of state values.

```
$ tail -f /tmp/completer.log

(empty input) matches: ['list', 'print', 'start', 'stop']
complete('', 0) => 'list'
complete('', 1) => 'print'
complete('', 2) => 'start'
complete('', 3) => 'stop'
complete('', 4) => None
(empty input) matches: ['list', 'print', 'start', 'stop']
complete('', 0) => 'list'
complete('', 1) => 'print'
complete('', 2) => 'start'
complete('', 3) => 'stop'
complete('', 4) => None
```

The first sequence is from the first tab key-press. The completion algorithm asks for all candidates but does not expand the empty input line. Upon the second tab key-press, the list of candidates is recalculated so it can be printed for the user.

If the next input is l followed by another tab, the following output is generated:

```
Prompt ("stop" to quit): list
```

The log reflects the different arguments to `complete()`:

```
'l' matches: ['list']
complete('l', 0) => 'list'
complete('l', 1) => None
```

Pressing enter now causes `input()` to return the value, and the `while` loop cycles.

```
Dispatch list
Prompt ("stop" to quit):
```

There are two possible ways to complete a command beginning with s. Typing s, then pressing tab, reveals that both `start` and `stop` are candidates, but the auto-completion feature only partially completes the text on the screen by adding a t.

The log file shows the following information:

```
's' matches: ['start', 'stop']
complete('s', 0) => 'start'
complete('s', 1) => 'stop'
complete('s', 2) => None
```

Output is also generated on the screen:

```
Prompt ("stop" to quit): st
```

NOTE

If a completer function raises an exception, it is ignored silently and `readline` assumes there are no matching completions.

14.3.3 Accessing the Completion Buffer

The completion algorithm in `SimpleCompleter` looks at only the text argument passed to the function, but does not use any other information about `readline`'s internal state. It is also possible to use `readline` functions to manipulate the text of the input buffer.

Listing 14.37: `readline_buffer.py`

```
try:
    import gnureadline as readline
except ImportError:
    import readline
import logging

LOG_FILENAME = '/tmp/completer.log'
```

```
logging.basicConfig(
    format='%(message)s',
    filename=LOG_FILENAME,
    level=logging.DEBUG,
)


class BufferAwareCompleter:

    def __init__(self, options):
        self.options = options
        self.current_candidates = []

    def complete(self, text, state):
        response = None
        if state == 0:
            # This is the first time for this text,
            # so build a match list.

            origline = readline.get_line_buffer()
            begin = readline.get_begidx()
            end = readline.get_endidx()
            being_completed = origline[begin:end]
            words = origline.split()

            logging.debug('origline=%s', repr(origline))
            logging.debug('begin=%s', begin)
            logging.debug('end=%s', end)
            logging.debug('being_completed=%s', being_completed)
            logging.debug('words=%s', words)

            if not words:
                self.current_candidates = sorted(
                    self.options.keys()
                )
            else:
                try:
                    if begin == 0:
                        # First word
                        candidates = self.options.keys()
                    else:
                        # Later word
                        first = words[0]
                        candidates = self.options[first]

                    if being_completed:
                        # Match options with portion of input
                        # being completed
                        self.current_candidates = [
```

```
                            w for w in candidates
                            if w.startswith(being_completed)
                        ]
                else:
                    # Matching empty string,
                    # use all candidates
                    self.current_candidates = candidates

                logging.debug('candidates=%s',
                              self.current_candidates)

            except (KeyError, IndexError) as err:
                logging.error('completion error: %s', err)
                self.current_candidates = []

        try:
            response = self.current_candidates[state]
        except IndexError:
            response = None
        logging.debug('complete(%s, %s) => %s',
                      repr(text), state, response)
        return response


def input_loop():
    line = ''
    while line != 'stop':
        line = input('Prompt ("stop" to quit): ')
        print('Dispatch {}'.format(line))


# Register our completer function.
completer = BufferAwareCompleter({
    'list': ['files', 'directories'],
    'print': ['byname', 'bysize'],
    'stop': [],
})
readline.set_completer(completer.complete)

# Use the tab key for completion.
readline.parse_and_bind('tab: complete')

# Prompt the user for text.
input_loop()
```

In this example, commands with sub-options are being completed. The `complete()` method needs to look at the position of the completion within the input buffer to determine whether it is part of the first word or a later word. If the target is the first word, the keys of the options dictionary are used as candidates. If it is not the first word, then the first word is used to find candidates from the options dictionary.

There are three top-level commands, two of which have subcommands.

- list

    - files

    - directories

- print

    - byname

    - bysize

- stop

Following the same sequence of actions as before, pressing tab twice gives the three top-level commands.

```
$ python3 readline_buffer.py

Prompt ("stop" to quit):
list    print   stop
Prompt ("stop" to quit):
```

The log includes the following information:

```
origline=''
begin=0
end=0
being_completed=
words=[]
complete('', 0) => list
complete('', 1) => print
complete('', 2) => stop
complete('', 3) => None
origline=''
begin=0
end=0
being_completed=
words=[]
complete('', 0) => list
complete('', 1) => print
complete('', 2) => stop
complete('', 3) => None
```

If the first word is 'list ' (with a space after the word), the candidates for completion are different.

```
Prompt ("stop" to quit): list
directories  files
```

The log shows that the text being completed is *not* the full line, but just the portion after
list.

```
origline='list '
begin=5
end=5
being_completed=
words=['list']
candidates=['files', 'directories']
complete('', 0) => files
complete('', 1) => directories
complete('', 2) => None
origline='list '
begin=5
end=5
being_completed=
words=['list']
candidates=['files', 'directories']
complete('', 0) => files
complete('', 1) => directories
complete('', 2) => None
```

14.3.4   Input History

readline tracks the input history automatically. Two different sets of functions may be
used when working with the history. The history for the current session can be accessed
with get_current_history_length() and get_history_item(). That same history can be
saved to a file and reloaded later using write_history_file() and read_history_file(),
respectively. By default, the entire history is saved but the maximum length of the file can
be set with set_history_length(). A value of −1 means there is no limit on this length.

Listing 14.38: **readline_history.py**

```
try:
    import gnureadline as readline
except ImportError:
    import readline
import logging
import os

LOG_FILENAME = '/tmp/completer.log'
HISTORY_FILENAME = '/tmp/completer.hist'

logging.basicConfig(
```

```
            format='%(message)s',
            filename=LOG_FILENAME,
            level=logging.DEBUG,
        )


def get_history_items():
    num_items = readline.get_current_history_length() + 1
    return [
        readline.get_history_item(i)
        for i in range(1, num_items)
    ]


class HistoryCompleter:

    def __init__(self):
        self.matches = []

    def complete(self, text, state):
        response = None
        if state == 0:
            history_values = get_history_items()
            logging.debug('history: %s', history_values)
            if text:
                self.matches = sorted(
                    h
                    for h in history_values
                    if h and h.startswith(text)
                )
            else:
                self.matches = []
            logging.debug('matches: %s', self.matches)
        try:
            response = self.matches[state]
        except IndexError:
            response = None
        logging.debug('complete(%s, %s) => %s',
                      repr(text), state, repr(response))
        return response


def input_loop():
    if os.path.exists(HISTORY_FILENAME):
        readline.read_history_file(HISTORY_FILENAME)
    print('Max history file length:',
          readline.get_history_length())
    print('Startup history:', get_history_items())
    try:
```

```
        while True:
            line = input('Prompt ("stop" to quit): ')
            if line == 'stop':
                break
            if line:
                print('Adding {!r} to the history'.format(line))
    finally:
        print('Final history:', get_history_items())
        readline.write_history_file(HISTORY_FILENAME)


# Register our completer function.
readline.set_completer(HistoryCompleter().complete)

# Use the tab key for completion.
readline.parse_and_bind('tab: complete')

# Prompt the user for text.
input_loop()
```

The HistoryCompleter remembers everything typed, and uses those values when completing subsequent inputs.

```
$ python3 readline_history.py

Max history file length: -1
Startup history: []
Prompt ("stop" to quit): foo
Adding 'foo' to the history
Prompt ("stop" to quit): bar
Adding 'bar' to the history
Prompt ("stop" to quit): blah
Adding 'blah' to the history
Prompt ("stop" to quit): b
bar     blah
Prompt ("stop" to quit): b
Prompt ("stop" to quit): stop
Final history: ['foo', 'bar', 'blah', 'stop']
```

The log shows the following output when the b is followed by two tab key-presses.

```
history: ['foo', 'bar', 'blah']
matches: ['bar', 'blah']
complete('b', 0) => 'bar'
complete('b', 1) => 'blah'
complete('b', 2) => None
history: ['foo', 'bar', 'blah']
matches: ['bar', 'blah']
complete('b', 0) => 'bar'
```

```
complete('b', 1) => 'blah'
complete('b', 2) => None
```

When the script is run the second time, all of the history is read from the file.

```
$ python3 readline_history.py

Max history file length: -1
Startup history: ['foo', 'bar', 'blah', 'stop']
Prompt ("stop" to quit):
```

Functions are also available for removing individual history items and clearing the entire history.

14.3.5   Hooks

Several hooks can be used to trigger actions as part of the interaction sequence. The *start-up* hook is invoked immediately before printing the prompt, and the *pre-input* hook is run after the prompt, but before reading text from the user.

Listing 14.39: readline_hooks.py

```python
try:
    import gnureadline as readline
except ImportError:
    import readline


def startup_hook():
    readline.insert_text('from startup_hook')


def pre_input_hook():
    readline.insert_text(' from pre_input_hook')
    readline.redisplay()

readline.set_startup_hook(startup_hook)
readline.set_pre_input_hook(pre_input_hook)
readline.parse_and_bind('tab: complete')

while True:
    line = input('Prompt ("stop" to quit): ')
    if line == 'stop':
        break
    print('ENTERED: {!r}'.format(line))
```

Either hook is a potentially good place to use insert_text() to modify the input buffer.

```
$ python3 readline_hooks.py

Prompt ("stop" to quit): from startup_hook from pre_input_hook
```

If the buffer is modified inside the pre-input hook, `redisplay()` must be called to update the screen.

TIP

Related Reading

- Standard library documentation for `readline`.[4]
- GNU `readline`[5]: Documentation for the GNU readline library.
- `readline` init file format[6]: The initialization and configuration file format.
- effbot: The `readline` module[7]: Effbot's guide to the `readline` module.
- `gnureadline`[8]: A statically linked version of `readline` available for many platforms and installable via `pip`.
- `pyreadline`[9]: A Python-based replacement for `readline` to be used on Windows.
- cmd (page 938): The `cmd` module uses `readline` extensively to implement tab completion in the command interface. Some of the examples in this section were adapted from the code in the `cmd` section.
- `rlcompleter`: Uses `readline` to add tab completion to the interactive Python interpreter.

14.4   getpass: Secure Password Prompt

Many programs that interact with the user via the terminal need to ask the user for password values without showing what the user types on the screen. The `getpass` module provides a portable way to handle such password prompts securely.

14.4.1   Example

The `getpass()` function prints a prompt, then reads input from the user until the user presses the enter key. The input is returned as a string to the caller.

---

[4] https://docs.python.org/3.5/library/readline.html
[5] http://tiswww.case.edu/php/chet/readline/readline.html
[6] http://tiswww.case.edu/php/chet/readline/readline.html#SEC10
[7] http://sandbox.effbot.org/librarybook/readline.htm
[8] https://pypi.python.org/pypi/gnureadline
[9] http://ipython.org/pyreadline.html

Listing 14.40: `getpass_defaults.py`

```
import getpass

try:
    p = getpass.getpass()
except Exception as err:
    print('ERROR:', err)
else:
    print('You entered:', p)
```

The default prompt, if the caller does not specify another one, is "`Password:`".

```
$ python3 getpass_defaults.py

Password:
You entered: sekret
```

The prompt can be changed to any value needed.

Listing 14.41: `getpass_prompt.py`

```
import getpass

p = getpass.getpass(prompt='What is your favorite color? ')
if p.lower() == 'blue':
    print('Right.  Off you go.')
else:
    print('Auuuuugh!')
```

Some programs ask for a passphrase instead of a simple password, to give better security.

```
$ python3 getpass_prompt.py

What is your favorite color?
Right.  Off you go.

$ python3 getpass_prompt.py

What is your favorite color?
Auuuuugh!
```

By default, `getpass()` uses `sys.stdout` to print the prompt string. For a program that may produce useful output on `sys.stdout`, it is frequently a better choice to send the prompt to another stream such as `sys.stderr`.

Listing 14.42: `getpass_stream.py`

```
import getpass
import sys
```

```
p = getpass.getpass(stream=sys.stderr)
print('You entered:', p)
```

Using `sys.stderr` for the prompt means standard output can be redirected (to a pipe or file) without seeing the password prompt. The value entered by the user is not echoed back to the screen.

```
$ python3 getpass_stream.py >/dev/null

Password:
```

14.4.2   Using getpass without a Terminal

Under Unix, `getpass()` always requires a tty it can control via `termios`, so input echoing can be disabled. With this approach, values will not be read from a non-terminal stream redirected to standard input. Instead, `getpass` tries to get to the tty for a process, and no error is raised if the function can access it.

```
$ echo "not sekret" | python3 getpass_defaults.py

Password:
You entered: sekret
```

The caller is responsible for detecting when the input stream is not a tty, and using an alternative method for reading in that case.

Listing 14.43: **getpass_noterminal.py**

```
import getpass
import sys

if sys.stdin.isatty():
    p = getpass.getpass('Using getpass: ')
else:
    print('Using readline')
    p = sys.stdin.readline().rstrip()

print('Read: ', p)
```

Output with a tty:

```
$ python3 ./getpass_noterminal.py

Using getpass:
Read:  sekret
```

Output without a tty:

```
$ echo "sekret" | python3 ./getpass_noterminal.py

Using readline
Read:   sekret
```

TIP

Related Reading

- Standard library documentation for getpass.[10]
- readline (page 922): Interactive prompt library.

14.5   cmd: Line-Oriented Command Processors

The cmd module contains one public class, Cmd, which is designed to be used as a base class for interactive shells and other command interpreters. By default, cmd uses readline (page 922) for interactive prompt handling, command-line editing, and command completion.

14.5.1   Processing Commands

A command interpreter created with cmd uses a loop to read all lines from its input, parse them, and then dispatch the command to an appropriate *command handler*. Input lines are parsed into two parts: the command, and any other text on the line. For example, if the user enters foo bar, and the interpreter class includes a method named do_foo(), it is called with "bar" as the only argument.

The end-of-file marker is dispatched to do_EOF(). If a command handler returns a value that evaluates to true, the program will exit cleanly. Thus, to provide a clean way to exit the interpreter, make sure to implement do_EOF() and have it return True.

The following simple example program supports the "greet" command.

Listing 14.44: cmd_simple.py

```
import cmd


class HelloWorld(cmd.Cmd):

    def do_greet(self, line):
        print("hello")
```

---

[10] https://docs.python.org/3.5/library/getpass.html

```
        def do_EOF(self, line):
            return True

if __name__ == '__main__':
    HelloWorld().cmdloop()
```

Running it interactively demonstrates how commands are dispatched and shows off some of the features included in Cmd.

```
$ python3 cmd_simple.py

(Cmd)
```

The first thing to notice is the command prompt, (Cmd). This prompt can be configured through the attribute prompt. The prompt value is dynamic; in other words, if a command handler changes the prompt attribute, the new value is used to query for the next command.

```
Documented commands (type help <topic>):
========================================
help

Undocumented commands:
======================
EOF  greet
```

The help command is built into the Cmd class. With no arguments, help shows the list of commands available. If the input includes a command name, the output is more verbose and restricted to details of that command, when available.

If the command is greet, do_greet() is invoked to handle it.

```
(Cmd) greet
hello
```

If the class does not include a specific handler for a command, the method default() is called with the entire input line as an argument. The built-in implementation of default() reports an error.

```
(Cmd) foo
*** Unknown syntax: foo
```

Since do_EOF() returns True, typing Ctrl-D causes the interpreter to exit.

```
(Cmd) ^D$
```

No newline is printed on exit, so the results are a little messy.

14.5.2 Command Arguments

The next example includes a few enhancements to eliminate some of the annoying aspects and add help for the greet command.

<hr/>

Listing 14.45: cmd_arguments.py

```python
import cmd


class HelloWorld(cmd.Cmd):

    def do_greet(self, person):
        """greet [person]
        Greet the named person"""
        if person:
            print("hi,", person)
        else:
            print('hi')

    def do_EOF(self, line):
        return True

    def postloop(self):
        print()


if __name__ == '__main__':
    HelloWorld().cmdloop()
```

<hr/>

The docstring added to do_greet() becomes the help text for the command.

```
$ python3 cmd_arguments.py

(Cmd) help

Documented commands (type help <topic>):
========================================
greet  help

Undocumented commands:
======================
EOF

(Cmd) help greet
greet [person]
        Greet the named person
```

The output shows that greet has one optional argument: person. Although the argument is optional to the command, a distinction is evident between the command and the callback method. The method always takes the argument, but sometimes the value is an empty string. The command handler is responsible for determining whether an empty argument is valid, or whether it should do any further parsing and processing of the command. In this example, if a person's name is provided, then the greeting is personalized.

```
(Cmd) greet Alice
hi, Alice
(Cmd) greet
hi
```

Whether or not an argument is given by the user, the value passed to the command handler does not include the command itself. That simplifies parsing in the command handler, especially if multiple arguments are needed.

14.5.3   Live Help

In the previous example, the formatting of the help text leaves something to be desired. Since it comes from the docstring, it retains the indentation from the source file. The source could be changed to remove the extra whitespace, but that would leave the application code looking poorly formatted. A better solution is to implement a help handler for the greet command, named help_greet(). The help handler is called to produce help text for the named command.

Listing 14.46: cmd_do_help.py

```python
# Set up gnureadline as readline if installed.
try:
    import gnureadline
    import sys
    sys.modules['readline'] = gnureadline
except ImportError:
    pass

import cmd


class HelloWorld(cmd.Cmd):

    def do_greet(self, person):
        if person:
            print("hi,", person)
        else:
            print('hi')

    def help_greet(self):
        print('\n'.join([
            'greet [person]',
            'Greet the named person',
        ]))

    def do_EOF(self, line):
```

```
        return True

if __name__ == '__main__':
    HelloWorld().cmdloop()
```

In this example, the text is static but formatted more nicely. It would also be possible to use previous command state to tailor the contents of the help text to the current context.

```
$ python3 cmd_do_help.py

(Cmd) help greet
greet [person]
Greet the named person
```

It is up to the help handler to actually output the help message, and not simply return the help text for handling elsewhere.

14.5.4   Auto-Completion

Cmd includes support for command completion based on the names of the commands with handler methods. The user triggers completion by pressing the tab key at an input prompt. When multiple completions are possible, pressing tab twice prints a list of the options.

NOTE

The GNU libraries needed for readline are not available on all platforms by default. In those cases, tab completion may not work. See readline (page 922) for tips on installing the necessary libraries if your Python installation does not have them.

```
$ python3 cmd_do_help.py

(Cmd) <tab><tab>
EOF     greet   help
(Cmd) h<tab>
(Cmd) help
```

Once the command is known, argument completion is handled by methods with the prefix complete_. This allows new completion handlers to assemble a list of possible completions by using arbitrary criteria (i.e., querying a database or looking at a file or directory on the file system). In this case, the program has a hard-coded set of "friends" who receive a less formal greeting than named or anonymous strangers. A real program would probably save the list somewhere, read it once, and then cache the contents to be scanned as needed.

Listing 14.47: cmd_arg_completion.py

```
# Set up gnureadline as readline if installed.
try:
    import gnureadline
```

```
        import sys
        sys.modules['readline'] = gnureadline
    except ImportError:
        pass

import cmd


class HelloWorld(cmd.Cmd):

    FRIENDS = ['Alice', 'Adam', 'Barbara', 'Bob']

    def do_greet(self, person):
        "Greet the person"
        if person and person in self.FRIENDS:
            greeting = 'hi, {}!'.format(person)
        elif person:
            greeting = 'hello, {}'.format(person)
        else:
            greeting = 'hello'
        print(greeting)

    def complete_greet(self, text, line, begidx, endidx):
        if not text:
            completions = self.FRIENDS[:]
        else:
            completions = [
                f
                for f in self.FRIENDS
                if f.startswith(text)
            ]
        return completions

    def do_EOF(self, line):
        return True


if __name__ == '__main__':
    HelloWorld().cmdloop()
```

When there is input text, `complete_greet()` returns a list of friends that match the input. Otherwise, the full list of friends is returned.

```
$ python3 cmd_arg_completion.py

(Cmd) greet <tab><tab>
Adam     Alice     Barbara   Bob
(Cmd) greet A<tab><tab>
Adam   Alice
(Cmd) greet Ad<tab>
```

```
(Cmd) greet Adam
hi, Adam!
```

If the name given does not appear in the list of friends, the formal greeting is output.

```
(Cmd) greet Joe
hello, Joe
```

14.5.5   Overriding Base Class Methods

Cmd includes several methods that can be overridden as hooks for taking actions or altering the base class behavior. This example is not exhaustive, but contains many of the methods that are useful on a routine basis.

Listing 14.48: <code>cmd_illustrate_methods.py</code>

```python
# Set up gnureadline as readline if installed.
try:
    import gnureadline
    import sys
    sys.modules['readline'] = gnureadline
except ImportError:
    pass

import cmd


class Illustrate(cmd.Cmd):
    "Illustrate the base class method use."

    def cmdloop(self, intro=None):
        print('cmdloop({})'.format(intro))
        return cmd.Cmd.cmdloop(self, intro)

    def preloop(self):
        print('preloop()')

    def postloop(self):
        print('postloop()')

    def parseline(self, line):
        print('parseline({!r}) =>'.format(line), end='')
        ret = cmd.Cmd.parseline(self, line)
        print(ret)
        return ret

    def onecmd(self, s):
        print('onecmd({})'.format(s))
```

```
            return cmd.Cmd.onecmd(self, s)

        def emptyline(self):
            print('emptyline()')
            return cmd.Cmd.emptyline(self)

        def default(self, line):
            print('default({})'.format(line))
            return cmd.Cmd.default(self, line)

        def precmd(self, line):
            print('precmd({})'.format(line))
            return cmd.Cmd.precmd(self, line)

        def postcmd(self, stop, line):
            print('postcmd({}, {})'.format(stop, line))
            return cmd.Cmd.postcmd(self, stop, line)

        def do_greet(self, line):
            print('hello,', line)

        def do_EOF(self, line):
            "Exit"
            return True

    if __name__ == '__main__':
        Illustrate().cmdloop('Illustrating the methods of cmd.Cmd')
```

cmdloop() is the main processing loop of the interpreter. Overriding it is usually not necessary, since the preloop() and postloop() hooks are available.

Each iteration through cmdloop() calls onecmd() to dispatch the command to its handler. The actual input line is parsed with parseline() to create a tuple containing the command and the remaining portion of the line.

If the line is empty, emptyline() is called, and the default implementation runs the previous command again. If the line contains a command, first precmd() is called, and then the handler is looked up and invoked. If a handler is not found, default() is called instead. Finally, postcmd() is called.

The following output shows an example session with print statements added.

```
$ python3 cmd_illustrate_methods.py

cmdloop(Illustrating the methods of cmd.Cmd)
preloop()
Illustrating the methods of cmd.Cmd
(Cmd) greet Bob
precmd(greet Bob)
onecmd(greet Bob)
parseline(greet Bob) => ('greet', 'Bob', 'greet Bob')
```

```
hello, Bob
postcmd(None, greet Bob)
(Cmd) ^Dprecmd(EOF)
onecmd(EOF)
parseline(EOF) => ('EOF', '', 'EOF')
postcmd(True, EOF)
postloop()
```

14.5.6   Configuring Cmd Through Attributes

In addition to the methods described earlier, several attributes can be specified to control command interpreters. prompt can be set to a string that is printed each time the user is asked for a new command. intro is the "welcome" message printed when the program begins running. cmdloop() takes an argument for this value, or it can be set on the class directly. When printing help, the doc_header, misc_header, undoc_header, and ruler attributes are used to format the output.

Listing 14.49: cmd_attributes.py

```
import cmd


class HelloWorld(cmd.Cmd):

    prompt = 'prompt: '
    intro = "Simple command processor example."

    doc_header = 'doc_header'
    misc_header = 'misc_header'
    undoc_header = 'undoc_header'

    ruler = '-'

    def do_prompt(self, line):
        "Change the interactive prompt"
        self.prompt = line + ': '

    def do_EOF(self, line):
        return True

if __name__ == '__main__':
    HelloWorld().cmdloop()
```

This example class shows a command handler that lets the user control the prompt for the interactive session.

```
$ python3 cmd_attributes.py

Simple command processor example.
```

```
prompt: prompt hello
hello: help

doc_header
----------
help  prompt

undoc_header
------------
EOF

hello:
```

14.5.7   Running Shell Commands

To supplement the standard command processing, Cmd includes two special command prefixes. A question mark (?) is equivalent to the built-in help command, and can be used in
the same way. An exclamation point (!) maps to do_shell(), and is intended for "shelling
out" to run other commands, as in this example.

Listing 14.50: cmd_do_shell.py

```python
import cmd
import subprocess


class ShellEnabled(cmd.Cmd):

    last_output = ''

    def do_shell(self, line):
        "Run a shell command"
        print("running shell command:", line)
        sub_cmd = subprocess.Popen(line,
                                   shell=True,
                                   stdout=subprocess.PIPE)
        output = sub_cmd.communicate()[0].decode('utf-8')
        print(output)
        self.last_output = output

    def do_echo(self, line):
        """Print the input, replacing '$out' with
        the output of the last shell command
        """
        # Obviously not robust
        print(line.replace('$out', self.last_output))

    def do_EOF(self, line):
        return True
```

```
if __name__ == '__main__':
    ShellEnabled().cmdloop()
```

This echo command implementation replaces the string $out in its argument with the output from the previous shell command.

```
$ python3 cmd_do_shell.py

(Cmd) ?

Documented commands (type help <topic>):
========================================
echo   help   shell

Undocumented commands:
======================
EOF

(Cmd) ? shell
Run a shell command
(Cmd) ? echo
Print the input, replacing '$out' with
        the output of the last shell command
(Cmd) shell pwd
running shell command: pwd
.../pymotw-3/source/cmd

(Cmd) ! pwd
running shell command: pwd
.../pymotw-3/source/cmd

(Cmd) echo $out
.../pymotw-3/source/cmd
```

14.5.8   Alternative Inputs

While the default mode for Cmd() is to interact with the user through readline (page 922), it is also possible to pass a series of commands to standard input using standard Unix shell redirection.

```
$ echo help | python3 cmd_do_help.py

(Cmd)
Documented commands (type help <topic>):
========================================
greet   help

Undocumented commands:
```

```
=======================
EOF

(Cmd)
```

To have the program read a script file directly, a few other changes may be needed. Since readline (page 922) interacts with the terminal/tty device, rather than the standard input stream, it should be disabled when the script will read from a file. Also, to avoid printing superfluous prompts, the prompt can be set to an empty string. The next example shows how to open a file and pass it as input to a modified version of the HelloWorld example.

Listing 14.51: cmd_file.py

```python
import cmd


class HelloWorld(cmd.Cmd):

    # Disable rawinput module use.
    use_rawinput = False

    # Do not show a prompt after each command read.
    prompt = ''

    def do_greet(self, line):
        print("hello,", line)

    def do_EOF(self, line):
        return True

if __name__ == '__main__':
    import sys
    with open(sys.argv[1], 'rt') as input:
        HelloWorld(stdin=input).cmdloop()
```

With use_rawinput set to False and prompt set to an empty string, the script can be called on an input file with one command on each line.

Listing 14.52: cmd_file.txt

```
greet
greet Alice and Bob
```

Running the example script with the example input produces the following output.

```
$ python3 cmd_file.py cmd_file.txt

hello,
hello, Alice and Bob
```

14.5.9   Commands from sys.argv

Command-line arguments to the program can also be processed as commands for the interpreter class, instead of reading commands from the console or a file. To use the command-line
arguments, call onecmd() directly, as in this example.

Listing 14.53: cmd_argv.py

```python
import cmd


class InteractiveOrCommandLine(cmd.Cmd):
    """Accepts commands via the normal interactive
    prompt or on the command line.
    """

    def do_greet(self, line):
        print('hello,', line)

    def do_EOF(self, line):
        return True

if __name__ == '__main__':
    import sys
    if len(sys.argv) > 1:
        InteractiveOrCommandLine().onecmd(' '.join(sys.argv[1:]))
    else:
        InteractiveOrCommandLine().cmdloop()
```

Since onecmd() takes a single string as input, the arguments to the program need to be
joined together before being passed in.

```
$ python3 cmd_argv.py greet Command-Line User

hello, Command-Line User

$ python3 cmd_argv.py

(Cmd) greet Interactive User
hello, Interactive User
(Cmd)
```

TIP

Related Reading

- Standard library documentation for cmd.[11]
- cmd2[12]: Drop-in replacement for cmd with additional features.

---

[11] https://docs.python.org/3.5/library/cmd.html
[12] http://pypi.python.org/pypi/cmd2

- GNU readline[13]: This library provides functions that allow users to edit input lines as they are typed.
- `readline` (page 922): The Python standard library interface to GNU readline.
- `subprocess` (page 535): Used to manage other processes and their output.

14.6   shlex: Parse Shell-Style Syntaxes

The `shlex` module implements a class for parsing simple shell-like syntaxes. It can be used for writing a domain-specific language or for parsing quoted strings (a task that is more complex than it seems on the surface).

14.6.1   Parsing Quoted Strings

A problem that often arises when working with input text is to identify a sequence of quoted words as a single entity. Splitting the text based on quotation marks does not always work as expected, especially if there are nested levels of quotes. Consider the following text as an example:

```
This string has embedded "double quotes" and
'single quotes' in it, and even "a 'nested example'".
```

A naive approach would be to construct a regular expression to find the parts of the text outside the quotes and separate them from the text inside the quotes, or vice versa. That regular expression would be unnecessarily complex and prone to errors resulting from edge cases such as apostrophes or even typos. A better solution is to use a true parser, such as the one provided by the `shlex` module. The next simple example prints the tokens identified in the input file using the `shlex` class.

Listing 14.54: **shlex_example.py**

```python
import shlex
import sys

if len(sys.argv) != 2:
    print('Please specify one filename on the command line.')
    sys.exit(1)

filename = sys.argv[1]
with open(filename, 'r') as f:
    body = f.read()
print('ORIGINAL: {!r}'.format(body))
print()

print('TOKENS:')
```

---

[13] http://tiswww.case.edu/php/chet/readline/rltop.html

```
lexer = shlex.shlex(body)
for token in lexer:
    print('{!r}'.format(token))
```

When run with data containing embedded quotes as the input, this parser produces the list of expected tokens.

```
$ python3 shlex_example.py quotes.txt

ORIGINAL: 'This string has embedded "double quotes" and\n\'singl
e quotes\' in it, and even "a \'nested example\'".\n'

TOKENS:
'This'
'string'
'has'
'embedded'
'"double quotes"'
'and'
"'single quotes'"
'in'
'it'
','
'and'
'even'
'"a \'nested example\'"'
'.'
```

This parser also handles isolated quotes such as apostrophes correctly. Consider this input file:

```
This string has an embedded apostrophe, doesn't it?
```

The token with the embedded apostrophe is no problem.

```
$ python3 shlex_example.py apostrophe.txt

ORIGINAL: "This string has an embedded apostrophe, doesn't it?"

TOKENS:
'This'
'string'
'has'
'an'
'embedded'
'apostrophe'
```

```
' , '
"doesn't"
'it'
'?'
```

14.6.2 Making Safe Strings for Shells

The `quote()` function performs the inverse operation, escaping existing quotes and adding missing quotes for strings to make them safe to use in shell commands.

Listing 14.55: shlex_quote.py

```python
import shlex

examples = [
    "Embedded'SingleQuote",
    'Embedded"DoubleQuote',
    'Embedded Space',
    '~SpecialCharacter',
    r'Back\slash',
]

for s in examples:
    print('ORIGINAL : {}'.format(s))
    print('QUOTED   : {}'.format(shlex.quote(s)))
    print()
```

It is still usually safer to use a list of arguments when using `subprocess.Popen`. Nevertheless, in situations where that is not possible, `quote()` provides some protection by ensuring that special characters and whitespace are quoted properly.

```
$ python3 shlex_quote.py

ORIGINAL : Embedded'SingleQuote
QUOTED   : 'Embedded'"'"'SingleQuote'

ORIGINAL : Embedded"DoubleQuote
QUOTED   : 'Embedded"DoubleQuote'

ORIGINAL : Embedded Space
QUOTED   : 'Embedded Space'

ORIGINAL : ~SpecialCharacter
QUOTED   : '~SpecialCharacter'

ORIGINAL : Back\slash
QUOTED   : 'Back\slash'
```

14.6.3   Embedded Comments

Since the parser is intended to be used with command languages, it needs to handle comments. By default, any text following a # is considered part of a comment and ignored. Due to the nature of the parser, only single-character comment prefixes are supported. The set of comment characters used can be configured through the `commenters` property.

```
$ python3 shlex_example.py comments.txt

ORIGINAL: 'This line is recognized.\n# But this line is ignored.
\nAnd this line is processed.'

TOKENS:
'This'
'line'
'is'
'recognized'
'.'
'And'
'this'
'line'
'is'
'processed'
'.'
```

14.6.4   Splitting Strings into Tokens

The function `split()` is provided as a convenient wrapper around the parser. It can be used to split an existing string into component tokens.

Listing 14.56: shlex_split.py

```python
import shlex

text = """This text has "quoted parts" inside it."""
print('ORIGINAL: {!r}'.format(text))
print()

print('TOKENS:')
print(shlex.split(text))
```

The result is a list.

```
$ python3 shlex_split.py

ORIGINAL: 'This text has "quoted parts" inside it.'

TOKENS:
['This', 'text', 'has', 'quoted parts', 'inside', 'it.']
```

14.6.5 Including Other Sources of Tokens

The shlex class includes several configuration properties that control its behavior. The
source property supports code (or configuration) reuse by allowing one token stream to
include another. This feature is similar to the Bourne shell source operator—hence the
name.

Listing 14.57: shlex_source.py

```
import shlex

text = "This text says to source quotes.txt before continuing."
print('ORIGINAL: {!r}'.format(text))
print()

lexer = shlex.shlex(text)
lexer.wordchars += '.'
lexer.source = 'source'

print('TOKENS:')
for token in lexer:
    print('{!r}'.format(token))
```

The string source quotes.txt in the original text receives special handling. Since the
source property of the lexer is set to "source", when the keyword is encountered, the
filename appearing on the next line is automatically included. To cause the filename to
appear as a single token, the . (period) character needs to be added to the list of characters
that are included in words; otherwise, quotes.txt becomes three tokens—quotes, ., and
txt. The output is shown here.

```
$ python3 shlex_source.py

ORIGINAL: 'This text says to source quotes.txt before
continuing.'

TOKENS:
'This'
'text'
'says'
'to'
'This'
'string'
'has'
'embedded'
'"double quotes"'
'and'
"'single quotes'"
'in'
'it'
```

```
','
'and'
'even'
'"a \'nested example\'"'
'.'
'before'
'continuing.'
```

The source feature uses a method called `sourcehook()` to load the additional input source. As a consequence, a subclass of `shlex` can provide an alternative implementation that loads data from locations other than files.

14.6.6　Controlling the Parser

An earlier example demonstrated changing the `wordchars` value to control which characters are included in words. It is also possible to set the `quotes` character to use additional or alternative quotes. Each quote must be a single character, so it is not possible to have different open and close quotes (parsing on parentheses, for example, is not allowed).

Listing 14.58: `shlex_table.py`

```
import shlex

text = """|Col 1||Col 2||Col 3|"""
print('ORIGINAL: {!r}'.format(text))
print()

lexer = shlex.shlex(text)
lexer.quotes = '|'

print('TOKENS:')
for token in lexer:
    print('{!r}'.format(token))
```

In this example, each table cell is wrapped in vertical bars.

```
$ python3 shlex_table.py

ORIGINAL: '|Col 1||Col 2||Col 3|'

TOKENS:
'|Col 1|'
'|Col 2|'
'|Col 3|'
```

It is also possible to control the whitespace characters used to split words.

Listing 14.59: shlex_whitespace.py

```
import shlex
import sys

if len(sys.argv) != 2:
    print('Please specify one filename on the command line.')
    sys.exit(1)

filename = sys.argv[1]
with open(filename, 'r') as f:
    body = f.read()
print('ORIGINAL: {!r}'.format(body))
print()

print('TOKENS:')
lexer = shlex.shlex(body)
lexer.whitespace += '.,'
for token in lexer:
    print('{!r}'.format(token))
```

Now, if the example in shlex_example.py is modified to include a period and a comma, the results also change.

```
$ python3 shlex_whitespace.py quotes.txt

ORIGINAL: 'This string has embedded "double quotes" and\n\'singl
e quotes\' in it, and even "a \'nested example\'".\n'

TOKENS:
'This'
'string'
'has'
'embedded'
'"double quotes"'
'and'
'"\'single quotes\'"'
'in'
'it'
'and'
'even'
'"a \'nested example\'"'
```

14.6.7 Error Handling

When the parser encounters the end of its input before all quoted strings are closed, it raises ValueError. In such a case, it is useful to examine some of the properties maintained by the parser as it processes the input. For example, infile refers to the name of the file being processed (which might be different from the original file, if one file sources another). The `lineno` value reports the line that was being processed when the error was discovered; it is typically the end of the file, which may be far away from the first quote. The `token` attribute contains the buffer of text not already included in a valid token. The `error_leader()` method produces a message prefix in a style similar to Unix compilers, which enables editors such as `emacs` to parse the error and take the user directly to the invalid line.

Listing 14.60: `shlex_errors.py`

```
import shlex

text = """This line is OK.
This line has an "unfinished quote.
This line is OK, too.
"""

print('ORIGINAL: {!r}'.format(text))
print()

lexer = shlex.shlex(text)

print('TOKENS:')
try:
    for token in lexer:
        print('{!r}'.format(token))
except ValueError as err:
    first_line_of_error = lexer.token.splitlines()[0]
    print('ERROR: {} {}'.format(lexer.error_leader(), err))
    print('following {!r}'.format(first_line_of_error))
```

The example produces this output.

```
$ python3 shlex_errors.py

ORIGINAL: 'This line is OK.\nThis line has an "unfinished quote.
\nThis line is OK, too.\n'

TOKENS:
'This'
'line'
'is'
'OK'
'.'
'This'
'line'
'has'
'an'
ERROR: "None", line 4:  No closing quotation
following '"unfinished quote.'
```

14.6.8 POSIX Versus Non-POSIX Parsing

The default behavior for the parser is to use a backward-compatible style that is not POSIX-compliant. For POSIX behavior, set the `posix` argument when constructing the parser.

Listing 14.61: **shlex_posix.py**

```
import shlex

examples = [
    'Do"Not"Separate',
    '"Do"Separate',
    'Escaped \e Character not in quotes',
    'Escaped "\e" Character in double quotes',
    "Escaped '\e' Character in single quotes",
    r"Escaped '\'' \"\'\" single quote",
    r'Escaped "\"" \'\"\' double quote',
    "\"'Strip extra layer of quotes'\"",
]

for s in examples:
    print('ORIGINAL : {!r}'.format(s))
    print('non-POSIX: ', end='')

    non_posix_lexer = shlex.shlex(s, posix=False)
    try:
        print('{!r}'.format(list(non_posix_lexer)))
    except ValueError as err:
        print('error({})'.format(err))

    print('POSIX    : ', end='')
    posix_lexer = shlex.shlex(s, posix=True)
    try:
        print('{!r}'.format(list(posix_lexer)))
    except ValueError as err:
        print('error({})'.format(err))

    print()
```

Here are a few examples of the differences in parsing behavior.

```
$ python3 shlex_posix.py

ORIGINAL : 'Do"Not"Separate'
non-POSIX: ['Do"Not"Separate']
POSIX    : ['DoNotSeparate']

ORIGINAL : '"Do"Separate'
non-POSIX: ['"Do"', 'Separate']
POSIX    : ['DoSeparate']
```

```
ORIGINAL : 'Escaped \\e Character not in quotes'
non-POSIX: ['Escaped', '\\', 'e', 'Character', 'not', 'in',
'quotes']
POSIX    : ['Escaped', 'e', 'Character', 'not', 'in', 'quotes']

ORIGINAL : 'Escaped "\\e" Character in double quotes'
non-POSIX: ['Escaped', '"\\e"', 'Character', 'in', 'double',
'quotes']
POSIX    : ['Escaped', '\\e', 'Character', 'in', 'double',
'quotes']

ORIGINAL : "Escaped '\\e' Character in single quotes"
non-POSIX: ['Escaped', "'\\e'", 'Character', 'in', 'single',
'quotes']
POSIX    : ['Escaped', '\\e', 'Character', 'in', 'single',
'quotes']

ORIGINAL : 'Escaped \'\\\'\' \\"\\\'\\" single quote'
non-POSIX: error(No closing quotation)
POSIX    : ['Escaped', '\\ \\"\\"', 'single', 'quote']

ORIGINAL : 'Escaped "\\"" \\\'\\"\\\' double quote'
non-POSIX: error(No closing quotation)
POSIX    : ['Escaped', '"', '\'"\'', 'double', 'quote']

ORIGINAL : '"\'Strip extra layer of quotes\'"'
non-POSIX: ['"\'Strip extra layer of quotes\'"']
POSIX    : ["'Strip extra layer of quotes'"]
```

TIP

Related Reading

- Standard library documentation for shlex.[14]
- cmd (page 938): Tools for building interactive command interpreters.
- argparse (page 888): Command-line option parsing.
- subprocess (page 535): Run commands after parsing the command line.

14.7   configparser: Work with Configuration Files

Use the configparser module to manage user-editable configuration files for an application using a format similar to Windows INI files. The contents of the configuration files can

---

[14] https://docs.python.org/3.5/library/shlex.html

be organized into groups and several option value types are supported, including integers, floating-point values, and booleans. Option values can be combined using Python formatting strings to build longer values such as URLs from shorter values such as hostnames and port numbers.

14.7.1 Configuration File Format

The file format used by configparser is similar to the format used by older versions of Microsoft Windows. It consists of one or more named *sections*, each of which can contain individual *options* with names and values.

The parser identifies config file sections by looking for lines starting with [and ending with]. The value between the square brackets is the section name, and can contain any characters except square brackets.

Options are listed one per line within a section. The line starts with the name of the option, which is separated from the value by a colon (:) or equal sign (=). Whitespace around the separator is ignored when the file is parsed.

Lines starting with a semicolon (;) or an octothorpe (#) are treated as comments. They are ignored when the contents of the configuration file are accessed programmatically.

The following sample configuration file contains a section named bug_tracker with three options: url, username, and password.

```
# This is a simple example with comments.
[bug_tracker]
url = http://localhost:8080/bugs/
username = dhellmann
; You should not store passwords in plain text
; configuration files.
password = SECRET
```

14.7.2 Reading Configuration Files

A user or system administrator often edits a configuration file with a regular text editor to set application behavior defaults, with the application then reading the file, parsing it, and acting based on its contents. Use the read() method of ConfigParser to read the configuration file.

Listing 14.62: configparser_read.py

```
from configparser import ConfigParser

parser = ConfigParser()
parser.read('simple.ini')

print(parser.get('bug_tracker', 'url'))
```

This program reads the simple.ini file from the previous section and prints the value of the url option from the bug_tracker section.

```
$ python3 configparser_read.py

http://localhost:8080/bugs/
```

The read() method also accepts a list of filenames. Each name in the list is scanned, and if the file exists it is opened and read.

Listing 14.63: configparser_read_many.py

```
from configparser import ConfigParser
import glob

parser = ConfigParser()

candidates = ['does_not_exist.ini', 'also-does-not-exist.ini',
              'simple.ini', 'multisection.ini']

found = parser.read(candidates)

missing = set(candidates) - set(found)

print('Found config files:', sorted(found))
print('Missing files    :', sorted(missing))
```

read() returns a list containing the names of the files that were successfully loaded. By examining this list, the program can discover which configuration files are missing and decide whether to ignore them or to treat the condition as an error.

```
$ python3 configparser_read_many.py

Found config files: ['multisection.ini', 'simple.ini']
Missing files    : ['also-does-not-exist.ini',
'does_not_exist.ini']
```

14.7.2.1   Unicode Configuration Data

Configuration files containing Unicode data should be read using the proper encoding value. The following example file changes the password value of the original input to contain Unicode characters and is encoded using UTF-8.

Listing 14.64: unicode.ini

```
[bug_tracker]
url = http://localhost:8080/bugs/
username = dhellmann
password = †ßéç®é
```

The file is opened with the appropriate decoder, converting the UTF-8 data to native Unicode strings.

Listing 14.65: **configparser_unicode.py**

```
from configparser import ConfigParser
import codecs

parser = ConfigParser()
# Open the file with the correct encoding.
parser.read('unicode.ini', encoding='utf-8')

password = parser.get('bug_tracker', 'password')

print('Password:', password.encode('utf-8'))
print('Type     :', type(password))
print('repr()   :', repr(password))
```

The value returned by get() is a Unicode string. To print it safely, the string must be re-encoded as UTF-8.

```
$ python3 configparser_unicode.py

Password: b'\xc3\x9f\xc3\xa9\xc3\xa7\xc2\xae\xc3\xa9\xe2\x80\xa0
'
Type     : <class 'str'>
repr()   : 'ßéç®é'
```

14.7.3 Accessing Configuration Settings

ConfigParser includes methods for examining the structure of the parsed configuration, including listing the sections and options, and getting their values. The following configuration file includes two sections for separate web services.

```
[bug_tracker]
url = http://localhost:8080/bugs/
username = dhellmann
password = SECRET

[wiki]
url = http://localhost:8080/wiki/
username = dhellmann
password = SECRET
```

The next sample program exercises some of the methods for looking at the configuration data, including sections(), options(), and items().

Listing 14.66: `configparser_structure.py`

```
from configparser import ConfigParser

parser = ConfigParser()
parser.read('multisection.ini')

for section_name in parser.sections():
    print('Section:', section_name)
    print('  Options:', parser.options(section_name))
    for name, value in parser.items(section_name):
        print('  {} = {}'.format(name, value))
    print()
```

Both `sections()` and `options()` return lists of strings, while `items()` returns a list of tuples containing the name–value pairs.

```
$ python3 configparser_structure.py

Section: bug_tracker
  Options: ['url', 'username', 'password']
  url = http://localhost:8080/bugs/
  username = dhellmann
  password = SECRET

Section: wiki
  Options: ['url', 'username', 'password']
  url = http://localhost:8080/wiki/
  username = dhellmann
  password = SECRET
```

A `ConfigParser` also supports the same mapping API as *dict*, with the `ConfigParser` acting as one dictionary containing separate dictionaries for each section.

Listing 14.67: `configparser_structure_dict.py`

```
from configparser import ConfigParser

parser = ConfigParser()
parser.read('multisection.ini')

for section_name in parser:
    print('Section:', section_name)
    section = parser[section_name]
    print('  Options:', list(section.keys()))
    for name in section:
        print('  {} = {}'.format(name, section[name]))
    print()
```

Using the mapping API to access the same configuration file produces the same output.

```
$ python3 configparser_structure_dict.py

Section: DEFAULT
  Options: []

Section: bug_tracker
  Options: ['url', 'username', 'password']
  url = http://localhost:8080/bugs/
  username = dhellmann
  password = SECRET

Section: wiki
  Options: ['url', 'username', 'password']
  url = http://localhost:8080/wiki/
  username = dhellmann
  password = SECRET
```

14.7.3.1   Testing Whether Values Are Present

To test whether a section exists, use has_section(), passing the section name as the argument to the method.

Listing 14.68: **configparser_has_section.py**

```python
from configparser import ConfigParser

parser = ConfigParser()
parser.read('multisection.ini')

for candidate in ['wiki', 'bug_tracker', 'dvcs']:
    print('{:<12}: {}'.format(
        candidate, parser.has_section(candidate)))
```

Testing whether a section exists before calling get() can prevent exceptions being generated for missing data.

```
$ python3 configparser_has_section.py

wiki         : True
bug_tracker  : True
dvcs         : False
```

Use has_option() to test whether an option exists within a section.

Listing 14.69: **configparser_has_option.py**

```python
from configparser import ConfigParser

parser = ConfigParser()
```

```
parser.read('multisection.ini')

SECTIONS = ['wiki', 'none']
OPTIONS = ['username', 'password', 'url', 'description']

for section in SECTIONS:
    has_section = parser.has_section(section)
    print('{} section exists: {}'.format(section, has_section))
    for candidate in OPTIONS:
        has_option = parser.has_option(section, candidate)
        print('{}.{:<12}  : {}'.format(
            section, candidate, has_option))
    print()
```

If the section does not exist, has_option() returns False.

```
$ python3 configparser_has_option.py

wiki section exists: True
wiki.username      : True
wiki.password      : True
wiki.url           : True
wiki.description   : False

none section exists: False
none.username      : False
none.password      : False
none.url           : False
none.description   : False
```

14.7.3.2 Value Types

All section and option names are treated as strings, but option values can be strings, integers, floating-point numbers, or booleans. Several different string values can be used to represent boolean values in the configuration file; they are converted to True or False when accessed. The following file includes examples of the numeric types and all of the values that are recognized by the parser as boolean values.

Listing 14.70: types.ini

```
[ints]
positive = 1
negative = -5

[floats]
positive = 0.2
negative = -3.14

[booleans]
```

```
number_true = 1
number_false = 0
yn_true = yes
yn_false = no
tf_true = true
tf_false = false
onoff_true = on
onoff_false = false
```

ConfigParser does not make any attempt to understand the option type. Instead, the application is expected to use the correct method to fetch the value as the desired type. get() always returns a string. Use getint() to fetch integers, getfloat() for floating-point numbers, and getboolean() for boolean values.

Listing 14.71: configparser_value_types.py

```
from configparser import ConfigParser

parser = ConfigParser()
parser.read('types.ini')

print('Integers:')
for name in parser.options('ints'):
    string_value = parser.get('ints', name)
    value = parser.getint('ints', name)
    print('  {:<12} : {!r:<7} -> {}'.format(
        name, string_value, value))

print('\nFloats:')
for name in parser.options('floats'):
    string_value = parser.get('floats', name)
    value = parser.getfloat('floats', name)
    print('  {:<12} : {!r:<7} -> {:0.2f}'.format(
        name, string_value, value))

print('\nBooleans:')
for name in parser.options('booleans'):
    string_value = parser.get('booleans', name)
    value = parser.getboolean('booleans', name)
    print('  {:<12} : {!r:<7} -> {}'.format(
        name, string_value, value))
```

Running this program with the example input produces the following output.

```
$ python3 configparser_value_types.py

Integers:
  positive     : '1'     -> 1
  negative     : '-5'    -> -5
```

```
Floats:
  positive      : '0.2'    -> 0.20
  negative      : '-3.14' -> -3.14

Booleans:
  number_true   : '1'      -> True
  number_false  : '0'      -> False
  yn_true       : 'yes'    -> True
  yn_false      : 'no'     -> False
  tf_true       : 'true'   -> True
  tf_false      : 'false' -> False
  onoff_true    : 'on'     -> True
  onoff_false   : 'false' -> False
```

Custom type converters can be added by passing conversion functions in the `converters` argument to `ConfigParser`. Each converter receives a single input value, which it then transforms into the appropriate return type.

Listing 14.72: <code>configparser_custom_types.py</code>

```python
from configparser import ConfigParser
import datetime


def parse_iso_datetime(s):
    print('parse_iso_datetime({!r})'.format(s))
    return datetime.datetime.strptime(s, '%Y-%m-%dT%H:%M:%S.%f')


parser = ConfigParser(
    converters={
        'datetime': parse_iso_datetime,
    }
)
parser.read('custom_types.ini')

string_value = parser['datetimes']['due_date']
value = parser.getdatetime('datetimes', 'due_date')
print('due_date : {!r} -> {!r}'.format(string_value, value))
```

Adding a converter causes `ConfigParser` to automatically create a retrieval method for that type, using the name of the type as specified in `converters`. In this example, the `'datetime'` converter causes a new `getdatetime()` method to be added.

```
$ python3 configparser_custom_types.py

parse_iso_datetime('2015-11-08T11:30:05.905898')
due_date : '2015-11-08T11:30:05.905898' -> datetime.datetime(201
5, 11, 8, 11, 30, 5, 905898)
```

It is also possible to add converter methods directly to a subclass of `ConfigParser`.

14.7.3.3 Options as Flags

Usually, the parser requires an explicit value for each option. With the `ConfigParser` parameter `allow_no_value` set to `True`, however, an option can appear by itself on a line in the input file, and can be used as a flag.

<hr/>

Listing 14.73: **configparser_allow_no_value.py**

<hr/>

```python
import configparser

# Require values.
try:
    parser = configparser.ConfigParser()
    parser.read('allow_no_value.ini')
except configparser.ParsingError as err:
    print('Could not parse:', err)

# Allow stand-alone option names.
print('\nTrying again with allow_no_value=True')
parser = configparser.ConfigParser(allow_no_value=True)
parser.read('allow_no_value.ini')
for flag in ['turn_feature_on', 'turn_other_feature_on']:
    print('\n', flag)
    exists = parser.has_option('flags', flag)
    print('  has_option:', exists)
    if exists:
        print('         get:', parser.get('flags', flag))
```

<hr/>

When an option has no explicit value, `has_option()` reports that the option exists and `get()` returns `None`.

<hr/>

```
$ python3 configparser_allow_no_value.py

Could not parse: Source contains parsing errors:
'allow_no_value.ini'
        [line  2]: 'turn_feature_on\n'

Trying again with allow_no_value=True

 turn_feature_on
  has_option: True
         get: None

 turn_other_feature_on
  has_option: False
```

<hr/>

14.7.3.4   Multiline Strings

String values can span multiple lines, if subsequent lines are indented.

```
[example]
message = This is a multiline string.
  With two paragraphs.

  They are separated by a completely empty line.
```

Within the indented multiline values, blank lines are treated as part of the value and preserved.

```
$ python3 configparser_multiline.py

This is a multiline string.
With two paragraphs.

They are separated by a completely empty line.
```

14.7.4   Modifying Settings

While ConfigParser is primarily intended to be configured by reading settings from files, settings can also be populated by calling add_section() to create a new section, and set() to add or change an option.

Listing 14.74: **configparser_populate.py**

```
import configparser

parser = configparser.SafeConfigParser()

parser.add_section('bug_tracker')
parser.set('bug_tracker', 'url', 'http://localhost:8080/bugs')
parser.set('bug_tracker', 'username', 'dhellmann')
parser.set('bug_tracker', 'password', 'secret')

for section in parser.sections():
    print(section)
    for name, value in parser.items(section):
        print('  {} = {!r}'.format(name, value))
```

All options must be set as strings, even if they will be retrieved as integer, float, or boolean values.

```
$ python3 configparser_populate.py

bug_tracker
  url = 'http://localhost:8080/bugs'
```

```
  username = 'dhellmann'
  password = 'secret'
```

To remove sections and options from a `ConfigParser`, use `remove_section()` and `remove_option()`, respectively.

Listing 14.75: **configparser_remove.py**

```python
from configparser import ConfigParser

parser = ConfigParser()
parser.read('multisection.ini')

print('Read values:\n')
for section in parser.sections():
    print(section)
    for name, value in parser.items(section):
        print('  {} = {!r}'.format(name, value))

parser.remove_option('bug_tracker', 'password')
parser.remove_section('wiki')

print('\nModified values:\n')
for section in parser.sections():
    print(section)
    for name, value in parser.items(section):
        print('  {} = {!r}'.format(name, value))
```

Removing a section deletes any options it contains.

```
$ python3 configparser_remove.py

Read values:

bug_tracker
  url = 'http://localhost:8080/bugs/'
  username = 'dhellmann'
  password = 'SECRET'
wiki
  url = 'http://localhost:8080/wiki/'
  username = 'dhellmann'
  password = 'SECRET'

Modified values:

bug_tracker
  url = 'http://localhost:8080/bugs/'
  username = 'dhellmann'
```

14.7.5   Saving Configuration Files

Once a ConfigParser is populated with the desired data, it can be saved to a file by calling the write() method. This approach can be used to provide a user interface for editing the configuration settings, without the need to write any code to manage the file.

Listing 14.76: **configparser_write.py**

```
import configparser
import sys

parser = configparser.ConfigParser()

parser.add_section('bug_tracker')
parser.set('bug_tracker', 'url', 'http://localhost:8080/bugs')
parser.set('bug_tracker', 'username', 'dhellmann')
parser.set('bug_tracker', 'password', 'secret')

parser.write(sys.stdout)
```

The write() method takes a file-like object as argument. It writes the data out in the INI format so it can be parsed again by the ConfigParser.

```
$ python3 configparser_write.py

[bug_tracker]
url = http://localhost:8080/bugs
username = dhellmann
password = secret
```

WARNING

Comments in the original configuration file are not preserved when reading, modifying, and rewriting a configuration file.

14.7.6   Option Search Path

ConfigParser uses a multistep search process when looking for an option. First, before starting the option search, the section name is tested. If the section does not exist, and the name is not the special value DEFAULT, then NoSectionError is raised.

1. If the option name appears in the vars dictionary passed to get(), the value from vars is returned.

2. If the option name appears in the specified section, the value from that section is returned.

3. If the option name appears in the `DEFAULT` section, that value is returned.

4. If the option name appears in the `defaults` dictionary passed to the constructor, that value is returned.

If the name is not found in any of those locations, `NoOptionError` is raised.

The search path behavior can be demonstrated using the following configuration file.

```
[DEFAULT]
file-only = value from DEFAULT section
init-and-file = value from DEFAULT section
from-section = value from DEFAULT section
from-vars = value from DEFAULT section

[sect]
section-only = value from section in file
from-section = value from section in file
from-vars = value from section in file
```

The test program in the following listing includes default settings for options not specified in the configuration file, and overrides some values that are defined in the file.

Listing 14.77: configparser_defaults.py

```
import configparser

# Define the names of the options.
option_names = [
    'from-default',
    'from-section', 'section-only',
    'file-only', 'init-only', 'init-and-file',
    'from-vars',
]

# Initialize the parser with some defaults.
DEFAULTS = {
    'from-default': 'value from defaults passed to init',
    'init-only': 'value from defaults passed to init',
    'init-and-file': 'value from defaults passed to init',
    'from-section': 'value from defaults passed to init',
    'from-vars': 'value from defaults passed to init',
}
parser = configparser.ConfigParser(defaults=DEFAULTS)

print('Defaults before loading file:')
defaults = parser.defaults()
for name in option_names:
    if name in defaults:
        print('  {:<15} = {!r}'.format(name, defaults[name]))
```

```
# Load the configuration file.
parser.read('with-defaults.ini')

print('\nDefaults after loading file:')
defaults = parser.defaults()
for name in option_names:
    if name in defaults:
        print('  {:<15} = {!r}'.format(name, defaults[name]))

# Define some local overrides.
vars = {'from-vars': 'value from vars'}

# Show the values of all the options.
print('\nOption lookup:')
for name in option_names:
    value = parser.get('sect', name, vars=vars)
    print('  {:<15} = {!r}'.format(name, value))

# Show error messages for options that do not exist.
print('\nError cases:')
try:
    print('No such option :', parser.get('sect', 'no-option'))
except configparser.NoOptionError as err:
    print(err)

try:
    print('No such section:', parser.get('no-sect', 'no-option'))
except configparser.NoSectionError as err:
    print(err)
```

The output shows where the value of each option originates and illustrates the way defaults from different sources override existing values.

```
$ python3 configparser_defaults.py

Defaults before loading file:
  from-default    = 'value from defaults passed to init'
  from-section    = 'value from defaults passed to init'
  init-only       = 'value from defaults passed to init'
  init-and-file   = 'value from defaults passed to init'
  from-vars       = 'value from defaults passed to init'

Defaults after loading file:
  from-default    = 'value from defaults passed to init'
  from-section    = 'value from DEFAULT section'
  file-only       = 'value from DEFAULT section'
  init-only       = 'value from defaults passed to init'
  init-and-file   = 'value from DEFAULT section'
  from-vars       = 'value from DEFAULT section'
```

```
Option lookup:
  from-default    = 'value from defaults passed to init'
  from-section    = 'value from section in file'
  section-only    = 'value from section in file'
  file-only       = 'value from DEFAULT section'
  init-only       = 'value from defaults passed to init'
  init-and-file   = 'value from DEFAULT section'
  from-vars       = 'value from vars'

Error cases:
No option 'no-option' in section: 'sect'
No section: 'no-sect'
```

14.7.7 Combining Values with Interpolation

ConfigParser provides a feature called *interpolation* that can be used to combine values. The retrieval of values containing standard Python format strings triggers this interpolation feature. Each of the options named within the value being fetched is replaced with its value in turn, until no more substitutions are necessary.

The URL examples from earlier in this section can be rewritten to use interpolation, thereby making it easier to change only part of the value. For example, the following configuration file separates the protocol, hostname, and port from the URL as separate options.

```
[bug_tracker]
protocol = http
server = localhost
port = 8080
url = %(protocol)s://%(server)s:%(port)s/bugs/
username = dhellmann
password = SECRET
```

Interpolation is performed by default each time get() is called. To retrieve the original value, without interpolation, pass a true value in the raw argument.

Listing 14.78: **configparser_interpolation.py**

```
from configparser import ConfigParser

parser = ConfigParser()
parser.read('interpolation.ini')

print('Original value        :', parser.get('bug_tracker', 'url'))

parser.set('bug_tracker', 'port', '9090')
print('Altered port value   :', parser.get('bug_tracker', 'url'))

print('Without interpolation:', parser.get('bug_tracker', 'url',
                                           raw=True))
```

Because the value is computed by `get()`, changing one of the settings being used by the `url` value changes the return value.

```
$ python3 configparser_interpolation.py

Original value      : http://localhost:8080/bugs/
Altered port value  : http://localhost:9090/bugs/
Without interpolation: %(protocol)s://%(server)s:%(port)s/bugs/
```

14.7.7.1   Using Defaults

Values for interpolation do not need to appear in the same section as the original option. Defaults can be mixed with override values.

```
[DEFAULT]
url = %(protocol)s://%(server)s:%(port)s/bugs/
protocol = http
server = bugs.example.com
port = 80

[bug_tracker]
server = localhost
port = 8080
username = dhellmann
password = SECRET
```

With this configuration, the value for `url` comes from the DEFAULT section, and the substitution starts by looking in `bug_tracker` and falling back to DEFAULT for pieces not found in the first location.

Listing 14.79: **configparser_interpolation_defaults.py**

```
from configparser import ConfigParser

parser = ConfigParser()
parser.read('interpolation_defaults.ini')

print('URL:', parser.get('bug_tracker', 'url'))
```

The `hostname` and `port` values come from the `bug_tracker` section, but the `protocol` comes from DEFAULT.

```
$ python3 configparser_interpolation_defaults.py

URL: http://localhost:8080/bugs/
```

14.7.7.2 Substitution Errors

Substitution stops after `MAX_INTERPOLATION_DEPTH` steps, so as to avoid problems due to recursive references.

Listing 14.80: **configparser_interpolation_recursion.py**

```
import configparser

parser = configparser.ConfigParser()

parser.add_section('sect')
parser.set('sect', 'opt', '%(opt)s')

try:
    print(parser.get('sect', 'opt'))
except configparser.InterpolationDepthError as err:
    print('ERROR:', err)
```

An `InterpolationDepthError` exception is raised if too many substitution steps are attempted.

```
$ python3 configparser_interpolation_recursion.py

ERROR: Recursion limit exceeded in value substitution: option 'o
pt' in section 'sect' contains an interpolation key which cannot
 be substituted in 10 steps. Raw value: '%(opt)s'
```

Missing values result in an `InterpolationMissingOptionError` exception.

Listing 14.81: **configparser_interpolation_error.py**

```
import configparser

parser = configparser.ConfigParser()

parser.add_section('bug_tracker')
parser.set('bug_tracker', 'url',
           'http://%(server)s:%(port)s/bugs')

try:
    print(parser.get('bug_tracker', 'url'))
except configparser.InterpolationMissingOptionError as err:
    print('ERROR:', err)
```

Since no `server` value is defined, the `url` cannot be constructed.

```
$ python3 configparser_interpolation_error.py

ERROR: Bad value substitution: option 'url' in section
```

```
'bug_tracker' contains an interpolation key 'server' which is
not a valid option name. Raw value:
'http://%(server)s:%(port)s/bugs'
```

14.7.7.3 Escaping Special Characters

Since % starts the interpolation instructions, a literal % in a value must be escaped as %%.

```
[escape]
value = a literal %% must be escaped
```

Reading the value does not require any special consideration.

Listing 14.82: configparser_escape.py

```
from configparser import ConfigParser
import os

filename = 'escape.ini'
config = ConfigParser()
config.read([filename])

value = config.get('escape', 'value')

print(value)
```

When the value is read, the %% is converted to % automatically.

```
$ python3 configparser_escape.py

a literal % must be escaped
```

14.7.7.4 Extended Interpolation

ConfigParser supports alternative interpolation implementations through its interpolation parameter. The object given as the interpolation argument should implement the API defined by the Interpolation class. For example, using ExtendedInterpolation instead of the default BasicInterpolation supports a different syntax that uses ${} to indicate variables.

Listing 14.83: configparser_extendedinterpolation.py

```
from configparser import ConfigParser, ExtendedInterpolation

parser = ConfigParser(interpolation=ExtendedInterpolation())
parser.read('extended_interpolation.ini')

print('Original value      :', parser.get('bug_tracker', 'url'))
```

```
parser.set('intranet', 'port', '9090')
print('Altered port value    :', parser.get('bug_tracker', 'url'))

print('Without interpolation:', parser.get('bug_tracker', 'url',
                                            raw=True))
```

With extended interpolation, values from other sections of the configuration file can be accessed by prefixing the variable name with the section name and a colon (:).

```
[intranet]
server = localhost
port = 8080

[bug_tracker]
url = http://${intranet:server}:${intranet:port}/bugs/
username = dhellmann
password = SECRET
```

Referring to values in other sections of the file makes it possible to share a hierarchy of values, without placing all of the default values in the DEFAULTS section.

```
$ python3 configparser_extendedinterpolation.py

Original value       : http://localhost:8080/bugs/
Altered port value   : http://localhost:9090/bugs/
Without interpolation: http://${intranet:server}:${intranet:port
}/bugs/
```

14.7.7.5 Disabling Interpolation

To disable interpolation, pass None instead of an Interpolation object.

Listing 14.84: configparser_nointerpolation.py

```
from configparser import ConfigParser

parser = ConfigParser(interpolation=None)
parser.read('interpolation.ini')

print('Without interpolation:', parser.get('bug_tracker', 'url'))
```

With interpolation disabled, any syntax that might have been processed by the interpolation object is safely ignored.

```
$ python3 configparser_nointerpolation.py

Without interpolation: %(protocol)s://%(server)s:%(port)s/bugs/
```

TIP

Related Reading

- Standard library documentation for `configparser`.[15]
- `ConfigObj`[16]: An advanced configuration file parser with support for features such as content validation.
- Python 2 to 3 porting notes for `configparser` (page 1358).

14.8   logging: Report Status, Error, and Informational Messages

The `logging` module defines a standard API for reporting errors and status information from applications and libraries. The key benefit of having a standard library module provide the logging API is that all Python modules can participate in logging, so an application's log can include messages from third-party modules.

14.8.1   Logging Components

The logging system consists of four interacting types of objects. Each module or application that wants to log some activity uses a `Logger` instance to add information to the logs. Invoking the logger creates a `LogRecord`, which holds the information in memory until it is processed. A `Logger` may have a number of `Handler` objects configured to receive and process log records. The `Handler` uses a `Formatter` to turn the log records into output messages.

14.8.2   Logging in Applications Versus Libraries

Application developers and library authors can both use `logging`, but each audience has different considerations to keep in mind.

Application developers configure the `logging` module, directing the messages to appropriate output channels. For example, they may seek to log messages with different verbosity levels or to different destinations. Handlers for writing log messages to files, HTTP GET/POST locations, email via SMTP, generic sockets, and OS-specific logging mechanisms are all included in `logging`, but developers can also create custom log destination classes for special requirements not handled by any of the built-in classes.

Developers of libraries can also use `logging` for their own purposes, but need to do even less work to utilize this module. Simply create a logger instance for each context, using an appropriate name, and then log messages using the standard levels. As long as a library uses the logging API with consistent naming and level selections, the application can be configured to show or hide messages from the library, as desired.

---

[15] https://docs.python.org/3.5/library/configparser.html
[16] http://configobj.readthedocs.org/en/latest/configobj.html

14.8.3   Logging to a File

Most applications are configured to log to a file. Use the `basicConfig()` function to set up the default handler so that debug messages are written to a file.

Listing 14.85: `logging_file_example.py`

```
import logging

LOG_FILENAME = 'logging_example.out'
logging.basicConfig(
    filename=LOG_FILENAME,
    level=logging.DEBUG,
)

logging.debug('This message should go to the log file')

with open(LOG_FILENAME, 'rt') as f:
    body = f.read()

print('FILE:')
print(body)
```

When the script is run, the log message is written to `logging_example.out`.

```
$ python3 logging_file_example.py

FILE:
DEBUG:root:This message should go to the log file
```

14.8.4   Rotating Log Files

Running the script in the previous listing repeatedly causes more messages to be appended to the file. To create a new file each time the program runs, pass a `filemode` argument to `basicConfig()` with a value of `'w'`. Rather than managing the creation of files this way, though, it is better to use a `RotatingFileHandler`, which creates new files automatically and preserves the old log file at the same time.

Listing 14.86: `logging_rotatingfile_example.py`

```
import glob
import logging
import logging.handlers

LOG_FILENAME = 'logging_rotatingfile_example.out'

# Set up a specific logger with the desired output level.
my_logger = logging.getLogger('MyLogger')
my_logger.setLevel(logging.DEBUG)
```

```
# Add the log message handler to the logger.
handler = logging.handlers.RotatingFileHandler(
    LOG_FILENAME,
    maxBytes=20,
    backupCount=5,
)
my_logger.addHandler(handler)

# Log some messages.
for i in range(20):
    my_logger.debug('i = %d' % i)

# See which files are created.
logfiles = glob.glob('%s*' % LOG_FILENAME)
for filename in logfiles:
    print(filename)
```

The result is six separate files, each with part of the log history for the application.

```
$ python3 logging_rotatingfile_example.py

logging_rotatingfile_example.out
logging_rotatingfile_example.out.1
logging_rotatingfile_example.out.2
logging_rotatingfile_example.out.3
logging_rotatingfile_example.out.4
logging_rotatingfile_example.out.5
```

In this example, the most current file is always `logging_rotatingfile_example.out`. Each time it reaches the size limit, this file is renamed with the suffix `.1`. Each of the existing backup files is renamed to increment the suffix (`.1` becomes `.2`, and so on) and the `.5` file is erased.

NOTE

Obviously, this example sets the log length much too small as an extreme example. Set `maxBytes` to a more appropriate value in a real program.

14.8.5   Verbosity Levels

Another useful feature of the `logging` API is the ability to produce different messages at different *log levels*. This means code can be instrumented with debug messages, for example, and the log level can be set so that those debug messages are not written on a production system. Table 14.2 lists the logging levels defined by `logging`.

The log message is shown only if the handler and the logger are configured to emit messages of that level or higher. For example, if a message is `CRITICAL`, and the logger is set to `ERROR`, the message is generated $(50 > 40)$. If a message is a `WARNING`, and the logger is set to produce only messages set to `ERROR`, the message is not generated $(30 < 40)$.

Table 14.2: Logging Levels

Level	Value
CRITICAL	50
ERROR	40
WARNING	30
INFO	20
DEBUG	10
UNSET	0

Listing 14.87: `logging_level_example.py`

```python
import logging
import sys

LEVELS = {
    'debug': logging.DEBUG,
    'info': logging.INFO,
    'warning': logging.WARNING,
    'error': logging.ERROR,
    'critical': logging.CRITICAL,
}

if len(sys.argv) > 1:
    level_name = sys.argv[1]
    level = LEVELS.get(level_name, logging.NOTSET)
    logging.basicConfig(level=level)

logging.debug('This is a debug message')
logging.info('This is an info message')
logging.warning('This is a warning message')
logging.error('This is an error message')
logging.critical('This is a critical error message')
```

Run the script with an argument such as debug or warning to see which messages show up at different levels.

```
$ python3 logging_level_example.py debug

DEBUG:root:This is a debug message
INFO:root:This is an info message
WARNING:root:This is a warning message
ERROR:root:This is an error message
CRITICAL:root:This is a critical error message

$ python3 logging_level_example.py info

INFO:root:This is an info message
WARNING:root:This is a warning message
```

```
ERROR:root:This is an error message
CRITICAL:root:This is a critical error message
```

14.8.6   Naming Logger Instances

The word `root` was embedded in all of the previous log messages because the code uses the root logger. An easy way to tell where a specific log message originates is to use a separate logger object for each module; log messages sent to a logger include the name of that logger. The following example illustrates logging from different modules in a way that makes it easy to trace the source of the message.

Listing 14.88: `logging_modules_example.py`

```python
import logging

logging.basicConfig(level=logging.WARNING)

logger1 = logging.getLogger('package1.module1')
logger2 = logging.getLogger('package2.module2')

logger1.warning('This message comes from one module')
logger2.warning('This comes from another module')
```

The output shows the different module names for each output line.

```
$ python3 logging_modules_example.py

WARNING:package1.module1:This message comes from one module
WARNING:package2.module2:This comes from another module
```

14.8.7   The Logging Tree

The `Logger` instances are configured in a tree structure, based on their names, as illustrated in Figure 14.1. Typically each application or library defines a base name, with loggers for individual modules set as children. The root logger has no name.

The tree structure is useful for configuring logging because it eliminates the need for each logger to have its own set of handlers. If a logger does not have any handlers, the message is handed to its parent for processing. Thus, for most applications, it is necessary to configure handlers only on the root logger, and all log information will be collected and sent to the same place, as shown in Figure 14.2.

The tree structure also allows different verbosity levels, handlers, and formatters to be set for different parts of the application or library. This flexibility allows the programmer to control which messages are logged and where they go, as shown in Figure 14.3.

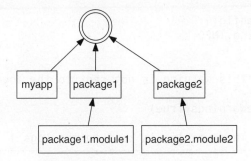

Figure 14.1: Example Logger Tree

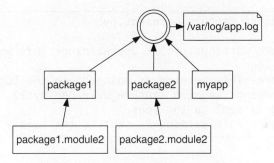

Figure 14.2: One Logging Handler

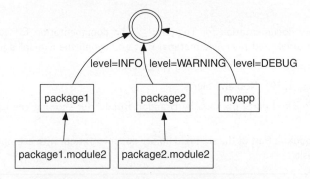

Figure 14.3: Different Levels and Handlers

14.8.8   Integration with the warnings Module

The logging module is integrated with warnings (page 1279) through the capture-Warnings() function, which configures warnings to send messages through the logging system instead of outputting them directly.

Listing 14.89: logging_capture_warnings.py

```
import logging
import warnings
```

```
logging.basicConfig(
    level=logging.INFO,
)

warnings.warn('This warning is not sent to the logs')

logging.captureWarnings(True)

warnings.warn('This warning is sent to the logs')
```

The warning message is sent to a logger named py.warnings using the WARNING level.

```
$ python3 logging_capture_warnings.py

logging_capture_warnings.py:13: UserWarning: This warning is not
  sent to the logs
  warnings.warn('This warning is not sent to the logs')
WARNING:py.warnings:logging_capture_warnings.py:17: UserWarning:
  This warning is sent to the logs
  warnings.warn('This warning is sent to the logs')
```

TIP

Related Reading

- Standard library documentation for logging[17]: The documentation for logging is extensive, and includes tutorials and reference material that go beyond the exmaples presented here.
- Python 2 to 3 porting notes for logging (page 1360).
- warnings (page 1279): Nonfatal alerts.
- logging_tree[18]: Third-party package by Brandon Rhodes for showing the logger tree for an application.
- Logging Cookbook[19]: Part of the standard library documentation, with examples of using logging for different tasks.

14.9   fileinput: Command-Line Filter Framework

The fileinput module is a framework for creating command-line programs for processing text files as a filter.

---

[17] https://docs.python.org/3.5/library/logging.html
[18] https://pypi.python.org/pypi/logging_tree
[19] https://docs.python.org/3.5/howto/logging-cookbook.html

14.9.1   Converting M3U Files to RSS

An example of a filter is m3utorss,[20] a program to convert a set of MP3 files into an RSS feed that can be shared as a podcast. The inputs to the program are one or more m3u files listing the MP3 files to be distributed. The output is an RSS feed printed to the console. To process the input, the program needs to iterate over the list of filenames and perform the following steps:

1. Open each file.

2. Read each line of the file.

3. Figure out if the line refers to an mp3 file.

4. If it does, add a new item to the RSS feed.

5. Print the output.

All of this file handling could have been coded by hand. It is not overly complicated and, with some testing, even the error handling would be right. Because `fileinput` handles all of the details, however, the program is greatly simplified.

```
for line in fileinput.input(sys.argv[1:]):
    mp3filename = line.strip()
    if not mp3filename or mp3filename.startswith('#'):
        continue
    item = SubElement(rss, 'item')
    title = SubElement(item, 'title')
    title.text = mp3filename
    encl = SubElement(item, 'enclosure',
                      {'type': 'audio/mpeg',
                       'url': mp3filename})
```

The `input()` function takes as an argument a list of filenames to examine. If the list is empty, the module reads data from standard input. The function returns an iterator that produces individual lines from the text files being processed. The caller just needs to loop over each line, skipping blanks and comments, to find the references to MP3 files.

The following listing provides the complete program.

Listing 14.90: `fileinput_example.py`

```
import fileinput
import sys
import time
from xml.etree.ElementTree import Element, SubElement, tostring
from xml.dom import minidom
```

---

[20] https://pypi.python.org/pypi/m3utorss

```
# Establish the RSS and channel nodes.
rss = Element('rss',
              {'xmlns:dc': "http://purl.org/dc/elements/1.1/",
               'version': '2.0'})
channel = SubElement(rss, 'channel')
title = SubElement(channel, 'title')
title.text = 'Sample podcast feed'
desc = SubElement(channel, 'description')
desc.text = 'Generated for PyMOTW'
pubdate = SubElement(channel, 'pubDate')
pubdate.text = time.asctime()
gen = SubElement(channel, 'generator')
gen.text = 'https://pymotw.com/'

for line in fileinput.input(sys.argv[1:]):
    mp3filename = line.strip()
    if not mp3filename or mp3filename.startswith('#'):
        continue
    item = SubElement(rss, 'item')
    title = SubElement(item, 'title')
    title.text = mp3filename
    encl = SubElement(item, 'enclosure',
                      {'type': 'audio/mpeg',
                       'url': mp3filename})

rough_string = tostring(rss)
reparsed = minidom.parseString(rough_string)
print(reparsed.toprettyxml(indent="  "))
```

The sample input file in the following listing contains the names of several MP3 files.

Listing 14.91: sample_data.m3u

```
# This is a sample m3u file.
episode-one.mp3
episode-two.mp3
```

Running `fileinput_example.py` with the sample input produces XML data using the RSS format.

```
$ python3 fileinput_example.py sample_data.m3u

<?xml version="1.0" ?>
<rss version="2.0" xmlns:dc="http://purl.org/dc/elements/1.1/">
  <channel>
    <title>Sample podcast feed</title>
    <description>Generated for PyMOTW</description>
    <pubDate>Sun Jul 10 10:45:01 2016</pubDate>
    <generator>https://pymotw.com/</generator>
```

```
        </channel>
        <item>
          <title>episode-one.mp3</title>
          <enclosure type="audio/mpeg" url="episode-one.mp3"/>
        </item>
        <item>
          <title>episode-two.mp3</title>
          <enclosure type="audio/mpeg" url="episode-two.mp3"/>
        </item>
      </rss>
```

14.9.2 Progress Metadata

In the previous example, the filename and the line number being processed were not important. Sometimes, however, tools such as grep-like search tools might need that information. fileinput includes functions for accessing all of the metadata about the current line (filename(), filelineno(), and lineno()).

Listing 14.92: fileinput_grep.py

```python
import fileinput
import re
import sys

pattern = re.compile(sys.argv[1])

for line in fileinput.input(sys.argv[2:]):
    if pattern.search(line):
        if fileinput.isstdin():
            fmt = '{lineno}:{line}'
        else:
            fmt = '{filename}:{lineno}:{line}'
        print(fmt.format(filename=fileinput.filename(),
                         lineno=fileinput.filelineno(),
                         line=line.rstrip()))
```

A basic pattern-matching loop can be used to find the occurrences of the string "fileinput" in the source for these examples.

```
$ python3 fileinput_grep.py fileinput *.py

fileinput_change_subnet.py:10:import fileinput
fileinput_change_subnet.py:17:for line in fileinput.input(files,
 inplace=True):
fileinput_change_subnet_noisy.py:10:import fileinput
fileinput_change_subnet_noisy.py:18:for line in fileinput.input(
files, inplace=True):
fileinput_change_subnet_noisy.py:19:    if fileinput.isfirstline
```

```
():
fileinput_change_subnet_noisy.py:21:              fileinput.filena
me()))
fileinput_example.py:6:"""Example for fileinput module.
fileinput_example.py:10:import fileinput
fileinput_example.py:30:for line in fileinput.input(sys.argv[1:]
):
fileinput_grep.py:10:import fileinput
fileinput_grep.py:16:for line in fileinput.input(sys.argv[2:]):
fileinput_grep.py:18:         if fileinput.isstdin():
fileinput_grep.py:22:          print(fmt.format(filename=fileinput
.filename(),
fileinput_grep.py:23:                        lineno=fileinput.f
ilelineno(),
```

Text can also be read from standard input.

```
$ cat *.py | python fileinput_grep.py fileinput

10:import fileinput
17:for line in fileinput.input(files, inplace=True):
29:import fileinput
37:for line in fileinput.input(files, inplace=True):
38:    if fileinput.isfirstline():
40:            fileinput.filename()))
54:"""Example for fileinput module.
58:import fileinput
78:for line in fileinput.input(sys.argv[1:]):
101:import fileinput
107:for line in fileinput.input(sys.argv[2:]):
109:        if fileinput.isstdin():
113:        print(fmt.format(filename=fileinput.filename(),
114:                        lineno=fileinput.filelineno(),
```

14.9.3   In-Place Filtering

Another common file-processing operation is to modify the content of a file where it is,
rather than creating a new file with the modified content. For example, a Unix hosts file
might need to be updated if a subnet range changes.

Listing 14.93: **etc_hosts.txt before modifications**

```
##
# Host Database
#
# localhost is used to configure the loopback interface
# when the system is booting.  Do not change this entry.
##
```

```
127.0.0.1           localhost
255.255.255.255 broadcasthost
::1                 localhost
fe80::1%lo0         localhost
10.16.177.128   hubert hubert.hellfly.net
10.16.177.132   cubert cubert.hellfly.net
10.16.177.136   zoidberg zoidberg.hellfly.net
```

The safe way to make the change automatically is to create a new file based on the input and then replace the original with the edited copy. fileinput supports this approach using the inplace option.

Listing 14.94: **fileinput_change_subnet.py**

```
import fileinput
import sys

from_base = sys.argv[1]
to_base = sys.argv[2]
files = sys.argv[3:]

for line in fileinput.input(files, inplace=True):
    line = line.rstrip().replace(from_base, to_base)
    print(line)
```

Although the preceding script uses print(), no output is produced because fileinput redirects standard output to the file being overwritten.

```
$ python3 fileinput_change_subnet.py 10.16 10.17 etc_hosts.txt
```

The updated file holds the changed IP addresses of all of the servers on the 10.16.0.0/16 network.

Listing 14.95: **etc_hosts.txt after modifications**

```
##
# Host Database
#
# localhost is used to configure the loopback interface
# when the system is booting.  Do not change this entry.
##
127.0.0.1           localhost
255.255.255.255 broadcasthost
::1                 localhost
fe80::1%lo0         localhost
10.17.177.128   hubert hubert.hellfly.net
10.17.177.132   cubert cubert.hellfly.net
10.17.177.136   zoidberg zoidberg.hellfly.net
```

Before processing begins, a backup file is created using the original name plus the extension .bak.

Listing 14.96: fileinput_change_subnet_noisy.py

```
import fileinput
import glob
import sys

from_base = sys.argv[1]
to_base = sys.argv[2]
files = sys.argv[3:]

for line in fileinput.input(files, inplace=True):
    if fileinput.isfirstline():
        sys.stderr.write('Started processing {}\n'.format(
            fileinput.filename()))
        sys.stderr.write('Directory contains: {}\n'.format(
            glob.glob('etc_hosts.txt*')))
    line = line.rstrip().replace(from_base, to_base)
    print(line)

sys.stderr.write('Finished processing\n')
sys.stderr.write('Directory contains: {}\n'.format(
    glob.glob('etc_hosts.txt*')))
```

The backup file is removed when the input is closed.

```
$ python3 fileinput_change_subnet_noisy.py 10.16. 10.17. etc_hosts.txt

Started processing etc_hosts.txt
Directory contains: ['etc_hosts.txt', 'etc_hosts.txt.bak']
Finished processing
Directory contains: ['etc_hosts.txt']
```

TIP

Related Reading

- Standard library documentation for fileinput.[21]
- m3utorss[22]: Script to convert m3u files listing MP3s to RSS files suitable for use as a podcast feed.
- xml.etree: More details of using ElementTree to produce XML.

---

[21] https://docs.python.org/3.5/library/fileinput.html
[22] https://pypi.python.org/pypi/m3utorss

14.10   atexit: Program Shutdown Callbacks

The `atexit` module provides an interface to register functions to be called when a program closes down normally.

14.10.1   Registering Exit Callbacks

The next example registers a function explicitly by calling `register()`.

Listing 14.97: atexit_simple.py

```
import atexit


def all_done():
    print('all_done()')


print('Registering')
atexit.register(all_done)
print('Registered')
```

Because the program does not do anything else, `all_done()` is called right away.

```
$ python3 atexit_simple.py

Registering
Registered
all_done()
```

It is also possible to register more than one function and to pass arguments to the registered functions. That approach can be useful to cleanly disconnect from databases and remove temporary files, among other things. Instead of keeping a list of resources that need to be freed, a separate cleanup function can be registered for each resource.

Listing 14.98: atexit_multiple.py

```
import atexit


def my_cleanup(name):
    print('my_cleanup({})'.format(name))


atexit.register(my_cleanup, 'first')
atexit.register(my_cleanup, 'second')
atexit.register(my_cleanup, 'third')
```

The exit functions are called in the reverse of the order in which they are registered. This method allows modules to be cleaned up in the reverse order from which they are imported (and therefore register their `atexit` functions), which should reduce dependency conflicts.

```
$ python3 atexit_multiple.py

my_cleanup(third)
my_cleanup(second)
my_cleanup(first)
```

14.10.2   Decorator Syntax

Functions that do not require any arguments can be registered by using `register()` as a decorator. This alternative syntax is convenient for cleanup functions that operate on module-level global data.

Listing 14.99: atexit_decorator.py

```
import atexit


@atexit.register
def all_done():
    print('all_done()')

print('starting main program')
```

Because the function is registered as it is defined, it is also important to ensure that it works properly even if the module does not perform any other work. If the resources it is supposed to clean up were never initialized, calling the exit callback should not produce an error.

```
$ python3 atexit_decorator.py

starting main program
all_done()
```

14.10.3   Canceling Callbacks

To cancel an exit callback, remove it from the registry using `unregister()`.

Listing 14.100: atexit_unregister.py

```
import atexit


def my_cleanup(name):
    print('my_cleanup({})'.format(name))

atexit.register(my_cleanup, 'first')
```

```
atexit.register(my_cleanup, 'second')
atexit.register(my_cleanup, 'third')

atexit.unregister(my_cleanup)
```

All calls to the same callback are canceled, regardless of how many times it has been registered.

```
$ python3 atexit_unregister.py
```

Removing a callback that was not previously registered is not considered an error.

Listing 14.101: atexit_unregister_not_registered.py

```
import atexit


def my_cleanup(name):
    print('my_cleanup({})'.format(name))

if False:
    atexit.register(my_cleanup, 'never registered')

atexit.unregister(my_cleanup)
```

Because it silently ignores unknown callbacks, `unregister()` can be used even when the sequence of registrations is not known.

```
$ python3 atexit_unregister_not_registered.py
```

14.10.4 When Are atexit Callbacks Not Called?

The callbacks registered with `atexit` are not invoked if any of the following conditions is met:

- The program dies because of a signal.

- `os._exit()` is invoked directly.

- A fatal error is detected in the interpreter.

An example from the `subprocess` (page 535) section can be updated to show what happens when a program is killed by a signal. Two files are involved—the parent and the child programs. The parent starts the child, pauses, and then kills the child.

Listing 14.102: atexit_signal_parent.py

```
import os
import signal
```

```
import subprocess
import time

proc = subprocess.Popen('./atexit_signal_child.py')
print('PARENT: Pausing before sending signal...')
time.sleep(1)
print('PARENT: Signaling child')
os.kill(proc.pid, signal.SIGTERM)
```

The child sets up an atexit callback, and then sleeps until the signal arrives.

Listing 14.103: **atexit_signal_child.py**

```
import atexit
import time
import sys


def not_called():
    print('CHILD: atexit handler should not have been called')

print('CHILD: Registering atexit handler')
sys.stdout.flush()
atexit.register(not_called)

print('CHILD: Pausing to wait for signal')
sys.stdout.flush()
time.sleep(5)
```

When this script is run, it produces the following output.

```
$ python3 atexit_signal_parent.py

CHILD: Registering atexit handler
CHILD: Pausing to wait for signal
PARENT: Pausing before sending signal...
PARENT: Signaling child
```

The child does not print the message embedded in not_called().

By using os._exit(), the programmer can avoid invoking the atexit callbacks.

Listing 14.104: **atexit_os_exit.py**

```
import atexit
import os


def not_called():
    print('This should not be called')

print('Registering')
```

```
atexit.register(not_called)
print('Registered')

print('Exiting...')
os._exit(0)
```

Because this example bypasses the normal exit path, the callback does not run. In addition, the print output is not flushed, so the example is run with the -u option to enable unbuffered I/O.

```
$ python3 -u atexit_os_exit.py

Registering
Registered
Exiting...
```

To ensure that the callbacks are run, allow the program to terminate by running out of statements to execute or by calling sys.exit().

Listing 14.105: atexit_sys_exit.py

```
import atexit
import sys


def all_done():
    print('all_done()')

print('Registering')
atexit.register(all_done)
print('Registered')

print('Exiting...')
sys.exit()
```

This example calls sys.exit(), so the registered callbacks are invoked.

```
$ python3 atexit_sys_exit.py

Registering
Registered
Exiting...
all_done()
```

14.10.5 Handling Exceptions

Tracebacks for exceptions raised in atexit callbacks are printed to the console. The last exception raised is raised again and serves as the final error message of the program.

Listing 14.106: **atexit_exception.py**

```
import atexit


def exit_with_exception(message):
    raise RuntimeError(message)


atexit.register(exit_with_exception, 'Registered first')
atexit.register(exit_with_exception, 'Registered second')
```

The registration order controls the execution order. If an error in one callback introduces an error in another (registered earlier, but called later), the final error message might not be the most useful error message to show the user.

```
$ python3 atexit_exception.py

Error in atexit._run_exitfuncs:
Traceback (most recent call last):
  File "atexit_exception.py", line 11, in exit_with_exception
    raise RuntimeError(message)
RuntimeError: Registered second
Error in atexit._run_exitfuncs:
Traceback (most recent call last):
  File "atexit_exception.py", line 11, in exit_with_exception
    raise RuntimeError(message)
RuntimeError: Registered first
```

The best approach is usually to handle and quietly log all exceptions in cleanup functions: It is messy to have a program dump errors on exit.

TIP

Related Reading

- Standard library documentation for atexit.[23]
- Section 17.2.4, "Exception Handling" (page 1194): Global handling for uncaught exceptions.
- Python 2 to 3 porting notes for atexit (page 1357).

14.11   sched: Timed Event Scheduler

The sched module implements a generic event scheduler for running tasks at specific times. The scheduler class uses a time function to learn the current time, and a delay function

---

[23] https://docs.python.org/3.5/library/atexit.html

to wait for a specific period of time. The actual units of time are not important, so the interface is flexible enough to be used for many purposes.

The `time` function is called without any arguments, and should return a number representing the current time. The `delay` function is called with a single integer argument, using the same scale as the time function, and should wait that many time units before returning. By default, `monotonic()` and `sleep()` from the `time` (page 211) module are used, but the examples in this section use `time.time()`, which also meets the requirements, because it makes the output easier to understand.

To support multithreaded applications, the delay function is called with argument 0 after each event is generated, to ensure that other threads also have a chance to run.

14.11.1   Running Events with a Delay

Events can be scheduled to run after a delay, or at a specific time. To schedule them with a delay, use the `enter()` method, which takes four arguments:

- A number representing the delay

- A priority value

- The function to call

- A tuple of arguments for the function

This example schedules two different events to run after 2 and 3 seconds, respectively. When the event's time comes up, `print_event()` is called and prints the current time and the name argument passed to the event.

Listing 14.107: sched_basic.py

```
import sched
import time

scheduler = sched.scheduler(time.time, time.sleep)


def print_event(name, start):
    now = time.time()
    elapsed = int(now - start)
    print('EVENT: {} elapsed={} name={}'.format(
        time.ctime(now), elapsed, name))

start = time.time()
print('START:', time.ctime(start))
scheduler.enter(2, 1, print_event, ('first', start))
scheduler.enter(3, 1, print_event, ('second', start))

scheduler.run()
```

Running this program produces the following output.

```
$ python3 sched_basic.py

START: Sun Sep  4 16:21:01 2016
EVENT: Sun Sep  4 16:21:03 2016 elapsed=2 name=first
EVENT: Sun Sep  4 16:21:04 2016 elapsed=3 name=second
```

The time printed for the first event is 2 seconds after start, and the time for the second event is 3 seconds after start.

14.11.2 Overlapping Events

The call to run() blocks until all of the events have been processed. Each event runs in the same thread, so if an event takes longer to run than the delay between events, overlap will occur. The overlap is resolved by postponing the later event. No events are lost, but some events may be called later than they were scheduled. In the next example, long_event() sleeps, but it could just as easily delay the processing by performing a long calculation or by blocking on I/O.

Listing 14.108: sched_overlap.py

```python
import sched
import time

scheduler = sched.scheduler(time.time, time.sleep)


def long_event(name):
    print('BEGIN EVENT :', time.ctime(time.time()), name)
    time.sleep(2)
    print('FINISH EVENT:', time.ctime(time.time()), name)

print('START:', time.ctime(time.time()))
scheduler.enter(2, 1, long_event, ('first',))
scheduler.enter(3, 1, long_event, ('second',))

scheduler.run()
```

The result is that the second event runs immediately after the first finishes, since the first event took long enough to push the clock past the desired starting time of the second event.

```
$ python3 sched_overlap.py

START: Sun Sep  4 16:21:04 2016
BEGIN EVENT : Sun Sep  4 16:21:06 2016 first
FINISH EVENT: Sun Sep  4 16:21:08 2016 first
BEGIN EVENT : Sun Sep  4 16:21:08 2016 second
FINISH EVENT: Sun Sep  4 16:21:10 2016 second
```

14.11.3 Event Priorities

If more than one event is scheduled for the same time, those events' priority values are used to determine the order in which they run.

Listing 14.109: **sched_priority.py**

```
import sched
import time

scheduler = sched.scheduler(time.time, time.sleep)


def print_event(name):
    print('EVENT:', time.ctime(time.time()), name)

now = time.time()
print('START:', time.ctime(now))
scheduler.enterabs(now + 2, 2, print_event, ('first',))
scheduler.enterabs(now + 2, 1, print_event, ('second',))

scheduler.run()
```

This example needs to ensure that the events are scheduled for the exact same time, so the enterabs() method is used instead of enter(). The first argument to enterabs() is the time to run the event, instead of the amount of time to delay its start.

```
$ python3 sched_priority.py

START: Sun Sep  4 16:21:10 2016
EVENT: Sun Sep  4 16:21:12 2016 second
EVENT: Sun Sep  4 16:21:12 2016 first
```

14.11.4 Canceling Events

Both enter() and enterabs() return a reference to the event that can be used to cancel that event later. Because run() blocks, the event must be canceled in a different thread. In this example, a thread is started to run the scheduler and the main processing thread is used to cancel the event.

Listing 14.110: **sched_cancel.py**

```
import sched
import threading
import time

scheduler = sched.scheduler(time.time, time.sleep)

# Set up a global to be modified by the threads.
```

```
counter = 0


def increment_counter(name):
    global counter
    print('EVENT:', time.ctime(time.time()), name)
    counter += 1
    print('NOW:', counter)

print('START:', time.ctime(time.time()))
e1 = scheduler.enter(2, 1, increment_counter, ('E1',))
e2 = scheduler.enter(3, 1, increment_counter, ('E2',))

# Start a thread to run the events.
t = threading.Thread(target=scheduler.run)
t.start()

# Back in the main thread, cancel the first scheduled event.
scheduler.cancel(e1)

# Wait for the scheduler to finish running in the thread.
t.join()

print('FINAL:', counter)
```

Two events were scheduled, but the first was later canceled. Only the second event runs, so the counter variable is incremented only one time.

```
$ python3 sched_cancel.py

START: Sun Sep  4 16:21:13 2016
EVENT: Sun Sep  4 16:21:16 2016 E2
NOW: 1
FINAL: 1
```

TIP

Related Reading

- Standard library documentation for sched.[24]
- time (page 211): The time module.

[24] https://docs.python.org/3.5/library/sched.html

Chapter 15

Internationalization and Localization

Python comes with two modules for preparing an application to work with multiple natural languages and cultural settings. gettext (page 1003) is used to create message catalogs in different languages, so that prompts and error messages can be displayed in a language that the user can understand. locale (page 1012) changes the way numbers, currency, dates, and times are formatted to take into account cultural differences such as how negative values are indicated and what the local currency symbol is. Both modules interface with other tools and the operating environment so that the Python application will fit in with all of the other programs on the system.

15.1 gettext: Message Catalogs

The gettext module provides a pure-Python implementation that is compatible with the GNU gettext library for message translation and catalog management. The tools available with the Python source distribution enable you to extract messages from a set of source files, build a message catalog containing translations, and use that message catalog to display an appropriate message for the user at runtime.

Message catalogs can be used to provide internationalized interfaces for a program, showing messages in a language appropriate to the user. They can also be used for other message customizations, including "skinning" an interface for different wrappers or partners.

NOTE

Although the standard library documentation says all of the necessary tools are included with Python, pygettext.py failed to extract messages wrapped in the ngettext call, even with the appropriate command-line options. These examples use xgettext from the GNU gettext tool set, instead of pygettext.py.

15.1.1 Translation Workflow Overview

The process for setting up and using translations includes five steps:

1. *Identify and mark up literal strings in the source code that contain messages to translate.*

   Start by identifying the messages within the program source that need to be translated and marking the literal strings so the extraction program can find them.

2. *Extract the messages.*

   After identifying the translatable strings in the source, use xgettext to extract them and create a .pot file, or *translation template.* The template is a text file with copies of all of the strings identified and placeholders for their translations.

3. *Translate the messages.*

   Give a copy of the .pot file to the translator, changing the extension to .po. The .po file is an editable source file used as input for the compilation step. The translator should update the header text in the file and provide translations for all of the strings.

4. *"Compile" the message catalog from the translation.*

   When the translator sends back the completed .po file, compile the text file to the binary catalog format using msgfmt. The binary format is used by the runtime catalog's lookup code.

5. *Load and activate the appropriate message catalog at runtime.*

   The final step is to add a few lines to the application to configure and load the message catalog and install the translation function. There are a few ways to do that, though all have associated trade-offs.

The rest of this section will examine these steps in a little more detail, starting with the code modifications needed.

15.1.2 Creating Message Catalogs from Source Code

gettext works by looking up literal strings in a database of translations and pulling out the appropriate translated string. The usual pattern is to bind the appropriate lookup function to the name _ (a single underscore character) so that the code is not cluttered with multiple calls to functions with longer names.

The message extraction program, xgettext, looks for messages embedded in calls to the catalog lookup functions. It understands different source languages and uses an appropriate parser for each. If the lookup functions are aliased, or if extra functions are added, give xgettext the names of additional symbols to consider when extracting messages.

This script has a single message that is ready to be translated.

Listing 15.1: gettext_example.py

```
import gettext

# Set up message catalog access.
t = gettext.translation(
    'example_domain', 'locale',
    fallback=True,
)
_ = t.gettext

print(_('This message is in the script.'))
```

The text "This message is in the script." is the message to be substituted from the catalog. Fallback mode is enabled, so if the script is run without a message catalog, the inline message is printed.

```
$ python3 gettext_example.py

This message is in the script.
```

The next step is to extract the message and create the .pot file, using pygettext.py or xgettext.

```
$ xgettext -o example.pot gettext_example.py
```

The output file produced contains the following content.

Listing 15.2: example.pot

```
# SOME DESCRIPTIVE TITLE.
# Copyright (C) YEAR THE PACKAGE'S COPYRIGHT HOLDER
# This file is distributed under the same license as the PACKAGE package.
# FIRST AUTHOR <EMAIL@ADDRESS>, YEAR.
#
#, fuzzy
msgid ""
msgstr ""
"Project-Id-Version: PACKAGE VERSION\n"
"Report-Msgid-Bugs-To: \n"
"POT-Creation-Date: 2016-07-10 10:45-0400\n"
"PO-Revision-Date: YEAR-MO-DA HO:MI+ZONE\n"
"Last-Translator: FULL NAME <EMAIL@ADDRESS>\n"
"Language-Team: LANGUAGE <LL@li.org>\n"
"Language: \n"
"MIME-Version: 1.0\n"
"Content-Type: text/plain; charset=CHARSET\n"
"Content-Transfer-Encoding: 8bit\n"

#: gettext_example.py:19
msgid "This message is in the script."
msgstr ""
```

Message catalogs are installed into directories organized by *domain* and *language*. The domain is provided by the application or library, and is usually a unique value like the application name. In this case, the domain in gettext_example.py is example_domain. The language value is provided by the user's environment at runtime, through one of the environment variables LANGUAGE, LC_ALL, LC_MESSAGES, or LANG, depending on the configuration and platform. The examples in this chapter were all run with the language set to en_US.

Now that the template is ready, the next step is to create the required directory structure and copy the template to the right spot. The locale directory inside the PyMOTW source tree will serve as the root of the message catalog directory for these examples, but it is typically better to use a directory that is accessible system-wide so that all users have access to the message catalogs. The full path to the catalog input source is `$localedir/$language/LC_MESSAGES/$domain.po`, and the actual catalog has the filename extension .mo.

To create the catalog, copy `example.pot` to `locale/en_US/LC_MESSAGES/example.po` and edit it to change the values in the header and set the alternate messages. The result is shown in the following listing.

Listing 15.3: **locale/en_US/LC_MESSAGES/example.po**

```
# Messages from gettext_example.py.
# Copyright (C) 2009 Doug Hellmann
# Doug Hellmann <doug@doughellmann.com>, 2016.
#
msgid ""
msgstr ""
"Project-Id-Version: PyMOTW-3\n"
"Report-Msgid-Bugs-To: Doug Hellmann <doug@doughellmann.com>\n"
"POT-Creation-Date: 2016-01-24 13:04-0500\n"
"PO-Revision-Date: 2016-01-24 13:04-0500\n"
"Last-Translator: Doug Hellmann <doug@doughellmann.com>\n"
"Language-Team: US English <doug@doughellmann.com>\n"
"MIME-Version: 1.0\n"
"Content-Type: text/plain; charset=UTF-8\n"
"Content-Transfer-Encoding: 8bit\n"


#: gettext_example.py:16
msgid "This message is in the script."
msgstr "This message is in the en_US catalog."
```

The catalog is built from the `.po` file using `msgformat`.

```
$ cd locale/en_US/LC_MESSAGES; msgfmt -o example.mo example.po
```

The domain in `gettext_example.py` is `example_domain`, but the file is called `example.pot`. To have `gettext` find the right translation file, the names need to match.

Listing 15.4: **gettext_example_corrected.py**

```
t = gettext.translation(
    'example', 'locale',
    fallback=True,
)
```

Now when the script is run, the message from the catalog is printed instead of the inline string.

```
$ python3 gettext_example_corrected.py

This message is in the en_US catalog.
```

15.1.3   Finding Message Catalogs at Runtime

As described earlier, the *locale directory* containing the message catalogs is organized based on the language, with catalogs named for the *domain* of the program. Different operating systems define their own default values, but gettext does not know all of these defaults. It uses a default locale directory of sys.prefix + '/share/locale', but most of the time it is safer to explicitly give a localedir value than to depend on this default always being valid. The find() function is responsible for locating an appropriate message catalog at runtime.

Listing 15.5: **gettext_find.py**

```
import gettext

catalogs = gettext.find('example', 'locale', all=True)
print('Catalogs:', catalogs)
```

The language portion of the path is taken from one of several environment variables that can be used to configure localization features (LANGUAGE, LC_ALL, LC_MESSAGES, and LANG). The first variable that is found to be set is used for this purpose. To select multiple languages, separate the values with a colon (:). To show how that works, the following examples use gettext_find.py to run a few experiments.

```
$ cd locale/en_CA/LC_MESSAGES; msgfmt -o example.mo example.po
$ cd ../../..
$ python3 gettext_find.py

Catalogs: ['locale/en_US/LC_MESSAGES/example.mo']

$ LANGUAGE=en_CA python3 gettext_find.py

Catalogs: ['locale/en_CA/LC_MESSAGES/example.mo']

$ LANGUAGE=en_CA:en_US python3 gettext_find.py

Catalogs: ['locale/en_CA/LC_MESSAGES/example.mo',
'locale/en_US/LC_MESSAGES/example.mo']

$ LANGUAGE=en_US:en_CA python3 gettext_find.py

Catalogs: ['locale/en_US/LC_MESSAGES/example.mo',
'locale/en_CA/LC_MESSAGES/example.mo']
```

Although `find()` shows the complete list of catalogs, only the first one in the sequence is actually loaded for message lookups.

```
$ python3 gettext_example_corrected.py

This message is in the en_US catalog.

$ LANGUAGE=en_CA python3 gettext_example_corrected.py

This message is in the en_CA catalog.

$ LANGUAGE=en_CA:en_US python3 gettext_example_corrected.py

This message is in the en_CA catalog.

$ LANGUAGE=en_US:en_CA python3 gettext_example_corrected.py

This message is in the en_US catalog.
```

15.1.4   Plural Values

While simple message substitution will handle most translation needs, `gettext` treats pluralization as a special case. Depending on the language, the difference between the singular and plural forms of a message may vary only by the ending of a single word; alternatively, the entire sentence structure may be different. Different forms may also exist depending on the level of plurality. To make managing plurals easier (and, in some cases, possible), a separate set of functions is provided for asking for the plural form of a message.

Listing 15.6: `gettext_plural.py`

```
from gettext import translation
import sys

t = translation('plural', 'locale', fallback=False)
num = int(sys.argv[1])
msg = t.ngettext('{num} means singular.',
                 '{num} means plural.',
                 num)

# Still need to add the values to the message ourselves
print(msg.format(num=num))
```

Use `ngettext()` to access the plural substitution for a message. The arguments are the messages to be translated and the item count.

```
$ xgettext -L Python -o plural.pot gettext_plural.py
```

Since there are alternate forms to be translated, the replacements are listed in an array. Using an array facilitates translations for languages with multiple plural forms (e.g., Polish has different forms indicating the relative quantity).

Listing 15.7: `plural.pot`

```
# SOME DESCRIPTIVE TITLE.
# Copyright (C) YEAR THE PACKAGE'S COPYRIGHT HOLDER
# This file is distributed under the same license as the PACKAGE package.
# FIRST AUTHOR <EMAIL@ADDRESS>, YEAR.
#
#, fuzzy
msgid ""
msgstr ""
"Project-Id-Version: PACKAGE VERSION\n"
"Report-Msgid-Bugs-To: \n"
"POT-Creation-Date: 2016-07-10 10:45-0400\n"
"PO-Revision-Date: YEAR-MO-DA HO:MI+ZONE\n"
"Last-Translator: FULL NAME <EMAIL@ADDRESS>\n"
"Language-Team: LANGUAGE <LL@li.org>\n"
"Language: \n"
"MIME-Version: 1.0\n"
"Content-Type: text/plain; charset=CHARSET\n"
"Content-Transfer-Encoding: 8bit\n"
"Plural-Forms: nplurals=INTEGER; plural=EXPRESSION;\n"

#: gettext_plural.py:15
#, python-brace-format
msgid "{num} means singular."
msgid_plural "{num} means plural."
msgstr[0] ""
msgstr[1] ""
```

In addition to filling in the translation strings, the library needs to be told about the way plurals are formed so it knows how to index into the array for any given count value. The line `"Plural-Forms: nplurals=INTEGER; plural=EXPRESSION;\n"` includes two values that must be replaced manually: `nplurals`, which is an integer indicating the size of the array (the number of translations used), and `plural`, which is a C language expression for converting the incoming quantity to an index in the array when looking up the translation. The literal string n is replaced with the quantity passed to `ungettext()`.

As an example, consider that English includes two plural forms. A quantity of 0 is treated as plural ("0 bananas"). The `Plural-Forms` entry is

```
Plural-Forms: nplurals=2; plural=n != 1;
```

The singular translation would be placed in position 0, and the plural translation in position 1.

```
# Messages from gettext_plural.py
# Copyright (C) 2009 Doug Hellmann
# This file is distributed under the same license
# as the PyMOTW package.
# Doug Hellmann <doug@doughellmann.com>, 2016.
#
#, fuzzy
msgid ""
msgstr ""
"Project-Id-Version: PyMOTW-3\n"
"Report-Msgid-Bugs-To: Doug Hellmann <doug@doughellmann.com>\n"
"POT-Creation-Date: 2016-01-24 13:04-0500\n"
"PO-Revision-Date: 2016-01-24 13:04-0500\n"
"Last-Translator: Doug Hellmann <doug@doughellmann.com>\n"
"Language-Team: en_US <doug@doughellmann.com>\n"
"MIME-Version: 1.0\n"
"Content-Type: text/plain; charset=UTF-8\n"
"Content-Transfer-Encoding: 8bit\n"
"Plural-Forms: nplurals=2; plural=n != 1;"

#: gettext_plural.py:15
#, python-format
msgid "{num} means singular."
msgid_plural "{num} means plural."
msgstr[0] "In en_US, {num} is singular."
msgstr[1] "In en_US, {num} is plural."
```

Running the test script a few times after the catalog is compiled will demonstrate how different values of N are converted to indexes for the translation strings.

```
$ cd locale/en_US/LC_MESSAGES/; msgfmt -o plural.mo plural.po
$ cd ../../..
$ python3 gettext_plural.py 0

In en_US, 0 is plural.

$ python3 gettext_plural.py 1

In en_US, 1 is singular.

$ python3 gettext_plural.py 2

In en_US, 2 is plural.
```

15.1.5   Application Versus Module Localization

The scope of a translation effort defines how gettext is installed and used with a body of code.

15.1.5.1   Application Localization

For application-wide translations, it is acceptable for the author to install a function such as ngettext() globally using the __builtins__ namespace, because the author has control over the application's top-level code and understands the full set of requirements.

Listing 15.9: **gettext_app_builtin.py**

```
import gettext

gettext.install(
    'example',
    'locale',
    names=['ngettext'],
)

print(_('This message is in the script.'))
```

The install() function binds gettext() to the name _() in the __builtins__ namespace. It also adds ngettext() and other functions listed in names.

15.1.5.2   Module Localization

For a library or an individual module, modifying __builtins__ is not a good idea, because doing so may introduce conflicts with an application's global value. Instead, import or rebind the names of translation functions by hand at the top of the module.

Listing 15.10: **gettext_module_global.py**

```
import gettext

t = gettext.translation(
    'example',
    'locale',
    fallback=False,
)
_ = t.gettext
ngettext = t.ngettext

print(_('This message is in the script.'))
```

15.1.6   Switching Translations

The earlier examples all used a single translation for the duration of the program. In some situations, especially in web applications, different message catalogs should be used at different times, without exiting and resetting the environment. For those cases, the class-based API provided in `gettext` will be more convenient. The API calls are essentially the same as the global calls described in this section, but the message catalog object is exposed and can be manipulated directly, so that multiple catalogs can be used.

TIP

Related Reading

- Standard library documentation for `gettext`.[1]
- `locale` (page 1012): Other localization tools.
- GNU gettext[2]: The message catalog formats, API, and other ancillaries for this module are all based on the original gettext package from GNU. The catalog file formats are compatible, and the command-line scripts have similar options (if not identical). The GNU gettext manual[3] has a detailed description of the file formats and describes GNU versions of the tools for working with them.
- Plural forms[4]: Handling of plural forms of words and sentences in different languages.
- Internationalizing Python[5]: A paper by Martin von Löwis about techniques for internationalization of Python applications.
- Django Internationalization[6]: Another good source of information on using `gettext`, including real-life examples.

15.2   locale: Cultural Localization API

The `locale` module is part of Python's internationalization and localization support library. It provides a standard way to handle operations that may depend on the language or location of a user. For example, it handles formatting numbers as currency, comparing strings for sorting, and working with dates. It does not cover translation [see the `gettext` (page 1003) module] or Unicode encoding [see the `codecs` (page 365) module].

NOTE

Changing the locale can have application-wide ramifications, so the recommended practice is to avoid changing the value in a library and to let the application set it one time. In the examples in this section, the locale is changed several times within a short program to highlight the differences in the settings of various locales. It is far more likely that an application will set the locale once as it starts up or when a web request is received, and will not change it repeatedly.

---

[1] https://docs.python.org/3.5/library/gettext.html
[2] www.gnu.org/software/gettext/
[3] www.gnu.org/software/gettext/manual/gettext.html
[4] www.gnu.org/software/gettext/manual/gettext.html#Plural-forms
[5] http://legacy.python.org/workshops/1997-10/proceedings/loewis.html
[6] https://docs.djangoproject.com/en/dev/topics/i18n/

This section covers some of the high-level functions in the `locale` module. Other functions are lower level (`format_string()`) or relate to managing the locale for an application (`resetlocale()`).

15.2.1 Probing the Current Locale

The most common way to let the user change the locale settings for an application is through an environment variable (`LC_ALL`, `LC_CTYPE`, `LANG`, or `LANGUAGE`, depending on the platform). The application then calls `setlocale()` without a hard-coded value, and the environment value is used.

Listing 15.11: `locale_env.py`

```python
import locale
import os
import pprint

# Default settings based on the user's environment
locale.setlocale(locale.LC_ALL, '')

print('Environment settings:')
for env_name in ['LC_ALL', 'LC_CTYPE', 'LANG', 'LANGUAGE']:
    print('  {} = {}'.format(
        env_name, os.environ.get(env_name, ''))
    )

# What is the locale?
print('\nLocale from environment:', locale.getlocale())

template = """
Numeric formatting:

  Decimal point      : "{decimal_point}"
  Grouping positions : {grouping}
  Thousands separator: "{thousands_sep}"

Monetary formatting:

  International currency symbol  : "{int_curr_symbol!r}"
  Local currency symbol          : {currency_symbol!r}
  Symbol precedes positive value : {p_cs_precedes}
  Symbol precedes negative value : {n_cs_precedes}
  Decimal point                  : "{mon_decimal_point}"
  Digits in fractional values    : {frac_digits}
  Digits in fractional values,
                   international  : {int_frac_digits}
  Grouping positions             : {mon_grouping}
  Thousands separator            : "{mon_thousands_sep}"
  Positive sign                  : "{positive_sign}"
  Positive sign position         : {p_sign_posn}
  Negative sign                  : "{negative_sign}"
```

```
    Negative sign position            : {n_sign_posn}

"""

sign_positions = {
    0: 'Surrounded by parentheses',
    1: 'Before value and symbol',
    2: 'After value and symbol',
    3: 'Before value',
    4: 'After value',
    locale.CHAR_MAX: 'Unspecified',
}

info = {}
info.update(locale.localeconv())
info['p_sign_posn'] = sign_positions[info['p_sign_posn']]
info['n_sign_posn'] = sign_positions[info['n_sign_posn']]

print(template.format(**info))
```

The localeconv() method returns a dictionary containing the locale's conventions. The full list of value names and definitions is covered in the standard library documentation.

A Mac running OS X 10.11.6 with all of the variables unset produces the following output.

```
$ export LANG=; export LC_CTYPE=; python3 locale_env.py

Environment settings:
  LC_ALL =
  LC_CTYPE =
  LANG =
  LANGUAGE =

Locale from environment: (None, None)

Numeric formatting:

  Decimal point      : "."
  Grouping positions : []
  Thousands separator: ""

Monetary formatting:

  International currency symbol  : "'''"
  Local currency symbol         : ''
  Symbol precedes positive value : 127
  Symbol precedes negative value : 127
```

```
Decimal point                      : ""
Digits in fractional values        : 127
Digits in fractional values,
                   international    : 127
Grouping positions                 : []
Thousands separator                : ""
Positive sign                      : ""
Positive sign position               : Unspecified
Negative sign                      : ""
Negative sign position               : Unspecified
```

Running the same script with the LANG variable set shows how the locale and default encoding change.

United States (en_US):

```
$ LANG=en_US LC_CTYPE=en_US LC_ALL=en_US python3 locale_env.py

Environment settings:
  LC_ALL = en_US
  LC_CTYPE = en_US
  LANG = en_US
  LANGUAGE =

Locale from environment: ('en_US', 'ISO8859-1')

Numeric formatting:

  Decimal point     : "."
  Grouping positions : [3, 3, 0]
  Thousands separator: ","

Monetary formatting:

  International currency symbol   : "'USD '"
  Local currency symbol          : '$'
  Symbol precedes positive value  : 1
  Symbol precedes negative value  : 1
  Decimal point                  : "."
  Digits in fractional values    : 2
  Digits in fractional values,
                   international  : 2
  Grouping positions             : [3, 3, 0]
  Thousands separator            : ","
  Positive sign                  : ""
  Positive sign position         : Before value and symbol
  Negative sign                  : "-"
  Negative sign position         : Before value and symbol
```

France (fr_FR):

```
$ LANG=fr_FR LC_CTYPE=fr_FR LC_ALL=fr_FR python3 locale_env.py

Environment settings:
  LC_ALL = fr_FR
  LC_CTYPE = fr_FR
  LANG = fr_FR
  LANGUAGE =

Locale from environment: ('fr_FR', 'ISO8859-1')

Numeric formatting:

  Decimal point      : ","
  Grouping positions : [127]
  Thousands separator: ""

Monetary formatting:

  International currency symbol   : "'EUR '"
  Local currency symbol          : 'Eu'
  Symbol precedes positive value : 0
  Symbol precedes negative value : 0
  Decimal point                  : ","
  Digits in fractional values    : 2
  Digits in fractional values,
                    international : 2
  Grouping positions             : [3, 3, 0]
  Thousands separator            : " "
  Positive sign                  : ""
  Positive sign position         : Before value and symbol
  Negative sign                  : "-"
  Negative sign position         : After value and symbol
```

Spain (es_ES):

```
$ LANG=es_ES LC_CTYPE=es_ES LC_ALL=es_ES python3 locale_env.py

Environment settings:
  LC_ALL = es_ES
  LC_CTYPE = es_ES
  LANG = es_ES
  LANGUAGE =

Locale from environment: ('es_ES', 'ISO8859-1')

Numeric formatting:
```

```
    Decimal point       : ","
    Grouping positions : [127]
    Thousands separator: ""

Monetary formatting:

    International currency symbol  : "'EUR '"
    Local currency symbol         : 'Eu'
    Symbol precedes positive value : 0
    Symbol precedes negative value : 0
    Decimal point                 : ","
    Digits in fractional values   : 2
    Digits in fractional values,
                   international   : 2
    Grouping positions            : [3, 3, 0]
    Thousands separator           : "."
    Positive sign                 : ""
    Positive sign position        : Before value and symbol
    Negative sign                 : "-"
    Negative sign position        : Before value and symbol
```

Portugal (pt_PT):

```
$ LANG=pt_PT LC_CTYPE=pt_PT LC_ALL=pt_PT python3 locale_env.py

Environment settings:
  LC_ALL = pt_PT
  LC_CTYPE = pt_PT
  LANG = pt_PT
  LANGUAGE =

Locale from environment: ('pt_PT', 'ISO8859-1')

Numeric formatting:

  Decimal point       : ","
  Grouping positions : []
  Thousands separator: " "

Monetary formatting:

  International currency symbol  : "'EUR '"
  Local currency symbol         : 'Eu'
  Symbol precedes positive value : 0
  Symbol precedes negative value : 0
  Decimal point                 : "."
  Digits in fractional values   : 2
```

```
       Digits in fractional values,
                      international  : 2
       Grouping positions           : [3, 3, 0]
       Thousands separator          : "."
       Positive sign                : ""
       Positive sign position       : Before value and symbol
       Negative sign                : "-"
       Negative sign position       : Before value and symbol
```

Poland (pl_PL):

```
$ LANG=pl_PL LC_CTYPE=pl_PL LC_ALL=pl_PL python3 locale_env.py

Environment settings:
  LC_ALL = pl_PL
  LC_CTYPE = pl_PL
  LANG = pl_PL
  LANGUAGE =

Locale from environment: ('pl_PL', 'ISO8859-2')

Numeric formatting:

  Decimal point       : ","
  Grouping positions : [3, 3, 0]
  Thousands separator: " "

Monetary formatting:

  International currency symbol  : "'PLN '"
  Local currency symbol         : 'z'
  Symbol precedes positive value : 1
  Symbol precedes negative value : 1
  Decimal point                 : ","
  Digits in fractional values   : 2
  Digits in fractional values,
                   international : 2
  Grouping positions            : [3, 3, 0]
  Thousands separator           : " "
  Positive sign                 : ""
  Positive sign position        : After value
  Negative sign                 : "-"
  Negative sign position        : After value
```

15.2.2 Currency

The earlier example output shows that changing the locale updates the currency symbol setting and the character to separate whole numbers from decimal fractions. This example loops through several different locales to print positive and negative currency values formatted for each locale.

Listing 15.12: <code>locale_currency.py</code>

```
import locale

sample_locales = [
    ('USA', 'en_US'),
    ('France', 'fr_FR'),
    ('Spain', 'es_ES'),
    ('Portugal', 'pt_PT'),
    ('Poland', 'pl_PL'),
]

for name, loc in sample_locales:
    locale.setlocale(locale.LC_ALL, loc)
    print('{:>10}: {:>10}  {:>10}'.format(
        name,
        locale.currency(1234.56),
        locale.currency(-1234.56),
    ))
```

The output is this small table:

```
$ python3 locale_currency.py

     USA:    $1234.56    -$1234.56
  France: 1234,56 Eu   1234,56 Eu-
   Spain: 1234,56 Eu  -1234,56 Eu
Portugal: 1234.56 Eu  -1234.56 Eu
  Poland: łz 1234,56 ł z 1234,56-
```

15.2.3   Formatting Numbers

Numbers not related to currency are also formatted differently depending on the locale. In particular, the grouping character used to separate large numbers into readable chunks changes.

Listing 15.13: <code>locale_grouping.py</code>

```
import locale

sample_locales = [
    ('USA', 'en_US'),
    ('France', 'fr_FR'),
    ('Spain', 'es_ES'),
    ('Portugal', 'pt_PT'),
```

```
        ('Poland', 'pl_PL'),
    ]

print('{:>10} {:>10} {:>15}'.format(
    'Locale', 'Integer', 'Float')
)
for name, loc in sample_locales:
    locale.setlocale(locale.LC_ALL, loc)

    print('{:>10}'.format(name), end=' ')
    print(locale.format('%10d', 123456, grouping=True), end=' ')
    print(locale.format('%15.2f', 123456.78, grouping=True))
```

To format numbers without the currency symbol, use `format()` instead of `currency()`.

```
$ python3 locale_grouping.py

    Locale    Integer          Float
       USA    123,456     123,456.78
    France     123456     123456,78
     Spain     123456     123456,78
  Portugal     123456     123456,78
    Poland    123 456    123 456,78
```

To convert locale-formatted numbers to normalized locale-agnostic-formatted numbers, use `delocalize()`.

Listing 15.14: `locale_delocalize.py`

```
import locale

sample_locales = [
    ('USA', 'en_US'),
    ('France', 'fr_FR'),
    ('Spain', 'es_ES'),
    ('Portugal', 'pt_PT'),
    ('Poland', 'pl_PL'),
]

for name, loc in sample_locales:
    locale.setlocale(locale.LC_ALL, loc)
    localized = locale.format('%0.2f', 123456.78, grouping=True)
    delocalized = locale.delocalize(localized)
    print('{:>10}: {:>10}   {:>10}'.format(
        name,
        localized,
        delocalized,
    ))
```

Grouping punctuation is removed and the decimal separator is converted to always be a period (.).

```
$ python3 locale_delocalize.py

       USA: 123,456.78    123456.78
    France:  123456,78    123456.78
     Spain:  123456,78    123456.78
  Portugal:  123456,78    123456.78
    Poland: 123 456,78    123456.78
```

15.2.4   Parsing Numbers

Besides generating output in different formats, the locale module helps with parsing input. It includes atoi() and atof() functions for converting the strings to integer and floating-point values based on the locale's numerical formatting conventions.

Listing 15.15: locale_atof.py

```
import locale

sample_data = [
    ('USA', 'en_US', '1,234.56'),
    ('France', 'fr_FR', '1234,56'),
    ('Spain', 'es_ES', '1234,56'),
    ('Portugal', 'pt_PT', '1234.56'),
    ('Poland', 'pl_PL', '1 234,56'),
]

for name, loc, a in sample_data:
    locale.setlocale(locale.LC_ALL, loc)
    print('{:>10}: {:>9} => {:f}'.format(
        name,
        a,
        locale.atof(a),
    ))
```

The parser recognizes the grouping and decimal separator values of the locale.

```
$ python3 locale_atof.py

       USA:  1,234.56 => 1234.560000
    France:   1234,56 => 1234.560000
     Spain:   1234,56 => 1234.560000
  Portugal:   1234.56 => 1234.560000
    Poland:  1 234,56 => 1234.560000
```

15.2.5   Dates and Times

Another important aspect of localization is date and time formatting.

Listing 15.16: locale_date.py

```python
import locale
import time

sample_locales = [
    ('USA', 'en_US'),
    ('France', 'fr_FR'),
    ('Spain', 'es_ES'),
    ('Portugal', 'pt_PT'),
    ('Poland', 'pl_PL'),
]

for name, loc in sample_locales:
    locale.setlocale(locale.LC_ALL, loc)
    format = locale.nl_langinfo(locale.D_T_FMT)
    print('{:>10}: {}'.format(name, time.strftime(format)))
```

This example uses the date formatting string for the locale to print the current date and time.

```
$ python3 locale_date.py

      USA: Fri Aug  5 17:33:31 2016
   France: Ven  5 aoû 17:33:31 2016
    Spain: vie  5 ago 17:33:31 2016
 Portugal: Sex  5 Ago 17:33:31 2016
   Poland: ptk  5 sie 17:33:31 2016
```

TIP

Related Reading

- Standard library documentation for locale.[7]
- Python 2 to 3 porting notes for locale (page 1359).
- gettext (page 1003): Message catalogs for translations.

---

[7] https://docs.python.org/3.5/library/locale.html

Chapter 16

Developer Tools

Over the course of its lifetime, Python has evolved an extensive ecosystem of modules intended to make the lives of Python developers easier by eliminating the need to build everything from scratch. That same philosophy has been applied to the tools that developers rely on to do their work, even if they are not used in the final version of a program. This chapter covers the modules included with Python that facilitate common development tasks such as testing, debugging, and profiling.

The most basic form of help for developers is documentation of the code they are using. The `pydoc` (page 1024) module generates formatted reference documentation from the docstrings included in the source code for any importable module.

Python includes two testing frameworks for automatically exercising code and verifying that it works correctly. `doctest` (page 1026) extracts test scenarios from examples included in documentation, either inside the source or as stand-alone files. `unittest` (page 1051) is a full-featured automated testing framework with support for fixtures, predefined test suites, and test discovery.

The `trace` (page 1069) module monitors the way Python executes a program, producing a report that shows how many times each line was run. This information can be used to find code paths that are not being tested by an automated test suite, and to study the function call graph to find dependencies between modules.

Writing and running tests will uncover problems in most programs. Python makes debugging easier, because unhandled errors are typically printed to the console as tracebacks. When a program is not running in a text console environment, `traceback` (page 1078) can be used to prepare similar output for a log file or message dialog. When a standard traceback does not provide enough information, use `cgitb` (page 1089) to see details such as the local variable settings at each level of the stack and the source context. `cgitb` can also format tracebacks in HTML, for reporting errors in web applications.

Once the location of a problem is identified, stepping through the code using the interactive debugger in the `pdb` (page 1101) module can lead to a solution more quickly by showing which path through the code was followed to get to the error situation. This module also facilitates experimenting with changes using live objects and code, which can reduce the number of iterations needed to find the correct changes to remove an error.

After a program is tested and debugged so that it works correctly, the next step is to improve its performance. Using `profile` (page 1140) and `timeit` (page 1148), a developer can measure the speed of a program and find the slow parts so they can be isolated and enhanced.

It is important to indent source code consistently in a language like Python, where whitespace is part of the syntax. The `tabnanny` (page 1153) module provides a scanner that reports on ambiguous use of indentation; it can be used in tests to ensure that code meets a minimum standard before it is checked into the source repository.

Python programs are run by giving the interpreter a byte-compiled version of the original program source. The byte-compiled versions can be created either on the fly or just once when the program is packaged. The `compileall` (page 1155) module exposes the interface used by installation programs and packaging tools to create files containing the byte code for a module. It can be used in a development environment to make sure a file does not have any syntax errors and to build the byte-compiled files for packaging when the program is released.

At the source code level, the `pyclbr` (page 1160) module provides a class browser that can be used by a text editor or other program to scan Python source for interesting symbols such as functions and classes; this step occurs without importing the code and potentially triggering side effects.

Python virtual environments, which are managed by `venv` (page 1163), define isolated environments for installing packages and running programs. They make it easy to test the same program with different versions of dependencies, and to install different programs with conflicting dependencies on the same computer.

Taking advantage of the large ecosystem of extension modules, frameworks, and tools available through the Python Package Index requires a package installer. Python's package installer, pip, is not distributed with the interpreter, because of the long release cycle for the language compared to desired updates to the tool. The `ensurepip` (page 1167) module can be used to install the latest version of pip.

16.1   pydoc: Online Help for Modules

The `pydoc` module imports a Python module and uses the contents to generate help text at runtime. The output includes docstrings for any objects that have them. All of the classes, methods, and functions of the module are described.

16.1.1   Plain Text Help

Running `pydoc` as a command-line program and passing the name of a module produces help text for the module and its contents on the console, using a pager program if one is configured. For example, to see the help text for the `atexit` (page 993) module, run `pydoc atexit`.

```
$ pydoc atexit

Help on built-in module atexit:

NAME
    atexit - allow programmer to define multiple exit functions
to be executed upon normal program termination.
```

DESCRIPTION
    Two public functions, register and unregister, are defined.

FUNCTIONS
    register(...)
        register(func, *args, **kwargs) -> func

        Register a function to be executed upon normal program
termination

            func - function to be called at exit
            args - optional arguments to pass to func
            kwargs - optional keyword arguments to pass to func

            func is returned to facilitate usage as a decorator.

    unregister(...)
        unregister(func) -> None

        Unregister an exit function which was previously
registered using
        atexit.register

            func - function to be unregistered

FILE
    (built-in)

16.1.2 HTML Help

pydoc will also generate HTML output, either writing a static file to a local directory or
starting a web server to browse documentation online.

```
$ pydoc -w atexit
```

The preceding code creates atexit.html in the current directory, and

```
$ pydoc -p 5000
Server ready at http://localhost:5000/
Server commands: [b]rowser, [q]uit
server> q
Server stopped
```

starts a web server listening at http://localhost:5000/. The server generates documentation on the fly as you browse. Use the b command to open a browser window automatically,
and q to stop the server.

16.1.3 Interactive Help

pydoc also adds a function help() to the __builtins__ so the same information can be accessed from the Python interpreter prompt.

```
$ python

Python 3.5.2 (v3.5.2:4def2a2901a5, Jun 26 2016, 10:47:25)
[GCC 4.2.1 (Apple Inc. build 5666) (dot 3)] on darwin
Type "help", "copyright", "credits" or "license" for more
information.
>>> help('atexit')
Help on module atexit:

NAME
    atexit - allow programmer to define multiple exit functions
to be executed upon normal program termination.

...
```

TIP

Related Reading

- Standard library documentation for pydoc.[1]
- inspect (page 1311): The inspect module can be used to retrieve the docstrings for an object programmatically.

16.2   doctest: Testing Through Documentation

doctest tests source code by running examples embedded in the documentation and verifying that they produce the expected results. It works by parsing the help text to find examples, running them, and then comparing the output text with the expected value. Many developers find doctest easier to use than unittest (page 1051) because, in its simplest form, there is no API to learn before using it. However, as the examples become more complex, the lack of fixture management can make writing doctest tests more cumbersome than using unittest.

16.2.1 Getting Started

The first step to setting up doctests is to use the interactive interpreter to create examples and then copy and paste them into the docstrings in the module. In this example, two examples are given for my_function().

---

[1] https://docs.python.org/3.5/library/pydoc.html

Listing 16.1: `doctest_simple.py`

```python
def my_function(a, b):
    """
    >>> my_function(2, 3)
    6
    >>> my_function('a', 3)
    'aaa'
    """
    return a * b
```

To run the tests, use `doctest` as the main program by specifying the -m option. Usually no output is produced while the tests are running, so the next example includes the -v option to make the output more verbose.

```
$ python3 -m doctest -v doctest_simple.py

Trying:
    my_function(2, 3)
Expecting:
    6
ok
Trying:
    my_function('a', 3)
Expecting:
    'aaa'
ok
1 items had no tests:
    doctest_simple
1 items passed all tests:
    2 tests in doctest_simple.my_function
2 tests in 2 items.
2 passed and 0 failed.
Test passed.
```

Examples cannot usually stand on their own as explanations of a function, so `doctest` also allows for surrounding text. It looks for lines beginning with the interpreter prompt (>>>) to find the beginning of a test case; the case is ended by a blank line or by the next interpreter prompt. Intervening text is ignored, and can have any format as long as it does not look like a test case.

Listing 16.2: `doctest_simple_with_docs.py`

```python
def my_function(a, b):
    """Returns a * b.

    Works with numbers:

    >>> my_function(2, 3)
```

```
    6

    and strings:

    >>> my_function('a', 3)
    'aaa'
    """
    return a * b
```

The surrounding text in the updated docstring makes it more useful to a human reader. Because it is ignored by doctest, the results are the same.

```
$ python3 -m doctest -v doctest_simple_with_docs.py

Trying:
    my_function(2, 3)
Expecting:
    6
ok
Trying:
    my_function('a', 3)
Expecting:
    'aaa'
ok
1 items had no tests:
    doctest_simple_with_docs
1 items passed all tests:
    2 tests in doctest_simple_with_docs.my_function
2 tests in 2 items.
2 passed and 0 failed.
Test passed.
```

16.2.2   Handling Unpredictable Output

In some other cases, the exact output may not be predictable, but should still be testable. For example, local date and time values and object IDs change on every test run, the default precision used in the representation of floating-point values depends on the compiler options, and string representations of container objects such as dictionaries may not be deterministic. Although these conditions cannot be controlled, certain techniques can be applied to deal with them.

For example, in CPython, object identifiers are based on the memory address of the data structure holding the object.

Listing 16.3: **doctest_unpredictable.py**

```
class MyClass:
    pass
```

```
def unpredictable(obj):
    """Returns a new list containing obj.

    >>> unpredictable(MyClass())
    [<doctest_unpredictable.MyClass object at 0x10055a2d0>]
    """
    return [obj]
```

These ID values change each time a program runs, because it is loaded into a different part of memory.

```
$ python3 -m doctest -v doctest_unpredictable.py

Trying:
    unpredictable(MyClass())
Expecting:
    [<doctest_unpredictable.MyClass object at 0x10055a2d0>]
**********************************************************************
File ".../doctest_unpredictable.py", line 17, in doctest_unpredi
ctable.unpredictable
Failed example:
    unpredictable(MyClass())
Expected:
    [<doctest_unpredictable.MyClass object at 0x10055a2d0>]
Got:
    [<doctest_unpredictable.MyClass object at 0x1016a4160>]
2 items had no tests:
    doctest_unpredictable
    doctest_unpredictable.MyClass
**********************************************************************
1 items had failures:
    1 of    1 in doctest_unpredictable.unpredictable
1 tests in 3 items.
0 passed and 1 failed.
***Test Failed*** 1 failures.
```

When the tests include values that are likely to change in unpredictable ways, and if the actual value is not important to the test results, use the ELLIPSIS option to tell doctest to ignore portions of the verification value.

Listing 16.4: **doctest_ellipsis.py**

```
class MyClass:
    pass


def unpredictable(obj):
    """Returns a new list containing obj.
```

```
>>> unpredictable(MyClass()) #doctest: +ELLIPSIS
[<doctest_ellipsis.MyClass object at 0x...>]
"""
    return [obj]
```

The #doctest: +ELLIPSIS comment after the call to unpredictable() tells doctest to turn on the ELLIPSIS option for that test. The ... replaces the memory address in the object ID, so that portion of the expected value is ignored. The actual output matches and the test passes.

```
$ python3 -m doctest -v doctest_ellipsis.py

Trying:
    unpredictable(MyClass()) #doctest: +ELLIPSIS
Expecting:
    [<doctest_ellipsis.MyClass object at 0x...>]
ok
2 items had no tests:
    doctest_ellipsis
    doctest_ellipsis.MyClass
1 items passed all tests:
    1 tests in doctest_ellipsis.unpredictable
1 tests in 3 items.
1 passed and 0 failed.
Test passed.
```

Sometimes the unpredictable value cannot be ignored, because that would make the test incomplete or inaccurate. For example, simple tests quickly become more complex when they must deal with data types whose string representations are inconsistent. The string form of a dictionary, for example, may change based on the order in which the keys are added.

Listing 16.5: doctest_hashed_values.py

```
keys = ['a', 'aa', 'aaa']

print('dict:', {k: len(k) for k in keys})
print('set :', set(keys))
```

Because of hash randomization and key collision, the internal key list order may differ for the dictionary each time the script runs. Sets use the same hashing algorithm, and exhibit the same behavior.

```
$ python3 doctest_hashed_values.py

dict: {'aa': 2, 'a': 1, 'aaa': 3}
set : {'aa', 'a', 'aaa'}

$ python3 doctest_hashed_values.py
```

```
dict: {'a': 1, 'aa': 2, 'aaa': 3}
set : {'a', 'aa', 'aaa'}
```

The best way to deal with these potential discrepancies is to create tests that produce values that are not likely to change. In the case of dictionaries and sets, that might mean looking for specific keys individually, generating a sorted list of the contents of the data structure, or comparing against a literal value for equality instead of depending on the string representation.

Listing 16.6: doctest_hashed_values_tests.py

```
import collections


def group_by_length(words):
    """Returns a dictionary grouping words into sets by length.

    >>> grouped = group_by_length([ 'python', 'module', 'of',
    ... 'the', 'week' ])
    >>> grouped == { 2:set(['of']),
    ...              3:set(['the']),
    ...              4:set(['week']),
    ...              6:set(['python', 'module']),
    ...              }
    True

    """
    d = collections.defaultdict(set)
    for word in words:
        d[len(word)].add(word)
    return d
```

The single example in the preceding code is actually interpreted as two separate tests, with the first expecting no console output and the second expecting the boolean result of the comparison operation.

```
$ python3 -m doctest -v doctest_hashed_values_tests.py

Trying:
    grouped = group_by_length([ 'python', 'module', 'of',
    'the', 'week' ])
Expecting nothing
ok
Trying:
    grouped == { 2:set(['of']),
                 3:set(['the']),
                 4:set(['week']),
                 6:set(['python', 'module']),
                 }
```

```
Expecting:
    True
ok
1 items had no tests:
    doctest_hashed_values_tests
1 items passed all tests:
    2 tests in doctest_hashed_values_tests.group_by_length
2 tests in 2 items.
2 passed and 0 failed.
Test passed.
```

16.2.3 Tracebacks

Tracebacks are a special case involving changing data. Since the paths in a traceback depend on the location where a module is installed on the file system, it would be impossible to write portable tests if they were treated the same as other output.

Listing 16.7: doctest_tracebacks.py

```
def this_raises():
    """This function always raises an exception.

    >>> this_raises()
    Traceback (most recent call last):
      File "<stdin>", line 1, in <module>
      File "/no/such/path/doctest_tracebacks.py", line 14, in
      this_raises
        raise RuntimeError('here is the error')
    RuntimeError: here is the error
    """
    raise RuntimeError('here is the error')
```

doctest makes a special effort to recognize tracebacks, and ignore the parts that might change from system to system.

```
$ python3 -m doctest -v doctest_tracebacks.py

Trying:
    this_raises()
Expecting:
    Traceback (most recent call last):
      File "<stdin>", line 1, in <module>
      File "/no/such/path/doctest_tracebacks.py", line 14, in
      this_raises
        raise RuntimeError('here is the error')
    RuntimeError: here is the error
ok
1 items had no tests:
```

```
    doctest_tracebacks
1 items passed all tests:
   1 tests in doctest_tracebacks.this_raises
1 tests in 2 items.
1 passed and 0 failed.
Test passed.
```

In fact, the entire body of the traceback is ignored and can be omitted.

Listing 16.8: doctest_tracebacks_no_body.py

```python
def this_raises():
    """This function always raises an exception.

    >>> this_raises()
    Traceback (most recent call last):
    RuntimeError: here is the error

    >>> this_raises()
    Traceback (innermost last):
    RuntimeError: here is the error
    """
    raise RuntimeError('here is the error')
```

When doctest sees a traceback header line (either Traceback (most recent call last): or Traceback (innermost last):, to support different versions of Python), it skips ahead to find the exception type and message, ignoring the intervening lines entirely.

```
$ python3 -m doctest -v doctest_tracebacks_no_body.py

Trying:
    this_raises()
Expecting:
    Traceback (most recent call last):
    RuntimeError: here is the error
ok
Trying:
    this_raises()
Expecting:
    Traceback (innermost last):
    RuntimeError: here is the error
ok
1 items had no tests:
    doctest_tracebacks_no_body
1 items passed all tests:
   2 tests in doctest_tracebacks_no_body.this_raises
2 tests in 2 items.
2 passed and 0 failed.
Test passed.
```

16.2.4 Working Around Whitespace

In real-world applications, output usually includes whitespace such as blank lines, tabs, and extra spacing to make it more readable. Blank lines, in particular, cause issues with doctest because they are used to delimit tests.

Listing 16.9: doctest_blankline_fail.py

```
def double_space(lines):
    """Prints a list of double-spaced lines.

    >>> double_space(['Line one.', 'Line two.'])
    Line one.

    Line two.

    """
    for l in lines:
        print(l)
        print()
```

double_space() takes a list of input lines, and prints them double-spaced with blank lines in between.

```
$ python3 -m doctest -v doctest_blankline_fail.py

Trying:
    double_space(['Line one.', 'Line two.'])
Expecting:
    Line one.
**********************************************************************
File ".../doctest_blankline_fail.py", line 12, in doctest_blankl
ine_fail.double_space
Failed example:
    double_space(['Line one.', 'Line two.'])
Expected:
    Line one.
Got:
    Line one.
    <BLANKLINE>
    Line two.
    <BLANKLINE>
1 items had no tests:
    doctest_blankline_fail
**********************************************************************
1 items had failures:
   1 of   1 in doctest_blankline_fail.double_space
1 tests in 2 items.
0 passed and 1 failed.
***Test Failed*** 1 failures.
```

In the preceding example, the test fails, because it interprets the blank line after the line containing Line one. in the docstring as the end of the sample output. To match the blank lines, replace them in the sample input with the string <BLANKLINE>.

Listing 16.10: doctest_blankline.py

```
def double_space(lines):
    """Prints a list of double-spaced lines.

    >>> double_space(['Line one.', 'Line two.'])
    Line one.
    <BLANKLINE>
    Line two.
    <BLANKLINE>
    """
    for l in lines:
        print(l)
        print()
```

In this example, doctest replaces the actual blank lines with the same literal before performing the comparison. The actual and expected values now match, and the test passes.

```
$ python3 -m doctest -v doctest_blankline.py

Trying:
    double_space(['Line one.', 'Line two.'])
Expecting:
    Line one.
    <BLANKLINE>
    Line two.
    <BLANKLINE>
ok
1 items had no tests:
    doctest_blankline
1 items passed all tests:
    1 tests in doctest_blankline.double_space
1 tests in 2 items.
1 passed and 0 failed.
Test passed.
```

Whitespace within a line can also cause tricky problems with tests. The next example has a single extra space after the 6.

Listing 16.11: doctest_extra_space.py

```
def my_function(a, b):
    """
    >>> my_function(2, 3)
    6
    >>> my_function('a', 3)
```

```
'aaa'
"""
return a * b
```

Extra spaces can find their way into code via copy-and-paste errors. When they come at the end of the line, they can go unnoticed in the source file and will be invisible in the test failure report as well.

```
$ python3 -m doctest -v doctest_extra_space.py

Trying:
    my_function(2, 3)
Expecting:
    6
**************************************************************
File ".../doctest_extra_space.py", line 15, in doctest_extra_spa
ce.my_function
Failed example:
    my_function(2, 3)
Expected:
    6
Got:
    6
Trying:
    my_function('a', 3)
Expecting:
    'aaa'
ok
1 items had no tests:
    doctest_extra_space
**************************************************************
1 items had failures:
   1 of   2 in doctest_extra_space.my_function
2 tests in 2 items.
1 passed and 1 failed.
***Test Failed*** 1 failures.
```

Using one of the difference-based reporting options, such as REPORT_NDIFF, shows the difference between the actual and expected values with more detail, and the extra space becomes visible.

Listing 16.12: doctest_ndiff.py

```
def my_function(a, b):
    """
    >>> my_function(2, 3) #doctest: +REPORT_NDIFF
    6
    >>> my_function('a', 3)
```

```
    'aaa'
    """
    return a * b
```

Unified (`REPORT_UDIFF`) and context (`REPORT_CDIFF`) diffs are also available.

```
$ python3 -m doctest -v doctest_ndiff.py

Trying:
    my_function(2, 3) #doctest: +REPORT_NDIFF
Expecting:
    6
****************************************************************
File ".../doctest_ndiff.py", line 16, in doctest_ndiff.my_functi
on
Failed example:
    my_function(2, 3) #doctest: +REPORT_NDIFF
Differences (ndiff with -expected +actual):
    - 6
    ?  -
    + 6
Trying:
    my_function('a', 3)
Expecting:
    'aaa'
ok
1 items had no tests:
    doctest_ndiff
****************************************************************
1 items had failures:
   1 of   2 in doctest_ndiff.my_function
2 tests in 2 items.
1 passed and 1 failed.
***Test Failed*** 1 failures.
```

It is sometimes beneficial to add extra whitespace in the sample output for the test, but to have doctest ignore it. For example, data structures can be easier to read when they are spread across several lines, even if their representation would fit on a single line.

```
def my_function(a, b):
    """Returns a * b.

    >>> my_function(['A', 'B'], 3) #doctest: +NORMALIZE_WHITESPACE
    ['A', 'B',
     'A', 'B',
     'A', 'B']
```

```
This does not match because of the extra space after the [ in
the list.

>>> my_function(['A', 'B'], 2) #doctest: +NORMALIZE_WHITESPACE
[ 'A', 'B',
  'A', 'B', ]
"""
    return a * b
```

When `NORMALIZE_WHITESPACE` is turned on, any whitespace in the actual and expected values is considered a match. Whitespace cannot be added to the expected value where none exists in the output, but the length of the whitespace sequence and the actual whitespace characters do not need to match. The first test example gets this rule correct, and passes, even though the input contains extra spaces and newlines. The second example includes extra whitespace after [and before], so the test fails.

```
$ python3 -m doctest -v doctest_normalize_whitespace.py

Trying:
    my_function(['A', 'B'], 3) #doctest: +NORMALIZE_WHITESPACE
Expecting:
    ['A', 'B',
     'A', 'B',
     'A', 'B',]
**********************************************************************
File "doctest_normalize_whitespace.py", line 13, in doctest_nor
malize_whitespace.my_function
Failed example:
    my_function(['A', 'B'], 3) #doctest: +NORMALIZE_WHITESPACE
Expected:
    ['A', 'B',
     'A', 'B',
     'A', 'B',]
Got:
    ['A', 'B', 'A', 'B', 'A', 'B']
Trying:
    my_function(['A', 'B'], 2) #doctest: +NORMALIZE_WHITESPACE
Expecting:
    [ 'A', 'B',
      'A', 'B', ]
**********************************************************************
File "doctest_normalize_whitespace.py", line 21, in doctest_nor
malize_whitespace.my_function
Failed example:
    my_function(['A', 'B'], 2) #doctest: +NORMALIZE_WHITESPACE
Expected:
    [ 'A', 'B',
      'A', 'B', ]
```

```
Got:
    ['A', 'B', 'A', 'B']
1 items had no tests:
    doctest_normalize_whitespace
***************************************************************
1 items had failures:
    2 of   2 in doctest_normalize_whitespace.my_function
2 tests in 2 items.
0 passed and 2 failed.
***Test Failed*** 2 failures.
```

16.2.5 Test Locations

All of the tests in the examples so far have been written in the docstrings of the functions they are testing. That approach is convenient for users who examine the docstrings for help using the function (especially with pydoc (page 1024)), but doctest looks for tests in other places, too. The most obvious locations for additional tests are in the docstrings found elsewhere in the module.

Listing 16.13: doctest_docstrings.py

```python
"""Tests can appear in any docstring within the module.

Module-level tests cross class and function boundaries.

>>> A('a') == B('b')
False
"""


class A:
    """Simple class.

    >>> A('instance_name').name
    'instance_name'
    """

    def __init__(self, name):
        self.name = name

    def method(self):
        """Returns an unusual value.

        >>> A('name').method()
        'eman'
        """
        return ''.join(reversed(self.name))
```

```
class B(A):
    """Another simple class.

    >>> B('different_name').name
    'different_name'
    """
```

Docstrings at the module, class, and function levels can all contain tests.

```
$ python3 -m doctest -v doctest_docstrings.py

Trying:
    A('a') == B('b')
Expecting:
    False
ok
Trying:
    A('instance_name').name
Expecting:
    'instance_name'
ok
Trying:
    A('name').method()
Expecting:
    'eman'
ok
Trying:
    B('different_name').name
Expecting:
    'different_name'
ok
1 items had no tests:
    doctest_docstrings.A.__init__
4 items passed all tests:
    1 tests in doctest_docstrings
    1 tests in doctest_docstrings.A
    1 tests in doctest_docstrings.A.method
    1 tests in doctest_docstrings.B
4 tests in 5 items.
4 passed and 0 failed.
Test passed.
```

In some cases, tests should be included with the source code but not in the help text for a module. In that scenario, the tests need to be placed somewhere other than the docstrings. doctest looks for a module-level variable called __test__ as a way to locate other tests. The value of __test__ should be a dictionary that maps test set names (as strings) to strings, modules, classes, or functions.

Listing 16.14: `doctest_private_tests.py`

```
import doctest_private_tests_external

__test__ = {
    'numbers': """
>>> my_function(2, 3)
6

>>> my_function(2.0, 3)
6.0
""",

    'strings': """
>>> my_function('a', 3)
'aaa'

>>> my_function(3, 'a')
'aaa'
""",

    'external': doctest_private_tests_external,
}


def my_function(a, b):
    """Returns a * b
    """
    return a * b
```

If the value associated with a key is a string, it is treated as a docstring and scanned for
tests. If the value is a class or function, `doctest` searches it recursively for docstrings, which
are then scanned for tests. In the next example, the module `doctest_private_tests_external`
has a single test in its docstring.

Listing 16.15: `doctest_private_tests_external.py`

```
"""External tests associated with doctest_private_tests.py.

>>> my_function(['A', 'B', 'C'], 2)
['A', 'B', 'C', 'A', 'B', 'C']
"""
```

After scanning the example file, `doctest` finds a total of five tests to run.

```
$ python3 -m doctest -v doctest_private_tests.py

Trying:
    my_function(['A', 'B', 'C'], 2)
```

```
Expecting:
    ['A', 'B', 'C', 'A', 'B', 'C']
ok
Trying:
    my_function(2, 3)
Expecting:
    6
ok
Trying:
    my_function(2.0, 3)
Expecting:
    6.0
ok
Trying:
    my_function('a', 3)
Expecting:
    'aaa'
ok
Trying:
    my_function(3, 'a')
Expecting:
    'aaa'
ok
2 items had no tests:
    doctest_private_tests
    doctest_private_tests.my_function
3 items passed all tests:
   1 tests in doctest_private_tests.__test__.external
   2 tests in doctest_private_tests.__test__.numbers
   2 tests in doctest_private_tests.__test__.strings
5 tests in 5 items.
5 passed and 0 failed.
Test passed.
```

16.2.6 External Documentation

Mixing tests in with regular code is not the only way to use `doctest`. Examples embedded in external project documentation files, such as reStructuredText files, can be used as well.

Listing 16.16: `doctest_in_help.py`

```python
def my_function(a, b):
    """Returns a*b
    """
    return a * b
```

The help for this sample module is saved to a separate file, `doctest_in_help.txt`. The examples illustrating how to use the module are included with the help text, and `doctest` can be used to find and run them.

Listing 16.17: `doctest_in_help.txt`

```
================================
 How to Use doctest_in_help.py
================================

This library is very simple, since it only has one function called
''my_function()''.

Numbers
=======

''my_function()'' returns the product of its arguments.  For numbers,
that value is equivalent to using the ''*'' operator.

::

    >>> from doctest_in_help import my_function
    >>> my_function(2, 3)
    6

It also works with floating-point values.

::

    >>> my_function(2.0, 3)
    6.0

Non-Numbers
===========

Because ''*'' is also defined on data types other than numbers,
''my_function()'' works just as well if one of the arguments is a
string, a list, or a tuple.

::

    >>> my_function('a', 3)
    'aaa'

    >>> my_function(['A', 'B', 'C'], 2)
    ['A', 'B', 'C', 'A', 'B', 'C']
```

The tests in the text file can be run from the command line, just as with the Python source modules.

```
$ python3 -m doctest -v doctest_in_help.txt

Trying:
    from doctest_in_help import my_function
```

```
Expecting nothing
ok
Trying:
    my_function(2, 3)
Expecting:
    6
ok
Trying:
    my_function(2.0, 3)
Expecting:
    6.0
ok
Trying:
    my_function('a', 3)
Expecting:
    'aaa'
ok
Trying:
    my_function(['A', 'B', 'C'], 2)
Expecting:
    ['A', 'B', 'C', 'A', 'B', 'C']
ok
1 items passed all tests:
   5 tests in doctest_in_help.txt
5 tests in 1 items.
5 passed and 0 failed.
Test passed.
```

Normally `doctest` sets up the test execution environment to include the members of the module being tested, so the tests do not need to import the module explicitly. In this case, however, the tests are not defined in a Python module, and `doctest` does not know how to set up the global namespace. As a consequence, the examples need to do the import work themselves. All of the tests in a given file share the same execution context, so importing the module once at the top of the file is enough.

16.2.7 Running Tests

The previous examples all used the command-line test runner built into `doctest`. This approach is easy and convenient when testing a single module, but quickly becomes tedious as a package spreads out into multiple files. For those cases, several alternative approaches can prove more efficient.

16.2.7.1 By Module

The instructions to run `doctest` against the source can be included at the end of the modules.

Listing 16.18: `doctest_testmod.py`

```
def my_function(a, b):
    """
    >>> my_function(2, 3)
```

```
        6
        >>> my_function('a', 3)
        'aaa'
        """
        return a * b

if __name__ == '__main__':
    import doctest
    doctest.testmod()
```

Calling `testmod()` only if the current module name is `__main__` ensures that the tests are run only when the module is invoked as a main program.

```
$ python3 doctest_testmod.py -v

Trying:
    my_function(2, 3)
Expecting:
    6
ok
Trying:
    my_function('a', 3)
Expecting:
    'aaa'
ok
1 items had no tests:
    __main__
1 items passed all tests:
   2 tests in __main__.my_function
2 tests in 2 items.
2 passed and 0 failed.
Test passed.
```

The first argument to `testmod()` is a module containing code to be scanned for tests. A separate test script can use this feature to import the real code and run the tests in each of the modules, one after another.

Listing 16.19: doctest_testmod_other_module.py

```
import doctest_simple

if __name__ == '__main__':
    import doctest
    doctest.testmod(doctest_simple)
```

A test suite can be constructed for the project by importing each module and running its tests.

```
$ python3 doctest_testmod_other_module.py -v

Trying:
    my_function(2, 3)
Expecting:
    6
ok
Trying:
    my_function('a', 3)
Expecting:
    'aaa'
ok
1 items had no tests:
    doctest_simple
1 items passed all tests:
    2 tests in doctest_simple.my_function
2 tests in 2 items.
2 passed and 0 failed.
Test passed.
```

16.2.7.2   By File

testfile() works in a way similar to testmod(), allowing the tests to be invoked explicitly in an external file from within the test program.

Listing 16.20: doctest_testfile.py

```
import doctest

if __name__ == '__main__':
    doctest.testfile('doctest_in_help.txt')
```

Both testmod() and testfile() include optional parameters to control the behavior of the tests through the doctest options. Refer to the standard library documentation for more details about those features—but note that most of the time they are not needed.

```
$ python3 doctest_testfile.py -v

Trying:
    from doctest_in_help import my_function
Expecting nothing
ok
Trying:
    my_function(2, 3)
Expecting:
    6
ok
```

```
Trying:
    my_function(2.0, 3)
Expecting:
    6.0
ok
Trying:
    my_function('a', 3)
Expecting:
    'aaa'
ok
Trying:
    my_function(['A', 'B', 'C'], 2)
Expecting:
    ['A', 'B', 'C', 'A', 'B', 'C']
ok
1 items passed all tests:
   5 tests in doctest_in_help.txt
5 tests in 1 items.
5 passed and 0 failed.
Test passed.
```

16.2.7.3   Unittest Suite

When both unittest (page 1051) and doctest are used for testing the same code in different situations, the unittest integration in doctest can be used to run the tests together. Two classes, DocTestSuite and DocFileSuite, can be applied to create test suites compatible with the test-runner API of unittest.

Listing 16.21: **doctest_unittest.py**

```python
import doctest
import unittest

import doctest_simple

suite = unittest.TestSuite()
suite.addTest(doctest.DocTestSuite(doctest_simple))
suite.addTest(doctest.DocFileSuite('doctest_in_help.txt'))

runner = unittest.TextTestRunner(verbosity=2)
runner.run(suite)
```

The tests from each source are collapsed into a single outcome, instead of being reported individually.

```
$ python3 doctest_unittest.py

my_function (doctest_simple)
```

```
Doctest: doctest_simple.my_function ... ok
doctest_in_help.txt
Doctest: doctest_in_help.txt ... ok


----------------------------------------------------------------
Ran 2 tests in 0.002s

OK
```

16.2.8   Test Context

The execution context created by `doctest` as it runs tests contains a copy of the module-level global values for the test module. Each test source (e.g., function, class, module) has its own set of global values that isolate the tests to some extent, so they are less likely to interfere with one another.

Listing 16.22: `doctest_test_globals.py`

```python
class TestGlobals:

    def one(self):
        """
        >>> var = 'value'
        >>> 'var' in globals()
        True
        """

    def two(self):
        """
        >>> 'var' in globals()
        False
        """
```

`TestGlobals` has two methods: `one()` and `two()`. The tests in the docstring for `one()` set a global variable, and the test for `two()` looks for this variable (but does not expect to find it).

```
$ python3 -m doctest -v doctest_test_globals.py

Trying:
    var = 'value'
Expecting nothing
ok
Trying:
    'var' in globals()
Expecting:
    True
ok
```

```
Trying:
    'var' in globals()
Expecting:
    False
ok
2 items had no tests:
    doctest_test_globals
    doctest_test_globals.TestGlobals
2 items passed all tests:
    2 tests in doctest_test_globals.TestGlobals.one
    1 tests in doctest_test_globals.TestGlobals.two
3 tests in 4 items.
3 passed and 0 failed.
Test passed.
```

That does not mean the tests *cannot* interfere with each other, though, if they change the contents of mutable variables defined in the module.

Listing 16.23: doctest_mutable_globals.py

```python
_module_data = {}


class TestGlobals:

    def one(self):
        """
        >>> TestGlobals().one()
        >>> 'var' in _module_data
        True
        """
        _module_data['var'] = 'value'

    def two(self):
        """
        >>> 'var' in _module_data
        False
        """
```

The module variable _module_data is changed by the tests for one(), causing the test for two() to fail.

```
$ python3 -m doctest -v doctest_mutable_globals.py

Trying:
    TestGlobals().one()
Expecting nothing
ok
Trying:
    'var' in _module_data
```

```
Expecting:
    True
ok
Trying:
    'var' in _module_data
Expecting:
    False
*****************************************************************
File ".../doctest_mutable_globals.py", line 25, in doctest_mutab
le_globals.TestGlobals.two
Failed example:
    'var' in _module_data
Expected:
    False
Got:
    True
2 items had no tests:
    doctest_mutable_globals
    doctest_mutable_globals.TestGlobals
1 items passed all tests:
    2 tests in doctest_mutable_globals.TestGlobals.one
*****************************************************************
1 items had failures:
    1 of   1 in doctest_mutable_globals.TestGlobals.two
3 tests in 4 items.
2 passed and 1 failed.
***Test Failed*** 1 failures.
```

If global values are needed for the tests—to parameterize them for an environment, for example—values can be passed to `testmod()` and `testfile()` to set up the context using data controlled by the caller.

TIP

Related Reading

- Standard library documentation for `doctest`.[2]

- The Mighty Dictionary[3]: Presentation by Brandon Rhodes at PyCon 2010 about the internal operations of the `dict`.

- `difflib` (page 58): Python's sequence difference computation library, used to produce the `ndiff` output.

- Sphinx[4]: As well as being the documentation processing tool for Python's standard library, Sphinx has been adopted by many third-party projects because it is easy to use and produces clean output in several digital and print formats. Sphinx includes an extension for running doctests as its processes' documentation source files, so the examples are always accurate.

---

[2] https://docs.python.org/3.5/library/doctest.html
[3] www.youtube.com/watch?v=C4Kc8xzcA68
[4] www.sphinx-doc.org

- py.test[5]: Third-party test runner with `doctest` support.
- nose2[6]: Third-party test runner with `doctest` support.
- Manuel[7]: Third-party documentation-based test runner with more advanced test case extraction and integration with Sphinx.

16.3   unittest: Automated Testing Framework

The automated testing framework in `unittest` is based on the XUnit framework design by Kent Beck and Erich Gamma. The same pattern is repeated in many other languages, including C, Perl, Java, and Smalltalk. The framework implemented by `unittest` supports fixtures, test suites, and a test runner to enable automated testing.

16.3.1   Basic Test Structure

Tests, as defined by `unittest`, have two parts: code to manage test dependencies (called *fixtures*) and the test itself. Individual tests are created by subclassing `TestCase` and overriding or adding appropriate methods. In the following example, the `SimplisticTest` has a single `test()` method, which would fail if `a` is ever different from `b`.

Listing 16.24: **unittest_simple.py**

```
import unittest


class SimplisticTest(unittest.TestCase):

    def test(self):
        a = 'a'
        b = 'a'
        self.assertEqual(a, b)
```

16.3.2   Running Tests

The easiest way to run `unittest` tests is use the automatic discovery available through the command-line interface.

```
$ python3 -m unittest unittest_simple.py

.
----------------------------------------------------------------------
Ran 1 test in 0.000s

OK
```

---

[5] http://doc.pytest.org/en/latest/
[6] https://nose2.readthedocs.io/en/latest/
[7] https://pythonhosted.org/manuel/

This abbreviated output includes the amount of time the tests took, along with a status indicator for each test (the . on the first line of output means that a test passed). For more detailed test results, include the -v option.

```
$ python3 -m unittest -v unittest_simple.py

test (unittest_simple.SimplisticTest) ... ok

----------------------------------------------------------------
Ran 1 test in 0.000s

OK
```

16.3.3   Test Outcomes

Tests have three possible outcomes, as described in Table 16.1. There is no explicit way to cause a test to "pass," so a test's status depends on the presence (or absence) of an exception.

Listing 16.25: unittest_outcomes.py

```
import unittest


class OutcomesTest(unittest.TestCase):

    def testPass(self):
        return

    def testFail(self):
        self.assertFalse(True)

    def testError(self):
        raise RuntimeError('Test error!')
```

When a test fails or generates an error, the traceback is included in the output.

```
$ python3 -m unittest unittest_outcomes.py

EF.
================================================================
```

Table 16.1: Test Case Outcomes

Outcome	Description
ok	The test passes.
FAIL	The test does not pass, and raises an AssertionError exception.
ERROR	The test raises any exception other than AssertionError.

```
ERROR: testError (unittest_outcomes.OutcomesTest)
----------------------------------------------------------------
Traceback (most recent call last):
  File ".../unittest_outcomes.py", line 18, in testError
    raise RuntimeError('Test error!')
RuntimeError: Test error!


================================================================
FAIL: testFail (unittest_outcomes.OutcomesTest)
----------------------------------------------------------------
Traceback (most recent call last):
  File ".../unittest_outcomes.py", line 15, in testFail
    self.assertFalse(True)
AssertionError: True is not false


----------------------------------------------------------------
Ran 3 tests in 0.001s

FAILED (failures=1, errors=1)
```

In the previous example, `testFail()` fails and the traceback shows the line with the failure code. It is up to the person reading the test output to look at the code and figure out the meaning of the failed test, though.

Listing 16.26: unittest_failwithmessage.py

```python
import unittest


class FailureMessageTest(unittest.TestCase):

    def testFail(self):
        self.assertFalse(True, 'failure message goes here')
```

To make it easier to understand the nature of a test failure, the `fail*()` and `assert*()` methods accept an argument `msg`, which can be used to produce a more detailed error message.

```
$ python3 -m unittest -v unittest_failwithmessage.py

testFail (unittest_failwithmessage.FailureMessageTest) ... FAIL

================================================================
FAIL: testFail (unittest_failwithmessage.FailureMessageTest)
----------------------------------------------------------------
Traceback (most recent call last):
  File ".../unittest_failwithmessage.py", line 12, in testFail
    self.assertFalse(True, 'failure message goes here')
AssertionError: True is not false : failure message goes here
```

```
--------------------------------------------------------------
Ran 1 test in 0.000s

FAILED (failures=1)
```

16.3.4   Asserting Truth

Most tests assert the truth of some condition. Truth-checking tests can be written in two different ways, depending on the perspective of the test author and the desired outcome of the code being tested.

Listing 16.27: `unittest_truth.py`

```python
import unittest


class TruthTest(unittest.TestCase):

    def testAssertTrue(self):
        self.assertTrue(True)

    def testAssertFalse(self):
        self.assertFalse(False)
```

If the code produces a value that can be evaluated as true, the method `assertTrue()` should be used. If the code produces a false value, the method `assertFalse()` makes more sense.

```
$ python3 -m unittest -v unittest_truth.py

testAssertFalse (unittest_truth.TruthTest) ... ok
testAssertTrue (unittest_truth.TruthTest) ... ok

--------------------------------------------------------------
Ran 2 tests in 0.000s

OK
```

16.3.5   Testing Equality

As a special case, `unittest` includes methods for testing the equality of two values.

Listing 16.28: `unittest_equality.py`

```python
import unittest


class EqualityTest(unittest.TestCase):

    def testExpectEqual(self):
```

```
        self.assertEqual(1, 3 - 2)

    def testExpectEqualFails(self):
        self.assertEqual(2, 3 - 2)

    def testExpectNotEqual(self):
        self.assertNotEqual(2, 3 - 2)

    def testExpectNotEqualFails(self):
        self.assertNotEqual(1, 3 - 2)
```

When they fail, these special test methods produce error messages that identify the values being compared.

```
$ python3 -m unittest -v unittest_equality.py

testExpectEqual (unittest_equality.EqualityTest) ... ok
testExpectEqualFails (unittest_equality.EqualityTest) ... FAIL
testExpectNotEqual (unittest_equality.EqualityTest) ... ok
testExpectNotEqualFails (unittest_equality.EqualityTest) ...
FAIL

======================================================================
FAIL: testExpectEqualFails (unittest_equality.EqualityTest)
----------------------------------------------------------------------
Traceback (most recent call last):
  File ".../unittest_equality.py", line 15, in
testExpectEqualFails
    self.assertEqual(2, 3 - 2)
AssertionError: 2 != 1


======================================================================
FAIL: testExpectNotEqualFails (unittest_equality.EqualityTest)
----------------------------------------------------------------------
Traceback (most recent call last):
  File ".../unittest_equality.py", line 21, in
testExpectNotEqualFails
    self.assertNotEqual(1, 3 - 2)
AssertionError: 1 == 1


----------------------------------------------------------------------
Ran 4 tests in 0.001s

FAILED (failures=2)
```

16.3.6   Almost Equal?

In addition to strict equality, it is possible to test for near equality of floating-point numbers using assertAlmostEqual() and assertNotAlmostEqual().

Listing 16.29: <code>unittest_almostequal.py</code>

```
import unittest


class AlmostEqualTest(unittest.TestCase):

    def testEqual(self):
        self.assertEqual(1.1, 3.3 - 2.2)

    def testAlmostEqual(self):
        self.assertAlmostEqual(1.1, 3.3 - 2.2, places=1)

    def testNotAlmostEqual(self):
        self.assertNotAlmostEqual(1.1, 3.3 - 2.0, places=1)
```

The arguments are the values to be compared and the number of decimal places to use for the test.

```
$ python3 -m unittest unittest_almostequal.py

.F.
======================================================================
FAIL: testEqual (unittest_almostequal.AlmostEqualTest)
----------------------------------------------------------------------
Traceback (most recent call last):
  File ".../unittest_almostequal.py", line 12, in testEqual
    self.assertEqual(1.1, 3.3 - 2.2)
AssertionError: 1.1 != 1.0999999999999996


----------------------------------------------------------------------
Ran 3 tests in 0.001s

FAILED (failures=1)
```

16.3.7   Containers

In addition to the generic `assertEqual()` and `assertNotEqual()` methods, special methods are available for comparing containers such as `list`, `dict`, and `set` objects.

Listing 16.30: <code>unittest_equality_container.py</code>

```
import textwrap
import unittest


class ContainerEqualityTest(unittest.TestCase):

    def testCount(self):
```

```
            self.assertCountEqual(
                [1, 2, 3, 2],
                [1, 3, 2, 3],
            )

    def testDict(self):
        self.assertDictEqual(
            {'a': 1, 'b': 2},
            {'a': 1, 'b': 3},
        )

    def testList(self):
        self.assertListEqual(
            [1, 2, 3],
            [1, 3, 2],
        )

    def testMultiLineString(self):
        self.assertMultiLineEqual(
            textwrap.dedent("""
            This string
            has more than one
            line.
            """),
            textwrap.dedent("""
            This string has
            more than two
            lines.
            """),
        )

    def testSequence(self):
        self.assertSequenceEqual(
            [1, 2, 3],
            [1, 3, 2],
        )

    def testSet(self):
        self.assertSetEqual(
            set([1, 2, 3]),
            set([1, 3, 2, 4]),
        )

    def testTuple(self):
        self.assertTupleEqual(
            (1, 'a'),
            (1, 'b'),
        )
```

Each of these methods reports inequality using a format that is meaningful for the input type, thereby making test failures easier to understand and correct.

```
$ python3 -m unittest unittest_equality_container.py

FFFFFFF
======================================================================
FAIL: testCount
(unittest_equality_container.ContainerEqualityTest)
----------------------------------------------------------------------
Traceback (most recent call last):
  File ".../unittest_equality_container.py", line 15, in
testCount
    [1, 3, 2, 3],
AssertionError: Element counts were not equal:
First has 2, Second has 1:  2
First has 1, Second has 2:  3


======================================================================
FAIL: testDict
(unittest_equality_container.ContainerEqualityTest)
----------------------------------------------------------------------
Traceback (most recent call last):
  File ".../unittest_equality_container.py", line 21, in
testDict
    {'a': 1, 'b': 3},
AssertionError: {'b': 2, 'a': 1} != {'b': 3, 'a': 1}
- {'a': 1, 'b': 2}
?                 ^

+ {'a': 1, 'b': 3}
?                 ^


======================================================================
FAIL: testList
(unittest_equality_container.ContainerEqualityTest)
----------------------------------------------------------------------
Traceback (most recent call last):
  File ".../unittest_equality_container.py", line 27, in
testList
    [1, 3, 2],
AssertionError: Lists differ: [1, 2, 3] != [1, 3, 2]

First differing element 1:
2
3

- [1, 2, 3]
```

```
+ [1, 3, 2]


======================================================================
FAIL: testMultiLineString
(unittest_equality_container.ContainerEqualityTest)
----------------------------------------------------------------------
Traceback (most recent call last):
  File ".../unittest_equality_container.py", line 41, in
testMultiLineString
    """),
AssertionError: '\nThis string\nhas more than one\nline.\n' !=
'\nThis string has\nmore than two\nlines.\n'

- This string
+ This string has
?             ++++
- has more than one
? ----          --
+ more than two
?            ++
- line.
+ lines.
?      +



======================================================================
FAIL: testSequence
(unittest_equality_container.ContainerEqualityTest)
----------------------------------------------------------------------
Traceback (most recent call last):
  File ".../unittest_equality_container.py", line 47, in
testSequence
    [1, 3, 2],
AssertionError: Sequences differ: [1, 2, 3] != [1, 3, 2]

First differing element 1:
2
3

- [1, 2, 3]
+ [1, 3, 2]

======================================================================
FAIL: testSet
(unittest_equality_container.ContainerEqualityTest)
----------------------------------------------------------------------
Traceback (most recent call last):
  File ".../unittest_equality_container.py", line 53, in testSet
    set([1, 3, 2, 4]),
```

```
AssertionError: Items in the second set but not the first:
4


================================================================
FAIL: testTuple
(unittest_equality_container.ContainerEqualityTest)
----------------------------------------------------------------
Traceback (most recent call last):
  File ".../unittest_equality_container.py", line 59, in
testTuple
    (1, 'b'),
AssertionError: Tuples differ: (1, 'a') != (1, 'b')

First differing element 1:
'a'
'b'

- (1, 'a')
?      ^

+ (1, 'b')
?      ^



----------------------------------------------------------------
Ran 7 tests in 0.004s

FAILED (failures=7)
```

Use assertIn() to test container membership.

Listing 16.31: **unittest_in.py**

```python
import unittest


class ContainerMembershipTest(unittest.TestCase):

    def testDict(self):
        self.assertIn(4, {1: 'a', 2: 'b', 3: 'c'})

    def testList(self):
        self.assertIn(4, [1, 2, 3])

    def testSet(self):
        self.assertIn(4, set([1, 2, 3]))
```

Any object that supports the in operator or the container API can be used with assertIn().

```
$ python3 -m unittest unittest_in.py

FFF
================================================================
FAIL: testDict (unittest_in.ContainerMembershipTest)
----------------------------------------------------------------
Traceback (most recent call last):
  File ".../unittest_in.py", line 12, in testDict
    self.assertIn(4, {1: 'a', 2: 'b', 3: 'c'})
AssertionError: 4 not found in {1: 'a', 2: 'b', 3: 'c'}


================================================================
FAIL: testList (unittest_in.ContainerMembershipTest)
----------------------------------------------------------------
Traceback (most recent call last):
  File ".../unittest_in.py", line 15, in testList
    self.assertIn(4, [1, 2, 3])
AssertionError: 4 not found in [1, 2, 3]


================================================================
FAIL: testSet (unittest_in.ContainerMembershipTest)
----------------------------------------------------------------
Traceback (most recent call last):
  File ".../unittest_in.py", line 18, in testSet
    self.assertIn(4, set([1, 2, 3]))
AssertionError: 4 not found in {1, 2, 3}


----------------------------------------------------------------
Ran 3 tests in 0.001s

FAILED (failures=3)
```

16.3.8 Testing for Exceptions

As previously mentioned, if a test raises an exception other than `AssertionError`, it is treated as an error. This behavior can be used to uncover mistakes while modifying code that has existing test coverage. In some circumstances, however, the test should verify that some code does produce an exception. For example, if an invalid value is given to an attribute of an object, `assertRaises()` leads to clearer code than trapping the exception in the test. The next example includes two tests that can be compared on this basis.

Listing 16.32: **unittest_exception.py**

```
import unittest


def raises_error(*args, **kwds):
```

```
        raise ValueError('Invalid value: ' + str(args) + str(kwds))


class ExceptionTest(unittest.TestCase):

    def testTrapLocally(self):
        try:
            raises_error('a', b='c')
        except ValueError:
            pass
        else:
            self.fail('Did not see ValueError')

    def testAssertRaises(self):
        self.assertRaises(
            ValueError,
            raises_error,
            'a',
            b='c',
        )
```

The results for both tests are the same, but the second test using `assertRaises()` is more succinct.

```
$ python3 -m unittest -v unittest_exception.py

testAssertRaises (unittest_exception.ExceptionTest) ... ok
testTrapLocally (unittest_exception.ExceptionTest) ... ok


----------------------------------------------------------------
Ran 2 tests in 0.000s

OK
```

16.3.9   Test Fixtures

Fixtures are the outside resources that a test needs. For example, tests for one class may all need an instance of another class that provides configuration settings or another shared resource. Other test fixtures include database connections and temporary files. (Many people would argue that using external resources makes such tests not "unit" tests, but they are still tests and still useful.)

unittest includes special hooks to configure and clean up any fixtures needed by tests. To establish fixtures for each individual test case, override `setUp()` on the `TestCase`. To clean them up, override `tearDown()`. To manage one set of fixtures for all instances of a test class, override the class methods `setUpClass()` and `tearDownClass()` for the `TestCase`. Finally, to handle especially expensive setup operations for all of the tests within a module, use the module-level functions `setUpModule()` and `tearDownModule()`.

Listing 16.33: unittest_fixtures.py

```python
import random
import unittest


def setUpModule():
    print('In setUpModule()')


def tearDownModule():
    print('In tearDownModule()')


class FixturesTest(unittest.TestCase):

    @classmethod
    def setUpClass(cls):
        print('In setUpClass()')
        cls.good_range = range(1, 10)

    @classmethod
    def tearDownClass(cls):
        print('In tearDownClass()')
        del cls.good_range

    def setUp(self):
        super().setUp()
        print('\nIn setUp()')
        # Pick a number sure to be in the range. The range is
        # defined as not including the "stop" value, so this
        # value should not be included in the set of allowed
        # values for our choice.
        self.value = random.randint(
            self.good_range.start,
            self.good_range.stop - 1,
        )

    def tearDown(self):
        print('In tearDown()')
        del self.value
        super().tearDown()

    def test1(self):
        print('In test1()')
        self.assertIn(self.value, self.good_range)

    def test2(self):
        print('In test2()')
        self.assertIn(self.value, self.good_range)
```

When this sample test is run, the order of execution of the fixture and test methods is apparent.

```
$ python3 -u -m unittest -v unittest_fixtures.py

In setUpModule()
In setUpClass()
test1 (unittest_fixtures.FixturesTest) ...
In setUp()
In test1()
In tearDown()
ok
test2 (unittest_fixtures.FixturesTest) ...
In setUp()
In test2()
In tearDown()
ok
In tearDownClass()
In tearDownModule()


----------------------------------------------------------------
Ran 2 tests in 0.001s

OK
```

The tearDown methods may not all be invoked if errors occur during the process of cleaning up fixtures. To ensure that a fixture is always released correctly, use addCleanup().

Listing 16.34: unittest_addcleanup.py

```
import random
import shutil
import tempfile
import unittest


def remove_tmpdir(dirname):
    print('In remove_tmpdir()')
    shutil.rmtree(dirname)


class FixturesTest(unittest.TestCase):

    def setUp(self):
        super().setUp()
        self.tmpdir = tempfile.mkdtemp()
        self.addCleanup(remove_tmpdir, self.tmpdir)

    def test1(self):
```

```
          print('\nIn test1()')

      def test2(self):
          print('\nIn test2()')
```

This example test creates a temporary directory and then uses shutil (page 337) to clean it up when the test is complete.

```
$ python3 -u -m unittest -v unittest_addcleanup.py

test1 (unittest_addcleanup.FixturesTest) ...
In test1()
In remove_tmpdir()
ok
test2 (unittest_addcleanup.FixturesTest) ...
In test2()
In remove_tmpdir()
ok

----------------------------------------------------------------
Ran 2 tests in 0.003s

OK
```

16.3.10 Repeating Tests with Different Inputs

It is frequently useful to run the same test logic with different inputs. Rather than defining a separate test method for each small case, a commonly used technique is to create one test method containing several related assertion calls. The problem with this approach is that as soon as one assertion fails, the rest are skipped. A better solution is to use subTest() to create a context for a test within a test method. If the test then fails, the failure is reported and the remaining tests continue.

Listing 16.35: **unittest_subtest.py**

```
import unittest


class SubTest(unittest.TestCase):

    def test_combined(self):
        self.assertRegex('abc', 'a')
        self.assertRegex('abc', 'B')
        # The next assertions are not verified!
        self.assertRegex('abc', 'c')
        self.assertRegex('abc', 'd')

    def test_with_subtest(self):
```

```
        for pat in ['a', 'B', 'c', 'd']:
            with self.subTest(pattern=pat):
                self.assertRegex('abc', pat)
```

In this example, the `test_combined()` method never runs the assertions for the patterns `'c'` and `'d'`. The `test_with_subtest()` method does, and correctly reports the additional failure. Note that the test runner still perceives that only two test cases exist, even though three failures are reported.

```
$ python3 -m unittest -v unittest_subtest.py

test_combined (unittest_subtest.SubTest) ... FAIL
test_with_subtest (unittest_subtest.SubTest) ...
================================================================
FAIL: test_combined (unittest_subtest.SubTest)
----------------------------------------------------------------
Traceback (most recent call last):
  File ".../unittest_subtest.py", line 13, in test_combined
    self.assertRegex('abc', 'B')
AssertionError: Regex didn't match: 'B' not found in 'abc'


================================================================
FAIL: test_with_subtest (unittest_subtest.SubTest) (pattern='B')
----------------------------------------------------------------
Traceback (most recent call last):
  File ".../unittest_subtest.py", line 21, in test_with_subtest
    self.assertRegex('abc', pat)
AssertionError: Regex didn't match: 'B' not found in 'abc'


================================================================
FAIL: test_with_subtest (unittest_subtest.SubTest) (pattern='d')
----------------------------------------------------------------
Traceback (most recent call last):
  File ".../unittest_subtest.py", line 21, in test_with_subtest
    self.assertRegex('abc', pat)
AssertionError: Regex didn't match: 'd' not found in 'abc'


----------------------------------------------------------------
Ran 2 tests in 0.001s

FAILED (failures=3)
```

16.3.11 Skipping Tests

It is frequently useful to be able to skip a test if some external condition is not met. For example, if writing tests to check the behavior of a library under a specific version of Python, there is no reason to run those tests under other versions of Python. Test classes and methods can be decorated with `skip()` to always skip the tests. The decorators `skipIf()` and `skipUnless()` can be used to check a condition before skipping tests.

Listing 16.36: **unittest_skip.py**

```python
import sys
import unittest


class SkippingTest(unittest.TestCase):

    @unittest.skip('always skipped')
    def test(self):
        self.assertTrue(False)

    @unittest.skipIf(sys.version_info[0] > 2,
                     'only runs on python 2')
    def test_python2_only(self):
        self.assertTrue(False)

    @unittest.skipUnless(sys.platform == 'Darwin',
                         'only runs on macOS')
    def test_macos_only(self):
        self.assertTrue(True)

    def test_raise_skiptest(self):
        raise unittest.SkipTest('skipping via exception')
```

For complex conditions that are difficult to express in a single expression to be passed to `skipIf()` or `skipUnless()`, a test case may raise `SkipTest` directly to cause the test to be skipped.

```
$ python3 -m unittest -v unittest_skip.py

test (unittest_skip.SkippingTest) ... skipped 'always skipped'
test_macos_only (unittest_skip.SkippingTest) ... skipped 'only
runs on macOS'
test_python2_only (unittest_skip.SkippingTest) ... skipped 'only
runs on python 2'
test_raise_skiptest (unittest_skip.SkippingTest) ... skipped
'skipping via exception'

----------------------------------------------------------------
Ran 4 tests in 0.000s

OK (skipped=4)
```

16.3.12   Ignoring Failing Tests

Rather than deleting tests that are persistently broken, these tests can be marked with the expectedFailure() decorator so that their failure is ignored.

Listing 16.37: unittest_expectedfailure.py

```
import unittest


class Test(unittest.TestCase):

    @unittest.expectedFailure
    def test_never_passes(self):
        self.assertTrue(False)

    @unittest.expectedFailure
    def test_always_passes(self):
        self.assertTrue(True)
```

If a test that is expected to fail actually passes, that condition is treated as a special sort of failure and reported as an "unexpected success."

```
$ python3 -m unittest -v unittest_expectedfailure.py

test_always_passes (unittest_expectedfailure.Test) ...
unexpected success
test_never_passes (unittest_expectedfailure.Test) ... expected
failure

----------------------------------------------------------------
Ran 2 tests in 0.001s

FAILED (expected failures=1, unexpected successes=1)
```

TIP

Related Reading

- Standard library documentation for unittest.[8]
- doctest (page 1026): An alternative means of running tests embedded in docstrings or external documentation files.
- nose[9]: Third-party test runner with sophisticated discovery features.
- pytest[10]: A popular third-party test runner with support for distributed execution and an alternative fixture management system.

---

[8] https://docs.python.org/3.5/library/unittest.html
[9] https://nose.readthedocs.io/en/latest/
[10] http://doc.pytest.org/en/latest/

- testrepository[11]: Third-party test runner used by the OpenStack project, with support for parallel execution and tracking failures.

16.4   trace: Follow Program Flow

The trace module is useful for understanding the way a program runs. It watches the statements executed, produces coverage reports, and helps investigate the relationships between functions that call each other.

16.4.1   Example Program

This program will be used in the examples in the rest of the section. It imports another module called recurse and then runs a function from it.

Listing 16.38: trace_example/main.py

```
from recurse import recurse


def main():
    print('This is the main program.')
    recurse(2)


if __name__ == '__main__':
    main()
```

The recurse() function invokes itself until the level argument reaches 0.

Listing 16.39: trace_example/recurse.py

```
def recurse(level):
    print('recurse({})'.format(level))
    if level:
        recurse(level - 1)


def not_called():
    print('This function is never called.')
```

16.4.2   Tracing Execution

It is easy to use trace directly from the command line. The statements being executed as the program runs are printed when the --trace option is given. This example also ignores

---

[11] http://testrepository.readthedocs.io/en/latest/

the location of the Python standard library to avoid tracing into `importlib` (page 1329) and other modules that might be more interesting in another example, but that clutter up the output in this simple example.

```
$ python3 -m trace --ignore-dir=.../lib/python3.5 \
--trace trace_example/main.py

 --- modulename: main, funcname: <module>
main.py(7): """
main.py(10): from recurse import recurse
 --- modulename: recurse, funcname: <module>
recurse.py(7): """
recurse.py(11): def recurse(level):
recurse.py(17): def not_called():
main.py(13): def main():
main.py(17): if __name__ == '__main__':
main.py(18):     main()
 --- modulename: main, funcname: main
main.py(14):     print('This is the main program.')
This is the main program.
main.py(15):     recurse(2)
 --- modulename: recurse, funcname: recurse
recurse.py(12):     print('recurse({})'.format(level))
recurse(2)
recurse.py(13):     if level:
recurse.py(14):         recurse(level - 1)
 --- modulename: recurse, funcname: recurse
recurse.py(12):     print('recurse({})'.format(level))
recurse(1)
recurse.py(13):     if level:
recurse.py(14):         recurse(level - 1)
 --- modulename: recurse, funcname: recurse
recurse.py(12):     print('recurse({})'.format(level))
recurse(0)
recurse.py(13):     if level:
 --- modulename: trace, funcname: _unsettrace
trace.py(77):             sys.settrace(None)
```

The first part of the output shows the setup operations performed by `trace`. The rest of the output shows the entry into each function, including the module where the function is located, and then the lines of the source file as they are executed. `recurse()` is entered three times, as expected based on the way it is called in `main()`.

16.4.3 Code Coverage

Running `trace` from the command line with the `--count` option will produce a code coverage report detailing which lines are run and which are skipped. Since a complex program usually consists of multiple files, a separate coverage report is produced for each. By default, the coverage report files are written to the same directory as the module, named after the module but with a .cover extension instead of .py.

```
$ python3 -m trace --count trace_example/main.py

This is the main program.
recurse(2)
recurse(1)
recurse(0)
```

Two output files are produced: trace_example/main.cover,

Listing 16.40: trace_example/main.cover

```
1: from recurse import recurse

1: def main():
1:     print 'This is the main program.'
1:     recurse(2)
1:     return

1: if __name__ == '__main__':
1:     main()
```

and trace_example/recurse.cover,

Listing 16.41: trace_example/recurse.cover

```
1: def recurse(level):
3:     print 'recurse(%s)' % level
3:     if level:
2:         recurse(level-1)
3:     return

1: def not_called():
       print 'This function is never called.'
```

NOTE

Although the line def recurse(level): has a count of 1, that count does not mean the function was run only once. Rather, it means the function *definition* was executed only once. The same applies to def not_called():, because the function definition is evaluated even though the function itself is never called.

It is also possible to run the program several times, perhaps with different options, to save the coverage data and produce a combined report. The first time trace is run with an output file, it reports an error when it tries to load any existing data to merge with the new results before creating the file.

```
$ python3 -m trace --coverdir coverdir1 --count \
--file coverdir1/coverage_report.dat trace_example/main.py

This is the main program.
recurse(2)
recurse(1)
recurse(0)
Skipping counts file 'coverdir1/coverage_report.dat': [Errno 2]
No such file or directory: 'coverdir1/coverage_report.dat'

$ python3 -m trace --coverdir coverdir1 --count \
--file coverdir1/coverage_report.dat trace_example/main.py

This is the main program.
recurse(2)
recurse(1)
recurse(0)

$ python3 -m trace --coverdir coverdir1 --count \
--file coverdir1/coverage_report.dat trace_example/main.py

This is the main program.
recurse(2)
recurse(1)
recurse(0)

$ ls coverdir1

coverage_report.dat
```

To produce reports once the coverage information is recorded to the .cover files, use the --report option.

```
$ python3 -m trace --coverdir coverdir1 --report --summary \
--missing --file coverdir1/coverage_report.dat \
trace_example/main.py

lines   cov%   module   (path)
 537     0%    trace    (.../lib/python3.5/trace.py)
   7   100%    trace_example.main   (trace_example/main.py)
   7    85%    trace_example.recurse
(trace_example/recurse.py)
```

Since the program ran three times, the coverage report shows values three times higher than those in the first report. The --summary option adds the percent covered information to the output. The recurse module is only 87% covered. The cover file for recurse shows that the body of not_called is never executed, as indicated by the >>>>>> prefix.

Listing 16.42: **coverdir1/trace_example.recurse.cover**

```
3: def recurse(level):
9:     print('recurse({})'.format(level))
9:     if level:
6:         recurse(level - 1)


3: def not_called():
>>>>>>     print('This function is never called.')
```

16.4.4 Calling Relationships

In addition to coverage information, trace will collect and report on the relationships between functions that call each other. For a simple list of the functions called, use --listfuncs.

```
$ python3 -m trace --listfuncs trace_example/main.py | \
grep -v importlib

This is the main program.
recurse(2)
recurse(1)
recurse(0)

functions called:
filename: .../lib/python3.5/trace.py, modulename: trace,
funcname: _unsettrace
filename: trace_example/main.py, modulename: main, funcname:
<module>
filename: trace_example/main.py, modulename: main, funcname:
main
filename: trace_example/recurse.py, modulename: recurse,
funcname: <module>
filename: trace_example/recurse.py, modulename: recurse,
funcname: recurse
```

For more details about who is doing the calling, use --trackcalls.

```
$ python3 -m trace --listfuncs --trackcalls \
trace_example/main.py | grep -v importlib

This is the main program.
recurse(2)
```

```
    recurse(1)
    recurse(0)

    calling relationships:

    *** .../lib/python3.5/trace.py ***
        trace.Trace.runctx -> trace._unsettrace
     --> trace_example/main.py
        trace.Trace.runctx -> main.<module>

     --> trace_example/recurse.py


    *** trace_example/main.py ***
        main.<module> -> main.main
     --> trace_example/recurse.py
        main.main -> recurse.recurse

    *** trace_example/recurse.py ***
        recurse.recurse -> recurse.recurse
```

NOTE

Neither `--listfuncs` nor `--trackcalls` honors the `--ignore-dirs` or `--ignore-mods` arguments, so part of the output from this example is stripped using `grep` instead.

16.4.5   Programming Interface

To exert more control over the `trace` interface, invoke it from within a program using a `Trace` object. `Trace` supports setting up fixtures and other dependencies before running a single function or executing a Python command to be traced.

Listing 16.43: **trace_run.py**

```
import trace
from trace_example.recurse import recurse

tracer = trace.Trace(count=False, trace=True)
tracer.run('recurse(2)')
```

Since the example traces into just the `recurse()` function, no information from `main.py` is included in the output.

```
$ python3 trace_run.py

 --- modulename: trace_run, funcname: <module>
```

```
<string>(1):   --- modulename: recurse, funcname: recurse
recurse.py(12):      print('recurse({})'.format(level))
recurse(2)
recurse.py(13):      if level:
recurse.py(14):          recurse(level - 1)
 --- modulename: recurse, funcname: recurse
recurse.py(12):      print('recurse({})'.format(level))
recurse(1)
recurse.py(13):      if level:
recurse.py(14):          recurse(level - 1)
 --- modulename: recurse, funcname: recurse
recurse.py(12):      print('recurse({})'.format(level))
recurse(0)
recurse.py(13):      if level:
 --- modulename: trace, funcname: _unsettrace
trace.py(77):            sys.settrace(None)
```

The same output can be produced with the runfunc() method.

Listing 16.44: trace_runfunc.py

```python
import trace
from trace_example.recurse import recurse

tracer = trace.Trace(count=False, trace=True)
tracer.runfunc(recurse, 2)
```

runfunc() accepts arbitrary positional and keyword arguments, which are passed to the
function when it is called by the tracer.

```
$ python3 trace_runfunc.py

 --- modulename: recurse, funcname: recurse
recurse.py(12):      print('recurse({})'.format(level))
recurse(2)
recurse.py(13):      if level:
recurse.py(14):          recurse(level - 1)
 --- modulename: recurse, funcname: recurse
recurse.py(12):      print('recurse({})'.format(level))
recurse(1)
recurse.py(13):      if level:
recurse.py(14):          recurse(level - 1)
 --- modulename: recurse, funcname: recurse
recurse.py(12):      print('recurse({})'.format(level))
recurse(0)
recurse.py(13):      if level:
```

16.4.6   Saving Result Data

Counts and coverage information can be recorded as well, just as with the command-line interface. The data must be saved explicitly, using the `CoverageResults` instance from the `Trace` object.

Listing 16.45: trace_CoverageResults.py

```
import trace
from trace_example.recurse import recurse

tracer = trace.Trace(count=True, trace=False)
tracer.runfunc(recurse, 2)

results = tracer.results()
results.write_results(coverdir='coverdir2')
```

This example saves the coverage results to the directory `coverdir2`.

```
$ python3 trace_CoverageResults.py

recurse(2)
recurse(1)
recurse(0)

$ find coverdir2

coverdir2
coverdir2/trace_example.recurse.cover
```

The output file contains the following information.

```
        #!/usr/bin/env python
        # encoding: utf-8
        #
        # Copyright (c) 2008 Doug Hellmann All rights reserved.
        #
        """
>>>>>>  """

        #end_pymotw_header

>>>>>> def recurse(level):
    3:      print('recurse({})'.format(level))
    3:      if level:
    2:          recurse(level - 1)
```

```
>>>>>> def not_called():
>>>>>>      print('This function is never called.')
```

To save the counts data for generating reports, use the `infile` and `outfile` arguments
to `Trace`.

Listing 16.46: `trace_report.py`

```
import trace
from trace_example.recurse import recurse

tracer = trace.Trace(count=True,
                     trace=False,
                     outfile='trace_report.dat')
tracer.runfunc(recurse, 2)

report_tracer = trace.Trace(count=False,
                            trace=False,
                            infile='trace_report.dat')
results = tracer.results()
results.write_results(summary=True, coverdir='/tmp')
```

Pass a filename to `infile` to read previously stored data, and a filename to `outfile` to write
new results after tracing. If `infile` and `outfile` are the same, the preceding code has the
effect of updating the file with cumulative data.

```
$ python3 trace_report.py

recurse(2)
recurse(1)
recurse(0)
lines   cov%   module    (path)
   7    42%    trace_example.recurse
(.../trace_example/recurse.py)
```

16.4.7 Options

The constructor for `Trace` takes several optional parameters to control runtime behavior:

count Boolean. Turns on line number counting. Defaults to `True`.

countfuncs Boolean. Turns on the list of functions called during the run. Defaults to `False`.

countcallers Boolean. Turns on tracking for callers and callees. Defaults to `False`.

ignoremods Sequence. List of the modules or packages to ignore when tracking coverage.
     Defaults to an empty tuple.

ignoredirs Sequence. List of the directories containing modules or packages to be ignored. Defaults to an empty tuple.

infile Name of the file containing cached count values. Defaults to None.

outfile Name of the file to use for storing cached count files. Defaults to None, and data is not stored.

TIP

Related Reading

- Standard library documentation for trace.[12]
- Section 17.2.7, "Tracing a Program as It Runs" (page 1221): The sys module includes facilities for adding a custom tracing function to the interpreter at runtime.
- coverage.py[13]: Ned Batchelder's coverage module.
- figleaf[14]: Titus Brown's coverage application.

16.5   traceback: Exceptions and Stack Traces

The traceback module works with the call stack to produce error messages. A *traceback* is a stack trace from the point of an exception handler down the call chain to the point where the exception was raised. Tracebacks also can be accessed from the current call stack up from the point of a call (and without the context of an error), which is useful for determining the paths being followed into a function.

The high-level API in traceback uses StackSummary and FrameSummary instances to hold the representation of the stack. These classes can be constructed from a traceback or the current execution stack, and then processed in the same ways.

The low-level functions in traceback can be classified into several categories. Some functions extract raw tracebacks from the current runtime environment (either an exception handler for a traceback, or the regular stack). The extracted stack trace is a sequence of tuples containing the filename, line number, function name, and text of the source line.

Once extracted, the stack trace can be formatted using functions such as format_exception() and format_stack(). The format functions return a list of strings with messages formatted to be printed. Shorthand functions for printing the formatted values are available as well.

Although the functions in traceback mimic the behavior of the interactive interpreter by default, they can also handle exceptions in situations where dumping the full stack trace to the console is not desirable. For example, a web application may need to format the traceback so it looks good in HTML, and an IDE may convert the elements of the stack trace into a clickable list that lets the user browse the source.

---

[12] https://docs.python.org/3.5/library/trace.html
[13] http://nedbatchelder.com/code/modules/coverage.html
[14] http://darcs.idyll.org/~t/projects/figleaf/doc/

16.5.1   Supporting Functions

The examples in this section use the module `traceback_example.py`.

Listing 16.47: **traceback_example.py**

```
import traceback
import sys


def produce_exception(recursion_level=2):
    sys.stdout.flush()
    if recursion_level:
        produce_exception(recursion_level - 1)
    else:
        raise RuntimeError()


def call_function(f, recursion_level=2):
    if recursion_level:
        return call_function(f, recursion_level - 1)
    else:
        return f()
```

16.5.2   Examining the Stack

To examine the current stack, construct a StackSummary from walk_stack().

Listing 16.48: **traceback_stacksummary.py**

```
import traceback
import sys

from traceback_example import call_function


def f():
    summary = traceback.StackSummary.extract(
        traceback.walk_stack(None)
    )
    print(''.join(summary.format()))


print('Calling f() directly:')
f()

print()
print('Calling f() from 3 levels deep:')
call_function(f)
```

The `format()` method produces a sequence of formatted strings that are ready to be printed.

```
$ python3 traceback_stacksummary.py

Calling f() directly:
  File "traceback_stacksummary.py", line 18, in f
    traceback.walk_stack(None)
  File "traceback_stacksummary.py", line 24, in <module>
    f()


Calling f() from 3 levels deep:
  File "traceback_stacksummary.py", line 18, in f
    traceback.walk_stack(None)
  File ".../traceback_example.py", line 26, in call_function
    return f()
  File ".../traceback_example.py", line 24, in call_function
    return call_function(f, recursion_level - 1)
  File ".../traceback_example.py", line 24, in call_function
    return call_function(f, recursion_level - 1)
  File "traceback_stacksummary.py", line 28, in <module>
    call_function(f)
```

The `StackSummary` is an iterable container holding `FrameSummary` instances.

Listing 16.49: traceback_framesummary.py

```python
import traceback
import sys

from traceback_example import call_function

template = (
    '{fs.filename:<26}:{fs.lineno}:{fs.name}:\n'
    '    {fs.line}'
)


def f():
    summary = traceback.StackSummary.extract(
        traceback.walk_stack(None)
    )
    for fs in summary:
        print(template.format(fs=fs))


print('Calling f() directly:')
f()

print()
```

```
print('Calling f() from 3 levels deep:')
call_function(f)
```

Each `FrameSummary` describes a frame of the stack, including the location of the execution context within the program source files.

```
$ python3 traceback_framesummary.py

Calling f() directly:
traceback_framesummary.py :23:f:
    traceback.walk_stack(None)
traceback_framesummary.py :30:<module>:
    f()

Calling f() from 3 levels deep:
traceback_framesummary.py :23:f:
    traceback.walk_stack(None)
.../traceback_example.py:26:call_function:
    return f()
.../traceback_example.py:24:call_function:
    return call_function(f, recursion_level - 1)
.../traceback_example.py:24:call_function:
    return call_function(f, recursion_level - 1)
traceback_framesummary.py :34:<module>:
    call_function(f)
```

16.5.3 TracebackException

The `TracebackException` class is a high-level interface for building a `StackSummary` while processing a traceback.

Listing 16.50: **traceback_tracebackexception.py**

```
import traceback
import sys

from traceback_example import produce_exception

print('with no exception:')
exc_type, exc_value, exc_tb = sys.exc_info()
tbe = traceback.TracebackException(exc_type, exc_value, exc_tb)
print(''.join(tbe.format()))

print('\nwith exception:')
try:
    produce_exception()
except Exception as err:
    exc_type, exc_value, exc_tb = sys.exc_info()
```

```
    tbe = traceback.TracebackException(
        exc_type, exc_value, exc_tb,
    )
    print(''.join(tbe.format()))

    print('\nexception only:')
    print(''.join(tbe.format_exception_only()))
```

The `format()` method produces a formatted version of the full traceback, while
`format_exception_only()` shows only the exception message.

```
$ python3 traceback_tracebackexception.py

with no exception:
None


with exception:
Traceback (most recent call last):
  File "traceback_tracebackexception.py", line 22, in <module>
    produce_exception()
  File ".../traceback_example.py", line 17, in produce_exception
    produce_exception(recursion_level - 1)
  File ".../traceback_example.py", line 17, in produce_exception
    produce_exception(recursion_level - 1)
  File ".../traceback_example.py", line 19, in produce_exception
    raise RuntimeError()
RuntimeError


exception only:
RuntimeError
```

16.5.4   Low-Level Exception APIs

Another way to handle exception reporting is with `print_exc()`. This method uses
`sys.exc_info()` to obtain the exception information for the current thread, formats the
results, and prints the text to a file handle (`sys.stderr`, by default).

Listing 16.51: **traceback_print_exc.py**

```
import traceback
import sys

from traceback_example import produce_exception

print('print_exc() with no exception:')
```

```
traceback.print_exc(file=sys.stdout)
print()

try:
    produce_exception()
except Exception as err:
    print('print_exc():')
    traceback.print_exc(file=sys.stdout)
    print()
    print('print_exc(1):')
    traceback.print_exc(limit=1, file=sys.stdout)
```

In this example, the file handle for sys.stdout is substituted so the informational and traceback messages are mingled correctly.

```
$ python3 traceback_print_exc.py

print_exc() with no exception:
NoneType

print_exc():
Traceback (most recent call last):
  File "traceback_print_exc.py", line 20, in <module>
    produce_exception()
  File ".../traceback_example.py", line 17, in produce_exception
    produce_exception(recursion_level - 1)
  File ".../traceback_example.py", line 17, in produce_exception
    produce_exception(recursion_level - 1)
  File ".../traceback_example.py", line 19, in produce_exception
    raise RuntimeError()
RuntimeError

print_exc(1):
Traceback (most recent call last):
  File "traceback_print_exc.py", line 20, in <module>
    produce_exception()
RuntimeError
```

print_exc() is just a shortcut for print_exception(), which requires explicit arguments.

Listing 16.52: **traceback_print_exception.py**

```
import traceback
import sys

from traceback_example import produce_exception

try:
```

```
        produce_exception()
    except Exception as err:
        print('print_exception():')
        exc_type, exc_value, exc_tb = sys.exc_info()
        traceback.print_exception(exc_type, exc_value, exc_tb)
```

The arguments to print_exception() are produced by sys.exc_info().

```
$ python3 traceback_print_exception.py

Traceback (most recent call last):
  File "traceback_print_exception.py", line 16, in <module>
    produce_exception()
  File ".../traceback_example.py", line 17, in produce_exception
    produce_exception(recursion_level - 1)
  File ".../traceback_example.py", line 17, in produce_exception
    produce_exception(recursion_level - 1)
  File ".../traceback_example.py", line 19, in produce_exception
    raise RuntimeError()
RuntimeError
print_exception():
```

print_exception() uses format_exception() to prepare the text.

Listing 16.53: traceback_format_exception.py

```
import traceback
import sys
from pprint import pprint

from traceback_example import produce_exception

try:
    produce_exception()
except Exception as err:
    print('format_exception():')
    exc_type, exc_value, exc_tb = sys.exc_info()
    pprint(
        traceback.format_exception(exc_type, exc_value, exc_tb),
        width=65,
    )
```

The same three arguments—exception type, exception value, and traceback—are used with format_exception().

```
$ python3 traceback_format_exception.py

format_exception():
```

```
['Traceback (most recent call last):\n',
 '  File "traceback_format_exception.py", line 17, in
<module>\n'
 '    produce_exception()\n',
 '  File '
 '".../traceback_example.py", '
 'line 17, in produce_exception\n'
 '    produce_exception(recursion_level - 1)\n',
 '  File '
 '".../traceback_example.py", '
 'line 17, in produce_exception\n'
 '    produce_exception(recursion_level - 1)\n',
 '  File '
 '".../traceback_example.py", '
 'line 19, in produce_exception\n'
 '    raise RuntimeError()\n',
 'RuntimeError\n']
```

To process the traceback in some other way, such as by formatting it differently, use
extract_tb() to fetch the data in a usable form.

Listing 16.54: traceback_extract_tb.py

```python
import traceback
import sys
import os
from traceback_example import produce_exception

template = '{filename:<23}:{linenum}:{funcname}:\n    {source}'

try:
    produce_exception()
except Exception as err:
    print('format_exception():')
    exc_type, exc_value, exc_tb = sys.exc_info()
    for tb_info in traceback.extract_tb(exc_tb):
        filename, linenum, funcname, source = tb_info
        if funcname != '<module>':
            funcname = funcname + '()'
        print(template.format(
            filename=os.path.basename(filename),
            linenum=linenum,
            source=source,
            funcname=funcname)
        )
```

The return value is a list of entries from each level of the stack represented by the traceback.
Each entry is a tuple with four parts: the name of the source file, the line number in that file,

the name of the function, and the source text from that line with all whitespace stripped out (if the source is available).

```
$ python3 traceback_extract_tb.py

format_exception():
traceback_extract_tb.py:18:<module>:
    produce_exception()
traceback_example.py   :17:produce_exception():
    produce_exception(recursion_level - 1)
traceback_example.py   :17:produce_exception():
    produce_exception(recursion_level - 1)
traceback_example.py   :19:produce_exception():
    raise RuntimeError()
```

16.5.5   Low-Level Stack APIs

A similar set of functions is available for performing the same operations with the current call stack instead of a traceback. print_stack() prints the current stack, without generating an exception.

Listing 16.55: **traceback_print_stack.py**

```
import traceback
import sys

from traceback_example import call_function


def f():
    traceback.print_stack(file=sys.stdout)


print('Calling f() directly:')
f()

print()
print('Calling f() from 3 levels deep:')
call_function(f)
```

The output looks like a traceback without an error message.

```
$ python3 traceback_print_stack.py

Calling f() directly:
  File "traceback_print_stack.py", line 21, in <module>
    f()
  File "traceback_print_stack.py", line 17, in f
```

```
    traceback.print_stack(file=sys.stdout)

Calling f() from 3 levels deep:
  File "traceback_print_stack.py", line 25, in <module>
    call_function(f)
  File ".../traceback_example.py", line 24, in call_function
    return call_function(f, recursion_level - 1)
  File ".../traceback_example.py", line 24, in call_function
    return call_function(f, recursion_level - 1)
  File ".../traceback_example.py", line 26, in call_function
    return f()
  File "traceback_print_stack.py", line 17, in f
    traceback.print_stack(file=sys.stdout)
```

format_stack() prepares the stack trace in the same way that format_exception() prepares the traceback.

Listing 16.56: traceback_format_stack.py

```python
import traceback
import sys
from pprint import pprint

from traceback_example import call_function


def f():
    return traceback.format_stack()


formatted_stack = call_function(f)
pprint(formatted_stack)
```

It returns a list of strings, each of which makes up one line of the output.

```
$ python3 traceback_format_stack.py

['  File "traceback_format_stack.py", line 21, in <module>\n'
 '    formatted_stack = call_function(f)\n',
 '  File '
 '".../traceback_example.py", '
 'line 24, in call_function\n'
 '    return call_function(f, recursion_level - 1)\n',
 '  File '
 '".../traceback_example.py", '
 'line 24, in call_function\n'
 '    return call_function(f, recursion_level - 1)\n',
 '  File '
 '".../traceback_example.py", '
```

```
'line 26, in call_function\n'
'    return f()\n',
'  File "traceback_format_stack.py", line 18, in f\n'
'    return traceback.format_stack()\n']
```

The extract_stack() function works like extract_tb().

Listing 16.57: **traceback_extract_stack.py**

```python
import traceback
import sys
import os

from traceback_example import call_function

template = '{filename:<26}:{linenum}:{funcname}:\n    {source}'


def f():
    return traceback.extract_stack()


stack = call_function(f)
for filename, linenum, funcname, source in stack:
    if funcname != '<module>':
        funcname = funcname + '()'
    print(template.format(
        filename=os.path.basename(filename),
        linenum=linenum,
        source=source,
        funcname=funcname)
    )
```

It also accepts arguments, not shown here, to start from an alternative place in the stack frame or to limit the depth of traversal.

```
$ python3 traceback_extract_stack.py

traceback_extract_stack.py:23:<module>:
    stack = call_function(f)
traceback_example.py      :24:call_function():
    return call_function(f, recursion_level - 1)
traceback_example.py      :24:call_function():
    return call_function(f, recursion_level - 1)
traceback_example.py      :26:call_function():
    return f()
traceback_extract_stack.py:20:f():
    return traceback.extract_stack()
```

Related Reading

- Standard library documentation for traceback.[15]
- sys (page 1178): The sys module includes singletons that hold the current exception.
- inspect (page 1311): The inspect module includes other functions for probing the frames on the stack.
- cgitb (page 1089): Another module for formatting tracebacks nicely.

16.6   cgitb: Detailed Traceback Reports

cgitb is a valuable debugging tool in the standard library. It was originally designed for showing errors and debugging information in web applications. Although it was later updated to include plain text output as well, unfortunately the module was never renamed. Consequently, the module is not used as often as it could be, even though it includes more detailed traceback information than traceback (page 1078).

16.6.1   Standard Traceback Dumps

Python's default exception handling behavior is to print a traceback to the standard error output stream with the call stack leading up to the error position. This basic output frequently contains enough information to identify the cause of the exception and fix the problem.

Listing 16.58: cgitb_basic_traceback.py

```
def func2(a, divisor):
    return a / divisor


def func1(a, b):
    c = b - 5
    return func2(a, c)

func1(1, 5)
```

This example program has a subtle error in func2().

```
$ python3 cgitb_basic_traceback.py

Traceback (most recent call last):
```

[15] https://docs.python.org/3.5/library/traceback.html

```
    File "cgitb_basic_traceback.py", line 18, in <module>
      func1(1, 5)
    File "cgitb_basic_traceback.py", line 16, in func1
      return func2(a, c)
    File "cgitb_basic_traceback.py", line 11, in func2
      return a / divisor
ZeroDivisionError: division by zero
```

16.6.2   Enabling Detailed Tracebacks

While the basic traceback includes enough information to spot the error, enabling `cgitb` gives more detail. `cgitb` replaces `sys.excepthook` with a function that gives extended tracebacks.

Listing 16.59: cgitb_local_vars.py

```
import cgitb
cgitb.enable(format='text')
```

The error report produced by this example is much more extensive than the original report. Each frame of the stack is listed, along with the following information:

- The full path to the source file, instead of just the base name

- The values of the arguments to each function in the stack

- A few lines of source context from around the line in the error path

- The values of variables in the expression causing the error

Having access to the variables involved in the error stack can help the programmer find a logical error that occurs somewhere higher in the stack than the line where the actual exception is generated.

```
$ python3 cgitb_local_vars.py

ZeroDivisionError
Python 3.5.2: .../bin/python3
Thu Dec 29 09:30:37 2016

A problem occurred in a Python script.  Here is the sequence of
function calls leading up to the error, in the order they
occurred.

 .../cgitb_local_vars.py in <module>()
   18 def func1(a, b):
   19     c = b - 5
```

```
 20        return func2(a, c)
 21
 22 func1(1, 5)
func1 = <function func1>

  .../cgitb_local_vars.py in func1(a=1, b=5)
 18 def func1(a, b):
 19        c = b - 5
 20        return func2(a, c)
 21
 22 func1(1, 5)
global func2 = <function func2>
a = 1
c = 0


  .../cgitb_local_vars.py in func2(a=1, divisor=0)
 13
 14 def func2(a, divisor):
 15        return a / divisor
 16
 17
a = 1
divisor = 0
ZeroDivisionError: division by zero
    __cause__ = None
    __class__ = <class 'ZeroDivisionError'>
    __context__ = None
    __delattr__ = <method-wrapper '__delattr__' of
ZeroDivisionError object>
    __dict__ = {}
    __dir__ = <built-in method __dir__ of ZeroDivisionError
object>
    __doc__ = 'Second argument to a division or modulo operation
was zero.'
    __eq__ = <method-wrapper '__eq__' of ZeroDivisionError
object>
    __format__ = <built-in method __format__ of
ZeroDivisionError object>
    __ge__ = <method-wrapper '__ge__' of ZeroDivisionError
object>
    __getattribute__ = <method-wrapper '__getattribute__' of
ZeroDivisionError object>
    __gt__ = <method-wrapper '__gt__' of ZeroDivisionError
object>
    __hash__ = <method-wrapper '__hash__' of ZeroDivisionError
object>
    __init__ = <method-wrapper '__init__' of ZeroDivisionError
object>
    __le__ = <method-wrapper '__le__' of ZeroDivisionError
```

```
object>
__lt__ = <method-wrapper '__lt__' of ZeroDivisionError
object>
__ne__ = <method-wrapper '__ne__' of ZeroDivisionError
object>
__new__ = <built-in method __new__ of type object>
__reduce__ = <built-in method __reduce__ of
ZeroDivisionError object>
__reduce_ex__ = <built-in method __reduce_ex__ of
ZeroDivisionError object>
__repr__ = <method-wrapper '__repr__' of ZeroDivisionError
object>
__setattr__ = <method-wrapper '__setattr__' of
ZeroDivisionError object>
__setstate__ = <built-in method __setstate__ of
ZeroDivisionError object>
__sizeof__ = <built-in method __sizeof__ of
ZeroDivisionError object>
__str__ = <method-wrapper '__str__' of ZeroDivisionError
object>
__subclasshook__ = <built-in method __subclasshook__ of type
object>
__suppress_context__ = False
__traceback__ = <traceback object>
args = ('division by zero',)
with_traceback = <built-in method with_traceback of
ZeroDivisionError object>

The above is a description of an error in a Python program.
Here is
the original traceback:

Traceback (most recent call last):
  File "cgitb_local_vars.py", line 22, in <module>
    func1(1, 5)
  File "cgitb_local_vars.py", line 20, in func1
    return func2(a, c)
  File "cgitb_local_vars.py", line 15, in func2
    return a / divisor
ZeroDivisionError: division by zero
```

In the case of this code with a `ZeroDivisionError`, it is apparent that the problem is introduced in the computation of the value of `c` in `func1()`, rather than where the value is used in `func2()`.

The end of the output also includes the full details of the exception object (in case it has attributes other than `message` that would be useful for debugging) and the original form of the traceback dump.

16.6.3   Local Variables in Tracebacks

The code in cgitb that examines the variables used in the stack frame leading to the error
is smart enough to evaluate object attributes and display them, too.

Listing 16.60: cgitb_with_classes.py

```
import cgitb
cgitb.enable(format='text', context=12)


class BrokenClass:
    """This class has an error.
    """

    def __init__(self, a, b):
        """Be careful passing arguments in here.
        """
        self.a = a
        self.b = b
        self.c = self.a * self.b
        # Really
        # long
        # comment
        # goes
        # here.
        self.d = self.a / self.b
        return


o = BrokenClass(1, 0)
```

If a function or method includes a lot of inline comments, whitespace, or other code that
makes it very long, then having the default of five lines of context may not provide enough
direction. When the body of the function is pushed out of the code window so that it is no
longer visible on-screen, the context available is not sufficient to understand the location of
the error. Using a larger context value with cgitb solves this problem. Passing an integer
as the context argument to enable() controls the amount of code that is displayed for each
line of the traceback.

The following output shows that self.a and self.b are involved in the error-prone code.

```
$ python3 cgitb_with_classes.py

ZeroDivisionError
Python 3.5.2: .../bin/python3
Thu Dec 29 09:30:37 2016

A problem occurred in a Python script.  Here is the sequence of
function calls leading up to the error, in the order they
```

occurred.

```
.../cgitb_with_classes.py in <module>()
   21          self.a = a
   22          self.b = b
   23          self.c = self.a * self.b
   24          # Really
   25          # long
   26          # comment
   27          # goes
   28          # here.
   29          self.d = self.a / self.b
   30          return
   31
   32 o = BrokenClass(1, 0)
o undefined
BrokenClass = <class '__main__.BrokenClass'>

.../cgitb_with_classes.py in
__init__(self=<__main__.BrokenClass object>, a=1, b=0)
   21          self.a = a
   22          self.b = b
   23          self.c = self.a * self.b
   24          # Really
   25          # long
   26          # comment
   27          # goes
   28          # here.
   29          self.d = self.a / self.b
   30          return
   31
   32 o = BrokenClass(1, 0)
self = <__main__.BrokenClass object>
self.d undefined
self.a = 1
self.b = 0
ZeroDivisionError: division by zero
    __cause__ = None
    __class__ = <class 'ZeroDivisionError'>
    __context__ = None
    __delattr__ = <method-wrapper '__delattr__' of
    ZeroDivisionError object>
    __dict__ = {}
    __dir__ = <built-in method __dir__ of ZeroDivisionError
    object>
    __doc__ = 'Second argument to a division or modulo operation
    was zero.'
    __eq__ = <method-wrapper '__eq__' of ZeroDivisionError
    object>
```

```
    __format__ = <built-in method __format__ of
    ZeroDivisionError object>
    __ge__ = <method-wrapper '__ge__' of ZeroDivisionError
    object>
    __getattribute__ = <method-wrapper '__getattribute__' of
    ZeroDivisionError object>
    __gt__ = <method-wrapper '__gt__' of ZeroDivisionError
    object>
    __hash__ = <method-wrapper '__hash__' of ZeroDivisionError
    object>
    __init__ = <method-wrapper '__init__' of ZeroDivisionError
    object>
    __le__ = <method-wrapper '__le__' of ZeroDivisionError
    object>
    __lt__ = <method-wrapper '__lt__' of ZeroDivisionError
    object>
    __ne__ = <method-wrapper '__ne__' of ZeroDivisionError
    object>
    __new__ = <built-in method __new__ of type object>
    __reduce__ = <built-in method __reduce__ of
    ZeroDivisionError object>
    __reduce_ex__ = <built-in method __reduce_ex__ of
    ZeroDivisionError object>
    __repr__ = <method-wrapper '__repr__' of ZeroDivisionError
    object>
    __setattr__ = <method-wrapper '__setattr__' of
    ZeroDivisionError object>
    __setstate__ = <built-in method __setstate__ of
    ZeroDivisionError object>
    __sizeof__ = <built-in method __sizeof__ of
    ZeroDivisionError object>
    __str__ = <method-wrapper '__str__' of ZeroDivisionError
    object>
    __subclasshook__ = <built-in method __subclasshook__ of type
    object>
    __suppress_context__ = False
    __traceback__ = <traceback object>
    args = ('division by zero',)
    with_traceback = <built-in method with_traceback of
    ZeroDivisionError object>

The above is a description of an error in a Python program.
Here is
the original traceback:

Traceback (most recent call last):
  File "cgitb_with_classes.py", line 32, in <module>
    o = BrokenClass(1, 0)
  File "cgitb_with_classes.py", line 29, in __init__
```

```
    self.d = self.a / self.b
ZeroDivisionError: division by zero
```

16.6.4   Exception Properties

In addition to displaying the attributes of the local variables from each stack frame, cgitb shows all properties of the exception object. Extra properties on custom exception types are printed as part of the error report.

Listing 16.61: **cgitb_exception_properties.py**

```python
import cgitb
cgitb.enable(format='text')


class MyException(Exception):
    """Add extra properties to a special exception
    """

    def __init__(self, message, bad_value):
        self.bad_value = bad_value
        Exception.__init__(self, message)
        return


raise MyException('Normal message', bad_value=99)
```

In this example, the bad_value property is included along with the standard message and args values.

```
$ python3 cgitb_exception_properties.py

MyException
Python 3.5.2: .../bin/python3
Thu Dec 29 09:30:37 2016

A problem occurred in a Python script.  Here is the sequence of
function calls leading up to the error, in the order they
occurred.

 .../cgitb_exception_properties.py in <module>()
   19        self.bad_value = bad_value
   20        Exception.__init__(self, message)
   21        return
   22
   23 raise MyException('Normal message', bad_value=99)
MyException = <class '__main__.MyException'>
bad_value undefined
```

```
MyException: Normal message
    __cause__ = None
    __class__ = <class '__main__.MyException'>
    __context__ = None
    __delattr__ = <method-wrapper '__delattr__' of MyException
object>
    __dict__ = {'bad_value': 99}
    __dir__ = <built-in method __dir__ of MyException object>
    __doc__ = 'Add extra properties to a special exception\n
'
    __eq__ = <method-wrapper '__eq__' of MyException object>
    __format__ = <built-in method __format__ of MyException
object>
    __ge__ = <method-wrapper '__ge__' of MyException object>
    __getattribute__ = <method-wrapper '__getattribute__' of
MyException object>
    __gt__ = <method-wrapper '__gt__' of MyException object>
    __hash__ = <method-wrapper '__hash__' of MyException object>
    __init__ = <bound method MyException.__init__ of
MyException('Normal message',)>
    __le__ = <method-wrapper '__le__' of MyException object>
    __lt__ = <method-wrapper '__lt__' of MyException object>
    __module__ = '__main__'
    __ne__ = <method-wrapper '__ne__' of MyException object>
    __new__ = <built-in method __new__ of type object>
    __reduce__ = <built-in method __reduce__ of MyException
object>
    __reduce_ex__ = <built-in method __reduce_ex__ of
MyException object>
    __repr__ = <method-wrapper '__repr__' of MyException object>
    __setattr__ = <method-wrapper '__setattr__' of MyException
object>
    __setstate__ = <built-in method __setstate__ of MyException
object>
    __sizeof__ = <built-in method __sizeof__ of MyException
object>
    __str__ = <method-wrapper '__str__' of MyException object>
    __subclasshook__ = <built-in method __subclasshook__ of type
object>
    __suppress_context__ = False
    __traceback__ = <traceback object>
    __weakref__ = None
    args = ('Normal message',)
    bad_value = 99
    with_traceback = <built-in method with_traceback of
MyException object>

The above is a description of an error in a Python program.
Here is
```

the original traceback:

```
Traceback (most recent call last):
  File "cgitb_exception_properties.py", line 23, in <module>
    raise MyException('Normal message', bad_value=99)
MyException: Normal message
```

16.6.5 HTML Output

Because `cgitb` was originally developed for handling exceptions in web applications, no discussion would be complete without mentioning its original HTML output format. The earlier examples all showed plain text output. To produce HTML instead, leave out the `format` argument (or specify `"html"`). Most modern web applications are constructed using a framework that includes an error reporting facility, so the HTML form is largely obsolete.

16.6.6 Logging Tracebacks

In many situations, printing the traceback details to standard error is the best option. In a production system, however, logging the errors is even better. The `enable()` function includes an optional argument, `logdir`, to enable error logging. When a directory name is provided to the method, each exception is logged to its own file in the given directory.

Listing 16.62: `cgitb_log_exception.py`

```python
import cgitb
import os

LOGDIR = os.path.join(os.path.dirname(__file__), 'LOGS')

if not os.path.exists(LOGDIR):
    os.makedirs(LOGDIR)

cgitb.enable(
    logdir=LOGDIR,
    display=False,
    format='text',
)


def func(a, divisor):
    return a / divisor

func(1, 0)
```

Even though the error display is suppressed, a message is printed that indicates the location of the error log.

```
$ python3 cgitb_log_exception.py

<p>A problem occurred in a Python script.
.../LOGS/tmptxqq_6yx.txt contains the description of this error.

$ ls LOGS

tmptxqq_6yx.txt

$ cat LOGS/*.txt

ZeroDivisionError
Python 3.5.2: .../bin/python3
Thu Dec 29 09:30:38 2016

A problem occurred in a Python script.  Here is the sequence of
function calls leading up to the error, in the order they
occurred.

 .../cgitb_log_exception.py in <module>()
   24
   25 def func(a, divisor):
   26     return a / divisor
   27
   28 func(1, 0)
func = <function func>

 .../cgitb_log_exception.py in func(a=1, divisor=0)
   24
   25 def func(a, divisor):
   26     return a / divisor
   27
   28 func(1, 0)
a = 1
divisor = 0
ZeroDivisionError: division by zero
    __cause__ = None
    __class__ = <class 'ZeroDivisionError'>
    __context__ = None
    __delattr__ = <method-wrapper '__delattr__' of
    ZeroDivisionError object>
    __dict__ = {}
    __dir__ = <built-in method __dir__ of ZeroDivisionError
    object>
    __doc__ = 'Second argument to a division or modulo operation
    was zero.'
    __eq__ = <method-wrapper '__eq__' of ZeroDivisionError
    object>
```

```
__format__ = <built-in method __format__ of
ZeroDivisionError object>
__ge__ = <method-wrapper '__ge__' of ZeroDivisionError
object>
__getattribute__ = <method-wrapper '__getattribute__' of
ZeroDivisionError object>
__gt__ = <method-wrapper '__gt__' of ZeroDivisionError
object>
__hash__ = <method-wrapper '__hash__' of ZeroDivisionError
object>
__init__ = <method-wrapper '__init__' of ZeroDivisionError
object>
__le__ = <method-wrapper '__le__' of ZeroDivisionError
object>
__lt__ = <method-wrapper '__lt__' of ZeroDivisionError
object>
__ne__ = <method-wrapper '__ne__' of ZeroDivisionError
object>
__new__ = <built-in method __new__ of type object>
__reduce__ = <built-in method __reduce__ of
ZeroDivisionError object>
__reduce_ex__ = <built-in method __reduce_ex__ of
ZeroDivisionError object>
__repr__ = <method-wrapper '__repr__' of ZeroDivisionError
object>
__setattr__ = <method-wrapper '__setattr__' of
ZeroDivisionError object>
__setstate__ = <built-in method __setstate__ of
ZeroDivisionError object>
__sizeof__ = <built-in method __sizeof__ of
ZeroDivisionError object>
__str__ = <method-wrapper '__str__' of ZeroDivisionError
object>
__subclasshook__ = <built-in method __subclasshook__ of type
object>
__suppress_context__ = False
__traceback__ = <traceback object>
args = ('division by zero',)
with_traceback = <built-in method with_traceback of
ZeroDivisionError object>
```

The above is a description of an error in a Python program.
Here is
the original traceback:

```
Traceback (most recent call last):
  File "cgitb_log_exception.py", line 28, in <module>
    func(1, 0)
  File "cgitb_log_exception.py", line 26, in func
```

```
    return a / divisor
ZeroDivisionError: division by zero
```

TIP

Related Reading

- Standard library documentation for cgitb.[16]
- traceback (page 1078): Standard library module for working with tracebacks.
- inspect (page 1311): The inspect module includes more functions for examining the stack.
- sys (page 1178): The sys module provides access to the current exception value and the excepthook handler that is invoked when an exception occurs.
- Improved traceback module[17]: Discussion on the Python development mailing list about improvements to the traceback module and related enhancements other developers use locally.

16.7   pdb: Interactive Debugger

pdb implements an interactive debugging environment for Python programs. It includes features to pause a program, look at the values of variables, and watch program execution unfold step by step, so you can understand what the program actually does and find bugs in the logic.

16.7.1   Starting the Debugger

The first step when using pdb is to prompt the interpreter to enter the debugger at the right time. That goal can be accomplished in a few different ways, depending on the starting conditions and what is being debugged.

16.7.1.1   From the Command Line

The most straightforward way to use the debugger is to run it from the command line, giving it the program as input so it knows what to run.

Listing 16.63: **pdb_script.py**

```
1  #!/usr/bin/env python3
2  # encoding: utf-8
3  #
4  # Copyright (c) 2010 Doug Hellmann.  All rights reserved.
5  #
6
```

---

[16] https://docs.python.org/3.5/library/cgitb.html
[17] https://lists.gt.net/python/dev/802870

```
7
8   class MyObj:
9
10      def __init__(self, num_loops):
11          self.count = num_loops
12
13      def go(self):
14          for i in range(self.count):
15              print(i)
16          return
17
18  if __name__ == '__main__':
19      MyObj(5).go()
```

Running the debugger from the command line causes it to load the source file and stop execution at the first statement it finds. In this case, it stops before evaluating the definition of the class MyObj on line 8.

```
$ python3 -m pdb pdb_script.py

> .../pdb_script.py(8)<module>()
-> class MyObj(object):
(Pdb)
```

NOTE

Normally pdb includes the full path to each module in the output when printing a filename. To simplify the examples in this section, the path in the sample output has been replaced with an ellipsis (. . .).

16.7.1.2   From within the Interpreter

Many Python developers work with the interactive interpreter while developing early versions of modules because it lets them experiment more iteratively without the save/run/repeat cycle needed when creating stand-alone scripts. To run the debugger from within an interactive interpreter, use run() or runeval().

```
$ python3

Python 3.5.1 (v3.5.1:37a07cee5969, Dec  5 2015, 21:12:44)
[GCC 4.2.1 (Apple Inc. build 5666) (dot 3)] on darwin
Type "help", "copyright", "credits" or "license" for more information.
>>> import pdb_script
>>> import pdb
>>> pdb.run('pdb_script.MyObj(5).go()')
> <string>(1)<module>()
(Pdb)
```

The argument to `run()` is a string expression that can be evaluated by the Python interpreter. The debugger will parse it, then pause execution just before the first expression is evaluated. The debugger commands described here can be used to navigate and control the execution.

16.7.1.3   From within a Program

Both of the previous examples started the debugger at the beginning of a program. For a long-running process where the problem appears much later in the program execution, it is more convenient to start the debugger from inside the program using `set_trace()`.

Listing 16.64: pdb_set_trace.py

```
 1  #!/usr/bin/env python3
 2  # encoding: utf-8
 3  #
 4  # Copyright (c) 2010 Doug Hellmann.  All rights reserved.
 5  #
 6
 7  import pdb
 8
 9
10  class MyObj:
11
12      def __init__(self, num_loops):
13          self.count = num_loops
14
15      def go(self):
16          for i in range(self.count):
17              pdb.set_trace()
18              print(i)
19          return
20
21  if __name__ == '__main__':
22      MyObj(5).go()
```

Line 17 of the sample script triggers the debugger at that point in execution, pausing it on line 18.

```
$ python3 ./pdb_set_trace.py

> .../pdb_set_trace.py(18)go()
-> print(i)
(Pdb)
```

`set_trace()` is just a Python function, so it can be called at any point in a program. As a consequence, it becomes possible to enter the debugger based on conditions inside the program, including from an exception handler or via a specific branch of a control statement.

16.7.1.4 After a Failure

Debugging a failure after a program terminates is called *postmortem* debugging. pdb supports postmortem debugging through the pm() and post_mortem() functions.

Listing 16.65: **pdb_post_mortem.py**

```
 1  #!/usr/bin/env python3
 2  # encoding: utf-8
 3  #
 4  # Copyright (c) 2010 Doug Hellmann.  All rights reserved.
 5  #
 6
 7
 8  class MyObj:
 9
10      def __init__(self, num_loops):
11          self.count = num_loops
12
13      def go(self):
14          for i in range(self.num_loops):
15              print(i)
16          return
```

In this example, the incorrect attribute name on line 14 triggers an AttributeError exception, causing execution to stop. pm() looks for the active traceback and starts the debugger at the point in the call stack where the exception occurred.

```
$ python3
Python 3.5.1 (v3.5.1:37a07cee5969, Dec  5 2015, 21:12:44)
[GCC 4.2.1 (Apple Inc. build 5666) (dot 3)] on darwin
Type "help", "copyright", "credits" or "license" for more information.
>>> from pdb_post_mortem import MyObj
>>> MyObj(5).go()
Traceback (most recent call last):
  File "<stdin>", line 1, in <module>
  File ".../pdb_post_mortem.py", line 14, in go
    for i in range(self.num_loops):
AttributeError: 'MyObj' object has no attribute 'num_loops'
>>> import pdb
>>> pdb.pm()
> .../pdb/pdb_post_mortem.py(14)go()
-> for i in range(self.num_loops):
(Pdb)
```

16.7.2 Controlling the Debugger

The interface for the debugger is a small command language that lets you move around the call stack, examine and change the values of variables, and control how the debugger executes the program. The interactive debugger uses `readline` (page 922) to accept commands, and it supports tab completion for commands, filenames, and function names. Entering a blank line causes the previous command to be run again, unless it was a `list` operation.

16.7.2.1   Navigating the Execution Stack

At any point while the debugger is running, the `where` (abbreviated w) command can be given to find out exactly which line is being executed and where on the call stack the program is. In this case, execution is stopped at the module pdb_set_trace.py line 18 in the go() method.

```
$ python3 pdb_set_trace.py
> .../pdb_set_trace.py(18)go()
-> print(i)
(Pdb) where
  .../pdb_set_trace.py(22)<module>()
-> MyObj(5).go()
> .../pdb_set_trace.py(18)go()
-> print(i)
(Pdb)
```

To add more context around the current location, use `list` (l).

```
(Pdb) l
 13             self.count = num_loops
 14
 15     def go(self):
 16         for i in range(self.count):
 17             pdb.set_trace()
 18  ->         print(i)
 19         return
 20
 21  if __name__ == '__main__':
 22      MyObj(5).go()
[EOF]
(Pdb)
```

The default is to list 11 lines around the current line (5 lines before and 5 lines after). Using `list` with a single numerical argument lists 11 lines around that line instead of the current line.

```
(Pdb) list 14
  9
 10  class MyObj(object):
 11
 12      def __init__(self, num_loops):
 13          self.count = num_loops
 14
 15      def go(self):
```

```
16              for i in range(self.count):
17                  pdb.set_trace()
18  ->              print(i)
19          return
```

If `list` receives two arguments, it interprets them as the first and last lines, respectively, to include in its output.

```
(Pdb) list 7, 19
  7  import pdb
  8
  9
 10  class MyObj(object):
 11
 12      def __init__(self, num_loops):
 13          self.count = num_loops
 14
 15      def go(self):
 16          for i in range(self.count):
 17              pdb.set_trace()
 18  ->          print(i)
 19          return
```

The `longlist` (`ll`) command prints the source for the current function or frame, without having to determine the line numbers in advance. The command is named "longlist" because for long functions it may produce considerably more output than the default for `list`.

```
(Pdb) longlist
 15      def go(self):
 16          for i in range(self.count):
 17              pdb.set_trace()
 18  ->          print(i)
 19          return
```

The `source` command loads and prints the full source for an arbitrary class, function, or module.

```
(Pdb) source MyObj
 10  class MyObj:
 11
 12      def __init__(self, num_loops):
 13          self.count = num_loops
 14
 15      def go(self):
 16          for i in range(self.count):
 17              pdb.set_trace()
 18              print(i)
 19          return
```

To move between frames within the current call stack, use up and down. up (abbreviated u) moves toward older frames on the stack; down (d) moves toward newer frames. Each time you move up or down the stack, the debugger prints the current location in the same format used in the output produced by where.

```
(Pdb) up
> .../pdb_set_trace.py(22)<module>()
-> MyObj(5).go()

(Pdb) down
> .../pdb_set_trace.py(18)go()
-> print(i)
```

Pass a numerical argument to either up or down to move that many steps up or down the stack at one time.

16.7.2.2   Examining Variables on the Stack

Each frame on the stack maintains a set of variables, including both values local to the function being executed and global state information. pdb provides several ways to examine the contents of those variables.

Listing 16.66: **pdb_function_arguments.py**

```
1  #!/usr/bin/env python3
2  # encoding: utf-8
3  #
4  # Copyright (c) 2010 Doug Hellmann.  All rights reserved.
5  #
6
7  import pdb
8
9
10 def recursive_function(n=5, output='to be printed'):
11     if n > 0:
12         recursive_function(n - 1)
13     else:
14         pdb.set_trace()
15         print(output)
16     return
17
18 if __name__ == '__main__':
19     recursive_function()
```

The args command (abbreviated a) prints all of the arguments to the function that is active in the current frame. This example also uses a recursive function to show what a deeper stack looks like when where prints its contents.

```
$ python3 pdb_function_arguments.py
> .../pdb_function_arguments.py(15)recursive_function()
-> print(output)
(Pdb) where
  .../pdb_function_arguments.py(19)<module>()
-> recursive_function()
  .../pdb_function_arguments.py(12)recursive_function()
-> recursive_function(n - 1)
  .../pdb_function_arguments.py(12)recursive_function()
-> recursive_function(n - 1)
  .../pdb_function_arguments.py(12)recursive_function()
-> recursive_function(n - 1)
  .../pdb_function_arguments.py(12)recursive_function()
-> recursive_function(n - 1)
  .../pdb_function_arguments.py(12)recursive_function()
-> recursive_function(n - 1)
> .../pdb_function_arguments.py(15)recursive_function()
-> print(output)

(Pdb) args
n = 0
output = to be printed

(Pdb) up
> .../pdb_function_arguments.py(12)recursive_function()
-> recursive_function(n - 1)

(Pdb) args
n = 1
output = to be printed
```

The p command evaluates an expression given as an argument and prints the result. Python's print() function is also available, but it is passed through to the interpreter to be executed, rather than running as a command in the debugger.

```
(Pdb) p n
1

(Pdb) print(n)
1
```

Similarly, when an expression is prefixed with !, it is passed to the Python interpreter to be evaluated. This feature can be used to execute arbitrary Python statements, including modifying variables. This example changes the value of output before letting the debugger continue running the program. The statement after the call to set_trace() prints the value of output, showing the modified value.

```
$ python3 pdb_function_arguments.py

> .../pdb_function_arguments.py(14)recursive_function()
-> print(output)

(Pdb) !output
'to be printed'

(Pdb) !output='changed value'

(Pdb) continue
changed value
```

For more complicated values such as nested or large data structures, use pp to "pretty-print" them. The next program reads several lines of text from a file.

Listing 16.67: pdb_pp.py

```
 1  #!/usr/bin/env python3
 2  # encoding: utf-8
 3  #
 4  # Copyright (c) 2010 Doug Hellmann.  All rights reserved.
 5  #
 6
 7  import pdb
 8
 9  with open('lorem.txt', 'rt') as f:
10      lines = f.readlines()
11
12  pdb.set_trace()
```

Printing the variable lines with p results in output that is difficult to read because it may wrap awkwardly. pp uses pprint (page 136) to format the value for cleaner printing.

```
$ python3 pdb_pp.py

> .../pdb_pp.py(12)<module>()->None
-> pdb.set_trace()
(Pdb) p lines
['Lorem ipsum dolor sit amet, consectetuer adipiscing elit.
\n', 'Donec egestas, enim et consecte tuer ullamcorper, lect
us \n', 'ligula rutrum leo, a elementum el it tortor eu quam
.\n']

(Pdb) pp lines
['Lorem ipsum dolor sit amet, consectetuer adipiscing elit. \n',
 'Donec egestas, enim et consectetuer ullamcorper, lectus \n',
```

```
    'ligula rutrum leo, a elementum elit tortor eu quam.\n']

(Pdb)
```

For interactive exploration and experimentation purposes, it is possible to drop from the debugger into a standard Python interactive prompt, with the globals and locals from the current frame already being populated.

```
$ python3 -m pdb pdb_interact.py
> .../pdb_interact.py(7)<module>()
-> import pdb
(Pdb) break 14
Breakpoint 1 at .../pdb_interact.py:14

(Pdb) continue
> .../pdb_interact.py(14)f()
-> print(l, m, n)

(Pdb) p l
['a', 'b']

(Pdb) p m
9

(Pdb) p n
5

(Pdb) interact
*interactive*

>>> l
['a', 'b']

>>> m
9

>>> n
5
```

Mutable objects such as lists can be changed from the interactive interpreter. In contrast, immutable objects cannot be changed, and names cannot be rebound to new values.

```
>>> l.append('c')
>>> m += 7
>>> n = 3

>>> l
['a', 'b', 'c']
```

```
>>> m
16

>>> n
3
```

Use the end-of-file sequence Ctrl-D to exit the interactive prompt and return to the debugger. In this example, the list l has been changed but the values of m and n are unchanged.

```
>>> ^D

(Pdb) p l
['a', 'b', 'c']

(Pdb) p m
9

(Pdb) p n
5

(Pdb)
```

16.7.2.3   Stepping Through a Program

In addition to navigating up and down the call stack when the program is paused, it is possible to step through execution of the program past the point where it enters the debugger.

Listing 16.68: pdb_step.py

```python
1   #!/usr/bin/env python3
2   # encoding: utf-8
3   #
4   # Copyright (c) 2010 Doug Hellmann.  All rights reserved.
5   #
6
7   import pdb
8
9
10  def f(n):
11      for i in range(n):
12          j = i * n
13          print(i, j)
14      return
15
16  if __name__ == '__main__':
17      pdb.set_trace()
18      f(5)
```

Use step (abbreviated s) to execute the current line and then stop at the next execution point—either the first statement inside the function being called or the next line of the current function.

```
$ python3 pdb_step.py

> .../pdb_step.py(18)<module>()
-> f(5)
```

The interpreter pauses after the call to set_trace() and gives control to the debugger. The first step causes the execution to enter f().

```
(Pdb) step
--Call--
> .../pdb_step.py(10)f()
-> def f(n):
```

One more step moves execution to the first line of f() and starts the loop.

```
(Pdb) step
> .../pdb_step.py(11)f()
-> for i in range(n):
```

Stepping again moves to the first line inside the loop, where j is defined.

```
(Pdb) step
> .../pdb_step.py(12)f()
-> j = i * n

(Pdb) p i
0
```

The value of i is 0, so after one more step the value of j should also be 0.

```
(Pdb) step
> .../pdb_step.py(13)f()
-> print(i, j)

(Pdb) p j
0

(Pdb)
```

Stepping one line at a time in this way can become tedious if a large amount of code appears before the point at which the error occurs, or if the same function is called repeatedly.

Listing 16.69: pdb_next.py

```
1  #!/usr/bin/env python3
2  # encoding: utf-8
3  #
4  # Copyright (c) 2010 Doug Hellmann.  All rights reserved.
5  #
6
7  import pdb
8
9
10 def calc(i, n):
11     j = i * n
12     return j
13
14
15 def f(n):
16     for i in range(n):
17         j = calc(i, n)
18         print(i, j)
19     return
20
21 if __name__ == '__main__':
22     pdb.set_trace()
23     f(5)
```

In this example, there is nothing wrong with calc(). Thus, stepping through it each time it is called in the loop in f() obscures the useful output by showing all of the lines of calc() as they are executed.

```
$ python3 pdb_next.py

> .../pdb_next.py(23)<module>()
-> f(5)
(Pdb) step
--Call--
> .../pdb_next.py(15)f()
-> def f(n):

(Pdb) step
> .../pdb_next.py(16)f()
-> for i in range(n):

(Pdb) step
> .../pdb_next.py(17)f()
-> j = calc(i, n)

(Pdb) step
```

```
--Call--
> .../pdb_next.py(10)calc()
-> def calc(i, n):

(Pdb) step
> .../pdb_next.py(11)calc()
-> j = i * n

(Pdb) step
> .../pdb_next.py(12)calc()
-> return j

(Pdb) step
--Return--
> .../pdb_next.py(12)calc()->0
-> return j

(Pdb) step
> .../pdb_next.py(18)f()
-> print(i, j)

(Pdb) step
0 0

> .../pdb_next.py(16)f()
-> for i in range(n):
(Pdb)
```

The next command (abbreviated n) is like step, but does not enter functions called from the statement being executed. In effect, it steps all the way through the function call to the next statement in the current function in a single operation.

```
> .../pdb_next.py(16)f()
-> for i in range(n):
(Pdb) step
> .../pdb_next.py(17)f()
-> j = calc(i, n)

(Pdb) next
> .../pdb_next.py(18)f()
-> print(i, j)

(Pdb)
```

The until command is like next, except that it explicitly continues until execution reaches a line in the same function with a line number higher than the current value. That means, for example, that until can be used to step past the end of a loop.

```
$ python3 pdb_next.py

> .../pdb_next.py(23)<module>()
-> f(5)
(Pdb) step
--Call--
> .../pdb_next.py(15)f()
-> def f(n):

(Pdb) step
> .../pdb_next.py(16)f()
-> for i in range(n):

(Pdb) step
> .../pdb_next.py(17)f()
-> j = calc(i, n)

(Pdb) next
> .../pdb_next.py(18)f()
-> print(i, j)

(Pdb) until
0 0
1 5
2 10
3 15
4 20
> .../pdb_next.py(19)f()
-> return

(Pdb)
```

Before the until command was run, the current line was 18, the last line of the loop. After until ran, execution was on line 19, and the loop had been exited.

To let execution run until a specific line, pass the line number to the until command. Unlike when setting a breakpoint, the line number passed to until must be higher than the current line number, so this command is most useful for navigating within a function by skipping over long blocks.

```
$ python3 pdb_next.py
> .../pdb_next.py(23)<module>()
-> f(5)
(Pdb) list
 18            print(i, j)
 19        return
 20
 21  if __name__ == '__main__':
```

```
 22        pdb.set_trace()
 23  ->      f(5)
[EOF]

(Pdb) until 18
*** "until" line number is smaller than current line number

(Pdb) step
--Call--
> .../pdb_next.py(15)f()
-> def f(n):

(Pdb) step
> .../pdb_next.py(16)f()
-> for i in range(n):

(Pdb) list
 11        j = i * n
 12        return j
 13
 14
 15  def f(n):
 16  ->    for i in range(n):
 17            j = calc(i, n)
 18            print(i, j)
 19        return
 20
 21  if __name__ == '__main__':

(Pdb) until 19
0 0
1 5
2 10
3 15
4 20
> .../pdb_next.py(19)f()
-> return

(Pdb)
```

The return command is another shortcut for bypassing parts of a function. It continues executing until the function is ready to execute a return statement; it then pauses, providing time to look at the return value before the function returns.

```
$ python3 pdb_next.py

> .../pdb_next.py(23)<module>()
-> f(5)
(Pdb) step
--Call--
```

```
> .../pdb_next.py(15)f()
-> def f(n):

(Pdb) step
> .../pdb_next.py(16)f()
-> for i in range(n):

(Pdb) return
0 0
1 5
2 10
3 15
4 20
--Return--
> .../pdb_next.py(19)f()->None
-> return

(Pdb)
```

16.7.3 Breakpoints

As programs grow longer, even using next and until will become slow and cumbersome.
Instead of stepping through the program by hand, a better solution is to let it run normally
until it reaches a point where the debugger should interrupt it. set_trace() can start the
debugger, but that approach works only if there is a single point in the program where it
should pause. It is more convenient to run the program through the debugger, but tell the
debugger where to stop in advance using *breakpoints*. The debugger monitors the program,
and when it reaches the location described by a breakpoint, the program pauses before the
line executes.

Listing 16.70: pdb_break.py

```
1   #!/usr/bin/env python3
2   # encoding: utf-8
3   #
4   # Copyright (c) 2010 Doug Hellmann.  All rights reserved.
5   #
6
7
8   def calc(i, n):
9       j = i * n
10      print('j =', j)
11      if j > 0:
12          print('Positive!')
13      return j
14
15
16  def f(n):
17      for i in range(n):
18          print('i =', i)
```

```
19          j = calc(i, n)  # noqa
20      return
21
22  if __name__ == '__main__':
23      f(5)
```

Several options to the `break` command (abbreviated `b`) can be used when setting breakpoints, including the line number, file, and function where processing should pause. To set a breakpoint on a specific line of the current file, use `break lineno`.

```
$ python3 -m pdb pdb_break.py

> .../pdb_break.py(8)<module>()
-> def calc(i, n):
(Pdb) break 12
Breakpoint 1 at .../pdb_break.py:12

(Pdb) continue
i = 0
j = 0
i = 1
j = 5
> .../pdb_break.py(12)calc()
-> print('Positive!')

(Pdb)
```

The command `continue` (abbreviated `c`) tells the debugger to keep running the program until it reaches the next breakpoint. In this example, it runs through the first iteration of the `for` loop in `f()` and stops inside `calc()` during the second iteration.

Breakpoints can also be set to the first line of a function by specifying the function name instead of a line number. The next example shows what happens if a breakpoint is added for the `calc()` function.

```
$ python3 -m pdb pdb_break.py

> .../pdb_break.py(8)<module>()
-> def calc(i, n):
(Pdb) break calc
Breakpoint 1 at .../pdb_break.py:8

(Pdb) continue
i = 0
> .../pdb_break.py(9)calc()
-> j = i * n

(Pdb) where
  .../pdb_break.py(23)<module>()
-> f(5)
```

```
    .../pdb_break.py(19)f()
-> j = calc(i, n)
> .../pdb_break.py(9)calc()
-> j = i * n

(Pdb)
```

To specify a breakpoint in another file, prefix the line or function argument with a filename.

Listing 16.71: pdb_break_remote.py

```
1  #!/usr/bin/env python3
2  # encoding: utf-8
3
4  from pdb_break import f
5
6  f(5)
```

Here a breakpoint is set for line 12 of pdb_break.py after starting the main program pdb_break_remote.py.

```
$ python3 -m pdb pdb_break_remote.py

> .../pdb_break_remote.py(4)<module>()
-> from pdb_break import f
(Pdb) break pdb_break.py:12
Breakpoint 1 at .../pdb_break.py:12

(Pdb) continue
i = 0
j = 0
i = 1
j = 5
> .../pdb_break.py(12)calc()
-> print('Positive!')

(Pdb)
```

The filename can be either a full path to the source file, or a relative path to a file available on sys.path.

To list the breakpoints currently set, give the break command without any arguments. The output includes the file and line number of each breakpoint, as well as information about how many times it has been encountered.

```
$ python3 -m pdb pdb_break.py

> .../pdb_break.py(8)<module>()
-> def calc(i, n):
```

```
(Pdb) break 12
Breakpoint 1 at .../pdb_break.py:12

(Pdb) break
Num Type          Disp Enb   Where
1   breakpoint    keep yes   at .../pdb_break.py:12

(Pdb) continue
i = 0
j = 0
i = 1
j = 5
> .../pdb/pdb_break.py(12)calc()
-> print('Positive!')

(Pdb) continue
Positive!
i = 2
j = 10
> .../pdb_break.py(12)calc()
-> print('Positive!')

(Pdb) break
Num Type          Disp Enb   Where
1   breakpoint    keep yes   at .../pdb_break.py:12
        breakpoint already hit 2 times

(Pdb)
```

16.7.3.1 Managing Breakpoints

As each new breakpoint is added, it is assigned a numerical identifier. These ID numbers are used to enable, disable, and remove the breakpoints interactively. Turning off a breakpoint with `disable` tells the debugger not to stop when that line is reached. In such a case, the breakpoint is remembered, but ignored.

```
$ python3 -m pdb pdb_break.py

> .../pdb_break.py(8)<module>()
-> def calc(i, n):
(Pdb) break calc
Breakpoint 1 at .../pdb_break.py:8

(Pdb) break 12
Breakpoint 2 at .../pdb_break.py:12

(Pdb) break
Num Type          Disp Enb   Where
1   breakpoint    keep yes   at .../pdb_break.py:8
```

```
2    breakpoint    keep yes    at .../pdb_break.py:12

(Pdb) disable 1

(Pdb) break
Num Type            Disp Enb    Where
1    breakpoint    keep no     at .../pdb_break.py:8
2    breakpoint    keep yes    at .../pdb_break.py:12

(Pdb) continue
i = 0
j = 0
i = 1
j = 5
> .../pdb_break.py(12)calc()
-> print('Positive!')

(Pdb)
```

The next debugging session sets two breakpoints in the program, then disables one. The program runs until the remaining breakpoint is encountered, and then the other breakpoint is turned back on with enable before execution continues.

```
$ python3 -m pdb pdb_break.py

> .../pdb_break.py(8)<module>()
-> def calc(i, n):
(Pdb) break calc
Breakpoint 1 at .../pdb_break.py:8

(Pdb) break 18
Breakpoint 2 at .../pdb_break.py:18

(Pdb) disable 1

(Pdb) continue
> .../pdb_break.py(18)f()
-> print('i =', i)

(Pdb) list
 13        return j
 14
 15
 16  def f(n):
 17      for i in range(n):
 18 B->      print('i =', i)
 19          j = calc(i, n)
 20      return
 21
 22  if __name__ == '__main__':
```

```
 23          f(5)

(Pdb) continue
i = 0
j = 0
> .../pdb_break.py(18)f()
-> print('i =', i)

(Pdb) list
 13          return j
 14
 15
 16   def f(n):
 17          for i in range(n):
 18 B->          print('i =', i)
 19              j = calc(i, n)
 20          return
 21
 22   if __name__ == '__main__':
 23          f(5)

(Pdb) p i
 1

(Pdb) enable 1
Enabled breakpoint 1 at .../pdb_break.py:8

(Pdb) continue
i = 1
> .../pdb_break.py(9)calc()
-> j = i * n

(Pdb) list
  4  # Copyright (c) 2010 Doug Hellmann.  All rights reserved.
  5  #
  6
  7
  8 B   def calc(i, n):
  9  ->     j = i * n
 10         print('j =', j)
 11         if j > 0:
 12             print('Positive!')
 13         return j
 14

(Pdb)
```

The lines prefixed with B in the output from list show where the breakpoints are set in the program (lines 8 and 18).

Use clear to delete a breakpoint entirely.

```
$ python3 -m pdb pdb_break.py

> .../pdb_break.py(8)<module>()
-> def calc(i, n):
(Pdb) break calc
Breakpoint 1 at .../pdb_break.py:8

(Pdb) break 12
Breakpoint 2 at .../pdb_break.py:12

(Pdb) break 18
Breakpoint 3 at .../pdb_break.py:18

(Pdb) break
Num Type          Disp Enb   Where
1   breakpoint    keep yes   at .../pdb_break.py:8
2   breakpoint    keep yes   at .../pdb_break.py:12
3   breakpoint    keep yes   at .../pdb_break.py:18

(Pdb) clear 2
Deleted breakpoint 2

(Pdb) break
Num Type          Disp Enb   Where
1   breakpoint    keep yes   at .../pdb_break.py:8
3   breakpoint    keep yes   at .../pdb_break.py:18

(Pdb)
```

The other breakpoints retain their original identifiers and are not renumbered.

16.7.3.2 Temporary Breakpoints

A temporary breakpoint is automatically cleared the first time program execution hits it.
Using a temporary breakpoint makes it easy to reach a particular spot in the program flow
quickly, just as with a regular breakpoint. Because it is cleared immediately, however, the
breakpoint does not interfere with subsequent progress if that part of the program is run
repeatedly.

```
$ python3 -m pdb pdb_break.py

> .../pdb_break.py(8)<module>()
-> def calc(i, n):
(Pdb) tbreak 12
Breakpoint 1 at .../pdb_break.py:12

(Pdb) continue
```

```
i = 0
j = 0
i = 1
j = 5
Deleted breakpoint 1 at .../pdb_break.py:12
> .../pdb_break.py(12)calc()
-> print('Positive!')

(Pdb) break

(Pdb) continue
Positive!
i = 2
j = 10
Positive!
i = 3
j = 15
Positive!
i = 4
j = 20
Positive!
The program finished and will be restarted
> .../pdb_break.py(8)<module>()
-> def calc(i, n):

(Pdb)
```

After the program reaches line 12 the first time, the breakpoint is removed. Execution does not stop again until the program finishes.

16.7.3.3 Conditional Breakpoints

Rules can be applied to breakpoints so that execution stops only when the conditions are met. Using conditional breakpoints gives finer control over how the debugger pauses the program compared to enabling and disabling breakpoints by hand. Conditional breakpoints can be set in two ways. The first option is to specify the condition when the breakpoint is set using break.

```
$ python3 -m pdb pdb_break.py

> .../pdb_break.py(8)<module>()
-> def calc(i, n):
(Pdb) break 10, j>0
Breakpoint 1 at .../pdb_break.py:10

(Pdb) break
Num Type          Disp Enb   Where
1   breakpoint    keep yes   at .../pdb_break.py:10
        stop only if j>0
```

```
(Pdb) continue
i = 0
j = 0
i = 1
> .../pdb_break.py(10)calc()
-> print('j =', j)

(Pdb)
```

The condition argument must be an expression using values that are visible in the stack frame where the breakpoint is defined. If the expression evaluates as true, execution stops at the breakpoint.

Alternatively, a condition can be applied to an existing breakpoint using the condition command. The arguments to this command are the breakpoint ID and the expression.

```
$ python3 -m pdb pdb_break.py

> .../pdb_break.py(8)<module>()
-> def calc(i, n):
(Pdb) break 10
Breakpoint 1 at .../pdb_break.py:10

(Pdb) break
Num Type          Disp Enb   Where
1   breakpoint    keep yes   at .../pdb_break.py:10

(Pdb) condition 1 j>0

(Pdb) break
Num Type          Disp Enb   Where
1   breakpoint    keep yes   at .../pdb_break.py:10
        stop only if j>0

(Pdb)
```

16.7.3.4 Ignoring Breakpoints

Programs that loop or use a large number of recursive calls to the same function can often be debugged more easily by skipping ahead in the execution, instead of watching every call or breakpoint. The ignore command tells the debugger to pass over a breakpoint without stopping. Each time processing encounters the breakpoint, it decrements the ignore counter. When the counter reaches zero, the breakpoint is reactivated.

```
$ python3 -m pdb pdb_break.py

> .../pdb_break.py(8)<module>()
-> def calc(i, n):
```

```
(Pdb) break 19
Breakpoint 1 at .../pdb_break.py:19

(Pdb) continue
i = 0
> .../pdb_break.py(19)f()
-> j = calc(i, n)

(Pdb) next
j = 0
> .../pdb_break.py(17)f()
-> for i in range(n):

(Pdb) ignore 1 2
Will ignore next 2 crossings of breakpoint 1.

(Pdb) break
Num Type          Disp Enb   Where
1   breakpoint    keep yes   at .../pdb_break.py:19
        ignore next 2 hits
        breakpoint already hit 1 time

(Pdb) continue
i = 1
j = 5
Positive!
i = 2
j = 10
Positive!
i = 3
> .../pdb_break.py(19)f()
-> j = calc(i, n)

(Pdb) break
Num Type          Disp Enb   Where
1   breakpoint    keep yes   at .../pdb_break.py:19
        breakpoint already hit 4 times
```

Explicitly resetting the ignore count to zero reactivates the breakpoint immediately.

```
$ python3 -m pdb pdb_break.py

> .../pdb_break.py(8)<module>()
-> def calc(i, n):
(Pdb) break 19
Breakpoint 1 at .../pdb_break.py:19

(Pdb) ignore 1 2
Will ignore next 2 crossings of breakpoint 1.
```

```
(Pdb) break
Num Type         Disp Enb   Where
1   breakpoint   keep yes   at .../pdb_break.py:19
        ignore next 2 hits

(Pdb) ignore 1 0
Will stop next time breakpoint 1 is reached.

(Pdb) break
Num Type         Disp Enb   Where
1   breakpoint   keep yes   at .../pdb_break.py:19
```

16.7.3.5 Triggering Actions on a Breakpoint

In addition to the purely interactive mode, pdb supports basic scripting. Using commands, a series of interpreter commands—including Python statements—can be executed when a specific breakpoint is encountered. When commands is run with the breakpoint number as its argument, the debugger prompt changes to (com). Enter the desired commands one a time, and finish the list with end to save the script and return to the main debugger prompt.

```
$ python3 -m pdb pdb_break.py

> .../pdb_break.py(8)<module>()
-> def calc(i, n):
(Pdb) break 10
Breakpoint 1 at .../pdb_break.py:10

(Pdb) commands 1
(com) print('debug i =', i)
(com) print('debug j =', j)
(com) print('debug n =', n)
(com) end

(Pdb) continue
i = 0
debug i = 0
debug j = 0
debug n = 5
> .../pdb_break.py(10)calc()
-> print('j =', j)

(Pdb) continue
j = 0
i = 1
debug i = 1
debug j = 5
debug n = 5
> .../pdb_break.py(10)calc()
```

```
-> print 'j =', j

(Pdb)
```

This feature is especially useful for debugging code that uses a lot of data structures or variables. The debugger can be made to print out all of their values automatically, instead of manually printing the values each time the breakpoint is encountered.

16.7.3.6 Watching Data Change

It is also possible to watch as values change during the course of program execution without scripting explicit `print` commands. To do so, use the `display` command.

```
$ python3 -m pdb pdb_break.py
> .../pdb_break.py(8)<module>()
-> def calc(i, n):
(Pdb) break 18
Breakpoint 1 at .../pdb_break.py:18

(Pdb) continue
> .../pdb_break.py(18)f()
-> print('i =', i)

(Pdb) display j
display j: ** raised NameError: name 'j' is not defined **

(Pdb) next
i = 0
> .../pdb_break.py(19)f()
-> j = calc(i, n)   # noqa

(Pdb) next
j = 0
> .../pdb_break.py(17)f()
-> for i in range(n):
display j: 0  [old: ** raised NameError: name 'j' is not defined **]

(Pdb)
```

Each time execution stops in the frame, the expression is evaluated. If it has changed, the result is printed along with the old value. Giving the `display` command with no argument prints a list of the displays that are active for the current frame.

```
(Pdb) display
Currently displaying:
j: 0

(Pdb) up
```

```
> .../pdb_break.py(23)<module>()
-> f(5)

(Pdb) display
Currently displaying:

(Pdb)
```

To remove a display expression, use undisplay.

```
(Pdb) display
Currently displaying:
j: 0

(Pdb) undisplay j

(Pdb) display
Currently displaying:

(Pdb)
```

16.7.4   Changing Execution Flow

The jump command alters the flow of the program at runtime, but without modifying the
code. It can skip forward to avoid running some code, or it can jump backward to run some
code again. The following example program generates a list of numbers.

Listing 16.72: **pdb_jump.py**

```
1   #!/usr/bin/env python3
2   # encoding: utf-8
3   #
4   # Copyright (c) 2010 Doug Hellmann.  All rights reserved.
5   #
6
7
8   def f(n):
9       result = []
10      j = 0
11      for i in range(n):
12          j = i * n + j
13          j += n
14          result.append(j)
15      return result
16
17   if __name__ == '__main__':
18       print(f(5))
```

When run without interference, the output from this example is a sequence of increasing numbers that are divisible by 5.

```
$ python3 pdb_jump.py

[5, 15, 30, 50, 75]
```

16.7.4.1   Jump Ahead

Jumping ahead moves the point of execution past the current location without evaluating any of the statements in between the old and new locations. Skipping over line 13 in the example means that the value of j is not incremented, so all of the subsequent values that depend on it are a little smaller.

```
$ python3 -m pdb pdb_jump.py

> .../pdb_jump.py(8)<module>()
-> def f(n):
(Pdb) break 13
Breakpoint 1 at .../pdb_jump.py:13

(Pdb) continue
> .../pdb_jump.py(13)f()
-> j += n

(Pdb) p j
0

(Pdb) step
> .../pdb_jump.py(14)f()
-> result.append(j)

(Pdb) p j
5

(Pdb) continue
> .../pdb_jump.py(13)f()
-> j += n

(Pdb) jump 14
> .../pdb_jump.py(14)f()
-> result.append(j)

(Pdb) p j
10

(Pdb) disable 1

(Pdb) continue
```

```
[5, 10, 25, 45, 70]

The program finished and will be restarted
> .../pdb_jump.py(8)<module>()
-> def f(n):
(Pdb)
```

16.7.4.2   Jump Back

Jumps can also move the program execution to a statement that has already been executed, so that the code can be run again. In this example, the value of j is incremented an extra time, so the numbers in the result sequence are all larger than they would otherwise be.

```
$ python3 -m pdb pdb_jump.py

> .../pdb_jump.py(8)<module>()
-> def f(n):
(Pdb) break 14
Breakpoint 1 at .../pdb_jump.py:14

(Pdb) continue
> .../pdb_jump.py(14)f()
-> result.append(j)

(Pdb) p j
5

(Pdb) jump 13
> .../pdb_jump.py(13)f()
-> j += n

(Pdb) continue
> .../pdb_jump.py(14)f()
-> result.append(j)

(Pdb) p j
10

(Pdb) disable 1

(Pdb) continue
[10, 20, 35, 55, 80]

The program finished and will be restarted
> .../pdb_jump.py(8)<module>()
-> def f(n):
(Pdb)
```

16.7.4.3 Illegal Jumps

Jumping in and out of certain flow control statements is dangerous or undefined. Such behavior is not allowed by the debugger.

Listing 16.73: pdb_no_jump.py

```
 1  #!/usr/bin/env python3
 2  # encoding: utf-8
 3  #
 4  # Copyright (c) 2010 Doug Hellmann.  All rights reserved.
 5  #
 6
 7
 8  def f(n):
 9      if n < 0:
10          raise ValueError('Invalid n: {}'.format(n))
11      result = []
12      j = 0
13      for i in range(n):
14          j = i * n + j
15          j += n
16          result.append(j)
17      return result
18
19
20  if __name__ == '__main__':
21      try:
22          print(f(5))
23      finally:
24          print('Always printed')
25
26      try:
27          print(f(-5))
28      except:
29          print('There was an error')
30      else:
31          print('There was no error')
32
33      print('Last statement')
```

Although jump can be used to enter a function, the arguments are not defined and the code is unlikely to work.

```
$ python3 -m pdb pdb_no_jump.py

> .../pdb_no_jump.py(8)<module>()
-> def f(n):
(Pdb) break 22
```

```
Breakpoint 1 at .../pdb_no_jump.py:22

(Pdb) jump 9
> .../pdb_no_jump.py(9)<module>()
-> if n < 0:

(Pdb) p n
*** NameError: NameError("name 'n' is not defined",)

(Pdb) args

(Pdb)
```

jump will not enter the middle of a block, such as a for loop or a try:except statement.

```
$ python3 -m pdb pdb_no_jump.py

> .../pdb_no_jump.py(8)<module>()
-> def f(n):
(Pdb) break 22
Breakpoint 1 at .../pdb_no_jump.py:22

(Pdb) continue
> .../pdb_no_jump.py(22)<module>()
-> print(f(5))

(Pdb) jump 27
*** Jump failed: can't jump into the middle of a block

(Pdb)
```

The code in a finally block must all be executed, so jump will not leave the block.

```
$ python3 -m pdb pdb_no_jump.py

> .../pdb_no_jump.py(8)<module>()
-> def f(n):
(Pdb) break 24
Breakpoint 1 at .../pdb_no_jump.py:24

(Pdb) continue
[5, 15, 30, 50, 75]
> .../pdb_no_jump.py(24)<module>()
-> print 'Always printed'

(Pdb) jump 26
*** Jump failed: can't jump into or out of a 'finally' block

(Pdb)
```

The most basic restriction is that jumping is constrained to the bottom frame on the call stack. The execution flow cannot be changed if the debugging context has been changed using the up command.

```
$ python3 -m pdb pdb_no_jump.py

> .../pdb_no_jump.py(8)<module>()
-> def f(n):
(Pdb) break 12
Breakpoint 1 at .../pdb_no_jump.py:12

(Pdb) continue
> .../pdb_no_jump.py(12)f()
-> j = 0

(Pdb) where
  .../lib/python3.5/bdb.py(
431)run()
-> exec cmd in globals, locals
    <string>(1)<module>()
  .../pdb_no_jump.py(22)<module>()
-> print(f(5))
> .../pdb_no_jump.py(12)f()
-> j = 0

(Pdb) up
> .../pdb_no_jump.py(22)<module>()
-> print(f(5))

(Pdb) jump 25
*** You can only jump within the bottom frame

(Pdb)
```

16.7.4.4   Restarting a Program

When the debugger reaches the end of the program, the program is automatically restarted. Alternatively, the program can be restarted explicitly without leaving the debugger and losing the current breakpoints or other settings.

Listing 16.74: **pdb_run.py**

```
1  #!/usr/bin/env python3
2  # encoding: utf-8
3  #
4  # Copyright (c) 2010 Doug Hellmann.  All rights reserved.
5  #
```

```
 6
 7  import sys
 8
 9
10  def f():
11      print('Command-line args:', sys.argv)
12      return
13
14  if __name__ == '__main__':
15      f()
```

Running the preceding program to completion within the debugger causes the name of the script file to be printed, since no other arguments were given on the command line.

```
$ python3 -m pdb pdb_run.py

> .../pdb_run.py(7)<module>()
-> import sys
(Pdb) continue

Command line args: ['pdb_run.py']
The program finished and will be restarted
> .../pdb_run.py(7)<module>()
-> import sys

(Pdb)
```

The program can be restarted using run. Arguments passed to run are parsed with shlex (page 951) and passed to the program as though they were command-line arguments, so the program can be restarted with different settings.

```
(Pdb) run a b c "this is a long value"
Restarting pdb_run.py with arguments:
        a b c this is a long value
> .../pdb_run.py(7)<module>()
-> import sys

(Pdb) continue
Command line args: ['pdb_run.py', 'a', 'b', 'c',
'this is a long value']
The program finished and will be restarted
> .../pdb_run.py(7)<module>()
-> import sys

(Pdb)
```

run can also be used at any other point during processing to restart the program.

```
$ python3 -m pdb pdb_run.py

> .../pdb_run.py(7)<module>()
-> import sys
(Pdb) break 11
Breakpoint 1 at .../pdb_run.py:11

(Pdb) continue
> .../pdb_run.py(11)f()
-> print('Command line args:', sys.argv)

(Pdb) run one two three
Restarting pdb_run.py with arguments:
        one two three
> .../pdb_run.py(7)<module>()
-> import sys

(Pdb)
```

16.7.5   Customizing the Debugger with Aliases

Avoid typing complex commands repeatedly by using `alias` to define a shortcut. Alias expansion is applied to the first word of each command. The body of the alias can consist of any command that is legal to type at the debugger prompt, including other debugger commands and pure Python expressions. Recursion is allowed in alias definitions, so one alias can even invoke another.

```
$ python3 -m pdb pdb_function_arguments.py

> .../pdb_function_arguments.py(7)<module>()
-> import pdb
(Pdb) break 11
Breakpoint 1 at .../pdb_function_arguments.py:11

(Pdb) continue
> .../pdb_function_arguments.py(11)recursive_function()
-> if n > 0:

(Pdb) pp locals().keys()
dict_keys(['output', 'n'])

(Pdb) alias pl pp locals().keys()

(Pdb) pl
dict_keys(['output', 'n'])
```

Running `alias` without any arguments shows the list of defined aliases. A single argument is assumed to be the name of an alias, and its definition is printed.

```
(Pdb) alias
pl = pp locals().keys()

(Pdb) alias pl
pl = pp locals().keys()

(Pdb)
```

Arguments to the alias are referenced using %n, where n is replaced with a number indicating the position of the argument, starting with 1. To consume all of the arguments, use %*.

```
$ python3 -m pdb pdb_function_arguments.py

> .../pdb_function_arguments.py(7)<module>()
-> import pdb
(Pdb) alias ph !help(%1)

(Pdb) ph locals
Help on built-in function locals in module builtins:

locals()
    Return a dictionary containing the current scope's local
    variables.

    NOTE: Whether or not updates to this dictionary will affect
    name lookups in the local scope and vice-versa is
    *implementation dependent* and not covered by any backwards
    compatibility guarantees.
```

Clear the definition of an alias with `unalias`.

```
(Pdb) unalias ph

(Pdb) ph locals
*** SyntaxError: invalid syntax (<stdin>, line 1)

(Pdb)
```

16.7.6   Saving Configuration Settings

Debugging a program involves a lot of repetition: running the code, observing the output, adjusting the code or inputs, and running the code again. pdb attempts to cut down on the amount of repetition needed to control the debugging experience, thereby letting you concentrate on the code instead of the debugger. To help reduce the number of times you issue the same commands to the debugger, pdb can read a saved configuration from text files that are interpreted as it starts.

The file ~/.pdbrc is read first; it establishes any global personal preferences for all debugging sessions. Then ./.pdbrc is read from the current working directory, to set local preferences for a particular project.

```
$ cat ~/.pdbrc

# Show python help
alias ph !help(%1)
# Overridden alias
alias redefined p 'home definition'

$ cat .pdbrc

# Breakpoints
break 11
# Overridden alias
alias redefined p 'local definition'

$ python3 -m pdb pdb_function_arguments.py

Breakpoint 1 at .../pdb_function_arguments.py:11
> .../pdb_function_arguments.py(7)<module>()
-> import pdb
(Pdb) alias
ph = !help(%1)
redefined = p 'local definition'

(Pdb) break
Num Type           Disp Enb   Where
1   breakpoint     keep yes   at .../pdb_function_arguments.py:11

(Pdb)
```

Any configuration commands that can be typed at the debugger prompt can be saved in one of the start-up files. Some commands that control the execution (e.g., continue, next) can be saved in the same way as well.

```
$ cat .pdbrc
break 11
continue
list

$ python3 -m pdb pdb_function_arguments.py
Breakpoint 1 at .../pdb_function_arguments.py:11
   6
   7  import pdb
```

```
   8
   9
  10   def recursive_function(n=5, output='to be printed'):
  11 B->     if n > 0:
  12             recursive_function(n - 1)
  13         else:
  14             pdb.set_trace()
  15             print(output)
  16         return
> .../pdb_function_arguments.py(11)recursive_function()
-> if n > 0:
(Pdb)
```

Especially useful is saving run commands. Doing so means the command-line arguments for a debugging session can be set in ./.pdbrc so they are consistent across several runs.

```
$ cat .pdbrc
run a b c "long argument"

$ python3 -m pdb pdb_run.py
Restarting pdb_run.py with arguments:
     a b c "long argument"
> .../pdb_run.py(7)<module>()
-> import sys

(Pdb) continue
Command-line args: ['pdb_run.py', 'a', 'b', 'c',
'long argument']
The program finished and will be restarted
> .../pdb_run.py(7)<module>()
-> import sys

(Pdb)
```

TIP

Related Reading

- Standard library documentation for pdb.[18]
- readline (page 922): Interactive prompt editing library.
- cmd (page 938): Build interactive programs.
- shlex (page 951): Shell command-line parsing.
- Python issue 26053[19]: If the output of run does not match the values presented here, refer to this bug for details about a regression in pdb output between 2.7 and 3.5.

---

[18] https://docs.python.org/3.5/library/pdb.html
[19] http://bugs.python.org/issue26053

16.8   profile and pstats: Performance Analysis

The profile module provides APIs for collecting and analyzing statistics about how Python code consumes processor resources.

NOTE

The output reports in this section have been reformatted to fit on the page. Lines ending with a backslash (\) are continued on the next line.

16.8.1   Running the Profiler

The most basic starting point in the profile module is run(). It takes a string statement as its argument, and creates a report of the time spent executing different lines of code while running the statement.

Listing 16.75: profile_fibonacci_raw.py

```
import profile


def fib(n):
    # from literateprograms.org
    # http://bit.ly/hl0Q5m
    if n == 0:
        return 0
    elif n == 1:
        return 1
    else:
        return fib(n - 1) + fib(n - 2)


def fib_seq(n):
    seq = []
    if n > 0:
        seq.extend(fib_seq(n - 1))
    seq.append(fib(n))
    return seq


profile.run('print(fib_seq(20)); print()')
```

This recursive version of a Fibonacci sequence calculator is especially useful for demonstrating the profile module, because the program's performance can be improved significantly. The standard report format shows a summary and then details for each function executed.

```
$ python3 profile_fibonacci_raw.py

[0, 1, 1, 2, 3, 5, 8, 13, 21, 34, 55, 89, 144, 233, 377, 610, 98\
7, 1597, 2584, 4181, 6765]

        57359 function calls (69 primitive calls) in 0.127 seco\
nds

   Ordered by: standard name

   ncalls  tottime  percall  cumtime  percall filename:lineno(fu\
nction)
       21    0.000    0.000    0.000    0.000 :0(append)
        1    0.000    0.000    0.127    0.127 :0(exec)
       20    0.000    0.000    0.000    0.000 :0(extend)
        2    0.000    0.000    0.000    0.000 :0(print)
        1    0.001    0.001    0.001    0.001 :0(setprofile)
        1    0.000    0.000    0.127    0.127 <string>:1(<module\
>)
        1    0.000    0.000    0.127    0.127 profile:0(print(fi\
b_seq(20))); print())
        0    0.000             0.000          profile:0(profiler\
)
 57291/21    0.126    0.000    0.126    0.006 profile_fibonacci_\
raw.py:11(fib)
     21/1    0.000    0.000    0.127    0.127 profile_fibonacci_\
raw.py:22(fib_seq)
```

The raw version takes 57,359 separate function calls and 0.127 seconds to run. The fact that there are only 69 *primitive* calls says that the vast majority of those 57,359 calls were recursive. The details about where time was spent are broken out by function in the listing showing the number of calls, total time spent in the function, time per call (`tottime/ncalls`), cumulative time spent in a function, and ratio of cumulative time to primitive calls.

Not surprisingly, most of the time here is spent calling `fib()` repeatedly. Adding a cache decorator reduces the number of recursive calls, and has a dramatic impact on the performance of this function.

Listing 16.76: `profile_fibonacci_memoized.py`

```python
import functools
import profile


@functools.lru_cache(maxsize=None)
def fib(n):
    # from literateprograms.org
    # http://bit.ly/hlOQ5m
    if n == 0:
```

```
            return 0
        elif n == 1:
            return 1
        else:
            return fib(n - 1) + fib(n - 2)


def fib_seq(n):
    seq = []
    if n > 0:
        seq.extend(fib_seq(n - 1))
    seq.append(fib(n))
    return seq


if __name__ == '__main__':
    profile.run('print(fib_seq(20)); print()')
```

By remembering the Fibonacci value at each level, most of the recursion is avoided and the run drops down to 89 calls that take only 0.001 seconds. The ncalls count for fib() shows that it *never* recurses.

```
$ python3 profile_fibonacci_memoized.py

[0, 1, 1, 2, 3, 5, 8, 13, 21, 34, 55, 89, 144, 233, 377, 610, 98\
7, 1597, 2584, 4181, 6765]

         89 function calls (69 primitive calls) in 0.001 seconds

   Ordered by: standard name

   ncalls  tottime  percall  cumtime  percall filename:lineno(fu\
nction)
       21    0.000    0.000    0.000    0.000 :0(append)
        1    0.000    0.000    0.000    0.000 :0(exec)
       20    0.000    0.000    0.000    0.000 :0(extend)
        2    0.000    0.000    0.000    0.000 :0(print)
        1    0.001    0.001    0.001    0.001 :0(setprofile)
        1    0.000    0.000    0.000    0.000 <string>:1(<module\
>)
        1    0.000    0.000    0.001    0.001 profile:0(print(fi\
b_seq(20)); print())
        0    0.000             0.000          profile:0(profiler\
)
       21    0.000    0.000    0.000    0.000 profile_fibonacci_\
memoized.py:12(fib)
     21/1    0.000    0.000    0.000    0.000 profile_fibonacci_\
memoized.py:24(fib_seq)
```

16.8.2 Running in a Context

Sometimes, instead of constructing a complex expression for `run()`, it is easier to build a simple expression and pass it parameters through a context, using `runctx()`.

Listing 16.77: **profile_runctx.py**

```
import profile
from profile_fibonacci_memoized import fib, fib_seq

if __name__ == '__main__':
    profile.runctx(
        'print(fib_seq(n)); print()',
        globals(),
        {'n': 20},
    )
```

In this example, the value of n is passed through the local variable context instead of being embedded directly in the statement passed to `runctx()`.

```
$ python3 profile_runctx.py

[0, 1, 1, 2, 3, 5, 8, 13, 21, 34, 55, 89, 144, 233, 377, 610,
987, 1597, 2584, 4181, 6765]

        148 function calls (90 primitive calls) in 0.002 seconds

   Ordered by: standard name

   ncalls  tottime  percall  cumtime  percall filename:lineno(\
function)
       21    0.000    0.000    0.000    0.000 :0(append)
        1    0.000    0.000    0.001    0.001 :0(exec)
       20    0.000    0.000    0.000    0.000 :0(extend)
        2    0.000    0.000    0.000    0.000 :0(print)
        1    0.001    0.001    0.001    0.001 :0(setprofile)
        1    0.000    0.000    0.001    0.001 <string>:1(<module\
>)
        1    0.000    0.000    0.002    0.002 profile:0(print(fi\
b_seq(n)); print())
        0    0.000             0.000          profile:0(profiler\
)
    59/21    0.000    0.000    0.000    0.000 profile_fibonacci_\
memoized.py:19(__call__)
       21    0.000    0.000    0.000    0.000 profile_fibonacci_\
memoized.py:27(fib)
     21/1    0.000    0.000    0.001    0.001 profile_fibonacci_\
memoized.py:39(fib_seq)
```

16.8.3   pstats: Saving and Working with Statistics

The standard report created by the `profile` functions is not very flexible. However, custom reports can be produced by saving the raw profiling data from `run()` and `runctx()` and processing it separately with the `pstats.Stats` class.

The next example runs several iterations of the same test and combines the results.

Listing 16.78: `profile_stats.py`

```python
import cProfile as profile
import pstats
from profile_fibonacci_memoized import fib, fib_seq

# Create 5 sets of stats.
for i in range(5):
    filename = 'profile_stats_{}.stats'.format(i)
    profile.run('print({}, fib_seq(20))'.format(i), filename)

# Read all 5 stats files into a single object.
stats = pstats.Stats('profile_stats_0.stats')
for i in range(1, 5):
    stats.add('profile_stats_{}.stats'.format(i))

# Clean up filenames for the report.
stats.strip_dirs()

# Sort the statistics by the cumulative time spent
# in the function.
stats.sort_stats('cumulative')

stats.print_stats()
```

The output report is sorted in descending order of cumulative time spent in the function. The directory names are removed from the printed filenames to conserve horizontal space on the page.

```
$ python3 profile_stats.py

0 [0, 1, 1, 2, 3, 5, 8, 13, 21, 34, 55, 89, 144, 233, 377, 610, \
987, 1597, 2584, 4181, 6765]
1 [0, 1, 1, 2, 3, 5, 8, 13, 21, 34, 55, 89, 144, 233, 377, 610, \
987, 1597, 2584, 4181, 6765]
2 [0, 1, 1, 2, 3, 5, 8, 13, 21, 34, 55, 89, 144, 233, 377, 610, \
987, 1597, 2584, 4181, 6765]
3 [0, 1, 1, 2, 3, 5, 8, 13, 21, 34, 55, 89, 144, 233, 377, 610, \
987, 1597, 2584, 4181, 6765]
4 [0, 1, 1, 2, 3, 5, 8, 13, 21, 34, 55, 89, 144, 233, 377, 610, \
987, 1597, 2584, 4181, 6765]
Sat Dec 31 07:46:22 2016    profile_stats_0.stats
Sat Dec 31 07:46:22 2016    profile_stats_1.stats
```

```
Sat Dec 31 07:46:22 2016     profile_stats_2.stats
Sat Dec 31 07:46:22 2016     profile_stats_3.stats
Sat Dec 31 07:46:22 2016     profile_stats_4.stats

         351 function calls (251 primitive calls) in 0.000 secon\
ds

    Ordered by: cumulative time

    ncalls  tottime  percall  cumtime  percall filename:lineno(fu\
nction)
         5    0.000    0.000    0.000    0.000 {built-in method b\
uiltins.exec}
         5    0.000    0.000    0.000    0.000 <string>:1(<module\
>)
     105/5    0.000    0.000    0.000    0.000 profile_fibonacci_\
memoized.py:24(fib_seq)
         5    0.000    0.000    0.000    0.000 {built-in method b\
uiltins.print}
       100    0.000    0.000    0.000    0.000 {method 'extend' o\
f 'list' objects}
        21    0.000    0.000    0.000    0.000 profile_fibonacci_\
memoized.py:12(fib)
       105    0.000    0.000    0.000    0.000 {method 'append' o\
f 'list' objects}
         5    0.000    0.000    0.000    0.000 {method 'disable' \
of '_lsprof.Profiler' objects}
```

16.8.4 Limiting Report Contents

The output can be restricted by function. This version shows information about the performance of only fib() and fib_seq() by using a regular expression to match the desired filename:lineno(function) values.

Listing 16.79: profile_stats_restricted.py

```python
import profile
import pstats
from profile_fibonacci_memoized import fib, fib_seq

# Read all 5 stats files into a single object.
stats = pstats.Stats('profile_stats_0.stats')
for i in range(1, 5):
    stats.add('profile_stats_{}.stats'.format(i))
stats.strip_dirs()
stats.sort_stats('cumulative')

# Limit output to lines with "(fib" in them.
stats.print_stats('\(fib')
```

The regular expression includes a literal left parenthesis (() to match against the function name portion of the location value.

```
$ python3 profile_stats_restricted.py

Sat Dec 31 07:46:22 2016      profile_stats_0.stats
Sat Dec 31 07:46:22 2016      profile_stats_1.stats
Sat Dec 31 07:46:22 2016      profile_stats_2.stats
Sat Dec 31 07:46:22 2016      profile_stats_3.stats
Sat Dec 31 07:46:22 2016      profile_stats_4.stats

         351 function calls (251 primitive calls) in 0.000 secon\
ds

   Ordered by: cumulative time
   List reduced from 8 to 2 due to restriction <'\\(fib'>

   ncalls  tottime  percall  cumtime  percall filename:lineno(fu\
nction)
      105/5    0.000    0.000    0.000    0.000 profile_fibonacci_\
memoized.py:24(fib_seq)
         21    0.000    0.000    0.000    0.000 profile_fibonacci_\
memoized.py:12(fib)
```

16.8.5   Caller/Callee Graphs

Stats also includes methods for printing the callers and callees of functions.

Listing 16.80: **profile_stats_callers.py**

```
import cProfile as profile
import pstats
from profile_fibonacci_memoized import fib, fib_seq

# Read all 5 stats files into a single object.
stats = pstats.Stats('profile_stats_0.stats')
for i in range(1, 5):
    stats.add('profile_stats_{}.stats'.format(i))
stats.strip_dirs()
stats.sort_stats('cumulative')

print('INCOMING CALLERS:')
stats.print_callers('\(fib')

print('OUTGOING CALLEES:')
stats.print_callees('\(fib')
```

The arguments to print_callers() and print_callees() work the same way as the restriction arguments to print_stats(). The output shows the caller, callee, number of calls, and cumulative time.

```
$ python3 profile_stats_callers.py

INCOMING CALLERS:
   Ordered by: cumulative time
   List reduced from 8 to 2 due to restriction <'\\(fib'>

Function                                      was called by...
                                                  ncalls  tottime  \
cumtime
profile_fibonacci_memoized.py:24(fib_seq)  <-        5    0.000  \
   0.000   <string>:1(<module>)
                                                    100/5    0.000  \
   0.000   profile_fibonacci_memoized.py:24(fib_seq)
profile_fibonacci_memoized.py:12(fib)      <-       21    0.000  \
   0.000   profile_fibonacci_memoized.py:24(fib_seq)


OUTGOING CALLEES:
   Ordered by: cumulative time
   List reduced from 8 to 2 due to restriction <'\\(fib'>

Function                                      called...
                                                  ncalls  tottime  \
cumtime
profile_fibonacci_memoized.py:24(fib_seq)  ->       21    0.000  \
   0.000   profile_fibonacci_memoized.py:12(fib)
                                                    100/5    0.000  \
   0.000   profile_fibonacci_memoized.py:24(fib_seq)
                                                     105    0.000  \
   0.000   {method 'append' of 'list' objects}
                                                     100    0.000  \
   0.000   {method 'extend' of 'list' objects}
profile_fibonacci_memoized.py:12(fib)      ->
```

TIP

Related Reading

- Standard library documentation for profile.[20]
- functools.lru_cache() (page 155): The cache decorator used to improve performance in this example.

---

[20] https://docs.python.org/3.5/library/profile.html

- The Stats Class[21]: Standard library documentation for `pstats.Stats`.
- Gprof2Dot[22]: Visualization tool for profile output data.
- Smiley[23]: Python Application Tracer.

16.9   timeit: Time the Execution of Small Bits of Python Code

The `timeit` module provides a simple interface for determining the execution time of small bits of Python code. It uses a platform-specific time function to provide the most accurate time calculation possible, and reduces the impact of start-up or shutdown costs on the time calculation by executing the code repeatedly.

16.9.1   Module Contents

`timeit` defines a single public class, `Timer`. The constructor for `Timer` takes a statement to be timed and a "setup" statement (used to initialize variables, for example). The Python statements should be strings and can include embedded newlines.

The `timeit()` method runs the setup statement one time, then executes the primary statement repeatedly. It returns the amount of time that passes. The argument to `timeit()` controls how many times to run the statement; the default is 1,000,000.

16.9.2   Basic Example

To illustrate how the various arguments to `Timer` are used, here is a simple example that prints an identifying value when each statement is executed.

Listing 16.81: **timeit_example.py**

```
import timeit

# Using setitem
t = timeit.Timer("print('main statement')", "print('setup')")

print('TIMEIT:')
print(t.timeit(2))

print('REPEAT:')
print(t.repeat(3, 2))
```

---

[21] https://docs.python.org/3.5/library/profile.html#the-stats-class
[22] http://code.google.com/p/jrfonseca/wiki/Gprof2Dot
[23] https://github.com/dhellmann/smiley

The output shows the results of the repeated calls to print().

```
$ python3 timeit_example.py

TIMEIT:
setup
main statement
main statement
3.7070130929350853e-06
REPEAT:
setup
main statement
main statement
setup
main statement
main statement
setup
main statement
main statement
[1.4499528333544731e-06, 1.1939555406570435e-06,
1.1870870366692543e-06]
```

timeit() runs the setup statement one time, then calls the main statement count times. It returns a single floating-point value representing the cumulative amount of time spent running the main statement.

When repeat() is used, it calls timeit() several times (three times in this case). All of the responses are returned in a list.

16.9.3   Storing Values in a Dictionary

The next, more complex example compares the amount of time it takes to populate a dictionary with a large number of values using a variety of methods. First, a few constants are needed to configure the Timer. The setup_statement variable initializes a list of tuples containing strings and integers that will be used by the main statements to build dictionaries; the strings are used as keys, and the integers are stored as their associated values.

```
# A few constants
range_size = 1000
count = 1000
setup_statement = ';'.join([
    "l = [(str(x), x) for x in range(1000)]",
    "d = {}",
])
```

A utility function, show_results(), is defined to print the results in a useful format. The timeit() method returns the amount of time it takes to execute the statement repeatedly. The output of show_results() converts that value into the amount of time it takes per iteration, and then further reduces the value to the average amount of time it takes to store one item in the dictionary.

```python
def show_results(result):
    "Print microseconds per pass and per item."
    global count, range_size
    per_pass = 1000000 * (result / count)
    print('{:6.2f} usec/pass'.format(per_pass), end=' ')
    per_item = per_pass / range_size
    print('{:6.2f} usec/item'.format(per_item))


print("{} items".format(range_size))
print("{} iterations".format(count))
print()
```

To establish a baseline, the first configuration tested uses __setitem__(). All of the other variations avoid overwriting values that are already in the dictionary, so this simple version should be the fastest.

The first argument to Timer is a multiline string, with whitespace preserved to ensure that the function parses the string correctly when run. The second argument is a constant established to initialize the list of values and the dictionary.

```python
# Using __setitem__ without checking for existing values first
print('__setitem__:', end=' ')
t = timeit.Timer(
    textwrap.dedent(
        """
        for s, i in l:
            d[s] = i
        """),
    setup_statement,
)
show_results(t.timeit(number=count))
```

The next variation uses setdefault() to ensure that values already in the dictionary are not overwritten.

```python
# Using setdefault
print('setdefault :', end=' ')
t = timeit.Timer(
    textwrap.dedent(
        """
        for s, i in l:
            d.setdefault(s, i)
        """),
```

```
        setup_statement,
    )
    show_results(t.timeit(number=count))
```

This method adds the value only if a `KeyError` exception is raised when looking for the existing value.

```
# Using exceptions
print('KeyError    :', end=' ')
t = timeit.Timer(
    textwrap.dedent(
        """
        for s, i in l:
            try:
                existing = d[s]
            except KeyError:
                d[s] = i
        """),
    setup_statement,
)
show_results(t.timeit(number=count))
```

The last method uses in to determine whether a dictionary has a particular key.

```
# Using "in"
print('"not in"    :', end=' ')
t = timeit.Timer(
    textwrap.dedent(
        """
        for s, i in l:
            if s not in d:
                d[s] = i
        """),
    setup_statement,
)
show_results(t.timeit(number=count))
```

When run, the script produces the following output.

```
$ python3 timeit_dictionary.py

1000 items
1000 iterations

__setitem__ :  91.79 usec/pass    0.09 usec/item
setdefault  : 182.85 usec/pass    0.18 usec/item
KeyError    :  80.87 usec/pass    0.08 usec/item
"not in"    :  66.77 usec/pass    0.07 usec/item
```

The times in this output are for a MacMini. The results will, of course, vary depending on which hardware is used and which other programs are running on the system. Experiment with the `range_size` and `count` variables, since different combinations will produce different results.

16.9.4   From the Command Line

In addition to the programmatic interface, `timeit` provides a command-line interface for testing modules without instrumentation.

To run the module, use the `-m` option to the Python interpreter to find the module and treat it as the main program.

```
$ python3 -m timeit
```

For example, to get help, give the following command.

```
$ python3 -m timeit -h

Tool for measuring execution time of small code snippets.

This module avoids a number of common traps for measuring execution
times.  See also Tim Peters' introduction to the Algorithms chapter in
the Python Cookbook, published by O'Reilly.

...
```

The `statement` argument works a little differently on the command line than does the argument to `Timer`. Instead of using one long string, pass each line of the instructions as a separate command-line argument to the method. To indent lines (such as inside a loop), embed spaces in the string by enclosing it in quotes.

```
$ python3 -m timeit -s \
"d={}" \
"for i in range(1000):" \
"  d[str(i)] = i"

1000 loops, best of 3: 306 usec per loop
```

It is also possible to define a function with more complex code, and then call the function from the command line.

Listing 16.82: `timeit_setitem.py`

```
def test_setitem(range_size=1000):
    l = [(str(x), x) for x in range(range_size)]
    d = {}
```

```
    for s, i in l:
        d[s] = i
```

To run the test, pass in code that imports the modules and runs the test function.

```
$ python3 -m timeit \
"import timeit_setitem; timeit_setitem.test_setitem()"

1000 loops, best of 3: 401 usec per loop
```

TIP

Related Reading

- Standard library documentation for `timeit`.[24]
- `profile` (page 1140): The `profile` module is also useful for performance analysis.
- Monotonic Clocks (page 214): Discussion of the monotonic clock from the `time` module.

16.10   tabnanny: Indentation Validator

Consistent use of indentation is important in a language like Python, where whitespace is significant. The `tabnanny` module provides a scanner that reports on ambiguous use of indentation.

16.10.1   Running from the Command Line

The simplest way to use `tabnanny` is to run it from the command line, passing it the names of files to check. If you pass directory names, the directories are scanned recursively to find `.py` files to check.

Running `tabnanny` across the PyMOTW source code exposed one old module with tabs instead of spaces.

```
$ python3 -m tabnanny .
./source/queue/fetch_podcasts.py 65 "    \t\tparsed_url = \
urlparse(enclosure['url'])\n"
```

Line 65 of `fetch_podcasts.py` included two tabs instead of eight spaces. The tabs were not readily apparent in a text editor that was configured with tabstops set to four spaces, such that visually there was no difference between the two tabs and the eight spaces.

```
        for enclosure in entry.get('enclosures', []):
            parsed_url = urlparse(enclosure['url'])
```

---

[24] https://docs.python.org/3.5/library/timeit.html

```
message('queuing {}'.format(
    parsed_url.path.rpartition('/')[-1]))
enclosure_queue.put(enclosure['url'])
```

Correcting line 65 and running tabnanny again showed another error on line 66. One last problem showed up on line 67.

If you want to scan files, but not see the details about the error, use the -q option to suppress all information except the filename.

```
$ python3 -m tabnanny -q .
./source/queue/fetch_podcasts.py
```

To see more information about the files being scanned, use the -v option.

```
'source/queue/': listing directory
'source/queue/fetch_podcasts.py': *** Line 65: trouble in tab
city! ***
offending line: "    \t\tparsed_url = urlparse(enclosure['url'])
\n"
indent not greater e.g. at tab sizes 1, 2
'source/queue/queue_fifo.py': Clean bill of health.
'source/queue/queue_lifo.py': Clean bill of health.
'source/queue/queue_priority.py': Clean bill of health.
```

NOTE

Running these examples against the PyMOTW source files will not lead to the same errors being reported, because the issues have been fixed.

TIP

Related Reading

- Standard library documentation for tabnanny.[25]
- tokenize: Lexical scanner for Python source code.
- flake8[26]: Modular source code checker.
- pycodestyle[27]: Python style guide checker.
- pylint[28]: Python code static checker.

---

[25] https://docs.python.org/3.5/library/tabnanny.html
[26] https://pypi.python.org/pypi/flake8
[27] https://pycodestyle.readthedocs.io/en/latest/
[28] https://pypi.python.org/pypi/pylint

16.11   compileall: Byte-Compile Source Files

The compileall module finds Python source files and compiles them to the byte-code representation, saving the results in .pyc.

16.11.1   Compiling One Directory

compile_dir() is used to recursively scan a directory and byte-compile the files within it.

Listing 16.83: **compileall_compile_dir.py**

```
import compileall
import glob


def show(title):
    print(title)
    for filename in glob.glob('examples/**',
                              recursive=True):
        print('  {}'.format(filename))
    print()

show('Before')

compileall.compile_dir('examples')

show('\nAfter')
```

By default, all of the subdirectories are scanned to a depth of 10. The output files are written to a __pycache__ directory and named based on the Python interpreter version.

```
$ python3 compileall_compile_dir.py

Before
  examples/
  examples/README
  examples/a.py
  examples/subdir
  examples/subdir/b.py

Listing 'examples'...
Compiling 'examples/a.py'...
Listing 'examples/subdir'...
Compiling 'examples/subdir/b.py'...

After
  examples/
```

```
examples/README
examples/__pycache__
examples/__pycache__/a.cpython-35.pyc
examples/a.py
examples/subdir
examples/subdir/__pycache__
examples/subdir/__pycache__/b.cpython-35.pyc
examples/subdir/b.py
```

16.11.2   Ignoring Files

To filter directories out, use the rx argument to provide a regular expression that matches
the names to be excluded.

Listing 16.84: **compileall_exclude_dirs.py**

```
import compileall
import re

compileall.compile_dir(
    'examples',
    rx=re.compile(r'/subdir'),
)
```

This version excludes files in the subdir subdirectory.

```
$ python3 compileall_exclude_dirs.py

Listing 'examples'...
Compiling 'examples/a.py'...
Listing 'examples/subdir'...
```

The maxlevels argument controls the depth of recursion. For example, to avoid recursion
entirely, pass 0 as the value of this argument.

Listing 16.85: **compileall_recursion_depth.py**

```
import compileall
import re

compileall.compile_dir(
    'examples',
    maxlevels=0,
)
```

In this case, only files within the directory passed to compile_dir() are compiled.

```
$ python3 compileall_recursion_depth.py

Listing 'examples'...
Compiling 'examples/a.py'...
```

16.11.3   Compiling sys.path

All of the Python source files found in sys.path can be compiled with a single call to
compile_path().

Listing 16.86: compileall_path.py

```
import compileall
import sys

sys.path[:] = ['examples', 'notthere']
print('sys.path =', sys.path)
compileall.compile_path()
```

This example replaces the default contents of sys.path to avoid permission errors while
running the script, but still illustrates the default behavior. Note that the value of maxlevels
defaults to 0.

```
$ python3 compileall_path.py

sys.path = ['examples', 'notthere']
Listing 'examples'...
Compiling 'examples/a.py'...
Listing 'notthere'...
Can't list 'notthere'
```

16.11.4   Compiling Individual Files

To compile a single file, rather than an entire directory of files, use compile_file().

Listing 16.87: compileall_compile_file.py

```
import compileall
import glob


def show(title):
    print(title)
    for filename in glob.glob('examples/**',
                              recursive=True):
        print('  {}'.format(filename))
    print()
```

```
show('Before')

compileall.compile_file('examples/a.py')

show('\nAfter')
```

The first argument should be the name of the file, in the form of either a full path or a relative path.

```
$ python3 compileall_compile_file.py

Before
  examples/
  examples/README
  examples/a.py
  examples/subdir
  examples/subdir/b.py

Compiling 'examples/a.py'...

After
  examples/
  examples/README
  examples/__pycache__
  examples/__pycache__/a.cpython-35.pyc
  examples/a.py
  examples/subdir
  examples/subdir/b.py
```

16.11.5 From the Command Line

It is also possible to invoke compileall from the command line, so it can be integrated with a build system via a Makefile. For example:

```
$ python3 -m compileall -h

usage: compileall.py [-h] [-l] [-r RECURSION] [-f] [-q] [-b] [-d DESTDIR]
                     [-x REGEXP] [-i FILE] [-j WORKERS]
                     [FILE|DIR [FILE|DIR ...]]

Utilities to support installing Python libraries.

positional arguments:
  FILE|DIR            zero or more file and directory names to compile; if
                     no arguments given, defaults to the
equivalent of -l
                     sys.path
```

```
optional arguments:
  -h, --help             show this help message and exit
  -l                     don't recurse into subdirectories
  -r RECURSION           control the maximum recursion level. if
'-l' and '-r'

                         options are specified, then '-r' takes
precedence.
  -f                     force rebuild even if timestamps are up
to date
  -q                     output only error messages; -qq will
suppress the

                         error messages as well.
  -b                     use legacy (pre-PEP3147) compiled file
locations
  -d DESTDIR             directory to prepend to file paths for
use in compile-

                         time tracebacks and in runtime
tracebacks in cases

                         where the source file is unavailable
  -x REGEXP              skip files matching the regular
expression; the regexp

                         is searched for in the full path of each
file

                         considered for compilation
  -i FILE                add all the files and directories listed
in FILE to

                         the list considered for compilation; if
"-", names are

                         read from stdin
  -j WORKERS, --workers WORKERS
                         Run compileall concurrently
```

To recreate the earlier example that skips the subdir directory, run the following command.

```
$ python3 -m compileall -x '/subdir' examples

Listing 'examples'...
Compiling 'examples/a.py'...
Listing 'examples/subdir'...
```

TIP

Related Reading

- Standard library documentation for compileall.[29]

---

[29] https://docs.python.org/3.5/library/compileall.html

16.12   pyclbr: Class Browser

pyclbr can scan Python source files to find both classes and stand-alone functions. The information about class, method, and function names and line numbers is gathered by using tokenize *without* importing the code.

The examples in this section use the following source file as input.

Listing 16.88: `pyclbr_example.py`

```python
"""Example source for pyclbr.
"""


class Base:
    """This is the base class.
    """

    def method1(self):
        return


class Sub1(Base):
    """This is the first subclass.
    """


class Sub2(Base):
    """This is the second subclass.
    """


class Mixin:
    """A mixin class.
    """

    def method2(self):
        return


class MixinUser(Sub2, Mixin):
    """Overrides method1 and method2
    """

    def method1(self):
        return

    def method2(self):
        return
```

```
        def method3(self):
            return


    def my_function():
        """Stand-alone function.
        """
        return
```

16.12.1 Scanning for Classes

There are two public functions exposed by pyclbr. The first, readmodule(), takes the name of the module as an argument and returns a mapping of class names to Class objects containing the metadata for the class source.

Listing 16.89: pyclbr_readmodule.py

```
import pyclbr
import os
from operator import itemgetter


def show_class(name, class_data):
    print('Class:', name)
    filename = os.path.basename(class_data.file)
    print('  File: {0} [{1}]'.format(
        filename, class_data.lineno))
    show_super_classes(name, class_data)
    show_methods(name, class_data)
    print()


def show_methods(class_name, class_data):
    for name, lineno in sorted(class_data.methods.items(),
                               key=itemgetter(1)):
        print('  Method: {0} [{1}]'.format(name, lineno))


def show_super_classes(name, class_data):
    super_class_names = []
    for super_class in class_data.super:
        if super_class == 'object':
            continue
        if isinstance(super_class, str):
            super_class_names.append(super_class)
        else:
            super_class_names.append(super_class.name)
    if super_class_names:
```

```
        print('  Super classes:', super_class_names)


example_data = pyclbr.readmodule('pyclbr_example')

for name, class_data in sorted(example_data.items(),
                               key=lambda x: x[1].lineno):
    show_class(name, class_data)
```

The metadata for the class includes the file and line number where it is defined, as well as the names of super classes. The methods of the class are saved as a mapping between the method name and the line number. The output shows the classes and methods listed in order based on their line number in the source file.

```
$ python3 pyclbr_readmodule.py

Class: Base
  File: pyclbr_example.py [11]
  Method: method1 [15]

Class: Sub1
  File: pyclbr_example.py [19]
  Super classes: ['Base']

Class: Sub2
  File: pyclbr_example.py [24]
  Super classes: ['Base']

Class: Mixin
  File: pyclbr_example.py [29]
  Method: method2 [33]

Class: MixinUser
  File: pyclbr_example.py [37]
  Super classes: ['Sub2', 'Mixin']
  Method: method1 [41]
  Method: method2 [44]
  Method: method3 [47]
```

16.12.2 Scanning for Functions

The other public function in pyclbr is readmodule_ex(). It does everything that readmodule() does, and adds functions to the result set.

Listing 16.90: pyclbr_readmodule_ex.py

```
import pyclbr
import os
```

```
from operator import itemgetter

example_data = pyclbr.readmodule_ex('pyclbr_example')

for name, data in sorted(example_data.items(),
                         key=lambda x: x[1].lineno):
    if isinstance(data, pyclbr.Function):
        print('Function: {0} [{1}]'.format(name, data.lineno))
```

Each `Function` object has properties much like the `Class` object.

```
$ python3 pyclbr_readmodule_ex.py

Function: my_function [51]
```

TIP

Related Reading

- Standard library documentation for `pyclbr`.[30]
- `inspect` (page 1311): The `inspect` module can discover more metadata about classes and functions, but requires importing the code.
- `tokenize`: The `tokenize` module parses Python source code into tokens.

16.13   venv: Create Virtual Environments

Python virtual environments, which are managed by `venv`, are set up for installing packages and running programs in a way that isolates them from other packages installed on the rest of the system. Because each environment has its own interpreter executable and directory for installing packages, it is easy to create multiple environments configured with various combinations of Python and package versions on the same computer.

16.13.1   Creating Environments

The primary command-line interface to `venv` relies on Python's ability to run a "main" function in a module using the `-m` option.

```
$ python3 -m venv /tmp/demoenv
```

A separate `pyvenv` command-line application may be installed, depending on how the Python interpreter was built and packaged. The following command has the same effect as that in the previous example.

---

[30] https://docs.python.org/3.5/library/pyclbr.html

```
$ pyvenv /tmp/demoenv
```

Using -m venv is preferred because it requires explicitly selecting a Python interpreter. This approach ensures that there is no confusion about the version number or import path assocated with the resulting virtual environment.

16.13.2   Contents of a Virtual Environment

Each virtual environment contains a bin directory, where the local interpreter and any executable scripts are installed; an include directory for files related to building C extensions; and a lib directory, with a separate site-packages location for installing packages.

```
$ ls -F /tmp/demoenv

bin/
include/
lib/
pyvenv.cfg
```

The default bin directory contains "activation" scripts for several Unix shell variants. These can be used to install the virtual environment on the shell's search path, thereby ensuring the shell picks up programs installed in the environment. Although it is not necessary to activate an environment to use programs installed into it, that technique can be more convenient.

```
$ ls -F /tmp/demoenv/bin

activate
activate.csh
activate.fish
easy_install*
easy_install-3.5*
pip*
pip3*
pip3.5*
python@
python3@
```

On platforms that support them, symbolic links are used rather than copying the executables like the Python interpreter. In this environment, pip is installed as a local copy but the interpreter is a symlink.

Finally, the environment includes a pyvenv.cfg file with settings describing how the environment is configured and should behave. The home variable points to the location of the Python interpreter where venv was run to create the environment. include-system-site-packages is a boolean variable indicating whether the packages that are installed outside the virtual environment, at the system level, should be visible inside the virtual environment. `version` is the Python version used to create the environment.

Listing 16.91: `pyvenv.cfg`

```
home = /Library/Frameworks/Python.framework/Versions/3.5/bin
include-system-site-packages = false
version = 3.5.2
```

A virtual environment is more useful when combined with tools such as `pip` and `setup-tools`, which are available to install other packages, so `pyvenv` installs them by default. To create a bare environment without these tools, pass `--without-pip` on the command line.

16.13.3 Using Virtual Environments

Virtual environments are commonly used to run different versions of programs or to test a given version of a program with different versions of its dependencies. For example, before upgrading from one version of Sphinx to another, it is useful to test the input documentation files using both the old and new versions. To do so, first create two virtual environments.

```
$ python3 -m venv /tmp/sphinx1
$ python3 -m venv /tmp/sphinx2
```

Then install the versions of the tools to test.

```
$ /tmp/sphinx1/bin/pip install Sphinx==1.3.6

Collecting Sphinx==1.3.6
  Using cached Sphinx-1.3.6-py2.py3-none-any.whl
Collecting Jinja2>=2.3 (from Sphinx==1.3.6)
  Using cached Jinja2-2.8-py2.py3-none-any.whl
Collecting Pygments>=2.0 (from Sphinx==1.3.6)
  Using cached Pygments-2.1.3-py2.py3-none-any.whl
Collecting babel!=2.0,>=1.3 (from Sphinx==1.3.6)
  Using cached Babel-2.3.4-py2.py3-none-any.whl
Collecting snowballstemmer>=1.1 (from Sphinx==1.3.6)
  Using cached snowballstemmer-1.2.1-py2.py3-none-any.whl
Collecting alabaster<0.8,>=0.7 (from Sphinx==1.3.6)
  Using cached alabaster-0.7.9-py2.py3-none-any.whl
Collecting six>=1.4 (from Sphinx==1.3.6)
  Using cached six-1.10.0-py2.py3-none-any.whl
Collecting sphinx-rtd-theme<2.0,>=0.1 (from Sphinx==1.3.6)
  Using cached sphinx_rtd_theme-0.1.9-py3-none-any.whl
Collecting docutils>=0.11 (from Sphinx==1.3.6)
  Using cached docutils-0.13.1-py3-none-any.whl
Collecting MarkupSafe (from Jinja2>=2.3->Sphinx==1.3.6)
Collecting pytz>=0a (from babel!=2.0,>=1.3->Sphinx==1.3.6)
  Using cached pytz-2016.10-py2.py3-none-any.whl
```

```
Installing collected packages: MarkupSafe, Jinja2, Pygments,
pytz, babel, snowballstemmer, alabaster, six, sphinx-rtd-theme,
docutils, Sphinx
Successfully installed Jinja2-2.8 MarkupSafe-0.23 Pygments-2.1.3
Sphinx-1.3.6 alabaster-0.7.9 babel-2.3.4 docutils-0.13.1
pytz-2016.10 six-1.10.0 snowballstemmer-1.2.1 sphinx-rtd-
theme-0.1.9

$ /tmp/sphinx2/bin/pip install Sphinx==1.4.4

Collecting Sphinx==1.4.4
  Using cached Sphinx-1.4.4-py2.py3-none-any.whl
Collecting Jinja2>=2.3 (from Sphinx==1.4.4)
  Using cached Jinja2-2.8-py2.py3-none-any.whl
Collecting imagesize (from Sphinx==1.4.4)
  Using cached imagesize-0.7.1-py2.py3-none-any.whl
Collecting Pygments>=2.0 (from Sphinx==1.4.4)
  Using cached Pygments-2.1.3-py2.py3-none-any.whl
Collecting babel!=2.0,>=1.3 (from Sphinx==1.4.4)
  Using cached Babel-2.3.4-py2.py3-none-any.whl
Collecting snowballstemmer>=1.1 (from Sphinx==1.4.4)
  Using cached snowballstemmer-1.2.1-py2.py3-none-any.whl
Collecting alabaster<0.8,>=0.7 (from Sphinx==1.4.4)
  Using cached alabaster-0.7.9-py2.py3-none-any.whl
Collecting six>=1.4 (from Sphinx==1.4.4)
  Using cached six-1.10.0-py2.py3-none-any.whl
Collecting docutils>=0.11 (from Sphinx==1.4.4)
  Using cached docutils-0.13.1-py3-none-any.whl
Collecting MarkupSafe (from Jinja2>=2.3->Sphinx==1.4.4)
Collecting pytz>=0a (from babel!=2.0,>=1.3->Sphinx==1.4.4)
  Using cached pytz-2016.10-py2.py3-none-any.whl
Installing collected packages: MarkupSafe, Jinja2, imagesize,
Pygments, pytz, babel, snowballstemmer, alabaster, six,
docutils, Sphinx
Successfully installed Jinja2-2.8 MarkupSafe-0.23 Pygments-2.1.3
Sphinx-1.4.4 alabaster-0.7.9 babel-2.3.4 docutils-0.13.1
imagesize-0.7.1 pytz-2016.10 six-1.10.0 snowballstemmer-1.2.1
```

At this point, the different versions of Sphinx from the virtual environments can be run separately, so as to test them with the same input files.

```
$ /tmp/sphinx1/bin/sphinx-build --version

Sphinx (sphinx-build) 1.3.6

$ /tmp/sphinx2/bin/sphinx-build --version

Sphinx (sphinx-build) 1.4.4
```

TIP

Related Reading

- Standard library documentation for venv.[31]
- **PEP 405**[32]: Python Virtual Environments.
- virtualenv[34]: A version of the Python virtual environments that works for Python 2 and 3.
- virtualenvwrapper[34]: A set of shell wrappers for virtualenv that make it easier to manage a large number of environments.
- Sphinx[35]: Tool for converting reStructuredText input files to HTML, LaTeX, and other formats for consumption.

16.14 ensurepip: Install the Python Package Installer

While Python is the "batteries included" programming language and comes with a wide variety of modules in its standard library, even more libraries, frameworks, and tools are available to be installed from the Python Package Index.[36] To install those packages, a developer needs the installer tool `pip`. Installing a tool that is meant to install other tools presents an interesting bootstrapping issue, which `ensurepip` solves.

16.14.1 Installing pip

This example uses a virtual environment configured without `pip` installed.

```
$ python3 -m venv --without-pip /tmp/demoenv
$ ls -F /tmp/demoenv/bin

activate
activate.csh
activate.fish
python@
python3@
```

Run `ensurepip` from the command line using the `-m` option to the Python interpreter. By default, a copy of `pip` that is delivered with the standard library is installed. This version can then be used to install an updated version of `pip`. To ensure a recent version of `pip` is installed immediately, use the `--upgrade` option with `ensurepip`.

---

[31] https://docs.python.org/3.5/library/venv.html
[32] www.python.org/dev/peps/pep-0405
[34] https://pypi.python.org/pypi/virtualenv
[34] https://pypi.python.org/pypi/virtualenvwrapper
[35] www.sphinx-doc.org/en/stable/
[36] https://pypi.python.org/pypi

```
$ /tmp/demoenv/bin/python3 -m ensurepip --upgrade

Ignoring indexes: https://pypi.python.org/simple
Collecting setuptools
Collecting pip
Installing collected packages: setuptools, pip
Successfully installed pip-8.1.1 setuptools-20.10.1
```

This command installs pip3 and pip3.5 as separate programs in the virtual environment, with the setuptools dependency needed to support them.

```
$ ls -F /tmp/demoenv/bin

activate
activate.csh
activate.fish
easy_install-3.5*
pip3*
pip3.5*
python@
python3@
```

TIP

Related Reading

- Standard library documentation for ensurepip.[37]

- venv (page 1163): Virtual environments.

- **PEP 453**[38]: Explicit bootstrapping of pip in Python installations.

- Installing Python Modules[39]: Instructions for installing extra packages for use with Python.

- Python Package Index[40]: Hosting site for extension modules for Python programmers.

- pip[41]: Tool for installing Python packages.

---

[37] https://docs.python.org/3.5/library/ensurepip.html
[38] www.python.org/dev/peps/pep-0453
[39] https://docs.python.org/3.5/installing/index.html#installing-index
[40] https://pypi.python.org/pypi
[41] https://pypi.python.org/pypi/pip

Chapter 17

Runtime Features

This chapter covers the features of the Python standard library that allow a program to interact with the interpreter or the environment in which it runs.

During start-up, the interpreter loads the `site` (page 1169) module to configure settings specific to the current installation. The import path is constructed from a combination of environment settings, interpreter build parameters, and configuration files.

The `sys` (page 1178) module is one of the largest in the standard library. It includes functions for accessing a broad range of interpreter and system settings, including interpreter build settings and limits; command-line arguments and program exit codes; exception handling; thread debugging and control; the import mechanism and imported modules; runtime control-flow tracing; and standard input and output streams for the process.

While `sys` is focused on interpreter settings, `os` (page 1227) provides access to operating system information. It can be used for portable interfaces to system calls that return details about the running process such as its owner and environment variables. The `os` module also includes functions for working with the file system and process management.

Python is often used as a cross-platform language for creating portable programs. Even in a program intended to run anywhere, it is occasionally necessary to know the operating system or hardware architecture of the current system. The `platform` (page 1246) module provides functions to retrieve those settings.

The limits for system resources such as the maximum process stack size or number of open files can be probed and changed through the `resource` (page 1251) module. It also reports the current consumption rates, so a process can be monitored for resource leaks.

The `gc` (page 1254) module gives access to the internal state of Python's garbage collection system. It includes information useful for detecting and breaking object cycles, turning the collector on and off, and adjusting thresholds that automatically trigger collection sweeps.

The `sysconfig` (page 1270) module holds the compile-time variables from the build scripts. It can be used by build and packaging tools to generate paths and other settings dynamically.

17.1 site: Site-Wide Configuration

The `site` module handles site-specific configuration, especially the import path.

17.1.1 Import Path

`site` is automatically imported each time the interpreter starts up. As it is being imported, it extends `sys.path` with site-specific names that are constructed by combining the prefix values sys.prefix and sys.exec_prefix with several suffixes. The prefix values used are saved in the module-level variable PREFIXES for later reference. Under Windows, the suffixes are an empty string and lib/site-packages. For Unix-like platforms, the values are lib/python$version/site-packages (where $version is replaced by the major and minor version numbers of the interpreter, such as 3.5) and lib/site-python.

Listing 17.1: site_import_path.py

```
import sys
import os
import site

if 'Windows' in sys.platform:
    SUFFIXES = [
        '',
        'lib/site-packages',
    ]
else:
    SUFFIXES = [
        'lib/python{}/site-packages'.format(sys.version[:3]),
        'lib/site-python',
    ]

print('Path prefixes:')
for p in site.PREFIXES:
    print('  ', p)

for prefix in sorted(set(site.PREFIXES)):
    print()
    print(prefix)
    for suffix in SUFFIXES:
        print()
        print(' ', suffix)
        path = os.path.join(prefix, suffix).rstrip(os.sep)
        print('   exists :', os.path.exists(path))
        print('   in path:', path in sys.path)
```

Each of the paths resulting from the combinations is tested, and those that exist are added to sys.path. The following output shows the framework version of Python installed on a Mac OS X system.

```
$ python3 site_import_path.py

Path prefixes:
    /Library/Frameworks/Python.framework/Versions/3.5
    /Library/Frameworks/Python.framework/Versions/3.5

/Library/Frameworks/Python.framework/Versions/3.5
```

```
lib/python3.5/site-packages
  exists : True
  in path: True

lib/site-python
  exists : False
  in path: False
```

17.1.2   User Directories

In addition to the global site-packages paths, site is responsible for adding the user-specific locations to the import path. The user-specific paths are all based on the USER_BASE directory, which is usually located in a part of the file system owned (and writable) by the current user. Inside the USER_BASE directory is a site-packages directory, with the path being accessible as USER_SITE.

Listing 17.2: site_user_base.py

```
import site

print('Base:', site.USER_BASE)
print('Site:', site.USER_SITE)
```

The USER_SITE path name is created using the same platform-specific suffix values described earlier.

```
$ python3 site_user_base.py

Base: /Users/dhellmann/.local
Site: /Users/dhellmann/.local/lib/python3.5/site-packages
```

The user base directory can be set through the PYTHONUSERBASE environment variable, and has platform-specific defaults (~/Python$version/site-packages for Windows and ~/.local for non-Windows).

```
$ PYTHONUSERBASE=/tmp/$USER python3 site_user_base.py

Base: /tmp/dhellmann
Site: /tmp/dhellmann/lib/python3.5/site-packages
```

The user directory is disabled under some circumstances that would pose security issues (for example, if the process is running with a different effective user or group ID than the actual user who started it). An application can check the setting by examining ENABLE_USER_SITE.

Listing 17.3: `site_enable_user_site.py`

```
import site

status = {
    None: 'Disabled for security',
    True: 'Enabled',
    False: 'Disabled by command-line option',
}

print('Flag   :', site.ENABLE_USER_SITE)
print('Meaning:', status[site.ENABLE_USER_SITE])
```

The user directory can also be explicitly disabled on the command line with -s.

```
$ python3 site_enable_user_site.py

Flag   : True
Meaning: Enabled

$ python3 -s site_enable_user_site.py

Flag   : False
Meaning: Disabled by command-line option
```

17.1.3   Path Configuration Files

As paths are added to the import path, they are also scanned for *path configuration files*. A path configuration file is a plain text file with the extension .pth. Each line in the file can take one of four forms:

- A full or relative path to another location that should be added to the import path.

- A Python statement to be executed. All such lines must begin with an import statement.

- A blank line that is ignored.

- A line starting with # that is treated as a comment and ignored.

   Path configuration files can be used to extend the import path to look in locations that would not have been added automatically. For example, the setuptools package adds a path to easy-install.pth when it installs a package in development mode using python setup.py develop.

   The function for extending sys.path is public, and it can be used in example programs to show how the path configuration files work. Suppose a directory named with_modules contains the file mymodule.py, with the following print statement showing how the module was imported.

Listing 17.4: with_modules/mymodule.py

```
import os
print('Loaded {} from {}'.format(
    __name__, __file__[len(os.getcwd()) + 1:])
)
```

This script shows how `addsitedir()` extends the import path so the interpreter can find the desired module.

Listing 17.5: site_addsitedir.py

```
import site
import os
import sys

script_directory = os.path.dirname(__file__)
module_directory = os.path.join(script_directory, sys.argv[1])

try:
    import mymodule
except ImportError as err:
    print('Could not import mymodule:', err)

print()
before_len = len(sys.path)
site.addsitedir(module_directory)
print('New paths:')
for p in sys.path[before_len:]:
    print(p.replace(os.getcwd(), '.'))  # Shorten dirname

print()
import mymodule
```

After the directory containing the module is added to `sys.path`, the script can import `mymodule` without issue.

```
$ python3 site_addsitedir.py with_modules

Could not import mymodule: No module named 'mymodule'

New paths:
./with_modules

Loaded mymodule from with_modules/mymodule.py
```

The path changes made by `addsitedir()` go beyond simply appending the argument to `sys.path`. If the directory given to `addsitedir()` includes any files matching the pattern `*.pth`, they are loaded as path configuration files. With a directory structure like

```
with_pth
 pymotw.pth
 subdir
     mymodule.py
```

if with_pth/pymotw.pth contains

```
# Add a single subdirectory to the path.
./subdir
```

then with_pth/subdir/mymodule.py can be imported by adding with_pth as a site directory, even though the module is not in that directory, because both with_pth and with_pth/subdir are added to the import path.

```
$ python3 site_addsitedir.py with_pth

Could not import mymodule: No module named 'mymodule'

New paths:
./with_pth
./with_pth/subdir

Loaded mymodule from with_pth/subdir/mymodule.py
```

If a site directory contains multiple .pth files, they are processed in alphabetical order.

```
$ ls -F multiple_pth

a.pth
b.pth
from_a/
from_b/

$ cat multiple_pth/a.pth

./from_a

$ cat multiple_pth/b.pth

./from_b
```

In this case, the module is found in multiple_pth/from_a because a.pth is read before b.pth.

```
$ python3 site_addsitedir.py multiple_pth

Could not import mymodule: No module named 'mymodule'

New paths:
```

```
./multiple_pth
./multiple_pth/from_a
./multiple_pth/from_b

Loaded mymodule from multiple_pth/from_a/mymodule.py
```

17.1.4   Customizing Site Configuration

The site module is responsible for loading site-wide customization defined by the local site owner in a sitecustomize module. Uses for sitecustomize include extending the import path and enabling coverage, profiling, or other development tools.

For example, the sitecustomize.py script in the following listing extends the import path with a directory based on the current platform. The platform-specific path in /opt/python is added to the import path, so any packages installed there can be imported. This kind of system is useful for sharing packages containing compiled extension modules between hosts on a network via a shared file system. Only the sitecustomize.py script needs to be installed on each host; the other packages can be accessed from the file server.

Listing 17.6: **with_sitecustomize/sitecustomize.py**

```
print('Loading sitecustomize.py')

import site
import platform
import os
import sys

path = os.path.join('/opt',
                    'python',
                    sys.version[:3],
                    platform.platform(),
                    )
print('Adding new path', path)

site.addsitedir(path)
```

A simple script can be used to show that sitecustomize.py is imported before Python starts running the programmer's own code.

Listing 17.7: **with_sitecustomize/site_sitecustomize.py**

```
import sys

print('Running main program from\n{}'.format(sys.argv[0]))

print('End of path:', sys.path[-1])
```

Since sitecustomize is meant for system-wide configuration, it should be installed somewhere in the default path (usually in the site-packages directory). This example sets PYTHONPATH explicitly to ensure the module is picked up.

```
$ PYTHONPATH=with_sitecustomize python3 with_sitecustomize/sit\
e_sitecustomize.py

Loading sitecustomize.py
Adding new path /opt/python/3.5/Darwin-15.6.0-x86_64-i386-64bit
Running main program from
with_sitecustomize/site_sitecustomize.py
End of path: /opt/python/3.5/Darwin-15.6.0-x86_64-i386-64bit
```

17.1.5 Customizing User Configuration

Similar to `sitecustomize`, the `usercustomize` module can be used to establish user-specific settings each time the interpreter starts up. `usercustomize` is loaded after `sitecustomize`, so site-wide customizations can be overridden.

In environments where a user's home directory is shared on several servers running different operating systems or versions, the standard user directory mechanism may not work for user-specific installations of packages. In these cases, a platform-specific directory tree can be used instead.

Listing 17.8: `with_usercustomize/usercustomize.py`

```python
print('Loading usercustomize.py')

import site
import platform
import os
import sys

path = os.path.expanduser(os.path.join('~',
                                       'python',
                                       sys.version[:3],
                                       platform.platform(),
                                       ))
print('Adding new path', path)

site.addsitedir(path)
```

Another simple script, similar to the one used for `sitecustomize`, can be used to show that `usercustomize.py` is imported before Python starts running other code.

Listing 17.9: `with_usercustomize/site_usercustomize.py`

```python
import sys

print('Running main program from\n{}'.format(sys.argv[0]))

print('End of path:', sys.path[-1])
```

Since `usercustomize` is meant for user-specific configuration for a user, it should be installed somewhere in the user's default path, but not in the site-wide path. The default `USER_BASE` directory is a good location. The next example sets `PYTHONPATH` explicitly to ensure the module is picked up.

```
$ PYTHONPATH=with_usercustomize python3 with_usercustomize/site\
_usercustomize.py

Loading usercustomize.py
Adding new path /Users/dhellmann/python/3.5/Darwin-15.5.0-x86_64\
-i386-64bit
Running main program from
with_usercustomize/site_usercustomize.py
End of path: /Users/dhellmann/python/3.5/Darwin-15.5.0-x86_64\
-i386-64bit
```

When the user site directory feature is disabled, `usercustomize` is not imported, whether it is located in the user site directory or elsewhere.

```
$ PYTHONPATH=with_usercustomize python3 -s with_usercustomize/s\
ite_usercustomize.py

Running main program from
with_usercustomize/site_usercustomize.py
End of path: /Users/dhellmann/Envs/pymotw35/lib/python3.5/site-
packages
```

17.1.6 Disabling the site Module

To maintain backward-compatibility with versions of Python that predate the addition of the automatic import functionality, the interpreter accepts an `-S` option.

```
$ python3 -S site_import_path.py

Path prefixes:
   /Users/dhellmann/Envs/pymotw35/bin/..
   /Users/dhellmann/Envs/pymotw35/bin/..

/Users/dhellmann/Envs/pymotw35/bin/..

   lib/python3.5/site-packages
    exists : True
    in path: False

   lib/site-python
    exists : False
    in path: False
```

TIP

Related Reading

- Standard library documentation for site.[1]
- Section 17.2.6, "Modules and Imports" (page 1200): Description of how the import path defined in sys works.
- setuptools[2]: Packaging library and installation tool easy_install.
- Running code at Python startup[3]: Post from Ned Batchelder discussing ways to cause the Python interpreter to run custom initialization code before starting the main program execution.

17.2   sys: System-Specific Configuration

The sys module includes a collection of services for probing or changing the configuration of the interpreter at runtime as well as resources for interacting with the operating environment outside the current program.

17.2.1   Interpreter Settings

sys contains attributes and functions for accessing compile-time or runtime configuration settings for the interpreter.

17.2.1.1   Build-Time Version Information

The version used to build the C interpreter is available in a few forms. sys.version is a human-readable string that usually includes the full version number as well as information about the build date, compiler, and platform. sys.hexversion is easier to use for checking the interpreter version because it is a simple integer. When this value is formatted using hex(), it is clear that parts of sys.hexversion come from the version information that is also visible in the more readable sys.version_info (a five-part namedtuple representing just the version number). The separate C API version used by the current interpreter is saved in sys.api_version.

Listing 17.10: sys_version_values.py

```python
import sys

print('Version info:')
print()
print('sys.version      =', repr(sys.version))
print('sys.version_info =', sys.version_info)
print('sys.hexversion   =', hex(sys.hexversion))
print('sys.api_version  =', sys.api_version)
```

---

[1] https://docs.python.org/3.5/library/site.html
[2] https://setuptools.readthedocs.io/en/latest/index.html
[3] http://nedbatchelder.com/blog/201001/running_code_at_python_startup.html

All of the values depend on the actual interpreter used to run the sample program.

```
$ python3 sys_version_values.py

Version info:

sys.version      = '3.5.2 (v3.5.2:4def2a2901a5, Jun 26 2016,
10:47:25) \n[GCC 4.2.1 (Apple Inc. build 5666) (dot 3)]'
sys.version_info = sys.version_info(major=3, minor=5, micro=2,
releaselevel='final', serial=0)
sys.hexversion   = 0x30502f0
sys.api_version  = 1013
```

The operating system platform used to build the interpreter is saved as `sys.platform`.

Listing 17.11: sys_platform.py

```
import sys

print('This interpreter was built for:', sys.platform)
```

For most Unix systems, this value is created by combining the output of uname -s with the first part of the version in uname -r. For other operating systems, a hard-coded table of values is used.

```
$ python3 sys_platform.py

This interpreter was built for: darwin
```

TIP

Related Reading

- Platform values[4]: Hard-coded values of `sys.platform` for systems without uname.

17.2.1.2 Interpreter Implementation

The CPython interpreter is one of several implementations of the Python language. `sys.implementation` is provided to detect the current implementation for libraries that need to work around any differences in interpreters.

Listing 17.12: sys_implementation.py

```
import sys


print('Name:', sys.implementation.name)
```

---

[4] https://docs.python.org/3/library/sys.html#sys.platform

```
print('Version:', sys.implementation.version)
print('Cache tag:', sys.implementation.cache_tag)
```

sys.implementation.version is the same as sys.version_info for CPython, but will be different for other interpreters.

```
$ python3 sys_implementation.py

Name: cpython
Version: sys.version_info(major=3, minor=5, micro=2, releaseleve
l='final', serial=0)
Cache tag: cpython-35
```

TIP

Related Reading

- **PEP 421**[5]: Adding sys.implementation.

17.2.1.3   Command Line Options

The CPython interpreter accepts several command-line options to control its behavior, listed in Table 17.1. Some of these options are available for programs to check through sys.flags.

Table 17.1: CPython Command-Line Option Flags

Option	Meaning
-B	Do not write .py[co] files on import.
-b	Issue warnings about converting bytes to strings without decoding properly and comparing bytes with strings.
-bb	Convert warnings from manipulating bytes objects into errors.
d	Debug output from parser.
-E	Ignore PYTHON* environment variables (such as PYTHONPATH).
-i	Inspect interactively after running script.
-0	Optimize generated byte-code slightly.
-00	Remove docstrings in addition to performing the -0 optimizations.
-s	Do not add user site directory to sys.path.
-S	Do not run "import site" on initialization.
-t	Issue warnings about inconsistent tab usage.
-tt	Issue errors for inconsistent tab usage.
-v	Verbose.

---

[5] www.python.org/dev/peps/pep-0421

Listing 17.13: sys_flags.py

```
import sys

if sys.flags.bytes_warning:
    print('Warning on bytes/str errors')
if sys.flags.debug:
    print('Debuging')
if sys.flags.inspect:
    print('Will enter interactive mode after running')
if sys.flags.optimize:
    print('Optimizing byte-code')
if sys.flags.dont_write_bytecode:
    print('Not writing byte-code files')
if sys.flags.no_site:
    print('Not importing "site"')
if sys.flags.ignore_environment:
    print('Ignoring environment')
if sys.flags.verbose:
    print('Verbose mode')
```

Experiment with sys_flags.py to learn how the command-line options map to the flags settings.

```
$ python3 -S -E -b sys_flags.py

Warning on bytes/str errors
Not importing "site"
Ignoring environment
```

17.2.1.4   Unicode Defaults

To get the name of the default Unicode encoding that the interpreter is using, call getdefaultencoding(). This value is set during start-up, and cannot be changed during a session.

The internal encoding default and the file system encoding may be different for some operating systems, so there is a separate way to retrieve the file system setting. getfilesystemencoding() returns an OS-specific (*not* file system–specific) value.

Listing 17.14: sys_unicode.py

```
import sys

print('Default encoding     :', sys.getdefaultencoding())
print('File system encoding :', sys.getfilesystemencoding())
```

Rather than relying on the global default encoding, most Unicode experts recommend making an application explicitly Unicode-aware. This approach provides two benefits: Different Unicode encodings for different data sources can be handled more cleanly, and the number of assumptions about encodings in the application code is reduced.

```
$ python3 sys_unicode.py

Default encoding     : utf-8
File system encoding : utf-8
```

17.2.1.5   Interactive Prompts

The interactive interpreter uses two separate prompts for indicating the default input level (ps1) and the "continuation" of a multiline statement (ps2). These values are used only by the interactive interpreter.

```
>>> import sys
>>> sys.ps1
'>>> '
>>> sys.ps2
'... '
>>>
```

Either or both prompts can be changed to a different string.

```
>>> sys.ps1 = '::: '
::: sys.ps2 = '~~~ '
::: for i in range(3):
~~~     print i
~~~
0
1
2
:::
```

Alternatively, any object that can be converted to a string (via __str__) can be used for the prompt.

Listing 17.15: sys_ps1.py

```
import sys


class LineCounter:

    def __init__(self):
        self.count = 0

    def __str__(self):
```

```
        self.count += 1
        return '({:3d})> '.format(self.count)
```

The `LineCounter` keeps track of how many times the prompt has been used, so the number in the prompt increases each time.

```
$ python
Python 3.4.2 (v3.4.2:ab2c023a9432, Oct  5 2014, 20:42:22)
[GCC 4.2.1 (Apple Inc. build 5666) (dot 3)] on darwin
Type "help", "copyright", "credits" or "license" for more
information.
>>> from sys_ps1 import LineCounter
>>> import sys
>>> sys.ps1 = LineCounter()
(  1)>
(  2)>
(  3)>
```

17.2.1.6 Display Hook

`sys.displayhook` is invoked by the interactive interpreter each time the user enters an expression. The result of evaluating the expression is passed as the only argument to the function.

Listing 17.16: sys_displayhook.py

```
import sys


class ExpressionCounter:

    def __init__(self):
        self.count = 0
        self.previous_value = self

    def __call__(self, value):
        print()
        print('  Previous:', self.previous_value)
        print('  New     :', value)
        print()
        if value != self.previous_value:
            self.count += 1
            sys.ps1 = '({:3d})> '.format(self.count)
        self.previous_value = value
        sys.__displayhook__(value)


print('installing')
sys.displayhook = ExpressionCounter()
```

The default value (saved in `sys.__displayhook__`) prints the result to stdout and saves it in _ for easy reference later.

```
$ python3
Python 3.4.2 (v3.4.2:ab2c023a9432, Oct  5 2014, 20:42:22)
[GCC 4.2.1 (Apple Inc. build 5666) (dot 3)] on darwin
Type "help", "copyright", "credits" or "license" for more
information.
>>> import sys_displayhook
installing
>>> 1 + 2

  Previous: <sys_displayhook.ExpressionCounter
  object at 0x1021035f8>
  New     : 3

3
(  1)> 'abc'

  Previous: 3
  New     : abc

'abc'
(  2)> 'abc'

  Previous: abc
  New     : abc

'abc'
(  2)> 'abc' * 3

  Previous: abc
  New     : abcabcabc

'abcabcabc'
(  3)>
```

17.2.1.7 Install Location

The path to the actual interpreter program is available in `sys.executable` on all systems for which having a path to the interpreter makes sense. This information can be examined to ensure that the correct interpreter is being used, and it gives clues about paths that might be set based on the interpreter location.

`sys.prefix` refers to the parent directory of the interpreter installation. It usually includes `bin` and `lib` directories for executables and installed modules, respectively.

Listing 17.17: sys_locations.py

```
import sys

print('Interpreter executable:')
print(sys.executable)
print('\nInstallation prefix:')
print(sys.prefix)
```

The following output was produced on a Mac running a framework build installed from python.org.

```
$ python3 sys_locations.py

Interpreter executable:
/Library/Frameworks/Python.framework/Versions/3.5/bin/python3

Installation prefix:
/Library/Frameworks/Python.framework/Versions/3.5
```

17.2.2   Runtime Environment

sys provides low-level APIs for interacting with the system outside of an application, by accepting command-line arguments, accessing user input, and passing messages and status values to the user.

17.2.2.1   Command-Line Arguments

The arguments captured by the interpreter are processed there; they are not passed to the program being run. Any remaining options and arguments, including the name of the script itself, are saved to sys.argv in case the program does need to use them.

Listing 17.18: sys_argv.py

```
import sys

print('Arguments:', sys.argv)
```

In the third example shown here, the -u option is understood by the interpreter; it is not passed to the program being run.

```
$ python3 sys_argv.py

Arguments: ['sys_argv.py']

$ python3 sys_argv.py -v foo blah
```

```
Arguments: ['sys_argv.py', '-v', 'foo', 'blah']

$ python3 -u sys_argv.py

Arguments: ['sys_argv.py']
```

Related Reading

- argparse (page 888): Module for parsing command-line arguments.

17.2.2.2 Input and Output Streams

Following the Unix paradigm, Python programs can access three file descriptors by default.

Listing 17.19: sys_stdio.py

```python
import sys

print('STATUS: Reading from stdin', file=sys.stderr)

data = sys.stdin.read()

print('STATUS: Writing data to stdout', file=sys.stderr)

sys.stdout.write(data)
sys.stdout.flush()

print('STATUS: Done', file=sys.stderr)
```

stdin is the standard way to read input, usually from a console but also from other programs via a pipeline. stdout is the standard way to write output for a user (to the console) or to be sent to the next program in a pipeline. stderr is intended for use with warning or error messages.

```
$ cat sys_stdio.py | python3 -u sys_stdio.py

STATUS: Reading from stdin
STATUS: Writing data to stdout
#!/usr/bin/env python3

#end_pymotw_header
import sys

print('STATUS: Reading from stdin', file=sys.stderr)
```

```
data = sys.stdin.read()

print('STATUS: Writing data to stdout', file=sys.stderr)

sys.stdout.write(data)
sys.stdout.flush()

print('STATUS: Done', file=sys.stderr)
STATUS: Done
```

TIP

Related Reading

- subprocess (page 535) and pipes: Both of these modules have features for pipelining programs together.

17.2.2.3 Returning Status

To return an exit code from a program, pass an integer value to sys.exit().

Listing 17.20: sys_exit.py

```
import sys

exit_code = int(sys.argv[1])
sys.exit(exit_code)
```

A nonzero value means the program exited with an error.

```
$ python3 sys_exit.py 0 ; echo "Exited $?"

Exited 0

$ python3 sys_exit.py 1 ; echo "Exited $?"

Exited 1
```

17.2.3 Memory Management and Limits

sys includes several functions for understanding and controlling memory usage.

17.2.3.1 Reference Counts

The primary implementation of Python (CPython) uses *reference counting* and *garbage collection* to perform automatic memory management. An object is automatically marked

to be collected when its reference count drops to zero. To examine the reference count of
an existing object, use getrefcount().

Listing 17.21: **sys_getrefcount.py**

```
import sys

one = []
print('At start           :', sys.getrefcount(one))

two = one

print('Second reference :', sys.getrefcount(one))

del two

print('After del          :', sys.getrefcount(one))
```

The count reported is actually one higher than the expected value because there is a temporary reference to the object held by getrefcount() itself.

```
$ python3 sys_getrefcount.py

At start          : 2
Second reference : 3
After del         : 2
```

TIP

Related Reading

- gc (page 1254): Control the garbage collector via the functions exposed in gc.

17.2.3.2   Object Size

Knowing how many references an object has may help the developer find cycles or identify
the source of a memory leak, but it is not enough information to determine which objects
are consuming the *most* memory. That requires knowledge about the sizes of the objects.

Listing 17.22: **sys_getsizeof.py**

```
import sys


class MyClass:
    pass
```

```
objects = [
    [], (), {}, 'c', 'string', b'bytes', 1, 2.3,
    MyClass, MyClass(),
]

for obj in objects:
    print('{:>10} : {}'.format(type(obj).__name__,
                               sys.getsizeof(obj)))
```

getsizeof() reports the size of an object in bytes.

```
$ python3 sys_getsizeof.py

      list : 64
     tuple : 48
      dict : 288
       str : 50
       str : 55
     bytes : 38
       int : 28
     float : 24
      type : 1016
   MyClass : 56
```

The reported size for a custom class does not include the size of the attribute values.

Listing 17.23: sys_getsizeof_object.py

```
import sys


class WithoutAttributes:
    pass


class WithAttributes:
    def __init__(self):
        self.a = 'a'
        self.b = 'b'
        return


without_attrs = WithoutAttributes()
print('WithoutAttributes:', sys.getsizeof(without_attrs))

with_attrs = WithAttributes()
print('WithAttributes:', sys.getsizeof(with_attrs))
```

This can give a false impression of the amount of memory actually being consumed.

```
$ python3 sys_getsizeof_object.py

WithoutAttributes: 56
WithAttributes: 56
```

For a more complete estimate of the space used by a class, provide a `__sizeof__()` method to compute the value by aggregating the sizes of the various objects' attributes.

Listing 17.24: sys_getsizeof_custom.py

```python
import sys


class WithAttributes:
    def __init__(self):
        self.a = 'a'
        self.b = 'b'
        return

    def __sizeof__(self):
        return object.__sizeof__(self) + \
            sum(sys.getsizeof(v) for v in self.__dict__.values())


my_inst = WithAttributes()
print(sys.getsizeof(my_inst))
```

This version adds the base size of the object to the sizes of all of the attributes stored in the internal `__dict__`.

```
$ python3 sys_getsizeof_custom.py

156
```

17.2.3.3 Recursion

Allowing infinite recursion in a Python application may introduce a stack overflow in the interpreter itself, leading to a crash. To eliminate this situation, the interpreter provides a way to control the maximum recursion depth using `setrecursionlimit()` and `getrecursionlimit()`.

Listing 17.25: sys_recursionlimit.py

```python
import sys

print('Initial limit:', sys.getrecursionlimit())
```

```
sys.setrecursionlimit(10)

print('Modified limit:', sys.getrecursionlimit())


def generate_recursion_error(i):
    print('generate_recursion_error({})'.format(i))
    generate_recursion_error(i + 1)


try:
    generate_recursion_error(1)
except RuntimeError as err:
    print('Caught exception:', err)
```

Once the stack size reaches the recursion limit, the interpreter raises a RuntimeError exception so the program has an opportunity to handle the situation.

```
$ python3 sys_recursionlimit.py

Initial limit: 1000
Modified limit: 10
generate_recursion_error(1)
generate_recursion_error(2)
generate_recursion_error(3)
generate_recursion_error(4)
generate_recursion_error(5)
generate_recursion_error(6)
generate_recursion_error(7)
generate_recursion_error(8)
Caught exception: maximum recursion depth exceeded while calling
a Python object
```

17.2.3.4   Maximum Values

Along with the runtime configurable values, sys includes variables defining the maximum values for types that vary from system to system.

Listing 17.26: sys_maximums.py

```
import sys

print('maxsize   :', sys.maxsize)
print('maxunicode:', sys.maxunicode)
```

maxsize is the maximum size of a list, dictionary, string, or other data structure dictated by the C interpreter's size type. maxunicode is the largest integer Unicode point supported by the interpreter as currently configured.

```
$ python3 sys_maximums.py

maxsize    : 9223372036854775807
maxunicode: 1114111
```

17.2.3.5   Floating-Point Values

The structure `float_info` contains information about the floating-point type representation used by the interpreter, based on the underlying system's `float` implementation.

Listing 17.27: **sys_float_info.py**

```python
import sys

print('Smallest difference (epsilon):', sys.float_info.epsilon)
print()
print('Digits (dig)                :', sys.float_info.dig)
print('Mantissa digits (mant_dig):', sys.float_info.mant_dig)
print()
print('Maximum (max):', sys.float_info.max)
print('Minimum (min):', sys.float_info.min)
print()
print('Radix of exponents (radix):', sys.float_info.radix)
print()
print('Maximum exponent for radix (max_exp):',
      sys.float_info.max_exp)
print('Minimum exponent for radix (min_exp):',
      sys.float_info.min_exp)
print()
print('Max. exponent power of 10 (max_10_exp):',
      sys.float_info.max_10_exp)
print('Min. exponent power of 10 (min_10_exp):',
      sys.float_info.min_10_exp)
print()
print('Rounding for addition (rounds):', sys.float_info.rounds)
```

These values depend on the compiler and the underlying system. The following output was produced on OS X 10.9.5 on an Intel Core i7.

```
$ python3 sys_float_info.py

Smallest difference (epsilon): 2.220446049250313e-16

Digits (dig)              : 15
Mantissa digits (mant_dig): 53

Maximum (max): 1.7976931348623157e+308
Minimum (min): 2.2250738585072014e-308
```

Radix of exponents (radix): 2

Maximum exponent for radix (max_exp): 1024
Minimum exponent for radix (min_exp): -1021

Max. exponent power of 10 (max_10_exp): 308
Min. exponent power of 10 (min_10_exp): -307

Rounding for addition (rounds): 1

TIP

Related Reading

- The float.h C header file for the local compiler contains more details about these settings.

17.2.3.6 Integer Values

The structure int_info holds information about the internal representation of integers used by the interpreter.

Listing 17.28: sys_int_info.py

```
import sys

print('Number of bits used to hold each digit:',
      sys.int_info.bits_per_digit)
print('Size in bytes of C type used to hold each digit:',
      sys.int_info.sizeof_digit)
```

The following output was produced on OS X 10.9.5 on an Intel Core i7.

```
$ python3 sys_int_info.py

Number of bits used to hold each digit: 30
Size in bytes of C type used to hold each digit: 4
```

The C type used to store integers internally is determined when the interpreter is built. By default, 64-bit architectures automatically use 30-bit integers, but they can be enabled for 32-bit architectures by setting the configuration flag --enable-big-digits.

TIP

Related Reading

- Build and C API Changes[6] from *What's New in Python 3.1.*

---

[6] https://docs.python.org/3.1/whatsnew/3.1.html#build-and-c-api-changes

17.2.3.7 Byte Ordering

byteorder is set to the native byte order.

Listing 17.29: **sys_byteorder.py**

```
import sys

print(sys.byteorder)
```

The value is either big for big-endian or little for little-endian.

```
$ python3 sys_byteorder.py

little
```

TIP

Related Reading

- Wikipedia: Endianness[7]: Description of big-endian and little-endian memory systems.
- array (page 98) and struct (page 117): Other modules that depend on the byte order of data.
- float.h: The C header file for the local compiler contains more details about these settings.

17.2.4 Exception Handling

sys includes features for trapping and working with exceptions.

17.2.4.1 Unhandled Exceptions

Many applications are structured with a main loop that wraps execution in a global exception handler to trap errors that are not otherwise handled at a lower level. Another way to achieve the same end is to set sys.excepthook to a function that takes three arguments (the error type, error value, and traceback) and let it deal with unhandled errors.

Listing 17.30: **sys_excepthook.py**

```
import sys


def my_excepthook(type, value, traceback):
    print('Unhandled error:', type, value)

sys.excepthook = my_excepthook
```

---

[7] https://en.wikipedia.org/wiki/Byte_order

```
print('Before exception')

raise RuntimeError('This is the error message')

print('After exception')
```

Since there is no `try:except` block around the line where the exception is raised, the following call to `print()` is not executed, even though the `excepthook` is set.

```
$ python3 sys_excepthook.py

Before exception
Unhandled error: <class 'RuntimeError'> This is the error
message
```

17.2.4.2 Current Exception

On some occasions, an explicit exception handler is preferred, either for code clarity or to avoid conflicts with libraries that try to install their own `excepthook`. In these cases, the programmer can create a handler function that does not need to have the exception object passed to it explicitly by calling `exc_info()` to retrieve the current exception for a thread.

The return value of `exc_info()` is a three-member tuple containing the exception class, an exception instance, and a traceback. Using `exc_info()` is preferred over the previously used form (with `exc_type`, `exc_value`, and `exc_traceback`) because it is thread-safe.

Listing 17.31: sys_exc_info.py

```
import sys
import threading
import time


def do_something_with_exception():
    exc_type, exc_value = sys.exc_info()[:2]
    print('Handling {} exception with message "{}" in {}'.format(
        exc_type.__name__, exc_value,
        threading.current_thread().name))


def cause_exception(delay):
    time.sleep(delay)
    raise RuntimeError('This is the error message')


def thread_target(delay):
    try:
        cause_exception(delay)
```

```
        except:
            do_something_with_exception()


    threads = [
        threading.Thread(target=thread_target, args=(0.3,)),
        threading.Thread(target=thread_target, args=(0.1,)),
    ]

    for t in threads:
        t.start()
    for t in threads:
        t.join()
```

This example avoids introducing a circular reference between the traceback object and a local variable in the current frame by ignoring that part of the return value from exc_info(). If the traceback is needed (for example, so it can be logged), explicitly delete the local variable (using del) to avoid cycles.

```
$ python3 sys_exc_info.py

Handling RuntimeError exception with message "This is the error
message" in Thread-2
Handling RuntimeError exception with message "This is the error
message" in Thread-1
```

17.2.4.3 Previous Interactive Exception

The interactive interpreter includes only one thread of interaction. Unhandled exceptions in that thread are saved to three variables in sys (last_type, last_value, and last_traceback), thereby making it easy to retrieve them for debugging purposes. Using the postmortem debugger in pdb (page 1101) avoids any need to use the values directly.

```
$ python3
Python 3.4.2 (v3.4.2:ab2c023a9432, Oct  5 2014, 20:42:22)
[GCC 4.2.1 (Apple Inc. build 5666) (dot 3)] on darwin
Type "help", "copyright", "credits" or "license" for more information.
>>> def cause_exception():
...     raise RuntimeError('This is the error message')
...
>>> cause_exception()
Traceback (most recent call last):
  File "<stdin>", line 1, in <module>
  File "<stdin>", line 2, in cause_exception
RuntimeError: This is the error message
>>> import pdb
>>> pdb.pm()
> <stdin>(2)cause_exception()
```

```
(Pdb) where
  <stdin>(1)<module>()
> <stdin>(2)cause_exception()
(Pdb)
```

TIP

Related Reading

- exceptions: Built-in errors.
- pdb (page 1101): Python debugger.
- traceback (page 1078): Module for working with tracebacks.

17.2.5 Low-Level Thread Support

sys includes low-level functions for controlling and debugging thread behavior.

17.2.5.1 Switch Interval

Python 3 uses a global lock to prevent separate threads from corrupting the interpreter state. After a configurable time interval, byte-code execution pauses and the interpreter checks whether any signal handlers need to be executed. During the same check, the global interpreter lock (GIL) is released by the current thread and then reacquired, with other threads being given priority over the thread that has just released the lock.

The default switch interval is 5 milliseconds, and the current value can always be retrieved with sys.getswitchinterval(). Changing the interval with sys.setswitchinterval() may affect the performance of an application, depending on the nature of the operations being performed.

Listing 17.32: **sys_switchinterval.py**

```
import sys
import threading
from queue import Queue


def show_thread(q):
    for i in range(5):
        for j in range(1000000):
            pass
        q.put(threading.current_thread().name)
    return


def run_threads():
    interval = sys.getswitchinterval()
```

```
    print('interval = {:0.3f}'.format(interval))
    q = Queue()
    threads = [
        threading.Thread(target=show_thread,
                         name='T{}'.format(i),
                         args=(q,))
        for i in range(3)
    ]
    for t in threads:
        t.setDaemon(True)
        t.start()
    for t in threads:
        t.join()
    while not q.empty():
        print(q.get(), end=' ')
    print()
    return


for interval in [0.001, 0.1]:
    sys.setswitchinterval(interval)
    run_threads()
    print()
```

When the switch interval is less than the amount of time a thread takes to run to completion, the interpreter gives another thread control so that it runs for a while. This behavior is illustrated in the first set of output that follows, where the interval is set to 1 millisecond.

With longer intervals, the active thread will be able to complete more work before it is forced to release control. This case is illustrated by the order of the name values in the queue in the second example, which uses an interval of 10 milliseconds.

```
$ python3 sys_switchinterval.py

interval = 0.001
T0 T1 T2 T1 T0 T2 T0 T1 T2 T1 T0 T2 T1 T0 T2

interval = 0.100
T0 T0 T0 T0 T0 T1 T1 T1 T1 T1 T2 T2 T2 T2 T2
```

Many factors other than the switch interval may control the context switching behavior of Python's threads. For example, when a thread performs I/O, it releases the GIL and, therefore, may allow another thread to take over execution.

17.2.5.2 Debugging

Identifying deadlocks can be one of the most difficult aspects of working with threads. `sys._current_frames()` can help by showing exactly where a thread is stopped.

Listing 17.33: `sys_current_frames.py`

```
1  import sys
2  import threading
3  import time
4
5  io_lock = threading.Lock()
6  blocker = threading.Lock()
7
8
9  def block(i):
10     t = threading.current_thread()
11     with io_lock:
12         print('{} with ident {} going to sleep'.format(
13             t.name, t.ident))
14     if i:
15         blocker.acquire()  # Acquired but never released
16         time.sleep(0.2)
17     with io_lock:
18         print(t.name, 'finishing')
19     return
20
21  # Create and start several threads that "block."
22  threads = [
23      threading.Thread(target=block, args=(i,))
24      for i in range(3)
25  ]
26  for t in threads:
27      t.setDaemon(True)
28      t.start()
29
30  # Map the threads from their identifier to the thread object.
31  threads_by_ident = dict((t.ident, t) for t in threads)
32
33  # Show where each thread is "blocked."
34  time.sleep(0.01)
35  with io_lock:
36      for ident, frame in sys._current_frames().items():
37          t = threads_by_ident.get(ident)
38          if not t:
39              # Main thread
40              continue
41          print('{} stopped in {} at line {} of {}'.format(
42              t.name, frame.f_code.co_name,
43              frame.f_lineno, frame.f_code.co_filename))
```

The dictionary returned by `sys._current_frames()` is keyed on the thread identifier, rather than its name. A little work is needed to map those identifiers back to the thread object.

Since Thread-1 does not sleep, it finishes before its status is checked. This thread is no longer active, so it does not appear in the output. Thread-2 acquires the lock `blocker`, then sleeps for a short period. Meanwhile, Thread-3 tries to acquire `blocker` but cannot because Thread-2 already has it.

```
$ python3 sys_current_frames.py

Thread-1 with ident 123145307557888 going to sleep
Thread-1 finishing
Thread-2 with ident 123145307557888 going to sleep
Thread-3 with ident 123145312813056 going to sleep
Thread-3 stopped in block at line 18 of sys_current_frames.py
Thread-2 stopped in block at line 19 of sys_current_frames.py
```

TIP

Related Reading

- threading (page 560): The threading module includes classes for creating Python threads.
- Queue: The Queue module provides a thread-safe implementation of a FIFO data structure.
- Reworking the GIL[8]: Email from Antoine Pitrou to the python-dev mailing list describing the GIL implementation changes to introduce the switch interval.

17.2.6 Modules and Imports

Most Python programs end up as a combination of several modules with a main application importing them. Whether using the features of the standard library or organizing custom code in separate files to make it easier to maintain, understanding and managing the dependencies for a program is an important aspect of development. `sys` includes information about the modules available to an application, either as built-ins or after being imported. It also defines hooks for overriding the standard import behavior for special cases.

17.2.6.1 Imported Modules

`sys.modules` is a dictionary mapping the names of imported modules to the module objects holding their code.

Listing 17.34: `sys_modules.py`

```
import sys
import textwrap
```

---

[8] https://mail.python.org/pipermail/python-dev/2009-October/093321.html

```
names = sorted(sys.modules.keys())
name_text = ', '.join(names)

print(textwrap.fill(name_text, width=64))
```

The contents of `sys.modules` change as new modules are imported.

```
$ python3 sys_modules.py

__main__, _bootlocale, _codecs, _collections_abc,
_frozen_importlib, _frozen_importlib_external, _imp, _io,
_locale, _signal, _sre, _stat, _thread, _warnings, _weakref,
_weakrefset, abc, builtins, codecs, copyreg, encodings,
encodings.aliases, encodings.latin_1, encodings.utf_8, errno,
genericpath, io, marshal, os, os.path, posix, posixpath, re,
site, sre_compile, sre_constants, sre_parse, stat, sys,
textwrap, zipimport
```

17.2.6.2 Built-In Modules

The Python interpreter can be compiled with some C modules built into it, so they do not need to be distributed as separate shared libraries. These modules do not appear in the list of imported modules managed in `sys.modules` because they were not technically imported. The only way to find the available built-in modules is by using `sys.builtin_module_names`.

Listing 17.35: `sys_builtins.py`

```
import sys
import textwrap

name_text = ', '.join(sorted(sys.builtin_module_names))

print(textwrap.fill(name_text, width=64))
```

The output of this script will vary, especially if it is run with a custom-built version of the interpreter. The following output was created using a copy of the interpreter installed from the standard python.org installer for OS X.

```
$ python3 sys_builtins.py

_ast, _codecs, _collections, _functools, _imp, _io, _locale,
_operator, _signal, _sre, _stat, _string, _symtable, _thread,
_tracemalloc, _warnings, _weakref, atexit, builtins, errno,
faulthandler, gc, itertools, marshal, posix, pwd, sys, time,
xxsubtype, zipimport
```

TIP

Related Reading

- Build Instructions[9]: Instructions for building Python, from the README file distributed with the source.

17.2.6.3 Import Path

The search path for modules is managed as a Python list saved in `sys.path`. The default contents of the path include the directory of the script used to start the application and the current working directory.

Listing 17.36: sys_path_show.py

```python
import sys

for d in sys.path:
    print(d)
```

The first directory in the search path is the home of the sample script itself. That location is followed by a series of platform-specific paths indicating where compiled extension modules (written in C) might be installed. The global `site-packages` directory is listed last.

```
$ python3 sys_path_show.py

/Users/dhellmann/Documents/PyMOTW/pymotw-3/source/sys
.../python35.zip
.../lib/python3.5
.../lib/python3.5/plat-darwin
.../python3.5/lib-dynload
.../lib/python3.5/site-packages
```

The import search-path list can be modified before starting the interpreter by setting the shell variable `PYTHONPATH` to a colon-separated list of directories.

```
$ PYTHONPATH=/my/private/site-packages:/my/shared/site-packages \
> python3 sys_path_show.py

/Users/dhellmann/Documents/PyMOTW/pymotw-3/source/sys
/my/private/site-packages
/my/shared/site-packages
.../python35.zip
.../lib/python3.5
.../lib/python3.5/plat-darwin
```

---

[9] https://hg.python.org/cpython/file/tip/README

```
.../python3.5/lib-dynload
.../lib/python3.5/site-packages
```

A program can also modify its path by adding elements to sys.path directly.

Listing 17.37: sys_path_modify.py

```python
import imp
import os
import sys

base_dir = os.path.dirname(__file__) or '.'
print('Base directory:', base_dir)

# Insert the package_dir_a directory at the front of the path.
package_dir_a = os.path.join(base_dir, 'package_dir_a')
sys.path.insert(0, package_dir_a)

# Import the example module.
import example
print('Imported example from:', example.__file__)
print('   ', example.DATA)

# Make package_dir_b the first directory in the search path.
package_dir_b = os.path.join(base_dir, 'package_dir_b')
sys.path.insert(0, package_dir_b)

# Reload the module to get the other version.
imp.reload(example)
print('Reloaded example from:', example.__file__)
print('   ', example.DATA)
```

Reloading an imported module re-imports the file, and uses the same module object to hold the results. Changing the path between the initial import and the call to reload() means a different module may be loaded the second time.

```
$ python3 sys_path_modify.py

Base directory: .
Imported example from: ./package_dir_a/example.py
    This is example A
Reloaded example from: ./package_dir_b/example.py
    This is example B
```

17.2.6.4 Custom Importers

Modifying the search path lets a programmer control how standard Python modules are found. But what if a program needs to import code from somewhere other than the

usual .py or .pyc files on the file system? **PEP 302**[10] solves this problem by introducing
import hooks, which can trap an attempt to find a module on the search path and take
alternative measures to load the code from somewhere else or apply preprocessing to it.

Custom importers are implemented in two separate phases. The *finder* is responsible
for locating a module and providing a *loader* to manage the actual import. To add custom
module finders, append a factory to the sys.path_hooks list. On import, each part of the
path is given to a finder until one claims support (by not raising ImportError). That finder is
then responsible for searching data storage represented by its path entry for named modules.

Listing 17.38: sys_path_hooks_noisy.py

```python
import sys


class NoisyImportFinder:

    PATH_TRIGGER = 'NoisyImportFinder_PATH_TRIGGER'

    def __init__(self, path_entry):
        print('Checking {}:'.format(path_entry), end=' ')
        if path_entry != self.PATH_TRIGGER:
            print('wrong finder')
            raise ImportError()
        else:
            print('works')
        return

    def find_module(self, fullname, path=None):
        print('Looking for {!r}'.format(fullname))
        return None


sys.path_hooks.append(NoisyImportFinder)

for hook in sys.path_hooks:
    print('Path hook: {}'.format(hook))

sys.path.insert(0, NoisyImportFinder.PATH_TRIGGER)

try:
    print('importing target_module')
    import target_module
except Exception as e:
    print('Import failed:', e)
```

This example illustrates how the finders are instantiated and queried. NoisyImportFinder
raises ImportError when it is instantiated with a path entry that does not match its special

---

[10] www.python.org/dev/peps/pep-0302

trigger value, which is obviously not a real path on the file system. This test prevents `NoisyImportFinder` from breaking imports of real modules.

```
$ python3 sys_path_hooks_noisy.py

Path hook: <class 'zipimport.zipimporter'>
Path hook: <function
FileFinder.path_hook.<locals>.path_hook_for_FileFinder at
0x100734950>
Path hook: <class '__main__.NoisyImportFinder'>
importing target_module
Checking NoisyImportFinder_PATH_TRIGGER: works
Looking for 'target_module'
Import failed: No module named 'target_module'
```

17.2.6.5 Importing from a Shelf

When the finder locates a module, it is responsible for returning a *loader* capable of importing that module. The example in this section illustrates a custom importer that saves its module contents in a database created by `shelve` (page 405).

First, a script is used to populate the shelf with a package containing a submodule and subpackage.

Listing 17.39: **sys_shelve_importer_create.py**

```
import shelve
import os

filename = '/tmp/pymotw_import_example.shelve'
if os.path.exists(filename + '.db'):
    os.unlink(filename + '.db')
with shelve.open(filename) as db:
    db['data:README'] = b"""
===============
package README
===============

This is the README for "package".
"""
    db['package.__init__'] = b"""
print('package imported')
message = 'This message is in package.__init__'
"""
    db['package.module1'] = b"""
print('package.module1 imported')
message = 'This message is in package.module1'
"""
    db['package.subpackage.__init__'] = b"""
```

```
    print('package.subpackage imported')
message = 'This message is in package.subpackage.__init__'
"""
    db['package.subpackage.module2'] = b"""
print('package.subpackage.module2 imported')
message = 'This message is in package.subpackage.module2'
"""
    db['package.with_error'] = b"""
print('package.with_error being imported')
raise ValueError('raising exception to break import')
"""
    print('Created {} with:'.format(filename))
    for key in sorted(db.keys()):
        print('  ', key)
```

A real packaging script would read the contents from the file system, but using hard-coded values is sufficient for a simple example like this.

```
$ python3 sys_shelve_importer_create.py

Created /tmp/pymotw_import_example.shelve with:
    data:README
    package.__init__
    package.module1
    package.subpackage.__init__
    package.subpackage.module2
    package.with_error
```

The custom importer needs to provide finder and loader classes that know how to look in a shelf for the source of a module or a package.

Listing 17.40: **sys_shelve_importer.py**

```
import imp
import os
import shelve
import sys


def _mk_init_name(fullname):
    """Return the name of the __init__ module
    for a given package name.
    """
    if fullname.endswith('.__init__'):
        return fullname
    return fullname + '.__init__'


def _get_key_name(fullname, db):
```

```
        """Look in an open shelf for fullname or
        fullname.__init__, and return the name found.
        """
        if fullname in db:
            return fullname
        init_name = _mk_init_name(fullname)
        if init_name in db:
            return init_name
        return None


class ShelveFinder:
    """Find modules collected in a shelve archive."""

    _maybe_recursing = False

    def __init__(self, path_entry):
        # Loading shelve creates an import recursive loop when it
        # imports dbm, and we know we will not load the
        # module being imported. Thus, when we seem to be
        # recursing, just ignore the request so another finder
        # will be used.
        if ShelveFinder._maybe_recursing:
            raise ImportError
        try:
            # Test the path_entry to see if it is a valid shelf.
            try:
                ShelveFinder._maybe_recursing = True
                with shelve.open(path_entry, 'r'):
                    pass
            finally:
                ShelveFinder._maybe_recursing = False
        except Exception as e:
            print('shelf could not import from {}: {}'.format(
                path_entry, e))
            raise
        else:
            print('shelf added to import path:', path_entry)
            self.path_entry = path_entry
        return

    def __str__(self):
        return '<{} for {!r}>'.format(self.__class__.__name__,
                                      self.path_entry)

    def find_module(self, fullname, path=None):
        path = path or self.path_entry
        print('\nlooking for {!r}\n  in {}'.format(
            fullname, path))
```

```
                with shelve.open(self.path_entry, 'r') as db:
                    key_name = _get_key_name(fullname, db)
                    if key_name:
                        print('  found it as {}'.format(key_name))
                        return ShelveLoader(path)
            print('  not found')
            return None


class ShelveLoader:
    """Load source for modules from shelve databases."""

    def __init__(self, path_entry):
        self.path_entry = path_entry
        return

    def _get_filename(self, fullname):
        # Make up a fake filename that starts with the path entry
        # so pkgutil.get_data() works correctly.
        return os.path.join(self.path_entry, fullname)

    def get_source(self, fullname):
        print('loading source for {!r} from shelf'.format(
            fullname))
        try:
            with shelve.open(self.path_entry, 'r') as db:
                key_name = _get_key_name(fullname, db)
                if key_name:
                    return db[key_name]
                raise ImportError(
                    'could not find source for {}'.format(
                        fullname)
                )
        except Exception as e:
            print('could not load source:', e)
            raise ImportError(str(e))

    def get_code(self, fullname):
        source = self.get_source(fullname)
        print('compiling code for {!r}'.format(fullname))
        return compile(source, self._get_filename(fullname),
                       'exec', dont_inherit=True)

    def get_data(self, path):
        print('looking for data\n  in {}\n  for {!r}'.format(
            self.path_entry, path))
        if not path.startswith(self.path_entry):
            raise IOError
        path = path[len(self.path_entry) + 1:]
```

```python
        key_name = 'data:' + path
        try:
            with shelve.open(self.path_entry, 'r') as db:
                return db[key_name]
        except Exception:
            # Convert all errors to IOError.
            raise IOError()

    def is_package(self, fullname):
        init_name = _mk_init_name(fullname)
        with shelve.open(self.path_entry, 'r') as db:
            return init_name in db

    def load_module(self, fullname):
        source = self.get_source(fullname)

        if fullname in sys.modules:
            print('reusing module from import of {!r}'.format(
                fullname))
            mod = sys.modules[fullname]
        else:
            print('creating a new module object for {!r}'.format(
                fullname))
            mod = sys.modules.setdefault(
                fullname,
                imp.new_module(fullname)
            )

        # Set a few properties required by PEP 302.
        mod.__file__ = self._get_filename(fullname)
        mod.__name__ = fullname
        mod.__path__ = self.path_entry
        mod.__loader__ = self
        # PEP-366 specifies that packages set __package__ to
        # their name, and modules have it set to their parent
        # package (if any).
        if self.is_package(fullname):
            mod.__package__ = fullname
        else:
            mod.__package__ = '.'.join(fullname.split('.')[:-1])

        if self.is_package(fullname):
            print('adding path for package')
            # Set __path__ for packages
            # so we can find the submodules.
            mod.__path__ = [self.path_entry]
        else:
            print('imported as regular module')
```

```
    print('execing source...')
    exec(source, mod.__dict__)
    print('done')
    return mod
```

Now `ShelveFinder` and `ShelveLoader` can be used to import code from a shelf. For example, the `package` just created can be imported with the following code.

Listing 17.41: **`sys_shelve_importer_package.py`**

```
import sys
import sys_shelve_importer


def show_module_details(module):
    print('  message    :', module.message)
    print('  __name__   :', module.__name__)
    print('  __package__:', module.__package__)
    print('  __file__   :', module.__file__)
    print('  __path__   :', module.__path__)
    print('  __loader__ :', module.__loader__)

filename = '/tmp/pymotw_import_example.shelve'
sys.path_hooks.append(sys_shelve_importer.ShelveFinder)
sys.path.insert(0, filename)

print('Import of "package":')
import package

print()
print('Examine package details:')
show_module_details(package)

print()
print('Global settings:')
print('sys.modules entry:')
print(sys.modules['package'])
```

The shelf is added to the import path the first time an import occurs after the path is modified. The finder recognizes the shelf and returns a loader, which is used for all imports from that shelf. The initial package-level import creates a new module object and then uses `exec` to run the source loaded from the shelf. The new module is used as the namespace, so that names defined in the source are preserved as module-level attributes.

```
$ python3 sys_shelve_importer_package.py

Import of "package":
```

```
shelf added to import path: /tmp/pymotw_import_example.shelve

looking for 'package'
  in /tmp/pymotw_import_example.shelve
  found it as package.__init__
loading source for 'package' from shelf
creating a new module object for 'package'
adding path for package
execing source...
package imported
done

Examine package details:
  message    : This message is in package.__init__
  __name__   : package
  __package__: package
  __file__   : /tmp/pymotw_import_example.shelve/package
  __path__   : ['/tmp/pymotw_import_example.shelve']
  __loader__ : <sys_shelve_importer.ShelveLoader object at
0x101467860>

Global settings:
sys.modules entry:
<module 'package' (<sys_shelve_importer.ShelveLoader object at
0x101467860>)>
```

17.2.6.6   Custom Package Importing

Loading other modules and subpackages proceeds in the same way.

Listing 17.42: **sys_shelve_importer_module.py**

```python
import sys
import sys_shelve_importer


def show_module_details(module):
    print('  message    :', module.message)
    print('  __name__   :', module.__name__)
    print('  __package__:', module.__package__)
    print('  __file__   :', module.__file__)
    print('  __path__   :', module.__path__)
    print('  __loader__ :', module.__loader__)


filename = '/tmp/pymotw_import_example.shelve'
sys.path_hooks.append(sys_shelve_importer.ShelveFinder)
sys.path.insert(0, filename)
```

```
print('Import of "package.module1":')
import package.module1

print()
print('Examine package.module1 details:')
show_module_details(package.module1)

print()
print('Import of "package.subpackage.module2":')
import package.subpackage.module2

print()
print('Examine package.subpackage.module2 details:')
show_module_details(package.subpackage.module2)
```

The finder receives the entire dotted name of the module to load, and returns a ShelveLoader configured to load modules from the path entry pointing to the shelf file. The fully qualified module name is passed to the loader's load_module() method, which constructs and returns a module instance.

```
$ python3 sys_shelve_importer_module.py

Import of "package.module1":
shelf added to import path: /tmp/pymotw_import_example.shelve

looking for 'package'
  in /tmp/pymotw_import_example.shelve
  found it as package.__init__
loading source for 'package' from shelf
creating a new module object for 'package'
adding path for package
execing source...
package imported
done

looking for 'package.module1'
  in /tmp/pymotw_import_example.shelve
  found it as package.module1
loading source for 'package.module1' from shelf
creating a new module object for 'package.module1'
imported as regular module
execing source...
package.module1 imported
done

Examine package.module1 details:
  message    : This message is in package.module1
  __name__   : package.module1
  __package__: package
```

```
    __file__    : /tmp/pymotw_import_example.shelve/package.module1
    __path__    : /tmp/pymotw_import_example.shelve
    __loader__  : <sys_shelve_importer.ShelveLoader object at
0x101376e10>

Import of "package.subpackage.module2":

looking for 'package.subpackage'
  in /tmp/pymotw_import_example.shelve
  found it as package.subpackage.__init__
loading source for 'package.subpackage' from shelf
creating a new module object for 'package.subpackage'
adding path for package
execing source...
package.subpackage imported
done

looking for 'package.subpackage.module2'
  in /tmp/pymotw_import_example.shelve
  found it as package.subpackage.module2
loading source for 'package.subpackage.module2' from shelf
creating a new module object for 'package.subpackage.module2'
imported as regular module
execing source...
package.subpackage.module2 imported
done

Examine package.subpackage.module2 details:
  message    : This message is in package.subpackage.module2
  __name__   : package.subpackage.module2
  __package__: package.subpackage
  __file__   :
/tmp/pymotw_import_example.shelve/package.subpackage.module2
  __path__   : /tmp/pymotw_import_example.shelve
  __loader__ : <sys_shelve_importer.ShelveLoader object at
0x1013a6c88>
```

17.2.6.7   Reloading Modules in a Custom Importer

Reloading a module is handled slightly differently. Instead of creating a new module object,
the existing object is reused.

Listing 17.43: `sys_shelve_importer_reload.py`

```
import importlib
import sys
import sys_shelve_importer

filename = '/tmp/pymotw_import_example.shelve'
```

```
sys.path_hooks.append(sys_shelve_importer.ShelveFinder)
sys.path.insert(0, filename)

print('First import of "package":')
import package

print()
print('Reloading "package":')
importlib.reload(package)
```

By reusing the same object, existing references to the module are preserved even if the reload step modifies class or function definitions.

```
$ python3 sys_shelve_importer_reload.py

First import of "package":
shelf added to import path: /tmp/pymotw_import_example.shelve

looking for 'package'
  in /tmp/pymotw_import_example.shelve
  found it as package.__init__
loading source for 'package' from shelf
creating a new module object for 'package'
adding path for package
execing source...
package imported
done

Reloading "package":

looking for 'package'
  in /tmp/pymotw_import_example.shelve
  found it as package.__init__
loading source for 'package' from shelf
reusing module from import of 'package'
adding path for package
execing source...
package imported
done
```

17.2.6.8   Handling Import Errors

When a module cannot be located by any finder, ImportError is raised by the main import code.

Listing 17.44: sys_shelve_importer_missing.py

```
import sys
import sys_shelve_importer
```

```
filename = '/tmp/pymotw_import_example.shelve'
sys.path_hooks.append(sys_shelve_importer.ShelveFinder)
sys.path.insert(0, filename)

try:
    import package.module3
except ImportError as e:
    print('Failed to import:', e)
```

Other errors during the import are propagated.

```
$ python3 sys_shelve_importer_missing.py

shelf added to import path: /tmp/pymotw_import_example.shelve

looking for 'package'
  in /tmp/pymotw_import_example.shelve
  found it as package.__init__
loading source for 'package' from shelf
creating a new module object for 'package'
adding path for package
execing source...
package imported
done

looking for 'package.module3'
  in /tmp/pymotw_import_example.shelve
  not found
Failed to import: No module named 'package.module3'
```

17.2.6.9 Package Data

In addition to defining the API for loading executable Python code, **PEP 302** defines an optional API for retrieving package data intended to be used when distributing data files, documentation, and other non-code resources required by a package. By implementing get_data(), a loader can allow calling applications to support retrieval of data associated with the package without considering how the package is actually installed (especially without assuming that the package is stored as files on a file system).

Listing 17.45: **sys_shelve_importer_get_data.py**

```
import sys
import sys_shelve_importer
import os
import pkgutil

filename = '/tmp/pymotw_import_example.shelve'
sys.path_hooks.append(sys_shelve_importer.ShelveFinder)
```

```
sys.path.insert(0, filename)

import package

readme_path = os.path.join(package.__path__[0], 'README')

readme = pkgutil.get_data('package', 'README')
# Equivalent to:
#   readme = package.__loader__.get_data(readme_path)
print(readme.decode('utf-8'))

foo_path = os.path.join(package.__path__[0], 'foo')
try:
    foo = pkgutil.get_data('package', 'foo')
    # Equivalent to:
    #   foo = package.__loader__.get_data(foo_path)
except IOError as err:
    print('ERROR: Could not load "foo"', err)
else:
    print(foo)
```

get_data() takes a path based on the module or package that owns the data. It either returns the contents of the resource "file" as a byte string, or raises IOError if the resource does not exist.

```
$ python3 sys_shelve_importer_get_data.py

shelf added to import path: /tmp/pymotw_import_example.shelve

looking for 'package'
  in /tmp/pymotw_import_example.shelve
  found it as package.__init__
loading source for 'package' from shelf
creating a new module object for 'package'
adding path for package
execing source...
package imported
done
looking for data
  in /tmp/pymotw_import_example.shelve
  for '/tmp/pymotw_import_example.shelve/README'

==============
package README
==============

This is the README for "package".

looking for data
```

```
        in /tmp/pymotw_import_example.shelve
        for '/tmp/pymotw_import_example.shelve/foo'
ERROR: Could not load "foo"
```

TIP

Related Reading

- pkgutil (page 1334): Includes get_data() for retrieving data from a package.

17.2.6.10   Importer Cache

Searching through all of the hooks each time a module is imported can be time-consuming. To save time, sys.path_importer_cache is maintained as a mapping between a path entry and the loader that can use the value to find modules.

Listing 17.46: **sys_path_importer_cache.py**

```python
import os
import sys

prefix = os.path.abspath(sys.prefix)

print('PATH:')
for name in sys.path:
    name = name.replace(prefix, '...')
    print(' ', name)

print()
print('IMPORTERS:')
for name, cache_value in sys.path_importer_cache.items():
    if '..' in name:
        name = os.path.abspath(name)
    name = name.replace(prefix, '...')
    print('  {}: {!r}'.format(name, cache_value))
```

A FileFinder is used to identify path locations found on the file system. Locations on the path not supported by any finder are associated with a None value, since they cannot be used to import modules. The following output showing cache importing has been truncated due to formatting constraints.

```
$ python3 sys_path_importer_cache.py

PATH:
  /Users/dhellmann/Documents/PyMOTW/Python3/pymotw-3/source/sys
  .../lib/python35.zip
  .../lib/python3.5
```

```
.../lib/python3.5/plat-darwin
.../lib/python3.5/lib-dynload
.../lib/python3.5/site-packages

IMPORTERS:
  sys_path_importer_cache.py: None
  .../lib/python3.5/encodings: FileFinder(
  '.../lib/python3.5/encodings')
  .../lib/python3.5/lib-dynload: FileFinder(
  '.../lib/python3.5/lib-dynload')
  .../lib/python3.5/lib-dynload: FileFinder(
  '.../lib/python3.5/lib-dynload')
  .../lib/python3.5/site-packages: FileFinder(
  '.../lib/python3.5/site-packages')
  .../lib/python3.5: FileFinder(
  '.../lib/python3.5/')
  .../lib/python3.5/plat-darwin: FileFinder(
  '.../lib/python3.5/plat-darwin')
  .../lib/python3.5: FileFinder(
  '.../lib/python3.5')
  .../lib/python35.zip: None
  .../lib/python3.5/plat-darwin: FileFinder(
  '.../lib/python3.5/plat-darwin')
```

17.2.6.11   Meta-path

The sys.meta_path further extends the sources of potential imports by allowing a finder to be searched *before* the regular sys.path is scanned. The API for a finder on the meta-path is the same as that for a regular path, except that the meta-finder is not limited to a single entry in sys.path—it can search anywhere at all.

Listing 17.47: sys_meta_path.py

```python
import sys
import imp


class NoisyMetaImportFinder:

    def __init__(self, prefix):
        print('Creating NoisyMetaImportFinder for {}'.format(
            prefix))
        self.prefix = prefix
        return

    def find_module(self, fullname, path=None):
        print('looking for {!r} with path {!r}'.format(
            fullname, path))
```

```
            name_parts = fullname.split('.')
            if name_parts and name_parts[0] == self.prefix:
                print(' ... found prefix, returning loader')
                return NoisyMetaImportLoader(path)
            else:
                print(' ... not the right prefix, cannot load')
            return None


class NoisyMetaImportLoader:

    def __init__(self, path_entry):
        self.path_entry = path_entry
        return

    def load_module(self, fullname):
        print('loading {}'.format(fullname))
        if fullname in sys.modules:
            mod = sys.modules[fullname]
        else:
            mod = sys.modules.setdefault(
                fullname,
                imp.new_module(fullname))

        # Set a few properties required by PEP 302.
        mod.__file__ = fullname
        mod.__name__ = fullname
        # Always looks like a package
        mod.__path__ = ['path-entry-goes-here']
        mod.__loader__ = self
        mod.__package__ = '.'.join(fullname.split('.')[:-1])

        return mod


# Install the meta-path finder.
sys.meta_path.append(NoisyMetaImportFinder('foo'))

# Import some modules that are "found" by the meta-path finder.
print()
import foo

print()
import foo.bar

# Import a module that is not found.
print()
try:
    import bar
```

```
except ImportError as e:
    pass
```

Each finder on the meta-path is interrogated before sys.path is searched, so there is always an opportunity to have a central importer load modules without explicitly modifying sys.path. Once the module is "found," the loader API works in the same way as for regular loaders (although this example is truncated for simplicity).

```
$ python3 sys_meta_path.py

Creating NoisyMetaImportFinder for foo

looking for 'foo' with path None
    ... found prefix, returning loader
loading foo

looking for 'foo.bar' with path ['path-entry-goes-here']
    ... found prefix, returning loader
loading foo.bar

looking for 'bar' with path None
    ... not the right prefix, cannot load
```

TIP

Related Reading

- importlib (page 1329): Base classes and other tools for creating custom importers.
- zipimport (page 1344): Implements importing Python modules from inside ZIP archives.
- The Internal Structure of Python Eggs[11]: setuptools documentation for the egg format.
- Wheel[12]: Documentation for wheel archive format for installable Python code.
- **PEP 302**[13]: Import Hooks.
- **PEP 366**[14]: Main module explicit relative imports.
- **PEP 427**[15]: The Wheel Binary Package Format 1.0.
- Import this, that, and the other thing: custom importers[16]: Brett Cannon's PyCon 2010 presentation.

---

[11] http://setuptools.readthedocs.io/en/latest/formats.html?highlight=egg
[12] http://wheel.readthedocs.org/en/latest/
[13] www.python.org/dev/peps/pep-0302
[14] www.python.org/dev/peps/pep-0366
[15] www.python.org/dev/peps/pep-0427
[16] http://pyvideo.org/pycon-us-2010/pycon-2010--import-this--that--and-the-other-thin.html

Table 17.2: Event Hooks for settrace()

Event	When It Occurs	Argument Value
call	Before a line is executed	None
line	Before a line is executed	None
return	Before a function returns	The value being returned
exception	After an exception occurs	The (exception, value, traceback) tuple
c_call	Before a C function is called	The C function object
c_return	After a C function returns	None
c_exception	After a C function throws an error	None

17.2.7   Tracing a Program as It Runs

There are two ways to inject code that watches a program run: *tracing* and *profiling*. These techniques are similar, but intended for different purposes and so have different constraints. The easiest, albeit least efficient, way to monitor a program is through a *trace hook*, which can be used to write a debugger, monitor code coverage, or achieve many other purposes.

The trace hook is modified by passing a callback function to sys.settrace(). The callback takes three arguments: the stack frame from the code being run, a string naming the type of notification, and an event-specific argument value. Table 17.2 lists the seven event types for different levels of information that occur as a program is being executed.

17.2.7.1   Tracing Function Calls

A call event is generated before every function call. The frame passed to the callback can be used to determine which function is being called and from where.

Listing 17.48: **sys_settrace_call.py**

```python
#!/usr/bin/env python3
# encoding: utf-8

import sys


def trace_calls(frame, event, arg):
    if event != 'call':
        return
    co = frame.f_code
    func_name = co.co_name
    if func_name == 'write':
        # Ignore write() calls from printing.
        return
    func_line_no = frame.f_lineno
    func_filename = co.co_filename
    caller = frame.f_back
    caller_line_no = caller.f_lineno
    caller_filename = caller.f_code.co_filename
    print('* Call to', func_name)
```

```
21      print('*  on line {} of {}'.format(
22          func_line_no, func_filename))
23      print('*  from line {} of {}'.format(
24          caller_line_no, caller_filename))
25      return
26
27
28  def b():
29      print('inside b()\n')
30
31
32  def a():
33      print('inside a()\n')
34      b()
35
36  sys.settrace(trace_calls)
37  a()
```

This example ignores calls to `write()`, as used by `print` to write to `sys.stdout`.

```
$ python3 sys_settrace_call.py

* Call to a
*  on line 32 of sys_settrace_call.py
*  from line 37 of sys_settrace_call.py
inside a()

* Call to b
*  on line 28 of sys_settrace_call.py
*  from line 34 of sys_settrace_call.py
inside b()
```

17.2.7.2 Tracing Inside Functions

The trace hook can return a new hook to be used inside the new scope (the *local* trace function). It is possible, for instance, to control tracing so that it runs line-by-line within only certain modules or functions.

Listing 17.49: sys_settrace_line.py

```
1  #!/usr/bin/env python3
2  # encoding: utf-8
3
4  import functools
5  import sys
6
7
8  def trace_lines(frame, event, arg):
```

```
 9      if event != 'line':
10          return
11      co = frame.f_code
12      func_name = co.co_name
13      line_no = frame.f_lineno
14      print('* {} line {}'.format(func_name, line_no))
15
16
17  def trace_calls(frame, event, arg, to_be_traced):
18      if event != 'call':
19          return
20      co = frame.f_code
21      func_name = co.co_name
22      if func_name == 'write':
23          # Ignore write() calls from printing.
24          return
25      line_no = frame.f_lineno
26      filename = co.co_filename
27      print('* Call to {} on line {} of {}'.format(
28          func_name, line_no, filename))
29      if func_name in to_be_traced:
30          # Trace into this function.
31          return trace_lines
32      return
33
34
35  def c(input):
36      print('input =', input)
37      print('Leaving c()')
38
39
40  def b(arg):
41      val = arg * 5
42      c(val)
43      print('Leaving b()')
44
45
46  def a():
47      b(2)
48      print('Leaving a()')
49
50
51  tracer = functools.partial(trace_calls, to_be_traced=['b'])
52  sys.settrace(tracer)
53  a()
```

In this example, the list of functions is kept in the variable to_be_traced. Thus, when
trace_calls() runs, it can return trace_lines() to enable tracing inside of b().

```
$ python3 sys_settrace_line.py

* Call to a on line 46 of sys_settrace_line.py
* Call to b on line 40 of sys_settrace_line.py
*   b line 41
*   b line 42
* Call to c on line 35 of sys_settrace_line.py
input = 10
Leaving c()
*   b line 43
Leaving b()
Leaving a()
```

17.2.7.3   Watching the Stack

Another useful application for hooks is keeping up with which functions are being called and what their return values are. To monitor return values, watch for the return event.

Listing 17.50: **sys_settrace_return.py**

```
1  #!/usr/bin/env python3
2  # encoding: utf-8
3
4  import sys
5
6
7  def trace_calls_and_returns(frame, event, arg):
8      co = frame.f_code
9      func_name = co.co_name
10     if func_name == 'write':
11         # Ignore write() calls from printing.
12         return
13     line_no = frame.f_lineno
14     filename = co.co_filename
15     if event == 'call':
16         print('* Call to {} on line {} of {}'.format(
17             func_name, line_no, filename))
18         return trace_calls_and_returns
19     elif event == 'return':
20         print('* {} => {}'.format(func_name, arg))
21     return
22
23
24 def b():
25     print('inside b()')
26     return 'response_from_b '
27
28
```

```
29   def a():
30       print('inside a()')
31       val = b()
32       return val * 2
33
34
35   sys.settrace(trace_calls_and_returns)
36   a()
```

The local trace function is used for watching return events. `trace_calls_and_returns()` needs to return a reference to itself when a function is called, so the return value can be monitored.

```
$ python3 sys_settrace_return.py

* Call to a on line 29 of sys_settrace_return.py
inside a()
* Call to b on line 24 of sys_settrace_return.py
inside b()
* b => response_from_b
* a => response_from_b response_from_b
```

17.2.7.4   Exception Propagation

To monitor exceptions, look for `exception` events in a local trace function. When an exception occurs, the trace hook is called with a tuple containing the type of exception, the exception object, and a traceback object.

Listing 17.51: **sys_settrace_exception.py**

```
1    #!/usr/bin/env python3
2    # encoding: utf-8
3
4    import sys
5
6
7    def trace_exceptions(frame, event, arg):
8        if event != 'exception':
9            return
10       co = frame.f_code
11       func_name = co.co_name
12       line_no = frame.f_lineno
13       exc_type, exc_value, exc_traceback = arg
14       print(('* Tracing exception:\n'
15              '* {} "{}"\n'
16              '* on line {} of {}\n').format(
17                  exc_type.__name__, exc_value, line_no,
18                  func_name))
```

```
19
20
21 def trace_calls(frame, event, arg):
22     if event != 'call':
23         return
24     co = frame.f_code
25     func_name = co.co_name
26     if func_name in TRACE_INTO:
27         return trace_exceptions
28
29
30 def c():
31     raise RuntimeError('generating exception in c()')
32
33
34 def b():
35     c()
36     print('Leaving b()')
37
38
39 def a():
40     b()
41     print('Leaving a()')
42
43
44 TRACE_INTO = ['a', 'b', 'c']
45
46 sys.settrace(trace_calls)
47 try:
48     a()
49 except Exception as e:
50     print('Exception handler:', e)
```

Take care to limit where the local function is applied, because some of the internals of formatting error messages generate—and ignore—their own exceptions. Every exception is seen by the trace hook, regardless of whether the caller catches and ignores it.

```
$ python3 sys_settrace_exception.py

* Tracing exception:
* RuntimeError "generating exception in c()"
* on line 31 of c

* Tracing exception:
* RuntimeError "generating exception in c()"
* on line 35 of b

* Tracing exception:
```

```
* RuntimeError "generating exception in c()"
* on line 40 of a

Exception handler: generating exception in c()
```

TIP

Related Reading

- `profile` (page 1140): The `profile` module documentation shows how to use a ready-made profiler.
- `trace` (page 1069): The `trace` module implements several code analysis features.
- Types and members[17]: Descriptions of frame and code objects and their attributes.
- Tracing Python code[18]: Another `settrace()` tutorial.
- Wicked hack: Python bytecode tracing[19]: Ned Batchelder's experiments with tracing with more granularity than source line level.
- smiley[20]: Python application tracer.

TIP

Related Reading for the sys Module

- Standard library documentation for `sys`.[21]
- Python 2 to 3 porting notes for `sys` (page 1363).

17.3 os: Portable Access to Operating System–Specific Features

The `os` module provides a wrapper for platform-specific modules such as `posix`, `nt`, and `mac`. The API for functions available on all platforms should be the same, so using the `os` module offers some measure of portability. Not all functions are available on every platform, however. Notably, many of the process management functions described in this summary are not available for Windows.

The Python documentation for the `os` module is subtitled "Miscellaneous Operating System Interfaces." The module consists mostly of functions for creating and managing running processes or file system content (files and directories), with a few other bits of functionality thrown in as well.

---

[17] https://docs.python.org/3/library/inspect.html#types-and-members
[18] www.dalkescientific.com/writings/diary/archive/2005/04/20/tracing_python_code.html
[19] http://nedbatchelder.com/blog/200804/wicked_hack_python_bytecode_tracing.html
[20] https://pypi.python.org/pypi/smiley
[21] https://docs.python.org/3.5/library/sys.html

17.3.1 Examining the File System Contents

To prepare a list of the contents of a directory on the file system, use `listdir()`.

Listing 17.52: **os_listdir.py**

```
import os
import sys

print(os.listdir(sys.argv[1]))
```

The return value is a list of all of the named members of the directory given. No distinction is made among files, subdirectories, and symlinks.

```
$ python3 os_listdir.py .

['index.rst', 'os_access.py', 'os_cwd_example.py',
'os_directories.py', 'os_environ_example.py',
'os_exec_example.py', 'os_fork_example.py',
'os_kill_example.py', 'os_listdir.py', 'os_listdir.py~',
'os_process_id_example.py', 'os_process_user_example.py',
'os_rename_replace.py', 'os_rename_replace.py~',
'os_scandir.py', 'os_scandir.py~', 'os_spawn_example.py',
'os_stat.py', 'os_stat_chmod.py', 'os_stat_chmod_example.txt',
'os_strerror.py', 'os_strerror.py~', 'os_symlinks.py',
'os_system_background.py', 'os_system_example.py',
'os_system_shell.py', 'os_wait_example.py',
'os_waitpid_example.py', 'os_walk.py']
```

The function `walk()` traverses a directory recursively. For each subdirectory, it generates a `tuple` containing the directory path, any immediate subdirectories of that path, and a list containing the names of any files in that directory.

Listing 17.53: **os_walk.py**

```
import os
import sys

# If we are not given a path to list, use /tmp.
if len(sys.argv) == 1:
    root = '/tmp'
else:
    root = sys.argv[1]

for dir_name, sub_dirs, files in os.walk(root):
    print(dir_name)
    # Make the subdirectory names stand out with /.
    sub_dirs = [n + '/' for n in sub_dirs]
    # Mix the directory contents together.
    contents = sub_dirs + files
    contents.sort()
```

```
    # Show the contents.
    for c in contents:
        print('  {}'.format(c))
    print()
```

This example shows a recursive directory listing.

```
$ python3 os_walk.py ../zipimport

../zipimport
  __init__.py
  example_package/
  index.rst
  zipimport_example.zip
  zipimport_find_module.py
  zipimport_get_code.py
  zipimport_get_data.py
  zipimport_get_data_nozip.py
  zipimport_get_data_zip.py
  zipimport_get_source.py
  zipimport_is_package.py
  zipimport_load_module.py
  zipimport_make_example.py

../zipimport/example_package
  README.txt
  __init__.py
```

If more information is needed than the names of the files, it is likely to be more efficient to use scandir() than listdir(): More information is collected in one system call when the directory is scanned.

Listing 17.54: os_scandir.py

```
import os
import sys

for entry in os.scandir(sys.argv[1]):
    if entry.is_dir():
        typ = 'dir'
    elif entry.is_file():
        typ = 'file'
    elif entry.is_symlink():
        typ = 'link'
    else:
        typ = 'unknown'
    print('{name} {typ}'.format(
        name=entry.name,
        typ=typ,
    ))
```

scandir() returns a sequence of DirEntry instances for the items in the directory. This object has several attributes and methods for accessing metadata about the file.

```
$ python3 os_scandir.py .

index.rst file
os_access.py file
os_cwd_example.py file
os_directories.py file
os_environ_example.py file
os_exec_example.py file
os_fork_example.py file
os_kill_example.py file
os_listdir.py file
os_listdir.py~ file
os_process_id_example.py file
os_process_user_example.py file
os_rename_replace.py file
os_rename_replace.py~ file
os_scandir.py file
os_scandir.py~ file
os_spawn_example.py file
os_stat.py file
os_stat_chmod.py file
os_stat_chmod_example.txt file
os_strerror.py file
os_strerror.py~ file
os_symlinks.py file
os_system_background.py file
os_system_example.py file
os_system_shell.py file
os_wait_example.py file
os_waitpid_example.py file
os_walk.py file
```

17.3.2   Managing File System Permissions

Detailed information about a file can be accessed using stat() or lstat() (for checking the status of something that might be a symbolic link).

Listing 17.55: os_stat.py

```python
import os
import sys
import time

if len(sys.argv) == 1:
    filename = __file__
```

```
else:
    filename = sys.argv[1]

stat_info = os.stat(filename)

print('os.stat({}):'.format(filename))
print('  Size:', stat_info.st_size)
print('  Permissions:', oct(stat_info.st_mode))
print('  Owner:', stat_info.st_uid)
print('  Device:', stat_info.st_dev)
print('  Created      :', time.ctime(stat_info.st_ctime))
print('  Last modified:', time.ctime(stat_info.st_mtime))
print('  Last accessed:', time.ctime(stat_info.st_atime))
```

The output will vary depending on how the example code was installed. To experiment with this function, try passing different filenames on the command line to os_stat.py.

```
$ python3 os_stat.py

os.stat(os_stat.py):
  Size: 593
  Permissions: 0o100644
  Owner: 527
  Device: 16777218
  Created      : Sat Dec 17 12:09:51 2016
  Last modified: Sat Dec 17 12:09:51 2016
  Last accessed: Sat Dec 31 12:33:19 2016

$ python3 os_stat.py index.rst

os.stat(index.rst):
  Size: 26878
  Permissions: 0o100644
  Owner: 527
  Device: 16777218
  Created      : Sat Dec 31 12:33:10 2016
  Last modified: Sat Dec 31 12:33:10 2016
  Last accessed: Sat Dec 31 12:33:19 2016
```

On Unix-like systems, file permissions can be changed using chmod(), with the mode being passed as an integer. Mode values can be constructed using constants defined in the stat module. The next example toggles the user's execute permission bit.

Listing 17.56: os_stat_chmod.py

```
import os
import stat

filename = 'os_stat_chmod_example.txt'
```

```
if os.path.exists(filename):
    os.unlink(filename)
with open(filename, 'wt') as f:
    f.write('contents')

# Determine which permissions are already set using stat.
existing_permissions = stat.S_IMODE(os.stat(filename).st_mode)

if not os.access(filename, os.X_OK):
    print('Adding execute permission')
    new_permissions = existing_permissions | stat.S_IXUSR
else:
    print('Removing execute permission')
    # Use xor to remove the user execute permission.
    new_permissions = existing_permissions ^ stat.S_IXUSR

os.chmod(filename, new_permissions)
```

This script assumes it has the permissions necessary to modify the mode of the file when run.

```
$ python3 os_stat_chmod.py

Adding execute permission
```

Use the function access() to test the access rights that a process has for a file.

Listing 17.57: **os_access.py**

```
import os

print('Testing:', __file__)
print('Exists:', os.access(__file__, os.F_OK))
print('Readable:', os.access(__file__, os.R_OK))
print('Writable:', os.access(__file__, os.W_OK))
print('Executable:', os.access(__file__, os.X_OK))
```

The results will vary depending on how the example code is installed, but the output will be similar to this:

```
$ python3 os_access.py

Testing: os_access.py
Exists: True
Readable: True
Writable: True
Executable: False
```

The library documentation for `access()` includes two special warnings. First, it makes little sense to call `access()` to test whether a file can be opened before actually calling `open()` on that file. There is a small, but real, window of time between the two calls during which the permissions on the file could change. The second warning applies mostly to networked file systems that extend the POSIX permission semantics. Some file system types may respond to the POSIX call that a process has permission to access a file, then report a failure when the attempt is made using `open()` for some reason not tested via the POSIX call. A better strategy is to call `open()` with the required mode and catch the `IOError` raised if there is a problem.

17.3.3   Creating and Deleting Directories

Several functions are available for working with directories on the file system, including functions for creating directories, listing their contents, and removing directories.

Listing 17.58: os_directories.py

```python
import os

dir_name = 'os_directories_example'

print('Creating', dir_name)
os.makedirs(dir_name)

file_name = os.path.join(dir_name, 'example.txt')
print('Creating', file_name)
with open(file_name, 'wt') as f:
    f.write('example file')

print('Cleaning up')
os.unlink(file_name)
os.rmdir(dir_name)
```

Two sets of functions are available for creating and deleting directories. When creating a new directory with `mkdir()`, all of the parent directories must already exist. When a directory is removed with `rmdir()`, only the leaf directory (the last part of the path) is actually removed. In contrast, `makedirs()` and `removedirs()` operate on all of the nodes in the path. `makedirs()` will create any parts of the path that do not exist, and `removedirs()` will remove all of the parent directories, as long as they are empty.

```
$ python3 os_directories.py

Creating os_directories_example
Creating os_directories_example/example.txt
Cleaning up
```

17.3.4   Working with Symbolic Links

For platforms and file systems that support them, functions are available for working with symlinks.

Listing 17.59: os_symlinks.py

```
import os

link_name = '/tmp/' + os.path.basename(__file__)

print('Creating link {} -> {}'.format(link_name, __file__))
os.symlink(__file__, link_name)

stat_info = os.lstat(link_name)
print('Permissions:', oct(stat_info.st_mode))

print('Points to:', os.readlink(link_name))

# Clean up.
os.unlink(link_name)
```

Use `symlink()` to create a symbolic link and `readlink()` to read a link and determine the original file pointed to by the link. The `lstat()` function is like `stat()`, but it operates on symbolic links.

```
$ python3 os_symlinks.py

Creating link /tmp/os_symlinks.py -> os_symlinks.py
Permissions: 0o120755
Points to: os_symlinks.py
```

17.3.5   Safely Replacing an Existing File

Replacing or renaming an existing file is not idempotent and may expose applications to race conditions. The `rename()` and `replace()` functions implement safe algorithms for these actions, using atomic operations on POSIX-compliant systems when possible.

Listing 17.60: os_rename_replace.py

```
import glob
import os


with open('rename_start.txt', 'w') as f:
    f.write('starting as rename_start.txt')

print('Starting:', glob.glob('rename*.txt'))
```

```
os.rename('rename_start.txt', 'rename_finish.txt')

print('After rename:', glob.glob('rename*.txt'))

with open('rename_finish.txt', 'r') as f:
    print('Contents:', repr(f.read()))

with open('rename_new_contents.txt', 'w') as f:
    f.write('ending with contents of rename_new_contents.txt')

os.replace('rename_new_contents.txt', 'rename_finish.txt')

with open('rename_finish.txt', 'r') as f:
    print('After replace:', repr(f.read()))

for name in glob.glob('rename*.txt'):
    os.unlink(name)
```

The `rename()` and `replace()` functions work across file systems, most of the time. Renaming a file may fail if that file is moved to a new file system or if the destination already exists.

```
$ python3 os_rename_replace.py

Starting: ['rename_start.txt']
After rename: ['rename_finish.txt']
Contents: 'starting as rename_start.txt'
After replace: 'ending with contents of rename_new_contents.txt'
```

17.3.6 Detecting and Changing the Process Owner

The next set of functions provided by `os` is used for determining and changing the process owner IDs. These functions are most frequently used by authors of daemons or special system programs that need to change the permission level rather than running as root. This section does not try to explain all of the intricate details of Unix security, process owners, and other process-related issues. See the references list at the end of this section for more details.

The following example shows the real and effective user and group information for a process, and then changes the effective values. This is similar to what a daemon would need to do when it starts as root during a system boot, so as to lower the privilege level and run as a different user.

NOTE

Before running the example, change the `TEST_GID` and `TEST_UID` values to match a real user defined on the system.

Listing 17.61: os_process_user_example.py

```python
import os

TEST_GID = 502
TEST_UID = 502


def show_user_info():
    print('User (actual/effective)  : {} / {}'.format(
        os.getuid(), os.geteuid()))
    print('Group (actual/effective) : {} / {}'.format(
        os.getgid(), os.getegid()))
    print('Actual Groups    :', os.getgroups())


print('BEFORE CHANGE:')
show_user_info()
print()

try:
    os.setegid(TEST_GID)
except OSError:
    print('ERROR: Could not change effective group. '
          'Rerun as root.')
else:
    print('CHANGE GROUP:')
    show_user_info()
    print()

try:
    os.seteuid(TEST_UID)
except OSError:
    print('ERROR: Could not change effective user. '
          'Rerun as root.')
else:
    print('CHANGE USER:')
    show_user_info()
    print()
```

When run as the user with ID 502 and group 502 on OS X, this code produces the following output.

```
$ python3 os_process_user_example.py

BEFORE CHANGE:
User (actual/effective)  : 527 / 527
Group (actual/effective) : 501 / 501
Actual Groups    : [501, 701, 402, 702, 500, 12, 61, 80, 98, 398,
```

```
399, 33, 100, 204, 395]

ERROR: Could not change effective group. Rerun as root.
ERROR: Could not change effective user. Rerun as root.
```

The values do not change because when it is not running as root, a process cannot change its effective owner value. Any attempt to set the effective user ID or group ID to anything other than that of the current user causes an OSError. Running the same script using sudo so that it starts out with root privileges is a different story.

```
$ sudo python3 os_process_user_example.py

BEFORE CHANGE:

User (actual/effective)  : 0 / 0
Group (actual/effective) : 0 / 0
Actual Groups : [0, 1, 2, 3, 4, 5, 8, 9, 12, 20, 29, 61, 80,
702, 33, 98, 100, 204, 395, 398, 399, 701]

CHANGE GROUP:
User (actual/effective)  : 0 / 0
Group (actual/effective) : 0 / 502
Actual Groups  : [0, 1, 2, 3, 4, 5, 8, 9, 12, 20, 29, 61, 80,
702, 33, 98, 100, 204, 395, 398, 399, 701]

CHANGE USER:
User (actual/effective)  : 0 / 502
Group (actual/effective) : 0 / 502
Actual Groups  : [0, 1, 2, 3, 4, 5, 8, 9, 12, 20, 29, 61, 80,
702, 33, 98, 100, 204, 395, 398, 399, 701]
```

In this case, since it starts as root, the script can change the effective user and group for the process. Once the effective UID is changed, the process is limited to the permissions of that user. Because non-root users cannot change their effective group, the program needs to change the group before changing the user.

17.3.7 Managing the Process Environment

Another feature of the operating system that is exposed to a program though the os module is the environment. Variables set in the environment are visible as strings that can be read through os.environ or getenv(). Environment variables are commonly used for configuration values such as search paths, file locations, and debug flags. The next example shows how to retrieve an environment variable and pass a value through it to a child process.

Listing 17.62: os_environ_example.py

```
import os

print('Initial value:', os.environ.get('TESTVAR', None))
```

```
print('Child process:')
os.system('echo $TESTVAR')

os.environ['TESTVAR'] = 'THIS VALUE WAS CHANGED'

print()
print('Changed value:', os.environ['TESTVAR'])
print('Child process:')
os.system('echo $TESTVAR')

del os.environ['TESTVAR']

print()
print('Removed value:', os.environ.get('TESTVAR', None))
print('Child process:')
os.system('echo $TESTVAR')
```

The os.environ object follows the standard Python mapping API for retrieving and setting values. Changes to os.environ are exported for child processes.

```
$ python3 -u os_environ_example.py

Initial value: None
Child process:


Changed value: THIS VALUE WAS CHANGED
Child process:
THIS VALUE WAS CHANGED

Removed value: None
Child process:
```

17.3.8   Managing the Process Working Directory

Operating systems with hierarchical file systems have a concept of the *current working directory*—that is, the directory on the file system that the process uses as the starting location when files are accessed with relative paths. The current working directory can be retrieved with getcwd() and changed with chdir().

Listing 17.63: os_cwd_example.py

```
import os

print('Starting:', os.getcwd())

print('Moving up one:', os.pardir)
os.chdir(os.pardir)

print('After move:', os.getcwd())
```

os.curdir and os.pardir are used to refer to the current and parent directories, respectively, in a portable manner.

```
$ python3 os_cwd_example.py

Starting: .../pymotw-3/source/os
Moving up one: ..
After move: .../pymotw-3/source
```

17.3.9   Running External Commands

WARNING

Many of these functions for working with processes have limited portability. For a more consistent way to work with processes in a platform-independent manner, see the subprocess (page 535) module instead.

The most basic way to run a separate command, without interacting with it at all, is via the system() function. It takes a single string argument, which is the command line to be executed by a subprocess running a shell.

Listing 17.64: os_system_example.py

```
import os

# Simple command
os.system('pwd')
```

The return value of system() is the exit value of the shell running the program packed into a 16-bit number. The high byte of this number is the exit status, and the low byte is either the signal number that caused the process to die or zero.

```
$ python3 -u os_system_example.py

.../pymotw-3/source/os
```

Because the command is passed directly to the shell for processing, it can include shell syntax such as globbing or environment variables.

Listing 17.65: os_system_shell.py

```
import os

# Command with shell expansion
os.system('echo $TMPDIR')
```

The environment variable $TMPDIR in this string is expanded when the shell runs the command line.

```
$ python3 -u os_system_shell.py

/var/folders/5q/8gk0wq888xlggz008k8dr7180000hg/T/
```

Unless the command is explicitly run in the background, the call to `system()` blocks until it is complete. Standard input, output, and error from the child process are tied to the appropriate streams owned by the caller by default, but can be redirected using shell syntax.

Listing 17.66: os_system_background.py

```
import os
import time

print('Calling...')
os.system('date; (sleep 3; date) &')

print('Sleeping...')
time.sleep(5)
```

This is getting into shell trickery, though, and there are better ways to accomplish the same thing.

```
$ python3 -u os_system_background.py

Calling...
Sat Dec 31 12:33:20 EST 2016
Sleeping...
Sat Dec 31 12:33:23 EST 2016
```

17.3.10   Creating Processes with os.fork()

The POSIX functions `fork()` and `exec()` (available under Mac OS X, Linux, and other Unix variants) are exposed via the `os` module. Entire books have been written about reliably using these functions, so check the library or bookstore for more details than are presented here in this introduction.

To create a new process as a clone of the current process, use `fork()`.

Listing 17.67: os_fork_example.py

```
import os

pid = os.fork()

if pid:
    print('Child process id:', pid)
```

```
else:
    print('I am the child')
```

The output will vary based on the state of the system each time the example is run, but it will look something like this:

```
$ python3 -u os_fork_example.py

Child process id: 29190
I am the child
```

After the fork, there are two processes running the same code. For a program to tell whether it is running in the parent process or the child process, it needs to check the return value of fork(). If the value is 0, the current process is the child. If it is not 0, the program is running in the parent process and the return value is the process ID of the child process.

Listing 17.68: os_kill_example.py

```
import os
import signal
import time


def signal_usr1(signum, frame):
    "Callback invoked when a signal is received"
    pid = os.getpid()
    print('Received USR1 in process {}'.format(pid))


print('Forking...')
child_pid = os.fork()
if child_pid:
    print('PARENT: Pausing before sending signal...')
    time.sleep(1)
    print('PARENT: Signaling {}'.format(child_pid))
    os.kill(child_pid, signal.SIGUSR1)
else:
    print('CHILD: Setting up signal handler')
    signal.signal(signal.SIGUSR1, signal_usr1)
    print('CHILD: Pausing to wait for signal')
    time.sleep(5)
```

The parent can send signals to the child process using kill() and the signal (page 553) module. First, define a signal handler to be invoked when the signal is received. Then call fork(), and in the parent pause a short amount of time before sending a USR1 signal using kill(). This example uses a short pause to give the child process time to set up the signal handler. A real application would not need (or want) to call sleep(). In the child, set up the signal handler and go to sleep for a while to give the parent enough time to send the signal.

```
$ python3 -u os_kill_example.py

Forking...
PARENT: Pausing before sending signal...
CHILD: Setting up signal handler
CHILD: Pausing to wait for signal
PARENT: Signaling 29193
Received USR1 in process 29193
```

An easy way to handle separate behavior in the child process is to check the return value of fork() and branch. More complex behavior may call for more code separation than a simple branch can deliver. In other cases, an existing program might need to be wrapped. In both of these situations, the exec*() series of functions can be used to run another program.

Listing 17.69: **os_exec_example.py**

```
import os

child_pid = os.fork()
if child_pid:
    os.waitpid(child_pid, 0)
else:
    os.execlp('pwd', 'pwd', '-P')
```

When a program is run by exec(), the code from that program replaces the code from the existing process.

```
$ python3 os_exec_example.py

.../pymotw-3/source/os
```

Many variations of exec() can be applied, depending on the form in which the arguments are available, whether the path and environment of the parent process should be copied to the child, and other factors. For all variations, the first argument is a path or filename, and the remaining arguments control how that program runs. The arguments either are passed in via the command line or override the process "environment" (see os.environ and os.getenv). Refer to the library documentation for complete details.

17.3.11   Waiting for Child Processes

Many computationally intensive programs use multiple processes to work around the threading limitations of Python and the global interpreter lock. When starting several processes to run separate tasks, the master will need to wait for one or more of them to finish before starting new ones, so as to avoid overloading the server. To do so, wait() and related functions can be used, depending on the cirumstances.

When it does not matter which child process might exit first, use wait(). It returns as soon as any child process exits.

Listing 17.70: **os_wait_example.py**

```
import os
import sys
import time

for i in range(2):
    print('PARENT {}: Forking {}'.format(os.getpid(), i))
    worker_pid = os.fork()
    if not worker_pid:
        print('WORKER {}: Starting'.format(i))
        time.sleep(2 + i)
        print('WORKER {}: Finishing'.format(i))
        sys.exit(i)

for i in range(2):
    print('PARENT: Waiting for {}'.format(i))
    done = os.wait()
    print('PARENT: Child done:', done)
```

The return value from wait() is a tuple containing the process ID and the exit status combined into a 16-bit value. The low byte is the number of the signal that killed the process, and the high byte is the status code returned by the process when it exited.

```
$ python3 -u os_wait_example.py

PARENT 29202: Forking 0
PARENT 29202: Forking 1
PARENT: Waiting for 0
WORKER 0: Starting
WORKER 1: Starting
WORKER 0: Finishing
PARENT: Child done: (29203, 0)
PARENT: Waiting for 1
WORKER 1: Finishing
PARENT: Child done: (29204, 256)
```

To wait for a specific process, use waitpid().

Listing 17.71: **os_waitpid_example.py**

```
import os
import sys
import time

workers = []
```

```
    for i in range(2):
        print('PARENT {}: Forking {}'.format(os.getpid(), i))
        worker_pid = os.fork()
        if not worker_pid:
            print('WORKER {}: Starting'.format(i))
            time.sleep(2 + i)
            print('WORKER {}: Finishing'.format(i))
            sys.exit(i)
        workers.append(worker_pid)

    for pid in workers:
        print('PARENT: Waiting for {}'.format(pid))
        done = os.waitpid(pid, 0)
        print('PARENT: Child done:', done)
```

Pass the process ID of the target process, and `waitpid()` blocks until that process exits.

```
$ python3 -u os_waitpid_example.py

PARENT 29211: Forking 0
PARENT 29211: Forking 1
PARENT: Waiting for 29212
WORKER 0: Starting
WORKER 1: Starting
WORKER 0: Finishing
PARENT: Child done: (29212, 0)
PARENT: Waiting for 29213
WORKER 1: Finishing
PARENT: Child done: (29213, 256)
```

`wait3()` and `wait4()` work in a similar manner, but return more detailed information about the child process with the process ID, exit status, and resource usage.

17.3.12   Spawning New Processes

As a convenience, the `spawn()` family of functions handles the `fork()` and `exec()` actions in a single statement.

Listing 17.72: os_spawn_example.py

```
import os

os.spawnlp(os.P_WAIT, 'pwd', 'pwd', '-P')
```

The first argument is a mode indicating whether the function should wait for the process to finish before returning. This example waits. Use `P_NOWAIT` to let the other process start, but then resume in the current process.

```
$ python3 os_spawn_example.py

.../pymotw-3/source/os
```

17.3.13   Operating System Error Codes

Error codes defined by the operating system and managed in the `errno` module can be translated to message strings using `strerror()`.

Listing 17.73: os_strerror.py

```
import errno
import os

for num in [errno.ENOENT, errno.EINTR, errno.EBUSY]:
    name = errno.errorcode[num]
    print('[{num:>2}] {name:<6}: {msg}'.format(
        name=name, num=num, msg=os.strerror(num)))
```

The following output shows the messages associated with some error codes that are frequently encountered.

```
$ python3 os_strerror.py

[ 2] ENOENT: No such file or directory
[ 4] EINTR : Interrupted system call
[16] EBUSY : Resource busy
```

TIP

Related Reading

- Standard library documentation for os.[22]
- Python 2 to 3 porting notes for os (page 1360).
- signal (page 553): The section on the signal module covers signal handling techniques in more detail.
- subprocess (page 535): The subprocess module supersedes os.popen().
- multiprocessing (page 586): The multiprocessing module makes working with extra processes easier.
- tempfile (page 330): The tempfile module for working with temporary files.
- Section 6.7.3, "Working with Directory Trees" (page 342): The shutil (page 337) module also includes functions for working with directory trees.

---

[22] https://docs.python.org/3.5/library/os.html

- Speaking UNIX, Part 8[23]: Learn how UNIX multitasks.
- Wikipedia: Standard streams[24]: For more discussion of stdin, stdout, and stderr.
- Delve into Unix Process Creation[25]: Explains the life cycle of a Unix process.
- *Advanced Programming in the UNIX Environment* by W. Richard Stevens and Stephen A. Rago. Addison-Wesley, 2005. ISBN-10: 0201433079. This book covers working with multiple processes, such as handling signals, closing duplicated file descriptors, and more.

17.4   platform: System Version Information

Although Python is often used as a cross-platform language, it is occasionally necessary to know which sort of system a program is running on. Build tools need that information, but an application might also know that some of the libraries or external commands it uses have different interfaces on different operating systems. For example, a tool to manage the network configuration of an operating system can define a portable representation of network interfaces, aliases, IP addresses, and other OS-specific information. When the time comes to edit the configuration files, however, it must know more about the host so it can use the correct operating system configuration commands and files. The platform module includes the tools for learning about the interpreter, operating system, and hardware platform where a program is running.

NOTE

The example output in this section was generated on three systems: a Mac mini running OS X 10.11.6, a Dell PC running Ubuntu Linux 14.04, and a VirtualBox VM running Windows 10. Python was installed on the OS X and Windows systems using the precompiled installers from python.org. The Linux system is running a version in a system package.

17.4.1   Interpreter

Four functions are used to obtain information about the current Python interpreter. python_version() and python_version_tuple() return different forms of the interpreter version with major, minor, and patch-level components. python_compiler() reports on the compiler used to build the interpreter. python_build() gives a version string for the build of the interpreter.

Listing 17.74: platform_python.py

```
import platform

print('Version        :', platform.python_version())
```

---
[23] www.ibm.com/developerworks/aix/library/au-speakingunix8/index.html
[24] https://en.wikipedia.org/wiki/Standard_streams
[25] www.ibm.com/developerworks/aix/library/au-unixprocess.html

```
print('Version tuple:', platform.python_version_tuple())
print('Compiler    :', platform.python_compiler())
print('Build       :', platform.python_build())
```

OS X:

```
$ python3 platform_python.py

Version      : 3.5.2
Version tuple: ('3', '5', '2')
Compiler     : GCC 4.2.1 (Apple Inc. build 5666) (dot 3)
Build        : ('v3.5.2:4def2a2901a5', 'Jun 26 2016 10:47:25')
```

Linux:

```
$ python3 platform_python.py

Version      : 3.5.2
Version tuple: ('3', '5', '2')
Compiler     : GCC 4.8.4
Build        : ('default', 'Jul 17 2016 00:00:00')
```

Windows:

```
C:\>Desktop\platform_python.py

Version      : 3.5.1
Version tuple: ('3', '5', '1')
Compiler     : MSC v.1900 64 bit (AMD64)
Build        : ('v3.5.1:37a07cee5969', 'Dec  6 2015 01:54:25')
```

17.4.2 Platform

The platform() function returns a string containing a general-purpose platform identifier. This function accepts two optional boolean arguments. If aliased is True, the names in the return value are converted from formal names to their more common forms. When terse is True, a minimal value with some parts dropped is returned instead of the full string.

Listing 17.75: platform_platform.py

```
import platform

print('Normal :', platform.platform())
print('Aliased:', platform.platform(aliased=True))
print('Terse  :', platform.platform(terse=True))
```

OS X:

```
$ python3 platform_platform.py

Normal : Darwin-15.6.0-x86_64-i386-64bit
Aliased: Darwin-15.6.0-x86_64-i386-64bit
Terse   : Darwin-15.6.0
```

Linux:

```
$ python3 platform_platform.py

Normal : Linux-3.13.0-55-generic-x86_64-with-Ubuntu-14.04-trusty
Aliased: Linux-3.13.0-55-generic-x86_64-with-Ubuntu-14.04-trusty
Terse   : Linux-3.13.0-55-generic-x86_64-with-glibc2.9
```

Windows:

```
C:\>platform_platform.py

Normal : Windows-10-10.0.10240-SP0
Aliased: Windows-10-10.0.10240-SP0
Terse   : Windows-10
```

17.4.3 Operating System and Hardware Information

More detailed information about the operating system and hardware on which the interpreter is running can be retrieved as well. uname() returns a tuple containing the system, node, release, version, machine, and processor values. Individual values can be accessed through functions of the same names, listed in Table 17.3.

Listing 17.76: platform_os_info.py

```
import platform

print('uname:', platform.uname())

print()
```

Table 17.3: Platform Information Functions

Function	Return Value
system()	Operating system name
node()	Hostname of the server, not fully qualified
release()	Operating system release number
version()	More detailed system version
machine()	A hardware-type identifier, such as 'i386'
processor()	A real identifier for the processor (the same value as machine() in many cases)

```
print('system    :', platform.system())
print('node      :', platform.node())
print('release   :', platform.release())
print('version   :', platform.version())
print('machine   :', platform.machine())
print('processor:', platform.processor())
```

OS X:

```
$ python3 platform_os_info.py

uname: uname_result(system='Darwin', node='hubert.local',
release='15.6.0', version='Darwin Kernel Version 15.6.0: Thu Jun
23 18:25:34 PDT 2016; root:xnu-3248.60.10~1/RELEASE_X86_64',
machine='x86_64', processor='i386')

system    : Darwin
node      : hubert.local
release   : 15.6.0
version   : Darwin Kernel Version 15.6.0: Thu Jun 23 18:25:34 PDT
2016; root:xnu-3248.60.10~1/RELEASE_X86_64
machine   : x86_64
processor: i386
```

Linux:

```
$ python3 platform_os_info.py

uname: uname_result(system='Linux', node='apu',
release='3.13.0-55-generic', version='#94-Ubuntu SMP Thu Jun 18
00:27:10 UTC 2015', machine='x86_64', processor='x86_64')

system    : Linux
node      : apu
release   : 3.13.0-55-generic
version   : #94-Ubuntu SMP Thu Jun 18 00:27:10 UTC 2015
machine   : x86_64
processor: x86_64
```

Windows:

```
C:\>Desktop\platform_os_info.py

uname: uname_result(system='Windows', node='IE11WIN10',
release='10', version='10.0.10240', machine='AMD64',
processor='Intel64 Family 6 Model 70 Stepping 1, GenuineIntel')

system    : Windows
```

```
node     : IE11WIN10
release  : 10
version  : 10.0.10240
machine  : AMD64
processor: Intel64 Family 6 Model 70 Stepping 1, GenuineIntel
```

17.4.4   Executable Architecture

Individual program architecture information can be probed using the architecture() function. The first argument is the path to an executable program (defaulting to sys.executable, the Python interpreter). The return value is a tuple containing the bit architecture and the linkage format used.

Listing 17.77: **platform_architecture.py**

```
import platform

print('interpreter:', platform.architecture())
print('/bin/ls    :', platform.architecture('/bin/ls'))
```

OS X:

```
$ python3 platform_architecture.py

interpreter: ('64bit', '')
/bin/ls    : ('64bit', '')
```

Linux:

```
$ python3 platform_architecture.py

interpreter: ('64bit', 'ELF')
/bin/ls    : ('64bit', 'ELF')
```

Windows:

```
C:\>Desktop\platform_architecture.py

interpreter: ('64bit', 'WindowsPE')
/bin/ls    : ('64bit', '')
```

TIP

Related Reading

- Standard library documentation for platform.[26]
- Python 2 to 3 porting notes for platform (page 1362).

---

[26] https://docs.python.org/3.5/library/platform.html

17.5   resource: System Resource Management

The functions in resource probe the current system resources consumed by a process, and place limits on them to control how much load a program can impose on a system.

17.5.1   Current Usage

Use getrusage() to probe the resources used by the current process and/or its children. The return value is a data structure containing several resource metrics based on the current state of the system.

NOTE

Not all of the resource values collected are displayed here. Refer to the standard library documentation for resource for a more complete list.

Listing 17.78: **resource_getrusage.py**

```python
import resource
import time

RESOURCES = [
    ('ru_utime', 'User time'),
    ('ru_stime', 'System time'),
    ('ru_maxrss', 'Max. Resident Set Size'),
    ('ru_ixrss', 'Shared Memory Size'),
    ('ru_idrss', 'Unshared Memory Size'),
    ('ru_isrss', 'Stack Size'),
    ('ru_inblock', 'Block inputs'),
    ('ru_oublock', 'Block outputs'),
]

usage = resource.getrusage(resource.RUSAGE_SELF)

for name, desc in RESOURCES:
    print('{:<25} ({:<10}) = {}'.format(
        desc, name, getattr(usage, name)))
```

Because the test program is extremely simple, it does not use very many resources.

```
$ python3 resource_getrusage.py

User time                 (ru_utime  ) = 0.021876
System time               (ru_stime  ) = 0.0067269999999999995
Max. Resident Set Size    (ru_maxrss ) = 6479872
Shared Memory Size        (ru_ixrss  ) = 0
Unshared Memory Size      (ru_idrss  ) = 0
```

```
Stack Size              (ru_isrss  ) = 0
Block inputs            (ru_inblock) = 0
Block outputs           (ru_oublock) = 0
```

17.5.2 Resource Limits

Apart from determining the current actual usage, it is possible to check the *limits* imposed on the application, and then change them.

Listing 17.79: resource_getrlimit.py

```
import resource

LIMITS = [
    ('RLIMIT_CORE', 'core file size'),
    ('RLIMIT_CPU', 'CPU time'),
    ('RLIMIT_FSIZE', 'file size'),
    ('RLIMIT_DATA', 'heap size'),
    ('RLIMIT_STACK', 'stack size'),
    ('RLIMIT_RSS', 'resident set size'),
    ('RLIMIT_NPROC', 'number of processes'),
    ('RLIMIT_NOFILE', 'number of open files'),
    ('RLIMIT_MEMLOCK', 'lockable memory address'),
]

print('Resource limits (soft/hard):')
for name, desc in LIMITS:
    limit_num = getattr(resource, name)
    soft, hard = resource.getrlimit(limit_num)
    print('{:<23} {}/{}'.format(desc, soft, hard))
```

The return value for each limit is a tuple containing the *soft* limit imposed by the current configuration and the *hard* limit imposed by the operating system.

```
$ python3 resource_getrlimit.py

Resource limits (soft/hard):
core file size          0/9223372036854775807
CPU time                9223372036854775807/9223372036854775807
file size               9223372036854775807/9223372036854775807
heap size               9223372036854775807/9223372036854775807
stack size              8388608/67104768
resident set size       9223372036854775807/9223372036854775807
number of processes     709/1064
number of open files    7168/9223372036854775807
lockable memory address 9223372036854775807/9223372036854775807
```

To change the limits, use setrlimit().

Listing 17.80: **resource_setrlimit_nofile.py**

```python
import resource
import os

soft, hard = resource.getrlimit(resource.RLIMIT_NOFILE)
print('Soft limit starts as  :', soft)

resource.setrlimit(resource.RLIMIT_NOFILE, (4, hard))

soft, hard = resource.getrlimit(resource.RLIMIT_NOFILE)
print('Soft limit changed to :', soft)

random = open('/dev/random', 'r')
print('random has fd =', random.fileno())
try:
    null = open('/dev/null', 'w')
except IOError as err:
    print(err)
else:
    print('null has fd =', null.fileno())
```

This example uses `RLIMIT_NOFILE` to control the number of open files allowed, changing it to a smaller soft limit than the default.

```
$ python3 resource_setrlimit_nofile.py

Soft limit starts as  : 7168
Soft limit changed to : 4
random has fd = 3
[Errno 24] Too many open files: '/dev/null'
```

It can also be useful to limit the amount of CPU time a process should consume, to avoid using too much. When the process runs past the allotted amount of time, it receives a `SIGXCPU` signal.

Listing 17.81: **resource_setrlimit_cpu.py**

```python
import resource
import sys
import signal
import time


# Set up a signal handler to notify us
# when we run out of time.
def time_expired(n, stack):
    print('EXPIRED :', time.ctime())
    raise SystemExit('(time ran out)')
```

```
signal.signal(signal.SIGXCPU, time_expired)

# Adjust the CPU time limit.
soft, hard = resource.getrlimit(resource.RLIMIT_CPU)
print('Soft limit starts as  :', soft)

resource.setrlimit(resource.RLIMIT_CPU, (1, hard))

soft, hard = resource.getrlimit(resource.RLIMIT_CPU)
print('Soft limit changed to :', soft)
print()

# Consume some CPU time in a pointless exercise.
print('Starting:', time.ctime())
for i in range(200000):
    for i in range(200000):
        v = i * i

# We should never make it this far.
print('Exiting :', time.ctime())
```

Under normal circumstances, the signal handler should flush all open files and close them, but in this case it just prints a message and exits.

```
$ python3 resource_setrlimit_cpu.py

Soft limit starts as  : 9223372036854775807
Soft limit changed to : 1

Starting: Sun Aug 21 19:18:51 2016
EXPIRED : Sun Aug 21 19:18:52 2016
(time ran out)
```

TIP

Related Reading

- Standard library documentation for resource.[27]
- signal (page 553): For details on registering signal handlers.

17.6　gc: Garbage Collector

gc exposes the underlying memory management mechanism of Python—namely, the automatic garbage collector. The module includes functions for controlling how the collector

---

[27] https://docs.python.org/3.5/library/resource.html

operates and examining the objects known to the system, which are either pending collection
or stuck in reference cycles and unable to be freed.

17.6.1   Tracing References

With gc, the incoming and outgoing references between objects can be used to find cycles in
complex data structures. If a data structure is known to have a cycle, custom code can be
used to examine its properties. If the cycle appears in unknown code, the get_referents()
and get_referrers() functions can be used to build generic debugging tools.

For example, get_referents() shows the objects *referred to* by the input arguments.

Listing 17.82: gc_get_referents.py

```python
import gc
import pprint


class Graph:

    def __init__(self, name):
        self.name = name
        self.next = None

    def set_next(self, next):
        print('Linking nodes {}.next = {}'.format(self, next))
        self.next = next

    def __repr__(self):
        return '{}({})'.format(
            self.__class__.__name__, self.name)


# Construct a graph cycle.
one = Graph('one')
two = Graph('two')
three = Graph('three')
one.set_next(two)
two.set_next(three)
three.set_next(one)

print()
print('three refers to:')
for r in gc.get_referents(three):
    pprint.pprint(r)
```

In this case, the Graph instance three holds references to its instance dictionary (in the
__dict__ attribute) and its class.

```
$ python3 gc_get_referents.py

Linking nodes Graph(one).next = Graph(two)
```

```
Linking nodes Graph(two).next = Graph(three)
Linking nodes Graph(three).next = Graph(one)

three refers to:
{'name': 'three', 'next': Graph(one)}
<class '__main__.Graph'>
```

The next example uses a `Queue` to perform a breadth-first traversal of all of the object references looking for cycles. The items inserted into the queue are tuples containing the reference chain so far plus the next object to examine. The inspection starts with `three`, and looks at everything it refers to. Skipping classes means that their methods, modules, and other components are not examined.

Listing 17.83: gc_get_referents_cycles.py

```python
import gc
import pprint
import queue


class Graph:

    def __init__(self, name):
        self.name = name
        self.next = None

    def set_next(self, next):
        print('Linking nodes {}.next = {}'.format(self, next))
        self.next = next

    def __repr__(self):
        return '{}({})'.format(
            self.__class__.__name__, self.name)


# Construct a graph cycle.
one = Graph('one')
two = Graph('two')
three = Graph('three')
one.set_next(two)
two.set_next(three)
three.set_next(one)

print()

seen = set()
to_process = queue.Queue()

# Start with an empty object chain and Graph three.
```

```
    to_process.put(([], three))

    # Look for cycles, building the object chain for each object
    # found in the queue so the full cycle can be printed at the
    # end.
    while not to_process.empty():
        chain, next = to_process.get()
        chain = chain[:]
        chain.append(next)
        print('Examining:', repr(next))
        seen.add(id(next))
        for r in gc.get_referents(next):
            if isinstance(r, str) or isinstance(r, type):
                # Ignore strings and classes.
                pass
            elif id(r) in seen:
                print()
                print('Found a cycle to {}:'.format(r))
                for i, link in enumerate(chain):
                    print('  {}: '.format(i), end=' ')
                    pprint.pprint(link)
            else:
                to_process.put((chain, r))
```

The cycle in the nodes is easily found by watching for objects that have already been processed. So that references to those objects will not be collected, their id() values are cached in a set. The dictionary objects found in the cycle are the __dict__ values for the Graph instances, and hold their instance attributes.

```
$ python3 gc_get_referents_cycles.py

Linking nodes Graph(one).next = Graph(two)
Linking nodes Graph(two).next = Graph(three)
Linking nodes Graph(three).next = Graph(one)

Examining: Graph(three)
Examining: {'next': Graph(one), 'name': 'three'}
Examining: Graph(one)
Examining: {'next': Graph(two), 'name': 'one'}
Examining: Graph(two)
Examining: {'next': Graph(three), 'name': 'two'}

Found a cycle to Graph(three):
  0:  Graph(three)
  1:  {'name': 'three', 'next': Graph(one)}
  2:  Graph(one)
  3:  {'name': 'one', 'next': Graph(two)}
  4:  Graph(two)
  5:  {'name': 'two', 'next': Graph(three)}
```

17.6.2   Forcing Garbage Collection

Although the garbage collector runs automatically as the interpreter executes a program, it can be triggered to run at a specific time when many objects need to be freed or when little work is happening and the collector will not hurt application performance. To trigger garbage collection, use collect().

Listing 17.84: gc_collect.py

```
import gc
import pprint


class Graph:

    def __init__(self, name):
        self.name = name
        self.next = None

    def set_next(self, next):
        print('Linking nodes {}.next = {}'.format(self, next))
        self.next = next

    def __repr__(self):
        return '{}({})'.format(
            self.__class__.__name__, self.name)


# Construct a graph cycle.
one = Graph('one')
two = Graph('two')
three = Graph('three')
one.set_next(two)
two.set_next(three)
three.set_next(one)

# Remove references to the graph nodes in this module's namespace.
one = two = three = None

# Show the effect of garbage collection.
for i in range(2):
    print('\nCollecting {} ...'.format(i))
    n = gc.collect()
    print('Unreachable objects:', n)
    print('Remaining Garbage:', end=' ')
    pprint.pprint(gc.garbage)
```

In this example, the cycle is cleared as soon as collection runs the first time, since nothing refers to the Graph nodes except themselves. collect() returns the number of "unreachable" objects it found. In this case, the value is 6, representing the three objects with their instance attribute dictionaries.

```
$ python3 gc_collect.py

Linking nodes Graph(one).next = Graph(two)
Linking nodes Graph(two).next = Graph(three)
Linking nodes Graph(three).next = Graph(one)

Collecting 0 ...
Unreachable objects: 34
Remaining Garbage: []

Collecting 1 ...
Unreachable objects: 0
Remaining Garbage: []
```

17.6.3   Finding References to Objects That Cannot Be Collected

Looking for the object holding a reference to another object is a little trickier than seeing what an object references. Because the code asking about the reference needs to hold a reference itself, some of the referrers need to be ignored. The next example creates a graph cycle, then works through the Graph instances and removes the reference in the "parent" node.

Listing 17.85: **gc_get_referrers.py**

```
import gc
import pprint


class Graph:

    def __init__(self, name):
        self.name = name
        self.next = None

    def set_next(self, next):
        print('Linking nodes {}.next = {}'.format(self, next))
        self.next = next

    def __repr__(self):
        return '{}({})'.format(
            self.__class__.__name__, self.name)

    def __del__(self):
        print('{}.__del__()'.format(self))


# Construct a graph cycle.
```

```
one = Graph('one')
two = Graph('two')
three = Graph('three')
one.set_next(two)
two.set_next(three)
three.set_next(one)

# Collecting now keeps the objects as uncollectable,
# but not garbage.
print()
print('Collecting...')
n = gc.collect()
print('Unreachable objects:', n)
print('Remaining Garbage:', end=' ')
pprint.pprint(gc.garbage)

# Ignore references from local variables in this module, global
# variables, and from the garbage collector's bookkeeping.
REFERRERS_TO_IGNORE = [locals(), globals(), gc.garbage]


def find_referring_graphs(obj):
    print('Looking for references to {!r}'.format(obj))
    referrers = (r for r in gc.get_referrers(obj)
                 if r not in REFERRERS_TO_IGNORE)
    for ref in referrers:
        if isinstance(ref, Graph):
            # A graph node
            yield ref
        elif isinstance(ref, dict):
            # An instance or other namespace dictionary
            for parent in find_referring_graphs(ref):
                yield parent


# Look for objects that refer to the objects in the graph.
print()
print('Clearing referrers:')
for obj in [one, two, three]:
    for ref in find_referring_graphs(obj):
        print('Found referrer:', ref)
        ref.set_next(None)
        del ref  # Remove reference so the node can be deleted.
    del obj  # Remove reference so the node can be deleted.

# Clear references held by gc.garbage.
print()
print('Clearing gc.garbage:')
del gc.garbage[:]
```

```
# Everything should have been freed this time.
print()
print('Collecting...')
n = gc.collect()
print('Unreachable objects:', n)
print('Remaining Garbage:', end=' ')
pprint.pprint(gc.garbage)
```

This sort of logic is overkill if the cycles are understood. Nevertheless, for an unexplained cycle in data, using `get_referrers()` can expose the unexpected relationship.

```
$ python3 gc_get_referrers.py

Linking nodes Graph(one).next = Graph(two)
Linking nodes Graph(two).next = Graph(three)
Linking nodes Graph(three).next = Graph(one)

Collecting...
Unreachable objects: 28
Remaining Garbage: []

Clearing referrers:
Looking for references to Graph(one)
Looking for references to {'next': Graph(one), 'name': 'three'}
Found referrer: Graph(three)
Linking nodes Graph(three).next = None
Looking for references to Graph(two)
Looking for references to {'next': Graph(two), 'name': 'one'}
Found referrer: Graph(one)
Linking nodes Graph(one).next = None
Looking for references to Graph(three)
Looking for references to {'next': Graph(three), 'name': 'two'}
Found referrer: Graph(two)
Linking nodes Graph(two).next = None

Clearing gc.garbage:

Collecting...
Unreachable objects: 0
Remaining Garbage: []
Graph(one).__del__()
Graph(two).__del__()
Graph(three).__del__()
```

17.6.4 Collection Thresholds and Generations

The garbage collector maintains three lists of objects that it sees as it runs—one for each "generation" tracked by the collector. As objects are examined in each generation, either

they are collected or else they age into subsequent generations until they finally reach the
stage where they are kept permanently.

The collector routines can be tuned to occur at different frequencies based on the difference between the number of object allocations and deallocations between runs. When the
number of allocations minus the number of deallocations is greater than the threshold for
the generation, the garbage collector runs. The current thresholds can be examined with
get_threshold().

Listing 17.86: gc_get_threshold.py

```
import gc

print(gc.get_threshold())
```

The return value is a tuple with the threshold for each generation.

```
$ python3 gc_get_threshold.py

(700, 10, 10)
```

To change the thresholds, use set_threshold(). The next example program uses a
command-line argument to set the threshold for generation 0, then allocates a series of
objects.

Listing 17.87: gc_threshold.py

```
import gc
import pprint
import sys

try:
    threshold = int(sys.argv[1])
except (IndexError, ValueError, TypeError):
    print('Missing or invalid threshold, using default')
    threshold = 5


class MyObj:

    def __init__(self, name):
        self.name = name
        print('Created', self.name)


gc.set_debug(gc.DEBUG_STATS)

gc.set_threshold(threshold, 1, 1)
print('Thresholds:', gc.get_threshold())
```

```
print('Clear the collector by forcing a run')
gc.collect()
print()

print('Creating objects')
objs = []
for i in range(10):
    objs.append(MyObj(i))
print('Exiting')

# Turn off debugging.
gc.set_debug(0)
```

Different threshold values introduce the garbage collection sweeps at different times. These values are shown here because debugging is enabled.

```
$ python3 -u gc_threshold.py 5

gc: collecting generation 1...
gc: objects in each generation: 240 1439 4709
gc: done, 0.0013s elapsed
Thresholds: (5, 1, 1)
Clear the collector by forcing a run
gc: collecting generation 2...
gc: objects in each generation: 1 0 6282
gc: done, 0.0025s elapsed

gc: collecting generation 0...
gc: objects in each generation: 5 0 6275
gc: done, 0.0000s elapsed
Creating objects
gc: collecting generation 0...
gc: objects in each generation: 8 0 6275
gc: done, 0.0000s elapsed
Created 0
Created 1
Created 2
gc: collecting generation 1...
gc: objects in each generation: 9 2 6275
gc: done, 0.0000s elapsed
Created 3
Created 4
Created 5
gc: collecting generation 0...
gc: objects in each generation: 9 0 6280
gc: done, 0.0000s elapsed
Created 6
Created 7
```

```
Created 8
gc: collecting generation 0...
gc: objects in each generation: 9 3 6280
gc: done, 0.0000s elapsed
Created 9
Exiting
```

A smaller threshold causes the sweeps to run more frequently.

```
$ python3 -u gc_threshold.py 2

gc: collecting generation 1...
gc: objects in each generation: 240 1439 4709
gc: done, 0.0003s elapsed
Thresholds: (2, 1, 1)
Clear the collector by forcing a run
gc: collecting generation 2...
gc: objects in each generation: 1 0 6282
gc: done, 0.0010s elapsed
gc: collecting generation 0...
gc: objects in each generation: 3 0 6275
gc: done, 0.0000s elapsed

Creating objects
gc: collecting generation 0...
gc: objects in each generation: 6 0 6275
gc: done, 0.0000s elapsed
gc: collecting generation 1...
gc: objects in each generation: 3 4 6275
gc: done, 0.0000s elapsed
Created 0
Created 1
gc: collecting generation 0...
gc: objects in each generation: 4 0 6277
gc: done, 0.0000s elapsed
Created 2
gc: collecting generation 0...
gc: objects in each generation: 8 1 6277
gc: done, 0.0000s elapsed
Created 3
Created 4
gc: collecting generation 1...
gc: objects in each generation: 4 3 6277
gc: done, 0.0000s elapsed
Created 5
gc: collecting generation 0...
gc: objects in each generation: 8 0 6281
gc: done, 0.0000s elapsed
```

```
Created 6
Created 7
gc: collecting generation 0...
gc: objects in each generation: 4 2 6281
gc: done, 0.0000s elapsed
Created 8
gc: collecting generation 1...
gc: objects in each generation: 8 3 6281
gc: done, 0.0000s elapsed
Created 9
Exiting
```

17.6.5 Debugging

Debugging memory leaks can be challenging. gc includes several options to expose the inner workings of code to make this job easier. The options are bit-flags that are meant to be combined and passed to set_debug() to configure the garbage collector while the program is running. Debugging information is printed to sys.stderr.

The DEBUG_STATS flag turns on statistics reporting, causing the garbage collector to report when it is running, how many objects were tracked for each generation, and how much time it took to perform the sweep.

Listing 17.88: gc_debug_stats.py

```
import gc

gc.set_debug(gc.DEBUG_STATS)

gc.collect()
print('Exiting')
```

The following output shows two separate runs of the collector: It runs once when it is invoked explicitly, and a second time when the interpreter exits.

```
$ python3 gc_debug_stats.py

gc: collecting generation 2...
gc: objects in each generation: 123 1063 4711
gc: done, 0.0008s elapsed
Exiting
gc: collecting generation 2...
gc: objects in each generation: 1 0 5880
gc: done, 0.0007s elapsed
gc: collecting generation 2...
gc: objects in each generation: 99 0 5688
gc: done, 2114 unreachable, 0 uncollectable, 0.0011s elapsed
gc: collecting generation 2...
```

```
gc: objects in each generation: 0 0 3118
gc: done, 292 unreachable, 0 uncollectable, 0.0003s elapsed
```

Enabling `DEBUG_COLLECTABLE` and `DEBUG_UNCOLLECTABLE` causes the collector to report on whether each object it examines can or cannot be collected. If seeing the objects that cannot be collected is not enough information to understand where data is being retained, enable `DEBUG_SAVEALL` to cause gc to preserve all objects it finds without any references in the garbage list.

Listing 17.89: **gc_debug_saveall.py**

```python
import gc

flags = (gc.DEBUG_COLLECTABLE |
         gc.DEBUG_UNCOLLECTABLE |
         gc.DEBUG_SAVEALL
         )

gc.set_debug(flags)


class Graph:

    def __init__(self, name):
        self.name = name
        self.next = None

    def set_next(self, next):
        self.next = next

    def __repr__(self):
        return '{}({})'.format(
            self.__class__.__name__, self.name)


class CleanupGraph(Graph):

    def __del__(self):
        print('{}.__del__()'.format(self))


# Construct a graph cycle.
one = Graph('one')
two = Graph('two')
one.set_next(two)
two.set_next(one)

# Construct another node that stands on its own.
three = CleanupGraph('three')
```

```
# Construct a graph cycle with a finalizer.
four = CleanupGraph('four')
five = CleanupGraph('five')
four.set_next(five)
five.set_next(four)

# Remove references to the graph nodes in this module's namespace.
one = two = three = four = five = None

# Force a sweep.
print('Collecting')
gc.collect()
print('Done')

# Report on what was left.
for o in gc.garbage:
    if isinstance(o, Graph):
        print('Retained: {} 0x{:x}'.format(o, id(o)))

# Reset the debug flags before exiting to avoid dumping a lot
# of extra information and making the example output more
# confusing.
gc.set_debug(0)
```

This code allows the objects to be examined after garbage collection, which is helpful if, for example, the constructor cannot be changed to print the object ID when each object is created.

```
$ python3 -u gc_debug_saveall.py

CleanupGraph(three).__del__()
Collecting
gc: collectable <Graph 0x101be7240>
gc: collectable <Graph 0x101be72e8>
gc: collectable <dict 0x101994108>
gc: collectable <dict 0x101994148>
gc: collectable <CleanupGraph 0x101be73c8>
gc: collectable <CleanupGraph 0x101be7400>
gc: collectable <dict 0x101bee548>
gc: collectable <dict 0x101bee488>
CleanupGraph(four).__del__()
CleanupGraph(five).__del__()
Done
Retained: Graph(one) 0x101be7240
Retained: Graph(two) 0x101be72e8
Retained: CleanupGraph(four) 0x101be73c8
Retained: CleanupGraph(five) 0x101be7400
```

For simplicity, DEBUG_LEAK is defined as a combination of all of the other options.

Listing 17.90: gc_debug_leak.py

```python
import gc

flags = gc.DEBUG_LEAK

gc.set_debug(flags)


class Graph:

    def __init__(self, name):
        self.name = name
        self.next = None

    def set_next(self, next):
        self.next = next

    def __repr__(self):
        return '{}({})'.format(
            self.__class__.__name__, self.name)


class CleanupGraph(Graph):

    def __del__(self):
        print('{}.__del__()'.format(self))


# Construct a graph cycle.
one = Graph('one')
two = Graph('two')
one.set_next(two)
two.set_next(one)

# Construct another node that stands on its own.
three = CleanupGraph('three')

# Construct a graph cycle with a finalizer.
four = CleanupGraph('four')
five = CleanupGraph('five')
four.set_next(five)
five.set_next(four)

# Remove references to the graph nodes in this module's namespace.
one = two = three = four = five = None

# Force a sweep.
```

```
print('Collecting')
gc.collect()
print('Done')

# Report on what was left.
for o in gc.garbage:
    if isinstance(o, Graph):
        print('Retained: {} 0x{:x}'.format(o, id(o)))

# Reset the debug flags before exiting to avoid dumping a lot
# of extra information and making the example output more
# confusing.
gc.set_debug(0)
```

Keep in mind that because DEBUG_SAVEALL is enabled by DEBUG_LEAK, even the unreferenced objects that would normally have been collected and deleted during garbage collection are retained.

```
$ python3 -u gc_debug_leak.py

CleanupGraph(three).__del__()
Collecting
gc: collectable <Graph 0x1013e7240>
gc: collectable <Graph 0x1013e72e8>
gc: collectable <dict 0x101194108>
gc: collectable <dict 0x101194148>
gc: collectable <CleanupGraph 0x1013e73c8>
gc: collectable <CleanupGraph 0x1013e7400>
gc: collectable <dict 0x1013ee548>
gc: collectable <dict 0x1013ee488>
CleanupGraph(four).__del__()
CleanupGraph(five).__del__()
Done
Retained: Graph(one) 0x1013e7240
Retained: Graph(two) 0x1013e72e8
Retained: CleanupGraph(four) 0x1013e73c8
Retained: CleanupGraph(five) 0x1013e7400
```

TIP

Related Reading

- Standard library documentation for gc.[28]
- Python 2 to 3 porting notes for gc (page 1358).
- weakref (page 121): The weakref module provides a way to create references to objects without increasing their reference count, so they can still be garbage collected.

---

[28] https://docs.python.org/3.5/library/gc.html

- Supporting Cyclic Garbage Collection[29]: Background material from Python's C API documentation.

- How does Python manage memory?[30]: An article on Python memory management by Fredrik Lundh.

17.7   sysconfig: Interpreter Compile-Time Configuration

The features of sysconfig have been extracted from distutils to create a stand-alone module. This module includes functions for determining the settings used to compile and install the current interpreter.

17.7.1   Configuration Variables

Access to the build-time configuration settings is provided through two functions: get_config_vars() and get_config_var(). get_config_vars() returns a dictionary mapping the configuration variable names to values.

Listing 17.91: sysconfig_get_config_vars.py

```
import sysconfig

config_values = sysconfig.get_config_vars()
print('Found {} configuration settings'.format(
    len(config_values.keys())))

print('\nSome highlights:\n')

print(' Installation prefixes:')
print('  prefix={prefix}'.format(**config_values))
print('  exec_prefix={exec_prefix}'.format(**config_values))

print('\n Version info:')
print('  py_version={py_version}'.format(**config_values))
print('  py_version_short={py_version_short}'.format(
    **config_values))
print('  py_version_nodot={py_version_nodot}'.format(
    **config_values))

print('\n Base directories:')
print('  base={base}'.format(**config_values))
print('  platbase={platbase}'.format(**config_values))
print('  userbase={userbase}'.format(**config_values))
print('  srcdir={srcdir}'.format(**config_values))
```

---

[29] https://docs.python.org/3/c-api/gcsupport.html
[30] http://effbot.org/pyfaq/how-does-python-manage-memory.htm

```
print('\n Compiler and linker flags:')
print(' LDFLAGS={LDFLAGS}'.format(**config_values))
print(' BASECFLAGS={BASECFLAGS}'.format(**config_values))
print(' Py_ENABLE_SHARED={Py_ENABLE_SHARED}'.format(
    **config_values))
```

The level of detail available through the sysconfig API depends on the platform on which a program is running. On POSIX systems such as Linux and OS X, the Makefile used to build the interpreter and the config.h header file generated for the build are parsed, and all of the variables found within each file are available. On non-POSIX systems such as Windows, the settings are limited to a few paths, filename extensions, and version details.

```
$ python3 sysconfig_get_config_vars.py

Found 665 configuration settings

Some highlights:

 Installation prefixes:
  prefix=/Library/Frameworks/Python.framework/Versions/3.5
  exec_prefix=/Library/Frameworks/Python.framework/Versions/3.5

 Version info:
  py_version=3.5.2
  py_version_short=3.5
  py_version_nodot=35

 Base directories:
  base=/Users/dhellmann/Envs/pymotw35
  platbase=/Users/dhellmann/Envs/pymotw35
  userbase=/Users/dhellmann/Library/Python/3.5
  srcdir=/Library/Frameworks/Python.framework/Versions/3.5/lib/p
ython3.5/config-3.5m

 Compiler and linker flags:
  LDFLAGS=-arch i386 -arch x86_64  -g
  BASECFLAGS=-fno-strict-aliasing -Wsign-compare -fno-common
-dynamic
  Py_ENABLE_SHARED=0
```

Passing variable names to get_config_vars() changes the return value to a list, which is created by appending all of the values for those variables together.

Listing 17.92: sysconfig_get_config_vars_by_name.py

```
import sysconfig

bases = sysconfig.get_config_vars('base', 'platbase', 'userbase')
print('Base directories:')
```

```
for b in bases:
    print('  ', b)
```

This example builds a list of all of the installation base directories where modules can be found on the current system.

```
$ python3 sysconfig_get_config_vars_by_name.py

Base directories:
    /Users/dhellmann/Envs/pymotw35
    /Users/dhellmann/Envs/pymotw35
    /Users/dhellmann/Library/Python/3.5
```

When only a single configuration value is needed, use `get_config_var()` to retrieve it.

Listing 17.93: sysconfig_get_config_var.py

```
import sysconfig

print('User base directory:',
      sysconfig.get_config_var('userbase'))
print('Unknown variable   :',
      sysconfig.get_config_var('NoSuchVariable'))
```

If the variable is not found, `get_config_var()` returns None instead of raising an exception.

```
$ python3 sysconfig_get_config_var.py

User base directory: /Users/dhellmann/Library/Python/3.5
Unknown variable   : None
```

17.7.2 Installation Paths

sysconfig is primarily meant to be used by installation and packaging tools. As a result, while it provides access to general configuration settings such as the interpreter version, it is focused on the information needed to locate parts of the Python distribution currently installed on a system. The locations used for installing a package depend on the *scheme* used.

A scheme is a set of platform-specific default directories organized based on the platform's packaging standards and guidelines. Different schemes are used for installing into a site-wide location or a private directory owned by the user. The full set of schemes can be accessed with `get_scheme_names()`.

Listing 17.94: **sysconfig_get_scheme_names.py**

```
import sysconfig

for name in sysconfig.get_scheme_names():
    print(name)
```

There is no concept of a "current scheme" per se. Instead, the default scheme depends on the platform, and the actual scheme used depends on options given to the installation program. If the current system is running a POSIX-compliant operating system, the default is posix_prefix. Otherwise, the default is the operating system name, as defined by os.name.

```
$ python3 sysconfig_get_scheme_names.py

nt
nt_user
osx_framework_user
posix_home
posix_prefix
posix_user
```

Each scheme defines a set of paths used for installing packages. For a list of the path names, use get_path_names().

Listing 17.95: **sysconfig_get_path_names.py**

```
import sysconfig

for name in sysconfig.get_path_names():
    print(name)
```

Some of the paths may be the same for a given scheme, but installers should not make any assumptions about what the actual paths are. Each name has a particular semantic meaning, so the correct name should be used to find the path for a given file during installation. Refer to Table 17.4 for a complete list of the path names and their meanings.

Table 17.4: Path Names Used in sysconfig

Name	Description
stdlib	Standard Python library files, not platform-specific
platstdlib	Standard Python library files, platform-specific
platlib	Site-specific, platform-specific files
purelib	Site-specific, non-platform-specific files
include	Header files, not platform-specific
platinclude	Header files, platform-specific
scripts	Executable script files
data	Data files

```
$ python3 sysconfig_get_path_names.py

stdlib
platstdlib
purelib
platlib
include
scripts
data
```

Use `get_paths()` to retrieve the actual directories associated with a scheme.

Listing 17.96: sysconfig_get_paths.py

```python
import sysconfig
import pprint
import os

for scheme in ['posix_prefix', 'posix_user']:
    print(scheme)
    print('=' * len(scheme))
    paths = sysconfig.get_paths(scheme=scheme)
    prefix = os.path.commonprefix(paths.values())
    print('prefix = {}\n'.format(prefix))
    for name, path in sorted(paths.items()):
        print('{}\n  .{}'.format(name, path[len(prefix):]))
    print()
```

This example shows the difference between the system-wide paths used for `posix_prefix` under a framework build on Mac OS X, and the user-specific values for `posix_user`.

```
$ python3 sysconfig_get_paths.py

posix_prefix
============
prefix = /Users/dhellmann/Envs/pymotw35

data
  .
include
  ./include/python3.5m
platinclude
  ./include/python3.5m
platlib
  ./lib/python3.5/site-packages
platstdlib
  ./lib/python3.5
```

```
purelib
  ./lib/python3.5/site-packages
scripts
  ./bin
stdlib
  ./lib/python3.5

posix_user
==========
prefix = /Users/dhellmann/Library/Python/3.5

data
  .
include
  ./include/python3.5
platlib
  ./lib/python3.5/site-packages
platstdlib
  ./lib/python3.5
purelib
  ./lib/python3.5/site-packages
scripts
  ./bin
stdlib
  ./lib/python3.5
```

For an individual path, call get_path().

Listing 17.97: sysconfig_get_path.py

```python
import sysconfig
import pprint

for scheme in ['posix_prefix', 'posix_user']:
    print(scheme)
    print('=' * len(scheme))
    print('purelib =', sysconfig.get_path(name='purelib',
                                           scheme=scheme))
    print()
```

Using get_path() is equivalent to saving the value of get_paths() and looking up the individual key in the dictionary. If several paths are needed, get_paths() is more efficient because it does not recompute all of the paths each time.

```
$ python3 sysconfig_get_path.py

posix_prefix
============
purelib = /Users/dhellmann/Envs/pymotw35/lib/python3.5/site-pack
ages
```

```
posix_user
==========
purelib = /Users/dhellmann/Library/Python/3.5/lib/python3.5/site
-packages
```

17.7.3   Python Version and Platform

While sys (page 1178) includes some basic platform identification [see Section 17.2.1.1, "Build-Time Version Information" (page 1178)], it is not specific enough to be used for installing binary packages, because sys.platform does not always include information about hardware architecture, instruction size, or other values that affect the compatibility of binary libraries. For a more precise platform specifier, use get_platform().

Listing 17.98: sysconfig_get_platform.py

```
import sysconfig

print(sysconfig.get_platform())
```

The interpreter used to prepare this sample output was compiled for Mac OS X 10.6 compatibility, so that is the version number included in the platform string.

```
$ python3 sysconfig_get_platform.py

macosx-10.6-intel
```

As a convenience, the interpreter version from sys.version_info is also available through get_python_version() in sysconfig.

Listing 17.99: sysconfig_get_python_version.py

```
import sysconfig
import sys

print('sysconfig.get_python_version():',
      sysconfig.get_python_version())
print('\nsys.version_info:')
print('  major      :', sys.version_info.major)
print('  minor      :', sys.version_info.minor)
print('  micro      :', sys.version_info.micro)
print('  releaselevel:', sys.version_info.releaselevel)
print('  serial     :', sys.version_info.serial)
```

get_python_version() returns a string suitable for use when building a version-specific path.

```
$ python3 sysconfig_get_python_version.py

sysconfig.get_python_version(): 3.5

sys.version_info:
  major      : 3
  minor      : 5
  micro      : 2
  releaselevel: final
  serial     : 0
```

TIP

Related Reading

- Standard library documentation for sysconfig.[31]
- distutils: sysconfig used to be part of the distutils package.
- site (page 1169): The site module describes the paths searched when importing in more detail.
- os (page 1227): Includes os.name, the name of the current operating system.
- sys (page 1178): Includes other build-time information such as the platform.

---

[31] https://docs.python.org/3.5/library/sysconfig.html

Chapter 18
Language Tools

In addition to the developer tools covered in an earlier chapter, Python includes modules that provide access to its internal features. This chapter covers some of the tools for working in Python, regardless of the application area.

The warnings (page 1279) module is used to report non-fatal conditions or recoverable errors. A common example of a warning is the DeprecationWarning that is generated when a feature of the standard library has been superseded by a new class, interface, or module. Use warnings to report conditions that may need user attention, but are not fatal.

Defining a set of classes that conform to a common API can be a challenge when the API is defined by someone else or uses a lot of methods. A popular way to work around this problem is to derive all of the new classes from a common base class, but it is not always obvious which methods should be overridden and which can fall back on the default behavior. Abstract base classes from the abc (page 1287) module formalize an API by explicitly marking the methods a class must provide in a way that prevents the class from being instantiated if it is not completely implemented. For example, many of Python's container types have abstract base classes defined in abc or collections (page 75).

The dis (page 1296) module can be used to disassemble the byte-code version of a program so as to understand the steps the interpreter takes to run it. Looking at disassembled code can be useful when debugging performance or concurrency issues, since it exposes the atomic operations executed by the interpreter for each statement in a program.

The inspect (page 1311) module provides introspection support for all objects in the current process. That includes imported modules, class and function definitions, and the objects instantiated from them. Introspection can be used to generate documentation for source code, adapt behavior at runtime dynamically, or examine the execution environment for a program.

18.1 warnings: Non-fatal Alerts

The warnings module was introduced by **PEP 230**[1] as a way to warn programmers about changes in language or library features in anticipation of backward-incompatible changes coming with Python 3.0. It can also be used to report recoverable configuration errors or feature degradation owing to missing libraries. It is better to deliver user-facing messages via the logging (page 980) module, though, because warnings sent to the console may be lost.

Given that warnings are not fatal, a program may encounter the same warn-able situation many times in the course of its execution. The warnings module suppresses repeated messages from the same source to cut down on the annoyance of seeing the same warning over and over. The output can be controlled on a case-by-case basis, using the command-line options to the interpreter or by calling functions found in warnings.

---

[1] www.python.org/dev/peps/pep-0230

18.1.1   Categories and Filtering

Warnings are categorized using subclasses of the built-in exception class `Warning`. Several standard values are described in the online documentation for the `exceptions` module, and custom warnings can be added by subclassing from `Warning`.

Warnings are processed based on *filter* settings. A filter consists of five parts: the `action`, `message`, `category`, `module`, and `line number`. The `message` portion of the filter is a regular expression that is used to match the warning text. The `category` is the name of an exception class. The `module` contains a regular expression to be matched against the module name generating the warning. The `line number` can be used to change the handling on specific occurrences of a warning.

When a warning is generated, it is compared against all of the registered filters. The first filter that matches it controls the action taken for the warning. If no filter matches the warning, the default action is taken. The actions understood by the filtering mechanism are listed in Table 18.1.

18.1.2   Generating Warnings

The simplest way to emit a warning is to call `warn()` with the message as an argument.

Listing 18.1: `warnings_warn.py`

```
import warnings

print('Before the warning')
warnings.warn('This is a warning message')
print('After the warning')
```

Then, when the program runs, the message is printed.

```
$ python3 -u warnings_warn.py

Before the warning
warnings_warn.py:13: UserWarning: This is a warning message
  warnings.warn('This is a warning message')
After the warning
```

Table 18.1: Warning Filter Actions

Action	Meaning
error	Turn the warning into an exception.
ignore	Discard the warning.
always	Always emit a warning.
default	Print the warning the first time it is generated from each location.
module	Print the warning the first time it is generated from each module.
once	Print the warning the first time it is generated.

Even though the warning is printed, the default behavior is to continue past that point and run the rest of the program. This behavior can be changed with a filter.

Listing 18.2: **warnings_warn_raise.py**

```
import warnings

warnings.simplefilter('error', UserWarning)

print('Before the warning')
warnings.warn('This is a warning message')
print('After the warning')
```

In this example, the `simplefilter()` function adds an entry to the internal filter list to tell the `warnings` module to raise an exception when a `UserWarning` warning is issued.

```
$ python3 -u warnings_warn_raise.py

Before the warning
Traceback (most recent call last):
  File "warnings_warn_raise.py", line 15, in <module>
    warnings.warn('This is a warning message')
UserWarning: This is a warning message
```

The filter behavior can also be controlled from the command line by using the `-W` option to the interpreter. Specify the filter properties as a string with the five parts (action, message, category, module, and line number) separated by colons (:). For example, if warnings_warn.py is run with a filter set to raise an error on `UserWarning`, an exception is produced.

```
$ python3 -u -W "error::UserWarning::0" warnings_warn.py

Before the warning
Traceback (most recent call last):
  File "warnings_warn.py", line 13, in <module>
    warnings.warn('This is a warning message')
UserWarning: This is a warning message
```

When the fields for `message` and `module` are left blank, they are interpreted as matching anything.

18.1.3 Filtering with Patterns

To filter on more complex rules programmatically, use `filterwarnings()`. For example, to filter based on the content of the message text, give a regular expression pattern as the `message` argument.

Listing 18.3: `warnings_filterwarnings_message.py`

```
import warnings

warnings.filterwarnings('ignore', '.*do not.*',)

warnings.warn('Show this message')
warnings.warn('Do not show this message')
```

The pattern contains `do not`, but the actual message uses `Do not`. The pattern matches because the regular expression is always compiled to look for case-insensitive matches.

```
$ python3 warnings_filterwarnings_message.py

warnings_filterwarnings_message.py:14: UserWarning: Show this
message
  warnings.warn('Show this message')
```

The next example program generates two warnings.

Listing 18.4: `warnings_filter.py`

```
import warnings

warnings.warn('Show this message')
warnings.warn('Do not show this message')
```

One of the warnings can be ignored using the filter argument on the command line.

```
$ python3 -W "ignore:do not:UserWarning::0" warnings_filter.py

warnings_filter.py:12: UserWarning: Show this message
  warnings.warn('Show this message')
```

The same pattern matching rules apply to the name of the source module containing the call generating the warning. Suppress all messages from the `warnings_filter` module by passing the module name as the pattern in the `module` argument.

Listing 18.5: `warnings_filterwarnings_module.py`

```
import warnings

warnings.filterwarnings(
    'ignore',
    '.*',
    UserWarning,
    'warnings_filter',
)

import warnings_filter
```

Since the filter is in place, no warnings are emitted when `warnings_filter` is imported.

```
$ python3 warnings_filterwarnings_module.py
```

To suppress only the message on line 13 of `warnings_filter`, include the line number as the last argument to `filterwarnings()`. Use the actual line number from the source file to limit the filter, or `0` to have the filter apply to all occurrences of the message.

Listing 18.6: **warnings_filterwarnings_lineno.py**

```
import warnings

warnings.filterwarnings(
    'ignore',
    '.*',
    UserWarning,
    'warnings_filter',
    13,
)

import warnings_filter
```

The pattern matches any message, so the important arguments are the module name and the line number.

```
$ python3 warnings_filterwarnings_lineno.py

.../warnings_filter.py:12: UserWarning: Show this message
  warnings.warn('Show this message')
```

18.1.4   Repeated Warnings

By default, most types of warnings are printed just the first time they occur in a given location, with "location" defined by the combination of module and line number where the warning is generated.

Listing 18.7: **warnings_repeated.py**

```
import warnings


def function_with_warning():
    warnings.warn('This is a warning!')


function_with_warning()
function_with_warning()
function_with_warning()
```

This example calls the same function several times, but produces a single warning.

```
$ python3 warnings_repeated.py

warnings_repeated.py:14: UserWarning: This is a warning!
  warnings.warn('This is a warning!')
```

The `"once"` action can be used to suppress instances of the same message from different locations.

Listing 18.8: `warnings_once.py`

```
import warnings

warnings.simplefilter('once', UserWarning)

warnings.warn('This is a warning!')
warnings.warn('This is a warning!')
warnings.warn('This is a warning!')
```

The message text for all warnings is saved and only unique messages are printed.

```
$ python3 warnings_once.py

warnings_once.py:14: UserWarning: This is a warning!
  warnings.warn('This is a warning!')
```

Similarly, `"module"` will suppress repeated messages from the same module, no matter which line number they appear in.

18.1.5   Alternative Message Delivery Functions

Normally warnings are printed to `sys.stderr`. To change that behavior, replace the `showwarning()` function inside the `warnings` module. For example, to send warnings to a log file instead of standard error, replace `showwarning()` with a function that logs the warning.

Listing 18.9: `warnings_showwarning.py`

```
import warnings
import logging


def send_warnings_to_log(message, category, filename, lineno,
                         file=None):
    logging.warning(
        '%s:%s: %s:%s',
        filename, lineno,
        category.__name__, message,
    )
```

```
logging.basicConfig(level=logging.INFO)

old_showwarning = warnings.showwarning
warnings.showwarning = send_warnings_to_log

warnings.warn('message')
```

The warnings are emitted with the rest of the log messages when `warn()` is called.

```
$ python3 warnings_showwarning.py

WARNING:root:warnings_showwarning.py:28: UserWarning:message
```

18.1.6 Formatting

If warnings should go to standard error, but they need to be reformatted, replace `formatwarning()`.

Listing 18.10: warnings_formatwarning.py

```
import warnings


def warning_on_one_line(message, category, filename, lineno,
                        file=None, line=None):
    return '-> {}:{}: {}:{}'.format(
        filename, lineno, category.__name__, message)

warnings.warn('Warning message, before')
warnings.formatwarning = warning_on_one_line
warnings.warn('Warning message, after')
```

The format function must return a single string containing the representation of the warning to be displayed to the user.

```
$ python3 -u warnings_formatwarning.py

warnings_formatwarning.py:18: UserWarning: Warning message,
before
  warnings.warn('Warning message, before')
-> warnings_formatwarning.py:20: UserWarning:Warning message,
after
```

18.1.7   Stack Level in Warnings

By default, the warning message includes the source line that generated it, when available. It is not always useful to see the line of code with the actual warning message, though. Instead, `warn()` can be told how far up the stack it must go to find the line that called the function containing the warning. That way, users of a deprecated function can see where the function is called, instead of the implementation of the function.

Listing 18.11: `warnings_warn_stacklevel.py`

```
1   #!/usr/bin/env python3
2   # encoding: utf-8
3
4   import warnings
5
6
7   def old_function():
8       warnings.warn(
9           'old_function() is deprecated, use new_function()',
10          stacklevel=2)
11
12
13  def caller_of_old_function():
14      old_function()
15
16
17  caller_of_old_function()
```

In this example, `warn()` needs to go up the stack two levels—one for itself and one for `old_function()`.

```
$ python3 warnings_warn_stacklevel.py

warnings_warn_stacklevel.py:14: UserWarning: old_function() is deprecated,
 use new_function()
  old_function()
```

TIP

Related Reading

- Standard library documentation for `warnings`.[2]
- **PEP 230**[3]: Warning Framework.
- `exceptions`: Base classes for exceptions and warnings.
- `logging` (page 980): An alternative mechanism for delivering warnings is to write to the log.

---

[2] https://docs.python.org/3.5/library/warnings.html
[3] www.python.org/dev/peps/pep-0230

18.2 abc: Abstract Base Classes

Abstract base classes are a form of interface checking that is stricter than individual `hasattr()` checks for particular methods. By defining an abstract base class, a common API can be established for a set of subclasses. This capability is especially useful in situations where someone less familiar with the source for an application will provide plug-in extensions, but it can also offer advantages when working on a large team or with a large code-base where keeping track of all of the classes at the same time is difficult or not possible.

18.2.1 How ABCs Work

`abc` works by marking methods of the base class as abstract, and then registering concrete classes as implementations of the abstract base. If an application or library requires a particular API, use `issubclass()` or `isinstance()` to check an object against the abstract class.

To use the `abc` module, begin by defining an abstract base class to represent the API of a set of plug-ins for saving and loading data. Set the metaclass for the new base class to `ABCMeta`, and use decorators to establish the public API for the class. The following examples use `abc_base.py`.

Listing 18.12: abc_base.py

```
import abc


class PluginBase(metaclass=abc.ABCMeta):

    @abc.abstractmethod
    def load(self, input):
        """Retrieve data from the input source
        and return an object.
        """

    @abc.abstractmethod
    def save(self, output, data):
        """Save the data object to the output."""
```

18.2.2 Registering a Concrete Class

There are two ways to indicate that a concrete class implements an abstract API: either explicitly register the class or create a new subclass directly from the abstract base. Use the `register()` class method as a decorator on a concrete class to add it explicitly when the class provides the required API, but is not part of the inheritance tree of the abstract base class.

Listing 18.13: abc_register.py

```
import abc
from abc_base import PluginBase


class LocalBaseClass:
    pass


@PluginBase.register
class RegisteredImplementation(LocalBaseClass):

    def load(self, input):
        return input.read()

    def save(self, output, data):
        return output.write(data)


if __name__ == '__main__':
    print('Subclass:', issubclass(RegisteredImplementation,
                                  PluginBase))
    print('Instance:', isinstance(RegisteredImplementation(),
                                  PluginBase))
```

In this example, RegisteredImplementation is derived from LocalBaseClass, but is registered as implementing the PluginBase API. Consequently, issubclass() and isinstance() treat it as though it is derived from PluginBase.

```
$ python3 abc_register.py

Subclass: True
Instance: True
```

18.2.3   Implementation Through Subclassing

Subclassing directly from the base avoids the need to register the class explicitly.

Listing 18.14: abc_subclass.py

```
import abc
from abc_base import PluginBase


class SubclassImplementation(PluginBase):
```

```
        def load(self, input):
            return input.read()

        def save(self, output, data):
            return output.write(data)


    if __name__ == '__main__':
        print('Subclass:', issubclass(SubclassImplementation,
                                      PluginBase))
        print('Instance:', isinstance(SubclassImplementation(),
                                      PluginBase))
```

In this case, normal Python class management features are used to recognize
SubclassImplementation as implementing the abstract PluginBase.

```
$ python3 abc_subclass.py

Subclass: True
Instance: True
```

A side effect of using direct subclassing is that it becomes possible to find all of the
implementations of a plug-in by asking the base class for the list of known classes derived
from it. (This is not an abc feature—all classes can do this.)

Listing 18.15: abc_find_subclasses.py

```
import abc
from abc_base import PluginBase
import abc_subclass
import abc_register

for sc in PluginBase.__subclasses__():
    print(sc.__name__)
```

Even though abc_register() is imported, RegisteredImplementation is not among the list
of subclasses found because it is not actually derived from the base.

```
$ python3 abc_find_subclasses.py

SubclassImplementation
```

18.2.4 Helper Base Class

If the metaclass is not set properly, the APIs will not be enforced for the concrete implementations. To make it easier to set up the abstract class properly, a base class is provided
that specifies the metaclass automatically.

Listing 18.16: **abc_abc_base.py**

```python
import abc


class PluginBase(abc.ABC):

    @abc.abstractmethod
    def load(self, input):
        """Retrieve data from the input source
        and return an object.
        """

    @abc.abstractmethod
    def save(self, output, data):
        """Save the data object to the output."""


class SubclassImplementation(PluginBase):

    def load(self, input):
        return input.read()

    def save(self, output, data):
        return output.write(data)


if __name__ == '__main__':
    print('Subclass:', issubclass(SubclassImplementation,
                                  PluginBase))
    print('Instance:', isinstance(SubclassImplementation(),
                                  PluginBase))
```

To create a new abstract class, simply inherit from `ABC`.

```
$ python3 abc_abc_base.py

Subclass: True
Instance: True
```

18.2.5   Incomplete Implementations

Another benefit of subclassing directly from the abstract base class is that the subclass cannot be instantiated unless it fully implements the abstract portion of the API.

Listing 18.17: **abc_incomplete.py**

```python
import abc
from abc_base import PluginBase
```

```
@PluginBase.register
class IncompleteImplementation(PluginBase):

    def save(self, output, data):
        return output.write(data)


if __name__ == '__main__':
    print('Subclass:', issubclass(IncompleteImplementation,
                                  PluginBase))
    print('Instance:', isinstance(IncompleteImplementation(),
                                  PluginBase))
```

This keeps incomplete implementations from triggering unexpected errors at runtime.

```
$ python3 abc_incomplete.py

Subclass: True
Traceback (most recent call last):
  File "abc_incomplete.py", line 24, in <module>
    print('Instance:', isinstance(IncompleteImplementation(),
TypeError: Can't instantiate abstract class
IncompleteImplementation with abstract methods load
```

18.2.6   Concrete Methods in ABCs

Although a concrete class must provide implementations of all abstract methods, the abstract base class can also provide implementations that can be invoked via super(). Common logic can then be reused by placing it in the base class, but subclasses are forced to provide an overriding method with (potentially) custom logic.

Listing 18.18: **abc_concrete_method.py**

```
import abc
import io


class ABCWithConcreteImplementation(abc.ABC):

    @abc.abstractmethod
    def retrieve_values(self, input):
        print('base class reading data')
        return input.read()


class ConcreteOverride(ABCWithConcreteImplementation):

    def retrieve_values(self, input):
```

```
        base_data = super(ConcreteOverride,
                          self).retrieve_values(input)
        print('subclass sorting data')
        response = sorted(base_data.splitlines())
        return response


input = io.StringIO("""line one
line two
line three
""")

reader = ConcreteOverride()
print(reader.retrieve_values(input))
print()
```

Since `ABCWithConcreteImplementation()` is an abstract base class, it is not possible to instantiate it so as to use it directly. Subclasses *must* provide an override for `retrieve_values()`, and in this case the concrete class sorts the data before returning it.

```
$ python3 abc_concrete_method.py

base class reading data
subclass sorting data
['line one', 'line three', 'line two']
```

18.2.7 Abstract Properties

If an API specification includes attributes in addition to methods, it can require the attributes in concrete classes by combining `abstractmethod()` with `property()`.

Listing 18.19: abc_abstractproperty.py

```
import abc


class Base(abc.ABC):

    @property
    @abc.abstractmethod
    def value(self):
        return 'Should never reach here'

    @property
    @abc.abstractmethod
    def constant(self):
        return 'Should never reach here'
```

```
class Implementation(Base):

    @property
    def value(self):
        return 'concrete property'

    constant = 'set by a class attribute'


try:
    b = Base()
    print('Base.value:', b.value)
except Exception as err:
    print('ERROR:', str(err))

i = Implementation()
print('Implementation.value   :', i.value)
print('Implementation.constant:', i.constant)
```

The Base class in the example cannot be instantiated because it has only an abstract version of the property getter methods for value and constant. The value property is given a concrete getter in Implementation, and constant is defined using a class attribute.

```
$ python3 abc_abstractproperty.py

ERROR: Can't instantiate abstract class Base with abstract
methods constant, value
Implementation.value   : concrete property
Implementation.constant: set by a class attribute
```

Abstract read-write properties can also be defined.

Listing 18.20: abc_abstractproperty_rw.py

```
import abc


class Base(abc.ABC):

    @property
    @abc.abstractmethod
    def value(self):
        return 'Should never reach here'

    @value.setter
    @abc.abstractmethod
    def value(self, new_value):
        return
```

```
class PartialImplementation(Base):

    @property
    def value(self):
        return 'Read-only'


class Implementation(Base):

    _value = 'Default value'

    @property
    def value(self):
        return self._value

    @value.setter
    def value(self, new_value):
        self._value = new_value


try:
    b = Base()
    print('Base.value:', b.value)
except Exception as err:
    print('ERROR:', str(err))

p = PartialImplementation()
print('PartialImplementation.value:', p.value)

try:
    p.value = 'Alteration'
    print('PartialImplementation.value:', p.value)
except Exception as err:
    print('ERROR:', str(err))

i = Implementation()
print('Implementation.value:', i.value)

i.value = 'New value'
print('Changed value:', i.value)
```

The concrete property must be defined the same way as the abstract property, as either read-write or read-only. Overriding a read-write property in `PartialImplementation` with one that is read-only leaves the property read-only; that is, the property's setter method from the base class is not reused.

```
$ python3 abc_abstractproperty_rw.py

ERROR: Can't instantiate abstract class Base with abstract
```

```
methods value
PartialImplementation.value: Read-only
ERROR: can't set attribute
Implementation.value: Default value
Changed value: New value
```

To use the decorator syntax with read-write abstract properties, the methods to get and set the value must have the same names.

18.2.8   Abstract Class and Static Methods

Class and static methods can also be marked as abstract.

Listing 18.21: abc_class_static.py

```python
import abc


class Base(abc.ABC):

    @classmethod
    @abc.abstractmethod
    def factory(cls, *args):
        return cls()

    @staticmethod
    @abc.abstractmethod
    def const_behavior():
        return 'Should never reach here'


class Implementation(Base):

    def do_something(self):
        pass

    @classmethod
    def factory(cls, *args):
        obj = cls(*args)
        obj.do_something()
        return obj

    @staticmethod
    def const_behavior():
        return 'Static behavior differs'


try:
    o = Base.factory()
    print('Base.value:', o.const_behavior())
```

```
    except Exception as err:
        print('ERROR:', str(err))

i = Implementation.factory()
print('Implementation.const_behavior :', i.const_behavior())
```

Although the class method is invoked on the class rather than an instance, it still prevents the class from being instantiated if it is not defined.

```
$ python3 abc_class_static.py

ERROR: Can't instantiate abstract class Base with abstract
methods const_behavior, factory
Implementation.const_behavior : Static behavior differs
```

TIP

Related Reading

- Standard library documentation for abc.[4]
- **PEP 3119**[5]: Introducing Abstract Base Classes.
- collections (page 75): The collections module includes abstract base classes for several collection types.
- **PEP 3141**[6]: A Type Hierarchy for Numbers.
- Wikipedia: Strategy pattern[7]: Description and examples of the strategy pattern, a commonly used plug-in implementation pattern.
- Dynamic Code Patterns: Extending Your Applications with Plugins[8]: PyCon 2013 presentation by Doug Hellmann.
- Python 2 to 3 porting notes for abc (page 1356).

18.3   dis: Python Byte-Code Disassembler

The dis module includes functions for working with Python byte-code by *disassembling* it into a more human-readable form. Reviewing the byte-code being executed by the interpreter is a good way to hand-tune tight loops and perform other kinds of optimizations. It is also useful for finding race conditions in multithreaded applications, since it can be used to estimate the point in the code where thread control may switch.

---

[4] https://docs.python.org/3.5/library/abc.html
[5] www.python.org/dev/peps/pep-3119
[6] www.python.org/dev/peps/pep-3141
[7] https://en.wikipedia.org/wiki/Strategy_pattern
[8] http://pyvideo.org/pycon-us-2013/dynamic-code-patterns-extending-your-application.html

WARNING

The use of byte-codes is a version-specific implementation detail of the CPython interpreter. Refer to `Include/opcode.h` in the source code for the version of the interpreter you are using to find the canonical list of byte-codes.

18.3.1   Basic Disassembly

The function `dis()` prints the disassembled representation of a Python code source (module, class, method, function, or code object). A module such as `dis_simple.py` can be disassembled by running `dis` from the command line.

Listing 18.22: `dis_simple.py`

```
1  #!/usr/bin/env python3
2  # encoding: utf-8
3
4  my_dict = {'a': 1}
```

The output is organized into columns with the original source line number, the instruction address within the code object, the opcode name, and any arguments passed to the opcode.

```
$ python3 -m dis dis_simple.py

    4           0 LOAD_CONST            0 ('a')
                3 LOAD_CONST            1 (1)
                6 BUILD_MAP             1
                9 STORE_NAME            0 (my_dict)
               12 LOAD_CONST            2 (None)
               15 RETURN_VALUE
```

In this case, the source translates the code into four different operations to create and populate the dictionary, then save the results to a local variable. Since the Python interpreter is stack-based, the first steps are to put the constants onto the stack in the correct order with `LOAD_CONST`, and then use `BUILD_MAP` to pop off the new key and value to be added to the dictionary. The resulting `dict` object is bound to the name `my_dict` with `STORE_NAME`.

18.3.2   Disassembling Functions

Unfortunately, disassembling an entire module does not recurse into functions automatically.

Listing 18.23: `dis_function.py`

```
1  #!/usr/bin/env python3
2  # encoding: utf-8
3
4
```

```
 5  def f(*args):
 6      nargs = len(args)
 7      print(nargs, args)
 8
 9
10  if __name__ == '__main__':
11      import dis
12      dis.dis(f)
```

The results of disassembling `dis_function.py` show the operations for loading the function's code object onto the stack and then turning it into a function (`LOAD_CONST`, `MAKE_FUNCTION`), but *not* the body of the function.

```
$ python3 -m dis dis_function.py

  5           0 LOAD_CONST               0 (<code object f at
0x10141ba50, file "dis_function.py", line 5>)
              3 LOAD_CONST               1 ('f')
              6 MAKE_FUNCTION            0
              9 STORE_NAME               0 (f)

 10          12 LOAD_NAME                1 (__name__)
             15 LOAD_CONST               2 ('__main__')
             18 COMPARE_OP               2 (==)
             21 POP_JUMP_IF_FALSE       49

 11          24 LOAD_CONST               3 (0)
             27 LOAD_CONST               4 (None)
             30 IMPORT_NAME              2 (dis)
             33 STORE_NAME               2 (dis)

 12          36 LOAD_NAME                2 (dis)
             39 LOAD_ATTR                2 (dis)
             42 LOAD_NAME                0 (f)
             45 CALL_FUNCTION            1 (1 positional, 0
keyword pair)
             48 POP_TOP
        >>   49 LOAD_CONST               4 (None)
             52 RETURN_VALUE
```

To see inside the function, the function itself must be passed to `dis()`.

```
$ python3 dis_function.py

  6           0 LOAD_GLOBAL              0 (len)
              3 LOAD_FAST                0 (args)
              6 CALL_FUNCTION            1 (1 positional, 0
keyword pair)
```

```
          9 STORE_FAST              1 (nargs)

 7       12 LOAD_GLOBAL             1 (print)
         15 LOAD_FAST               1 (nargs)
         18 LOAD_FAST               0 (args)
         21 CALL_FUNCTION           2 (2 positional, 0
keyword pair)
         24 POP_TOP
         25 LOAD_CONST              0 (None)
         28 RETURN_VALUE
```

To print a summary of the function, including information about the arguments and names it uses, call show_code(), passing the function as the first argument.

```python
#!/usr/bin/env python3
# encoding: utf-8


def f(*args):
    nargs = len(args)
    print(nargs, args)


if __name__ == '__main__':
    import dis
    dis.show_code(f)
```

The argument to show_code() is passed to code_info(), which returns a nicely formatted summary of the function, method, code string, or other code object, ready to be printed.

```
$ python3 dis_show_code.py

Name:              f
Filename:          dis_show_code.py
Argument count:    0
Kw-only arguments: 0
Number of locals:  2
Stack size:        3
Flags:             OPTIMIZED, NEWLOCALS, VARARGS, NOFREE
Constants:
   0: None
Names:
   0: len
   1: print
Variable names:
   0: args
   1: nargs
```

18.3.3 Classes

Classes can be passed to dis(), in which case all of the methods are disassembled in turn.

Listing 18.24: **dis_class.py**

```
1  #!/usr/bin/env python3
2  # encoding: utf-8
3
4  import dis
5
6
7  class MyObject:
8      """Example for dis."""
9
10     CLASS_ATTRIBUTE = 'some value'
11
12     def __str__(self):
13         return 'MyObject({})'.format(self.name)
14
15     def __init__(self, name):
16         self.name = name
17
18
19 dis.dis(MyObject)
```

The methods are listed in alphabetical order, not in the order in which they appear in the file.

```
$ python3 dis_class.py

Disassembly of __init__:
  16          0 LOAD_FAST               1 (name)
              3 LOAD_FAST               0 (self)
              6 STORE_ATTR              0 (name)
              9 LOAD_CONST              0 (None)
             12 RETURN_VALUE

Disassembly of __str__:
  13          0 LOAD_CONST              1 ('MyObject({})')
              3 LOAD_ATTR               0 (format)
              6 LOAD_FAST               0 (self)
              9 LOAD_ATTR               1 (name)
             12 CALL_FUNCTION           1 (1 positional, 0
keyword pair)
             15 RETURN_VALUE
```

18.3.4   Source Code

It is often more convenient to work with the source code for a program than with the code
objects themselves. The functions in dis accept string arguments containing source code,
and convert them into code objects before producing the disassembly or other output.

Listing 18.25: dis_string.py

```python
import dis

code = """
my_dict = {'a': 1}
"""

print('Disassembly:\n')
dis.dis(code)

print('\nCode details:\n')
dis.show_code(code)
```

Passing a string means that the step of compiling the code and holding a reference to
the results can be skipped. That approach is more convenient when statements outside of
a function are being examined.

```
$ python3 dis_string.py

Disassembly:

  2           0 LOAD_CONST               0 ('a')
              3 LOAD_CONST               1 (1)
              6 BUILD_MAP                1
              9 STORE_NAME               0 (my_dict)
             12 LOAD_CONST               2 (None)
             15 RETURN_VALUE

Code details:

Name:              <module>
Filename:          <disassembly>
Argument count:    0
Kw-only arguments: 0
Number of locals:  0
Stack size:        2
Flags:             NOFREE
Constants:
   0: 'a'
   1: 1
```

```
    2: None
Names:
    0: my_dict
```

18.3.5   Using Disassembly to Debug

Sometimes when debugging an exception, it can be useful to see which byte-code caused
a problem. There are several options for disassembling the code around an error. The first
strategy is to use dis() in the interactive interpreter to report on the last exception. If no
argument is passed to dis(), then it looks for an exception and shows the disassembly of
the top of the stack that caused it.

```
$ python3
Python 3.5.1 (v3.5.1:37a07cee5969, Dec  5 2015, 21:12:44)
[GCC 4.2.1 (Apple Inc. build 5666) (dot 3)] on darwin
Type "help", "copyright", "credits" or "license" for more information.
>>> import dis
>>> j = 4
>>> i = i + 4
Traceback (most recent call last):
  File "<stdin>", line 1, in <module>
NameError: name 'i' is not defined
>>> dis.dis()
  1 -->         0 LOAD_NAME                0 (i)
                3 LOAD_CONST               0 (4)
                6 BINARY_ADD
                7 STORE_NAME               0 (i)
               10 LOAD_CONST               1 (None)
               13 RETURN_VALUE
>>>
```

The --> after the line number indicates the opcode that caused the error. There is no i
variable defined, so the value associated with the name cannot be loaded onto the stack.

A program can also print the information about an active traceback by passing it to
distb() directly. In the next example, a DivideByZero exception is identified, but because
the formula includes two divisions it may not be clear which part is zero.

Listing 18.26: dis_traceback.py

```
1  #!/usr/bin/env python3
2  # encoding: utf-8
3
4  i = 1
5  j = 0
6  k = 3
7
8  try:
9      result = k * (i / j) + (i / k)
```

```
10   except:
11       import dis
12       import sys
13       exc_type, exc_value, exc_tb = sys.exc_info()
14       dis.distb(exc_tb)
```

The error is easy to spot when it is loaded onto the stack in the disassembled version. The bad operation is highlighted with the `-->`, and the previous line pushes the value for j onto the stack.

```
$ python3 dis_traceback.py

  4            0 LOAD_CONST               0 (1)
               3 STORE_NAME               0 (i)

  5            6 LOAD_CONST               1 (0)
               9 STORE_NAME               1 (j)

  6           12 LOAD_CONST               2 (3)
              15 STORE_NAME               2 (k)

  8           18 SETUP_EXCEPT            26 (to 47)

  9           21 LOAD_NAME                2 (k)
              24 LOAD_NAME                0 (i)
              27 LOAD_NAME                1 (j)
      -->     30 BINARY_TRUE_DIVIDE
              31 BINARY_MULTIPLY
              32 LOAD_NAME                0 (i)
              35 LOAD_NAME                2 (k)
              38 BINARY_TRUE_DIVIDE
              39 BINARY_ADD
              40 STORE_NAME               3 (result)

...trimmed...
```

18.3.6 Performance Analysis of Loops

Besides debugging errors, `dis` can help identify performance issues. Examining the disassembled code is especially useful with tight loops where the number of Python instructions is small, but those instructions translate into an inefficient set of byte-codes. The helpfulness of the disassembly can be seen by examining a few different implementations of a class, `Dictionary`, that reads a list of words and groups the words by their first letter.

Listing 18.27: `dis_test_loop.py`

```
import dis
import sys
```

```
import textwrap
import timeit

module_name = sys.argv[1]
module = __import__(module_name)
Dictionary = module.Dictionary

dis.dis(Dictionary.load_data)
print()
t = timeit.Timer(
    'd = Dictionary(words)',
    textwrap.dedent("""
    from {module_name} import Dictionary
    words = [
        l.strip()
        for l in open('/usr/share/dict/words', 'rt')
    ]
    """).format(module_name=module_name)
)
iterations = 10
print('TIME: {:0.4f}'.format(t.timeit(iterations) / iterations))
```

The test driver application dis_test_loop.py can be used to run each incarnation of the Dictionary class, starting with a straightforward, but slow, implementation.

Listing 18.28: dis_slow_loop.py

```
1  #!/usr/bin/env python3
2  # encoding: utf-8
3
4
5  class Dictionary:
6
7      def __init__(self, words):
8          self.by_letter = {}
9          self.load_data(words)
10
11     def load_data(self, words):
12         for word in words:
13             try:
14                 self.by_letter[word[0]].append(word)
15             except KeyError:
16                 self.by_letter[word[0]] = [word]
```

Running the test program with this version shows the disassembled program and the amount of time it takes to run.

```
$ python3 dis_test_loop.py dis_slow_loop

12            0 SETUP_LOOP              83 (to 86)
```

```
                  3 LOAD_FAST              1 (words)
                  6 GET_ITER
          >>      7 FOR_ITER              75 (to 85)
                 10 STORE_FAST             2 (word)

     13          13 SETUP_EXCEPT          28 (to 44)

     14          16 LOAD_FAST              0 (self)
                 19 LOAD_ATTR              0 (by_letter)
                 22 LOAD_FAST              2 (word)
                 25 LOAD_CONST             1 (0)
                 28 BINARY_SUBSCR
                 29 BINARY_SUBSCR
                 30 LOAD_ATTR              1 (append)
                 33 LOAD_FAST              2 (word)
                 36 CALL_FUNCTION          1 (1 positional, 0
keyword pair)
                 39 POP_TOP
                 40 POP_BLOCK
                 41 JUMP_ABSOLUTE          7

     15  >>      44 DUP_TOP
                 45 LOAD_GLOBAL            2 (KeyError)
                 48 COMPARE_OP            10 (exception match)
                 51 POP_JUMP_IF_FALSE     81
                 54 POP_TOP
                 55 POP_TOP
                 56 POP_TOP

     16          57 LOAD_FAST              2 (word)
                 60 BUILD_LIST             1
                 63 LOAD_FAST              0 (self)
                 66 LOAD_ATTR              0 (by_letter)
                 69 LOAD_FAST              2 (word)
                 72 LOAD_CONST             1 (0)
                 75 BINARY_SUBSCR
                 76 STORE_SUBSCR
                 77 POP_EXCEPT
                 78 JUMP_ABSOLUTE          7
          >>     81 END_FINALLY
                 82 JUMP_ABSOLUTE          7
          >>     85 POP_BLOCK
          >>     86 LOAD_CONST             0 (None)
                 89 RETURN_VALUE

TIME: 0.0568
```

As the output shows, dis_slow_loop.py takes 0.0568 seconds to load the 235,886 words in the copy of /usr/share/dict/words on OS X. That performance is not too bad, but the accompanying disassembly shows that the loop is doing more work than strictly necessary. As it enters the loop in opcode 13, the program sets up an exception context (`SETUP_EXCEPT`). Then it takes six opcodes to find `self.by_letter[word[0]]` before appending `word` to the list. If an exception is generated because `word[0]` is not in the dictionary yet, the exception handler does all of the same work to determine `word[0]` (three opcodes) and sets `self.by_letter[word[0]]` to a new list containing the word.

One technique to eliminate the exception setup is to prepopulate `self.by_letter` with one list for each letter of the alphabet. That means the list for the new word should always be found, and the value can be saved after the lookup.

Listing 18.29: `dis_faster_loop.py`

```
1   #!/usr/bin/env python3
2   # encoding: utf-8
3
4   import string
5
6
7   class Dictionary:
8
9       def __init__(self, words):
10          self.by_letter = {
11              letter: []
12              for letter in string.ascii_letters
13          }
14          self.load_data(words)
15
16      def load_data(self, words):
17          for word in words:
18              self.by_letter[word[0]].append(word)
```

This change cuts the number of opcodes in half, but only shaves the time down to 0.0567 seconds. Obviously the exception handling had some overhead, but not a significant amount.

```
$ python3 dis_test_loop.py dis_faster_loop

17              0 SETUP_LOOP              38 (to 41)
                3 LOAD_FAST                1 (words)
                6 GET_ITER
        >>      7 FOR_ITER                30 (to 40)
               10 STORE_FAST               2 (word)

18             13 LOAD_FAST                0 (self)
               16 LOAD_ATTR                0 (by_letter)
               19 LOAD_FAST                2 (word)
               22 LOAD_CONST               1 (0)
               25 BINARY_SUBSCR
               26 BINARY_SUBSCR
```

```
                    27 LOAD_ATTR           1 (append)
                    30 LOAD_FAST           2 (word)
                    33 CALL_FUNCTION       1 (1 positional, 0
keyword pair)
                    36 POP_TOP
                    37 JUMP_ABSOLUTE       7
            >>      40 POP_BLOCK
            >>      41 LOAD_CONST          0 (None)
                    44 RETURN_VALUE

TIME: 0.0567
```

The performance can be improved further by moving the lookup for self.by_letter outside of the loop (the value does not change, after all).

Listing 18.30: **dis_fastest_loop.py**

```
1  #!/usr/bin/env python3
2  # encoding: utf-8
3
4  import collections
5
6
7  class Dictionary:
8
9      def __init__(self, words):
10         self.by_letter = collections.defaultdict(list)
11         self.load_data(words)
12
13     def load_data(self, words):
14         by_letter = self.by_letter
15         for word in words:
16             by_letter[word[0]].append(word)
```

Opcodes 0–6 now find the value of self.by_letter and save it as a local variable by_letter. Using a local variable takes just a single opcode, instead of two (statement 22 uses LOAD_FAST to place the dictionary onto the stack). After this change, the running time is down to 0.0473 seconds.

```
$ python3 dis_test_loop.py dis_fastest_loop

    14          0 LOAD_FAST           0 (self)
                3 LOAD_ATTR           0 (by_letter)
                6 STORE_FAST          2 (by_letter)

    15          9 SETUP_LOOP         35 (to 47)
               12 LOAD_FAST           1 (words)
               15 GET_ITER
```

```
      >>    16 FOR_ITER              27 (to 46)
            19 STORE_FAST             3 (word)

 16         22 LOAD_FAST              2 (by_letter)
            25 LOAD_FAST              3 (word)
            28 LOAD_CONST             1 (0)
            31 BINARY_SUBSCR
            32 BINARY_SUBSCR
            33 LOAD_ATTR              1 (append)
            36 LOAD_FAST              3 (word)
            39 CALL_FUNCTION          1 (1 positional, 0
keyword pair)
            42 POP_TOP
            43 JUMP_ABSOLUTE         16
      >>    46 POP_BLOCK
      >>    47 LOAD_CONST             0 (None)
            50 RETURN_VALUE
```

```
TIME: 0.0473
```

A further optimization, suggested by Brandon Rhodes, is to eliminate the Python version of the `for` loop entirely. If `itertools.groupby()` is used to arrange the input, the iteration is moved to C. This transition is safe because the inputs are known to be sorted. If that was not the case, the program would need to sort them first.

Listing 18.31: **dis_eliminate_loop.py**

```python
1  #!/usr/bin/env python3
2  # encoding: utf-8
3
4  import operator
5  import itertools
6
7
8  class Dictionary:
9
10     def __init__(self, words):
11         self.by_letter = {}
12         self.load_data(words)
13
14     def load_data(self, words):
15         # Arrange by letter.
16         grouped = itertools.groupby(
17             words,
18             key=operator.itemgetter(0),
19         )
20         # Save arranged sets of words.
21         self.by_letter = {
```

```
 22            group[0][0]: group
 23            for group in grouped
 24        }
```

The `itertools` version takes only 0.0332 seconds to run, or approximately 60% of the running time for the original program.

```
$ python3 dis_test_loop.py dis_eliminate_loop

 16          0 LOAD_GLOBAL           0 (itertools)
             3 LOAD_ATTR             1 (groupby)

 17          6 LOAD_FAST             1 (words)
             9 LOAD_CONST            1 ('key')

 18         12 LOAD_GLOBAL           2 (operator)
            15 LOAD_ATTR             3 (itemgetter)
            18 LOAD_CONST            2 (0)
            21 CALL_FUNCTION         1 (1 positional, 0
keyword pair)
            24 CALL_FUNCTION       257 (1 positional, 1
keyword pair)
            27 STORE_FAST            2 (grouped)

 21         30 LOAD_CONST            3 (<code object
<dictcomp> at 0x101517930, file ".../dis_eliminate_loop.py",
line 21>)
            33 LOAD_CONST            4
('Dictionary.load_data.<locals>.<dictcomp>')
            36 MAKE_FUNCTION         0

 23         39 LOAD_FAST             2 (grouped)
            42 GET_ITER
            43 CALL_FUNCTION         1 (1 positional, 0
keyword pair)
            46 LOAD_FAST             0 (self)
            49 STORE_ATTR            4 (by_letter)
            52 LOAD_CONST            0 (None)
            55 RETURN_VALUE

TIME: 0.0332
```

18.3.7 Compiler Optimizations

Disassembling compiled source also exposes some of the optimizations made by the compiler. For example, literal expressions are folded during compilation, when possible.

Listing 18.32: `dis_constant_folding.py`

```
1  #!/usr/bin/env python3
2  # encoding: utf-8
3
4  # Folded
5  i = 1 + 2
6  f = 3.4 * 5.6
7  s = 'Hello,' + ' World!'
8
9  # Not folded
10 I = i * 3 * 4
11 F = f / 2 / 3
12 S = s + '\n' + 'Fantastic!'
```

None of the values in the expressions on lines 5–7 can change the way the operation is performed, so the result of the expressions can be computed at compilation time and collapsed into single `LOAD_CONST` instructions. In contrast, because a variable is involved in the expressions on lines 10–12, and because the variable might refer to an object that overloads the operator involved, the evaluation must be delayed until runtime.

```
$ python3 -m dis dis_constant_folding.py

  5           0 LOAD_CONST              11 (3)
              3 STORE_NAME               0 (i)

  6           6 LOAD_CONST              12 (19.04)
              9 STORE_NAME               1 (f)

  7          12 LOAD_CONST              13 ('Hello, World!')
             15 STORE_NAME               2 (s)

 10          18 LOAD_NAME                0 (i)
             21 LOAD_CONST               6 (3)
             24 BINARY_MULTIPLY
             25 LOAD_CONST               7 (4)
             28 BINARY_MULTIPLY
             29 STORE_NAME               3 (I)

 11          32 LOAD_NAME                1 (f)
             35 LOAD_CONST               1 (2)
             38 BINARY_TRUE_DIVIDE
             39 LOAD_CONST               6 (3)
             42 BINARY_TRUE_DIVIDE
             43 STORE_NAME               4 (F)

 12          46 LOAD_NAME                2 (s)
             49 LOAD_CONST               8 ('\n')
```

```
        52 BINARY_ADD
        53 LOAD_CONST              9 ('Fantastic!')
        56 BINARY_ADD
        57 STORE_NAME              5 (S)
        60 LOAD_CONST             10 (None)
        63 RETURN_VALUE
```

TIP

Related Reading

- Standard library documentation for dis[9]: Includes the list of byte-code instructions.[10]

- Include/opcode.h: The source code for the CPython interpreter defines the byte-codes in opcode.h.

- *Python Essential Reference, Fourth Edition*, by David M. Beazley.

- thomas.apestaart.org: Python Disassembly[11]: A short discussion of the difference between storing values in a dictionary between Python 2.5 and 2.6.

- Why is looping over range() in Python faster than using a while loop?[12]: A discussion on Stack Overflow comparing two looping examples via their disassembled byte-codes.

- Decorator for binding constants at compile time[13]: Python Cookbook recipe by Raymond Hettinger and Skip Montanaro with a function decorator that rewrites the byte-codes for a function to insert global constants to avoid runtime name lookups.

18.4 inspect: Inspect Live Objects

The inspect module provides functions for learning about live objects, including modules, classes, instances, functions, and methods. The functions in this module can be used to retrieve the original source code for a function, look at the arguments to a method on the stack, and extract the sort of information useful for producing library documentation for source code.

18.4.1 Example Module

The rest of the examples for this section use this example file, example.py.

---

[9] https://docs.python.org/3.5/library/dis.html
[10] https://docs.python.org/3.5/library/dis.html#python-bytecode-instructions
[11] http://thomas.apestaart.org/log/?p=927
[12] http://stackoverflow.com/questions/869229/why-is-looping-over-range-in-python-faster-than-using-a-while-loop
[13] http://code.activestate.com/recipes/277940/

Listing 18.33: `example.py`

```python
# This comment appears first
# and spans 2 lines.

# This comment does not show up in the output of getcomments().

"""Sample file to serve as the basis for inspect examples.
"""


def module_level_function(arg1, arg2='default', *args, **kwargs):
    """This function is declared in the module."""
    local_variable = arg1 * 2
    return local_variable


class A(object):
    """The A class."""

    def __init__(self, name):
        self.name = name

    def get_name(self):
        "Returns the name of the instance."
        return self.name

instance_of_a = A('sample_instance')


class B(A):
    """This is the B class.
    It is derived from A.
    """

    # This method is not part of A.
    def do_something(self):
        """Does some work"""

    def get_name(self):
        "Overrides version from A"
        return 'B(' + self.name + ')'
```

18.4.2   Inspecting Modules

The first kind of inspection probes live objects to learn about them. Use `getmembers()` to discover the member attributes of objects. The types of members that might be returned depend on the type of object scanned. Modules can contain classes and functions, classes can contain methods and attributes, and so on.

The arguments to getmembers() are an object to scan (a module, class, or instance) and an optional predicate function that is used to filter the objects returned. The return value is a list of tuples with two values: the name of the member and the type of the member. The inspect module includes several such predicate functions with names like ismodule(), isclass(), and so on.

Listing 18.34: **inspect_getmembers_module.py**

```
import inspect

import example

for name, data in inspect.getmembers(example):
    if name.startswith('__'):
        continue
    print('{} : {!r}'.format(name, data))
```

This example program prints the members of the example module. Modules have several private attributes that are used as part of the import implementation as well as a set of __builtins__. All of these are ignored in the output for this example because they are not actually part of the module and the list is long.

```
$ python3 inspect_getmembers_module.py

A : <class 'example.A'>
B : <class 'example.B'>
instance_of_a : <example.A object at 0x1014814a8>
module_level_function : <function module_level_function at
0x10148bc80>
```

The predicate argument can be used to filter the types of objects returned.

Listing 18.35: **inspect_getmembers_module_class.py**

```
import inspect

import example

for name, data in inspect.getmembers(example, inspect.isclass):
    print('{} : {!r}'.format(name, data))
```

Now only classes are included in the output.

```
$ python3 inspect_getmembers_module_class.py

A : <class 'example.A'>
B : <class 'example.B'>
```

18.4.3   Inspecting Classes

Classes are scanned using `getmembers()` in the same way as modules are inspected, though the types of members are different.

Listing 18.36: `inspect_getmembers_class.py`

```python
import inspect
from pprint import pprint

import example

pprint(inspect.getmembers(example.A), width=65)
```

Because no filtering is applied, the output shows the attributes, methods, slots, and other members of the class.

```
$ python3 inspect_getmembers_class.py

[('__class__', <class 'type'>),
 ('__delattr__',
  <slot wrapper '__delattr__' of 'object' objects>),
 ('__dict__',
  mappingproxy({'__dict__': <attribute '__dict__' of 'A'
objects>,
                '__doc__': 'The A class.',
                '__init__': <function A.__init__ at
0x101c99510>,
                '__module__': 'example',
                '__weakref__': <attribute '__weakref__' of 'A'
objects>,
                'get_name': <function A.get_name at
0x101c99598>})),
 ('__dir__', <method '__dir__' of 'object' objects>),
 ('__doc__', 'The A class.'),
 ('__eq__', <slot wrapper '__eq__' of 'object' objects>),
 ('__format__', <method '__format__' of 'object' objects>),
 ('__ge__', <slot wrapper '__ge__' of 'object' objects>),
 ('__getattribute__',
  <slot wrapper '__getattribute__' of 'object' objects>),
 ('__gt__', <slot wrapper '__gt__' of 'object' objects>),
 ('__hash__', <slot wrapper '__hash__' of 'object' objects>),
 ('__init__', <function A.__init__ at 0x101c99510>),
 ('__le__', <slot wrapper '__le__' of 'object' objects>),
 ('__lt__', <slot wrapper '__lt__' of 'object' objects>),
 ('__module__', 'example'),
 ('__ne__', <slot wrapper '__ne__' of 'object' objects>),
 ('__new__',
```

```
        <built-in method __new__ of type object at 0x10022bb20>),
  ('__reduce__', <method '__reduce__' of 'object' objects>),
  ('__reduce_ex__', <method '__reduce_ex__' of 'object'
objects>),
  ('__repr__', <slot wrapper '__repr__' of 'object' objects>),
  ('__setattr__',
   <slot wrapper '__setattr__' of 'object' objects>),
  ('__sizeof__', <method '__sizeof__' of 'object' objects>),
  ('__str__', <slot wrapper '__str__' of 'object' objects>),
  ('__subclasshook__',
   <built-in method __subclasshook__ of type object at
0x10061fba8>),
  ('__weakref__', <attribute '__weakref__' of 'A' objects>),
  ('get_name', <function A.get_name at 0x101c99598>)]
```

To find the methods of a class, use the isfunction() predicate. The ismethod() predicate recognizes only bound methods of instances.

Listing 18.37: **inspect_getmembers_class_methods.py**

```
import inspect
from pprint import pprint

import example

pprint(inspect.getmembers(example.A, inspect.isfunction))
```

Now only unbound methods are returned.

```
$ python3 inspect_getmembers_class_methods.py

[('__init__', <function A.__init__ at 0x10139d510>),
 ('get_name', <function A.get_name at 0x10139d598>)]
```

The output for B includes the override for get_name() as well as the new method, and the inherited __init__() method implemented in A.

Listing 18.38: **inspect_getmembers_class_methods_b.py**

```
import inspect
from pprint import pprint

import example

pprint(inspect.getmembers(example.B, inspect.isfunction))
```

Methods inherited from A, such as __init__(), are identified as being methods of B.

```
$ python3 inspect_getmembers_class_methods_b.py

[('__init__', <function A.__init__ at 0x10129d510>),
 ('do_something', <function B.do_something at 0x10129d620>),
 ('get_name', <function B.get_name at 0x10129d6a8>)]
```

18.4.4   Inspecting Instances

Inspecting instances works in the same way as inspecting other objects.

Listing 18.39: **inspect_getmembers_instance.py**

```
import inspect
from pprint import pprint

import example

a = example.A(name='inspect_getmembers')
pprint(inspect.getmembers(a, inspect.ismethod))
```

The predicate `ismethod()` recognizes two bound methods from `A` in the example instance.

```
$ python3 inspect_getmembers_instance.py

[('__init__', <bound method A.__init__ of <example.A object at 0
x101ab1ba8>>),
 ('get_name', <bound method A.get_name of <example.A object at 0
x101ab1ba8>>)]
```

18.4.5   Documentation Strings

To retrieve the docstring for an object, use `getdoc()`. The return value is the `__doc__` attribute with tabs expanded to spaces and with indentation made uniform.

Listing 18.40: **inspect_getdoc.py**

```
import inspect
import example

print('B.__doc__:')
print(example.B.__doc__)
print()
print('getdoc(B):')
print(inspect.getdoc(example.B))
```

The second line of the docstring is indented when it is retrieved through the attribute directly, but moved to the left margin by `getdoc()`.

```
$ python3 inspect_getdoc.py

B.__doc__:
This is the B class.
    It is derived from A.


getdoc(B):
This is the B class.
It is derived from A.
```

In addition to the actual docstring, it is possible to retrieve the comments from the source file where an object is implemented, if the source is available. The getcomments() function looks at the source of the object and finds comments on lines preceding the implementation.

Listing 18.41: **inspect_getcomments_method.py**

```
import inspect
import example

print(inspect.getcomments(example.B.do_something))
```

The lines returned include the comment prefix with any whitespace prefix stripped off.

```
$ python3 inspect_getcomments_method.py

# This method is not part of A.
```

When a module is passed to getcomments(), the return value is always the first comment in the module.

Listing 18.42: **inspect_getcomments_module.py**

```
import inspect
import example

print(inspect.getcomments(example))
```

Contiguous lines from the example file are included as a single comment, but as soon as a blank line appears the comment is stopped.

```
$ python3 inspect_getcomments_module.py

# This comment appears first
# and spans 2 lines.
```

18.4.6   Retrieving Source

If the .py file is available for a module, the original source code for the class or method can be retrieved using getsource() and getsourcelines().

Listing 18.43: **inspect_getsource_class.py**

```
import inspect
import example

print(inspect.getsource(example.A))
```

When a class is passed in, all of the methods for the class are included in the output.

```
$ python3 inspect_getsource_class.py

class A(object):
    """The A class."""

    def __init__(self, name):
        self.name = name

    def get_name(self):
        "Returns the name of the instance."
        return self.name
```

To retrieve the source for a single method, pass the method reference to getsource().

Listing 18.44: **inspect_getsource_method.py**

```
import inspect
import example

print(inspect.getsource(example.A.get_name))
```

The original indent level is retained in this case.

```
$ python3 inspect_getsource_method.py

    def get_name(self):
        "Returns the name of the instance."
        return self.name
```

Use getsourcelines() instead of getsource() to retrieve the lines of a source file and split them into individual strings.

Listing 18.45: **inspect_getsourcelines_method.py**

```
import inspect
import pprint
```

```
import example

pprint.pprint(inspect.getsourcelines(example.A.get_name))
```

The return value from `getsourcelines()` is a `tuple` containing a list of strings (the lines from the source file) plus the line number in the file where the source begins.

```
$ python3 inspect_getsourcelines_method.py

(['    def get_name(self):\n',
  '        "Returns the name of the instance."\n',
  '        return self.name\n'],
 23)
```

If the source file is not available, `getsource()` and `getsourcelines()` raise an `IOError`.

18.4.7 Method and Function Signatures

In addition to the documentation for a function or method, a complete specification can be obtained for the arguments that the callable takes, including their default values. The `signature()` function returns a `Signature` instance containing information about the arguments to the function.

Listing 18.46: **inspect_signature_function.py**

```
import inspect
import example

sig = inspect.signature(example.module_level_function)
print('module_level_function{}'.format(sig))

print('\nParameter details:')
for name, param in sig.parameters.items():
    if param.kind == inspect.Parameter.POSITIONAL_ONLY:
        print('  {} (positional-only)'.format(name))
    elif param.kind == inspect.Parameter.POSITIONAL_OR_KEYWORD:
        if param.default != inspect.Parameter.empty:
            print('  {}={!r}'.format(name, param.default))
        else:
            print('  {}'.format(name))
    elif param.kind == inspect.Parameter.VAR_POSITIONAL:
        print('  *{}'.format(name))
    elif param.kind == inspect.Parameter.KEYWORD_ONLY:
        if param.default != inspect.Parameter.empty:
            print('  {}={!r} (keyword-only)'.format(
                name, param.default))
        else:
            print('  {} (keyword-only)'.format(name))
```

```
    elif param.kind == inspect.Parameter.VAR_KEYWORD:
        print('  **{}'.format(name))
```

The function arguments are available through the `parameters` attribute of the `Signature`. `parameters` is an ordered dictionary that maps the parameter names to `Parameter` instances describing the argument. In this example, the first argument to the function, `arg1`, does not have a default value, while `arg2` does.

```
$ python3 inspect_signature_function.py

module_level_function(arg1, arg2='default', *args, **kwargs)

Parameter details:
  arg1
  arg2='default'
  *args
  **kwargs
```

The `Signature` for a function can be used by decorators or other functions to validate inputs, provide different defaults, and perform other tasks. Writing a suitably generic and reusable validation decorator brings one special challenge, though: It can be complicated to match up incoming arguments with their names for functions that accept a combination of named and positional arguments. The `bind()` and `bind_partial()` methods provide the necessary logic to handle the mapping in such cases. They return a `BoundArguments` instance populated with the arguments associated with the names of the arguments of a specified function.

Listing 18.47: **inspect_signature_bind.py**

```
import inspect
import example

sig = inspect.signature(example.module_level_function)

bound = sig.bind(
    'this is arg1',
    'this is arg2',
    'this is an extra positional argument',
    extra_named_arg='value',
)

print('Arguments:')
for name, value in bound.arguments.items():
    print('{} = {!r}'.format(name, value))

print('\nCalling:')
print(example.module_level_function(*bound.args, **bound.kwargs))
```

The `BoundArguments` instance has attributes `args` and `kwargs` that can be used to call the function using the syntax to expand the tuple and dictionary onto the stack as the arguments.

```
$ python3 inspect_signature_bind.py

Arguments:
arg1 = 'this is arg1'
arg2 = 'this is arg2'
args = ('this is an extra positional argument',)
kwargs = {'extra_named_arg': 'value'}

Calling:
this is arg1this is arg1
```

If only some arguments are available, `bind_partial()` will still create a `BoundArguments` instance. It may not be fully usable until the remaining arguments are added.

Listing 18.48: **inspect_signature_bind_partial.py**

```
import inspect
import example

sig = inspect.signature(example.module_level_function)

partial = sig.bind_partial(
    'this is arg1',
)

print('Without defaults:')
for name, value in partial.arguments.items():
    print('{} = {!r}'.format(name, value))

print('\nWith defaults:')
partial.apply_defaults()
for name, value in partial.arguments.items():
    print('{} = {!r}'.format(name, value))
```

`apply_defaults()` will add any values from the parameter defaults.

```
$ python3 inspect_signature_bind_partial.py

Without defaults:
arg1 = 'this is arg1'

With defaults:
arg1 = 'this is arg1'
```

```
arg2 = 'default'
args = ()
kwargs = {}
```

18.4.8   Class Hierarchies

`inspect` includes two methods for working directly with class hierarchies. The first,
`getclasstree()`, creates a tree-like data structure based on the classes it is given and their
base classes. Each element in the list returned is either a tuple with a class and its base
classes, or another list containing tuples for subclasses.

Listing 18.49: inspect_getclasstree.py

```
import inspect
import example


class C(example.B):
    pass


class D(C, example.A):
    pass


def print_class_tree(tree, indent=-1):
    if isinstance(tree, list):
        for node in tree:
            print_class_tree(node, indent + 1)
    else:
        print('  ' * indent, tree[0].__name__)
    return

if __name__ == '__main__':
    print('A, B, C, D:')
    print_class_tree(inspect.getclasstree(
        [example.A, example.B, C, D])
    )
```

The output from this example is the tree of inheritance for the A, B, C, and D classes. D
appears twice, since it inherits from both C and A.

```
$ python3 inspect_getclasstree.py

A, B, C, D:
 object
   A
```

```
      D
      B
        C
          D
```

If getclasstree() is called with unique set to a true value, the output is different.

Listing 18.50: inspect_getclasstree_unique.py

```
import inspect
import example
from inspect_getclasstree import *

print_class_tree(inspect.getclasstree(
    [example.A, example.B, C, D],
    unique=True,
))
```

This time, D appears in the output only once.

```
$ python3 inspect_getclasstree_unique.py

 object
   A
     B
       C
         D
```

18.4.9 Method Resolution Order

The other function for working with class hierarchies is getmro(), which returns a tuple of classes in the order they should be scanned when resolving an attribute that might be inherited from a base class using the *method resolution order* (MRO). Each class in the sequence appears only once.

Listing 18.51: inspect_getmro.py

```
import inspect
import example


class C(object):
    pass


class C_First(C, example.B):
    pass
```

```
class B_First(example.B, C):
    pass


print('B_First:')
for c in inspect.getmro(B_First):
    print('   {}'.format(c.__name__))
print()
print('C_First:')
for c in inspect.getmro(C_First):
    print('   {}'.format(c.__name__))
```

The output from this example demonstrates the "depth-first" nature of the MRO search. For B_First, A also comes before C in the search order, because B is derived from A.

```
$ python3 inspect_getmro.py

B_First:
  B_First
  B
  A
  C
  object

C_First:
  C_First
  C
  B
  A
  object
```

18.4.10   The Stack and Frames

In addition to functions for inspecting code objects, inspect includes functions for inspecting the runtime environment while a program is being executed. Most of these functions work with the call stack, and operate on *call frames*. Frame objects hold the current execution context, including references to the code being run, the operation being executed, and the values of local and global variables. Typically such information is used to build tracebacks when exceptions are raised. It can also be useful for logging or when debugging programs, since the stack frames can be interrogated to discover the argument values passed to the functions.

currentframe() returns the frame at the top of the stack (for the current function).

Listing 18.52: inspect_currentframe.py

```
import inspect
import pprint
```

```
def recurse(limit, keyword='default', *, kwonly='must be named'):
    local_variable = '.' * limit
    keyword = 'changed value of argument'
    frame = inspect.currentframe()
    print('line {} of {}'.format(frame.f_lineno,
                                 frame.f_code.co_filename))
    print('locals:')
    pprint.pprint(frame.f_locals)
    print()
    if limit <= 0:
        return
    recurse(limit - 1)
    return local_variable


if __name__ == '__main__':
    recurse(2)
```

The values of the arguments to recurse() are included in the frame's dictionary of local
variables.

```
$ python3 inspect_currentframe.py

line 14 of inspect_currentframe.py
locals:
{'frame': <frame object at 0x1022a7b88>,
 'keyword': 'changed value of argument',
 'kwonly': 'must be named',
 'limit': 2,
 'local_variable': '..'}

line 14 of inspect_currentframe.py
locals:
{'frame': <frame object at 0x102016b28>,
 'keyword': 'changed value of argument',
 'kwonly': 'must be named',
 'limit': 1,
 'local_variable': '.'}

line 14 of inspect_currentframe.py
locals:
{'frame': <frame object at 0x1020176b8>,
 'keyword': 'changed value of argument',
 'kwonly': 'must be named',
 'limit': 0,
 'local_variable': ''}
```

Using stack(), it is also possible to access all of the stack frames from the current frame
to the first caller. This example is similar to the one shown earlier, except that it waits until
reaching the end of the recursion to print the stack information.

Listing 18.53: **inspect_stack.py**

```
import inspect
import pprint


def show_stack():
    for level in inspect.stack():
        print('{}[{}]\n   -> {}'.format(
            level.frame.f_code.co_filename,
            level.lineno,
            level.code_context[level.index].strip(),
        ))
        pprint.pprint(level.frame.f_locals)
        print()


def recurse(limit):
    local_variable = '.' * limit
    if limit <= 0:
        show_stack()
        return
    recurse(limit - 1)
    return local_variable

if __name__ == '__main__':
    recurse(2)
```

The last part of the output represents the main program, outside of the recurse()
function.

```
$ python3 inspect_stack.py

inspect_stack.py[11]
  -> for level in inspect.stack():
{'level': FrameInfo(frame=<frame object at 0x10127e5d0>,
filename='inspect_stack.py', lineno=11, function='show_stack',
code_context=['    for level in inspect.stack():\n'], index=0)}

inspect_stack.py[24]
  -> show_stack()
{'limit': 0, 'local_variable': ''}

inspect_stack.py[26]
  -> recurse(limit - 1)
{'limit': 1, 'local_variable': '.'}

inspect_stack.py[26]
```

```
    -> recurse(limit - 1)
{'limit': 2, 'local_variable': '..'}

inspect_stack.py[30]
  -> recurse(2)
{'__builtins__': <module 'builtins' (built-in)>,
 '__cached__': None,
 '__doc__': 'Inspecting the call stack.\n',
 '__file__': 'inspect_stack.py',
 '__loader__': <_frozen_importlib_external.SourceFileLoader
object at 0x1007a97f0>,
 '__name__': '__main__',
 '__package__': None,
 '__spec__': None,
 'inspect': <module 'inspect' from
'.../lib/python3.5/inspect.py'>,
 'pprint': <module 'pprint' from '.../lib/python3.5/pprint.py'>,
 'recurse': <function recurse at 0x1012aa400>,
 'show_stack': <function show_stack at 0x1007a6a60>}
```

Other functions are available for building lists of frames in different contexts, such as when an exception is being processed. See the documentation for `trace()`, `getouterframes()`, and `getinnerframes()` for more details.

18.4.11   Command-Line Interface

The `inspect` module also includes a command-line interface for getting details about objects without having to write out the calls in a separate Python program. The input is a module name and optional object from within the module. The default output is the source code for the named object. Using the `--details` argument causes metadata to be printed instead of the source.

```
$ python3 -m inspect -d example

Target: example
Origin: .../example.py
Cached: .../__pycache__/example.cpython-35.pyc
Loader: <_frozen_importlib_external.SourceFileLoader object at 0
x101527860>



$ python3 -m inspect -d example:A

Target: example:A
Origin: .../example.py
Cached: .../__pycache__/example.cpython-35.pyc
Line: 16
```

```
$ python3 -m inspect example:A.get_name

def get_name(self):
    "Returns the name of the instance."
    return self.name
```

TIP

Related Reading

- Standard library documentation for `inspect`.[14]
- Python 2 to 3 porting notes for `inspect` (page 1359).
- Python 2.3 Method Resolution Order[15]: Documentation for the C3 method resolution order used by Python 2.3 and later.
- `pyclbr` (page 1160): The `pyclbr` module provides access to some of the same information as `inspect` by parsing the module without importing it.
- **PEP 362**[16]: Function Signature Object.

---

[14] https://docs.python.org/3.5/library/inspect.html
[15] www.python.org/download/releases/2.3/mro/
[16] www.python.org/dev/peps/pep-0362

Chapter 19

Modules and Packages

Python's primary extension mechanism uses source code saved to modules and incorporated into a program through the `import` statement. The features that most developers think of as "Python" are actually implemented as the collection of modules called the Standard Library, the subject of this book. Although the import feature is built into the interpreter itself, the library also includes several modules related to the import process.

The `importlib` (page 1329) module exposes the underlying implementation of the import mechanism used by the interpreter. It can be used to import modules dynamically at runtime, instead of using the `import` statement to load them during start-up. Dynamically loading modules is useful when the name of a module that needs to be imported is not known in advance, such as for plug-ins or extensions to an application.

Python packages can include supporting resource files such as templates, default configuration files, images, and other data, along with source code. The interface for accessing resource files in a portable way is implemented in the `pkgutil` (page 1334) module. It also includes support for modifying the import path for a package, so that the contents can be installed into multiple directories but appear as part of the same package.

`zipimport` (page 1344) provides a custom importer for modules and packages saved to ZIP archives. It is used to load Python EGG files, for example, and can also be used as a convenient way to package and distribute an application.

19.1 importlib: Python's Import Mechanism

The `importlib` module includes functions that implement Python's import mechanism for loading code in packages and modules. It is one access point to importing modules dynamically, and is useful in some cases where the name of the module that needs to be imported is unknown when the code is written (for example, for plug-ins or extensions to an application).

19.1.1 Example Package

The examples in this section use a package called `example` with `__init__.py`.

Listing 19.1: example/__init__.py

```
print('Importing example package')
```

This package also contains `submodule.py`.

Listing 19.2: **example/submodule.py**

```
print('Importing submodule')
```

Watch for the text from the `print()` calls in the sample output when the package or module are imported.

19.1.2   Module Types

Python supports several styles of modules. Each requires its own handling when opening the module and adding it to the namespace, and support for the formats varies by platform. For example, under Microsoft Windows, shared libraries are loaded from files with the extensions `.dll` and `.pyd`, instead of `.so`. The extensions for C modules may also change when using a debug build of the interpreter instead of a normal release build, since they can be compiled with debug information included as well. If a C extension library or other module is not loading as expected, use the constants defined in `importlib.machinery` to find the supported types for the current platform, as well as the parameters for loading them.

Listing 19.3: **importlib_suffixes.py**

```
import importlib.machinery

SUFFIXES = [
    ('Source:', importlib.machinery.SOURCE_SUFFIXES),
    ('Debug:',
     importlib.machinery.DEBUG_BYTECODE_SUFFIXES),
    ('Optimized:',
     importlib.machinery.OPTIMIZED_BYTECODE_SUFFIXES),
    ('Bytecode:', importlib.machinery.BYTECODE_SUFFIXES),
    ('Extension:', importlib.machinery.EXTENSION_SUFFIXES),
]


def main():
    tmpl = '{:<10}  {}'
    for name, value in SUFFIXES:
        print(tmpl.format(name, value))

if __name__ == '__main__':
    main()
```

The return value is a sequence of tuples containing the file extension, the mode to use for opening the file containing the module, and a type code from a constant defined in the module. The following output is incomplete, because some of the importable module or package types do not correspond to single files.

```
$ python3 importlib_suffixes.py

Source:    ['.py']
```

```
Debug:        ['.pyc']
Optimized:    ['.pyc']
Bytecode:     ['.pyc']
Extension:    ['.cpython-35m-darwin.so', '.abi3.so', '.so']
```

19.1.3   Importing Modules

The high-level API in `importlib` simplifies the process of importing a module given an absolute or relative name. When using a relative module name, specify the package containing the module as a separate argument.

Listing 19.4: **importlib_import_module.py**

```
import importlib


m1 = importlib.import_module('example.submodule')
print(m1)

m2 = importlib.import_module('.submodule', package='example')
print(m2)

print(m1 is m2)
```

The return value from `import_module()` is the module object that was created by the import.

```
$ python3 importlib_import_module.py

Importing example package
Importing submodule
<module 'example.submodule' from '.../example/submodule.py'>
<module 'example.submodule' from '.../example/submodule.py'>
True
```

If the module cannot be imported, `import_module()` raises `ImportError`.

Listing 19.5: **importlib_import_module_error.py**

```
import importlib


try:
    importlib.import_module('example.nosuchmodule')
except ImportError as err:
    print('Error:', err)
```

The error message includes the name of the missing module.

```
$ python3 importlib_import_module_error.py

Importing example package
Error: No module named 'example.nosuchmodule'
```

To reload an existing module, use reload().

Listing 19.6: importlib_reload.py

```
import importlib


m1 = importlib.import_module('example.submodule')
print(m1)

m2 = importlib.reload(m1)
print(m1 is m2)
```

The return value from reload() is the new module. Depending on which type of loader was used, it may be the same module instance.

```
$ python3 importlib_reload.py

Importing example package
Importing submodule
<module 'example.submodule' from '.../example/submodule.py'>
Importing submodule
True
```

19.1.4 Loaders

The lower-level API in importlib provides access to the loader objects, as described in Section 17.2.6, "Modules and Imports" (page 1200) in the section on the sys module. To get a loader for a module, use find_loader(). Then, to retrieve the module, use the loader's load_module() method.

Listing 19.7: importlib_find_loader.py

```
import importlib

loader = importlib.find_loader('example')
print('Loader:', loader)

m = loader.load_module()
print('Module:', m)
```

This example loads the top level of the example package.

```
$ python3 importlib_find_loader.py

Loader: <_frozen_importlib_external.SourceFileLoader object at
0x101be0da0>
Importing example package
Module: <module 'example' from '.../example/__init__.py'>
```

Submodules within packages need to be loaded separately using the path from the package. In the following example, the package is loaded first, and then its path is passed to find_loader() to create a loader capable of loading the submodule.

Listing 19.8: **importlib_submodule.py**

```
import importlib

pkg_loader = importlib.find_loader('example')
pkg = pkg_loader.load_module()

loader = importlib.find_loader('submodule', pkg.__path__)
print('Loader:', loader)

m = loader.load_module()
print('Module:', m)
```

Unlike with import_module(), the name of the submodule should be given without any relative path prefix, since the loader will already be constrained by the package's path.

```
$ python3 importlib_submodule.py

Importing example package
Loader: <_frozen_importlib_external.SourceFileLoader object at
0x1012e5390>
Importing submodule
Module: <module 'submodule' from '.../example/submodule.py'>
```

TIP

Related Reading

- Standard library documentation for importlib.[1]
- Section 17.2.6, "Modules and Imports" (page 1200): Import hooks, the module search path, and other related machinery in the sys module.
- inspect (page 1311): Load information from a module programmatically.

---

[1] https://docs.python.org/3.5/library/importlib.html

- **PEP 302**[2]: New-import hooks.
- **PEP 369**[3]: Post-import hooks.
- **PEP 488**[4]: Elimination of PYO files.

19.2   pkgutil: Package Utilities

The `pkgutil` module includes functions for changing the import rules for Python packages and for loading non-code resources from files distributed within a package.

19.2.1   Package Import Paths

The `extend_path()` function is used to modify the search path and change the way sub-modules are imported from within a package so that several different directories can be combined as though they were one. This function can be used to override installed versions of packages with development versions, or to combine platform-specific and shared modules into a single package namespace.

The most common way to call `extend_path()` is by adding two lines to the `__init__.py` inside the package.

```
import pkgutil
__path__ = pkgutil.extend_path(__path__, __name__)
```

`extend_path()` scans `sys.path` for directories that include a subdirectory whose name is based on the package given as the second argument. The list of directories is combined with the path value passed as the first argument and returned as a single list, suitable for use as the package import path.

The example package called `demopkg` includes two files, `__init__.py` and `shared.py`. The `__init__.py` file in `demopkg1` contains `print` statements to show the search path before and after it is modified, to highlight the differences between these paths.

Listing 19.9: `demopkg1/__init__.py`

```
import pkgutil
import pprint

print('demopkg1.__path__ before:')
pprint.pprint(__path__)
print()

__path__ = pkgutil.extend_path(__path__, __name__)

print('demopkg1.__path__ after:')
```

---

[2] www.python.org/dev/peps/pep-0302
[3] www.python.org/dev/peps/pep-0369
[4] www.python.org/dev/peps/pep-0488

```
    pprint.pprint(__path__)
    print()
```

The extension directory, with add-on features for demopkg, contains three more source files. An __init__.py is present at each directory level, as well as a not_shared.py.

```
$ find extension -name '*.py'

extension/__init__.py
extension/demopkg1/__init__.py
extension/demopkg1/not_shared.py
```

The next simple test program imports the demopkg1 package.

Listing 19.10: pkgutil_extend_path.py

```
import demopkg1
print('demopkg1            :', demopkg1.__file__)

try:
    import demopkg1.shared
except Exception as err:
    print('demopkg1.shared    : Not found ({})'.format(err))
else:
    print('demopkg1.shared    :', demopkg1.shared.__file__)

try:
    import demopkg1.not_shared
except Exception as err:
    print('demopkg1.not_shared: Not found ({})'.format(err))
else:
    print('demopkg1.not_shared:', demopkg1.not_shared.__file__)
```

When this test program is run directly from the command line, the not_shared module is not found.

NOTE

The full file system paths in these examples have been shortened to emphasize the parts that change.

```
$ python3 pkgutil_extend_path.py

demopkg1.__path__ before:
['.../demopkg1']

demopkg1.__path__ after:
['.../demopkg1']

demopkg1            : .../demopkg1/__init__.py
```

```
demopkg1.shared    : .../demopkg1/shared.py
demopkg1.not_shared: Not found (No module named 'demopkg1.not_sh
ared')
```

However, if the extension directory is added to the PYTHONPATH and the program is run again, different results are produced.

```
$ PYTHONPATH=extension python3 pkgutil_extend_path.py

demopkg1.__path__ before:
['.../demopkg1']

demopkg1.__path__ after:
['.../demopkg1',
 '.../extension/demopkg1']

demopkg1           : .../demopkg1/__init__.py
demopkg1.shared    : .../demopkg1/shared.py
demopkg1.not_shared: .../extension/demopkg1/not_shared.py
```

The version of demopkg1 inside the extension directory has been added to the search path, so the not_shared module is found there.

Extending the path in this manner is useful for combining platform-specific versions of packages with common packages, especially if the platform-specific versions include C extension modules.

19.2.2   Development Versions of Packages

While creating enhancements to a project, a developer often needs to test changes to an installed package. Replacing the installed copy with a development version may be a bad idea, since that version is not necessarily correct and other tools on the system are likely to depend on the installed package.

A completely separate copy of the package could be configured in a development environment using virtualenv or venv (page 1163). For small modifications, however, the overhead of setting up a virtual environment with all of the dependencies may be excessive.

Another option is to use pkgutil to modify the module search path for modules that belong to the package under development. In this case, the path must be reversed so the development version will override the installed version.

Given a package demopkg2 containing an __init__.py and overloaded.py, with the function under development located in demopkg2/overloaded.py, the installed version contains

Listing 19.11: demopkg2/overloaded.py

```
def func():
    print('This is the installed version of func().')
```

and demopkg2/__init__.py contains

Listing 19.12: demopkg2/__init__.py

```
import pkgutil

__path__ = pkgutil.extend_path(__path__, __name__)
__path__.reverse()
```

reverse() is used to ensure that any directories added to the search path by pkgutil are scanned for imports *before* the default location.

The next program imports demopkg2.overloaded and calls func().

Listing 19.13: pkgutil_devel.py

```
import demopkg2
print('demopkg2             :', demopkg2.__file__)

import demopkg2.overloaded
print('demopkg2.overloaded:', demopkg2.overloaded.__file__)

print()
demopkg2.overloaded.func()
```

Running it without any special path treatment produces output from the installed version of func().

```
$ python3 pkgutil_devel.py

demopkg2             : .../demopkg2/__init__.py
demopkg2.overloaded: .../demopkg2/overloaded.py

This is the installed version of func().
```

A development directory containing

```
$ find develop/demopkg2 -name '*.py'

develop/demopkg2/__init__.py
develop/demopkg2/overloaded.py
```

and a modified version of overloaded,

Listing 19.14: develop/demopkg2/overloaded.py

```
def func():
    print('This is the development version of func().')
```

will be loaded when the test program is run with the `develop` directory in the search path.

```
$ PYTHONPATH=develop python3 pkgutil_devel.py

demopkg2           : .../demopkg2/__init__.py
demopkg2.overloaded: .../develop/demopkg2/overloaded.py

This is the development version of func().
```

19.2.3   Managing Paths with PKG Files

The first example illustrated how to extend the search path using extra directories included in the PYTHONPATH. It is also possible to extend the search path by using *.pkg files containing directory names. PKG files are similar to the PTH files used by the site (page 1169) module. They can contain directory names, one per line, to be added to the search path for the package.

Another way to structure the platform-specific portions of the application from the first example is to use a separate directory for each operating system, and include a .pkg file to extend the search path.

The next example uses the same demopkg1 files, and also includes the following files.

```
$ find os_* -type f

os_one/demopkg1/__init__.py
os_one/demopkg1/not_shared.py
os_one/demopkg1.pkg
os_two/demopkg1/__init__.py
os_two/demopkg1/not_shared.py
os_two/demopkg1.pkg
```

The PKG files are named demopkg1.pkg to match the package being extended. They both contain one line.

```
demopkg
```

This demonstration program shows the version of the module being imported.

Listing 19.15: pkgutil_os_specific.py

```
import demopkg1
print('demopkg1:', demopkg1.__file__)

import demopkg1.shared
print('demopkg1.shared:', demopkg1.shared.__file__)

import demopkg1.not_shared
print('demopkg1.not_shared:', demopkg1.not_shared.__file__)
```

A simple wrapper script can be used to switch between the two packages.

Listing 19.16: with_os.sh

```sh
#!/bin/sh

export PYTHONPATH=os_${1}
echo "PYTHONPATH=$PYTHONPATH"
echo

python3 pkgutil_os_specific.py
```

When this script is run with "one" or "two" as the argument, the path is adjusted.

```
$ ./with_os.sh one

PYTHONPATH=os_one

demopkg1.__path__ before:
['.../demopkg1']

demopkg1.__path__ after:
['.../demopkg1',
 '.../os_one/demopkg1',
 'demopkg']

demopkg1: .../demopkg1/__init__.py
demopkg1.shared: .../demopkg1/shared.py
demopkg1.not_shared: .../os_one/demopkg1/not_shared.py

$ ./with_os.sh two

PYTHONPATH=os_two

demopkg1.__path__ before:
['.../demopkg1']

demopkg1.__path__ after:
['.../demopkg1',
 '.../os_two/demopkg1',
 'demopkg']

demopkg1: .../demopkg1/__init__.py
demopkg1.shared: .../demopkg1/shared.py
demopkg1.not_shared: .../os_two/demopkg1/not_shared.py
```

PKG files can appear anywhere in the normal search path, so a single PKG file in the current working directory could also be used to include a development tree.

19.2.4   Nested Packages

For nested packages, only the path of the top-level package needs to be modified. As an example, consider the directory structure

```
$ find nested -name '*.py'

nested/__init__.py
nested/second/__init__.py
nested/second/deep.py
nested/shallow.py
```

where nested/__init__.py contains

Listing 19.17: nested/__init__.py

```
import pkgutil

__path__ = pkgutil.extend_path(__path__, __name__)
__path__.reverse()
```

and a development tree like

```
$ find develop/nested -name '*.py'

develop/nested/__init__.py
develop/nested/second/__init__.py
develop/nested/second/deep.py
develop/nested/shallow.py
```

Both the shallow and deep modules contain a simple function to print out a message indicating whether they come from the installed or development version. The following test program exercises the new packages.

Listing 19.18: pkgutil_nested.py

```
import nested

import nested.shallow
print('nested.shallow:', nested.shallow.__file__)
nested.shallow.func()

print()
import nested.second.deep
print('nested.second.deep:', nested.second.deep.__file__)
nested.second.deep.func()
```

When pkgutil_nested.py is run without any path manipulation, the installed versions of both modules are used.

```
$ python3 pkgutil_nested.py

nested.shallow: .../nested/shallow.py
This func() comes from the installed version of nested.shallow

nested.second.deep: .../nested/second/deep.py
This func() comes from the installed version of nested.second.de
ep
```

When the `develop` directory is added to the path, the development versions of both functions override the installed versions.

```
$ PYTHONPATH=develop python3 pkgutil_nested.py

nested.shallow: .../develop/nested/shallow.py
This func() comes from the development version of nested.shallow

nested.second.deep: .../develop/nested/second/deep.py
This func() comes from the development version of nested.second.
deep
```

19.2.5   Package Data

In addition to code, Python packages can contain data files such as templates, default configuration files, images, and other supporting files used by the code in the package. The `get_data()` function gives access to the data in the files in a format-agnostic way, so it does not matter if the package is distributed as an EGG, as part of a frozen binary, or as regular files on the file system.

Suppose the a package `pkgwithdata` contains a `templates` directory.

```
$ find pkgwithdata -type f

pkgwithdata/__init__.py
pkgwithdata/templates/base.html
```

The file `pkgwithdata/templates/base.html` contains a simple HTML template.

Listing 19.19: **pkgwithdata/templates/base.html**

```
<!DOCTYPE HTML PUBLIC "-//IETF//DTD HTML//EN">
<html> <head>
<title>PyMOTW Template</title>
</head>

<body>
<h1>Example Template</h1>
```

```
<p>This is a sample data file.</p>

</body>
</html>
```

The following program uses `get_data()` to retrieve the template contents and print them out.

Listing 19.20: pkgutil_get_data.py

```
import pkgutil

template = pkgutil.get_data('pkgwithdata', 'templates/base.html')
print(template.decode('utf-8'))
```

The arguments to `get_data()` are the dotted name of the package and a filename relative to the top of the package. The return value is a byte sequence, so it is decoded from UTF-8 before being printed.

```
$ python3 pkgutil_get_data.py

<!DOCTYPE HTML PUBLIC "-//IETF//DTD HTML//EN">
<html> <head>
<title>PyMOTW Template</title>
</head>

<body>
<h1>Example Template</h1>

<p>This is a sample data file.</p>

</body>
</html>
```

`get_data()` is distribution format-agnostic because it uses the import hooks defined in **PEP 302** to access the package contents. Any loader that provides the hooks can be used, including the ZIP archive importer in `zipfile` (page 511).

Listing 19.21: pkgutil_get_data_zip.py

```
import pkgutil
import zipfile
import sys

# Create a ZIP file with code from the current directory
# and the template using a name that does not appear on the
# local file system.
with zipfile.PyZipFile('pkgwithdatainzip.zip', mode='w') as zf:
    zf.writepy('.')
    zf.write('pkgwithdata/templates/base.html',
```

```
                    'pkgwithdata/templates/fromzip.html',
                    )

# Add the ZIP file to the import path.
sys.path.insert(0, 'pkgwithdatainzip.zip')

# Import pkgwithdata to show that it comes from the ZIP archive.
import pkgwithdata
print('Loading pkgwithdata from', pkgwithdata.__file__)

# Print the template body.
print('\nTemplate:')
data = pkgutil.get_data('pkgwithdata', 'templates/fromzip.html')
print(data.decode('utf-8'))
```

This example uses `PyZipFile.writepy()` to create a ZIP archive containing a copy of the `pkgwithdata` package, including a renamed version of the template file. It then adds the ZIP archive to the import path, before using `pkgutil` to load the template and print it. Refer to the discussion of `zipfile` (page 511) for more details about using `writepy()`.

```
$ python3 pkgutil_get_data_zip.py

Loading pkgwithdata from
pkgwithdatainzip.zip/pkgwithdata/__init__.pyc

Template:
<!DOCTYPE HTML PUBLIC "-//IETF//DTD HTML//EN">
<html> <head>
<title>PyMOTW Template</title>
</head>

<body>
<h1>Example Template</h1>

<p>This is a sample data file.</p>

</body>
</html>
```

TIP

Related Reading

- Standard library documentation for `pkgutil`.[5]
- `virtualenv`[6]: Ian Bicking's virtual environment script.
- `distutils`: Packaging tools from the Python standard library.

---

[5] https://docs.python.org/3.5/library/pkgutil.html
[6] http://pypi.python.org/pypi/virtualenv

- setuptools[7]: Next-generation packaging tools.
- **PEP 302**[8]: Import Hooks.
- zipfile (page 511): Create importable ZIP archives.
- zipimport (page 1344): Importer for packages in ZIP archives.

19.3   zipimport: Load Python Code from ZIP Archives

The zipimport module implements the zipimporter class, which can be used to find and load Python modules inside ZIP archives. The zipimporter supports the import hooks API specified in **PEP 302**; it is how Python Eggs work.

Using the zipimport module directly is rarely necessary, since importing directly from a ZIP archive is feasible as long as that archive appears in sys.path. Nevertheless, studying how the importer API can be used can help a programmer learn the features available and understand how module importing works. Knowing how the ZIP importer works will also help when debugging the issues that may come up when distributing applications packaged as ZIP archives created with zipfile.PyZipFile.

19.3.1   Example

The followiong examples reuse some of the code from the discussion of zipfile (page 511) to create an example ZIP archive containing a few Python modules.

Listing 19.22: **zipimport_make_example.py**

```
import sys
import zipfile

if __name__ == '__main__':
    zf = zipfile.PyZipFile('zipimport_example.zip', mode='w')
    try:
        zf.writepy('.')
        zf.write('zipimport_get_source.py')
        zf.write('example_package/README.txt')
    finally:
        zf.close()
    for name in zf.namelist():
        print(name)
```

Run zipimport_make_example.py before trying any of the other examples, so as to create a ZIP archive containing all of the modules in the example directory, along with some test data needed for the examples in this section.

---

[7] https://setuptools.readthedocs.io/en/latest/
[8] www.python.org/dev/peps/pep-0302

```
$ python3 zipimport_make_example.py

__init__.pyc
example_package/__init__.pyc
zipimport_find_module.pyc
zipimport_get_code.pyc
zipimport_get_data.pyc
zipimport_get_data_nozip.pyc
zipimport_get_data_zip.pyc
zipimport_get_source.pyc
zipimport_is_package.pyc
zipimport_load_module.pyc
zipimport_make_example.pyc
zipimport_get_source.py
example_package/README.txt
```

19.3.2 Finding a Module

Given the full name of a module, find_module() will try to locate that module inside the ZIP archive.

Listing 19.23: **zipimport_find_module.py**

```
import zipimport

importer = zipimport.zipimporter('zipimport_example.zip')

for module_name in ['zipimport_find_module', 'not_there']:
    print(module_name, ':', importer.find_module(module_name))
```

If the module is found, the zipimporter instance is returned. Otherwise, None is returned.

```
$ python3 zipimport_find_module.py

zipimport_find_module : <zipimporter object
"zipimport_example.zip">
not_there : None
```

19.3.3 Accessing Code

The get_code() method loads the code object for a module from the archive.

Listing 19.24: **zipimport_get_code.py**

```
import zipimport

importer = zipimport.zipimporter('zipimport_example.zip')
```

```
code = importer.get_code('zipimport_get_code')
print(code)
```

The code object is not the same as a `module` object, but is used to create one.

```
$ python3 zipimport_get_code.py

<code object <module> at 0x1012b4ae0, file
"./zipimport_get_code.py", line 6>
```

To load the code as a usable module, use `load_module()` instead.

Listing 19.25: `zipimport_load_module.py`

```
import zipimport

importer = zipimport.zipimporter('zipimport_example.zip')
module = importer.load_module('zipimport_get_code')
print('Name   :', module.__name__)
print('Loader :', module.__loader__)
print('Code   :', module.code)
```

The result is a module object configured as though the code had been loaded from a regular import.

```
$ python3 zipimport_load_module.py

<code object <module> at 0x1007b4c00, file
"./zipimport_get_code.py", line 6>
Name   : zipimport_get_code
Loader : <zipimporter object "zipimport_example.zip">
Code   : <code object <module> at 0x1007b4c00, file
"./zipimport_get_code.py", line 6>
```

19.3.4   Source

As with the `inspect` (page 1311) module, it is possible to retrieve the source code for a module from the ZIP archive with the `zipimport` module, if the archive includes the source. In the following example, only `zipimport_get_source.py` is added to `zipimport_example.zip`; the rest of the modules are just added as the `.pyc` files.

Listing 19.26: `zipimport_get_source.py`

```
import zipimport

modules = [
    'zipimport_get_code',
```

```
        'zipimport_get_source',
]

importer = zipimport.zipimporter('zipimport_example.zip')
for module_name in modules:
    source = importer.get_source(module_name)
    print('=' * 80)
    print(module_name)
    print('=' * 80)
    print(source)
    print()
```

If the source for a module is not available, get_source() returns None.

```
$ python3 zipimport_get_source.py

================================================================
zipimport_get_code
================================================================
None

================================================================
zipimport_get_source
================================================================
#!/usr/bin/env python3
#
# Copyright 2007 Doug Hellmann.
#
"""Retrieving the source code for a module within a zip archive.
"""

#end_pymotw_header
import zipimport

modules = [
    'zipimport_get_code',
    'zipimport_get_source',
]

importer = zipimport.zipimporter('zipimport_example.zip')
for module_name in modules:
    source = importer.get_source(module_name)
    print('=' * 80)
    print(module_name)
    print('=' * 80)
    print(source)
    print()
```

19.3.5   Packages

To determine whether a name refers to a package instead of a regular module, use
`is_package()`.

Listing 19.27: `zipimport_is_package.py`

```
import zipimport

importer = zipimport.zipimporter('zipimport_example.zip')
for name in ['zipimport_is_package', 'example_package']:
    print(name, importer.is_package(name))
```

In this case, `zipimport_is_package` came from a module and the `example_package` is a
package.

```
$ python3 zipimport_is_package.py

zipimport_is_package False
example_package True
```

19.3.6   Data

Sometimes source modules or packages need to be distributed with non-code data. Images,
configuration files, default data, and test fixtures are just a few examples of these types of
data. Frequently, the module `__path__` or `__file__` attributes are used to find these data
files relative to where the code is installed.

For example, with a "normal" module, the file system path can be constructed from the
`__file__` attribute of the imported package as in the following code.

Listing 19.28: `zipimport_get_data_nozip.py`

```
import os
import example_package

# Find the directory containing the imported
# package and build the data filename from it.
pkg_dir = os.path.dirname(example_package.__file__)
data_filename = os.path.join(pkg_dir, 'README.txt')

# Read the file and show its contents.
print(data_filename, ':')
print(open(data_filename, 'r').read())
```

The output will depend on where the sample code is located on the file system.

```
$ python3 zipimport_get_data_nozip.py

.../example_package/README.txt :
```

> This file represents sample data which could be embedded in the
> ZIP archive. You could include a configuration file, images, or
> any other sort of noncode data.

If the example_package is imported from the ZIP archive instead of the file system, using
__file__ does not work.

Listing 19.29: zipimport_get_data_zip.py

```
import sys
sys.path.insert(0, 'zipimport_example.zip')

import os
import example_package
print(example_package.__file__)
data_filename = os.path.join(
    os.path.dirname(example_package.__file__),
    'README.txt',
)
print(data_filename, ':')
print(open(data_filename, 'rt').read())
```

The __file__ of the package refers to the ZIP archive, rather than a directory, so building
up the path to the README.txt file gives the wrong value.

```
$ python3 zipimport_get_data_zip.py

zipimport_example.zip/example_package/__init__.pyc
zipimport_example.zip/example_package/README.txt :
Traceback (most recent call last):
  File "zipimport_get_data_zip.py", line 20, in <module>
    print(open(data_filename, 'rt').read())
NotADirectoryError: [Errno 20] Not a directory:
'zipimport_example.zip/example_package/README.txt'
```

A more reliable way to retrieve the file is to use the get_data() method. The zipimporter
instance that loaded the module can be accessed through the __loader__ attribute of the
imported module.

Listing 19.30: zipimport_get_data.py

```
import sys
sys.path.insert(0, 'zipimport_example.zip')

import os
import example_package
print(example_package.__file__)
data = example_package.__loader__.get_data(
```

```
        'example_package/README.txt')
    print(data.decode('utf-8'))
```

pkgutil.get_data() uses this interface to access data from within a package. The value
returned is a byte string, which needs to be decoded to a Unicode string before it is printed.

```
$ python3 zipimport_get_data.py

zipimport_example.zip/example_package/__init__.pyc
This file represents sample data which could be embedded in the
ZIP archive.  You could include a configuration file, images, or
any other sort of noncode data.
```

The __loader__ is not set for modules not imported via zipimport.

TIP

Related Reading

- Standard library documentation for zipimport.[9]
- Python 2 to 3 porting notes for zipimport (page 1365).
- imp: Other import-related functions.
- pkgutil (page 1334): Provides a more generic interface to get_data().
- zipfile (page 511): Read and write ZIP archive files.
- **PEP 302**[10]: New Import Hooks.

---

[9] https://docs.python.org/3.5/library/zipimport.html
[10] www.python.org/dev/peps/pep-0302

Appendix A
Porting Notes

This section includes notes and tips for updating from Python 2 to Python 3, including summaries of and references for the changes in each module.

A.1 References

The notes in this section are based on the *What's New* documents prepared by the Python development team and release manager for each release.

- What's New In Python 3.0[1]

- What's New In Python 3.1[2]

- What's New In Python 3.2[3]

- What's New In Python 3.3[4]

- What's New In Python 3.4[5]

- What's New In Python 3.5[6]

For more information about porting to Python 3, refer to the following documents:

- Porting Python 2 Code to Python 3[7]

- Porting to Python 3[8], by Lennart Regebro

- The python-porting[9] mailing list

---

[1] https://docs.python.org/3.0/whatsnew/3.0.html
[2] https://docs.python.org/3.1/whatsnew/3.1.html
[3] https://docs.python.org/3.2/whatsnew/3.2.html
[4] https://docs.python.org/3.3/whatsnew/3.3.html
[5] https://docs.python.org/3.4/whatsnew/3.4.html
[6] https://docs.python.org/3.5/whatsnew/3.5.html
[7] https://docs.python.org/3/howto/pyporting.html
[8] http://python3porting.com/
[9] http://mail.python.org/mailman/listinfo/python-porting

A.2   New Modules

Python 3 includes a number of new modules, providing features not present in Python 2:

asyncio (page 617) Asynchronous I/O, event loop, and other concurrency tools.

concurrent.futures (page 677) Managing pools of concurrent tasks.

ensurepip (page 1167) Install the Python Package Installer, pip.

enum (page 66) Defines enumeration type.

ipaddress (page 687) Classes for working with Internet Protocol (IP) addresses.

pathlib (page 305) An object-oriented API for working with file system paths.

selectors (page 724) I/O multiplexing abstractions.

statistics (page 290) Statistical calculations.

venv (page 1163) Create isolated installation and execution contexts.

A.3   Renamed Modules

Many standard library modules were renamed between Python 2 and 3 as part of **PEP 3108**. All of the new module names consistently use lowercase, and some have been moved into packages to better organize related modules. Often, code using these modules can be updated to work with Python 3 just by fixing the import statements. A complete list of the renamed modules can be found in the dictionary lib2to3.fixes.fix_imports.MAPPING (the keys are the Python 2 name and the values are the Python 3 name) and in Table A.1.

TIP

Related Reading

- The Six[10] package is useful for writing code that runs under both Python 2 and 3. In particular, the six.moves module allows your code to import renamed modules using a single import statement, automatically redirecting the import to the correct version of the name depending on the version of Python.
- **PEP 3108**[11]: Standard Library Reorganization.

---

[10] http://pythonhosted.org/six/
[11] www.python.org/dev/peps/pep-3108

Table A.1: Renamed Modules

Python 2 name	Python 3 name
`__builtin__`	`builtins`
`_winreg`	`winreg`
`BaseHTTPServer`	`http.server` (page 781)
`CGIHTTPServer`	`http.server` (page 781)
`commands`	`subprocess` (page 535)
`ConfigParser`	`configparser` (page 960)
`Cookie`	`http.cookies` (page 790)
`cookielib`	`http.cookiejar`
`copy_reg`	`copyreg`
`cPickle`	`pickle` (page 396)
`cStringIO`	`io` (page 390)
`dbhash`	`dbm.bsd`
`dbm`	`dbm.ndbm`
`Dialog`	`tkinter.dialog`
`DocXMLRPCServer`	`xmlrpc.server` (page 827)
`dumbdbm`	`dbm.dumb`
`FileDialog`	`tkinter.filedialog`
`gdbm`	`dbm.gnu`
`htmlentitydefs`	`html.entities`
`HTMLParser`	`html.parser`
`httplib`	`http.client`
`Queue`	`queue` (page 111)
`repr`	`reprlib`
`robotparser`	`urllib.robotparser` (page 773)
`ScrolledText`	`tkinter.scrolledtext`
`SimpleDialog`	`tkinter.simpledialog`
`SimpleHTTPServer`	`http.server` (page 781)
`SimpleXMLRPCServer`	`xmlrpc.server` (page 827)
`SocketServer`	`socketserver` (page 742)
`StringIO`	`io` (page 390)
`Tix`	`tkinter.tix`
`tkColorChooser`	`tkinter.colorchooser`
`tkCommonDialog`	`tkinter.commondialog`
`Tkconstants`	`tkinter.constants`
`Tkdnd`	`tkinter.dnd`
`tkFileDialog`	`tkinter.filedialog`
`tkFont`	`tkinter.font`
`Tkinter`	`tkinter`
`tkMessageBox`	`tkinter.messagebox`
`tkSimpleDialog`	`tkinter.simpledialog`
`ttk`	`tkinter.ttk`
`urlparse`	`urllib.parse` (page 753)
`UserList`	`collections` (page 75)
`UserString`	`collections` (page 75)
`xmlrpclib`	`xmlrpc.client` (page 816)

A.4   Removed Modules

These modules are either no longer present at all, or have had their features merged into other existing modules.

A.4.1   bsddb

The `bsddb` and `dbm.bsd` modules have been removed. Bindings for Berkeley DB are now maintained outside of the standard library as bsddb3.[12]

A.4.2   commands

The `commands` module was deprecated in Python 2.6 and removed in Python 3.0. See `subprocess` (page 535) instead.

A.4.3   compiler

The `compiler` module has been removed. See `ast` instead.

A.4.4   dircache

The `dircache` module has been removed, without a replacement.

A.4.5   EasyDialogs

The `EasyDialogs` module has been removed. See `tkinter` instead.

A.4.6   exceptions

The `exceptions` module has been removed because all of the exceptions defined there are available as built-in classes.

A.4.7   htmllib

The `htmllib` module has been removed. See `html.parser` instead.

A.4.8   md5

The implementation of the MD5 message digest algorithm has moved to `hashlib` (page 523).

A.4.9   mimetools, MimeWriter, mimify, multifile, and rfc822

The `mimetools`, `MimeWriter`, `mimify`, `multifile`, and `rfc822` modules have been removed. See `email` instead.

A.4.10   popen2

The `popen2` module has been removed. See `subprocess` (page 535) instead.

---

[12] `https://pypi.python.org/pypi/bsddb3`

A.4.11 posixfile

The posixfile module has been removed. See io (page 390) instead.

A.4.12 sets

The sets module was deprecated in Python 2.6 and removed in Python 3.0. Use the built-in types set and orderedset instead.

A.4.13 sha

The implementation of the SHA-1 message digest algorithm has moved to hashlib (page 523).

A.4.14 sre

The sre module was deprecated in Python 2.5 and removed in Python 3.0. Use re (page 13) instead.

A.4.15 statvfs

The statvfs module was deprecated in Python 2.6 and removed in Python 3.0. See os.statvfs() in the os (page 1227) module instead.

A.4.16 thread

The thread module has been removed. Use the higher-level API in threading (page 560) instead.

A.4.17 user

The user module was deprecated in Python 2.6 and removed in Python 3.0. See user-customization features provided by the site (page 1169) module instead.

A.5 Deprecated Modules

These modules are still present in the standard library, but are deprecated and should not be used in new Python 3 programs.

A.5.1 asyncore and asynchat

Asynchronous I/O and protocol handlers. See asyncio (page 617) instead.

A.5.2 formatter

Generic output formatter and device interface. See Python issue 18716[13] for details.

---

[13] http://bugs.python.org/issue18716

A.5.3 imp

Access the implementation of the import statement. See `importlib` (page 1329) instead.

A.5.4 optparse

Command-line option parsing library. The API for `argparse` (page 888) is similar to the one provided by `optparse`, and in many cases `argparse` can be used as a straightforward replacement by updating the names of the classes and methods used.

A.6 Summary of Changes to Modules
A.6.1 abc

The `abstractproperty()`, `abstractclassmethod()`, and `abstractstaticmethod()` decorators are deprecated. Combining `abstractmethod()` with the `property()`, `classmethod()`, and `staticmethod()` decorators works as expected (Python issue 11610[14]).

A.6.2 anydbm

The `anydbm` module has been renamed `dbm` (page 408) in Python 3.

A.6.3 argparse

The `version` argument to `ArgumentParser` has been removed in favor of a special `action` type (Python issue 13248[15]).

The old form passed `version` as an argument.

```
parser = argparse.ArgumentParser(version='1.0')
```

The new form requires adding an explicit argument definition.

```
parser = argparse.ArgumentParser()
parser.add_argument('--version', action='version',
                    version='%(prog)s 1.0')
```

The option name and version format string can be modified to suit the needs of the application.

In Python 3.4, the version action was changed to print the version string to stdout instead of stderr (Python issue 18920[16]).

---

[14] http://bugs.python.org/issue11610
[15] http://bugs.python.org/issue13248
[16] http://bugs.python.org/issue18920

A.6.4   array

The 'c' type used for character bytes in early version of Python 2 has been removed. Use 'b' or 'B' for bytes instead.

The 'u' type for characters from Unicode strings has been deprecated and will be removed in Python 4.0.

The methods tostring() and fromstring() have been renamed tobytes() and frombytes(), respectively, to eliminate ambiguity (Python issue 8990[17]).

A.6.5   atexit

When atexit (page 993) was updated to include a C implementation (Python issue 1680961[18]), a regression was introduced in the error handling logic that caused only the summary of the exception to be shown, without the traceback. This regression was fixed in Python 3.3 (Python issue 18776[19]).

A.6.6   base64

The encodestring() and decodestring() functions have been renamed encodebytes() and decodebytes(), respectively. The old names still work as aliases, but are deprecated (Python issue 3613[20]).

Two new encodings using 85-character alphabets have been added. b85encode() implements an encoding used in Mercurial and git, while a85encode() implements the Ascii85 format used by PDF files (Python issue 17618[21]).

A.6.7   bz2

BZ2File instances now support the context manager protocol, and do not need to be wrapped with contextlib.closing().

A.6.8   collections

The abstract base classes formerly defined in collections (page 75) moved to collections.abc (page 97), with backward-compatibility imports available in collections, for now (Python issue 11085[22]).

A.6.9   comands

The functions getoutput() and getstatusoutput() have been moved to subprocess (page 535) and commands has been deleted.

---

[17] http://bugs.python.org/issue8990
[18] http://bugs.python.org/issue1680961
[19] http://bugs.python.org/issue18776
[20] http://bugs.python.org/issue3613
[21] http://bugs.python.org/issue17618
[22] http://bugs.python.org/issue11085

A.6.10   configparser

The old `ConfigParser` module has been renamed to `configparser` (page 960).

The old `ConfigParser` class was removed in favor of `SafeConfigParser`, which has in turn been renamed to `ConfigParser`. The deprecated interpolation behavior is available via `LegacyInterpolation`.

The `read()` method now supports an `encoding` argument, so it is no longer necessary to use `codecs` (page 365) to read configuration files with Unicode values in them.

Use of the old `RawConfigParser` is discouraged. New projects should use `ConfigParser(interpolation=None)` instead to achieve the same behavior.

A.6.11   contextlib

`contextlib.nested()` has been removed. Pass multiple context managers to the same `with` statement instead.

A.6.12   csv

Instead of using the `next()` method of a reader directly, use the built-in `next()` function to invoke the iterator properly.

A.6.13   datetime

Starting with Python 3.3, equality comparisons between naive and time zone–aware `datetime` instances return `False` instead of raising `TypeError` (Python issue 15006[23]).

Prior to Python 3.5, a `datetime.time` object representing midnight evaluated to `False` when converted to a boolean value. This behavior has been removed in Python 3.5 (Python issue 13936[24]).

A.6.14   decimal

Python 3.3 incorporated a C implementation of `decimal` (page 239) based on `libmpdec`. This change improved performance, but also included some API changes and behavior differences from the pure-Python implementation. See the Python 3.3 release notes[25] for details.

A.6.15   fractions

The `from_float()` and `from_decimal()` class methods are no longer needed. Floating-point and `Decimal` values can be passed directly to the `Fraction` constructor.

A.6.16   gc

The flags `DEBUG_OBJECT` and `DEBUG_INSTANCE` have been removed. They are no longer needed to differentiate between new- and old-style classes.

---

[23] http://bugs.python.org/issue15006
[24] http://bugs.python.org/issue13936
[25] https://docs.python.org/3.3/whatsnew/3.3.html#decimal

A.6.17 gettext

All of the translation functions in `gettext` (page 1003) assume Unicode input and output, and the Unicode variants such as `ugettext()` have been removed.

A.6.18 glob

The new function `escape()` implements a work-around for searching for files containing meta-characters in their names (Python issue 8402[26]).

A.6.19 http.cookies

In addition to escaping quotes, SimpleCookie encodes commas and semicolons in values to better reflect the behavior of real browsers (Python issue 9824[27]).

A.6.20 imaplib

Under Python 3, `imaplib` (page 864) returns byte-strings encoded as UTF-8. There is support for accepting Unicode strings and encoding them automatically as outgoing commands are sent or as the username and password for logging in to the server.

A.6.21 inspect

The functions `getargspec()`, `getfullargspec()`, `getargvalues()`, `getcallargs()`, `getargvalues()`, `formatargspec()`, and `formatargvalues()` have been deprecated in favor of `signature()` (Python issue 20438[28]).

A.6.22 itertools

The functions `imap()`, `izip()`, and `ifilter()` have been replaced with versions of the built-in functions that return iterables instead of `list` objects (`map()`, `zip()`, and `filter:()` respectively).

The function `ifilterfalse()` has been renamed `filterfalse()`.

A.6.23 json

The `json` (page 803) API was updated to support only `str`, and not `bytes`, because the JSON specification is defined using Unicode.

A.6.24 locale

The normalized version of the name of the UTF-8 encoding was changed from "UTF8" to "UTF-8" because Mac OS X and OpenBSD do not support the use of "UTF8" (Python issue 10154[29] and Python issue 10090[30]).

---

[26] bugs.python.org/issue8402
[27] http://bugs.python.org/issue9824
[28] bugs.python.org/issue20438
[29] http://bugs.python.org/issue10154
[30] http://bugs.python.org/issue10090

A.6.25   logging

The logging (page 980) module now includes a lastResort logger that is used if no other logging configuration is performed by an application. This eliminates the need for an application to configure logging solely to avoid having a user see error messages in case a library imported by the application uses logging but the application itself does not.

A.6.26   mailbox

mailbox reads and writes mailbox files in binary mode, relying on the email package to parse messages. StringIO and text file input is deprecated (Python issue 9124[31]).

A.6.27   mmap

Values returned from read APIs are byte-strings, and need to be decoded before being treated as text.

A.6.28   operator

The div() function has been removed. Use either floordiv() or truediv(), depending on the desired semantics.

The repeat() function has been removed. Use mul() instead.

The functions getslice(), setslice(), and delslice() have been removed. Use getitem(), setitem(), and delitem(), respectively, with slice indexes instead.

The function isCallable() has been removed. Use the abstract base class collections.Callable instead.

```
isinstance(obj, collections.Callable)
```

The type checking functions isMappingType(), isSequenceType(), and isNumberType() have been removed. Use the relevant abstract base classes from collections (page 75) or numbers instead.

```
isinstance(obj, collections.Mapping)
isinstance(obj, collections.Sequence)
isinstance(obj, numbers.Number)
```

The sequenceIncludes() function has been removed. Use contains() instead.

A.6.29   os

The functions popen2(), popen3(), and popen4() have been removed. popen() is still available but is deprecated and emits warnings if used. Code using these functions should be rewritten to use subprocess (page 535) instead, to be more portable across operating systems.

The functions os.tmpnam(), os.tempnam(), and os.tmpfile() have been removed. Use the tempfile (page 330) module instead.

---

[31] http://bugs.python.org/issue9124

The function `os.stat_float_times()` is deprecated (Python issue 14711[32]).
`os.unsetenv()` no longer ignores errors (Python issue 13415[33]).

A.6.30   os.path

`os.path.walk()` has been removed. Use `os.walk()` instead.

A.6.31   pdb

The `print` command alias has been removed so that it does not shadow the `print()` function
(Python issue 18764[34]). The `p` shortcut is retained.

A.6.32   pickle

The C implementation of the `pickle` module from Python 2 has been moved to a new
module that is automatically used to replace the Python implementation when possible.
The old import idiom of looking for `cPickle` before `pickle` is no longer needed.

```
try:
    import cPickle as pickle
except:
    import pickle
```

With the automatic import of the C implementation, it is only necessary to import the
`pickle` module directly.

```
import pickle
```

Interoperability between Python 2.x and 3.x has been improved for pickled data using
the level 2 protocol or lower to resolve an issue introduced when a large number of standard
library modules were renamed during the transition to Python 3. Because pickled data
includes references to class and type names, and those names changed, it was difficult to
exchange pickled data between Python 2 and 3 programs. Now, for data pickled using
protocol level 2 or older, the old names of the classes are automatically used when writing
to and reading from a pickle stream.

This behavior is available by default, but can be turned off using the `fix_imports` option.
This change improves the situation, but does not completely eliminate incompatibilities. In
particular, data pickled under Python 3.1 may not be readable under Python 3.0. To ensure
maximum portability between Python 3 applications, use protocol level 3, which does not
include this compatibility feature.

The default protocol version has changed from `0`, the human-readable version, to `3`, the
binary format with the best interoperability when shared between Python 3 applications.

---

[32] http://bugs.python.org/issue14711
[33] http://bugs.python.org/issue13415
[34] http://bugs.python.org/issue18764

Byte-string data written to a pickle by a Python 2.x application is decoded when it is read back to create a Unicode string object. The encoding for the transformation defaults to ASCII, and can be changed by passing values to the `Unpickler`.

A.6.33   pipes

`pipes.quote()` has moved to `shlex` (page 951) (Python issue 9723[35]).

A.6.34   platform

`platform.popen()` has been deprecated. Use `subprocess.popen()` instead (Python issue 11377[36]).

`platform.uname()` now returns a `namedtuple`.

Because Linux distributions do not have a consistent way to describe themselves, the functions for getting the descriptions [`platform.dist()` and `platform.linux_distribution()`] are deprecated and scheduled to be removed in Python 3.7 (Python issue 1322[37]).

A.6.35   random

The function `jumpahead()` was removed in Python 3.0.

A.6.36   re

The `UNICODE` flag represents the default behavior. To restore the ASCII-specific behavior from Python 2, use the `ASCII` flag.

A.6.37   shelve

The default output format for `shelve` (page 405) may create a file with a `.db` extension added to the name given to `shelve.open()`.

A.6.38   signal

PEP 475[38] mandates that system calls interrupted and returning with `EINTR` be retried. This changes the behavior of signal handlers and other system calls. Now, after the signal handler returns, the interrupted call will be retried, unless the signal handler raises an exception. Refer to the PEP documentation for complete details.

A.6.39   socket

Under Python 2, typically `str` objects could be sent directly over a socket. Because `str` replaces `unicode`, in Python 3 the values must be encoded before being sent. The examples in the `socket` (page 693) section use byte-strings, which are already encoded.

---

[35] http://bugs.python.org/issue9723
[36] http://bugs.python.org/issue11377
[37] http://bugs.python.org/issue1322
[38] www.python.org/dev/peps/pep-0475

A.6.40   socketserver

The socketserver (page 742) module was named SocketServer under Python 2.

A.6.41   string

All functions from the string (page 1) module that are also methods of str objects have been removed.

The constants letters, lowercase, and uppercase have been removed. The new constants with similar names are limited to the ASCII character set.

The maketrans() function has been replaced by methods on str, bytes, and bytearray to clarify which input types are supported by each translation table.

A.6.42   struct

struct.pack() now supports only byte-strings when using the s string pack code, and no longer implicitly encodes string objects to UTF-8 (Python issue 10783[39]).

A.6.43   subprocess

The default value for the close_fds argument to subprocess.Popen has changed from always being False. It always defaults to True under Unix. It defaults to True under Windows if the standard I/O stream arguments are set to None; otherwise, it defaults to False.

A.6.44   sys

The variable sys.exitfunc is no longer checked for a cleanup action to be run when a program exits. Use atexit (page 993) instead.

The variable sys.subversion is no longer defined.

The flags sys.flags.py3k_warning, sys.flags.division_warning, sys.flags.division_new, sys.flags.tabcheck, and sys.flags.unicode are no longer defined.

The variable sys.maxint is no longer defined; use sys.maxsize instead. See **PEP 237**[40] (Unifying Long Integers and Integers).

The global exception tracking variables sys.exc_type, sys.exc_value, and sys.exc_traceback have been removed. The function sys.exc_clear() has also been removed.

The variable sys.version_info is now a namedtuple instance with attributes major, minor, micro, releaselevel, and serial (Python issue 4285[41]).

The check interval feature, which controls the number of opcodes that can execute before a thread context switch is allowed, has been replaced with an absolute time value, which is managed with sys.setswitchinterval(). The old functions for managing the check interval, sys.getcheckinterval() and sys.setcheckinterval(), are deprecated.

The sys.meta_path and sys.path_hooks variables now expose all of the path finders and entry hooks for importing modules. In earlier versions, only finders and hooks explicitly

---

[39] http://bugs.python.org/issue10783
[40] www.python.org/dev/peps/pep-0237
[41] http://bugs.python.org/issue4285

added to the path were exposed, and the C import used values in its implementation that could not be modified from the outside.

For Linux systems, `sys.platform` no longer includes the version number. The value is now just `linux` and not `linux2` or `linux3`.

A.6.45   threading

The `thread` module is deprecated in favor of the API in `threading` (page 560).

The debugging features of `threading`, including the "verbose" argument, have been removed from the APIs (Python issue 13550[42]).

Older implementations of `threading` used factory functions for some of the classes because they were implemented in C as extension types and could not be subclassed. That limitation of the language has been removed, so many of the old factory functions have been converted to standard classes, which allow subclassing (Python issue 10968[43]).

The public symbols exported from `threading` have been renamed to be **PEP 8**[44] compliant. The old names are retained for backward compatibility, but they will be removed in a future release.

A.6.46   time

`time.asctime()` and `time.ctime()` have been changed to not use the system functions of the same time to allow larger years to be used. `time.ctime()` now supports years from 1900 through `maxint`, although for values greater than `9999` the output string is longer than the standard 24 characters to allow for the extra year digits (Python issue 8013[45]).

A.6.47   unittest

The `TestCase` methods starting with "fail" (e.g., `failIf()`, `failUnless()`) have been deprecated. Use the alternative forms of the assert methods instead.

Several older method aliases have been deprecated and replaced with preferred names. Using the deprecated names produces a warning (Python issue 9424[46]). See Table A.2 for a mapping between the old and new names.

Table A.2: Deprecated unittest.TestCase Methods

Deprecated name	Preferred name
`assert_()`	`assertTrue()`
`assertEquals()`	`assertEqual()`
`assertNotEquals()`	`assertNotEqual()`
`assertAlmostEquals()`	`assertAlmostEqual()`
`assertNotAlmostEquals()`	`assertNotAlmostEqual()`

---

[42] http://bugs.python.org/issue13550
[43] http://bugs.python.org/issue10968
[44] www.python.org/dev/peps/pep-0008
[45] http://bugs.python.org/issue8013
[46] http://bugs.python.org/issue9424

A.6.48   UserDict, UserList, and UserString

The UserDict, UserList, and UserString classes have been moved out of their own modules and into the collections (page 75) module. dict, list, and str can be subclassed directly, but the classes in collections may make implementing the subclass simpler because the content of the container is available directly through an instance attribute. The abstract classes in collections.abc (page 97) are also useful for creating custom containers that follow the APIs of the built-in types.

A.6.49   uuid

uuid.getnode() now uses the PATH environment variable to find programs that can report the MAC address of the host under Unix (Python issue 19855[47]). It falls back to looking in /sbin and /usr/sbin if no program is found on the search path. This search behavior may give different results than with earlier versions of Python if alternative versions of programs such as netstat, ifconfig, ip, and arp are present.

A.6.50   whichdb

The functionality of whichdb has moved to the dbm (page 408) module.

A.6.51   xml.etree.ElementTree

XMLTreeBuilder has been renamed TreeBuilder, and the API has undergone several changes.

ElementTree.getchildren() has been deprecated. Use list(elem) to build a list of the children.

ElementTree.getiterator() has been deprecated. Use iter() to create an iterator using the normal iterator protocol instead.

When parsing fails, rather than raising xml.parsers.expat.ExpatError, XMLParser now raises xml.etree.ElementTree.ParseError.

A.6.52   zipimport

The data returned from get_data() is a byte-string, which needs to be decoded before being used as a Unicode string.

---

[47] http://bugs.python.org/issue19855

Appendix B

Outside of the Standard Library

Although the Python standard library is extensive, it is complemented by a robust ecosystem of modules provided by third-party developers and available from the Python Package Index.[1] This appendix describes some of these modules, and the situations in which you might want to use them to supplement or even replace the standard library.

B.1 Text

The string (page 1) module includes a very basic template tool. Many web frameworks include more powerful template tools, but Jinja[2] and Mako[3] are popular stand-alone alternatives. Both support looping and conditional control structures as well as other features for combining data with a template to produce text output.

The re (page 13) module includes functions for searching and parsing text using formally described patterns called regular expressions. It is not the only way to parse text, though.

The PLY[4] package supports building parsers in the style of the GNU tools lexx and yacc, which are often used for building language compilers. By providing inputs describing the valid tokens, a grammar, and actions to take when each token is encountered, it is possible to build fully functional compilers and interpreters, as well as more straightforward data parsers.

PyParsing[5] is a another tool for building parsers. The inputs are instances of classes that can be chained together using operators and method calls to build up a grammar.

Finally, NLTK[6] is a package for processing natural-language text—that is, human languages instead of computer languages. It supports parsing sentences into parts of speech, finding the root form of words, and basic semantic processing.

B.2 Algorithms

The functools (page 143) module includes some tools for creating decorators, which are functions that wrap other functions to change how they behave. The wrap[7] package goes

---

[1] https://pypi.python.org/pypi
[2] http://jinja.pocoo.org
[3] http://docs.makotemplates.org/en/latest/
[4] www.dabeaz.com/ply/
[5] http://pyparsing.wikispaces.com
[6] www.nltk.org
[7] http://wrapt.readthedocs.org/

further than `functools.wrap()`, by ensuring that a decorator is constructed properly and works for all edge-cases.

B.3   Dates and Times

The `time` (page 211) and `datetime` (page 221) modules provide functions and classes for manipulating time and date values. Both include functions for parsing strings to turn them into internal representations. The dateutil[8] package includes a more flexible parser that makes it easier to build robust applications that are more forgiving of different input formats.

The `datetime` module includes a time zone–aware class for representing a specific time on a specific day. It does not, however, include a full time zone database. The pytz[9] package does provide such a database. It is distributed separately from the standard library because it is maintained by other authors, and because it is updated frequently when time zone and daylight savings time values are changed by the political institutions that control them.

B.4   Mathematics

The `math` (page 264) module contains fast implementations of advanced mathematical functions. NumPy[10] expands the set of functions supported to include linear algebra and Fourier transform functions. It also includes a fast multidimensional array implementation, improving on the version in `array` (page 98).

B.5   Data Persistence and Exchange

The examples in the `sqlite3` (page 412) section run SQL statements directly and work with low-level data structures. For large applications, it is often desirable to map classes to tables in the database using an *object relational mapper* (ORM). The SQLAlchemy[11] ORM library provides APIs for associating classes with tables, building queries, and connecting to different types of production-grade relational databases.

The lxml[12] package wraps the libxml2 and libxslt libraries to create an alternative to the XML parser in `xml.etree.ElementTree` (page 445). Developers who are familiar with using those libraries from other languages may find lxml easier to adopt in Python.

---

[8] https://dateutil.readthedocs.io/
[9] http://pythonhosted.org/pytz/
[10] www.numpy.org
[11] www.sqlalchemy.org
[12] http://lxml.de

The defusedxml[13] package contains fixes for "billion laughs"[14] and other entity expansion denial-of-service vulnerabilities in Python's XML libraries and makes working with untrusted XML safer than using the standard library alone.

B.6   Cryptography

The team building the cryptography[15] package says, "Our goal is for it to be your 'cryptographic standard library.'" The cryptography package exposes high-level APIs to make it easy to add cryptographic features to applications. The package is actively maintained, with frequent releases being issued to address vulnerabilities in the underlying libraries such as OpenSSL.

B.7   Concurrency with Processes, Threads, and Coroutines

The event loop built into `asyncio` (page 617) is a reference implementation based on the abstract API defined by the module. It is possible to replace the event loop with a library such as uvloop,[16] which gives better performance in exchange for adding extra application dependencies.

The curio[17] package is another concurrency package that is similar to `asyncio` but with a smaller API that treats everything as a coroutine. It does not support callbacks in the same way that `asyncio` does.

The Twisted[18] library provides an extensible framework for Python programming, with special focus on event-based network programming and multiprotocol integration. It is mature, robust, and well documented.

B.8   The Internet

The requests[19] package is a very popular replacement for `urllib.request` (page 761). It provides a consistent API for working with remote resources that are addressable via HTTP, includes robust SSL support, and can use connection pooling for better performance in multi-threaded applications. It also provides features that make it well suited for accessing REST APIs, such as built-in JSON parsing.

---

[13] `https://pypi.python.org/pypi/defusedxml`
[14] `http://en.wikipedia.org/wiki/Billion_laughs`
[15] `https://cryptography.io/en/latest/`
[16] `http://uvloop.readthedocs.io`
[17] `https://github.com/dabeaz/curio`
[18] `https://twistedmatrix.com/`
[19] `http://docs.python-requests.org/`

Python's `html` module includes a basic parser for well-formed HTML data. However, real-world data is rarely well structured, making parsing it problematic. The BeautifulSoup[20] and PyQuery[21] libraries are alternatives to `html` that are more robust in the face of messy data. Both define APIs for parsing, modifying, and constructing HTML.

The built-in `http.server` (page 781) package includes base classes for creating simple HTTP servers from scratch. It does not offer much support beyond that for building web-based applications, though. The Django[22] and Pyramid[23] packages are two popular web application frameworks that provide more support for advanced features such as request parsing, URL routing, and cookie handling.

Many existing libraries do not work with `asyncio` (page 617) because they have not been updated to work with the event loop. A new set of libraries, including those such as aiohttp,[24] is being created to fill this gap as part of the aio-libs[25] project.

B.9   Email

The API for `imaplib` (page 864) is relatively low level, requiring the caller to understand the IMAP protocol to build queries and parse results. The imapclient[26] package provides a higher-level API that is easier to work with when building applications that need to manipulate IMAP mailboxes.

B.10   Application Building Blocks

The two standard library modules for building command-line interfaces, `argparse` (page 888) and `getopt` (page 916), both separate the definition of command-line arguments from their parsing and value processing. An alternative, click[27] (the "Command-Line Interface Construction Kit"), defines command processing functions and then associates option and prompt definitions with those commands using decorators.

cliff[28] ("Command-Line Interface Formulation Framework") provides a set of base classes for defining commands and a plug-in system for extending applications with multiple subcommands that can be distributed in separate packages. It uses `argparse` (page 888) to build the help text and argument parser, so the command-line processing is familiar.

---

[20] `www.crummy.com/software/BeautifulSoup/`
[21] `http://pyquery.rtfd.org/`
[22] `www.djangoproject.com/`
[23] `https://trypyramid.com/`
[24] `http://aiohttp.readthedocs.io/`
[25] `https://github.com/aio-libs`
[26] `http://imapclient.freshfoo.com/`
[27] `http://click.pocoo.org`
[28] `http://docs.openstack.org/developer/cliff/`

The docopt[29] package reverses the typical flow by asking the developer to write the help text for a program, which it then parses to understand the valid combinations of options and subcommands.

For interactive terminal–based programs, prompt_toolkit[30] includes advanced features such as color support, syntax highlighting, input editing, mouse support, and searchable history. It can be used to build command-oriented programs with a prompt loop like the `cmd` (page 938) module, or full-screen applications like text editors.

While INI files such as those used by `configparser` (page 960) continue to be popular for application configuration, the YAML[31] file format is also widely used for this purpose. YAML provides many of the data structure features of JSON in a format that is easier for people to read. The PyYAML[32] library provides access to a YAML parser and serializer.

B.11 Developer Tools

The standard library module `venv` (page 1163) is new in Python 3. For similar application isolation under both Python 2 and 3, use virtualenv.[33]

The fixtures[34] package provides several test resource management classes tailor-made to work with the `addCleanup()` method of test cases from the `unittest` (page 1051) module. The fixture classes can manage loggers, environment variables, temporary files, and more in a consistent and safe way that ensures each test case is completely isolated from others in the suite.

The `distutils` module in the standard library for packaging Python modules for distribution and reuse is deprecated. Its replacement, setuptools,[35] is packaged separately from the standard library to make it easier to deliver new versions at frequent intervals. The API for setuptools includes tools for building the list of files to include in a package. Extensions are available that automatically build the list from the set of files managed by a version control system. For example, using setuptools-git[36] with sourcecode in a git[37] repository causes all of the tracked files to be included in the package by default. After a package is built, the twine[38] application will upload it to the package index to be shared with other developers.

Tools such as `tabnanny` (page 1153) are good at finding common formatting mistakes in Python code. The Python Code Quality Authority[39] maintains an extensive range of more

---

[29] http://docopt.org
[30] http://python-prompt-toolkit.readthedocs.io/en/stable/
[31] http://yaml.org
[32] http://pyyaml.org
[33] https://virtualenv.pypa.io/
[34] https://pypi.python.org/pypi/fixtures
[35] https://setuptools.readthedocs.io/en/latest/
[36] https://pypi.python.org/pypi/setuptools-git
[37] https://git-scm.com
[38] https://pypi.python.org/pypi/twine
[39] http://meta.pycqa.org/en/latest/

advanced *static analysis tools*, including tools that enforce style guidelines, find common programming errors, and even help avoid excessive complexity.

TIP
_____

Related Reading

- Python Package Index[40] (PyPI): The site for finding and downloading extension modules distributed separately from the Python runtime.

_____

_____

[40] https://pypi.python.org/pypi

Index of Python Modules

A

abc, 1287
argparse, 888
array, 98
asyncio, 617
atexit, 993

B

base64, 776
bisect, 109
bz2, 491

C

calendar, 233
cgitb, 1089
cmd, 938
codecs, 365
collections, 75
collections.abc, 97
compileall, 1155
concurrent.futures, 677
configparser, 960
contextlib, 191
copy, 130
csv, 466

D

datetime, 221
dbm, 408
decimal, 239
difflib, 58
dis, 1296
doctest, 1026

E

ensurepip, 1167
enum, 66

F

filecmp, 351
fileinput, 986
fnmatch, 323
fractions, 250
functools, 143

G

gc, 1254
getopt, 916
getpass, 935
gettext, 1003
glob, 319
gzip, 486

H

hashlib, 523
heapq, 103
hmac, 528
http.cookies, 790
http.server, 781

I

imaplib, 864
importlib, 1329
inspect, 1311
io, 390
ipaddress, 687
itertools, 163

J

json, 803

L

linecache, 326
locale, 1012
logging, 980

M

mailbox, 852
math, 264
mmap, 361
multiprocessing, 586

O

operator, 183
os, 1227
os.path, 296

P

pathlib, 305
pdb, 1101
pickle, 396
pkgutil, 1334
platform, 1246
pprint, 136
profile, 1140
pstats, 1144
pyclbr, 1160
pydoc, 1024

Q

queue, 111

R

random, 254
re, 13
readline, 922
resource, 1251

S

sched, 998
select, 728
selectors, 724
shelve, 405
shlex, 951
shutil, 337
signal, 553
site, 1169
sitecustomize, 1175
smtpd, 847
smtplib, 841
socket, 693
socketserver, 742
sqlite3, 412
statistics, 290
string, 1
struct, 117
subprocess, 535
sys, 1178
sysconfig, 1270

T

tabnanny, 1153
tarfile, 503
tempfile, 330
textwrap, 7
threading, 560
time, 211
timeit, 1148
trace, 1069
traceback, 1078

U

unittest, 1051
urllib.parse, 753
urllib.request, 761
urllib.robotparser, 773
usercustomize, 1176
uuid, 797

V

venv, 1163

W

warnings, 1279
weakref, 121
webbrowser, 796

X

xml.etree.ElementTree, 445
xmlrpc.client, 816
xmlrpc.server, 827

Z

zipfile, 511
zipimport, 1344
zlib, 477

Index

A

Abbreviations, regular expression flags, 43

abc module
   abstract properties, 1292–1295
   avoiding incomplete implementation, 1290–1291
   changes in Python 3, 1356
   concrete methods in, 1291–1292
   helper base classes, 1289–1290
   marking class and static methods as abstract, 1295–1296
   overview of, 1279, 1287
   registering concrete classes, 1287–1288
   subclassing from base class, 1288–1289

abort() method, Barrier, 580–581

Absolute value, math, 272–274

abspath() function, os.path, 302

abs_tol keyword argument, math, 268–269

Abstract base classes. See abc module

Abstract properties, abc, 1292–1295

accept() function, selectors, 705, 724

Access control
   concurrent resources in multiprocessing, 605–607
   concurrent resources in threading, 581–583
   configuration files, 963–970
   Internet spider. See urllib.robotparser
   resources in multiprocessing, 603–604
   resources in threading, 572–576
   in sqlite3, 442–443

ACCESS_COPY argument, memory-map files, 363–364

access()function, file permissions, 1232–1233

ACCESS_READ argument, memory-map files, 362

ACCESS_WRITE argument, memory-map files, 362–363

accumulate() function, itertools, 176–182

acosh()function, math, 288

acquire() method, threading, 574, 576, 579

Actions, argparse argument, 891–894

Actions, argument
   customizing, 913–915
   defining, 888

Active Pool instance, shared state, 608

add() method
   mbox mailbox, 852–853
   new archive, tarfile, 508

add_argument(), argparse
   argument types, 910–912
   conflict resolution, 903–904
   customizing argument actions, 913–915
   nesting parsers, 907–908
   variable argument lists, 908–910

add_argument_group(), argparse, 905

addCleanup(), fixtures package, 1371

add_done_callback() method, 680–681

addfile() method, tarfile, 509

add_flag() method, mailbox, 862–863

add_header() method, urllib.request, 765–766

add_help argument, ArgumentParser, 897

Address families, socket, 693–694

Address(es)
   choosing for listening, socket, 708–711
   IP. See ipaddress module
   IP address representations, socket, 702–703
   looking up server, socket, 700–702
   lookup by name, asyncio, 658–659
   for multicast groups, socket, 718
   verifying email, smtplib, 846–847

add_section() method, configparser, 970–971

add_signal_handler(), asyncio, 668

adler32() function, computing checksums, 481–482

AF_INET address family, IPv4, 693–694

AF_INET6 address family, IPv6, 693–694

AF_UNIX address family, UDS, 694, 714

Aggregation functions, sqlite3, 440–441

aiohttp library, 1370

Alarms, signal, 556–557, 559–560

Algorithms
   context manager utilities. See contextlib module
   cryptogaphic. See hashlib module; hmac module
   customizing debugger, 1136–1137
   functional interface to built-in operators. See operator module
   iterator functions. See itertools module
   manipulating functions, see functools module

Algorithms (*continued*)
  overview of, 143
  supplements to standard
    library, 1367–1368
Alternate API names,
  `xmlrpc.server`, 829–830
Anchoring codes, regular
  expressions, 26–27
Angles, `math`, 282–284
Angular distribution, `random`,
  264
`anydbm` module, changes in
  Python 3, 1356
APIs
  abstract base classes,
    `collections.abc`, 97–98
  alternate names for,
    `xmlrpc.server`,
    829–830
  arbitrary names for,
    `xmlrpc.server`,
    831–832
  context manager, 191–192
  dotted names for,
    `xmlrpc.server`, 830–831
  as event based, `selectors`,
    724
  in `subprocess`, 535–536
`append` action, arguments,
  891–892
`append()` method, `imaplib`,
  881–883
`append_const` action,
  arguments, 891–892
Appending to archives
  `tarfile`, 510
  `zipfile`, 518–519
Application building blocks
  command-line filter. *See*
    `fileinput` module
  command-line option parsing.
    See `getopt` module
  configuration files. *See*
    `configparser` module
  GNU readline library. *See*
    `readline` module
  line-oriented command
    processors. *See* `cmd` module
  overview of, 887–888
  parsing shell-style syntaxes.
    See `shlex` module
  parsing/validating
    command-line arguments.
    See `argparse` module
  program shutdown callbacks.
    See `atexit` module

secure password prompt. *See*
    `getpass` module
  supplements to standard
    library, 1370–1371
  timed event scheduler,
    998–1002
Application threads. *See*
    `threading` module
Applications
  configuring `logging` for,
    980–981
  localization, 1011
Approximation distribution,
    `random`, 263
Arbitrary API names,
    `xmlrpc.server`, 831–832
Arbitrary classes, `pprint`,
    138–139
Arbitrary context callbacks,
    `contextlib`, 206–207
Archives
  accessing tar. *See* `tarfile`
    module
  managing in `shutil`, 346–350
  manipulating email. *See*
    `mailbox` module
  ZIP. *See* ZIP archive;
    `zipfile` module
`argparse` module
  advanced argument
    processing, 908–916
  argument actions, 891–894
  changes in Python 3, 1356
  defining arguments, 888
  help output, 897–901
  interface-related supplements
    to standard library, 1370
  option prefixes, 894–895
  overview of, 887
  parser organization, 901–908
  parsing command line, 889
  parsing/validating
    command-line arguments,
    888
  setting up parser, 888
  simple examples, 889–892
  sources of arguments, 895–897
`args` command, `pdb`, 1107–1108
`ArgumentParser`. *See*
    `argparse` module
Arguments
  `chain()` taking iterators as,
    `itertools`, 164–166
  command, 939–940
  command-line option parsing.
    See `getopt` module

encoding, `urllib.request`,
    763–764
  mail server base class, `smtpd`,
    848
  parsing/validating
    command-line. *See*
    `argparse` module
  passing to registered
    functions, `atexit`,
    993–994
Arithmetic
  aggregating results, `counter`,
    82–83
  calculating `timedeltas`,
    `datetime`, 225–226
  date, 226–227
  decimal, 242–243
  fractions, 252–253
  operators, 184–186
`array` module
  alternative byte ordering,
    101–102
  arrays and files, 100–101
  changes in Python 3, 1357
  defined, 65
  initialization, 98–99
  manipulating arrays, 99–100
  sequence of fixed-type
    data, 98
  supplements to standard
    library, 1368
ASCII
  encoding binary data with.
    See `base64` module
  restricting escape codes to, 38
  `string` constants, 6
`asinh()` function, `math`, 288
`astimezone()`, `datetime`
    conversion, 232
`asynchat` module, deprecated,
    1355
Asynchronous I/O
  with protocol class
    abstractions, 644–650
  using coroutines and streams,
    650–655
Asynchronous system events.
    See `signal` module
`asyncio` module
  asynchronous concurrency
    concepts, 618
  asynchronous I/O using
    coroutines/streams,
    650–655
  asynchronous I/O using
    protocol class abstractions,
    644–650

combining coroutines with
threads/processes, 670–673
composing coroutines with
control structures, 632–637
cooperative multitasking with
coroutines, 618–622
debugging with, 673–675
executing tasks concurrently,
628–632
interacting with DNS,
658–660
Internet-related supplements
to standard library, 1370
loop supplements to standard
library, 1369
new in Python 3, 1352
overview of, 617
producing results
asynchronously, 625–628
receiving Unix signals,
668–670
scheduling calls to regular
functions, 622–625
subprocesses, 661–668
synchronization primitives.
See Synchronization
primitives, asyncio
using SSL, 656–658
asyncio_executor_thread.py,
670–673
asyncore module, deprecated,
1355
atanh() function, math, 288
atexit module
canceling callbacks, 994–995
changes in Python 3, 1357
decorator syntax, 994
getting plain text help,
1024–1026
handling exceptions, 997–998
program shutdown callbacks
with, 993
registering exit callbacks,
993–994
when callbacks are not called,
995–997
atexit property, weakref,
124–125
atof() function, locale, 1021
atoi() function, locale, 1021
Attribute getters, operator,
188–189
AttributeError,
namedtuple, 91
Attributes
configuring cmd through,
946–947

IEEE 802 MAC Address,
UUID 1, 799
namedtuple special, 92–94
objects with non-picklable,
400
XML element property,
459–461
XML parsed node, 449–450
Authentication
create argument group for,
905
email, in smtplib, 843–846
failure, in imaplib,
865–866
Authorizer function, sqlite3,
442–443
Auto-completion, command,
942–944
Autocommit mode, sqlite3,
434
Automatically generated help,
argparse, 897–901
Averages, statistics, 290–291
await keyword, asyncio
asynchronous I/O using, 651,
653–654
chaining coroutines, 621
composing coroutines,
632–637
coroutines pausing execution
with, 618
using Future with, 626–627

B

backslashreplace, lossless
error handling, 374
Backup file, fileinput, 992
Barrier, synchronizing threads,
579–581
Base classes
implementing Web servers.
See http.server module
overriding methods in cmd,
944–946
Base16 encoded data, 778–779
Base32 encoded data, 778
base64 module
Base64 decoding, 778
Base64 encoding, 777
changes in Python 3, 1357
encode binary data with
ASCII using, 776
other encodings, 779–781
URL-safe variations, 778–779
Base85 encoded data, 778–780

BaseHTTPRequestHandler
class, http.server,
781–786
basename() function, parsing
paths in os.path, 297–298
BaseServer class,
socketserver, 742–743
basicConfig() function, log
files, 981–982
BCC (blind carbon-copy),
smtplib, 843
BeautifulSoup library, 1370
Beta distribution, random, 264
betavariate() function, Beta
distribution, 264
Bidirectional process
communication,
subprocess, 543
Binary class, passing in
XML-RPC, 823–825
Binary data
encoding with ASCII. *See*
base64 module
passing in XML-RPC,
823–825
sending, socket, 721–723
structures. *See* struct
module
Binary digests, hmac, 529–530
Binary heap, 103
bind() function
choosing address for listening,
711
socket echo server, 704–705
bisect module, 109–111
Blank lines, managing in
doctest, 1034–1035
Blind carbon-copy (BCC),
smtplib, 843
BOM (byte order marker),
codecs, 370–372
Boolean values
in configparser, 966–968
testing files in os.path,
303–304
trace options, 1077
braced patterns, advanced
string templates, 5–6
break command, breakpoints,
1118–1120, 1124–1125
Breakpoints, pdb
changing execution flow,
1129–1130
conditional breakpoints,
1124–1125
ignoring, 1125–1127

Breakpoints, pdb (*continued*)
  jumps forward or backward,
    1130–1134
  managing, 1120–1123
  temporary breakpoints,
    1123–1124
  triggering actions, 1127–1128
  using, 1117–1120
  watching data change,
    1128–1129
BrokenBarrierError, threads,
  580
BROWSER variable, webbrowser,
  797
Browser, webbrowser, 796
BSD socket interface. *See*
  socket module
bsddb module, removed from
  Python 3, 1354
BufferedIncrementalDecoder,
  389
BufferedIncrementalEncoder,
  389
Buffers, struct, 120–121
Building paths
  os.path, 300–301
  pathlib, 305–307
Building trees,
  xml.etree.ElementTree
    module, 461–464
Built-in modules, 1201–1202
Bulk loading, sqlite3, 421–422
Byte code, compiling source files
  to, 1155–1159
Byte order
  alternative arrays, 101–102
  codecs, 370–372
  memory management, 1194
Byte order marker (BOM),
  codecs, 370–372
Bytes
  raw, 391
  understanding encodings
    through, 366–368
  Unicode, 365–366
BytesIO buffer
  file-like streams in pickle,
    398
  message signatures, 531–532
  streams in gzip, 490–491
  wrapping byte streams for
    text data, 392–393
byteswap() method, arrays,
  102
bz2 module
  bzip2 compression via, 491
  changes in Python 3, 1357

compressing network data,
    499–503
  incremental compression and
    decompression, 493–494
  mixed-content streams,
    494–495
  one-shot operations in
    memory, 492–493
  reading and writing Unicode
    data, 498–499
  reading compressed files,
    497–498
  tarfile using compressed
    archives of, 510–511
  writing compressed files,
    495–497
BZ2Compressor object,
  493–494, 499
BZ2Decompressor object,
  493–495, 501
Bz2RequestHandler, 500
bzip2 compression. *See* bz2
  module

C

C modules, as built-in,
  1201–1202
Cache
  functools, 155–158
  importer, 1217–1218
  weakref, 127–130
Calculations, commonly used
  math, 274–277
Calendar date values, 222–225
calendar module
  calculating dates, 236–238
  defined, 211
  formatting examples, 233–236
  locales, 236
  overview of, 233
  working with dates, 236
call() function, subprocess,
  535
Callable objects, functools
  acquiring function properties,
    145–147
  acquiring function properties
    for decorators, 149–151
  partial objects working
    with any, 147–148
  wrapping with partial class,
    143–145
Callbacks
  arbitrary context,
    contextlib, 206–207

Future,
  concurrent.futures,
    680–681
  program shutdown. *See*
    atexit module
  receiving signals, 554–555
  weakref, 122–123
Callbacks, asyncio
  concept of, 618
  Future invoking, 627–628
  scheduling for soon, 622–623
  scheduling for specific time,
    624–625
  scheduling with delay,
    623–625
CalledProcessError
  exception, subprocess,
    537–538
call_later function,
  scheduling callbacks in
    asyncio, 623–625
call_soon function, scheduling
  callbacks in asyncio,
    622–623, 624
Cancel events, sched,
  1001–1002
cancel() method,
  concurrent.futures,
    681–683
cancel_task() method,
  asyncio, 629–631
capwords() function, string
  module, 1–2
Case-insensitive matching,
  regular expression search,
    36–37
ceil() function, math, 270
cgitb module
  command-line interface,
    1152–1153
  detailed tracebacks,
    1090–1092
  examining local variables in
    tracebacks, 1093–1096
  exception properties,
    1096–1098
  HTML output format, 1098
  logging tracebacks, 1098–1101
  overview of, 1023, 1089
  standard traceback dump,
    1089–1090
chain() function, itertools,
  164–167
chain.from_iterable(),
  itertools, 164–165
Chaining coroutines, asyncio,
  620–621

ChainMap class, search multiple dictionaries, 75–79

Changes, preserving in sqlite3, 428–430

Channels, managing registered data, 737–738

Character map–based codecs, 383–384

Character ranges
   filename pattern matching in glob, 322
   regular expression character sets, 21–22

Character sets, regular expression, 20–23, 38–39

charmap_decode(), 389

charmap_encode(), 389

charset, regular expression, 20–23

check_output() function, subprocess, 535, 539–541

Checksums, computing, 481–482

chmod() method, file permissions, 317–318, 1231–1232

choice() function, random, 258

Circular references, pickle, 401–402

Class browser, pyclbr, 1160–1163

class syntax, creating enumerations, 66

Classes
   abstract base. See abc module
   disassembling methods, 1300
   helper base, 1289–1290
   implementing Web servers with base. See http.server module
   inspecting, 1314–1316
   inspecting method resolution order, 1323–1324
   json encoder and decoder, 810–812
   mail server base, 847–850
   managing file system paths, 305
   marking class and static methods as abstract, 1295–1296
   operator combined with custom, 190–191
   registering concrete, for use with abc, 1287–1288

retrieving source code for, 1318–1319
   scanning for, 1161–1162
   in socketserver, 742–743
   subclassing from base, 1288–1289
   working with hierarchies, 1322–1324

clear command, deleting breakpoints, 1123

clear() method, threading, 572

click (Command-Line Interface Construction Kit), 1370

Client
   I/O multiplexing abstractions in selectors, 726–728
   library, IMAP4. See imaplib module
   library, XML-RPC. See xmlrpc.client module
   sending binary data, 722
   TCP/IP, 704–711
   UDP, 711–713
   UDS, 714–716

cliff (Command-Line Interface Formulation Framework), 1370

Clock time. See time module

clock() function, 211, 214–216

Closing
   open handles, contextlib, 198–199
   partial stacks, contextlib, 208–209
   TCP/IP server, socket, 705

Cmd (command prompt), 938–939

cmd module
   alternative inputs, 948–949
   auto-completion, 942–944
   command arguments, 940–941
   commands from sys.argv, 950
   configuring through attributes, 946–947
   defined, 887
   line-oriented command processors with, 938
   live help, 941–942
   overriding base class methods, 944–946
   processing commands, 938–939
   running shell commands, 947–948

cmdloop() method, cmd, 945

Code coverage, 1070–1073, 1076–1077

Code, source. See Source code

CodecInfo instance, custom encoding, 387

codecs module
   byte order, 370–372
   defining custom encoding, 383–389
   encoding translation, 376–377
   encodings, 366–368
   error handling, 372–376
   incremental encoding, 378–380
   non-Unicode encodings, 377–378
   as string encoding and decoding, 365
   Unicode data and network communication, 380–383
   Unicode primer, 365–366
   working with files, 368–370

collections module
   ChainMap, 75–79
   changes in Python 3, 1357
   collections.abc, 97–98
   container data types, 65, 75
   Counter, 79–82
   defaultdict, 82–84
   deque, 84–89
   namedtuple, 89–94
   OrderedDict, 94–97

collections.abc module, 97–98

Columns, in sqlite3
   defining new types, 422–425
   determining types, 426–427
   restricting access, 442–443

Combining dates and times, datetime, 228–230

Command handler, cmd, 938–939

Command-Line Interface Construction Kit (click), 1370

Command-Line Interface Formulation Framework (cliff), 1370

Command-line programs
   arguments captured by interpreter, 1185–1186
   building, 1370–1371
   compiling files from, 1158–1159
   CPython, 1180–1181
   filter framework for text files, 987–992

Command-line programs
(*continued*)
`http.server`, 789–790
`inspect`, 1327–1328
`json`, 815
option parsing. *See* `getopt`
module
parsing, 889
parsing/validating arguments
in. *See* `argparse` module
running `unittest` tests,
1051–1052
starting `pdb` from, 1101–1102
`timeit`, 1152–1153
`trace`, 1069–1070
`webbrowser`, 797
Commands
auto-completion for, 942
breakpoints triggering
actions, 1127
processing in `cmd`, 938–939
running external, 1239–1240
`commands` module, 1354, 1357
Comments
parsing embedded, 954
in verbose regular
expressions, 42
`commit()` method, transactions
in `sqlite3`, 428–429
`communicate()` method
`asyncio`, 667
`subprocess`, 546–548
Communication
bi-directional process, 543
capturing error output,
543–544
interprocess, 398–399
network. *See* `socket` module
non-blocking, 723
one-way process, 542–543
Unicode and network,
380–383
`compact` flag, `pprint()`,
140–142
Compact vs. human-consumable
output, `json`, 805–807
`compare_digest()` method,
message signatures, 532–533
Comparison
bodies of text, 59
of clocks, 211–213
`enum`, 67
file. *See* `filecmp` module
functions, `functools`,
151–155
functions, `math`, 267–269
operators, 183, 228

sequences. *See* `difflib`
module
of values, `datetime`, 228
`compileall` module
compiling from command
line, 1158–1159
compiling individual files,
1157–1158
compiling source files to
byte-code, 1155–1157
compiling `sys.path`, 1157
overview of, 1024
Compiled expressions, 15
`compiler` module, removed
from Python 3, 1354
Compilers, 1004, 1309–1311
`complete()` method,
`readline`, 925–931
`complete_` prefix,
auto-completion for
commands, 942
`CompletedProcess`,
`subprocess`, 536–538
Completion buffer, `readline`,
927–931
`Compress` class, `zlib`, 479–480
Compression
adding for new archive in
`zipfile`, 515–516
bz2. *See* `bz2` module
GNU zlib. *See* `zlib` module
levels, `gzip`, 488
levels, `zlib`, 479
read and write GNU zip files.
See `gzip` module
Concrete paths, `pathlib`, 309
Concurrency
asynchronous system events.
See `signal` module
concurrency/asynchronous
I/O management. *See*
`asyncio` module
managing concurrent
operations within process.
See `threading` module
managing pools of concurrent
tasks. *See*
`concurrent.futures`
module
managing processes like
threads. *See*
`multiprocessing`
module
overview of, 535
spawning additional
processes. *See*
`subprocess` module

supplements to standard
library, 1369
`concurrent` module, new in
Python 3, 1352
`concurrent.futures` module
canceling tasks, 681–683
context manager, 683–684
exceptions in tasks, 683
future callbacks, 680–681
managing pools of concurrent
tasks, 677
process pools, 685–686
scheduling individual tasks,
678–679
using `map()` with basic
thread pool, 677–678
waiting for tasks in any order,
679–680
`Condition` objects
synchronizing in
`multiprocessing`,
604–605
synchronizing in `threading`,
578–581
`configparser` module
accessing configuration
settings, 963–970
application construction
supplements to standard
library, 1371
changes in Python 3, 1358
combining values with
interpolation, 975–979
configuration file format, 961
modifying settings, 970–972
option search path, 972–975
reading configuration files,
961–963
saving configuration files, 972
sources of arguments in
`argparse`, 895–896
working with configuration
files, 960–961
Configuration
customizing site, 1175–1176
customizing user, 1176–1177
files. *See* `configparser`
module
properties in `shlex`, 955–956
`readline` library, 923–924
saving settings in `pdb`,
1137–1139
site-wide, 1169
system-specific, 1178
variables, 1270–1272
Conflicting options, `argparse`,
902–904

Connections
  create database, `sqlite3`,
    413
  echo client, `socket`, 705
  to IMAP server, 864–865
  managing multiple at same
    time with `select()`,
    732–733
  send email message,
    `smtplib`, 841
  sharing in `sqlite3`, 441–442
  TCP/IP easy client, 707–708
Constants
  compiler optimizations,
    1309–1311
  quoting options in CSV files
    as, 469
  `string` module, 6–7
Consuming deque, 85–87
Containers
  abstract base classes for, 236
  comparing in `unittest`,
    1056–1061
  data types. *See* `collections`
    module
Context managers
  executors working as, 683–684
  locks as, 577–578
  utilities. *See* `contextlib`
    module
`ContextDecorator` class,
  194–195
`context_diff()` function,
  `difflib`, 61
`contextlib` module
  changes in Python 3, 1358
  closing open handles, 198–199
  context manager API,
    191–194
  as context manager utilities,
    202
  context manager utilities, 191
  context managers as function
    decorators, 194–195
  defined, 143
  dynamic context manager
    stacks, 202–209
  from generator to context
    manager, 196–198
  ignoring exceptions, 199–201
  redirecting output streams,
    201
Contexts, `decimal`
  current context, 244–245
  local context, 247–248
  overview of, 244
  per-instance context, 248

precision, 245
rounding, 245–247
threads, 248–249
`continue` command, breakpoint
  in `pdb`, 1118–1120
Conversion
  functions, `configparser`,
    968–969
  inputs, `itertools`, 167–169
  new column types, `sqlite3`,
    424
`convert_to_builtin_type()`,
  `json`, 808, 812
Cookies. *See* `http.cookies`
  module
Cooperative multitasking,
  coroutines in `asyncio`,
  618–622
`copy` module
  customizing copy behavior,
    132–133
  deep copies, 131–132
  duplicate objects, 130
  recursion in deep copy,
    133–136
  shallow copies, 130–131
Copying files
  duplicate objects, memory
    management, 65
  memory-map, 363–364
  messages, `imaplib`, 883–884
  metadata, 340–341
  shallow copies, 130–131
  in `shutil`, 337–342
`copysign()` function, `math`,
  273
`copytree()` function, `shutil`,
  342–343
Coroutines, `asyncio`
  asynchronous I/O using
    streams and, 650–655
  calling subprocesses in
    `asyncio` with, 664–666
  chaining, 620–621
  combining with
    threads/processes in
    `asyncio`, 670–673
  concept of, 618
  cooperative multitasking
    with, 618
  creating tasks from, 631–632
  `Future` acting like, 625–626
  gathering results from,
    635–636
  generators instead of, 621–622

handling background
  operations as they finish,
  636–637
returning values from,
  619–620
starting, 619
supplements to standard
  library, 1369
waiting for multiple, 632–635
Cosine functions, `math`, 284, 288
`count()` function, new values in
  `itertools`, 169–172
`--count` option, code coverage
  report, 1070–1072
`Counter` module
  accessing counts, 81–82
  arithmetic, 82–83
  as counting hashable objects,
    79–82
  defined, 79
  initializing, 80
`count_words()` function,
  MapReduce in
  `multiprocessing`, 616
CPU time. *See* Processor clock
  time
CPython, 1179–1181
`crc32()` function, computing
  checksums, 481–482
Create database
  `dbm`, 409–410
  `sqlite3`, 412–415
`create_connection()`
  method, asynchronous I/O,
  648
Cryptography
  hashing. *See* `hashlib` module
  message signing/verification.
    See `hmac` module
  supplements to standard
    library, 1369
  UUID 3 and 5, name-based
    values, 800–801
`csv` module
  bulk loading in `sqlite3`,
    421–422
  changes in Python 3, 1358
  comma-separated values, 466
  dialects, 469–474
  event-style processing in
    XML, 452–453
  handling XML parse events,
    453–455
  quoting, 468–469
  reading, 466–467
  setting XML element
    properties, 459–461

csv module (*continued*)
  using field names, 474–476
  writing, 467–468
ctime() function
  logging or printing time,
    213–214
  processor clock time, 215–216
Cultural localization API. *See*
  locale module
curio package, supplements to
  standard library, 1369
curl, http.server, 783, 785
Currency, updating when
  changing locale, 1018–1019
Current context, decimal,
  244–245
Current date, datetime_date,
  222–223
Current locale, probing,
  1013–1018
Current thread, determining,
  562
Current working directory,
  1238–1239
currentframe(), inspecting at
  top of stack, 1324
Cursor, sqlite3, 415, 417
Customizing
  aggregation, sqlite3,
    440–441
  argument actions, argparse,
    913–915
  classes, operator, 190–191
  copy behavior, copy, 132–133
  encoding, codecs, 383–389
  help, argparse, 898–901
  mail server, stmpd, 847–851
  TreeBuilder, 453–455
  types, json, 807–810
CustomSMTPServer, 847–850
cycle() function, values in
  itertools, 170

D

Daemon processes,
  multiprocessing, 589–593
Daemon threads, 564–567
Data
  communication, in Unicode,
    380–383
  finding non-code, during
    import, 1348–1350
  sending to subprocess in
    asyncio, 666–668

Data compression and archiving
  bzip2 compression. *See* bz2
    module
  GNU zlib compression. *See*
    zlib module
  overview of, 477
  read and write GNU zip files.
    See gzip module
  tar archive access. *See*
    tarfile module
  ZIP archive access. *See*
    zipfile module
data definition language (DDL)
  statements, database in
    sqlite3, 413
Data files, in packages,
  1341–1344
Data persistence and exchange
  comma-separated values. *See*
    csv module
  embedded relational database.
    See sqlite3 module
  object serialization. *See*
    pickle module
  overview of, 395–396
  persistent storage of objects.
    See shelve module
  supplements to standard
    library, 1368–1369
  Unix key-value databases. *See*
    dbm module
  XML manipulation API. *See*
    xml.etree.ElementTree
    module
Data sets, reducing in
  functools, 158–160
Data structures
  binary data structures. *See*
    struct module
  bisect module, 109–111
  container data types. *See*
    collections module
  duplicate objects. *See* copy
    module
  enumeration types. *See* enum
    module
  heap-sort algorithm. *See*
    heapq module
  impermanent references to
    objects. *See* weakref
    module
  overview of, 65–66
  pretty-print. *See* pprint
    module
  sequence of fixed-type data,
    see array module

thread-safe FIFO
    implementation. *See*
    queue module
Data types
  customizing, in json, 807–810
  encoding/decoding in json,
    804–805
  XML-RPC server, 819–822
Databases
  embedded relational. *See*
    sqlite3 module
  Unix key-value dbm, 408–411
Datagram sockets, 694
Dates
  date/time value manipulation.
    See datetime module
  formatting in locale, 1022
  overview, 211
  supplements to standard
    library, 1368
  as supported data type in
    XML-RPC, 822
  working with. *See* calendar
    module
datetime module
  changes in Python 3, 1358
  combining dates and times,
    228–230
  comparing values, 228
  date arithmetic, 226–227
  as date-time value
    manipulation, 221
  dates as supported data type
    in XML-RPC, 822
  defined, 211
  formatting and parsing,
    230–231
  new column types in
    sqlite3, 423
  supplements to standard
    library, 1368
  time, 221–225
  time zones, 231–232
  timedeltas, 225–226
dateutil package, date/time
  supplements, 1368
DbfilenameShelf class,
  405–406, 408
dbm module
  creating new database,
    409–410
  creating new shelf, 406
  database types, 408–409
  error cases, 411
  opening existing database,
    410

Unix key-value databases via, 408

dbm.dumb module, 409–410

dbm.gnu module, 409–410

dbm.ndbm module, 409–410

DDL (data definition language) statements, database in sqlite3, 413

Deadlocks, debugging threads, 1198–1200

Debugging
built-in, asnycio, 673–675
data structures, pprint, 65
detailed tracebacks. See cgitb module
interactive. See pdb module
memory leaks, 1265–1270
multiprocessing, 594–596
server, stmpd, 850
threads, 1198–1200
tracebacks for. See traceback module
using disassembly for, 1302–1303

DebuggingServer, stmpd, 850

decimal module
arithmetic, 242–243
changes in Python 3, 1358
context, 244–249
creating fraction instances, 252
Decimals, 239–241
formatting, 241–242
overview of, 239
special values, 243–244

Decoding
binary data with base64, 778
creating map for, codecs, 384–386
data in strings, pickle, 396–397
error handling, codecs, 372–376
incremental classes, 389
simple data types, json, 804–805
string. See codecs module
understanding, codecs, 367–368
working with files, codecs, 368–370

Decompression, zlib
incremental, 479–480
mixed content streams, 480–481
of network data, 483–486

working with data in memory, 477–479

Decorator syntax, atexit, 994

Decorators
algorithms supplementing standard library, 1367–1368
context managers, as function, 194–195

Decorators, functools
acquiring function properties, 145–147
acquiring function properties for decorators, 149–151
methods and functions, 148–149
other callables, 147–148
overview of, 143
partial objects, 144–145

Dedented text, 8–10

Deep copies
duplicate objects, 131–132
making recursive copies, 65, 133–136

deep module, printing messages, 1340

default() method, cmd, 939, 945

DEFAULT_COMPRESSION level, zlib, 479

defaultdict, 65, 82–84

Defaults, interpolation using, 976

DefaultSelector, 724

DEFERRED isolation level, sqlite3, 432–433

DefragResult value, urllib.parse, 756

defusedxml package, 1369

degrees() function, math angles, 283

Delay
running events with, 999
sched module, 998–999

Deleting from file system, pathlib, 318–319

Deleting messages
imaplib, 884–885
from Maildir mailbox, 858–860
from mbox mailbox, 854

delimiter class attribute, advanced string templates, 4–5

delitem() function, sequence operators, 187

delocalize() method, locale, 1020

Deltas, human-readable, 58

depth argument, pprint, 139–140

deque module
constraining queue size, 88–89
consuming, 85–87
defined, 65
as double-ended queue, 84–85
populating, 85
rotating, 87–88

description attribute, cursor in sqlite3, 417

dest argument, 888

detect_types flag, sqlite3, 422, 427

Developer tools
automated tests. See unittest module
class browser, 1160–1163
collecting and analyzing statistics. See profile module
compiling source files to byte-code, 1155–1159
creating virtual environments, 1163–1167
detailed tracebacks. See cgitb module
following program flow. See trace module
interactive debugging. See pdb module
online help, 1023–1026
stack traces and exceptions. See traceback module
supplements to standard library, 1371–1372
testing through documentation. See doctest module
timing execution of code. See timeit module
validating indentation, 1153–1155
working with Python package installer, 1167–1169

Development, managing package versions in, 1336–1338

DEVNULL, suppressing output in subprocesses, 541–542

Dialects, csv module
automatically detecting, 472–474
creating, 469–470
overview of, 469
parameters, 470–472

dict, OrderedDict vs., 93–94
Dictionaries
    encoding, json, 807
    initialization, Counter, 80
    non-integer member values
        using, enum, 75
    remember order that keys are
        added to, 94–97
    retrieving values, Counter,
        81
    search multiple, ChainMap,
        75–79
    using field names, cvs,
        474–476
    values stored in, timeit,
        1149–1152
DictReader class, cvs, 474–476
DictWriter class, cvs, 474–476
Differ class, difflib, 58–60
Difference-based reporting,
    managing blank lines,
    1036–1037
Differences in programs, using,
    356
difflib module
    compare bodies of text, 58–61
    comparing arbitrary types,
        62–64
    comparing sequences with, 58
    defined, 1
    junk data, 61–62
    overview of, 58
Digests
    applications of message
        signatures, 530–533
    hashlib MD5 hash example,
        524–525
    hashlib SHA1 example, 525
    hmac alternative types,
        528–529
    hmac binary, 529–530
dircache module, removed
    from Python 3, 1354
dircmp class, comparing large
    directory trees, 355–356
Directories
    accessing contents, pathlib,
        309–312
    comparing, filecmp, 354,
        355–356
    creating/deleting, 1233
    creating temporary, filecmp,
        335
    examining file system
        contents, 1228–1230
    installing message catalogs
        into, 1005–1006

managing process working
    directory, 1238–1239
managing user, 1171–1172
manipulating, pathlib,
    312–313
moving, shutil, 345
removing empty, pathlib,
    318
removing, shutil, 344–345
Directory trees
    recursive comparison of large,
        355–356
    working in shutil with,
        342–345
dirname() function, parsing
    paths in os.path, 297–298
dis(), basic dissasembly, 1297
dis module
    analyzing compiler
        optimizations, 1309–1311
    analyzing loop performance,
        1303–1309
    applying to class methods,
        1300
    applying to functions,
        1297–1299
    applying to source code,
        1301–1302
    basic dissasembly, 1297
    overview of, 1279, 1296–1297
    using for debugging,
        1302–1303
Disabling interpolation,
    configparser, 979
Disassembler/disassembling. See
    dis module
disk_usage() function,
    shutil, 350–351
display command, breakpoints
    for watching data change,
    1128–1129
Display hook, interpreter,
    1183–1184
distutils module, supplement
    to standard library, 1371
Django package, 1370
DNS (domain name services)
    asyncio, 658–660
    name lookups using UDP, 694
    network hostname lookup,
        socket, 695
DocFileSuite class, 1047–1048
docopt package, 1371
docstring, retrieving for
    objects, 1316–1317
doctest module
    execution context, 1048–1051

for external documentation,
    1042–1043
integration with unittests,
    1047–1048
overview of, 1023, 1026–1028
running by file, 1046–1047
running by module
    (testmod()), 1044–1046
test locations, 1039–1042
for tracebacks, 1032–1033
for unpredictable output,
    1028–1032
for whitespace management,
    1034–1039
DocTestSuite class,
    1047–1048
Documentation
    external, using doctest,
        1042–1043
    retrieving docstring for an
        object, 1316–1317
Domain, creating message
    catalogs, 1005–1006
Domain name services. See DNS
    (domain name services)
DOTALL flag, search for multiline
    text, 37–38
Dotted API names,
    xmlrpc.server, 830–831
Dotted notation, accessing fields
    of namedtuple, 90
Double-ended queue. See deque
    module
download_enclosures()
    function, threaded podcast
    client, 115
dropwhile() function, filtering
    iterable contents, 172–173
dumps() function
    encoding/decoding data in
        strings, pickle, 396–397
    human-readable output,
        json, 805–807
    working with streams/files,
        json, 813
dup list, shallow copies, 131–132
Duplicate
    lists in sorted order, 110–111
    objects. See copy module
dynamic context manager stacks
    arbitrary context callbacks,
        206–207
    overview of, 202
    partial stacks, 207–209
    stacking context managers,
        202–206

E

EasyDialogs module, removed
   from Python 3, 1354
Echo client
   asynchronous I/O, asyncio,
      646–649, 652–654
   enabling SSL on sockets,
      asyncio, 652–654
   example, socketserver,
      744–749
   I/O multiplexing
      abstractions, selectors,
      726–728
   TCP/IP, socket, 705–711
   UDP, socket, 712–713
Echo server
   asynchronous I/O, asyncio,
      644–646, 650–652
   enabling SSL on sockets,
      asyncio, 650–652
   example, socketserver,
      743–749
   I/O multiplexing
      abstractions, selectors,
      724–728
   TCP/IP, socket, 704–711
   UDP, socket, 712–713
   using select() with, 729–730
EchoRequestHandler,
   socketserver, 743–748
ehlo(),
   authentication/encryption in
      smtplib, 843–845
Element nodes, building XML
   documents from, 457–458
ElementTree library, see
   xml.etree.ElementTree
   module
Email
   IMAP4 client library. See
      imaplib module
   manipulate email archives.
      See mailbox module
   overview of, 841
   sample mail servers. See
      smtpd module
   SMTP. See smtplib module
   supplements to standard
      library, 1370
Embedded comments, parsing in
   shlex, 954
Embedded relational database.
   See sqlite3 module
emptyline() method,
   overriding base class
   methods in cmd, 945

Encoded value, http.cookies,
   793–794
Encoder/decoder classes, json,
   810
Encoding
   arguments,
      urllib.request,
      763–764
   binary data with ASCII. See
      base64 module
   connecting to XML-RPC
      server, 818
   data in strings, pickle,
      396–397
   defining custom, codecs,
      383–389
   dictionaries, json, 807
   error handling, codecs,
      372–373
   errors, in codec, 373–374
   files, codecs, 368–370
   files for upload,
      urllib.request,
      767–768
   incremental, bz2, 378–380
   maps, 384–386
   non-Unicode, 377–378
   query arguments,
      urllib.parse, 759–760
   simple data types, json,
      804–805
   strings. See codecs module
   translation, codecs, 376–377
   understanding, 366–368
   values in cookie header,
      793–794
   Western languages, 366
Encryption
   email, smtplib, 843–846
   enabling SSL on sockets in
      asyncio, 656
Endianness, 118–120, 370–372
Ending argument processing,
   getopt, 922
ensurepip module
   new in Python 3, 1352
   overview of, 1024
   working with Python package
      installer, 1167–1169
enter_context(), stacking
   context managers, 202–206
enter() function
   canceling events in sched,
      1001–1002
   running events with delay,
      999

enterabs() function, canceling
   events in sched, 1001–1002
enum module
   creating enumerations, 66
   creating enumerations
      programmatically, 71–72
   defined, 65
   enumeration type, 66
   iteration, 67–69
   new in Python 3, 1352
   non-integer member values,
      72–75
   unique enumeration values,
      69–71
Enumeration
   of all threads, 567–568
   enum. See enum module
Environment variables, process
   environment, 1237–1238
Equality-checking
   almost equal in unittests,
      1055–1056
   comparing in unittests,
      1056–1061
   unittest for, 1054–1055
Equality, OrderedDict, 94
erf(-x) error function, math,
   289
erfc() error function, math,
   289–290
error, conflict_handler,
   argparse, 903
Error handling
   capturing output,
      subprocess, 543–545
   in codecs, 372–376
   in http.server, 787–788
   read text in linecache,
      328–329
   running external command in
      subprocess, 537–538
   in shlex, 957–958
Errors. See also Exceptions
   in dbm, 411
   operating system codes for,
      1245–1246
   recoverable. See warnings
      module
Escape
   codes, 23–26, 39
   meta-characters in glob,
      322–323
escape() function,
   meta-characters, 322–323
Event loop, asyncio
   chaining coroutines, 620–621
   concept of, 618

Event loop, asyncio
  (continued)
  scheduling calls to regular
    functions, 622–625
  starting coroutine, 619
Events
  asynchronous system. See
    signal module
  timed event scheduler. See
    sched module
  XML parse, 451–455
Exception handling
  program shutdown callbacks,
    atexit, 997–998
  in XML-RPC, 825–826
Exceptional sockets, 732
Exceptional values, testing in
  math, 265–267
Exceptions
  applied to low-level exception
    APIs, 1082–1086
  applied to low-level stack
    APIs, 1086–1089
  applying dis to, 1302–1303
  argument types, argparse,
    911
  authentication failure,
    imaplib, 865–866
  causing, argparse, 902
  current, sys, 1195–1196
  detailed tracebacks, cgitb,
    1090–1092
  exception properties, cgitb,
    1096–1098
  handling, sys, 1194
  handling module import
    errors, sys, 1214–1215
  HTML output format, cgitb,
    1098
  ignoring, 199–201
  local variables in tracebacks,
    cgitb, 1093–1096
  logging tracebacks, cgitb,
    1098–1101
  monitoring, sys, 1225–1227
  previous interactive, sys,
    1196–1197
  in tasks,
    concurrent.futures,
    683
  testing for, unittest,
    1061–1062
  TracebackException class,
    1081–1082
  unhandled, 1194–1195
exceptions module, removed
  from Python 3, 1354

Exclusive mode isolation level,
  sqlite3, 433–434
exec()method, creating
  processes, 1240
execute() method
  autocommit mode, 434
  positional parameters in
    sqlite3, 419
  sqlite3, 415
  using variables with queries in
    sqlite3, 419
executemany() method, bulk
  loading in sqlite3, 421–422
executescript() method,
  create database in sqlite3,
  414
Executors
  managing pools of workers,
    677
  working as context managers,
    683–684
Exit callbacks, registering,
  994–997
exit(), sys, 1187
exitcode, multiprocessing,
  594–596
ExitStack
  arbitrary context callbacks,
    206–207
  dynamic context manager
    stacks, 202
  partial stacks, 208–209
  stacking context managers,
    202–206
exp() function, math, 282
expanduser() function,
  os.path, 300–301
expandvars() function,
  os.path, 301
expectedFailure(),
  unittest, 1068–1069
expm1() function, math, 282
Exponent, math functions,
  278–282
Exponential distribution,
  random, 263–264
Exponentiation operator (**),
  278
Exporting database contents,
  sqlite3, 435
expovariate() function,
  exponential distribution, 263
EXPUNGE command, imaplib,
  884–885
ExtendedInterpolation,
  configparser, 978–979

External command,
  subprocess
  capturing output, 538–541
  error handling, 537–538
  overview of, 536–537
  suppressing output, 541–542
Extremes, heap data, 107–108

F

fabs() function, math, 272–274
factorial() function, math,
  274–275
Fault objects, XML-RPC,
  825–827
FauxNFSHandler class,
  urrlib.request, 771–772
feedparser module, threaded
  podcast client, 116
fetch() method, messages in
  imaplib, 874–881
fetchall() method, sqlite3,
  415
fetchmany() method,
  sqlite3, 416
fetchone() method, sqlite3,
  416
fetch_podcasts, threaded
  podcast client, 114–115
Fibonacci sequence, profile
  applied to, 1140–1142
Field names, 91–92, 474–476
FIFO (first-in, first-out) queue.
  See queue module
File arguments, 912–913
File extensions, 1330–1331
File system
  comparing files. See filecmp
    module
  filename pattern matching.
    See glob module
  high level file operations. See
    shutil module
  memory-map files. See mmap
    module
  overview of, 295–296
  parsing paths. See os.path
    module
  as paths. See pathlib
    module
  read text files efficiently. See
    linecache module
  string encoding/decoding. See
    codecs module
  temporary file system objects.
    See tempfile module

text, binary, and raw stream
i/o tools. *See* `io` module
Unix-style glob pattern
matching. *See* `fnmatch`
module
File system space, `shutil`,
350–351
File systems
creating/deleting directories,
1233
examination of file system
contents, 1228–1230
managing file system
permissions, 1230–1233
rename/replace files,
1234–1235
symbolic links, 1234
File times, `os.path`, 302–303
File types, `pathlib`, 313–315
`filecmp` module
comparing directories,
355–356
comparing files, 353–355
example data, 351–353
using differences in program,
357–360
`fileinput` module
command-line filter
framework with, 986
converting M3U files to RSS,
987–989
in-place filtering, 990–992
progress metadata, 989–990
Filenames
changing archive, `tarfile`,
508–509
changing archive, `zipfile`,
516
pattern matching, 319–323
platform-independent
manipulation of. *See*
`os.path` module
`fileno()` method, 334, 729–734
`FileNotFoundError`
exception, `pathlib`, 318
Files
arrays and, 100–101
configuring logs to, 981
encoding/decoding strings,
368–370
working with `json`, 813
`FileType`, file arguments,
912–913
`fill()` function
combining `dedent()` with,
9–10
paragraphs, 8

Filters
command-line framework for
text files, 987–992
`fnmatch` glob pattern
matching, 325
in `itertools`, 172–174
in `warnings`, 1280–1283
`finalize()` method, custom
aggregation in `sqlite3`,
440–441
`finalize` objects, `weakref`,
123–126
Finding
files, `shutil`, 345–346
message catalogs at runtime,
1007–1008
multiple matches in text, 16
nodes in XML document,
447–448
paragraphs, 55
`find_module()`, inside ZIP
archive, 1345
First-in, first-out (FIFO) queue.
See `queue` module
Fixtures
package, 1371
`unittest` applied to,
1062–1065
in `unittest` structure, 1051
Flags
mailbox message, 862–864
options as, `configparser`,
969–970
registered data channels,
737–741
regular expressions. *See* `re`
module, search options
Float representation, wall clock
time, 213
Floating-point values, `math`,
966–968
Floating-point values, `math`
alternative representations,
271–272
calculate absolute value,
272–274
commonly used calculations,
274–277
comparisons involving,
267–269
converting to integers,
270–271
division, 185–186
fixed- and floating-point
math. *See* `decimal`
module
`fraction` module, 251–254

`random()` generating, 257
testing for exceptional,
265–267
Floating-point values, memory
management, 1192–1193
`floor()` function, converting
floating-point values, 270
`floordiv()` operator, 185–186
`flush()` method
incremental compression,
`zlib`, 480
messages, `mbox` mailbox, 854
`fmod()` function, `math`, 276–277
`fnmatch` module
filtering, 325
simple matching, 323–324
translating patterns, 325–326
as Unix-style glob pattern
matching, 325
Folders, Maildir mailbox,
860–862
Forking
adding in `http.server`,
786–787
adding to server in
`socketserver`, 749–751
creating processes in
`os.fork`, 1240–1242
`ForkingMixIn`
`http.server`, 787
`socket.server`, 750–751
`formatter` module, deprecated,
1355
Formatting
`calendar`, 233–236
configuration files, 975–979
`datetime`, 230–231
`decimal`, 241–242
numbers, `locale`, 1019–1021
`pprint`, 137–138
stack, traceback, 1087–1088
`string`, 6
`time`, clock time, 219–220
traceback exception,
1084–1085
`warnings`, 1285
`fractions` module
approximating values, 253
arithmetic, 252–253
changes in Python 3, 1358
creating fraction instances,
250–252
as rational numbers, 250
Frames, inspecting stacks and,
1324–1327
`frexp()` function, `math`,
271–272

`frombytes()` method, arrays and files, 101

`fromfile()` method, arrays and files, 101

`fromfile_prefix_chars`, `arparse`, 896–897

`from_float()` method, `decimal`, 239

`fromordinal()` function, `datetime`, 224, 229

`fromtimestamp()` function, `datetime`, 224, 229

`fsum()` function, `math`, 274

`fullmatch()` function, search constraints in `re`, 29

Fully qualified domain name, `socket`, 697

Function decorators, 194–195, 197–198

Functions
  `asyncio` event loop scheduling calls to, 622–625
  disassembling, 1297–1299
  examining stack variables in `pdb`, 1107–1111
  mathematical. *See* `math` module
  printing, 1146–1148
  Python, `sqlite3`, 436–438
  report on relationships between, `trace`, 1073–1074
  scanning for, 1162–1163
  signatures for, 1319–1322
  `string` module, 1–2
  `Struct` class vs., 117
  tools for manipulating. *See* `functools` module
  tracing, 1221–1224

`functools` module
  caching, 155–158
  comparison, 151–155
  creating decorators, 1367–1368
  decorators. *See* decorators, `functools`
  defined, 143
  generic functions, 161–163
  reducing data set, 158–160
  as tools for manipulating functions, 143

`Future`, `asyncio`
  callbacks, 627–628
  concept of, 618
  producing results asynchronously, 625

running client in asynchronous I/O, 647–648
  waiting for a, 625–627

`Future`, `concurrent.futures`
  callbacks, 680–681
  canceling tasks, 681–682
  exceptions in tasks, 683
  managing results by workers, 677

G

Gamma distribution, `random`, 264

`gamma()` function, `math`, 275

Garbage collection. *See also* `gc` module
  caching objects, 127–128
  memory management, `sys`, 1187–1188

Gauss error function, `statistics`, 289

`gc` module
  caching objects, `weakref`, 127–130
  changes in Python 3, 1358
  collection thresholds and generations, 1261–1265
  debugging memory leaks, 1265–1270
  finalizing objects, `weakref`, 125–126
  finding references to uncollectable objects, 1259–1261
  forcing garbage collection, 1258–1259
  overview of, 1169, 1254
  tracing references, 1255–1257

`gcd()` function, `math`, 277

Generator functions
  converting into context manager, 196–198
  instead of coroutines in `asyncio`, 621

Generator sequences, 188

Generic functions, `functools`, 161–163

`get()` method
  basic FIFO queue, 112
  basic LIFO queue, 112
  calling interpolation by default, `configparser`, 975–976
  options as flags, `configparser`, 969–970

testing if section exists, `configparser`, 965
  using specific browser in `webbrowser`, 796
  value types, `configparser`, 967

`getaddrinfo()`
  DNS, `asyncio`, 658–659
  server addresses, `socket`, 700–702
  TCP/IP client connections, `socket`, 708

`getmember()` method, `tarfile`, 505

`getmembers()` method
  inspecting classes, 1314–1316
  inspecting instances, 1316
  inspecting modules, 1312–1313
  load metadata from archive, `tarfile`, 505

`getopt` module
  abbreviating long-form options, 920
  command-line option parsing with, 916
  complete example, 918–920
  ending argument processing, 922
  function arguments, 916–917
  GNU-style option parsing, 920–922
  interface-related supplements to standard library, 1370
  long-form options, 917–918
  replace by `argparse` for newer applications, 922
  short-form options, 917

`getpass` module
  defined, 887
  example, 935–937
  secure password prompt with, 935
  use without terminal, 937–938

Getters, `operator`
  module/attribute/item, 188–190

`gettext` module
  application vs. module localization, 1012
  changes in Python 3, 1359
  creating message catalogs from source code, 1004–1007
  finding message catalogs at runtime, 1007–1008
  message catalogs with, 1003

plural values, 1008–1010
translation workflow
overview, 1003–1004
geturl() method, 756–758,
770–773
GIL (global interpreter lock),
threads, 1197
glob() method, 310–311
glob module
changes in Python 3, 1359
character ranges, 322
escaping meta-characters,
322–323
example data, 320
filename pattern matching,
319–320
fnmatch Unix-style, 323–326
single-character wildcard,
321–322
wildcards, 320–321
global interpreter lock (GIL),
controlling/debugging
threads, 1197
gmtime() function, 217
GNU
option parsing, 920–922
read and write zip files. See
gzip module
readline library. See
readline module
zlib compression. See zlib
module
Graph class, 134–136
Greediness, regular expressions,
18–19, 20–23
group() method, 32, 316
groupby() function,
itertools, 175–176
groupdict() method, regular
expression groups, 33
grouping character, formatting
numbers in locale,
1018–1019
Groups
argument, argparse,
904–905
data, itertools, 175–176
dissecting matches in regular
expressions, 30–36
mutually exclusive options,
argparse, 906
splitting with patterns, 56–57
traversing parsed tree, 447
groups() method, regular
expressions, 31, 33–35

gzip module
read and write GNU zip files,
486
reading compressed data,
489–490
tarfile using compressed
archives of, 510–511
working with streams,
490–491
writing compressed files,
486–488

H
handle() method,
socketserver, 743
Handler objects, 980, 984–985
handle_request() method,
socketserver, 743
Handles, contextlib closing
open, 198–199
Hanging indents, 12
Hardware, obtaining operating
information, 1248–1250
hasattr(), interface checking
alternatives, 1287
Hashable keys, functools
caching, 157–158
Hashable objects, counting,
79–83
Hashed values, doctests for
unpredictable, 1030–1032
Hashing, cryptographic. See
hashlib module
hashlib module
creating hash by name,
525–526
cryptographic hashing with,
523
hash algorithms, 523–524
incremental updates, 526–527
MD5 hash example, 524–525
sample data, 524
SHA1 digest example, 525
has_option() method,
configparser, 965–966,
969–970
has_section() method,
configparser, 965
Headers
adding outgoing,
urllib.request,
765–766
encoding values, cookie,
793–794
receiving and parsing,
cookie, 794–795

send email message,
smtplib, 841–843
setting, http.server,
788–789
Heap. See heapq module
Heap sort algorithm. See heapq
module
heapify() method, 105, 106
heappop() method, 105–106
heappush() method, 104–105
heapq module
accessing contents of heap,
104–106
creating heap, 103–104
data extremes from heaps,
106–108
defined, 65
example data, 103
as heap sort algorithm, 103
heapreplace() method,
106–107
Help
in argparse, 897–901
HTML, 1025–1026
live, 941–942
online, 1024–1026
output, argparse, 897–901
plain text, in atexit,
1024–1026
help command, Cmd class,
938–939
Helper base classes, 1289–1290
hexdigest() method
MD5 hash, 524–525
using Base64 version of
binary digest vs., 529–530
High-level file operations. See
shutil module
HistoryCompleter, 933
HMAC authentication, 530–533
hmac module
alternative digest types,
528–529
applications of message
signatures, 530–533
binary digests, 529–530
cryptographic message
signing/verification, 528
signing messages, 528
Hooks, readline, 934–935
Hostname, looking up network,
694–697
Hosts, in sqlite3, 419
hosts() method, ipaddress,
689–691

HTML
  formatting HTMLCalendar, 234
  getting help, 1025–1026
  html module, 1370
  htmlib module, removed from Python, 1354
  output format, 1098
HTTP cookies. *See* http.cookies module
HTTP GET operation
  http.server, 781–783
  urllib.request, 761–763
HTTP POST operation
  http.server, 784–786
  posting form data, urllib.request, 766–767
  urllib.request, 764–765
http.cookies module
  alternative output formats, 795–796
  changes in Python 3, 1359
  creating and setting cookies, 790–791
  encoded values, 793–794
  HTTP cookies, 790
  morsels, 791–793
  receiving and parsing cookie headers, 794–795
http.server module
  base classes implementing Web servers with, 781
  command-line use, 789–790
  handling errors, 787–788
  HTTP GET, 781–783
  HTTP POST, 784–786
  setting headers, 788–789
  threading and forking, 786–787
http.server package, 1370
Human-consumable vs. compact output, json, 805–807
Hyperbolic functions, math, 288
hypot() function, math trigonometry, 285–287

I

I/O operations
  asynchronous, in asyncio, 644–650
  encoding and decoding strings in codecs, 368–370
  multiplexing abstractions. *See* selectors module

text, binary and raw stream tools for, 390–393
waiting efficiently for with select. *See* select module
ID numbers, managing breakpoints, 1120–1121
Identation validator, tabnanny, 1153–1154
idpattern class attribute, advanced string templates, 4–5
IDs, detect/change process owner, 1235–1237
IEEE 802 MAC Address, UUID 1, 798–800
ignore command
  decoding errors, codecs, 375
  encoding errors, codecs, 374
  ignoring breakpoints, pdb, 1125–1127
Ignore signals, 557–558
IGNORECASE flag, regular expressions, 36–37, 49–51
ignore_patterns() function, directory trees in shutil, 342–343
IMAP4 client class, using clear text sockets, 864
IMAP4 client library. *See* imaplib module
IMAP4_SSL client class, 864
IMAP4_stream client class, 864
imapclient package, 1370
imaplib module
  changes in Python 3, 1359
  connecting to server, 864–866
  deleting messages, 884–885
  email supplements to standard library, 1370
  example configuration, 866
  fetching messages, 874–880
  IMAP4 client library with, 864
  listing mailboxes, 866–869
  mailbox status, 869–871
  moving and copying messages, 883–884
  search criteria, 872–874
  searching for messages, 872
  selecting mailbox, 871
  uploading messages, 881–883
  variations, 864
  whole messages, 880–881
Immediate mode isolation level, sqlite3, 433

Immutable, tuple and namedtuple as, 90–91
imp module, deprecated, 1356
Import hooks, custom importers, 1204–1205
Import path
  backward compatibility and, 1177–1178
  modules, 1202–1203
  packages, 1334–1336
  scanning for path configuration files, 1172–1175
  site, 1169–1170
import statement, 1329
Importable target functions, multiprocessing, 587–588
Importers. *See also* zipimport module, 1344
Importing modules. *See also* importlib module
  custom importers, 1203–1205
  custom package, 1211–1213
  handling import errors, 1214–1215
  importer cache, 1217–1218
  mapping to module objects, 1200–1201
  meta-path, 1218–1221
  retrieving import package data, 1215–1217
  from shelf, 1205–1211
importlib module
  accessing loaders, 1332–1334
  example, 1329–1330
  importing modules, 1331–1332
  overview of, 1329
  Python supported module styles, 1330–1331
import_module(), 1331–1332
In-memory approach
  bz2 compression, 492–493
  io streams, 390–391
  sqlite3 databases, 434–435
  zlib compression, 477–479
in operator, ipaddress, 691
In-place filtering, fileinput, 990–992
In-place operators, functional interface, 187–188
INADDR_ANY address, choosing for listening, 710–711
Incremental compression/decompression
  bz2, 493
  zlib, 479–480

Incremental encoding, `codecs`, 378–380

Incremental updates, hash calculators, 526–527

`IncrementalDecoder`, 378–380, 389

`IncrementalEncoder`, 378–380, 389

Indents, text paragraph
 block, 10–11
 combining `dedent()` and `fill()`, 9–10
 hanging, 12
 removing existing, 8–9

`inf` special value, `math`, 265–267, 269

`infolist()` method, `zipfile`, 512–514

Initialization
 `array`, 98–99
 `Counter`, 80

`initializer` argument, `functools`, 159–160

`input()` function, converting M3U files to RSS, 987–989

Input history, tracked in `readline`, 931–934

Input/output streams (stdin/stdout), `sys`, 1186–1187

`input_loop()` function, `readline`, 925

Inputs
 alternative, in `cmd`, 948–949
 combining in `itertools`, 176–182

`insert` statements, `sqlite3`, 415, 421

`insert_text()`, `readline`, 934

`insort()` method, 109–111

`inspect` module
 changes in Python 3, 1359
 command-line interface for, 1327–1328
 example, 1311–1312
 inspecting classes, 1314–1316
 inspecting instances, 1316
 inspecting method resolution order, 1323–1324
 inspecting modules, 1312–1313
 inspecting stack and frames, 1324–1327
 overview of, 1279, 1311
 retrieving docstring for an object, 1316–1317

retrieving source code for class or method, 1318–1319

returning specifcation of method or function arguments, 1319–1322

working with class hierarchies, 1322–1324

`install()` function, application localization, 1011

Installation paths, managing, 1272–1276

Instances, creating `fraction`, 250–252

Instances, inspecting, 1316

Integer division, `floordiv()` operator, 185–186

Integers
 converting floating-point values to, `math`, 270–271
 creating fraction, 253
 parsing command line arguments with, 889–891
 value types, `configparser`, 966–967
 values, memory management, 1193

`IntEnum` class, 68–69

Interactive prompts, Interpreter, 1182–1183

Interfaces
 network `ipaddress`, 692–693
 `pdb`, 1104–1105
 `trace` programming, 1074–1075

Internationalization and localization
 cultural localization API. *See* `locale` module
 message catalogs. *See* `gettext` module
 overview of, 1003

Internet
 addresses. *See* `ipaddress` module
 base classes implementing Web servers. *See* `http.server` module
 display Web pages via `webbrowser`, 796–797
 encode binary data with ASCII. *See* `base64` module
 HTTP cookies. *See* `http.cookies` module
 JavaScript Object Notation. *See* `json` module

network resource access. *See* `urllib.request` module

overview of, 753

spider access control. *See* `urllib.robotparser`

split URLs into components. *See* `urllib.parse` module

supplements to standard library, 1369–1370

Universally Unique Identifiers. *See* `uuid` module

XML-RPC client library. *See* `xmlrpc.client` module

XML-RPC server. *See* `xmlrpc.server` module

Interpolation
 `configparser`, 975–979
 `string.Template`, 2–4

Interpreter
 build-time version information, 1178–1179
 command-line arguments captured by, 1185–1186
 display hook, 1183–1184
 implementation, 1179–1180
 install location, 1184–1185
 interactive prompts, 1182–1183
 obtaining operating information, 1246–1247
 Unicode defaults, 1181–1182

Introspection API, `xmlrpc.server`, 837–839

Inverse `math` functions, 287, 288

Invertcaps
 character map-based codecs, 383–384
 define custom encoding, 384–389

`io` module
 in-memory streams, 390–392
 text, binary and raw stream I/O tools, 390
 wrapping byte streams for text data, 392–393

`IOError`
 copying files in `shutil`, 337
 testing tar files, 504

`ipaddress` module
 addresses, 687–688
 interfaces, 692–693
 networks, 688–692
 new in Python 3, 1352
 working with IPv4 and IPv6 addresses, 687

IPv4 and IPv6 addresses. *See*
  `ipaddress` module; `socket`
  module
`isclose()` function,
  comparisons in `math`,
  267–269
`isfinite()` function, `math`,
  267
`islice()` function,
  `itertools`, 166
`isnan`, `math`, 266–267
ISO-8601 format, datetime
  objects, 230–231
Isolation levels, `sqlite3`
  autocommit mode, 434
  `DEFERRED`, 432–433
  exclusive mode, 433–434
  immediate mode, 433
  overview of, 431–432
`is_()` function, 183
`is_not()` function, 183
`is_tarfile()` function,
  503–504
`is_zipfile()` function, 512
Item getters, `operator`,
  188–190
`items()` method, 859, 964
`iter()` function, traversing
  parsed tree, 446–447
`iterall()` function, regular
  expression search, 29
Iteration
  `enum`, 67
  over networks, 689–691
Iterators
  functions for. *See* `itertools`
    module
  using getters with, 188
`itertools` module
  changes in Python 3, 1359
  combining inputs, 176–182
  converting inputs, 167–169
  defined, 143
  filtering, 172–175
  grouping data, 175–176
  merging and splitting
    iterators, 164–167
  overview of, 163–164
  producing new values,
    169–172

J

JavaScript Object Notation. *See*
  `json` module
`join()` method

building paths in `os.path`,
  300
daemon threads, 565–567
join process after terminating
  it, 594
normalizing paths in
  `os.path`, 301
threaded podcast client, 116
waiting for processes,
  `multiprocessing`,
  591–593
`joinpath()`method, `pathlib`,
  306
`json` module
  changes in Python 3, 1359
  encoder and decoder classes,
    810–812
  encoding/decoding simple
    data types, 804–805
  encoding dictionaries, 807
  human-consumable vs.
    compact output, 805–807
  JavaScript Object Notation
    with, 803–804
  JSON at command-line, 815
  mixed data streams, 813–814
  working with custom types,
    807–810
  working with streams and
    files, 813
JSON, YAML and, 1371
`JSONDecoder` class, 812–814
`JSONEncoder` class, 810–811
`json.tool` module, 815
`js_output()` method,
  `http.cookie`, 795–796
`jump` command, breakpoints,
  1130–1134
Junk data, `difflib`, 61–64

K

Key-value databases, Unix, 408
`KeyError`
  `Counter`, 81
  `tarfile`, 505
Keys, `Morsel`, 793
`Kill` command, sending signals,
  554

L

Language, creating message
  catalogs, 1005–1006
Language tools
  abstract base classes. *See* `abc`
    module
  disassembler. *See* `dis` module

inspecting live objects. *See*
  `inspect` module
non-fatal alerts/recoverable
  errors. *See* `warnings`
  module
  overview of, 1279
`ldexp()` function, `math`, 272
Length, constraining queue,
  88–89
Levels
  logging tree structure,
    984–985
  verbosity, `logging` API,
    982–984
`lgamma()` function, `math`, 276
Libraries
  configuring `logging` for, 980
  runtime. *See* Runtime
LIFO (last-in, first-out) queue,
  112
`LifoQueue`, 112
Limiting concurrent access to
  resources, `threading`,
  581–583
Line-oriented command
  processors. *See* `cmd` module
`linecache` module
  error handling, 328–329
  handling blank lines, 328
  overview of, 326
  reading Python source files,
    329–330
  reading specific lines, 327–328
  test data, 326–327
Lines, in `linecache`, 327–328
`lineterm` argument,
  `unified_diff()`, 60
Linux, operating information
  functions, 1249
`list_contents()`,
  `xmlrpc.server`, 828–830
`list_dialects()` method,
  `csv`, 469
`listdir()`, examine file system
  contents, 1228–1229
`listen()`, socket echo server,
  705
`--listfuncs`, calling
  relationships in `trace`,
  1073–1074
Lists
  `hashlib` algorithms, 524
  of mailboxes, in `imaplib`,
    866–869
  maintain in sorted order with
    `bisect`, 109–111

of nodes, building XML trees, 461–464

passing to select(), 730

variable argument, 908–910

Literal expressions, compiler optimization, 1309–1310

Literal strings, 1003–1007

load() method

decoding cookie headers in http.cookie, 794–795

file-like streams in pickle, 398

streams/files in json, 813

Loaders

accessing, 1332–1334

importing modules, 1205

load_module(), 1332–1334

local() class, thread specific data, 583–585

local_data list, pprint recursion, 139

Locale

calendar formatting for, 236

directory, 1005–1008

locale module

changes in Python 3, 1359

currency, 1018–1019

dates and times, 1022

formatting numbers, 1019–1021

overview of, 1012–1013

parsing numbers, 1021

probing current locale, 1013–1018

Localization and internationalization

cultural localization API. See locale module

message catalogs. See gettext module

localtime() function, 217

Location, temporary file, 336–337

lock() method, remove messages from mbox mailbox, 854

Lock object, resource access control in multiprocessing, 603–604

Lock object, threading

as context managers, 577–578

controlling access to resources, 572–576

re-entrant locks, 576–577

RLock, 576–577

synchronizing threads, 578–581

log() function, math, 279–281

log1p() function, math, 281

Logarithms, math, 278–282

Logger, 980, 984–985

Logging

multiprocessing, 596–597

tracebacks, 1098–1101

xmlrpc.server, 829

logging module

asynchronous I/O using, 644–647, 650–653

changes in Python 3, 1360

combining coroutines with threads in asyncio, 671–672

debugging with asyncio, 673–674

embedding thread name in, 563–564

integration with warning module, 985–986

logging components, 980

logging in applications vs. libraries, 980

logging to file, 981

logging tree, 984–985

naming logger instances, 984

report status, error, informational messages with, 980

rotating log files, 981–982

verbosity levels, 982–984

Logical operations, functional interface, 183–184

LogRecord, as logging component, 980

log_to_stderr(), multiprocessing, 596–597

Long-form options, getopt, 917–918

Long-lived spiders, urllib.robotparser, 775–776

longlist, navigating execution stack, 1106

Look ahead assertion syntax, regular expressions, 44–46

Look behind assertion syntax, regular expressions, 46–48

Loops, analyzing performance, 1303–1309

lru_cache() decorator, functools, 155–158

lstat() method, 315, 1230

lxml package, 1368

M

M3U files, converting to RSS, 987–989

m3utorss, converting M3U files to RSS, 987–989

MAC address, UUID 1, 798–800

Mail server base class, smtpd, 847–850

mailbox module

changes in Python 3, 1360

Maildir format. See Maildir format

manipulating email archives, 852

mbox format, 852–855

message flags, 862–864

other formats, 862

mailbox status, imaplib, 869–871

Mailboxes

IMAP4 client library. See imaplib module

mailbox module. See mailbox module

Maildir format

create Maildir mailbox, 854–858

Maildir folders, 860–862

overview of, 854

read from Maildir mailbox, 858

remove messages from Maildir mailbox, 858–860

MaildirMessage, 857

make_archive()function, shutil, 347–348

make_encoding_map(), custom encoding, 384–385

makefile(), Unicode data/network communication, 381, 383

Manager, shared namespaces, 608–610

Manipulating arrays, 99–100

map() method

converting inputs in itertools, 167–168

new values in itertools, 171–172

process pools in multiprocessing, 611–613

using with basic thread pool, 677–678

Mapping
　accessing configuration
　　settings, 964–965
　using `poll()` in `select`, 738
MapReduce,
　`multiprocessing`, 613–617
`Maps` attribute, `ChainMap`,
　75–76
Masks, network, 688, 691–692
`match()` function, regular
　expression search, 28, 39
`Match` object
　find multiple matches in text,
　　16
　regular expression groups,
　　30–36
　search for patterns in text,
　　14–15
`math` module
　angles, 282–284
　commonly used calculations,
　　274–277
　comparing, 267–269
　converting floating-point
　　values to integers, 270–271
　exponents and logarithms,
　　278–282
　hyperbolic functions, 288
　as mathematical functions,
　　264
　positive and negative signs,
　　272–274
　representations of
　　floating-point values,
　　271–272
　special constants, 265
　special functions, 289–290
　supplements to standard
　　library, 1368
　testing for exceptional values,
　　265–267
　trigonometry, 284–288
Mathematics
　fixed- and floating-point
　　math. *See* `decimal`
　　module
　mathematical functions. *See*
　　`math` module
　overview of, 239
　pseudorandom number
　　generators. *See* `random`
　　module
　rational numbers. *See*
　　`fractions` module
　statistical calculations,
　　290–294

supplements to standard
　library, 1368
`max` attribute
　`datetime_date`, 224
　`datetime_time`, 222
　random numbers, 254
Max-heap, 103
`maxsize` argument, caching in
　`functools`, 156–158
`maxtasksperchild` parameter,
　process pools, 612–613
mbox, `mailbox`, 852–855
MD5 algorithm
　`hashlib` module, 524–525
　`hmac` module, 528–529
　UUID 3 and 5, name-based
　　values, 800–801
`md5` module, removed from
　Python 3, 1354
`mean()` function, `statistics`,
　290–291
`median()` function,
　`statistics`, 291–292
`median_grouped()` function,
　`statistics`, 292
`median_high()` function,
　`statistics`, 292
`median_low()` function,
　`statistics`, 292
Memory
　debugging leaks, 1265–1270
　holding data in, `zlib`,
　　477–479
　modules for managing, 65
Memory management
　byte ordering in, 1194
　controlling recursion,
　　1190–1191
　defining maximum values,
　　1191
　determining object size,
　　1188–1190
　floating-point values,
　　1192–1193
　integer values, 1193
　reference counts for,
　　1187–1188
　`sys` features, 1187
Memory-map files. *See* `mmap`
　module
`merge()` method, `heapq`,
　108–109
Merging iterators, `itertools`,
　164–167
Message catalogs. *See* `gettext`
　module

Message flags, `mailbox`,
　862–864
Messages
　cryptographic signatures for.
　　See `hmac` module
　multicast, 718–720
　passing to processes,
　　`multiprocessing`,
　　598–599
　remove from Maildir mailbox,
　　858–860
　remove from `mbox` mailbox,
　　854–855
　sending, `smtplib`, 841–843
Meta-characters
　escaping in `glob`, 322–323
　regular expressions. *See* `re`
　　module, pattern syntax
Meta-path, module import and,
　1218–1221
Metaclasses, helper base classes
　specifying, 1289–1290
Metadata
　copying file, in `shutil`,
　　340–342
　progress, in `fileinput`,
　　989–990
　querying, in `sqlite3`, 417
　reading from archive, in
　　`tarfile`, 504–505
　reading from archive, in
　　`zipfile`, 512–514
Method resolution order (MRO),
　inspecting, 1323–1324
Methods
　accessing configuration
　　settings, 963–970
　concrete methods in `abc`,
　　1291–1292
　disassembling class methods,
　　1300
　exposing object,
　　`xmlrpc.server`, 832–834
　marking class/static methods
　　as abstract, 1295–1296
　overriding base class, in `cmd`,
　　944–946
　retrieving source code for
　　class/method, 1318–1319
　returning specification of
　　method/function
　　arguments, 1319–1322
Microsoft Windows, 305
`mimetools` module, removed
　from Python 3, 1354
`MimeWriter` module, removed
　from Python 3, 1354

`mimify` module, removed from Python 3, 1354
`min` attribute
  `datetime_date`, 224
  `datetime_time`, 222
  generating random numbers, 254
Min-heap, 103
`mkdir()` method, `pathlib`, 312–313
`mktime()` function, 217
`mmap` module
  changes in Python 3, 1360
  copy mode, 363–364
  as memory-map files, 361
  reading, 361–362
  regular expressions, 364–365
  writing, 362–363
`mode()` function, `statistics`, 291
`mod()` function, `math`, 271
Module localization, 1011–1012
Modules. *See also* by individual types
  built-in modules, 1201–1202
  custom importers, 1203–1205
  determining if package or regular module, 1348
  handling of import errors, 1214–1215
  import path, 1202–1203
  imported modules, 1200–1201
  importing from shelf, 1205–1211
  inspecting, 1312–1313
  new in Python 3, 1352
  Python supported module styles, 1330–1331
  reloading, 1213–1214
  removed from Python 3, 1354–1355
  renamed in Python 3, 1352–1353
  third party, 1367
Modules, porting Python 2 to Python 3
  deprecated modules, 1355–1356
  new modules, 1352
  removed modules, 1354–1355
  renamed modules, 1352–1353
  summarizing changes to modules, 1356–1365
Monotonic clocks
  comparing, 212–213
  defined, 211
  overview of, 214

scheduling callback for specific time, 624–625
`monotonic()` function, `sched`, 999
`monthCalendar()` method, formatting `calendar`, 234, 237
`Morsel` object, RFC attributes for cookies, 791–793
`most_common()` method, `Counter`, 81–82
`move()` function
  file or directory in `shutil`, 345
  messages in `imaplib`, 883–884
`move_to_end()` method, `OrderedDict`, 96–97
MRO (method resolution order), inspecting, 1323–1324
`msgformat`, building message catalogs, 1006
`Multicall`, XML-RPC, 826–827
Multicasting
  groups, 718
  `socket`, 717–718
  UDP used for, 694
`multifile` module, removed from Python 3, 1354
Multiline strings, `configparser`, 970
Multiline text, regular expression search for, 37–38
`MultiPartForm` class, encoding files for upload, 767–770
Multiple matches, finding in text, 16
Multiple simultaneous generators, `random`, 261–262
multiplexing abstractions, I/O. *See* `selectors` module
`multiprocessing` module
  controlling access to resources, 603–604
  controlling concurrent access to resources, 605–607
  daemon processes, 589–591
  determining current process, 588–589
  implementing MapReduce, 613–617
  importable target functions, 587–588
  logging, 596–597
  managing processes like threads, 586

managing shared state, 608
multiprocessing basics, 586–587
passing messages to processes, 598–602
process exit status, 594–596
process pools, 611–613
shared namespaces, 608–610
signaling between processes, 602–603
subclassing `Process`, 597–598
synchronizing operations, 604–605
terminating processes, 593–594
waiting for processes, 591–593
Mutually exclusive options, `argparse`, 906
`MyThreadWithArgs`, 569

N
Name
  current process in `multiprocessing`, 588–589
  DNS address lookup in `asyncio` by, 658–660
  DNS address lookups in UDP by, 694
  hash in `hlib`, 525–526
  `Logger` instances, 984
  predicting `tempfile`, 335–336
  renaming `namedtuple` invalid fields, 70
  temporary files, 333
  threads, in server processes, 562–564
  UUID 3 and 5 values based on, 800–801
`name` property
  enumerations, 66
  parsing paths in `pathlib`, 308
Named groups
  modify strings with patterns, 53
  regular expressions, 32–33
  test matching, 51–52
Named parameters, `sqlite3`, 420–421
`NamedTemporaryFile()` function, 333
`namedtuple()` factory function, 90

`namedtuple` module
  invalid field names, 91–92
  overview of, 89–90
  special attributes, 92–94
  as tuple subclass with named
    fields, 90–91
`names` argument, enumerations,
  71
Namespaces
  `Manager` creating shared, 608
  parsing command line
    arguments with, 889–891
  UUID 3 and 5, name-based
    values, 800–801
`nan` special value, `math`,
  266–267, 269
`nargs`, variable argument lists
  in `argparse`, 908–910
`ndiff()` function, `difflib`, 60,
  62
Negative look ahead assertion
  (`?!pattern`), `re`, 45–46
Negative look behind assertion
  (`?<!pattern`), `re`, 46–47
Nesting
  data types in XML-RPC
    server, 820–822
  `for` loops, 177–178
  output in `pprint`, 139–140
  packages, 1340–1341
  parsers, 906–908
Networking
  communication, Unicode,
    380–383
  compressing data, `bz2`,
    499–503
  compressing data, `zlib`,
    482–486
  creating network servers. *See*
    `socketserver` module
  I/O multiplexing
    abstractions. *See*
    `selectors` module
  Internet addresses. *See*
    `ipaddress` module
  network communication. *See*
    `socket` module
  overview of, 687
  resource access. *See*
    `urllib.request` module
  wait for I/O efficiently. *See*
    `select` module
`new_child()`, `ChainMap`, 77
`new()`function
  creating hash by name,
    `hashlib`, 525–526
  SHA1 algorithm in `hmac`, 529

signing cryptographic
  messages, `hmac`, 528
Newton-Mercator series,
  281–282
`next`, stepping through program
  in `pdb`, 1114–1115
`NFSFile` class,
  `urrlib.request`, 770–773
`ngettext()` function,
  1008–1011
`nlargest()` method, heap,
  107–108
NLTK package, 1367
`nmap()` function, reading
  memory-map files, 361–362
`no-expression`, regular
  expressions, 51–52
Nodes
  building XML documents
    from Element, 457–458
  building XML trees from lists
    of, 461–464
  finding in XML document,
    447–448
  traversing parsed tree,
    446–447
  XML attributes of, 449–450
Non-blocking communication
  and timeouts, `socket`, 723
Non-blocking I/O with
  timeouts, `select`, 734–737
Non-capturing groups, regular
  expressions, 35–36
Non-daemon processes,
  `multiprocessing`, 591–593
Non-daemon threads,
  `threading`, 564–567
Non-integer member values,
  `enum`, 72–75
Non-Unicode encodings,
  `codecs`, 377–378
Non-uniform distributions,
  `random`, 263–264
`None` value
  alternative regular expression
    patterns, 35
  disabling interpolation,
    `configparser`, 979
  retrieving registered handlers,
    555–556
  search for patterns in text, 14
`NoOptionError`, option search
  in `configparser`, 973–974
Normal distribution, `random`,
  263
Normalizing paths, `os.path`,
  301–302

`normpath()` function,
  `os.path`, 301
`NoSectionError`,
  `configparser`, 972, 974
`not_()` function, logical
  operations, 183
`NotADirectoryError`,
  `pathlib`, 309
`not_called()`, callbacks,
  995–996
`nsmallest()` method, heap,
  107–108
NULL byte, 653, 824
Number generators, multiple
  random, 261–262
Numbers
  arithmetic operator functions
    for, 184–185
  formatting in `locale`,
    1019–1021
  numeric types in
    `configparser`, 966–967
  parsing in `locale`, 1021
  rational. *See* `fractions`
    module
NumPly, math supplement to
  standard library, 1368

O

Object relational mapper
  (ORM), 1368–1369
`object_hook` argument,
  customizing types in `json`,
  809–810
Objects
  correcting problems
    reconstructing, in `pickle`,
    399–400
  determining size of,
    1188–1190
  exposing methods in
    `xmlrpc.server`, 832–834
  file system paths as. *See*
    `pathlib` module
  impermanent references to.
    See `weakref` module
  inspecting live. *See* `inspect`
    module
  passing in XML-RPC,
    822–823
  persistent storage of. *See*
    `shelve` module
  retrieving docstring for,
    1316–1317
  serializing. *See* `pickle`
    module

server, in `socketserver`, 743
`sqlite3` row, 417–419
temporary file system. *See*
  `tempfile` module
types of logging component,
  980
unpicklable, 400–402
working with UUID, 802–803
One-way process
  communication,
  `subprocess`, 542–543
`onecmd()` method, `sys.argv`,
  950–951
Online help, `pydoc`, 1024–1026
`open()` function
  creating new database,
    409–410
  customizing protocol handlers
    in `urrlib.request`,
    770–773
  reading/writing files in
    `pathlib`, 312
  `webbrowser` example using,
    796
  working with files in `codecs`,
    368–370
  writing compressed files in
    `gzip`, 486–488
`open_connection()`
  asynchronous I/O using
    coroutines/streams, 653
  connecting to IMAP server,
    864–865
  enabling SSL on sockets,
    652–654
`open_new()` function,
  `webbrowser`, 796
`openssl` command, enabling
  SSL on sockets, 656
Operating systems. *See also* `os`
  module
  error codes, 1245–1246
  obtaining operating
    information, 1248–1250
`operator` module
  arithmetic operators, 184–186
  attribute and item getters,
    188–190
  changes in Python 3, 1360
  combining operators/custom
    classes, 190–191
  comparison operators, 184
  as functional interface to
    built-in operators, 183
  logical operations, 183–184
  in-place operators, 187–188
  sequence operators, 186–187

Optimization
  analyzing compiler
    optimizations, 1309–1311
  analyzing loop performance,
    1303–1309
Options
  argument groups in
    `argparse`, 904
  configuration file format in
    `configparser`, 961
  as flags in `configparser`,
    969–970
  modifying settings in
    `configparser`, 970–971
  mutually exclusive, in
    `argparse`, 906
  parsing in command-line. *See*
    `getopt` module
  prefixes in `argparse`,
    894–895
  search path in
    `configparser`, 972–975
  searching for in
    `configparser`, 972–975
  testing if present in
    `configparser`, 965–966
  value types in
    `configparser`, 966–969
`optparse` module, deprecated,
  1356
`OrderedDict` subclass
  changing `namedtuple`
    instances to, 93
  defined, 65
  equality, 95
  remembers order that keys
    are added to dictionary,
    94–95
  reordering, 96
ORM (object relational
  mapper), 1368–1369
`os` module
  changes in Python 3,
    1360–1361
  creating/deleting directories,
    1233
  creating processes, 1240–1242
  detect/change process owner,
    1235–1237
  error codes, 1245–1246
  examination of file system
    contents, 1228–1230
  management of file system
    permissions, 1230–1233
  management of process
    environment, 1237–1238

management of process
  working directory,
  1238–1239
overview of, 1227
rename/replace files,
  1234–1235
running external commands,
  1239–1240
signaling between processes,
  `subprocess`, 548–553
spawning new processes,
  1244–1245
symbolic links, 1234
waiting for child processes,
  1242–1244
OS X, operating information
  functions, 1249
`os.curdir` variable, 296
`os._exit()`, avoid `atexit`
  callbacks, 996–997
`os.extsep` variable, 296
`os.fork()`, interprocess
  communication, 398–399
`os.kill()` method, sending
  signals, 554, 556
`os.pardir` variable, `os.path`,
  296
`os.path` module
  building paths, 300–301
  changes in Python 3, 1361
  file times, 302–303
  normalizing paths, 301–302
  parsing paths, 296–300
  as platform-independent
    manipulation of filenames,
    296
  testing files, 303–304
`os.pipe()`, interprocess
  communication in `pickles`,
  398–399
`os.sep` variable, parsing paths
  in `os.path`, 296
`os.stat()`, comparing files in
  `filecmp`, 354
`os.urandom()` function,
  `SystemRandom` class,
  261–262
Outcomes, `unittest`,
  1052–1054
Outline nodes, finding in XML
  document, 447–448
Output
  alternative cookie formats,
    794–795
  asynchronous I/O, 649–650

Output (*continued*)
  asynchronous I/O using
    coroutines/streams,
    654–655
  capturing error, `subprocess`,
    543–545
  capturing, `subprocess`,
    538–541
  human-consumable vs.
    compact, in `json`, 805–807
  multicast messages, 720
  redirecting streams,
    `contextlib`, 201
  suppressing, `subprocess`,
    541–542
Overlapping events, `sched`, 1000
`owner()` method, `pathlib` file
  properties, 316

P

Package installer (pip), 1024,
  1167–1168
Packages. *See also* `pkgutil`
  module
  custom package importing,
    1211–1213
  data files in, 1341–1344
  determining if package or
    regular module, 1348
  development versions of,
    1336–1338
  import paths, 1334–1336
  importing modules from shelf,
    1205–1211
  managing installation paths,
    1272–1276
  managing path with PKG
    files, 1338–1339
  nested packages, 1340–1341
  retrieving import package
    data, 1215–1217
  submodules within, 1333
Packing data into strings, in
  `struct`, 117
`pack_into()` method, `struct`
  buffers, 120–121
Paragraph formatting. *See*
  `textwrap` module
Parameters
  CSV dialect, 470–472
  named, `sqlite3`, 420–421
  positional, `sqlite3`, 419–420
`parent` property, parsing paths
  in `pathlib`, 307
`parents` property, parsing
  paths in `pathlib`, 307–308

`parse()` function, configuring
  GNU readline library,
  923–924
`parse_args()`, command line
  in `argparse`, 889
`PARSE_COLNAMES`, column types
  in `sqlite3`, 427
Parsed node attributes,
  `xml.etree.ElementTree`,
  449–450
`PARSE_DECLTYPES`, new column
  types in `sqlite3`, 422
`parse_qs()` method,
  `urllib.parse`, 759–760
`parse_qsl()` method,
  `urllib.parse`, 759–760
Parser, `argparse`
  argument groups, 904–905
  conflicting options, 902–904
  mutually exclusive options,
    906
  nesting parsers, 906–908
  setting up, 888
  sharing parser rules, 901–902
Parsing
  command line in `argparse`,
    889
  command line in `getopt`. *See*
    `getopt` module
  cookie headers in
    `http.cookie`, 794–795
  creating UUID objects,
    802–803
  `datetime`, 230–231
  manipulating URLs in
    `urllib.parse`, 754–756
  numbers in `locale`, 1021
  paths in `os.path`, 296–300
  paths in `pathlib`, 307–308
  POSIX vs. non-POSIX,
    959–960
  reading data from CSV files,
    467
  shell-style syntaxes. *See*
    `shlex` module
  strings in XML text, 455–457
  `time`, clock time, 219–220
  unparsing URLs in
    `urllib.parse`, 756–758
  and validating command-line
    arguments. *See* `argparse`
    module
  watching events in XML
    while, 451–453
  XML document, 445–446
  XML parsed tree, 446–447

`partial()` method
  algorithms in `functools`,
    148–149
  `Future` callbacks in
    `asyncio`, 627–628
  receiving Unix signals in
    `asyncio`, 668
  scheduling callbacks soon in
    `asyncio`, 622–623
`partial` objects
  acquiring function properties,
    145–147
  `functools` primarily using,
    143
  overview of, 144–145
  working with any callable
    object, 147–148
`parts` property, parsing paths
  in `pathlib`, 307
`PassThrough`, Unicode
  data/network
  communication, 382–383
Password prompt security. *See*
  `getpass` module
`pathlib` module
  building paths, 305–307
  creating concrete paths, 309
  deleting from file system,
    318–319
  directory contents, 309–312
  file properties, 315–317
  file types, 313–315
  manipulating directories and
    symbolic links, 312–313
  new in Python 3, 1352
  parsing paths, 307–308
  path representations, 305
  permissions, 317–318
  reading and writing files, 312
Paths
  file system paths as objects.
    See `pathlib` module
  platform-independent
    manipulation of filenames.
    See `os.path` module
  representations in `pathlib`,
    305
  scanning for configuration
    files, 1172–1175
Pattern matching
  `fnmatch` Unix-style glob,
    323–326
  `glob` filename, 319–323
Patterns, regular expressions.
  See `re` module
`pdb` module
  breakpoint jumps, 1130–1134

breakpoint management, 1120–1123

breakpoint use, 1117–1120

breakpoints for changing execution flow, 1129–1130

breakpoints for watching data change, 1128–1129

breakpoints triggering actions, 1127–1128

changes in Python 3, 1361

conditional breakpoints, 1124–1125

control interface, 1104–1105

customization using aliases, 1136–1137

debugging after failure, 1104

examining of stack variables, 1107–1111

ignoring breakpoints, 1125–1127

for interactive debugging, 1101

navigating execution stack, 1105–1107

overview of, 1023

program restart, 1134–1136

saving configuration settings, 1137–1139

startup from command line, 1101–1102

startup within interactive interpreter, 1102–1103

startup within program, 1103

stepping through a program, 1111–1117

temporary breakpoints, 1123–1124

peer argument, process_message()in smtpd, 848

PEP 230, warnings, 1279

Per-instance context, decimal, 248

perf_counter()
clock time, 211

comparing clocks, 212–213

determining best clock data source, 216–217

Performance analysis
compiler optimizations, 1309–1311

loop performance, 1303–1309

Permissions, file
changing in pathlib, 317–318

copying from one file to another, 340–342

managing, 1230–1233

removing file system object in pathlib, 319

testing, urllib.robotparser, 774–775

UDS, 716–717

permutations() function, itertools, 180–181

Permutations, random, 258–260

permutations_with_replacement() function, itertools, 182

Persistent storage of objects. See shelve module

pformat() function, pprint, 138–139

Pi character, handling encoding errors, 374

Picking random items, random, 258

pickle module
applications of message signatures, 530–533

changes in Python 3, 1361–1362

circular references, 402–404

encoding/decoding data in strings, 396–397

json module vs., 803–804

new column types in sqlite3, 424–425

object serialization via, 396

passing arguments to multiprocessing process, 587

problems reconstructing objects, 399–400

sending binary objects in XML-RPC, 824–825

unpicklable objects, 400–402

working with streams, 397–399

pip (package installer), 1024, 1167–1168

PIPE, subprocess
capturing output, 538–540

connecting segments, 545–546

select() function monitoring, 729–734

working directly with, 542–545

pipe_data_received(), protocol abstraction with subprocesses, 662

pipes module, changes in Python 3, 1362

PKG files, managing paths, 1338–1339

pkgutil module
data files in packages, 1341–1344

development versions of packages, 1336–1338

import paths for packages, 1334–1336

nested packages, 1340–1341

overview of, 1329, 1332–1334

Plain text help, 1024–1025

platform module
basic FIFO queue, 112

changes in Python 3, 1362

executable architecture, 1250

interpreter, 1246–1247

operating system/hardware information, 1248–1250

overview of, 1169, 1246

platform() function, 1247–1248

platform(), as identifier of platform, 1247–1248

Platforms
filename manipulation independent of. See os.path module

getting version/platform information, 1276–1277

module styles supported by Python, 1330–1331

obtaining information about architecture, 1250

specific options in select, 742

symbolic links and, 1234

system version information. See platform module

Plural values, in gettext, 1008–1010

PLY package, text-related supplements to standard library, 1367

Podcast-feed URLs, traversing parsed tree, 447

Podcasting client, building threaded, 114–117

POLLERR error, using poll() in select, 740

poll()function, select, 737–741

Pool class
managing concurrent tasks. See concurrent.futures module

multiprocessing, 611–617

pop_all() method, ExitStack, 208–209

Popen class, subprocess, 535–536

popen2 module, removed from Python 3, 1354

Populating deque, 85

Port numbers, socket addresses, 697–700

Porting Python 2 to Python 3
deprecated modules, 1355–1356
new modules, 1352
references, 1351
removed modules, 1354–1355
renamed modules, 1352–1353
summarizing changes to modules, 1356–1365

Positional arguments, in argparse, 904–905

Positional parameters, in sqlite3, 419–420

Positive and negative signs, math, 272–274

Positive look ahead assertion (?=pattern), regular expressions, 44–45

Positive look behind assertion (?<=pattern), regular expressions, 47–48

POSIX
managing file system paths in pathlib, 305
timestamps in datetime_date, 223–224
vs. non-POSIX parsing in shlex, 959–960

Posixfile module, 1355

postcmd() method, overriding base class methods, 945–946

Posting form data, urllib.request, 766–767

postloop() method, overriding base class methods in cmd, 945–946

Postmortem debugging, pdb, 1104

pow() function, math exponents, 278

pprint() function, 136–137

pprint module
arbitrary classes, 138–139
controlling output width, 140–142
debugging with, 65
formatting, 137–138

limiting nested output, 139–140
pretty-print data structures, 136
printing, 136–137
recursion, 139

Pre-input hook, readline, 934

prec attribute of context, 244–245

Precision context, decimal, 245

precmd() method, overriding base class methods in cmd, 945

predicate, textwrap_indent_predicate.py, 10–11

Predicting names, tempfile, 335–336

preloop() method, overriding base class methods in cmd, 945

Pretty-print data structures. See pprint module

Pretty-printing XML, 458–459

print() call, printing time, 214

print_event(), running events with delay, 999–1000

print_exc(), traceback exception reporting, 1082–1084

print_stack(), traceback applied to low-level stack APIs, 1086–1087

Priorities for events, in sched, 1001

PriorityQueue, 112–113

prmonth(), formatting calendar, 233

Process pools
concurrent.futures, 685–686
multiprocessing, 611–613

Processes
combining coroutines with threads and, 670–673
concurrency using system. See multiprocessing module
creating, 1240–1242
detect/change process owner, 1235–1237
determining current, multiprocessing, 588–589
exit status, multiprocessing, 594–596

managing concurrent operations within. See threading module

managing environment of, 1237–1238

managing like threads. See multiprocessing module

managing working directory for, 1238–1239

multiprocessing basics, 586–587

signaling between, subprocess, 550–553

spawning additional. See subprocess module

spawning new, 1244–1245

subclassing, multiprocessing, 597–598

supplements to standard library, 1369

UDS socket communication, 717

waiting for child, 1242–1244

process_exited() method, protocol abstraction, 662

process_message() method, smtpd, 847–848

Processor clock time, 211, 214–216

ProcessPoolExecutor, 672–673, 684–685

process_time(), CPU time via, 211

product() function, itertools, 177–180

profile module
overview of, 1023, 1140
run method, 1140–1142
statistics (pstats), 1144–1148

Programmatically, creating enumerations, 71–72

Programming interface, trace, 1074–1075

Programs
restarting using pdb, 1134–1136
shutdown callbacks. See atexit module
stepping through using pdb, 1111–1117

Progress metadata, fileinput, 989–990

Prompts, interactive, 1182–1183

prompt_toolkit, 1371

Properties
  abstract, 1292–1295
  file, in `os.path`, 302–303
  function, 145–147, 149–151
  parsing paths in `pathlib`, 307–308
  `pathlib` file, 315
  setting element, 459–461
  `shlex`, 955–956
  socket, 693
Protocol abstraction, with subprocesses in `asyncio`, 661–664
Protocol class, asynchronous I/O, 644–650
Protocol handlers, customizing in `urrlib.request`, 770–773
Proxies, `weakref`, 126–127
Proxy server, `stmpd`, 851
Pseudorandom numbers. *See* `random` module
`pstats`
  limiting report contents, 1145–1146
  printing callers and callees of functions, 1146–1148
  profiling and, 1144–1145
`pstdev()` function, `statistics` variance, 293–294
`PurePosixPath` class, managing file paths in `pathlib`, 305
`PureProxy` class, proxy server in `stmpd`, 851
`PureWindowsPath` class, managing file paths in `pathlib`, 305
`put()` method, basic FIFO queue, 112
`pvariance()` function, `statistics` variance, 293–294
`pyclbr` module
  class browser, 1160–1161
  overview of, 1024
  scanning for classes, 1161–1162
  scanning for functions, 1162–1163
`pydoc` module, 1023–1026
PyParsing tool, 1367
PyQuery library, 1370
Pyramid package, 1370

Python
  Code Quality Authority, 1371–1372
  ZIP archives, 519–521
pytz package, 1368
`pytz`, time zone support via, 232
pyvenu, virtual environments, 1163–1164
PyYAML, 1371
PyZipFile class, Python ZIP archives, 519–521

Q

Queries, `sqlite3`
  calling functions during, 436–438
  with regular expressions, 439–440
  retrieving data, 415
  using variables with, 419
Queue, double-ended. *See* `deque` module
`queue` module
  building threaded podcast client, 114–117
  defined, 65
  LIFO queue, 112
  priority queue, 113–114
  as thread-safe FIFO implementation, 111
`quote()` function, 760, 953
Quoted strings, parsing in `shlex`, 951–953
`quote_plus()` function, 760
Quoting options, CSV files, 468–469

R

Race conditions, searching readable files, 346
`radians()` function, `math` angles, 282
`randint()` function, random integers, 257
`random()` function. *See* `random` module
Random integers, 257
`random` module
  changes in Python 3, 1362
  as generating random numbers, 254
  multiple simultaneous generators, 261–262
  non-uniform distributions, 263–264
  permutations, 258–260

picking random items, 258
  as pseudorandom number generators, 254
  random integers, 257
  sampling, 260–261
  saving state, 255–256
  seeding, 255
  `SystemRandom`, 262–263
Random values, UUID 4, 802
`randrange()` function, random integers, 257
Rational numbers. *See* `fractions` module
`raw` argument, 975–976
Raw bytes, 391–393
`raw_decode` method, `JSONDecoder`, 813–814
Re-entrant locks, `threading`, 576–578
`re` module
  changes in Python 3, 1362
  compiling expressions, 15
  constraining search, 28–29
  dissecting matches with groups, 30–36
  finding patterns in text, 14–15
  listing mailboxes, `imaplib`, 867–868
  looking ahead or behind, 44–48
  matching files using, 1156–1157
  memory-map files used with, 364–365
  modifying string with patterns, 53–54
  multiple matches, 16
  queryies in `sqlite3` with, 439–440
  as regular expressions, 13–14
  searching and parsing text, 1367
  self-referencing, 48–53
  splitting with patterns, 55–57
  translating patterns in `fnmatch`, 325–326
`re` module, pattern syntax
  anchoring, 26–27
  character sets, 20–23
  escape codes, 23–26
  overview, 17
  repetition, 18–20
`re` module, search options
  case-insensitive matching, 36–37
  embedding flags in patterns, 43

re module, search options
    (*continued*)
    input with multiple lines,
        37–38
    overview of, 14
    Unicode, 38–39
    verbose expression syntax,
        39–43
read() method
    access data from archive, 514
    asynchronous I/O, 651, 654
    calling subprocesses, 664–666
    customizing protocol
        handlers, 770–773
    I/O multiplexing
        abstractions, 724–725
    reading configuration files,
        961–963
readable sockets, 730–731,
    738–739
Reading
    compressed data in gzip,
        489–490
    compressed files in bz2,
        497–498
    configuration files, 961
    files in pathlib, 312
    GNU zip files, gzip, 486
    from Maildir mailbox, 858
    mbox mailbox, 853–854
    memory-map files, 361–362
    metadata from archive,
        tarfile, 504–505
    metadata from archive,
        zipfile, 512–514
    read text efficiently. *See*
        linecache module
    Unicode data, 498–499
readline module
    accessing completion buffer,
        927–931
    auto-completion for
        commands, 942–944
    cmd module using, 938
    completing text, 924–927
    configuring readline, 923–924
    GNU readline library with,
        922–923
    hooks, 934–935
    input history, 931–934
    overview of, 887
readmodule(), 1161–1163
Receiving signals, 554–555
Recursion
    controlling, 1190–1191
    deep copy, 133–136

examining file system
    contents, 1228–1229
pprint, 139
    in substitution errors during
        interpolation, 977
Redirecting output streams,
    contextlib, 201
Reducing data sets, functools,
    158–160
ref class, reference callbacks,
    122–123
Reference counts, memory
    management, 1187–1188
ReferenceError exception,
    weakref proxies, 127
References
    circular, 402–404
    finding to uncollectable
        objects, 1259–1261
    impermanent object. *See*
        weakref module
    tracing, 1255–1257
register() attribute, of
    generic functions, 161–163
Registering
    alternate API names,
        xmlrpc.server, 831–832
    arbitrary API names,
        xmlrpc.server, 831–832
    concrete classes, abc,
        1287–1288
    custom encoding, codecs,
        386–389
    data channels using poll(),
        737–738
    decorator syntax, atexit,
        994
    dispatching calls,
        xmlrpc.server, 835–836
    dotted API names,
        xmlrpc.server, 830–831
    exit callbacks, atexit,
        993–994
    introspection API,
        xmlrpc.server, 837–839
    new column types, sqlite3,
        424
Registry, shutil-managed
    archive, 348–349
Regular expressions. *See* re
    module
Relational database, embedded.
    See sqlite3 module
Reload modules, 1213–1214
Removing
    directory contents, 344–345
    empty directory, 318

messages from Maildir
    mailbox, 858–860
messages from mbox mailbox,
    854
sections/options from
    ConfigParser, 971
Reordering
    keys in OrderedDict, 96–97
    mappings with ChainMap,
        76–77
repeat() function, values in
    itertools, 170–172
Repetition
    regular expression character
        sets, 23
    regular expression escape
        codes, 24–26
    regular expression patterns,
        18–20
    of warnings, 1283–1284
replace() method, dates,
    224–225
replace mode, decoding errors,
    375
Request handlers
    creating network servers,
        socketserver, 742–744,
        748
    implementing web servers,
        http.server, 781–783
requests package, Internet,
    1369
Resolution, datetime, 221–222,
    224
resolve() method,
    normalizing path, 306, 313
resource module, 1169,
    1251–1254
Resources
    controlling access to,
        multiprocessing,
        603–604
    controlling access to,
        threading, 572–576
    controlling concurrent access
        to, multiprocessing,
        605–607
    limiting access to concurrent,
        threading, 581–583
    thread specific data, 583–585
ResourceWarning warnings,
    debugging with asyncio,
        673
Restricting access to data,
    sqlite3, 442–444

Results
  gathering from coroutines,
    635–636
  of tasks,
    concurrent.futures,
    679–680, 683
Retrieving data, sqlite3, 415
return command, stepping
  through program in pdb,
  1116–1117
Reverse lookups, socket, 697,
  698–699
rfc822 module, removed from
  Python 3, 1354
rglob() method, directory
  contents in pathlib,
  311–312
Rich comparison methods,
  functools, 151–153
Rich comparison operators, 184
RLock, re-entrant locks, 576–577
RobotFileParser.can_fetch(),
  testing access permissions,
  774–775
robots.txt, urllib.
  robotparser, 773–776
rollback() method, preserve
  changes in transactions,
  429–430
rollover() method,
  temporary spooled files, 334
Rotation
  double-ended queue, 87–88
  of log files, 981–982
Rounding, decimal, 245–247
Row objects, sqlite3, 417–419
RSS feed, converting M3U files
  to, 987–989
Rules, sharing parser (in
  argparse), 901–902
Runtime
  accessing operating system
    features. See os module
  accessing system version
    information. See
    platform module
  determining interpreter
    settings. See sysconfig
    module
  finding message catalogs at,
    1007–1008
  garbage collection. See gc
    module
  load and activate message
    catalog in gettext, 1004
  managing system resources.
    See Resources

overview of, 1169
system-specific configuration.
  See sys module
rx argument, matching files
  with regular expression,
  1156–1157

S
safe_substitute() method,
  string.Template, 3
Sampling, random, 260–261
Saving
  configuration files, 972
  state, random, 255–256
scandir, examining file system
  contents, 1229–1230
sched module
  canceling events, 1001–1002
  event priorities, 1001
  implementing timed event
    scheduler, 998–999
  overlapping events, 1000
  running events with delay,
    999–1000
  timed event scheduler using,
    998–999
Scheduling
  callbacks in asyncio,
    622–623
  implementing timed event
    scheduler. See sched
    module
  individual tasks in
    concurrent.futures,
    678–679
Schema, database in sqlite3,
  413
Search. See also re module,
  search options
  constraints in regular
    expressions, 28–29
  criteria in imaplib, 872–874
  files in shutil, 345–346
  messages in imaplib, 872
  options in configparser,
    972–975
Sections, configparser
  configuration file format, 961
  modifying settings, 970–971
  option search path, 972–975
  testing if present, 965
Secure password prompt. See
  getpass module
Seeding, in random, 255
seek() method
  in-memory streams, io, 391

reading compressed data,
  gzip, 489–490
reading compressed files, bz2,
  497–498
reading/writing Unicode
  data, bz2, 499
temporary files, tempfile,
  332
select module
  non-blocking I/O with
    timeouts, 734–737
  platform-specific options, 742
  using poll(), 737–741
  using select(), 729–734
  wait for I/O efficiently with,
    728–729
select statements, query
  parameters in sqlite3, 421
select() function, calling
  programs in selectors, 724
Selecting mailbox, imaplib, 871
selectors module
  Echo client, 726–727
  Echo server, 724–725
  I/O multiplexing abstractions
    with, 724
  new in Python 3, 1352
  operating model, 724
  server and client together,
    727–728
Self-referencing regular
  expressions, 48–53
Semaphore
  multiprocessing, 605–607
  threading, 581–583
Sequence operators, functional
  interface for, 186–187
SequenceMatcher class,
  difflib, 61–64
Sequences
  comparing. See difflib
    module
  Counter initialization via
    data, 80
  deques as type of container
    for, 84
  efficiently merging sorted,
    108–109
  of fixed type data. See array
    module
  reducing data set in
    functools, 160
Serialization
  object. See also pickle
    module, 587
  XML to stream, 464–466

`ServerProxy` object,
connecting to XML-RPC
server, 817–819
Server(s)
connecting to IMAP, 864–866
connecting to XML-RPC,
817–819
creating network. *See*
`socketserver` module
I/O multiplexing
abstractions, `selectors`,
724–728
implementing web. *See*
`http.server` module
looking up addresses in
network, 700–702
sample mail. *See* `smtpd`
module
sending binary data to, 722
TCP/IP, 704–711
types, `socketserver`,
742–743
UDP, 711–713
UDS, 714–716
Service information, `socket`,
697
Sessions, signaling between
processes, 550–553
`set()` method
modifying settings in
`ConfigParser`, 970–971
signaling between threads,
571–572
`sets` module, removed from
Python 3, 1355
Settings
accessing configuration,
963–970
modifying `configparser`,
970–971
setuptools-git, 1371
`setuptools` module, 1371
`sha` module, removed from
Python 3, 1355
SHA1 algorithm
in `hashlib`, 525
in `hmac`, 529
UUID 3 and 5, name-based
values, 800–801
`shallow` argument, comparing
files in `filecmp`, 354
Shallow copies, duplicate
objects, 130–131
`shallow` module, 1340
Shared namespaces,
`multiprocessing`, 608–610

Shared state,
`multiprocessing`, 608
Sharing parser rules, `argparse`,
901–902
`shell` argument, `subprocess`,
537
Shell commands, running,
947–948
Shell-style syntaxes, parsing. *See*
`shlex` module
`shelve` module, 405–408, 1362
ShelveLoader
custom package importing,
1211–1213
importing modules from shelf,
1205–1211
reloading modules, 1213–1214
`shlex` module
controlling parser, 956–957
embedded comments, 954
error handling, 957–958
including other sources of
tokens, 955–956
making safe strings for shells,
953
parse-style syntaxes with, 951
parsing quoted strings,
951–953
POSIX vs. non-POSIX
parsing, 959–960
splitting strings into tokens,
954
Short-form options, `getopt`, 917
`shorten()` function, truncating
long text, 12–13
`show_code`, printing summary
of function, 1299
`showwarning()`, warning
message delivery, 1284
`shuffle()` function, `random`,
258–260
`shutdown()` method,
`concurrent.futures`,
683–684
`shutil` module
archives, 346–350
copying file metadata,
340–342
copying files, 337–340
file system space, 350–351
finding files, 345–346
as high level file operations,
337
working with directory trees,
342–345
SIGINT. *See* `signal` module

Sign flag, creating `Decimals`
from, 240
Signal handlers
mixing signals and threads,
558–560
receiving signals via, 554–555
retrieving registered, 555–556
`signal` module
alarms, 556–557
asynchronous system events
via, 553
changes in Python 3, 1362
ignoring signals, 557–558
receiving signals, 554–555
retrieving registered handlers,
555–556
signaling between processes,
`subprocess`, 548–553
signals and threads, 558–560
Signals
mixing threads and, 558–560
between processes, 602–603
between threads, 571–572
Signals, receiving Unix, 668–670
`signature()`, method or
function arguments,
1319–1322
Signing cryptographic messages,
`hmac`, 528
Simple Mail Transport Protocol
(SMTP)
email. *See* `smtplib` module
sample mail servers. *See*
`smtpd` module
`SimpleCompleter` class,
autocompletion of text in
`readline`, 925–927
`SimpleObject`, reconstructing
objects in `pickle`, 400
`SimpleXMLRPCServer`,
828–829, 835–836
Sine function, `math`, 284, 288
Single-character wildcards,
321–322
`singledispatch()` decorator,
generic functions, 161–163
`site` module
customizing site
configuration, 1175–1176
customizing user
configuration, 1176–1177
import path, 1169–1170
managing user directories,
1171–1172
overview of, 1169, 1177–1178

scanning for path
  configuration files,
  1172–1175
site-wide configuration, 1169
Size
  caching in functools,
    156–158
  constraining queue, 88–89,
    111
  struct buffer. *See* weakref
    module
skipkeys argument, encoding
  dictionaries, 807
skipping unittests for unmet
  conditions, 1067
sleep() function
  alarms in signal, 557
  mixing signals and threads,
    559–560
  processor clock time, 216
  sched using, 999
  using map() with basic
    thread pool, 677–678
SMTP (Simple Mail Transport
  Protocol)
  email. *See* smtplib module
  sample mail servers. *See*
    smtpd module
smtpd module
  create custom mail server, 847
  debugging server, 850
  mail server base class,
    847–850
  proxy server, 851
smtplib module
  authentication and
    encryption, 843–846
  create client to send data to
    test server, 848–849
  sending email message,
    841–843
  verifying email address,
    846–847
SMTP_SSL, email encryption
  in smtplib, 843
Sniffer class, detecting CSV
  dialects, 472–474
SOCK_DGRAM sockets, 694
socket module
  changes in Python 3, 1362
  finding service information,
    697–700
  IP address representations,
    702–703
  looking up hosts on network,
    694–697

looking up server addresses,
  700–702
multicast, 717–721
network communication with,
  693
non-blocking communication
  and timeouts, 723
sending binary data, 721–723
TCP/IP client and server,
  704–711
user datagram client and
  server, 711–717
socket.error exception, 695,
  723
socketpair() function, UDS
  sockets, 717
Sockets
  enabling SSL in asyncio on,
    656–658
  monitoring using
    select()function,
    729–734
  using poll() in select,
    737–741
socketserver module
  changes in Python 3, 1363
  compressing network data in
    bz2, 499–500
  creating network servers with,
    742
  Echo example, 744–749
  implementing server, 743
  request handlers, 743
  server objects, 743
  server types, 742–743
  threading and forking,
    749–751
socketserver.TCPServer, 786
SOCK_STREAM sockets, 694
Sort algorithm. *See* heapq
  module
Sorted order
  queue. *See* queue module
  use bisect to maintain lists
    in, 109–111
Source code
  creating message catalogs
    from, 1004–1007
  disassembling, 1301–1302
  retrieving for class or method,
    1318–1319
  retrieving from ZIP archive,
    1346–1347
Source files
  compiling to byte-code,
    1155–1159
  reading Python, 329–330

Sources of arguments,
  argparse, 895–897
spawning new processes,
  1244–1245
Special constants, math, 265
Special values, decimal,
  243–244
Spider access control, Internet,
  773–776
Splitting
  iterators, itertools,
    164–167
  parsing paths, os.path,
    296–298
  with patterns, re, 55–57
  strings into tokens, shlex,
    954
Spooled files, tempfile,
  333–334
SQL-injection attacks, 419
sqlalchemy ORM, 1368
sqlite3 module
  bulk loading, 421–422
  creating database, 412–415
  custom aggregation, 440–441
  defining new column types,
    422–425
  determining types for
    columns, 426–427
  embedded relational database
    via, 412
  exporting contents of
    database, 435–436
  isolation levels, 431–434
  in-memory databases,
    434–435
  query metadata, 417
  querying with regular
    expressions, 439–440
  restricting access to data,
    442–444
  retrieving data, 415–417
  row objects, 417–419
  threading and connection
    sharing, 441–442
  transactions, 428–430
  using Python functions in
    SQL, 436–438
  using variables with queries,
    419–421
Square root, computing in math,
  278–279
sre module, removed from
  Python 3, 1355
SSL communication, enabling on
  sockets, 656–658
SSLContext, encryption, 656

Stack
  controlling recursion,
    1190–1191
  examination of variables in,
    1107–1111
  examining, 1079–1081
  inspecting frames and,
    1324–1327
  stack level in warnings, 1286
  traces. *See* traceback
    module
  watching with trace hooks,
    1224–1225
Stacking behavior, ChainMap,
  77
Stacks, dynamic context
  manager, 202–209
Standard deviation,
  statistics variance,
  292–294
starmap() function, converting
  inputs in itertools, 169
start argument, 170, 257
start() method, search for
  patterns in text, 14
Start-up hook, readline, 934
start_server() method,
  652, 656
STARTTLS extension, email
  authentication/encryption,
  844–845
stat() method
  managing file system
    permissions, 1230–1231
  pathlib file properties,
    315–316
Static analysis tool, Python
  Code Quality Authority,
  1372
Static methods, marking as
  abstract, 1295–1296
statistics module
  averages, 290–292
  new in Python 3, 1352
  variance, 292–294
Statistics, profiling and, 1140,
  1144–1148
Status conditions, IMAP4
  mailbox, 869–871
status(), mailbox in imaplib,
  869–871
statvfs module, removed from
  Python 3, 1355
stddev() function,
  statistics variance,
  293–294

stderr attribute, subprocess
  capturing error output,
    543–544
  capturing output, 538–541
  interaction with another
    command, 546–548
stdin attribute, subprocess,
  542–543, 546–548
stdin attribute, sys,
  1186–1187
stdout attribute, subprocess
  capturing error output,
    543–544
  capturing output, 538–541
  connecting segments of pipe,
    545–546
  interaction with another
    command, 546–548
  working with pipes, 542–543
stdout attribute, sys,
  1186–1187
step argument
  new values, itertools, 170
  random integers, math, 257
  stepping through program,
    pdb, 1111–1114
step() method, custom
  aggregation in sqlite3,
  440–441
stop argument, random
  integers in math, 257
Storage of objects, persistent.
  See shelve module
store action, arguments, 891
str class
  modify strings with patterns,
    53–54
  as text processing tool, 1
Stream-oriented transport,
  SOCK_STREAM sockets, 694
StreamReader instance,
  asynchronous I/O, 651, 653
Streams
  asynchronous IO, in
    asyncio, 650–655
  calling subprocesses with, in
    asyncio, 664–666
  mixed-content, in bz2, 495
  mixed content, in zlib,
    480–481
  serializing XML to, 464–466
  working with file-like, in
    pickle, 397–399
  working with, in gzip,
    490–491
  working with, in json,
    813–814

wrapping byte, in io, 392–393
StreamWriter instance,
  asynchronous I/O, 651, 653
strftime() function, 219–220,
  230–231
strict mode
  handling decoding errors, 375
  handling encoding errors, 373
string module
  advanced templates, 4–6
  changes in Python 3, 1363
  constants, 1, 6–7
  formatter, 6
  functions, 1–2
  template tool, 1, 2–4, 1367
StringIO buffers, in-memory
  streams, 390–391
Strings
  configuration settings, 964
  converting in argparse,
    910–912
  creating fractions, 251
  dis accepting string
    arguments, 1301–1302
  encoding and decoding. *See*
    codecs module
  encoding/decoding data in,
    396–397
  making safe for shells, 953
  multiliner, 970
  packing/unpacking data into,
    117–118
  parsing command line
    arguments with, 889–890
  parsing in XML, 455–457
  parsing quoted, 951–953
  retrieving docstring for
    object, 1316–1317
  splitting into tokens, 954
  Unicode primer, 365–366
  value types, 966–969
string.Template, 1–6
strptime() function
  datetime, 230–231
  time, 218–219
Struct class, 117–121
struct module
  as binary data structures, 117
  buffers, 120–121
  changes in Python 3, 1363
  defined, 65
  endianness, 118–120
  functions vs. Struct class,
    117
  packing and unpacking,
    117–118
  sending binary data, 721–723

struct_time, 217–220
sub(), modify strings with
    patterns, 53–54
Subclasses
    from abstract base class,
        1289–1291
    from base class, 1288–1289
    creating Process,
        multiprocessing,
        597–598
    creating Thread, threading,
        568–569
Subdirectory, listing files in, 321
Submodules, within packages,
    1333
subn(), modify strings with
    patterns, 54
subprocess module
    changes in Python 3, 1363
    connecting segments of pipe,
        545–546
    interacting with another
        command, 546–548
    running external command,
        536–542
    signaling between processes,
        548–553
    spawning additional
        processes, 535–536
    working with pipes directly,
        542–545
subprocesses, asyncio
    calling with
        coroutines/streams,
        664–666
    sending data to, 666–668
    using protocol abstraction
        with, 661–664
SubprocessProtocol,
    asyncio, 661–664
Substitution errors,
    interpolation in
    configparser, 977–978
subTest(), repeating unitests
    with different inputs,
    1065–1066
suffix property, parsing paths
    in pathlib, 308
Switch interval,
    controlling/debugging
    threads, 1197–1198
Switching translations,
    gettext, 1012
Symbolic links
    creating in pathlib, 313
    functions for, 1234

removing in pathlib,
    318–319
Synchronization primitives,
    asyncio
    Condition, 640–641
    Event, 639–640
    Lock, 637–639
    overview of, 637
    Queue, 642–644
Synchronizing operations,
    multiprocessing, 604–605
Synchronizing threads,
    threading, 578–581
sys module
    applied to build-time version
        information, 1178–1179
    built-in modules, 1201–1202
    byte ordering, 1194
    changes in Python 3,
        1363–1364
    command-line arguments
        captured by interpreter,
        1185–1186
    CPython command-line flags,
        1180–1181
    custom importers, 1203–1205
    custom package importing,
        1211–1213
    debugging threads, 1198–1200
    defining maximum values in
        memory, 1191
    determining object size,
        1188–1190
    exception handling,
        1194–1197
    exception monitoring,
        1225–1227
    floating-point values,
        1192–1193
    handling of import errors,
        1214–1215
    imported modules, 1200–1201
    importer cache, 1217–1218
    importing from shelf,
        1205–1211
    input/output streams
        (stdin/stdout),
        1186–1187
    integer values in memory
        management, 1193
    interactive prompts,
        1182–1183
    interpreter install location,
        1184–1185
    interpreter display hook,
        1183–1184

memory management
    features, 1187
    meta-path, 1218–1221
    module import path,
        1202–1203
    module reload, 1213–1214
    overview of, 1169
    recursion, 1190–1191
    reference counts and garbage
        collection, 1187–1188
    retrieval of import package
        data, 1215–1217
    returning exit code (exit()),
        1187
    switch interval for threads,
        1197–1198
    for system-specific
        configuration, 1178
    thread support, 1197
    tracing function calls,
        1221–1222
    tracing inside functions,
        1222–1224
    Unicode defaults, 1181–1182
    watching the stack, 1224–1225
sys.argv, commands from,
    950–951
sysconfig module
    configuration variables,
        1270–1272
    getting version and platform
        information, 1276–1277
    management of installation
        paths, 1272–1276
    overview of, 1169, 1270
sys.exit(), invoking
    registered callbacks, 997
sys.path, compiling, 1157
sys.stderr, getpass(),
    936–937
sys.stdout, getpass(), 936
sys.stdout.buffer, 464–466
System clock, 214
system(), running external
    commands, 1239–1240
SystemRandom class, random,
    262–263

T

Tab completion
    GNU readline library, 923
    text in readline, 924–927
tabnanny module
    indentation validator,
        1153–1154

tabnanny module (*continued*)
overview of, 1023–1024
supplements to standard
library, 1371
Tabs vs. windows, **webbrowser**,
796
Tangent
hyperbolic functions, 288
trigonometric functions, 284
tar archive access. *See* **tarfile**
module
tarfile module
appending to archives, 510
creating new archives, 508
extracting files from archive,
506–507
reading metadata from
archive, 504–505
tar archive access via, 503
testing tar files, 503–504
using alternative archive
member names, 508–509
working with compressed
archives, 510–512
writing data from sources
other than files, 509
Tasks
duration modeling, 264
executing concurrently,
asyncio, 628–632
managing pools of concurrent.
See **concurrent.futures**
module
as subclass of **Future**,
asyncio, 618
timed event scheduler, **sched**,
998–1002
TCP/IP (Transmission Control
Protocol/Internet Protocol)
socket
choosing address for listening,
708–711
as client, 705–706
client and server together,
706–707
easy client connections,
707–708
as server, 704–705
UDS vs., 714
TCP (Transmission Control
Protocol), 694
TCPServer class,
socketserver, 742–743
tempfile module
named files, 333
predicting names, 335–336
spooled files, 333–334

temporary directories, 335
temporary file location,
336–337
as temporary file system
objects, 330
temporary files, 331–332
Templates
advanced string, 4–6
string, 1–2
using **ChainMap** instances as,
77
Temporary directories,
tempfile, 335
Temporary files, **tempfile**,
331–332, 336–337
Terminal, using **getpass()**
without, 937–938
Terminating processes,
multiprocessing, 564–567
Testing
access permissions,
urllib.robotparser,
774–775
with **doctest**. *See* **doctest**
module
exceptional values, **math**,
265–267
file types, **pathlib**, 313–314
files, **os.path**, 303–304
in-memory databases,
sqlite3, 434–435
tar files, 503–504
with **unittest**. *See*
unittest module
ZIP files, 512
test_patterns() function,
regular expressions, 17,
33–34
Text
command-line filter
framework for, 987–992
comparing. *See* **difflib**
module
completing in **readline**,
924–927
constants and templates. *See*
string module
content of nodes, 449–450
formatting paragraphs. *See*
textwrap module
getting help with plain,
1024–1025
overview of, 1
reading efficiently. *See*
linecache module
regular expressions. *See* **re**
module

supplements to standard
library, 1367
wrapping byte streams for,
392–393
TextIOWrapper
reading compressed data in
gzip, 489–490
reading compressed files in
bz2, 495
reading/writing Unicode data
in **bz2**, 498–499
wrapping byte streams for
text data, 392–393
textwrap module
combining dedent and
fill(), 9–10
defined, 1
example data, 8
filling paragraphs, 8
as formatting text
paragraphs, 7
hanging indents, 12
indenting blocks, 10–11
removing existing
indentation, 8–9
truncating long text, 12–13
Thread context, **decimal**,
248–249
thread module, removed from
Python 3, 1355
Thread objects, 560–561
Thread-safe FIFO
implementation. *See* **queue**
module
Thread-specific data,
threading module, 583–585
Threading
adding in **http.server**,
786–787
adding in **socketserver**,
749–751
combining coroutines with,
asyncio, 670–673
and connection sharing,
sqlite3, 441–442
debugging, 1198–1200
managing processes like. *See*
multiprocessing
module
mixing signals and, 558–560
supplements to standard
library, 1369
switch interval for, 1197–1198
sys support for, 1197
threading module
changes in Python 3, 1364

controlling access to resources, 572–576

daemon versus non-daemon threads, 564–567

determining current thread, 562–564

enumerating all threads, 567–568

isolation levels, `sqlite3`, 432

limiting concurrent access to resources, 581–583

managing concurrent operations within process via, 560

re-entrant locks, 576–578

signaling between threads, 571–572

subclassing Thread, 568–569

synchronizing threads, 578–581

`Thread` objects, 560–562

thread-specific data, 583–585

Timer threads, 570

`ThreadingMixIn`, 749–750, 787

`ThreadPoolExecutor`, 670–673, 677–678

Thresholds, garbage collection, 1261–1265

Time

clock time. *See* `time` module

components, 217–218

`datetime`. *See* `datetime` module

event scheduler to run tasks at specific, 998–1002

execution, for small bits of Python code, 1148–1153

formatting in `locale`, 1022

overview, 211

scheduling callback for specific, 624–625

supplements to standard library, 1368

zones, 218–219, 231–232

`time` class, `datetime_time`, 221–222

`time` module

changes in Python 3, 1364

as clock time, 211

comparing clocks, 211–213

defined, 211

monotonic clocks, 214

parsing and formatting times, 219–220

performance counter, 216–217

processor clock time, 214–216

supplements to standard library, 1368

time components, 217–218

wall clock time, 213–214

working with time zones, 218–219

time-to-live value (TTL), sending multicast messages, 720

`timedelta` objects, `datetime`, 225–227

`time()function`, clock time, 211, 213–214

`timeit` module

contents of, 1148

example, 1148–1149

overview of, 1023

values stored in dictionary, 1149–1152

Timeouts

non-blocking I/O with, 734–735

socket operations, 723

using `poll()`, 737

`Timer` class, `timeit`, 1148–1151

TLS (transport layer security) encryption, email in `smtplib`, 843–846

`today()` class method, `datetime_date`, 222–223

`tofile()` method, arrays and files, 101

Tokens

including other sources of, `shlex`, 955–956

splitting strings into, `shlex`, 954

Trace hooks

overview of, 1221

tracing inside functions, 1222–1224

watching stack, 1224–1225

`trace` module

applied to execution, 1069–1070

code coverage report, 1070–1073

example program, 1069

function relationship report, 1073–1074

options, 1077–1078

overview of, 1023

programming interface, 1074–1075

saving data, 1076–1077

`Trace` object, 1074–1075

`traceback` module

applied to low-level exception APIs, 1082–1086

applied to low-level stack APIs, 1086–1089

examining stack (`FrameSummary`), 1080–1081

examining stack (`StackSummary`), 1079–1080

example, 1079

exceptions, 1081–1082

overview of, 1023, 1078

stack summary, 1079–1081

`TracebackException` class, 1081–1082

Tracebacks. *See also* `traceback` module

applying `dis` to, 1302–1303

detailed tracebacks, `cgitb`, 1090–1092

`doctest` for, 1032–1033

examining local variables, `cgitb`, 1093–1096

logging tracebacks, `cgitb`, 1098–1101

traceback dump, `cgitb`, 1089–1090

Tracing

exception monitoring, 1225–1227

function calls, 1221–1222

inside functions, 1222–1224

references, 1255–1257

`--trackcalls`, function calls report, 1073–1074

Transactions

database, `sqlite3`, 428

discarding changes, `sqlite3`, 429–430

preserving changes, `sqlite3`, 428–429

Translations

`codec` used for many data, 377–378

encoding, 376–377

message catalog. *See* `gettext` module

pattern, 325–326

Transmission Control Protocol/Internet Protocol. *See* TCP/IP (Transmission Control Protocol/Internet Protocol) socket

Transmission Control Protocol (TCP), 694

Transport argument, `asyncio`, 662

Transport classes, asynchronous I/O, 644–645

Transport layer security (TLS) encryption, email in `smtplib`, 843–846

Transport protocol, retrieve port number to, 699–700

Tree structure, logging, 984–985

TreeBuilder, customizing, 453–455

Triangular distribution, `random`, 263

Trigonometry, `math`, 284–288

`truediv()` function, operator, 185–186

`trunc()` function, `math`, 270–271

Truncating long text, 12–13

Truth-checking, `unittest` for, 1054

`truth()` function, logical operations, 183

`try:except` statement, ignoring exceptions in `contextlib`, 199–200

`try:finally` block, context manager API, 192

TTL (time-to-live value), sending multicast messages, 720

tty, using `getpass()` without terminal, 937–938

Tuples
  as convenient containers for simple uses, 89
  encoding/decoding simple data types in `json`, 804–805
  Enum non-integer member values, 72–75
  row objects in `sqlite3`, 417–419
  subclass with named fields. See `namedtuple` module

Twisted library, 1369

`TypeError` exceptions
  caching in `functools`, 158
  comparing enums, 68
  `dbm` module, 411
  reducing data set in `functools`, 160

Types, specific shelve, 408

`TZ` environment variable, time zones, 218–219

`tzinfo` abstract base class, `datetime_timezone`, 231–232

`tzset()` function, time zones, 218–219

U

UDP (user datagram protocol)
  datagram sockets associated with, 694
  sending multicast messages via, 718–720
  `UDPServer` class, `socketserver`, 743

UDS (Unix Domain Sockets), 694, 714–717

Unicode
  data and network communication, `codecs`, 380–383
  decoding errors, `codecs`, 374–376
  defaults, 1181–1182
  encoding errors, `codecs`, 373–374
  primer, `codecs`, 365–366
  reading and writing , `bz2`, 498–499
  reading configuration files, `config`, 962–963
  regular expression search, `re`, 38–39

Unique values, Enum, 69–71

`unittest` module
  `addCleanup()`, 1371
  basic test structure, 1051
  changes in Python 3, 1364
  containers, 1056–1061
  doctests compared with, 1026
  equality-checking, 1054–1056
  exceptions, 1061–1062
  fixtures tests, 1062–1065
  ignoring test failure, 1068–1069
  integrating doctests with, 1047–1048
  outcomes, 1052–1054
  overview of, 1023
  repeating tests with different inputs, 1065–1066
  running, 1051–1052
  skipping tests for unmet conditions, 1067
  truth-checking, 1054

Universally Unique Identifiers. See `uuid` module

Unix
  key-value databases. See `dbm` module
  receiving signals with `asyncio`, 668–670

Unix Domain Sockets (UDS), 694, 714–717

`UnixDatagramServer` class, `socketserver`, 743

`UnixStreamServer` class, `socketserver`, 743

`unlink()` method, removing file system object in `pathlib`, 318–319

`unlock()` method, remove messages from `mbox` mailbox, 854

Unpacking
  archive files, `shutil`, 349–350
  data into strings, `struct`, 117–118
  pre-allocated buffers, `struct`, 120–121

Unparsing URLs, `urllib.parse`, 756–758

Unpicklable objects, 400–402

Unregister, canceling exit callbacks in `atexit`, 994–995

`until` command, stepping through program in `pdb`, 1115–1116

`unused_data` attribute, mixed-content streams, 481, 495

Updates
  incremental, `hashlib`, 526–527
  initialization, `Counter`, 80
  query parameters, `sqlite3`, 421
  wrapper, `functools`, 145–147

Upload
  files for encoding, `urllib.request`, 767–770
  messages, `imaplib`, 881–883

`urllib.parse` module
  encoding query arguments, 759–761
  joining, 758
  parsing, 754–756
  split URLs into components with, 753
  unparsing, 756–758

`urllib.request` module

adding outgoing headers,
    765–766
creating custom protocol
    handlers, 770–773
encoding arguments, 763–764
HTTP GET, 761–763
HTTP POST, 764–765
Internet-related supplements
    to standard library, 1369
network resource access with,
    761
posting form data from
    request, 766–767
uploading files, 767–770
urllib.robotparser
    Internet spider access control
        with, 773
    long-lived spiders, 775–776
    robots.txt, 773–774
    testing access permissions,
        774–775
urlopen() function,
    urllib.request, 761–766
urlparse() function,
    urllib.parse, 754–758
URLs
    building threaded podcast
        client, 114–117
    finding nodes in XML
        document, 447–448
    network resource access. See
        urllib.request module
    safe variations for Base64
        encoding, 778–780
    splitting into components. See
        urllib.parse module
    traversing parsed tree, 447
User datagram protocol. See
    UDP (user datagram
    protocol)
user module, removed from
    Python 3, 1355
use_rawinput, cmd, 949
USER_BASE directory,
    1171–1172
UserDict module, changes in
    Python 3, 1365
UserList module, changes in
    Python 3, 1365
Users
    customizing configuration of,
        1176–1177
    managing directories,
        1171–1172
UserString module, changes in
    Python 3, 1365

UTC, time zones, datetime,
    231–232
UTF-16 encoding
    byte order in codecs,
        370–372
    understanding encodings, 366
    Western languages, 366
UTF-32 encoding, codecs,
    370–372
UTF-8 encoding
    Base64 encoding, 777
    loading standard codecs from,
        387
    reading Unicode configuration
        files, 962–963
    understanding encodings, 367
    Western languages, 366
uuid module
    changes in Python 3, 1365
    implementing UUIDs,
        797–798
    UUID 1, IEEE 802 MAC
        Address, 798–800
    UUID 3 and 5, name-based
        values, 800–801
    UUID 4, random values, 802
    working with UUID objects,
        802–803
uvloop library, 1369

V

value property, enumerations,
    66, 71
Value types, configparser,
    966–969
ValueError exception
    Enum, 70
    handling in shlex, 957–958
    namedtuple invalid field
        names, 91–92
    square root of negative value,
        279
Values
    accessing existing, ChainMap,
        75–76
    approximating, fraction,
        253
    combining with interpolation,
        configparser, 975–979
    duplicate, bisect, 110–111
    encoding, http.cookies,
        793–794
    floating-point, math, 271–272
    floating-point, memory
        management, 1192–1193

integer, memory
    management, 1193
manipulating date and time,
    datetime, 221–222
maximum, memory
    management, 1191
missing keys returning
    default, Counter, 82–84
new iterator, itertools,
    169–172
retrieving, Counter, 81
returning from coroutines,
    asyncio, 619–620
special, decimal, 243–244
testing for exceptional, math,
    265–267
unique enumeration, enum,
    69–75
updating, ChainMap, 77–78
Variable argument lists,
    argparse, 908–910
Variables
    compiler optimizations,
        1309–1311
    configuration, 1270–1272
    environment, managing
        process environment,
        1237–1238
    examining local, in
        tracebacks, 1093–1096
    examining stack, pdb,
        1107–1111
    parsing paths in os.path,
        296
    using with queries, sqlite3,
        419
variable_stack() method,
    contextlib, 204, 209
Variance, statistics,
    292–294
variations, IMAP4 client library,
    864
venv module
    contents of virtual
        environment, 1164–1165
    creating virtual environments,
        1163–1164
    managing package versions
        during development,
        1336–1338
    new in Python 3, 1352
    supplements to standard
        library, 1371
    using virtual environments,
        1165–1167

Verbosity
   levels, `logging` API, 982–984
   regular expression syntax,
    39–43
`verbose` option, connecting
   to XML-RPC server, 818
`verbose_copy()`, directory
   trees in `shutil`, 342–343
Verify email address, `smtplib`,
   846–847
`version` action, arguments,
   891–892
Versions
   build-time information,
    1178–1179
   getting platform information
    and, 1276–1277
   site disabled for backward
    compatibility, 1177–1178
Virtual environments
   creating, 1163–1167
   `venv` module. *See* `venv`
    module
   `virtualenv` module,
    1336–1338, 1371
`virtualenv` module,
   1336–1338, 1371
von Mises, or circular normal,
   distribution, `random`, 264
`vonmisesvariate()` function,
   angular distribution, 264

W

wait for I/O efficiently. *See*
   `select` module
`wait()` method
   child processes, 1242–1244
   multiple coroutines, 632–635
   signaling between threads,
    571–572
   synchronizing threads,
    580–581
`walk()`, examine file system
   contents, 1228–1229
Wall clock time. *See also* `time`
   module, 213–214
`warn()`, generating warnings,
   1280–1281
`warnings` module
   alternatives for message
    delivery, 1284–1285
   categories and filtering, 1280
   filtering with patterns,
    1281–1283
   formatting, 1285
   generating, 1280–1281

`logging` integration with,
   985–986
   overview of, 1279
   repeated, 1283–1284
   stack level in, 1286
`wc()` function, `statistics`
   variance, 293
`WeakKeyDictionary` class,
   caching objects, 127
`weakref` module
   caching objects, 127–130
   finalizing objects, 123–126
   as impermanent references to
    objects, 121
   memory management with, 65
   proxies, 126–127
   reference callbacks, 122–123
   references, 122
`WeakValueDictionary` class,
   caching objects, 127–130
Web Robots Page, `robots.txt`,
   774
`webbrowser` module, displaying
   Web pages, 796–797
`weekheader()` method,
   `calendar`, 234
Weibull distribution, `random`,
   264
`weibullvariate()` function,
   Weibull distribution, 264
What's New, Python
   documentation, 1351
`which()` function, finding files
   in `shutil`, 345–346
`whichdb` module, 408–411,
   1365
Whitespace
   difference-based reporting
    (`REPORT_NDIFF`),
    1036–1037
   managing blank lines in
    `doctest`, 1034–1036
   `NORMALIZE_WHITESPACE`,
    1037–1039
`width` argument, `pprint`,
   140–142
Wildcards, filename pattern
   matching in `glob`, 320–322
Windows OS
   obtaining operating
    information, 1249–1250
   vs. tabs, `webbrowser`, 796
`with` statement
   context manager enabled by,
    191–194

   converting generator function
    into context manager,
    196–198
   `deci-`
    `mal_context_manager`,
    247–248
   stacking context managers,
    202–206
`WRAPPER_ASSIGNMENTS`,
   `functools`, 146
`WRAPPER_UPDATES`,
   `functools`, 146–147
`wrapt` package, 1367–1368
`writable` sockets, 730–732,
   738–739
`write()` method
   alternative archive member
    names, `zipfile`, 516
   creating new archive,
    `zipfile`, 514–516
   saving configuration files in
    `config`, 972
   serializing XML to stream,
    464–466
`Writeback`, shelves, 406–408
`writepy()` method, Python
   ZIP archives, 519–521
`writer()` function, `sqlite3`,
   432
Writing
   compressed files in `bz2`,
    495–497
   compressed files in `gzip`,
    486–488
   data from sources other than
    files, `tarfile`, 509
   data from sources other than
    files, `zipfile`, 517–518
   files in `pathlib`, 312
   GNU zip files, `gzip`, 486
   Unicode data, 498–499

X

`xgettext`, message catalogs,
   1004–1005
XML manipulation API. *See*
   `xml.etree.ElementTree`
   module
XML-RPC
   client library for. *See*
    `xmlrpc.client` module
   server. *See* `xmlrpc.server`
    module
`xmlcharrefreplace`, lossless
   error handling, 374

`xml.dom.minidom`,
pretty-printing XML,
458–459
`xml.etree.ElementTree`
module
building documents with
element nodes, 457–458
building trees from lists of
nodes, 461–464
changes in Python 3, 1365
creating custom TreeBuilder,
453–455
data supplements to standard
library, 1368
`ElementTree` library, 445
finding nodes in document,
447–448
parsed node attributes,
449–450
parsing strings, 455–457
parsing XML document,
445–446
pretty-printing XML, 458–459
serializing XML to stream,
464–466
setting element properties,
459–461
traversing parsed tree,
446–447
watching events while
parsing, 451–453
XML manipulation API via,
445
`xmlrpc.client` module
binary data, 823–825
combining calls into one
message, 826–827
connecting to server, 817–819
data types, 819–822
exception handling, 825–826
passing objects, 822–823

XML-RPC client library,
816–817
`xmlrpc.server` module
alternate API names, 829–830
arbitrary API names, 831–832
dispatching calls, 835–836
dotted API names, 830–831
exposing methods of objects,
832–834
introspection API, 837–839
simple server, 828–829
XML-RPC server, 827

Y

YAML, application
configuration, 1371

Z

ZIP archive. *See also*
`zipimport` module
accessing code from,
1345–1346
example, 1344–1345
finding modules in, 1345
retrieving source code from,
1346–1347
Zip files, read and write GNU.
See `gzip` module
`zip()` function, `itertools`,
165, 171
`zipfile` module
appending to files, 518–519
creating new archives,
514–516
extracting archived files from
archive, 514
limitations, 521
Python ZIP archives, 519–521
reading metadata from
archive, 512–514

testing ZIP files, 512
using alternative archive
member names, 516
writing data from sources
other than files, 517
writing with `ZipInfo`
instance, 517–518
ZIP archive access with, 511
`zipimport` module
accessing code from ZIP
archive, 1345–1346
changes in Python 3, 1365
determining if package or
regular module, 1348
example, 1344–1345
finding modules inside ZIP
archive, 1345
finding non-code data,
1348–1350
overview of, 1329, 1344
retrieving source code from
ZIP archive, 1346–1347
`ZipInfo` instance, `zipfile`,
517–518
`zip_longest()` function,
`itertools`, 165
`zlib` module
checksums, 481–482
compressing network data,
482–486
GNU zlib compression via,
477
GZipFile vs., 490
incremental compression/
decompression, 479–480
mixed content streams,
480–481
working with data in memory,
477–479